The Beach Boys

The Complete History

Wiki Editors

Published by

Transactual Systems
Minneapolis, Minnesota
United States of America

www.transactual.com/wikibits/

ISBN: 1453603565
EAN-13: 9781453603567

Printed in the United States of America by CreateSpace

Bulk purchases and reseller discounts, contact dave@transactual.com

WikiBits Books

WikiBits books are “snapshots” of a Wikipedia subject taken at a specific moment in time. Because Wikipedia is a publicly editable online encyclopedia, some of the contents in this book may change over time. However, the topic of this book was carefully chosen as a historical set of facts that are generally not in dispute, so the information is unlikely to change.

Acknowledgements

With tremendous gratitude to the millions of Wikipedia editors who contribute their time and knowledge for the benefit of the entire world.

Contents

The Beach Boys

The Beach Boys	
The Beach Boys in 1964.	
Background information	
Origin	Hawthorne, California, United States
Genres	Surf rock, sunshine pop, psychedelic pop, psychedelic rock, baroque pop, art rock, traditional pop
Years active	1961–present
Labels	Capitol, Brother, Reprise, Caribou, X Records, Ariola, Columbia
Associated acts	Kenny & The Cadets, The Survivors, Jan and Dean, Glen Campbell, The Honeys, The Flames
Website	www.thebeachboys.com [1]
Members	
Al Jardine Bruce Johnston Mike Love Brian Wilson	
Former members	
Carl Wilson Dennis Wilson David Marks Ricky Fataar Blondie Chaplin Glen Campbell	

The Beach Boys are an American rock band, formed in 1961, who gained popularity for their close vocal harmonies and lyrics reflecting a Southern California youth culture of cars, surfing, and romance. Brian Wilson's growing creative ambitions later transformed them into a more artistically innovative group that earned critical praise and influenced many later musicians.[2]

The group was initially composed of singer-musician-composer Brian Wilson, his brothers, Carl and Dennis, their cousin Mike Love, and friend Al Jardine. This core quintet was inducted into the Rock and Roll Hall of Fame Class of 1988.

The Beach Boys have often been called "America's Band",[3] [4] [5] and Allmusic has stated that "the band's unerring ability... made them America's first, best rock band."[2] The group has had thirty-six U.S. Top 40 hits (the most of any U.S. rock band) and fifty-six Hot 100 hits, including four number-one singles.[2] Rolling Stone magazine listed The Beach Boys as number 12 in the 100 Greatest Artists of All Time [6].[7] According to *Billboard*, in terms of singles and album sales, The Beach Boys are the No.-1-selling American band of all time.[8]

Many changes in both musical styles and personnel have occurred during their career, notably because of Brian Wilson's mental illness and recreational drug use (leading to his eventual withdrawal from the group) and the deaths of Dennis and Carl Wilson in 1983 and 1998, respectively. Extensive legal battles between members of the group have also played their part. After the death of Carl Wilson, founding member Al Jardine left to pursue a solo career. Currently, the surviving members of The Beach Boys continue to tour in three separate bands: "The Beach Boys Band" with Love, Bruce Johnston, and a rotation of backing musicians; Al Jardine's "Endless Summer Band" with Jardine, his sons, and several former Beach Boys backup musicians; and Brian Wilson with a 10-piece band including members of The Wondermints and Jeff Foskett, who toured with the Beach Boys in the 1980s and 1990s as a backing guitarist/singer.[9]

History

Formative years

Brian Wilson was born in Inglewood, California, in 1942, and his family moved to nearby Hawthorne when Brian was two years old. At the age of 16, Brian shared a bedroom with his two brothers, Dennis and Carl. He watched his father, Murry Wilson, play piano and listened intently to the harmonies of vocal groups like The Four Freshmen. One night he taught his brothers a song called "Ivory Tower" and how to sing the background harmonies. "We practiced night after night, singing softly, hoping we wouldn't wake our Dad." [10] For his 16th birthday, Brian had received a reel-to-reel tape recorder. He learned how to overdub, using his vocals and those of Carl and his mother. He would play piano and later added Carl playing the Rickenbacker guitar he got as a Christmas present.[11]

The first Beach Boys record (released December 1961) after having their band name changed from *The Pendletones*: this is the record's first pressing, on X Records

Soon Brian was avidly listening to Johnny Otis on his KFOX radio show, a favorite station of Carl's. Inspired by the simple structure and vocals of the rhythm and blues songs he heard, he changed his piano-playing style and started writing songs. His enthusiasm interfered with his music studies at school. He failed to complete a twelfth-grade piano sonata, but did submit an original composition, called "Surfin'".[12]

Family gatherings brought the Wilsons in contact with cousin Mike Love. Brian taught Love's sister Maureen and a friend harmonies. Later, Brian, Mike and two friends performed at Hawthorne High School, drawing tremendous applause for their version of The Olympics' (doo-wop group) "Hully Gully".[13] Brian also knew Al Jardine, a high school classmate, who had already played guitar in a folk group called The Islanders. One day, on the spur of the moment, they asked a couple of football players in the school training room to learn harmony parts, but it wasn't a success — the bass singer was flat.[14]

Brian suggested to Jardine that they team up with his cousin and brother Carl. It was at these sessions, held in Brian's bedroom, that "the Beach Boys sound" began to form. Brian says: "Everyone contributed something. Carl kept us hip to the latest tunes, Al taught us his repertoire of folk songs, and Dennis, though he didn't [at the time] play anything, added a combustible spark just by his presence." It was Love who encouraged Brian to write songs and he also gave the fledgling band its first name: The Pendletones. The Pendletones name was derived from the Pendleton woolen shirts popular at that time. In their earliest performances, the band wore the heavy wool jacket-like shirts, which were favored by surfers in the South Bay. In 1962, the Beach Boys began wearing blue/gray-striped button-down shirts tucked into white pants as their touring "uniforms." This was the band's signature look through to 1966.[15]

Although surfing motifs were very prominent in their early songs, Dennis was the only member of the group who surfed. He suggested that his brothers compose some songs celebrating his hobby and the lifestyle which had developed around it in Southern California.[16]

Jardine and a singer friend, Gary Winfrey, went to Brian's to see if he could help out with a version of a folk song they wanted to record - "Sloop John B." In Brian's absence, the two spoke with his father, Murry, who was a music industry veteran of modest success. In September 1961, Murry arranged for The Pendletones to meet publishers Hite and Dorinda Morgan at Stereo Masters in Hollywood.[17] The group performed a straightforward rendition of "Sloop John B.", but failed to impress the Morgans. After an awkward pause, Dennis mentioned they had an original song, called "Surfin'". Brian was taken aback — he had not finished writing the song — but Hite Morgan was interested and asked them to call back when the song was complete.[16]

With help from Mike, Brian finished the song and the group rented guitars, drums, amplifiers and microphones. They practiced for three days while the Wilsons' parents were on a short vacation. A few days later they auditioned for the Morgans again and Hite Morgan declared: "That's a smash!"[18]

On October 3, 1961, The Pendletones recorded twelve takes of "Surfin'" in the Morgans' cramped offices (Dennis was deemed not yet good enough to play drums, much to his chagrin). A small quantity of singles was pressed. When the boys eagerly unpacked the first box of singles, on the Candix Records label, they were surprised and angered to see their band name had been changed to "Beach Boys". Murry Wilson, now intimately involved with the band's fortunes, called the Morgans. Apparently a young promotion worker, Russ Regan, had decided on the change to more obviously tie the group in with other surf bands of the time (his original name for the band was The Surfers). The limited budget meant the labels could not be reprinted.[19]

Released mid-November, 1961, "Surfin'" was soon aired on KFWB and KDAY, two of Los Angeles' most influential radio stations. It was a hit on the West Coast, and peaked at #75 on the national pop charts.

Influence of Murry Wilson

As an eight-year-old, Brian Wilson says his "young life was already being shaped and influenced by music... None affected me more than the music I heard when my father played the family piano... I watched how his fingers made chords and memorized the positions".[20]

Murry had limited success as a songwriter, peaking with "Two Step Side Step" when it was recorded for a Bachelors album in 1952. Despite his musical ability and any wish to educate Brian in particular, Murry "was a tyrant", quick to offer discouraging criticism and who "abused [his sons] psychologically and physically, creating wounds that never healed."[21] Carl found comfort in food and Dennis rebelled against the world to express his anger.[22] Brian would immerse himself in music to cope, but though he longed to learn piano as a child, he was too frightened to ask and even too scared to press the keys when his father was at work.[21]

Eventually Brian surprised his parents by showing he had learned how to play the piano by watching his father. Thereafter, "playing the piano... literally saved my ass. I recall playing one time while my dad flung Dennis against the wall... That was just one of many incidents when I didn't miss a note, supplying background music to the hell that often substituted for a family life..."[23]

At first, Murry steered the Beach Boys' career, engineering their signing with Capitol Records in 1962. In 1964, Brian ousted his father after a violent confrontation in the studio. Over the next few years, they became increasingly estranged; when Murry died of a heart attack in June 1973, Brian and Dennis did not attend the funeral.

Early career

German 1962 single release of *Surfin' Safari*

Murry Wilson told the boys he did not like "Surfin'". However, "he smelled money to be made and jumped on the promotional bandwagon, calling every radio station..."[24] He got the group's first paying gig on New Year's Eve, 1961, at the Ritchie Valens Memorial Dance in Long Beach, headlined by Ike and Tina Turner. Brian recalls how he wondered what they were doing there; "five clean-cut, unworldly white boys from a conservative white suburb, in an auditorium full of black kids". Brian describes the night as an "education" - he knew afterwards that success was all about "R&B, rock and roll, and money." The boys went home with $50 apiece. In February 1962, Al Jardine left the band to continue his college studies.[25] David Marks, a thirteen-year-old neighbor and friend of Carl's, replaced him (Jardine, at Brian's request, rejoined the group in July 1963).[26] .

Though Murry effectively seized managerial control of the band without consultation, Brian acknowledges that he "deserves credit for getting us off the ground... he hounded us mercilessly... [but] also worked hard himself". He was the first to stress the importance of having a follow-up hit.[27] They duly recorded four more originals, on June 13 at Western Studios, Los Angeles, including "Surfer Girl", "409" and "Surfin' Safari". The session ended on a bitter note, however: Murry Wilson unsuccessfully suggested and then demanded that the Beach Boys record some of his own songs, saying "My songs are better than yours."[28]

On July 16, on the strength of the June demo session, the Beach Boys were signed to Capitol Records. By November, their first album was ready - "Surfin' Safari". Their song output continued along the same commercial line, focusing on California youth lifestyle. The early Beach Boys' hits helped raise both the profile of the state of California and of surfing. The group also celebrated the Golden State's obsession with hot-rod racing ("Shut Down," "409," "Little Deuce Coupe") and the pursuit of happiness by carefree teens in less complicated times ("Be True to Your School," "Fun, Fun, Fun," "I Get Around").

Their early hits made them major pop stars in the United States, the United Kingdom, and other countries, with sixteen hit singles in 1962-1965. After the British Invasion in 1964, some British groups, in particular The Beatles, eclipsed their success.

Apart from the Wilsons' father and the close vocal harmonies of Brian's favorite groups, early inspiration came from the driving rock-and-roll sound of Chuck Berry and Phil Spector's Wall of Sound. Musically, their early songs are often based on those of others; for instance, "Surfer Girl" shares its rhythmic melody with "When You Wish Upon a Star", while "Surfin' USA" is a slight variation of Berry's "Sweet Little Sixteen". However, Brian Wilson rapidly progressed as a composer, arranger and producer; the *Pet Sounds* album in particular is recognized for the quality and originality of its melodies, harmonies, and arrangements.[29] In his autobiography, Brian states that the melody of "God Only Knows" was inspired by a John Sebastian record.

Brian's innovations and personal difficulties

The stress of road travel, composing, producing and maintaining a high level of creativity was too much for Brian Wilson to bear. On December 23, 1964, while on a flight to Houston, Brian suffered from an anxiety attack and left the tour. Shortly afterward, he announced his withdrawal from touring to concentrate entirely on songwriting and record production. This wasn't the first time Brian had stopped touring. In 1963, when Al Jardine returned, Brian left the road; but when David Marks quit, Brian had to return in his place. For the rest of 1964 and into 1965, Glen Campbell served as Wilson's replacement in concert, until his own career success required him to leave the group. Bruce Johnston was asked to locate a replacement for Campbell; having failed to find one, Johnston himself

subsequently became a full-time member of the band, first replacing Wilson on the road and later contributing his own talents in the studio beginning with the sessions for "California Girls."

Jan & Dean, close friends with the band and opening act for them in concert in 1963 and 1964, encouraged Brian to use session musicians in the studio. This, along with Brian's withdrawal from touring, permitted him to expand his role as a producer. Wilson also wrote "Surf City" for the Jan & Dean opening act. Their recording hit #1 on the U.S. charts in the summer of 1963, a development that pleased Brian but angered father/manager Murry, who felt his son had "given away" what should have been the Beach Boys' first chart-topper. A year later, the Beach Boys would notch their first #1 single with "I Get Around."

By 1964, traces of Brian Wilson's increasing studio productivity and ideas were noticeable: "Drive-In," an album track from *All Summer Long* features bars of silence between two verses while "Denny's Drums," the last track on *Shut Down, Vol. II*, is a two-minute drum solo. As Wilson's musical efforts became more ambitious, the group relied more on nimble session players, on tracks such as "I Get Around" and "When I Grow Up (To Be a Man)." "Help Me, Rhonda" became the band's second #1 single in the spring of 1965.

1965 led to greater experimentation behind the soundboard with Wilson. The album *Today!* featured less focus on guitars, more emphasis on keyboards and percussion, as well as volume experiments and increased lyrical maturity. Side A of the album was devoted to sunnier pop tunes, with darker ballads on the reverse side. This pattern was also evident on some of the band's singles, with songs such as "Kiss Me, Baby" released on the B-side to "Help Me, Rhonda" and "Let Him Run Wild" on the B-side to "California Girls", each featuring Brian Wilson's lead vocals and foreshadowing the youthful angst that would later pervade *Pet Sounds*.

In November 1965 the group followed up their #3 summer smash "California Girls," with another top 20 single, "The Little Girl I Once Knew." It is considered to be the band's most experimental statements prior to *Pet Sounds*, using silence as a pre-chorus, clashing keyboards, moody brass, and vocal tics. Perhaps too extreme an arrangement to go much higher than its modest #20 peak, it was only the band's second single not to reach the top 10 since their 1962 breakthrough. In December they would score an unexpected #2 hit (#3 in the UK) with the single "Barbara Ann", which Capitol Records released as a single without input from any of the Beach Boys. It has become one of their most recognized hits over the years and was a cover of a 1961 song by The Regents.

It was during this time that the Beatles' *Rubber Soul* came out, and Brian Wilson was enthralled with it. Until then, each Beach Boys album (and most pop albums of the day) contained a few "filler tracks" like cover songs or even stitched-together comedy bits. Brian found *Rubber Soul* filled with all-original songs and, more importantly, all good ones, none of them filler. Inspired, he rushed to his wife and proclaimed, "Marilyn, I'm gonna make the greatest album! The greatest rock album ever made!"[30]

Pet Sounds and *Good Vibrations*

Wilson's growing mastery of studio recording and his increasingly sophisticated songs and complex arrangements would reach a creative peak with the acclaimed LP *Pet Sounds* (1966). *Pet Sounds* is on many music lists as one of the greatest albums of all time, including those of *TIME*,[31] *Rolling Stone*, *New Musical Express*, *Mojo*, and *The Times*. According to Acclaimedmusic.net, Pet Sounds is the most acclaimed album of all time by music journalists.[32] . Among other accolades, Paul McCartney has named it one of his favorite albums of all time (with "God Only Knows" as his all-time favorite song). McCartney has frequently said that it was the inspiration behind the seminal Beatles' album, *Sgt. Pepper's Lonely Hearts Club Band*. Echoing this sentiment, Beatles producer George Martin is quoted saying, "Pepper was an attempt to equal *Pet Sounds*."[33]

The album's meticulously layered harmonies and inventive instrumentation (performed by the cream of Los Angeles session musicians known among themselves as The Wrecking Crew) set a new standard for popular music. It remains one of the most evocative releases of the decade, with distinctive strains of lushness, melancholy, and nostalgia for youth. The tracks "Wouldn't It Be Nice" and "God Only Knows", showcased Wilson's growing mastery as a composer, arranger, and producer. "Caroline, No," also taken from *Pet Sounds*, was issued as a Brian Wilson

solo single, the only time Brian was credited as a solo artist during the early Capitol years. The album also included two sophisticated instrumental tracks, the quiet and wistful "Let's Go Away for Awhile" and the brittle brassy surf of the title track, "Pet Sounds". Despite the critical praise it received, the album was indifferently promoted by Capitol Records and failed to become the major hit Brian had hoped it would be (only reaching #10). Its failure to gain wider recognition hurt him deeply.[34]

Because of his withdrawal from touring, Wilson was able to complete almost all the backing tracks for the album while the Beach Boys were on tour in Japan. They returned to find a substantially complete album, requiring only their vocals to finish it off. There was some resistance from within the band to this new direction. Lead singer Mike Love is reported to have been strongly opposed to it, calling it "Brian's ego music," and warning the composer not to "fuck with the formula."[35] Other group members also fretted that the band would lose its core audience if they changed their successful musical blueprint. At Love's insistence, Brian changed the title and lyrics of one song from "Hang On to Your Ego" to "I Know There's an Answer." Another likely factor in Love's antipathy to *Pet Sounds* was that Wilson worked extensively on it with outside lyricist Tony Asher rather than with Love, even though Love had co-written the lyrics for many of their earlier songs and was the lead vocalist on most of their early hits.

Seeking to expand on the advances made on *Pet Sounds*, Wilson began an even more ambitious project, originally dubbed *Dumb Angel*. Its first fruit was "Good Vibrations," which Brian described as "a pocket symphony". The song became the Beach Boys' biggest hit to date and a U.S. and U.K. No. 1 single in 1966 — many critics consider it to be one of the best rock singles of all time. In 1997, it was named the "Greatest Single of All Time" by *Mojo* music magazine. In 2000, VH1 placed it at number 8 on their "100 Greatest Rock Songs" list, and in late 2004, *Rolling Stone* magazine placed it at number 6 on their "500 Greatest Songs of All Time" list. It was also one of the most complex pop productions ever undertaken, and was reputed to have been the most expensive American single ever recorded at that time. Costing a reported $16,000, more than most pop *albums*, sessions for the song stretched over several months in at least three major studios.

In contrast to his work on *Pet Sounds*, Wilson adopted a modular approach to "Good Vibrations" — he broke the song into sections and taped multiple versions of each at different studios to take advantage of the different sound and ambience of each facility. He then assembled his favorite sections into a master backing track and added vocals. The song's innovative instrumentation included drums, organ, piano, tack piano, two basses, guitars, electro-theremin, harmonica, and cello. The group members recall the "Good Vibrations" vocal sessions as among the most demanding of their career.[34]

Even as his personal life deteriorated, Wilson's musical output remained remarkable. The exact nature of his mental problems was a topic of much speculation. He abused drugs heavily, gained an enormous amount of weight, suffered long bouts of depression, and became paranoid. Several biographies have suggested that his father may have had bipolar disorder and after years of suffering, Wilson's own condition was eventually diagnosed as schizoaffective disorder.[34]

Smile

While putting the finishing touches on *Pet Sounds,* and just beginning work on "Good Vibrations," Brian met fellow musician and songwriter Van Dyke Parks. In late 1966, Brian and Parks began an intense collaboration that resulted in a suite of challenging new songs for the Beach Boys' next album, which was eventually named *Smile*.[37] Using the same techniques as on "Good Vibrations," recording began in August 1966 and carried on into early 1967. Although the structure of the album and the exact running order of the songs have been the subjects of endless speculation, it is known that Wilson and Parks intended *Smile* to be a continuous suite of songs that were linked both thematically and musically, with the main songs being linked together by small vocal pieces and instrumental segments that elaborated upon the musical themes of the major songs.

The original cover of *Smile*. More than 400,000 *Smile* covers were produced; they were kept in a warehouse in Pennsylvania before being destroyed in the late 80s. Today, there are reportedly fewer than a dozen original *Smile* covers in existence.[36]

But some of the other Beach Boys, especially Love, found the new music too difficult and too far removed from their established style. Another serious concern was that the new music was simply not feasible for live performance by the current Beach Boys lineup. Love was bitterly opposed to *Smile* and was particularly critical of Parks' lyrics; he has also since stated that he was deeply concerned about Wilson's escalating drug intake. The problems came to a head during the recording of "Cabin Essence," when Love demanded that Parks explain the meaning of the closing refrain of the song, "Over and over the crow cries uncover the cornfield." After a heated argument, Parks walked out of the session, and shortly thereafter his creative partnership with Wilson came to an equally abrupt end.

Many factors combined to put intense pressure on Brian Wilson as *Smile* neared completion: Wilson's own mental instability, the pressure to create against fierce internal opposition to his new music, the relatively unenthusiastic response to *Pet Sounds*, Carl Wilson's draft resistance, and a major dispute with Capitol Records. Matters were complicated by Wilson's reliance on both prescription and illegal drugs, amphetamines in particular, which only exacerbated his underlying mental health problems.

Also at this time the Beach Boys management (Nick Grillo and David Anderle) started work on developing and implementing the band's own record label, Brother. The intent of the label was for side projects and an invitation for new talent. The Beach Boys became one of the first rock bands to create their own label (shortly afterwards, The Beatles followed with Apple). The output of the label, however, was limited to one album and two singles and with the subsequent failure of the second *Smiley Smile* single "Getting Hungry", the band decided to shelve the Brother label until 1970.

In May 1967, *Smile* was shelved, and over the next thirty years, the legends surrounding *Smile* grew until it became the most famous unreleased album in the history of popular music.[38]

However, some of the tracks were salvaged and re-recorded at Brian's new home studio, albeit in drastically scaled-down versions. These were released, along with the completed versions of "Good Vibrations" and "Heroes and Villains", on the 1967 LP *Smiley Smile*, which would prove to be a critical and commercial disaster for the group.

Despite the cancellation of *Smile,* interest in the work remained high and versions of several major tracks — including "Our Prayer", "Cabin Essence", "Cool, Cool Water", and "Surf's Up" — continued to trickle out. Many

were assembled by Carl Wilson over the next few years and included on later albums. The band was still expecting to complete and release *Smile* as late as 1972, before it became clear that Brian had been the only one who could have made sense out of the endless fragments that were recorded. A substantial number of original tracks and linking fragments were included on the group's 30th anniversary CD boxed set in 1993. The full *Smile* project did not surface until Wilson and Parks completed the writing, aided by Darian Sanahaja who helped in sequencing, and Brian re-recorded it as Brian Wilson Presents "Smile" in 2004.

Mid-career changes

After the popularity of the song "Good Vibrations" came a period of declining commercial success. *Smiley Smile* and subsequent albums performed poorly on the U.S. charts (although they fared better in the UK). The group's image problems took a further hit following their withdrawal from the bill of the 1967 Monterey International Pop Festival.

The 1967 album *Wild Honey*, regarded by some as another classic, features songs written by Wilson and Love, including the hit "Darlin'" and a rendition of Stevie Wonder's "I Was Made to Love Her". *Friends* (1968) is a largely acoustic album, influenced by the group's adoption of the practice of Transcendental Meditation. The title single was their least successful single since 1962. This was followed by the single "Do It Again," a return to their earlier-style formula. Moderately successful in the US at #20, the single went to #1 in the UK.

As Brian's mental and physical health deteriorated in the late 1960s and early 1970s, his song output diminished; he eventually became withdrawn and detached from the band. To fill his creative void, the other members began writing and producing songs. Carl Wilson gradually took over leadership of the band, developing into an accomplished producer. To complete their contract with Capitol Records before signing with Reprise Records, they produced one more album, *20/20* (1969), primarily a collection of leftovers (including remnants from *Smile*), old songs by outside writers, and several new songs by Dennis Wilson. One of those songs, "Never Learn Not to Love", featured uncredited lyrics by Charles Manson[39] and was originally titled "Cease to Exist". Besides "Do It Again", the album included Carl's production of the Ronettes' "I Can Hear Music".

In 1969, the Beach Boys reactivated their Brother Records label and signed with Reprise Records. With the new contract, the band appeared rejuvenated, releasing the album *Sunflower* to critical acclaim. The album was and still is recognized as a complete group effort, with all band members contributing significant material, such as "Add Some Music to Your Day", Brian's "This Whole World", Dennis' "Forever" and Bruce Johnston's "Tears in the Morning". The album, like *Pet Sounds*, was ignored by the public. The band experienced their worst chart performance ever, not even making the top 100, although the single "Cottonfields"—which appeared on non-US releases of *Sunflower* as a re-vamped version of a track that first appeared on *20/20*—did become a Top 5 hit in the UK.

After *Sunflower*, the band hired Jack Rieley as their manager. Rieley chose a different direction for the group, emphasizing, among other things, political and social awareness. The result was 1971's *Surf's Up*, featuring Brian's *Smile* centerpiece, "Surf's Up". The song itself was virtually the same arrangement of Brian performing in the studio in 1966, with Carl adding vocals and the "Child is Father of the Man" overdubs. Carl's "Long Promised Road" and "Feel Flows" are standouts. Brian contributed one of his best songs, "'Til I Die", which almost did not make the album sequencing. Bruce Johnston produced the classic "Disney Girls (1957)", a throwback to the easier, simpler times they remembered. Johnston ended his first stint with the band shortly after the record's release, reportedly because of friction between him and Jack Rieley. The album was moderately successful, reaching the US top 30. While the record made its run on the charts, the Beach Boys added to their refound fame by performing a near-sellout concert at Carnegie Hall, and following that with the famous appearance with the Grateful Dead at Fillmore East on April 27, 1971.

The addition of Ricky Fataar and Blondie Chaplin in February, 1972, led to a dramatic departure in sound for the band. The album *Carl and the Passions - "So Tough"* was an uncharacteristic mix that included several songs drawn from Fataar and Chaplin's previous group, Flame, which are nearly unrecognizable as Beach Boys songs. Although it has its supporters, the album is widely considered to be one of the group's most unfocused and inconsistent. It did not

make an impact on the charts.

The Beach Boys came up with an ambitious (and expensive) plan in developing their next project, *Holland*. The band, their families, assorted associates and technicians moved to the Netherlands for the summer of 1972, renting a farmhouse to convert into a makeshift studio. By the end of their adventure the band felt they had come up with one of their best efforts yet. Reprise, however, felt that the album was weak, and after some wrangling between the camps, the band asked Brian to come up with commercial material. This resulted in the song "Sail On, Sailor", a collaboration between Brian Wilson and Van Dyke Parks, became one of the most emblematic Beach Boys songs. Reprise approved and the album was released early 1973, peaking at #37 on the Billboard album chart. *Holland* was also popular on FM radio, which embraced tracks like Mike Love and Al Jardine's "California Saga". Included as a "bonus" EP was Brian's storytale Mount Vernon and Fairway (A Fairy Tale), which was directly influenced by Randy Newman's *Sail Away* LP. *Holland* proved that the band could still produce contemporary songs with wide (if not mass) appeal.

Despite the indifference displayed by the record label, the band's concert audience started to grow. *The Beach Boys in Concert*, a double album documenting the 1972 and 1973 US tours, became the band's first gold record for Reprise.

Endless Summer

In the summer of 1974, Capitol, in consultation with Love, released a double album compilation of the Beach Boys' pre-*Pet Sounds* hits. *Endless Summer,* helped by a sunny, colorful graphic cover, caught the mood of the country and surged to #1 on the Billboard album chart. It was the group's first multi-million selling record since "Good Vibrations", and remained on the album chart for three years.[40] The following year Capitol released another compilation, *Spirit of America*, which also sold well. With both compilations, the Beach Boys suddenly became relevant again to the American musical landscape, propelling themselves from being the opening act for Crosby, Stills, Nash and Young to headliners selling out basketball arenas. Manager Jack Rieley, who remained in the Netherlands after *Holland*'s release, was relieved of his managerial duties in late 1973. Rolling Stone awarded the band the distinction of 1974's "Band of The Year", based solely on the their juggernaut touring schedule and the material written and produced by Brian over a decade earlier.

Blondie Chaplin left the band in late 1973 after an argument with Steve Love, the band's business manager (and Mike's brother), Ricky Fataar stayed until fall 1974, when he was offered a chance to join a new group being formed by Joe Walsh. Chaplin's replacement, James William Guercio, started offering the group career advice that turned out to be so smart and sensible that eventually he became the band's new manager.

Under Guercio, The Beach Boys staged a highly successful 1975 joint concert tour with Chicago, with each group performing some of the other's songs, including their previous year's collaboration on Chicago's hit "Wishing You Were Here". Beach Boy vocals were also heard on Elton John's 1974 hit "Don't Let the Sun Go Down on Me."

Nostalgia had settled into the Beach Boys' hype; the group had not officially released any albums of new material since 1973's *Holland*. While their concerts continuously sold out, the stage act slowly changed from contemporary presentation/oldies encores to an entire show composed of mostly pre-1967 music. Performances of *Smiley Smile* to *Holland* material would eventually be phased out, replaced by their hits from 1961 to 1966. This decision frustrated serious fans of the band for many years to come.

Brian's return

15 Big Ones marked the return of Brian Wilson as a major force in the group in that it was the first album he produced since *Pet Sounds*. This album included several new songs composed by Brian, and several of his arrangements of favorite old songs by other artists, including "Rock and Roll Music" (which made #5), "Blueberry Hill", and "In the Still of the Night". Brian and Mike's "It's OK" was yet another return to their earlier "summertime fun" style, and was a moderate hit. The album was publicized by an NBC-TV special, telecast on August 4, 1976,

simply entitled "The Beach Boys", which was produced by *Saturday Night Live* creator Lorne Michaels and featured appearances by *SNL* cast members John Belushi and Dan Aykroyd. Another project included singing back-up for Eric Carmen on his Top 40 hit, "She Did It" in 1977.

For the remainder of 1976 to early 1977, Brian Wilson spent his time making sporadic public appearances and producing the band's next LP *Love You*, a quirky collection of 14 songs mostly written by Brian alone, including more "fun" songs ("Honkin' Down the Highway"), a mature love song ("The Night Was So Young")—a mix ranging from infectious to touching to downright silly. The songs were delivered to the Beach Boys only as demo versions, mostly with only Brian's vocals and Moog synth and drum-machine backing tracks. The Beach Boys were expected to finish them, but because of time constraints the majority of the material was released as Brian's originally recorded demos. The result was an uneven, incomplete effort and not a commercial success. Despite its flaws, the album is one of the more popular offerings in the Beach Boys' later oeuvre. Many sources cited the album as a return to the group's roots.

After *Love You*, Brian's contributions began to decline over the next several albums until he again virtually withdrew from the group. His appearances with the band in concert diminished. His performances became erratic, his recordings uninspired. Despite the much-publicized "Brian's Back" campaign in the late '70s, most critics believed the group was past its prime. Many expected that at some point Brian Wilson would eventually become the latest in a long line of celebrity drug casualties.

During this period the band put out two further studio efforts: *M.I.U.* and *L.A. Light Album*. *M.I.U.* was recorded at Maharishi International University in Iowa (now Maharishi University of Management) at the insistence of Mike Love. Dennis and Carl made limited contributions to the project; the album was mostly produced by Alan Jardine and Ron Altbach, with Brian appearing as the role of "Executive Producer". Regardless, despite a handful of interesting tracks, the album was largely a contractual obligation to finish out their association with Reprise Records. Reprise likewise did not promote the album.

At the same time of the M.I.U. album release, The Beach Boys signed with CBS Records (now part of Sony/BMG). They received a substantial advance and reportedly agreed to a guaranteed minimum of one million dollars per album. However, CBS was not satisfied with preliminary reviews of their first product-*L.A. Light Album*. The band realized at this point that Brian either could not or would not write and produce the required material. As a stop-gap measure, Bruce Johnston returned to the group as both a member and this time as a producer. The Brian and Carl song "Good Timin'" became a US top 40 single. The album featured outstanding performances by both Dennis (cuts intended for his second solo effort *Bambu*) and Carl ("Full Sail"). The group also enjoyed moderate success (if not indifferently received) with a disco reworking of the song "Here Comes the Night", originally on the *Wild Honey* album.

In 1980, the band recorded and released *Keeping the Summer Alive*. Again, Bruce Johnston was in the producer's role as well as performing on the album. Sessions took place at Western Recorders, the site where Brian produced many of his most enduring songs as well as Al Jardine's barn studio in Big Sur and Rumbo Studios in Los Angeles. Brian contributed some inspired production ideas occasionally as seen in the television special the band made for the album's release. Even though Dennis Wilson was credited,(his drumming is heard on the group's cover version of Chuck Berry's "School Days") this was the first *Beach Boys* album not to feature Dennis (due to his ongoing personal problems). He was not in the *Going Platinum* television special and was asked not to participate in the recording project. Carl Wilson had discovered a young talented drummer, vocalist and multi-instrumentalist by the name of Scott Mathews and though Mathews was signed to Capitol Records, Carl asked him to join the band. Mathews jumped at the chance to record with his long-time heroes but ultimately chose not to join the band because of his blossoming career in the studio as a producer and songwriter plus (much like Brian), his dislike for touring.

Late 1970s – present

In the late 1970s, Dennis Wilson increasingly indulged in drug and alcohol abuse. Some of the group's concert appearances were marred when he and other band members showed up on stage drunk or stoned. The band was forced to publicly apologize after a poor performance in Perth, Australia in 1978, during which several members of the group appeared to be drunk.

The current touring line-up of The Beach Boys, 2008

Dennis Wilson was the first Beach Boy to release a solo album, entitled *Pacific Ocean Blue*, on August 22, 1977. A follow-up album entitled *Bambu* was recorded with friend and musician Carli Muñoz but remained unfinished and unreleased until *Pacific Ocean Blue* was re-issued in 2008.

From 1980 through 1982, The Beach Boys and The Grass Roots performed Independence Day concerts on the National Mall in Washington, D.C., attracting large crowds.[41] [42] However, in April 1983, James G. Watt, President Ronald Reagan's Secretary of the Interior, banned Independence Day concerts on the Mall by such groups. Watt said that "rock bands" that had performed on the Mall on Independence Day in 1981 and 1982 had encouraged drug use and alcoholism and had attracted "the wrong element", who would mug people and families attending any similar events in the future.[42] During the ensuing uproar, The Beach Boys stated that the Soviet Union, which had invited them to perform in Leningrad in 1978, "obviously .... did not feel that the group attracted the wrong element".[42] Vice President George H. W. Bush said of The Beach Boys, "They're my friends and I like their music".[42] Watt apologized to The Beach Boys after learning that President Reagan and First Lady Nancy Reagan were fans of The Beach Boys.[43] Nancy Reagan apologized for Watt.[44] White House staff presented Watt with a plaster foot with a hole in it, symbolizing his having shot himself in the foot with his decision.[45] In 1984, The Beach Boys gave an Independence Day concert on the Mall to an audience of 750,000 people.[46] [47] Love and Johnston most recently appeared on the Mall in 2005 for the Fourth of July concert.

Meanwhile, Dennis Wilson's personal problems continued to escalate, and on December 28, 1983, he drowned while diving from a friend's boat, trying to recover items he had previously thrown overboard in fits of rage.

Despite Dennis's death, the Beach Boys soldiered on as a successful touring act. On July 4, 1985, the Beach Boys played to an afternoon crowd of one million in Philadelphia and the same evening they performed for over 750,000 people on the Mall in Washington (the day's historic achievement was recorded in the Guinness Book of World Records). They also appeared nine days later at the Live Aid concert. That year, they released an eponymous album and enjoyed a resurgence of interest later in the 1980s, assisted by tributes such as David Lee Roth's hit version of "California Girls." In 1987, they played with the rap group The Fat Boys, performing the song "Wipe Out" and filming a video for it.

In 1988, they unexpectedly scored their first #1 hit in 22 years with the song "Kokomo" which was written for the movie *Cocktail*, becoming their biggest-selling hit ever. It was written by John Phillips, Scott McKenzie, Mike Love, and Terry Melcher. As well as producing and co-writing several of the band's later songs and albums, Melcher was a long-time friend of Bruce Johnston, and the duo recorded together as Bruce & Terry and The Rip Chords, both surf acts with a very similar California sound, before Johnston formally joined The Beach Boys. Riding on "Kokomo"'s steam, the Beach Boys quickly put out the album *Still Cruisin'*, which went gold in the U.S. and gave them their best chart showing since 1976. In 1990, the band, featuring John Stamos on drums, recorded the title track of the comedy *Problem Child*. Stamos later appeared singing lead vocals on the song "Forever" (written by Dennis Wilson) on their 1992 album *Summer in Paradise*.

Members of the band appeared on television shows such as *Full House*, *Home Improvement (TV series)*, and *Baywatch* in the late 1980s and 1990s, as well as touring regularly. In 1995, Brian Wilson appeared in the critically

acclaimed documentary *I Just Wasn't Made for These Times*, which saw him performing for the first time with his now-adult daughters, Wendy and Carnie of the group Wilson Phillips. The documentary also included glowing tributes to his talents from a host of major music stars of the '60s, '70s and '80s. In 1996, the Beach Boys guested with Status Quo on a re-recording of "Fun, Fun, Fun," which was a British Top 30 hit.

After years of heavy smoking, Carl Wilson succumbed to lung cancer on February 6, 1998 after a long battle with the disease. Although Love and Johnston continued to tour as the Beach Boys, Jardine did not participate and no other original members accompanied them. Their tours remained reliable draws, even as they came to be viewed as a nostalgia act. Meanwhile, Brian Wilson and Al Jardine (both still legally members of the Beach Boys organization) each pursued solo careers with their new bands.

On June 13, 2006, the major surviving Beach Boys (Brian Wilson, Mike Love, Al Jardine, Bruce Johnston, and David Marks) all set aside their differences and reunited for a celebration of the 40th anniversary of the album *Pet Sounds* and the double-platinum certification of their greatest hits compilation, *Sounds of Summer: The Very Best of the Beach Boys*, in a ceremony atop the Capitol Records building in Hollywood. Plaques were awarded for their efforts to all major members, with Brian Wilson accepting for his late brothers Carl and Dennis. Wilson himself implied there was a chance that all the living members (not having performed together since September 1996) would reunite again.

Court battles

Many legal difficulties developed from Brian Wilson's psychological problems. In the early 1980s, the band hired controversial therapist Eugene Landy in an attempt to help him. Landy did achieve some significant improvements in Wilson's overall condition; from his own admissions about his massive drug intake, it was highly likely that Wilson would have died if Landy had not intervened. Landy successfully treated Wilson's drug dependence, and by 1988 Wilson had recovered sufficiently to record his first solo album, *Brian Wilson.* But Landy became increasingly possessive of his star patient. After accusations that Landy was using his control over Wilson for his own benefit, the band successfully entreated the courts to separate Landy from Wilson.

In addition to the challenges over the use of the band's name and over the best way to care for Wilson, there have been three significant legal cases involving the Beach Boys in recent years. The first was Wilson's suit to reclaim the rights to his songs and the group's publishing company, Sea of Tunes, which he had signed away to his father in 1969. He successfully argued that he had not been mentally fit to make an informed decision. While Wilson failed to regain his copyrights, he was awarded $25 million for unpaid royalties.

The second lawsuit stemmed from Wilson's reclamation of his publishing rights. Soon after Wilson won his Sea of Tunes case in 1989, Mike Love discovered Murry Wilson did not properly credit him as co-writer on dozens of Beach Boys songs, including "California Girls", "Catch a Wave," "I Get Around," "When I Grow Up (To Be a Man)," "Be True to Your School," "Help Me, Rhonda," "I Know There's an Answer," and numerous others. With Mike and Brian unable to determine exactly what Mike was properly owed, Mike sued Brian in 1992 to gain credit for his co-authorship of a number of important Beach Boys songs, winning $13 million in 1994 for lost royalties. In interviews, Mike revealed that on some songs he wrote most of the lyrics, on others only a line or two. Even though Mike sued Brian, both parties said in interviews that there was no malice between them; they simply couldn't come up with an agreeable settlement by themselves.

However in November 2005, Love filed yet another lawsuit against Brian Wilson and his management. Love alleged that the UK publication *The Mail on Sunday* and Wilson's representatives gave the false impression to the readers of *The Mail on Sunday* that their joint promotional giveaway of nearly three million copies of the CD called *Good Vibrations* was authorized by Mike Love and the Beach Boys. This free CD, Love alleged, includes five of Love and Wilson's co-authored hit Beach Boys songs, and was done to promote Wilson's solo CD, *Smile*. Love also claimed that *Smile* and *Good Vibrations* were marketed using the Beach Boys' names and images without permission. The complaint sought several million dollars in damages, and also a million dollars to cover costs of advertising to

correct the perceived "damage to the band's reputation".

Love stated at the time: "Once again the people around Brian, my cousin and collaborator on many hits, who I love and care about, have used him for their own financial gain without regard to his rights, or my rights, or even the rights of the estates of his deceased brothers, Carl and Dennis, and their children... Unfortunately, history repeats itself. Because of Brian's mental issues he has always been vulnerable to manipulation. I simply want to stop the infringers and stop the deception!"[48]

There has been speculation that Love's lawsuit was an attempt to pressure Wilson into agreeing to let him continue to use the profitable Beach Boys name for his and Johnston's touring efforts.[48] Wilson's lawyers suggested in legal filings that Love was seeking to assert as personal claims the rights of the corporate holder of the Beach Boys trademark, Brother Records International, in which Love and Wilson are both shareholders.[49]

Wilson's website listed the following statement in response: "The lawsuit against Brian is meritless. While he will vigorously defend himself he is deeply saddened that his cousin Mike Love has sunk to these depths for his own financial gain."

Love's 2005 lawsuit was dismissed with prejudice on May 10, 2007 as to all the defendants, including Wilson. In a series of rulings, the court rejected all of Love's claims, including the claim that Smile was a Beach Boys project as to which Love deserved compensation from Wilson directly.[50] The court subsequently ruled that Love had to pay the legal fees of all the defendants as well.[51]

Legacy

The Beach Boys with President Ronald and First Lady Nancy Reagan, 1983

The group was inducted into the Rock and Roll Hall of Fame in 1988,[52] with Mike Love delivering a speech that assailed Mick Jagger, Paul McCartney and the Beatles, Bruce Springsteen, Billy Joel and Diana Ross.[53] The band was chosen for the Vocal Group Hall of Fame in 1998.[54] In 2001, the group received the Grammy Lifetime Achievement Award. Brian Wilson was inducted into the UK Rock and Roll Hall of Fame in November 2006.[55] In 2004, Rolling Stone Magazine ranked the Beach Boys #12 on their list of the 100 Greatest Artists of All Time [56], .[57]

In 2007, the Beach Boys were inducted into the Hit Parade Hall of Fame.[54]

The group is frequently referred to when the topic of summertime songs comes up. About.com listed *Sounds of Summer: The Very Best of The Beach Boys*, a 2003 compilation CD, as the greatest summertime hits CD.[58]

Richard Daniel Roman's Latin pop summer classic "Vive El Verano" is dedicated to the Beach Boys.

Toni Tennille, of the duo Captain & Tennille, remains the only known "Beach Girl", having once sung with the Beach Boys while on tour.

The Wilsons' Hawthorne, California house, where the Wilson brothers grew up and the group began, was demolished in 1986 to make way for Interstate 105, the Century Freeway. A Beach Boys Historic Landmark (California Landmark #1041 at 3701 West 119th Street), dedicated on May 20, 2005, marks the location. The Beach Boys continue to tour, with a backing band accompanying original members Mike Love and Bruce Johnston. Other "honorary Beach Boys", such as John Stamos and former member David Marks also make guest appearances on their tours.[59]

As of 2010, the remaining Beach Boys (Love and Johnston, minus Brian and Jardine) continue to tour.[60]

The Beach Boys logo was created by artist Jim Evans, and was originally used on the "15 Big Ones" record sleeve.

Band members

When the band first formed in 1961, it consisted of the Wilson brothers, their cousin Mike Love, and their friend Al Jardine. Jardine quickly left and was replaced by David Marks. After 16 months or so, Jardine came back, and Marks would quit soon thereafter.

Brian Wilson quit touring in 1965, and at first, Glen Campbell filled in for him. Later, when it became clear that Campbell's other commitments would interfere with The Beach Boys' touring schedule, Bruce Johnston became the permanent fill-in. Johnston would soon become a full-fledged member of the band, starting with providing backing vocals for *Summer Days (And Summer Nights!!)*.

In the early 1970s, Ricky Fataar and Blondie Chaplin, both members of The Flame, joined the band. Chaplin lasted for just under two years, with Fataar departing a year later.

With the deaths of Dennis and Carl Wilson, surviving Beach Boys include Brian Wilson, Mike Love, Al Jardine, David Marks and Bruce Johnston. However, Love has licensed the name 'The Beach Boys' for his touring group, which consists of himself, Johnston, Love's son Christian Love, Scott Totten, Randell Kirsch, John Cowsill, and Tim Bonhomme.

Discography

- *Surfin' Safari* (1962)
- *Surfin' USA* (1963)
- *Surfer Girl* (1963)
- *Little Deuce Coupe* (1963)
- *Shut Down Volume 2* (1964)
- *All Summer Long* (1964)
- *The Beach Boys' Christmas Album* (1964)
- *Today!* (1965)
- *Summer Days (and Summer Nights!!)* (1965)
- *Beach Boys' Party!* (1965)
- *Pet Sounds* (1966)
- *Smiley Smile* (1967)
- *Wild Honey* (1967)
- *Friends* (1968)
- *20/20* (1969)
- *Sunflower* (1970)
- *Surf's Up* (1971)
- *Carl and the Passions - "So Tough"* (1972)
- *Holland* (1973)
- *15 Big Ones* (1976)
- *Love You* (1977)
- *M.I.U. Album* (1978)
- *L.A. (Light Album)* (1979)
- *Keepin' the Summer Alive* (1980)
- *The Beach Boys* (1985)
- *Still Cruisin'* (1989)
- *Summer in Paradise* (1992)
- *Stars and Stripes Vol. 1* (1996)

See also

- List of songs by The Beach Boys
- *Smile*

Films

1. "Cute Mario Bros: The Blue Terror" (2008) Heroes and Villains
2. "Happy Feet" (2006) Do It Again
3. "Fantastic Mr. Fox" (2009) Heroes and Villains
4. "Hotel For Dogs" (2009) Fun, Fun, Fun
5. "Open Season 2" (2008) Shut Down Surfin' Safari
6. "Pingu Goes Ice Surfing" (2006) Surfin' USA
7. "Tomcats" (2001) I Get Around
8. "You Don't Mess With The Zohan" (2008) God Only Knows
9. "The Shaggy Dog" (2006) Pet Sounds
10. "Surf's Up" (2007) Surfin' USA Surfer Girl

Videography

- *The Beach Boys: An American Band*, High Ridge Productions (1985) Biography of the band, notable for the first commercial release of excerpts from *Smile*, including "Mrs. O'Leary's Cow". During the research for the film, the Beach Boys' recordings were copied to digital audio tape, many of which surfaced years later on bootleg CDs. Running time: 103 minutes.
- *Brian Wilson: I Just Wasn't Made for These Times*, Palomar Picture (1995) Running Time: 69 minutes.
- *Brian Wilson: A Beach Boys Story*, Biography (1999) Produced for A&E's *Biography* series. Running time: 100 minutes.
- *Endless Harmony: The Beach Boys Story*, Delilah Films (2000) Documentary produced for VH1. Includes five bonus video clips and seven 5.1 surround sound audio mixes of "California Girls", "Kiss Me, Baby", "God Only Knows", "Surf's Up", "Long Promised Road", "Sail On, Sailor", and "Do It Again". Running time: 141 minutes.

References

- Whitburn, Joel, *The Billboard Book of Top 40 Hits*, 1992.
- Wilson, Brian (with Todd Gold), *Wouldn't It Be Nice, My Own Story*, 1991. Nota Bene: It has been documented by numerous Beach Boys authors, including Andrew G. Doe, that Brian Wilson did not actually write this book and his participation in its creation was minimal. Please see http://www.esquarterly.com/bellagio/1991.html for details.
- *Complete Guide To The Music Of The Beach Boys*, a book updated in 2004 as *Brian Wilson & The Beach Boys: The Complete Guide To Their Music*, author Andrew Grayham Doe.

External links

- Official site [1]
- Brian Wilson's official site [61]
- Al Jardine's official site [62]

References

[1] http://thebeachboys.com/
[2] allmusic "The Beach Boys - Overview" (http://www.allmusic.com/cg/amg.dll?p=amg&sql=11:3ifrxqw5ldse). John Bush. Allmusic. Accessed July 12, 2008.
[3] "Still America's Band: The Beach Boys Today" (http://www.nationalreview.com/comment/comment-cherry070802.asp) Kevin M. Cherry. *National Review*. Published July 8, 2002. Accessed July 12, 2008.
[4] The Beach Boys: It must be summer, the Beach Boys are in town! (http://www.toronto.com/concerts/event/609670) *toronto.com* (http://www.toronto.com/). Accessed July 12, 2008.
[5] "Beach Boys: Sunny pop veterans are still shining" (http://news.scotsman.com/entertainment/Beach-Boys-Sunny-pop-.4091152.jp). Martin Lennon. *Scotsman.com* (http://news.scotsman.com/). Published May 16, 2008. Accessed July 12, 2008.
[6] http://www.rollingstone.com/news/story/5939214/the_idgjmmortals_the_first_fifty/
[7] "The Immortals: The First Fifty" (http://www.rollingstone.com/news/story/5939214/the_immortals_the_first_fifty). *Rolling Stone Issue 946*. Rolling Stone. . Retrieved 2008-07-08.
[8] "The Record Setters: Top 10 American Bands" (http://www.recordresearch.com/record_setters.php?id=1)
[9] (http://www.beachboysfanclub.com/bbtours.htm)
[10] Wilson, Brian (with Todd Gold), *Wouldn't It Be Nice: My Own Story*, p. 34
[11] Wilson, Brian (with Todd Gold), 1996. *Wouldn't It Be Nice: My Own Story*, Bloomsbury Paperbacks, p. 35
[12] Wilson, Brian (with Todd Gold), *Wouldn't It Be Nice: My Own Story*, p. 37-39
[13] Wilson, Brian (with Todd Gold), *Wouldn't It Be Nice: My Own Story*, p. 41
[14] Wilson, Brian (with Todd Gold), *Wouldn't It Be Nice: My Own Story*, p. 43
[15] Wilson, Brian (with Todd Gold), *Wouldn't It Be Nice: My Own Story*, p. 44.
[16] Wilson, Brian (with Todd Gold), *Wouldn't It Be Nice: My Own Story*, p. 46
[17] Wilson, Brian (with Todd Gold), *Wouldn't It Be Nice: My Own Story*, p. 45
[18] Wilson, Brian (with Todd Gold), *Wouldn't It Be Nice: My Own Story*, p. 48
[19] Wilson, Brian (with Todd Gold), *Wouldn't It Be Nice: My Own Story*, p. 51
[20] Wilson, Brian (with Todd Gold), 1996. *Wouldn't It Be Nice: My Own Story*, p. 30
[21] Wilson, Brian (with Todd Gold), *Wouldn't It Be Nice: My Own Story*, p. 30
[22] Wilson, Brian (with Todd Gold), *Wouldn't It Be Nice: My Own Story*, p. 26
[23] Wilson, Brian (with Todd Gold), *Wouldn't It Be Nice: My Own Story*, p. 32
[24] Wilson, Brian (with Todd Gold), *Wouldn't It Be Nice: My Own Story*, p. 52
[25] Wilson, Brian (with Todd Gold), *Wouldn't It Be Nice: My Own Story*, p. 53
[26] The Beach Boys (http://www.thebeachboys.com/home.aspx)
[27] Wilson, Brian (with Todd Gold), *Wouldn't It Be Nice: My Own Story*, p. 54
[28] Wilson, Brian (with Todd Gold), *Wouldn't It Be Nice: My Own Story*, p. 55
[29] The Beach Boys (http://www.rockhall.com/inductee/the-beach-boys)
[30] Carlin, Peter Ames (2006). Catch a Wave: The Rise, Fall, & Redemption of the Beach Boys' Brian Wilson. Rodale Books (New York). ISBN 13-978-1-59486-320-2.
[31] The All-TIME 100 Albums (http://www.time.com/time/2006/100albums/)
[32] (http://acclaimedmusic.net/Current/1948-02a.htm)
[33] Abbott, Kingsley (2001). The Beach Boys Pet Sounds: The Greatest Album of the Twentieth Century. Helter Skelter Pub. (London). ISBN 1-9000924-30-7.
[34] Carlin, Peter Ames (2006). 'Catch a Wave: The Rise, Fall, & Redemption of the Beach Boys' Brian Wilson', n. 27 supra.
[35] musicangle.com - By Michael Fremer - Music * Reviews * Audio * Sound * Vinyl (http://www.musicangle.com/feat.php?id=58)
[36] Psychedelicatessen, Topic: Smile Booklet? (http://smiledeli.tripod.com/smbook.html), *tripod.com*, retrieved on 2007-01-15
[37] The unusual capitalization of the title, "SMiLE", is an accident of Capitol Records' mid-1960s graphic design. Brian himself wrote it as "Smile" on his own message board.
[38] Priore, Dominic (1997), Look Listen Vibrate Smile, Last Gasp pub., collects much of the "Smile" legend in historical articles and reviews.
[39] Urban Legends Reference Page: All I Want to Do (http://www.snopes.com/risque/tattled/alliwant.asp), *snopes.com*, retrieved on 2007-01-15
[40] Endless Summer, The Beach Boys (http://www.mp3.com/albums/1194/summary.html), *mp3.com*, retrieved on 2007-01-15
[41] "July 4: Day of Music, Parades, Fireworks", *The Washington Post*, Washington, D.C., July 3, 1982, p. D1.

[42] Phil McCombs, "Watt Outlaws Rock Music on Mall for July 4", *The Washington Post*, Washington, D.C., April 6, 1983, p. A1; Phil McCombs and Richard Harrington, "Watt Sets Off Uproar with Music Ban", *The Washington Post*, Washington, D.C., April 7, 1983, pp. A1, A17.

[43] Tim Ahern, Associated Press, "Newton concert goes off despite rain", *Gettysburg Times*, Gettysburg, Pennsylvania, July 5, 1983, p. 7 (http://news.google.com/newspapers?id=soE0AAAAIBAJ&sjid=AegFAAAAIBAJ&pg=2280,5284705&hl=en) *in* Google news (http://news.google.com/). Retrieved 2010-02-18.

[44] "The Beach Boys Bio" (http://www.yuddy.com/celebrity/the-beach-boys/bio) *in* website of yuddy.com (http://www.yuddy.com) by Yuddy, LLC. © and TM Yuddy, LLC. Retrieved 2010-01-29.

[45] Associated Press, "Newton Performance Dampened by Rain", *Reading Eagle*, Reading, Pennsylvania, July 5, 1983, p. 27 (http://news.google.com/newspapers?id=SdcxAAAAIBAJ&sjid=muMFAAAAIBAJ&pg=3000,2778153&hl=en),*in* Google news (http://news.google.com/). Retrieved 2010-02-18.

[46] Richard Harrington, "Back to the Beach Boys: Rock Returns to Mall For the Fourth of July; Beach Boys to Perform On the Mall July 4", *The Washington Post*, Washington, D.C., June 6, 1984, p. B1.

[47] Timeline (http://thebeachboys.com/timeline.aspx) on website of The Beach Boys (http://thebeachboys.com) by Capitol Records. Retrieved 2010-01-29.

[48] Brian Wilson and Mike Love: More bad vibrations (http://enjoyment.independent.co.uk/music/features/article327663.ece), *independent.co.uk*, retrieved on 2007-01-15

[49] Love v. Mail on Sunday and Brian Wilson, U.S. District Court, Cent. Dist. CA, civil no. 2:05-7798, 2007 WL 4928035 (Westlaw citation, available by subscription).

[50] Love v. Mail On Sunday and Brian Wilson, et als., U.S. District Court, Cent. Dist. CA, civil no. 2:05-7798, docket entries 193 (opinion) and 197 (modified judgment May 29, 2007). In paragraph 1 of his original complaint, Love stated that "This action arises out of an international advertising and marketing scheme organized and orchestrated by Brian Wilson and his agents to promote the release of The Beach Boys' long-awaited Smile album, at the expense of fellow Beach Boy Mike Love and The Beach Boys corporate entity, Brother Records, Inc. ("BRI")."

[51] Id., 2008 WL 4678714 (9th Cir. Court of Appeals, reply brief of Brian Wilson) at pp. 27-28, summarizing District Court orders (Westlaw citation).

[52] Rock and Roll Hall of Fame Inductees: The Beach Boys (http://www.rockhall.com/hof/inductee.asp?id=65), *rockhall.com*, retrieved on 2007-01-15

[53] I Know There´s An Answer (http://www.mountvernonandfairway.de/answer2.htm)

[54] Vocal Group Hall of Fame Inductees: The Beach Boys (http://www.vocalgroup.org/inductees/beach_boys.htm), *vocalgroup.org*, retrieved on 2007-01-15

[55] Led Zeppelin make UK Hall of Fame (http://news.bbc.co.uk/1/hi/entertainment/5338196.stm), *bbc.co.uk*, retrieved on 2007-01-15

[56] http://www.rollingstone.com/news/story/5939214/the_immortals_the_first_fifty/

[57] "The Immortals: The First Fifty" (http://www.rollingstone.com/news/story/5939214/the_immortals_the_first_fifty). *Rolling Stone Issue 946*. Rolling Stone. .

[58] Top 10 Summer Pop Albums: The Beach Boys (http://top40.about.com/od/top10lists/tp/summermus.htm)- Sounds Of Summer, retrieved on 2008-01-27

[59] http://www.beachboysband.net

[60] Beach Boys på Pite Havsbad (http://www.blt.se/noje_o_kultur__/tt_noje/beach-boys-pa-pite-havsbad(1008873).gm), *BLT.se (Swedish)*, retrieved on 2008-12-02

[61] http://Brianwilson.com

[62] http://www.aljardine.com

Band Members

Blondie Chaplin

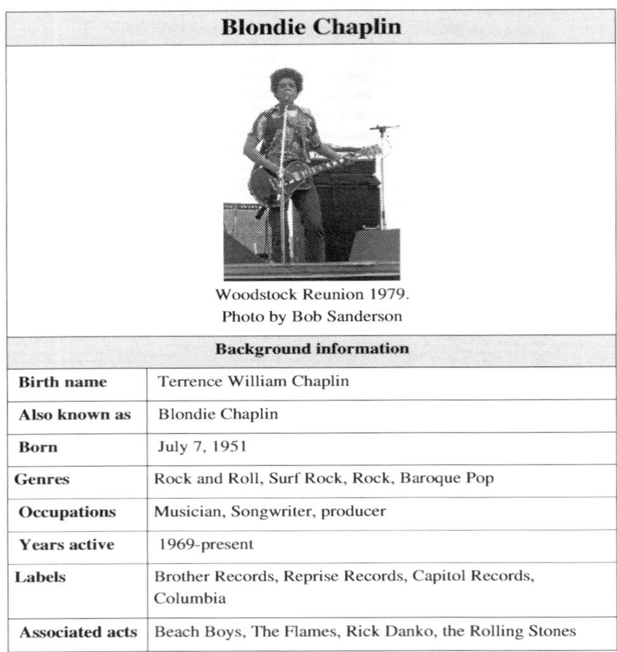

Blondie Chaplin	
Woodstock Reunion 1979. Photo by Bob Sanderson	
Background information	
Birth name	Terrence William Chaplin
Also known as	Blondie Chaplin
Born	July 7, 1951
Genres	Rock and Roll, Surf Rock, Rock, Baroque Pop
Occupations	Musician, Songwriter, producer
Years active	1969-present
Labels	Brother Records, Reprise Records, Capitol Records, Columbia
Associated acts	Beach Boys, The Flames, Rick Danko, the Rolling Stones

Terence William 'Blondie' Chaplin is a musician from Durban, South Africa who first became known to international audiences through his brief stint in the early 1970s as a singer and guitarist for The Beach Boys.[1] Chaplin was also listed as a co-producer, sang lead vocals with fellow South African musician Ricky Fataar (drummer) and composed, with Fataar, "Here She Comes" and "Hold On Dear Brother" on the twenty-third official Beach Boys album, *Carl and the Passions - "So Tough"*, released in 1972. He is well known in recent years as a long term backing vocalist and acoustic rhythm guitarist for the Rolling Stones on their tours.

Blondie Chaplin, along with drummer Ricky Fataar, joined the Beach Boys when original drummer Dennis Wilson suffered a hand injury which left him unable to play the drums for almost two years. For the Beach Boys, it was a period in which long-time member Bruce Johnston had departed the band, and one-time leader Brian Wilson's participation in the group was very limited. As a result, Chaplin and Fataar joined the Beach Boys as full-fledged members and not merely as backing musicians. Chaplin left the group in 1973 after a dispute with the Beach Boys' management; Fataar remained with the band until the following year.

Both Chaplin and Fataar were members of South African rock band The Flame before joining The Beach Boys. The Flame were discovered by Beach Boy Carl Wilson while performing in London. Wilson signed the band to the Beach Boys' Brother Records label and produced their self-titled album which featured soulful rock/pop songs in the

vein of The Beach Boys and Badfinger. The Flame were the only band aside from The Beach Boys to record for Brother Records.

Chaplin sang lead on at least three Beach Boys songs, "Sail On, Sailor," "Leaving This Town" and "Funky Pretty" (all from the 1973 album *Holland*). During the late 1980s Chaplin toured with The Band, replacing some of Richard Manuel's vocals and playing guitar. Chaplin was also a featured player in former Byrds members Gene Clark and Michael Clarke's new band, titled "The 20th Anniversary Celebration of the Byrds". Chaplin then appeared on the Jennifer Warnes albums *The Hunter* and *The Well*. Since the late 1990s and the Bridges to Babylon Tour, Chaplin has been a backing vocalist and occasional guitar player for The Rolling Stones.

Chaplin has released three solo albums, most recently *Between Us* in 2006.

Discography

Other albums from the Blondie Chaplin catalogue:

- The Flames - Burning Soul/Soulfire! - 1968/69
- The Flames - The Best of the Flames, Teal Records, 1994
- The Flame - *The Flame*, Brother Records, 1970
- Blondie Chaplin - *Blondie Chaplin*, Asylum Records, 1977
- David Johansen - *Here Comes The Night*, Blue Sky Records, 1981
- Skollie, *Ostrich Man*, PVB Records, 1992
- Blondie Chaplin, *Fragile Thread*, unreleased(but in circulation), 2001
- Rick Danko, *Cryin Heart Blues*, 2005
- Anton Fig, *Figments*, 2002

External links

Official Website
[2]

References

[1] Harris, Craig. "Biography: Blondie Chaplin" (http://www.allmusic.com/cg/amg.dll?p=amg&searchlink=BLONDIE). Allmusic. . Retrieved 26 April 2010.
[2] http://www.blondiechaplin.com

Ricky Fataar

Ricky Fataar (born September 5, 1952) is a South African multi-instrumentalist of Malay descent, who has performed as both a drummer, and a guitarist. He gained fame as an actor in the comedic television movie, *The Rutles: All You Need Is Cash*, a spoof on the actual history of The Beatles, and for his performance as a member of The Beach Boys. Fataar may also be recognized for his contributions as a record producer, and has worked on projects scoring music to film and television.

Ricky Fataar behind the drums in 2008.

Music career

The Flames

Fataar's first childhood band was The Flames, a band from his birthplace of Durban, South Africa that began in 1963. He joined the band at the age of nine. The band made several recordings as well as touring all over Southern Africa and before long they became quite popular in South Africa. By the time he was twelve years old he had already won the honour of being voted as the "Best Rock Drummer in South Africa."

In 1968 the band moved to London and began touring in the United Kingdom. On one of their tours, they were spotted by a member of The Beach Boys, Carl Wilson. He was impressed by their talent and offered to sign them to the Beach Boys new record label, Brother Records.[1] The band moved to Los Angeles, US, and they recorded and released their 1970 album *The Flame* with Carl Wilson producing the album.

Beach Boys

The Flames dissolved in late 1970. Fataar and his fellow former Flame bandmate Blondie Chaplin were recruited by the Beach Boys, in 1971. Fataar was asked to play drums for the band after drummer Dennis Wilson suffered a debilitating hand accident. The duo recorded two albums with the Beach Boys, and began touring with them in 1970. The 1972 Beach Boys album *Carl and the Passions - "So Tough"* featured musical and vocal contributions from Chaplin and Fataar. It also included two songs written by the duo, "Here She Comes" and "Hold On Dear Brother". On the band's next album, *Holland*, released a year later, both musicians recorded, and provided backing vocals, including the hit single "Sail On, Sailor", on which Chaplin sang as lead vocalist. They additionally collaborated with Carl Wilson and Mike Love on the song "Leaving This Town". 1973 saw the first live album *The Beach Boys in Concert*, upon which Fataar performed. It featured a live version of the previously unreleased Chaplin/Fataar/Love collaboration "We Got Love", which was originally intended to be released on the *Holland* album, but was considered too weak a song to be included at that time.

Rutles

In 1978, Fataar starred in *All You Need Is Cash*, a mockumentary film known more commonly as "*The Rutles*", a spoof on the real life history of The Beatles, which had a follow up to a *Saturday Night Live* television sketch, which is a popular comedy show in the United States. His character was Stig O'Hara, the band's guitarist (analogous to George Harrison). He has no speaking part in the film, and indeed he is sent up as "the quiet one" in it.[1] Rikki's then wife , Penelope Tree, also appeared in *All You Need Is Cash* , as Stig's wife "Penelope". *(This in itself being a spoof of George's first wife Patti Boyd , whom was also a teen model in the 1960's.)*

Fataar is less than quiet on the two albums produced by The Rutles: **"The Rutles"** & **"Archeology"** which feature him playing guitar , bass , sitar, drums , and even singing. He would also go on to record a single with Eric Idle as **"Dirk & Stig"** titled , "Mr.Sheene" / "Ging Gang Goolie".

Other projects

Film and television scores

Fataar has also combined his talents as an actor and a musician, developing musical scores for both film and television. An example includes the composition of the score for an Australian film *Spotswood*.

As recording producer

Working in his capacity as producer, Fataar has produced the music for various films that include *High Tide*, *Les Patterson Saves the World*, and *The Coca-Cola Kid*, in which he makes a cameo appearance as an actor as well.

Other work

Fataar has worked as a session musician, notably for Ian McLagan as well as other artists, as a drummer. Fataar emigrated to Australia in 1978 where he recorded with and co-produced albums for Tim Finn, Crowded House, Jenny Morris, Peter Blakeley, and Wendy Matthews as well as various other artists.[1]

In 1979 Fataar was introduced to Bonnie Raitt, and recorded on her *Green Light* album. In 2002, he joined up with Raitt, and has been a member of Raitt's band.[2] Fataar continued to work in between other projects as a sideman for many artists, usually as a drummer.

Personal life

Richard Fataar was married to the fashion model Penelope Tree with whom he had one child, Paloma Fataar.

References

[1] Falaar Biography (http://www.imdb.com/name/nm0268813/bio)
[2] Fataar's biography as part of Bonnie Raitt's band (http://www.bonnieraitt.com/theband.php)

Al Jardine

Al Jardine	
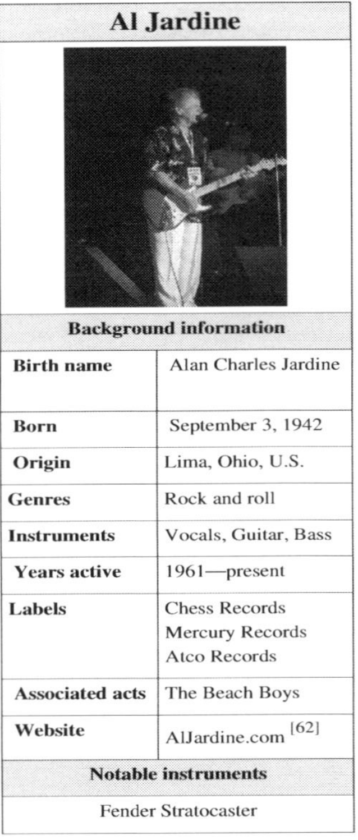	
Background information	
Birth name	Alan Charles Jardine
Born	September 3, 1942
Origin	Lima, Ohio, U.S.
Genres	Rock and roll
Instruments	Vocals, Guitar, Bass
Years active	1961—present
Labels	Chess Records Mercury Records Atco Records
Associated acts	The Beach Boys
Website	AlJardine.com [62]
Notable instruments	
Fender Stratocaster	

Alan Charles "Al" Jardine (born September 3, 1942) is a founding member of top-selling American music group The Beach Boys, their occasional lead vocalist, and one of their guitarists. He was inducted into the Rock and Roll Hall of Fame in 1988.

Early life

Jardine was born in Lima, Ohio. His family moved from Ohio to San Francisco, California, and later to Hawthorne, California. In high school, he met a fellow student, Brian Wilson, and played stand up bass on The Beach Boys' first recording, the 1961 song "Surfin'." It was long assumed that he quit soon after its release to attend college (pre-dental), but recent research has established that he attended Ferris State College (now Ferris State University) in Big Rapids, Michigan in 1960/61, prior to the formation of The Beach Boys. Following his leaving the band in early 1962, he worked in the air industry in Los Angeles. He was replaced by David Marks. The long-held belief that Jardine returned to the band as a full-fledged member when Marks quit the band in 1963 is also inaccurate. He rejoined the band in summer 1963 at the request of Brian Wilson and until October, he toured with and worked in the studio with David, until the latter left the band.

With The Beach Boys

Jardine, a member of the band for over 35 years, was the band's rhythm guitarist and harmony vocalist, and sang lead on songs such as the number one hit "Help Me, Rhonda," as well as "Come Go With Me," "Susie Cincinnati," "Then I Kissed Her," and "Lookin' at Tomorrow (A Welfare Song)," and shared the lead with other members of the band on tracks including "Break Away" and "I Know There's an Answer." Despite being the only non-family original band member, Jardine's falsetto was similar to Brian Wilson's and his voice was often substituted for Brian's in the studio and in concert.

Beginning with the *Friends* album, Jardine also wrote or co-wrote a number of songs for the band, the most notable of which is probably "California Saga: California" from the *Holland* album, which charted in early 1973. Jardine's song "Lady Lynda" was one of the band's biggest hits outside the USA. After Jardine's divorce from his wife, the song was re-written and re-titled "Lady Liberty" in honor of the centennial of the Statue Of Liberty in 1986. During the *Pet Sounds* sessions, he was the one that suggested to Brian Wilson that the group record "Sloop John B."

He also shared production credits with Ron Altbach on 1978's *M.I.U. Album*. Two of the band's late-period hits ("Lady Lynda" and "Come Go with Me") were Jardine productions, as was his 1969 rewrite of Leadbelly's "Cotton Fields," which sold successfully in the UK but only reached #103 in the US.

Post-Beach Boy career

Jardine left the touring version of the Beach Boys in 1998 after Carl Wilson died of lung cancer. Jardine remains a member of the Beach Boys corporation Brother Records and tours with his Endless Summer Band containing many of the stage musicians who toured with The Beach Boys, including Billy Hinsche of Dino, Desi and Billy, Ed Carter, Bobby Figueroa, and Jardine's son Matt Jardine, who sang with the Beach Boys during much of their later career.

In the fall of 2006, Jardine joined the band of Brian Wilson for a short tour celebrating the 40th anniversary of *Pet Sounds*.

In March 2008, Jardine settled a suit brought against him by Mike Love and the estate of Carl Wilson regarding use of the "Beach Boys" name.[1]

Recently, Jardine has been putting finishing touches to what will be his first full-length solo studio album, with contributions from fellow Beach Boys Brian Wilson, David Marks, and Mike Love - along with guest appearances from Steve Miller, Gerry Beckley, Dewey Bunnell (members of America). It will also feature a cover of "Honkin' Down the Highway" from the 1977 album *The Beach Boys Love You*.

External links

- Al Jardine's official site [2]

References

[1] http://www.tmz.com/2008/03/20/beach-boys-wouldnt-it-be-nice-to-settle-lawsuit/
[2] http://www.aljardine.com/

Bruce Johnston

Bruce Arthur Johnston	
Bruce Johnston, 2006	
Background information	
Birth name	Benjamin Baldwin
Born	June 27, 1942 Peoria, Illinois, U.S.
Origin	Los Angeles, California
Years active	Late 1950s–Present
Associated acts	The Rip Chords, The Beach Boys

Bruce Arthur Johnston (born **Benjamin Baldwin** on June 27, 1942 in Peoria, Illinois) is a member of The Beach Boys and a songwriter, remembered especially for composing "I Write the Songs".[1] Johnston was not one of the original members of the band. He joined the band on April 9, 1965 after Glen Campbell (who was substituting on stage for the group's chief song writer Brian Wilson) decided to embark on a solo career. Johnston's first vocal recording with the Beach Boys was "California Girls."

Biography

As a child Johnston was adopted by William and Irene Johnston of Chicago, and grew up on the West side of Los Angeles in Brentwood and Bel-Air. His adoptive father was president of the Owl Rexall Drug Company in Los Angeles after moving from Walgreens in Chicago. Johnston attended private school in Los Angeles and also studied classical piano in his early years. In high school, Johnston switched to contemporary music. He performed in a few "beginning" bands during this time and then moved on to working with young musicians such as Sandy Nelson, Kim Fowley and Phil Spector. Soon Johnston began backing people such as Ritchie Valens, the Everly Brothers, and even Eddie Cochran. In 1959 while still in high school, Johnston arranged and played on his first hit record called "Teenbeat" by Sandy Nelson. The single record reached the Billboard Top Ten. The same year Johnston made his first single under his own name, "Take This Pearl" on Arwin Records (a record label owned by Doris Day) as part of the Bruce & Terry duo.

In 1960 Johnston started his record production career at Del-Fi Records, producing five singles and an album — *Love You So* — by Ron Holden (for good measure, all but two of the album's eleven tracks were written or co-written by him). In 1962 and 1963 Johnston resurrected his recording career with a series of surfin' singles (vocal & instrumental) and an album, *Surfin Around The World*, credited to Bruce Johnston and another "live" album, The Bruce Johnston Surfin' Band's *Surfer's Pajama Party*. In 1963 came the first collaboration with his friend Terry Melcher, a mostly instrumental covers album credited to The Hot Doggers. The first artist the pair produced was a group called The Rip Chords. Johnston and Melcher were now working as staff producers at Columbia Records, Hollywood and by the time they were producing the million selling "Hey Little Cobra," a knock-off of the Beach

Boys car song vocal style, they also wound up singing every layered vocal part for the recording using an Ampex three track recording machine (without sel-sync!). The two of them made a few recordings as Bruce & Terry, or The Rogues, but Terry Melcher began to focus more on his production career (The Byrds, Paul Revere and The Raiders). On April 9, 1965, Johnston joined the Beach Boys, replacing Glen Campbell who was playing bass on the road and singing Brian Wilson's vocal parts. Johnston did not start playing bass until his first tenure with the Beach Boys, and the very first vocal recording Johnston made as one of the Beach Boys was *California Girls*. On his solo album from 1977, *Going Public*, he recorded a version of the Lynsey De Paul-penned "Won't Somebody Dance With Me". He also scored a hit on the disco charts with a dance-oriented remake of the Chantays' hit "Pipeline". Also in 1977 he sang back-up vocals on Eric Carmen's LP, *Boats Against the Current*, and can be clearly heard on the hit single, "She Did It."

Johnston is frequently credited as one of the original greatest supporters of the Beach Boys' 1966 signature album *Pet Sounds*. He flew to London in May 1966 and played the album for John Lennon and Paul McCartney. He wrote several Beach Boy songs, notably 1971's "Disney Girls (1957)", a favorite of Brian Wilson's, which was covered by both Captain & Tennille and Art Garfunkel.

He wrote the Billboard number one, Barry Manilow hit ("I Write the Songs") for which he won a Grammy. "I Write The Songs" has been recorded by over two hundred artists (including Frank Sinatra) and it currently has a cumulative singles/albums worldwide sales figure of twenty-five million copies. In addition, Johnston wrote backing vocal arrangements and also sang on the recordings for Elton John's "Don't Let The Sun Go Down On Me" and Pink Floyd's album *The Wall."*

Johnston left the Beach Boys in 1972, returning to the fold in 1979 to appear on (and produce) the album *L.A. (Light Album)*. As of 2010, Johnston is still a member of the touring version of The Beach Boys, performing 170 concerts a year. Despite his long involvement with the band he no longer has a full membership in Brother Records having traded his shares (but not his artist royalties) in 1972. Johnston still retains his equal ownership of the band's ASCAP publishing company, Wilojarston, and is the only member of the band to have earned a Song of the Year Grammy.

See also

- The Beach Boys

External links

- Bruce Johnston [2] at the Internet Movie Database
- Bruce Johnston solo discography (very basic) [3]
- Beach Boys Band [4] — current touring band

References

[1] Ankeny, Jason. "Biography: Bruce Johnston" (http://www.allmusic.com/cg/amg.dll?p=amg&searchlink=BRUCE). Allmusic. . Retrieved 21 May 2010.

[2] http://www.imdb.com/name/nm0426552/

[3] http://www.btinternet.com/~bellagio/bruce.html

[4] http://BeachBoysBand.net/

Mike Love

Mike Love	
 Mike Love in concert, June 2006.	
Background information	
Birth name	Michael Edward Love
Born	March 15, 1941
Origin	Los Angeles, CA, U.S.
Genres	Pop Rock Surf
Occupations	Vocalist
Instruments	Vocals Saxophone Electro-Theremin

Michael Edward "Mike" Love (born March 15, 1941) is an American singer/songwriter and musician with The Beach Boys. He formed the band along with his cousins Brian, Carl, and Dennis Wilson, and their friend Al Jardine.

Role in The Beach Boys

Although Love played the saxophone in the early days, he was mainly the co-lead singer, along with Brian Wilson, of the Beach Boys. Love sang the lead vocal on many of the Beach Boys' biggest hits, including, "Surfin' Safari", "Surfin' USA", "Little Deuce Coupe", "Be True to Your School", "Fun, Fun, Fun", "Little Saint Nick", "I Get Around", "When I Grow Up (To Be a Man)" and "California Girls". His lead vocal roles later diminished as other members' voices began to be heard more, but he remained one of the most recognized voices in the group, due in part to his nasal sound, on songs such as "Do It Again". He is also known for his bass vocals, such as the vocal break in "I Can Hear Music" and the bass line in "Good Vibrations". Onstage, Love has always served as the Beach Boys' MC, introducing songs and band members.

Love also wrote or co-wrote lyrics to many of the Beach Boys songs, mostly with the themes of surfing, cars or love, but also memorable ballads such as "The Warmth of the Sun". In the 1990's he initiated and won a legal proceeding to gain co-authorship credit for many of the Beach Boys hits.

Love was one of the first pop musicians to become involved in the practice of Transcendental Meditation, through his meeting with the Maharishi Mahesh Yogi. As a result he accompanied The Beatles, Donovan, Prudence Farrow, and Mia Farrow on their famous trip to the guru's ashram at Rishikesh in India in early 1968. Love remains an advocate and teacher of the benefits of Transcendental Meditation.

In 1988 the Beach Boys had a US number-one hit with "Kokomo", the only number-one song the band had without Brian Wilson's involvement. Mike Love (along with "Kokomo" co-writers Scott McKenzie, Terry Melcher, and John Phillips) was nominated for a Golden Globe Award (1988) in the Original Song category, and was nominated for a Grammy Award as well.

As of 2009, Love continues to tour with The Beach Boys, along with Bruce Johnston and a supporting band of new musicians. He is the only original member in the current lineup.

Smile

Love is reported to have vehemently objected to Van Dyke Parks' oblique lyrics to *Smile*, reserving particular scorn for the song "Cabinessence." During a heated argument at a recording session, Love demanded that Parks explain the song's meaning; Parks demurred and walked out; some few weeks later he officially terminated his partnership with Wilson. Although Love allegedly had nothing personal against Parks, he apparently feared the lyrics were too abstract for a Beach Boys record.[1]

Love contributed lyrics to their famous 1966 single "Good Vibrations", although the song also has an earlier set of lyrics written by Wilson's main *Pet Sounds* collaborator, Tony Asher, which Wilson restored on the 2004 *Smile* version.

Legal controversies

In the late 1990s Brian Wilson went to court to regain his rights to the publishing company, Sea of Tunes, which owned the copyrights to most of the Beach Boys' hit songs. The suit stemmed from Wilson's forced decision to sign over his publishing rights to his father Murry Wilson in 1969, but when the suit came to court it was found that the contract Wilson had signed was not valid because of the mental problems he was suffering from at the time. (It was even suggested that Murry had signed his son's name on the document.) Wilson failed to regain the copyrights, but won a $25 million settlement.

Following Wilson's win, Love launched his own lawsuit, claiming that he had made significant writing contributions to many Beach Boys songs, including two titles on *Pet Sounds* and "California Girls", and never received due credit (or the accompanying royalties). Love won the case, due in no small part to Brian's statements that Mike's assertions were correct (although Tony Asher has unequivocally stated that Love had no input into at least one song involved, "Wouldn't It Be Nice"). As a result, he was granted $13 million of Wilson's award, and his name was retroactively added to the writing credits on all subsequent releases of those songs. (Love and Wilson reportedly had no malice toward each other in the lawsuit; unable to come to terms, they resorted to going to court to settle matters.)

Love has also initiated successful lawsuits against Al Jardine (mostly the Beach Boys' company, Brother Records, suing Jardine at Love's instigation, but also personal lawsuits) for Jardine's use of the band name *Beach Boys Family And Friends* in his solo work.

Most recently, Love initiated a lawsuit on November 3, 2005 against Brian Wilson and the Mail On Sunday newspaper, arguing that both misused the Beach Boys' name and Love's image in a promotional CD that was given with the paper to promote the 2004 *Smile* release, and also arguing that Wilson has misused the Beach Boys' name in other promotions relating to *Smile*, resulting in loss of income for the band. He sought several million dollars in damages plus a million dollars to cover costs of advertising to correct the perceived damage to the band's reputation.

The lawsuit was thrown out of court on May 16, 2007 on the grounds that it was meritless.[2]

Solo career

Love has attempted several times to have a career outside the Beach Boys. In the mid 1970s he recorded and released two albums with side band Celebration, including the top 30 hit single "Almost Summer" (co-written with Brian Wilson and Jardine), along with further songwriting contributions to the band's third (unreleased) album "Disco Celebration". In the late 1970s he also recorded two unreleased solo albums, *First Love* and *Country Love*. Some tracks from *First Love* were used on later Beach Boys releases.

In 1981 he released a solo album, *Looking Back With Love*. Consisting mostly of cover versions, the album was neither critically nor commercially successful.

After that point he confined himself to guest spots on recordings alongside artists such as Dean Torrence of Jan And Dean and The Association, contributing to the albums "Rock'n'Roll City", "Rock 'n Roll Again," "Winter Party On The Beach (aka "Scrooge's Rock'n'Roll Christmas")" and "New Memories". He also developed a penchant for re-recording old Beach Boys' hits, released on packages like "Catch a Wave" and "Salute Nascar" with Adrian Baker. He has also lent his vocal abilities to a 2003 Bruce Springsteen tribute CD (singing "Hungry Heart"), and a Bruce Johnston–produced album for the Kings Singers, amongst others.

Also, in 2003 he announced plans for a new solo album. This album, which has been announced under the working titles *Unleash The Love* and *Mike Love, Not War* (not to be confused with the Beach Boys bootleg of the same name), is still a work in progress (although bootleg recordings have appeared) and, to date, one new track from these sessions, "Cool Head, Warm Heart", has appeared on an official Beach Boys–related collection.

Discography

- *Looking Back with Love* (1981)
- Mike Love: *Catch a Wave* (Limited Edition CD 1996) MELECO - MEL CD 101 - 1996
- Mike Love, Bruce Johnston & David Marks: *Salute NASCAR* (Limited Edition)
- Mike Love & Bruce Johnston: *Summertime Cruisin'* (Limited Edition CD 2001)
- "Santa's Goin' To Kokomo" (single) (iTunes download 2006)
- "Hungry Heart" (single) (iTunes download 2007)

Family

Love was born in Los Angeles, California, the son of Emily Glee (née Wilson) and Edwin Milton Love. In addition to being cousin to the Wilson brothers, Love is the brother of former NBA basketball player Stan Love and of Pink Martini harpist Maureen Love, and the uncle of Minnesota Timberwolves basketball player Kevin Love, who was named Naismith Male Prep Player of the Year in 2007. Love's son Christian Love tours with The Beach Boys in their backing band.

See also

- The Beach Boys
- List of songs by Mike Love
- Beach Boys Historic Landmark

External links

- Mike Love Fan Club [3]
- Beach Boys Band - Current Touring Band [4]
- Jan & Dean Official Site (Mike & Dean era related) [5]

References

[1] The Beach Boys: Endless Harmony Documentary

[2] Beach Boys lawsuit dismissed - Los Angeles Times (http://www.latimes.com/entertainment/news/business/la-et-quick16.1may16,1,6718298.story?ctrack=1&cset=true)

[3] http://www.mikelovefanclub.com/bio.html

[4] http://www.BeachBoysBand.net/

[5] http://www.jananddean.moonfruit.com/

David Marks

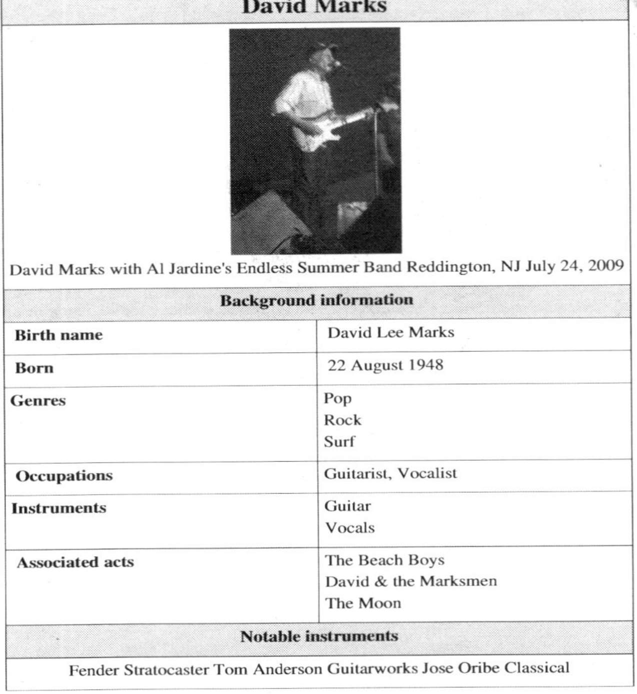

David Marks	
David Marks with Al Jardine's Endless Summer Band Reddington, NJ July 24, 2009	
Background information	
Birth name	David Lee Marks
Born	22 August 1948
Genres	Pop Rock Surf
Occupations	Guitarist, Vocalist
Instruments	Guitar Vocals
Associated acts	The Beach Boys David & the Marksmen The Moon
Notable instruments	
Fender Stratocaster Tom Anderson Guitarworks Jose Oribe Classical	

David Lee Marks (born August 22, 1948) is a songwriter and musician. He is best known as being a member of The Beach Boys from February 1962 to October 1963, a period of time that established the band as a top-rate American rock group.

Early Biography

Sometimes referred to by Beach Boys historians as the "Lost" Beach Boy, Marks was part of the group's line-up when they signed with Capitol Records on July 16, 1962 - he played rhythm guitar and sang harmony vocals.

As a child, David had moved in across the street from the family home of the three Wilson brothers in 1956, and as the 50s progressed began singing and playing music with them on their family Sunday night singalongs.[1] Inspired by seeing a 1958 performance by guitarist John Maus (later of the 60s hit-making group the Walker Brothers) David asked his parents to buy him a guitar. His wish came true on Christmas Eve, 1958. He began taking lessons from Maus (who had himself been a student of legendary early rocker Ritchie Valens) almost at once.[1]

In 1959, David Marks and Brian Wilson's youngest brother Carl had begun to develop their own style of playing electric guitars (David having introduced Maus to Carl, they both had the same teacher.)[1] Brian eventually realized that the combination of Carl and David could bring a rock guitar sound to his original compositions, and the two then-teenagers were participants in Brian's first songwriting efforts that led to the later hit single Surfer Girl.[1]

However, David was not on the Beach Boys first recording Surfin' for Candix Records on October 16, 1961; this roster included the nearly six year older Al Jardine, a high school classmate of Brian's who had been singing and playing stand-up bass with the Wilson brothers and their cousin Mike Love. [2] Over the next couple of months, Brian experimented with various combinations of musicians, including his mother Audree Wilson, but was not able to secure interest from a major label.

David Marks, Beach Boy

In mid-February 1962, a new line-up, which included then 13 year old David Marks, was established. On April 16, 1962, the newly electrified Beach Boys recorded a demo session at Western Recorders that produced the masters for the songs, “Surfin’ Safari” and “409” that would became the band’s first double-sided hit, landing them a long-term contract with Capitol Records.

David's guitar chemistry with Carl notably changed the sound of the band, notes his biographer Jon Stebbins. Writing about the difference between The Beach Boy's Candix Records single and their first Capitol Records release, Stebbins states

> Compared to 'Surfin', this was metal. No sign of stand-up bass or folk sensibility on this recording. And the tiny amateurish guitar sound and lazy feel of the [earlier demo] World Pacific version of 'Surfin' Safari' had now transformed into something crisp and modern. "It was Carl and Dave who brought that electric guitar drive into the band," says Al Jardine."And because of that, Brian was able to expand a little bit."

David Marks would continue to sing and play rhythm guitar with the Beach Boys long enough to record on the first four (plus) albums, as well as early hits such as "Surfin Safari", “409”, "Surfin USA", “Shut Down”, "Surfer Girl", "In My Room" and "Be True to Your School". David also played well over 100 live performances with The Beach Boys, touring across the United States from Hawaii to New York and appeared on their first string of National TV appearances. While his time in the band may have been relatively short, David Marks contributed to the foundational sound of one of America's most influential pop groups and the iconic image of 5 Pendelton clad teens holding a surf board on a California beach would forever be engrained in American pop culture.

Although it is often assumed that David Marks left the Beach Boys because Al Jardine wanted to return to the band, this is not the case. Marks and Jardine were both part of the 1963 Beach Boys touring line-up. Al Jardine initially returned on a part-time basis to fill-in on bass for Brian Wilson, who had already begun to detach himself from the touring band as early as the spring of 1963.

At the height of their first initial wave of International success, Marks quit The Beach Boys in late August 1963 toward the end of the group's summer tour during an argument with Murry Wilson, but did not immediately leave the band until later that year when his parents and Murry came to blows over financial and managerial issues. The first show without David Marks on guitar was Oct 31, 1963, though he would stay friends and be in close contact with various band members for many years, and he would remain, unbeknown to him, a legal member of the Beach Boys until September 27, 1967.[1]

Post-Beach Boys Career in the 60s

In February 1963, Dennis Wilson was injured in a car accident and his replacement was a Hawthorne High friend of Carl Wilson's named Mark Groseclose. David and Mark became fast friends and David eventually took over Mark's garage band, The Jaguars - which he quickly renamed The Marksmen. The band was initially a side project for the aspiring songwriter, who was growing tired of his songs being passed over for Beach Boys records by Murry Wilson.

After Marks left the Beach Boys, The Marksmen became his full-time focus - becoming one of the first acts to be signed to Herb Alpert's A&M Records in 1964. Reportedly, still-hostile Murry Wilson had threatened radio deejays in order to keep them from playing The Marksmen's records.[1] Later, the group signed with (and released a single on) Warner Bros. Records, but in spite of packed concert venues up and down the State of California, lack of air play precluded any further releases. The 2009 release of David Marks & the Marksmen Ultimate Collector's Edition 1963 – 1965 marks the first-time the entire Marksmen catalog was made available to the public.

In 1966 Marks played with Casey Kasem's Band Without a Name. He then worked with the late 60s psych-pop band, The Moon along with Matt Moore, Larry Brown and David Jackson. The band signed a production deal with producer Mike Curb and released two under-promoted albums on the Imperial label, which are nevertheless regarded as 60s classics. [1] He also performed with Delaney and Bonnie, Colours (recording lead guitar on their second album), and Warren Zevon.[1] By the time David Marks was 21 years old, he'd been signed to five major label deals and had grown disillusioned with the LA music scene. In 1969 he relocated to the Boston area from L.A., where he studied jazz and classical guitar as a private student at the Berklee College of Music and the New England Conservatory, in 1970-71.

1971-Present

In early 1971, after reuniting onstage in Boston with The Beach Boys, Marks received an offer from Mike Love to rejoin the band; however, he declined. [1] Instead, he spent the next 25 years playing with artists like Buzz Clifford (Baby Sittin' Boogie) Daniel Moore (writer of My Maria, Shambala) Gary Montgomery (Colours), Jim Keltner, Carl Radle, Leon Russell, drummer-turned-actor, Gary Busey, Delbert Mc Clinton and many others, earning a reputation as a solid session guitarist without cashing in on his notoriety as having been a Beach Boy. In 1988, when The Beach Boys were inducted into The Rock and Roll Hall of Fame, David Marks was neither invited nor acknowledged at the ceremony – an oversight which was finally rectified in 2007.

Marks eventually rejoined The Beach Boys as a full time member on lead guitar in 1997 when Carl Wilson, fighting cancer, was unable to continue touring with the group. After playing another 300 shows as an official "Beach Boy" again, Marks left the band for a second time in 1999 due to his own health issues when he was diagnosed with Hepatitis C.

David became a leading light in the bid to raise awareness of this disease, often appearing in the media to highlight the cause.[1] , and during 2007, working alongside aforementioned noted author Jon Stebbins, David published his autobiography "The Lost Beach Boy", which detailed his early career as a member of America's most famous band, as well as uncovering the dramatic truth about his 'lost years', the fight against his illness, his musical wanderings and his ultimate recovery and acceptance within the Beach Boys community.

On May 20, 2005 the original Beach Boys six man line-up (including both Marks & Jardine) was memorialized on the Beach Boys Historic Landmark in Hawthorne, California literally and forever cementing David Marks' place in history as one of the founding members of The Beach Boys. The following year, on June 13, 2006 Marks gathered with surviving Beach Boys Brian Wilson, Al Jardine, Mike Love and Bruce Johnston on the roof of the landmark Capitol Records building in Hollywood, where all five were presented with an RIAA Platinum record Award in recognition of two million in sales of The Beach Boys CD song collection Sounds of Summer: The Very Best of The Beach Boys.[1]

Now free of the threat of the Hepatitis C virus, and happily married to wife Carrie, he spends his time exploring new musical ventures, whilst regularly acknowledging the contributions he made in the past to the many hits by the Beach Boys by appearing onstage alongside his former band members in various off-shoots of the original line-up. In 2008, following the release of a career retrospective, "The Lost Years" (released to coincide with his autobiography), he toured the UK as a 'special guest' with the Beach Boys. He still occasionally performs with them as well as Al Jardine and Dean Torrence of Jan & Dean, as the Legends of Surf Music.

Solo discography

- Work Tapes (Compiled 1992 / Released 2000)
- Something Funny Goin' On (2003) Quiver Records
- The Marks-Clifford Band "Live At The Blue Dolphin '77" (2006)
- I Think About You Often (2006) Quiver Records
- The Lost Years : Limited Edition 3-CD Set (2008) Quiver Records
- The Marksmen : The Ultimate Collectors Edition (2008) Quiver Records

Published Biography

- 'The Lost Beach Boy', Jon Stebbins with David Marks, Virgin Books 2007

See also

- Beach Boys Historic Landmark

External links

- Official website [3]
- David Marks 2008 Interview on ilikemusic.com [4]

References

[1] Stebbins, Jon (2007). *The Lost Beach Boy*. London: Virgin Books Ltd. pp. 18. ISBN 978 1 8522 7391 0.
[2] Leaf, David (1978). *The Beach Boys and the California Myth*. Kingsport,Tennessee: Kingsport Press. pp. 27. ISBN 0 89471 412 0.
[3] http://www.davidleemarks.com/
[4] http://www.ilikemusic.com/interviews/The_Beach_Boys_David_Marks_Interview_2008-5009

Brian Wilson

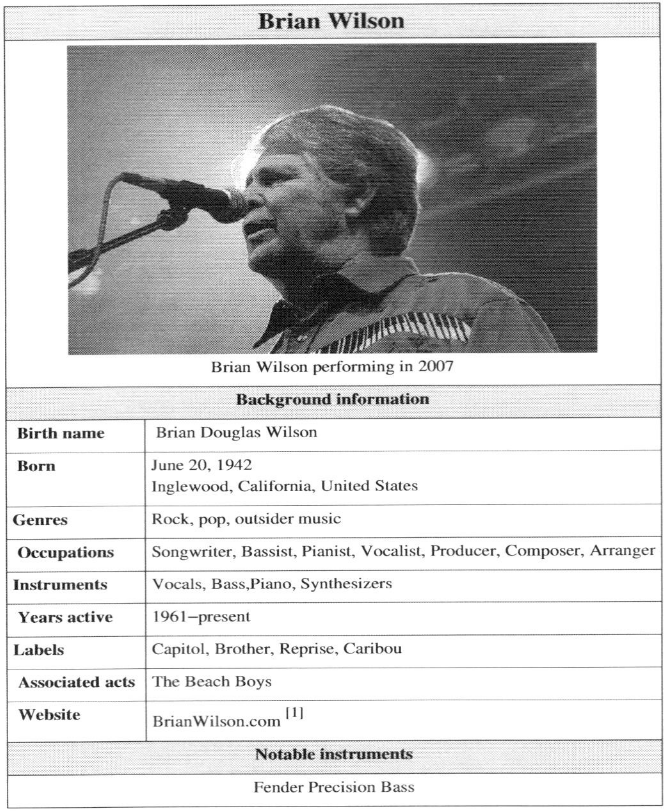

Brian Wilson	
Brian Wilson performing in 2007	
Background information	
Birth name	Brian Douglas Wilson
Born	June 20, 1942 Inglewood, California, United States
Genres	Rock, pop, outsider music
Occupations	Songwriter, Bassist, Pianist, Vocalist, Producer, Composer, Arranger
Instruments	Vocals, Bass,Piano, Synthesizers
Years active	1961–present
Labels	Capitol, Brother, Reprise, Caribou
Associated acts	The Beach Boys
Website	BrianWilson.com [1]
Notable instruments	
Fender Precision Bass	

Brian Douglas Wilson (born June 20, 1942 in Inglewood, California) is an American musician, best known as the leader and chief songwriter of the rock group The Beach Boys. Within the band, Wilson played bass and keyboards, also providing part-time lead vocals and, more often, backing vocals, harmonizing in falsetto with the group.

Wilson was the primary songwriter in The Beach Boys, also functioning as the band's main producer, composer, and arranger. In 1988, Wilson and his band-mates were inducted into the Rock and Roll Hall of Fame, which refers to Wilson on its website as "One of the few undisputed geniuses in popular music".[2] In 2008, *Rolling Stone* magazine published a list of the "100 Greatest Singers of All Time", and ranked Wilson number 52.[3] Wilson won a Grammy Award in 2005 for "Mrs. O'Leary's Cow (Fire)" as Best Rock Instrumental. He is also an occasional actor and voice actor, having appeared in television shows, films, and other music artist music videos.

Life and career

Early years

Wilson was born June 20, 1942 at Centinela Hospital in Inglewood, California.[4] When Brian was two,[5] the Wilson family moved from Inglewood to 3701 West 119th Street in nearby Hawthorne, California, a town in the greater Los Angeles urban area about five miles inland from the Pacific Ocean. He spent his entire subsequent childhood years in this middle-class family home.[6]

Brian Wilson's father Murry Wilson told of Brian's unusual musical abilities prior to his first birthday, observing that the baby could repeat the melody from "When the Caissons Go Rolling Along" after only a few verses had been sung by the father. Murry stated, "He was very clever and quick. I just fell in love with him."[7]

At about age two, Brian heard George Gershwin's "Rhapsody in Blue", which had an enormous emotional impact on him.[8] A few years later Brian was discovered to have extremely diminished hearing in his right ear. The exact cause of this hearing loss is unclear, though theories range from Brian's simply being born partially deaf, to a blow to the head from Brian's father, or a neighborhood bully, being to blame.[9]

While father Murry was ostensibly a reasonable provider, he was abusive and hard to please, liable to dispense harsh punishments for minor or perceived misdeeds. But Murry, a minor musician and songwriter, also encouraged his children in this field in numerous ways. At a young age, Brian was given six weeks of lessons on a "toy accordion", and at seven and eight sang solos in church with a choir behind him.[10]

By most accounts a natural leader by the time he began attending Hawthorne High School, Brian was on the football team as a quarterback, played baseball and was a cross-country runner in his senior year.[11] However, most of his energy was directed toward music. He sang with various students at school functions and with his family and friends at home. Brian taught his two brothers harmony parts that all three would then practice when they were supposed to be asleep. He also played piano obsessively after school, deconstructing the harmonies of The Four Freshmen by listening to short segments of their songs on a phonograph, then working to recreate the blended sounds note by note on the keyboard.[12] Brian received a Wollensak tape recorder on his sixteenth birthday, allowing him to experiment with audio overdubs and early group vocals.[13]

First steps: Carl and the Passions

Wilson's surviving home tapes document his initial musical efforts singing with various buddies and family, including a song that would later be recorded in the studio by The Beach Boys, "Sloop John B", as well as "Bermuda Shorts" and a hymn titled "Good News". In his senior year at Hawthorne High, in addition to his classroom music studies, he would gather at lunchtime to sing with friends like Keith Lent, Bruce Griffin, and Robin Hood. Brian and Lent worked on a revised version of the tune "Hully Gully" to support the campaign of a classmate named Carol Hess who was running for senior class president. When performed for a full high school gathering, Brian's revised arrangement received a warm round of applause from the student audience.[14]

Enlisting his cousin and often-time singing partner Mike Love, and Wilson's reluctant youngest brother Carl Wilson, Brian's next public performance featured more ambitious arrangements at a fall arts program at his high school. To entice Carl into the group, Wilson named the newly-formed membership "Carl and the Passions". The performance featured tunes by Dion and the Belmonts and The Four Freshmen ("It's a Blue World"), the latter of which proved difficult for the ensemble to carry off. However, the event was notable for the impression it made on another musician and classmate of Brian's who was in the audience that night, Al Jardine, later to join the three Wilson brothers and Mike Love in The Beach Boys.[15]

Initial compositions and the Pendletones

Brian enrolled at El Camino Community College in Los Angeles, majoring in psychology, in September 1960. However, he continued his music studies at the college as well.[16] At some point in the year 1961 Brian wrote his first all-original melody, loosely based on a Dion and the Belmonts version of "When You Wish Upon a Star". Brian's tune would eventually be known as "Surfer Girl". Brian has commented that he wrote the melody in his car, then later at home finished the bridge and harmonies. Although an early demo of the song was recorded in Feb. 1962 at World-Pacific Studios, it was not re-recorded and released until 1963, when it became a top ten hit.[17]

Brian and his brothers Carl and Dennis Wilson along with Mike Love and Al Jardine first jelled as a music group in the summer of 1961, initially named the Pendeltones. After being prodded by Dennis to write a song about the local water sports craze, Brian and Mike Love together created what would become the first single for the band, "Surfin'". Recorded by Hite and Dorinda Morgan and released on the small Candix label, the song became a top local hit in Los Angeles and reached number seventy-five on the national *Billboard* sales charts.[18]

Dennis later described the first time Brian heard their song on the radio as the three Wilson brothers (and soon-to-be-band member David Marks) drove in Brian's 1957 Ford in the rain: "Nothing will ever top the expression on Brian's face, ever ... THAT was the all-time moment."

However, the Pendletones were no more. Without the band's knowledge or permission, Candix Records had changed their name to The Beach Boys.[19]

First performances and the quest for a major label

Brian Wilson and his bandmates, following a set by Ike and Tina Turner, performed their first major live show at The Ritchie Valens Memorial Dance on New Year's Eve, 1961. Three days previously, Brian's father had bought him an electric bass and amplifier; Brian had learned to play the instrument in that short period of time, with Al Jardine moving to rhythm guitar.

Looking for a followup single for their radio hit, Brian and Mike wrote "Surfin' Safari," and attempts were made to record a usable take at World Pacific, including overdubs, on February 8, 1962, along with several other tunes including an early version of "Surfer Girl". Only a few days later, discouraged about the band's financial prospects, and objecting to adding some Chubby Checker songs to The Beach Boys live setlist, Al Jardine abruptly left the group.[20]

Murry Wilson had become The Beach Boys manager, and when Candix Records ran into money problems and sold the group's master recordings to another label, Murry terminated the contract. Brian, worried about The Beach Boys' future, asked his father to help his group make more recordings. But Murry and Hite Morgan (who at this point was their music publisher) were turned down by a number of Los Angeles record companies.

As "Surfin'" faded from the charts, Brian, who had forged a songwriting partnership with Gary Usher, created several new tunes, including a car song, "409", that Usher had helped write. Recruiting Carl and Dennis' friend, thirteen-year-old neighbor David Marks, who had been playing electric guitar (and practicing with Carl) for years, Brian and the revamped Beach Boys cut new tracks on April 19 at Western Recorders including an updated "Surfin' Safari" and "409". These tunes convinced Capitol Records to release the demos as a single; they became a double-sided national hit.[21]

The Beach Boys and first success with Capitol Records

After signing with Capitol Records in mid-1962, Brian Wilson wrote or co-wrote (most often with Mike Love) a series of hit singles including the aforementioned "Surfin' Safari", "Surfin' USA", "Shut Down", "Little Deuce Coupe", "Be True to Your School", "In My Room", "Fun, Fun, Fun", "I Get Around", "Dance, Dance, Dance", "Help Me Rhonda", "California Girls" and "Good Vibrations". These songs and their accompanying albums were internationally popular, making The Beach Boys one of the biggest acts of their time.[22]

Recording sessions for the band's first album took place in Capitol's basement studios (in the famous tower building) in August 1962, but early on Brian lobbied for a different place to cut Beach Boy tracks. The large rooms were built to record the big orchestras and ensembles of the 50s, not small rock groups. At Brian's insistence, Capitol agreed to let The Beach Boys pay for their own outside recording sessions, which Capitol would own all the rights to, and in return the band would receive a higher royalty rate on their record sales. Additionally, although it was very rare at the time for rock and roll band members to have a say in the process of making their records, during the taping of their first LP Brian fought for, and won, the right to be totally in charge of the production- though his first acknowledged liner notes production credit did not come until the band's third album *Surfer Girl*, in 1963.[23]

January 1963 saw the recording of the first top-ten (cresting at #3 in the United States) Beach Boys single, "Surfin' USA", which began their long run of highly successful recording efforts at Hollywood's Western Recorders on Sunset Boulevard. It was during the sessions for this single that Brian made the production decision from that point on to use doubletracking on the group's vocals, resulting in a deeper and more resonant sound.[24]

The tune, adapted from (and eventually partially credited to) Chuck Berry, is widely seen as emblematic of the early 60s American rock cultural experience.[25] The Surfin' USA album was also a big hit in the United States, reaching number two on the national sales charts by early July, 1963. Brian and his group had become a top-rank recording and touring music band.[4]

Early era as writer/producer

As previously mentioned, Brian was first credited as The Beach Boys' producer on the *Surfer Girl* album, recorded in June and July 1963 and released in September 1963. This LP reached #7 on the national charts on the strength of songs like the ballad "In My Room", later released as a single; "Catch a Wave"; and "Little Deuce Coupe", which was released as a double-sided single with the album's title track, both top-15 hits.

He also began working with other artists in this period. On July 20, 1963, "Surf City", which he had co-written with Jan and Dean, was the first surfing song to reach the pinnacle of the sales charts. While Brian was excited and happy, his father (and still-manager) Murry and Capitol Records were less than thrilled. Indeed, openly enraged by Brian's chart-topping effort for what he saw as a rival band, Murry went so far as to order his oldest son to sever any further efforts with Jan and Dean.

Brian's other non-Beach Boy work in this period included tracks by The Honeys, Sharon Marie, The Timers, and The Survivors. Feeling that surfing songs had become limiting, Brian decided to produce a set of largely car-oriented tunes for The Beach Boys' fourth album *Little Deuce Coupe*, which was released in October 1963, only three weeks after the *Surfer Girl* LP. The departure of guitarist David Marks from the band that month meant that Brian was forced to resume touring with The Beach Boys, for a time reducing his availability in the recording studio.[26]

Artistic growth

Brian became known for his unique use of vocal harmonies, his trademark style of lyrics and incessant studio perfectionism. Early influences on his music included not only the previously mentioned Four Freshmen and Chuck Berry, but also the work of record producer Phil Spector, the latter of whom obsessed Wilson for years.[27] He later considered The Beatles to be his chief rivals, and they in turn would cite his work as a major influence. Wilson also produced records for other artists, but to much lesser success, with the exception of Jan and Dean, for whom Wilson co-wrote several hit songs. Following a nervous breakdown onboard a flight from L.A. to Houston in 1964,[28] Wilson stopped performing live with the Beach Boys in an effort to concentrate solely on songwriting[29] and studio production.[28] Glen Campbell was called in as his temporary stand-in for live performances,[27] before Wilson chose Bruce Johnston as a long-term replacement—a band member who remains with the Beach Boys today. In late 1965, Wilson began working on material for a new album after hearing The Beatles' 1965 album, *Rubber Soul*.[30]

"With the 1966 Pet Sounds album, and then songs like Good Vibrations and Heroes and Villains, Wilson had become America's equivalent of The Beatles with his ability to expand the limits of popular taste."

Robin Denselow writing for *The Guardian*, September 1976[29]

As he began work on the new project, *Pet Sounds*, Wilson formed a temporary songwriting partnership with lyricist Tony Asher. Wilson, who had recorded the album's instrumentation with The Wrecking Crew, then gathered with The Beach Boys to record vocal overdubs, following their return from a tour of Japan. Upon hearing what Wilson had created for the first time in 1965,[28] the group, particularly Mike Love, was somewhat critical of their leader's music,[27] and expressed their dislike.[28] At this time, Wilson still had considerable control within the group and, according to Wilson, they eventually overcame their initial negative reaction, as his newly created music began to near completion; "They thought it was too far-out to do, you know?... But then when it was all done, they liked it. They started liking it."[28] The album was released in July 1966 and, despite modest sales figures at the time, has since become widely critically acclaimed, often being cited among the all-time greatest albums. Although the record was issued under the group's name, *Pet Sounds* is arguably seen as a Brian Wilson solo album—Wilson even toyed with the idea by releasing "Caroline, No" as a solo single in March 1966, reaching no. 32 on the *Billboard* charts.[31]

During the *Pet Sounds* sessions, Wilson had been working on another song, which was held back from inclusion on the record as he felt that it was not sufficiently complete. The song, "Good Vibrations", set a new standard for musicians, and what could be achieved in the recording studio. Recorded in multiple sessions and in numerous studios, the song eventually cost $50,000 to record within a six month period.[30] In October 1966, the song was released as a single, giving The Beach Boys their third U.S. number-one hit—alongside "I Get Around" and "Help Me, Rhonda"—and it sold over a million copies.

Smile, group tension, and Brother Records

With the surprising success of "Good Vibrations", Capitol Records had no choice but to back Wilson up for his next project, originally called *Dumb Angel*[27] but soon re-titled *Smile,* which he described as a "teenage symphony to God".[27] The album's approach was similar to "Good Vibrations" in the style of recording, which, at the time, was called modular music. This was vastly different compared to the standard live performances that were typically done in a studio at the time. After having been introduced to each other at a party, Wilson sought the lyrical assistance of L.A.-based folk singer, Van Dyke Parks, who had made a profound impression on Wilson with the "visionary eloquence" of his lyrics.[32] During the album's songwriting sessions, they collaborated on "Heroes and Villains", "Surf's Up", "Wonderful", "Vegetables" and "Mrs. O Leary's Cow". However, between December 1966 and May 1967, the *Smile* sessions fell apart due to conflict within the group and Wilson's own growing personal problems. As a result, Wilson was having problems completing the album towards the end of the recording sessions. Originally slated to be released in January 1967, the date was continually pushed back until its eventual cancellation—even "Heroes and Villains" and "Vegetables" were planned as singles within that time, but nothing appeared.

The original cover of *Smile*.

Another source of problems came from The Beach Boys deciding to file a lawsuit against Capitol Records to start their own label, Brother Records. This came at a terrible time when Wilson was trying to finish the album and, right along the way, The Beatles were working on *Sgt. Pepper's Lonely Hearts Club Band.* In April 1967, Wilson—who was suffering growing mental problems—was "deeply affected by hearing a tape of the Pepper song "A Day in the Life", which Paul McCartney played to him in Los Angeles.[33] Soon after, *Smile* was abandoned, and Wilson would not return to complete it until 2003. Van Dyke Parks later noted, "...Brian had a nervous collapse. What broke his heart was Sgt. Pepper."[32] Writing for *The Guardian* in December 1999, Will Hodgkinson summarized the main reasons for the eventual demise of Wilson's ambitious project;[32]

> [A] combination of factors, including litigations against the record company and increasing animosity between Wilson and the rest of the band, meant that in May 1967 Wilson pulled the plug on the record... [Mike] Love had already dismissed Good Vibrations as "avant-garde shit" and objected to the way Wilson, Parks and a group of highly skilled session musicians were creating music way beyond his understanding... By March 1967, the bad feeling got too much for Parks and, having no desire to break up The Beach Boys, he walked out.

Following the cancellation of *Smile*, The Beach Boys relocated to a recording studio within the confines of Brian Wilson's mansion, where the hastily compiled *Smiley Smile* album was assembled, along with a number of future Beach Boys records. This marked the end of Wilson's leadership within the band, and has been seen to be "the moment when the Beach Boys first started slipping from the vanguard to nostalgia."[28]

Mental illness

Psychologically overwhelmed by the cancellation of *Smile*, the release of The Beatles' album *Sgt. Pepper's Lonely Hearts Club Band*, and the birth of his first child Carnie in 1968, Wilson began having a diminished creative role with The Beach Boys. Until about 1970 he remained the group's principal songwriter, but increasingly production reins were handed to younger brother Carl. Carl Wilson mostly oversaw the albums *Smiley Smile*, *Wild Honey*, and *Friends*, which only performed modestly on the charts. After that, Brian Wilson all but stopped writing songs and was frequently seen partying in the company of songwriter Tandyn Almer and Three Dog Night singer Danny Hutton. It was during this period that he was introduced to cocaine. The 1969 album *20/20* was made mostly without Wilson's participation, although the Wilson/Love-authored "Do It Again" was a major hit, topping the charts in the UK.

Wilson spent the majority of the following three years in his bedroom sleeping, taking drugs, and overeating. During this time, his voice deteriorated significantly as a result of chain smoking, drug ingestion and neglect. Many of his "new" contributions to Beach Boys albums were remnants of *Smile* (e.g., "Cabinessence", "Surf's Up"), and those that were genuinely new reflected his depression and growing detachment from the world ("'Til I Die", the EP "Mount Vernon and Fairway"). Reportedly, Warner Bros. Records was so desperate for material from Wilson that the single "We Got Love" (co-written by Ricky Fataar, Blondie Chaplin, and Love) was scrapped from the *Holland* album in favor of "Sail On, Sailor", a song mostly written by committee (including Chaplin, Almer and Parks) that happened to draw its initial germ from a Wilson chord sequence.

In 1975, Brian's wife and family enlisted the services of controversial therapist Eugene Landy in a bid to help Brian, and hopefully help revive the group's ailing profile. Brian did not stay under Landy's care for long, but during this short period, the doctor managed to help him into a more productive, social frame of mind. The new album *15 Big Ones*, consisting of oldies and some new songs was released in 1976 and Brian began to regularly appear live on stage with the band. A Love-orchestrated publicity campaign announced that "Brian is Back". Brian was also deemed to be well enough to do a solo performance on *Saturday Night Live* in November 1976. In 1977, the cult favorite *Love You* was released, consisting entirely of new material written and performed by Wilson. He continues to say it is his favorite Beach Boys album.

By 1982 Eugene Landy was once more called into action, and a more radical program was undertaken to try to restore Brian to health. This involved firing him from The Beach Boys, isolating him from his family on Hawaii, and putting him onto a rigorous diet and health regimen. This, coupled with long, extreme counseling sessions, and bringing Brian back to reality. He lost a tremendous amount of weight, was certainly healthier and more conversant than previously, but he was also under a strict level of control by Landy. Brian's recovery continued as he joined the band on stage in Live Aid in 1985, and recorded the album *The Beach Boys* with the group.

Dr. Landy provided a Svengali-like environment for Wilson, controlling his every movement in his life, including his musical direction. Landy's misconduct would eventually lead to the loss of his psychologist license, [34] as well as a court-ordered removal and restraining order from Wilson.[35]

Some years later, during his second marriage, Wilson was diagnosed with schizoaffective disorder, bipolar type which supposedly caused him to hear voices in his head. By 1989 the rumor was that Brian either had a stroke or had abused too many drugs and was permanently "fried".[7] One biographer reported that the actual problem was that Wilson, who had been prescribed antipsychotic medicine by Landy since 1983, had developed tardive dyskinesia,[36] a neurological condition marked by involuntary, repetitive movements, that develops in about 20% of patients treated with antipsychotic drugs for a long period of time.[37] Wilson's drug regimen has now been reduced to a mild combination of antidepressants, and he has resumed recording and performing.

The effects of Brian Wilson's mental illness on his parenting skills were discussed by Wilson's daughter Wendy during her appearance in an episode of the British reality television program, *Supernanny*.[38] Wilson's daughter Carnie and granddaughter Lola also made an appearance on the episode.

Solo career

Wilson launched a career as a solo artist in 1988 with limited success. It is possible that his efforts in this regard were both encouraged and hampered by Landy's influence. Partly due to the control that Landy exercised on his life, Wilson stopped working with The Beach Boys on a regular basis after the release of *The Beach Boys* in 1985. He had been signed to a solo record deal with Sire Records by label boss Seymour Stein.

Wilson released a solo album, *Brian Wilson*, in 1988 and a memoir, *Wouldn't It Be Nice - My Own Story*, in which he spoke for the first time about his troubled relationship with his abusive father Murry and his "lost years" of mental illness. Although it was written following interviews with Brian and others, Landy was largely responsible for the book, in conjunction with *People* magazine writer Todd Gold. The book describes Landy in terms that could be called messianic. In a later lawsuit over the book, Wilson testified in court that he hadn't even read the final manuscript. As a result, the book was taken out of press some years later.

A second solo album made for Sire, entitled *Sweet Insanity*, was never released. Landy's illegal use of psychotropic drugs on Wilson and his influence over Wilson's financial affairs was legally ended by Carl Wilson. In 1995, Wilson married Melinda Ledbetter. The couple adopted two girls, Daria Rose and Delanie Rae, in 1998; a boy, Dylan, in 2004; and a boy, Dash Tristan[39] , in 2009. Wilson has two daughters from his first marriage to Marilyn Rovell: Carnie Wilson and Wendy Wilson, who would go on to musical success of their own in the early 1990s as two-thirds of Wilson Phillips.

Also in 1995, he released two albums, albeit neither containing any new original Wilson material, almost simultaneously. The first, the soundtrack to Don Was's documentary *I Just Wasn't Made for These Times*, consists of re-recorded versions of songs from his Beach Boys and solo catalogue produced by Was, along with a 1976-vintage demo recording. The second, *Orange Crate Art*, saw Wilson as lead vocalist, multitracked many times over, on an album of songs produced, arranged and (mostly) written by Van Dyke Parks, and was released as a duo album under both men's names.

His final release as part of the group was on the 1996 album *Stars and Stripes Vol. 1*, a group collaboration with select country music artists singing the lead vocals. After considerable mental recovery, he mended his relationship with his daughters Carnie and Wendy and the three of them released an album in 1997 titled *The Wilsons*.

Wilson released a second solo album of mostly new material, *Imagination*, in 1998. Following this, he received extensive vocal coaching to improve his voice, and learned to cope with his stage fright and started to play live for the first time in decades, going on to play the whole *Pet Sounds* album live on his tours of the United States, United Kingdom, and Europe.

A new studio album, *Gettin' in Over My Head*, was released on June 22, 2004. It featured collaborations with Elton John, Paul McCartney, Eric Clapton, and Wilson's deceased brother Carl. Clapton played on the track "City Blues." The album was almost entirely composed of re-recordings of unreleased material, and received mixed reviews.

Smile resurrected

With the improvements in his mental health, Wilson found himself able to contemplate returning to the *Smile* project. Aided by musician and long time fan Darian Sahanaja of The Wondermints, and lyricist Van Dyke Parks, Brian painstakingly worked throughout 2003 to realize the album. In February 2004, 37 years after it was conceived, Wilson debuted the newly completed *Smile* at the Royal Festival Hall in London and throughout a subsequent UK tour.

The debut performance at the RFH was a defining moment for Brian. The documentary DVD of the event shows Brian preparing for the big day and, right up to show time, expressing doubts over the concept of putting this legendary work before the public. After an opening set of Beach Boys classics, he climbed back on stage for a rousing performance of the album. A 10-minute standing ovation followed the concert; the DVD shows a sprinkling of rock luminaries in the crowd, such as Roger Daltrey, Paul Weller, Sir George Martin and Sir Paul McCartney.

Smile was then recorded through April to June and released in September, to wide critical acclaim. The release hit #13 on the Billboard chart. The 2004 recording featured his backup/touring band, including Beach Boys guitarist Jeff Foskett, members of the Wondermints and backup singer Taylor Mills. In this version, "Good Vibrations" features Tony Asher's original lyrics in the verses, instead of Mike Love's lyrics from the released 1966 version.

Wilson won his only Grammy Award in 2005 for the track "Mrs. O'Leary's Cow (Fire)" as Best Rock Instrumental. In 2004 *Smile* was taken on the road for a thorough tour of Australia, New Zealand and Europe. In December 2005, he also released *What I Really Want for Christmas* for Arista Records. The release hit #200 on the Billboard chart, though sales were modest. Wilson's remake of the classic "Deck The Halls" became a surprise Top 10 Adult Contemporary hit.

Though no longer a part of The Beach Boys touring band, Brian Wilson remains a member of the Beach Boys corporation, Brother Records Incorporated.

Recent events/*That Lucky Old Sun*

In February 2005, Wilson had a cameo in the TV series *Duck Dodgers in the 24½th Century* as Daffy Duck's spiritual surfing advisor.[40] He also appeared in the 2005 holiday episode of *Extreme Makeover: Home Edition*, performing "Deck the Halls" for a group of children with xeroderma pigmentosum (hypersensitivity to sunlight) at Walt Disney World Resort. On July 2, 2005, Wilson performed for the Live 8 concert in Berlin, Germany.

In September 2005, Wilson arranged a charity drive to aid victims of Hurricane Katrina, wherein people who donated $100 or more would receive a personal phone call from Wilson. According to the website, over $250K was raised.[41] In November 2005, former bandmate Mike Love sued Wilson over "shamelessly misappropriating... Love's songs, likeness, and the Beach Boys trademark, as well as the 'Smile' album itself" in the promotion of *Smile*.[42] The lawsuit was ultimately thrown out of court on grounds that it was meritless.[43]

On November 1, 2006, Wilson kicked off a small but highly anticipated tour celebrating the 40th anniversary of *Pet Sounds*.[44] He was joined by Al Jardine.

Wilson released a new album *That Lucky Old Sun* on September 2, 2008. The piece originally debuted in a series of September 2007 concerts at London's Royal Festival Hall, and in January 2008 at Sydney's State Theatre while headlining the Sydney Festival.[45] Wilson describes the piece as "consisting of five 'rounds', with interspersed spoken word".[46] A series of US and UK concerts led up to its release.

On September 30, 2008, Seattle's Light in the Attic Records released *A World of Peace Must Come*, a collaboration between Wilson and Stephen Kalinich, originally recorded in 1969, but later lost in Kalinich's closet.[47]

It was reported by *Rolling Stone* that Wilson is completing at least two unfinished compositions by George Gershwin for possible release in 2010.[48]

Awards and recognitions

- Brian and the Beach Boys were inducted into the Rock Hall of Fame in January 1988, alongside The Beatles and Bob Dylan.
- In 2000, Brian was inducted into the Songwriters Hall of Fame. Paul McCartney introduced Brian, referring to him as "one of the great American geniuses."[49]
- In March 2001, TNT and Radio City Music Hall hosted "An All-Star Tribute to Brian Wilson." This event featured performances and appearances by Elton John, Billy Joel, David Crosby, Paul Simon, Carly Simon, The Go-Go's, Cameron Crowe, Sir George Martin and others.
- *Pet Sounds* has been ranked as one of the most influential records in western pop music, and has been ranked #1 on several music magazines' lists of the greatest albums of all time. It is ranked #2 on Rolling Stone's 500 Greatest Albums of All Time.
- A 2005 concert, "Musicares: A Tribute to Brian Wilson," was held in Wilson's honor, during which he was named MusiCares Person of the Year. Performers included Jeff Beck, the Red Hot Chili Peppers, Earth Wind & Fire, Barenaked Ladies, and The Backstreet Boys, among others.
- On May 20, 2005, Wilson and the five other original-era Beach Boys were honored with the unveiling of the Beach Boys Historic Landmark on the former site of the Wilson family home in Hawthorne, California.
- In 2005, Wilson won the Grammy Award for Best Rock Instrumental Performance for Mrs. O'Leary's Cow.
- In November 2006, Wilson was inducted into the UK Music Hall of Fame by Pink Floyd guitarist David Gilmour. Wilson performed "God Only Knows" and "Good Vibrations" at the ceremony.
- On December 2, 2007, the prestigious Kennedy Center Honors committee recognized Brian for a lifetime of contributions to American culture through the performing arts in music.

Discography

- *Brian Wilson* (July 12, 1988)
- *I Just Wasn't Made for These Times* (August 15, 1995)
- *Orange Crate Art* (with Van Dyke Parks) (October 24, 1995)
- *Imagination* (June 16, 1998)
- *Live at the Roxy Theatre* (June, 2000)
- *Pet Sounds Live* (June 11, 2002)
- *Gettin' in Over My Head* (June 22, 2004)
- *Smile* (September 28, 2004)
- *What I Really Want for Christmas* (October 18, 2005)
- *That Lucky Old Sun* (September 2, 2008)

See also

- List of songs by Brian Wilson
- Beach Boys Historic Landmark

References

- Badman, Keith. *The Beach Boys: The Definitive Diary of America's Greatest Band on Stage and in the Studio* (Backstreet Books, 2004). ISBN 0-87930-818-4.
- Carlin, Peter Ames. *Catch a Wave: The Rise, Fall and Redemption of the Beach Boys' Brian Wilson* (Rodale Inc., 2006). ISBN 13 978-1-59486-749-1.
- Leaf, David. *The Beach Boys and the California Myth* (Kingsport Press, 1978). ISBN 0 89471 412 0.
- Lambert, Philip. *Inside the Music of Brian Wilson: the songs, sounds and influences of the Beach Boys' founding genius* (Continuum International Publishing Group Inc., 2007). ISBN 13 978 0 8264 1877 7.
- Stebbins, Jon. *The Lost Beach Boy* (Virgin Books Ltd, 2007). ISBN 978 1 8522 7391 0.

External links

- Official site [1]
- 2004 Larry King Transcript where they speak about Wilson's mental illness [50]
- "After the wipe out" by Ginny Dougary in *The Guardian* (June 1, 2002) [51]
- "Four Decades Later, Wilson's 'Smile' Hits London" Audio review at NPR (February 25, 2004) [52]
- SMiLE Timeline [53]
- Brian Wilson Pictures from 2007 Consumer Electronics Show performance [54]
- Works by or about Brian Wilson [55] in libraries (WorldCat catalog)
- January 2009 Interview [56] with L.A. Record
- This list of "outside productions" by members of the Beach Boys includes records Brian produced and-or wrote for other artists throughout his career [57]
- Cabin Essence, Web Page for Brian Wilson [58]

References

[1] http://www.brianwilson.com

[2] "Rock and Roll Hall of Fame - The Beach Boys" (http://www.rockhall.com/inductee/the-beach-boys). . Retrieved 2009-12-04.

[3] "The 100 Greatest Singers of All Time" (http://www.rollingstone.com/news/coverstory/24161972/page/103). *1060*. Jann Wenner. November, 2008. pp. 52. . Retrieved 2009-02-03.

[4] Gaines, Steven (1986). *Heroes and Villains: the true story of the Beach Boys*. New York: New American Library. p. 40. ISBN 0 306 80647 9.

[5] Leaf, p. 14

[6] Stebbins, p. 14

[7] Carlin, p. 11

[8] Carlin, p. 10

[9] Carlin, p. 12

[10] Leaf, pp. 15–17

[11] Carlin, p. 15

[12] Stebbins, p. 18

[13] Badman, p. 14

[14] Carlin, p. 23

[15] Carlin, p. 24

[16] Badman, p. 15

[17] Lambert, pp. 27–31

[18] Carlin, pp. 30–31

[19] Badman, pp. 16–17

[20] Badman, p. 20

[21] Badman, pp. 22–23

[22] Badman, pp. 34–150
[23] Badman, p. 26
[24] Badman, p. 32
[25] Lambert, pp. 64–65
[26] Badman, pp. 39–42
[27] O'Hagan, Sean. "Feature: *A Boy's own story*". *Review, The Observer* (Guardian Media Group) (January 6, 2002): 1–3.
[28] Beets, Greg (July 21, 2000). "Review: *Pet Sounds: Fifteen Minutes With Brian Wilson*" (http://www.austinchronicle.com/gyrobase/Issue/story?oid=oid:77984). Nick Barbaro. . Retrieved 29 August 2009.
[29] Denselow, Robin. "Feature: *Riding a wave*". *The Guardian* (Guardian Media Group) (September 1, 1976): 8.
[30] O'Hagan, Sean. "Feature: *The nutty producers*". *G2* (Guardian Media Group) (December 16, 1999): 10.
[31] "Review: *Pet Sounds, Charts & Awards, Billboard Singles*" (http://www.allmusic.com/cg/amg.dll?p=amg&sql=10:3ifwxql5ld0e). Macrovision Corporation. . Retrieved 28 August 2009.
[32] Hodgkinson, Will. "Feature: *The unknown surfer*". *Friday Review* (Guardian Media Group) (December 10, 1999): 16–17.
[33] "Feature: *Reactions to Sgt. Pepper*" (http://www.icons.org.uk/theicons/collection/sgt-pepper/features/reactions-to-sergeant-pepper). . Retrieved 28 August 2009.
[34] http://www.people.com/people/archive/article/0,,20120051,00.html People Magazine, Vol. 31, No. 15, April 17, 1989
[35] http://www.newsweek.com/id/107279 Newsweek, September 4, 1995
[36] Catch a Wave (http://www.aarpmagazine.org/books/catch_wave.html)
[37] Sweet, R.A., Mulsant, B. H. Gupta, B., Rifai, A.H., Pasternak, R.E., et al. (1995). Duration of neuroleptic treatment and prevalence of tardive dyskinesia in late life. Archives of General Psychiatry, 52, 478-486.
[38] "I Like to Watch" by Heather Havrilesky, March 2, 2008, [[Salon.com (http://www.salon.com/ent/tv/iltw/2008/03/02/supernanny/)]]
[39] "Brian Wilson Official Website: News" (http://www.brianwilson.com/news/index.html). 11 October 2009. . Retrieved 22 December 2009.
[40] Duck Dodgers: Surf the Stars / Samurai Quack - TV.com (http://www.tv.com/duck-dodgers/surf-the-stars---samurai-quack/episode/355094/summary.html)
[41] "Donate to hurricane relief and Brian Wilson will say hi" usatoday.com (http://www.usatoday.com/life/people/2005-09-24-brian-wilson-website_x.htm)
[42] ABC News: ABC News (http://abcnews.go.com/Entertainment/wireStory?id=1281384)
[43] However, a documentary on the Biography Channel reported that Love actually WON this lawsuit. Beach Boys lawsuit dismissed - Los Angeles Times (http://www.latimes.com/entertainment/news/business/la-et-quick16.1may16,1,6718298.story?ctrack=1&cset=true)
[44] Two Beach Boys to reunite - Listen Up - USATODAY.com (http://blogs.usatoday.com/listenup/2006/09/two_beach_boys_.html)
[45] Brian Wilson to headline Sydney Festival - Arts - Entertainment - smh.com.au (http://www.smh.com.au/news/arts/brian-wilson-to-headline-sydney-festival/2007/09/12/1189276795807.html)
[46] Uncut.co.uk - News (http://www.uncut.co.uk/news/brian_wilson/news/9313)
[47] "Seattle Weekly: The Lost Brian Wilson Album" (http://www.seattleweekly.com/2008-10-08/music/finding-peace/). . Retrieved 2008-10-13.
[48] " Brian Wilson Will Complete Unfinished Gershwin Compositions (http://www.rollingstone.com/rockdaily/index.php/2009/10/08/brian-wilson-will-complete-unfinished-gershwin-compositions/)". *Rolling Stone*.
[49] Kennedy Center: Biographical information for Brian Wilson (http://www.kennedy-center.org/calendar/index.cfm?fuseaction=showIndividual&entitY_id=18317&source_type=A)
[50] http://www.brianwilson.com/media/words/larry_king.html
[51] http://www.ginnydougary.co.uk/2002/06/01/after-the-wipe-out/
[52] http://www.npr.org/templates/story/story.php?storyId=1700586
[53] http://pages.cthome.net/tobelman/The_Out-Of-Sight_SMiLE_Site.html
[54] http://www.pbase.com/rking401/brian_wilson
[55] http://worldcat.org/identities/lccn-no90-21396
[56] http://larecord.com/issues/2009/01/15/brian-wilson-write-rock-n-roll-music/
[57] http://www.btinternet.com/~bellagio/productions.html
[58] http://www.cabinessence.net/

Carl Wilson

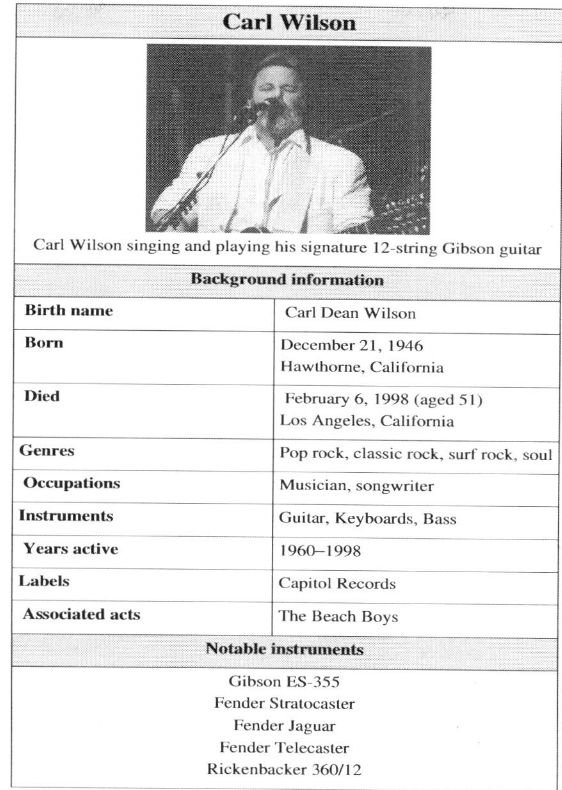

Carl Wilson	
Carl Wilson singing and playing his signature 12-string Gibson guitar	
Background information	
Birth name	Carl Dean Wilson
Born	December 21, 1946 Hawthorne, California
Died	February 6, 1998 (aged 51) Los Angeles, California
Genres	Pop rock, classic rock, surf rock, soul
Occupations	Musician, songwriter
Instruments	Guitar, Keyboards, Bass
Years active	1960–1998
Labels	Capitol Records
Associated acts	The Beach Boys
Notable instruments	
Gibson ES-355 Fender Stratocaster Fender Jaguar Fender Telecaster Rickenbacker 360/12	

Carl Dean Wilson (December 21, 1946 – February 6, 1998) was an American rock and roll singer and guitarist, best known as a founding member, lead guitarist and sometime lead vocalist of The Beach Boys. He was inducted into the Rock and Roll Hall of Fame in 1988. He was the younger brother of fellow Beach Boys Brian Wilson and Dennis Wilson.

Beach Boys career

Wilson played the Chuck Berry-esque guitar parts on many of the band's early hits. Because the band first became successful when he was in his teens, he was still developing as a musician and singer. His lead vocals in the band's first three years included "Summertime Blues" (duet with David Marks), "Louie, Louie" (splitting the lead with Mike Love), "Pom Pom Play Girl," "All Dressed Up for School", and "Girl Don't Tell Me". When the band started being augmented or replaced by session musicians on many of their mid-'60s recordings (they contributed the majority of the instrumental work themselves on the early-'60s recordings), unlike the other members of the band Carl often played side by side in the studio with the session pros that Brian increasingly turned to from 1964 onward, or recorded his guitar leads during the Beach Boys vocal sessions, with his guitar plugged directly into the soundboard.

Following his performance of the lead vocal on "God Only Knows" in 1966, Carl was increasingly featured as lead vocalist for the band (a role previously dominated by Mike Love and Brian Wilson), singing many leads on the *Smiley Smile* and *Wild Honey* albums, including the hit singles "Good Vibrations," "Darlin'," and "Wild Honey," then on 1969's "I Can Hear Music," which served as Carl's first major studio production. He is widely recognized as an important singer in popular music. The presenter Mark Lawson on BBC Radio 4's Front Row from 16 December 2009 referred to Wilson's lead in Good Vibrations as "[that] wonderful male alto solo; exactly the same sound you'd hear from a good singer in a cathedral or on a Baroque opera stage. It's a wonderful sound".

After his elder brother Brian's retirement from the stage in 1965, Carl became the de facto leader of the band onstage (contracts at that time reading that promoters hired 'Carl Wilson plus four other musicians'), and shortly after became the band's in-studio leader, producing the bulk of the albums *20/20*, *Sunflower*, *Surf's Up*, *Carl and the Passions - "So Tough"* (named in honour of his effective leadership of the band at this point) and *Holland*.

In 1967, Wilson also made headlines as a conscientious objector to the Vietnam War, at one point having to let the rest of the band tour the UK without him while he was up before the draft board.

Never a prolific songwriter, Wilson's first solo composing contributions to the band, other than a handful of early surf instrumentals, came with 1971's *Surf's Up*, on which he composed "Long Promised Road" and "Feel Flows" to lyrics by the band's then manager Jack Rieley. He had earlier been given cowriting credits on a few songs, but these appear to have been for arrangement ideas contributed to others' songs - he considered "Long Promised Road" his first real song. On the immediately following Beach Boys albums, he would average one or two songs, cowritten with various lyricists or other members of the band. Carl's leadership role in the band diminished somewhat in the late '70s, both due to Brian's brief reemergence as the band's producer and substance abuse problems. He nonetheless remained a prominent and recognizable voice in the band, taking lead vocals on many songs and serving as "mixdown producer" on the Brian-produced *Love You* album.

By the time of recording of 1979's *L.A. (Light Album)*, Carl again found himself filling the vocal and songwriting gap left by a retreating Brian Wilson. A song he wrote with Brian in 1974 and sang lead on, "Good Timin'", was a Top 40 American hit from that album.

During the 1970s Wilson also produced records for several other artists, notably Ricci Martin (son of Dean Martin, not to be confused with the late-'90s pop star) and South African group The Flame (two members of which later joined The Beach Boys for a couple of years). His voice appears as a backing vocal on many recordings by groups and solo singers. Examples include Chicago's hit "Baby, What A Big Surprise", Chicago's Wishing You Were Here (with Al Jardine and his brother Dennis Wilson), Elton John's "Don't Let The Sun Go Down On Me" (with Bruce Johnston), David Lee Roth's hit cover of "California Girls," Warren Zevon's "Desperados Under the Eaves" and the Carnie & Wendy Wilson holiday track "Hey Santa!".

Solo records

By the early 1980s the Beach Boys were in disarray - the band had split into several camps. Frustrated with the band's sluggishness to record new material and reluctance to rehearse for live shows, Wilson took a leave of absence in 1981, rather than remain as part of what he saw increasingly becoming a nostalgia act.

He released a solo album, *Carl Wilson*, which was well received by reviewers, in 1981, made up of songs co-written with Myrna Smith-Schilling (former backing vocalist for Elvis Presley and Aretha Franklin and wife of Wilson's then-manager Jerry Schilling). The album briefly made the charts, and the second single, "Heaven", hit the top 20 on Billboard's Adult Contemporary chart. He also undertook a solo tour to promote the album that same year, the first member of the band to do so (not counting Mike Love's various side projects in the late '70s). Initially, Carl and his band played clubs like The Bottom Line in New York City, and the Roxy in Los Angeles, then joined the Doobie Brothers as opening act on their 1981 summer tour.

He recorded a second solo album, *Youngblood*, in a similar vein, but by the time it was released in 1983 he had already rejoined The Beach Boys. Although *Youngblood* did not chart, a single, the John Hall-penned "What You Do To Me," did, making Carl only the second Beach Boy to land a solo single on the Billboard Hot 100, and again, hit the top 20 on their AC chart. Carl frequently performed that song and "Rockin' All Over the World" from the album, as well as "Heaven" from the 1981 album at Beach Boys concerts in the '80s, the latter being cast as a tribute to brother Dennis after his death in December 1983. The Beach Boys' 1985 eponymous album was dominated by Carl's lead vocals and songwriting, highlighted by his "It's Gettin' Late" (another top 20 AC hit) and the "Heaven"-like "Where I Belong". After this, though, Mike Love increasingly came to dominate the group's recorded output, and Carl stepped aside.

He still remained an important part of the band as a performer, singing lead on the chorus of the band's last big success, 1988's US number one "Kokomo". He carried on touring with the band until the last months of his life.

Death

Wilson was diagnosed with brain and lung cancer in early 1997. Despite his illness and chemotherapy treatments, Carl continued to perform after diagnosis. Carl played through the Beach Boys' entire summer tour which ended in the fall of 1997. He sat down most of the time and needed oxygen after every song, but he still had his unique voice. The only time he stood during concerts was when he sang "God Only Knows" to his fans.

Carl Wilson lost his battle with cancer on February 6, 1998, just two months after the death of his mother, Audree Wilson. He was survived by his brother Brian, wife Gina (daughter of Dean Martin), and two sons by his first marriage, Justyn and Jonah.

A handful of recordings of Wilson have been released - notably the album *Like a Brother*, by a "supergroup" Wilson formed with Gerry Beckley of America and Robert Lamm of Chicago. He also appeared posthumously on his brother Brian's album *Gettin' in Over My Head*, which used his vocal from the unreleased Beach Boys song "Soul Searchin'" put to a new backing track. He also appears on the many Beach Boys archival releases that have come out since his death.

Solo discography

- *Carl Wilson* (1981)
- *Youngblood* (1983)

External links

- Carl Wilson Foundation [1]

References

[1] http://www.carlwilsonfoundation.org/

Dennis Wilson

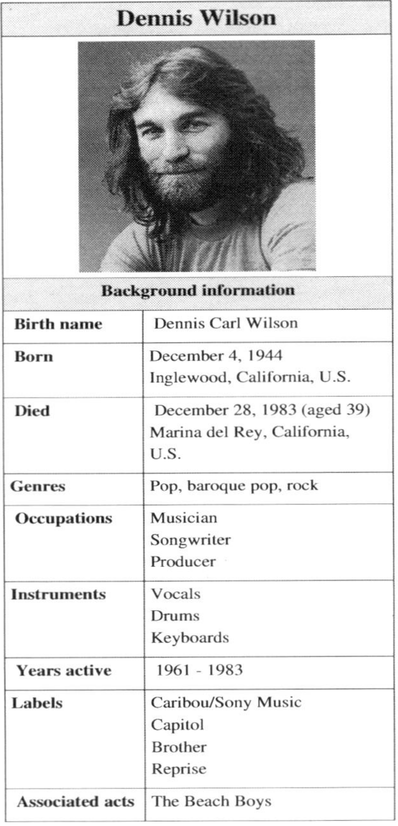

Dennis Wilson	
Background information	
Birth name	Dennis Carl Wilson
Born	December 4, 1944 Inglewood, California, U.S.
Died	December 28, 1983 (aged 39) Marina del Rey, California, U.S.
Genres	Pop, baroque pop, rock
Occupations	Musician Songwriter Producer
Instruments	Vocals Drums Keyboards
Years active	1961 - 1983
Labels	Caribou/Sony Music Capitol Brother Reprise
Associated acts	The Beach Boys

Dennis Carl Wilson (December 4, 1944 – December 28, 1983) was an American rock and roll musician best known as a founding member and the drummer of The Beach Boys. He was a member of the group from its formation until his death in 1983.

Compared to his bandmates, which included his brothers Brian and Carl, and his cousin Mike Love, Dennis often did not sing backup vocals at live performances, though he did so in the studio. His prominence in the group increased as their careers went on, sometimes singing lead, and as a writer towards and into the 1970s.

The Beach Boys

Born in Inglewood, California, Dennis was the second oldest of the three Wilson brothers. Their mother, Audree, forced Brian to include Dennis in the earliest lineup of the Beach Boys. Urged by older cousin Mike Love, Dennis had approached Brian to form a group and compose a song about surfing. The Beach Boys formed in August 1961 under the guidance of father Murry Wilson, meeting immediate success. Though the Beach Boys were named for and developed an image based on the California surfing culture, Dennis was the only real surfer in the band.

During the first few years of The Beach Boys, Wilson was given the role of the drummer. Wilson had little musical experience at the outset but quickly learned to play the drums. Although he rarely sang on stage, his raspy-sounding vocals were a key ingredient to the group's vocal blend in the studio.

Though given few important lead vocals on the early Beach Boys recordings ("Little Girl (You're My Miss America)" and "This Car of Mine" as well as the bridge verse on "Girls On The Beach") he sang lead on "Do You Wanna Dance?" in February 1965. Later that year on *Beach Boys' Party!*, Dennis sang a rendition of The Beatles' "You've Got to Hide Your Love Away". He accompanied himself on guitar, and like the other Beach Boys, became a multi-instrumentalist. His piano playing in particular was showcased on his *Pacific Ocean Blue* album.

Dennis Wilson's first major released composition was "Little Bird", the B-side of the "Friends" single, though he had already helped Brian write a few other songs dating back to 1963.

Wilson had further compositions featured on later Beach Boys albums such as *20/20* (1969), *Sunflower* (1970), *Carl and the Passions - "So Tough"* (1972), *Holland* (1973) as well as others. *Sunflower* included the track "Forever", not only popular with fans, but also earned him some much sought praise from brother Brian and father Murry. The album included three other songs written by Wilson which were not originally recorded for the album.

The 1973 live album *The Beach Boys In Concert* features only Dennis onstage among thousands of fans on the album cover, however none of his songs were included in the lineup.

During the three-year recording hiatus following *Holland*, Dennis's voice deteriorated markedly. By then his onstage antics (including streaking) occasionally disrupted the Beach Boys' live shows.

In 1974, concurrent with the success of the '60s hits compilation *Endless Summer*, Wilson returned to his role behind the drums.

Charles Manson

In 1968, Dennis Wilson was driving through Malibu when he noticed two female hitchhikers. He picked them up and dropped them off at their destination.[1] Later on, Wilson noticed the same two girls hitchhiking again. This time, he took them to his home at 14400 Sunset Boulevard, near Will Rogers Park. Wilson then went to a recording session. When he returned at around 3 a.m., he was met in his driveway by a stranger, Charles Manson. When he walked into his home, there were about a dozen people occupying the premises, most of them female. Wilson became fascinated by Manson and his followers. The "Manson Family" lived with Wilson for a period of time afterwards, at his expense.

Initially impressed by Manson's songwriting talent, Wilson introduced him to a few friends in the music business, including Terry Melcher, whose home on Cielo Drive would later be rented by director Roman Polanski and his wife, actress Sharon Tate; Tate and several others would later be murdered at the home by Manson Family members. Recording sessions for Manson were held at Brian Wilson's home studio. Those recordings, if existent, have never been released. The Beach Boys released a Manson song, originally titled "Cease To Exist", but reworked as "Never Learn Not To Love", as a single B-side.

As Wilson became increasingly aware of Manson's volatile nature and growing tendency to violence, he finally made a break from the friendship by simply moving out of the house, and leaving Manson there. When Manson subsequently sought further contact (and money), he left a bullet with Wilson's housekeeper to be delivered with a

cryptic message, which was perceived by Wilson as a threat.

In August 1969, the Tate/LaBianca murders occurred. He rarely discussed his involvement with the Manson Family and he usually became upset when the subject was broached. He was upset in regard to Charles Manson and his 'family' and did mention that he felt it was his 'fault' for introducing him to the music world.

Movie role

Dennis Wilson starred alongside James Taylor and Warren Oates in the critically acclaimed film *Two-Lane Blacktop* (1971) as "The Mechanic". It depicts "The Driver" (Taylor) and "The Mechanic" driving aimlessly across the United States in their '55 Chevy surviving on money made by street drag-racing.

Solo career

On December 4, 1970, Wilson released his first piece of solo material, a little-known single released under the name "Dennis Wilson & Rumbo." The single featured "Sound of Free" on the A-side with "Lady" (also known as "Fallin' In Love") on the B-side. The song was later covered by American Spring and released as the B-side to their single "Shyin' Away."

Pacific Ocean Blue

Wilson released his debut solo album *Pacific Ocean Blue* in 1977. His collaborators on the album included Daryl Dragon (the 'Captain' of Captain & Tennille) and Gregg Jakobson. The album peaked at #96 in the US and sold around 300,000 copies, matching that year's Beach Boys album *Love You*. Dates were booked for a Dennis Wilson solo tour but these were ultimately cancelled, however Wilson did occasionally perform his solo material on the 1977 Beach Boys tour.[2] Despite Wilson himself claiming the album had "no substance",[3] *Pacific Ocean Blue* performed well critically and continues to maintain a cult following. The album was out of print and difficult to obtain for more than a decade, but has been reissued as of June 2008. The expanded Sony Legacy edition of Pacific Ocean Blue was voted the 2008 Reissue of the Year in both Rolling Stone and Mojo magazines, and made #16 on the British LP charts and #8 and both the Billboard Catalog chart and the Billboard Internet Sales chart.[4]

Bambu

Pacific Ocean Blue's follow-up, *Bambu*, was initially scuttled by lack of financing and the distractions of simultaneous Beach Boys projects. A sampling of its music was officially released in 2008 as bonus material with the *Pacific Ocean Blue* reissue.

Two songs from the *Bambu* sessions - "Love Surrounds Me" and "Baby Blue" - were lifted for the Beach Boys 1979 *L.A. (Light Album)*. Wilson and brother Brian also recorded together apart from the Beach Boys in 1980 and 1981. These sessions remain unreleased though widely bootlegged.

Personal life

At the time of his death, he was married to Shawn Marie Love, (allegedly an illegitimate child of cousin and fellow Beach Boy Mike Love) with whom he had a son, Gage Dennis Wilson (born September 3, 1982). Shawn Wilson died after a 15-year battle with cancer shortly after Gage's 21st birthday.

Wilson's previous marriages include Carole Freedman, with whom he had a daughter, Jennifer (born December 21, 1966) and whose son, Scott, he adopted, and Barbara Charren, with whom he had two sons, Michael (born February 19, 1971) and Carl (born December 31, 1972). Wilson was married twice to Karen Lamm, the ex-wife of Robert Lamm. Wilson was quoted in the sleeve notes for the album *All Summer Long*:

> They say I live a fast life. Maybe I just like a fast life. I wouldn't give it up for anything in the world. It won't last forever, either. But the memories will.

Dennis also had a significant relationship with Christine McVie for a couple of years from 1979.

Death

Succeeding years saw Wilson battling alcohol abuse. On December 28, 1983, shortly after his 39th birthday, Wilson drowned at Marina Del Rey, Los Angeles after drinking all day and diving in the afternoon to recover items he had thrown overboard at the marina from his yacht back in 1980. On January 4, 1984 he was buried at sea off the California coast by the U.S. Coast Guard.

Solo discography

Albums

- *Pacific Ocean Blue* (1977)
- *Bambu* (1978-79-uncompleted, released 2008)

Singles

- "Sound of Free"/"Lady" (1970) (as Dennis Wilson & Rumbo)
- "River Song"/"Farewell My Friend" (1977)
- "You and I"/"Friday Night" (1977)

See also

- The Beach Boys
- List of songs by Dennis Wilson
- Beach Boys Historic Landmark

Further reading

- Jon Stebbins, "Dennis Wilson - The Real Beach Boy". ECW Press 2000. ISBN 1-55022-404-2
- Adam Webb, *Dumb Angel: the life and music of Dennis Wilson*. Creation Books, 2001. ISBN 1-84068-051-2

External links

- The Beach Boys [5]
- "Sea of Heartbreak: Dennis Wilson's Majestic Solo Work," [6], at Pop Matters, 2007, by Tony Sclafani
- The Official Site of Pacific Ocean Blue [7]
- Dennis Wilson [8] at Find a Grave

References

[1] *Helter Skelter* by Vincent Bugliosi, pg. 338, published March 1975

[2] "Dennis Wilson solo recordings" (http://www.webcitation.org/5lo4bdOSY). Local Gentry. Archived from the original (http://therecordroom.informe.com/forum/dennis-wilson-solo-recordings-dt336.html) on 2009-12-05. . Retrieved 2009-12-05.

[3] Leaf, David. "Dennis Wilson Interview, 1977" (http://www.webcitation.org/5lo51rI3X). Dan Addington.com. Archived from the original (http://www.danaddington.com/denny/interview.html) on 2009-12-05. . Retrieved 2009-12-05.

[4] "Wilson's 'Ocean' Set For Expanded Reissue" (http://www.webcitation.org/5lo5Chxk7). Billboard.com. Archived from the original (http://www.billboard.com/bbcom/search/google/article_display.jsp?vnu_content_id=1003701480) on 2009-12-05. . Retrieved 2009-12-05.

[5] http://www.thebeachboys.com/

[6] http://www.popmatters.com/pm/features/article/48236/sea-of-heartbreak/

[7] http://www.pacificoceanblue.net/

[8] http://www.findagrave.com/cgi-bin/fg.cgi?page=gr&GRid=2011

Albums

15 Big Ones

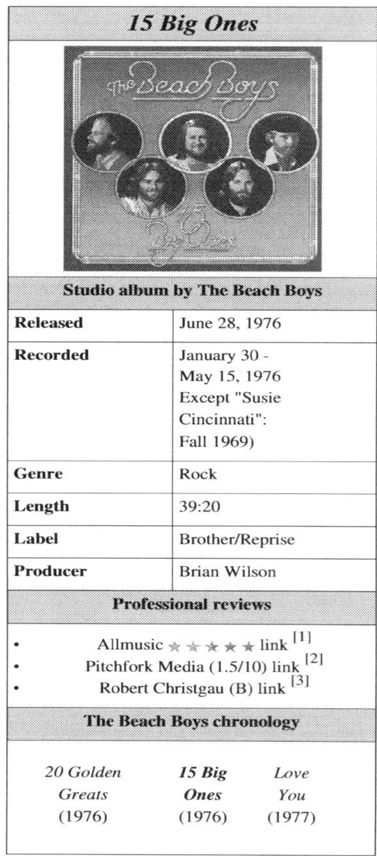

15 Big Ones	
Studio album by The Beach Boys	
Released	June 28, 1976
Recorded	January 30 - May 15, 1976 Except "Susie Cincinnati": Fall 1969)
Genre	Rock
Length	39:20
Label	Brother/Reprise
Producer	Brian Wilson
Professional reviews	
• Allmusic ★★★★★ link [1] • Pitchfork Media (1.5/10) link [2] • Robert Christgau (B) link [3]	
The Beach Boys chronology	
20 Golden Greats (1976) · ***15 Big Ones*** (1976) · *Love You* (1977)	

15 Big Ones is the twentieth studio album by The Beach Boys, released in 1976. It was their first studio album in three years and the first Brian Wilson-produced album released by the band since *Pet Sounds*, ten years earlier.

In the fall of 1974, sessions were held at Caribou Ranch studio (owned by James William Guercio) in Colorado and Brother Studio in Santa Monica for an album set to be released in early 1975. It was reported that Brian was actively involved in the proceedings but no release occurred. Many of the tapes were allegedly destroyed when the Caribou Ranch and its studio burned down, with only the tapes taken to Brother Studio surviving.

By 1975, The Beach Boys' *Endless Summer* compilation was selling well and the band (without Wilson) was touring non-stop, making them the biggest live draw in the US.

At the end of January 1976, The Beach Boys were back in the studio, with Brian Wilson producing once again. He decided the band should do an "oldies" album, but brothers Carl and Dennis disagreed, feeling that an album of originals was far more ideal. Mike Love and Al Jardine reportedly wanted the album out as quickly as possible to take advantage of their resurgence of popularity. At one point during the recordings, it was decided that a double album was to be released: one album of oldies and another of original material. In the end, a compromise of both new originals and covers was decided upon, though Brian's younger brothers were displeased. Whatever the case, it was a radical shift from previous albums such as *Sunflower* and *Holland*.

With media coverage in high gear, The Beach Boys were given an NBC TV special heralding their return. One of the highlights of the special is a rendition of That Same Song with the Alexander Hamilton Double Rock Baptist Choir, where Brian looks to be more at ease than he really was. More at ease than the "Failure To Surf" comedy skit that enlisted the help of Dan Aykroyd and John Belushi as "surf cops".

The group also embarked on a large US tour, several of the performances included Brian. Although Dennis Wilson suggested calling the album *Group Therapy*, and rejecting *Pick Ya Up At 8* (after the song "I Wanna Pick You Up") *15 Big Ones*, was named for their fifteen years in the business and for the fact that it had the same number of tracks. It was released in late June, reaching #8 in the US and going gold. It was the most successful Beach Boys studio album in over ten years, though the critical reaction of the album was not strong.

Album cover, art direction and logo was done by Jim Evans

Track listing

Side one				
No.	**Title**	**Writer(s)**	**Lead Vocals**	**Length**
1.	"Rock and Roll Music"	Chuck Berry	Mike Love	2:29
2.	"It's OK"	Brian Wilson/Mike Love	Love/Dennis Wilson	2:12
3.	"Had To Phone Ya"	B. Wilson/Love/Diane Rovell	Love/Al Jardine/D. Wilson/Carl Wilson/Brian Wilson	1:43
4.	"Chapel of Love"	Jeff Barry/Ellie Greenwich/Phil Spector	B. Wilson	2:34
5.	"Everyone's in Love with You"	Love	Love	2:42
6.	"Talk to Me"	Joe Seneca	C. Wilson	2:14
7.	"That Same Song"	B. Wilson/Love	B. Wilson	2:16
8.	"TM Song"	B. Wilson	Jardine	1:34

Side two				
No.	**Title**	**Writer(s)**	**Lead Vocals**	**Length**
1.	"Palisades Park"	Chuck Barris	C. WIlson	2:27
2.	"Susie Cincinnati"	Al Jardine	Jardine	2:57
3.	"A Casual Look"	Ed Wells	Love/Jardine	2:45
4.	"Blueberry Hill"	Al Lewis/Larry Stock/Vincent Rose	Love	3:01
5.	"Back Home"	B. Wilson/Bob Norberg	B. Wilson	2:49
6.	"In the Still of the Night"	Fred Parris	D. Wilson	3:03
7.	"Just Once in My Life"	Gerry Goffin/Carole King/Phil Spector	C. Wilson/B. Wilson	3:47

Singles

- "Rock And Roll Music" b/w "TM Song" (Brother 1354), 24 May 1976 **US #5**; **UK #36**
- "It's O.K." b/w "Had to Phone Ya" (Brother 1368), 9 August 1976 **US #29**
- "Everyone's In Love With You" b/w "Susie Cincinnati" (Brother 1375), 1 November 1976

15 Big Ones is now paired on CD with *Love You*.

15 Big Ones (Brother/Reprise MS 2251) hit **#8** in the US during a chart stay of 27 weeks. It reached **#31** in the UK.

Sources

- *Surf's Up: The Beach Boys On Record* Brad Elliott
- *15 Big Ones/Love You* CD booklet notes, Dennis Diken and Peter Buck, c.2000.
- "The Nearest Faraway Place: Brian Wilson, The Beach Boys and the Southern California Experience", Timothy White, c. 1994.
- "Wouldn't It Be Nice - My Own Story", Brian Wilson and Todd Gold, c. 1991.
- "Top Pop Singles 1955-2001", Joel Whitburn, c. 2002.
- "Top Pop Albums 1955-2001", Joel Whitburn, c. 2002.
- Allmusic.com

References

[1] http://www.allmusic.com/cg/amg.dll?p=amg&sql=10:diftxql5ld0e
[2] http://www.pitchforkmedia.com/article/record_review/15337-15-big-oneslove-you
[3] http://www.robertchristgau.com/get_artist.php?name=beach+boys

20/20

This is an article about The Beach Boys' album 20/20. *For other albums with the title* 20/20, *see 20/20 (disambiguation).*

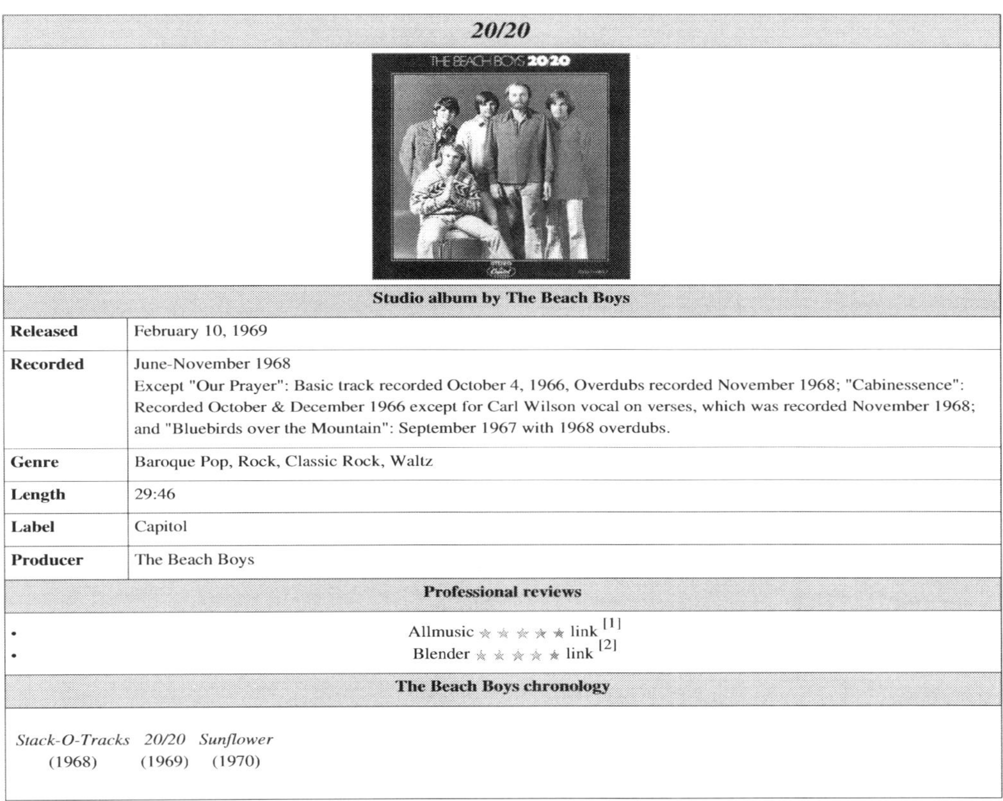

20/20	
Studio album by The Beach Boys	
Released	February 10, 1969
Recorded	June-November 1968 Except "Our Prayer": Basic track recorded October 4, 1966, Overdubs recorded November 1968; "Cabinessence": Recorded October & December 1966 except for Carl Wilson vocal on verses, which was recorded November 1968; and "Bluebirds over the Mountain": September 1967 with 1968 overdubs.
Genre	Baroque Pop, Rock, Classic Rock, Waltz
Length	29:46
Label	Capitol
Producer	The Beach Boys
Professional reviews	
• Allmusic ☆☆☆☆★ link [1]	
• Blender ☆☆☆☆★ link [2]	
The Beach Boys chronology	
Stack-O-Tracks (1968) *20/20* (1969) *Sunflower* (1970)	

20/20 is the sole 1969 album release by The Beach Boys, and their last studio album to be released with Capitol Records for the next seventeen years. As a mixed bag of recent singles, new studio recordings and two exhumed *Smile* tracks, *20/20* turned out to be one of The Beach Boys' most artistically interesting albums, and - in retrospect - can now be seen as a dry run for the creative re-birth that resulted in *Sunflower* the following year.

Recording

20/20 got its name from its distinction of being The Beach Boys' 20th official album release (counting the three "Best of..." packages and *Stack-O-Tracks*). Brian Wilson poked fun at the title by hiding behind an eye examination chart inside the gatefold cover's photo. Otherwise, Wilson's involvement in the album was far less than perceived at the time.

With increasing emotional problems, Brian Wilson began to withdraw from the band's recording sessions. He did participate on over half of the songs, but Wilson's only "new" contributions to *20/20* was a soothing waltz entitled (rather prophetically) "I Went to Sleep" and his and Mike Love's "Do It Again". It had been a summer of 1968 hit and was added on as commercial insurance, although a small snatch of the *Smile*-era "Workshop" session was hidden at the track's fade-out.

In the wake of the elder Wilson's partial absence, younger siblings Dennis Wilson and Carl Wilson began to take the helm both inside and outside of the studio's control room. Carl produced a version of Phil Spector's "I Can Hear Music," giving The Beach Boys their last original Top 40 US hit for the next seven years. Dennis progressed from his contributions on *Friends* to deliver the dramatic and dynamic "Be with Me" and the somewhat racy "All I Want to Do," sung by Mike and featuring a quick X-rated interlude at the fade-out. Undeniably, the most controversial moment on *20/20* is Dennis' "Never Learn Not to Love".

Before the album commenced recording, Dennis had befriended a struggling musician named Charles Manson and decided to help him in the music industry by recording his song "Cease to Exist" for the Beach Boys, under the new title "Never Learn Not to Love". Manson explicitly told Wilson that the words were not to be altered, though he could do what he liked with the music (in the event, the basic melody was largely unchanged). When "Never Learn Not to Love" was first released by the Beach Boys as a B-side in late 1968, and credited solely to Dennis Wilson—with altered lyrics and a new bridge—Manson threatened Wilson with murder. According to Brian's collaborator Van Dyke Parks, when Manson once showed up to make good on his threat, Dennis beat him up. The Manson incident gave everyone a scare in the Beach Boys' camp—especially after his well-known crimes came to light. Some fans have also suggested that Charles Manson wrote "Be with Me", but this is likely due to a simple misunderstanding: "Never Learn Not to Love" has a line containing the words, "be with me". Furthermore, unlike "Never Learn Not to Love", the Beach Boys' "Be with Me" does not resemble any of Manson's own recordings.

Bruce Johnston had been waiting for his moment after years of supporting the others on stage and in the studio. He was finally able to release one of his compositions on *20/20*, the lush instrumental "The Nearest Faraway Place." The composition was reportedly inspired by Brian Wilson's work on *Pet Sounds*, and its title was based on an article found in Life magazine. His second contribution was a cover of Ersel Hickey's "Bluebirds over the Mountain". Begun in the Fall of 1967 as a potential solo single, it was completed with Carl Wilson's help during the album's sessions. Perhaps reflecting on "Sloop John B" and feeling that lightning could strike twice, Al Jardine suggested to Brian that they work on another folk standard, "Cotton Fields." Wilson produced a recording, but feeling that Brian was holding back again, Jardine went ahead and rerecorded the song six months after Brian's version was released on *20/20.* Al's instincts were on the ball, as it turned out, for while the retitled "Cottonfields" (the last Capitol Records single) was a US flop, it became a huge hit internationally in the Spring of 1970.

After all the admirable work by his bandmates, it was ironic that Brian Wilson would steal the show with three older compositions. "Cabinessence" (re-spelled as one word on *20/20*) and "Our Prayer" derived from the mythical *Smile* sessions. "Time to Get Alone," begun during the *Wild Honey* sessions but was newly recorded here. Initally intended for Three Dog Night, when they were known as "Redwood", it became a major highlight of *20/20* (Although Stephen Desper claims the song is a complete re-recording and not the original late 1967 track).

Released in February 1969, *20/20* sold better than *Friends*, reaching a still underwhelming #68 in the US, but it went as high as #3 in the UK. It was followed up by the single-only release of "Break Away" (co-authored under a pseudonym by Murry Wilson with son Brian), a serious attempt at a hit, which only succeeded in the UK. Undeterred, and booming with confidence and the sense that they were on the verge of a major creative renaissance,

The Beach Boys began formulating what would prove to be one of the most acclaimed albums of their career.

Track listing

Side one				
No.	**Title**	**Writer(s)**	**Lead Vocals**	**Length**
1.	"Do It Again"	Brian Wilson/Mike Love	Mike Love/Carl Wilson	2:25
2.	"I Can Hear Music"	Jeff Barry/Ellie Greenwich/Phil Spector	C. Wilson	2:36
3.	"Bluebirds Over the Mountain"	Ersel Hickey	Love/C. Wilson/Bruce Johnston	2:51
4.	"Be with Me"	Dennis Wilson	Dennis Wilson	3:08
5.	"All I Want to Do"	D. Wilson/Steve Kalinich	Love	2:02
6.	"The Nearest Faraway Place"	Bruce Johnston	instrumental	2:39

Side two				
No.	**Title**	**Writer(s)**	**Lead Vocals**	**Length**
1.	"Cotton Fields (The Cotton Song)"	Huddie Ledbetter	Al Jardine	2:21
2.	"I Went to Sleep"	B. Wilson/Carl Wilson	Brian Wilson/C. Wilson	1:36
3.	"Time to Get Alone"	B. Wilson	C. Wilson/B. Wilson/Jardine	2:40
4.	"Never Learn Not to Love"	D. Wilson	D. Wilson	2:31
5.	"Our Prayer"	B. Wilson	group	1:07
6.	"Cabinessence"	B. Wilson/Van Dyke Parks	C. Wilson/Love	3:34

Singles

- "Do it Again" b/w "Wake the World" (from *Friends*) (Capitol 2239), 8 July 1968 **US #20**; **UK #1**
- "Bluebirds over the Mountain" b/w "Never Learn Not to Love" (Capitol 2360), 2 December 1968 **US #61**; **UK #33**
- "I Can Hear Music" b/w "All I Want to Do" (Capitol 2432), 3 March 1969 **US #24**; **UK #10**
- "Break Away" b/w "Celebrate the News" (Capitol 2530), 16 June 1969 **US #63**; **UK #6** (Non-LP single)
- "Cottonfields" (Single Version) b/w "The Nearest Faraway Place" (Capitol 2765), 20 April 1970 **US #103**; **UK #2**

20/20 is now paired on CD with *Friends*, with bonus tracks from that period.

20/20 (Capitol SKAO 133) hit **#68** in the US during a chart stay of 11 weeks. It reached **#3** in the UK.

- In May 1970, EMI issued *Live in London*, a live album that captured 1968 performances in the UK. It wouldn't surface in the US until the Fall of 1976 as *Beach Boys '69* released by Capitol Records. It never charted in the UK, but reached **#75** during its US release. *Live in London* has been paired up with 1964's *Beach Boys Concert* on CD.

References

- *Friends/20/20* CD booklet notes, David Leaf, c.1990.
- "The Nearest Faraway Place: Brian Wilson, The Beach Boys and the Southern California Experience", Timothy White, c. 1994.
- "Wouldn't It Be Nice - My Own Story", Brian Wilson and Todd Gold, c. 1991.
- "Top Pop Singles 1955-2001", Joel Whitburn, c. 2002.
- "Top Pop Albums 1955-2001", Joel Whitburn, c. 2002.
- Allmusic.com

References

[1] http://www.allmusic.com/cg/amg.dll?p=amg&sql=10:af47gjlrj6ib

[2] http://www.blender.com/guide/reviews.aspx?id=2248

All Summer Long

All Summer Long	
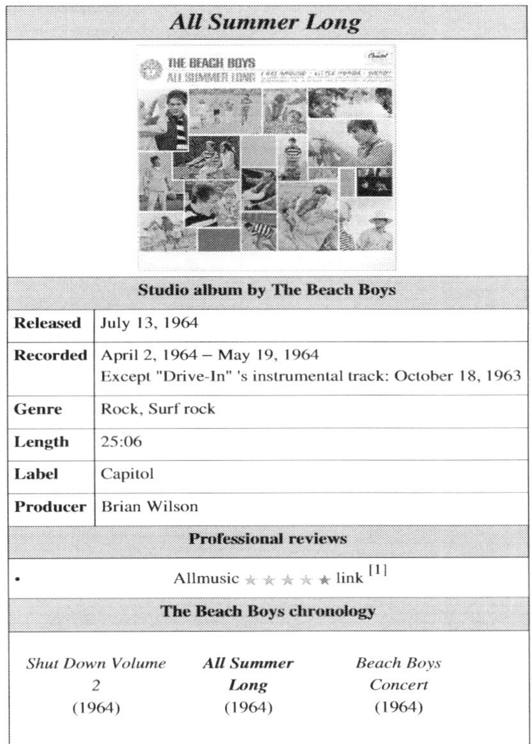	
Studio album by The Beach Boys	
Released	July 13, 1964
Recorded	April 2, 1964 – May 19, 1964 Except "Drive-In" 's instrumental track: October 18, 1963
Genre	Rock, Surf rock
Length	25:06
Label	Capitol
Producer	Brian Wilson
Professional reviews	
• Allmusic ★★★★★ link [1]	
The Beach Boys chronology	
Shut Down Volume 2 (1964) · ***All Summer Long*** (1964) · *Beach Boys Concert* (1964)	

All Summer Long is the sixth studio album by The Beach Boys and their second in 1964. Recorded in the aftermath of the British Invasion, spearheaded by The Beatles, the album marked a major turning point in The Beach Boys' career, and in leader/prime songwriter Brian Wilson as an artist.

All Summer Long hit **#4** in the US during a 49 week chart stay. *All Summer Long* (Capitol (S) T 2110) is now paired on CD with *Little Deuce Coupe*, with bonus tracks from that period.

Songs from this album are also featured on the EP *Four*.

Album history

Beginning in February 1964, Wilson engaged in a rigorous period of songwriting, emerging some weeks afterwards with songs including "I Get Around", "All Summer Long", "Wendy" and "Girls on the Beach". The Beach Boys dubbed their vocals over the instrumental tracks performed by session musicians, all produced by the 21-year-old Wilson.

"I Get Around" preceded the album's release by some two months and quickly raced to become their first #1 single in the United States; they also had a UK Top 10 debut with a #7 peak. The album was released in July, peaking at #4 in the United States, and being certified gold; the album did not make the UK charts, however.

But there was one major change in the internal structure of The Beach Boys during the making of *All Summer Long*. After enduring father and manager Murry Wilson's domineering ways for over two years, the band had reached the breaking point. .

Front cover artwork

A summer feel permeates the cover of this album, with a series of candid snapshots mounted into a montage. Photography was credited to both Kenneth Veeder and George Jerman (who had taken the photographs for the bands earlier albums) but it remains unclear as to who took the color pictures on the front of the sleeve, or the black and white studio shots on the reverse. The location for the shoot was once again Paradise Cove, north of Malibu, the same location used for the *Surfin' Safari* sleeve. However, whilst it appears that all five band members were present for the session only Brian, Carl, Dennis and Mike were photographed on the sand (along with the two girls, in various outfits) - Al was absent that day for unknown reasons and his images were added at a later date.

On first pressings of the LP, the song "Don't Back Down" is misprinted as "Don't Break Down" on the front cover - ironic considering Brian Wilson's nervous breakdown later in the year and subsequent mental problems. This version of the LP sleeve also has the song titles printed in the same mustard-colored ink as the album title. Subsequent printings with the typo corrected have the song titles printed in black.

Track listing

Side one				
No.	**Title**	**Writer(s)**	**Lead Vocals**	**Length**
1.	"I Get Around"	Brian Wilson/Mike Love	Brian Wilson/Mike Love	2:12
2.	"All Summer Long"	B. Wilson/Love	Love	2:06
3.	"Hushabye"	Doc Pomus/Mort Shuman	B. Wilson/Love	2:40
4.	"Little Honda"	B. Wilson/Love	Love	1:52
5.	"We'll Run Away"	B. Wilson/Gary Usher	B. Wilson	2:00
6.	"Carl's Big Chance"	B. Wilson/Carl Wilson	instrumental	2:25

Side two				
No.	**Title**	**Writer(s)**	**Lead Vocals**	**Length**
1.	"Wendy"	B. Wilson/Love	B. Wilson/Love	2:19
2.	"Do You Remember?"	B. Wilson/Love	Love/B. Wilson	1:40
3.	"Girls on the Beach"	B. Wilson	B. Wilson/Dennis Wilson	2:24
4.	"Drive-In"	B. Wilson/Love	Love	1:51
5.	"Our Favorite Recording Sessions"	B. Wilson/Dennis Wilson/C. Wilson/Love/Al Jardine	spoken word	1:59
6.	"Don't Back Down"	B. Wilson/Love	Love/B. Wilson	1:44

Singles

- "I Get Around" b/w "Don't Worry Baby" (from *Shut Down Volume 2*) (Capitol 5174), 23 May 1964 **US #1**; **UK #7** ("Don't Worry Baby" **US #24**)

References

- *Little Deuce Coupe/All Summer Long* CD booklet notes, David Leaf, c.1990.
- *The Nearest Faraway Place: Brian Wilson, The Beach Boys and the Southern California Experience*, Timothy White, c. 1994.
- *Wouldn't It Be Nice - My Own Story*, Brian Wilson and Todd Gold, c. 1991.
- *Top Pop Singles 1955-2001*, Joel Whitburn, c. 2002.
- *Top Pop Albums 1955-2001*, Joel Whitburn, c. 2002.
- Allmusic.com

References

[1] http://www.allmusic.com/cg/amg.dll?p=amg&sql=10:hxkzikp6bb89

The Beach Boys

The Beach Boys	
Studio album by The Beach Boys	
Released	June 10, 1985
Recorded	June 1984–March 1985
Genre	Rock
Length	40:31
Label	Brother/Caribou/CBS
Producer	Steve Levine
Professional reviews	
• Allmusic ★★★★ link [1]	
• Robert Christgau (C) link [3]	
The Beach Boys chronology	

Ten Years of Harmony (1981)	*The Beach Boys* (1985)	*Made in U.S.A.* (1986)

The Beach Boys is the twenty-fifth studio album by The Beach Boys, released in 1985. This album is notable for several reasons:

- It was the band's first album to be recorded after the death of Dennis Wilson.
- It was the first of the band's albums to be released on CD.
- It was the band's last album for CBS Records (now Sony Music).
- It was the first album for which Brian Wilson's Svengali, Eugene Landy, was noted as a collaborating songwriter with Brian.
- It was the band's last album with all new compositions.

For the album, the band hired Culture Club producer Steve Levine, who took them into the world of drum machines, synthesizers, sampling, and hi-tech recording technology. All the members – Brian Wilson, Carl Wilson, Mike Love, Bruce Johnston, and Al Jardine – took an active role in the project, writing several new songs for it, with Stevie Wonder and Culture Club each donating a song.

Although "Getcha Back" (composed by Love and his new musical partner, former Byrds producer Terry Melcher), was a top 30 hit, the album only reached #52 in the U.S. (making it their highest charting album since the release of 1976's album *15 Big Ones*). After the album, CBS Records let the band's contract expire, leaving them without a record deal for the first time in years.

Brian Wilson contributed a song written in 1982 by himself and Dennis Wilson called "Oh Lord", but the song did not make the final cut. Also cut from the album was a cover of "At The Hop" with lead vocals by Mike Love.

Promotional videos

Two videos were produced to promote the album: "Getcha Back" and "It's Gettin' Late". Both videos featured a stereotypical nerd as the central character who socializes near the beach. In "Getcha Back", all (then-surviving) Beach Boys were featured in a story of childhood love separated until the couple reaches their teen years. The second video, "It's Gettin' Late", the central character is learning about the trials and tribulations of dating. The only Beach Boys member to be appear in "It's Gettin' Late" is Brian Wilson, who has a cameo at the end of the video where he picks up a seashell and listens to the song, "California Calling".

Track listing

1. "Getcha Back" (Mike Love/Terry Melcher) – 3:02
   - *Features Mike Love on lead vocals, w/ Brian Wilson on the chorus falsetto as well as the ending lines to the song*
2. "It's Gettin' Late" (Carl Wilson/Myrna Smith Schilling/Robert White Johnson) – 3:27
   - *Features Carl Wilson on lead vocals*
3. "Crack at Your Love" (Brian Wilson/Al Jardine) – 3:40
   - *Features Brian Wilson and Alan Jardine on lead vocals*
4. "Maybe I Don't Know" (Carl Wilson/Myrna Smith Schilling/Steve Levine/Julian Stewart Lindsay) – 3:54
   - *Features Carl Wilson on lead vocals, w/ Gary Moore on rhythm and lead guitars*
5. "She Believes in Love Again" (Bruce Johnston) – 3:29
   - *Features Carl Wilson and Bruce Johnston on lead vocals, w/ Gary Moore on guitar and synthaxe*
6. "California Calling" (Al Jardine/Brian Wilson) – 2:50
   - *Features Mike Love and Al Jardine on lead vocals, w/ Ringo Starr on drums and timpani*
7. "Passing Friend" (George O'Dowd/Roy Hay) – 5:00
   - *Features Carl Wilson on lead vocals, w/Roy Hay on all instrumentation*
8. "I'm So Lonely" (Brian Wilson/Eugene E. Landy) – 2:52
   - *Features Brian Wilson and Carl Wilson [middle-8] on lead vocals*
9. "Where I Belong" (Carl Wilson/Robert White Johnson) – 2:58
   - *Features Carl Wilson [verses] and Al Jardine [chorus] on lead vocals*
10. "I Do Love You" (Stevie Wonder) – 4:20
    - *Features Carl Wilson and Al Jardine on lead vocals, w/ Stevie Wonder on drums, bass, Fender rhodes and harmonica*
11. "It's Just a Matter of Time" (Brian Wilson/Eugene E. Landy) – 2:23
    - *Features Brian Wilson and Mike Love on lead vocals*
12. "Male Ego" (Brian Wilson/Mike Love/Eugene E. Landy) – 2:32
    - *Features Brian Wilson and Mike Love on lead vocals*
      This song was included as a bonus track on all CD releases of "The Beach Boys"

Singles

- "Getcha Back" b/w "Male Ego" (Brother/Caribou), May 8, 1985 US #26
- "It's Gettin' Late" b/w "It's OK" (Brother/Caribou), July 17, 1985 US #82
- "She Believes in Love Again" b/w "It's Just a Matter of Time" (Caribou), October 2, 1985

The Beach Boys is now paired on CD with *Keepin' the Summer Alive*.

The Beach Boys (Brother/Caribou/CBS BFZ 39946) reached #52 in the U.S. during a chart stay of 14 weeks. It reached #60 in the UK

Sources

- *Keepin' the Summer Alive/The Beach Boys* CD booklet notes, Andrew G. Doe, c.2000.
- "The Nearest Faraway Place: Brian Wilson, The Beach Boys and the Southern California Experience", Timothy White, c. 1994.
- "Wouldn't It Be Nice - My Own Story", Brian Wilson and Todd Gold, c. 1991.
- "Top Pop Singles 1955-2001", Joel Whitburn, c. 2002.
- "Top Pop Albums 1955-2001", Joel Whitburn, c. 2002.
- Allmusic.com

References

[1] http://www.allmusic.com/cg/amg.dll?p=amg&sql=10:0m5zefwkhgfj

Beach Boys Concert

Beach Boys Concert	
Live album by The Beach Boys	
Released	October 19, 1964
Recorded	December 21, 1963 August 1, 1964 Civic Memorial Auditorium, Sacramento, CA August 31, 1964 Western Studios
Genre	Rock
Length	32:07
Label	Capitol
Producer	Brian Wilson
Professional reviews	
•	Allmusic ★★★★★ link [1]
The Beach Boys chronology	
All Summer Long (1964)	***Beach Boys Concert*** (1964) · *The Beach Boys' Christmas Album* (1964)

Beach Boys Concert is a live album by The Beach Boys, released in 1964. It is their seventh album in all, and their third alone in the same year. What is perhaps most notable about the album is that it provided The Beach Boys with their first #1 album in the US, remaining at the top for four weeks and becoming another gold seller.

Beach Boys Concert proves to be a timely release because leader and producer Brian Wilson was about to vacate his position in the live group, and would only perform sporadically with them over the course of the next three decades. It is also the only live document of the original five members of The Beach Boys in officially released LP form. It was recorded live at the Memorial Auditorium in Sacramento, CA.

The album includes several songs that The Beach Boys regularly performed live but had not previously included on an album, such as "Papa-Oom-Mow-Mow", "The Wanderer" and "Monster Mash". "The Little Old Lady From Pasadena" was actually a Jan & Dean hit. Alongside those were a sampling of their favorites, such as "Hawaii", "In My Room", "Fun, Fun, Fun" and "I Get Around".

Studio doctoring on *Beach Boys Concert* is very evident, from the overdubbed vocals, and the fact that the concert also featured recordings from December 1963 (also where announcer Fred Vail's introduction comes from). Most obviously, Brian Wilson used the original music tracks for both "Fun, Fun, Fun" (which was sped up) and "I Get Around", both of which had elements removed to make them appear as though they were new performances.

Despite the shady circumstances surrounding its post-production (as is the case with many live albums), *Beach Boys Concert* is still an edgy live document and a missing link in their early discography, which captured The Beach Boys in a context that was about to change forever.

A truncated version was released on Pickwick Records as *Wow, Great Concert!*

Track listing

Side one

1. "Fun, Fun, Fun" (Brian Wilson/Mike Love) – 2:26
2. "The Little Old Lady From Pasadena" (Don Altfeld/Jan Berry/Roger Christian) – 3:00
3. "Little Deuce Coupe" (Brian Wilson/Roger Christian) – 2:27
4. "Long, Tall Texan" (Henry Strezlecki) – 2:32
5. "In My Room" (Brian Wilson/Gary Usher) – 2:25
6. "Monster Mash" (Boris Pickett/Lenny Capizzi) – 2:27
7. "Let's Go Trippin'" (Dick Dale) – 2:34

Side two

- "Papa-Oom-Mow-Mow" (Carl White/Al Frazier/Sonny Harris/Turner Wilson Jr.) – 2:18

2. "The Wanderer" (Ernest Maresca) – 2:00
3. "Hawaii" (Brian Wilson/Mike Love) – 1:51
4. "Graduation Day" (Joe Sherman/Noel Sherman) – 3:29
5. "I Get Around" (Brian Wilson/Mike Love) – 2:42
6. "Johnny B. Goode" (Chuck Berry) – 1:56

Beach Boys Concert (Capitol (S)TAO 2198) is now paired on CD with *Live in London*, with bonus tracks from both periods.

Beach Boys Concert hit **#1** in the US during a 62 week chart stay.

Sources

- *Beach Boys Concert/Live In London* CD booklet notes, David Leaf, c.1990.
- "The Nearest Faraway Place: Brian Wilson, The Beach Boys and the Southern California Experience", Timothy White (editor) lTimothy White, c. 1994.
- "Wouldn't It Be Nice - My Own Story", Brian Wilson and Todd Gold, c. 1991.
- "Top Pop Singles 1955-2001", Joel Whitburn, c. 2002.
- "Top Pop Albums 1955-2001", Joel Whitburn, c. 2002.
- Allmusic.com

References

[1] http://www.allmusic.com/cg/amg.dll?p=amg&sql=10:ozkqoalabijd

The Beach Boys Today!

The Beach Boys Today!	
Studio album by The Beach Boys	
Released	8 March 1965
Recorded	Main Recording: January 7-19, 1965 Sporadically: June 8 & 22, August 5 & 8, October 9, and December 16, 1964
Genre	Rock, Surf rock, Baroque Pop, Sunshine Pop
Length	28:54
Label	Capitol
Producer	Brian Wilson
Professional reviews	
• Allmusic ★★★★★ link [1] • Blender ★★★★★ link [2] • Rolling Stone ★★★★★ [3]	
The Beach Boys chronology	

The Beach Boys' Christmas Album (1964)	***The Beach Boys Today!*** (1965)	*Summer Days (and Summer Nights!!)* (1965)

The Beach Boys Today! is the eighth studio album by The Beach Boys, and their first of three in 1965. Although few realized the significance of the album at the time, *The Beach Boys Today!* marked a major turning point inside the band's world, and in particular, leader Brian Wilson's personal life.[4]

After *Pet Sounds*, the album is arguably the most acclaimed album of the Beach Boys' career. The album includes the original version of the classic hit, "Help Me, Rhonda" (titled on this album as "Help Me, Ronda").

In 1965 *The Beach Boys Today!* (Capitol (D) T 2269) hit **#4** in the US during a chart stay of 50 weeks.[5] It reached **#6** in the UK in the summer of 1966.[6]

History

By the end of a particularly stressful 1964, The Beach Boys had released four albums in the preceding twelve months, in addition to beginning this album by recording two advance singles—"When I Grow Up (To Be a Man)" and "Dance, Dance, Dance."[4] As the man in charge, Wilson was both physically and emotionally exhausted, yet the Beatles' ever-increasing popularity and influence ensured that Brian kept slogging to keep afloat. On December 23, 1964, Brian had an anxiety attack due to the strain and realized that something was going to have to give; and that was touring.[7]

While the bulk of *The Beach Boys Today!* was being recorded in January 1965, he informed the rest of the band that he wanted to stay in the studio and create their music while the Boys went on the road and played it to audiences.[4] The band reluctantly agreed, and after a brief alliance with Glen Campbell in Wilson's place, Bruce Johnston, a musician (and ex-partner, with Terry Melcher in The Ripchords) and major admirer of the band, became the Beach Boys' live bassist in April 1965 as *The Beach Boys Today!* was rising the charts.[8] Many consider this album to mark the beginning of Brian Wilson's artistic maturation.

The album is famous for having one side of up-beat songs and a second side of melancholic ballads.[8] On the first half, "When I Grow Up (To Be a Man)," "Dance, Dance, Dance" and "Do You Wanna Dance?" were all hits, and "Help Me, Ronda" would be worked on further to deliver the Beach Boys their second #1 hit in May.[9] (amid a small spelling change in the title). The second side, in retrospect, was an indicator to where Brian Wilson was going musically. Considered darker and more meaningful than previous softer works, alongside Wilson's increasing productivity in the studio, the ballads on the second side are thought of as a precursor to *Pet Sounds*' technical triumphs, including strings, horns, piano and keyboards, more percussion, and volume tricks.

However, the shift in style appeared to have little detrimental effect, concerning sales; *The Beach Boys Today!* was a #4 gold-selling smash in the US, and the following year it would reach #6 in the UK. In 2003, the album was ranked number 270 on *Rolling Stone* magazine's list of the 500 greatest albums of all time.

The front cover lists nine of the album's selections, followed by "plus three great new songs written by Brian Wilson." However, the remaining three tracks include a cover, "I'm So Young"; and the interview track "Bull Session with the "Big Daddy"". Only "In The Back Of My Mind" was a Brian Wilson composition.

It has since come to light - and been acknowledged by Brian Wilson - that he had begun using marijuana during December 1964 as a stress reliever, and once he realized the profound effect it had on the way he perceived music, Wilson became a regular user.[10]

Track listing

All songs written and composed by Brian Wilson/Mike Love, except where noted.

Side one			
No.	**Title**	**Lead vocals**	**Length**
1.	"Do You Wanna Dance?" (Freeman)	Dennis Wilson	2:19
2.	"Good to My Baby"	Brian Wilson/Mike Love	2:16
3.	"Don't Hurt My Little Sister"	Love/B. Wilson	2:07
4.	"When I Grow Up (To Be a Man)"	Love/B. Wilson	2:01
5.	"Help Me, Ronda"	Al Jardine	3:08
6.	"Dance, Dance, Dance"	Love/B. Wilson	1:59

Side two			
No.	**Title**	**Lead vocals**	**Length**
1.	"Please Let Me Wonder"	B. Wilson/Love	2:45
2.	"I'm So Young" (Tyrus)	B. Wilson	2:30
3.	"Kiss Me, Baby"	Love/B. Wilson	2:35
4.	"She Knows Me Too Well"	B. Wilson	2:27
5.	"In the Back of My Mind"	D. Wilson	2:07
6.	"Bull Session with the "Big Daddy"" (Wilson/Wilson/Love/Jardine)	n/a	2:10

Singles

- "When I Grow Up" b/w "She Knows Me Too Well" (Capitol 5245), 17 August 1964 **US #9**; **UK #27**
- "Dance, Dance, Dance" b/w "The Warmth of the Sun" (from *Shut Down Volume 2*) (Capitol 5306), 26 October 1964 **US #8**; **UK #24**
- "Do You Wanna Dance?" b/w "Please Let Me Wonder" (Capitol 5372), 8 February 1965 **US #12** ("Please Let Me Wonder" **US #52**)
- "Kiss Me, Baby" featured as the B-side to "Help Me, Rhonda"

References

[1] http://www.allmusic.com/cg/amg.dll?p=amg&sql=10:4sr9286c052a
[2] http://www.blender.com/guide/reviews.aspx?id=2246
[3] http://www.rollingstone.com/artists/thebeachboys
[4] Leaf, David (1990).*The Beach Boys Today!/Summer Days (and Summer Nights!!)* (1990 CD liner notes)
[5] www.billboard.com (http://www.billboard.com/bbcom/esearch/chart_display.jsp?cfi=305&cfgn=Albums&cfn=The+Billboard+200&ci=3068661&cdi=8717551&cid=05/08/1965)
[6] Brown, Tony (2000). "The Complete Book of the British Charts"
[7] White, Timothy (1994). "The Nearest Faraway Place: Brian Wilson, The Beach Boys and the Southern California Experience"
[8] www.allmusic.com (http://www.allmusic.com/cg/amg.dll?p=amg&sql=11:3ifrxqw5ldse~T1)
[9] Whitburn, Joel (2002). "Top Pop Singles 1955-2001"
[10] Wilson, Brian/Gold, Todd (1991). "Wouldn't It Be Nice - My Own Story"

The Beach Boys in Concert

The Beach Boys in Concert	
Live album by The Beach Boys	
Released	November 19, 1973
Recorded	Winter 1972 and Summer 1973
Genre	Rock
Length	75:49
Label	Brother/Reprise
Producer	The Beach Boys
Professional reviews	
• Allmusic ★★★★★ [1] • *Rolling Stone* (Positive)[2]	
The Beach Boys chronology	
Holland (1973) · ***The Beach Boys in Concert*** (1973) · *Good Vibrations - Best of The Beach Boys* (1975)	

The Beach Boys in Concert is the second official live album by The Beach Boys, nine years after *Beach Boys Concert* (*Live in London* released in the UK in 1970 and the US in 1976). Released in late 1973, the set proved to be a healthy seller in the US, giving the band their best chart peak since early 1968 with *Wild Honey* by reaching #24, and earning them their first gold record since 1966's *Best of The Beach Boys*. The album is now available on a single-disc CD.

Background

Compiled from two separate US jaunts in late 1972 and mid-1973, *The Beach Boys In Concert* was initially submitted to Reprise Records as a single live disc and was rejected, before expanding into a double album. Highlights include updated interpretations of "Caroline, No", "You Still Believe in Me", "Heroes and Villains", "Don't Worry Baby" and "Surfer Girl". Of the newer material, "Marcella", "Sail On, Sailor", "Funky Pretty" and "The Trader" are joined, among others, with *Holland* out-take "We Got Love", which makes its debut here on a Beach Boys album. *The Beach Boys in Concert* (Brother/Reprise 2RS 6484) hit #25 in the US during a chart stay of 24 weeks.

Both Blondie Chaplin and Ricky Fataar would depart the band's line-up, in late 1973 and late 1974 respectively, making this the last album on which they appeared as official members.

Track listing

All tracks written by Brian Wilson, Mike Love, unless otherwise noted.

1. "Sail On, Sailor" (Brian Wilson, Tandyn Almer, Ray Kennedy, Jack Rieley, Van Dyke Parks) – 3:21
2. "Sloop John B" (Trad., Arr. Brian Wilson) – 3:12
3. "The Trader" (Carl Wilson, Rieley) – 4:46
4. "You Still Believe in Me" (Brian Wilson, Tony Asher) – 2:58
5. "California Girls" – 2:57
6. "Darlin'" – 2:21
7. "Marcella" (Brian Wilson, Almer, Rieley) – 3:55
8. "Caroline, No" (Brian Wilson, Asher) – 3:04
9. "Leaving This Town" (Carl Wilson, Ricky Fataar, Blondie Chaplin, Love) – 6:59
10. "Heroes and Villains" (Brian Wilson, Parks) – 3:51
11. "Funky Pretty" (Brian Wilson, Rieley, Love) – 4:04
12. "Let the Wind Blow" – 4:22
13. "Help Me, Rhonda" – 4:59
14. "Surfer Girl" (Brian Wilson) – 2:35
15. "Wouldn't It Be Nice?" (Brian Wilson, Asher, Love) – 2:45
16. "We Got Love" (Fataar, Chaplin, Love) – 5:25
17. "Don't Worry Baby" (Brian Wilson, Roger Christian) – 3:11
18. "Surfin' USA" (Chuck Berry, Brian Wilson) – 2:49
19. "Good Vibrations" – 4:49
20. "Fun, Fun, Fun" – 3:16

Personnel

The Beach Boys

- Carl Wilson – vocals, lead guitar, electric piano
- Dennis Wilson – vocals, electric piano, Moog synthesizer
- Mike Love – vocals, tambourine, electro-Theremin
- Alan Jardine – vocals, rhythm guitar
- Blondie Chaplin – lead guitar, bass guitar, vocals
- Ricky Fataar – drums, rhythm guitar, pedal steel guitar, flute, vocals

Additional musicians

- Ed Carter – bass guitar, lead guitar
- Billy Hinsche – piano, electric piano, guitar
- Robert Kenyatta – percussion
- Mike Kowalski – drums, percussion
- Carli Muñoz – organ, electric piano

Unreleased Version

The original version of *The Beach Boys In Concert* was a single disc set, not a two-record set like the one that came out. The track lineup was as follows:

Side 1

1. "Wouldn't It Be Nice"
2. "Leaving This Town"
3. "Heroes and Villains"
4. "Marcella"
5. "You Need a Mess of Help To Stand Alone"

Side 2

1. "Let the Wind Blow"
2. "Do It Again"
3. "Wild Honey"
4. "Fun Fun Fun"
5. "Jumpin' Jack Flash"

- The version of "Heroes and Villains" from this album was later released on the *Endless Harmony Soundtrack* CD.

Sources

- *The Beach Boys in Concert* CD booklet notes, Paul Williams, c.2000.
- "The Nearest Faraway Place: Brian Wilson, The Beach Boys and the Southern California Experience", Timothy White, c. 1994.
- "Wouldn't It Be Nice - My Own Story", Brian Wilson and Todd Gold, c. 1991.
- "Top Pop Singles 1955-2001", Joel Whitburn, c. 2002.
- "Top Pop Albums 1955-2001", Joel Whitburn, c. 2002.
- Allmusic.com

References

[1] Planer, Lindsay. "Review: *The Beach Boys in Concert*" (http://www.allmusic.com/cg/amg.dll?p=amg&sql=10:et7uak8k5m3c). Macrovision Corporation. . Retrieved 3 September 2009.

[2] Maslin, Janet (January 31, 1974). "Review: *The Beach Boys - The Beach Boys In Concert*" (http://www.rollingstone.com/artists/thebeachboys/albums/album/168579/review/5942456/the_beach_boys_in_concert). Jann Wenner. . Retrieved 3 September 2009.

The Beach Boys' Christmas Album

The Beach Boys' Christmas Album	
Studio album by The Beach Boys	
Released	November 16, 1964
Recorded	18 - 30 June 1964 Except "Little Saint Nick": 20 October 1963
Genre	Rock Christmas
Length	27:37
Label	Capitol
Producer	Brian Wilson
Professional reviews	
•	Allmusic ★★★★★ link [1]
The Beach Boys chronology	
Beach Boys Concert (1964)	***The Beach Boys' Christmas Album*** (1964)
The Beach Boys Today! (1965)	

The Beach Boys' Christmas Album is a Christmas album by The Beach Boys, released on November 16, 1964. Containing five original songs and seven standards, the album proved to be a long-running success during subsequent Christmas seasons, initially reaching #6 in the US Christmas album chart in its year of release and eventually going gold.

Of the original songs, "Little Saint Nick" was already famous, having been a hit single the year before. "The Man with All the Toys" was another hit during Christmastime 1964. "Christmas Day" is noteworthy for being the first Beach Boys song to feature a lead vocal from Al Jardine.

While leader Brian Wilson produced and arranged the "rock" songs, he left it to Dick Reynolds (an arranger of The Four Freshmen, a group Wilson idolized) to arrange the orchestral backings on the traditional songs to which The Beach Boys would apply their vocals.

Track listing

Side one				
No.	**Title**	**Writer(s)**	**Lead Vocals**	**Length**
1.	"Little Saint Nick"	Brian Wilson/Mike Love	Mike Love	1:59
2.	"The Man with All the Toys"	B. Wilson/Love	Brian Wilson/Love	1:32
3.	"Santa's Beard"	B. Wilson/Love	Love	1:59
4.	"Merry Christmas, Baby"	B. Wilson	Love	2:22
5.	"Christmas Day"	B. Wilson	Al Jardine	1:35
6.	"Frosty the Snowman"	Steve Nelson/Jack Rollins	B. Wilson	1:54

Side two				
No.	**Title**	**Writer(s)**	**Lead Vocals**	**Length**
1.	"We Three Kings of Orient Are"	John Henry Hopkins	Love/B. Wilson	4:03
2.	"Blue Christmas"	Billy Hayes/Jay W. Johnson	B. Wilson	3:09
3.	"Santa Claus Is Comin' to Town"	J. Fred Coots/Haven Gillespie	B. Wilson/Love	2:20
4.	"White Christmas"	Irving Berlin	B. Wilson	2:29
5.	"I'll Be Home for Christmas"	Kim Gannon/Walter Kent/Buck Ram	B. Wilson	2:44
6.	"Auld Lang Syne"	Trad. arr. B. Wilson	group	1:19

The Musicians

- Al Jardine - guitar, vocals
- Mike Love - vocals
- Brian Wilson - bass guitar, vocals
- Carl Wilson - guitar, vocals
- Dennis Wilson - drums, vocals

Orchestra

- Violins: Robert Barene, Arnold Belnick, Harry Bluestone, Jimmy Getzoff, Bernard Kundell, William Kurasch, Alfred Lustgarten, Lou Raderman, Henry Roth, Paul Shure, Marshall Sosson, Darrel Terwilliger
- Cellos: Jesse Ehrlich, Armand Kaproff, Raymond Kelley, Karl Rossner, Joseph Saxon, Frederick Seykora
- Harp: Dorothy Ramsen
- Woodwinds: Gene Cipriano, Billy Green, Robert Jung, Wilbur Schwartz
- Trumpets: Virgil Evans, Henry Laubach, Oliver Mitchell, Al Porcino
- Trombones: Urbie Green, Lew McCreary, Richard Nash
- French horns: David Duke, Arthur Maebe, Richard Perissi
- Tuba: George "Red" Callender
- Piano: Eugene DiNovi
- Guitar: Al Viola
- Bass: Clifford Hils
- Drums: Frankie Capp
- Percussion: Bones Howe
  - Orchestra Conducted by Benjamin Barrett

- Special Arrangements by Dick Reynolds

Singles

- "Little Saint Nick" b/w "The Lord's Prayer" (Capitol 5096), 2 December 1963 **US #3** (on Christmas chart)
- "The Man with All the Toys" b/w "Blue Christmas" (Capitol 5312), 16 November 1964 **US #3** (on Christmas chart)

The Beach Boys' Christmas Album (Capitol T-2164/ST-2164) hit **#6** in the US Christmas album chart during a 13 week chart stay spread out from 1964 to 1968.

Reissues

- *The Beach Boys' Christmas Album* was first issued on CD in 1988 with the single mix of "Little Saint Nick" as the first track, replacing the LP version. It was reissued on CD in 1991 with four bonus tracks: the single mix of "Little Saint Nick" (in mono and featuring additional instrumental overdubs not on the stereo album version), its B-side "The Lord's Prayer", and alternate takes of "Little Saint Nick" (utilizing the melody from the group's song "Drive-In") and "Auld Lang Syne".
- 1998 saw the release of *Ultimate Christmas*, a new CD compilation containing all of the tracks from the original LP, all of the bonus tracks from the previous CD except for "The Lord's Prayer", and 11 additional tracks including the 1974 single "Child of Winter" and several previously-unreleased tracks from an aborted 1977 Christmas album.
- *Christmas with the Beach Boys*, issued in 2004, is essentially a reissue of *Ultimate Christmas* with a new title and cover art and one song ("Christmas Time Is Here Again") deleted from the tracklist. Like *Ultimate Christmas*, it omits "The Lord's Prayer" from the "Little Saint Nick" single.

Sources

- *The Beach Boys' Christmas Album* CD booklet notes, David Leaf, c.1990.
- *Ultimate Christmas* CD booklet notes, Brad Elliott, c.1998
- "The Nearest Faraway Place: Brian Wilson, The Beach Boys and the Southern California Experience", Timothy White (editor) lTimothy White, c. 1994.
- "Wouldn't It Be Nice - My Own Story", Brian Wilson and Todd Gold, c. 1991.
- "Top Pop Singles 1955-2001", Joel Whitburn, c. 2002.
- "Top Pop Albums 1955-2001", Joel Whitburn, c. 2002.
- Allmusic.com

References

[1] http://www.allmusic.com/cg/amg.dll?p=amg&sql=10:2267gjyrj6ia

Beach Boys' Party!

Beach Boys' Party!	
Studio album by The Beach Boys	
Released	November 8, 1965
Recorded	September 8-27, 1965
Genre	Rock
Length	31:10
Label	Capitol
Producer	Brian Wilson
Professional reviews	
• Allmusic ★★★★★ link [1]	
• *warr.org* ★★★★★ link [2]	
The Beach Boys chronology	
Summer Days (And Summer Nights!!) (1965)	***Beach Boys' Party!*** (1965) — *Pet Sounds* (1966)

Beach Boys' Party! is an album of cover songs (featuring acoustic instruments) by American rock and roll band The Beach Boys that was marketed during the lucrative Christmas season. The original album release included a sheet of photographs of the band 'appearing' to be at the party at hand.[3] It was The Beach Boys' tenth album release, and their third in 1965. Although it was recorded in a music studio, it is presented as an impromptu live recording of a party.[4]

In August, after the release of *Summer Days (and Summer Nights!!)*, The Beach Boys' leader Brian Wilson was contemplating his next studio album, which would turn out to be *Pet Sounds*. Capitol Records requested a new album for the holiday season. Since a live album, *Beach Boys Concert*, had already been released the previous year, the "live party" idea was selected. (Also, the Beach Boys already had had a Christmas album, and it was felt that a "greatest hits" compilation would signal that the Beach Boys' career was coming to an end.) Sporadically during September, the band and their friends rehearsed current and older hits (including revisiting The Rivingtons' "Papa-Oom-Mow-Mow"). Although presented as a live recording, the individual songs were recorded carefully, and laughter and background chatter was mixed in during post-production.[3]

The album included versions of The Beatles' "Tell Me Why", "You've Got To Hide Your Love Away" and "I Should Have Known Better", The Everly Brothers' "Devoted To You", Phil Spector's "There's No Other (Like My Baby)" and a send-up of their own "I Get Around" and "Little Deuce Coupe". *Beach Boys' Party!* was meant as a fun album created without a single, because Wilson was readying "The Little Girl I Once Knew" for single release concurrently with the album. Several other songs were also recorded, but not put on the album. This included a rendition of The Beatles song Ticket To Ride, three takes of The Stones (I Can't Get No) Satisfaction, a version of Bob Dylan's Blowin' in the Wind, Riot In Cell Block#9 (which would later be played live in the early 70s, and then became Student Demonstration Time on their Surf's Up Lp), and several other songs, all of which can be found in the form of bootlegs on the internet.

The new single's inventive use of silence was disliked by radio programmers,[5] causing "The Little Girl I Once Knew" to stop at US #20. The last track of *Party!*, a cover of The Regents' "Barbara Ann", which radio disc jockeys around the country had started playing straight off the "Party" album and getting good listeners response was promptly issued as a single by Capitol when they started hearing from radio programmers, and became a #2 smash in early 1966.[3]

Beach Boys' Party! reached #6 in the US (though it never went gold). *Beach Boys' Party!* and its surprise hit single became The Beach Boys' biggest successes yet in the UK, both reaching #3 in early 1966 and making them stars in The Beatles' homeland.

Track listing

Side one

1. "Hully Gully" (Fred Smith/Cliff Goldsmith) – 2:22
   - *Lead Vocal - Mike Love*
2. "I Should Have Known Better" (John Lennon/Paul McCartney) – 1:40
   - *Lead Vocal - Carl Wilson and Al Jardine*
3. "Tell Me Why" (John Lennon/Paul McCartney) – 1:46
   - *Lead Vocal - Carl Wilson and Al Jardine*
4. "Papa-Oom-Mow-Mow" (Carl White/Al Frazier/Sonny Harris/Turner Wilson Jr.) – 2:18
   - *Lead Vocal - Brian Wilson, with Mike Love (bass)*
5. "Mountain of Love" (Harold Dorman) – 2:51
   - *Lead Vocal - Mike Love*
6. "You've Got to Hide Your Love Away" (John Lennon/Paul McCartney) – 2:56
   - *Lead Vocal - Dennis Wilson*
7. "Devoted To You" (Boudleaux Bryant) – 2:13
   - *Lead Vocal - Mike Love and Brian Wilson*

Side two

1. "Alley Oop" (Dallas Frazier) – 2:56
   - *Lead Vocal - Mike Love*
2. "There's No Other (Like My Baby)" (Phil Spector/Leroy Bates) – 3:05
   - *Lead Vocal - Brian Wilson*
3. "Medley: I Get Around/Little Deuce Coupe" (Brian Wilson/Mike Love/Roger Christian) – 3:12
   - *Lead vocals by Dennis, Mike, Brian, Al, Carl*
4. "The Times They Are a-Changin'" (Bob Dylan) – 2:23
   - *Lead Vocal - Al Jardine*
5. "Barbara Ann" (Fred Fassert) – 3:23
   - *Lead Vocal Brian Wilson and Dean Torrence of Jan and Dean*

Singles

- "The Little Girl I Once Knew" (non-LP track) b/w "There's No Other (Like My Baby)" (Capitol 5540), 8 November 1965 **#20**

  "The Little Girl I Once Knew" would not appear on a Beach Boys LP until 1968 as part of the Best of The Beach Boys Vol. 3 compilation

- "Barbara Ann" b/w "Girl Don't Tell Me" (from *Summer Days (and Summer Nights!!)* (Capitol 5561), 20 December 1965, **US #2**; **UK #3**

Beach Boys' Party! is now paired on CD with *Stack-O-Tracks* with bonus instrumental tracks.

Beach Boys' Party! (Capitol (D) MAS 2398) hit **#6** in the US during a chart stay of 24 weeks. It reached **#3** in the UK in March 1966.

Influence

- In 1997, the Canadian Indie Rock group Sloan, released an EP entitled "Recorded Live at a Sloan Party! (AKA The Party Album)" as a bonus disc to the U.S. release of "One Chord To Another" in homage to The Beach Boys' Party! LP, Like the Beach Boy's Party! LP, Live At A Sloan Party! mixes acoustic versions of old classics and songs originally written and recorded by other artists, and presents a supposed gathering that was actually constructed in the studio.
- Rivers Cuomo revealed that the Party! LP inspired Weezer's 2008 "Hootenanny Tour," in which fans would be invited to bring their own instruments to play along with the band. Cuomo also named it as his favorite all-time Summer album in a July 2008 issue of Entertainment Weekly.

Sources

- "The Nearest Faraway Place: Brian Wilson, The Beach Boys and the Southern California Experience", Timothy White (editor) ǀTimothy White, c. 1994.
- "Wouldn't It Be Nice - My Own Story", Brian Wilson and Todd Gold, c. 1991.
- "Top Pop Singles 1955-2001", Joel Whitburn, c. 2002.
- "Top Pop Albums 1955-2001", Joel Whitburn, c. 2002.

External links

- Rivers Cuomo's favorite Summer Album in Entertainment Weekly [6]

References

[1] http://www.allmusic.com/cg/amg.dll?p=amg&sql=10:jep1z81ajyvn
[2] http://www.warr.org/brian.html#Party
[3] Leaf, David (1990) *The Beach Boys' Party!/Stack-O-Tracks* (1990 CD liner notes)
[4] www.allmusic.com (http://www.allmusic.com/cg/amg.dll?p=amg&sql=10:hifoxql5ldke)
[5] Leaf, David (1990) *The Beach Boys Today!/Summer Days (And Summer Nights!!)* (1990 CD liner notes)
[6] http://www.ew.com/ew/gallery/0,,20205094_2,00.html

Best of The Beach Boys Vol. 2

Best of The Beach Boys Vol. 2	
Greatest hits by The Beach Boys	
Released	July 24, 1967
Recorded	April 1962 - September 1965
Genre	Rock
Length	28:43
Label	Capitol
Producer	Brian Wilson
Professional reviews	
• Allmusic ★★★★★ link [1]	
The Beach Boys chronology	

Best of The Beach Boys (1966)	***Best of The Beach Boys Vol. 2*** (1967)	*Smiley Smile* (1967)

Best of The Beach Boys Vol. 2 is the 1967 sequel to the previous year's hits package. It was compiled by Capitol Records rather hastily after Brian Wilson had announced the shelving of *Smile*, the album he had spent the better part of a year toiling on.

Released at a perilous moment in The Beach Boys' career, the appearance of their past glories on *Best of The Beach Boys Vol. 2* perhaps helped confirm to the general public that the band was not up to the challenge of the new psychedelic music, spearheaded by The Beatles' *Sgt. Pepper's Lonely Hearts Club Band* and The Jimi Hendrix Experience's radical debut *Are You Experienced*.

Although it is hard to argue with a line-up that includes "I Get Around", "California Girls", "Let Him Run Wild" and "Please Let Me Wonder", those songs were considered old hat in the face of psychedelia, and as a result *Best of The Beach Boys Vol. 2* initially flopped in the U.S., only reaching #50. In time, it would go on to sell over two million copies, but it was likely with the reaction to this album that The Beach Boys knew they were in trouble commercially in their homeland.

However, a reworked tracklist, issued under the same title in the UK in late 1967 proved to be another big success.

Like its predecessor, *Best of The Beach Boys Vol. 2* is out of print.

Track listing

1. "Barbara Ann" (Fred Fassert) – 2:11
2. "When I Grow Up" (Brian Wilson/Mike Love) – 2:01
3. "Long, Tall Texan" (Henry Strezlecki) – 2:30
4. "Please Let Me Wonder" (Brian Wilson/Mike Love) – 2:45
5. "409" (Brian Wilson/Mike Love/Gary Usher) – 1:59
6. "Let Him Run Wild" (Brian Wilson/Mike Love) – 2:20
7. "Don't Worry Baby" (Brian Wilson/Roger Christian) – 2:47
8. "Surfin' Safari" (Brian Wilson/Mike Love) – 2:05
9. "Little Saint Nick" (Brian Wilson/Mike Love) – 1:59
10. "California Girls" (Brian Wilson/Mike Love) – 2:38
11. "Help Me, Rhonda" (Brian Wilson/Mike Love) – 2:46
12. "I Get Around" (Brian Wilson/Mike Love) – 2:12

"Please Let Me Wonder" and "Little Saint Nick" do not appear on the cassette tape version.

Best of The Beach Boys Vol. 2 (Capitol (D) 2706) hit **#50** in the U.S. during a 22 week chart stay. In the UK, it reached **#3**.

British Version

The British version of ***Best of The Beach Boys Vol. 2*** was released in mid-1967 with 14 songs, instead of the usual 12 found on American albums.

The following songs were found on the British version of ***Best of The Beach Boys Vol. 2***:

1. "Surfer Girl" – 2:26
2. "Don't Worry Baby" – 2:51
3. "Wendy" – 2:22
4. "When I Grow Up (To Be A Man)" – 2:02
5. "Good to My Baby" – 2:16
6. "Dance, Dance, Dance" – 1:58
7. "Then I Kissed Her" – 2:15
8. "The Girl from New York City" – 1:53
9. "Girl Don't Tell Me" – 2:19
10. "The Little Girl I Once Knew" – 2:36
11. "Mountain of Love" – 2:47
12. "Here Today" – 2:52
13. "Wouldn't It Be Nice" – 2:22
14. "Good Vibrations" – 3:35

References

- *The Nearest Faraway Place: Brian Wilson, The Beach Boys and the Southern California Experience*, Timothy White, c. 1994.
- *Wouldn't It Be Nice - My Own Story*, Brian Wilson and Todd Gold, c. 1991.
- *Top Pop Singles 1955-2001*, Joel Whitburn, c. 2002.
- *Top Pop Albums 1955-2001*, Joel Whitburn, c. 2002.
- Allmusic.com

References

[1] http://www.allmusic.com/cg/amg.dll?p=amg&sql=10:3srj286c051a

Best of The Beach Boys

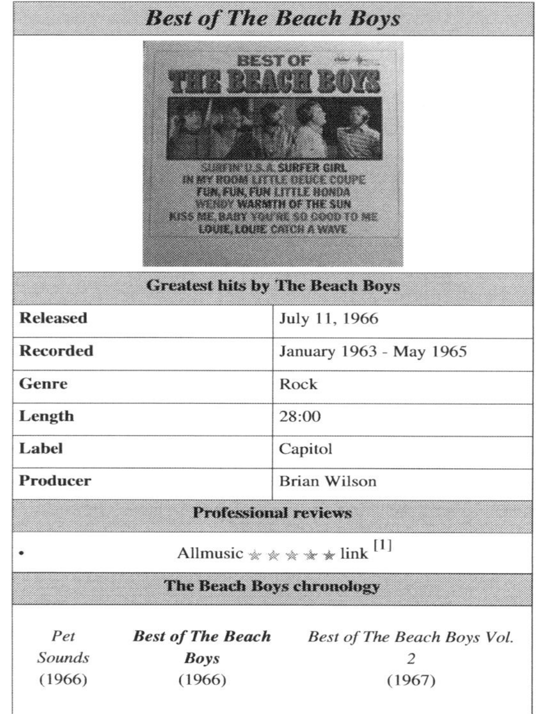

Best of The Beach Boys	
Greatest hits by The Beach Boys	
Released	July 11, 1966
Recorded	January 1963 - May 1965
Genre	Rock
Length	28:00
Label	Capitol
Producer	Brian Wilson
Professional reviews	
• Allmusic ★★★★★ link [1]	
The Beach Boys chronology	

Pet Sounds (1966)	***Best of The Beach Boys*** (1966)	*Best of The Beach Boys Vol. 2* (1967)

Best of The Beach Boys is the first compilation album by The Beach Boys, released in the summer of 1966 just two months after *Pet Sounds*. It includes many of their most popular songs from 1963 to 1965. The album reached #8 on U.S. charts and soon went gold. Brian Wilson is said to have been irritated by the label's decision to release a compilation of the group's older material at a time when the group's music was rapidly becoming more complex and sophisticated.

The UK edition of the album, with a revised track order, was issued later in the year, reaching #2 on British charts.

Although *Best of The Beach Boys* is currently certified double platinum in the US, it is now out of print, supplanted by more comprehensive compilation albums.

Track listing

1. "Surfin' USA" (Brian Wilson/Chuck Berry) – 2:28
2. "Catch a Wave" (Brian Wilson/Mike Love) – 2:18
3. "Surfer Girl" (Brian Wilson) – 2:26
4. "Little Deuce Coupe" (Brian Wilson/Roger Christian) – 1:50
5. "In My Room" (Brian Wilson/Gary Usher) – 2:13
6. "Little Honda" (Brian Wilson/Mike Love) – 1:51
7. "Fun, Fun, Fun" (Brian Wilson/Mike Love) – 2:18
8. "The Warmth of the Sun" (Brian Wilson/Mike Love) – 2:50
9. "Louie, Louie" (Richard Berry) – 2:23
10. "Kiss Me, Baby" (Brian Wilson/Mike Love) – 2:35
11. "You're So Good to Me" (Brian Wilson/Mike Love) – 2:13
12. "Wendy" (Brian Wilson/Mike Love) – 2:22

British version

The British version of ***Best of The Beach Boys*** was released in mid-1966 with 14 songs, instead of the usual 12 found on American albums.

The following songs were found on the British version of ***Best of The Beach Boys***:

1. "Surfin' Safari" – 2:05
2. "Surfin' USA" – 2:28
3. "Little Deuce Coupe" – 1:50
4. "Fun, Fun, Fun" – 2:18
5. "I Get Around" – 2:12
6. "All Summer Long" – 2:05
7. "In My Room" – 2:13
8. "Do You Wanna Dance?" – 2:18
9. "Help Me, Rhonda" – 2:45
10. "California Girls" – 2:37
11. "Barbara Ann" – 2:05
12. "You're So Good To Me" – 2:13
13. "Sloop John B" – 2:55
14. "God Only Knows" – 2:49

References

- *The Nearest Faraway Place: Brian Wilson, The Beach Boys and the Southern California Experience*, Timothy White, c. 1994.
- *Wouldn't It Be Nice - My Own Story*, Brian Wilson and Todd Gold, c. 1991.
- *Top Pop Singles 1955-2001*, Joel Whitburn, c. 2002.
- *Top Pop Albums 1955-2001*, Joel Whitburn, c. 2002.
- Allmusic.com

References

[1] http://www.allmusic.com/cg/amg.dll?p=amg&sql=10:z7d8vwvva9yk

Best of The Beach Boys Vol. 3

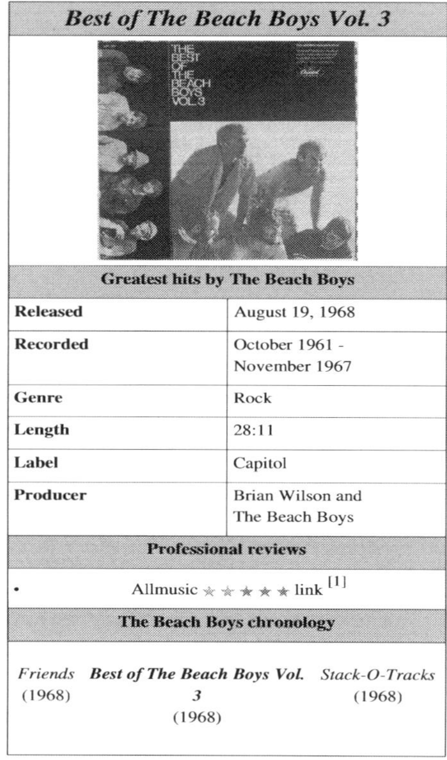

Best of The Beach Boys Vol. 3

Greatest hits by The Beach Boys

Released	August 19, 1968
Recorded	October 1961 - November 1967
Genre	Rock
Length	28:11
Label	Capitol
Producer	Brian Wilson and The Beach Boys

Professional reviews

- Allmusic ★★★★★ link [1]

The Beach Boys chronology

Friends (1968)	***Best of The Beach Boys Vol. 3*** (1968)	*Stack-O-Tracks* (1968)

Best of The Beach Boys Vol. 3 is the third in a series of hits compilations of music by The Beach Boys released by Capitol Records. It would prove to be the last official "best of" package by the band on their first record label.

Released in August 1968, *Best of The Beach Boys Vol. 3* was primarily put together to compensate for the disastrous U.S. sales of The Beach Boys' *Friends* album. Containing another helping of hits, the album had both its good points and bad.

This album was the LP debut of the pre-*Pet Sounds* single "The Little Girl I Once Knew". Also featured are "She Knows Me Too Well" from *The Beach Boys Today!*; their very first charted hit from 1962, "Surfin'"; and the passage of time that enabled the inclusions of "Good Vibrations", "Heroes and Villains" and "Darlin'". However, the appearance of "Frosty The Snowman" from *The Beach Boys' Christmas Album* is indeed puzzling and out of place. Another odd inclusion is "409", which had already been placed on *Vol. 2*. Among the hits that were not included in any of the original "best of" packages were: "Be True to Your School", "Shut Down", "Do You Wanna Dance?", "Sloop John B", and "Wouldn't It Be Nice". These (among many others) would appear later in several double-record compilations issued by Capitol in the 70s and 80s.

Long out of print, *Best of The Beach Boys Vol. 3* limped to an embarrassing #153 in the U.S.. UK fans were more charitable, sending it to #9.

Track listing

Side 1

1. "God Only Knows" (Brian Wilson/Tony Asher) – 2:49
2. "Dance, Dance, Dance" (Brian Wilson/Carl Wilson/Mike Love) – 1:59
3. "409" (Brian Wilson/Mike Love/Gary Usher) – 1:59
4. "The Little Girl I Once Knew" (Brian Wilson) – 2:36
5. "Frosty the Snowman" (Steve Nelson/Jack Rollins) – 1:54
6. "Girl Don't Tell Me" (Brian Wilson/Mike Love) – 2:19

Side 2

1. "Surfin'" (Brian Wilson/Mike Love) – 2:11
2. "Heroes and Villains" (Brian Wilson/Van Dyke Parks) – 3:37
3. "She Knows Me Too Well" (Brian Wilson/Mike Love) – 2:27
4. "Darlin'" (Brian Wilson/Mike Love) – 2:12
5. "Good Vibrations" (Brian Wilson/Mike Love) – 3:36

Best of The Beach Boys Vol. 3 (Capitol (D) T 2945) hit **#153** in the U.S. during a 6 week chart stay. In the UK, it reached **#9**.

British version

The British version of *Best of The Beach Boys Vol. 3* was released in mid-1968 with 14 songs, instead of the 12 found on American albums.

1. "409" – 1:58
2. "The Lonely Sea" – 2:23
3. "Catch a Wave" – 2:08
4. "The Warmth of the Sun" – 2:52
5. "Long Tall Texan" – 2:27
6. "Please Let Me Wonder" – 2:44
7. "Let Him Run Wild" – 2:21
8. "I Know There's an Answer" – 3:08
9. "Heroes and Villains" – 3:36
10. "Wild Honey" – 2:36
11. "Darlin'" – 2:11
12. "Country Air" – 2:19
13. "Friends" – 2:32
14. "Do It Again" – 2:18

References

- *Friends / 20/20* CD booklet notes, David Leaf, c.1990.
- *The Nearest Faraway Place: Brian Wilson, The Beach Boys and the Southern California Experience*, Timothy White, c. 1994.
- *Wouldn't It Be Nice - My Own Story*, Brian Wilson and Todd Gold, c. 1991.
- *Top Pop Singles 1955-2001*, Joel Whitburn, c. 2002.
- *Top Pop Albums 1955-2001*, Joel Whitburn, c. 2002.
- Allmusic.com

References

[1] http://www.allmusic.com/cg/amg.dll?p=amg&sql=10:sxkxikp6bb89

The Capitol Years

The Capitol Years	

Box set by The Beach Boys	
Genre	Pop
Label	Capitol
Producer	Brian Wilson
Professional reviews	
• Allmusic ★★★★★ link [1]	

The Capitol Years is a 4-CD box set which documents The Beach Boys' career with the Capitol Records label. It features 106 tracks from their time with Capitol.

Track listing

Disc one

1. "Surfin'"
2. "Surfin' Safari"
3. "Ten Little Indians"
4. "Surfin' U.S.A."
5. "Catch a Wave"
6. "Hawaii"
7. "Surfer's Rule"
8. "Surfer Girl"
9. "Don't Back Down"
10. "Little Deuce Coupe"
11. "409"
12. "In the Parkin' Lot"
13. "Car Crazy Cutie"
14. "Spirit of America"
15. "Shut Down"
16. "Custom Machine"
17. "Drive-In"
18. "Cherry, Cherry Coupe"
19. "Little Honda"
20. "Be True to Your School"
21. "Fun, Fun, Fun"
22. "Why Do Fools Fall in Love?"
23. "All Summer Long"
24. "I Get Around"

25. "Wendy"
26. "When I Grow Up (To Be a Man)"
27. "Little Saint Nick"
28. "Christmas Day"
29. "Auld Lang Syne"
30. "Don't Worry Baby"
31. "Your Summer Dream"

Disc two

1. "In My Room"
2. "The Warmth of the Sun"
3. "Keep an Eye on Summer"
4. "Girls on the Beach"
5. "Please Let Me Wonder"
6. "Hushabye"
7. "The Lord's Prayer"
8. "Dance, Dance, Dance"
9. "The Little Girl I Once Knew"
10. "Good to My Baby"
11. "Help Me, Rhonda"
12. "Do You Wanna Dance"
13. "You're So Good to Me"
14. "Don't Hurt My Little Sister"
15. "She Knows Me Too Well"
16. "California Girls"
17. "The Little Old Lady from Pasadena"
18. "Graduation Day"
19. "The Monster Mash"
20. "Johnny B. Goode"
21. "Barbara Ann"
22. "There's No Other (Like My Baby)"
23. "Devoted to You"
24. "Mountain of Love"
25. "Aren't You Glad"
26. "Their Hearts Were Full of Spring"

Disc three

1. "Then I Kissed Her"
2. "Kiss Me, Baby"
3. "Let Him Run Wild"
4. "Amusement Parks, U.S.A."
5. "I'm So Young"
6. "Girl Don't Tell Me"
7. "Salt Lake City"
8. "The Girl from New York City"
9. "Sloop John B"
10. "Here Today"

11. "Caroline No"
12. "I'm Waiting for the Day"
13. "You Still Believe in Me"
14. "I Know There's an Answer"
15. "Wouldn't It Be Nice"
16. "God Only Knows"
17. "I Just Wasn't Made for These Times"
18. "Good Vibrations"
19. "Wind Chimes"
20. "Cabin Essence"
21. "Vegetables"
22. "Wonderful"
23. "Our Prayer"
24. "Heroes and Villains"

Disc four

1. "Darlin'"
2. "Gettin' Hungry"
3. "Here Comes the Night"
4. "With Me Tonight"
5. "Wake the World"
6. "Country Air"
7. "You're Welcome"
8. "I'd Love Just Once to See You"
9. "Wild Honey"
10. "Do It Again"
11. "Little Bird"
12. "Let the Wind Blow"
13. "Busy Doin' Nothin'"
14. "Passing By"
15. "Time to Get Alone"
16. "Be Here in the Morning"
17. "Friends"
18. "I Can Hear Music"
19. "Never Learn Not to Love"
20. "Cotton Fields (The Cotton Song)"
21. "I Went to Sleep"
22. "Bluebirds over the Mountain"
23. "Celebrate the News"
24. "Be with Me"
25. "Break Away"

See also

- The Beach Boys
- Capitol Records

References

[1] http://www.allmusic.com/cg/amg.dll?p=amg&sql=10:rvse4j874wat

Carl and the Passions – "So Tough"

Carl and the Passions – "So Tough"	

Studio album by The Beach Boys	
Released	May 15, 1972
Recorded	December 4, 1971 – April 13, 1972
Genre	Rock, Soul, rhythm & blues, blues
Length	34:26
Label	Brother/Reprise
Producer	Carl Wilson, Brian Wilson, Dennis Wilson, Mike Love, Al Jardine, Ricky Fataar, Blondie Chaplin.
Professional reviews	
• Allmusic ★★★★★ link [1] • Robert Christgau (C+) link [3]	
The Beach Boys chronology	
Surf's Up (1971) · *Carl and the Passions – "So Tough"* (1972) · *Holland* (1973)	

Carl and the Passions – "So Tough" is the eighteenth studio album by The Beach Boys, released in 1972. Upon initial release, it was the second disc of a two-album set with *Pet Sounds* as the first of the set (which The Beach Boys were able to license from Capitol Records). Unfortunately, because *Carl and the Passions – "So Tough"* was a transitional album that saw the departure of one member and the introduction of two new ones (making it wildly inconsistent in terms of type of material present), it paled next to their 1966 classic and was seen as something of a disappointment at the time of release. The title of the album itself was a reference to an early band Carl Wilson had been in as a teenager (some say a possible early name for the Beach Boys). It was also the first album released under a new deal with Warner Bros. that allowed the company to distribute all future Beach Boys product in foreign as well as domestic markets.

In 1971, Carl (who served as the group's de facto musical director at this juncture) decided to spice up the structure of The Beach Boys by hiring third guitarist Blondie Chaplin, whose soulful singing brought a strong R&B element into the band's sound. Joining him was drummer Ricky Fataar after Dennis Wilson suffered a debilitating hand accident. Both had been discovered by Carl in 1969 while they were playing in a London band called The Flame.

Not long after the sessions began, Bruce Johnston had a falling out with manager Jack Rieley and quit the band (or was possibly fired). His main contribution, an early version of "Endless Harmony" entitled "Ten Years of Harmony", was re-recorded and eventually released in 1980 on *Keepin' the Summer Alive.* (Johnston recently confirmed that his only performance on the released album is as a background vocalist on "Marcella.") Johnston quit because he was unenthusiastic about Rieley's suggestion that the group adopt a hard rock approach and felt that Brian Wilson's prolonged lack of involvement had resulted in declining artistic quality. (However, Rieley claims he fired Johnston, and for two reasons: first, to prevent him from voting in the group's democratic processes and second, because of the supposed disrespect and contempt Johnston was showing the eldest Wilson at the time.) Brian Wilson himself barely contributed to the album's sessions, distracted by his personal demons and various extraneous side projects. These included the production of Spring's debut album (a reunion of The Honeys that included his wife and sister-in-law) and a projected trio with Tandyn Almer. Reportedly, their demo tape was rejected by A&M Records because Almer was considered a "troublemaker" by top brass. The executives also did not know who the lead singer on the tape was and were surprised when told it was Brian Wilson. Additionally, the executives were supposedly angered by the decision to use Wilson, as they feared he was so crazy he "would be pitching circus tents in [their] parking lots."

Brian Wilson's contributions consisted of collaborating on the writing of two songs and singing backing vocals on "Cuddle Up," "He Come Down," "Marcella" and, reportedly, "You Need A Mess Of Help To Stand Alone." The latter, credited to Wilson and Rieley, was Wilson and Almer's *Beatrice From Baltimore* with less tawdry lyrics. ("She's got some holes in her stockings/she do a whole lot of rockin'" is a couplet from the original lyrics.) "Marcella" was a song written about a masseuse/prostitute known by Wilson, before Rieley again replaced most of Almer's lyrics with his own. "Marcella" is a revamped version of a song left over from the *Today!* sessions called "All Dressed Up For School." This was first resurrected during the *Sunflower* sessions as "I Just Got My Pay." The song evolved such that, while the background of the songs "Marcella" and "All Dressed Up For School" are similar, the similarities between the melodies of the song are very removed.

It's been speculated that *Carl And The Passions – "So Tough"* was either scheduled to be released, or re-released, as a single album. A Warner/Reprise catalogue number, MS 2090, had been assigned to this single disc release, but nothing came of it. It should be noted that it was released as a stand-alone single album in Europe on Reprise Records.

The group photo on the inner sleeve was thought to have been doctored to show Brian with the rest of the Beach Boys, a fact confirmed when a picture featuring the same image of Brian appeared in a 2004 book by Keith Badman. This rare shot showed him surrounded by fellow band members including Bruce Johnston (in his final group picture), but not with either Ricky Fataar or Blondie Chaplin, both of whom are credited on the final album cover. This is the last known group photo taken with Brian before his massive weight gain.

It was because of the jarring stylistic clashing that *Carl and the Passions – "So Tough"* met with a less than rapturous response upon release, going as far as #50 in the US and #25 in the UK. Though still not considered to be among their finest albums, the passage of time has repaired *Carl And The Passions – "So Tough"*'s critical standing considerably.

English Britpop band Saint Etienne used the title *So Tough* for their 1993 album as an homage to the Beach Boys. Likewise, they also named their compilation of the same year You Need a Mess of Help to Stand Alone after the Beach Boys song.

Track listing

Side one				
No.	**Title**	**Writer(s)**	**Lead Vocals**	**Length**
1.	"You Need a Mess of Help to Stand Alone"	Brian Wilson/Jack Rieley	Carl Wilson	3:27
2.	"Here She Comes"	Ricky Fataar/Blondie Chaplin	Ricky Fataar/Blondie Chaplin	5:10
3.	"He Come Down"	Al Jardine/B. Wilson/Mike Love	Mike Love/Chaplin/Al Jardine/C. Wilson	4:41
4.	"Marcella"	B. Wilson/Tandyn Almer/Rieley	C. Wilson/Love	3:54

Side two				
No.	**Title**	**Writer(s)**	**Lead Vocals**	**Length**
1.	"Hold On Dear Brother"	Fataar/Chaplin	Chaplin	4:43
2.	"Make It Good"	Dennis Wilson/Daryl Dragon	Dennis Wilson	4:43
3.	"All This Is That"	Jardine/Carl Wilson/Love	C. Wilson/Jardine/Love	4:00
4.	"Cuddle Up"	D. Wilson/Dragon	D. Wilson	5:30

Singles

- "You Need a Mess of Help to Stand Alone" b/w "Cuddle Up" (Brother 1091), 15 May 1972
- "Marcella" b/w "Hold On Dear Brother" (Brother 1101), 26 June 1972) **US #110**

Carl and the Passions – "So Tough" is now paired on CD with *Holland*.

Carl and the Passions – "So Tough" (Brother/Reprise 2MS 2083) hit **#50** in the US during a 20 week chart stay. It reached **#25** in the UK.

Personnel

- Blondie Chaplin – Guitar, Bass, Vocals, Producer
- Ricky Fataar – Drums, Vocals, Producer
- Alan Jardine – Vocals, Producer
- Mike Love – Vocals
- Stephen Moffitt – Engineer
- Ed Thrasher – Art Direction
- Brian Wilson – Keyboards, Vocals, Producer
- Carl Wilson – Bass, Guitar, Keyboards, Vocals, Producer
- Dennis Wilson – Keyboards, Vocals, Producer

Sources

- *Carl and the Passions – "So Tough"/Holland* CD booklet notes, Elton John and Scott McCaughey, c.2000.
- "The Nearest Faraway Place: Brian Wilson, The Beach Boys and the Southern California Experience", Timothy White, c. 1994.
- "Wouldn't It Be Nice – My Own Story", Brian Wilson and Todd Gold, c. 1991.
- "Top Pop Singles 1955-2001", Joel Whitburn, c. 2002.
- "Top Pop Albums 1955-2001", Joel Whitburn, c. 2002.
- Allmusic.com

References

[1] http://www.allmusic.com/cg/amg.dll?p=amg&sql=10:45rx28gc058a

Classics Selected by Brian Wilson

Classics selected by Brian Wilson	
Greatest hits by The Beach Boys	
Released	July 2, 2002
Recorded	June 1963 - November 1972, Except "California Feelin' ": Spring 2002
Genre	Rock
Length	56:57
Label	Capitol
Producer	Brian Wilson and Carl Wilson
Professional reviews	
• Allmusic ★★★★★ link [1]	
The Beach Boys chronology	

Hawthorne, CA (2001)	*Classics selected by Brian Wilson* (2002)	*Good Timin': Live at Knebworth England 1980* (2002)

Classics selected by Brian Wilson is a unique compilation of songs by The Beach Boys and released through Capitol Records in mid-2002. Its main attraction is that it was compiled by the band's creative genius, Brian Wilson, that February, with the addition of a new recording of an unreleased 1970s track, "California Feelin' ", not by The Beach Boys, but Wilson and his live band.

Wilson's choices tend to favor his ballads, from "Surfer Girl" and "The Warmth of the Sun" to his *Pet Sounds* and *Smile* classics. Later song selections include "Til I Die" and "Sail On, Sailor".

A different spin on a Beach Boys compilation album, *Classics selected by Brian Wilson* briefly made the US charts, reaching #159.

Track listing

1. "Surfer Girl" (Brian Wilson) – 2:26
2. "The Warmth of the Sun" (Brian Wilson/Mike Love) – 2:52
3. "I Get Around" (Brian Wilson/Mike Love) – 2:12
4. "Don't Worry Baby" (Brian Wilson/Roger Christian) – 2:47
5. "In My Room" (Brian Wilson/Gary Usher) – 2:11
6. "California Girls" (Brian Wilson/Mike Love) – 2:45
7. "God Only Knows" (Brian Wilson/Tony Asher) – 2:52
   - *Uses The Pet Sounds Sessions stereo remix*
8. "Caroline, No" (Brian Wilson/Tony Asher) – 2:17
   - *Uses The Pet Sounds Sessions stereo remix, with passing train/barking dogs coda*
9. "Good Vibrations" (Brian Wilson/Mike Love) – 3:36
10. "Wonderful" (Brian Wilson/Van Dyke Parks) – 2:21
    - *Smiley Smile version*
11. "Heroes and Villains" (Brian Wilson/Van Dyke Parks) – 3:38
    - *Uses Hawthorne, CA stereo remix*
12. "Surf's Up" (Brian Wilson/Van Dyke Parks) – 4:12
13. "Busy Doin' Nothin'" (Brian Wilson) – 3:03
14. "We're Together Again" (Ron Wilson) – 1:46
    - *First heard on the Friends/20/20 two-fer CD release in 1990 (reissued in 2001)*
15. "Time to Get Alone" (Brian Wilson) – 2:37
16. "This Whole World" (Brian Wilson) – 1:56
17. "Marcella" (Brian Wilson/Jack Rieley) – 3:53
18. "Sail On, Sailor" (Brian Wilson/Van Dyke Parks/Tandyn Almer/Ray Kennedy/Jack Rieley) – 3:18
19. "Til I Die" (Brian Wilson) – 2:41
20. "California Feelin'" (Brian Wilson/Stephen Kalinich) – 2:49
    - *Written in 1974 and unreleased by The Beach Boys, this new version is by Brian Wilson in 2002 and backed by his live band*

Classics selected by Brian Wilson (Capitol 7243 5 40087 2) hit **#159** in the US during a chart stay of 1 week.

Personnel

- Herb Agner – Project Manager
- Kevin Flaherty – A&R
- Joe Gastwirt – Mastering
- Mark Linett – Compilation Engineer
- Kazunori Uemura – Package Design
- Brian Wilson – Producer, Selection
- Carl Wilson – Producer
- Satoru Yonekawa – Package Design

Sources

- *Classics selected by Brian Wilson* CD booklet notes, Brian Wilson, c. 2002
- Allmusic.com

References

[1] http://www.allmusic.com/cg/amg.dll?p=amg&sql=10:d7ozefwk2gf6

Endless Harmony Soundtrack

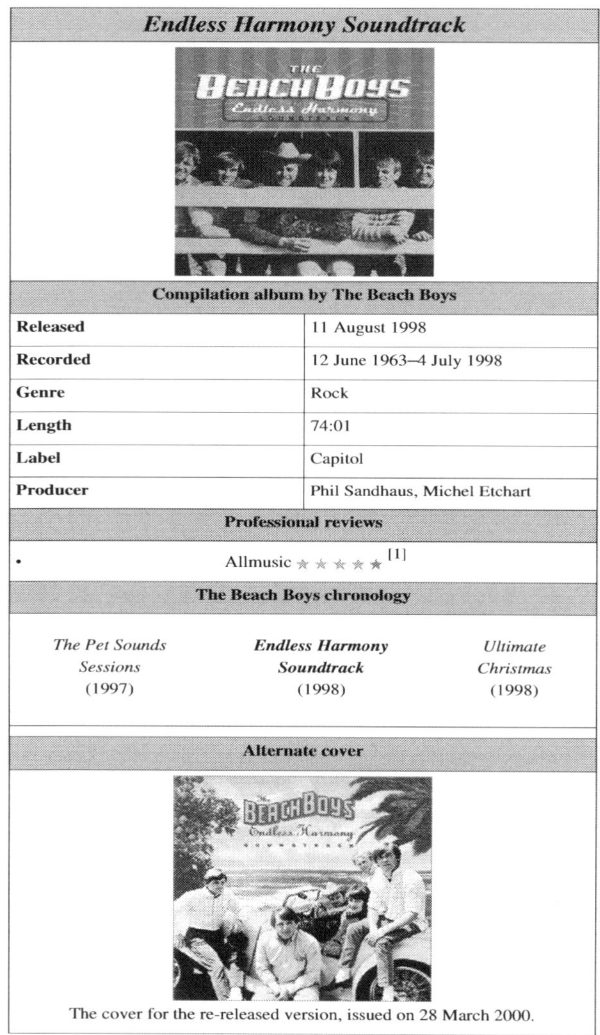

Endless Harmony Soundtrack	
Compilation album by The Beach Boys	
Released	11 August 1998
Recorded	12 June 1963–4 July 1998
Genre	Rock
Length	74:01
Label	Capitol
Producer	Phil Sandhaus, Michel Etchart
Professional reviews	
• Allmusic ★★★★★ [1]	
The Beach Boys chronology	
The Pet Sounds Sessions (1997) · ***Endless Harmony Soundtrack*** (1998) · *Ultimate Christmas* (1998)	
Alternate cover	
The cover for the re-released version, issued on 28 March 2000.	

Endless Harmony Soundtrack is an anthology album of previously unheard material by The Beach Boys, originally released by Capitol Records in August 1998. Named for Bruce Johnston's song on the 1980 album *Keepin' the Summer Alive*, it was designed as a tie-in with the band's biographical documentary of the same name. The soundtrack was re-issued in March 2000 with some remixing and different artwork, while the original 1998 edition (with the orange/yellow cover) was deleted shortly thereafter.

Background

This project was undertaken during a time when The Beach Boys fractured apart - irrevocably - after the death of 51-year-old Carl Wilson in February 1998 from lung cancer. Brian Wilson, a temporary member for several years by this time, decided that the band was over and disassociated himself from any further group activity. At odds with Mike Love in continuing on after Carl's passing, Al Jardine did the same. To the present day, while Wilson and Jardine are pursuing solo careers, both Love and Bruce Johnston (with their accompanying concert act) still perform live as The Beach Boys.

The *Endless Harmony Soundtrack* itself is patterned somewhat like The Beatles' *Anthology* albums, with, various alternate versions and live renditions of songs, as well as previously unreleased ones. Spanning from a stereo remix of 1963's "Surfer Girl" to the completion of the unreleased 1969 recording "Loop de Loop (Flip Flop Flyin' in an Aeroplane)" 29 years after it was started, the album also includes a brief snippet of both Brian Wilson and Van Dyke Parks routining three *Smile* songs in 1966.

Endless Harmony Soundtrack never charted in the U.S. or the UK. Although the album wasn't a commercial success, it did encourage Capitol Records to issue a more comprehensive archival package in *Hawthorne, CA*, released in May 2001.

Track listing

All tracks written by Brian Wilson/Mike Love, unless otherwise noted.

1. "Soulful Old Man Sunshine" (Writing session excerpt) (Brian Wilson/Rick Henn) – 0:42
2. "Soulful Old Man Sunshine" (Brian Wilson/Rick Henn) – 3:25
3. "Radio Concert Promo 1" – 0:15
4. "Medley: Surfin' Safari/Fun, Fun, Fun/Shut Down/Little Deuce Coupe/Surfin' USA" (Live) (Brian Wilson/Love/Roger Christian/Chuck Berry) – 3:33
   - *Recorded on 22 October 1966 in Michigan*
5. "Surfer Girl" (Binaural mix) (Brian Wilson) – 2:27
   - The version on the revised 2000 edition of the album is more of an a cappella mix
6. "Help Me, Rhonda" (Alternate single version) – 2:50
7. "Kiss Me, Baby" (Stereo remix) – 2:42
8. "California Girls" (Stereo remix) – 2:44
9. "Good Vibrations" (Live) – 3:40
   - *Recorded in rehearsal on 8 December 1968 in London*
10. "Heroes and Villains (Demo)" (Brian Wilson/Van Dyke Parks) – 2:27
    - *Recorded on 4 November 1966, this run through for Los Angeles DJ "Humble" Harve features, in addition to "Heroes and Villains", the fragments "I'm in Great Shape" and "Barnyard"*
11. "Heroes and Villains" (Live) (Brian Wilson/Parks) – 3:40
12. "God Only Knows" (Live) (Brian Wilson/Tony Asher) – 2:45
    - *Actually a live-in-the-studio recording in September 1967*
13. "Radio Concert Promo 2" – 0:15
14. "Darlin'" (Live) – 2:26
    - *Recorded on 21 June 1980 at Knebworth*
15. "Wonderful"/"Don't Worry Bill" (Brian Wilson/Parks/Ricky Fataar/Blondie Chaplin/Steve Fataar/Brother Fataar) – 5:52
    - *A medley of* Smile*'s "Wonderful" and a song released by The Flame (also known as "The Flames") called "Don't Worry Bill" recorded on 23 November 1972 at Carnegie Hall in New York City*

16. "Do It Again" (Early version) – 2:30
17. "Break Away" (Demo) (Brian Wilson/Reggie Dunbar) – 2:38
    - *"Reggie Dunbar" is a pseudonym for Murry Wilson*
18. "Sail Plane Song" (Brian Wilson/Carl Wilson) – 2:12
19. "Loop de Loop (Flip Flop Flyin' in an Aeroplane)" (Brian Wilson/Carl Wilson/Al Jardine) – 2:56
    - *Recording begun in March 1969, finished by Al Jardine in July 1998*
20. "Barbara" (Dennis Wilson) – 2:58
21. "'Til I Die" (Alternate mix) (Brian Wilson) – 4:52
22. "Long Promised Road" (Live) (Carl Wilson/Jack Rieley) – 4:17
    - *Recorded on 23 November 1972 at Carnegie Hall in New York City*
23. "All Alone" (Carli Muñoz) – 3:36
24. "Brian's Back" (Love) – 4:07
    - Written in response to Brian Wilson's 1976 return to the public eye
25. "Endless Harmony" (Bruce Johnston) – 3:29
    - *Includes a hidden a cappella sample of "Kiss Me, Baby" after the song ends*

Sources

- *Endless Harmony Soundtrack* CD booklet notes, Brad Elliott, c. 2000.
- Allmusic

References

[1] Eder, Bruce. "Review: *Endless Harmony*" (http://www.allmusic.com/cg/amg.dll?p=amg&sql=10:ccev97y0krst). Macrovision Corporation. . Retrieved 5 September 2009.

Endless Summer

This article is about the Beach Boys album. For other uses, including the Donna Summer album, see Endless Summer.

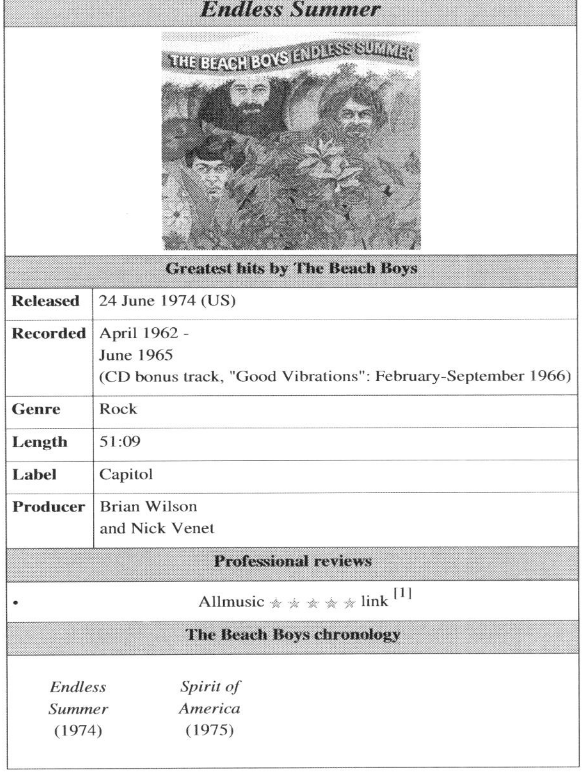

Endless Summer	
Greatest hits by The Beach Boys	
Released	24 June 1974 (US)
Recorded	April 1962 - June 1965 (CD bonus track, "Good Vibrations": February-September 1966)
Genre	Rock
Length	51:09
Label	Capitol
Producer	Brian Wilson and Nick Venet
Professional reviews	
• Allmusic link [1]	
The Beach Boys chronology	
Endless Summer (1974)	*Spirit of America* (1975)

Endless Summer is a pop compilation album by The Beach Boys, released on June 24, 1974.

A collection of hits from the pre-*Pet Sounds* period, *Endless Summer* (reportedly named by Mike Love), was compiled by their old label Capitol Records while The Beach Boys were contracted with Reprise Records. The compilation displays a number of oddities, including the inclusion of album versions of "Be True To Your School", "Help Me Ronda", and "Fun, Fun, Fun" instead of the hit-single versions, a difference which is subtle in the last case, but more prominent in the first two. Initial pressings of this album contained a poster depicting an airplane flying a Beach Boys banner. While the album is limited entirely to the band's sixties material, the cover artwork reflected the Beach Boys' seventies appearance. With vegetation in the foreground, it also seems to evoke images of the band's late 1960s *Smiley Smile* album, although none of the songs are from *Smiley Smile*.

Endless Summer is notable, however, for reclaiming the band's commercial glory at home, spending 155 weeks on the *Billboard* album chart, and peaking at #1, selling over three million copies.

Although released as a 'double album' (two LPs in a gatefold sleeve) in the USA, in the UK, the album was released on one LP with ten songs on each side.

Track listing

All songs by Brian Wilson/Mike Love, except where noted.

Side 1

1. "Surfin' Safari" – 2:05
2. "Surfer Girl" (Brian Wilson) – 2:26
3. "Catch a Wave" – 2:07
4. "The Warmth of the Sun" – 2:51
5. "Surfin' USA" (Chuck Berry/Brian Wilson) – 2:27

Side 2

1. "Be True to Your School" (Album Version) – 2:07
2. "Little Deuce Coupe" (Brian Wilson/Roger Christian) – 1:38
3. "In My Room" (Brian Wilson/Gary Usher) – 2:11
4. "Shut Down" (Brian Wilson/Roger Christian) – 1:49
5. "Fun, Fun, Fun" – 2:16

Side 3

1. "I Get Around" – 2:12
2. "Girls on the Beach" – 2:24
3. "Wendy" – 2:16
4. "Let Him Run Wild" – 2:20
5. "Don't Worry Baby" (Brian Wilson/Roger Christian) – 2:47

Side 4

1. "California Girls" – 2:38
2. "Girl Don't Tell Me" – 2:19
3. "Help Me, Ronda" – 3:08
4. "You're So Good to Me" – 2:14
5. "All Summer Long" – 2:06

Bonus CD track

1. "Good Vibrations", was added to the end of *Endless Summer* in the 1980s for its CD edition.

Endless Summer (Capitol SVBB 11307) hit **#1** in the US during a chart stay of 155 weeks.

The 2-record set was pressed with Side 1 backed with Side 4 and Side 2 backed with Side 3

The cassette version differs slightly as to the sequence of tracks. Side 1 features all tracks from Sides 1 & 2 in the same order plus "I Get Around" from Side 3. Side 2 includes the remaining tracks from Sides 3 & 4 in the same order with the exception of "Girls On The Beach" and "Wendy" which were 'swapped'.

The song "Help Me, Ronda" included in this album was also featured as one of 2 Beach Boys tracks in a promotional-only various artists compilation album issued by Capitol records entitled *The Greatest Music Ever Sold* (Capitol SPRO-8511/8512), that was distributed to record stores during the 1976 Holiday season as part of Capitol's "Greatest Music Ever Sold" campaign, which promoted 15 "Best Of" albums released by the record label. "Dance,

Dance, Dance" from *Spirit Of America* was the other Beach Boys song to be included.

Chart positions

Year	Chart	Position
1974	*Billboard* 200	1

References

[1] http://www.allmusic.com/cg/amg.dll?p=amg&sql=10:umf2zf0heh5k

Four by The Beach Boys

Four By The Beach Boys		
EP by The Beach Boys		
Released	September 21, 1964	
Recorded	April 10 & 29, 1964 Western Studios	
Genre	Pop music	
Length	8:31	
Label	Capitol	
Producer	Brian Wilson	
The Beach Boys chronology		
All Summer Long (1964)	***Four By The Beach Boys*** (EP) (1964)	*The Beach Boys' Christmas Album* (1964)

Four By The Beach Boys EP by The Beach Boys was the bands first and only EP. It contained only songs from the album *All Summer Long*. It charted at #44 in the US.

Track listing

Side one

1. "Little Honda" (B. Wilson/M. Love) – 2:33
2. "Wendy" (B. Wilson/M. Love) – 2:05

Side two

1. "Don't Back Down" (B. Wilson/M. Love) – 2:00
2. "Hushabye" (D. Pomus/M. Schuman) – 1:53

Friends

Friends	
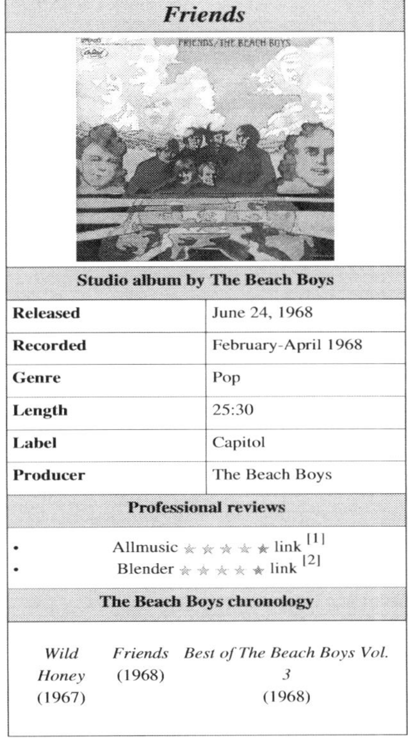	
Studio album by The Beach Boys	
Released	June 24, 1968
Recorded	February-April 1968
Genre	Pop
Length	25:30
Label	Capitol
Producer	The Beach Boys
Professional reviews	
• Allmusic ★★★★★ link [1]	
• Blender ★★★★★ link [2]	
The Beach Boys chronology	
Wild Honey (1967) *Friends* (1968) *Best of The Beach Boys Vol. 3* (1968)	

Friends is the fourteenth studio album by The Beach Boys, released in 1968.

As work on the album began in February 1968, Mike Love, a recent convert to transcendental meditation (TM), departed on a two week trip to India (alongside The Beatles and Donovan) to study TM further with his new master, Maharishi Mahesh Yogi. In his absence, the remaining Beach Boys, Brian Wilson, Dennis Wilson, Carl Wilson, Al Jardine and, now an official member, Bruce Johnston recorded the bulk of *Friends* along with selected members of The Wrecking Crew.

Friends was the first Beach Boys album to feature significant songwriting contributions from Dennis Wilson, "Little Bird" and "Be Still"; the former's bridge incorporated elements of "Child Is The Father Of The Man", a then-unreleased song from the aborted *Smile*. Although production was credited to the group as a whole, this was the band's last album until 1977's *Love You* to feature Brian Wilson as a dominant creative force, writing or co-writing every song with the exception of "Be Still" (he went uncredited on "Little Bird" so that Dennis and Stephen Kainich could collect more royalties), and actively participating in recording sessions.

In mid-March, Mike Love returned from his TM retreat and contributed to the subsequent vocal sessions, with leads on the brief "Meant for You", which opens the album, and the understated "Anna Lee, the Healer", who was in reality a spiritual healer and not a masseuse as has been claimed (that was Marcella, on a later album). Almost immediately, The Beach Boys embarked on two US tours, one with the Strawberry Alarm Clock, and another with, most controversially, Maharishi Mahesh Yogi himself (as a lecturer). Both were commercial failures, and were swiftly canceled (after they famously drew only 200 people in New York City).

The first Beach Boys album to be released only in stereo, *Friends* was issued in June. It reached only #126 on American charts, as an indication of the band's depleted commercial fortunes at the time, but its later UK release was more popular, reaching #13.

Track listing

Side one

1. "Meant for You" (Brian Wilson/Mike Love) – 0:38
   - *Features Mike Love on lead vocals*
2. "Friends" (Brian Wilson/Carl Wilson/Dennis Wilson/Al Jardine) – 2:30
   - *Features Carl Wilson on lead vocals*
3. "Wake the World" (Brian Wilson/Al Jardine) – 1:28
   - *Features Brian Wilson and Carl Wilson on lead vocals*
4. "Be Here in the Mornin' " (Brian Wilson/Carl Wilson/Mike Love/Dennis Wilson/Al Jardine) – 2:16
   - *Features Alan Jardine [sped-up], Brian Wilson and Carl Wilson on lead vocals*
5. "When a Man Needs a Woman" (Brian Wilson/Dennis Wilson/Carl Wilson/Al Jardine/Steve Korthof/Jon Parks) – 2:06
   - *Features Brian Wilson on lead vocals*
6. "Passing By" (Brian Wilson) – 2:23
   - *Features Brian Wilson and Al Jardine on lead vocals*

Side two

- "Anna Lee, the Healer" (Brian Wilson/Mike Love) – 1:51
- *Features Mike Love on lead vocals*

2. "Little Bird" (Dennis Wilson/Steve Kalinich/Brian Wilson [uncredited]) – 1:57
   - *Features Dennis Wilson on lead vocals*
3. "Be Still" (Dennis Wilson/Steve Kalinich) – 1:22
   - *Features Dennis Wilson on lead vocals*
4. "Busy Doin' Nothin'" (Brian Wilson) – 3:04
   - *Features Brian Wilson on lead vocals*
5. "Diamond Head" (Al Vescovo/Lyle Ritz/Jim Ackley/Brian Wilson) – 3:37
   - *Instrumental*
6. "Transcendental Meditation" (Brian Wilson/Mike Love/Al Jardine) – 1:49
   - *Features Brian Wilson on lead vocals*

Foreign editions

The Australian release of **Friends** had "Good Vibrations" replace "Diamond Head" on Side 2.

The Japanese release of **Friends** added "Do It Again" as the first song on Side 2.

Singles

- "Friends" b/w "Little Bird" (Capitol 2160), 8 April 1968 **US #47**; **UK #25**
- "Wake the World" featured as the B-side of "Do It Again"

Friends is now paired on CD with *20/20*, with bonus tracks from that period.

References

- *Friends / 20/20* CD booklet notes, David Leaf, c.1990.
- *The Nearest Faraway Place: Brian Wilson, The Beach Boys and the Southern California Experience*, Timothy White, c. 1994.
- *Wouldn't It Be Nice - My Own Story*, Brian Wilson and Todd Gold, c. 1991.
- *Top Pop Singles 1955-2001*, Joel Whitburn, c. 2002.
- *Top Pop Albums 1955-2001*, Joel Whitburn, c. 2002.
- Allmusic.com

References

[1] http://www.allmusic.com/cg/amg.dll?p=amg&sql=10:oz0qoaeabijb

Good Timin': Live at Knebworth England 1980

Good Timin': *Live at Knebworth England 1980*	
Live album by The Beach Boys	
Released	26 November 2002 (UK) 4 March 2003 (US)
Recorded	21 June 1980
Genre	Rock
Length	70:22
Label	Brother/ Eagle
Producer	Mark Linett
Professional reviews	
• Allmusic ★★★★★ link [1]	
The Beach Boys chronology	

Classics selected by Brian Wilson (2002)	*Good Timin': Live at Knebworth England 1980* (2002)	*Sounds of Summer: The Very Best of The Beach Boys* (2003)

Good Timin': Live at Knebworth England 1980 is a CD release of a concert performance by The Beach Boys at the aforementioned venue in June 1980. Featuring all six Beach Boys: Brian Wilson, Dennis Wilson, Carl Wilson, Mike Love, Al Jardine and Bruce Johnston, this was their last major UK performance together.

A nice overview of their career (the band's current album was *Keepin' the Summer Alive*), *Good Timin': Live at Knebworth England 1980* was first issued in the UK in 2002 and the following year in the US, both through the band's Brother Records imprint with independent distribution. It is also available on DVD.

The album included an impromptu version of "Happy Birthday", intended for Brian, whose birthday it had been the day before the concert was performed.

Aside from The Beach Boys themselves, the band included Bobby Figueroa on drums and percussion, Ed Carter on guitar, Joe Chemay on bass and Mike Meros on keyboards.

Track listing

1. "Intro" – 0:49
2. "California Girls" (Brian Wilson/Mike Love) – 3:10
3. "Sloop John B" (Trad. Arr. Brian Wilson) – 3:04
4. "Darlin' " (Brian Wilson/Mike Love) – 2:37
5. "School Days" (Chuck Berry) – 3:26
6. "God Only Knows" (Brian Wilson/Tony Asher) – 2:51
7. "Be True To Your School" (Brian Wilson/Mike Love) – 2:27
8. "Do It Again" (Brian Wilson/Mike Love) – 3:08
9. "Little Deuce Coupe" (Brian Wilson/Roger Christian) – 2:14
10. "Cotton Fields"/"Heroes And Villains" (Huddie Ledbetter/Brian Wilson/Van Dyke Parks) – 5:19
11. "Happy Birthday Brian" – 1:25
12. "Keepin' The Summer Alive (Carl Wilson/Randy Bachman) – 3:42
13. "Lady Lynda" (Al Jardine/Ron Altbach) – 5:01
14. "Surfer Girl" (Brian Wilson) – 2:39
15. "Help Me, Rhonda" (Brian Wilson/Mike Love) – 4:05
16. "Rock And Roll Music" (Chuck Berry) – 2:22
17. "I Get Around" (Brian Wilson/Mike Love) – 2:14
18. "Surfin' USA" (Brian Wilson/Chuck Berry) – 2:54
19. "You Are So Beautiful" (Billy Preston/Fisher) – 3:13
20. "Good Vibrations" (Brian Wilson/Mike Love) – 6:03
21. "Barbara Ann" (Fred Fassert) – 2:46
22. "Fun, Fun, Fun" (Brian Wilson/Mike Love) – 4:49

Good Timin': Live at Knebworth England 1980 (Brother/Eagle ER 20002) did not chart in the US or the UK.

Sources

- *Good Timin': Live at Knebworth England 1980* CD booklet notes, Mike Grant, c. 2002
- Allmusic.com

References

[1] http://www.allmusic.com/cg/amg.dll?p=amg&sql=10:yh9ds37wa3xg

Good Vibrations – Best of The Beach Boys

Good Vibrations – Best of The Beach Boys	
Greatest hits by The Beach Boys	
Released	June 30, 1975
Recorded	July 1965 - November 1972
Genre	Rock
Length	36:54
Label	Brother/Reprise
Producer	Brian Wilson and The Beach Boys
Professional reviews	
• Allmusic ★★★★★ link [1]	
The Beach Boys chronology	
The Beach Boys in Concert (1973) · ***Good Vibrations – Best of The Beach Boys*** (1975) · *20 Golden Greats* (1976)	

Good Vibrations – Best of The Beach Boys is the fourth official compilation album by The Beach Boys, and the first by their Brother Records imprint. In June 1974, The Beach Boys' old label, Capitol Records released a double-album compilation of the band's 1962-1965 hits called *Endless Summer*, to capitalize on their recent surge of success while the band toured incessantly. When the unofficial release turned out to be a surprise smash, a successor, *Spirit of America*, was rushed out in the spring of 1975 and was almost as successful. Deciding to issue an official compilation in the wake of their sudden commercial explosion at home, The Beach Boys opportunistically released *Good Vibrations – Best of The Beach Boys* to the public.

Having temporarily received the licensing rights to all their Capitol albums from *Pet Sounds* onwards, the band was able to exclusively use post-1965 material, including their contemporary works, to create a more diverse collection.

Released in June 1975, *Good Vibrations – Best of The Beach Boys* did well, reaching #25 in the US, but the two Capitol collections were more attractive to shoppers, and far outsold this collection.

Due to newer and more comprehensive compilations, *Good Vibrations – Best of The Beach Boys* has long since been deleted.

Track listing

Side 1

1. "Sail On, Sailor" (Brian Wilson/Tandyn Almer/Jack Rieley/Ray Kennedy/Van Dyke Parks) – 3:18
2. "Sloop John B" (Trad. Arr. Brian Wilson) – 2:56
3. "God Only Knows" (Brian Wilson/Tony Asher) – 2:50
4. "Darlin'" (Brian Wilson) – 2:12
5. "Add Some Music to Your Day" (Brian Wilson/Mike Love/Joe Knott) – 3:34
6. "Wouldn't It Be Nice" (Brian Wilson/Tony Asher/Mike Love) – 2:22

Side 2

1. "Good Vibrations" (Brian Wilson/Mike Love) – 3:36
2. "Do It Again" (Brian Wilson/Mike Love) – 2:25
3. "Caroline, No" (Brian Wilson/Tony Asher) – 2:18
4. "Friends" (Brian Wilson/Carl Wilson/Dennis Wilson/Al Jardine) – 2:30
5. "Surf's Up" (Brian Wilson/Van Dyke Parks) – 4:12
6. "Heroes and Villains" (Brian Wilson/Van Dyke Parks) – 3:37

Good Vibrations – The Very Best of The Beach Boys (Brother/Reprise MS 2223) hit **#25** in the US during a 23 week chart stay.

Sources

- "The Nearest Faraway Place: Brian Wilson, The Beach Boys and the Southern California Experience", Timothy White, c. 1994.
- "Top Pop Singles 1955–2001", Joel Whitburn, c. 2002.
- "Top Pop Albums 1955–2001", Joel Whitburn, c. 2002.

References

[1] http://www.allmusic.com/cg/amg.dll?p=amg&sql=10:krhqoawabij9

Good Vibrations: Thirty Years of The Beach Boys

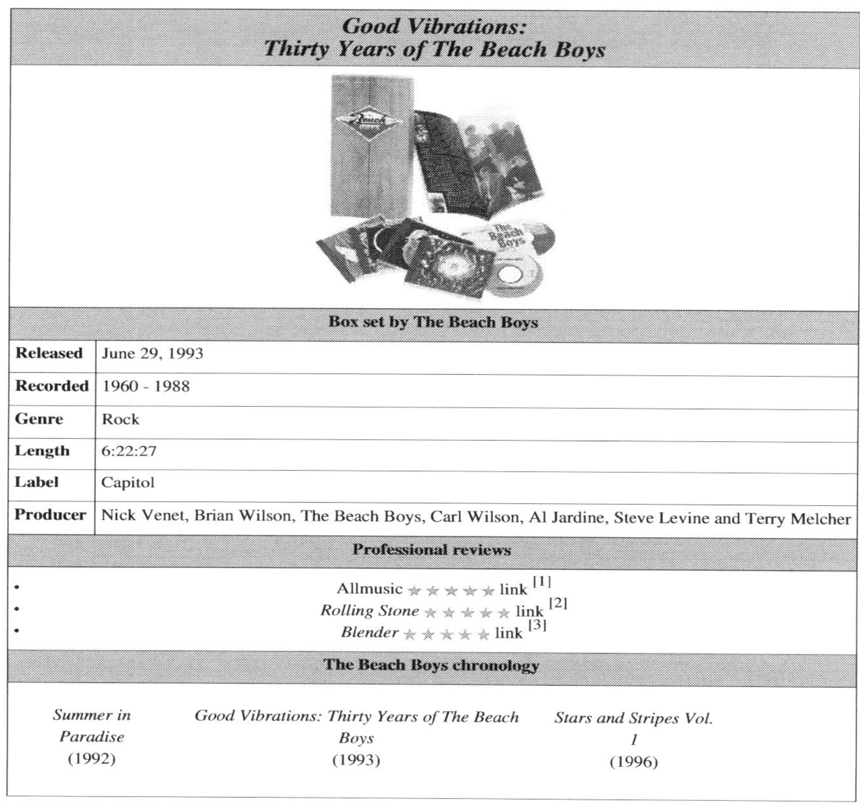

Good Vibrations: Thirty Years of The Beach Boys	
Box set by The Beach Boys	
Released	June 29, 1993
Recorded	1960 - 1988
Genre	Rock
Length	6:22:27
Label	Capitol
Producer	Nick Venet, Brian Wilson, The Beach Boys, Carl Wilson, Al Jardine, Steve Levine and Terry Melcher
Professional reviews	

- Allmusic ★★★★★ link [1]
- *Rolling Stone* ★★★★★ link [2]
- *Blender* ★★★★★ link [3]

The Beach Boys chronology		
Summer in Paradise (1992)	*Good Vibrations: Thirty Years of The Beach Boys* (1993)	*Stars and Stripes Vol. 1* (1996)

Good Vibrations: Thirty Years of The Beach Boys is a 1993 boxed set released by Capitol Records which collects tracks spanning The Beach Boys' entire career to that point on four CDs. A fifth disc contains mostly studio session tracks, complete vocal and instrumental tracks, and rare live performances. The set also includes a car window decal. Though it never charted, *Good Vibrations: Thirty Years of The Beach Boys* went gold in the US just over four months after its release.

The first four discs anthologize the band with mostly mono single versions, but also several demos and unreleased songs; the tracks are organized essentially in chronological order. Included is 30 minutes of music from the 1966/1967 *Smile* sessions, which had never been officially released, though had been heavily bootlegged for years. In addition, there is a hidden recording at the end of Disc 1 of a young Brian Wilson singing "Happy Birthday Four Freshmen" to his favorite vocal group into his multi-track tape recorder in 1960.

Track listing

All songs by Brian Wilson/Mike Love, except where noted.

Disc one

1. "Surfin' USA" (demo version) (Brian Wilson/Chuck Berry) – 1:49
2. "Little Surfer Girl" (Brian Wilson) – 0:31
3. "Surfin' (rehearsal)" – 1:31
4. "Surfin'" – 2:28
    - *Featuring Take 1, followed by Take 7 (master)*
5. "Their Hearts Were Full Of Spring (demo)" (Troup) – 2:35
    - *Murry Wilson is heard talking to engineer Nik Venet at the end of the track*
6. "Surfin' Safari" – 2:16
7. "409" (Brian Wilson/Mike Love/Gary Usher) – 2:09
8. "Punchline (Instrumental)" (Brian Wilson) – 1:52
9. "Surfin' USA" (Brian Wilson/Chuck Berry) – 2:29
10. "Shut Down" (Brian Wilson/Roger Christian) – 1:51
11. "Surfer Girl" (Brian Wilson) – 2:26
12. "Little Deuce Coupe" (Brian Wilson/Roger Christian) – 1:48
13. "In My Room" (Brian Wilson/Gary Usher) – 2:15
14. "Catch A Wave" (Brian Wilson/Mike Love) – 2:18
15. "The Surfer Moon" (Brian Wilson) – 2:18
16. "Be True to Your School" (single version) – 2:07
17. "Spirit Of America " (Brian Wilson/Roger Christian) – 2:20
18. "Little Saint Nick" – 1:59
19. "The Things We Did Last Summer" (J. Styne/S. Cahn) – 2:27
20. "Fun, Fun, Fun" – 2:19
21. "Don't Worry Baby" (Brian Wilson/Roger Christian) – 2:49
22. "Why Do Fools Fall In Love" (Frankie Lymon/Morris Levy) – 2:08
23. "The Warmth of the Sun" – 2:50
24. "I Get Around" – 2:13
25. "All Summer Long" – 2:07
26. "Little Honda" – 1:51
27. "Wendy" – 2:20
28. "Don't Back Down" – 1:53
29. "Do You Wanna Dance" (Bobby Freeman) – 2:17
30. "When I Grow Up (To Be a Man)" – 2:01
31. "Dance, Dance, Dance" (Brian Wilson/Carl Wilson/Mike Love) – 1:59
32. "Please Let Me Wonder" – 2:45
33. "She Knows Me Too Well" – 2:28
34. "Radio Station Jingles/Concert Promo" (Unknown) – 1:03
35. "Hushabye (live)" (D. Pomus/M. Shuman) – 3:56

Disc two

1. "California Girls" – 2:37
2. "Help Me, Rhonda" – 2:47
3. "Then I Kissed Her" (J. Barry, E. Greenwich, Phil Spector) – 2:15
4. "And Your Dream Comes True" – 1:06
5. "The Little Girl I Once Knew" (Brian Wilson) – 2:37
6. "Barbara Ann" (single version)(Fred Fassert) – 2:04
7. "Ruby Baby" (Jerry Leiber/Mike Stoller) – 2:10
8. "KOMA (Radio Promo Spot)" – 0:10
9. "Sloop John B" (Trad. Arr. Brian Wilson) – 2:57
10. "Wouldn't It Be Nice" (Brian Wilson/Tony Asher) – 2:23
11. "You Still Believe in Me" (Brian Wilson/Tony Asher) – 2:30
12. "God Only Knows" (Brian Wilson/Tony Asher) – 2:49
13. "Hang On to Your Ego" (Brian Wilson/Terry Sachen) – 3:13
14. "I Just Wasn't Made for These Times" (Brian Wilson/Tony Asher) – 3:12
15. "Pet Sounds" (Brian Wilson) – 2:22
16. "Caroline, No" (Brian Wilson/Tony Asher) – 2:52
    - *Features the barking dogs and oncoming train that close the* Pet Sounds *album*
17. "Good Vibrations" – 3:38
18. "Our Prayer" (Brian Wilson) – 1:07
19. "Heroes and Villains (Alternate Version) (Brian Wilson/Van Dyke Parks) – 2:56
20. "Heroes and Villains (Sections)" (Brian Wilson/Van Dyke Parks) – 6:40
21. "Wonderful" (Brian Wilson/Van Dyke Parks) – 2:02
22. "Cabinessence" (Brian Wilson/Van Dyke Parks) – 3:33
23. "Wind Chimes" (Brian Wilson/Van Dyke Parks) – 2:32
24. "Heroes and Villains (Intro) Parks, Wilson :35
25. "Do You Like Worms" (Brian Wilson/Van Dyke Parks) – 4:00
    - *Released with extra lyrics as "Roll Plymouth Rock" on Brian Wilson's 2004 Smile album*
26. "Vegetables" (Brian Wilson/Van Dyke Parks) – 3:29
27. "I Love To Say Da Da" (Brian Wilson) – 1:34
    - *Released with extra lyrics as "In Blue Hawaii" on Brian Wilson's 2004 Smile album*
28. "Surf's Up" (Brian Wilson/Van Dyke Parks) – 3:38
29. "With Me Tonight" (Brian Wilson) – 2:17

Disc three

1. "Heroes and Villains" (Brian Wilson/Van Dyke Parks) – 3:38
2. "Darlin'" – 2:12
3. "Wild Honey" – 2:37
4. "Let the Wind Blow" – 2:21
5. "Can't Wait Too Long (Previously unreleased)" (Brian Wilson) – 3:51
6. "Cool, Cool Water (Previously unreleased)" (Brian Wilson) – 1:12
7. "Meant for You" – 0:40
8. "Friends" (Brian Wilson/Carl Wilson/Dennis Wilson/Al Jardine) – 2:31
9. "Little Bird" (Dennis Wilson/Stephen Kalinich) – 1:58
10. "Busy Doin' Nothin'" (Brian Wilson) – 3:04
11. "Do It Again" – 2:28

12. "I Can Hear Music" (J. Barry/E. Greenwich/Phil Spector) – 2:38
13. "I Went to Sleep" (Brian Wilson/Carl Wilson) – 1:38
14. "Time to Get Alone" (Brian Wilson) – 2:43
15. "Break Away" (Brian Wilson/Reggie Dunbar) – 2:56
    - *"Reggie Dunbar" is a pseudonym for Murry Wilson*
16. "Cotton Fields (The Cotton Song) (45 Version)" (Huddie Ledbetter) – 3:03
17. "San Miguel" (Dennis Wilson/Gregg Jakobson) – 2:26
    - *First released on the 1981 compilation Ten Years of Harmony*
18. "Games Two Can Play" (Brian Wilson) – 2:01
19. "I Just Got My Pay" (Brian Wilson) – 2:20
    - *Re-written as "Marcella" for 1972's Carl and the Passions - "So Tough"*
20. "This Whole World" (Brian Wilson) – 1:57
21. "Add Some Music to Your Day" (Brian Wilson/Mike Love/Joe Knott) – 3:33
22. "Forever" (Dennis Wilson/Gregg Jakobson) – 2:41
23. "Our Sweet Love" (Brian Wilson/Carl Wilson/Al Jardine) – 2:38
24. "H.E.L.P. Is In The Way (Previously unreleased)" (Brian Wilson) – 2:30
25. "4th Of July (Previously unreleased)" (Dennis Wilson) – 2:44
26. "Long Promised Road" (Carl Wilson/Jack Rieley) – 3:27
27. "Disney Girls (1957)" (Bruce Johnston) – 4:08
28. "Surf's Up" (Brian Willson/Van Dyke Parks) – 4:13
29. "Til I Die" (Brian Wilson) – 2:30

Disc four

1. "Sail On, Sailor" (Brian Wilson/Van Dyke Parks/Tandyn Almer/Ray Kennedy/Jack Rieley) – 3:19
2. "California" (Al Jardine) – 3:20
3. "The Trader" (Carl Wilson/Jack Rieley) – 5:04
4. "Funky Pretty" (Brian Wilson/Mike Love/Jack Rieley) – 4:10
5. "Fairy Tale Music" (Brian Wilson) – 4:05
6. "You Need a Mess of Help to Stand Alone" (Brian Wilson/Jack Rieley) – 3:26
7. "Marcella" (Brian Wilson/Jack Rieley) – 3:52
8. "All This Is That" (Carl Wilson/Mike Love/Al Jardine) – 3:59
9. "Rock And Roll Music" (Chuck Berry) – 2:28
10. "It's O.K." – 2:11
11. "Had to Phone Ya" (Brian Wilson/Mike Love/Diane Rovell) – 1:44
12. "That Same Song" – 2:15
13. "It's Over Now (Previously unreleased)" (Brian Wilson) – 2:50
14. "Still I Dream of It" (Brian Wilson) – 3:26
    - *Above two songs from the aborted* Adult/Child *album*
15. "Let Us Go On This Way" – 1:59
16. "The Night Was So Young" (Brian Wilson) – 2:15
17. "I'll Bet He's Nice" (Brian Wilson) – 2:35
18. "Airplane" (Brian Wilson) – 3:04
19. "Come Go with Me" (C.E. Quick) – 2:03
20. "Our Team (Previously unreleased)" (Brian Wilson/Dennis Wilson/Carl Wilson/Mike Love/Al Jardine) – 2:33
21. "Baby Blue" (Dennis Wilson/Gregg Jakobson/Karen Lamm) – 3:18
22. "Good Timin'" (Brian Wilson/Carl Wilson) – 2:11

23. "Goin' On" – 3:03
24. "Getcha Back" (Mike Love/Terry Melcher) – 3:02
25. "Kokomo" (Mike Love/Scott McKenzie/John Phillips/Terry Melcher) – 3:37

Disc 5 "Sessions"

1. "In My Room (Demo)" (Brian Wilson/Gary Usher) – 2:33
2. "Radio Spot #1" – 0:09
3. "I Get Around (Track Only)" – 2:19
4. "Radio Spot #2" – 0:15
5. "Dance, Dance, Dance (Tracking Session)" (Brian Wilson/Carl Wilson/Mike Love) – 2:12
6. "Hang On to Your Ego (Sessions)" (Brian Wilson/Tony Asher) – 6:40
7. "God Only Knows (Tracking Session)" (Brian Wilson/Tony Asher) – 9:14
8. "Good Vibrations (Sessions)" – 15:18
   - *Included in the above two tracks are the final instrumental masters*
9. "Heroes and Villains (Track Only)" (Brian Wilson/Van Dyke Parks) – 0:47
10. "Cabinessence (Track Only)" (Brian Wilson/Van Dyke Parks) – 3:59
11. "Surf's Up (Track Only)" (Brian Wilson/Van Dyke Parks) – 1:40
12. "Radio Spot #3" – 0:06
13. "All Summer Long (Vocals)" – 2:12
14. "Wendy (Vocals)" – 2:27
15. "Hushabye (Vocals)" (D. Pomus/M. Shuman) – 2:42
16. "When I Grow Up (Vocals)" – 2:19
17. "Wouldn't It Be Nice (Vocals) (Brian Wilson/Tony Asher) – 2:43
   - *The above five tracks feature the vocals on one channel and the instrumental masters on the other channel so that listeners can hear one or the other or both, depending on the balance setting*
18. "California Girls (Vocals only)" – 2:34
19. "Radio Spot #4" – 0:11
20. "Concert Intro/Surfin' USA (Live 1964)" – 3:15
21. "Surfer Girl (Live 1964)" (Brian Wilson) – 2:52
22. "Be True to Your School (Live 1964)" – 2:29
23. "Good Vibrations (Live 1966)" – 5:14
24. "Surfer Girl (Live in Hawaii Rehearsals 1967)" (Brian Wilson) – 2:18

Good Vibrations: Thirty Years of The Beach Boys (Capitol 0777 7 81294 2) never charted in either the US or the UK.

Disc 6[4]

1. "Bluebirds Over The Mountain"
2. "Tears In The Morning"
3. "Here Comes The Night (12" version)"
4. "Lady Lynda"
5. "Sumahama"

Sources

- "The Nearest Faraway Place: Brian Wilson, The Beach Boys and the Southern California Experience", Timothy White (editor) lTimothy White, c. 1994.
- *Good Vibrations: Thirty Years of The Beach Boys* booklet notes, David Leaf, c.1993.
- Allmusic.com

External links

- *Good Vibrations: Thirty Years of The Beach Boys (disc one)* lyrics [5]
- *Good Vibrations: Thirty Years of The Beach Boys (disc two)* lyrics [6]
- *Good Vibrations: Thirty Years of The Beach Boys (disc three)* lyrics [7]
- *Good Vibrations: Thirty Years of The Beach Boys (disc four)* lyrics [8]
- *Good Vibrations: Thirty Years of The Beach Boys (bonus disc)* lyrics [9]

References

[1] http://www.allmusic.com/cg/amg.dll?p=amg&sql=10:kq7ibkg9hak9
[2] http://www.rollingstone.com/artists/thebeachboys/albums/album/211934/review/5942680/good_vibrations_thirty_years_of_the_beach_boys
[3] http://www.blender.com/guide/reviews.aspx?id=2245
[4] European edition only
[5] http://www.surfermoon.com/lyrics/box_set_1.html
[6] http://www.surfermoon.com/lyrics/box_set_2.html
[7] http://www.surfermoon.com/lyrics/box_set_3.html
[8] http://www.surfermoon.com/lyrics/box_set_4.html
[9] http://www.surfermoon.com/lyrics/box_set_bonus.html

The Greatest Hits – Volume 1: 20 Good Vibrations

The Greatest Hits – Volume 1: 20 Good Vibrations	
Greatest hits by The Beach Boys	
Released	September 21, 1999
Recorded	April 1962 - September 1966 Except "Kokomo": Spring 1988
Genre	Rock
Length	49:08
Label	Capitol
Producer	Murry Wilson, Brian Wilson and Terry Melcher
Professional reviews	
•	Allmusic ☆☆☆☆☆ link [1]
The Beach Boys chronology	

Ultimate Christmas (1998)	*The Greatest Hits – Volume 1: 20 Good Vibrations* (1999)	*The Greatest Hits – Volume 2: 20 More Good Vibrations* (1999)

The Greatest Hits – Volume 1: 20 Good Vibrations is a 1999 single disc compilation by The Beach Boys and released through Capitol Records. Initially, the collection was released in 1995 without its volume number and with a slight difference in sequencing. It was decided to create sequels to the original collection, so the 1995 release was updated accordingly to reflect this change. The updated version was re-issued the same day that its sequel, *The Greatest Hits – Volume 2: 20 More Good Vibrations*, appeared. The variation to the 1995 issue and the 1999 issue are the versions chosen for Be True To Your School and Help Me, Rhonda. The 1995 issue features the album version of both while the 1999 issue features the single version.

Featuring most of their classic—and biggest—hits during The Beach Boys' 1962-1966 golden streak, the album only breaks the period production by including the worthy 1988 #1 hit, "Kokomo".

The Greatest Hits – Volume 1: 20 Good Vibrations is also notable for crediting Murry Wilson, not Nick Venet, as producer of "Surfin' Safari" and "409", while also modifying "Surfin' USA" and "Shut Down"'s credits to reflect Brian Wilson as producer.

Released in September 1999, *The Greatest Hits – Volume 1: 20 Good Vibrations* charted at #95 US in March 2000 after a less-than-accurate Beach Boys ABC-TV movie was transmitted.

Track listing

1999 version. All songs by Brian Wilson/Mike Love, except where noted. All tracks are mono single mixes, except where noted.

1. "Surfin' Safari" – 2:05
2. "409" (Brian Wilson/Mike Love/Gary Usher) – 1:59
3. "Surfin' USA" (Brian Wilson/Chuck Berry) – 2:27
4. "Shut Down" (Brian Wilson/Roger Christian) – 1:49
5. "Surfer Girl" (Brian Wilson) – 2:26
6. "Little Deuce Coupe" (Brian Wilson/Roger Christian) – 1:48
7. "Catch a Wave" (mono album mix) – 2:17
8. "Be True to Your School" – 2:06
9. "Fun, Fun, Fun" – 2:18
10. "I Get Around" – 2:13
11. "Dance, Dance, Dance" (Brian Wilson/Carl Wilson/Mike Love) – 1:59
12. "Do You Wanna Dance?" (Bobby Freeman) – 2:18
13. "Help Me, Rhonda" – 2:46
14. "California Girls" – 2:44
15. "Barbara Ann" (Fred Fassert) – 2:07
16. "Sloop John B" (Trad. Arr. Brian Wilson) – 2:55
17. "Wouldn't It Be Nice" (Brian Wilson/Tony Asher/Mike Love) – 2:23
18. "God Only Knows" (Brian Wilson/Tony Asher) – 2:49
19. "Good Vibrations" – 3:36
20. "Kokomo" (stereo single mix) (John Phillips/Mike Love/Terry Melcher/Scott McKenzie) – 3:35

1995 version. All songs by Brian Wilson/Mike Love, except where noted.

1. "Surfin' Safari" – 2:05
2. "Surfin' USA" (Brian Wilson/Chuck Berry) – 2:27
3. "Surfer Girl" (Brian Wilson) – 2:26
4. "Little Deuce Coupe" (Brian Wilson/Roger Christian) – 1:48
5. "Be True to Your School" – 2:06
6. "Fun, Fun, Fun" – 2:18
7. "I Get Around" – 2:13
8. "Shut Down" (Brian Wilson/Roger Christian) – 1:49
9. "Dance, Dance, Dance" (Brian Wilson/Carl Wilson/Mike Love) – 1:59
10. "Do You Wanna Dance?" (Bobby Freeman) – 2:18
11. "Help Me, Rhonda" – 2:46
12. "California Girls" – 2:44
13. "Barbara Ann" (Fred Fassert) – 2:07
14. "Sloop John B" (Trad. Arr. Brian Wilson) – 2:55
15. "Wouldn't It Be Nice" (Brian Wilson/Tony Asher/Mike Love) – 2:23
16. "Good Vibrations" – 3:36
17. "409" (Brian Wilson/Mike Love/Gary Usher) – 1:59
18. "God Only Knows" (Brian Wilson/Tony Asher) – 2:49
19. "Catch a Wave" – 2:17

20. "Kokomo" (John Phillips/Mike Love/Terry Melcher/Scott McKenzie) – 3:35

The Greatest Hits – Volume 1: 20 Good Vibrations (Capitol 7243 5 21860 2) hit **#95** in the US during a chart stay of 11 weeks.

References

[1] http://www.allmusic.com/cg/amg.dll?p=amg&sql=10:5ms9keptaq7v

The Greatest Hits – Volume 2: 20 More Good Vibrations

The Greatest Hits – Volume 2: 20 More Good Vibrations	
Greatest hits by The Beach Boys	
Released	September 21, 1999
Recorded	July 1963 - August 1969
Genre	Rock
Length	51:12
Label	Capitol
Producer	Brian Wilson, Carl Wilson, Bruce Johnston, Murry Wilson and Al Jardine
Professional reviews	
• Allmusic link [1]	
The Beach Boys chronology	

The Greatest Hits – Volume 1: 20 Good Vibrations (1999)	*The Greatest Hits – Volume 2: 20 More Good Vibrations* (1999)	*Greatest Hits Volume Three: Best of the Brother Years 1970-1986* (2000)

The Greatest Hits – Volume 2: 20 More Good Vibrations is a 1999 single disc compilation by The Beach Boys and released through Capitol Records. It was released as the companion piece to *The Greatest Hits – Volume 1: 20 Good Vibrations* on the same day.

This CD basically mops up some of the early classics that were left behind on the first volume, such as "In My Room" and "Don't Worry Baby", but continues on to cover their commercially-lean but artistically-valid 1967-1970 period, going from "Heroes and Villains" to the Al Jardine-produced "Cottonfields", a European hit in the summer of 1970.

As on its earlier volume, the production credits on this album have been revised. Although originally credited to The Beach Boys, "Heroes and Villains", "Wild Honey", "Darlin' " and "Friends" are now credited as produced by Brian Wilson.

Released in September 1999, *The Greatest Hits – Volume 2: 20 More Good Vibrations* charted at #192 U.S. in March 2000 after a Beach Boys ABC-TV movie was transmitted.

Track listing

All songs by Brian Wilson/Mike Love, except where noted. All tracks are mono single mixes, except where noted.

1. "In My Room" (Brian Wilson/Gary Usher) – 2:11
2. "The Warmth of the Sun" – 2:50
3. "Don't Worry Baby" (Brian Wilson/Roger Christian) – 2:50
4. "All Summer Long" (mono album mix) – 2:06
5. "Wendy" – 2:23
6. "Little Honda" – 1:50
7. "When I Grow Up (To Be a Man)" – 2:02
8. "Please Let Me Wonder" – 2:45
9. "You're So Good to Me" – 2:14
10. "The Little Girl I Once Knew" – 2:36
11. "Caroline, No" (Brian Wilson/Tony Asher) – 2:17
    - *Single version, without passing train/barking dogs coda*
12. "Heroes and Villains" (Brian Wilson/Van Dyke Parks) – 3:37
13. "Wild Honey" – 2:37
14. "Darlin'" – 2:12
15. "Friends" (Brian Wilson/Dennis Wilson/Carl Wilson/Al Jardine) – 2:30
16. "Do It Again" – 2:18
    - *Single version, without workshop effects coda*
17. "Bluebirds over the Mountain" (Ersel Hickey) – 2:51
18. "I Can Hear Music" (stereo single mix) (Jeff Barry/Ellie Greenwich/Phil Spector) – 2:38
19. "Break Away" (stereo single mix) (Brian Wilson/Reggie Dunbar) – 2:55
    - *"Reggie Dunbar" is a pseudonym for Murry Wilson*
20. "Cottonfields" (Huddie Ledbetter) – 3:04

The Greatest Hits – Volume 2: 20 More Good Vibrations (Capitol 7243 5 20238 2) hit **#192** in the U.S. during a chart stay of 1 week.

References

[1] http://www.allmusic.com/cg/amg.dll?p=amg&sql=10:yj9ss39la3zg

Greatest Hits Volume Three: Best of the Brother Years 1970–1986

Greatest Hits Volume Three: Best of the Brother Years 1970–1986	
Greatest hits by The Beach Boys	
Released	February 1, 2000
Recorded	Autumn 1969 – Spring 1986
Genre	Rock
Length	61:52
Label	Capitol
Producer	Brian Wilson, Carl Wilson, Bruce Johnston, Al Jardine, Steve Levine and Terry Melcher
Professional reviews	
•	Allmusic ★★★★★ link [1]
The Beach Boys chronology	

The Greatest Hits – Volume 2: 20 More Good Vibrations (1999)	*Greatest Hits Volume Three: Best of the Brother Years 1970–1986* (2000)	*The Very Best of The Beach Boys* (2001)

Greatest Hits Volume Three: Best of the Brother Years 1970–1986 is a 2000 single disc compilation by The Beach Boys and released through Capitol Records. It was released several months after its predecessors, *The Greatest Hits – Volume 1: 20 Good Vibrations* and *The Greatest Hits – Volume 2: 20 More Good Vibrations*.

Track listing

1. "Add Some Music To Your Day" (Brian Wilson/Mike Love/Joe Knott) – 3:34
2. "Susie Cincinnati" (Al Jardine) – 2:57
   - *Single mix*
3. "This Whole World" (Brian Wilson) – 1:56
4. "Long Promised Road" (Carl Wilson/Jack Rieley) – 3:30
5. "Disney Girls (1957)" (Bruce Johnston) – 4:06
6. "Til I Die" (Brian Wilson) – 2:40
7. "Surf's Up" (Brian Wilson/Van Dyke Parks) – 4:12
8. "Marcella" (Brian Wilson/Jack Rieley) – 3:53

9. "Sail On, Sailor" (Brian Wilson/Van Dyke Parks/Tandyn Almer/Ray Kennedy/Jack Rieley) – 3:18
10. "The Trader" (Carl Wilson/Jack Rieley) – 5:05
11. "California Saga (On My Way To Sunny Californ-i-a)" (Al Jardine) – 3:15
    - *Single mix*
12. "Rock And Roll Music" (Chuck Berry) – 2:27
    - *Single version*
13. "It's OK" (Brian Wilson/Mike Love) – 2:07
    - *Marginally sped up single version*
14. "Honkin' Down The Highway" (Brian Wilson) – 2:47
15. "Peggy Sue" (Jerry Allison/Norman Petty/Buddy Holly) – 2:15
16. "Good Timin' " (Brian Wilson/Carl Wilson) – 2:12
17. "Goin' On" (Brian Wilson/Mike Love) – 2:59
18. "Come Go With Me" (C.E. Quick) – 2:07
19. "Getcha Back" (Mike Love/Terry Melcher) – 3:02
20. "California Dreamin' " (John Phillips/Michelle Phillips) – 3:12

The Beach Boys version of California Dreaming is worth the view. Roger McGuinn from The Byrds on 12-string. The single's producer, the late Terry Melcher, got John Phillips (on Sax), Michelle Phillips (Mama's and the Papa's) and McGuinn (The Byrds) to appear in this video. Denny Doherty (now deceased) was on the east coast and declined. Sadly, Cass Elliott had died years earlier.

Titled *The Best of the Beach Boys: 1970–1986* in England, it included three additional songs not issued on the U.S. version: "Tears In The Morning", the single-edit of "Here Comes The Night", and "Sumahama".

Greatest Hits Volume Three: Best of the Brother Years 1970–1986 (Capitol 7243 5 24511 2) never charted in the US or the UK.

References

[1] http://www.allmusic.com/cg/amg.dll?p=amg&sql=10:yxs9keptaq7v

Hawthorne, CA

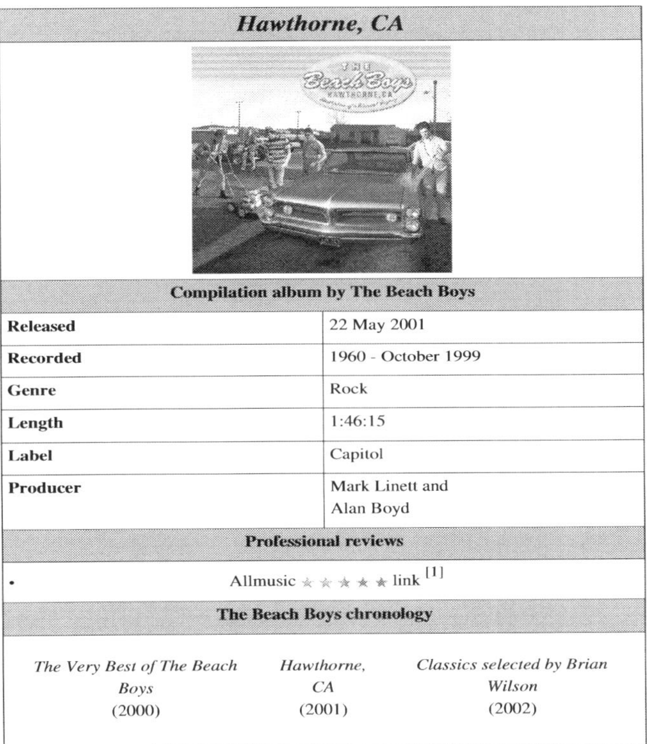

Hawthorne, CA	
Compilation album by The Beach Boys	
Released	22 May 2001
Recorded	1960 - October 1999
Genre	Rock
Length	1:46:15
Label	Capitol
Producer	Mark Linett and Alan Boyd
Professional reviews	
• Allmusic ★★★★★ link [1]	
The Beach Boys chronology	

The Very Best of The Beach Boys (2000)	*Hawthorne, CA* (2001)	*Classics selected by Brian Wilson* (2002)

Hawthorne, CA, subtitled *Birthplace of a Musical Legacy*, is the second anthology collection by The Beach Boys and released through Capitol Records. A double-CD, it was put together after the positive reaction to the *Endless Harmony Soundtrack* to give hardcore Beach Boys fans more rarities and alternate versions of well-known songs.

What is different about this set from its predecessor is that spoken word tracks from different band members in the mid to late 1990s (during the film production of the *Endless Harmony* documentary), as well as a 1969 radio show are salted throughout, letting *Hawthorne, CA* play more as an aural biography of the band, much like The Beatles' *Anthology 1* did.

Spanning from home recordings in the Wilsons' family home in 1960, to the cutting of the backing track of "Sail On, Sailor" in late 1972, *Hawthorne, CA* is a fascinating alternate view into The Beach Boys' long career.

Track listing

Disc one

1. "Mike Love Introduces 'Surfin' " – 0:48
2. "3701 West 119th Street, Hawthorne, California: The 'Surfin" Rehearsal (Brian Wilson/Mike Love) – 2:40
3. "Happy Birthday Four Freshman" (unknown) – 0:56
4. "Mike On Brian's Harmonies" – 0:45
5. "Their Hearts Were Full Of Spring" (Troup) – 2:31
   - *Live rehearsal for Hawaii performance, 25 August 1967*
6. "Surfin' USA" (demo) (Brian Wilson/Chuck Berry) – 2:03
7. "Surfin' USA" (Backing track) (Brian Wilson/Chuck Berry) – 2:35
8. "Carl Wilson Radio Promo" – 0:15
9. "Shut Down" (live) (Brian Wilson/Roger Christian) – 1:56
   - *Recorded in Chicago on 26 March 1965 with Brian Wilson*
10. "Little Deuce Coupe" (demo) (Brian Wilson/Roger Christian) – 1:51
11. "Murry Wilson Directs A Radio Promo" – 0:25
12. "Fun, Fun, Fun" (backing track) (Brian Wilson/Mike Love) – 2:26
13. "Brian's Message to 'Rog' - Take 22" – 0:29
14. "Dance, Dance, Dance" (stereo remix) (Brian Wilson/Carl Wilson/Mike Love) – 2:05
15. "Kiss Me, Baby" (a cappella mix) (Brian Wilson/Mike Love) -
16. "Good to My Baby" (backing track) (Brian Wilson/Mike Love) – 2:32
17. "Chuck Britz On Brian In The Studio" – 0:21
18. "Salt Lake City" (session highlights) (Brian Wilson/Mike Love) – 1:49
19. "Salt Lake City" (stereo remix) (Brian Wilson/Mike Love) – 2:08
20. "Wish That He Could Stay" (session excerpt) (Brian Wilson/Mike Love) – 1:12
21. "And Your Dream Comes True" (stereo remix) (Brian Wilson/Mike Love) – 1:06
22. "Carol K Session Highlights" – 2:12
23. "The Little Girl I Once Knew" (alternate version) (Brian Wilson) – 2:33
24. "Alan and Dennis Introduce 'Barbara Ann' " – 0:29
25. "Barbara Ann" (session excerpt) (Fred Fassert) – 2:52
26. "Barbara Ann" (master take without *Party* overdubs) (Fred Fassert) – 3:08
27. "Mike On The Everly Brothers" – 0:22
28. "Devoted To You" (master take without *Party* overdubs) (Bryant) – 2:19
29. "Dennis Thanks Everybody/In the Back of My Mind" (Brian Wilson/Mike Love) – 2:25
   - *Includes a hidden excerpt of The Beach Boys singing a brief tribute to KFWB radio station in concert*

Disc two

1. "Can't Wait Too Long" (a cappella mix) (Brian Wilson) – 0:50
2. "Dennis Introduces Carl" – 0:43
3. "Good Vibrations" (stereo track sections) (Brian Wilson/Mike Love) – 3:13
4. "Good Vibrations" (concert rehearsal) (Brian Wilson/Mike Love) – 4:09
   - *Recorded in Hawaii on 25 August 1967*
5. "Heroes and Villains" (stereo single version) (Brian Wilson/Van Dyke Parks) – 3:40
6. "Vegetables" (promo - instrumental section) (Brian Wilson/Van Dyke Parks) – 0:56
7. "Vegetables" (stereo extended mix) (Brian Wilson/Van Dyke Parks) – 3:01
8. "You're With Me Tonight" (Brian Wilson) – 0:49

9. "Lonely Days" (unknown) – 0:49
10. "Bruce on *Wild Honey*" – 0:14
11. "Let the Wind Blow" (stereo remix) (Brian Wilson/Mike Love) – 2:35
12. "I Went to Sleep" (a cappella mix) (Brian Wilson/Carl Wilson) – 1:35
13. "Time to Get Alone" (alternate version) (Brian Wilson) – 3:39
14. "Alan And Brian Talk About Dennis" – 0:19
15. "A Time to Live in Dreams" (Dennis Wilson/Stephen Kalinich) – 1:50
16. "Be With Me" (backing track) (Dennis Wilson) – 3:17
17. "Dennis Introduces 'Cotton Fields' " – 0:10
18. "Cottonfields (The Cotton Song)" (stereo single version) (Huddie Ledbetter) – 3:15
19. "Alan And Carl on 'Break Away' " – 0:21
20. "Break Away" (alternate version) (Brian Wilson/Reggie Dunbar) – 3:12
    - *"Reggie Dunbar" is a pseudonym for Murry Wilson*
21. "Add Some Music to Your Day" (a cappella mix) (Brian Wilson/Mike Love/Joe Knott) – 3:29
22. "Dennis Wilson" – 0:27
23. "Forever" (a cappella mix) (Dennis Wilson/Gregg Jakobson) – 2:51
24. "Sail On, Sailor" (backing track) (Brian Wilson/Van Dyke Parks/Tandyn Almer/Ray Kennedy/Jack Rieley) – 3:16
25. "Old Man River" (vocal section) (Kern/Hammerstein II) – 1:20
26. "Carl Wilson" – 0:39
27. "The Lord's Prayer" (stereo remix) (Malotte) – 2:33
28. "Carl Wilson - Coda" – 2:28
    - *Includes a hidden excerpt of background vocals from "Heroes and Villains"*

Hawthorne, CA (Capitol 7243 5 31583 2) never charted in the US or the UK.

References

- *Hawthorne, CA* CD booklet notes, Alan Boyd, c. 2001
- Allmusic.com

References

[1] http://www.allmusic.com/cg/amg.dll?p=amg&sql=10:jmknu3r0an6k

Holland

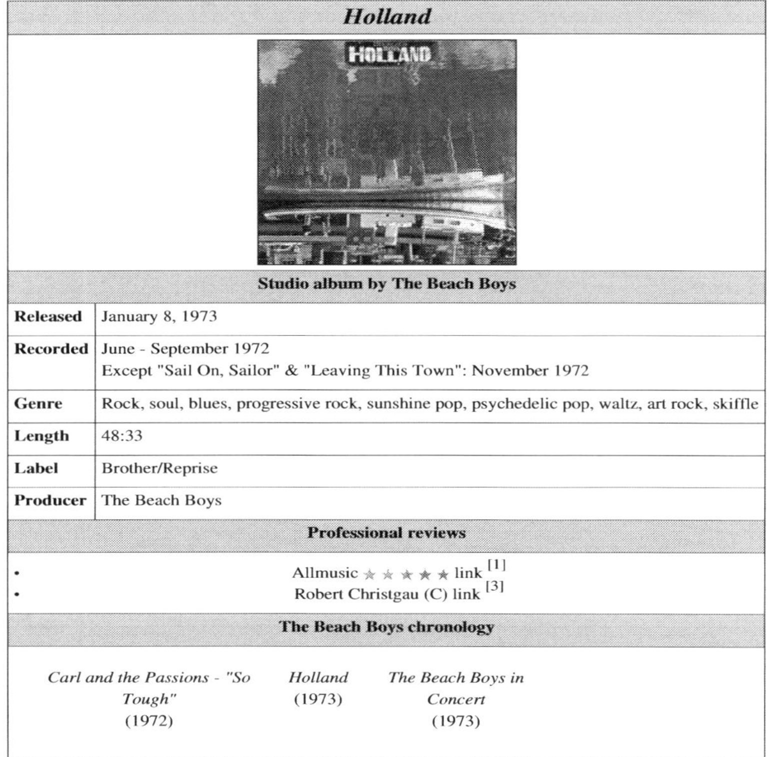

Holland	
Studio album by The Beach Boys	
Released	January 8, 1973
Recorded	June - September 1972 Except "Sail On, Sailor" & "Leaving This Town": November 1972
Genre	Rock, soul, blues, progressive rock, sunshine pop, psychedelic pop, waltz, art rock, skiffle
Length	48:33
Label	Brother/Reprise
Producer	The Beach Boys
Professional reviews	
• Allmusic ★★★★★ link [1]	
• Robert Christgau (C) link [3]	
The Beach Boys chronology	
Carl and the Passions - "So Tough" (1972) · *Holland* (1973) · *The Beach Boys in Concert* (1973)	

Holland is the sole 1973 studio release by The Beach Boys, their nineteenth studio album. It was famously (and expensively) recorded in Baambrugge, Netherlands over the summer of 1972 using a reconstructed studio sent from home, and with two Brian Wilson tracks rush-recorded in Los Angeles and added to the album at the last minute.

Just as *Carl and the Passions - "So Tough"* was coming to print, The Beach Boys, at manager Jack Rieley's urging, decided to pack up and record their next album in the Netherlands, feeling the change of scenery would add some inspiration to the sessions, and, over-optimistically, they also hoped that it would snap former leader Brian Wilson out of his deep depression.

By mid-1972, Wilson was well into mental illness. Keenly aware that he was creating less music than ever before, The Beach Boys were hoping to jump-start Brian's creative juices. Although he did make the trip (after three separate attempts to get on the plane), Wilson contributed little to the album, concentrating his musical efforts on "Mount Vernon and Fairway", a ten-minute long "musical fairy tale" which was later included with the album as a bonus EP. As a consequence, with Carl Wilson taking charge, the rest of the band had to carry the album, and as it turned out, *Holland* ended up as one of The Beach Boys' most respected 1970's releases.

Due to homesickness, Al Jardine and Mike Love conspired to create a three-part ode to California, resulting in a song cycle that ranks among both Jardine's and Love's best works. Mike donated the country-laced "Big Sur" (written three years earlier and here presented in 3/4 waltz time), while Mike and Al delivered the partially spoken-word of Robinson Jeffers' poem "Beaks of Eagles" and the shuffle-arranged "California", which features Brian on its first two lines. A remix of "California" was issued as the second single from the album and retitled "California Saga (On My Way To Sunny Californ-i-a)". Dennis, who was not given a lead vocal on *Holland*, offered up "Steamboat" and "Only with You". Carl included "The Trader": an anti-imperialist two-part epic that starts with a gleeful "Hi!" from his 3-year-old son, Jonah.

Upon the band's return from the Netherlands in the fall, *Holland* was rejected by Reprise Records for not having a potential hit single. It was decided to add an old unfinished Brian Wilson song, "Sail On, Sailor", which he had co-written with Ray Kennedy. After some re-working, Brian delivered what would become *Holland*'s most famous track. "Sail On, Sailor" was one of two songs recorded at home (the other was Ricky Fataar's and Chaplin's soulful and moog-tinged "Leaving This Town") and added at the last minute to a re-sequenced and re-submitted *Holland*. One of the casualties of this tracklist reshuffling proved to be another Fataar/Chaplin tune, written with Mike Love, called "We Got Love", which would resurface later in 1973 in a live context.

Early test pressings of Holland, made in the USA and in the UK feature the album in its original group-intended running order. Side one kicks off with "Steamboat", then the three-part Saga, followed by "We Got Love". The German distributor for Reprise records failed to implement the changed side-one line up correctly and mistakenly pressed 300-400 copies with the earlier running order. Early French and Canadian pressings of *Holland* still mention "We Got Love" on the sleeve, although the song is not on those albums.

Holland's bonus EP, entitled *Mount Vernon and Fairway (A Fairy Tale)*, was based on the intersection where the Love family lived in Los Angeles, and was primarily composed by Brian Wilson. Wilson originally intended it to be the centerpiece of a new Beach Boys album, consisting of the tracks from the EP and "Funky Pretty". It was initially rejected by the other band members, which effectively caused Brian to quit the sessions until Carl decided to include it as a separate EP. However, by that point, Wilson had lost interest in both the project and the Beach Boys; reportedly for denying his artistic output towards the group. Wilson would not record with the Beach Boys again as a group until 1974 for the aborted *Caribou* sessions. While narrated by Jack Rieley (as it was mostly unfinished when Wilson effectively walked away from the project), the voice of the Pied Piper was supplied by Brian.

Released in January 1973, *Holland* received mostly encouraging reviews and helped The Beach Boys improve their critical standing further. Reaching #36 in the US and #20 in the UK, the album still failed to go gold. At the end of the year which saw their US shows grow consistently in audience size, *Rolling Stone* named *Holland* as one of their picks for "album of the year", and The Beach Boys moved closer to widespread public re-acceptance.

Front cover artwork

The photograph on the front sleeve of the "Holland" album is an upside down image of the Kromme Waal, a canal that runs through the center of Amsterdam.

Track listing

Side one				
No.	**Title**	**Writer(s)**	**Lead Vocals**	**Length**
1.	"Sail On, Sailor"	Brian Wilson/Tandyn Almer/Ray Kennedy/Jack Rieley/Van Dyke Parks	Blondie Chaplin	3:19
2.	"Steamboat"	Dennis Wilson/Rieley	Carl Wilson/Dennis Wilson	4:33
3.	"California Saga: Big Sur"	Mike Love	Mike Love	2:56
4.	"California Saga: The Beaks of Eagles"	Robinson Jeffers/Al Jardine/Lynda Jardine	Love/Al Jardine	3:49
5.	"California Saga: California"	Jardine	Brian Wilson/Love/C. Wilson/Jardine	3:21

Side two				
No.	**Title**	**Writer(s)**	**Lead Vocals**	**Length**
1.	"The Trader"	Carl Wilson/Rieley	C. Wilson	5:04
2.	"Leaving This Town"	Ricky Fataar/Blondie Chaplin/C. Wilson/Love	Chaplin	5:49
3.	"Only with You"	D. Wilson/Love	C. Wilson	2:59
4.	"Funky Pretty"	B. Wilson/Love/Rieley	C. Wilson/Jardine/Chaplin/Ricky Fataar/Love	4:09

Mount Vernon and Fairway (A Fairy Tale)

All narration by Jack Rieley.

Side one				
No.	**Title**	**Writer(s)**	**Lead Vocals**	**Length**
1.	"Mt. Vernon and Fairway (Theme)"	B. Wilson		1:34
2.	"I'm the Pied Piper (Instrumental)"	B. Wilson/C. Wilson		2:20
3.	"Better Get Back in Bed"	B. Wilson	C. Wilson	1:39

Side two				
No.	**Title**	**Writer(s)**	**Lead Vocals**	**Length**
1.	"Magic Transistor Radio"	B. Wilson	B. Wilson	1:43
2.	"I'm the Pied Piper"	B. Wilson/C. Wilson	B. Wilson	2:09
3.	"Radio King Dom"	B. Wilson/Rieley		2:38

Singles

- "Sail On Sailor" b/w "Only with You" (Brother 1138), 29 January 1973) **US #79**
- "California Saga (On My Way To Sunny Californ-i-a)" b/w "Funky Pretty" (Brother 1156), 16 April 1973 **US #84**; **UK #37**
- "Sail On Sailor" b/w "Only with You" (re-release) (Brother 1325), 10 March 1975 **US #49**

Holland is now paired on CD with *Carl and the Passions - "So Tough"*.

Holland (Brother/Reprise MS 2118) hit **#36** in the US during a chart stay of 30 weeks. In the UK, it reached **#20**.

Early version

An early version of "Holland", scheduled to be released in November of 1972, was to have included the following songs:

1. "Steamboat"
2. "California Saga: Big Sur"
3. "California Saga: The Beaks of Eagles"
4. "California Saga: California"
5. "We Got Love"
6. "The Trader"
7. "Leaving This Town"
8. "Only with You"
9. "Funky Pretty"
10. "Mount Vernon And Fairway"

Warner Bros. rejected the album for being too weak, and had "We Got Love" replaced with "Sail On, Sailor".

Sources

- *Carl and the Passions - "So Tough"/Holland* CD booklet notes, Tom Petty and Scott McCaughey, c.2000.
- "The Nearest Faraway Place: Brian Wilson, The Beach Boys and the Southern California Experience", Timothy White, c. 1994.
- "Wouldn't It Be Nice - My Own Story", Brian Wilson and Todd Gold, c. 1991.
- "Top Pop Singles 1955-2001", Joel Whitburn, c. 2002.
- "Top Pop Albums 1955-2001", Joel Whitburn, c. 2002.
- Allmusic.com

References

[1] http://www.allmusic.com/cg/amg.dll?p=amg&sql=10:2q3tk6ax9krg

Keepin' the Summer Alive

Keepin' the Summer Alive	
Studio album by The Beach Boys	
Released	March 24, 1980
Recorded	July 1979–February 1980 Except: "When Girls Get Together": backing track recorded November 4, 1969, with overdubs in January 1970
Genre	Rock
Length	33:10
Label	Brother/Caribou/CBS
Producer	Bruce Johnston
Professional reviews	
•	Allmusic ★★★★★ link [1]
The Beach Boys chronology	
L.A. (Light Album) (1979) · *Keepin' the Summer Alive* (1980) · *Ten Years of Harmony* (1981)	

Keepin' the Summer Alive is the twenty-fourth studio album by The Beach Boys, their first released in the 1980s, and their second release under their contract with CBS Records (now Sony Music). After *L.A. (Light Album)* failed to live up to expectations, the executives at CBS expected Brian Wilson's full involvement, and thus, there was another attempt to lure him back into the producer's chair.

In July 1979, after Brian and Mike Love quickly composed some new original songs, the Beach Boys all reconvened at Western Recorders in Los Angeles (where most of the band's classic 1960s material had been produced by Brian) and hoped for the best. Things did not work out as planned, however. Dennis Wilson, at odds with the rest of the group, lasted a couple of sessions before leaving and taking no further part in the album. The initial sessions themselves were halted when Brian only wanted to work on oldies (hence the inclusion of a cover of Chuck Berry's "School Days").

The band took a small break to re-think the project, with Bruce Johnston taking complete control of the album's production, and placing the songs in a more contemporary-sounding context. The album was recorded at Al Jardine's recording studio in Big Sur and ended up as a mixture of brand new songs and older songs from the archives that hadn't been released up until that point. Of the new songs, "Keepin' the Summer Alive" and "Livin' With a Heartache" were written by Carl Wilson and Randy Bachman (of The Guess Who and Bachman-Turner Overdrive). The rest of the new songs, "Oh Darlin'", "Some of Your Love", "Goin' On" and "Sunshine" were written by Mike

Love and Brian Wilson. The older songs date back to 1970 ("When Girls Get Together"), 1972 ("Endless Harmony", the only track on the album where Dennis is heard) and 1978 ("Santa Ana Winds").

Keepin' the Summer Alive was released in March 1980, reaching #75 in the U.S. and #54 in the UK. After this, the Beach Boys would not release an album for another five years. Thus, this would become the last Beach Boys album to feature Dennis Wilson as he drowned in December 1983.

Track listing

Side one				
No.	**Title**	**Writer(s)**	**Lead Vocals**	**Length**
1.	"Keepin' the Summer Alive"	Carl Wilson/Randy Bachman	Carl Wilson	3:43
2.	"Oh Darlin'"	Brian Wilson/Mike Love	C. Wilson/Mike Love	3:52
3.	"Some of Your Love"	B. Wilson/Love	Love/C. Wilson	2:36
4.	"Livin' with a Heartache"	C. Wilson/Bachman	C. Wilson	4:06
5.	"School Day (Ring! Ring! Goes the Bell)"	Chuck Berry	Al Jardine	2:52

Side two				
No.	**Title**	**Writer(s)**	**Lead Vocals**	**Length**
1.	"Goin' On"	B. Wilson/Love	Love/C. Wilson/Brian Wilson	3:00
2.	"Sunshine"	B. Wilson/Love	Love/B. Wilson/C. Wilson	2:52
3.	"When Girls Get Together"	B. Wilson/Love	Love/B. Wilson	3:31
4.	"Santa Ana Winds"	B. Wilson/Al Jardine	Jardine/Love/C. Wilson	3:14
5.	"Endless Harmony"	Bruce Johnston	Bruce Johnston/C. Wilson	3:10

Singles

- "Goin' On" b/w "Endless Harmony" (Brother/Caribou), March 11, 1980 **US #83**
- "Livin' with a Heartache" b/w "Santa Ana Winds" (Brother/Caribou), May 20, 1980

Keepin' the Summer Alive is now paired on CD with *The Beach Boys*.

Keepin' the Summer Alive (Brother/Caribou/CBS JZ 36283) reached **#75** in the U.S. during a chart stay of 6 weeks. It reached **#54** in the UK

Sources

- *Keepin' the Summer Alive/The Beach Boys* CD booklet notes, Andrew G. Doe, c.2000.
- "The Nearest Faraway Place: Brian Wilson, The Beach Boys and the Southern California Experience", Timothy White, c. 1994.
- "Wouldn't It Be Nice - My Own Story", Brian Wilson and Todd Gold, c. 1991.
- "Top Pop Singles 1955-2001", Joel Whitburn, c. 2002.
- "Top Pop Albums 1955-2001", Joel Whitburn, c. 2002.
- Allmusic.com

References

[1] http://www.allmusic.com/cg/amg.dll?p=amg&sql=10:hz861vf8zzxa

L.A.

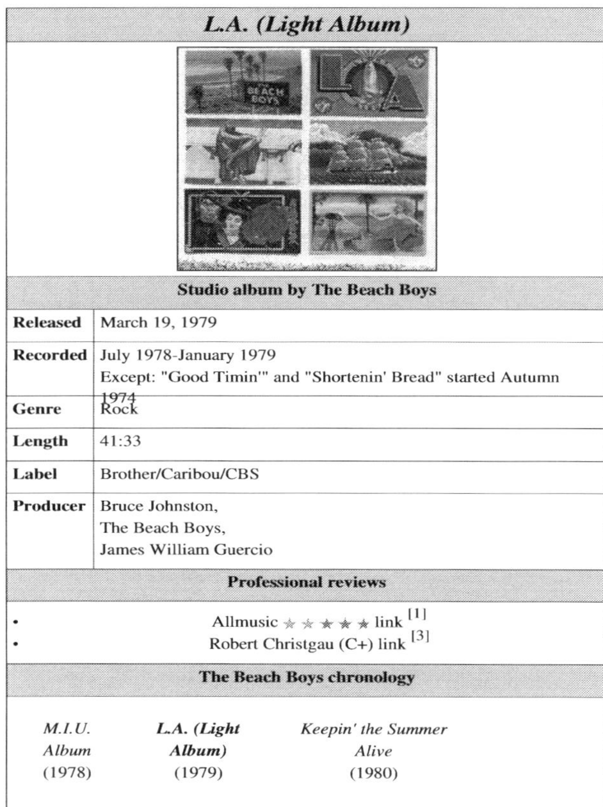

L.A. (Light Album)	
Studio album by The Beach Boys	
Released	March 19, 1979
Recorded	July 1978-January 1979 Except: "Good Timin'" and "Shortenin' Bread" started Autumn 1974
Genre	Rock
Length	41:33
Label	Brother/Caribou/CBS
Producer	Bruce Johnston, The Beach Boys, James William Guercio
Professional reviews	
• Allmusic ★★★★★ link [1] • Robert Christgau (C+) link [3]	
The Beach Boys chronology	
M.I.U. Album (1978) · ***L.A. (Light Album)*** (1979) · *Keepin' the Summer Alive* (1980)	

L.A. (Light Album) is the The Beach Boys' twenty-third studio album, their last released in the 1970s, and their first as part of their contract with CBS Records. Although Brother Records was still in operation, their manager at the time, former Chicago producer James William Guercio had his Caribou Records label distribute the album in conjunction with Brother.

Also co-producing with Guercio and The Beach Boys was Bruce Johnston, who had left the band in early 1972. Johnston was brought in when it became clear that the ailing Brian Wilson was in no fit state to produce the album. Johnston has been with the Beach Boys ever since.

L.A. (Light Album) (Brother/Caribou/CBS JZ 35752) reached #100 in the U.S. during a chart stay of thirteen weeks, and is now paired on CD with *M.I.U. Album*.

Track listing

Side one				
No.	**Title**	**Writer(s)**	**Lead Vocals**	**Length**
1.	"Good Timin'"	Brian Wilson/Carl Wilson	Carl Wilson	2:12
2.	"Lady Lynda"	Al Jardine/Ron Altbach	Al Jardine	3:58
3.	"Full Sail"	C. Wilson/Geoffrey Cushing-Murray	C. Wilson	2:56
4.	"Angel Come Home"	C. Wilson/Cushing-Murray	Dennis Wilson	3:39
5.	"Love Surrounds Me"	Dennis Wilson/Cushing-Murray	D. Wilson	3:41
6.	"Sumahama"	Mike Love	Mike Love	4:30

Side two				
No.	**Title**	**Writer(s)**	**Lead Vocals**	**Length**
1.	"Here Comes the Night"	B. Wilson/Love	C. Wilson/Jardine	10:51
2.	"Baby Blue"	D. WIlson/Gregg Jakobson/Karen Lamm	C. Wilson/D. Wilson	3:25
3.	"Goin' South"	C. Wilson/Cushing-Murray	C. WIlson	3:16
4.	"Shortnin' Bread"	trad. arr. B. Wilson	C. Wilson/D. Wilson	2:49

Singles

- "Here Comes the Night" (edit) b/w "Baby Blue" (Brother/Caribou ZS9 9026), February 19, 1979 US #44; UK #37
- "Good Timin' " b/w "Love Surrounds Me" (Brother/Caribou ZS9 9029), April 16, 1979 US #40
- "Lady Lynda" b/w "Full Sail" (Brother/Caribou ZS9 9030), June 1979 UK #6
- "Sumahama" b/w "It's a Beautiful Day" (Brother/Caribou ZS9 9031), September 1979 UK #45

Production Notes

Producers: Bruce Johnston/The Beach Boys/Jim Guercio/Curt Becher

Engineer: Bill Fletcher

Art Director/Designer: Tony Lane

Photographer: Ed Roach

The recording of *L.A. (Light Album)*

Despite a new $8 million contract with CBS Records calling for Brian Wilson to write and produce 75% of the songs on each new album, his contributions to *L.A. (Light Album)* are minimal. His presence on the album as a vocalist has only been confirmed on one song, "Angel Come Home," though he probably played piano on the single "Good Timin'" which was co-written by him with brother Carl, but had been recorded four years earlier. His arrangement of the traditional song "Shortenin' Bread" was also old. The vocals for both songs were recorded without Brian. "Good Timin'" hit #40 in the US.

Both "Baby Blue" and "Love Surrounds Me" were originally recorded for Dennis Wilson's never-released second solo album, *Bambu*. These would be the last Dennis Wilson songs released before his death in 1983.

L.A. (Light Album) spawned a top-ten hit in the UK with Al Jardine's Bach-inspired "Lady Lynda", written for his wife, and later rerecorded as "Lady Liberty" after their divorce. Jardine recently revealed that Dennis Wilson made an uncredited contribution to the song's lush string arrangement. Mike Love's Japanese-flavored "Sumahama" was also a UK single chart entry later in 1979.

Possibly the album's most controversial moment was an eleven-minute disco recasting of *Wild Honey*'s "Here Comes the Night" that caused considerable consternation among fans. The song was only played live during a few dates at New York City's Radio City Music Hall in March 1979 before being dropped from the live set due to adverse audience reaction. Nevertheless, an abridged 4:34 version made the charts in the U.S. as the lead single, peaking at #44.

L.A. (Light Album) peaked at #100 in the U.S. and at #32 in the UK.

Sources

- *M.I.U. Album/L.A. (Light Album)* CD booklet notes, Jeff Tamarkin, c.2000.
- "The Nearest Faraway Place: Brian Wilson, The Beach Boys and the Southern California Experience", Timothy White, c. 1994.
- "Wouldn't It Be Nice - My Own Story", Brian Wilson and Todd Gold, c. 1991.
- "Top Pop Singles 1955-2001", Joel Whitburn, c. 2002.
- "Top Pop Albums 1955-2001", Joel Whitburn, c. 2002.
- Allmusic.com
- Smiley Smile Message Board - "The Definitive Vocal Credits Thread," posts by Beach Boys archivist Alan Boyd and others

References

[1] http://www.allmusic.com/cg/amg.dll?p=amg&sql=10:et7uak5k5m3v

Little Deuce Coupe

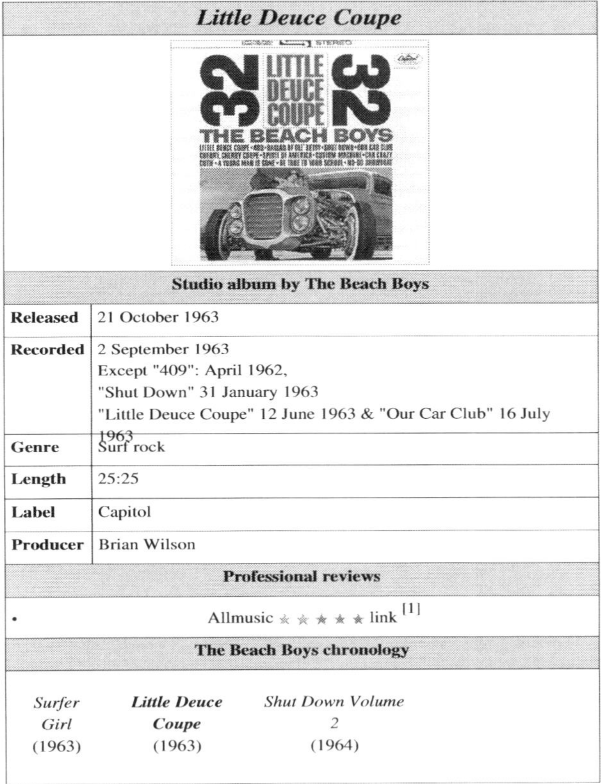

Little Deuce Coupe	
Studio album by The Beach Boys	
Released	21 October 1963
Recorded	2 September 1963 Except "409": April 1962, "Shut Down" 31 January 1963 "Little Deuce Coupe" 12 June 1963 & "Our Car Club" 16 July 1963
Genre	Surf rock
Length	25:25
Label	Capitol
Producer	Brian Wilson
Professional reviews	
•	Allmusic ★★★★★ link [1]
The Beach Boys chronology	
Surfer Girl (1963)	***Little Deuce Coupe*** (1963) · *Shut Down Volume 2* (1964)

Little Deuce Coupe is The Beach Boys' fourth album, and third overall LP release in 1963. Almost unintentionally, the album was rush-recorded and compiled when leader Brian Wilson sought to protect his band from exploitation from Capitol Records.

Little Deuce Coupe hit **#4** in the US during a 46-week chart stay. *Little Deuce Coupe* (Capitol (S) T 1998) is now paired on CD with *All Summer Long*, with bonus tracks from that period.

Production

In the summer of 1963, Capitol Records compiled a "hot rod" compilation album called *Shut Down*, including The Beach Boys' "Shut Down" itself and "409" - without their approval or involvement. Brian Wilson promptly readied several songs he had already been working on (mainly with radio DJ Roger Christian) and the band zipped through recording sessions to put *Little Deuce Coupe* on the record shop racks, remarkably, one month after *Surfer Girl* had come out. Eight of the tracks were new, while "Little Deuce Coupe", "Our Car Club", "Shut Down" and "409" had all come out on their last three albums.

Although it was a gamble putting so much vinyl out at once, *Little Deuce Coupe* became a big hit, reaching #4 in the US, and eventually going platinum. Because it mostly deals with cars as a subject matter (save "Be True to Your School", although even that has a mention of cruising), some observers have retroactively called *Little Deuce Coupe* an early rock example of what would become known as the concept album.

Although Nick Venet was listed as producer for "409" and "Shut Down", the official producer's credit for the entire *Little Deuce Coupe* album cites only Brian Wilson.

For an album recorded so quickly, the quality was amazingly high. In particular, Brian Wilson's songs and their arrangements were becoming more and more dazzling and complex, specifically "No-Go Showboat" and "Custom Machine".

After its recording, Brian Wilson re-recorded "Be True to Your School" for single release, resulting in another Top 10 hit. An original Christmas single, "Little Saint Nick" was also prepared.

This is the last Beach Boys album with which rhythm guitarist David Marks was involved. Original member Al Jardine made his permanent return preceding this album's sessions, and Marks departed shortly thereafter.

A 'Deuce Coupe' is a 1932 Ford Model B Coupe (*deuce* being for the year). This was the definitive hot-rod and featured an optional Ford flathead V8 engine when the car was introduced. A *pink slip* was the title to the car, named for the color of the paper used in Californian titles.

Front cover photo of the hot rod, and the story behind the vehicle

The picture featured on the front cover of the album was supplied by *Hot Rod* magazine, and features the body (with his head cropped in the photo) of hod-rod owner Clarence 'Chili' Catallo and his own customized four-window 1932 Ford Coupe - known forevermore amongst hot rod enthusiasts as "the lil' deuce coupe". A full shot of Catallo and his car from the same photo shoot appeared on the front cover of the July 1961 edition of *Hot Rod* magazine, and whilst Catallo himself died in 1998 the car still tours the showrooms and exhibitions to this day.

Catallo bought the vehicle in 1956 for 75 dollars in Michigan when he was 15 years old. Catallo replaced the original stock Ford engine (unlike The Beach Boys song lyrics, which mention "a flathead mill") with a newer Olsmobile V-8, as well as lowering the height of the coupe by six inches. Much of the original customizing work, including the stacked headlights, side trim, and front grille was done by an auto shop owned by Mike and Larry Alexander in the Detroit suburb of Southfield.

After Catallo moved to Southern California, additional work, including the 'chopping' or lowering of the roof, was done in 1960-61 at 'Kustom City', George Barris' noted North Hollywood auto customizing shop. This led to the magazine cover and two years later, the shot was featured as the cover for The Beach Boys' fourth album.

Catallo sold the coupe a few years later, but at the urging of his son Curt was able to buy it back in the late 90s for forty thousand dollars. The coupe had since been additionally modified but was restored by Curt Catallo with many of the original parts the coupe had in the early 1960s, so that it now is again virtually identical to the famous photo. In 2000, the hot rod won the 'People's Choice' award at the Meadow Brook Concours d'Elegance.

For a link to a *New York Times* article with additional details, including a photo gallery, see the 'External Links' section.

Track listing

Side one				
No.	**Title**	**Writer(s)**	**Lead Vocals**	**Length**
1.	"Little Deuce Coupe"	Brian Wilson/Roger Christian	Mike Love	1:38
2.	"Ballad of Ole' Betsy"	B. Wilson/Christian	Brian Wilson	2:15
3.	"Be True to Your School"	B. Wilson/Mike Love	Love	2:06
4.	"Car Crazy Cutie"	B. Wilson/Christian	B. Wilson	2:47
5.	"Cherry, Cherry Coupe"	B. Wilson/Christian	Love	1:47
6.	"409"	B. Wilson/Gary Usher/Love	Love	1:58

Side two				
No.	**Title**	**Writer(s)**	**Lead Vocals**	**Length**
1.	"Shut Down"	B. Wilson/Usher/Love	Love	1:48
2.	"Spirit of America"	B. Wilson/Christian	B. Wilson	2:23
3.	"Our Car Club"	B. Wilson/Love	Love/B. Wilson	2:21
4.	"No-Go Showboat"	B. Wilson/Christian	B. Wilson/Love	1:54
5.	"A Young Man is Gone"	Bobby Troup/Love	group	2:15
6.	"Custom Machine"	B. Wilson/Love	Love	1:38

Musicians

- Mike Love - Lead Vocals
- Brian Wilson - Bass Guitar, Vocals
- David Marks - Guitar, Vocals
- Carl Wilson - Guitar, Vocals
- Dennis Wilson - Drums

References

- *Little Deuce Coupe / All Summer Long* CD booklet notes, David Leaf, c.1990.
- *The Nearest Faraway Place: Brian Wilson, The Beach Boys and the Southern California Experience*, Timothy White, c. 1994.
- *Wouldn't It Be Nice - My Own Story*, Brian Wilson and Todd Gold, c. 1991.
- *Top Pop Singles 1955-2001*, Joel Whitburn, c. 2002.
- *Top Pop Albums 1955-2001*, Joel Whitburn, c. 2002.
- Allmusic.com

External links

- New York Times article (11-14-09) on the hot rod on the album cover [2]

References

[1] http://www.allmusic.com/cg/amg.dll?p=amg&sql=10:rmfjzf0heh5k
[2] http://www.nytimes.com/2009/08/30/automobiles/collectibles/30DEUCE.html?pagewanted=1&ei=5087&en=cc62eff02674b5b2&ex=1268539200

Live in London

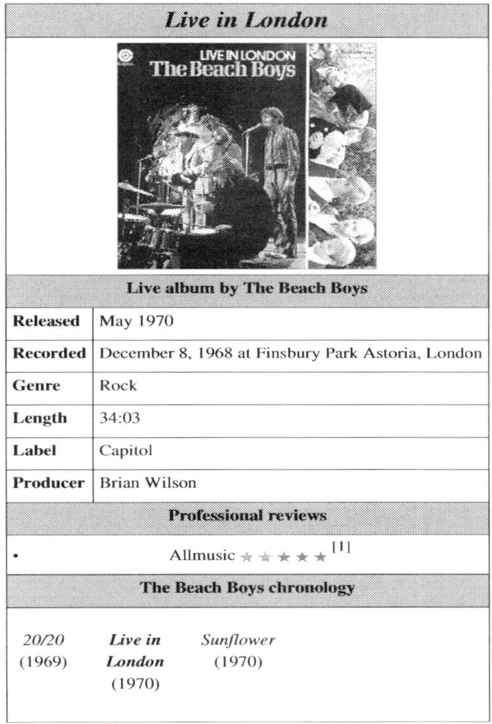

Live in London	
Live album by The Beach Boys	
Released	May 1970
Recorded	December 8, 1968 at Finsbury Park Astoria, London
Genre	Rock
Length	34:03
Label	Capitol
Producer	Brian Wilson
Professional reviews	
• Allmusic ★★★★★ [1]	
The Beach Boys chronology	
20/20 (1969) · ***Live in London*** (1970) · *Sunflower* (1970)	

Live in London (*Beach Boys '69* in North America) is a live album by The Beach Boys, initially released by EMI in the UK in May 1970, and in the US via Capitol Records on November 15, 1976.

Background

1968 was a very difficult year for The Beach Boys at home, where their reputation had soured considerably, yet their European success was still strong as evidenced by these confident performances recorded while the group were making their *20/20* album. After the surprise success of the *Endless Summer* and *Spirit of America* hits packages in 1974 and 1975, the Beach Boys enjoyed a resurgence of popularity at home, especially on the concert circuit. It was during this time that Capitol decided to strike while the iron was hot and issue a re-named edition of the album for the first time in the US. The reissue had art by rock artist Jim Evans, and a new title, ***Beach Boys '69***. Besides the fact that the live performance was actually recorded in December 1968, the LP's appearance added confusion to the marketplace as the group had recently issued a new, live double album—*The Beach Boys in Concert*—on their own Brother Records label, as part of a distribution deal with their new label, Reprise. Despite this, the record became a small chart success in the US, following the Top 10 placing of *15 Big Ones*, reaching #75 in the Fall of 1976 during a US chart stay of 10 weeks. The UK edition failed to chart.

It is believed that The Beach Boys owed Capitol one more album (this may have been it, instead of the *The Fading Rock Group Revival/Reverberation* project), and so, this release ended their relationship with the record label, and with EMI in the UK. When their albums were remastered for CD in 1990 (and again in 2001), *Live in London* was paired with their 1964 live release *Beach Boys Concert*.

Track listing

All tracks written by Brian Wilson/Mike Love, unless otherwise noted.

Side one

1. "Darlin'" – 2:41
2. "Wouldn't It Be Nice" (Brian Wilson/Tony Asher/Love) – 1:53
3. "Sloop John B" (Trad./Arr. Brian Wilson) – 2:30
4. "California Girls" – 2:19
5. "Do It Again" – 2:47
6. "Wake The World" (Brian Wilson/Al Jardine) – 2:26
7. "Aren't You Glad" – 3:09

Side two

- "Bluebirds Over The Mountain" (Ersel Hickey) – 2:53

2. "Their Hearts Were Full Of Spring" (Bobby Troup) – 2:49
3. "Good Vibrations" – 4:36
4. "God Only Knows" (Brian Wilson/Asher) – 3:27
5. "Barbara Ann" (Fred Fassert) – 2:32

- *Live in London* is now paired on CD with *Beach Boys Concert*, with bonus tracks from both periods.
- A live version of Dennis Wilson's "All I Want To Do" was recorded at these concerts, but was not included on the album. It remained unreleased until 1983's *Beach Boys Rarities* compilation album.
- "Aren't You Glad" is on the first side of the LP.

Sources

- *Surf's Up: The Beach Boys On Record* Brad Elliott c. 1981
- *Beach Boys Concert/Live in London* CD booklet notes, David Leaf, c. 1990.
- Allmusic

References

[1] Ruhlmann, William. "Review: *Live in London*" (http://www.allmusic.com/cg/amg.dll?p=amg&sql=10:utfnzfohehpk). Macrovision Corporation. . Retrieved 4 September 2009.

Lost & Found (1961–62)

Lost & Found (1961–62)	
Compilation album by The Beach Boys	
Released	February 1991
Recorded	September 15, 1961 – March 8, 1962
Genre	Rock
Length	37:48
Label	DCC Compact Classics
Producer	Brian Wilson
Professional reviews	
• Allmusic ★★★★★ link [1]	
The Beach Boys chronology	
Still Cruisin' (1989) *Lost & Found (1961-62)* (1991) *Summer in Paradise* (1992)	

Lost & Found (1961–62) is a Beach Boys compilation album which was released in 1991 under DCC Compact Classics record company. The album contains some of the early recordings the band did before they were signed to their first major record label, Capitol Records.

Track listing

1. "Luau" (Bruce Morgan) – 1:46
2. "Surfin'" (Brian Wilson/Mike Love) – 2:31
3. "Studio Chatter" – 0:16
4. "Surfin'" (Brian Wilson/Mike Love) – 2:29
5. "Studio Chatter" – 0:07
6. "Surfin'" (Brian Wilson/Mike Love) – 2:21
7. "Studio Chatter" – 0:23
8. "Luau" (Bruce Morgan) – 1:50
9. "Luau" (Bruce Morgan) – 1:49
10. "Barbie" (Bruce Morgan) – 2:23
11. "What Is a Young Girl Made Of" (Bruce Morgan) – 2:18
12. "Surfin' Safari" (Brian Wilson/Mike Love) – 2:06
13. "Studio Chatter" – 0:20
14. "Surfin' Safari" (Brian Wilson/Mike Love) – 2:05
15. "Studio Chatter" – 1:00
16. "Surfer Girl" (Brian Wilson) – 2:26
17. "Judy" (Brian Wilson) – 2:22
18. "Judy" (Brian Wilson) – 2:21
19. "Beach Boys Stomp (A.K.A. Karate)" (Carl Wilson) – 2:15
20. "Surfin' Safari" (Brian Wilson/Mike Love) – 2:09

21. "Lavender" (Bruce Morgan) – 2:31

References

[1] http://www.allmusic.com/cg/amg.dll?p=amg&sql=10:rmf5zf0heh5k

Love You

Love You	
Studio album by The Beach Boys	
Released	April 11, 1977
Recorded	Autumn 1976–January 1977 Except "Good Time": Autumn 1969, finished with overdubs by January 1977
Genre	Rock, Pop music
Length	34:50
Label	Brother/Reprise
Producer	Brian Wilson Mixdown producer: Carl Wilson
Professional reviews	
• Allmusic ★★★★★ link [1] • Pitchfork Media (7.8/10) link [2] • Robert Christgau (A) link [3]	
The Beach Boys chronology	
15 Big Ones (1976) · *Love You* (1977) · *M.I.U. Album* (1978)	

Love You is the 1977 follow-up to The Beach Boys' comeback album *15 Big Ones* and their twenty-first studio album overall. Almost entirely written and performed by Brian Wilson, it sharply divides critics' opinions from then and now on the project. Some feel that this record is Wilson's real return to form in the 1970s. Others feel it marks the point where Wilson seemingly lost the ability to produce and sing at a professional level.

A pop/rock album full of Brian's recent songs, *Love You* has a unique and distinct sound. It was during the album's recording that Wilson made his awkward Saturday Night Live appearance on November 27, introducing "Love Is a Woman" for the first time.

Many of the songs contained here have a very childish quality to them ("Roller Skating Child", "Airplane", and "Solar System" are examples of this) and, while attempting to be an up-beat album, it does conjure up a sense of melancholy when one considers that these naive songs are being created and performed by a man who had regressed to a child-like state in the wake of years of drug-affected emotional abuse.

Not all of the songs were strictly new, a few having been written during the *15 Big Ones* period, but more specifically "Good Time", which hailed from the 1970 *Sunflower* era, and "Ding Dang", which was co-written with The Byrds' former leader Roger McGuinn and recorded in late 1973. "Good Time" is a particularly anomalous inclusion because, unlike the rest of *Love You*, it features Brian's original sweet voice before that was lost in a haze of heavy tobacco and cocaine use in 1975. Indeed, on the other tracks Wilson's voice is so gruff that it can be difficult to distinguish him from his also newly hoarse brother Dennis.

A trilogy of love songs, "The Night Was So Young", "I'll Bet He's Nice" and "Let's Put Our Hearts Together" (with soon to be ex-wife Marilyn on co-lead) was a throwback to the topics of the *Pet Sounds* era without approaching their sophistication.

Considered by some to be The Beach Boys' last truly great album, others have found the release's unconventional sound difficult to swallow. Released just after announcing the band's new record deal with CBS Records (now Sony Music), Reprise Records put little promotion into the album, and with the advent of disco and punk, The Beach Boys' commercial steam had run out once again. Peaking at a disappointing fifty-three in the U.S. (and a marginally better twenty-eight in the UK), *Love You* was overlooked and soon forgotten by the mainstream pop music audience. However, many Brian Wilson fans all continue to claim for it an awkward beauty and high level of musical creativity. In recent years, Brian Wilson has called it his favourite Beach Boys album.

Track listing

All songs written and composed by Brian Wilson, except where noted.

Side one			
No.	**Title**	**lead vocals**	**Length**
1.	"Let Us Go On This Way" (B. Wilson/Mike Love)	Carl Wilson/Mike Love	1:58
2.	"Roller Skating Child"	Love/C. Wilson/Al Jardine/Brian Wilson	2:17
3.	"Mona"	Dennis Wilson/B. Wilson	2:06
4.	"Johnny Carson"	Love/C. Wilson	2:47
5.	"Good Time" (B. Wilson/Al Jardine)	B. Wilson	2:50
6.	"Honkin' Down the Highway"	Jardine	2:48
7.	"Ding Dang" (B. Wilson/Roger McGuinn)	Love/C. WIlson	0:57

Side two			
No.	**Title**	**lead vocals**	**Length**
1.	"Solar System"	B. Wilson	2:49
2.	"The Night Was So Young"	C. Wilson	2:15
3.	"I'll Bet He's Nice"	D. WIlson/B. Wilson/C. Wilson	2:36
4.	"Let's Put Our Hearts Together"	B. Wilson/Marilyn Wilson	2:14
5.	"I Wanna Pick You Up"	D. Wilson/B. Wilson	2:39
6.	"Airplane"	Love/B. WIlson/C. Wilson	3:05
7.	"Love Is a Woman"	B. Wilson/Love/Jardine	2:57

Singles

- "Honkin' Down the Highway" b/w "Solar System" (Brother 1389), May 30, 1977

Love You is now paired on CD with *15 Big Ones*.

Love You (Brother/Reprise MS 2258) reached **#53** in the U.S. during a chart stay of 7 weeks. It reached **#28** in the UK

New Album

In late 1976, Brian Wilson's original follow-up to *15 Big Ones* was titled "New Album". The album was to be made up of *15 Big Ones* outtakes, new songs recorded in late 1976, and songs from the group's library. The following songs were to be included on that album:

1. "My Diane"
2. "Marilyn Rovell"
3. "Hey Little Tomboy"
4. "Ruby Baby"
5. "You've Lost That Lovin' Feelin'"
6. "Sherry She Needs Me" (a 1965 track finished with a 1976 Brian Wilson vocal)
7. "Come Go with Me" (different from the one released on M.I.U. Album)
8. "Mony Mony"
9. "On Broadway"
10. "Sea Cruise"
11. "H.E.L.P. Is on the Way"
12. "Games Two Can Play"
13. "When Girls Get Together"

Adult Child

In 1977, Brian Wilson put together a proposed solo album to follow *Love You*. Called "Adult Child", group dynamics prevented its release. It included:

1. "Life Is For The Living"
2. "Hey Little Tomboy"
3. "Deep Purple"
4. "H.E.L.P. Is On The Way"
5. "It's Over Now"
6. "Everybody Wants To Live"
7. "Shortenin' Bread"
8. "Lines"
9. "On Broadway"
10. "Games Two Can Play"
11. "It's Trying To Say" (aka "Baseball")
12. "Still I Dream Of It"

Both unreleased albums have been heavily bootlegged, and padded out with other unrelated outtakes from the period

Sources

- *Surf's Up: The Beach Boys On Record* Brad Elliott
- *15 Big Ones/Love You* CD booklet notes, Dennis Diken and Peter Buck, c.2000.
- "The Nearest Faraway Place: Brian Wilson, The Beach Boys and the Southern California Experience", Timothy White, c. 1994.
- "Wouldn't It Be Nice - My Own Story", Brian Wilson and Todd Gold, c. 1991.
- "Top Pop Singles 1955-2001", Joel Whitburn, c. 2002.
- "Top Pop Albums 1955-2001", Joel Whitburn, c. 2002.
- Allmusic.com

References

[1] http://www.allmusic.com/cg/amg.dll?p=amg&sql=10:1tkvu3e5an7k

M.I.U. Album

M.I.U. Album	
Studio album by The Beach Boys	
Released	October 2, 1978
Recorded	Autumn 1977 and Spring 1978 except "Hey Little Tomboy" (1974) and "My Diane" (1976)
Genre	Rock
Length	32:19
Label	Brother/Reprise
Producer	Al Jardine Ron Altbach
Professional reviews	
• Allmusic ★★★★★ link [1] • Robert Christgau (C) link [3]	
The Beach Boys chronology	
Love You (1977) *M.I.U. Album* (1978) *L.A. (Light Album)* (1979)	

M.I.U. Album is the twenty-second studio album by The Beach Boys, released in 1978. Recorded at a fraught time for the band, only Mike Love, Al Jardine, and Brian Wilson appear throughout the album. Carl and Dennis Wilson are audible on only a few of the songs.

After the release of *Love You*, The Beach Boys fell into dispute over the direction of the band, and were close to breaking up. Brian Wilson began regressing back into drug use and mental illness. Dennis was readying his debut solo album, *Pacific Ocean Blue*, and was largely unavailable for the new project, of which he and brother Carl were not in favor. The idea, by staunch Transcendental Meditation follower Mike Love, was to record the new album – initially intended as a Christmas release – at the Maharishi International University in Fairfield, Iowa, (hence the 'M.I.U.' title). Consequently, when it was time to record the album in September 1977, only Love, Jardine and the eldest Wilson showed up.

The original intention was for Brian Wilson to produce the album, but it soon became clear he was either unable or unwilling to function in that role. The production credit on the album was given to Al Jardine and songwriting partner Ron Altbach, with Brian billed as "executive producer" - though the exact nature of this role was never clarified. The provisionally titled *Merry Christmas from the Beach Boys* was rejected by the record company, which demanded the band submit a regular studio album instead. New lyrics were overdubbed on to some of the original Christmas tracks the following spring, which, together with quickly-penned new material, formed the basis of the *M.I.U. Album*, the band's last for Reprise Records before embarking on their CBS Records (now Sony Music) contract.

When asked about *M.I.U. Album* in the British press, Dennis Wilson said that he "[doesn't] believe in that album" and that it was "an embarrassment to [his] life. It should self destruct.. I hope that the karma will fuck up Mike Love's meditation forever."[2]

Although the album peaked at only #151 in the US and became their first since 1964 to miss the UK chart completely, "Come Go With Me" would become a top 20 hit in late 1981 when it was released as a single from the *Ten Years of Harmony* compilation.

Track listing

Side one				
No.	**Title**	**Writer(s)**	**Lead Vocals**	**Length**
1.	"She's Got Rhythm"	Brian Wilson/Mike Love/Ron Altbach	Brian Wilson/Mike Love	2:27
2.	"Come Go with Me"	C.E. Quick	Al Jardine	2:06
3.	"Hey, Little Tomboy"	B. Wilson	Love/B. Wilson/Carl Wilson	2:25
4.	"Kona Coast"	Al Jardine/Love	Love/Jardine/B. Wilson	2:33
5.	"Peggy Sue"	Buddy Holly/Jerry Allison/Norman Petty	Jardine	2:15
6.	"Wontcha Come Out Tonight?"	B. Wilson/Love	B. Wilson/Love	2:30

Side two				
No.	**Title**	**Writer(s)**	**Lead Vocals**	**Length**
1.	"Sweet Sunday Kinda Love"	B. Wilson/Love	C. Wilson	2:42
2.	"Belles of Paris"	B. Wilson/Love/Altbach	Love	2:27
3.	"Pitter Patter"	B. Wilson/Love/Jardine	Love/Jardine	3:14
4.	"My Diane"	B. Wilson	Dennis Wilson/B. Wilson	2:37
5.	"Match Point of Our Love"	B. Wilson/Love	B. Wilson	3:29
6.	"Winds of Change"	Altbach/Ed Tuleja	Jardine/Love	3:14

Singles

- "Peggy Sue" b/w "Hey, Little Tomboy" (Brother 1394), 28 August 1978 **US #59**
- "Come Go with Me" b/w "Don't Go Near The Water" (from *Surf's Up*) (Brother/Caribou ZS4 02633), 2 November 1981 **US #18**

M.I.U. Album is now paired on CD with *L.A. (Light Album)*.

M.I.U. Album (Brother/Reprise MSK 2268) reached **# 151** in the U.S. during a chart stay of 4 weeks.

Merry Christmas From The Beach Boys

After signing with CBS Records in 1977, the Beach Boys wanted to satisfy the terms of their Warner/Reprise contract by releasing a Christmas album. Rejected by Warners, many of the tracks appeared on various bootlegs and on the 1998 release *Ultimate Christmas*. If released, the album would have had the following track listing:

Side 1:

1. "Christmastime Is Here Again" (The Peggy Sue track with new lyrics)
2. "Child Of Winter (Christmas Song)" (A remix of the 1974 single)
3. "Winter Symphony"
4. "Michael Row The Boat Ashore" (Outtake from *15 Big Ones*)
5. "Seasons In The Sun" (Recorded in 1970)

Side 2:

1. "Holy Evening" (a.k.a. "Morning Christmas")
2. "Christmas Day" (A new track, not the song from 1964's Christmas album)
3. "Go And Get That Girl"
4. "Santa's On His Way" ("H.E.L.P. Is On The Way" with new lyrics)
5. "I Saw Mommy Kissing Santa Claus" (not the seasonal standard)
6. "Medley: God Rest Ye Merry Gentlemen/Come All Ye Faithful/Hark The Herald Angels Sing/We Wish You A Merry Christmas"

outtakes include:

1. "Santa's Got An Airplane" ("Loop De Loop" with new lyrics)
2. "Belles of Christmas" (Rewritten as "Belles of Paris")
3. "Kona Christmas" (Rewritten as "Kona Coast")
4. "I Saw Mommy Kissing Santa Claus" (Lead vocals by Wendy and Carnie Wilson, backing vocals by the Beach Boys)

California Feeling

The non-seasonal album recorded in Iowa was delivered to Warner Bros. in the spring of 1978. It was originally titled "California Feeling", after a song which Brian demanded not be included on the album. The album was to be released with the following lineup:

1. "Match Point Of Our Love"
2. "Pitter Patter"
3. "Sweet Sunday Kind Of Love"
4. "Belles Of Paris"
5. "Winds Of Change"
6. "My Diane"
7. "She's Got Rhythm"
8. "Our Team"
9. "Hey Little Tomboy"
10. "Kona Coast"
11. "Wontcha Come Out Tonight"
12. "How's About A Little Bit Of Your Sweet Lovin'"

Also considered for the album were the 1969 Dennis Wilson song, "San Miguel," and an early version of Al Jardine's "Lady Lynda." This album was rejected by Warners.

Winds Of Change

The "California Feeling" album was overdubbed and "sweetened" for release. Two songs, "How's About A Little Bit Of Your Sweet Lovin'" and "Our Team", were replaced with "Peggy Sue" and a new version of "Come Go With Me." The album was retitled "Winds Of Change" and scheduled for release in the summer of 1978. "Winds Of Change" was to be released with the following lineup:

1. "Match Point Of Our Love"
2. "Pitter Patter"
3. "Sweet Sunday Kind Of Love"
4. "Belles Of Paris"
5. "Winds Of Change"
6. "My Diane"
7. "She's Got Rhythm"
8. "Peggy Sue"
9. "Hey Little Tomboy"
10. "Kona Coast"
11. "Wontcha Come Out Tonight"
12. "Come Go With Me"

Also considered for the album was the 1977 outtake, "Ruby Baby." This album was also rejected by Warners.

The album was finally released in October 1978 as "M.I.U. Album" with an alternate mix of "Hey Little Tomboy" used.

References

[1] http://www.allmusic.com/cg/amg.dll?p=amg&sql=10:v7yvad8kv8w3
[2] http://www.pipeline-operaglass.moonfruit.com/#/miu/4519796526

Sources

- *M.I.U. Album/L.A. (Light Album)* CD booklet notes, Jeff Tamarkin, c.2000.
- "The Nearest Faraway Place: Brian Wilson, The Beach Boys and the Southern California Experience", Timothy White, c. 1994.
- "Wouldn't It Be Nice — My Own Story", Brian Wilson and Todd Gold, c. 1991.
- "Top Pop Singles 1955–2001", Joel Whitburn, c. 2002.
- "Top Pop Albums 1955–2001", Joel Whitburn, c. 2002.
- Allmusic.com

Made in U.S.A.

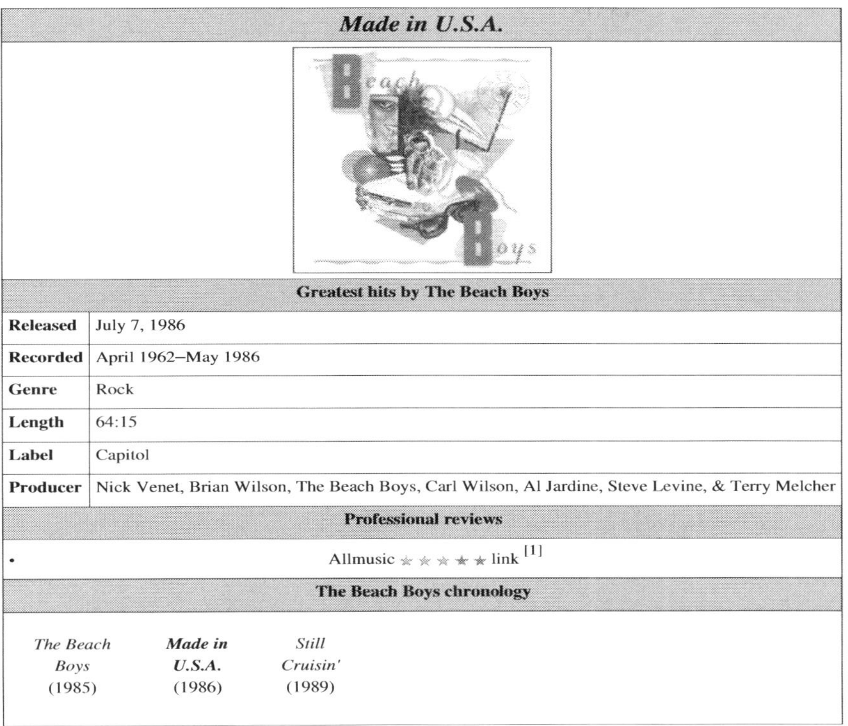

Made in U.S.A.	
Greatest hits by The Beach Boys	
Released	July 7, 1986
Recorded	April 1962–May 1986
Genre	Rock
Length	64:15
Label	Capitol
Producer	Nick Venet, Brian Wilson, The Beach Boys, Carl Wilson, Al Jardine, Steve Levine, & Terry Melcher
Professional reviews	
• Allmusic ★★★★★ link [1]	
The Beach Boys chronology	
The Beach Boys (1985)	***Made in U.S.A.*** (1986)
Still Cruisin' (1989)	

Made in U.S.A. is a 1986 double vinyl album (or one-CD) compilation of some of The Beach Boys' biggest successes. Released by their original label, Capitol Records, it marked a brief return to the label, with whom The Beach Boys released one further album, 1989's *Still Cruisin'*.

Featuring a number of their 1960s' classics, in addition to a sampling of their later hits, *Made in U.S.A.* also contains two new recordings made especially for this package, both produced by Terry Melcher. "Rock 'n' Roll to the Rescue" is a Mike Love/Melcher collaboration, and "California Dreamin'" is a cover of The Mamas & the Papas' late 1965 debut single. Both were released as singles and made the U.S. pop singles chart.

A slow seller, *Made in U.S.A.* reached #96 in the U.S. and ultimately went double platinum there, though with other compilations now available, *Made in U.S.A.* has since been deleted.

Promotional videos

The first video released for *Made in U.S.A.* was for the single, "Rock 'n' Roll to the Rescue". The video features a common Beach Boys theme of the beach, surfboards, and cars. The video features all (then-surviving) members of the Beach Boys (Brian Wilson, Carl Wilson, Mike Love, Al Jardine, and Bruce Johnston).

The second music video produced for the album was a black and white video of the song, "California Dreamin'". The video is predominantly filmed at a church and features all (then-surviving) members of the Beach Boys (Brian Wilson, Carl Wilson, Mike Love, Al Jardine, and Bruce Johnston). The Mamas & the Papas member and "California Dreamin'" songwriter John Phillips appears in the video as a preacher within the church.

Track listing

All songs by Brian Wilson/Mike Love, except where noted.

1. "Surfin' Safari" – 2:05
2. "409" (Brian Wilson/Mike Love/Gary Usher) – 1:58
3. "Surfin' USA" (Brian Wilson/Chuck Berry) – 2:27
4. "Be True to Your School" – 2:07
5. "Surfer Girl" (Brian Wilson) – 2:23
6. "Dance, Dance, Dance" (Brian Wilson/Carl Wilson/Mike Love) – 1:59
7. "Fun, Fun, Fun" – 2:16
8. "I Get Around" – 2:11
9. "Help Me, Rhonda" – 2:45
10. "Don't Worry Baby" (Brian Wilson/Roger Christian) – 2:42
11. "California Girls" – 2:37
12. "When I Grow Up (To Be a Man)" – 2:00
13. "Barbara Ann" (Fred Fassert) – 2:05
14. "Good Vibrations" – 3:36
15. "Heroes and Villains" (Brian Wilson/Van Dyke Parks) – 3:37
16. "Wouldn't It Be Nice" (Brian Wilson/Tony Asher/Mike Love) – 2:23

    Featuring alternative mono mix with more prominent lead vocal, due to original mix being temporarily lost
17. "Sloop John B" (trad., arr. Brian Wilson) – 2:56
18. "God Only Knows" (Brian Wilson/Tony Asher) – 2:48
19. "Caroline, No" (Brian Wilson/Tony Asher) – 2:17

    Single version without passing train/barking dogs coda
20. "Do It Again" – 2:18

    Single version without workshop effects coda
21. "Rock and Roll Music" (Chuck Berry) – 2:28
22. "Come Go with Me" (C.E. Quick) – 2:06
23. "Getcha Back" (Mike Love/Terry Melcher) – 3:01
24. "Rock 'n' Roll to the Rescue" (Mike Love/Terry Melcher) – 3:44
25. "California Dreamin'" (John Phillips/Michelle Phillips) – 3:10

    Roger McGuinn on electric guitar

Singles

- "Rock'n'Roll to the Rescue" b/w "Good Vibrations (Live in London)" (Capitol), June 9, 1986 *US #68*
- "California Dreamin'" b/w "Lady Liberty" (Capitol), September 1, 1986 *US #57*

Made in U.S.A. (Capitol) reached #96 in the U.S. during a chart stay of 12 weeks.

Sources

- "The Nearest Faraway Place: Brian Wilson, The Beach Boys and the Southern California Experience", Timothy White, c. 1994.
- "Wouldn't It Be Nice - My Own Story", Brian Wilson and Todd Gold, c. 1991.
- "Top Pop Singles 1955-2001", Joel Whitburn, c. 2002.
- "Top Pop Albums 1955-2001", Joel Whitburn, c. 2002.
- Allmusic.com

References

[1] http://www.allmusic.com/cg/amg.dll?p=amg&sql=10:6s220r8ac48i

The Original US Singles Collection The Capitol Years 1962–1965

The US Singles Collection was a boxset released in 2008 from Capitol Records, which features the original singles (in mono and stereo) from The Beach Boys from 1962–1965.

Track listing

CD SINGLE 1

1. Surfin' Safari - mono
2. 409 - mono
3. 409 (Live) mono / previously unreleased

CD SINGLE 2

1. Ten Little Indians - mono
2. County Fair - mono
3. Punchline - mono

CD SINGLE 3

1. Surfin' USA - mono
2. Shut Down - mono
3. Surfin' USA - stereo
4. Shut Down – stereo

CD SINGLE 4

1. Surfer Girl - mono
2. Little Deuce Coupe - mono
3. Surfer Girl - stereo
4. Little Deuce Coupe – stereo

CD SINGLE 5

1. Be True To Your School - mono single
2. In My Room - mono single
3. Be True To Your School - original mono mix from Little Deuce Coupe
4. In My Room – stereo mix from Surfer Girl

CD SINGLE 6

1. Little Saint Nick - mono
2. The Lord's Prayer - mono
3. Little Saint Nick - new stereo mix /previously unreleased
4. The Lord's Prayer – stereo

CD SINGLE 7

1. Fun, Fun, Fun - mono
2. Why Do Fools Fall In Love? - mono single
3. Fun, Fun, Fun - stereo
4. Why Do Fools Fall In Love? – alternate mono single edit / previously unreleased

CD SINGLE 8

1. I Get Around - mono
2. Don't Worry Baby - mono
3. I Get Around - stereo
4. Don't Worry Baby – stereo

CD SINGLE 9

1. When I Grow Up To Be A Man - mono
2. She Knows Me Too Well - mono
3. When I Grow Up To Be A Man - new stereo mix / previously unreleased
4. She Knows Me Too Well - new stereo mix /previously unreleased

CD EP/SINGLE 10

1. Wendy - mono
2. Don't Back Down - mono
3. Little Honda - mono
4. Hushabye - mono
5. Wendy - stereo
6. Don't Back Down - stereo
7. Little Honda - stereo
8. Hushabye – stereo

CD SINGLE 11

1. Dance, Dance, Dance - mono
2. The Warmth Of The Sun - mono
3. Dance, Dance, Dance - stereo
4. The Warmth Of The Sun – stereo

CD SINGLE 12

1. The Man With All The Toys - mono
2. Blue Christmas - mono
3. The Man With All The Toys - stereo
4. Blue Christmas – stereo

CD SINGLE 13

1. Do You Wanna Dance? - mono
2. Please Let Me Wonder - mono
3. Do You Wanna Dance? - new stereo Track mix /previously unreleased
4. Please Let Me Wonder

CD SINGLE 14

1. Help Me, Rhonda - mono
2. Kiss Me, Baby - mono
3. Help Me, Rhonda - mono backing track
4. Kiss Me Baby – stereo

CD SINGLE 15

1. California Girls - mono
2. Let Him Run Wild - mono
3. California Girls - stereo
4. Let Him Run Wild – stereo

CD BONUS SINGLE

1. All Dressed Up For School – previously unreleased original mono mix
2. I'm So Young - previously unreleased original mono mix
3. Graduation Day - stereo
4. Help Me, Rhonda - alternate mono mix

Pet Sounds

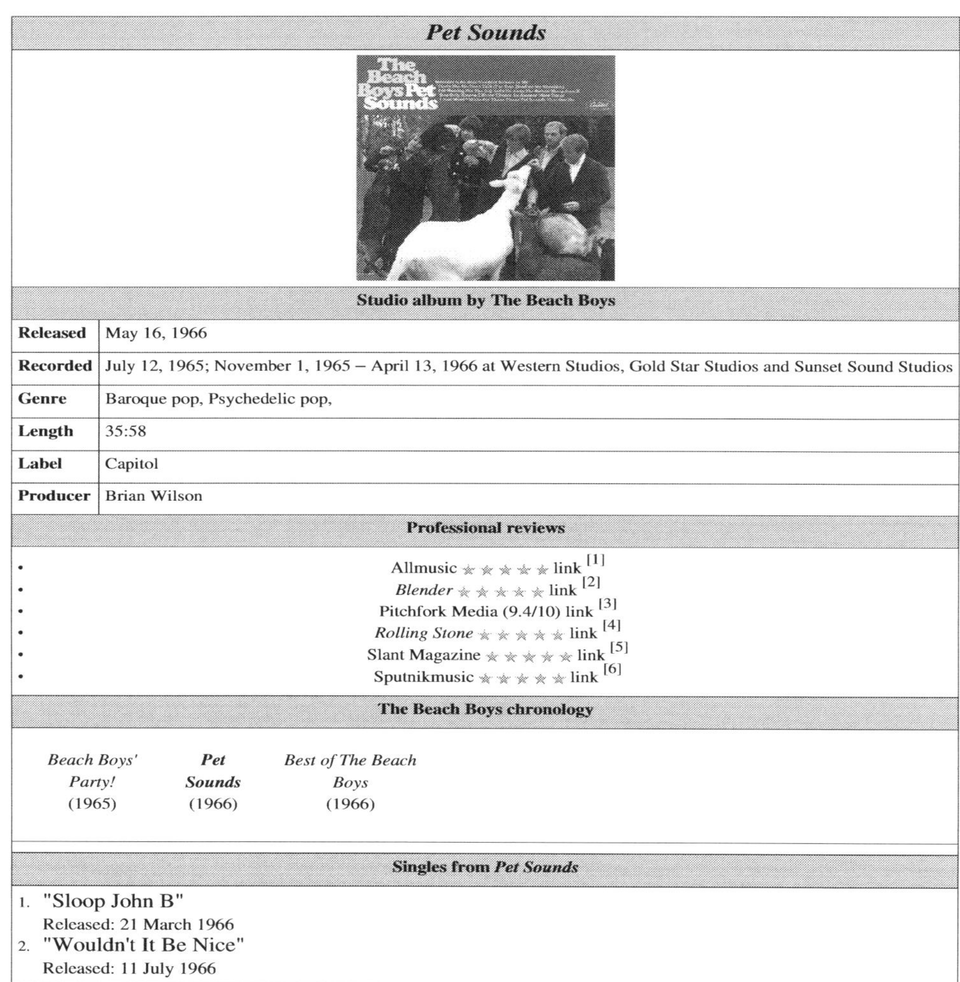

Pet Sounds	
Studio album by The Beach Boys	
Released	May 16, 1966
Recorded	July 12, 1965; November 1, 1965 – April 13, 1966 at Western Studios, Gold Star Studios and Sunset Sound Studios
Genre	Baroque pop, Psychedelic pop,
Length	35:58
Label	Capitol
Producer	Brian Wilson

Professional reviews

- Allmusic ★★★★★ link [1]
- *Blender* ★★★★★ link [2]
- Pitchfork Media (9.4/10) link [3]
- *Rolling Stone* ★★★★★ link [4]
- Slant Magazine ★★★★★ link [5]
- Sputnikmusic ★★★★★ link [6]

The Beach Boys chronology

Beach Boys' Party! (1965)	***Pet Sounds*** (1966)	*Best of The Beach Boys* (1966)

Singles from *Pet Sounds*

1. "Sloop John B"
   Released: 21 March 1966
2. "Wouldn't It Be Nice"
   Released: 11 July 1966

Pet Sounds is the eleventh studio album by the American rock band The Beach Boys, released May 16, 1966, on Capitol Records. It has been widely ranked as one of the most influential records ever released in pop music and has been ranked at number #1 in several music magazines' lists of greatest albums of all time, including *New Musical Express*, *The Times* and *Mojo* Magazine.[7] [8] [9] In 2003, it was ranked #2 in *Rolling Stone*'s 500 Greatest Albums of All Time list.[10]

Pet Sounds was created several months after Brian Wilson had quit touring with the band in order to focus his attention on writing and recording.[11] In it, he wove elaborate layers of vocal harmonies, coupled with sound effects and unconventional instruments such as bicycle bells, buzzing organs, harpsichords, flutes, the Electro-Theremin, and dog whistles, along with the more usual keyboards and guitars.[12]

Background

The track "Sloop John B" predated the recording of the rest of the LP by some months, but it proved to be a pivotal point in the album's development. It was a traditional Caribbean folk song that had been suggested to Wilson by group member Al Jardine.[13] Wilson recorded a backing track on July 12, 1965, but after laying down a rough lead vocal, he set the song aside for some time, concentrating on the recording of what became their next LP, the 'live in the studio' album *Beach Boys' Party!*, which was provided in response to their record company so the Beach Boys could have a new album ready for the Christmas 1965 market. What would become the Pet Sounds LP could not be finished in time for Christmas 1965.

The real catalyst for *Pet Sounds* was the U.S. version of The Beatles' new LP *Rubber Soul*, which was released that December in time for the Chrismas market. Wilson later recalled his first impressions of the groundbreaking album:

> I really wasn't quite ready for the unity. It felt like it all belonged together. *Rubber Soul* was a collection of songs ... that somehow went together like no album ever made before, and I was very impressed. I said, "That's it. I really am challenged to do a great album."[14]

As has been noted in discussions about the Rubber Soul album, the U.S. version (cited above) was revised (with respect to the British version of such) to provide more emphasis on folk sounds.

In early January 1966 Wilson contacted Tony Asher, a young lyricist and copywriter who had been working on advertising jingles, and whom Wilson had met in a Hollywood recording studio months earlier. Within ten days they were writing together. Wilson played him some of the music he had been recording, and gave him a cassette of the finished backing track for a piece with the working title "In My Childhood"; it had lyrics, but Wilson refused to show them to Asher, who took the music away and wrote new lyrics. The result was eventually retitled "You Still Believe in Me" and the success of the piece convinced Wilson that Tony Asher was the collaborator he was looking for.

"The general tenor of the lyrics was always his," Asher later recalled, "and the actual choice of words was usually mine. I was really just his interpreter."[15]

Writing and composition

Most of the songs on the album were written during December 1965 and January 1966. While most were composed with Tony Asher, "I Know There's an Answer" was co-written by another new associate, Terry Sachen.[16]

Mike Love is co-credited on the album's opening track, "Wouldn't It Be Nice", and on "I Know There's an Answer" but with the exception of his co-credit on "I'm Waiting for the Day,"[16] (originally copyrighted in February 1964, to Wilson alone) his contributions are thought to have been minimal. The exact degree of Love's contribution to "Wouldn't It Be Nice" is still hazy, but under oath in a court of law, Tony Asher has stated that it consisted of the tag "Good night my baby/Sleep tight, my baby."[16]

Love, in addition to Dennis Wilson and Al Jardine, was taken aback by Brian's new sound (and Asher's lyrics) when they returned from touring the Far East to record their vocals. Love in particular was nonplussed by Brian's complete abandonment of the "fast cars, cute girls, and sunny beaches" formula that had marked the group's hit-making career up to that point.

Love's main influence on "I Know There's an Answer" is reputed to have consisted of his strenuous opposition to the song's original title, "Hang On to Your Ego", and his insistence that it be partially rewritten and retitled. The original lyrics created quite a stir within the group. "I was aware that Brian was beginning to experiment with LSD and other psychedelics," explained Love. "The prevailing drug jargon at the time had it that doses of LSD would shatter your ego, as if that were a positive thing... I wasn't interested in taking acid or getting rid of my ego." Jardine recalled that the decision to change the lyrics was ultimately Wilson's. "Brian was very concerned. He wanted to know what we thought about it. To be honest, I don't think we even knew what an ego was... Finally Brian decided, 'Forget it. I'm changing the lyrics. There's too much controversy.'" Terry Sachen, who co-wrote the revised lyrics to this song, was the Beach Boys' road manager in 1966.[17]

The album included two sophisticated instrumental tracks, the wistful "Let's Go Away for Awhile" — with a working parenthetical title of "And Then We'll have World Peace"[16] [18] — and the brittle brassy surf of the title track, "Pet Sounds" (originally "Run James, Run", the suggestion being that it would be offered for use in a James Bond movie). The subtitle of "Let's Go Away For A While" was a catchphrase from one of Wilson's favorite comedy recordings, John Brent and Del Close's *How To Speak Hip* (1959) (which Wilson can be heard talking about in a session outtake included on the *Pet Sounds* boxed set). Both titles had been recorded as backing tracks for existing songs, but by the time the album neared completion Wilson had decided that the tracks worked better without vocals and so left them as such. A third instrumental, called "Trombone Dixie," had been fully recorded, but it remained in the vaults until its inclusion on the album's 1990 remastered CD release.

Recording process

With writing well under way, Wilson worked rapidly through January and early February 1966, recording six backing tracks for the new material. When the other Beach Boys returned from a three-week tour of Japan and Hawaii, they were presented with a substantial portion of a new album, with music that was in many ways a radical departure from their earlier attempts. Both Asher and Wilson state that there was resistance to the project from within the group, but on this occasion, Wilson's belief in his new work convinced the other members of the group.[15]

The backing tracks for *Pet Sounds* were recorded over a four-month period, using major Los Angeles studios (Gold Star Studios, Western Studios and Sunset Sound) and an ensemble that included some highly regarded session musicians, including jazz guitarist Barney Kessel, bassist Carol Kaye, and session drummer Hal Blaine. The tracks were produced and arranged by Brian Wilson. He also wrote or co-wrote every track except "Sloop John B."

Wilson had developed his production methods over several years, bringing them to their zenith with the recording of *Pet Sounds* during late 1965 and early 1966. Wilson's approach was in some respects a refinement and development of the famous "Wall of Sound" technique created by his mentor and rival Phil Spector. In fact Wilson has stated that he named the album using Spector's initials.[19] With new Ampex 8-track recorders, Wilson produced tracks of great complexity using his regular team of 'first call' players, sometimes known collectively as "The Wrecking Crew".[20] Wilson's typical production method on *Pet Sounds* was to record the instrumental backing tracks for each song as a live ensemble performance direct onto a 4-track recorder. His engineer Larry Levine has reported that Wilson also typically mixed these backing tracks live, as they were being taped. Like Spector, Wilson was a pioneer of the 'studio as instrument' concept, exploiting novel combinations of sounds that sprang from the use of multiple electric instruments and voices in an ensemble and combining them with echo and reverberation. He often doubled bass, guitar and keyboard parts, blending them with reverberation and adding other unusual instruments.[21] The deceptive simplicity of Brian's music often veiled the fact that his arrangements were among the most musically adventurous and complex in pop music.

Although the self-taught Wilson often had entire arrangements worked out in his head (which were usually written in a shorthand form for the other players by one of his session musicians), surviving tapes of his recording sessions show that he was remarkably open to input from his musicians, often taking advice and suggestions from them and even incorporating apparent 'mistakes' if they provided a useful or interesting alternative.

In spite of the availability of complex multitrack recording, Wilson always mixed the final version of his recordings in mono, as did Phil Spector. He did this for several reasons; one of which was that he felt that mono mastering provided more sonic control over the final result that the listener heard, regardless of the vagaries of speaker placement and sound system quality. It was also motivated by the knowledge that, back then, radio and TV were broadcast in mono, and most domestic and automotive radios and record players were monophonic. Another and more personal reason for Wilson's preference of recording in mono was due to his being almost totally deaf in his right ear, rumored to be the result of childhood injury to his eardrum caused by a blow from his violent father Murry Wilson, although Wilson has claimed that he was born deaf in one ear.[22]

These backing tracks were then dubbed down onto one track of an 8-track recorder (at Columbia studio, the only facility in LA with an 8-track), and, although much of the fine detail in the arrangements was often covered by the group's rich vocal harmonies, they interacted effectively with the vocal tracks. This mono recording meant that a stereo mixdown could not be achieved. Wilson's partial deafness made him indifferent to stereo and it was not until the advent of digital recording that it was possible to combine the instrumental and vocal session-tapes to achieve a true stereo release.[23]

Six of the remaining seven tracks were usually dedicated to each of the Beach Boys' vocals (the five-piece group was by then being regularly augmented by singer Bruce Johnston, who later became a permanent member). The last track was usually reserved for additional vocals and/or instruments and other 'sweetening' elements.

On February 15, the group traveled to the San Diego Zoo to shoot the photographs for the cover of the new album, which had already been titled *Pet Sounds*.[15] According to the Pet Sounds' liner notes, "The photos of The Beach Boys feeding an assortment of goats was a play on the album's chosen title, *Pet Sounds*. The title came from Brian's wish to pay tribute to Phil Spector by naming the album using his initials, and the idea that the sounds heard on the album were Brian's 'pet,' or favorite, sounds."[15] Two days later, Wilson was back in the studio with his session band, laying down the first takes for a new composition, "Good Vibrations."[15] Around February 23, Wilson gave Capitol a provisional track listing for the new LP, which included both "Sloop John B" and "Good Vibrations." This contradicts the long held misconception that "Sloop John B" was a forced inclusion as the hit single at Capitol's insistence: in late February, the song was weeks away from release.[15]

Wilson worked through February and into March fine-tuning the backing tracks. To the group's surprise he also dropped "Good Vibrations" from the running order, telling them that he wanted to spend more time on it. Al Jardine remembers:

> “At the time, we all had assumed that "Good Vibrations" was going to be on the album, but Brian decided to hold it out. It was a judgment call on his part; we felt otherwise but left the ultimate decision up to him.[15]”

Most of March and early April was devoted to recording the remaining backing tracks and to the crucial recording of vocals, a process which proved to be the most exacting work the group had hitherto undertaken, as Mike Love later recalled:

> “We worked and worked on the harmonies and, if there was the slightest little hint of a sharp or a flat, it wouldn't go on. We would do it over again until it was right. [Brian] was going for every subtle nuance that you could conceivably think of. Every voice had to be right, every voice and its resonance and tonality had to be right. The timing had to be right. The timbre of the voices just had to be correct, according to how he felt. And then he might, the next day, completely throw that out and we might have to do it over again.[15]”

Release

By mid-April *Pet Sounds* was finished and had been submitted to Capitol. "Caroline, No," released as a solo single; it was credited to Brian Wilson alone, leading to speculation that he was considering leaving the band. The single reached #32 in the United States.[24]

"Sloop John B" was extremely successful, scoring a #3 hit in the U.S.[24] and #2 in Great Britain.[25] "Wouldn't It Be Nice" reached #8 in the U.S.[24] Its flip side, "God Only Knows," was another #2 single in Britain,[25] but reached only #39 in the States.[24] The LP broke into the Top Ten in the U.S., belying its reputation as a commercial failure there. In Australia, the album was only released under the title *The Fabulous Beach Boys* on the Music for Pleasure label.

Pet Sounds' greatest success was in the UK, where it reached #2 in the LP charts.[25] Its success there was aided by considerable support from the British music industry, who embraced the record warmly; Paul McCartney spoke often about the album's influence on The Beatles. But although it's been claimed that the Rolling Stones manager Andrew Oldham placed unsolicited advertisements lauding the album in British music papers, a search of the UK pop press for 1966 fails to uncover any such advert.

However, like *Beach Boys' Party!*, *Pet Sounds* failed to reach gold status on its initial release in the U.S., where it reached #10, which deeply disappointed Wilson. Much of the blame for its lukewarm commercial fortunes has been laid with Capitol Records, which did not promote the album as heavily as the band's earlier releases. *Pet Sounds* eventually went gold and platinum in 2000.[26]

Re-issues

In 1990, Pet Sounds was released in CD format with three bonus tracks: "Unreleased Backgrounds" (actually an unused vocal section for "Don't Talk (Put Your Head on My Shoulder"), "Hang On to Your Ego" and "Trombone Dixie" all of which were described as unreleased.[27]

In 1997, *The Pet Sounds Sessions* box set was released which included the original mono release, the first stereo release and three CDs of out-takes and rehearsals.[28] The stereo mix was released in 1999 on vinyl and on CD and again in 2001 along with the CD release having the mono mix as well, with "Hang On to Your Ego" (the original version of "I Know There's an Answer") as a bonus track.[28]

Recordings from Brian Wilson's 2002 concert tour, in which he reproduced the whole album live on stage, were released as *Pet Sounds Live*.[29]

On August 29, 2006, Capitol released the 40th Anniversary edition of *Pet Sounds*. The new compilation contains a new 2006 mono mix, DVD mixes (stereo and Surround Sound), and a "making of" documentary.[30] The discs were released in a regular jewel box and a deluxe edition was released in a green fuzzy box. A two disk colored gatefold vinyl set was released with green and yellow disks with the yellow one having the mono mix on it and the green disc having the stereo version.

On September 2, 2008, Capitol reissued a single LP version replicating the original artwork (including the inner sleeve) with the original mono mix on 180 gram vinyl.[31]

Reception

Although not a big seller for the band originally, *Pet Sounds* has been influential since the day it was released. Rapturously received in Britain, it was lauded in the music press and championed by many top pop stars. The Beatles, for example, have said that *Pet Sounds* was a major influence on their album *Sgt. Pepper's Lonely Hearts Club Band*, and Paul McCartney has repeatedly named it as one of his favorite albums (with "God Only Knows" as his favorite song) — completing a circle begun by The Beatles' influence on Wilson. McCartney stated that:

> “It was *Pet Sounds* that blew me out of the water. I love the album so much. I've just bought my kids each a copy of it for their education in life ... I figure no one is educated musically 'til they've heard that album ... I love the orchestra, the arrangements ... it may be going overboard to say it's the classic of the century ... but to me, it certainly is a total, classic record that is unbeatable in many ways ... I've often played *Pet Sounds* and cried. I played it to John [Lennon] so much that it would be difficult for him to escape the influence ... it was the record of the time. The thing that really made me sit up and take notice was the bass lines ... and also, putting melodies in the bass line. That I think was probably the big influence that set me thinking when we recorded *Pepper*, it set me off on a period I had then for a couple of years of nearly always writing quite melodic bass lines. "God Only Knows" is a big favourite of mine ... very emotional, always a bit of a choker for me, that one. On "You Still Believe in Me", I love that melody - that kills me ... that's my favourite, I think ... it's so beautiful right at the end ... comes surging back in these multi-coloured harmonies ... sends shivers up my spine.[32]”

Other artists have also cited *Pet Sounds* as one of the all time classic albums. Eric Clapton stated that "I consider *Pet Sounds* to be one of the greatest pop LPs to ever be released. It encompasses everything that's ever knocked me out and rolled it all into one."[33]

Elton John has said of the album, "For me to say that I was enthralled would be an understatement. I had never heard such magical sounds, so amazingly recorded. It undoubtedly changed the way that I, and countless others, approached recording. It is a timeless and amazing recording of incredible genius and beauty."[30]

Beatles producer George Martin stated that "Without *Pet Sounds*, *Sgt. Pepper* wouldn't have happened... *Pepper* was an attempt to equal *Pet Sounds*."[34]

Bob Dylan has said of Brian Wilson's talents, "That ear — I mean, Jesus, he's got to will that to the Smithsonian."[35]

In 1995, nearly thirty years after its release, a panel of top musicians, songwriters and producers assembled by *MOJO* magazine voted it "The Greatest Album Ever Made." It was number one in New Musical Express's list "The 100 Best Albums". In 1997, *Pet Sounds* was named the 26th greatest album of all time in a *Music of the Millennium* [36] poll conducted in the United Kingdom by HMV, Channel 4, *The Guardian* and Classic FM. In 2006 *Q* magazine readers voted it the 18th greatest album of all time; critics of German magazine *Spex* voted it the best album of the 20th Century; in 2001 the TV channel VH1 placed it at #3. *The Times* magazine ranked it the greatest album of all time. It also placed #2 on *Rolling Stone*'s list of the 500 greatest albums of all time behind only *Sgt. Pepper's Lonely Hearts Club Band* by The Beatles. In 2004, it was one of 50 recordings chosen by the Library of Congress to be added to the National Recording Registry.

In 2006, the album was chosen by *TIME* as one of the 100 best albums of all time.[37]

Track listing

Side one

No.	Title	Writer(s)	Lead Vocals	Length
1.	"Wouldn't It Be Nice"	Brian Wilson/Tony Asher/Mike Love	Brian Wilson/Mike Love	2:22
2.	"You Still Believe in Me"	B. Wilson/Asher	B. Wilson	2:30
3.	"That's Not Me"	B. Wilson/Asher	Love/B. Wilson	2:27
4.	"Don't Talk (Put Your Head on My Shoulder)"	B. Wilson/Asher	B. Wilson	2:51
5.	"I'm Waiting for the Day"	B. Wilson/Love	B. Wilson	3:03
6.	"Let's Go Away for Awhile"	B. Wilson	instrumental	2:18
7.	"Sloop John B"	trad. arr. B. Wilson	B. Wilson/Love	2:56

Side two

No.	Title	Writer(s)	Lead Vocals	Length
1.	"God Only Knows"	B. Wilson/Asher	Carl Wilson	2:49
2.	"I Know There's an Answer"	B. Wilson/Terry Sachen/Love	Love/Al Jardine/B. Wilson	3:08
3.	"Here Today"	B. Wilson/Asher	Love	2:52
4.	"I Just Wasn't Made for These Times"	B. Wilson/Asher	B. Wilson	3:11
5.	"Pet Sounds"	B. Wilson	instrumental	2:20
6.	"Caroline, No"	B. Wilson/Asher	B. Wilson	2:52

Personnel

Band members

- Al Jardine - vocals, tambourine
- Bruce Johnston - vocals
- Mike Love - vocals
- Brian Wilson - vocals, organ, piano
- Carl Wilson - vocals, guitar
- Dennis Wilson - vocals, drums

Session musicians

- Arnold Belnick - violin
- Chuck Berghofer - upright bass
- Hal Blaine - drums, percussion
- Norman Botnick - viola
- Glen Campbell - guitar
- Frank Capp - percussion
- Al Casey - guitar
- Ray Caton - trumpet
- Jerry Cole - guitar
- Kyle Burkett - guitar
- Andrew Maxson - bass
- Gary Coleman - percussion
- Mike Deasy - guitar
- Al de Lory - piano, harpsichord, organ
- Joseph DiFiore - viola
- Justin DiTullio - cello
- Steve Douglas - saxophones, clarinet, percussion, flute
- Jesse Erlich - cello
- Ritchie Frost - drums, percussion
- Carl Fortina - accordion
- James Getzoff - violin
- Jim Gordon - drums, percussion
- Bill Green - saxophone, flute, percussion
- Leonard Hartman - English horn, clarinets
- Jim Horn - saxophones, flute
- Paul Horn - saxophone
- Harry Hyams - viola
- Jules Jacob - flute
- Plas Johnson - saxophones, percussion
- Carol Kaye - electric bass
- Barney Kessel - mandolin, guitar
- Bobby Klein - saxophone
- Larry Knechtel - organ
- William Kurasch - violin
- Leonard Malarsky - violin
- Frank Marocco - accordion
- Gail Martin - trombone

- Nick Martinis - drums
- Terry Melcher - tambourine
- Mike Melvoin - harpsichord
- Jay Migliori - saxophones, clarinets, flute
- Tommy Morgan - harmonica
- Jack Nimitz - saxophone
- Bill Pitman - guitar
- Ray Pohlman - mandolin, guitar, electric bass
- Don Randi - piano
- Jerome Reisler - violin
- Lyle Ritz - upright bass, ukulele
- Alan Robinson - French horn
- Joseph Saxon - cello
- Ralph Schaffer - violin
- Sid Sharp - violin
- Billy Strange - guitar
- Ron Swallow - tambourine
- Ernie Tack - trombone
- Paul Tanner - electrotheremin
- Darrel Terwilliger - viola
- Tommy Tedesco - guitar
- Julius Wechter - percussion
- Jerry Williams - percussion
- Tibor Zelig - violin

Other staff

- Ralph Balantin - Engineer
- Bruce Botnick - Engineer
- Chuck Britz - Engineer
- H. Bowen David - Engineer
- Larry Levine - Engineer

References

- *Pet Sounds* CD booklet notes, David Leaf, c.1990 and 2001.
- *The Pet Sounds Sessions* box set notes, David Leaf, c.1997.
- "The Nearest Faraway Place: Brian Wilson, The Beach Boys and the Southern California Experience", Timothy White, c. 1994.
- "Wouldn't It Be Nice - My Own Story", Brian Wilson and Todd Gold, c. 1991.
- "Top Pop Singles 1955-2001", Joel Whitburn, c. 2002.
- "Top Pop Albums 1955-2001", Joel Whitburn, c. 2002.
- *Pet Sounds* on Allmusic.com [38]
- Badman, Keith; Bacon, Tony *The Beach Boys: The Definitive Diary of America's Greatest Band on Stage*, Backbeat Books, 2004 ISBN 0879308184
- Doe, Andrew; Tobler, John *Brian Wilson and The Beach Boys: The Complete Guide to Their Music*, Omnibus Press, 2004 ISBN 1844494268 c. 46-53

External links

- *Rolling Stone* voted the album the second greatest album ever [39].
- *Out-Of-Sight!* SMiLE Timeline [53]

References

[1] http://www.allmusic.com/cg/amg.dll?p=amg&sql=10:hnfpxqrkldte
[2] http://www.blender.com/guide/back-catalogue/52789/pet-sounds.html
[3] http://pitchfork.com/reviews/albums/9371-pet-sounds-40th-anniversary/
[4] http://www.rollingstone.com/reviews/album/112386/review/6068244/petsounds
[5] http://www.slantmagazine.com/music/music_review.asp?ID=435
[6] http://www.sputnikmusic.com/album.php?albumid=1380
[7] "New Musical Express Writers Top 100 Albums" (http://www.rocklistmusic.co.uk/nme_writers.htm#100_93). NME. 1993-10-02. . Retrieved 2009-03-03.
[8] "The 100 Greatest Albums Ever Made" (http://www.rocklistmusic.co.uk/mojo.html). Mojo. . Retrieved 2009-03-03.
[9] "The Times All Time Top 100 Albums" (http://www.rocklistmusic.co.uk/times100.htm). The Times. . Retrieved 2009-03-03.
[10] "The 500 Greatest Albums of All Time" (http://www.rollingstone.com/news/story/5938174/the_rs_500_greatest_albums_of_all_time). Rolling Stone. 2003-11-18. . Retrieved 2009-11-03.
[11] Katz, Larry (1998-01-25). "A 'Pet Sounds' Apotheosis" (http://archive.southcoasttoday.com/daily/01-98/01-25-98/e07ae207.htm). Entertainment News Service. . Retrieved 2009-03-03.
[12] Cobley, Mike (2007-09-09). "Brighton Beach Boys: 'Getting Better' All The Time!" (http://magazine.brighton.co.uk/index.asp?art_id=2369&cat_id=21&sec_id=1&sub_id=45). The Brighton Magazine. . Retrieved 2009-03-03.
[13] *The Pet Sounds Sessions: "The Making Of Pet Sounds"* booklet page 25-26
[14] Stevens, Robert (2007-10-24). "An Evening with Brian Wilson: The Palace Theatre in Manchester, England—September 23, 2007" (http://www.wsws.org/articles/2007/oct2007/wils-o24.shtml). wsws.org. . Retrieved 2009-03-03.
[15] *Pet Sounds* booklet and liner notes (http://www.beachboysfanclub.com/ps-liner.html)
[16] Elliott, Brad (1999-08-31). "Pet Sounds Track Notes" (http://www.beachboysfanclub.com/ps-tracks.html). beachboysfanclub.com. . Retrieved 2009-03-03.
[17] Tobler, John. *Brian Wilson and The Beach Boys: The Complete Guide to Their Music*. Omnibus Press, 2004, ISBN 1844494268 p. 50 (http://books.google.com/books?id=km5OFb6eEYcC&pg=PA50&lpg=PA50&dq=terry+sachen+road+manager&source=web&ots=_ZEs-AUBJt&sig=94XPck1EFKOEtZ9CvWaJsyqqWFU)
[18] Tobler, John. Omnibus Press, 2004, ISBN 1844494268 p. 49 (http://books.google.com/books?id=km5OFb6eEYcC&pg=PA49&lpg=PA49&dq=let's+go+away+for+a+while+and+then+"we+ll"+have+world+peace&source=web&ots=_ZEs-AVEMq&sig=nUQ9WSdnF_3-0h-vSBM4-w2ztQc)
[19] Phil Gallo, *The Set List* (http://weblogs.variety.com/thesetlist/brian_wilson/) blog on variety.com, January 16, 2009
[20] Hartman, Kent. "The Wrecking Crew" (http://www.americanheritage.com/articles/web/20070212-rock-n-roll-brian-wilson-beach-boys-glen-campbell-monkees-hal-blaine-carol-kaye-leon-russell.shtml). American Heritage.com. . Retrieved 2009-03-03.
[21] Booklet notes, *Pet Sounds* stereo/mono CD release.
[22] Schinder, Scott (2007). Icons of Rock [Two Volumes]: An Encyclopedia of the Legends Who Changed Music Forever. Greenwood Press (Santa Barbara, CA).
[23] David Leaf, Booklet notes, *Pet Sounds* stereo/mono CD release.
[24] "Beach Boys Singles Chart History" (http://www.allmusic.com/cg/amg.dll?p=amg&sql=10:3ifwxql5ld0e~T31). *Billboard*. . Retrieved 2009-03-03.
[25] "UK Top 40 Singles Chart" (http://www.everyhit.com/). Everyhit.com. . Retrieved 2009-03-03.
[26] "Gold & Platinum" (http://www.riaa.com/). RIAA. . Retrieved 2009-03-03.
[27] Hilburn, Robert (1990-05-11). "'Pet Sounds' Finally Reissued" (http://pqasb.pqarchiver.com/latimes/access/60052630.xml?dids=60052630:60052630&FMT=ABS&FMTS=ABS:FT&type=current&date=May+11,+1990&author=ROBERT+HILBURN&pub=Los+Angeles+Times+(pre-1997+Fulltext)&desc=`Pet+Sounds'+Finally+Reissued&pqatl=google). Los Angeles Times. . Retrieved 2009-03-03.
[28] Crowe, Jerry (1997-11-01). "'Pet Sounds Sessions': Body of Influence Put in a Box" (http://pqasb.pqarchiver.com/latimes/access/21696821.html?dids=21696821:21696821&FMT=ABS&FMTS=ABS:FT&date=Nov+01,+1997&author=JERRY+CROWE&pub=Los+Angeles+Times&desc='Pet+Sounds+Sessions':+Body+of+Influence+Put+in+a+Box;+Pop+Beat:+A+four-CD+compilation+of+the+Beach+Boys'+1966+album+regarded+as+an+artistic+masterpiece+is+being+released+for+fans+new+and+old.&pqatl=google). Los Angeles Times. . Retrieved 2009-03-03.
[29] Page, Tim (2002-11-19). "Crossing Over, Looking Back, Tripping Up" (http://pqasb.pqarchiver.com/washingtonpost/access/234822711.html?dids=234822711:234822711&FMT=ABS&FMTS=ABS:FT&type=current&date=Nov+10,+2002&author=Tim+Page&pub=The+Washington+Post&desc=Crossing+Over,+Looking+Back,+Tripping+Up&pqatl=google). The Washington Post. . Retrieved 2009-11-03.

[30] "The Beach Boys' Pet Sounds and "Good Vibrations 40 Anniversaries Feted by Capitol/EMI" (http://www.emission-online.com/issues/2006-06-23/news2.asp). EMIssion-online.com. 2006-06-23. . Retrieved 2009-03-03.
[31] Kreps, Daniel (2008-06-12). "EMI/Capitol Catch Vinyl Fever with Radiohead, "Pet Sounds" Reissues" (http://www.rollingstone.com/rockdaily/index.php/2008/06/12/emicapitol-catch-vinyl-fever-with-radiohead-pet-sounds-reissues/). Rolling Stone. . Retrieved 2009-03-03.
[32] "Musicians on Brian: Paul McCartney" (http://www.brianwilson.com/brian/musicians.html). Brian Wilson.com. . Retrieved 2009-03-03.
[33] Bacon, Tony and Badman, Keith. *The Beach Boys: The Definitive Diary of America's Greatest Band, on Stage and in the Studio*. Backbeat Books, 2004, ISBN 0879308184 p. 139 (http://books.google.com/books?id=sLEMdjRhDgQC)
[34] http://www.brianwilson.com/brian/musicians.html
[35] http://www.newsweek.com/id/97107
[36] http://news.bbc.co.uk/1/hi/uk/50266.stm
[37] "The All-Time 100 Albums" (http://www.time.com/time/2006/100albums/index.html). Time. 2006-11-13. . Retrieved 2009-03-03.
[38] http://www.allmusic.com/cg/amg.dll?p=amg&sql=10:cx8m96ho3ep6%7ET1
[39] http://www.rollingstone.com/news/story/_/id/6553833

The Pet Sounds Sessions

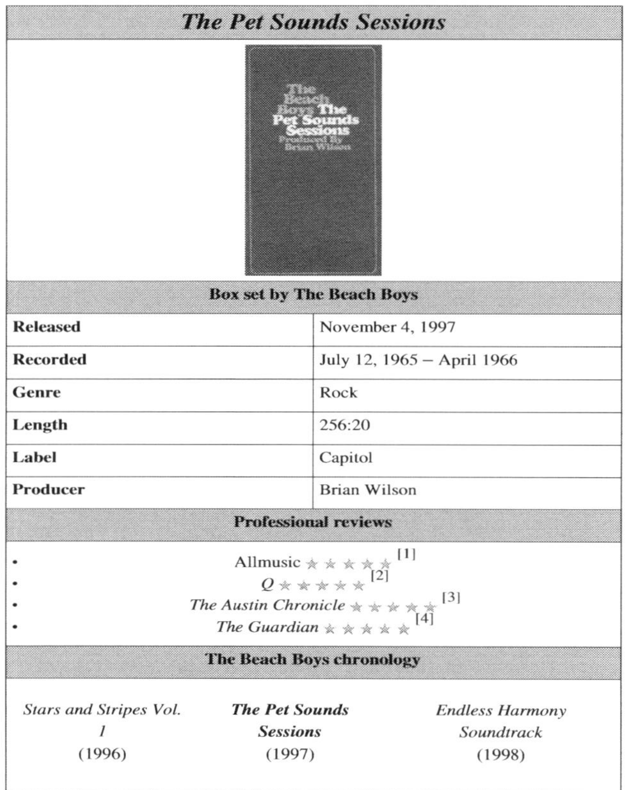

The Pet Sounds Sessions	
Box set by The Beach Boys	
Released	November 4, 1997
Recorded	July 12, 1965 – April 1966
Genre	Rock
Length	256:20
Label	Capitol
Producer	Brian Wilson

Professional reviews

- Allmusic ★★★★★ [1]
- *Q* ★★★★★ [2]
- *The Austin Chronicle* ★★★★★ [3]
- *The Guardian* ★★★★★ [4]

The Beach Boys chronology

Stars and Stripes Vol. 1 (1996)	***The Pet Sounds Sessions*** (1997)	*Endless Harmony Soundtrack* (1998)

The Pet Sounds Sessions is a 4-CD boxed set released in 1997 which compiles tracks from The Beach Boys' 1966 album *Pet Sounds*, and its recording sessions. The album is included in its entirety in its original mono mix, as well as a stereo mix. The set also contains instrumental tracks, vocals-only tracks, alternate mixes, and edited highlights from the recording sessions for many of the album's songs, as well as several songs not included on the album.

Background

Overseen by producer Brian Wilson, the set includes a new stereo mix of *Pet Sounds* by engineer Mark Linett. These new mixes would also be made available on the 1999 and 2001 re-issues of the regular album. *The Pet Sounds Sessions* was nominated for "Best Historical Album" at the Grammy Awards of 1999[5] .

The stereo mix of the album contains some notable differences from the original mono mix. Among them, alternate vocal parts used for the bridge of "Wouldn't It Be Nice?" and the end of "God Only Knows" due to the original tracks no longer existing. "You Still Believe In Me" also features a single tracked vocal instead of the doubled vocal of the original due to a missing tape. Other differences are also noted in the booklet.

There was a minor controversy regarding a significant 18-month delay in the release of the box set (originally planned for May 1996 to coincide with the 30th anniversary of the album's original issue). Reportedly, Mike Love was dissatisfied with the accompanying essays that undermined his involvement in the album's making.

Track listing

All songs by Brian Wilson/Tony Asher, except where noted.

Disc one

1. "Wouldn't It Be Nice" (Stereo Mix) (Brian Wilson/Tony Asher/Mike Love) – 2:33
2. "You Still Believe in Me" (Stereo Mix) – 2:36
3. "That's Not Me" (Stereo Mix) – 2:31
4. "Don't Talk (Put Your Head on My Shoulder)" (Stereo Mix) – 2:58
5. "I'm Waiting for the Day" (Stereo Mix) (Brian Wilson/Mike Love) – 3:06
6. "Let's Go Away For Awhile" (Stereo Mix) (Brian Wilson) – 2:24
7. "Sloop John B" (Stereo Mix) (Trad. Arr. Brian Wilson) – 2:59
8. "God Only Knows" (Stereo Mix) – 2:54
9. "I Know There's an Answer" (Stereo Mix) (Brian Wilson/Mike Love/Terry Sachen) – 3:18
10. "Here Today" (Stereo Mix) – 3:07
11. "I Just Wasn't Made for These Times" (Stereo Mix) – 3:21
12. "Pet Sounds" (Stereo Mix) (Brian Wilson) – 2:37
13. "Caroline, No" (Stereo Mix) – 2:53
14. "Sloop John B" (Highlights from tracking date) (Trad. Arr. Brian Wilson) – 1:04
15. "Sloop John B" (Stereo backing track) (Trad. Arr. Brian Wilson) – 3:18
16. "Trombone Dixie" (Highlights from tracking date) (Brian Wilson) – 1:26
17. "Trombone Dixie" (Stereo backing track) (Brian Wilson) – 2:50
18. "Pet Sounds" (Highlights from tracking date) (Brian Wilson) – 0:57
19. "Pet Sounds" (Stereo backing track) (Brian Wilson) – 2:48
20. "Let's Go Away For Awhile" (Highlights from tracking date) (Brian Wilson) – 2:20
21. "Let's Go Away For Awhile" (Stereo backing track) (Brian Wilson) – 2:51
22. "Wouldn't It Be Nice" (Highlights from tracking date) (Brian Wilson/Tony Asher/Mike Love) – 7:20
23. "Wouldn't It Be Nice" (Stereo backing track) (Brian Wilson/Tony Asher/Mike Love) – 2:34
24. "Wouldn't It Be Nice" (Stereo track with background vocals) (Brian Wilson/Tony Asher/Mike Love) – 2:34
25. "You Still Believe in Me" (Intro - session) – 1:39
26. "You Still Believe in Me" (Intro - master take) – 0:15
27. "You Still Believe in Me" (Highlights from tracking date) – 1:11
28. "You Still Believe in Me" (Stereo backing track) – 2:37

Disc two

1. "Caroline, No" (Highlights from tracking date) – 4:16
2. "Caroline, No" (Stereo backing track) – 2:53
3. "Hang On to Your Ego" (Highlights from tracking date) (Brian Wilson/Terry Sachen) – 4:47
4. "Hang On to Your Ego" (Stereo backing track) (Brian Wilson/Terry Sachen) – 3:23
5. "Don't Talk (Put Your Head on My Shoulder)" (Brian's instrumental demo) – 2:20
6. "Don't Talk (Put Your Head on My Shoulder)" (Stereo backing track) – 3:11
7. "Don't Talk (Put Your Head on My Shoulder)" (String overdub) – 1:48
8. "I Just Wasn't Made for These Times" (Highlights from tracking date) – 2:59
9. "I Just Wasn't Made for These Times" (Stereo backing track) – 3:47
10. "That's Not Me" (Highlights from tracking date) – 1:52
11. "That's Not Me" (Stereo backing track) – 2:46
12. "Good Vibrations" (Highlights from tracking date) (Brian Wilson/Mike Love) – 2:41
13. "Good Vibrations" (Stereo backing track) (Brian Wilson/Mike Love) – 3:15
14. "I'm Waiting for the Day" (Highlights from tracking date) (Brian Wilson/Mike Love) – 5:25
15. "I'm Waiting for the Day" (Stereo backing track) (Brian Wilson/Mike Love) – 3:14
16. "God Only Knows" (Highlights from tracking date) – 9:25
17. "God Only Knows" (Stereo backing track) – 3:06
18. "Here Today" (Highlights from tracking date) – 6:37
19. "Here Today" (Stereo backing track) – 4:55

Disc three

1. "Wouldn't It Be Nice" (A cappella) (Brian Wilson/Tony Asher/Mike Love) – 2:37
2. "You Still Believe in Me" (A cappella) – 2:47
3. "That's Not Me" (A cappella) – 2:28
4. "Don't Talk (Put Your Head on My Shoulder)" (A cappella) – 3:07
5. "I'm Waiting for the Day" (A cappella) (Brian Wilson/Mike Love) – 3:02
6. "Sloop John B" (A cappella) (Trad. Arr. Brian Wilson) – 3:09
7. "God Only Knows" (A cappella) – 2:49
8. "I Know There's an Answer" (A cappella) (Brian Wilson/Mike Love/Terry Sachen) – 2:19
9. "Here Today" (A cappella) – 3:29
10. "I Just Wasn't Made for These Times" (A cappella) – 3:22
11. "Caroline, No" (A cappella) – 1:54
12. "Caroline, No" (Promotional Spot #1) :32
13. "Wouldn't It Be Nice" (Mono alternate mix) (Brian Wilson/Tony Asher/Mike Love) – 2:29
14. "You Still Believe in Me" (Mono alternate mix) – 2:23
15. "Don't Talk (Put Your Head on My Shoulder)" (Vocal snippet) – 0:56
16. "I'm Waiting for the Day" (Mono alternate mix, Mike sings lead) - (Brian Wilson/Mike Love) – 3:02
17. "Sloop John B" (Mono alternate mix, Carl sings lead) (Trad. Arr. Brian Wilson) – 3:05
18. "God Only Knows (Mono alternate mix, with sax solo) – 2:49
19. "Hang On to Your Ego" (Brian Wilson/Terry Sachen) – 3:13
20. "Here Today" (Mono alternate mix, Brian sings lead) – 3:07
21. "I Just Wasn't Made for These Times (Mono alternate mix) – 3:11
22. "Banana & Louie" – 0:05
23. "Caroline, No" (Original speed, stereo mix) – 2:24
24. "Dog Barking Session" (Outtakes) – 0:34
25. "Caroline, No" (Promotional spot #2) – 0:28

26. "God Only Knows" (with a cappella tag) – 2:56
27. "Wouldn't It Be Nice" (Mono alternate mix) (Brian Wilson/Tony Asher/Mike Love) – 2:28
28. "Sloop John B" (Brian sings lead throughout) (Trad. Arr. Brian Wilson) – 3:04
29. "God Only Knows" (Mono alternate mix, Brian sings lead) – 2:42
30. "Caroline, No" (Original speed, mono mix) – 3:03

Disc four (Original mono *Pet Sounds*)

1. "Wouldn't It Be Nice" (Brian Wilson/Tony Asher/Mike Love) – 2:33
2. "You Still Believe in Me" – 2:36
3. "That's Not Me" – 2:31
4. "Don't Talk (Put Your Head on My Shoulder)" – 2:58
5. "I'm Waiting for the Day" (Brian Wilson/Mike Love) – 3:06
6. "Let's Go Away For Awhile" (Brian Wilson) – 2:24
7. "Sloop John B" (Trad. Arr. Brian Wilson) – 2:59
8. "God Only Knows" – 2:54
9. "I Know There's an Answer" (Brian Wilson/Mike Love/Terry Sachen) – 3:18
10. "Here Today" – 3:07
11. "I Just Wasn't Made for These Times" – 3:21
12. "Pet Sounds" (Brian Wilson) – 2:37
13. "Caroline, No" – 2:53

The Pet Sounds Sessions (Capitol 7243 8 37662 2) never charted in either the US or the UK.

Sources

- *The Pet Sounds Sessions* booklet notes, David Leaf, c.1997.
- Allmusic

References

[1] Erlewine, Stephen Thomas. "Review: *The Pet Sounds Sessions*" (http://www.allmusic.com/cg/amg.dll?p=amg&sql=10:00q5g4smtvnz). Macrovision Corporation. . Retrieved 26 August 2009.

[2] Cavanagh, David. "Review: *The Beach Boys, The Pet Sounds Sessions - A 30th Anniversary Collection*". *Q* (EMAP Metro Ltd) (Q118, July 1996): 133.

[3] Beets, Greg (December 12, 1997). "Review: *THE BEACH BOYS: The Pet Sounds Sessions (Capitol)*" (http://www.austinchronicle.com/gyrobase/Issue/story?oid=oid:519069). Nick Barbaro. . Retrieved 29 August 2009.

[4] Bennun, David. "Review: *The Beach Boys, The Pet Sounds Sessions (Capitol)*". *The Guardian Review* (Guardian Media Group) (October 24, 1997): 24.

[5] 1999 Grammy Nominations (http://www.thefreelibrary.com/1999+GRAMMY+NOMINATIONS-a083603629)

Rarities

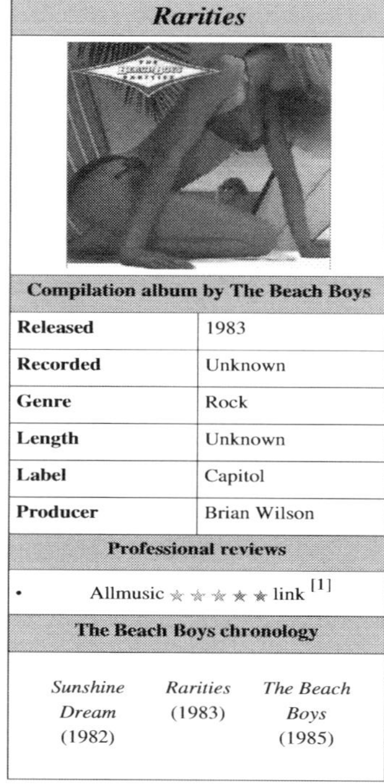

Rarities	
Compilation album by The Beach Boys	
Released	1983
Recorded	Unknown
Genre	Rock
Length	Unknown
Label	Capitol
Producer	Brian Wilson
Professional reviews	
• Allmusic ★★★★★ link [1]	
The Beach Boys chronology	

Sunshine Dream (1982)	*Rarities* (1983)	*The Beach Boys* (1985)

Rarities is a Beach Boys compilation album which was released in 1983 under Capitol Records record company.

Track listing

1. "With a Little Help from My Friends" (Lennon/McCartney) – 2:22
2. "The Letter" (Carson) – 1:47
3. "I Was Made to Love Her" (Cosby/Hardaway/Moy/Wonder) – 2:34
4. "You're Welcome" (B. Wilson) – 1:06
5. "The Lord's Prayer" (Malotte) – 2:31
6. "Bluebirds over the Mountain" (Hickey) – 2:49
7. "Celebrate the News" (D. Wilson/Jakobson) – 3:03
8. "Good Vibrations" (B. Wilson/Love) – 3:33
9. "Land Ahoy" (B. Wilson) – 1:42
10. "In My Room [German Version]" (B. Wilson/Usher) – 2:15
11. "Cottonfields" (Leadbelly) – 3:02
12. "All I Want to Do" (D. Wilson) – 2:30
13. "Auld Lang Syne" (Traditional) – 1:11
14. "Medley: Good Vibrations/Help Me, Rhonda/I Get Around/Little Deuce Coupe"
15. "Medley: Surfer Girl/Girls on the Beach/Ballad of Ole' Betsy/We'll Run Away"

16. "Beach Boys Medley: Good Vibrations/Help Me, Rhonda/I Get Around/Shut Down"

References

[1] http://www.allmusic.com/cg/amg.dll?p=amg&sql=10:px8ibka96akn

Shut Down Volume 2

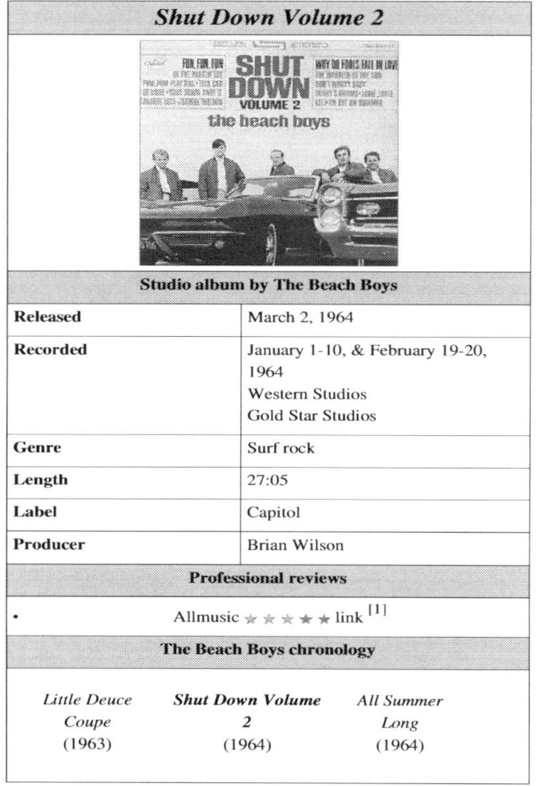

Shut Down Volume 2	
Studio album by The Beach Boys	
Released	March 2, 1964
Recorded	January 1-10, & February 19-20, 1964 Western Studios Gold Star Studios
Genre	Surf rock
Length	27:05
Label	Capitol
Producer	Brian Wilson
Professional reviews	
•	Allmusic ★★★★★ link [1]
The Beach Boys chronology	
Little Deuce Coupe (1963)	***Shut Down Volume 2*** (1964) · *All Summer Long* (1964)

Shut Down Volume 2 is the fifth studio album by The Beach Boys, and the first of four they would release in 1964. The album's "Volume 2" refers to the 1963 hot rod compilation *Shut Down*, released by the band's label, Capitol Records, which included "409" and "Shut Down" but was not a Beach Boys album.

Shut Down Volume 2 hit **#13** in the US charts during a chart stay of 38 weeks. *Shut Down Volume 2* (Capitol (S) T 2027) is now paired on CD with *Surfer Girl*, with bonus tracks from that period.

Album History

Recorded just as "Beatlemania" was beginning to reach American shores (and would soon profoundly affect leader Brian Wilson's writing and career goals for The Beach Boys) *Shut Down Volume 2* was meant to cement the band's position as the biggest band in America. Instead, The Beatles' invasion was so overpowering that the album peaked at US #13 (though it eventually went gold).

Part of the blame for the album's less than stellar performance was due to possibly the weakest ending to any Beach Boys album, with the last three tracks being considered, by common consent, filler. And although humorous, the addition of " "Cassius" Love Vs. "Sonny" Wilson" (a mock-fight between Brian and Mike) served to illustrate the need to fill up the album.

However, the high points of *Shut Down Volume 2* are arguably among the strongest moments in The Beach Boys' saga thus far: "Fun, Fun, Fun", "Don't Worry Baby" (Brian's response to Phil Spector's "Be My Baby"), "The Warmth of the Sun" (written just hours after JFK's assassination) and a cover of Frankie Lymon's "Why Do Fools Fall In Love". "Pom, Pom Play Girl" also features Carl Wilson's first official lead vocal on a Beach Boys song.

Shut Down Volume 2 was marketed as a "hot rod" collection after predecessor *Little Deuce Coupe* had performed so successfully, but The Beach Boys were not able to maintain the theme as consistently this time around, signaling that prime songwriter Brian Wilson was already running out of car songs and would need to shift gears, subject-wise, soon.

Cover art

The front sleeve photograph, taken by Capitol staff photographer George Jerman, shows the band (now with Al Jardine making his cover debut) posing next to a selection of cool cars - notably, a blue Corvette Sting Ray owned by Dennis and Pontiac Grand Prix owned by Carl.

Track listing

Side one				
No.	**Title**	**Writer(s)**	**Lead Vocals**	**Length**
1.	"Fun, Fun, Fun"	Brian Wilson/Mike Love	Mike Love	2:03
2.	"Don't Worry Baby"	B. Wilson/Roger Christian	Brian Wilson	2:47
3.	"In the Parkin' Lot"	B. Wilson/Christian	Love	2:01
4.	"Cassius Love vs. Sonny Wilson"	Love/B. Wilson	group - spoken word	3:30
5.	"The Warmth of the Sun"	B. WIlson/Love	B. Wilson	2:51
6.	"This Car of Mine"	B. Wilson/Love	Dennis Wilson	1:35

Side two				
No.	**Title**	**Writer(s)**	**Lead Vocals**	**Length**
1.	"Why Do Fools Fall in Love"	Frankie Lymon/Morris Levy	B. Wilson	2:07
2.	"Pom Pom Play Girl"	B. Wilson/Gary Usher	Carl Wilson/Love	1:30
3.	"Keep an Eye on Summer"	B. Wilson/Bob Norberg/Love	B. Wilson/Love	2:21
4.	"Shut Down, Part II"	Carl Wilson	instrumental	2:07
5.	"Louie Louie"	Richard Berry	C. WIlson/Love	2:17
6.	"Denny's Drums"	Dennis Wilson	instrumental	1:56

Singles

- "Fun, Fun, Fun" b/w "Why Do Fools Fall In Love" (Capitol 5118), 3 February 1964 **US #5**
- "Don't Worry Baby" featured as the B-side to "I Get Around" **US #24**
- "The Warmth of the Sun" featured as the B-side to "Dance, Dance, Dance"

Sources

- *Surfer Girl/Shut Down Volume 2* CD booklet notes, David Leaf, c.1990.
- "The Nearest Faraway Place: Brian Wilson, The Beach Boys and the Southern California Experience", Timothy White, c. 1994.
- "Wouldn't It Be Nice - My Own Story", Brian Wilson and Todd Gold, c. 1991.
- "Top Pop Singles 1955-2001", Joel Whitburn, c. 2002.
- "Top Pop Albums 1955-2001", Joel Whitburn, c. 2002.
- Allmusic.com

References

[1] http://www.allmusic.com/cg/amg.dll?p=amg&sql=10:fcd7ylkjxpbb

Smile

Smile	
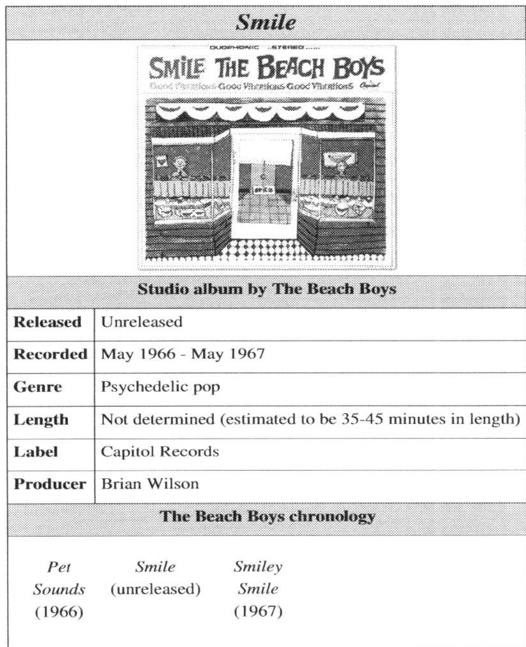	
Studio album by The Beach Boys	
Released	Unreleased
Recorded	May 1966 - May 1967
Genre	Psychedelic pop
Length	Not determined (estimated to be 35-45 minutes in length)
Label	Capitol Records
Producer	Brian Wilson
The Beach Boys chronology	
Pet Sounds (1966) — *Smile* (unreleased) — *Smiley Smile* (1967)	

Smile (sometimes typeset with the idiosyncratic partial capitalization ***SMiLE***) is an unreleased album by The Beach Boys, and perhaps the most famous unreleased rock and roll album of all time. Recorded throughout 1966 and 1967, the project was intended by its creator Brian Wilson as the follow-up to The Beach Boys' influential album *Pet Sounds*, but was never completed in its original form. The project was resurrected in 2003, and a newly recorded version was released by Beach Boys composer and leader Wilson in 2004. During the 37 years from its cancellation to the release of Wilson's version, *Smile* acquired considerable mystique, and bootlegged tracks from the never-completed album are circulated widely among Beach Boys collectors. Many of the tracks which were originally recorded for *Smile* eventually found their way onto subsequent Beach Boys albums.

Conception

In an October 1966 interview, Brian Wilson dubbed the work "a teenage symphony to God".[1] His plan was to take his work on *Pet Sounds* to a new level, with an album-length suite of specially-written songs which were both thematically and musically linked, and would be recorded using the unusual sounds and innovative production techniques which had made their recent hit "Good Vibrations" so successful.

The *Smile* story begins during the recording of *Pet Sounds*. On February 17, 1966, during the sessions for *Pet Sounds*, Brian Wilson started work on a new single, "Good Vibrations". The most expensive—at a cost of more than $50,000—and complex pop recording ever made (at the time), it still stands as a milestone in recording history. "Good Vibrations" was created by an unprecedented recording technique: nearly 30 minutes of barely-related musical sections were recorded, then painstakingly spliced together and reduced into a three-minute pop song. Many within The Beach Boys' camp were skeptical, but the song quickly became the band's biggest hit yet, which went to #1 in both Britain and the USA. *Smile* was intended to be an entire album produced in the same fashion.

Crucial to the inception and creation of *Smile* was Wilson's collaboration with singer, musician, composer and lyricist Van Dyke Parks, whom Wilson invited to write lyrics for the new album in the Spring of 1966; at the time, the project was provisionally entitled *Dumb Angel*. The two quickly formed a close and fruitful working relationship, and between April and September 1966 they co-wrote a number of major songs, including "Surf's Up", "Heroes and Villains", "Wonderful", "Cabin Essence" and "Wind Chimes", all of which were written in the famous sandbox that Brian had installed in his home. Their first collaboration was "Heroes and Villains", and it is reported that when Wilson played the song's descending melody line to him, Parks devised the opening line on the spot. Their most acclaimed song, "Surf's Up", was written in one night.

Pet Sounds lyricist Tony Asher wrote the original lyrics for "Good Vibrations." The hit version released in October 1966 featured a new set of lyrics co-written by Brian Wilson and the Beach Boys' Mike Love. Wilson had in fact asked Parks to write new lyrics for "Good Vibrations", but Parks declined, preferring not to enter a project which was already underway.

Although the precise nature of its original conception is still hotly debated, several key features of *Smile* are generally acknowledged: both musically and lyrically, Wilson and Parks intended *Smile* to be explicitly American in style and subject, a direct reaction to the British dominance of popular music at the time. It was supposedly conceived as a musical journey across America from east to west, beginning at Plymouth Rock and ending in Hawaii, as well as traversing some of the great themes of modern American history and culture, including the impact of white settlement on native Americans, the influence of the Spanish, the Wild West, and the opening up of the country by railroad and highway.

As the name implies, humour was a key ingredient, and the *Smile* songs are replete with wordplay, puns and multiple meanings. A good example is "Vega-Tables", which includes the lines "I'm gonna do well, my vegetables, cart off and sell my vegetables"; the phrase "...cart off and..." is a bilingual pun on the word *Kartoffeln*, which is German for potatoes. At one stage, Wilson apparently toyed with the idea of expanding *Smile* to include an additional "humour" record, and a number of recordings were made in this vein, although they were apparently unsuccessful, so the idea was dropped. One of the possible remnants of this aspect of the project is the track "She's Goin' Bald", which was recorded after the main *Smile* sessions and included on *Smiley Smile* (the original *Smile* track circulated amongst bootleggers is sometimes titled "He Gives Speeches").

Wilson is known to have been deeply influenced by the music of George Gershwin at an early age (especially "Rhapsody in Blue"), and *Smile* contains echoes of Gershwin's emphatic American-ness, and the episodic and programmatic characteristics of the composer's works. A short scene featuring Brian at the piano in the DVD documentary on the making of *Smile* 2003 suggests that Brian may have directly based the main riff of "Heroes and Villains" on a variation or inversion of a fragment of "Rhapsody in Blue".

Smile also drew heavily on American popular music of the past; Wilson's innovative original compositions were interwoven with snippets of significant songs of yesteryear, including "The Old Master Painter" (made famous by Peggy Lee), the perennial "You Are My Sunshine", Johnny Mercer's jazz standard "I Wanna Be Around" (recorded by Tony Bennett), the song "Gee" by noted '50s doo-wop group The Crows, as well as quotations from other pop-culture reference points, such as the Woody Woodpecker theme.

The cut-up structure of *Smile* was certainly unique for its time in mainstream popular music, and it indicates that Brian was familiar with the techniques of *musique concrète* and the usage of chance operations in making art—an approach which, according to musicologist Ian MacDonald, was also exerting a strong influence on the Beatles at this point.

Wilson's experiments with LSD were undoubtedly a significant influence on the texture and structure of the work, and one of the strongest intellectual influences on his thinking at this time was his friend Loren Schwartz, who is said to have introduced Brian to both marijuana and LSD.

Writer Bill Tobelman suggests that *Smile* is filled with coded references to Brian's life and his recent LSD experiences (a presumed Lake Arrowhead, CA trip being the most important), and that it was heavily influenced by his interest in Zen philosophy — especially in that Zen teaching uses absurd humour and the paradoxical riddle, the *koan*, to liberate the mind from preconceptions — and that *Smile* as a whole can be interpreted as an extended Zen koan.[2] Tobelman notes that Wilson's autobiography recounts an acid flashback which Wilson interprets as a Zen riddle and suggests that this same riddle, when contemplated upon, helped Wilson attain spiritual enlightenment. By presenting this riddle in the form of Smile, Wilson is promoting spiritual enlightenment.

Studio techniques

Brian Wilson developed his 'classic' production method over several years, perfecting it with the recording of *Pet Sounds* during 1965 and 1966. In this period it was still common for mainstream pop recordings to be recorded 'live' in the studio in a single take, but Wilson developed a more 'modular' approach that relied on recent advances in recording technology, using both 4-track and the newer 8-track audio recorders. He produced the tracks for *Pet Sounds* in two major 'blocks' -- while the rest of the group were away on tour he recorded the elaborate instrumental backing tracks using a band of "first-call" Los Angeles session players (now often referred to as "The Wrecking Crew") and these backing tracks were typically recorded live in a single take onto a 4-track recorder. By the time the group returned from touring, the backing tracks were virtually complete and had been mixed down onto one track of an 8-track master tape. Wilson then recorded the group vocals, often assigning an entire track on the 8-track tape to each voice; the remaining eighth track was reserved for additional "sweetening" overdubs.

With "Good Vibrations", Wilson took this 'modular' approach to recording even further, experimenting with radical editing of his work. Now, instead of taping each backing track as a complete performance (as had been the case for all previous Beach Boys recordings) he began to break the arrangements into sections, recording multiple 'takes' of each section. He also recorded the same section at several different studios, to exploit the unique sonic characteristics or special effects available in each. Then, he would select the best performances of each section and edit these different segments together to create a composite which combined the best features of production and performance.

Wilson continued this exploration with the songs on *Smile*. Working mainly at Gold Star Studios in Los Angeles (Phil Spector's favorite studio), he began a long and complex series of sessions in late 1966 that continued until early 1967. He also frequently used Sunset Sound Studios and United Western Recorders on Sunset Boulevard, and Capitol's own renowned in-house studio.

Much of *Smile* was recorded in this piecemeal manner; each of the finished tracks is a heavily-edited composite recording, and most of the unreleased *Smile* fragments are either alternate versions of backing tracks, alternate sections of these tracks, or passages intended to provide transitions between the main songs.

Despite the availability of stereo recording, Wilson always made his final mixes in mono, as did rival producer Phil Spector. Wilson did so for several reasons -- he personally felt that mono mixing provided more sonic control over what the listener heard, minimizing the vagaries of speaker placement and sound system quality. It was also motivated by the knowledge that pop radio broadcast in mono, and most domestic and car radios and record players were monophonic. Another, more personal reason for Wilson's preference was deafness in his right ear.

Recordings

Recording for the new LP, now officially named *Smile*, began in earnest in August 1966 and continued until mid-December.

In early December, Capitol Records was given a handwritten list of twelve tracks planned for *Smile*, for use on the LP back cover. This list was long considered crucial evidence of Wilson's intentions for the piece, but since the track listing (as printed by Capitol on the never-used album covers) carried the standard advisory "see label for correct playing order", it can only be taken as confirming Brian's apparent choice of songs at that time, and not their exact sequence. However, in 2006 it was realized that the handwriting on the list was not Brian's, but someone else's; furthermore, when shown a copy of the list, Brian himself stated that he had never seen it before. A comparison of the handwriting indicates that it may have been written by Carl Wilson, or possibly Brian's sister-in-law, Diane Rovell.

Capitol began production on a lavish gatefold cover with a 12-page booklet. Cover artwork was commissioned from Frank Holmes, a friend of Van Dyke Parks, and colour photographs of the group were taken by Guy Webster. 466,000 covers and 419,000 booklets were printed by early January 1967; promotional materials were sent to record distributors and dealers, and ads were placed in *Billboard* and teenage magazines including *Teen Set*.

Some time in December, Brian informed Capitol that *Smile* would not be ready that month, but he advised that he would deliver it "prior to January 15". Wilson's conception of the work evidently changed around this time, probably as a result of disagreements within the band. Early in 1967, work was halted on all the *Smile* tracks except for "Heroes and Villains" and "Vega-Tables".

"Heroes and Villains"

"Heroes and Villains" was a semi-autobiographical piece couched as a Wild West fantasy, and featured some of Parks' most intriguing lyrics. It is the keystone for the musical structure of the album, and like "Good Vibrations", it was edited together from several discrete sections.

Like most of the *Smile* songs, "Heroes and Villains" is based around a deceptively simple three-chord pattern. It encapsulates Wilson's musical approach for the project, which was to create songs that were (for the most part) structurally simple, but overlaid with extremely complex and often highly chromatic vocal and instrumental arrangements, and capped by Parks' lyrics.

The considerable time and effort that Wilson devoted to "Heroes and Villains" is indicative of its importance, both as a single and as part of *Smile* - sessions for the various versions and sections extended over more than a year, from May 1966 to July 1967.

Capitol Records had scheduled January 13 1967 as the release date for the single. Yet, although he was renowned for his efficiency in the studio, Brian Wilson clearly struggled to complete "Heroes and Villains", and despite devoting more than twenty sessions to it between October 1966 and March 1967, he was unable to complete it to his satisfaction.

It now appears that the song underwent many changes during its production, and that several important elements, including the so-called "Cantina scene" and the segment commonly known as "Bicycle Rider", were taken out of the finished single and album versions, although they were retained in other (unreleased) mixes. A single version of the song was released in mid-1967, but rumours persist of a far longer edit, and it is known that several alternate versions were put together. Both Brian Wilson and The Beach Boys frequently included "Bicycle Rider" when performing the song in concert.

"Surf's Up"

Smile's centerpiece, "Surf's Up", was written in one night and was certainly fully composed by November 1966, when Brian Wilson was filmed performing the song on piano for a CBS news special on popular music, hosted by Leonard Bernstein and David Oppenheim; "Surf's Up" was featured on Oppenheim's portion of the show. Wilson also made a studio demo with solo vocal and piano around this time, which was eventually released on the Beach Boys' 30th anniversary boxed set.

A nearly or fully completed backing track for the first (2:20) section was recorded and mixed in November 1966, but vocals and other overdubs were still to be added, and work on the middle and closing sections was either never undertaken or never finished. It is notable that the flourishes played on muted trumpet in the verses of "Surf's Up" are almost identical to the familiar 'laughing' refrain of the theme for the cartoon series *Woody Woodpecker*. This musical reference recurs in the instrumental piece "Fall Breaks And Back To Winter" on the album *Smiley Smile* (which was in fact subtitled "W. Woodpecker Symphony").

A full-length version of "Surf's Up" was eventually assembled by Carl Wilson and released on the 1971 Beach Boys album *Surf's Up*. The 1971 track was edited together from the two major basic tracks - Carl and the group recorded new vocals over the original 1966 "Part 1" backing track, which was edited together with the 1966 studio demo of Brian performing the second half solo on a piano, with new group vocals and additional instrumental overdubs in the closing section.

Other songs

The following is based upon the handwritten note given to Capitol Records in December 1966. It was given to Capitol in order for the track titles to be included on the album cover; however, the original cover states "see record for running order". It has not been conclusively proven whose handwriting is actually on the note.

All the evidence, including interviews with Brian himself, state that a final definitive running order was never decided upon until the release of the 2004 *Smile*.

- "Do You Like Worms?"
- "Wind Chimes"
- "Heroes and Villains"
- "Surf's Up"
- "Good Vibrations"
- "Cabin Essence"
- "Wonderful"
- "I'm in Great Shape"
- "Child Is Father of the Man"
- "The Elements"
- "Vega-Tables"
- "The Old Master Painter"

Certain songs have been renamed. "The Elements" was a suite which encompassed the four elements: Air, Fire, Earth, and Water. The songs were all retitled: "Wind Chimes" (for Air), "Mrs O'Leary's Cow" (for Fire), "Vega-Tables" (for Earth), "In Blue Hawaii" (for Water).

Project collapse

According to most sources, Brian Wilson began to encounter serious problems with *Smile* around late November 1966; some of this can be ascribed to his increasingly fragile mental state (by then, he was beginning to exhibit signs of depression and paranoia), but it is now evident that there was vehement opposition to the project from within the band.

It is reported that, during the recording session for the "Fire" section of the "Elements Suite" at Gold Star Studios on November 28, Brian became irrationally concerned that the music had been responsible for starting several fires in the neighborhood of the studio.

For many years, it was rumoured that Wilson had tried to burn the tapes of this session, but that was not the case, although he did abandon the "Fire" piece for good. No recording of anything but the introduction to the original "Fire" tapes has been released, nor is it likely to be. It has also been noted, in several accounts, that Parks deliberately stayed away from the session (during which Wilson encouraged the musicians to wear toy firemen hats), and that he later described Wilson's behaviour as "regressive".

In addition to Brian's possible mental health problems, and his many personal, family and creative pressures, there were other significant business and legal pressures surrounding the Beach Boys during the recording of *Smile*. These included Carl Wilson's call-up notice for the draft (which he was to fight as a conscientious objector), plus the commencement of the group's contractual dispute with Capitol over royalty payments. In addition, there was the band's attempt to terminate their then-present contract, which was a legacy of Murry's management, and establish their own label, Brother Records.

During early 1967, Brian's behaviour became increasingly erratic, and his use of drugs escalated, but while this was a concern for some of his friends, he was still completely functional in the studio. Although stories of his sometimes bizarre "off-duty" behaviour became the stuff of legend, the session musicians who worked with him during this period have stated that he was totally professional in the studio.

In retrospect, arguably the most significant reason why *Smile* was repeatedly postponed, and finally scrapped, was conflict within the group, particularly the increasing antagonism between Mike Love and the Wilson/Parks partnership, although Bruce Johnston has also indicated in a web forum discussion that there was also opposition to the project from Capitol Records and from Murry Wilson.

The growing conflict within the Beach Boys about *Smile* came to a head during December 1966. The December 6, 1966 session for "Cabin Essence" was apparently the scene of a climactic argument between Van Dyke Parks and Mike Love about the song's lyrics, and the situation evidently worsened during the 15 December vocal sessions for "Surf's Up" and "Wonderful". The group was filmed by CBS during this session which, according to Jules Siegel, went "very badly". Later the same day, Wilson recorded his now-legendary solo piano demo of "Surf's Up". Although there were more *Smile* sessions (on December 23, January 9, and January 23), work on the major tracks effectively stopped after 15 December.

Love later stated that he was suspicious of the new friends with whom Brian was associating, and that his opposition to these people whom he regarded as hangers-on, who were exploiting Brian and supplying him with 'hard' drugs, was another major source of conflict. Love has suggested that some of those who have since been critical of him did so because he had told them to "take a hike".

Love denied disliking *Pet Sounds*, also claiming that he liked the *Smile* music and only disliked the lyrics. However, this is strongly disputed by several other participants, most notably Van Dyke Parks. Responding to Love's claims in a letter to the editor of UK music magazine *Mojo*, Parks was strongly critical of Love's comments—which he described as "revisionism" -- and he was unequivocal in citing Love's hostility to "Smile" as one of the major factors in Brian's decision to abandon the project. On the DVD that accompanied the 2004 *Smile* release, Brian himself also makes it clear that Love's antagonism was one of the major deciding factors in the cancellation of the album:

> "The reasons that I didn't release *Smile*: One, Mike didn't like it...".[3]

Wilson continued work on "Heroes and Villains" and other cuts, including "Do You Like Worms" and "Vega-Tables", as well as taping numerous musical fragments which were probably intended to serve as links between the main songs. Throughout the first half of 1967, the album's release date was repeatedly postponed as Wilson tinkered with the recordings, experimenting with different takes and mixes, unable or unwilling to supply a completed version of the album.

Another significant event, cited in the *Beautiful Dreamer* documentary, was Brian's first hearing of The Beatles' new single "Strawberry Fields Forever". He heard the song while driving his car, and was so struck by it that he had to pull over and listen; he then commented to his companion that The Beatles had "got there first". Although he apparently later laughed about that comment, the stunning new Beatles production had affected him deeply. The final, irrevocable blow came in early March 1967 when, after gradually distancing himself from Wilson and the group, Van Dyke Parks finally quit the project.

Capitol evidently still hoped to the last that *Smile* might eventually appear, but on 6 May, only a few weeks before the release of The Beatles' groundbreaking *Sgt. Pepper's Lonely Hearts Club Band* album, The Beach Boys' press officer Derek Taylor ruefully announced to the British press that the *Smile* project had been shelved, and that the album would not be released.

Fame and reception

Following the stillbirth of *Smile* and the release of the poorly-received *Smiley Smile* (which Carl Wilson described as "a bunt instead of a grand-slam"[4]) that September, Brian Wilson retreated from the public eye, increasingly hampered by mental health problems, but his legend grew, and the *Smile* period came to be seen as the pivotal episode in his decline; Wilson would become tagged as one of the most notorious celebrity drug casualties of the rock era.

By the beginning of the 1990s, *Smile* had earned its place as the most famous unreleased album in the rock era, and was a focal point for bootleg album makers and collectors. A 1988 proposed sequencing of the album by engineer Mark Linett eventually leaked to the public in stunning sound quality. In 1993, fans were treated to a goldmine of official archival *Smile* material included on the 5CD boxed set *Good Vibrations - 30 Years of the Beach Boys*. The second disc of the set included almost thirty minutes of original *Smile* recordings including versions of "Our Prayer", "Wonderful", "Cabin Essence", "Wind Chimes", "Do You Like Worms", "Vege-Tables", "I Love to Say Da-Da", an alternate version of "Heroes and Villains" and numerous linking segments built around the "Heroes and Villains" theme, plus Brian's fabled demo recording of "Surf's Up", which Elvis Costello famously compared to discovering an original recording of Mozart in performance.

These recordings, sequenced by David Leaf, made it clear that *Smile* had been much closer to completion than had previously been thought, and this prompted much excitement by fans over what additional songs might exist, and debate about how the songs fitted into the *Smile* running order. There was hope that the box set would be followed by an official *Smile* release, but this did not materialize.

With the emerging popularity of the Internet in the mid 1990's, the original, bootlegged, Smile recordings became more widely available through a series of websites and "tape trees". A few websites actually offered full downloads of the tracks, and fan edits and arrangements started to appear.

Project resurrection

Brian Wilson and Van Dyke Parks would eventually revisit and complete the *Smile* project with Brian's touring musicians in 2004, 37 years after its conception. First, in a series of concerts (debuting at London's Royal Festival Hall on February 20, 2004), then as the solo album *Brian Wilson Presents Smile*, released in September 2004. The album debuted at number 13 on the *Billboard* 200 chart, and later earned 3 Grammy nominations, winning Brian Wilson his first solo Grammy award for Best Rock Instrumental Performance ("Mrs. O'Leary's Cow"). In 2005, the album won graphic artist Mark London and Nonesuch/Elektra Records the 2005 ALEX award for Best Vinyl Package.

iTunes Store released a playlist of Smile [5] comprising the songs that were released on later Beach Boys albums in 2006.

Further reading

One of the principal sources of original information on *Smile*, and the basis for much of its legendary status, was Jules Siegel's article "Goodbye Surfing, Hello God!" [6] which appeared in the first issue of *Cheetah Magazine* in October 1967. Almost equally influential was Domenic Priore's 1987 book *Look, Listen, Vibrate, Smile*.

In Lewis Shiner's novel *Glimpses*, the mental time-traveling protagonist meets and befriends Brian Wilson, and encourages Wilson to complete *Smile* over the objections of his bandmates. *Glimpses* won the 1994 World Fantasy Award for Best Novel.

External links

- Rockument-Beach Boy's Smile Sessions [7] with commentary and links to music
- http://theelements.ca/hnv/heroesandvillains.htm
- *Stylus Magazine* article [8]
- The Smile Shop - The Smile Sessions Information Site [9]
- Wilson explains SMiLE [53]
- An interview with "Smile" historian Domenic Priore [10]
- Background information and essays on the making of [11]

References

[1] Wilson's SMiLE / Brian Wilson finally finishes his 'teenage symphony to God' (http://sfgate.com/cgi-bin/article.cgi?file=/gate/archive/2004/10/28/derk.DTL)

[2] Bill Tobelman - *The Zen Interpretation of Brian Wilson & Van Dyke Parks' SMiLE* (http://pages.cthome.net/tobelman/page001.htm)

[3] Brian Wilson, quoted in *Beautiful Dreamer: Brian Wilson & the story of Smile* (Warner Vision/LSL Productions, 2005)

[4] http://www.cokemachineglow.com/reviews/beachboys_smileysmile1967.html

[5] http://phobos.apple.com/WebObjects/MZStore.woa/wa/viewMix?id=160932941&s=143441

[6] http://www.cafecancun.com/bookarts/wilson.htm

[7] http://www.rockument.com/smilesessions.html

[8] http://www.stylusmagazine.com/feature.php?ID=59

[9] http://www.thesmileshop.net/index.php/Main_Page

[10] http://www.gadflyonline.com/05-06-02/ftr-smile.html

[11] http://www.bradcoweb.com/smile/smilealbum.htm

Smiley Smile

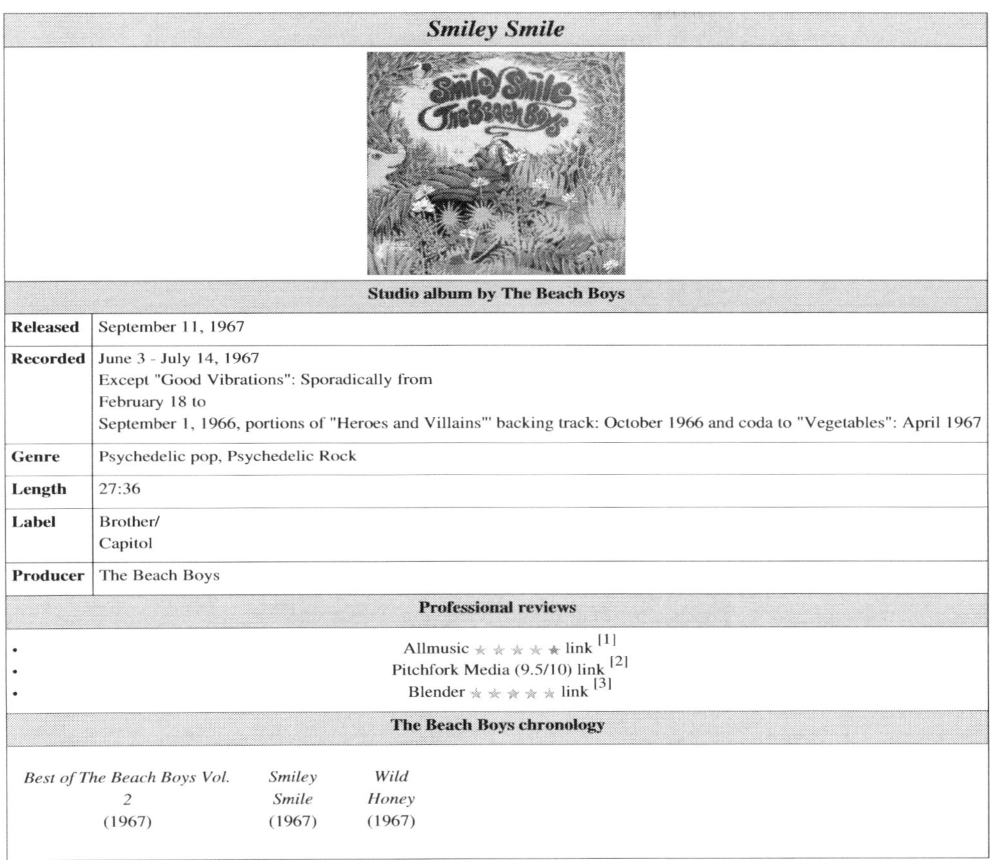

Smiley Smile	
Studio album by The Beach Boys	
Released	September 11, 1967
Recorded	June 3 - July 14, 1967 Except "Good Vibrations": Sporadically from February 18 to September 1, 1966, portions of "Heroes and Villains"' backing track: October 1966 and coda to "Vegetables": April 1967
Genre	Psychedelic pop, Psychedelic Rock
Length	27:36
Label	Brother/ Capitol
Producer	The Beach Boys
Professional reviews	
• Allmusic ★★★★★ link [1] • Pitchfork Media (9.5/10) link [2] • Blender ★★★★★ link [3]	
The Beach Boys chronology	
Best of The Beach Boys Vol. 2 (1967) · *Smiley Smile* (1967) · *Wild Honey* (1967)	

Smiley Smile is the twelfth studio album by The Beach Boys, issued in 1967. Released in the place of the much-touted *Smile*, *Smiley Smile* is widely considered to be under-produced, and it was received with indifference and confusion upon its unveiling.[4] However, *Smiley Smile* has managed to grow in stature over the years to become a cult favorite in The Beach Boys' recorded catalog.[4]

History

After "Good Vibrations" topped the singles charts in late 1966, the reported *Smile* project was eagerly anticipated.[5] However, in May 1967, the album was cancelled, and The Beach Boys pulled out of their headlining spot at the Monterey Pop Festival. The original project (which took longer to record than any other Beach Boys album) was scrapped. Cut largely at Brian Wilson's new home studio in Bel Air during June and July, the album includes alternate versions of songs originally intended for *Smile* ("Heroes and Villains", "Wind Chimes", "Vegetables", and "Wonderful") and quickly recorded new material. Only "Good Vibrations" appears in its original version. "Good

Vibrations" was included to help bolster sales, even though Brian was strongly against its inclusion.

When *Smiley Smile* was finally released in September, after months of hype, its critical reception was unenthusiastic, peaking at only #41 in the US.[6] Its commercial reception a few months later in the UK was better; it reached #9 on British charts. Carl Wilson is reported to have called it "a bunt instead of a grand slam"[4] comparing *Smiley Smile* to the much-fabled unreleased album that it eventually replaced.

Smiley Smile is generally considered the most controversial Beach Boys album; many fans consider it a massive failure while others consider it among the most distinctive albums of the sixties. Pete Townshend of The Who is a known admirer of the record, as well as Robbie Robertson of The Band.

Smiley Smile marked the beginning of the end of Brian Wilson as the creative leader of The Beach Boys. Although the album was mostly produced by him, the production was for the first time credited to the group. The following years and albums had Wilson less and less involved in music production. It would not be until 1976's *15 Big Ones* that Wilson was credited as producer again.

Quotes

> In Fort Worth, Texas there is a drug clinic which takes people off the streets and helps them get over bad LSD trips. They don't use any traditional medical treatment whatsoever. All they do is play the patient our *Smiley Smile* album and apparently this acts as a soothing remedy which relaxes them and helps them to recover completely from their trip. - Carl Wilson, (1970) [7]

- "*Smiley Smile* was an album that marked the end of an era." - Bruce Johnston[8]
- "*Smiley Smile* was just something we were going through at that time connected with drugs, love, and everything." - Dennis Wilson[8]

Track listing

Side one				
No.	**Title**	**Writer(s)**	**Lead Vocals**	**Length**
1.	"Heroes and Villains"	Brian Wilson/Van Dyke Parks	Brian Wilson/Al Jardine	3:37
2.	"Vegetables"	B. Wilson/Parks	Jardine/B. Wilson/Mike Love	2:07
3.	"Fall Breaks and Back to Winter (Woody Woodpecker Symphony)"	B. Wilson	instrumental	2:15
4.	"She's Goin' Bald"	B. Wilson/Mike Love/Parks	B. Wilson/Love/Dennis Wilson/Jardine	2:15
5.	"Little Pad"	B. Wilson	Love/Carl Wilson/B. Wilson	2:30

Side two				
No.	**Title**	**Writer(s)**	**Lead Vocals**	**Length**
1.	"Good Vibrations"	B. Wilson/Love	C. Wilson/B. Wilson/Love	3:36
2.	"With Me Tonight"	B. Wilson	C. Wilson	2:17
3.	"Wind Chimes"	B. Wilson	Love/B. Wilson/C. Wilson/D. Wilson	2:36
4.	"Gettin' Hungry"	B. Wilson/Love	Love/B. Wilson	2:27
5.	"Wonderful"	B. Wilson/Parks	C. Wilson	2:21
6.	"Whistle In"	B. Wilson	C. Wilson/Love	1:04

Singles

- "Good Vibrations" b/w "Let's Go Away for Awhile" (from *Pet Sounds*) (Capitol 5676), 10 October 1966 **US #1**; **UK #1**. (UK B-side was "Wendy" from *All Summer Long*)
- "Heroes and Villains" b/w "You're Welcome" (Brother 1001), 31 July 1967 **US #12**; **UK #8**; **CAN #5**
- "Gettin' Hungry" b/w "Devoted to You" (Brother 1002), 28 August 1967. (Credited to "Brian and Mike")

Smiley Smile is now paired on CD with *Wild Honey*, with bonus tracks from that period. In Australia, *Smiley Smile* was released on the Music for Pleasure label as *The Beach Boys*.

Personnel

- Alan Jardine - vocals, bass, guitar
- Bruce Johnston - vocals, bass, keyboards
- Mike Love - vocals
- Brian Wilson - bass, keyboards, vocals
- Carl Wilson - vocals, guitars, bass
- Dennis Wilson - drums, vocals
- Mike Deasy Sr. - guitar
- Lyle Ritz - upright bass

Sources

- *Smiley Smile / Wild Honey* CD booklet notes, David Leaf, c.1990.
- *Look! Listen! Vibrate! Smile!*, Domenic Priore, c.1995
- *Catch a Wave*, Carlin, c. 2006
- *The Nearest Faraway Place: Brian Wilson, The Beach Boys and the Southern California Experience*, Timothy White, c. 1994.
- *The Beach Boys - The Definitive Diary of America's Greatest Band on Stage and in the Studio*, Keith Badman, c. 2004
- *Wouldn't It Be Nice - My Own Story*, Brian Wilson and Todd Gold, c. 1991.
- *Top Pop Singles 1955–2001*, Joel Whitburn, c. 2002.
- *Top Pop Albums 1955–2001*, Joel Whitburn, c. 2002.
- Allmusic.com

External links

- *Smiley Smile* [9] at MusicBrainz

References

[1] http://www.allmusic.com/cg/amg.dll?p=amg&sql=10:hq6ftr29kl3x
[2] http://www.pitchforkmedia.com/article/record_review/15335-smiley-smilewild-honey
[3] http://www.blender.com/guide/reviews.aspx?id=2244
[4] Carlin A., Peter. *Catch a Wave: The Rise, Fall Redemption of the Beach Boys' Brian Wilson*. Rodale Inc, 2006, ISBN 1-59486-320-2 p. 129
[5] allmusic (((Smiley Smile > Charts & Awards > Billboard Singles))) (http://www.allmusic.com/cg/amg.dll?p=amg&sql=10:fifwxql5ld0e~T31)
[6] allmusic (((Smiley Smile > Charts & Awards > Billboard Albums))) (http://www.allmusic.com/cg/amg.dll?p=amg&sql=10:fifwxql5ld0e~T3)
[7] http://surfermoon.com/essays/quotes.shtml#carl_wilson
[8] Priore, Domenic. *Look! Listen! Vibrate! Smile!*. Last Gap, 1995, ISBN 0-86719-417-0 p. 194
[9] http://musicbrainz.org/release/67bb98fb-2d80-4636-9d7b-aebd5ecd455b.html

Songs from Here & Back

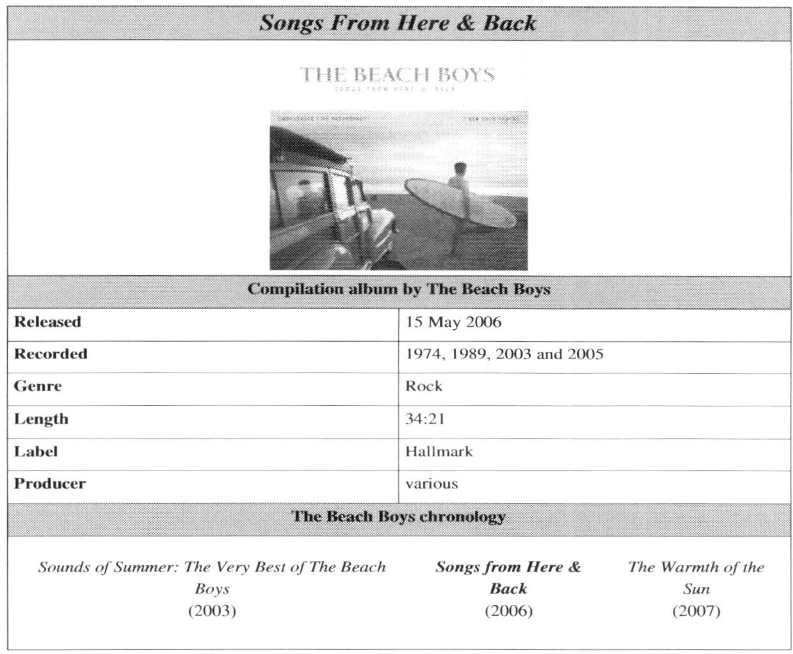

Songs From Here & Back	
THE BEACH BOYS	
Compilation album by The Beach Boys	
Released	15 May 2006
Recorded	1974, 1989, 2003 and 2005
Genre	Rock
Length	34:21
Label	Hallmark
Producer	various
The Beach Boys chronology	

Sounds of Summer: The Very Best of The Beach Boys (2003)	***Songs from Here & Back*** (2006)	*The Warmth of the Sun* (2007)

Songs From Here & Back is a 2006 live album by The Beach Boys released through Hallmark Gold Crown Stores and only available for two months. The album contains nine never-before-released live recordings, as well as three solo studio recordings, one by each surviving member of the Beach Boys.

Track listing

1. "Intro" – 0:27
2. "Dance, Dance, Dance" – 2:08
3. "Wouldn't It Be Nice" – 2:42
4. "Surfer Girl" – 3:01
5. "Kokomo" – 4:33
6. "Car Medley Intro" – 1:18
7. "Little Deuce Coupe" – 1:46
8. "I Get Around" – 2:26
9. "Good Vibrations" – 4:38
10. "Spirit of Rock & Roll" (Brian Wilson) – 3:09
11. "PT Cruiser" (Al Jardine) – 2:47
12. "Cool Head, Warm Heart" (Mike Love) – 3:15

Sounds of Summer: The Very Best of The Beach Boys

Sounds of Summer: The Very Best of The Beach Boys	
Greatest hits by The Beach Boys	
Released	June 10, 2003
Recorded	April 1962 - Spring 1988
Genre	Rock
Length	75:58
Label	Capitol
Producer	Brian Wilson, Murry Wilson, Nick Venet, The Beach Boys, Carl Wilson, Al Jardine, Ron Altbach, Bruce Johnston, James William Guercio, Steve Levine and Terry Melcher
Professional reviews	
•	Allmusic ★★★★★ link [1]
The Beach Boys chronology	
Good Timin': Live at Knebworth England 1980 (2002)	*Sounds of Summer: The Very Best of The Beach Boys* (2003) — *Songs from Here & Back* (2006)

Sounds of Summer: The Very Best of The Beach Boys is a 2003 compilation of music by The Beach Boys released through Capitol Records. This collection is the most expansive compilation ever issued of their music, with 30 tracks clocking in at over 76 minutes and grabbing nearly every US Top 40 hit of their career, except for 1965's #20 hit "The Little Girl I Once Knew" and the 1976 top-30 hit "It's OK".

Sounds of Summer: The Very Best of The Beach Boys was released in a market already containing the three volumes of hits issued during 1999 and 2000, but that did little to deter shoppers, who were responsible for shooting the CD into the US charts at a remarkable #16 (their highest peak since 1976's *15 Big Ones*) and a lengthy 104-week stay. Currently certified double platinum, *Sounds of Summer: The Very Best of The Beach Boys* was re-issued with a DVD component in 2004 with the regular edition remaining available.

In 2007, the album was succeeded by *The Warmth of the Sun*, which is composed of fan favorites and hits that were left off *Sounds of Summer*.

Track listing

1. "California Girls" (Brian Wilson/Mike Love [1965]) – 2:44
   - *Stereo remix from Endless Harmony Soundtrack*
2. "I Get Around" (Brian Wilson/Mike Love [1964]) – 2:13
3. "Surfin' Safari" (Brian Wilson/Mike Love [1962]) – 2:05
4. "Surfin' USA" (Brian Wilson/Chuck Berry [1963]) – 2:27
5. "Fun, Fun, Fun" (Brian Wilson/Mike Love [1964]) – 2:18
6. "Surfer Girl" (Brian Wilson [1963]) – 2:27
7. "Don't Worry Baby" (Brian Wilson/Roger Christian [1964]) – 2:47
8. "Little Deuce Coupe" (Brian Wilson/Roger Christian [1963]) – 1:38
9. "Shut Down" (Brian Wilson/Roger Christian [1963]) – 1:48
   - *Exclusive new stereo remix*
10. "Help Me, Rhonda" (Brian Wilson/Mike Love [1965]) – 2:46
11. "Be True to Your School" (Brian Wilson/Mike Love [1963]) – 2:08
12. "When I Grow Up (To Be a Man)" (Brian Wilson/Mike Love [1964]) – 2:02
13. "In My Room" (Brian Wilson/Gary Usher [1963]) – 2:12
14. "God Only Knows" (Brian Wilson/Tony Asher [1966]) – 2:51
15. "Sloop John B" (Trad. Arr. Brian Wilson [1966]) – 2:57
   - *Above two: stereo remixes from The Pet Sounds Sessions box set*
16. "Wouldn't It Be Nice" (Brian Wilson/Tony Asher/Mike Love [1966]) – 2:31
   - *Revised stereo remix from 2001 re-issue of Pet Sounds*
17. "Getcha Back" (Mike Love/Terry Melcher [1985]) – 3:00
18. "Come Go with Me" (C.E. Quick [1978]) – 2:05
19. "Rock and Roll Music" (Chuck Berry [1976]) – 2:27
20. "Dance, Dance, Dance" (Brian Wilson/Carl Wilson/Mike Love [1964]) – 2:00
   - *Exclusive new stereo remix*
21. "Barbara Ann" (Fred Fassert [1965]) – 2:11
22. "Do You Wanna Dance?" (Bobby Freeman [1965]) – 2:18
23. "Heroes and Villains" (Brian Wilson/Van Dyke Parks [1967]) – 3:38
24. "Good Timin'" (Brian Wilson/Carl Wilson [1979]) – 2:12
25. "Kokomo" (John Phillips/Mike Love/Scott McKenzie/Terry Melcher [1988])3:35
26. "Do It Again" (Brian Wilson/Mike Love [1968]) – 2:18
   - *Single version, without workshop effects coda*
27. "Wild Honey" (Brian Wilson/Mike Love [1967]) – 2:37
28. "Darlin'" (Brian Wilson/Mike Love [1967]) – 2:12
29. "I Can Hear Music" (Jeff Barry/Ellie Greenwich/Phil Spector [1969]) – 2:36
30. "Good Vibrations" (Brian Wilson/Mike Love [1966]) – 3:36

Sounds of Summer: The Very Best of The Beach Boys (Capitol 72435 82710 2) hit **#16** in the US during a chart stay of 104 weeks.

DVD: Sights of Summer

1. "Surfin' USA"
2. "I Get Around"
3. "Surfer Girl"
4. "Dance, Dance, Dance"
5. "Little Deuce Coupe"
6. "Sloop John B"
7. "Pet Sounds promo film"
8. "God Only Knows"
9. "Good Vibrations"
10. "Do It Again"

- 1-4 Live on *The T.A.M.I. Show*, 1964
- 5 Live from the Lost Concert, 1964
- 6 Promotional Video, 1966
- 7 Promo film, 1966
- 8 Live montage, 1967 & 1968
- 9-10 Live on *The Ed Sullivan Show*, 1968

References

- *Sounds of Summer: The Very Best of The Beach Boys* CD booklet notes, Anthony DeCurtis, c.2003
- Allmusic.com

References

[1] http://www.allmusic.com/cg/amg.dll?p=amg&sql=10:hy66mpnk9f7o

Spirit of America

Spirit of America	
Greatest hits by The Beach Boys	
Released	April 14, 1975
Recorded	April 1962 - April 1969
Genre	Rock
Length	51:09
Label	Capitol
Producer	Brian Wilson, The Beach Boys and Nick Venet
Professional reviews	
• Allmusic ★★★★★ link [1]	
The Beach Boys chronology	
Endless Summer (1974) · *Spirit of America* (1975) · *Good Vibrations - Best of The Beach Boys* (1975)	

Spirit of America is the 1975 follow-up to the Capitol Records compilation of music by The Beach Boys, *Endless Summer*, released the previous year. After the enormous success of its predecessor, Capitol rounded up the few remaining early hits that weren't released on *Endless Summer*, as well as some worthy album tracks, in addition to two rare singles, "The Little Girl I Once Knew" and "Break Away". Although it features only a handful genuine hits, *Spirit of America* proved to be another success for The Beach Boys' former label, reaching #8 at home and going gold.

As with *Endless Summer*, *Spirit of America* was compiled and released while The Beach Boys were contracted with Reprise Records and, as such, is not considered an "official" album of theirs.

Due to the appearance of more comprehensive and updated hit packages, *Endless Summer*, *Spirit of America*, and the 1982 followup *Sunshine Dream* have long since been deleted from the group's catalog.

Track listing

All songs by Brian Wilson/Mike Love, except where noted.

Side 1

1. Dance, Dance, Dance (Brian Wilson/Carl Wilson/Mike Love) – 1:59
2. Break Away (Brian Wilson/Reggie Dunbar) – 2:54
   - Reggie Dunbar is a pseudonym for Murry Wilson
3. A Young Man is Gone (Bobby Troup/Mike Love) – 2:15
4. 409 (Brian Wilson/Mike Love/Gary Usher) – 2:00
5. The Little Girl I Once Knew (Brian Wilson) – 2:36
6. Spirit Of America (Brian Wilson/Roger Christian) – 2:23

Side 2

1. Little Honda – 1:51
2. Hushabye (D. Pomus/M. Shuman) – 2:40
3. Hawaii – 1:59
4. Drive-In – 1:50
5. Good to My Baby – 2:17
6. Tell Me Why (John Lennon/Paul McCartney) – 1:38

Side 3

1. Do You Remember? – 1:37
2. This Car of Mine – 1:35
3. Please Let Me Wonder – 2:45
4. Why Do Fools Fall In Love? (Frankie Lymon/Morris Levy) – 1:58
5. Custom Machine – 1:38

Side 4

1. Barbara Ann (Fred Fassert) – 3:07
   - *Full length Beach Boys' Party! version*
2. Salt Lake City – 2:00
3. Don't Back Down – 1:44
4. When I Grow Up (To Be a Man) – 2:02
5. Do You Wanna Dance? (Bobby Freeman) – 2:18
6. Graduation Day (J. Sherman/N. Sherman) – 2:17

Spirit of America (Capitol SVBB 11384) hit **#8** in the US during a chart stay of 43 weeks.

As with the *Endless Summer* compilation, the 2-record set was pressed with Sides 1 & 4 on one disc and Sides 2 & 3 on the other.

Side 1 of the cassette version features all tracks from Sides 1 & 2 except "Tell Me Why", which was placed on Side 2 as the first track, followed by Sides 3 & 4

The song "Dance, Dance, Dance" featured in this album was also one of 2 Beach Boys tracks included in a promotional-only various artists compilation album issued by Capitol records entitled "The Greatest Music Ever Sold" (Capitol SPRO-8511/8512), which was distributed to record stores during the 1976 Holiday season, as part of Capitol's "Greatest Music Ever Sold" campaign which promoted 15 "Best Of" albums that were released by the record label. "Help Me, Rhonda" from "Endless Summer" was the other Beach Boys song included.

References

[1] http://www.allmusic.com/cg/amg.dll?p=amg&sql=10:w1uh6j2h71e0

Stack-O-Tracks

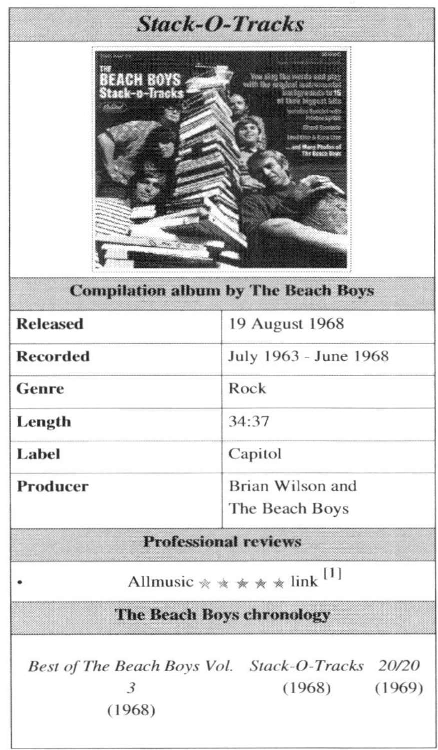

Stack-O-Tracks	
Compilation album by The Beach Boys	
Released	19 August 1968
Recorded	July 1963 - June 1968
Genre	Rock
Length	34:37
Label	Capitol
Producer	Brian Wilson and The Beach Boys
Professional reviews	
• Allmusic ★★★★★ link [1]	
The Beach Boys chronology	
Best of The Beach Boys Vol. 3 (1968)	*Stack-O-Tracks* (1968) *20/20* (1969)

Stack-O-Tracks is an album release by The Beach Boys containing the backing tracks to fifteen of their songs spanning their career to that point. Considered little more than a penny pincher when it came out, *Stack-O-Tracks* turned out to be a very educational album for those wanted to know what went into the making of a Beach Boys music track. This type of release was unique for the band, and generally was and still is relatively unique throughout the music industry where backing tracks, in the rare event of their commercial release, are generally bonus tracks or b-sides to singles.

The Beach Boys third and final album release of 1968, coming after *Friends* and released the same day as the quickly cobbled-together *Best of The Beach Boys Vol. 3*, *Stack-O-Tracks* was seen by many at the time as a desperate last-ditch effort by Capitol Records to try *anything* to sell Beach Boys records. The strategy backfired, however; issued at one of their lowest commercial ebbs in the U.S., *Stack-O-Tracks* became the first Beach Boys album to fail to reach the U.S. or UK charts. Until 1992's much-maligned *Summer in Paradise*, it would remain their only official release to have this distinction.

Nonetheless, featuring instrumental highlights from the past studio albums, and including a booklet with the bass lines, lead lines, chords and lyrics (to sing along with), *Stack-O-Tracks* was clearly a gift to those who wanted to hear what was going on beneath the lush harmonies. *Stack-O-Tracks* quickly disappeared and was out of print for two decades. In 1990, Capitol Records saw fit to re-issue it on CD, and again in 2001 - both releases without the handy booklet that accompanied the vinyl edition.

Track listing

All songs by Brian Wilson/Mike Love, except where noted.

1. "Darlin' " – 2:12
2. "Salt Lake City" – 1:58
3. "Sloop John B" (Trad. arr. Brian Wilson) – 3:04
4. "In My Room" (Brian Wilson/Gary Usher) – 2:13
5. "Catch A Wave" – 2:00
6. "Wild Honey" – 2:35
7. "Little Saint Nick" – 1:49
8. "Do It Again" – 2:11
9. "Wouldn't It Be Nice" (Brian Wilson/Tony Asher/Mike Love) – 2:11
10. "God Only Knows" (Brian Wilson/Tony Asher) – 2:37
11. "Surfer Girl" (Brian Wilson) – 2:16
12. "Little Honda" – 1:36
13. "Here Today" (Brian Wilson/Tony Asher) – 3:06
14. "You're So Good To Me" – 1:55
15. "Let Him Run Wild" – 2:13

Stack-O-Tracks is now paired on CD with *Beach Boys' Party!*, with bonus instrumental tracks.

Stack-O-Tracks (Capitol (D) KAO 2893) failed to chart in either the U.S. or the UK.

References

- *Beach Boys' Party! / Stack-O-Tracks* CD booklet notes, David Leaf, c.1990.
- *The Nearest Faraway Place: Brian Wilson, The Beach Boys and the Southern California Experience*, Timothy White, c. 1994.
- *Wouldn't It Be Nice - My Own Story*, Brian Wilson and Todd Gold, c. 1991.
- *Top Pop Singles 1955-2001*, Joel Whitburn, c. 2002.
- *Top Pop Albums 1955-2001*, Joel Whitburn, c. 2002.
- Allmusic.com

References

[1] http://www.allmusic.com/cg/amg.dll?p=amg&sql=10:hzfrxq95ldhe

Stars and Stripes Vol. 1

Stars and Stripes Vol. 1	
Studio album by The Beach Boys	
Released	19 August 1996
Recorded	5 October 1995 - 12 June 1996
Genre	Country
Length	37:47
Label	River North Records
Producer	Joe Thomas Brian Wilson
Professional reviews	
• Allmusic ★★★★★ link [1]	
The Beach Boys chronology	

Good Vibrations: Thirty Years of The Beach Boys (1993)	***Stars and Stripes Vol. 1*** (1996)	*The Pet Sounds Sessions* (1997)

Stars and Stripes Vol. 1 is an album by The Beach Boys. Released in 1996, it is, despite its 'Volume 1' sub-title, their only venture into the genre of country music.

The album contains new recordings of a number of the group's best-known songs, with stars of the country scene featured as guest artists. In the mid-1990s, country music was enjoying a new popularity and increased record sales (partly due to the success of Garth Brooks), and after the extremely poor sales of the previous Beach Boys album *Summer in Paradise*, it was hoped the project would revive their commercial fortunes.

Brian Wilson, at the time recently remarried and in his best mental state for many years, was persuaded to re-join the group and act as co-producer. In the event, it was to be the group's last recording with either Brian, Carl Wilson or Al Jardine, making *Stars and Stripes Vol. 1*, in all likelihood, the Beach Boys' final studio album.

Most of the guests were not mainstream country superstars who had crossed over into the pop market, although Toby Keith has done so since. Willie Nelson was easily the most recognizable name among them, and Timothy B. Schmit was known for his time in The Eagles. Tammy Wynette had recorded a version of "In My Room" with Brian Wilson, but it was saved for the projected *Stars and Stripes Vol. 2*, which never appeared (although her performance is included in the television documentary).

When it was released, *Stars and Stripes Vol. 1* easily outsold *Summer in Paradise*, but overall was not a major hit and was poorly received by critics. Consequently, further volumes in the series were scrapped.

The album went out of print for some years, but was reissued on CD in May 2008. The TV documentary *Beach Boys: Nashville Sounds* features studio footage of its making and interviews with participants.

Track listing

1. "Don't Worry Baby" (Brian Wilson/Roger Christian) – 3:16
    - **with Lorrie Morgan**
2. "Little Deuce Coupe" (Brian Wilson/Roger Christian) – 2:50
    - **with James House**
3. "409" (Brian Wilson/Mike Love/Gary Usher) – 2:20
    - **with Junior Brown**
4. "Long Tall Texan" (Henry Strzelecki) – 4:02
    - **with Doug Supernaw**
5. "I Get Around" (Brian Wilson/Mike Love) – 2:29
    - **with Sawyer Brown**
6. "Be True to Your School" (Brian Wilson/Mike Love) – 3:18
    - **with Toby Keith**
7. "Fun, Fun, Fun" (Brian Wilson/Mike Love) – 2:20
    - **with Ricky Van Shelton**
8. "Help Me, Rhonda" (Brian Wilson/Mike Love) – 3:10
    - **with T. Graham Brown**
9. "The Warmth of the Sun" (Brian Wilson/Mike Love) – 3:18
    - **with Willie Nelson**
10. "Sloop John B" (Trad. Arr. Brian Wilson) – 3:45
    - **with Collin Raye**
11. "I Can Hear Music" (Jeff Barry/Ellie Greenwich/Phil Spector) – 3:14
    - **with Kathy Troccoli**
12. "Caroline, No" (Brian Wilson/Tony Asher) – 3:19
    - **with Timothy B. Schmit**

Sales chart positions

Album

Chart (1996)	Peak Position
U.S. *Billboard* Billboard 200	101
U.S. *Billboard* Top Country Albums	12
Canadian *RPM* Country Albums	11

Singles

Year	Single	Chart Positions		
		US AC	US Country	CAN Country
1996	"I Can Hear Music" (with Kathy Troccoli)	16		
	"Don't Worry Baby" (with Lorrie Morgan)		73	
	"Little Deuce Coupe" (with James House)		69	41
	"Long Tall Texan" (with Doug Supernaw)		69	82

Sources

- *Stars and Stripes Vol. 1* CD booklet notes, Robert K. Oermann
- Allmusic.com

References

[1] http://www.allmusic.com/cg/amg.dll?p=amg&sql=10:rtkmikkjbbf9

Still Cruisin'

Still Cruisin'	
Studio album by The Beach Boys	
Released	August 28, 1989
Recorded	1987–1989, Except "I Get Around": April 1964, "Wouldn't It Be Nice": January–April 1966, and "California Girls": April & June 1965
Genre	Rock
Length	33:44
Label	Capitol
Producer	Brian Wilson, Terry Melcher, Al Jardine, Albert Calbrera and Tony Moran
Professional reviews	
• Allmusic ★★★★★ link [1] • *Rolling Stone* ★★★★★ link [2]	
The Beach Boys chronology	
Made in U.S.A. (1986)	***Still Cruisin'*** (1989)	*Summer in Paradise* (1992)

Still Cruisin' is the twenty-sixth studio album by The Beach Boys, their thirty-fifth official album (counting compilations and live packages), and their last release of the 1980s. It is also the last album of new material released during a brief return to Capitol Records.

After "Kokomo" (when released as a single from the *Cocktail* film soundtrack) gave the Beach Boys their first number-one hit in the U.S. since 1966's "Good Vibrations", the band decided to put together an album of recent and classic songs. The classic songs included had been heard in recent films. The songs "Still Cruisin'", "Somewhere Near Japan" and "Island Girl" were recorded for the album by the touring Beach Boys band as well as studio musicians and producer Terry Melcher. Due to his ongoing relationship with Dr. Eugene Landy, Brian Wilson's lone contribution to this album was "In My Car", a song credited as being co-written by Landy and girlfriend Alexandra Morgan. However, as subsequent court cases have seen Landy's name removed from other period songs[3] , such as those on Wilson's 1988 album, these credits may be negated. "Kokomo" was a recent single, as was "Wipe Out", a duet with American rap group the Fat Boys. (The song was originally to be recorded with Run-DMC, but Mike Love apparently struck a deal with the other group.)[3] "Make It Big" was recorded for the film *Troop Beverly Hills*, and the remaining three songs- "I Get Around", "Wouldn't It Be Nice" and "California Girls" - were the 'classic' recordings, ones from the group's earlier period, that had been used in recent films.

The Australian issue of the album adds the Spanish language version of "Kokomo".

Riding on the coattails of "Kokomo", *Still Cruisin'* went gold in the U.S., and gave The Beach Boys their best chart showing since 1976. During Capitol's Beach Boys re-issue campaign in 2000 and 2001 however, *Still Cruisin'* was left behind and allowed to go out of print. The album is available to download though on iTunes and other music downloading sites.

Promotional videos

Four music videos were produced for *Still Crusin*'

- "Still Cruisin'"
- "Somewhere Near Japan"
- "Kokomo"
- "Wipe Out"

Track listing

No.	Title	Writer(s)	Lead Vocals	Length
1.	"Still Cruisin'" (from Lethal Weapon 2)	Mike Love/Terry Melcher	Mike Love/Carl Wilson/Al Jardine/Bruce Johnston	3:35
2.	"Somewhere Near Japan"	Bruce Johnston/Love/Melcher/John Phillips	Love/C. Wilson/Jardine/Johnston	4:48
3.	"Island Girl"	Al Jardine	C. Wilson/Jardine/Love	3:49
4.	"In My Car"	Brian Wilson/Eugene Landy/Alexandra Morgan	Brian Wilson/C. Wilson/Jardine	3:21
5.	"Kokomo" (from Cocktail)	Love/Scott McKenzie/Melcher/Phillips	Love/C. Wilson	3:35
6.	"Wipe Out"	Bob Berryhill/Pat Connolly/Jim Fuller/Ron Wilson	The Fat Boys/B. Wilson	4:00
7.	"Make It Big" (from Troop Beverly Hills)	Love/Bob House/Melcher	C. Wilson/Love/Jardine/B. Wilson	3:08
8.	"I Get Around" (from Good Morning Vietnam)	B. Wilson/Love	B. Wilson/Love	2:09
9.	"Wouldn't It Be Nice" (from The Big Chill)	B. Wilson/Tony Asher	B. Wilson/Love	2:22
10.	"California Girls" (from Soul Man)	B. Wilson/Love	Love	2:35

Singles

- "Kokomo" b/w "Tutti Frutti" (Little Richard) (Elektra), July 18, 1988 **US #1**; **UK #25**
- "Still Cruisin' " b/w "Kokomo" (Capitol), August 7, 1989 **US #93**
- "Somewhere Near Japan" b/w "Kokomo" (Capitol), January 1990

Still Cruisin' (Capitol) reached **#46** in the U.S. during a chart stay of 22 weeks.

References

[1] http://www.allmusic.com/cg/amg.dll?p=amg&sql=10:x9508qbtbtv4
[2] http://www.rollingstone.com/artists/thebeachboys/albums/album/171139/review/5946315/still_cruisin
[3] Doe, Andrew and Tobler, John G. *Brian Wilson and the Beach Boys- The Complete Guys to Their Music*. Omnibus Press, 1997.

- *The Nearest Faraway Place: Brian Wilson, The Beach Boys and the Southern California Experience*, Timothy White, c. 1994.
- *Wouldn't It Be Nice - My Own Story*, Brian Wilson and Todd Gold, c. 1991.
- *Top Pop Singles 1955-2001*, Joel Whitburn, c. 2002.
- *Top Pop Albums 1955-2001*, Joel Whitburn, c. 2002.
- Allmusic.com

Summer Days (And Summer Nights!!)

Summer Days (And Summer Nights!!)	
Studio album by The Beach Boys	
Released	June 28, 1965
Recorded	February 26 - May 24, 1965
Genre	Rock, pop, sunshine pop, baroque pop
Length	26:42
Label	Capitol
Producer	Brian Wilson
Professional reviews	
• Allmusic ★★★★★ link [1]	
• Blender ★★★★★ link [2]	
• *warr.org* ★★★★★ link [2]	
The Beach Boys chronology	

The Beach Boys Today! (1965)	***Summer Days (and Summer Nights!!)*** (1965)	*Beach Boys' Party!* (1965)

Summer Days (And Summer Nights!!) is the ninth studio album by The Beach Boys and their second in 1965.

Summer Days (And Summer Nights!!) hit #2 in the US during a chart stay of 33 weeks. It reached #4 in the UK in the summer of 1966. The album was eventually rereleased on CD, paired with *The Beach Boys Today!* as well as bonus tracks from that period.

History

After the dramatic and highly sophisticated shift in style on Side 2 of *The Beach Boys Today!*, leader Brian Wilson reportedly was questioned by Mike Love and Capitol Records as to what his musical intentions were, and encouraged to make more "Beach Boys-type music" for the next release. It was clear that the band was, at this point, stereotyped as a happy "fun in the sun" band that sang about the beach, girls and good times. While on the surface *Summer Days (And Summer Nights!!)* appeared to be a throwback to the carefree ideals of *All Summer Long*, Brian Wilson had carefully woven intricate music tracks beneath the lighthearted words of "Amusement Parks USA" and "Salt Lake City". He also devised a successful instrumental with strings ("Summer Means New Love") and even composed a symphonic intro to their new, and sensational, US #3 hit single "California Girls" (that intro being Brian's personal favorite of his entire songwriting career). In hindsight, it's clear that Wilson was building towards what would become *Pet Sounds* the following year.

Of the many highlights on the album, "The Girl from New York City" was a response to "The Boy From New York City", a hit by The Ad Libs earlier that year, and "Then I Kissed Her" was Brian's attempt to beat his hero Phil Spector at his own game. A successful recording (and an unlikely Top 5 UK hit in 1967), it was Al Jardine's second lead vocal on the album. The first was a re-recording of a *The Beach Boys Today!* track which was now called "Help Me, Rhonda" and was recently The Beach Boys' second US #1 hit. "Girl Don't Tell Me", with Carl on lead, featured none other than the five Beach Boys themselves on instruments (in lieu of the usual session musicians), playing a track that was deliberately modeled after The Beatles' "Ticket To Ride". Besides "California Girls", the other major progression on *Summer Days (And Summer Nights!!)* was "Let Him Run Wild", a Burt Bacharach-style track.

Of course there had to be a little silliness on the album, and it was saved almost to the end with the tongue-in-cheek "I'm Bugged at My Ol' Man", a none-too-subtle poke at the Wilsons' father Murry, who had been fired from his post as manager the previous year, though he did still occasionally show up to either support, or badger, Brian in the studio.

Summer Days (And Summer Nights!!) proved to be Bruce Johnston's first appearance on a Beach Boys album. As Brian's stage replacement, he was not an "official" member yet, but Brian Wilson appreciated Johnston's skills enough to have him contribute vocally. Bruce would often accompany the group on photo shoots, but he was prohibited from having those pictures published due to a preexisting contract with Columbia Records. His face would not grace the cover of a Beach Boys' album until *Friends* in 1968. (Along with Johnston, Al Jardine is also missing from the *Summer Days* cover photo depicting the group on a sailboat; he had to miss the shoot due to illness.)

The album proved to be another gold-selling success in the US, where it hit #2 (behind The Rolling Stones's *Out of Our Heads*) and the following year, *Summer Days (And Summer Nights!!)* would reach #4 in the UK.

In the early 1980s, as part of Capitol Records' reissue series of their Beach Boys albums, *Summer Days (And Summer Nights!!)* was retitled *California Girls* and had two tracks removed: "Amusement Parks, USA" and "I'm Bugged at My Ol' Man".

Track listing

All songs written and composed by Brian Wilson/Mike Love, except where noted.

Side one			
No.	**Title**	**Lead Vocals**	**Length**
1.	"The Girl from New York City"	Mike Love	1:54
2.	"Amusement Parks U.S.A."	Love/Brian Wilson	2:29
3.	"Then I Kissed Her" (Phil Spector/Ellie Greenwich/Jeff Barry)	Al Jardine	2:15
4.	"Salt Lake City"	Love/B. Wilson	2:00
5.	"Girl Don't Tell Me" (B. Wilson)	Carl Wilson	2:19
6.	"Help Me, Rhonda"	Jardine	2:46

Side two			
No.	**Title**	**Lead Vocals**	**Length**
1.	"California Girls"	Love	2:38
2.	"Let Him Run Wild"	B. Wilson	2:20
3.	"You're So Good to Me"	B. Wilson	2:14
4.	"Summer Means New Love" (B. Wilson)	instrumental	1:59
5.	"I'm Bugged at My Ol' Man" (B. Wilson)	B. Wilson	2:17
6.	"And Your Dream Comes True"	group	1:04

Singles

- "Help Me, Rhonda" b/w "Kiss Me Baby" (from *The Beach Boys Today!*) (Capitol 5395), 5 April 1965 US #1; UK #27
- "California Girls" b/w "Let Him Run Wild (Capitol 5464), 12 July 1965 US #3; UK #26

References

- *The Beach Boys Today! / Summer Days (and Summer Nights!!)* CD booklet notes, David Leaf, c.1990.
- *The Nearest Faraway Place: Brian Wilson, The Beach Boys and the Southern California Experience", Timothy White (editor) |Timothy White, c. 1994.*
- *Wouldn't It Be Nice - My Own Story*, Brian Wilson and Todd Gold, c. 1991.
- *Top Pop Singles 1955-2001*, Joel Whitburn, c. 2002.
- *Top Pop Albums 1955-2001*, Joel Whitburn, c. 2002.
- Allmusic.com

References

[1] http://www.allmusic.com/cg/amg.dll?p=amg&sql=10:17d8vwvva9yk
[2] http://www.warr.org/brian.html#Summer

Summer in Paradise

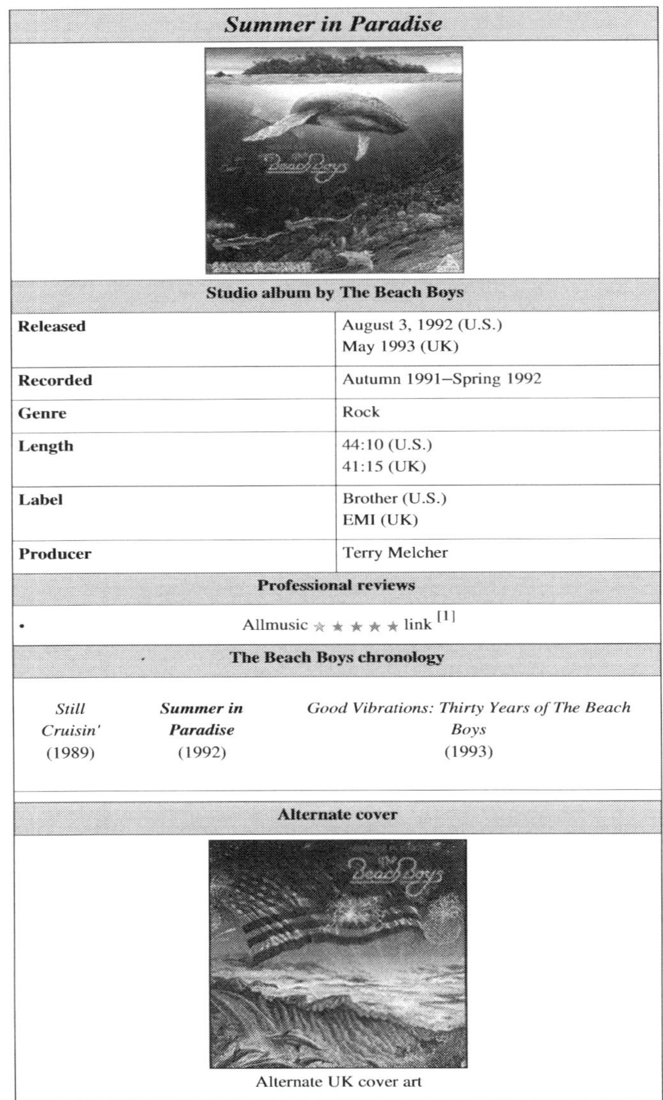

Summer in Paradise	
Studio album by The Beach Boys	
Released	August 3, 1992 (U.S.) May 1993 (UK)
Recorded	Autumn 1991–Spring 1992
Genre	Rock
Length	44:10 (U.S.) 41:15 (UK)
Label	Brother (U.S.) EMI (UK)
Producer	Terry Melcher
Professional reviews	
• Allmusic ★★★★★ link [1]	
The Beach Boys chronology	
Still Cruisin' (1989) · ***Summer in Paradise*** (1992) · *Good Vibrations: Thirty Years of The Beach Boys* (1993)	
Alternate cover	

Alternate UK cover art

Summer in Paradise is The Beach Boys' twenty-seventh studio album, their first release of the 1990s and the band's last full album of new, original material. It was released in the United States in 1992 on Brother Records (through an independent distributor, Navarre) and in the United Kingdom in 1993 on EMI. It has been reported that Navarre went bankrupt after distributing the album.[2]

Background

The entire album was recorded using Pro Tools on a Macintosh Quadra computer, being one of the first albums to do so. Musically, it continued in the vein of *The Beach Boys* and *Still Cruisin'* by having an abundance of electronic instrumentation. The entire rhythm section was electronic on most songs, with all the drum parts being programmed (although not credited as such) and most of the bass parts being synthesized as well.

The only band member to actually play was Bruce Johnston, although Terry Melcher played many keyboard parts, and Van Dyke Parks played accordion on two tracks. Touring "regulars" such as Bobby Figueroa, Ed Carter, Mike Kowalski and Matt Jardine did not contribute to the album either. Al Jardine's son Adam did sing backup vocals on the title track, and touring musician Adrian Baker contributed background vocals. All the surviving original band members (except Brian Wilson, who was being removed from the care of Eugene Landy) contributed to this project, though the contributions from Carl Wilson and Al Jardine are purely vocals as they have no songwriting credits here. Jardine had been "suspended" from the band prior to the album's recording (apparently due to Love taking issue with his attitude) and for a while into it, and so he only sings the chorus on two songs.

The idea of this album, in Mike Love's words was to create "the quintessential soundtrack of summer". Every song on the album, with the exception of a cover of their 1970 song "Forever" and the original song "Strange Things Happen", deals with summer in one way or another. Of the album's twelve tracks, two songs are straight-up covers ("Hot Fun in the Summertime" originally by Sly & the Family Stone, and "Remember (Walking in the Sand)" originally by The Shangri-Las); two are new versions of older Beach Boys songs, "Surfin'" and "Forever", the latter with a vocal by John Stamos); one combines a classic song ("One Summer Night") with a new Bruce Johnston song ("Slow Summer Dancing"); and one takes an old song ("Under the Boardwalk") and adds new lyrics. The rest are original songs, all containing both titular and lyrical references to summer and/or surfing, with the exception of the Transcendental Meditation-influenced "Strange Things Happen". The quasi-rap number "Summer of Love" was originally intended to be a duet, albeit one with Bart Simpson. (The song was also used in an episode of "Baywatch".)

Since Navarre and EMI only did one print run each, *Summer in Paradise* has technically been out of print since its release. Copies have become somewhat rare, fetching upwards of $25 USD on eBay for a U.S. pressing and upwards of $40 USD for UK pressings.

The album sold very badly (reportedly less than 10,000 copies) [2] and was received less favorably than any album put out by the band to date. Critics attacked the album upon release and are still going at it today. In their book "The Beach Boys and Brian Wilson: The Complete Guide to Their Music", Andrew G. Doe and John Tobler call the album "the absolute nadir of their recording career", "pointless, vapid and soulless" and "utterly disposable" (the latter in reference to the songs). In "Catch a Wave", Peter Ames Carlin speaks especially disparagingly about "Summer of Love", referencing its overtly sexual lyrics.

The band never again released an album of original material. The last official group project was *Stars and Stripes Vol. 1*, an album of Beach Boys classics performed by country stars with the Boys on backup vocals.

Front cover artwork

The artwork that features prominently on the front of this release, and indeed the similar pieces that feature throughout the package, were painted by fellow Californian artist Robert Lyn Nelson. The original U.S. front sleeve utilises the painting "Elements Of The Universe", whilst inside the gatefold casing were further Nelson works, notably "Ring Of Life" (used for the alternate UK pressing), "Embraced By The Sea" and "Amethyst Dawn At Kipahulu"

Track listing

No.	Title	Writer(s)	Lead Vocals	Length
1.	"Hot Fun in the Summertime"	Sylvester Stewart	Mike Love/Carl Wilson	3:29
2.	"Surfin'"	Brian Wilson/Mike Love	Love/C. Wilson	3:45
3.	"Summer of Love"	Love/Terry Melcher	Love	2:51
4.	"Island Fever"	Love/Melcher	Love/C. Wilson	3:27
5.	"Still Surfin'"	Love/Melcher	Love	4:03
6.	"Slow Summer Dancin' (One Summer Night)"	Bruce Johnston/Danny Webb	Bruce Johnston/Al Jardine	3:23
7.	"Strange Things Happen"	Love/Melcher	Love/Jardine	4:42
8.	"Remember (Walking in the Sand)"	George Morton	C. Wilson	3:31
9.	"Lahaina Aloha"	Love/Melcher	Love/C. Wilson	3:44
10.	"Under the Boardwalk"	Artie Resnick/Kenny Young/Love	Love/C. Wilson	4:07
11.	"Summer in Paradise"	Love/Melcher/Fall	Love	3:52
12.	"Forever"	Dennis Wilson/Gregg Jakobson	John Stamos	3:05

UK CD tracks

The UK CD release - in a numbered, limited edition gatefold digipack, was released in the summer of 1992 - though it has the same track order as the U.S. CD, features different versions of five songs:

- "Island Fever" – 3:11
  - Completely re-recorded and features new music and different lyrics.
  - Features Mike Love and Al Jardine on lead vocals
- "Strange Things Happen" – 3:17
  - Remixed and shortened considerably.
  - Features Mike Love and Al Jardine on lead vocals
- "Under the Boardwalk" – 3:28
  - Remixed and shortened considerably, although the bridge was restored.
  - Features Mike Love and Carl Wilson on lead vocals
- "Summer in Paradise" – 3:27
  - Completely re-recorded and features new music, different lyrics, and Roger McGuinn singing lead vocals on one verse.
  - Features Mike Love and Roger McGuinn on lead vocals
- "Forever" – 2:58
  - Remixed and shortened slightly.
  - Features John Stamos on lead vocals

- *Remember (Walking in the Sand)* was remixed for the UK CD but the new mix was left off in favor of the U.S. version.

The US CD version was also available in the UK (released a year later).

Singles

- "Hot Fun in the Summertime" b/w "Summer of Love" (Brother), July 1992

Summer in Paradise (Brother BBR 727-2 and EMI 0777 7 81036 2 2) failed to chart in either the U.S. or the UK.

"Forever" was released as a promotional single to US radio stations. The promotional single included a "CHR mix" that is different from both the standard CD version (also on the promotional single) and the UK CD version.

"Summer Of Love" was released before the album came out on the "Baywatch" TV series soundtrack on Sept. 22, 1989.

Musicians

- Adrian Baker - vocals
- Rod Clark - bass guitar
- Craig Fall - guitar, mandolin, keyboard bass
- Al Jardine - vocals
- Bruce Johnston - keyboard, vocals
- Danny Kortchmar - guitar
- Mike Love - vocals
- Sal Marullo - conga drums
- Roger McGuinn - Rickenbacker 12-string guitar - (vocals UK version only)
- Terry Melcher - keyboard, vocals
- Sammy Merendino - drums
- Van Dyke Parks - accordion, keyboard
- Joel Peskin - saxophone
- Richard Titus - keyboards, keyboard programming
- Keith Wechsler - keyboard, drums
- John Weston - pedal steel guitar
- Carl Wilson - vocals
- John Stamos - Drums, Vocals
- Adam Jardine - Vocals

Notes

[1] http://www.allmusic.com/cg/amg.dll?p=amg&sql=10:ofd6vwrva92k
[2] Doe, Andrew and Tobler, John G. Brian Wilson and the Beach Boys- The Complete Guide to Their Music. Omnibus Press, 1997.

Sources

- *Summer in Paradise* CD booklet notes, Mike Love
- "The Nearest Faraway Place: Brian Wilson, The Beach Boys and the Southern California Experience", Timothy White, c. 1994.
- Allmusic.com

Sunflower

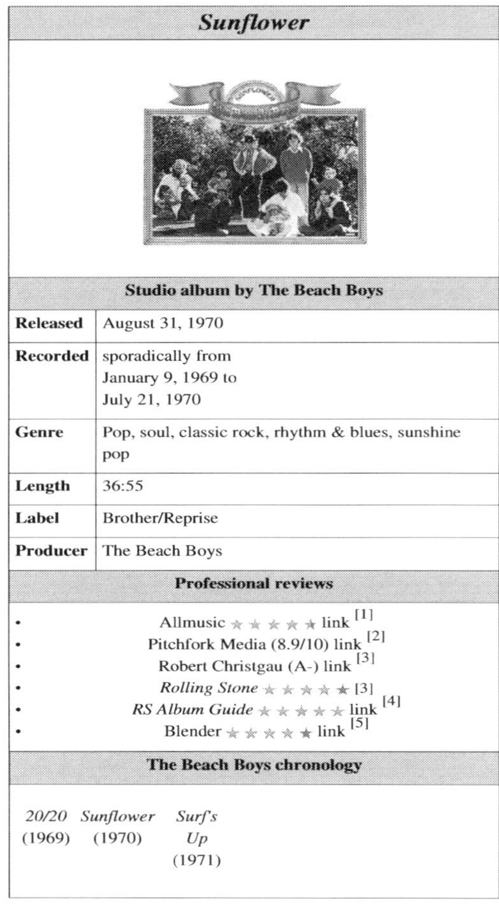

Sunflower	
Studio album by The Beach Boys	
Released	August 31, 1970
Recorded	sporadically from January 9, 1969 to July 21, 1970
Genre	Pop, soul, classic rock, rhythm & blues, sunshine pop
Length	36:55
Label	Brother/Reprise
Producer	The Beach Boys

Professional reviews

- Allmusic ★★★★★ link [1]
- Pitchfork Media (8.9/10) link [2]
- Robert Christgau (A-) link [3]
- *Rolling Stone* ★★★★★ [3]
- *RS Album Guide* ★★★★★ link [4]
- Blender ★★★★★ link [5]

The Beach Boys chronology

20/20 (1969)	*Sunflower* (1970)	*Surf's Up* (1971)

Sunflower is The Beach Boys' sixteenth studio album, 21st official album release, and their first under their contract with Reprise Records. Issued in August 1970, *Sunflower* is often regarded as among The Beach Boys' very best releases.

Sunflower (Brother/Reprise RS 6382) hit **#151** in the US charts during a four week stay, becoming the lowest charting Beach Boys album until 1978's M.I.U. Album equalled it. It reached **#29** in the UK.

The album's critical reputation has grown since its original appearance. In 2003, the album was ranked number 380 on *Rolling Stone* magazine's list of the 500 greatest albums of all time.[6] *Sunflower* is now paired on CD with *Surf's Up*.

The recording of *Sunflower*

Early Sessions

After their last album, *20/20*, Dennis Wilson was the first Beach Boy to head back into the recording studio, producing five tracks in the first two months of 1969: "Forever", "San Miguel", "Got To Know The Woman", "What Can The Matter Be?", and "Celebrate The News". Bruce Johnston's "Deirdre" was also recorded during these sessions. In early March the entire band went into the studio to record "Loop de Loop" and "All I Wanna Do", and also finish up Dennis's "Forever".

On April 12, The Beach Boys sued Capitol Records for unpaid royalties and unpaid production fees in the amount of two million dollars. This was the second time that they have sued Capitol (the first being in the spring of 1967), and it may have contributed to a lack of promotion by Capitol of The Beach Boys' final releases for them.

They then turned their attention to "Break Away", written by Brian Wilson and his father Murry, who used the pseudonym Reggie Dunbar. At the time, it was thought that it would be their last single for Capitol and was a very small hit in the U.S. (It reached #63). It did much better overseas, peaking at #6 in the UK. "Celebrate The News" was the b-side, and neither song was released on a Beach Boys album.

After they were done recording "Break Away", the band went on a tour of Europe. When they got back, they recorded two more Dennis Wilson songs, "Slip On Through" and "I'm Going Your Way". Next on the agenda was a rerecording of "Cotton Fields" (retitled on the single as "Cottonfields"), a Huddie Ledbetter (Lead Belly) song that was released on The Beach Boys previous album, *20/20*. Al Jardine was the producer for this recording of the song.

The Fading Rock Group Revival

After the new "Cotton Fields" was finished, they started to try to put an album together which would finish their commitment to Capitol. It had working titles of *Reverberation* and *The Fading Rock Group Revival*. A master tape was put together with these songs:

- "Cotton Fields"
- "Loop de Loop"
- "San Miguel"
- "Deirdre"
- "Forever"
- "The Lord's Prayer"
- "Break Away"
- "Celebrate The News"
- "All I Wanna Do"
- "Got To Know The Woman"

track sequence unknown

"The Lord's Prayer" was the B-side to their 1963 single "Little Saint Nick", and was remixed to be in Duophonic sound on this album. This album was never released, and it is unknown if Capitol rejected the album or if the Beach Boys never submitted it. The Beach Boys fulfilled their contract with *Live in London*. Capitol had such little faith in the album, they chose to release it only where the Beach Boys' records were still selling respectably well—the UK. That business decision forced diehard fans around the world into record stores to 'special order' the import version. The live album finally appeared as an official American release in 1976.

A new record label

After giving *Live in London* to Capitol, the band began to work seriously on a new album. In October and November 1969, they started recording "Walkin'", "Games Two Can Play", "Add Some Music To Your Day", "When Girls Get Together", "Soulful Old Man Sunshine", "Raspberries, Strawberries", "This Whole World", and "Tears In The Morning". They also continued work on Dennis's "Slip On Through".

In fall of 1969, The Beach Boys intensified work on their new project. Their reputation had fallen sharply in the US since 1967, but Mo Ostin decided to sign them in November(reportedly on Van Dyke Parks' urging despite Brian Wilson's personal attempts at sabotage by meeting Warner executives, promising to behave but also painting his face green). Part of the deal was to revive their Brother Records imprint, initially founded during the *Smile* era and used only for the *Smiley Smile* album, and the "Heroes and Villains" and "Gettin' Hungry" singles before becoming dormant.

Add Some Music sessions

After signing their new contracts, The Beach Boys redoubled their efforts in the studio, finishing up "Tears In The Morning" and "Add Some Music To Your Day", the latter of which was going to serve as the title of the new album. In addition, they recorded nine new songs: "Susie Cincinnati", "Fallin' In Love", "Carnival", "I Just Got My Pay", "Take A Load Off Your Feet", "Good Time", "Back Home", and "Our Sweet Love". A rough piano run-through of The Beatles' "You Never Give Me Your Money" was also taped.

Add Some Music To Your Day

After the final session (on February 2, to add car sound effects to "Susie Cincinnati"), they started to assemble the album, and released the lead single, "Add Some Music To Your Day". Reprise was so excited about the single that they convinced retailers to carry more copies of it than they ever had for any other Reprise single. Unfortunately for the band, the single (with the b-side "Susie Cincinnati") did not sell as well as they had hoped, only reaching #64 on the Billboard top 100 chart.

After the Reprise single failed, Capitol Records released their last Beach Boys single, Cotton Fields. While it failed to chart in the US, the song hit #1 in Australia, Sweden, and Norway, and hit #5 in the UK.

Before leaving for a tour of Australia and New Zealand, they finished putting the album together and submitted it to the label. Entitled *Add Some Music*, it consisted of these tracks:

1. "Susie Cincinnati"
2. "Good Time"
3. "Our Sweet Love"
4. "Tears In The Morning"
5. "When Girls Get Together"
6. "Slip On Through"
7. "Add Some Music To Your Day"
8. "Take A Load Off Your Feet"
9. "This Whole World"
10. "I Just Got My Pay"
11. "At My Window"
12. "Fallin' In Love"

It was rejected. After listening to the album, and after the failure of the lead single, Mo Ostin suggested that they come up with a few stronger tracks or their days at Reprise Records would be short-lived. The band was unhappy, but went into the studio one last time.

Final Sunflower sessions

The Beach Boys recorded the last two *Sunflower* songs in July 1970. The first, recorded at the behest of Lenny Waronker, was "Cool, Cool Water". Waronker, then an A&R executive at Warner Music, heard the unfinished tape, and convinced Wilson to finish the track for *Sunflower* (Wilson later reworked the original version of the song *I Love to Say Dada* as "In Blue Hawaii" for his 2004 solo release). Waronker was so impressed with the song's inspired simplicity, that he noted:

> *If I ever get the opportunity to produce Brian, I'd encourage him to do something that combined the vividness of Good Vibrations with the non-commercial gentleness of Cool, Cool Water.*

Eighteen years later, in 1988, Waronker would produce Brian's "Rio Grande" for Wilson's self-titled solo album.

The other song that they recorded was "It's About Time", a rocker that briefly became a concert staple for them.

Bruce Johnston also rerecorded his vocal to "Tears In The Morning".

After recording over 30 different songs, and going through several different album titles, The Beach Boys' *Sunflower* was finally released in August 1970.

Recorded But Not Included

The sessions that led to Sunflower provided a lot of material for future Beach Boys albums and compilations.

"Break Away" and "Celebrate The News" were released as a single, and reissued on the *Friends/20/20* twofer. "Loop de Loop" and "Soulful Old Man Sunshine" were unreleased until 1998's *Endless Harmony Soundtrack*. "San Miguel" was released on the 1970s compilation *Ten Years of Harmony*. After "Cotton Fields" became a big European hit, it was added to *Sunflower* overseas. In the US, it wouldn't be released on an album until the 1983's *Rarities* came out. Dennis Wilson released "Fallin' In Love", now retitled "Lady", as the b-side to his European single "Sound of Free" in December 1970.

"Games Two Can Play" and "I Just Got My Pay" were released on the *Good Vibrations: Thirty Years of The Beach Boys* box set. "When Girls Get Together" was on the 1980 album *Keepin' the Summer Alive*. "Raspberries, Strawberries" was a working title for "At My Window", which was on the *Sunflower* album. "Susie Cincinnati" was the b-side to the ill-fated "Add Some Music To Your Day" single, then again used as the b-side for a rare 1974 Christmas single, "Child of Winter", and was then released in 1976 on *15 Big Ones*, which also included "Back Home". "Take A Load Off Your Feet" was on the next album, *Surf's Up*. "Good Time" stayed in the vaults until 1977's *Love You*.

"What Can The Matter Be?", "Walkin'", "Carnival", and "You Never Give Me Your Money" have never been released.

Track listing

Side one				
No.	**Title**	**Writer(s)**	**Lead Vocals**	**Length**
1.	"Slip On Through"	Dennis Wilson	Dennis Wilson	2:17
2.	"This Whole World"	Brian Wilson	Brian and Carl Wilson	1:56
3.	"Add Some Music to Your Day"	B. Wilson/Joe Knott/Mike Love	Mike Love, Bruce Johnston, C. Wilson, B. Wilson, and Al Jardine	3:34
4.	"Got to Know the Woman"	D. Wilson	D. Wilson	2:41
5.	"Deirdre"	Bruce Johnston/B. Wilson	Johnston	3:27
6.	"It's About Time"	D. Wilson/Carl Wilson/Bob Burchman/Al Jardine	C. Wilson	2:55

Side two				
No.	**Title**	**Writer(s)**	**Lead Vocals**	**Length**
1.	"Tears in the Morning"	Johnston	Johnston	4:07
2.	"All I Wanna Do"	B. Wilson/Love	Love	2:34
3.	"Forever"	D. Wilson/Gregg Jakobson	D. Wilson	2:40
4.	"Our Sweet Love"	B. Wilson/C. Wilson/Jardine	C. Wilson	2:38
5.	"At My Window"	B. Wilson/Jardine	Johnston	2:30
6.	"Cool, Cool Water"	B. Wilson/Love	B. Wilson and Love	5:03

European track listing

This variation of the album was released by EMI subsidiary, Stateside Records, in November, 1970. Its opening track was "Cottonfields." "Got to Know the Woman" and "Deirdre" were placed in inverse order on side 1. The contents of the individual tracks were unchanged. This track listing has been superseded with the regular Sunflower running order, now released worldwide.

Singles

- "Add Some Music to Your Day" b/w "Susie Cincinnati" (Brother 0894), 23 February 1970; **US #64**
- "Cottonfields" b/w "The Nearest Faraway Place" (Capitol 2765), 20 April 1970; **US #103**, **UK #5**
- "Slip On Through" b/w "This Whole World" (Brother 0929), 29 June 1970
- "Tears in the Morning" b/w "It's About Time" (Brother 0957), November 1970
- "Cool, Cool Water" b/w "Forever" (Brother 0998), February 1971

Production notes

producer: The Beach Boys
chief engineer and mixer: Steve Desper
cover photo: Ricci Martin
other photos: Ed Thrasher

The vast majority of the album was recorded at Brian Wilson's home studio in Bel Air.

Artwork

The picture of the band on the front sleeve, featuring all six group members, was taken on the golf course at the family ranch owned by Dean Martin (named The Hidden Valley Ranch) near Thousand Oaks in Ventura County, CA. Dean's son Ricci Martin, a friend of the band, took the photograph, also featuring Brian's daughter Carnie, Alan's first son Matthew (later an auxiliary Beach Boy himself), Mike's children Hayleigh and Christian (the latter a current touring member of the Beach Boys Band), and Carl's son Jonah.

The inner gatefold spread on the original vinyl LP featured a series of photographs taken by designer/photographer Ed Thrasher at the Warner Brothers studio backlot.

Critical Reaction

Despite not being the hit it was expected to be, *Sunflower* has been received well by critics. Rolling Stone magazine gave the album four stars, saying it is one of the Beach Boys' best albums. Music critic Robert Christgau gave it an A-. The album has gained more popularity since its release. In 2003, Rolling Stone named it the 380th Best Album of All Time in its 500 Greatest Albums of All Time list.

Sources

- Badman, Keith; Bacon, Tony. *The Beach Boys: The Definitive Diary of America's Greatest Band on Stage and in the Studio* (San Francisco: Backbeat Books, 2004) ISBN 0-87930-818-4
- Bush, John. 'Sunflower', *All Music* (2005) [1] Retrieved July 24 2005.
- Elliott, Brad. *Surf's Up: The Beach Boys On Record* (1981)
- Whitburn, Joel. "Top Pop Albums 1955-2001", (Menomonee Falls, Wisconsin: Record Research, 2002) ISBN 0-89820-147-0
- Whitburn, Joel. "Top Pop Singles 1955-2001", (Menomonee Falls, Wisconsin: Record Research, 2002)
- White, Timothy. *The Nearest Faraway Place: Brian Wilson, The Beach Boys and the Southern California Experience* (1994)
- White, Timothy. CD booklet notes, *Sunflower/Surf's Up* (2000)
- Wilson, Brian; Gold, Todd. *Wouldn't It Be Nice - My Own Story* (1991).

References

[1] http://www.allmusic.com/cg/amg.dll?p=amg&sql=10:16msa9rgb23a
[2] http://www.pitchforkmedia.com/article/record_review/15334-sunflowersurfs-up
[3] http://www.rollingstone.com/artists/thebeachboys/albums/album/141828/review/5943283/sunflowelink
[4] http://www.acclaimedmusic.net/
[5] http://www.blender.com/guide/reviews.aspx?id=2249
[6] 380) Sunflower : Rolling Stone (http://www.rollingstone.com/news/story/6626203/380_sunflower)

Sunshine Dream

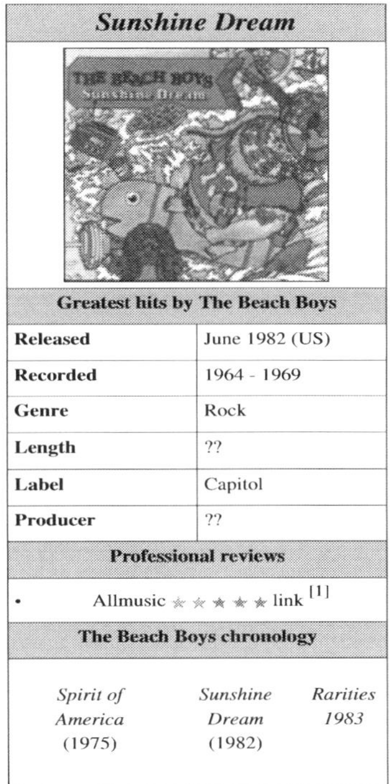

Sunshine Dream	
Greatest hits by The Beach Boys	
Released	June 1982 (US)
Recorded	1964 - 1969
Genre	Rock
Length	??
Label	Capitol
Producer	??
Professional reviews	
• Allmusic ★★★★★ link [1]	
The Beach Boys chronology	
Spirit of America (1975) · *Sunshine Dream* (1982) · *Rarities 1983*	

Sunshine Dream is the third double-album compilation of The Beach Boys' music to be compiled by their former label, Capitol Records (following the earlier *Endless Summer* and *Spirit of America*). Released in 1982, the album features singles and album tracks ranging from 1964 to 1969, and also includes "The Beach Boys Medley", which reached #12 in 1981. The album was compiled and released while The Beach Boys were contracted with CBS Records and, as such, is not considered an "official" release.

Due to the appearance of more recent compilations, *Sunshine Dream* has long since been deleted.

Track listing

All songs by Brian Wilson/Mike Love, except where noted.

1. "I Can Hear Music" (Jeff Barry/Ellie Greenwich/Phil Spector) – 2:36
2. "Here Today" (Brian Wilson/Tony Asher) – 2:52
3. "Darlin'" – 2:12
4. "Caroline, No" (Brian Wilson/Tony Asher) – 2:52
5. "Aren't You Glad" – 2:16
6. "Good Vibrations" – 3:36
7. "Wouldn't It Be Nice" (Brian Wilson/Tony Asher/Mike Love) – 2:22
8. "Friends" (Brian Wilson/Carl Wilson/Dennis Wilson/Al Jardine) – 2:30

9. "God Only Knows" (Brian Wilson/Tony Asher) – 2:49
10. "Vegetables" (Brian Wilson/Van Dyke Parks) – 2:07
11. "How She Boogalooed It" (Mike Love/Bruce Johnston/Al Jardine/Carl Wilson) – 1:56
12. "There's No Other (Like You Baby)" (Phil Spector/Leroy Bates) – 3:05
13. "Heroes and Villains" (Brian Wilson/Van Dyke Parks) – 3:37
14. "All I Want To Do" (Dennis Wilson/Steve Kalinich) – 2:02
15. "Wild Honey" – 2:37
16. "I'm Waiting for the Day" – 3:03
17. "Cottonfields" (Huddie Ledbetter) – 3:02
18. "Then I Kissed Her" (Phil Spector/Ellie Greenwich/Jeff Barry) – 2:15
19. "Sloop John B" (Trad. arr. by Brian Wilson) – 2:56
20. "Be Here in the Morning" (Brian Wilson/Carl Wilson/Mike Love/Dennis Wilson/Al Jardine) – 2:16
21. "Bluebirds Over the Mountain" (Ersel Hickey) – 2:51
22. "Keep an Eye on Summer" (Brian Wilson/Bob Norman) – 2:21
23. "Do It Again" – 2:25
24. The Beach Boys Medley

Singles

"The Beach Boys Medley" b/w "God Only Knows" (Capitol A-5030), October, 1981 **US #12**

Sunshine Dream (Capitol SVBB 12220) hit **#180** in the US.

References

[1] http://www.allmusic.com/cg/amg.dll?p=amg&sql=10:li0xlfje5cqy~T00

Surf's Up

Surf's Up	
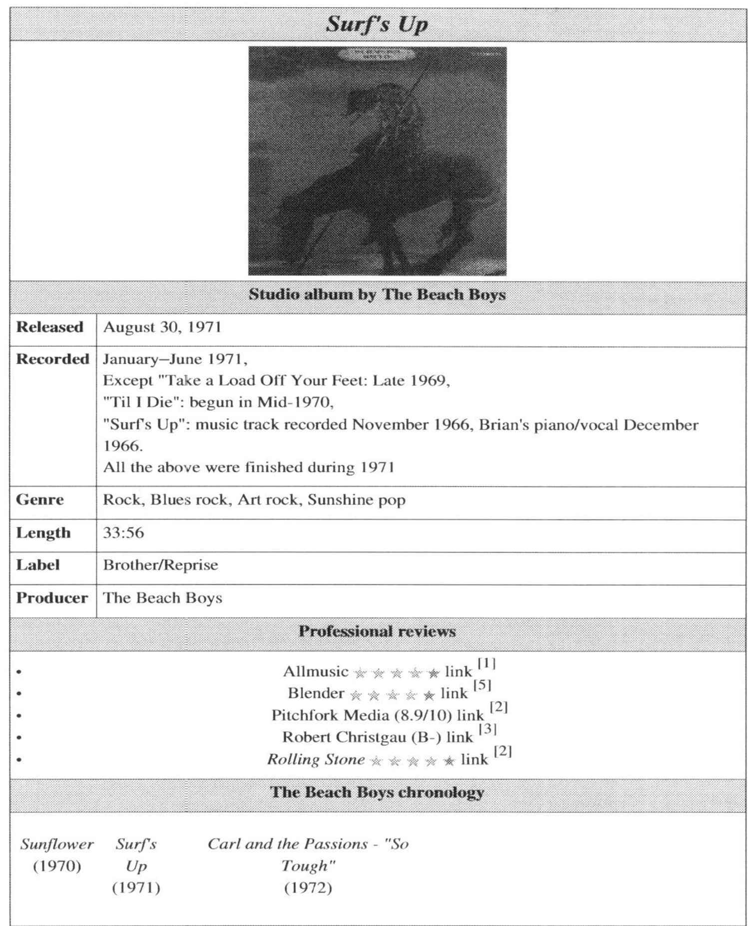	
Studio album by The Beach Boys	
Released	August 30, 1971
Recorded	January–June 1971, Except "Take a Load Off Your Feet: Late 1969, "Til I Die": begun in Mid-1970, "Surf's Up": music track recorded November 1966, Brian's piano/vocal December 1966. All the above were finished during 1971
Genre	Rock, Blues rock, Art rock, Sunshine pop
Length	33:56
Label	Brother/Reprise
Producer	The Beach Boys
Professional reviews	
• Allmusic link [1] • Blender link [5] • Pitchfork Media (8.9/10) link [2] • Robert Christgau (B-) link [3] • *Rolling Stone* link [2]	
The Beach Boys chronology	
Sunflower (1970) — *Surf's Up* (1971) — *Carl and the Passions - "So Tough"* (1972)	

Surf's Up is an album title for The Beach Boys based on a song with the same title written by Brian Wilson and Van Dyke Parks for the abandoned 1966–1967 Beach Boys *Smile* album. The song was reworked and used as the title track for the seventeenth studio album by The Beach Boys, released in 1971. *Smile*, including the original version of the song 'Surf's Up,' was finally completed and released by Brian Wilson and his band in 2004.

Album history

In the fall of 1970, after the commercial failure of the *Sunflower* album, The Beach Boys hired Jack Rieley as their manager. Rieley, a DJ, had impressed the band with his falsified credentials (a supposed Peabody Award-winning stint as NBC bureau chief in Puerto Rico) and ideas on how to regain respect from American music fans and critics. His first initiative was to have The Beach Boys record songs with more socially aware lyrics. Rieley also insisted that the band officially appoint Carl Wilson "musical director" in recognition of the integral role he had played keeping the group together since 1967. Most importantly, he demanded the completion of "Surf's Up" for release by composer and erstwhile bandleader Brian Wilson, a song that had taken on mythical proportions in the underground press since the demise of *Smile* three years earlier. He also organized a guest appearance at a Grateful Dead concert in April 1971, further enhancing the Beach Boys' once-lacking hip credentials.

According to Rieley in 1996 posts to the "Smiley Smile" message board, the band had split into two camps: the artistically inclined, drug using, bashful Wilson brothers and the commercially-oriented, teetotalling triumvirate of Mike Love, Al Jardine, and Bruce Johnston. In his opinion, if the group were to return to their mid-60s heights, the former group would have to fully assert itself. To this end, Rieley all but ordered Al Jardine to stop work on "Loop de Loop", an intentionally juvenile and childlike collaboration with Brian Wilson that Jardine thought would revive the band's commercial prospects.

Haunted by memories of the *Smile* era, Brian Wilson initially refused to work on "Surf's Up", now the eponymous track of the band's new album. Nevertheless, an undaunted Carl Wilson overdubbed a new vocal in the song's first part, a backing track dating from 1966. The second movement was composed of a 1966 solo piano demo recorded by Brian Wilson augmented with vocal and Moog bass overdubs.

To the surprise and glee of his associates, Wilson emerged near the end of the sessions to aid his brother and engineer Stephen Desper in the completion of the third movement, which combined the end of the 1966 demo with the "Child Is Father Of The Man" vocal tag and a final lyrical couplet possibly written by Rieley. The newly recorded lead vocals - sung by Al Jardine over a choral backdrop featuring all the Beach Boys - were sped up by Desper for continuity purposes in an attempt to make them sound more like they did in 1966.

The album also included "'Til I Die" a song Brian had been working on for well over a year. Though there was some alleged dislike of the ballad by Mike Love, he has praised and performed the song in recent years. Wilson spent weeks arranging the song, crafting a harmony-driven, vibraphone and organ-laden background that closely resembled the halcyon-era sonic tapestries of *Pet Sounds*.

"Long Promised Road" and "Feel Flows" were Carl Wilson's first significant solo compositions; both songs were almost entirely recorded by him. "Student Demonstration Time" (essentially the R&B classic "Riot In Cell Block #9") and "Don't Go Near the Water" found Love and Jardine eagerly embracing the group's new topical-oriented direction. "A Day in the Life of a Tree" was Brian Wilson's sole new contribution. Although it is often dismissed by fans as a throwaway effort, several attempts at recording the song were made before the pump organ-led arrangement was nailed. The slightly off-key lead vocal from Rieley (at Wilson's insistence) and equally jarring background vocals from Van Dyke Parks could be interpreted as perfectly befitting the song's weary tone or a joke on the part of the composer. Bruce Johnston's "Disney Girls (1957)" was hailed as a masterpiece by Brian Wilson and has been covered by Art Garfunkel and Cass Elliot.

The Dennis Wilson songs "4th of July", "Fallin' In Love" (also known as Lady), and "Wouldn't It Be Nice To Live Again" were excised from the final running order shortly before release. Although "4th of July"'s elagaic tone and lyrical relevance made it a logical thematic choice, Rieley has claimed that it was met with a reception of "glaring envy" by Wilson's bandmates. The song was duly replaced with Jardine's "Take A Load Off Your Feet", a novelty in the vein of "Loop De Loop". In the case of "Wouldn't It Be Nice To Live Again", a disagreement between the middle and younger Wilson brothers resulted in the song being left off the album. Dennis wanted the song to be the final track on the album, segueing out of "'Til I Die", while Carl felt "Surf's Up" should have that place. As a consequence, Dennis took the song out of the album's final running order. "Fallin' In Love" was released in late 1970 as the B-side of a solo single. It should be noted that Wilson (in collaboration with Beach Boys touring keyboardist Daryl Dragon) had been stockpiling songs for a potential solo album throughout the era and left the band on a provisional basis for a brief time in early 1971. Dennis's work during this period ultimately produced two songs for the next album, the solo single, "Lady," and the solo album itself finally came out in 1977 as *Pacific Ocean Blue*.

Surf's Up was released that August to more public anticipation than The Beach Boys had had for several years. It outperformed *Sunflower* commercially, reaching #29 in the US (their first Top 40 album since *Wild Honey*) and #15 in the UK. Like *Sunflower*, *Surf's Up* was released on EMI's Stateside label internationally.

The album was ranked #61 on Pitchfork Media's The Top 100 Albums Of The 1970's list.

Artwork

The cover art is a painting based on the sculpture *End of The Trail* by James Earle Fraser (1876 – 1953).

This lone figure on his weary horse is one of the most recognized symbols of the American West. The title *Surf's Up* juxtaposed with what appears to be an exhausted and thirsty warrior adds an ironic quality to a title that only ten years before would have carried no hint of irony whatsoever.

Track listing

Side one

1. "Don't Go Near the Water" (Mike Love, /Al Jardine) – 2:39
   - *Features Mike Love and Al Jardine on lead vocals*
2. "Long Promised Road" (Carl Wilson, Jack Rieley) – 3:30
   - *Features Carl Wilson on lead vocals*
3. "Take a Load Off Your Feet" (Al Jardine, Brian Wilson, Gary Winfrey) – 2:29
   - *Features Al Jardine and Brian Wilson on lead vocals*
4. "Disney Girls (1957)" (Bruce Johnston) – 4:07
   - *Features Bruce Johnston on lead vocals*
5. "Student Demonstration Time" (Jerry Leiber, Mike Stoller, Mike Love) – 3:58
   - *Features Mike Love on lead vocals*

Side two

- "Feel Flows" (Carl Wilson, Jack Rieley) – 4:44
- *Features Carl Wilson on lead vocals*

2. "Lookin' at Tomorrow (A Welfare Song)" (Al Jardine, Gary Winfrey) – 1:55
   - *Features Al Jardine on lead vocals*
3. "A Day in the Life of a Tree" (Brian Wilson, Jack Rieley) – 3:07
   - *Features Jack Rieley on lead vocal, with Van Dyke Parks and Al Jardine on the tag*
4. "'Til I Die" (Brian Wilson) – 2:41
   - *Features Brian Wilson, Carl Wilson and Mike Love on lead vocals*
5. "Surf's Up" (Brian Wilson, Van Dyke Parks) – 4:12
   - *Features Carl Wilson on lead vocals on the first section (Recorded 1971) Brian Wilson on the second section (Recorded 1966 and 1971) Al Jardine on the tag (Recorded 1971)*

Singles

- "Long Promised Road" b/w "Deidre" (from *Sunflower* (Brother 1015), 24 May 1971
- "Long Promised Road" b/w "'Til I Die" (Brother 1047), 11 October 1971 **US #89**
- "Surf's Up" b/w "Don't Go Near The Water" (Brother 1058), 8 November 1971

Surf's Up is now paired on CD with *Sunflower*.

Landlocked (Second Warner Brothers Album)

Heavily bootlegged, it is commonly thought that the following songs were for an uncompleted album entitled *Landlocked*. It has since been discovered that the songs were part of a compilation reel of songs considered for the "Surf's Up" album. Part of the reason this is not spectacularly likely are the presence of "Fallin' In Love," "Susie Cincinnati," "Take A Load Off Your Feet," "I Just Got My Pay," "Good Time," and "When Girls Get Together" which were intended for the rejected Add Some Music album, but discarded when the album was reworked into *Sunflower*. Also, Jardine seems to have not been happy with "Loop De Loop." The version of "'Til I Die" featured here appears on Endless Harmony Soundtrack and the liner notes say it was definitely not intended for release but the engineer's own personal pleasure.

Nonetheless, this tape somehow made it to Jack Rieley with orders to submit to Warner for opinion (by whom is uncertain; Desper disputes the existence of *Landlocked* as intended for release). Rieley proposed that an appropriate title for a new Beach Boys album be called *Landlocked* before actually hearing it. He then decided that the album was completely inappropriate for the title (it is unknown who compiled it, and who ordered its submission, but what is clear is that no Wilson, engineer or Rieley approved the material). He then played the material he rejected to the executives for comments, perhaps without telling anyone (hence the album's myth).

1. "Loop De Loop"
2. "Susie Cincinnati"
3. "San Miguel"
4. "H. E. L. P. Is on the Way"
5. "Take A Load Off Your Feet"
6. "Carnival"
7. "I Just Got My Pay"
8. "Good Time"
9. "Big Sur"
10. "Fallin' In Love"
11. "When Girls Get Together"
12. "Lookin' at Tomorrow"
13. "'Til I Die"

Sources

- *Sunflower/Surf's Up* CD booklet notes, Timothy White, c.2000.
- "The Nearest Faraway Place: Brian Wilson, The Beach Boys and the Southern California Experience", Timothy White, c. 1994.
- "Wouldn't It Be Nice - My Own Story", Brian Wilson and Todd Gold, c. 1991.
- "Top Pop Singles 1955-2001", Joel Whitburn, c. 2002.
- "Top Pop Albums 1955-2001", Joel Whitburn, c. 2002.
- Allmusic.com

References

[1] http://www.allmusic.com/cg/amg.dll?p=amg&sql=10:hifexql5ld0e
[2] http://www.rollingstone.com/artists/thebeachboys/albums/album/175726/review/5945258/surfs_up

Surfer Girl

Surfer Girl	
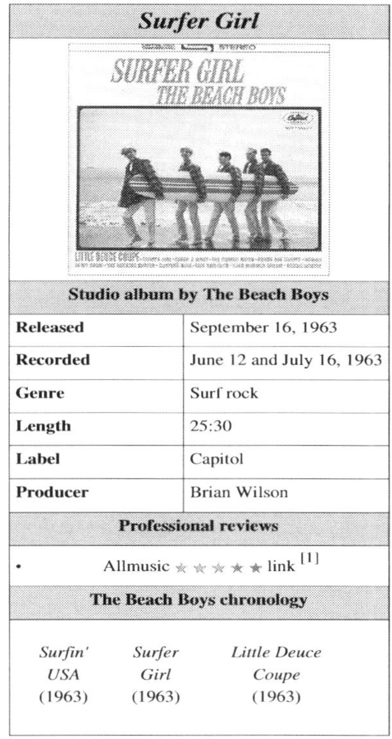	
Studio album by The Beach Boys	
Released	September 16, 1963
Recorded	June 12 and July 16, 1963
Genre	Surf rock
Length	25:30
Label	Capitol
Producer	Brian Wilson
Professional reviews	
• Allmusic ☆☆☆★★ link [1]	
The Beach Boys chronology	
Surfin' USA (1963) *Surfer Girl* (1963) *Little Deuce Coupe* (1963)	

Surfer Girl is the third studio album by The Beach Boys and their second longplayer in 1963. This was the first album by The Beach Boys for which Brian Wilson was given full production credit, a position Wilson would maintain until the end of the *Smile* sessions in 1967. ***Surfer Girl*** is also a 1973 repackaging of early 1960s The Beach Boys tracks by US budget label Pickwick Records.

Surfer Girl hit **#7** in the US during a chart stay of 56 weeks. In the UK, the album was re-released in spring 1967 and reached **#13**. *Surfer Girl* (Capitol (S) T 1981) is now paired on CD with *Shut Down Volume 2*, with bonus tracks from that period, including a German language version of "In my Room".

Album details

Brian Wilson himself turns in, along with, variously, Mike Love, Gary Usher and Roger Christian's help, some of his most cherished songs. The title track, a #7 US hit, was the first song Brian had ever composed, at the age of 19, using "When You Wish Upon A Star" as a guide while writing it. As a ballad, it was a risky move for a single, but its obvious quality overcame any potential commercial risks. Its flip-side, "Little Deuce Coupe", proved to be The Beach Boys' most successful B-side, reaching US #15 and becoming a hot rod staple. It also continued the band's current trend of putting a surf-related song on the A-side of singles, and car songs on the B-side. "Catch a Wave" featured Mike Love's sister, Maureen, on harp, while "The Surfer Moon" was the first Beach Boys song to have a string arrangement. "In My Room" was perhaps Brian Wilson's first personal song, a reflection on having a place to go to feel a sense of security and safety from the stress of one's life. Despite some slight material ("South Bay Surfer", "Boogie Woodie"), it was clear that *Surfer Girl* was a giant step forward for The Beach Boys - and the first of many.

"South Bay Surfer" is co-credited to Al Jardine, who had recently rejoined The Beach Boys in the summer of 1963.

Coming after their breakthrough *Surfin' USA* album, *Surfer Girl* hit #7 in the US (where it went gold) and, later in 1967, #13 in the UK.

The music title of the album, Surfer Girl, was featured in Charlie's Angels Full Throttle's soundtrack.

Front cover artwork

The front cover of *Surfer Girl* features (from right to left), Dennis Wilson, David Marks, Carl Wilson, Mike Love and Brian Wilson holding a surfboard from the same 1962 photo shoot that produced the cover of their album debut *Surfin' Safari*. The picture was taken by Capitol photographer Kenneth Veeder at Paradise Cove, north of Malibu.

Track listing

Side one				
No.	**Title**	**Writer(s)**	**Lead Vocals**	**Length**
1.	"Surfer Girl"	Brian Wilson	Brian Wilson	2:26
2.	"Catch a Wave"	B. Wilson/Mike Love	Mike Love/B. Wilson	2:07
3.	"The Surfer Moon"	B. Wilson	B. Wilson	2:11
4.	"South Bay Surfer"	B. Wilson/Carl Wilson/Al Jardine	Love/B. Wilson	1:45
5.	"The Rocking Surfer"	trad. arr. B. Wilson	instrumental	2:00
6.	"Little Deuce Coupe"	B. Wilson/Roger Christian	Love	1:38

Side two				
No.	**Title**	**Writer(s)**	**Lead Vocals**	**Length**
1.	"In My Room"	B. Wilson/Gary Usher	B. Wilson	2:11
2.	"Hawaii"	B. Wilson/Love	Love/B. Wilson	1:59
3.	"Surfers Rule"	B. WIlson/Love	Dennis Wilson/B. Wilson	1:54
4.	"Our Car Club"	B. WIlson/Love	Love/B. Wilson	2:22
5.	"Your Summer Dream"	B. Wilson/Bob Norberg	B. Wilson	2:27
6.	"Boogie Woodie"	trad. arr. B. Wilson	instrumental	1:56

Singles

- "Surfer Girl" b/w "Little Deuce Coupe" (Capitol 5009), 22 July 1963 **US #7** ("Little Deuce Coupe" **US #15**).
- "In My Room" featured as the B-side of "Be True to Your School" **US #23**

Musicians

The Beach Boys

- Al Jardine - bass guitar, vocals
- Mike Love - vocals
- David Marks - rhythm guitar, vocals
- Brian Wilson - piano, organ, bass guitar, vocals
- Carl Wilson - lead guitar, vocals
- Dennis Wilson - drums

others

- Hal Blaine - drums

References

- *Surfer Girl / Shut Down Volume 2* CD booklet notes, David Leaf, c.1990.
- *The Nearest Faraway Place: Brian Wilson, The Beach Boys and the Southern California Experience*, Timothy White, c. 1994.
- *Wouldn't It Be Nice - My Own Story*, Brian Wilson and Todd Gold, c. 1991.
- *Top Pop Singles 1955-2001*, Joel Whitburn, c. 2002.
- *Top Pop Albums 1955-2001*, Joel Whitburn, c. 2002.
- Allmusic.com

References

[1] http://www.allmusic.com/cg/amg.dll?p=amg&sql=10:px8ibkk96akq~T0

Surfin' Safari

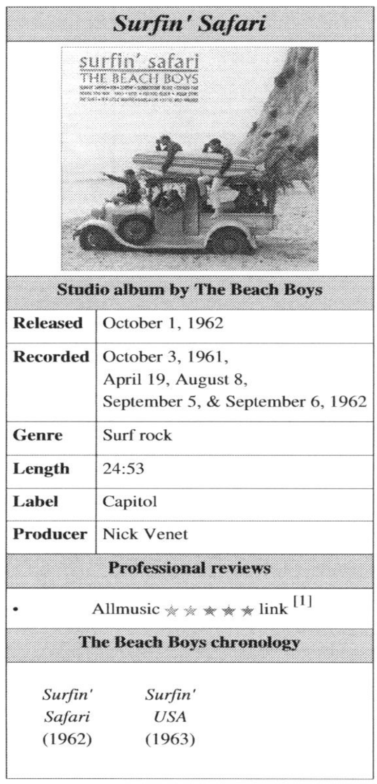

Surfin' Safari	
Studio album by The Beach Boys	
Released	October 1, 1962
Recorded	October 3, 1961, April 19, August 8, September 5, & September 6, 1962
Genre	Surf rock
Length	24:53
Label	Capitol
Producer	Nick Venet
Professional reviews	
• Allmusic ★★★★★ link [1]	
The Beach Boys chronology	
Surfin' Safari (1962)	*Surfin' USA* (1963)

Surfin' Safari is the debut album by The Beach Boys, released in 1962. *Surfin' Safari* is now paired on CD with *Surfin' USA* with bonus tracks from the period. *Surfin' Safari* peaked at #32 in its 37-week run on the US charts. It would be the lowest charting Beach Boys album until *Smiley Smile* in 1967.

History

In the autumn of 1961, cousins Brian Wilson and Mike Love composed a song on surfing, titled "Surfin'" at the behest of Brian's younger sibling, Dennis Wilson. They quickly formed a band, bringing in youngest Wilson brother Carl on lead guitar and Brian's high school friend Al Jardine on rhythm guitar. Brian took up bass, Dennis the drums and Mike would be the frontman, while they all would harmonize vocals arranged by Brian. Released that December, produced by Hite & Dorinda Morgan, and backed by the rarest Beach Boys' B-side, "Luau", "Surfin'" made #75 in the US Top 100 in early 1962.

Father Murry Wilson became the band's manager. He submitted a professionally-recorded demo tape to Capitol Records that spring. The Beach Boys were signed and "Surfin' Safari" b/w "409" (from the April 1962 demo tape) was released as a single that June. Al Jardine left the band before the demo session, to be replaced by a friend of Carl's, David Marks, until the fall of 1963.

With both "Surfin' Safari" and "409" becoming hits (the former reaching US #14), Capitol Records approved a full album. Brian Wilson, who regularly collaborated with Mike Love and Gary Usher, contributed the songs that made up the bulk of the LP.

Surfin' Safari, despite the official credit to Nick Venet, was reportedly produced by Brian Wilson. The second single, "Ten Little Indians", was less successful, reaching only #49, with Brian feeling that "Chug-A-Lug" would have made a far better follow-up. Though Mike and Brian are the most prominent singers (as they would be throughout most of The Beach Boys' career), Dennis makes his first vocal appearance on "Little Girl (You're My Miss America)".

Front cover artwork

The front sleeve features the five-piece band on the beach at Paradise Cove, north of Malibu. The picture was taken by in-house Capitol photographer Kenneth Veeder

Track listing

Side one				
No.	**Title**	**Writer(s)**	**Lead Vocals**	**Length**
1.	"Surfin' Safari"	Brian Wilson/Mike Love	Love	2:05
2.	"County Fair"	B. Wilson/Gary Usher	Love	2:15
3.	"Ten Little Indians"	B. Wilson/Usher	Love	1:26
4.	"Chug-A-Lug"	B. Wilson/Usher/Love	Love	1:59
5.	"Little Girl (You're My Miss America)"	Vincent Catalano/Herb Alpert	Dennis Wilson	2:04
6.	"409"	B. Wilson/Usher/Love	Love	1:59

Side two				
No.	**Title**	**Writer(s)**	**Lead Vocals**	**Length**
1.	"Surfin'"	B. Wilson/Love	Love	2:10
2.	"Heads You Win - Tails I Lose"	B. Wilson/Usher	Love	2:17
3.	"Summertime Blues"	Eddie Cochran/Jerry Capehart	Carl Wilson and David Marks	2:09
4.	"Cuckoo Clock"	B. Wilson/Usher	B. Wilson	2:08
5.	"Moon Dawg"	Derry Weaver	instrumental	2:00
6.	"The Shift"	B. Wilson/Love	Love	1:52

Musicians

- Mike Love - vocals
- David Marks - rhythm guitar, vocals
- Brian Wilson - bass guitar, piano, vocals
- Carl Wilson - lead guitar, vocals
- Dennis Wilson - drums, vocals

Sources

- *Surfin' Safari/Surfin' USA* CD booklet notes, David Leaf, c.1990.
- "The Nearest Faraway Place: Brian Wilson, The Beach Boys and the Southern California Experience", Timothy White, c. 1994.
- "Wouldn't It Be Nice - My Own Story", Brian Wilson and Todd Gold, c. 1991.
- "Top Pop Singles 1955-2001", Joel Whitburn, c. 2002.
- "Top Pop Albums 1955-2001", Joel Whitburn, c. 2002.
- Allmusic.com

References

[1] http://www.allmusic.com/cg/amg.dll?p=amg&sql=10:et7uak3k5m3l

Surfin' USA

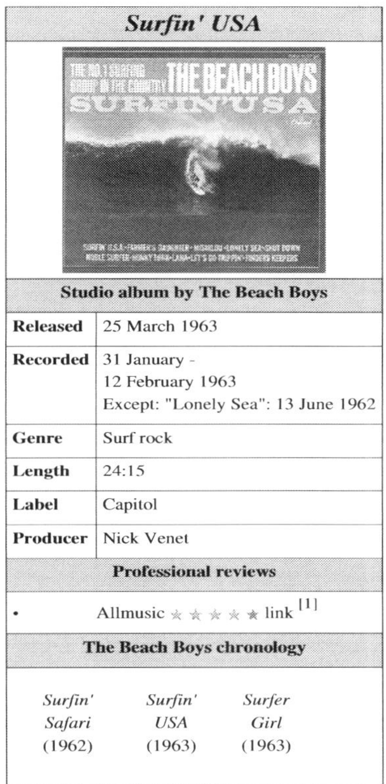

Surfin' USA	
Studio album by The Beach Boys	
Released	25 March 1963
Recorded	31 January - 12 February 1963 Except: "Lonely Sea": 13 June 1962
Genre	Surf rock
Length	24:15
Label	Capitol
Producer	Nick Venet
Professional reviews	
• Allmusic ★★★★★ link [1]	
The Beach Boys chronology	
Surfin' Safari (1962) *Surfin' USA* (1963) *Surfer Girl* (1963)	

Surfin' USA is the second album released by The Beach Boys and was released in early 1963. This was the group's second album to be credited with production from Capitol's Nick Venet, Capitol Records' representative for Artists and Repertoire.

Surfin' USA (Capitol (S) T 1890) reached **#2** in the US, lasting 78 weeks in the charts. It reached **#17** in the UK in late 1965. *Surfin' USA* is now paired on CD with *Surfin' Safari*, with bonus tracks from that period.

Impact, details and featured instrumentals

Surfin' USA is notable for giving The Beach Boys their first widespread success with its title track, and for Brian Wilson's increasing prowess in songwriting, as well as vocal arrangement. The fuller-sounding vocals were achieved using double tracking, creating The Beach Boys' own unique sound. As with *Surfin' Safari*, some have speculated that it was not Nick Venet, the officially-listed producer, but rather Brian, who produced *Surfin' USA*. The title track, "Surfin' USA", credited as composed by Brian Wilson, was a note-for-note cover of Chuck Berry's "Sweet Little Sixteen". A lawsuit officially granted Berry writing credit and royalties from the record.[2] Additionally, the lyrics seem inspired by the Bobby Rydell 1959 hit "Kissin' Time" (mentions various cities across the USA), which melodically also borrows liberally from Berry's "Sweet Little Sixteen."[3]

What is also interesting about this particular album is that five of its twelve tracks are surf instrumentals, "Stoked" being Brian Wilson's first of many instrumental songs he composed over the years for The Beach Boys. In addition, "Surf Jam" marks the first time Carl Wilson, aged 16 at the time, received a songwriting credit.

Notable vocal tracks

While the title track of the album was the center of attention (with its B-side "Shut Down" receiving some notice in the process), there were other highlights to be found. "Farmer's Daughter", the first of many Brian Wilson falsetto lead vocals, was affecting enough that Fleetwood Mac covered it live in 1980, while "Lonely Sea" (an outtake from the *Surfin' Safari* sessions and the first song Wilson wrote with Gary Usher) is the earliest glimpse of Brian Wilson's melancholic side. "Lana" and "Finders Keepers" (with its Four Seasons-esque hook) are also acclaimed tracks from *Surfin' USA*.

The title track, "Surfin' USA", became The Beach Boys' first big hit in the US and took its parent album into gold record status and the Top 10, peaking at #2. In 1965, upon re-release in the UK, *Surfin' USA* would reach #17.

The song "Surfin' USA" is part of the The Rock and Roll Hall of Fame's 500 Songs that Shaped Rock and Roll list.[4]

Front cover artwork

The photograph that adorns the front sleeve was taken by artist/photographer/surfer John Severson during January 1960, showing California-based waverider Leslie Williams riding the winter swell at Sunset Beach (Oahu) in Hawaii. Intended for the front cover of Severson's legendary *Surfer* magazine, the original negative was damaged during the color separation process and never appeared in print, until Capitol Records requested a suitable photograph for the new Beach Boys album. Severson fixed the damaged image and sold it to Capitol.

Track listing

Side one				
No.	**Title**	**Writer(s)**	**Lead Vocals**	**Length**
1.	"Surfin' USA"	Brian Wilson/Chuck Berry	Mike Love	2:27
2.	"Farmer's Daughter"	B. Wilson/Love	B. Wilson	1:49
3.	"Misirlou"	Roubanis/Wise/Leeds/Russell	instrumental	2:03
4.	"Stoked"	B. Wilson	instrumental	1:59
5.	"Lonely Sea"	B. Wilson/Gary Usher	B. Wilson	2:21
6.	"Shut Down"	B. Wilson/Roger Christian	Love	1:49

Side two				
No.	**Title**	**Writer(s)**	**Lead Vocals**	**Length**
1.	"Noble Surfer"	B. Wilson/Love	Love	1:51
2.	"Honky Tonk"	Doggett/Scott/Butler/Sheper/Glover	instrumental	2:01
3.	"Lana"	B. Wilson	B. Wilson	1:39
4.	"Surf Jam"	Carl Wilson	instrumental	2:10
5.	"Let's Go Trippin'"	Dick Dale	instrumental	1:57
6.	"Finders Keepers"	B. Wilson/Love	Love	1:38

Singles

- "Surfin' USA" b/w "Shut Down" (Capitol 4932), 4 March 1963, **US #3**; **#34 UK** ("Shut Down" **US #23**)

Personnel

- Brian Wilson - Vocals, bass, keyboards
- Mike Love - Vocals, saxophone
- Dennis Wilson - Vocals, drums
- Carl Wilson - Vocals, lead guitar
- David Marks - Rhythm guitar

Sources

- *Surfin' Safari / Surfin' USA* CD booklet notes, David Leaf, c.1990.
- *The Nearest Faraway Place: Brian Wilson, The Beach Boys and the Southern California Experience*, Timothy White, c. 1994.
- *Wouldn't It Be Nice - My Own Story*, Brian Wilson and Todd Gold, c. 1991.
- *Top Pop Singles 1955-2001*, Joel Whitburn, c. 2002.
- *Top Pop Albums 1955-2001*, Joel Whitburn, c. 2002.
- *The Lost Beach Boy*, Jon Stebbins and David Marks, 2008
- http://www.Allmusic.com

References

[1] http://www.allmusic.com/cg/amg.dll?p=amg&sql=10:0m5zefykhgf8
[2] "SURFIN USA" (http://repertoire.bmi.com/title.asp?blnWriter=True&blnPublisher=True&blnArtist=True&keyID=1434720&ShowNbr=0&ShowSeqNbr=0&querytype=WorkID). *BMI Repertoire*. Broadcast Music Incorporated. . Retrieved 16 November 2008.
[3] http://www.songfacts.com/detail.php?id=1771
[4] Rock and Roll Hall of Fame "500 songs that shaped rock and roll" (http://www.rockhall.com/exhibithighlights/500-songs/)

Ten Years of Harmony

Ten Years of Harmony	
Greatest hits by The Beach Boys	
Released	December 7, 1981
Recorded	Autumn 1969–February 1980 Except: "Surf's Up": backing track recorded November 1966
Genre	Rock
Length	1:34:34
Label	Brother/Caribou/CBS
Producer	The Beach Boys, Brian Wilson, James William Guercio, Bruce Johnston, (except "River Song": Dennis Wilson and Gregg Jakobson)
Professional reviews	
•	Allmusic ★★★★★ link [1]
The Beach Boys chronology	

Keepin' the Summer Alive (1980)	*Ten Years of Harmony* (1981)	*The Beach Boys* (1985)

Ten Years of Harmony is an official double album compilation album released by The Beach Boys in 1981, and spanning their entire Brother Records-era up to that point, (1970–1980), including some unreleased or rare material.

The Beach Boys had more or less splintered in 1981. Far from lucid, Brian Wilson would occasionally appear on stage, primarily as a replacement for brother Carl, who was concurrently embarking on a solo career. Dennis Wilson would show up to occasional concerts, but would usually be argumentative and disruptive. Mike Love, Al Jardine, and Bruce Johnston were the only stable members of a band who now had a whole cast of supporting musicians when they performed live. But the release of *Ten Years of Harmony* kept the pretense going and, unexpectedly, the *M.I.U. Album* cover of "Come Go with Me" became a U.S. top-twenty hit when released as a single from this collection.

While taking tracks from 1970's *Sunflower* to the previous year's *Keepin' the Summer Alive*, the compilers also included some oddities, rarities, and unreleased tracks. First, a handful of the songs, namely "Rock and Roll Music" and "California Saga: California" are presented in their original single mix. Moreover, *Ten Years of Harmony* includes a 1979 A-side "It's a Beautiful Day" (which failed to chart), a Dennis Wilson-written track called "San Miguel" (which was a *Sunflower*-era outtake from 1969), a cover of "Sea Cruise", which was a rejected track from the *15 Big Ones* sessions, and a selection from Dennis' solo album, *Pacific Ocean Blue*, "River Song".

Only the five original Beach Boys (Jardine, Brian, Carl, and Dennis Wilson, and Love) appear on the gatefold cover on the original LP issue. The group vetoed the use of a photo with Bruce Johnston, who had rejoined the group in 1978 after a six-year absence, and also declined a suggestion that Johnston appear in an inset on the already-chosen photo.

Ten Years of Harmony, now deleted, sold enough in its release to make #156 in the U.S.

Track listing

Disc one

1. "Add Some Music to Your Day" (Brian Wilson/Mike Love/Joe Knott) – 3:34
2. "Roller Skating Child" (Brian Wilson) – 2:16
3. "Disney Girls (1957)" (Bruce Johnston) – 4:06
4. "It's a Beautiful Day" (Mike Love/Al Jardine) – 3:15

   The longer version of this song was on the soundtrack to the film Americathon.
5. "California Saga: California" (Al Jardine) – 3:13

   The original LP contains the single mix whereas the US CD reissue contains the album version.
6. "Wontcha Come Out Tonight" (Brian Wilson/Mike Love) – 2:29
7. "Marcella" (Brian Wilson/Jack Rieley) – 3:52
8. "Rock and Roll Music" (Chuck Berry) – 2:26

   The original LP contains the single mix whereas the US CD reissue contains the album version.
9. "Goin' On" (Brian Wilson/Mike Love) – 3:01
10. "It's OK" (Brian Wilson/Mike Love) – 2:08
11. "Cool, Cool Water" (Brian Wilson/Mike Love) – 3:24
12. "San Miguel" (Dennis Wilson/Gregg Jakobson) – 2:25

    This song was recorded in 1969 during the very early sessions for Sunflower, *but was unreleased until 1981.*
13. "School Day (Ring! Ring! Goes the Bell)" (Chuck Berry) – 2:46
14. "Good Timin'" (Brian Wilson/Carl Wilson) – 2:10
15. "Sail On, Sailor" (Brian Wilson/Ray Kennedy/Jack Rieley/Tandyn Almer/Van Dyke Parks) – 3:17

Disc two

1. "Darlin'" (Brian Wilson/Mike Love) – 2:22

   This is the live version from the 1973 double album The Beach Boys in Concert. *The original studio version appears on the 1967 album* Wild Honey.
2. "Lady Lynda" (Al Jardine/Ron Altbach) – 3:56
3. "Sea Cruise" (H.P. Smith/Frankie Ford) – 3:25

   This was originally an outtake from the 15 Big Ones *sessions.*
4. "The Trader" (Carl Wilson/Jack Rieley) – 5:04
5. "This Whole World" (Brian Wilson) – 1:55
6. "Don't Go Near the Water" (Al Jardine/Mike Love) – 2:38
7. "Surf's Up" (Brian Wilson/Van Dyke Parks) – 4:10
8. "Come Go with Me (C.E. Quick) – 2:06

   The original LP contains the correct album mix from M.I.U. Album *whereas the US CD reissue contains a previously and since unreleased version originally recorded during the sessions for* 15 Big Ones.
9. "Deirdre" (Bruce Johnston/Brian Wilson) – 3:26
10. "She's Got Rhythm" (Brian Wilson/Mike Love/Ron Altbach) – 2:26

11. "River Song" (Dennis Wilson/Carl Wilson) – 3:44

    This is a Dennis Wilson recording from his 1977 Pacific Ocean Blue *solo album.*
12. "Long Promised Road" (Carl Wilson/Jack Rieley) – 3:29
13. "Feel Flows" (Carl Wilson/Jack Rieley) – 4:44
14. "Til I Die" (Brian Wilson) – 2:39

Singles

- "Come Go with Me" (from *M.I.U. Album*) b/w "Don't Go near the Water" (from *Surf's Up*) (Brother/Caribou), November 2, 1981 US #18

Ten Years of Harmony (Brother/Caribou/CBS Z2X 37445) reached **#156** in the U.S. during a chart stay of 6 weeks.

Sources

- "The Nearest Faraway Place: Brian Wilson, The Beach Boys and the Southern California Experience", Timothy White, c. 1994.
- "Wouldn't It Be Nice - My Own Story", Brian Wilson and Todd Gold, c. 1991.
- "Top Pop Singles 1955-2001", Joel Whitburn, c. 2002.
- "Top Pop Albums 1955-2001", Joel Whitburn, c. 2002.
- Allmusic.com

References

[1] http://www.allmusic.com/cg/amg.dll?p=amg&sql=10:jez1z8oajyv4

Ultimate Christmas

Ultimate Christmas	
Compilation album (Christmas) by The Beach Boys	
Released	22 September 1998
Recorded	October 1963 - November 1977
Genre	Rock
Length	61:58
Label	Capitol
Producer	Brian Wilson, Al Jardine and Dennis Wilson
Professional reviews	
• Allmusic ★★★★★ link [1]	
The Beach Boys chronology	
Endless Harmony Soundtrack (1998) (2000)	*Ultimate Christmas* (1998)
The Greatest Hits - Volume 1: 20 Good Vibrations (1999)	

Ultimate Christmas is a 1998 seasonal compilation of music by The Beach Boys released on Capitol Records. It rounds up all of the tracks from 1964's *The Beach Boys' Christmas Album*, including alternate versions of its lead single, "Little Saint Nick", while also including the extremely rare 1974 holiday single, "Child of Winter (Christmas Song)". In addition, there are a handful of unreleased tracks from the aborted *Merry Christmas From The Beach Boys* album in 1977, some of which were revised to be included on *M.I.U. Album* the following year.

As a collection of the Beach Boys' Christmas tunes, *Ultimate Christmas* manages to round up virtually every song the band recorded and released on the subject. In 2004 Capitol took it out of print and replaced it with *Christmas with the Beach Boys*, essentially the same compilation with new cover art and one song ("Christmas Time Is Here Again") removed from the tracklist.

Track listing

1. "Little Saint Nick" (Brian Wilson/Mike Love) – 2:01
   - *Features Mike Love on lead vocals*
   - *Album version; different mix from the 1963 mono single*
2. "The Man With All The Toys" (Brian Wilson/Mike Love) – 1:32
   - *Features Brian Wilson and Mike Love on lead vocals*
3. "Santa's Beard" (Brian Wilson/Mike Love) – 2:00
   - *Features Mike Love on lead vocals*
4. "Merry Christmas, Baby" (Brian Wilson) – 2:21
   - *Features Mike Love on lead vocals*
5. "Christmas Day" (Brian Wilson) – 1:47
   - *Features Al Jardine on lead vocals*
6. "Frosty The Snowman" (including the frosty the snowman handjive)(Steve Nelson/Jack Rollins) – 1:54
   - *Features Brian Wilson on lead vocals*
7. "We Three Kings Of Orient Are" (John Henry Hopkins) – 4:03
   - *Features Brian Wilson and Mike Love on lead vocals*
8. "Blue Christmas" (Billy Hayes/Jay W. Johnson) – 3:09
   - *Features Brian Wilson on lead vocals*
9. "Santa Claus Is Coming To Town" (J. Fred Coots/Haven Gillespie) – 2:20
   - *Features Brian Wilson and Mike Love on lead vocals*
10. "White Christmas" (Irving Berlin) – 2:29
    - *Features Brian Wilson on lead vocals*
11. "I'll Be Home For Christmas" (Kim Gannon/Walter Kent/Buck Ram) – 2:44
    - *Features Brian Wilson on lead vovals*
12. "Auld Lang Syne" (Trad. Arr. Brian Wilson) – 1:19
    - *Features Brian Wilson, Mike Love, Carl Wilson, Al Jardine and Dennis Wilson on lead vocals*
    - *Above 12 tracks originally released as The Beach Boys' Christmas Album in 1964*
13. "Little Saint Nick" (Single version) (Brian Wilson/Mike Love) – 2:08
    - *Features Mike Love on lead vocals*
14. "Auld Lang Syne" (Alternate mix) (Trad. Arr. Brian Wilson) – 1:23
    - *Features Brian Wilson, Mike Love, Carl Wilson, Al Jardine and Dennis Wilson on lead vocals*
15. "Little Saint Nick" (Alternate version) (Brian Wilson/Mike Love) – 2:04
    - *Features Brian Wilson and Mike Love on lead vocals*
    - *Utilizes the melody and backing track from All Summer Long's "Drive-In"*
16. "Child Of Winter (Christmas Song)" (Brian Wilson/Stephen Kalinich) – 2:49
    - *Features Brian Wilson and Mike Love on lead vocals*
    - *1974 single-only release*
17. "Santa's Got An Airplane" (Alan Jardine/Brian Wilson/Mike Love) – 3:09
    - *Features Mike Love and Al Jardine on lead vocals*
    - *Released as "Loop De Loop (Flip Flop Flyin' In An Aeroplane)" on* Endless Harmony Soundtrack *in 1998, and again in 2000*
18. "Christmas Time Is Here Again" (Buddy Holly/Norman Petty/Jerry Allison/new lyrics by Al Jardine) – 3:02
    - *Features Al Jardine on lead vocals*

- *Revised and released as "Peggy Sue" on M.I.U. Album in 1978*

19. "Winter Symphony" (Brian Wilson) – 3:00
    - *Features Brian Wilson on lead vocals*
20. "(I Saw Santa) Rockin' Around The Christmas Tree" (Brian Wilson/Al Jardine) – 2:23
    - *Features Al, Matt and Adam Jardine on lead vocals*
21. "Melekalikimaka" (aka "Kona Christmas") (Alan Jardine/Mike Love) – 2:34
    - *Features Mike Love and Al Jardine on lead vocals*
    - *Revised and released as "Kona Coast" on M.I.U. Album in 1978*
22. "Bells Of Christmas" (Alan Jardine/Ron Altbach/Mike Love) – 2:44
    - *Features Mike Love on lead vocals*
    - *Revised and released as "Belles Of Paris" on M.I.U. Album in 1978*
23. "Morning Christmas" (Dennis Wilson) – 3:22
    - *Features Dennis Wilson on lead vocals*
24. "Toy Drive Public Service Announcement" – 1:23
    - *Recorded in 1977*
25. "Dennis Wilson Christmas Message" – 0:31
    - *Recorded in 1977*
26. "Brian Wilson Christmas Interview" – 2:35
    - *Recorded in 1964*

Ultimate Christmas (Capitol 72434 95734 2 0) never charted in the US or the UK.

Sources

- *Ultimate Christmas* CD booklet notes, Brad Elliott, c.1998.
- Allmusic.com

References

[1] http://www.allmusic.com/cg/amg.dll?p=amg&sql=10:pi5m963ogepc

The Very Best of The Beach Boys

The Very Best of the Beach Boys	
Greatest hits by The Beach Boys	
Released	30 June 2001
Recorded	1961–2001
Genre	Rock
Length	1:17:58
Label	EMI
Producer	Brian Wilson, The Beach Boys
Professional reviews	
• Allmusic ☆☆☆☆☆ [1]	
The Beach Boys chronology	

Greatest Hits Volume Three: Best of the Brother Years 1970-1986 (2000)	***The Very Best of The Beach Boys*** (2001)	*Classics selected by Brian Wilson* (2002)

The Very Best of the Beach Boys is an album released by the American rock and roll band The Beach Boys. The album was released by EMI in 2001 and features 30 of their greatest hits digitally remastered. The album is the first compilation of The Beach Boys that makes a full retrospective of their career, displaying their greatest hit songs, during their 40-year career. Other compilations had already been released throughout the years, but only focusing on certain time periods of the band, or focusing on their complete career, but with several volumes.

Track listing

All tracks written by Brian Wilson/Mike Love, unless otherwise noted.

1. "Good Vibrations" – 3:37
2. "California Girls" – 2:43
3. "I Get Around" – 2:14
4. "Wouldn't It Be Nice" (Brian Wilson, Tony Asher, Love) – 2:25
5. "Surfin' Safari" – 2:07
6. "Fun, Fun, Fun" – 2:20
7. "Surfin' USA" (Brian Wilson, Chuck Berry) – 2:29
8. "Help Me Rhonda" – 2:47

9. "Don't Worry Baby" (Brian Wilson, Roger Christian) – 2:50
10. "When I Grow Up (To Be a Man)" – 2:04
11. "Little Deuce Coupe" (Brian Wilson, Christian) – 1:38
12. "Dance, Dance, Dance" (Brian Wilson, Carl Wilson, Love) – 2:00
13. "Little Honda" – 1:52
14. "Do You Wanna Dance?" (Bobby Freeman) – 2:21
15. "Surfer Girl" (Brian Wilson) – 2:27
16. "Then I Kissed Her" (Phil Spector, Ellie Greenwich, Jeff Barry) – 2:16
17. "God Only Knows" (Brian Wilson, Asher) – 2:50
18. "Caroline, No" (Brian Wilson, Asher) – 2:19
19. "Sloop John B" (Traditional, Brian Wilson) – 2:55
20. "Barbara Ann" (Fred Fassert) – 2:06
21. "Heroes and Villains" (Brian Wilson, Van Dyke Parks) – 3:38
22. "Do It Again" – 2:19
23. "Darlin'" – 2:13
24. "Wild Honey" – 2:38
25. "Break Away" (Brian Wilson, Murry Wilson) – 2:56
26. "Rock and Roll Music" (Berry) – 2:28
27. "I Can Hear Music" (Barry, Greenwich, Spector) – 2:37
28. "Cotton Fields (The Cotton Song)" (Huddie Ledbetter) – 3:02
29. "Lady Lynda" (Alan Jardine, Ron Altbach) – 3:58
30. "Kokomo" (Love, Scott McKenzie, Terry Melcher, John Phillips) – 3:37

References

[1] Prato, Greg. "Review: *The Very Best of The Beach Boys*" (http://www.allmusic.com/cg/amg.dll?p=amg&sql=10:0xfpxqe0ldse). Allmusic. . Retrieved 30 August 2009.

The Warmth of the Sun

The Warmth of the Sun	
Greatest hits by The Beach Boys	
Released	May 22, 2007
Recorded	1962 - 1986
Genre	Rock
Label	Capitol
Producer	Brian Wilson, Murry Wilson, Nick Venet, The Beach Boys, Carl Wilson, Al Jardine, Bruce Johnston and Terry Melcher
Professional reviews	
• Allmusic ★★★★★ link [1] • Music Box ★★★★★ link [2] • Pitchfork Media (8.6/10) link [3]	
The Beach Boys chronology	
Songs from Here & Back (2006)	*The Warmth of the Sun* (2007)

The Warmth of the Sun is a 2007 compilation of music by The Beach Boys released through Capitol Records. A successor to 2003's *Sounds of Summer: The Very Best of The Beach Boys*, *The Warmth of the Sun* is composed of fan favorites and hits that were left off its predecessor. Several songs were remixed in stereo for the first time. These are "All Summer Long", "You're So Good To Me", "Then I Kissed Her", "Please Let Me Wonder", and "Let Him Run Wild". The song "Wendy" appears as a new stereo remix with its middle eight cough edited out. This album also features an alternate mix of "Break Away" and the single versions of "Why Do Fools Fall In Love" and "Cool, Cool Water.".

The Warmth of the Sun debuted at #40 on the Billboard 200, selling a very strong 14,000 copies in its first week.[4]

Track listing

1. "All Summer Long" (Brian Wilson/Mike Love [1964]) - 2:09
2. "Catch a Wave" (Brian Wilson/Mike Love [1963]) - 2:08
3. "Hawaii" (Brian Wilson/Mike Love [1963]) - 2:00
4. "Little Honda" (Brian Wilson/Mike Love [1964]) - 1:52
5. "409" (Brian Wilson/Gary Usher/Mike Love [1962]) - 2:00
6. "It's OK" (Brian Wilson/Mike Love [1976]) - 2:12
7. "You're So Good to Me" (Brian Wilson/Mike Love [1965]) - 2:15
8. "Then I Kissed Her" (Barry/Greenwich/Phil Spector [1965]) - 2:16
9. "Kiss Me, Baby" (Brian Wilson/Mike Love [1965]) - 2:43
10. "Please Let Me Wonder" (Brian Wilson/Mike Love [1965]) - 2:50
11. "Let Him Run Wild" (Brian Wilson/Mike Love [1965]) - 2:20
12. "The Little Girl I Once Knew" (Brian Wilson [1965]) - 2:34
13. "Wendy" (Brian Wilson/Mike Love [1964]) - 2:20
14. "Disney Girls (1957)" (Bruce Johnston [1971]) - 4:07
15. "Forever" (Dennis Wilson/Gregg Jakobson [1970]) - 2:41

16. "Friends" (Brian Wilson/Dennis Wilson/Carl Wilson/Al Jardine [1968]) - 2:32
17. "Break Away" (Brian Wilson/Reggie Dunbar [1969]) - 3:05
18. "Why Do Fools Fall in Love" (Morris Levy/Frankie Lymon [1964]) - 2:07
19. "Surf's Up" (Brian Wilson/Van Dyke Parks [1971]) - 4:12
20. "Feel Flows" (Carl Wilson/Jack Rieley [1971]) - 4:46
21. "All This Is That" (Carl Wilson/Mike Love/Al Jardine [1972]) - 3:57
22. "'Til I Die" (Brian Wilson [1971]) - 2:40
23. "Sail On, Sailor" (Brian Wilson/Van Dyke Parks/Jack Rieley/Ray Kennedy/Tandyn Almer [1973]) - 3:16
24. "Cool, Cool Water" (Brian Wilson/Mike Love [1970]) - 3:24
25. "Don't Go Near the Water" (Mike Love/Al Jardine [1971]) - 2:39
26. "California Saga (On My Way To Sunny Californ-i-a) (Al Jardine [1973]) - 3:22
27. "California Dreamin'" (John Phillips/Michelle Phillips [1986]) - 3:24
28. "The Warmth of the Sun" (Brian Wilson/Mike Love [1964]) - 2:50

References

[1] http://www.allmusic.com/cg/amg.dll?p=amg&sql=10:gzfyxqedldfe
[2] http://www.musicbox-online.com/reviews-2007/beachboys-warmthofthesun-06172007.html
[3] http://www.pitchforkmedia.com/article/record_review/43229-the-warmth-of-the-sun
[4] Katie Hasty, "Maroon 5 Nudges Linkin Park From Atop Billboard 200" (http://www.billboard.com/bbcom/news/article_display.jsp?vnu_content_id=1003591609), Billboard.com, May 30, 2007.

Wild Honey

Wild Honey	
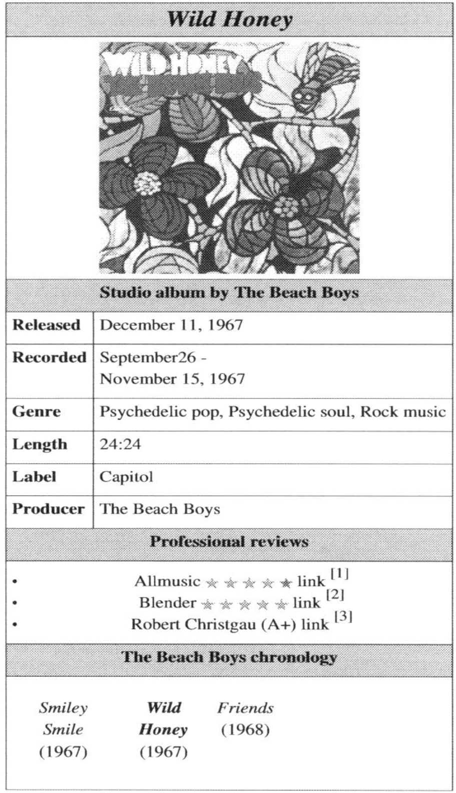	
Studio album by The Beach Boys	
Released	December 11, 1967
Recorded	September26 - November 15, 1967
Genre	Psychedelic pop, Psychedelic soul, Rock music
Length	24:24
Label	Capitol
Producer	The Beach Boys
Professional reviews	
• Allmusic ★★★★★ link [1] • Blender ★★★★★ link [2] • Robert Christgau (A+) link [3]	
The Beach Boys chronology	
Smiley Smile (1967) · ***Wild Honey*** (1967) · *Friends* (1968)	

Wild Honey is an album released by The Beach Boys in 1967. It was their thirteenth studio album and sixteenth overall, and, as a group production, was the first Beach Boy album since *Surfin' USA* not to be solely produced by Brian Wilson, who had gradually abdicated the band's musical leadership following the difficult sessions for the aborted *Smile* LP.

The closing track, "Mama Says", is a chant originally recorded for the abandoned *Smile* performance of "Vegetables". It was the first of several stray *Smile* tracks used to close a later Beach Boys album.

The title track became the first single, a minor hit with only a short chart stay. Its follow-up, "Darlin' ", reached the US Top 20, while the album itself (the last Beach Boys LP to be released in both mono and stereo) reached #24 in the US and #7 in the UK. The track "Here Comes the Night" was later redone as a disco song in the late 1970s but was not a hit. "How She Boogalooed It", co-written by Al Jardine, Mike Love, Bruce Johnston and Carl Wilson, was the first Beach Boys non-instrumental original not to be written or co-written by Brian Wilson.

In 1990 Capitol Records reissued *Wild Honey* on a Beach Boys double CD with *Smiley Smile* and bonus tracks including an alternate version of "Heroes and Villains" that contains the 'cantina section', two incomplete versions of "Good Vibrations", "You're Welcome", "Their Hearts Were Full Of Spring", and "Can't Wait Too Long". This printing of the CD also included in depth liner notes by David Leaf, as well as previously unreleased *Smile* session photos by Jasper Dailey.

Front cover artwork

The colorful image featured on the front of the album sleeve is, in fact, a photograph of a small section of an elaborate stained glass double-window that adorned Brian and Marilyn Wilson's house in Bel Air. Although the Wilson family no longer owns that property, the window itself was removed when they moved out and is currently to be found in Marilyn Wilson-Rutherford's present house.

Track listing

All songs by Brian Wilson/Mike Love, except where noted.

Side one

1. "Wild Honey" – 2:37
   - *Features Carl Wilson on lead vocals*
2. "Aren't You Glad" – 2:16
   - *Features Mike Love [verses], Brian Wilson [verses and chorus] and Carl Wilson [chorus] on lead vocals*
3. "I Was Made to Love Her" (Henry Cosby/Sylvia Moy/Lola Mae Hardaway/Stevie Wonder) – 2:05
   - *Features Carl Wilson on lead vocals*
4. "Country Air" – 2:20
   - *Features group vocals*
5. "A Thing or Two" – 2:40
   - *Features Mike Love, Carl Wilson, and Brian Wilson on lead vocals*

Side two

- "Darlin' " – 2:12
- *Features Carl Wilson on lead vocals*

2. "I'd Love Just Once to See You" – 1:48
   - *Features Brian Wilson on lead vocals*
3. "Here Comes the Night" – 2:41
   - *Features Brian Wilson on lead vocals*
4. "Let the Wind Blow" – 2:19
   - *Features Mike Love, Brian Wilson, and Carl Wilson on lead vocals*
5. "How She Boogalooed It" (Mike Love/Bruce Johnston/Al Jardine/Carl Wilson) – 1:56
   - *Features Carl Wilson on lead vocals* [3]
6. "Mama Says" – 1:05
   - *Features group vocals*

Singles

- "Wild Honey" b/w "Wind Chimes" (from *Smiley Smile*) (Capitol 2028), 23 October 1967 **US #31**; **UK #29**
- "Darlin'" b/w "Here Today" (from *Pet Sounds*) (Capitol 2068), 18 December 1967 **US #19**; **UK #11**. (UK B-side was "Country Air")

Wild Honey is now paired on CD with *Smiley Smile*, with bonus tracks from that period.

Early version

An early lineup of *Wild Honey* was sent to Capitol Records during fall/winter of 1967. If this version had been released, it would have been released as a Brother Records album distributed by Capitol. Its catalog number would have been "Brother ST-9003." If released, it would have had the following running order:

1. "Wild Honey"
2. "Here Comes the Night"
3. "Let the Wind Blow"
4. "I Was Made to Love Her"
5. "The Letter" (Cover of the Box Tops' hit)
6. "Darlin'"
7. "A Thing or Two"
8. "Aren't You Glad"
9. "Cool, Cool Water"
10. "Game of Love" (Cover of the Clint Ballard Jr./Wayne Fontana & the Mindbenders song)
11. "Lonely Days"
12. "Honey Get Home"

Trivia

The album is referenced in the lyrics of "Round The Bend" by The Beta Band on their self-titled album.

References

- *Smiley Smile / Wild Honey* CD booklet notes, David Leaf, c.1990.
- *Look! Listen! Vibrate! Smile!*, Domenic Priore, c.1995
- *The Nearest Faraway Place: Brian Wilson, The Beach Boys and the Southern California Experience*, Timothy White, c. 1994.
- *Wouldn't It Be Nice - My Own Story*, Brian Wilson and Todd Gold, c. 1991.
- *Top Pop Singles 1955-2001*, Joel Whitburn, c. 2002.
- *Top Pop Albums 1955-2001*, Joel Whitburn, c. 2002.
- Allmusic.com

[1] http://www.allmusic.com/cg/amg.dll?p=amg&sql=10:ox66mpc39f8o

[2] http://www.blender.com/guide/back-catalogue/52788/smiley-smilewild-honey.html

[3] Doe, Andrew G.: " ALBUMARCHIVE2 (http://www.btinternet.com/~bellagio/albumarchive2.html)." Bellagio 10452 (http://www.btinternet.com/~bellagio/). Retrieved on 2008-12-31.

Songs

409

"409"	
Single by The Beach Boys	
from the album *Surfin' Safari*	
A-side	"Surfin' Safari"
B-side	"409"
Released	June 4, 1962
Format	Vinyl
Recorded	April 19, 1962 Western Studios
Genre	Rock
Length	1:59
Label	Capitol Records
Writer(s)	Brian Wilson, Mike Love and Gary Usher
Producer	Murry Wilson
The Beach Boys singles chronology	

"Surfin'"/"Luau" (1961)	"Surfin' Safari"/ "409" (1962)	"Ten Little Indians"/"County Fair" (1962)

"**409**" is a song written by Brian Wilson, Mike Love and Gary Usher for the American rock and roll band, The Beach Boys. The song features Mike Love singing lead vocals. It was originally released as the b-side of the "Surfin' Safari" single. It was later released on their 1962 album, *Surfin' Safari*, and it was also on their 1963 album, *Little Deuce Coupe*.

"Surfin Safari" would reach #14 on the Billboard Hot 100, while 409 reached #76. Originally promoted as the A-side by Capitol, "409" went on to feature in many regional markets. It was the most popular song of 1962 in Dallas (KBOX chart) and, also in its own right, penetrated the top tens of Vancouver, Seattle and San Bernardino. It was co-hit with its later designated A-side near the top of playlists in most other areas.

Composition

The "409" of the song is the *Chevrolet 409*, a 409 cubic inch W-series V8 engine popular with "hot rodders" of the time. Gary Usher, who wrote the majority of the lyric for the song dreamed at that time of one day owning a Chevrolet 409.

The song was originally credited to just Wilson and Usher. Mike Love's name was added as a result of a lawsuit filed by him against Wilson in the 1990s.

Recording

"409" was recorded at the third Beach Boys recording session, on April 19, 1962, at Western Studios. The band's previous record label, Candix, had folded, and with the recordings made at this session, the band was able to sign with Capitol Records. This was David Marks's first session as a member of the band.

The engine noises heard at the beginning of the song were of Usher's Chevrolet 348, the W-series predecessor to the 409.

Musicians

- Mike Love - lead vocals
- David Marks - guitar
- Brian Wilson - bass guitar, vocals
- Carl Wilson - lead guitar, vocals
- Dennis Wilson - drums, vocals

See also

- List of songs by The Beach Boys
- *Surfin' Safari*

4th of July

"4th of July"	
Song by The Beach Boys from the album *Good Vibrations: Thirty Years of The Beach Boys*	
Released	June 29, 1993
Recorded	Brian Wilson's home studio track: April 3, 1971 vocals: June 20, 1971; July 1971
Genre	Pop music
Length	2:44
Composer	Dennis Wilson/Jack Rieley

"**4th of July**" is a song written by Dennis Wilson and Jack Rieley for the American pop band The Beach Boys. It was recorded for the band's 1971 allbum *Surf's Up* but was not released until 1993, on the box set *Good Vibrations: Thirty Years of The Beach Boys*.

The song was written in 1970 as a veiled comment on the alleged suppression of the NY Times by the US government. Originally intended for the 1971 *Surf's Up* album, it was pulled by Dennis after an argument with brother Carl over sequencing the album.

See also

- List of songs by The Beach Boys

Add Some Music to Your Day

"Add Some Music to Your Day"	
Single by The Beach Boys	
from the album *Sunflower*	
Released	February 23, 1970
Format	Vinyl
Recorded	Brian Wilson's home studio October 28 and December 1969, January 1970
Genre	Pop music
Length	3:34
Label	Brother/Reprise
Writer(s)	Brian Wilson, Joe Knott and Mike Love
Producer	The Beach Boys

The Beach Boys singles chronology		
"Break Away"/"Celebrate the News" (1969)	"Add Some Music to Your Day"/"Susie Cincinnati" (1970)	"Cottonfields"/"The Nearest Faraway Place" (1970)

"Add Some Music to Your Day" is a song written by Brian Wilson, Joe Knott and Mike Love for the American pop band The Beach Boys. It was first released as a single in February 1970. While making no impact overseas at all -- unusually for the Beach Boys -- early US orders were said to be at near-record levels for Warners and the song quickly entered top thirties in Los Angeles, New York, Boston, Salt Lake City, and climbed well into the top twenties of St Louis and Orlando. There it stopped, stalling nationally at #39 in *Record World*, #49 *Cash Box* and #64 in *Billboard*; #43 Canada. What might have been a prime peace anthem was then released on the band's 1970 album *Sunflower*.

Composer credit

According the liner notes of the 2000 re-issue of the *Sunflower* album, Joe Knott was not a professional songwriter. In the liner notes, Brian Wilson said of the song, "It was written by me and Mike and Joe Knott, who was a friend of mine who wasn't a songwriter but he contributed a couple of lines. But I can't remember which ones!".

Details

- Written by: Brian Wilson/Joe Knott/Mike Love
- Album: *Sunflower*
- Time: 3:34
- Produced by: The Beach Boys

Musicians

- Al Jardine - guitars, vocals
- Bruce Johnston - bass guitar, vocals
- Mike Love - vocals
- Brian Wilson - Roxichord, vocals
- Carl Wilson - guitars, vocals
- Dennis Wilson - drums, vocals

The lead vocal is shared between all of the band members except for Dennis.

See also

- The Beach Boys
- Sunflower
- List of songs by The Beach Boys

Airplane

"Airplane"	
Song by The Beach Boys from the album *The Beach Boys Love You*	
Released	April 11, 1977
Recorded	Brother Studio October-November 1976, January 12, 1977
Genre	Pop music
Length	3:05
Label	Brother/Reprise
Composer	Brian Wilson
Producer	Brian Wilson Mixdown producer: Carl Wilson
***The Beach Boys Love You* track listing**	
"I Wanna Pick You Up" (12) "**Airplane**" (13) "Love Is a Woman" (14)	

"Airplane" is a song written by Brian Wilson for the American pop band The Beach Boys. It was released on their 1977 album *Love You*.

Details

- *Written by:* Brian Wilson
- *Album:* Love You
- *Time:* 3 min 06 sec
- *Produced by:* Brian Wilson

Performers

- *Brian Wilson:* Lead Vocals
- *Carl Wilson:* Lead Vocals
- *Mike Love:* Lead Vocals

See also

- List of songs by The Beach Boys

All Alone

"All Alone" is the title of a song written by Carli Muñoz. It was recorded by Dennis Wilson and released on The Beach Boys' 1998 anthology album, *Endless Harmony Soundtrack*. It was later released on the 2008 reissue of *Pacific Ocean Blue*.

See also

- List of songs by The Beach Boys

All Dressed Up for School

"All Dressed Up for School"	
Song by The Beach Boys from the album *Little Deuce Coupe/All Summer Long* twofer	
Released	1990
Recorded	Western Studios September 16, 1964
Genre	Pop music
Length	2:20
Label	Capitol
Composer	Brian Wilson
Producer	Brian Wilson

"**All Dressed Up for School**" is a song written by Brian Wilson for the American pop band The Beach Boys. It was recorded very early in the sessions for the 1965 album *The Beach Boys Today!*, but was not released until 1990.

Composition

"All Dressed Up for School" started life as a song called "What Will I Wear to School (Today)", a song which was written in early 1964 by Sharon Marie, but never recorded. That song had lyrics by Roger Christian.

Parts of the melody of "All Dressed Up for School" would be reused by Brian Wilson in "I Just Got My Pay", an outtake from 1970's *Sunflower*, which was released in 1993 on the box set. He again used part of the melody in "Marcella", a song released in 1972 on *Carl and the Passions - "So Tough"*. The chords in the opening *a capella* vocal passage would later show up in unreleased versions of "Heroes and Villains", and later in the 1980 single "Goin' On".

Recording

The song was recorded on September 16, 1964 at Western Studios, with Chuck Britz as the engineer. For its release in 1990, it was mixed by Mark Linett.

Musicians

- Jimmy Bond - upright bass
- Steve Douglas - tenor saxophone
- Carl Fortina - accordion
- Al Jardine - bass guitar, vocals
- Mike Love - vocals
- Melvin Pollan - upright bass
- Lyle Ritz - upright bass
- Brian Wilson - piano, vocals
- Carl Wilson - 12-string guitar, lead vocal
- Dennis Wilson - drum kit, vocals

See also

- List of songs by The Beach Boys

All I Wanna Do

"All I Wanna Do"	
Song by The Beach Boys from the album *Sunflower*	
Released	August 31, 1970
Recorded	March 19, 1969
Genre	Pop music
Length	2:34
Label	Brother Records/Reprise Records
Composer	Brian Wilson/Mike Love
Producer	The Beach Boys
***Sunflower* track listing**	
Tears In The Morning (7) / **"All I Wanna Do"** (8) / Forever (9)	

"All I Wanna Do" is a song written by Brian Wilson and Mike Love for the American pop band The Beach Boys. It was released on their 1970 album *Sunflower*. It should not be confused with the Dennis Wilson song "All I Want to Do", recorded four months hence and included on the *20/20* album.

Details

- *Written by:* Brian Wilson/Mike Love
- *Album:* Sunflower
- *Time:* 2:34
- *Produced by:* The Beach Boys

Performers

- *Mike Love:* Lead Vocals

See also

- The Beach Boys
- Sunflower
- List of songs by The Beach Boys

All I Want to Do

"All I Want to Do"	
Song by The Beach Boys from the album *20/20*	
Released	February 10, 1969
Recorded	Brian Wilson's home studio November 21, 1968 tag: Capitol Studios; November 12, 1968
Genre	hard rock
Length	2:02
Label	Capitol
Composer	Dennis Wilson
Producer	Dennis Wilson
***20/20* track listing**	
"Be With Me" (4) / **"All I Want to Do"** (5) / "The Nearest Faraway Place" (6)	

"All I Want to Do" is a song written by Dennis Wilson. It was recorded by The Beach Boys for their 1969 album *20/20*. It was later released as the b-side to "I Can Hear Music", a single which charted at #24 in the U.S. and at #10 in the U.K..

A live version of the song, recorded for *Live in London*, was released on *Rarities* in 1983.

Details

- written by - Dennis Wilson
- album - *20/20*
- length - 2:02
- produced by - Dennis Wilson
- lead vocals - Mike Love

See also

- List of songs by The Beach Boys

All Summer Long

"All Summer Long"	
Song by The Beach Boys from the album *All Summer Long*	
Released	July 13, 1964
Recorded	May 6 & 7 1964 Western Studios
Genre	Pop music
Length	2:06
Label	Capitol Records
Composer	Brian Wilson/Mike Love
Producer	Brian Wilson

***All Summer Long* track listing**		
"I Get Around" (1)	**"All Summer Long"** (2)	"Hushabye" (3)

"All Summer Long" is a song written by Brian Wilson and Mike Love for the American pop band The Beach Boys. It was released on their 1964 album *All Summer Long*, and as a single in the UK in February 1965 in place of Capitol's U.S. release, the Beach Boys' version of "Do You Wanna Dance?" -- perhaps a tactical move by EMI in London to avoid taking sales from its existing version by Cliff Richard, "Do You Want to Dance?". In the event, "All Summer Long" was no hit on the now hard-rock British scene, breaking the Beach Boys' string of three previous consecutive UK hits.

The song is featured in the 1973 film *American Graffiti* as the closing credits roll, although the movie is set in the summer of 1962, two years before the song's release.

It also appears as the closing credits roll on *The Simpsons* episode "Summer of 4 Ft. 2". The episode makes a number of *American Graffiti* references.

On disc 5 of *Good Vibrations: Thirty Years of The Beach Boys*, there is a version of "All Summer Long" where the backing track and the vocals are separated onto two different speakers.

Details

- Written by: Brian Wilson/Mike Love
- Album: *All Summer Long*
- Time: 2:06
- Produced by: Brian Wilson

Performers

- *Mike Love:* Lead Vocals

See also

- List of songs by The Beach Boys

All This Is That

"All This Is That" is a song written by Alan Jardine, Carl Wilson and Mike Love for the American pop band The Beach Boys. It was released on their 1972 album *Carl and the Passions - "So Tough"*.

Details

- Written by: Alan Jardine/Carl Wilson/Mike Love
- Album: Carl and the Passions - "So Tough"
- Time: 4 min 00 sec
- Produced by: The Beach Boys

Performers

- Carl Wilson: Lead Vocals
- Mike Love: Lead Vocals

See also

- List of songs by The Beach Boys

Alley Oop

"Alley Oop"	
Single by The Hollywood Argyles	
B-side	"Sho Know a Lot About Love"
Released	1960
Recorded	1960
Label	Lute 5905
Writer(s)	Dallas Frazier
Producer	Gary S. Paxton Kim Fowley

"Alley Oop"	
Song by The Beach Boys from the album *Beach Boys' Party!*	
Released	November 8, 1965
Recorded	September 16, 1965 Western Studios
Genre	Rock and roll
Length	2:56
Label	Capitol
Composer	Dallas Frazier
Producer	Brian Wilson
***Beach Boys' Party!* track listing**	
• "Hully Gully" • "I Should Have Known Better" • "Tell Me Why" • "Papa-Oom-Mow-Mow" • "Mountain of Love" • "You've Got to Hide Your Love Away" • "Devoted to You" • "Alley Oop" • "There's No Other (Like My Baby)" • "Medley:I Get Around/Little Deuce Coupe" • "The Times They Are a-Changin' " • "Barbara Ann"	

"**Alley Oop**" is a song written by Dallas Frazier. The song, heavily inspired by the V. T. Hamlin-created comic strip of the same name, was first recorded by Frazier as a country tune in 1957.

The Hollywood Argyles

The Hollywood Argyles recorded the song in 1960 and hit number one on the *Billboard* Hot 100. It was produced by Gary S. Paxton. The lead vocalist on the track was Norm Davis. He was paid a one-time fee of $25 for his work on the single. He is currently a poet and poetry teacher in Rochester, New York.

This version of the story is contested by Gary Paxton. Paxton writes:

> There were NO Hollywood Argyles at the very beginning. I [Paxton] was the only lead singer. Kim Fowley helped me produce it, because we were partners in Maverick Music International/BMI at the time... The drummer was Ronnie Silico (Lloyd Price's road drummer). The piano player was Gaynel Hodge of the Penguins. The bass player was Harper Cosby, a jazz bassist in L.A. Sandy Nelson (of "Teenbeat" fame) played the garbage can and screamed on the record. The background singers were: Dallas Frazier...Buddy Mize, Scotty Turner, Diane ?? (A friend I knew), and [myself]. It was recorded at American Recorders, next door to Lawrence Welk's Palladium, and across from the Moulin Rouge on Sunset Blvd. near Sunset and Vine Street. A little bitty street (Argyle Street) was next door to the studio, so I said, 'Let's call ourselves The Hollywood Argyles!'[1]

Other versions

Also in 1960, The Dyno-Sores and Dante & The Evergreens took versions of the song to numbers 59 and 15, respectively, on the Hot 100 chart.[2] Both Dante & The Evergreens' and the Argyles' versions were credited as number ones in Cashbox magazine's singles chart.

The Beach Boys recorded and released their version on their 1965 album *Beach Boys' Party!*. The British satirical art rock/pop group, The Bonzo Dog Doo-Dah Band, recorded a version of "Alley Oop", which was released as their second single in October 1966. It was also performed by Dave Van Ronk and the Hudson Dusters on their self-titled album, released in 1967.

Actress-singer Darlene Love recorded a version of the song for the 1984 film *Bachelor Party*.
George Thorogood also did a version of this song and was on the Live CD that was released February 15, 1989.

See also

- Alley Oop, 1932-1973 comic strip

References

[1] http://www.garyspaxton.net/Music1/AlleyOop.htm
[2] Ask "Mr. Music" - Jerry Osborne (http://www.jerryosborne.com/6-12-00.htm)

Amusement Parks USA

"Amusement Parks USA"	
Song by The Beach Boys from the album *Summer Days (and Summer Nights!!)*	
Released	July 5, 1965
Recorded	April 14 & May 5, 1965
Genre	Sunshine pop, Surf rock
Length	2:29
Label	Capitol
Composer	Brian Wilson/Mike Love
Producer	Brian Wilson
***Summer Days (and Summer Nights!!)* track listing**	
"The Girl From New York City" (1) **"Amusement Parks USA"** (2) "Then I Kissed Her" (3)	

"**Amusement Parks USA**" is a song written by Brian Wilson and Mike Love for the American pop band The Beach Boys. It was released on their 1965 album *Summer Days (and Summer Nights!!)*.

Details

- Written by: Brian Wilson/Mike Love
- Album: *Summer Days (and Summer Nights!!)*
- Time: 2 min 29 sec
- Produced by: Brian Wilson
- Recording date: April 14, 1965 & May 5, 1965

Musicians

- Charles Berghofer - upright bass
- Hal Blaine - drums, carnival barker
- Jerry Cole - bass guitar
- Steve Douglas - tenor saxophone
- Al Jardine - vocals
- Carol Kaye - bass guitar
- Mike Love - lead vocal
- Jay Migliori - baritone saxophone
- Leon Russell - organ
- Billy Strange - guitar
- Julius Wechter - vibraphone
- Brian Wilson - piano, lead vocal, laughter
- Carl Wilson - vocals
- Dennis Wilson - vocals

See also

- The Beach Boys
- Summer Days (and Summer Nights!!)
- List of songs by The Beach Boys

And Your Dream Comes True

"And Your Dream Comes True"	
Song by The Beach Boys from the album *Summer Days (and Summer Nights!!)*	
Released	July 5, 1965
Recorded	May 24, 1965 Columbia Recording Studio
Genre	Pop
Length	1:04
Label	Capitol
Composer	Brian Wilson/Mike Love
Producer	Brian Wilson
***Summer Days (and Summer Nights!!)* track listing**	
"I'm Bugged at My Ol' Man" (11)	"**And Your Dream Comes True**" (12)

"**And Your Dream Comes True**" is an a cappella song written by Brian Wilson and Mike Love for the American pop band The Beach Boys. It was released on their 1965 album *Summer Days (and Summer Nights!!)*. The melody of the song is the same as the melody to the first two lines of "Twinkle Twinkle Little Star", though the harmonic structure is very different. Even though the song is just over a minute long, it was recorded in five sections (each one double-tracked) and edited together. *Hawthorne, CA* features part of the recording process of this song (the track "Wish That He Could Stay") as well as a stereo version of the song.

Details

- Written by: Brian Wilson/Mike Love
- Album: *Summer Days (and Summer Nights!!)*
- Time: 1 min 04 sec
- Produced by: Brian Wilson

Musicians

- Al Jardine - vocals
- Mike Love - vocals
- Brian Wilson - vocals
- Carl Wilson - vocals
- Bruce Johnston - present at the session but did not sing on this song
- Chuck Britz- session engineer

See also

- List of songs by The Beach Boys

Angel Come Home

"Angel Come Home" is a song written by Carl Wilson and Geoffrey Cushing-Murray for the American pop band The Beach Boys. It was released on their 1979 album *L.A. (Light Album)*. Dennis Wilson sang lead vocal.

"Angel Come Home" was covered by Mick Fleetwood's Zoo in 1984 (RCA), and was a minor hit in the USA. Billy Burnette was the lead vocalist, and Christine McVie and Lindsey Buckingham also appeared on the record.

Details

- *Written by:* Carl Wilson/Geoffrey Cushing-Murray
- *Album:* L.A. (Light Album)
- *Time:* 3 min 39 sec
- *Produced by:* Bruce Johnston, The Beach Boys, James William Guercio

Performers

- *Dennis Wilson:* Lead Vocals

See also

- The Beach Boys
- L.A. (Light Album)
- List of songs by The Beach Boys

Anna Lee, the Healer

"**Anna Lee, the Healer**" is a song written by Brian Wilson and Mike Love for the American pop band The Beach Boys. The title refers to a disciple of the Maharishi Mahesh Yogi, the healer Anneliese Braun. It was released on their 1968 album *Friends*.

Details

- *Written by:* Brian Wilson/Mike Love
- *Album:* Friends
- *Time:* 1 min 51 sec
- *Produced by:* The Beach Boys

Performers

- Mike Love: Lead Vocals

See also

- List of songs by The Beach Boys

Aren't You Glad

"**Aren't You Glad**" is a song written by Brian Wilson and Mike Love for the American pop band The Beach Boys. It was released on their 1967 album *Wild Honey*.

Details

- *Written by:* Brian Wilson/Mike Love
- *Album:* Wild Honey
- *Time:* 2 min 16 sec
- *Produced by:* The Beach Boys

Performers

- *Mike Love:* Lead Vocals (verse)
- *Brian Wilson:* Lead Vocals (pre-chorus)
- *Carl Wilson:* Lead Vocals (chorus)

See also

- List of songs by The Beach Boys

At My Window

"At My Window"			
Song by The Beach Boys from the album *Sunflower*			
Released	August 31, 1970		
Recorded	November 11, 1969		
Genre	Pop		
Length	2:30		
Label	Brother Records/Reprise Records		
Composer	Brian Wilson/Al Jardine		
Producer	The Beach Boys		
***Sunflower* track listing**			
Our Sweet Love (10)	**"At My Window"** (11)	Cool Cool Water (12)	

"At My Window" is a song written by Brian Wilson and Al Jardine for the American pop band The Beach Boys. It was released on their 1970 album *Sunflower*.

"At My Window" was first recorded under the working title "Raspberries, Strawberries".

Details

- *Written by:* Brian Wilson/Al Jardine
- *Album:* Sunflower
- *Time:* 2:30
- *Produced by:* The Beach Boys

Performers

- *Bruce Johnston:* Lead Vocals
- *Brian Wilson:* French spoken interlude

See also

- The Beach Boys
- Sunflower
- List of songs by The Beach Boys

Baby Blue

"Baby Blue"	
Single by The Beach Boys	
from the album *L.A. (Light Album)*	
Released	February 19, 1979
Format	Vinyl
Recorded	Unknown
Genre	Rock
Length	3 min 25 sec
Label	Capitol Records
Producer	Bruce Johnston The Beach Boys James William Guercio

The Beach Boys singles chronology		
"Peggy Sue"/"Hey, Little Tomboy" (1978)	"Here Comes the Night"/"Baby Blue" (1979)	"Good Timin'"/"Love Surrounds Me" (1979)

"Baby Blue" is a song written by Dennis Wilson, Gregg Jakobson and Karen Lamm for the American pop band The Beach Boys. It was released on their 1979 album *L.A. (Light Album)*.

This song is unrelated to the hit by the doo-wop group The Echoes, which went to # 12 on the Billboard Top 100.

Details

- *Written by:* Dennis Wilson/Gregg Jakobson/Karen Lamm
- *Album:* L.A. (Light Album)
- *Time:* 3 min 25 sec
- *Produced by:* Bruce Johnston/The Beach Boys/James William Guercio

Performers

- *Carl Wilson:* Lead Vocals
- *Dennis Wilson:* Lead Vocals

See also

- The Beach Boys
- L.A. (Light Album)
- List of songs by The Beach Boys

Back Home

"Back Home"		
Song by The Beach Boys from the album *15 Big Ones*		
Released	June 28, 1976	
Recorded	May 1976	
Genre	Rock music	
Length	2:49	
Label	Brother Records Reprise Records	
Writer	Brian Wilson Bob Norberg	
Producer	Brian Wilson	
***15 Big Ones* track listing**		
Blueberry Hill (12)	**"Back Home"** (13)	In the Still of the Night (14)

"Back Home" is a song written by Brian Wilson and Bob Norberg for the American pop band The Beach Boys. It was written in 1963, but not released until their 1976 album *15 Big Ones*. The song also appears on Brian Wilson's first live album as a solo artist, Live at the Roxy Theatre.

Details

- *Written by:* Brian Wilson/Bob Norberg
- *Album:* 15 Big Ones
- *Time:* 2 min 49 sec
- *Produced by:* Brian Wilson
- *Arranged by:* Brian Wilson

Performers

- *Brian Wilson:* Lead Vocals, Piano, Organ, Bells
- *Al Jardine:* Backing Vocals
- *Carl Wilson:* Backing Vocals, Bass, Guitar, Harp, percussion
- *Mike Love:* Backing Vocals
- *Dennis Wilson:* drums

See also

- List of songs by The Beach Boys

The Baker Man

"The Baker Man" is a song written by Brian Wilson. The song was recorded by the American pop band The Beach Boys although the song remained unreleased for many years. The song was eventually released on the re-release of the *Surfin' Safari/Surfin' USA* albums.

Details

- *Written by*: Brian Wilson
- *Album*: bonus track on *Surfin' Safari/Surfin' USA* 2fer
- *Time*: 2:36
- *Produced by*: Nik Venet
- *Recording date*: March 7, 1963

Musicians

- Mike Love - vocals
- David Marks - guitar
- Brian Wilson - bass guitar, lead vocal
- Carl Wilson - guitar, vocals
- Dennis Wilson - drums, vocals

See also

- List of songs by The Beach Boys

Ballad of Ole' Betsy

"**Ballad of Ole' Betsy**" is a song written by Brian Wilson and Roger Christian for the American pop band The Beach Boys and is notable for the barbershop-style, a cappella ending. It was released on their 1963 album *Little Deuce Coupe*. Interestingly, the ballad is a love song about a car rather than a person.

Details

- *Written by:* Brian Wilson/Roger Christian
- *Album:* Little Deuce Coupe
- *Time:* 2 min 15 sec
- *Produced by:* Brian Wilson

Performers

- *Brian Wilson:* Lead Vocals

See also

- List of songs by The Beach Boys

Barbara

"**Barbara**" is a song written by Dennis Wilson for the American pop band The Beach Boys. It was released on their 1998 album *Endless Harmony Soundtrack*.

Details

- *Written by:* Dennis Wilson
- *Album:* Endless Harmony Soundtrack
- *Time:* 2 min 58 sec
- *Produced by:* Brian Wilson

Performers

- *Dennis Wilson:* Lead Vocals

See also

- List of songs by The Beach Boys

Barbara Ann

"Barbara Ann"	
 single sleeve	
Single by The Beach Boys	
from the album *Beach Boys' Party!*	
B-side	"Girl Don't Tell Me"
Released	December 20, 1965
Format	Vinyl
Recorded	September 23, 1965
Genre	Rockabilly
Length	3:23 (LP) 2:05 (single)
Label	Capitol 5561
Writer(s)	Fred Fassert
Producer	Brian Wilson
The Beach Boys singles chronology	

"The Little Girl I Once Knew"/"There's No Other (Like My Baby)" (1965)	"Barbara Ann"/"Girl Don't Tell Me" (1965)	"Sloop John B"/"You're So Good To Me" (1966)

***Beach Boys' Party!* track listing**

- "Hully Gully"
- "I Should Have Known Better"
- "Tell Me Why"
- "Papa-Oom-Mow-Mow"
- "Mountain of Love"
- "You've Got to Hide Your Love Away"
- "Devoted to You"
- "Alley Oop"
- "There's No Other (Like My Baby)"
- "Medley:I Get Around/Little Deuce Coupe"
- "The Times They Are a-Changin'"
- "Barbara Ann"

"Barbara Ann" is a song written by Fred Fassert and performed (as "Barbara Anne") by The Regents in 1961. The recording reached a peak position of #13 on the *Billboard Hot 100 record chart.*

The most famous cover version is by the American pop band The Beach Boys. The song was released as a single on December 20, 1965, with the B-side "Girl Don't Tell Me". The song peaked at #2 in the U.S. *Billboard* Hot 100 (#1 in Cash Box and Record World) and at #3 in the U.K. It also topped the charts in Germany, Switzerland and Norway. It was The Beach Boys' biggest hit in Italy, reaching #4. The song was also released on the 1965 album *Beach Boys' Party!*. Brian Wilson and Dean Torrence, who had previously recorded the song as one half of Jan and Dean, are featured on lead vocals. Dean is not credited on the album jacket but "Thanks, Dean" is said by Carl at the end of the track.

A version recorded by the Beach Boys without the *Beach Boys' Party!* effects can be found on the *Hawthorne, CA* album. The Beach Boys made a false start on the *Party!* album by singing "Baa Baa Black Sheep" instead of "Baa Baa Baa Baa Barbara Ann". The Beach Boys sang this song as an encore on their *Live In London* album. Brian Wilson has a rendition on his live *Roxy* CD, and in 2001, performed it himself, with the ensemble, on *An All-Star Tribute to Brian Wilson.*

Beach Boys version

- Written by: Fred Fassert
- Album: *Beach Boys' Party!*
- Time: 3 min 23 sec
- Produced by: Brian Wilson

Performers

- Brian Wilson: Lead Vocals,Bass
- Dean Torrence: Lead Vocals
- Al Jardine: Backing Vocals,Guitar
- Bruce Johnston: Backing Vocals
- Mike Love: Backing Vocals
- Carl Wilson: Backing Vocals,Guitar
- Dennis Wilson: Backing Vocals

Use in pop culture

The Beach Boys appeared in the television series *Home Improvement* as cousins of the character Wilson. They perform "Barbara Ann" in Wilson's backyard. In episode of *Full House* called "Beach Boy Bingo" the Tanner family went to a Beach Boys concert and got to sing this song with them on stage.

The song was also covered by The Who (released in November 1966 on the *Ready Steady Who* 7" EP), sung by Keith Moon, and was a highlight of the film *The Kids are Alright*. Blind Guardian also covered the song on the album *Follow the Blind*.

In the late 1970s series *Welcome Back Kotter*, the character Vinnie Barbarino (John Travolta) sings a version with the lyrics "Baa-baa-baa Baa-Barbarino". The song featured in the 1973 film *American Graffiti*. In 1975, the Martin Cicus group performed a French version named "Marylène". This was in turn made into a jingle for Babybel cheese.

In the early 1990s television series *Saved by the Bell* episode "House Party" Zach, Slater and Screech lip-sync to the song while "cutting loose" at Screech's house when his parents are away on vacation. The song was featured during the 4th season episode, "My Ocardial Infarction", of the sitcom *Scrubs*, being sung by The Janitor's fake band, "Hibbleton". Brian Griffin mentions the song in the *Family Guy* episode "Ocean's Three and a Half". The song is also used as a plot point in the film Surf Ninjas.

The song was used as walk-on song for John McCain on the Late Night With Jimmy Fallon.[1]

Parodies

The song was later parodied as "Bomb Iran" by Vince Vance and the Valiants, written during the 1979 Iran hostage crisis.[2]

John McCain also parodied the song, briefly singing "Bomb, bomb, bomb, bomb, bomb Iran" in response to a question at a campaign stop on April 19, 2007.[3]

See also

- List of songs by The Beach Boys

References

[1] ?uestlove's "Late Night With Jimmy Fallon" Countdown (http://www.rollingstone.com/news/story/30970253/uestloves_late_night_with_jimmy_fallon_countdown/4). November 20, 2009. *CBSNews/AP*. Accessed 2010-01-25.

[2] Declain McCullagh (April 22, 2007). McCain's 'Bomb Iran' song was anti-Muslim? (http://www.news.com/8301-10784_3-9711370-7.html) *News.com*. Accessed 2007-11-05.

[3] McCain's "Bomb Iran" Joke Draws Fire (http://www.cbsnews.com/stories/2007/04/20/politics/main2709937.shtml). April 20, 2007. *CBSNews/AP*. Accessed 2007-11-05.

Barbie

"Barbie" is a song written by Bruce Morgan. After already having the instrumental track recorded, the vocals were recorded Feb. 8, 1962 by American pop band The Beach Boys during their early years as a recording group. The song was never released on any of the bands albums due to being part of the Hite Morgan sessions before they joined Capitol Records. Mike Love and Dennis Wilson were not available for the session. Audree Wilson provided backing vocals and Val Poliuto contributed the bass vocal.

See also

- List of songs by The Beach Boys

Be Here in the Mornin'

"Be Here in the Mornin'" is a song written by Brian Wilson, Carl Wilson, Dennis Wilson, Mike Love and Al Jardine for the American pop band The Beach Boys. It was released on their 1968 album *Friends*. The song was recorded in March, 1968. The lyrics "No calls from Korthof, Parks or Grillo" is referring to the Wilson brothers' cousin Steve Korthof, the Beach Boys road manager Jon Parks and the Beach Boys lawyer and business manager Nick Grillo. This song is a Waltz.

Details

- *Written by:* Brian Wilson/Carl Wilson/Dennis Wilson/Mike Love/Al Jardine
- *Album:* Friends
- *Time:* 2 min 16 sec
- *Produced by:* The Beach Boys

Performers

- *Brian Wilson:* Lead Vocals (on the intro, chorus)
- *Carl Wilson:* Lead Vocals (chorus)
- *Al Jardine:* Lead Vocals (verses, chorus)

See also

- List of songs by The Beach Boys

Be Still

"Be Still" is a song written by Dennis Wilson and Stephen Kalinich for the American pop band The Beach Boys. It was released on their 1968 album *Friends*. The song features Dennis Wilson on lead vocal. [1]

The song is an important part of Dennis Wilson's composing career as it is believed by many historians of the band, along with his song "Little Bird", to be his first real composition. The song undoubtedly gave confidence to Dennis as he began regularly composing songs in years to come, some of which are regarded amongst the groups best efforts of the period. The only other composition that Dennis had composed by himself was the drum solo "Denny's Drums" from the 1964 Beach Boys album *Shut Down Volume 2*.

"Be Still" was recorded in April 1968 at Brian's home studio and I.D. Sound studios. The song features a simple instrumental backing with Dennis' lead vocal assisting by his brother Carl. The song was once thought to be a song co-written with Charles Manson, though this of course is false. He did, however, co-write one of the later Dennis Wilson compositions, "Never Learn Not to Love".

See also

- List of songs by The Beach Boys

External links

- Free song downloads (including "Be Still") [2]

References

[1] http://www.secondhandsongs.com/performance/69410
[2] http://www.stephenkalinich.com/sjkdennis.html

Be True to Your School

"Be True to Your School"	
Single by The Beach Boys	
from the album *Little Deuce Coupe*	
Released	October 14, 1963
Format	Vinyl
Recorded	September 1963 (album) September 2, 1963 (single)
Genre	Surf rock
Length	2:09
Label	Capitol Records
Writer(s)	Brian Wilson and Mike Love
Producer	Brian Wilson

The Beach Boys singles chronology		
"Surfer Girl"/"Little Deuce Coupe" (1963)	"Be True to Your School"/"In My Room" (1963)	"Little Saint Nick"/"The Lord's Prayer" (1963)

"**Be True to Your School**" is a song by The Beach Boys. The album version of this song was recorded on Monday, September 2, 1963. It appears on *Little Deuce Coupe* and *Endless Summer*.

The song features the University of Wisconsin's fight song "On Wisconsin." However, it's most likely a tribute to Hawthorne High School, whose school fight song uses the same melody as "On Wisconsin," as briefly explained by Al Jardine in the documentary *The Beach Boys: An American Band.* (1984) The Wilson brothers and Beach Boy Al Jardine attended that school.

The song was written by Brian Wilson and Mike Love (as established by Mike's lawsuit gaining rights to several co-written songs of the 1960s), and was first recorded on Session 1 of the recording of their 1964 album *Little Deuce Coupe*. On that day, they recorded "Ballad of Ole' Betsy", a cute melody about a classic car, co-written by Brian Wilson and former DJ Roger Christian, automobile ballads "Car Crazy Cutie" and "Cherry, Cherry Coupe", "Spirit of America", "No-Go Showboat" and "A Young Man is Gone".

The Beach Boys recorded two studio versions of this song. The original recording, which appeared on the album, was in a higher key and at a slower tempo than the second version which was released as a single. The second version features The Honeys chanting various "cheerleader yells" before the first chorus, and after the second and third. The concept for the single version, recorded later that week, was born in the same studio session that Brian and

Mike created the original idea for "Fun, Fun, Fun", backstage in Farmington, Utah.

The single version was backed with "In My Room", a collaboration between Brian and Gary Usher, released as Capitol 5069 and charting at number 6 in *Billboard*, number 4 in the UPI chart survey for newspapers across the United States. It rated number 3 in New Zealand's Lever Hit Parade, number 6 in Sweden, and number 10 in Australia as cited by a contemporary issue of *Billboard*. Rising to popularity when the Beach Boys were still thought of as a Southern California phenomenon, it did best best in Los Angeles: three weeks at #1.

Though David Marks was later to appear on the cover of the album *Little Deuce Coupe*, he played little part, being replaced by Al Jardine. This album was shortly shipped off to disc jockeys in the United States, coupled with a list of automobile-related terms to get them familiar with the language used on the songs, such as "Shut Down" and "Little Deuce Coupe".

The song is featured in an episode of *Gilmore Girls*, where the town troubadour (portrayed by Grant-Lee Phillips) is playing it during a pep rally.

Be with Me

"**Be with Me**" is a song written by Dennis Wilson for the American pop band The Beach Boys. It was released on their 1969 album *20/20*. The song was recorded on November 11, 1968.

Details

- Written by: Dennis Wilson
- Album: *20/20*
- Time: 3:08
- Produced by: Dennis Wilson

Performers

- Dennis Wilson: Lead Vocals

See also

- List of songs by The Beach Boys

The Beach Boys Medley

"The Beach Boys Medley"	
Single by The Beach Boys	
Released	1981
Format	Vinyl
Genre	Pop
Length	4:05
Label	Capitol
Writer(s)	Brian Wilson, Mike Love, Roger Christian, Fred Fassert, Chuck Berry

The Beach Boys singles chronology		
"Livin' with a Heartache"/"Santa Ana Winds" (1980)	**"The Beach Boys Medley"**/"God Only Knows" (1981)	"Come Go with Me"/"Don't Go Near the Water" (1981)

"**The Beach Boys Medley**" is a single containing a medley of popular Beach Boys songs from the 1960s, edited by John Palladino. Released in mid-1981, it capitalized on a medley craze begun by the Stars on 45 medleys. "The Beach Boys Medley" reached number 12 on the *Billboard* Hot 100, becoming the band's highest charting hit in the U.S. in over five years.

Songs in the medley

In order, the songs of the medley include:

- "Good Vibrations"
- "Help Me, Rhonda"
- "I Get Around"
- "Shut Down"
- "Surfin' Safari"
- "Barbara Ann"
- "Surfin' USA"
- "Fun, Fun, Fun"

The first three songs in the medley represent, in reverse chronological order, the group's three number one hits on the U.S. Billboard Hot 100 pop singles chart at the time. All other songs in the medley reached at least the Top 5 on that chart with the exception of Surfin' Safari.

See also

- The Beach Boys
- List of The Beach Boys songs

Belles of Paris

"**Belles of Paris**" is a song written by Brian Wilson, Mike Love and Ron Altbach for the American pop band The Beach Boys. It was released on their 1978 album *M.I.U. Album*.

Details

- *Written by:* Brian Wilson/Mike Love/Ron Altbach
- *Album:* M.I.U. Album
- *Time:* 2 min 27 sec
- *Produced by:* Al Jardine/Ron Altbach

Performers

- *Mike Love:* Lead Vocals

See also

- The Beach Boys
- M.I.U. Album
- List of songs by The Beach Boys

Bells of Christmas

"Bells of Christmas" is a Christmas song written by Al Jardine, Ron Altbach and Mike Love. The song was recorded by the American pop band The Beach Boys and was released on their 1998 Christmas album *Ultimate Christmas*.

See also

- List of songs by The Beach Boys

Better Get Back in Bed

"**Better Get Back in Bed**" is the third track on the Mount Vernon and Fairway (A Fairy Tale) album. It was written by Brian Wilson for the American pop band The Beach Boys. The track features Jack Rieley on narration with Carl Wilson on lead vocals.

Details

- *Written by:* Brian Wilson
- *Album:* Mount Vernon and Fairway (A Fairy Tale)
- *Time:* 1 min 39 sec
- *Produced by:* The Beach Boys

Performers

- *Carl Wilson:* Lead Vocals

See also

- The Beach Boys
- Mount Vernon and Fairway (A Fairy Tale)
- List of songs by The Beach Boys

Blue Christmas

"**Blue Christmas**" is a Christmas song written by Billy Hayes and Jay W. Johnson. The heart-broken tale of unrequited love during the holidays had long been considered a Christmas staple of country music, having been recorded by Ernest Tubb in 1948. In 1957, Elvis Presley effectively made "Blue Christmas" a steadfast rock-and-roll holiday classic by recording it in his signature style. The song has since been recorded by a host of rock and country artists alike, as well as those of other genres. The song was also featured in the children's Christmas special, *The Year Without a Santa Claus*. More recently, the song has been covered by Céline Dion as well as the indie band Bright Eyes and Billy Idol in his 2006 Christmas album *Happy Holidays*.

Elvis Presley's famous recording of the song appeared on his 1957 LP *Elvis' Christmas Album*. It was also released as a single. Ernest Tubb's version of the song included an extra verse not used by Elvis' later version.

In 2009, Elvis' version was used in a TV commercial for Verizon Wireless.

Beach Boys version

"Blue Christmas"		
Single by The Beach Boys		
from the album *The Beach Boys' Christmas Album*		
Format	Vinyl	
Recorded	Unknown	
Genre	Pop music	
Length	4 min 41 sec for both songs	
Label	Capitol Records	
Producer	Brian Wilson	
The Beach Boys singles chronology		
"Dance, Dance, Dance"/"The Warmth of the Sun" (1964)	**"The Man with All the Toys"/"Blue Christmas"** (1964)	"Do You Wanna Dance?"/"Please Let Me Wonder" (1965)

The song was covered by the American pop band The Beach Boys. The song was released as the B-side of the "The Man with All the Toys" single on November 16, 1964; it charted at #3 in the U.S. Christmas charts but did not chart in the U.K. The song was also released on the bands 1964 album *The Beach Boys' Christmas Album* on the same day. The song featured Brian Wilson on lead vocals.

Details

- *Time:* 3 minutes, 9 seconds.
- *Produced by* Brian Wilson.

See also

- The Beach Boys
- The Beach Boys' Christmas Album
- List of songs by The Beach Boys

Blueberry Hill

"**Blueberry Hill**" is a popular song published in 1940. The music was written by Vincent Rose, the lyrics by Al Lewis and Larry Stock. It was recorded six times in 1940. Victor released the recording by the Sammy Kaye Orchestra with vocals by Tommy Ryan on May 31, 1940 (catalog #26643, with the flip side "Maybe"; matrix #51050[1]). Gene Krupa's version was issued on the Okeh label (#5672) on June 3. Other 1940 recordings were by: Glenn Miller on Bluebird (10768), Kay Kyser, Russ Morgan, Gene Autry (also in the 1941 film *The Singing Hill*[2]), Connee Boswell, and Jimmy Dorsey.[3] The largest 1940 hit was Glenn Miller.

Louis Armstrong's 1949 recording charted in the Billboard Top 40. It was an international hit in 1956 for Fats Domino, and has become a rock and roll standard. It reached number two, for three weeks on the Billboard Top 40 charts, becoming his biggest pop hit, and spent eight non-consecutive weeks at number one on the R&B Best Sellers chart[4] . The version by Fats Domino was also ranked #81 in Rolling Stone magazine's list of the 500 Greatest Songs of All Time.

Selected list of recorded versions

- Gene Autry (1941) (the original version, from the movie *The Singing Hill* (1941)
- Glenn Miller & His Orch. (vocal by Ray Eberle) (1941) (the most famous version in the 1940s)
- Russ Morgan & His Orch. (vocal by Carol Kay) (1941)
- Kay Kyser & His Orch. (vocal by Harry Babbitt) (1941)
- Louis Armstrong with Gordon Jenkins' Orchestra and Choir (1949) (with different lyrics)
- Fats Domino (1956)
- Elvis Presley (1957)
- Little Richard (1958)
- Ricky Nelson (1958)
- Andy Williams (1959)
- Duane Eddy (1959)
- Bill Haley & His Comets (1960)
- John Barry Orchestra (1960)
- Buster Brown (1960)
- Cliff Richard (1962)
- San Remo Golden Strings (1966)
- The Loved Ones Australia (1966)
- The Everly Brothers (1967)
- Led Zeppelin (1970) on the Led Zeppelin bootleg recording *Live On Blueberry Hill*.
- Freddy Fender (1970s)
- Jerry Lee Lewis (1973, Southern Roots)
- Ellen McIlwaine (1975)
- The Beach Boys (1976)
- Billy "Crash" Craddock (1977)
- Adriano Celentano (1977)
- Link Wray (1982)
- Jah Wobble (1982, Betrayal - The Legend Lives On)
- Yellowman (1987)
- Jean Shy & The Real Climax Band Cologne, on the CD "The Night Time Is The Right Time," released in Germany in 1995 on King Edward Records.
- Bruce Cockburn with Margo Timmins (1999)[5]

- Jimmy Clanton (2006, played in Boomtown Casino)
- Johnny Hallyday (2006, Flashback Tour)
- Elton John (2007, Goin' Home: A Tribute to Fats Domino)
- Frantisek Havlicek & Jan Jankeje (2007, Jazzpoint Records)
- The Rolling Stones [6]

In popular culture

- In the popular 1970s sitcom *Happy Days*, set in the 1950s, lead character Richie Cunningham, played by Ron Howard, would often sing "I found my thrill..." (the first line of Domino's 1950s version of "Blueberry Hill") in reference to pretty girls he dated or wanted to date.
- It is one of the songs that the time traveling James Cole enjoys in the film, *Twelve Monkeys*, and the song is later sung by the scientists upon his return to the future.
- The song is purportedly named after a "make-out" spot in Taos, New Mexico.

External links

- SongFacts: Blueberry Hill [7]
- "Blueberry Hill" [8] - Lead sheet at wikifonia.org

It is used in the movie "Animal Farm"

References

[1] Victor records in the 26500 to 26799 series (http://78discography.com/vic26500.html)
[2] http://www.imdb.com/title/tt0034192/
[3] http://www.originals.be/eng/main.cfm?c=t_upd_show&id=621
[4] Whitburn, Joel (2004). *Top R&B/Hip-Hop Singles: 1942-2004*. Record Research. p. 167.
[5] http://cockburnproject.net/songs&music/bh.html
[6] http://www.rollingstone.com/news/story/6595926/blueberry_hill
[7] http://www.songfacts.com/detail.php?id=2078
[8] http://www.wikifonia.org/node/2838

Bluebirds over the Mountain

"Bluebirds over the Mountain"		
Single by The Beach Boys		
from the album *20/20*		
Released	December 2, 1968	
Format	Vinyl	
Recorded	September 29, 1967 and November 14, 1968	
Genre	Pop, soul	
Length	2:51	
Label	Capitol	
Writer(s)	Ersel Hickey Producer = Bruce Johnston and Carl Wilson	
The Beach Boys singles chronology		
"Do It Again"/"Wake the World" (1968)	**"Bluebirds over the Mountain"**/"Never Learn Not to Love" (1968)	"I Can Hear Music"/"All I Want to Do" (1969)

"Bluebirds over the Mountain" is a song written by Ersel Hickey. This is perhaps his best known song. The song was covered by notable artists such as The Beach Boys and Ritchie Valens. The Echoes 1962 version hit Billboard's Bubbling Under The Top 100 survey and was a top 20 hit on Chicago's WLS.

Beach Boys version

"Bluebirds over the Mountain" was also covered by The Beach Boys and it was released on their 1969 album "20/20". It was also released as a single on December 2, 1968 with the B-side of the single being "Never Learn Not to Love". The single charted at #61 in the United States and at #33 in the United Kingdom. The song features Mike Love on lead vocals and it also features Ed Carter on guitar.

A big comedown from the Beach Boys' usual international impact in the Sixties (a No. 9 placing in Holland was its only real success), the single's low *Billboard* peak was somewhat softened by a No. 36 recognition in the *Record World* national Top 40. It punched above its weight in climbing well into the top twenties of Los Angeles, San Diego, Boston, Detroit, Minneapolis and Columbus.

Performers

- Mike Love: Lead vocals (verses, bridge)
- Carl Wilson: Lead vocals (chorus)
- Ed Carter: Electric lead guitar

Other covers

West Virginian horror punk band Blitzkid covered this song on their 2002 split, "Exhuming Graves And Making Dates".

See also

- List of The Beach Boys songs

Boogie Woodie

"Boogie Woodie" is a traditional instrumental song. It has been recorded by many artists. The American pop band The Beach Boys released a version of the song on their 1963 album *Surfer Girl*.

Details

- *Written by:* Traditional. Arranged by Brian Wilson
- *Album:* Surfer Girl
- *Time:* 1 min 56 sec
- *Produced by:* Brian Wilson

See also

- The Beach Boys
- Surfer Girl
- List of songs by The Beach Boys

Break Away

"Break Away"		
Single by The Beach Boys		
Released	June 23, 1969	
Format	Vinyl	
Recorded	March 31, 1969 and April 23, 1969	
Genre	Pop music and Rock music	
Length	2:56	
Label	Capitol Records	
Producer	Brian Wilson	
The Beach Boys singles chronology		
"I Can Hear Music"/"All I Want to Do" (1969)	"Break Away"/"Celebrate the News" (1969)	"Add Some Music to Your Day"/"Susie Cincinnati" (1970)

"Break Away" (occasionally listed as **Breakaway**) is a song recorded by The Beach Boys in 1969. Written by Brian Wilson his father, Murry Wilson, is credited as lyricist using the pseudonym Reggie Dunbar. Sometimes ranked as one of the band's stronger songs, it was a relatively unsuccessful single, charting at #63 in the US, but stronger abroad.

After the *Smiley Smile* sessions, Brian Wilson served as less of a band leader in the studio. Between *Surfer Girl* and the "Heroes and Villains" single, Brian was credited as producer; thereafter production credits were assigned to "The Beach Boys". "Break Away" was the last release (aside from the single "Cool, Cool Water") on which he was named as producer until "Child of Winter" in 1974.

"Break Away" features Carl Wilson singing verses (with Mike Love) and Al Jardine on the chorus. Initially, the song was planned to be released with Brian Wilson singing the first verse, as included on the 2001 compilation, *Hawthorne, CA*. Early stereo studio mixes of this title provide verification, but these remixes are illicit.

Brian has said that The Monkees inspired him to write this song.

Many commentators point out that the title of the song is a hidden message of relief, as The Beach Boys break away from Capitol records with their final single. Capitol had been under promoting The Beach Boys (not knowing how to transition them from a purely street-surf-summer band) and under documenting their sales. Having sued their record company, The Beach Boys were glad to break away from that relationship.

Single release

The "Break Away" single backed with "Celebrate The News" was released through Capitol Records in the United States in June 1969. It was the band's final single of the 1960s and indeed was the band's penultimate single with Capitol Records before moving on to Warner Brothers. The single peaked at the number 63 spot spot on the *Billboard* charts, and placed at number 35 in *Record World* and number 38 in *Cash Box*. The single was also released through Capitol Records in the same month in the United Kingdom. It was the band's final single of the 1960s in Britain. Capitol re-released the single in Britain in June 1975, although on that occasion the single failed to make any impact on the charts.

On regional US charts the single made the Beach Boys' weakest showing in major markets since the christmas single "The Man With All the Toys" five years earlier. Isolated, qualified success was seen in Columbus (#11), Calgary (#14) and Council Bluffs (#4). Settling on the bottom rung of top twenty in Los Angeles and Fresno, it made just the top thirty in Chicago, Sacramento, areas of New England, but failing entirely elsewhere. It apparently made few or no showings on playlists throughout the entire Southern United States.

The single fared much better in Britain, peaking at the number 6 position. It was number 10 in Malaysia and Ireland, number 17 in The Netherlands, number 20 in New Zealand, number 29 in Germany and number 38 in Canada. It would be the band's last single to chart in Germany until 1987.

"Break Away" did not appear on a regular Beach Boys LP. It made its album debut in 1975 as part of the *Spirit of America* compilation.

Brian's Back

"Brian's Back" is a song written by Mike Love for the American pop band The Beach Boys. The song was released on The Beach Boys' 1998 anthology album release *Endless Harmony Soundtrack*.

Details

- *Written by:* Mike Love
- *Album:* Endless Harmony Soundtrack
- *Time:* 4 min 07 sec
- *Produced by:* Phil Sandhaus/Michel Etchart

Performers

- *Mike Love:* Lead Vocals
- *Carl Wilson:* Lead Vocals

Bull Session with the "Big Daddy"

"Bull Session with the 'Big Daddy'" is the last track on the American pop band The Beach Boys 1965 album *The Beach Boys Today!*. The track is a recording of an informal interview of the Beach Boys by Earl Leaf. Al Jardine is not present during the interview, although the other four members are. Mike Love makes fun of Earl Leaf's name calling him "Earl Fig".

The album version, which is 2 minutes and 10 seconds long, is actually an excerpt from the interview which lasts 20 minutes and 12 seconds. It is unreleased but has been made available through bootlegs.

Details

- *Written by:* Brian Wilson/Carl Wilson/Dennis Wilson/Mike Love/Al Jardine
- *Album:* The Beach Boys Today!
- *Time:* 2 min 10 sec
- *Produced by:* Brian Wilson

See also

- List of songs by The Beach Boys

Busy Doin' Nothin'

"Busy Doin' Nothin'" is a song written by Brian Wilson for the American pop band The Beach Boys. It was released on their 1968 album *Friends*. This song is a Bossa Nova

Details

- *Written by:* Brian Wilson
- *Album:* Friends
- *Time:* 3 min 04 sec
- *Produced by:* The Beach Boys

Performers

- *Brian Wilson:* Lead Vocals

See also

- List of songs by The Beach Boys

Cabinessence

"Cabinessence"	
Song by The Beach Boys from the album *20/20*	
Released	February 10, 1969
Recorded	October 3, October 11, December 6, & December 27, 1966 November 20, 1968
Genre	Pop music
Length	3:34
Label	Capitol
Composer	Brian Wilson/Van Dyke Parks
Producer	Brian Wilson
Cover versions	
Brian Wilson	
***20/20* track listing**	
"Our Prayer" (11)	**"Cabinessence"** (12)

"Cabinessence" (alternately spelled **"Cabin Essence"**) is a song written by Brian Wilson and Van Dyke Parks for the American pop band The Beach Boys. It was released on their 1969 album *20/20*. It was originally intended for release on the 1967 album *Smile*, a project Wilson scuttled then resuscitated and finally released in 2004.

Brian Wilson claims that he and Van Dyke Parks wrote the song along with "Heroes and Villains" "Wonderful" and "Surf's Up" in a giant sandbox with a piano in it that Wilson had built in his living room. Perhaps the most notorious line from the song is "over and over, the crow cries uncover the cornfield" which allegedly caused Mike Love to question Van Dyke Parks' lyrics and the entire direction of the *Smile* project. The song contains a majestic Beach Boys harmony segment in which the group repeats the line "Who ran the iron horse?" presented in such a way that the group gives the impression of a locomotive.

An instrumental version can be found on the Beach Boys' 1993 *Good Vibrations* box set. The song was re-recorded by Brian Wilson's band and released on his 2004 version of *Smile*.

Details

- *Written by:* Brian Wilson/Van Dyke Parks
- *Album:* 20/20 / Smile
- *Time:* 3 min 34 sec
- *Produced by:* Brian Wilson

Performers

Beach Boys version

- Jimmy Bond, Jr. - upright bass
- James Burton - guitar
- Jesse Ehrlich - cello
- Carl Fortina - accordion
- Jim Gordon - drums, tambourine
- Al Jardine - vocals
- Armand Kaproff - cello
- Carol Kaye - bass guitar
- Mike Love - lead vocal
- Jay Migliori - saxophone
- Oliver Mitchell - trumpet
- Tommy Morgan - harmonicas
- Van Dyke Parks - harmonium
- Bill Pitman - guitar
- Lyle Ritz - upright bass
- Tommy Tedesco - guitar, bouzouki
- Brian Wilson - vocals
- Carl Wilson - guitar, lead vocal
- Dennis Wilson - vocals

Brian Wilson version

- Brian Wilson - lead vocals, keyboards
- Scott Bennett - vocals, keyboards
- Nelson Bragg - vocals, percussion
- Jeffery Foskett - vocals, guitar
- Probyn Gregory - vocals, banjo
- Jim Hines - drums
- Bob Lizik - bass
- Paul Mertons - saxophone, harmonica
- Taylor Mills - vocals, percussion
- Darian Sahanaja - vocals, keyboards
- Nick Walusko - vocals, guitar
- Stockholm Strings 'N' Horns

See also

- The Beach Boys
- 20/20
- Smile (Beach Boys album)
- Smile (Brian Wilson album)
- List of songs by The Beach Boys

California Calling

"California Calling" is a song written by Al Jardine and Brian Wilson for the American pop band The Beach Boys. It was released on their 1985 album *The Beach Boys*. Notable for drumming by Ringo Starr and strong backing vocals by Brian Wilson.

Details

- *Written by:* Al Jardine/Brian Wilson
- *Album: The Beach Boys*
- *Time:* 2:46
- *Produced by:* Steve Levine

Musicians

- John Alder - guitar
- Simon Humphrey - bass
- Al Jardine - guitar, lead vocal
- Bruce Johnston - vocals
- Steve Levine - synthesizer
- Julian Lindsay - organ
- Mike Love - lead vocal
- Ringo Starr - drums, timpani
- Brian Wilson - piano, keyboard, vocals
- Carl Wilson - vocals

See also

- The Beach Boys
- The Beach Boys (album)
- List of songs by The Beach Boys

California Dreamin'

"California Dreamin'"	
Single by The Mamas & the Papas	
from the album *If You Can Believe Your Eyes and Ears*	
Released	November 1965
Format	Vinyl record (7") 45 RPM
Recorded	1965
Genre	Pop rock, folk rock
Length	2:42
Label	Dunhill Records
Writer(s)	John Phillips, Michelle Phillips
Producer	Lou Adler
The Mamas & the Papas singles chronology	

"Go Where You Wanna Go" (1965)	**"California Dreamin'"** (1965)	"Monday, Monday" (1966)

"California Dreamin'" is a popular song by The Mamas & the Papas, first released in 1965. The song is #89 in *Rolling Stone*'s list of The 500 Greatest Songs of All Time.[1] The lyrics of the song are about a man in a cold winter landscape longing for the warmth of California.

History

According to John Phillips in a Bravo documentary, and Michelle Phillips in an NPR piece, the song was written in 1963 while they were living in New York. He dreamed about the song and woke her up to help him write it. At the time, the Phillipses were members of the folk group The New Journeymen which evolved into The Mamas & the Papas.

They earned their first record contract after being introduced to Lou Adler, the head of Dunhill Records, by the singer Barry McGuire. In thanks to Adler, they sang the backing vocals to "California Dreamin'" on McGuire's album *This Precious Time*. The Mamas and the Papas then recorded their own version, using the same instrumental backing track to which they added new vocals and an alto flute solo by Bud Shank. McGuire's original vocal can be briefly heard on the left channel at the beginning of the record, having not been completely wiped.[2] The single was released in late 1965 but it was not an immediate breakthrough. After gaining little attention in Los Angeles upon its release, Michelle Phillips remembers that it took a radio station in Boston to break the song nationwide.[3] By early 1966, the song peaked at #4 and stayed on the charts for 17 weeks.

Cover versions

Some high profile artists who have covered this song include The Beach Boys, America, (two versions), Wes Montgomery, Jose Feliciano (B-side on his 1968 hit single Light My Fire), The Carpenters, Four Tops, Bobby Womack, Queen Latifah, Wes Montgomery, George Benson, Eddie Hazel, Raquel Welch, and John Phillips without The Mamas & the Papas. House versions are also covered by Royal Gigolos, Benny Benassi and DJ Sammy. The John Mayer Trio covered California Dreamin' on the June 4, 2009 episode of The Tonight Show with Conan O'Brien. A more up tempo version was recorded by the Japanese punk band Hi-Standard. Their California Dreamin' EP was released on Fat Wreck Chords in 1996. The Kings Of Leon covered California Dreamin' on their live DVD titled Live at the O2 London, England recorded in June 2009 and released in November 2009.

The Beach Boys recorded a second version of "California Dreamin'" in 1986 for their greatest hits compilation *Made in U.S.A.*. It was produced by Terry Melcher and featured Roger McGuinn from The Byrds on 12-string guitar and John Phillips on saxophone. Michelle Phillips and McGuinn appear in the video. Denny Doherty was on the East coast and declined; Cass Elliot had died in 1974.

Use in media

The song is used repeatedly in the 1994 Wong Kar-Wai film *Chungking Express*, in which a character played by singer Faye Wong obsessively listens to it. The original song by The Mamas & the Papas was also used in the soundtrack on the Academy Award and Golden Globe-winning film Forrest Gump. A version by the band The Bald Eagles was used for the remake of the movie The Hills Have Eyes.

"California Dreamin'", as covered by Bobby Womack (1968), features prominently in 2009 British film *Fish Tank* by Andrea Arnold, where the main character Mia dances to it and uses it as her audition piece. The collection CD on which the song appears also plays a role, and is "The Best of Bobby Womack" (2008), on which "California Dreamin'" appears on track 17, as Mia requests at her audition.

The song was also used in the South Park episode 201.

External links

- NPR's "Present at the Creation" segment on the origins of the song [4]
- Technical article describing how California Dreamin' was originally mixed [5]
- Facts and discussion about the song [6]

References

[1] "The RS 500 Greatest Songs of All Time" (http://www.rollingstone.com/news/story/11028260/the_rs_500_greatest_songs_of_all_time/1). *Rolling Stone*. . Retrieved 2007-06-02.

[2] Rock Family Trees, BBC, interview with McGuire, 1999. McGuire's original harmonica solo can also just be made out under the flute solo.

[3] NPR : California Dreamin', Present at the Creation (http://www.npr.org/programs/morning/features/patc/californiadreamin/index.html)

[4] http://www.npr.org/programs/morning/features/patc/californiadreamin/

[5] http://mixonline.com/mag/audio_mamas_papas_california/

[6] http://www.songfacts.com/detail.php?id=2016

California Feelin'

"California Feelin'" is a song written by Brian Wilson and Stephen Kalinich in the early to mid 1970's - believed to be 1974 - that was originally intended to be recorded by The Beach Boys. Brian Wilson has quoted the song as being "a favorite of mine".

It was first recorded in November 1974 by Brian Wilson in a session that was engineered by Chuck Britz, although this version has not been released and has not surfaced among fans. This is said by Beach Boys insiders to be the last instance of Brian's "classic" voice before the more gruff tone as heard on *15 Big Ones*.

It was recorded again in 1978 by the Beach Boys with Carl Wilson and Bruce Johnston on lead vocal. This version has not been released, but has been bootlegged and traded among fans.

The song was later recorded by Brian Wilson's touring band. The song was released on the 2002 compilation album *Classics selected by Brian Wilson*.

See also

- List of songs by The Beach Boys

External links

- Free song downloads (including "California Feelin'") [1]

References

[1] http://stephenkalinich.com/sjkbrian.html

California Girls

"California Girls"	
Single by The Beach Boys	
from the album *Summer Days (And Summer Nights!!)*	
B-side	"Let Him Run Wild"
Released	July 12, 1965
Format	Vinyl
Recorded	track: April 6, 1965; Western Studios vocals: June 4, 1965; Columbia Records Studio
Genre	Sunshine pop
Length	2:38
Label	Capitol
Writer(s)	Brian Wilson/Mike Love
Producer	Brian Wilson

The Beach Boys singles chronology		
"Help Me, Rhonda"/"Kiss Me, Baby" (1965)	"**California Girls**"/"Let Him Run Wild" (1965)	"The Little Girl I Once Knew"/"There's No Other (Like My Baby)" (1965)

"**California Girls**" is a song written by Brian Wilson and Mike Love and recorded by The Beach Boys in 1965. It features contrasting verse-chorus form. The song was released as a single, reaching #3 on the *Billboard* Hot 100. It also appeared on the album *Summer Days (And Summer Nights!!)*. It is one of The Beach Boys' most famous songs and has been included on countless greatest hits compilations.

The song "California Girls" is part of the The Rock and Roll Hall of Fame's 500 Songs that Shaped Rock and Roll list.[1] In 2004, it was ranked #71 on *Rolling Stone*'s list of The 500 Greatest Songs of All Time.[2]

Recording

The music for the song came from Brian Wilson's first LSD experience. [3] According to Brian Wilson himself in the Beautiful Dreamer documentary, shortly after taking LSD, he ran up to a bedroom and hid under a pillow, shouting "I'm afraid of my mom, I'm afraid of my dad." Some time later he left the room and went to a piano. He started playing in the bass the B-F#-G# pattern over and over, and then added in the right hand after a few minutes a B chord, moving to an A chord. Within a half hour, he had come up with the "well east-coast girls are hip, I really dig the styles they wear" part of the song. The next day, he and Mike Love supposedly finished off the remainder of the song.

"California Girls" was the first Beach Boys recording to feature vocals from Bruce Johnston, who had joined the group to substitute for Brian Wilson on concert tours.

Cultural impact

In addition to reaching #3 in the US, other countries where the song was highly popular include Canada (#2 in RPMs national chart), Rhodesia (also #2), and Sweden (#6). It peaked at #8 in Australia, and in South Africa it made one of the Beach Boys' best-ever international showings, staying six weeks at No. 1. Radio plays of the song in the United States alone are said to total between four and five million to date, thus making it the Beach Boys' biggest royalty earner.

The song has been prominently referenced by other artists on more than one occasion. Most notably, the Beatles' "Back in the U.S.S.R." is considered an homage to the song.

A 1980s series of adverts for the former airline British Caledonian were another notable homage to the song, twisting the lines about California to become "I wish they all could all be Caledonian", in reference to the airline's flight attendants.

On her 2005 album, *All Jacked Up*, Gretchen Wilson (no relation to the Wilson brothers) performs a song composed with John Rich entitled "California Girls". Her song, a unique composition rather than a cover of the Beach Boys original, is instead a country-styled retort to Beach Boys song, featuring a chorus that asks, "ain't you glad we ain't all California girls?".

In Brian Wilson's 1998 concert *Live at the Roxy* he referred to "California Girls" as the theme song of The Beach Boys. Ricky Martin sang a cover version on *An All-Star Tribute to Brian Wilson*. The song has been also heard in the pre-title sequence of the James Bond movie (starring Roger Moore) , *A View to a Kill* in 1985.

This song can be heard at the beginning of *Rush Hour 2* where main characters Lee (played by Jackie Chan) and Carter (played by Chris Tucker) sing along to the song as it plays on the radio. In *Rush Hour 3*, Lee uses it as his ringtone when Carter calls him at the beginning, and later on in the movie a French performer sings the song on the street where Carter is eating dinner.

Principal Belding from *Saved by the Bell* tells Zack that it is his all time favourite song and walks off screen, humming the song.

The song was sampled by rapper Tyga in his demo song titled "California Girls".

In 2004 the song was covered for a Cotton commercial featuring mannequins.

Musicians

- Hal Blaine - drums
- Frank Capp - vibraphone
- Roy Caton - trumpet
- Jerry Cole - 12-string guitar
- Al de Lory - organ
- Steve Douglas - tenor saxophone
- Al Jardine - vocals
- Bruce Johnston - vocals
- Carol Kaye - bass guitar
- Mike Love - lead vocals
- Jay Migliori - baritone saxophone
- Jack Nimitz - bass saxophone
- Lyle Ritz - upright bass

- Howard Roberts - guitar
- Leon Russell - piano
- Billy Strange - tambourine
- Brian Wilson - vocals
- Carl Wilson - 12-string guitar, vocals
- Dennis Wilson - vocals

David Lee Roth cover

"California Girls"	
Single by David Lee Roth	
from the album *Crazy from the Heat*	
Released	1985
Format	CD single
Recorded	1985
Genre	Pop
Length	2:50
Label	Warner Bros.
David Lee Roth singles chronology	
"California Girls" (1985)	"Just a Gigolo"/"I Ain't Got Nobody" (1985)

"California Girls" was covered by Van Halen lead singer David Lee Roth on his 1985 EP *Crazy from the Heat* (with background vocals contributed by Beach Boy Carl Wilson along with Christopher Cross), and like the original it topped at #3 on the *Billboard* Hot 100.

Music video

The iconic music video for the cover, directed by Pete Angelus and David Lee Roth, was released in February, 1985.[4] Roth stars as a tour guide, showing tourists the beach and the obligatory swimsuit models. One of these tourists is notably played by Jane Leeves who went on to play *Frasier*'s Daphne Moon. The scenes follow the lyrics with bikini-clad women from all regions of the United States. An often imitated scene has Roth dancing down a sidewalk bordered by models frozen in mannequin poses. It was nominated for several 1985 MTV Video Music Awards. The video was parodied in the video for Dresden Dolls' "Shores of California".

See also

- List of songs by The Beach Boys

References

[1] Rock and Roll Hall of Fame "500 songs that shaped rock and roll" (http://www.rockhall.com/exhibithighlights/500-songs/)
[2] "The RS 500 Greatest Songs of All Time" (http://www.rollingstone.com/news/story/6595916/california_girls/1). *Rolling Stone*. . Retrieved 2008-06-19.
[3] Boucher, Geoff (2007-08-12). "'California Girls' The Beach Boys" (http://articles.latimes.com/2007/aug/12/entertainment/ca-socalsong12). Los Angeles Times. pp. F-4. . Retrieved 2008-08-17.
[4] www.mvdbase.com (http://www.mvdbase.com/video.php?id=24052)

California Saga: California

"California Saga: California"	
Single by The Beach Boys	
from the album *Holland*	
Released	April 16, 1973
Format	Vinyl
Recorded	Unknown
Genre	Pop
Length	3:21
Label	Brother Records
Producer	Al Jardine
The Beach Boys singles chronology	

"Sail On, Sailor"/"Only with You" (1973)	"California Saga: California"/"Funky Pretty" (1973)	"Child of Winter"/"Susie Cincinnati" (1974)

"California Saga: California" is a song written by Al Jardine for the American pop band The Beach Boys. It was released on their 1973 album *Holland*.

Issued internationally as a single in early 1973, and performed in the same loping country-shuffle beat, it garnered great reviews likening it to classic "California Girls" status. The song reached #84 in *Billboard*, but performed better in the UK (#37) and New Zealand (#15).

The version released as a single is a different mix to the album track.

Personnel

- Brian Wilson: lead vocals (on the intro)
- Mike Love: lead vocals
- Carl Wilson: backup vocals, guitar, piano
- Dennis Wilson: backup vocals
- Alan Jardine: backup vocals, guitar
- Blondie Chaplin: backup vocals, bass guitar
- Ricky Fataar: drums, percussion
- Daryl Dragon: Moog bass
- Bruce Johnston: backup vocals
- unknown horns

See also

- List of songs by The Beach Boys

California Saga: The Beaks of Eagles

"California Saga: The Beaks of Eagles" is a song written by Al Jardine and his wife, Lynda Jardine for the American pop band The Beach Boys, released on their 1973 album *Holland*. It is based on a poem by Robinson Jeffers. This song is a Psychedelic pop and Art rock.

Details

- *Written by:* Al Jardine/Robinson Jeffers/Lynda Jardine
- *Album:* Holland
- *Time:* 3 min 49 sec
- *Produced by:* Al Jardine

Performers

- *Al Jardine*: Acoustic Guitar, Backup and Harmony Vocals
- *Mike Love*: Lead Vocals
- *Carl Wilson*: Lead Guitar, Piano, Backup Vocals
- *Blondie Chaplin*: Bass Guitar, Backup Vocals
- *Ricky Fataar*: Drums, Flute, Backup Vocals
- *Dennis Wilson*: Percussion, Backup Vocals
- *Daryl Dragon*: Organ

Narration by Al Jardine and Mike Love

See also

- The Beach Boys
- Holland
- List of songs by The Beach Boys

Can't Wait Too Long

"Can't Wait Too Long"	
Song by The Beach Boys from the album *Smiley Smile/Wild Honey*	
Released	September, 1990
Recorded	1967–68
Genre	Pop
Length	5:33
Label	Capitol
Composer	Brian Wilson
Producer	Brian Wilson

"**Can't Wait Too Long**" is an unfinished song written by Brian Wilson for the American popular music group The Beach Boys. The song dates from 1967–68, but was only officially released in September 1990 via Capitol Records.

Music and lyrics

The track consists of an elaborate collection of vocal and instrumental tracks comparable to the group's earlier hit "Good Vibrations". It includes a main melody line played instrumentally without sung lyrics, plus several sections of chorus and a vocal middle section. There are very few lyrics. A lead vocal track can faintly be heard, although no mixes of this version featuring the lead vocal exist. The title phrase is sung several dozen times, sometime alternating with "been away too long". Elsewhere is a simple couplet: "I miss you darlin' / I miss you so hard".

Towards the end of the master outtake, there is a bass riff that had been labeled for years as an edit piece that is part of the "Heroes and Villains" suite—consult the *Smile* bootleg album, *Unsurpassed Masters Vol. 17*.

Releases

The song was eventually released in an unfinished form in September 1990, as a bonus track on a CD reissue compiling two Beach Boys albums onto one disc—*Smiley Smile/Wild Honey*.[1] A shorter form of the song was also released in June 1993 on the group's 5-disc anthology, *Good Vibrations: Thirty Years of The Beach Boys*.[2] On the latter version, we hear Brian instructing brother Carl on some other lyrics which were never recorded.

In May 2001, a 51 second a cappella version of the song was issued on disc two of the Beach Boys rarities compilation album, *Hawthorne, CA*.[3]

Solo version

An excerpt of "Can't Wait Too Long" appears on the Brian Wilson album *That Lucky Old Sun* released on Capitol Records, the Beach Boys' old record label, on 19 August 2008.[4]

References

[1] Eder, Bruce. "Review: *Smiley Smile/Wild Honey - The Beach Boys*" (http://www.allmusic.com/cg/amg.dll?p=amg&sql=10:kifuxql5ld0e). Macrovision Corporation. . Retrieved 23 August 2009.

[2] Unterberger, Richie. "Review: *Good Vibrations: Thirty Years of the Beach Boys - The Beach Boys*" (http://www.allmusic.com/cg/amg.dll?p=amg&sql=10:dnfixq8gldke). Macrovision Corporation. . Retrieved 23 August 2009.

[3] Bush, John. "Review: *Hawthorne, CA - The Beach Boys*" (http://www.allmusic.com/cg/amg.dll?p=amg&sql=10:3zfuxqq0ldke). Macrovision Corporation. . Retrieved 23 August 2009.

[4] Bush, John. "Review: *That Lucky Old Sun - Brian Wilson*" (http://www.allmusic.com/cg/amg.dll?p=amg&sql=10:3zfuxqq0ldke). Macrovision Corporation. . Retrieved 23 August 2009.

Car Crazy Cutie

"Car Crazy Cutie" is a song written by Brian Wilson and Roger Christian for the American pop band The Beach Boys. It was released on their 1963 album *Little Deuce Coupe*.

Around the same time that **"Car Crazy Cutie"** was recorded (August/September 1963), Brian used the same melody for a song, **"Pamela Jean"** he recorded with friends Bob Norberg, Dave Nowlen, and Richard Alarian as The Survivors. **"Pamela Jean"** by The Survivors is credited only to Brian Wilson, and was released on Capitol Records in January 1964.

Details

- *Written by:* Brian Wilson/Roger Christian
- *Album:* Little Deuce Coupe
- *Time:* 2 min 47 sec
- *Produced by:* Brian Wilson

Performers

- *Brian Wilson:* Lead Vocals

See also

- List of songs by The Beach Boys

Carl's Big Chance

"Carl's Big Chance" is an instrumental song written by Brian Wilson and Carl Wilson for the American pop band The Beach Boys. It was released on their 1964 album *All Summer Long*.

Details

- *Written by:* Brian Wilson/Carl Wilson
- *Album:* All Summer Long
- *Time:* 2 min 25 sec
- *Produced by:* Brian Wilson

See also

- The Beach Boys
- All Summer Long
- List of songs by The Beach Boys

Caroline, No

"Caroline, No"	
Single by Brian Wilson	
from the album *Pet Sounds*	
B-side	"Summer Means New Love"
Released	March 7, 1966
Format	Vinyl
Recorded	Western Studios January 31, 1966
Genre	Pop
Length	2:53
Label	Capitol 5610
Writer(s)	Wilson/Asher
Producer	Brian Wilson
Brian Wilson singles chronology	
— "Caroline, No"/"Summer Means New Love" (1966)	"Let's Go to Heaven in My Car"/"Too Much Sugar" (1988)

Pet Sounds track listing
• "Wouldn't It Be Nice"
• "You Still Believe in Me"
• "That's Not Me"
• "Don't Talk (Put Your Head on My Shoulder)"
• "I'm Waiting for the Day"
• "Let's Go Away for Awhile"
• "Sloop John B"
• "God Only Knows"
• "I Know There's an Answer"
• "Here Today"
• "I Just Wasn't Made for These Times"
• "Pet Sounds"
• "**Caroline, No**"

"**Caroline, No**" is a song written by Brian Wilson and Tony Asher, recorded during the *Pet Sounds* sessions. It was released as a solo Brian Wilson single in March 1966 in advance of the album's release. The single was only a modest success, reaching number thirty-two in the US national chart and No. 16 in Canada's RPM chart. Later in the year it appeared on a Beach Boys album as the thirteenth track on *Pet Sounds* despite no other members of the band appearing on the track.

Title and subject matter

The song may have been inspired by a former girlfriend of lyricist Tony Asher, who had moved to New York and cut her hair. In high school, Wilson became obsessed with Carol Mountain, a classmate and unrequited love interest.

The song was initially written as "Carol, I Know". When spoken, however, Brian Wilson heard this as "Caroline, No." After the confusion was resolved, the pair decided to keep the new title, feeling that it brought a poignant earnestness to the song's sad melody.

Recording

The song's backing track was recorded on January 31, 1966 at Western Recorders in Hollywood, Los Angeles, California. Wilson produced the session, with Chuck Britz as the engineer. As with the rest of the *Pet Sounds* backing tracks, Wilson employed players from a select group of southern California session musicians, who were later nicknamed The Wrecking Crew. None of the other Beach Boys appeared on the record. Wilson chose the session players because of their work with Phil Spector. Although The Wrecking Crew were primarily younger musicians, most were formally trained and already veterans of session playing.

For "Caroline, No", harpsichord and bass flutes accompany more typical pop/rock instrumentation in a sound that, like other compositions from this period, reflects a jazz influence. The percussive exchange that opens the song features a tambourine and a large empty water bottle from the studio, played either by drummer Hal Blaine or percussionist Frankie Capp.

After Brian Wilson's double-tracked vocals were overdubbed, the entire recording was sped up by a half step. This was done at the suggestion of Brian Wilson's father Murry. Although Murry was no longer managing the Beach Boys, it is often speculated that Brian Wilson was pressured into this decision. Brian, however, maintains that he preferred the "sweeter" sound of the sped-up version.

Brian later stated, "'Caroline, No' was my favorite on the album, the prettiest ballad I've ever sung. Awfully pretty song. The melody and the chords were like Glenn Miller...a Glenn Miller-type bridge. The fade-out was like a 1944 kind of record...Listen for the flutes in the fadeout."

On the *Pet Sounds* LP, the sound of a passing train can be heard at the end of "Caroline, No", accompanied by barking from Brian's dogs, Banana and Louie. In the late 1990s, it was "rediscovered" that the train sound effect came from a sound effects LP titled *Mister D's Machine*, recorded in 1963 by Brad Miller. The album featured then-current recordings of various trains around the Southern Pacific system. The sounds that were lifted for the end of the Pet Sounds album were that of Train #58, "The Owl", speeding through at 70 mph through Edison, California. The sound effects (minus Banana and Louie, of course) are in true stereo on the original effects album. They appeared in mono on *Pet Sounds*, but were not remixed into stereo with the rest of the album in 1996.

Single

"Caroline, No" was Brian Wilson's first solo single, released on Capitol Records as Capitol 5610 on March 7, 1966. Although Brian Wilson was the driving force behind The Beach Boys at the time, the solo release of "Caroline, No" was perhaps his first official recognition as an individual outside the band. However, it was also released on The Beach Boys' *Pet Sounds* album (as well as on subsequent Beach Boys compilation albums), where it is credited as a Beach Boys recording, even though Brian Wilson is the only Beach Boy performing on the record.

Recognition and influence

- The song was named at #211 in *Rolling Stone* magazine's list of The 500 Greatest Songs of All Time.[1]
- A song entitled "Caroline, Yes" appears on the Kaiser Chiefs' 2005 album *Employment* in reference to Brian Wilson's song.
- Neil Young mentions the song in his own composition "Long May You Run".
- They Might Be Giants have covered this song on their *Indestructible Object* EP.
- "Caroline Knows" by Splitsville from *The Complete Pet Soul* derives its title from this song.

Album appearances

The song's first album appearance was on The Beach Boys classic 1966 album *Pet Sounds*.

The song appears on several occasions from different stages of the recording process and in different formats on *The Pet Sounds Sessions* box set:

1. It appears on disc one in the first original stereo mix of the song.
2. On disc 2, the 'Caroline, No' highlights from tracking date appears, which documents the progress of the recording of the instrumental track of the song. This track goes for over four minutes.
3. Again on disc 2, the complete backing track is featured.
4. On disc 3, an A cappella (or vocals only) version of the song is featured.
5. A 32 second 'Caroline, No' promotional spot is featured on disc 3
6. Also on disc 3 appears the song in stereo at its original speed.
7. A second 'Caroline, No' promotional spot is also featured on disc 3 which goes for 28 seconds.
8. Lastly on disc 3 appears the song in mono at its original speed.
9. The song also appears on the bonus disc, disc 4, in its original mono mix.

A live version of the song also appears on the band's 1973 live album *The Beach Boys In Concert*, with Carl Wilson taking lead vocals.

Details

The track was recorded on January 31, 1966 at Western Recorders, Hollywood, California and was engineered by Chuck Britz. It was released as a single on March 7, 1966 under Capitol Records as single 5610. It entered Billboard "Hot 100" on March 26, 1966; remained on chart 7 weeks; peaked at #32 on April 30, 1966. The B-side of the single was "Summer Means New Love"

Performers

- *Brian Wilson:* Lead vocals
- *Hal Blaine:* drums
- *Frank Capp:* Vibraphone
- *Carol Kaye:* Electric bass
- *Glen Campbell:* Guitar
- *Barney Kessel:* Guitar
- *Lyle Ritz:* Ukelele
- *Al de Lory:* Harpsichord
- *Bill Green:* Flute
- *Jim Horn:* Flute
- *Plas Johnson:* Flute
- *Jay Migliori:* Flute

Overdub session

- *Hal Blaine:* Drums (in vamp)
- *Carol Kaye:* Electric Bass
- *Al de Lory:* Harpsichord
- *Steve Douglas:* Tenor saxophone

References

[1] "The RS 500 Greatest Songs of All Time" (http://www.rollingstone.com/news/story/6596056/caroline_no/1). *Rolling Stone*. . Retrieved 2008-06-19.

- *Wouldn't It Be Nice: Brian Wilson and the Making of the Beach Boys' Pet Sounds* by Charles L. Granata. Chicago Review Press, 2003.
- *Pet Sounds* reissue liner notes, written by Brad Elliott, 1999
- *Pet Sounds*, The Beach Boys (sheet music), Warner Bros. Publications, Miami, Florida, publication PF9805, published 1998

See also

- List of songs by The Beach Boys
- Greg Panfile's Musical Analysis of "Caroline, No" (http://www.cabinessence.net/essays/mob8.html)

Cassius Love vs. Sonny Wilson

"Cassius Love vs. Sonny Wilson"	
Song by The Beach Boys from the album *Shut Down Volume 2*	
Released	1964
Genre	Pop Surf rock
Length	3:30
Label	Capitol Records
Writer	Brian Wilson/Mike Love
Producer	Brian Wilson
***Shut Down Volume 2* track listing**	
• "Fun, Fun, Fun" • "Don't Worry Baby" • "In the Parkin' Lot" • "Cassius Love vs. Sonny Wilson" • "The Warmth of the Sun" • "This Car of Mine" • "Why Do Fools Fall in Love" • "Pom Pom Play Girl" • "Keep an Eye on Summer" • "Shut Down, Part II" • "Louie Louie" • "Denny's Drums"	

"**Cassius Love vs. Sonny Wilson**" is a song written by Brian Wilson and Mike Love for the American pop band The Beach Boys. It was released on their 1964 album *Shut Down Volume 2*. The song features Brian Wilson and Mike Love on lead vocals but all group members are featured in spoken word parts. In this skit, Brian and Mike make fun of each other with Mike singing his version of "Farmer's Daughter" and Brian singing his version of "Fun Fun Fun".

Performers

- Brian Wilson: Lead Vocals
- Mike Love: Lead Vocals

See also

- List of songs by The Beach Boys

A Casual Look

"A Casual Look" is a song written by Ed Wells and recorded by his group Six Teens on 1956.

Beach Boys version

The song was covered by the American pop band The Beach Boys. It was released on their 1976 album *15 Big Ones* with Mike Love and Al Jardine singing lead vocals.

Details

- *Written by:* Ed Wells
- *Album:* 15 Big Ones
- *Time:* 2 min 45 sec
- *Produced by:* Brian Wilson
- *Arranged by:* Brian Wilson

Performers

- *Mike Love:* Lead Vocals, Backing Vocals
- *Al Jardine:* Lead Vocals, Backing Vocals
- *Brian Wilson:* Backing Vocals, Piano
- *Carl Wilson:* Backing Vocals, Bass
- *Dennis Wilson:* percussion, drums
- *Ed Carter:* Guitar
- *Billy Hinsche:* Guitar
- *Steve Douglas:* Horns
- *Jay Migliori:* Horns

See also

- The Beach Boys
- 15 Big Ones
- List of songs by The Beach Boys

Sources

- *15 Big Ones* reissue liner notes, written by Dennis Diken, 2000.

Catch a Wave

"Catch a Wave"	
Song by The Beach Boys from the album *Surfer Girl*	
Released	September 16, 1963
Recorded	Summer 1963 Western Studios
Genre	Surf music
Length	2:11
Label	Capitol
Composer	Brian Wilson Mike Love
Producer	Brian Wilson
***Surfer Girl* track listing**	
"Surfer Girl" (1) "**Catch a Wave**" (2) "The Surfer Moon" (3)	

"**Catch a Wave**" is a song written by Brian Wilson and Mike Love for the American singing group, The Beach Boys. It was released on their 1963 album *Surfer Girl*. This song was recorded on July 14 and 16, 1963. This song is notable for the use of a harp played by Mike Love's sister, Maureen. The lead vocal was originally thought to be Dennis Wilson's, but in actuality, it is that of Mike Love with a heavy cold.

The album track was re-released in 1968, minus vocals, for the sing-along *Stack-O-Tracks* album, which features all-instrumental versions of original Beach Boys recordings. In the liner notes for both CD versions of the albums the song appears on, Brian Wilson observes that "'Catch a Wave' was more rhythmic. The guitars (Carl Wilson and David Marks) were more clean and driving as if to say they didn't wanna stop. The piano was played by me and it was perfectly synchronized with the guitars. The 3 different sounds combined to make one unique sound. I was ecstatic about this."

As Al Jardine performs on bass and sings on the track, "Catch a Wave" is an example of the six-man lineup the band had at times in the summer and fall of 1963, prior to Marks' quitting the Beach Boys late in the year.

Despite never being released as a single, the track was included on the greatest-hits 1974 *Endless Summer* album that revived the commercial sales of the band. The track is also featured in the 1993 box set *Good Vibrations: Thirty Years of the Beach Boys* in a version that is about 11 seconds longer due to the 'fade' coming after the refrain is sung four times, not two, as is the case with the original releases.

Details

- Written by: Brian Wilson/Mike Love
- Album: *Surfer Girl*
- Time: 2 min 07 sec
- Produced by: Brian Wilson
- Recording date: July 14, 1963 & July 16, 1963

Musicians

- Al Jardine - bass guitar, vocals
- Maureen Love - harp
- Mike Love - lead vocal
- David Marks - guitar, vocals
- Brian Wilson - organ, piano, lead vocal
- Carl Wilson - guitar, vocals
- Dennis Wilson - drums, vocals

Other recordings

Al Jardine released a live version of "Catch a Wave" on his *Live in Las Vegas* album.

Jan and Dean re-worked the lyrics of this surfing song to become a song about skateboarding and called "Sidewalk Surfin'". It was released as a single in 1964 and charted at #25 in *Billboard*.

See also

- The Beach Boys
- Surfer Girl
- List of songs by The Beach Boys

Celebrate the News

"Celebrate the News"	
Single by The Beach Boys	
Released	June 23, 1969
Format	Vinyl
Recorded	February 25, 1969
Genre	Pop music
Length	3:07
Label	Capitol Records
Producer	The Beach Boys

The Beach Boys singles chronology		
"I Can Hear Music"/"All I Want to Do" (1969)	"Break Away"/"**Celebrate the News**" (1969)	"Add Some Music to Your Day"/"Susie Cincinnati" (1970)

"**Celebrate the News**" is a song written by Dennis Wilson and Gregg Jakobson for the American pop band The Beach Boys. It was originally only released as the B-side of the "Break Away" single on June 23, 1969. Since then the song has been issued as a bonus track on the re-release of the *Friends/20/20* two-LP-on-one-CD format in 1990. The song was recorded February 25, 1969

Details

- Written by: Dennis Wilson/Gregg Jakobson
- Album: re-released on *Friends/20/20* two-LP-on-one-CD format
- Time: 3 min 07 sec
- Produced by: The Beach Boys

Performers

- *Dennis Wilson:* Lead Vocals

See also

- List of songs by The Beach Boys

Chapel of Love

"Chapel of Love"	
Single by The Dixie Cups	
Released	1964
Label	Red Bird Records
Writer(s)	Jeff Barry, Ellie Greenwich and Phil Spector
Producer	Joe Jones

"**Chapel of Love**" is a song written by Jeff Barry, Ellie Greenwich and Phil Spector, and made famous by The Dixie Cups in 1964, spending three weeks at number one on the Billboard Hot 100. There have also been many other versions of this song. This was also the debut release of the new Red Bird Records run by Jerry Leiber and Mike Stoller along with George Goldner.

Dixie Cups version

The song tells of the happiness and excitement the narrator feels on her wedding day, for she and her love are going to the "chapel of love," and "we'll never be lonely anymore."

Previously recorded by The Ronettes and The Blossoms, the definitive version of the song was recorded by the Dixie Cups in 1964.

Although "many have been quite annoyed by the sing-songy, cloying, childish quality",[1] the song was ranked #279 on Rolling Stone's list of the 500 Greatest Songs of All Time, being the group's only song on the list.

This version was heard on the soundtrack to films ranging from *Full Metal Jacket* to *Father of the Bride*

Bette Midler version

Bette Midler featured "Chapel of Love" on her 1972 debut album, *The Divine Miss M*. The following year, Midler included her version as the B-side of her #40 Pop single, "Friends" (the single charted on the Billboard Hot 100 as a double A-side).

Beach Boys version

The song was covered by the American pop group, The Beach Boys. It was released on their 1976 album, *15 Big Ones*.

- *Time:* 2 min 34 sec
- *Produced by:* Brian Wilson
- *Arranged by:* Brian Wilson

- *Brian Wilson:* Lead Vocals, Backing Vocals, String Ensemble, Piano, Moog Bass
- *Mike Love:* Backing Vocals
- *Carl Wilson:* Guitar
- *Dennis Wilson:* drums
- *Al Jardine:* Backing Vocals

- *Steve Douglas:* Saxophone
- *Jack Nimitz:* Saxophone
- *Mike Altschol:* Saxophone
- *Dennis Dreith:* Saxophone
- *John J. Kelson Jr.:* Saxophone
- *Carol Lee Miller:* Auto Harp
- *Gene Estes:* percussion

Elton John version

This song was also covered by Elton John for the soundtrack of *Four Weddings and a Funeral*.

References

[1] (http://www.allmusic.com/cg/amg.dll?p=amg&sql=33:kcfyxc8rldse)

Cherry, Cherry Coupe

"Cherry, Cherry Coupe" is a song written by Brian Wilson and Roger Christian for the American pop band The Beach Boys. It was released on their 1963 album *Little Deuce Coupe*. An earlier unreleased version of this song called Land Ahoy was in the 1990s released on the Surfin' Safari/Surfin' U.S.A. twofer as a bonus track. That song had completely different lyrics.

Details

- *Written by:* Brian Wilson/Roger Christian
- *Album:* Little Deuce Coupe
- *Time:* 1 min 47 sec
- *Produced by:* Brian Wilson

Performers

- *Mike Love:* Lead Vocals

See also

- The Beach Boys
- Little Deuce Coupe
- List of songs by The Beach Boys

Child of Winter

"Child of Winter (Christmas Song)/Susie Cincinnati"	
Single by The Beach Boys	
Released	December 23, 1974
Format	Vinyl
Recorded	November 18, 1974
Genre	Rock music
Length	2:50
Label	Brother Records/Reprise (1321)
Writer(s)	Brian Wilson/Steve Kalinich
Producer	Brian Wilson

The Beach Boys singles chronology		
"California Saga: California"/"Funky Pretty (1973)	"Child of Winter (Christmas Song)"/"Susie Cincinnati" (1974)	"Sail On, Sailor"/"Only with You" (1975)

"Child of Winter (Christmas Song)" is a Christmas song written by Brian Wilson and Stephen Kalinich. The song was recorded by the American pop band The Beach Boys and was released as a single in 1974 backed with Susie Cincinnati (and with Good Vibrations in some other countries such as France). It was the only Beach Boys single between the albums *Holland* and *15 Big Ones*. It was re-released on their 1998 Christmas album *Ultimate Christmas*.

Performers

- *Mike Love:* Lead Vocals
- *Brian Wilson:* Spoken Word

See also

- List of songs by The Beach Boys

Christmas Day

"Christmas Day" is a song written by Brian Wilson for the American pop band The Beach Boys. It was released on their 1964 album *The Beach Boys' Christmas Album*.

Details

- *Written by:* Brian Wilson
- *Album:* The Beach Boys' Christmas Album
- *Time:* 1 min 47 sec
- *Produced by:* Brian Wilson

Performers

- *Al Jardine:* Lead Vocals, Bass Guitar
- *Mike Love:* Harmony Vocals
- *Brian Wilson:* Harmony Vocals, Electric Organ
- *Carl Wilson:* Harmony Vocals, Guitar
- *Dennis Wilson:* Harmony Vocals, Drums

Note: The above list of performers is assumed from the fact that this track was recorded on the same day as *The Man With All The Toys* and *Santa's Beard*, both of which featured The Beach Boys playing the instruments instead of *The Wrecking Crew*.

See also

- List of songs by The Beach Boys

Christmas Time Is Here Again

"Christmas Time Is Here Again" is an adaptation of the Buddy Holly song "Peggy Sue", originally written by Holly with Jerry Allison and Norman Petty. Al Jardine of The Beach Boys rearranged the song for the American pop band The Beach Boys and the song was released on their 1998 Christmas album *Ultimate Christmas*.

See also

- List of songs by The Beach Boys

Chug-A-Lug

"Chug-A-Lug" is a song written by Brian Wilson, Gary Usher and Mike Love for the American pop band The Beach Boys. It was released on their 1962 album *Surfin' Safari*. The lyrics of the song are about the members of the band hanging out at a root beer stand and drinking mugs of root beer.

The song was originally credited to just Wilson and Usher. Mike Love's name was added as a result of a lawsuit filed by him against Wilson in the 1990s.

Details

- *Written by:* Brian Wilson/Gary Usher/Mike Love
- *Album:* Surfin' Safari
- *Time:* 1 min 59 sec
- *Produced by:* Nick Venet
- *Recording date:* August 8, 1962

Musicians

- Mike Love - lead vocal
- David Marks - guitar
- Brian Wilson - bass guitar, organ, vocals
- Carl Wilson - guitar, vocals
- Dennis Wilson - drums, vocals

See also

- The Beach Boys
- Surfin' Safari
- List of songs by The Beach Boys

Cindy, Oh Cindy

"**Cindy, Oh Cindy**" is a song written by Robert Nemiroff and Burt D'Lugoff[1] [2] and credited to Robert Barron and Burt Long.

The song was originally recorded in 1956 by Vince Martin and The Tarriers, and quickly covered by Eddie Fisher. Both versions made the charts that year.

The song was covered by the American pop band The Beach Boys in 1962 although the song remained unreleased for many years. The song was eventually released on the re-release of the *Surfin' Safari/Surfin' USA* albums.

Other versions have been recorded by Tony Brent, by Perry Como, by The Highwaymen, and by Waylon Jennings.

The Beach Boys' version

- *Written by*: Robert Barron/Burt Long
- *Album*: bonus track on *Surfin' Safari/Surfin' USA* 2fer
- *Time*: 2:11
- *Produced by*: Nik Venet
- *Recording date*: September 13, 1962

Musicians

- Mike Love - vocals
- David Marks - guitar
- Brian Wilson - bass guitar, vocals
- Carl Wilson - guitar, vocals
- Dennis Wilson - drums, vocals

See also

- List of songs by The Beach Boys

References

[1] "Folk Era Records: The Tarriers" (http://www.folkera.com/Tarriers/bio.html). 2001-07. . Retrieved 2010-01-24.

[2] "You Can't Do That on Broadway!: A Raisin in the Sun and Other Theatrical Improbabilities, by Philip Rose" (http://books.google.com/books?id=aIiCEzvygpIC&pg=PA181&lpg=PA181&dq="cindy+oh+cindy"+nemiroff&source=bl&ots=drY0Lb_Qza&sig=GaLuPZ5QdCdKzq_ZoUtlR7JNL8o&hl=en&ei=LHJTS5LpNIyylAeA0YmrCg&sa=X&oi=book_result&ct=result&resnum=2&ved=0CA0Q6AEwATgK#v=onepage&q="cindy oh cindy" nemiroff&f=false). 2001. . Retrieved 2010-01-24.

Come Go with Me

"Come Go with Me"	
Single by The Del-Vikings	
Released	1956
Format	7" (45 rpm)
Genre	Doo-wop
Label	Dot Records
Writer(s)	Clarence Quick

"**Come Go with Me**" is a song written by C. E. Quick (aka Clarence Quick), an original member of the American doo-wop vocal group The Del-Vikings. The song was originally recorded by The Del-Vikings in 1956 and was released on Fee Bee Records. When the group signed with Dot Records in 1957, the song became a hit, peaking at #4 on the *Billboard* Hot 100 chart[1] and becoming the group's highest-charting song. The song was later featured in the films *American Graffiti* (1973) and *Stand by Me* (1986).

"Come Go with Me" was later covered by the American pop band The Beach Boys and was included on their 1978 album, *M.I.U. Album*. Although not released as a single at the time, the song was included on a Beach Boys compilation album, *Ten Years of Harmony*, in 1981. This version was then released as a single to promote the compilation album, and it then rose to #18 on the *Billboard* Hot 100 chart in January 1982.[2]

In 2004, *Rolling Stone* magazine ranked the song #441 on its list of The 500 Greatest Songs of All Time.

Trivia

- The song bears a noticeable resemblance to the 1954 hit "Oop Shoop" by Shirley Gunter and the Queens, especially in two crucial hooks: the end of the bridge melody and the backing vocal riff at the end of the choruses.
- When Paul McCartney saw John Lennon for the first time in 1957, Lennon was performing this song with his band the Quarrymen. According to McCartney's recollection in the *Beatles Anthology*, Lennon, who did not recall much of the song's lyrics, inserted lyrics from blues songs (including the line, "Down, down down to the penitentiary.")
- The sit-com *Saved By the Bell* also covered this song when Zack Morris and the gang performed this song at The Max, their local hangout.
- In 2007, the British newspaper *Liverpool Echo* released a one-off music magazine, *Sound 08*. Given away free was a CD containing The Coral covering the track.
- Sha Na Na, a '60s rock and roll revival act, sang *Come Go with Me* live at the Woodstock Festival in the summer of 1969.

References

[1] Whitburn, Joel (2004). *The Billboard Book of Top 40 Hits*, 8th Edition (Billboard Publications), page 172.
[2] Whitburn, Joel (2004). *The Billboard Book of Top 40 Hits*, 8th Edition (Billboard Publications), page 51.

Cool, Cool Water

"Cool, Cool Water"	
Single by The Beach Boys	
from the album *Sunflower*	
Released	February, 1971
Format	Vinyl
Recorded	July 1970
Genre	Pop
Length	5:03
Label	Brother Records/Reprise Records
Producer	Brian Wilson

The Beach Boys singles chronology		
"Tears in the Morning"/"It's About Time" (1970)	"Cool, Cool Water"/"Forever" (1971)	"Wouldn't It Be Nice (live)" (1971)

"Cool, Cool Water" is a song written by Brian Wilson and Mike Love for the American pop band The Beach Boys. Originating from the 1966/67 Smile sessions, it was eventually released in its final form on their 1970 album *Sunflower*. It was also released as an edited single, with the B-side of the single being "Forever". The single never charted in the U.S. or in the U.K. The single edit was released in 2007, on the group's *The Warmth of the Sun* compilation.

Performers

- *Brian Wilson:* Lead Vocals
- *Mike Love:* Lead Vocals

See also

- List of songs by The Beach Boys

Cotton Fields

"**Cotton Fields**" is a song written by blues musician Huddie Ledbetter, better known as Lead Belly. It was also a #13 pop hit for The Highwaymen in 1961.

The song mentions that the fields are "down in Louisiana, just about a mile from Texarkana". This is geographically impossible, as Texarkana is about 30 miles north of the Louisiana border.[1] While the meaning of the name is clear – a portmanteau of Texas and Arkansas, it must be noted that Louisiana represents the ANA in (TEX ARK ANA) – the actual origin is that when surveyors first surveyed the land they thought that the city would also be on the border of Louisiana. See Texarkana, History Section [2]

Beach Boys version

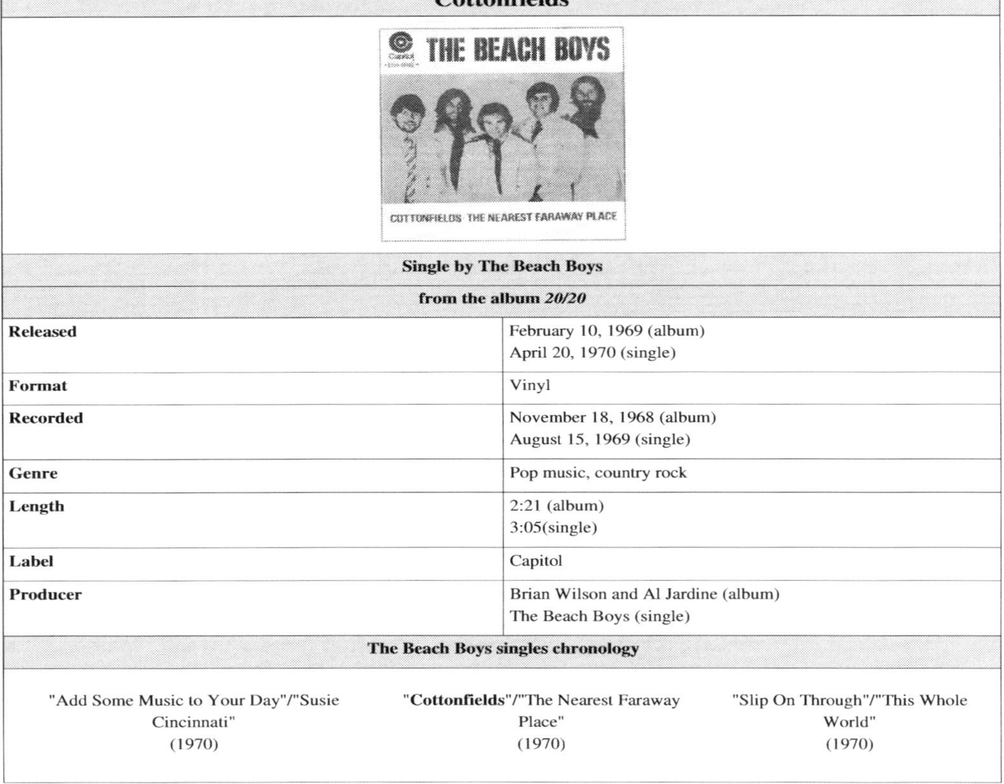

"Cottonfields"	
Single by The Beach Boys	
from the album *20/20*	
Released	February 10, 1969 (album) April 20, 1970 (single)
Format	Vinyl
Recorded	November 18, 1968 (album) August 15, 1969 (single)
Genre	Pop music, country rock
Length	2:21 (album) 3:05(single)
Label	Capitol
Producer	Brian Wilson and Al Jardine (album) The Beach Boys (single)

The Beach Boys singles chronology

"Add Some Music to Your Day"/"Susie Cincinnati" (1970)	"**Cottonfields**"/"The Nearest Faraway Place" (1970)	"Slip On Through"/"This Whole World" (1970)

American rock band The Beach Boys covered "Cotton Fields" in 1968. It was released on their 1969 album *20/20* with Al Jardine on lead vocals. The song was recorded on November 18, 1968.

Dissatisfied with Brian Wilson's arrangement, Jardine later led the group to record a more country-rock style version. The remake was recorded on August 15, 1969, with Orville "Red" Rhodes on steel pedal guitar. Released as

"Cottonfields", this remake, while not a hit in the U.S., was a Top 10 song around the world in the spring and summer of 1970. It was the group's last single for Capitol Records and the last released in mono.

While barely making a dent in the U.S. (#95 Record World, #103 *Billboard*) though promoted with an appearance on the network TV pop show *Something Else*, the song succeeded across the Atlantic, reaching number two in the UK's *Melody Maker* chart and listed as the tenth biggest seller of the year by the *New Musical Express*. Worldwide — outside North America — it virtually replicated the success of the group's "Do It Again" two years before. It was number 1 in Australia, South Africa, Sweden and Norway, number 2 in Denmark, number 3 in Ireland, similarly top 5 in Japan, Spain and Rhodesia; number 12 in Holland, number 13 in New Zealand and number 29 in Germany. Because of this popularity, it was placed on the international release of the group's *Sunflower* album.

Details

- *Album:* 20/20
- *Time:* 2 minutes 21 seconds (album version), 3 minutes 05 seconds (single version)
- *Produced and Arranged by:* Brian Wilson (album version)
- *Produced by:* The Beach Boys
- *Arranged by:* Al Jardine (single version)

Performers

- Al Jardine: Lead Vocals

Cover versions

- Creedence Clearwater Revival on their (1969) album *Willy and the Poor Boys*. This version hit #1 in Mexico in 1970.
- Esther Ofarim sang "Cottons Fields" live on television in 1969, with her then husband Abi Ofarim. They also recorded a German version, "Wenn ich bei Dir sein kann" in 1964.
- Elton John on *Reg Dwight's Piano Goes Pop*
- Harry Belafonte on his 1958 album *Belafonte Sings the Blues* and his 1959 album *Belafonte at Carnegie Hall*, attributing the song to C. C. Carter
- Harry Dean Stanton, in one scene of the film *Cool Hand Luke*, plays a sped-up version.
- Johnny Cash on his album *The Sound of Johnny Cash*
- Johnny Mann Singers on the album *Golden Folk Song Hits* - Liberty LST-7253
- New Christy Minstrels on the album *Chim-Chim-Cheree* - Columbia CS-9169
- Odetta on her 1963 album *One Grain Of Sand*
- Odetta and Larry on their 1954 album *The Tin Angel*
- Petula Clark in French as "L'enfant do" on a French EP released by Disques Vogue
- The Pogues on their 1989 album *Peace and Love* (while this version references the original in its lyrics, the song itself is not a cover per se)
- The Seekers on their 1964 album *The Seekers* (also known as *Roving With The Seekers*).
- Teresa Brewer on *The Muppet Show*
- The Springfields known as the launch pad for singer Dusty Springfield for a 1962 EP, their version is featured on the CD *On An Island Of Dreams: The Best Of The Springfields*.

Spanish version

The melody of "Cotton Fields" is also used in the Mexican song "Cuando Yo Era Jovencito" by Los Apson and Ramón Ayala.

References

[1] http://www.mapquest.com/maps?1s=LA&1y=US&1l=31.07095&1g=-92.0028&1v=STATE&2c=Texarkana&2s=TX&2y=US&2l=33.424999&2g=-94.047501&2v=CITY#a/maps/l::US-71:Doddridge:AR::US:33.024314:-93.892311:::1/l:::Texarkana:TX::US:33.424999:-94.047501:city::1/m:::::0:::::::::/io:1:::::f:EN:M:/e
[2] http://en.wikipedia.org/wiki/Texarkana

Country Air

"Country Air" is a song written by Brian Wilson and Mike Love for the American pop band The Beach Boys. It was released on their 1967 album *Wild Honey*.

Details

- Written by: Brian Wilson/Mike Love
- Album: *Wild Honey*
- Time: 2 min 20 sec
- Produced by: The Beach Boys

See also

- List of songs by The Beach Boys

County Fair

"County Fair"	
Single by The Beach Boys	
from the album *Surfin' Safari*	
Released	November 19, 1962
Format	Vinyl
Recorded	September 5, 1962
Genre	Rock
Length	3 min 41 sec for both songs
Label	Capitol Records
Producer	Nik Venet
The Beach Boys singles chronology	

"409"/"Surfin' Safari" (1962)	"Ten Little Indians"/"County Fair" (1962)	"Surfin' USA"/"Shut Down" (1963)

"County Fair" is a song written by Brian Wilson and Gary Usher for the American pop band The Beach Boys. It was released on their 1962 album *Surfin' Safari*. The melody was later recycled into the song I Do.

Details

- *Written by:* Brian Wilson/Gary Usher
- *Album:* Surfin' Safari
- *Time:* 2 min 15 sec
- *Produced by:* Nick Venet

Musicians

- Andrea Carlo - voice of girlfriend
- Mike Love - vocals
- David Marks - guitar
- Nik Venet - carnival barker
- Brian Wilson - bass guitar, organ, vocals
- Carl Wilson - guitar, vocals
- Dennis Wilson - drums, vocals

See also

- The Beach Boys
- Surfin' Safari
- List of songs by The Beach Boys

Crack at Your Love

"Crack at Your Love" is a song written by Al Jardine and Brian Wilson for the American pop band The Beach Boys. It was released on their 1985 album *The Beach Boys*.

Details

- *Written by:* Al Jardine/Brian Wilson
- *Album: The Beach Boys*
- *Time:* 3:36
- *Produced by:* Steve Levine

Musicians

- Al Jardine - lead vocal
- Bruce Johnston - vocals
- Steve Levine - synthesizer, drum programming
- Mike Love - vocals
- George McFarlaine - bass guitar
- Ian Ritchie - lyricon
- Brian Wilson - keyboards, lead vocal
- Carl Wilson - vocals

See also

- The Beach Boys
- The Beach Boys (album)
- List of songs by The Beach Boys

Cuckoo Clock

"Cuckoo Clock" is a song written by Brian Wilson and Gary Usher for the American pop band The Beach Boys. It was released on their 1962 album *Surfin' Safari*. The song was written about the myna bird of Brian's father Murry Wilson.

Details

- *Written by:* Brian Wilson/Gary Usher
- *Album:* Surfin' Safari
- *Time:* 2 min 08 sec
- *Produced by:* Nick Venet
- *Recording date*: September 6, 1962

Musicians

- Mike Love - vocals
- David Marks - guitar
- Brian Wilson - bass guitar, lead vocal
- Carl Wilson - guitar, vocals
- Dennis Wilson - drums, vocals

See also

- The Beach Boys
- Surfin' Safari
- List of songs by The Beach Boys

Cuddle Up

"Cuddle Up"	
Single by The Beach Boys	
from the album *Carl and the Passions - "So Tough"*	
Released	May 15, 1972
Format	Vinyl
Recorded	Unknown
Genre	Rock and Pop ballad
Length	5:30
Label	Brother/Reprise
Producer	The Beach Boys

The Beach Boys singles chronology		
"Surf's Up"/"Don't Go Near the Water" (1971)	"You Need a Mess of Help to Stand Alone"/"Cuddle Up" (1972)	"Marcella"/"Hold On Dear Brother" (1972)

"**Cuddle Up**" is a song written by Dennis Wilson and Daryl Dragon for the American pop band The Beach Boys. It was released on their 1972 album *Carl and the Passions - "So Tough"*. The track features Dennis Wilson on lead vocals and is produced by The Beach Boys.

A cover version was later released by the Captain and Tennille on their album Love Will Keep Us Together.

See also

- List of songs by The Beach Boys

Custom Machine

"Custom Machine" is a song written by Brian Wilson and Mike Love for the American pop band The Beach Boys. It was released on their 1963 album *Little Deuce Coupe*. It became a hit on the Billboard Hot 100 when released as a single by Bruce & Terry in 1964.

Details

- *Written by:* Brian Wilson/Mike Love
- *Album:* Little Deuce Coupe
- *Time:* 1 min 38 sec
- *Produced by:* Brian Wilson

Performers

- *Mike Love:* Lead Vocals

See also

- The Beach Boys
- Little Deuce Coupe
- List of songs by The Beach Boys

Dance, Dance, Dance

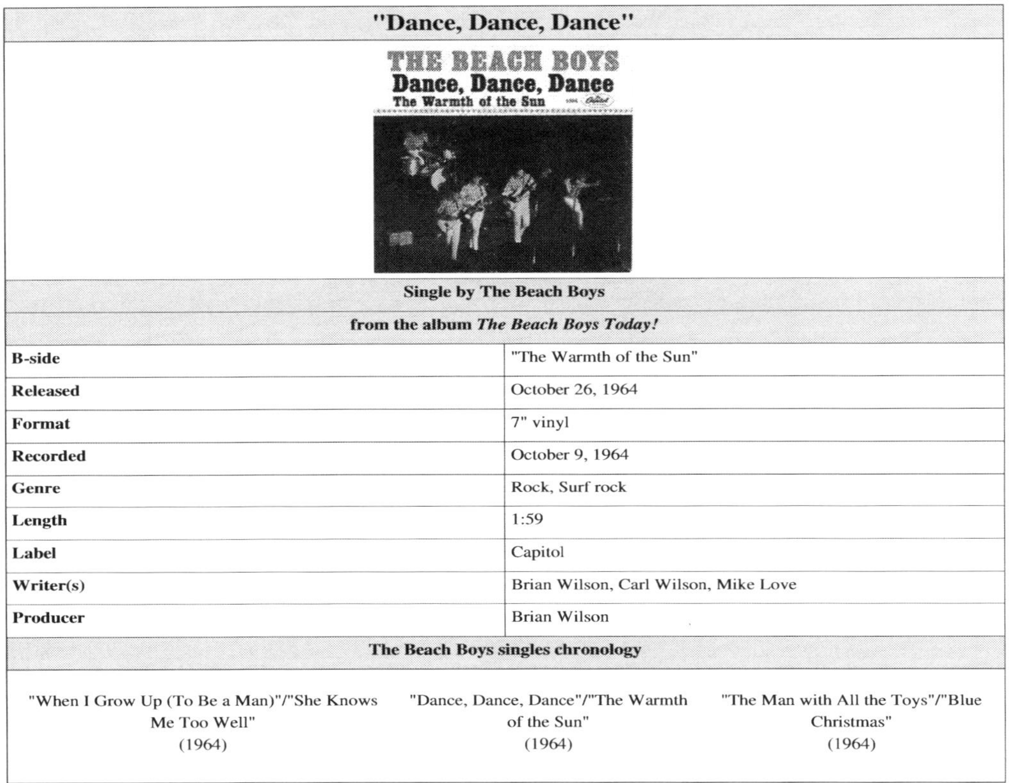

"Dance, Dance, Dance"	
Single by The Beach Boys	
from the album *The Beach Boys Today!*	
B-side	"The Warmth of the Sun"
Released	October 26, 1964
Format	7" vinyl
Recorded	October 9, 1964
Genre	Rock, Surf rock
Length	1:59
Label	Capitol
Writer(s)	Brian Wilson, Carl Wilson, Mike Love
Producer	Brian Wilson

The Beach Boys singles chronology		
"When I Grow Up (To Be a Man)"/"She Knows Me Too Well" (1964)	"Dance, Dance, Dance"/"The Warmth of the Sun" (1964)	"The Man with All the Toys"/"Blue Christmas" (1964)

For the Chic song see Dance, Dance, Dance (Yowsah, Yowsah, Yowsah).

"**Dance, Dance, Dance**" is a song written by Brian Wilson, Carl Wilson and Mike Love for the American singing group, The Beach Boys. It was released on their 1965 album *The Beach Boys Today!*. It was also released as a single in 1964, with the B-side of the single being "The Warmth of the Sun." The single peaked at #8 in the U.S. and #24 in the U.K. It was also #7 on Canada's national RPM chart, #6 in Sweden, and in France was their fourth song to place on the *Jukebox* chart.

Across the States, the single tended to be held out of the top five of regional playlists by a log-jam of British Invasion acts, and burst through to No. 1 only in Washington DC (WKMC), San Jose and Providence. It was #4 in San Francisco and Dallas.

The song was originally released in mono, while a remixed stereo version was released on the compilation *Hawthorne, CA*. An early version of the song, with different lyrics and arrangement, appears as a bonus track on the *Today!/Summer Days (And Summer Nights!!)* two-fer CD. Wilson Phillips -- featuring Brian Wilson's daughters Carnie and Wendy -- covered the song for their album *California*.

Musicians

- Hal Blaine - sleigh bells, triangle, tambourine, castanets
- Glen Campbell - guitar
- Steve Douglas - tenor saxophone
- Carl Fortina - accordion
- Al Jardine - guitar, vocals
- Mike Love - lead vocal
- Jay Migliori - baritone saxophone
- Ray Pohlman - bass guitar
- Brian Wilson - bass guitar, vocals
- Carl Wilson - 12 string guitar, vocals
- Dennis Wilson - drums, vocals

See also

- List of songs by The Beach Boys

External links

- "Dance, Dance, Dance" [1] review at Allmusic

References

[1] http://allmusic.com/cg/amg.dll?p=amg&sql=33:3ifixqrrldke

Darlin'

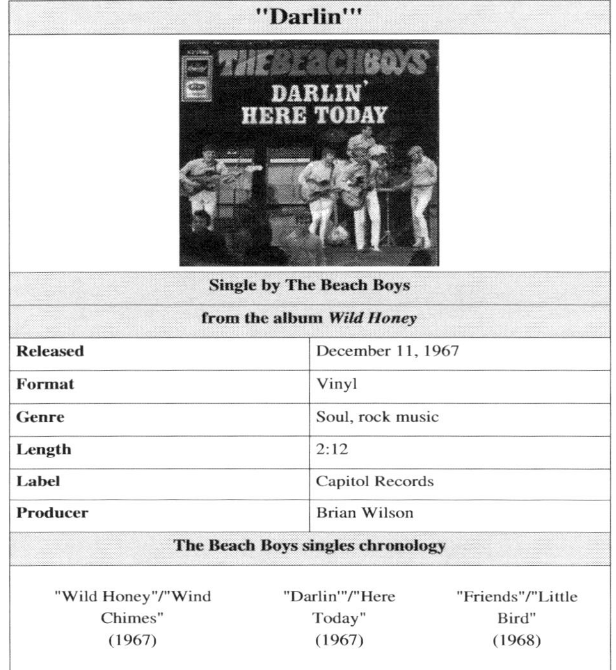

"Darlin'"	
Single by The Beach Boys	
from the album *Wild Honey*	
Released	December 11, 1967
Format	Vinyl
Genre	Soul, rock music
Length	2:12
Label	Capitol Records
Producer	Brian Wilson

The Beach Boys singles chronology		
"Wild Honey"/"Wind Chimes" (1967)	"Darlin'"/"Here Today" (1967)	"Friends"/"Little Bird" (1968)

"Darlin'" is a song written by Brian Wilson and Mike Love for the American pop band The Beach Boys. It was released on their 1967 album *Wild Honey*. It was also released as a single, with the B-side of the single being "Here Today". The single peaked at #19 in the United States and #11 in the United Kingdom. The song was produced by The Beach Boys and featured Carl Wilson on lead vocals.

Composition

The song "Darlin'" is a re-write of a song that Brian and Mike had written years earlier called "Thinkin' 'Bout You Baby" which was first recorded and released as a single in April 1964 by Sharon Marie - a previously unrecorded teenager who had informally auditioned for Brian and Mike (by singing opera standards) stageside after a Sacramento Beach Boys concert - with production by Brian himself. The song can be heard on the 2004 compilation *Pet Projects: The Brian Wilson Productions*. In 1972, Brian's wife at the time, Marilyn, as well as her sister Diane were known as the duo American Spring. On their one and only self-titled album they covered the song "Thinkin' 'Bout You Baby". After the song had been re-written as "Darlin'", Brian was planning to give the song to a band called Redwood (later to be known as Three Dog Night) as Danny Hutton was a friend of Brian's around that time, but the other Beach Boys members insisted that they should record the song.

Recording

The instrumental and vocal track was recorded under the production of Brian Wilson on October 27, 1967. The instrumental track of the song was released on the 1968 album *Stack-O-Tracks*.

Single release

The "Darlin'" single backed with "Here Today" was issued by Capitol Records in the United States in December, 1967. The single peaked at the number 19 position on the *Billboard* charts, but it placed at number 10 on the *Cash Box* sales chart. Radio station playlists indicated high popularity in Santa Barbara (#1), Los Angeles (#2), Baltimore and Norfolk (#4); Washington, Boston, Honolulu (all #5); San Diego, Fresno, Portland, Milwaukee, Louisville (all #6); #7 Vancouver, #9 Toronto, #14 in New York. And according to long-term popularity surveys conducted by Eastern Seaboard radio station networks over the following decade, the single showed no diminution in the group's sales.

In the United Kingdom the single was issued in January, 1968 with the B-side being "Country Air". The single peaked at the number 11 position. In New Zealand the single peaked at the number 10 position. In Sweden it placed number 15 and in the Dutch single charts the song peaked at number 21.

Live versions

After the song was released it became a regular song in The Beach Boys live set. The song has subsequently been released on three of the band's live albums. Firstly it was released on the band's original 1970 release *Live In London* in which it was the opening track on the album. It was then released in 1973 on the band's *The Beach Boys In Concert* live album. And then most recently it was released on the band's 2002 live album *Good Timin': Live At Knebworth England 1980*.

Cover versions

One of the song's earliest cover versions was by The Paper Dolls , a British girl group and featured on their debut 1968 album `Paper Dolls House`.

David Cassidy recorded *Darlin'* for his 1975 album, *The Higher They Climb (album)*. Although not an active member of the Beach Boys in 1975, Cassidy's album was produced by Beach Boys member Bruce Johnston. A live track of Cassidy's version is available on his album, *Daydreamer*.

Triumvirat recorded Darlin' on 'A la Carte' released in 1978.

Trivia

- The song later inspired a shortly lived indie-rock group of the same name which consisted of Thomas Bangalter, Guy-Manuel de Homem-Christo, and Laurent Brancowitz which would later become the band Daft Punk, without Brancowitz.

See also

- List of songs by The Beach Boys

A Day in the Life of a Tree

"A Day in the Life of a Tree"	
Song by The Beach Boys from the album *Surf's Up*	
Released	August 30, 1971
Recorded	April & June 1971 Brian Wilson's home studio
Genre	Pop
Length	3:07
Label	Brother/Reprise
Composer	Brian Wilson, Jack Rieley
Producer	The Beach Boys
***Surf's Up* track listing**	
"Lookin' at Tomorrow (A Welfare Song)" (7) · **"A Day in the Life of a Tree"** (8) · ""Til I Die" (9)	

"**A Day in the Life of a Tree**" is a song written by Brian Wilson and Jack Rieley for the American pop band The Beach Boys. It was released on their 1971 album *Surf's Up*. The lead vocals were performed by co-writer Rieley, who was also the Beach Boys' manager at the time.

The song was covered in 1996 by Matthew Sweet for an album benefiting the Honor The Earth campaign.

Performers

- Jack Rieley: lead vocals
- Van Dyke Parks: vocals towards the end of the song
- Al Jardine: vocals at the fade out

See also

- List of songs by The Beach Boys

Deirdre

"Deirdre"	
Single by The Beach Boys	
from the album *Sunflower*	
Released	May 24, 1971
Format	Vinyl
Recorded	February 21, 1969
Genre	Baroque Pop
Length	3:27
Label	Brother Records
Producer	The Beach Boys
The Beach Boys singles chronology	

"Wouldn't It Be Nice (live)" (1971)	"Long Promised Road"/"Deirdre" (1971)	"Long Promised Road"/""Til I Die" (1971)

"**Deirdre**" is a song written by Bruce Johnston and Brian Wilson for the American pop band The Beach Boys. It was released on their 1970 album *Sunflower*. It was also released as the B-side of the "Long Promised Road" single. The single never charted in the U.S. or the U.K. In 1977 Bruce Johnston covered the song in his solo album *Going Public*.

Details

- *Written by:* Bruce Johnston/Brian Wilson
- *Album:* Sunflower
- *Time:* 3:27
- *Produced by:* The Beach Boys

Performers

- *Bruce Johnston:* Lead Vocals

See also

- The Beach Boys
- Sunflower
- List of songs by The Beach Boys

Denny's Drums

"Denny's Drums"	
Song by The Beach Boys from the album *Shut Down Volume 2*	
Released	1964
Recorded	January 7, 1964 Western Studios
Genre	Pop Surf rock
Length	1:56
Label	Capitol Records
Writer	Dennis Wilson
Producer	Brian Wilson
***Shut Down Volume 2* track listing**	
• "Fun, Fun, Fun" • "Don't Worry Baby" • "In the Parkin' Lot" • "Cassius Love vs. Sonny Wilson" • "The Warmth of the Sun" • "This Car of Mine" • "Why Do Fools Fall in Love" • "Pom Pom Play Girl" • "Keep an Eye on Summer" • "Shut Down, Part II" • "Louie Louie" • "Denny's Drums"	

"Denny's Drums" is a drum solo written by Dennis Wilson and recorded by the American pop band The Beach Boys. It was released on their 1964 album *Shut Down Volume 2*. It features a number of rhythmic changes with an emphasis of accents on the tom toms.

Performers

- *Dennis Wilson:* Drums

See also

- The Beach Boys
- Shut Down Volume 2
- List of songs by The Beach Boys

Devoted to You

"**Devoted to You**" is a song written by Felice and Boudleaux Bryant.

The best-known version was recorded by The Everly Brothers, and released by Cadence Records as catalog number 1350. This version was issued as the flip side of "Bird Dog," but reached the charts on its own, at #10 on the United States pop charts, #25 in Australia, and #1 in Canada. In addition, the song reached #7 on the United States country music chart and #2 on the rhythm and blues chart.

It was also recorded by James Taylor and Carly Simon, appearing on Simon's 1978 album, *Boys in the Trees*. The song was also covered live by The Seekers on their 1993 *25 Year Reunion Celebration* album. The Beach Boys version was a part of their *Beach Boys' Party!* album and was sung by Mike Love and Brian Wilson. A version without the *Party!* sound effects can be found on their *Hawthorne, CA* compilation. Sandy Posey recorded an compelling cover on her *Sweet Dreams* album in which she emulated The Everly Brothers harmony using multi-track recording.

Beach Boys version

"Devoted to You"		
Single by The Beach Boys		
from the album *Beach Boys' Party!*		
Released	August 28, 1967	
Format	Vinyl	
Recorded	Unknown	
Genre	Pop music	
Length	2:13	
Label	Capitol Records	
Producer	Brian Wilson	
The Beach Boys singles chronology		
"Heroes and Villains"/"You're Welcome" (1967)	"Gettin' Hungry"/"Devoted to You" (1967)	"Wild Honey"/"Wind Chimes" (1967)

Beach Boys' Party! track listing

- "Hully Gully"
- "I Should Have Known Better"
- "Tell Me Why"
- "Papa-Oom-Mow-Mow"
- "Mountain of Love"
- "You've Got to Hide Your Love Away"
- "Devoted to You"
- "Alley Oop"
- "There's No Other (Like My Baby)"
- "Medley:I Get Around/Little Deuce Coupe"
- "The Times They Are a-Changin' "
- "Barbara Ann"

Details

- Album: *Beach Boys' Party!*
- Time: 2 min 13 sec
- Produced by: Brian Wilson

See also

- List of songs by The Beach Boys

Diamond Head

"**Diamond Head**" is an instrumental song written by Al Vescovo, Lyle Ritz, Jim Ackley and Brian Wilson. The song was recorded by The Beach Boys on their 1968 album *Friends*. The song from 1:54 is sampled by Kid Creole and the Coconuts in their hit "Annie I'm Not Your Daddy". This song is a hawaiian music and folk.

Ding Dang

"Ding Dang" is a song written by Brian Wilson and Roger McGuinn for the American pop band The Beach Boys. It was released on their 1977 album *Love You*.

Earlier, longer versions of the song were recorded earlier in the decade, one of which has been bootlegged under the unofficial titles "Hard Times" or "Rollin' Up to Heaven," although neither were real titles for the song at any point.

Details

- *Written by:* Brian Wilson/Roger McGuinn
- *Album:* Love You
- *Time:* 0 min 56 sec
- *Produced by:* Brian Wilson

Performers

- *Carl Wilson:* Lead Vocals
- *Mike Love:* Lead Vocals

See also

- The Beach Boys
- List of songs by The Beach Boys

"Ding Dang" is also song written by Les Claypool, played under the moniker of 'Les Claypool's Frog Brigade' on the 2002 concept album, "The Purple Onion".

Disney Girls

"Disney Girls (1957)"	
Song by The Beach Boys from the album *Surf's Up*	
Released	August 30, 1971
Recorded	June 3, 1971
Genre	Pop
Length	4:07
Label	Brother/Reprise
Composer	Bruce Johnston
Producer	The Beach Boys
***Surf's Up* track listing**	

Take a Load off Your Feet (3)	**"Disney Girls (1957)"** (4)	Student Demonstration Time (5)

"Disney Girls (1957)" is a song written by Bruce Johnston for the American pop band The Beach Boys. It was released on their 1971 album *Surf's Up*. The lead vocals are by Johnston, who also plays keyboards, moog bass, and mandolin.

"Disney Girls (1957)" has proven to be one of Bruce Johnston's most enduring songs, still occasionally performed by The Beach Boys in concert to this day. It has been covered by many artists, including Art Garfunkel, Cass Elliott, Jack Jones, Captain & Tennille, and even Johnston himself, on his 1977 solo album *Going Public*. Cass Elliot's version (from the album *Cass Elliot*) is notable for featuring both Johnston and Carl Wilson.

See also

- List of songs by The Beach Boys

Do It Again

"Do It Again"	
Single by The Beach Boys	
from the album *20/20*	
Released	July 15, 1968
Format	Vinyl
Recorded	June, 1968
Genre	Classic rock
Length	2:25
Label	Capitol Records
Producer	Brian and Carl Wilson
The Beach Boys singles chronology	

"Friends"/"Little Bird" (1968)	"Do It Again"/"Wake the World" (1968)	"Bluebirds over the Mountain"/"Never Learn Not to Love" (1968)

"Do It Again" is a song written by Brian Wilson and Mike Love for the American pop band The Beach Boys. It was first released as a single by The Beach Boys in 1968 on Capitol Records. The song was recorded in May and June 1968 and was included on the band's 1969 album *20/20*. On the song there are some hammering sounds at the end of the track that originated from the *Smile* workshop session. The B-side of the single release was "Wake the World". The song was produced by Brian and Carl Wilson. It features Mike Love on lead vocals.

Composition

The lyrics to the song, originally entitled "Rendezvous", were inspired after a day Mike had spent at the beach in which he had gone surfing with an old friend named Bill Jackson.[1] Mike then showed the lyrics to Brian, who proceeded to write the music to Mike's lyrics of nostalgia. Brian has stated in the past that he believes the song was the best collaboration that he and Mike ever did.[1]

Many critics and fans noted the return to the surfing style, which the band had generally avoided since 1964. Carl later explained the transition back to their old style in *Melody Maker*:

> "Yes, I suppose it has got the old Beach Boys surfing sound. It's back to that surfing idea with the voice harmony and the simple, direct melody and lyrics. We didn't plan the record as a return to the surf or anything. We just did it one day round a piano in the studio. Brian had the idea and played it over to us.

> We improved on that and recorded it very quickly, in about five minutes. It's certainly not an old track of ours; in fact it was recorded only a few weeks before it was released. We liked how it turned out and decided to release it."[1]

Recording

After six weeks of very little or no work done in the studio (as the band was busy touring), the band got back to work on May 26, 1968, when they first began working on "Do It Again" at Brian's home studio in Bel Air, California. The session, produced by Brian and Carl, first listed the song as being called "Rendezvous". After Brian had run the band through a demonstration of the song, the band begun recording the track using guitar, organ, bass and drums, with Mike singing his vocal during the initial takes of the track. At first Mike sings the lyric "and surf again", however this is later amended to "and do it again". After the band recorded the basic track, they overdubbed backing vocals as well as adding a guitar and organ insert and a new guitar solo. Further vocal work by Brian, Carl & Dennis Wilson and Bruce Johnston and Al Jardine was done on the track on June 6 again at Brian's home studio in Bel Air, California.

Further overdubs to the instrumental track are made at Brian's home studio on June 10. John Guerin playing drums, tambourine and wood blocks on the overdubs, Ernie Small provided saxophone overdubs and John E. Lowe provided woodwind overdubs.

Reportedly, during the mixdown Stephen Desper, the engineer on the album came up with the drum effect heard at the beginning of the track. Many believe that this sound added to the commercial success of the single. Desper explained that he had:

> "commissioned Philips, in Holland, to build two tape delay units for use on the road (to double live vocals). [he] moved four of the Philips PB heads very close together so that one drum strike was repeated four times about 10 milliseconds apart, and blended it with the original to give the effect you hear."

On the fade of the song there are some hammering sounds which originated from the *Smile* workshop session.

Single release

The "Do It Again" single backed with "Wake The World" was released in the United States on July 8, 1968. The single version was slightly different from the album version in that it didn't have the hammering sounds at the fade out of the song. The single hit the charts on July 27 and peaked at the number 20 position on September 14. It would be the band's last single to peak in the top twenty on the charts until "Rock And Roll Music" in 1976 (which is a total of 14 singles without charting inside the top 20), which peaked at the number 5 position.

Released on July 19, 1968 in the United Kingdom the single, forty days after its release, peaked at #1 on the chart on August 28, 1968, and thus becoming the band's second number one hit in the United Kingdom after "Good Vibrations" two years earlier. The single had knocked "Mony Mony" by Tommy James and the Shondells off the top position. However, the single only remained at the top position for one week after it was knocked off by the song "I've Gotta Get a Message to You" by The Bee Gees. Due to the single's success many years earlier, Capitol Records decided to re-issue the single in Britain in June 1991. The single, which featured both "Do It Again" and "Good Vibrations" (the band's only two number one hits in Britain) on the A-side and an extended version of "The Beach Boys Medley" on the B-side, peaked at number 61 on the charts.

In Australia the song became the band's first number one hit single. In Germany the single peaked at the number 4 position on the charts. On the Dutch, Swedish, Norwegian, Irish and Rhodesian (now known as Zimbabwe) charts the single peaked at number 5. It was number 4 in Malaysia, number 6 in Israel and number 7 in Denmark and Switzerland. It was the Beach Boys' last big national hit (of the Sixties) in Canada, placing at number 10 on the RPM Top 100. And on the New Zealand chart the single peaked at the number 14 position.

The impact of the single belied its relatively low position in *Billboard*, rising to number 7 and number 8 in the charts collated and published by rival trade papers *Record World* and *Cash Box*, respectively. It brought something of a media comeback for the Beach Boys, invited to appear on *The Johnny Carson Show* and several other New York talk shows. It placed at #8 on the major playlists of New York City, and did better than that in Chicago (#1), Calgary (#2), Los Angeles (#3), San Diego and Louisville (#4), Toronto (#5), Boston and Buffalo (#6), Washington DC (#7), Detroit and Cincinnati (#8).

As a solo artist, Brian Wilson also released a cover version off his 1995 album *I Just Wasn't Made For These Times* as a single in Britain. The single also featured his cover of ""Til I Die", which was also from *I Just Wasn't Made For These Times*, and a rare B-side "This Song Wants To Sleep With You Tonight". The single however failed to make any impact on the charts.

Promotional film

A promotional film, directed by Peter Clifton, was shot in Los Angeles. The film, shot in color, features the group pulling up in a van and visiting a surfing shop. The band then drives to the beach in their van and begin surfing. The first screenings of the promotional film were shown on BBC-1's *Top of the Pops* during broadcasts of the show on August 8, 22 and 29. In Germany the promotional film was shown in September during broadcasts of the *Hits A Go Go* show on ZDF TV. The clip was later featured in the 1969 Peter Clifton Australian surfing film *Fluid Journey*.[2] An alternate promotional film for "Do It Again" was planned with the idea to feature special guest, Beatles member Paul McCartney as a clerk. However the idea was abandoned due to his hectic schedule.[3]

Critical reception

After the release of the "Do It Again" single, many critics welcomed the return back to the band's former style. Penny Valentine noted the transition back to their former ways and gave a glowing review of the single in Britain's *Disc & Music Echo*:

> "This is a vast improvement on The Beach Boys' last single, and thank goodness for it. It sounds like bees humming on a summer breeze and is so completely solid; there isn't room for a fly to creep in. It goes on very gently and easily and is very, very pleasant. In a way it reminds me of one of the tracks off *Pet Sounds*, which is nice to say the least, and a hit it will most certainly be. I can imagine a few people will be muttering, 'Well, she said they were finished,' but I didn't. I said they should get back to their competent, commercial sound and they have. So there."[2]

Album and alternate releases

The song was first released on an album in 1969 on the band's *20/20* album. The song's backing track was released on the 1968 album *Stack-O-Tracks*. On the 1998 compilation album, *Endless Harmony Soundtrack*, an early incarnation of the song was released with slightly different lyrics. This early version of the song featured no drum intro and obviously wasn't as produced as the final version. Brian is also more prominent in the vocal mix on the chorus. The song is only available in mono (or rechanneled mono on the *20/20* LP) because the true stereo master was lost in the making of *Stack-O-Tracks*.

The song frequently appears on many of the groups greatest hits compilations including the 1975 compilation album *Good Vibrations - Best of The Beach Boys*; The single mix of the song, which doesn't feature the woodshop sounds on the fade out of the song, was released on the 1999 greatest hits compilation *The Greatest Hits - Volume 2: 20 More Good Vibrations*, the 2003 compilation *Sounds of Summer: The Very Best of The Beach Boys*, as well as the 1993 box set *Good Vibrations: Thirty Years of The Beach Boys*.

Do It Again! is also the title of a compilation album featuring the songs "California Girls", "I Get Around", "This Car Of Mine", "Fun, Fun, Fun", "Wendy", "Graduation Day", "Do It Again", "The Little Girl I Once Knew", and "Surfin'

Safari".

Live versions

The band performed a lip-synched version of the song on the *Dick Cavett Show* on August 12, 1968. Later that month on August 26, the band performed the song with a live vocal over a pre-recorded track on the *Mike Douglas Show*. The footage of this appearance was broadcast nationally in America on August 28. The band also performed the song soon after on the *Ed Sullivan Show* on October 13, 1968. The band sung live vocals over a pre-recorded track. The footage was shot in color in a special blue matte video montage. The footage from the show can be found on the DVD Sights of Summer which was included with the special 2004 edition of *Sounds of Summer: The Very Best of The Beach Boys*.

The first officially released live recording of the song was released on the 1970 live album *Live In London*. Brian Wilson, who sings falsetto on the studio track, had retired from touring by this time and in concert his part was replaced by horns as evident on the *Live In London* album version. In 1980, a live rendition was recorded, though not released until 2002 on the *Good Timin': Live at Knebworth England 1980* live album. Footage from the concert was also released on video and DVD format. The footage was also released on the 1998 documentary *Endless Harmony* with the sound re-mixed by Mark Linett into Dolby Digital 5.1 surround sound.

Brian Wilson performed a live version of the song which was released on his 2000 live solo album *Live at the Roxy Theatre*. Brian Wilson also performed the song at the Radio City Music Hall in New York City on March 29, 2001 along with his nephew Justyn Wilson (Carl's son) guesting on guitar on the song. The concert, billed as "An All-Star Tribute to Brian Wilson", was filmed and later released on DVD.

Cover versions

A Taste Of Honey and Ronnie Aldrich were the first artists to cover the song in 1969 just a year after the song had been released. Papa Doo Run Run later covered the song in 1983. Twist covered the song in 1985. Wall of Voodoo covered the track on their last studio album, *Happy Planet* in 1987. The band also recorded a promotional film for the song which featured a guest appearance by Brian Wilson himself.[4] Trygve Thue also covered the song in 1994. More recently, John Hunter Phillips covered the song on his 2000 album *Diamonds On The Beach*. The Spanish band Los Reactivos also made a cover, "Hazlo Otra Vez", on their 2008 EP *Split Single*.

Cultural references

The song was first featured on the 1986 film *One Crazy Summer*. The song was also featured in the 1996 film *Flipper* and the 2005 film *Life on the Longboard*. More recently the song was featured in the 2006 movie *Happy Feet* and subsequently was featured on the film's soundtrack. It was also the first song to be played after WCBS-FM reverted from the Jack FM format back to their oldies format on July 12, 2007.

Charts

Chart (1968)	Peak position
Australian Singles Chart[5]	1
Dutch Singles Chart[6]	5
German Singles Chart[7]	4
New Zealand Singles Chart[8]	14
Norwegian Singles Chart[9]	5
Rhodesian Singles Chart[10]	5
UK Singles Chart	1
U.S. *Billboard* Hot 100	20

See also

- List of songs by The Beach Boys

References

[1] Badman, Keith (2004). *The Beach Boys: The Definitive Diary of America's Greatest Band on Stage and in the Studio*. p. 221.
[2] Badman, Keith (2004). *The Beach Boys: The Definitive Diary of America's Greatest Band on Stage and in the Studio*. p. 223.
[3] Badman, Keith (2004). *The Beach Boys: The Definitive Diary of America's Greatest Band on Stage and in the Studio*. p. 224.
[4] Wall of Voodoo video clip featuring Brian Wilson (http://www.youtube.com/watch?v=bMx-2Aasrpg)
[5] "Australian Singles Charts" (http://www.mountvernonandfairway.de/charts10.htm). mountvernonandfairway.de. . Retrieved 13 November 2007.
[6] "Dutch Singles Charts" (http://www.mountvernonandfairway.de/charts6.htm). mountvernonandfairway.de. . Retrieved 13 November 2007.
[7] "German Singles Charts" (http://www.mountvernonandfairway.de/charts9.htm). mountvernonandfairway.de. . Retrieved 13 November 2007.
[8] "New Zealand Singles Charts" (http://www.mountvernonandfairway.de/charts5.htm). mountvernonandfairway.de. . Retrieved 13 November 2007.
[9] "Norwegian Singles Charts" (http://www.mountvernonandfairway.de/charts4.htm). mountvernonandfairway.de. . Retrieved 13 November 2007.
[10] "Rhodesian Singles Charts" (http://www.mountvernonandfairway.de/charts2.htm). mountvernonandfairway.de. . Retrieved 13 November 2007.

Do You Remember?

"**Do You Remember?**" is a song written by Brian Wilson and Mike Love for the American pop band The Beach Boys. It was released on their 1964 album *All Summer Long*.

Details

- *Written by:* Brian Wilson/Mike Love
- *Album:* All Summer Long
- *Time:* 1 min 37 sec
- *Produced by:* Brian Wilson

Performers

- *Brian Wilson:* Lead Vocals
- *Mike Love:* Lead Vocals

Plot

The song pays tribute to some of rock and roll's pioneers, including Little Richard, Chuck Berry and Elvis.

"Little Richard sang it and Dick Clark brought it to life. Danny and the Juniors hit a groove, stuck as sharp as a knife. Well now do you remember all the guys that gave us rock and roll..."

Chuck Berry's gotta be the greatest thing that's come along He made the guitar beats and wrote the all-time greatest song...

See also

- The Beach Boys
- All Summer Long
- List of songs by The Beach Boys

Do You Wanna Dance?

"**Do You Wanna Dance?**" is a song written by Bobby Freeman (as "Do You Want to Dance?"), and recorded by him in 1958. It is also popular in a version performed by the Beach Boys, which was released in 1965, and in a version recorded by Bette Midler in 1972. The Ramones also cover the song on *Rocket To Russia* and *It's Alive*.

Grateful Dead's Jerry Garcia recorded the guitar on the original Bobby Freeman version.

The Beach Boys version

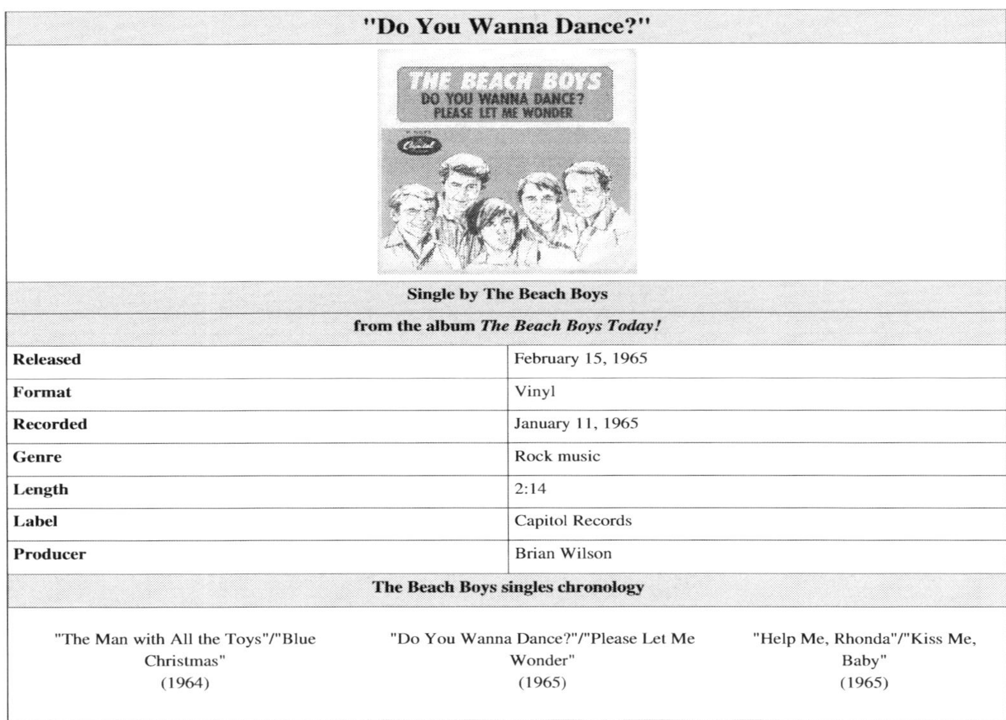

"Do You Wanna Dance?"		
Single by The Beach Boys		
from the album *The Beach Boys Today!*		
Released	February 15, 1965	
Format	Vinyl	
Recorded	January 11, 1965	
Genre	Rock music	
Length	2:14	
Label	Capitol Records	
Producer	Brian Wilson	
The Beach Boys singles chronology		
"The Man with All the Toys"/"Blue Christmas" (1964)	"Do You Wanna Dance?"/"Please Let Me Wonder" (1965)	"Help Me, Rhonda"/"Kiss Me, Baby" (1965)

"Do You Wanna Dance?" was a single released by The Beach Boys in 1965 through Capitol Records. It peaked at #12 on the Billboard Hot 100 and was the highest charted Beach Boys song to feature Dennis Wilson on lead vocals. According to the contemporary Gilbert Youth Survey conducted nationwide in April 1965, it was featured one week on its chart at No. 5. The B-side of this single was "Please Let Me Wonder". The song was also released on the band's 1965 album *The Beach Boys Today!*.

Musicians

The Beach Boys

- Al Jardine - backing vocals
- Mike Love - backing vocals
- Brian Wilson - piano, backing vocals
- Carl Wilson - guitars, backing vocals
- Dennis Wilson - lead vocals

Additional musicians

- Hal Blaine - drums, woodblocks
- Steve Douglas - tenor saxophone
- Plas Johnson - tenor saxophone
- Larry Knechtel - bass
- Jay Migliori - baritone saxophone
- Bill Pitman - guitar
- Leon Russell - organ
- Billy Strange - mandolin
- Tommy Tedesco - mandolin
- Julius Wechter - timpani, tambourine
- Marilyn Wilson - backing vocals

Bette Midler version

Bette Midler included the song — slightly retitled as "Do You Want to Dance" — on her 1972 debut album *The Divine Miss M*. Whereas the Bobby Freeman and Beach Boys versions are uptempo rock and roll, Midler slowed the tempo of the song down to a sultry-sounding ballad. As Midler's first single release, it was a hit, reaching #17 on the Billboard Hot 100 chart in early 1973.

In 1985, Ula Hedwig, a Bette Midler-soundalike and former backup singer, sang the song emulating Bette Midler's version for a Ford Lincoln Mercury television commercial. The Ninth Circuit Court of Appeals held that using this sound-alike version in a TV commercial violated Midler's right of publicity. *Midler v. Ford Motor Co.*, 849 F.2d 460 (9th Cir. 1988).

Other versions

1960s

- Eddie Cochran recorded a version of this song before his death.
- 1962 - Cliff Richard, b-side to "I'm Lookin' Out the Window" The single sold more than 1 million copies worldwide and reached #1 in Holland and Australia.
- 1964 - Del Shannon
- 1965 - The Beach Boys, the opening track on the album *The Beach Boys Today!*.
- 1966 - The Mamas & the Papas - debut album *If You Can Believe Your Eyes and Ears*. Part of the instrumental melody in this version is sampled in the Jens Lekman song "Maple Leaves".
- 1966 - Johnny Rivers album *Changes*

1970s

- 1974 - Hurriganes
- 1975 - John Lennon album *Rock 'n' Roll*.
- 1975 - T. Rex - bonus track on the album *Bolan's Zip Gun*.

- 1977 - The Ramones album *Rocket to Russia.*
- 1978 - Ray Stevens album *There is Something on Your Mind.* A portion of "Do You Wanna Dance" was featured as part of Ray's 'Dance Trilogy' medley of 1950's R&B songs with titles that had emphasis on dancing...the song samples: "Do You Wanna Dance/When You Dance/Save The Last Dance For Me")

1980s

- It was covered live during Neil Young's 1983 rockabilly period.
- 1987 - Barbie in the 'Rockin' Back to Earth' episode of her TV show.
- 1988 - David Lindley and El Rayo-X on their "Very Greasy"
- 1988 - A Swedish version, with lyrics by Keith Almgren, called "Säg, får jag lov min vän" was recorded by Tonix on the album *Bugga loss.*

1990s

- 1996 - Petty Booka on their album *Blue Lagoon of Petty Booka.*
- 1998 - The Queers on their Ramones tribute album *Rocket To Russia.*
- 1998 - Jazz saxophonist Walter Beasley on his release *For Your Pleasure.*
- 1998 - Attaque 77 in their CD of covers *Otras Canciones*; the version was in Spanish.

2000s

- 2006 - Laurent Voulzy album *La Septième Vague*
- 2008 - Energy album *Race the Sun.*
- 2008 - Andreas Johnson album *Rediscovered.*
- 2009 - Cliff Richard & The Shadows a track on the 250,000 selling album *Reunited*

In popular culture

- The original Bobby Freeman recording features in the film "American Graffiti" (1973).
- The Ramones's version of "Do You Wanna Dance?" was used in an American television advertisement for the release of Wall-E on DVD and in the popular cult film "*Rock 'n' Roll High School*"

Don't Back Down

"**Don't Back Down**" is a song written by Brian Wilson and Mike Love for the American pop band The Beach Boys. It was released on their 1964 album *All Summer Long*. It was also featured on their EP, Four. The subject matter of this song is surfing; this would be the group's last surfing-themed song until 1969's "Do It Again". An alternate take of this song is found on the *Little Deuce Coupe/All Summer Long* CD. The song was covered by The Queers on their album *Don't Back Down*.

Details

- *Written by:* Brian Wilson/Mike Love
- *Album:* All Summer Long
- *Time:* 1 min 44 sec
- *Produced by:* Brian Wilson

Performers

- *Brian Wilson:* Lead Vocals
- *Mike Love:* Lead Vocals

See also

- The Beach Boys
- All Summer Long
- List of songs by The Beach Boys

Don't Go Near the Water

"Don't Go Near the Water"	
Song by The Beach Boys from the album *Surf's Up*	
Released	August 30, 1971
Recorded	April 3, 1971
Genre	Pop
Length	2:39
Label	Brother/Reprise
Composer	Mike Love/Al Jardine
Producer	The Beach Boys
***Surf's Up* track listing**	
"Don't Go Near the Water" (1)	Long Promised Road (2)

"**Don't Go Near the Water**" is a song written by Mike Love and Al Jardine for the American pop band The Beach Boys. It was the first track on their 1971 album *Surf's Up*.

Composition

The Beach Boys hired Jack Rieley as their manager in 1970. In order to make the band more relevant, Rieley suggested that the band write songs that were more political. "Don't Go Near the Water" is the first example of this. The song puts an ironic, ecological spin on the traditional Beach Boys beach- and surf- based songs: instead of enjoying surfing and other fun activities, this time the listener is advised to avoid the water for environmental reasons.

Recording

The song was recorded at the same session as "Long Promised Road" and "4th of July", both also recorded for the Surf's Up album. The lead vocals are by the song's composers, Love and Jardine. Brian Wilson contributed the piano part.

Releases

The song was chosen to be the B-side of the "Surf's Up" single, released on November 8, 1971. It did not chart. It was later released on November 2, 1981 as the B-side of the "Come Go with Me" single. The single charted at #18 in the US but never charted in the UK.

See also

- List of songs by The Beach Boys

Don't Hurt My Little Sister

"Don't Hurt My Little Sister"	
Song by The Beach Boys from the album *The Beach Boys Today!*	
Released	March 8, 1965
Recorded	June 22, 1964
Length	2:07
Label	Capitol
Composer	Brian Wilson/Mike Love
Producer	Brian Wilson
***The Beach Boys Today!* track listing**	
"Good to My Baby" (2)	**"Don't Hurt My Little Sister"** (3) · "When I Grow Up (To Be a Man)" (4)

"Don't Hurt My Little Sister" is a song written by Brian Wilson and Mike Love for the American pop band The Beach Boys. It was released on their 1965 album *The Beach Boys Today!*.

Musicians

- Hal Blaine - drums
- John Gray - piano
- Al Jardine - bass guitar, backing vocals
- Mike Love - lead & backing vocals
- Ray Pohlman - guitar
- Tommy Tedesco - guitar
- Brian Wilson - piano, lead & backing vocals
- Carl Wilson - guitar, backing vocals
- Dennis Wilson - tambourine, backing vocals

See also

- List of songs by The Beach Boys

Don't Talk (Put Your Head on My Shoulder)

"Don't Talk (Put Your Head on My Shoulder)"	
Song by The Beach Boys from the album *Pet Sounds*	
Released	May 16, 1966
Recorded	Western Studios February 11, 1966 April 3, 1966
Genre	Sunshine pop
Length	2:51
Label	Capitol
Composer	Wilson/Asher
Producer	Brian Wilson
***Pet Sounds* track listing**	
• "Wouldn't It Be Nice" • "You Still Believe in Me" • "That's Not Me" • "Don't Talk (Put Your Head on My Shoulder)" • "I'm Waiting for the Day" • "Let's Go Away for Awhile" • "Sloop John B" • "God Only Knows" • "I Know There's an Answer" • "Here Today" • "I Just Wasn't Made for These Times" • "Pet Sounds" • "Caroline, No"	

"**Don't Talk (Put Your Head on My Shoulder)**" is a song written by Brian Wilson and Tony Asher for the American pop band The Beach Boys. It is the fourth track on the album *Pet Sounds*. It is one of four songs on the album on which no Beach Boys other than Brian appear.

On the line "Listen to my heart...beat", Brian stated "I felt very deeply about that line. One of the sweetest songs I ever sang. I have to say I'm proud of it. The innocence of youth in my voice, of being young and childlike. I think that's what people liked."

Elvis Costello has been quoted as saying, "Last summer, I heard 'Don't Talk (Put Your Head on My Shoulder)' played on the cello. It sounded beautiful and sad, just as it does on Pet Sounds. So now you know, if all the record players in the world get broken tomorrow, these songs could be heard a hundred years from now."

Recording

There were several early attempts at recording the song, including Brian playing the instrumental on an acoustic piano. Later he recorded a multitracked, instrumental a capella demo of himself singing all parts; this was released in the 1990 CD remaster, which erroneously claimed it was the entire band recording a scrapped overdub, as "Unreleased Backgrounds." Carol Kaye recalls Wilson playing the musicians this recording in order to give the musicians a feel for the song.

The first real attempt at recording the song was at a session held at 9am on February 11, 1966 at Western Studios in Hollywood, California. The session - engineered by Chuck Britz and produced by Brian Wilson - saw the recording of the basic instrumental track as well as Wilson's lead vocal. The song is one of the few Beach Boys records that features no backing vocals. However, a session on October 13 of the previous year did see backing vocals recorded, although it is unclear on whether or not they were to ever be included. A string overdub was later recorded on April 3, 1966 again at Western Studios although this time with H. Bowen David engineering the session.

Personnel

- Arnold Belnick - violin
- Hal Blaine - drums
- Norman Botnick - viola
- Glen Campbell - guitar
- Frank Capp - vibraphone, timpani
- Al de Lory - organ
- Steve Douglas - percussion
- Carol Kaye - bass guitar
- Lyle Ritz - upright bass
- Joseph Saxon - cello
- Ralph Schaeffer - violin
- Sid Sharp - violin
- Billy Strange - guitar
- Brian Wilson - lead vocal
- Tibor Zelig - violin

Cover versions

Linda Ronstadt covered the song on her 1991 album *Winter Light*. Anne Sofie von Otter covers the song on her disc with Elvis Costello, "For the Stars."

See also

- List of songs by The Beach Boys

Don't Worry Baby

"Don't Worry Baby"	
Single by The Beach Boys	
from the album *Shut Down Volume 2*	
Released	May 11, 1964
Format	Vinyl
Recorded	Unknown
Genre	Surf Pop
Length	2:47
Label	Capitol Records
Producer	Brian Wilson
The Beach Boys singles chronology	

"Fun, Fun, Fun"/"Why Do Fools Fall In Love" (1964)	"I Get Around"/"**Don't Worry Baby**" (1964)	"When I Grow Up (to be a man)"/"She Knows Me Too Well" (1964)

"**Don't Worry Baby**" is a song written by Brian Wilson and Roger Christian, produced by Wilson and first recorded by the Beach Boys. The band's version, a tender ballad with falsetto lead vocal by Brian, was first released on their 1964 album *Shut Down Volume 2*. It was also released as the B-side of The Beach Boys' first U.S. number-one hit single, "I Get Around", managing to reach number 24 on the U.S. Hot 100 in its own right. The single was released in the United States in May 1964 through Capitol Records. It was released a month later, in June 1964, in the United Kingdom.

Brian Wilson cited the song as his attempt to capture the essence of his all-time favourite record, "Be My Baby" by the Ronettes, who would later cover his song. At one time, Wilson listened to his 45 record of the song he "could never do" up to 100 times a day.

John Lennon's 1980 hit, "(Just Like) Starting Over", is considered by some to somewhat borrow from the chorus melody of "Don't Worry Baby", while Garbage's 1998 hit, "Push It", contains an interpolation of its chorus.

The song is prominently featured in the 2006 thriller, *Déjà Vu*.

The song "Don't Worry Baby" is part of the The Rock and Roll Hall of Fame's 500 Songs that Shaped Rock and Roll list.[1] , and ranked as the 176th greatest song of all time in Rolling Stone's 500 Greatest Songs of All Time.

Released versions

The stereo mix of the song had been used on "Shut Down- Vol.2" when it was released in 1990 and 2001. A single mono mix appeared on the "20 More Good Vibrations" compilation. On the 2008 Singles box set, a mono album version was used instead of the single mix. A big problem with the stereo mix was that on the left channel you could only hear Brian's lead vocal and on the right was the background vocals. Thanks to the discovery of the lost multi-track masters in 2009, a new stereo mix was created from the analog master. The track and Brian's lead vocal were placed in the middle while on the left and right channels you have the background vocals. This version fixed the previous stereo mix. The fixed stereo mix can be found on the 2009 compilation "Summer Love Songs".

Cover versions

Keith Moon, drummer for The Who, covered this song on his only solo album, *Two Sides of the Moon*, with Dick Dale on solo guitar. Bryan Ferry, B.J. Thomas, the Everly Brothers, the Bay City Rollers, the Fun & Games, and singer-songwriter Andy Pratt have also offered cover versions of "Don't Worry Baby". New Zealand band Zed performed an uptempo rock-oriented cover version in 2003 on their album *This Little Empire*.

The song as originally performed by the Beach Boys, is about a teenager who agrees to a challenge to race a rival in order to defend his honor after bragging about his car, and his girlfriend's plea to take her love with him when he races. The B.J. Thomas version has a more mature theme, as a man waking up to his partner every morning, thinking that her love for him is fading, but his spirits rise as she reminds him how much she believes in him and loves him.

Billy Joel performed the cover version of this song at "An All-Star Tribute to Brian Wilson (2001)". Before he sang, he mentioned that his daughter, Alexa Ray Joel, adored the song from *Never Been Kissed* and dedicated the song to her.

New York Rock and Soul Revue, with Donald Fagen and Walter Becker of Steely Dan, played this song live, with Boz Scaggs, Michael McDonald and Phoebe Snow featured on lead vocals.

Ronnie Spector covered the song on her *She Talks to Rainbows* EP.

Weezer frontman Rivers Cuomo in 1992 recorded a cover of the song which appears on *Alone II: The Home Recordings of Rivers Cuomo*.

See also

- List of songs by The Beach Boys

External links

- Greg Panfile's Musical Analysis of "Don't Worry Baby" [2]

References

[1] Rock and Roll Hall of Fame "500 songs that shaped rock and roll" (http://www.rockhall.com/exhibithighlights/500-songs/)

[2] http://www.cabinessence.net/essays/mob9.html

Drive-In

"Drive-In" is a song written by Brian Wilson and Mike Love for the American pop band The Beach Boys. It was released on their 1964 album *All Summer Long*.

Details

- *Written by:* Brian Wilson/Mike Love
- *Album:* All Summer Long
- *Time:* 1 min 51 sec
- *Produced by:* Brian Wilson

Performers

- *Mike Love:* Lead Vocals

See also

- The Beach Boys
- All Summer Long
- List of songs by The Beach Boys

The Elements

The Elements would have been a suite of short sections by The Beach Boys for the abandoned album *Smile* that represented the classical elements (earth, air, fire, and water). Most of this suite was recorded but never finalized in its original form. Brian Wilson resurrected this set for his re-recording of *Smile*.

The first section of the piece was an organ-and-bass driven section (which, in its original Beach Boys recorded form, was labeled as an intro to "Heroes and Villains") to represent the sound of fire engines. Another section was subtitled "Fire", with weird instrumentation to represent fire. It has been said that Wilson was so bothered by a series of fires in the Los Angeles area that were taking place at the time of the original recording that he later suffered a mental breakdown and burnt tapes of the sessions. Tapes from the session have survived, however, and the song can be heard on the "Beach Boys - An American Band" documentary. The musical motif of the "Fire" portion would be re-used for the *Smiley Smile* track "Fall Breaks and Back to Winter (Woody Woodpecker Symphony)".

Another section would be the "Water Chant", another abandoned section of *Smile*, and the fourth was what became "I Love to Say Da-Da" (aka "In Blue Hawaii").

Brian Wilson has said that the original air section is lost, but "Wind Chimes" is substituted. Earth is represented by "Vega-Tables".

Endless Harmony

"Endless Harmony"		
Single by The Beach Boys		
from the album *Keepin' the Summer Alive*		
A-side	"Goin' On"	
Released	March 11, 1980	
Format	Vinyl	
Genre	Pop	
Length	3:10	
Label	Caribou Records	
Writer(s)	Bruce Johnston	
Producer	Bruce Johnston	
The Beach Boys singles chronology		
"It's a Beautiful Day"/"Sumahama" (1979)	"Goin' On"/"**Endless Harmony**" (1980)	"Livin' with a Heartache"/"Santa Ana Winds" (1980)

"Endless Harmony" is a song written by Bruce Johnston for the American pop band The Beach Boys. It was released on their 1980 album *Keepin' the Summer Alive* and as the B-side to the single for "Goin' On". It is also the last new Beach Boys recording to feature Dennis Wilson (on percussion) and to feature the entire group recording as a band in the studio.

Performers

- Carl Wilson: Lead vocals, bass
- Bruce Johnston: Lead vocals, keyboards
- Brian Wilson: Organ
- Al Jardine: Guitar
- Dennis Wilson: Percussion
- Scott Matthews: Drums

See also

- The Beach Boys
- Keepin' the Summer Alive
- List of songs by The Beach Boys

Everyone's in Love with You

"Everyone's in Love with You"	
Single by The Beach Boys	
from the album *15 Big Ones*	
Released	November 1, 1976
Format	Vinyl
Recorded	Unknown
Genre	Rock and Pop ballad
Length	2 min 42 sec
Label	Brother Records
Producer	Brian Wilson
The Beach Boys singles chronology	

"It's O.K."/"Had to Phone Ya" (1976)	"Everyone's in Love with You"/"Susie Cincinnati" (1976)	"Honkin' Down the Highway"/"Solar System" (1977)

"Everyone's in Love with You" is a song written by Mike Love for the American pop band The Beach Boys. It was released on their 1976 album *15 Big Ones*. The subject of this song refers to the Maharishi. The song was later re-recorded in 2004 for Mike Love's abandoned Mike Love Not War album

Details

- *Written by:* Mike Love
- *Album:* 15 Big Ones
- *Time:* 2 min 42 sec
- *Produced by:* Brian Wilson
- *Arranged by:* Mike Love
- *Vocals Arranged by:* Daryl Dragon

Performers

- *Mike Love:* Lead Vocals, Backing Vocals
- *Al Jardine:* Backing Vocals
- *Carl Wilson:* Backing Vocals, Bass, Guitar
- *Toni Tennille:* Backing Vocals
- *Brian Wilson:* String Ensemble
- *Dennis Wilson:* drums
- *Maureen L. West:* Harp
- *Ron Altbach:* Piano, Harpsichord
- *Charles Lloyd:* Flute
- *Ed Carter:* Guitar
- *Steve Douglas:* Saxophone
- *Jay Migliori:* Saxophone

See also

- The Beach Boys
- 15 Big Ones
- List of songs by The Beach Boys

Fall Breaks and Back to Winter (Woody Woodpecker Symphony)

"Fall Breaks and Back to Winter (Woody Woodpecker Symphony)" is a song written by Brian Wilson for the American pop band The Beach Boys. It was released on their 1967 album *Smiley Smile*. It was a re-composed version of the song "The Elements" (aka "Mrs. O'Leary's Cow" and "Fire") intended for the shelved *Smile* album. The Mrs. O'Leary's Cow track eventually made it onto the 2004 release of *Smile*.

Details

- *Written by:* Brian Wilson
- *Album:* Smiley Smile
- *Time:* 2 min 15 sec
- *Produced by:* The Beach Boys

See also

- The Beach Boys
- Smiley Smile
- List of songs by The Beach Boys

Feel Flows

"Feel Flows"		
Song by The Beach Boys from the album *Surf's Up*		
Released	August 30, 1971	
Recorded	July 29, 1971	
Genre	Pop	
Length	4:44	
Label	Brother/Reprise	
Composer	Carl Wilson/Jack Rieley	
Producer	The Beach Boys	
***Surf's Up* track listing**		
Student Demonstration Time (5)	**"Feel Flows"** (6)	Lookin' at Tomorrow (A Welfare Song) (7)

"Feel Flows" is a song written by Carl Wilson and Jack Rieley for the American pop band The Beach Boys. It was released on their 1971 album *Surf's Up*.

Carl Wilson's lead vocals were recorded using reverse echo.

In 2000, movie director Cameron Crowe used this song in the Almost Famous soundtrack, and it played during the end credits of the film. Use of the song in the film may be indirectly attributed to Crowe's wife, Nancy Wilson of Heart,(no relation to the Beach Boys' family). In a syndicated "Guest DJ" 1 hour radio program that aired nationally in 1982, Nancy Wilson played it as one of her selections and offered high praise for the song. In 2005 it appeared on a compilation album of music that has inspired the Welsh indie-psychedelic pop band the Super Furry Animals titled "Under the Influence".

Musicians

- Charles Lloyd - saxophone, flute
- Woody Theus - percussion
- Carl Wilson - guitar, bass guitar, drums, keyboards, lead and backing vocals

See also

- List of songs by The Beach Boys

Finders Keepers

"Finders Keepers"	
Song by The Beach Boys from the album *Surfin' USA*	
Released	March 25, 1963
Recorded	February 12, 1963 Capitol Studios
Genre	Pop
Length	1:40
Label	Capitol
Composer	Brian Wilson/Mike Love
Producer	Brian Wilson
***Surfin' USA* track listing**	
"Let's Go Trippin'" (11)	**"Finders Keepers"** (12)

"**Finders Keepers**" is a song written by Brian Wilson and Mike Love for the American pop band The Beach Boys. It was released on their 1963 album *Surfin' USA*.

The song was originally credited to just Wilson. Mike Love's name was added as a result of a lawsuit filed by him against Wilson in the 1990s.

Details

- *Written by:* Brian Wilson/Mike Love
- *Album:* Surfin' USA
- *Time:* 1 min 38 sec
- *Produced by:* Nik Venet
- *Recording date*: February 12, 1963

Musicians

- Mike Love - vocals
- David Marks - guitar
- Brian Wilson - bass guitar, vocals
- Carl Wilson - guitar, vocals
- Dennis Wilson - drums, vocals

See also

- The Beach Boys
- Surfin' USA
- List of songs by The Beach Boys

Forever

"Forever"		
Single by The Beach Boys		
Released	February, 1971	
Format	Vinyl	
Recorded	January 9 and March 17, 1969	
Genre	Pop rock	
Length	2:40	
Label	Brother Records/Reprise Records	
Producer	The Beach Boys	
The Beach Boys singles chronology		
"Tears in the Morning"/"It's About Time" (1970)	"Cool, Cool Water"/"Forever" (1971)	"Wouldn't It Be Nice (live)" (1971)

"**Forever**" is a song written by Dennis Wilson and his close friend Gregg Jakobson. It was released in 1970 as the ninth track on The Beach Boys' *Sunflower* album and features Dennis on lead vocals. The song, along with the rest of the album was produced by The Beach Boys. Brian Wilson declared, "'Forever' has to be the most harmonically beautiful thing I've ever heard. It's a rock and roll prayer."

The lead vocal is sung by Dennis Wilson. With backing vocals sung by his brothers, Brian and Carl, his cousin Mike Love and Alan Jardine. An a cappella version of the song was included on The Beach Boys' *Hawthorne, CA* anthology album.

Cover versions

A cover version of the song by American Spring appeared on their début 1972 album, *Spring*, featuring Marilyn Wilson, wife of Brian Wilson, on lead vocal. It also featured a new instrumental and vocal arrangement by Brian as well as production by Brian Wilson, Stephen Desper and David Sandler as did the rest of the album. Although the album sold poorly, it has since become a sought-after collectible. The album was later re-issued by Rhino Records in 1988.

On The Beach Boys' 1992 album *Summer in Paradise*, "Forever" featured John Stamos on lead vocal. Stamos had previously sung the song on two occasions; both were on the television series *Full House*, in which he played the character Jesse Katsopolis. The first was a recording sung at his character's wedding, while the second was a recording sung for his character's twin sons.

The 1992 music video, titled "Forever by Jesse and the Rippers", featured Stamos predominantly. Three of The Beach Boys members are however briefly shown singing harmonies with Stamos: Carl Wilson, Bruce Johnston, and Mike Love. Brian Wilson and Al Jardine did not participate in the video because of their limited relationship with The Beach Boys at the time.

The 2005 Starbucks compilation album, *Sweetheart 2005: Love Songs*, features a cover by Dean Wareham.

In 2006, the song was also covered by American singer and television host Carnie Wilson. It's on an album of lullabies entitled *A Mother's Gift: Lullabies from the Heart*, created shortly after the birth of her daughter Lola. Carnie is Dennis Wilson's niece.

See also

- List of songs by The Beach Boys

Friends

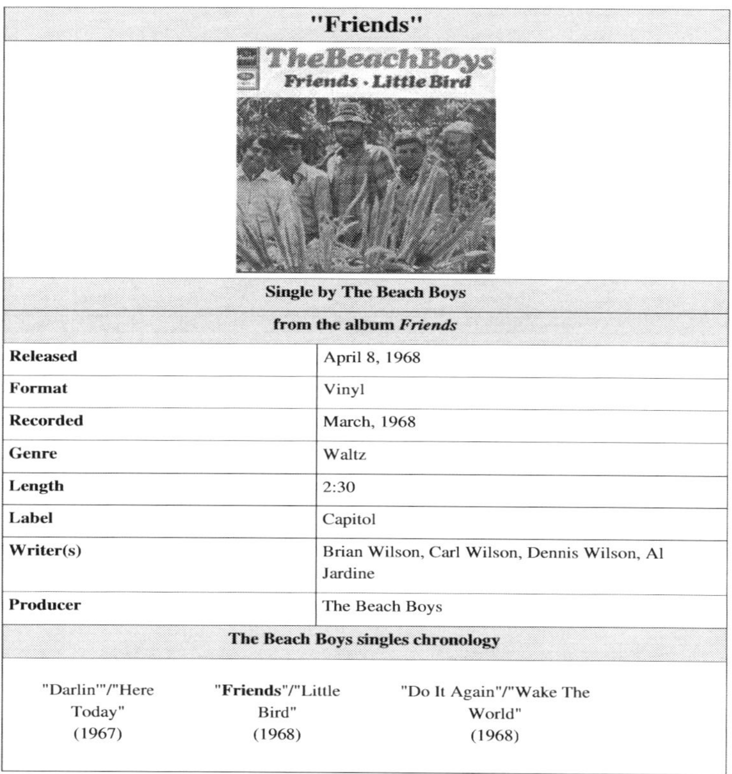

"Friends"	
Single by The Beach Boys	
from the album *Friends*	
Released	April 8, 1968
Format	Vinyl
Recorded	March, 1968
Genre	Waltz
Length	2:30
Label	Capitol
Writer(s)	Brian Wilson, Carl Wilson, Dennis Wilson, Al Jardine
Producer	The Beach Boys

The Beach Boys singles chronology		
"Darlin'"/"Here Today" (1967)	"**Friends**"/"Little Bird" (1968)	"Do It Again"/"Wake The World" (1968)

"**Friends**" is a song written by Brian Wilson, Carl Wilson, Dennis Wilson and Al Jardine for the American pop band The Beach Boys. It was released on their 1968 album *Friends*. It was also released as a single, with the B-side of the single being "Little Bird". The single peaked at #47 in the U.S. and #25 in the U.K. The song was recorded in March 1968.

Brian once stated, "The cut 'Friends' was, in my opinion, a good way to keep waltzes alive. Carl had sung...before and now he spearheaded this cut with a heavy vocal performance."

As Peter Reum, a Beach Boys historian, stated "'Friends' is a waltz, and it's been used at the Berklee College of Music to teach students how to write in 3/4 time."

Someone can be heard sneezing in the track at 2:01.

Performers

- *Carl Wilson:* Lead Vocals

See also

- List of songs by The Beach Boys

Frosty the Snowman

"Frosty the Snowman"	
Gene Autry & The Cass County Boys	
Released	December 14, 1950
Genre	Christmas Song
Label	Columbia Records
Writer	Jack Rollins and Steve Nelson

[[File:Frosty the Snowman GB.JPG|thumb|A Little Golden Book storybook edition of the popular song (1950). The illustrator was Corinne Malvern].]

"**Frosty the Snowman**" is a popular song written by Walter "Jack" Rollins and Steve Nelson, and first recorded by Gene Autry and the Cass County Boys in 1950. It was written after the success of Autry's recording of "Rudolph the Red-Nosed Reindeer" the previous year; Rollins and Nelson shipped the new song to Autry, who recorded "Frosty" in search of another seasonal hit. Like "Rudolph", "Frosty" was subsequently adapted to other media including a popular television special. The song was originally titled "Frosty the Snow Man".

Song

The song is about a snowman who came to life by some magical hat some children found;Jeremy brought him back to life and he then had playful adventures before he "hurried on his way." These included games, sports, and other jolly things. Near the end of their adventures together, the children are saddened by Frosty having to hurry on his way for the last time. However, Frosty reassures them by exclaiming, "I'll be back again some day." (Some versions of the song change the last line to "on Christmas Day!") It has been covered by many artists over the years, including The Jackson 5, The Ronettes, Bing Crosby, Nat King Cole, Ella Fitzgerald, Larry Groce, Ray Conniff, the Cocteau Twins, Alvin and the Chipmunks, The Beach Boys, Leon Redbone with Dr. John, Red Foley (and his daughters), Fiona Apple, Connie Talbot (2008 and 2009) and countless other musical acts (including a 2005 recording of the song by actor Burt Reynolds).

Jimmy Durante has recorded two versions, one with the earlier alternative lyric, and another for a television special of the same name (see below).

"Frosty" was recorded by Ella Fitzgerald on her Verve release Ella Wishes You a Swinging Christmas.

The Canadian Brass are known for a version that is both jazzy and darkly humorous ("One more time!" . . . "you know what happens when Frosty gets hot!"). Then he melted and faded away with the winter!

Charts

Gene Autry version	
Chart (1950)	**Peak position**
US Pop Singles	7

Perry Como version	
Chart (1957)	**Peak position**
US Pop Singles	74

Johnny Mathis version	
Chart (2003)	**Peak position**
US Adult Contemporary	29

Kimberley Locke version	
Chart (2007)	**Peak position**
US Hot Adult Contemporary Tracks	1
Canadian Adult Contemporary	40
Billboard Top AC Songs of 2008	46

Book

In 1950, Little Golden Books published "Frosty the Snow Man" as a children's book, adapted by Annie North Bedford and illustrated by Corinne Malvern.

1954 short film

In 1954, the UPA studio brought "Frosty" to life in a three-minute animated short which appears regularly on WGN-TV. This production included a bouncy, jazzy *a capella* version of the song and a limited animation style reminiscent of UPA's *Gerald McBoing-Boing*. The short, filmed entirely in black-and-white, has been a perennial WGN-TV Christmas classic, and was most recently broadcast on December 24 and 25, 2005, and every year since, as part of a WGN-TV children's programming retrospective, along with their two other short Christmas classics, "Suzy Snowflake" and "Hardrock, Coco and Joe".

The three cartoons are also a tradition on WJAC-TV in Johnstown, PA, which not only broadcasts the cartoons on their station, but also make it available on their website.

1969 Rankin-Bass television special

In 1969, the Rankin-Bass company produced a thirty-minute animated television special of *Frosty the Snowman* that featured the voices of comedians Jimmy Durante as narrator and Jackie Vernon as the title character. This was a story based on the discovery of Frosty the Snowman. Two sequels were produced, *Frosty's Winter Wonderland* (based upon the song Winter Wonderland) in 1976 in which Frosty got Married and *Rudolph and Frosty's Christmas in July* in 1979, followed by *The Legend of Frosty the Snowman* many years later, in 2005. A derivative work,

Frosty Returns, was broadcast on CBS in 1992.

Movie Connections

The version performed by The Ronettes is featured in the film *Goodfellas*, after the Lufthansa heist scene.

External links

- **Lyrics to** Frosty The Snowman [1]

References

[1] http://www.allchristmaslyrics.com/frosty-the-snowman-lyrics.htm

Full Sail

"Full Sail"	
Song by The Beach Boys from the album *L.A. (Light Album)*	
Released	March 19, 1979
Recorded	July-November, 1978
Genre	pop
Length	2:56
Label	Brother/Caribou/CBS
Composer	Carl Wilson, Geoffrey Cushing-Murray
Producer	Bruce Johnston, The Beach Boys, James William Guercio
L.A. (Light Album) **track listing**	
Lady Lynda (2) **"Full Sail"** (3) Angel Come Home (4)	

"Full Sail" is a song written by Carl Wilson and Geoffrey Cushing-Murray for the American pop band The Beach Boys. It was released on their 1979 album *L.A. (Light Album)*.

It was chosen to be the b-side to "Lady Lynda", a single released in the summer of 1979.

Details

- *Written by:* Carl Wilson/Geoffrey Cushing-Murray
- *Album:* L.A. (Light Album)
- *Time:* 2 min 56 sec
- *Produced by:* Bruce Johnston/The Beach Boys/James William Guercio

Performers

- *Carl Wilson:* Lead Vocals

See also

- The Beach Boys
- L.A. (Light Album)
- List of songs by The Beach Boys

Fun, Fun, Fun

"Fun, Fun, Fun"	
Single by The Beach Boys	
from the album *Shut Down Volume 2*	
Released	February 3, 1964
Format	Vinyl
Recorded	January 1, 1964
Genre	Sunshine pop
Length	2:16
Label	Capitol Records
Writer(s)	Brian Wilson/Mike Love
Producer	Brian Wilson

The Beach Boys singles chronology		
"Little Saint Nick"/"The Lord's Prayer" (1963)	**"Fun, Fun, Fun"**/"Why Do Fools Fall In Love" (1964)	"I Get Around"/"Don't Worry Baby" (1964)

"Fun, Fun, Fun", written by Brian Wilson and Mike Love, was a hit single by The Beach Boys that was released in 1964 on the band's album *Shut Down Volume 2*.

Composition

The song was written by Brian Wilson and Mike Love about Shirley England, the daughter of the owner of radio station KNAK in Salt Lake City, Utah (not to be confused with the call letters now assigned to a station in Delta, Utah) where she worked as a teenager. She borrowed her father's Ford Thunderbird to go study at the library. Instead of driving to the library, she ended up at a hamburger stand. When her father found out he took the car away. The next day she was at the radio station complaining about it to the staff while The Beach Boys were visiting and they were inspired to write this song.[1]

The Wilsons' father, Murry, always the critical conservative, denounced the whole idea for the song as immoral, and tried to prevent the group from recording it. The song, backed by a single-only mix of a cover version of Frankie Lymon and The Teenagers' "Why Do Fools Fall In Love", became a top-five hit. This argument set the seed for further deterioration in the family. It finally led to Murry being sacked as The Beach Boys manager a few months later when "I Get Around" was about to become the first number-one single for The Beach Boys.

The opening electric guitar introduction of the original version of the song was based on Chuck Berry's Johnny B. Goode, which was released in 1958.

Recording

The song was recorded on January 1, 1964 at Western Recorders. The instrumental track was released on the 2001 archival release *Hawthorne, CA*. The song features Mike Love on lead vocals.

The stereo and mono mixes stem from the same recording but have a significant difference: the fadeout on the stereo mix fades out early into the song's outro, with the instruments fading away before the vocals (and an overdubbed drum part). The mono mix, as heard on the 45 as well as mono copies of 'Shut Down Volume 2' has an extended outro.

The verse is taken from Chuck Berrys Carol.

Single release

The "Fun, Fun, Fun" single backed with "Why Do Fools Fall In Love" was released in the United States in February 1964. The single peaked at the number 5 spot on the *Billboard* chart.

In the United Kingdom the single was released in March 1964 through Capitol Records. However, the single failed to chart. In Australia, the single peaked at the number 6 position, which was the band's highest charting single in Australia at that time. In West Germany, the single became their first single to chart in the country when it peaked at the number 49 position. The single peaked at #4 in The Philippines (February 1965) with thirteen weeks in its top 10, and spent four weeks at #3 in Hong Kong (December 1965) with ten weeks in its top 10.

In February 1996, the Status Quo version of the song, featuring The Beach Boys, was released under Polygram Records as a single in the United Kingdom. The single, featuring another artist on the B-side, peaked at the number 24 position on the charts.

Album and alternate releases

The song was first released on an album in the United States in March 1964 on the band's *Shut Down Volume 2* album. In the United Kingdom the album was released in July 1964 and it was only the band's second album to be issued in the U.K. (as opposed to the fifth album in the U.S.) The song was also released in Britain on the *Fun, Fun, Fun EP* which included both "Fun, Fun, Fun" & "In My Room" on the A-side and "Little Deuce Coupe" and "Why Do Fools Fall In Love" on the B-side. The EP charted at the number 19 position.

The song was covered in 1996 by the then-current lineups of The Beach Boys and Status Quo (see *Don't Stop*), with a new verse written for the song. The Beach Boys sang mainly backing vocals, with Status Quo's Francis Rossi performing the lead vocal for the entire song, except the new verse, which was sung by Mike Love. The instrumental track was released on the 2001 album *Hawthorne, CA*.

The song is also regularly released on many of the band's greatest hits albums including the 1974 chart topping compilation *Endless Summer*; the 1986 compilation *Made in U.S.A.*; the 1993 box set *Good Vibrations: Thirty Years of The Beach Boys*; the 1999 compilation *The Greatest Hits - Volume 1: 20 Good Vibrations* and the 2003 compilation *Sounds of Summer: The Very Best of The Beach Boys*.

Live versions

After the song was released it immediately became a regular in The Beach Boys live set. In the early years when it was released it was sometimes used as the band's concert opener. However, in the mid-70's it regularly became the band's concert closer. Several live renditions of the song have been officially released on various Beach Boys releases. It was first released on their first live album *Beach Boys Concert* in 1964 as the opening track. It was later released on their 1973 live album *The Beach Boys in Concert* as the album closer. A concert from Anaheim Stadium on July 3, 1976 which featured the song was filmed and produced by Lorne Michaels for a Beach Boys television special which first aired in the United States in August, 1976. The TV special was later released on video and DVD as *Good Vibrations Tour*. In 1980, a live rendition was recorded, though not released until 2002 on the *Good Timin': Live at Knebworth England 1980* live album. Footage from the concert was also released on video and DVD format. The band also performed a live version of the song at the NBC Television Studios in Burbank, California which was filmed on March 14, 1964. Footage of the concert was later released on the DVD *The Lost Concert*.

Cover versions

Both the Boomerangs and Brendan Bower & His Royal Show Band Waterford covered the song in 1965.

Two french covers of the song have been released by Les Missiles in 1964 and Les Excentriques in 1965 under the title "Fume, Fume, Fume".

Dino, Desi, & Billy covered the song in 1966.

In 1967 The Surfriders covered the song.

During a concert at the Fillmore in 1970, New Riders of the Purple Sage performed a shortened rendition of the song.

The Carpenters did a cover of the song for their 1973 album, *Now & Then*.

In 1976 Adam Surf & The Pebble Beach Band covered the song.

Papa Doo Run Run covered the song on their 1985 album *California Project*.

In 1986, Joan Jett & The Blackhearts covered the song.

In 1994, both Cathedral City Project and Trygve Thue covered the song. In 2002, John B. & The Surfin´ Safaris covered the song on their 2002 album *A Tribute to the Beach Boys*.

In 1996 the British rock band Status Quo did a version of Fun, Fun, Fun with The Beach Boys.

This song was performed by Brian Wilson and the ensemble that performed for *An All-Star Tribute to Brian Wilson* in 2001, which was later released on DVD.

Caleigh Peters, a pop rock musician, performed a cover of this song for the soundtrack of *Herbie: Fully Loaded*, a Walt Disney Pictures movie released in 2005.

In 2000, Grandaddy covered the song on their album The Windfall Varietal. The track is labeled Fun x3.

Charts

Chart (1964)	Peak position
Australian Singles Chart[2]	10
German Singles Chart[3]	49
U.S. *Billboard* Hot 100	5

See also

- List of songs by The Beach Boys
- Greg Panfile's Musical Analysis of "Fun, Fun, Fun" [4]

References

[1] Beach Boys' Hit Inspired by a Utah Gal Having All the Fun (http://www.ksl.com/index.php?nid=148&sid=886044)
[2] "Australian Singles Charts" (http://www.mountvernonandfairway.de/charts10.htm). mountvernonandfairway.de. . Retrieved 12 November 2007.
[3] "German Singles Charts" (http://www.mountvernonandfairway.de/charts9.htm). mountvernonandfairway.de. . Retrieved 12 November 2007.
[4] http://www.cabinessence.net/essays/mob5.html

Funky Pretty

"California Saga: California/Funky Pretty"		
Single by The Beach Boys		
from the album *Holland*		
Released	April 16, 1973	
Format	Vinyl	
Genre	Pop, Rock music	
Length	4:09	
Label	Brother	
Writer(s)	Brian Wilson, Mike Love, Jack Rieley	
Producer	Brian and Carl Wilson	
The Beach Boys singles chronology		
"Sail On, Sailor"/"Only with You" (1973)	"California Saga: California"/"**Funky Pretty**" (1973)	"Child of Winter"/"Susie Cincinnati" (1974)

"Funky Pretty" is a song written by Brian Wilson, Mike Love and Jack Rieley for the American pop band The Beach Boys. It was released on their 1973 album *Holland*.

Performers

Alternating lead vocals between Carl Wilson, Al Jardine, Mike Love, and Blondie Chaplin, with the rest of the group doing backup vocals.

See also

- The Beach Boys
- Holland (album)
- List of The Beach Boys songs

Games Two Can Play

"Games Two Can Play" is a song written by Brian Wilson for the American pop band The Beach Boys. The song was released on the band's 1993 box set *Good Vibrations: Thirty Years of The Beach Boys*.

See also

- List of songs by The Beach Boys

Getcha Back

"Getcha Back/Male Ego"	
Single by The Beach Boys	
from the album *The Beach Boys*	
Released	May 8, 1985
Format	Vinyl
Genre	Pop music
Length	2:59
Label	Brother Records
Writer(s)	Mike Love, Terry Melcher
Producer	Steve Levine

The Beach Boys singles chronology		
"Come Go with Me"/"Don't Go Near the Water" (1981)	"**Getcha Back**"/"Male Ego" (1985)	"It's Gettin' Late"/"It's O.K." (1985)

"**Getcha Back**" is a song written by Mike Love and Terry Melcher for the American pop band The Beach Boys. It was released on their 1985 album *The Beach Boys*. It was the band's first release since the tragic drowning death of Dennis Wilson in 1983. While the song only peaked at number 26 nationally, "Getcha Back" managed to recapture the sound and feel of the Beach Boys' early hits.

The music video directed by Dominic Orlando, was filmed on location in Malibu and Venice, California. (1985). It featured a then-unknown Katherine Kelly Lang, who went on to play Brooke Logan on the soap opera *The Bold and the Beautiful*.

Mark McGrath, lead singer of the California rock band Sugar Ray, performed a cover of this song for the soundtrack of *Herbie: Fully Loaded*, a Walt Disney Pictures movie released in 2005. It appears at the beginning, during the flashback of Herbie's racing career.

Performers

- John Alder - guitars
- Graham Broad - percussion
- Steve Grainger - baritone saxophone
- Al Jardine - vocals
- Bruce Johnston - vocals
- Steve Levine - synth, drum programming
- Julian Lindsay - keyboards
- Mike Love - lead vocal
- Terry Melcher - keyboards
- Brian Wilson - lead vocal
- Carl Wilson - vocals

See also

- The Beach Boys
- The Beach Boys (album)
- List of The Beach Boys songs

Gettin' Hungry

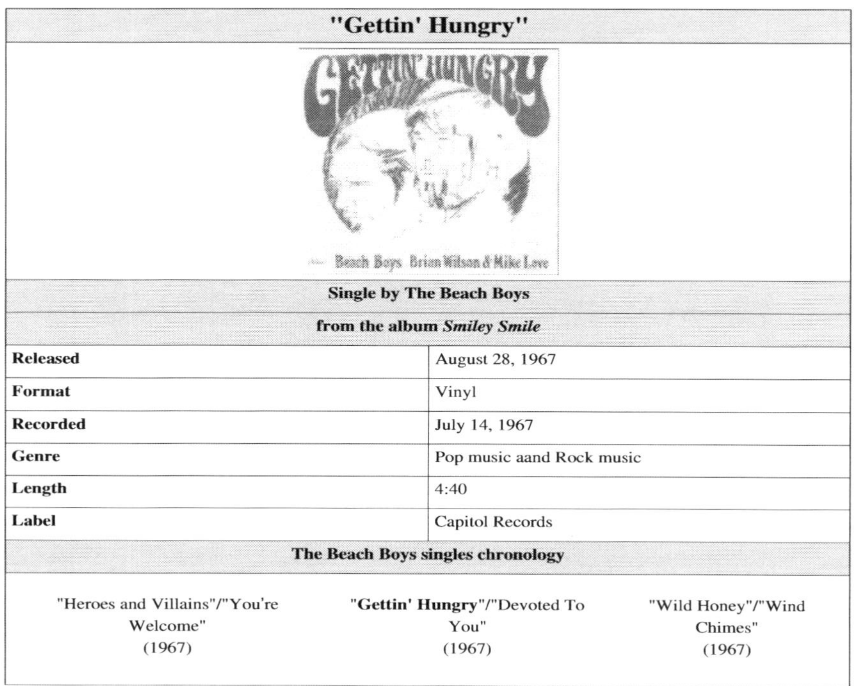

"Gettin' Hungry"	
Single by The Beach Boys	
from the album *Smiley Smile*	
Released	August 28, 1967
Format	Vinyl
Recorded	July 14, 1967
Genre	Pop music aand Rock music
Length	4:40
Label	Capitol Records

The Beach Boys singles chronology		
"Heroes and Villains"/"You're Welcome" (1967)	**"Gettin' Hungry"**/"Devoted To You" (1967)	"Wild Honey"/"Wind Chimes" (1967)

"Gettin' Hungry" is a song written by Brian Wilson and Mike Love for the American pop band The Beach Boys. It was released on their 1967 album *Smiley Smile*. It is one of the few songs on the album apparently unconnected with the aborted *Smile* project.

Performers

- Brian Wilson: Lead vocals
- Mike Love: Lead vocals

See also

- List of songs by The Beach Boys

Girl Don't Tell Me

"Girl Don't Tell Me"	
Song by The Beach Boys from the album *Summer Days (And Summer Nights!!)*	
Released	June 28, 1965
Genre	Pop music
Length	2:19
Label	Capitol Records
Writer	Brian Wilson/Mike Love
Producer	Brian Wilson
***Summer Days (And Summer Nights!!)* track listing**	
"Salt Lake City" (4) "**Girl Don't Tell Me**" (5) "Help Me, Rhonda" (6)	

"**Girl Don't Tell Me**" is a song written by Brian Wilson and Mike Love for the American pop band The Beach Boys. It was released on their 1965 album *Summer Days (and Summer Nights!!)*. In December 1965, it was chosen to be the B-side to The Beach Boys' "Barbara Ann" single, which would chart at #2 in the U.S. and #3 in the U.K. The song was originally credited to just Wilson. Mike Love's name was added as a result of a lawsuit filed by him against Wilson in the 1990s.

Brian Wilson claimed in his autobiography *Wouldn't It Be Nice* that he wrote this song for The Beatles to record, though there's no evidence he ever actually submitted the song to them.

Recording

The song was recorded on April 30, 1965 at Western Studios. Chuck Britz was the engineer. It is one of the first songs to feature Carl Wilson as the lead vocalist (his first unshared lead was on "Pom Pom Play Girl"), and is one of the few Beach Boys songs from the era to feature no backing vocals. It is also the first recording session that Bruce Johnston participated in as a member of The Beach Boys.

musicians

- Bruce Johnston - celesta
- Ron Swallow - tambourine
- Brian Wilson - bass guitar
- Carl Wilson - guitars, lead vocals
- Dennis Wilson - drums

Alternate versions

The song appears on Al Jardine's album, *Live in Las Vegas*, with Al's son Adam Jardine handling the lead vocals.

The song was covered with backing vocals on a 1966 Immediate single by the UK group Tony Rivers and the Castaways (not to be confused with the US band The Castaways who had the 1965 hit "Liar, Liar").

Indie-rock band The Shins covered the song and was part of their setlist for their 2009 tour.

Brooklyn lo-fi all-girl group Vivian Girls also covered the song on their "Surf's Up" 7".

A version of this song with French words was recorded by Souvenir, under the title "Ne de pas".

The Girl from New York City

"You're So Good to Me"	
Song by The Beach Boys from the album *Summer Days (And Summer Nights!!)*	
Released	June 28, 1965
Recorded	May 24, 1965
Genre	Rock, sunshine pop
Length	1:54
Label	Capitol
Composer	Brian Wilson/Mike Love
Producer	Brian Wilson
***Summer Days (And Summer Nights!!)* track listing**	
"You're So Good to Me" (1)	"Amusement Parks USA" (2)

"**The Girl from New York City**" is a song written by Brian Wilson and Mike Love for the American pop band The Beach Boys. It was released on their 1965 album *Summer Days (and Summer Nights!!)*. It was written as an answer song to The Ad Libs' hit from earlier that year, "The Boy from New York City".

Details

- Written by: Brian Wilson/Mike Love
- Album: *Summer Days (and Summer Nights!!)*
- Time: 1 min 54 sec
- Produced by: Brian Wilson
- Recording date: May 24, 1965

Musicians

- Hal Blaine - drums
- Steve Douglas - saxophone
- Al Jardine - guitar, vocals
- Bruce Johnston - vocals, piano
- Mike Love - lead vocal
- Jack Nimitz - saxophone
- Clifford Hils - upright bass
- Ray Pohlman - bass guitar
- Brian Wilson - vocals
- Carl Wilson - guitar, vocals

See also

- List of songs by The Beach Boys

Girls on the Beach

"**Girls on the Beach**" is a song written by Brian Wilson for the American pop band The Beach Boys. It was released on their 1964 album *All Summer Long*. The song also served as the title tune for the movie "The Girls On The Beach".

Details

- *Written by:* Brian Wilson
- *Album:* All Summer Long
- *Time:* 2 min 24 sec
- *Produced by:* Brian Wilson

Performers

- *Brian Wilson:* Lead Vocals
- *Dennis Wilson:* Lead Vocals

See also

- The Beach Boys
- All Summer Long
- List of songs by The Beach Boys

God Only Knows

"God Only Knows"	
Single by The Beach Boys	
from the album *Pet Sounds*	
A-side	"Wouldn't It Be Nice"
Released	July 11, 1966
Format	Vinyl
Recorded	Western Studios March 10, 1966 Columbia Studios March 10, 1966 April 11, 1966
Genre	Pop
Length	2:49
Label	Capitol (#5706)
Writer(s)	Brian Wilson, Tony Asher
Producer	Brian Wilson

The Beach Boys singles chronology		
"Sloop John B"/"You're So Good to Me" (1966	**"Wouldn't It Be Nice"/"God Only Knows"** (1966)	"Good Vibrations"/"Let's Go Away For Awhile" (1966)

Pet Sounds track listing		
"Sloop John B" (7)	**"God Only Knows"** (8)	"I Know There's an Answer" (9)

"God Only Knows" is a song by American surf rock band The Beach Boys. It is the eighth track on the group's 11th studio album, *Pet Sounds* (1966), and one of their most widely recognized songs. "God Only Knows" was composed and produced by Brian Wilson with lyrics by Tony Asher and lead vocal by Carl Wilson.

The song broke new ground in many ways. It was one of the first commercial pop songs to use the word 'God' in its title. The song was also far more technically sophisticated than anything the Beach Boys, or arguably any pop group, had ever attempted before — particularly the complicated melodic structure and vocal harmonies. As producer, Brian Wilson also used many unorthodox instruments for the genre, including the harpsichord and French horns that are heard in the song's famous introduction.

Mojo magazine ranked the song as the 13th greatest song of all time. Pitchfork Media named it the best song of the 1960s. The song is 25th on *Rolling Stone*'s list of the 500 greatest songs of all time.[1]

Writing

Brian Wilson explains in his autobiography ***Wouldn't It Be Nice: My Own Story*** that the melody of "God Only Knows" was inspired by a John Sebastian song that he had been listening to. However, the opening French horn motif bears a very close relationship to a motif, also stated by the French horns, in Act II Scene 2, the "Hagen" motif (itself a variation of the "nature" motif) of Richard Wagner's *Die Götterdämmerung* (Twilight of the Gods).

Wilson once described that the song "was a vision that Tony and I had. It's like being blind but in being blind, you can see more. You close your eyes; you're able to see a place or something that's happening." According to Wilson, "the idea summarized everything I was trying to express in a single song."

Tony Asher felt confident when writing the song that it would be a big hit. As he explains, "This is the one [song] that I thought would be a hit record because it was so incredibly beautiful. I was concerned that maybe the lyrics weren't up to the same level as the music; how many love songs start off with the line, 'I may not always love you'? I liked that twist, and fought to start the song that way. Working with Brian, I didn't have a whole lot of fighting to do, but I was certainly willing to fight to the end for that. I was probably saying to myself, 'God, I hope I'm right about this,' because you're never quite sure. But I knew that it would work, because by the second part, the real meaning of the song has come out: 'I'll love you till the sun burns out, then I'm gone,' ergo 'I'm gonna love you forever.' I guess that in the end, 'God Only Knows' is the song that most people remember, and love the most."[2]

Just as Tony Asher said, Wilson "hated the opening line" of the song as "it was too negative." He eventually gave in after hearing the following lines in the song.

Naming the song

"God Only Knows" was one of the first pop songs to use the word "God" in its title (a decision that Wilson and Asher agonized over, fearing it would not get airplay as a result). As Brian's former wife Marilyn describes, "The first time I heard it, Brian played it for me at the piano. And I went, 'Oh my God, he's talking about God in a record.' It was pretty daring to me. And it was another time I thought to myself, 'Oh, boy, he's really taking a chance.' I thought it was almost too religious. Too square. At that time. Yes, it was so great that he would say it and not be intimidated by what anybody else would think of the words or what he meant."[3]

Tony Asher also explains that he and Brian "had lengthy conversations during the writing of 'God Only Knows', because unless you were Kate Smith and you were singing 'God Bless America', no one thought you could say 'God' in a song. No one had done it, and Brian didn't want to be the first person to try it. He said, 'We'll just never get any air play.' Isn't it amazing that we thought that? But it worked, and 'God Only Knows' is, to me, one of the great songs of our time. I mean *the* great songs. Not because I wrote the lyrics, but because it is an amazing piece of music that we were able to write a very compelling lyric to. It's the simplicity — the inference that 'I am who I am because of you' — that makes it very personal and tender.[2]

Wilson explains that although he feared putting the word 'God' in the title of the song, he eventually agreed to keep it. He explains that he agreed to keep the word 'God' in the title firstly, "because God was a spiritual word, and secondly, because Brian and The Beach Boys would "be breaking ground."

Choosing the vocalists

Brian Wilson originally intended to sing lead vocal on "God Only Knows" but in the end sacrificed the lead vocal to his brother, Carl: "Well, I thought I was gonna do it. As the song progressed, I said, 'Hey, I feel kind of natural doing this.' But when we completed creating the song, I said my brother Carl will probably be able to impart the message better than I could, so I sacrificed that one. But he had a good time singing it."[3]

Carl Wilson later described how lucky he felt being given the opportunity to sing 'God Only Knows': "I was honored to be able to sing that one. It is so beautifully written, it sings itself. Brian said something like, 'Don't do anything with it. Just sing it real straight. No effort. Take in a breath. Let it go real easy.' I was really grateful to be the one to sing that song. I felt extremely lucky."[3]

Bruce Johnston explains that "Brian really worked a lot on 'God Only Knows', and at one point, he had all the Beach Boys, Terry Melcher and two of the Rovell sisters [Brian's wife Marilyn and her sister Diane] on it. It just got so overloaded; it was nuts. So he was smart enough to peel it all back, and he held voices back to the bridge, me at the top end, Carl in the middle and Brian on the bottom. At that point, Brian's right move was to get subtler. He had a very tender track here. 'God Only Knows' is a very small masterpiece with a major heartbeat, and he was right to peel everybody back and wind up with the three parts. In fact, it's probably the only well-known Beach Boys track that has just three voices on it."[3]

Recording

The instrumental section of the song was recorded on March 10, 1966, at Western Recorders, Hollywood, California, with the session engineered by Chuck Britz and produced by Brian Wilson. The instrumental part of the song took 20 takes to achieve what is the master take of the song. Present on the day of the instrumental recording were Hal Blaine on drums, Jim Gordon on percussion, Lyle Ritz on string bass, Carol Kaye on electric bass, Ray Pohlman on danelectro bass, Don Randi on piano, Larry Knechtel on organ, Carl Fortina and Frank Morocco on accordion, Leonard Hartman on clarinet and bass clarinet, Bill Green and Jim Horn on flute, Alan Robinson on French horn, Jay Migliori on baritone saxophone, Leonard Malarsky and Sid Sharp on violin, Darrel Terwilliger on viola and Jesse Erlich on cello.

According to Brian, many of the musicians who were present at the 'God Only Knows' sessions claim that those sessions were some of "the most magical, beautiful musical experiences they've ever heard." According to Brian there were 23 musicians present during the 'God Only Knows' sessions, though only 16 are credited as being present on the actual take that was used for the final song. At the time, 23 musicians was an astounding number of musicians for a pop record. All the musicians played simultaneously, creating "a rich, heavenly blanket of music."

The vocal track was recorded between March and April 1966 at Columbia Studios, Hollywood, California, with the session engineered by Ralph Balantin and produced by Brian Wilson. The song features three voices on the track. Carl Wilson is featured on lead vocals, with Brian Wilson and Bruce Johnston backing him. Bruce Johnston explained that, "The really cute thing is that at the end of the session, Carl was really tired, and he went home. So Brian ... remember, this was 8-track, so, he now has these extra tracks at his disposal. But there were just the two of us. So in the fade, he's singing two of the three parts. He sang the top and the bottom part and I sang in the middle."[3] Brian used the production technique of double-tracking Carl's voice, so that his voice is simultaneously singing the same part twice, to give the vocal a fuller and richer sound; Brian Wilson used this technique often during the recording of *Pet Sounds*.

Recognition and influence

While Mojo Magazine ranked the song 13th greatest song of all time, when first released it only reached No. 39 on the US charts in 1966. Treated as the A-side across Europe, it was a great success scoring No. 2 in the UK, and in national charts cited contemporarily by Billboard, No. 3 in Ireland, No. 4 in Holland and Belgium, No. 6 in Norway, No. 22 in Germany; and No. 2 in Australia. The song "God Only Knows" is part of the The Rock and Roll Hall of Fame's 500 Songs that Shaped Rock and Roll list.[4] The song was also recognized by Pitchfork Media as the number one "greatest song of the 1960s" in their feature on the 200 Best Songs of the 1960s.[5]

Paul McCartney has expressed on a number of occasions his love for the song. In an interview with David Leaf in 1990 he stated, "It's a really, really great song — it's a big favorite of mine. I was asked recently to give my top 10 favorite songs for a Japanese radio station ... I didn't think long and hard on it but I popped that [God Only Knows] on the top of my list. It's very deep. Very emotional, always a bit of a choker for me, that one. There are certain songs that just hit home with me, and they're the strangest collection of songs ... but that is high on the list, I must say ... God Only Knows' ' lyrics are great. Those do it to me every time."

Speaking on a special Radio 1 show to mark the British station's 40th anniversary, McCartney said "'God Only Knows' is one of the few songs that reduces me to tears every time I hear it. It's really just a love song, but it's brilliantly done. It shows the genius of Brian. "I've actually performed it with him and I'm afraid to say that during the sound check I broke down. It was just too much to stand there singing this song that does my head in and to stand there singing it with Brian."[3]

Bono said in October 2006 during Brian Wilson's induction into the UK Music Hall of Fame that "the string arrangement on 'God Only Knows' is fact and proof of angels". Jimmy Webb, an American popular music composer, has also stated his love for the song, stating, "I love 'God Only Knows' and its bow to the baroque that goes all the way back to 1740 and J.S. Bach. It represents the whole tradition of liturgical music that I feel is a spiritual part of Brian's music. And Carl's singing is pretty much at its pinnacle — as good as it ever got."[2]

Brian's mother, Audree Wilson, believes that "God Only Knows" was one of Brian's finest ever compositions as she stated in an interview: "'God Only Knows' ... What can you say about it? I still think it's one of his greatest pieces."[3]

In a 2003 solo concert in Tel Aviv, Steven Wilson, frontman of Porcupine Tree, declared "God Only Knows" as his favorite song of all time. On the insurgentes listening party that took place in Mexico City in 2009, Steven Wilson said it was a perfect song. In a poll on the MTV station, Vh1, it was placed No. 28 on the U.K's Nation's Favourite Lyric. It was voted by the Listeners of BBC Radio 2 as one of the three songs that changes people's lives.

Simon Neil of Scottish band Biffy Clyro has the lyrics "God only knows what I'd be without you" tattooed across his chest.

The song inspired songwriter Margo Guryan to move into writing "pop" music. She said: "I thought it was just gorgeous. I bought the record and played it a million times, then sat down and wrote 'Think of Rain.' That's really how I started writing that way. I just decided it was better than what was happening in jazz."

Jake Burns, the lead singer of Stiff Little Fingers, thinks "God Only Knows" is the best song of all time.

Album and alternate releases

The song first appeared on The Beach Boys classic 1966 album *Pet Sounds* in monophonic sound format. It was also released July 11, 1966, as the B-side of the "Wouldn't It Be Nice" single. The song appears in several stages of the recording process on *The Pet Sounds Sessions* box set, including its original monophonic mix; the first ever original stereo mix of the song, which was mixed by Mark Linett; highlights from the tracking dates, which documents the progress of the recording of the instrumental track; the finished instrumental track; an *a cappella* mix of the song; an alternate version, with a saxophone solo; another alternate version with an *a cappella* tag; and a version with Brian singing lead vocals.

Live versions appear on two of the band's albums: *Live In London* and *Good Timin': Live at Knebworth England 1980*.

In the documentary *I Just Wasn't Made for These Times*, there is a version of Brian Wilson playing the song at his piano with his mother by his side and with Carl Wilson singing lead vocals. Live versions of the song were also recorded and released on two of Brian Wilson's live albums: the 2000 release *Live At The Roxy Theatre* and the 2002 release *Pet Sounds Live*.

There is another live version of this song on Al Jardine's solo album, *Live in Las Vegas*, which has lead vocals by Carnie Wilson.

Musicians

- Hal Blaine — drums
- Jesse Erlich — cello
- Carl Fortina — accordion
- Jim Gordon — percussion
- Bill Green — flute
- Leonard Hartman — clarinet, bass clarinet
- Jim Horn — flute
- Bruce Johnston — backing vocals
- Carol Kaye — electric bass
- Larry Knechtel — organ
- Leonard Malarsky — violin
- Jay Migliori — baritone saxophone
- Frank Morocco — accordion
- Ray Pohlman — electric bass
- Don Randi — piano
- Lyle Ritz — upright bass
- Alan Robinson — French horn
- Sid Sharp — violin
- Darrel Terwilliger — viola
- Brian Wilson — backing vocals
- Carl Wilson — lead vocal, backing vocals

Cover versions

Cover versions of the song have been recorded by many artists, including Glen Campbell, Jack Jones, Claudine Longet, Andy Williams and Neil Diamond, David Bowie as well as many others. David Bowie recorded a version for his 1984 album *Tonight*. The 2004 film *Saved!* features a version by the film's star Mandy Moore over the opening credits, and a duet of the song by Moore and Michael Stipe (one of the film's producers) over the end credits. In 2005, Joss Stone recorded a version for a CD produced by Gap, on which various artists sang their own favourite songs. Brian Wilson also released a live CD version of Pet Sounds, Pet Sounds Live, which featured 'God Only Knows'. A Spanish version of the song by Charly García and Pedro Aznar is included in their 1991 album *Tango 4*.

Cultural references

The Beach Boys' version of the song appears on several movie releases. It underscores a lengthy montage sequence near the end of the Paul Thomas Anderson 1997 film *Boogie Nights* and it also appears on the *Boogie Nights Soundtrack*. It appears in the 2002 Raja Gosnell live-action film *Scooby Doo*. The song is the closing track of the Richard Curtis 2003 movie *Love Actually*, and hence it appears on the Love Actually Soundtrack. Two cover versions of the song were featured in the Brian Dannelly 2004 film *Saved!*. The song also served as the opening title credit score for the HBO series *Big Love* during the first three seasons. The song has also been featured in an episode of "The Wonder Years" and recently in a commercial for the Mastercard credit card company.

The song was featured in the film *My Life Without Me*. The main character (played by Sarah Polley) sings the song to her husband. "God Only Knows" was also featured prominently in the British drama/thriller entitled *Enduring Love*, in which one of the characters, Jed (Rhys Ifans), sings the song as he stalks Joe (Daniel Craig) in several of the film's creepier scenes.

'God Only Knows' was also featured in the British teen drama *Skins*, where it was sung in a choral style by Nicholas Hoult and Georgina Moffat as a way for Hoult's character Tony to emotionally damage his friend and girlfriend.

See also

- List of songs by The Beach Boys

References

[1] "The RS 500 Greatest Songs of All Time" (http://www.rollingstone.com/news/story/6595870/god_only_knows/1). *Rolling Stone*. . Retrieved 2008-09-21.

[2] *I Just Wasn't Made for These Times: Brian Wilson and the Making of Pet Sounds* by Charles L. Granata. Published by Unanimous Ltd, 2003. ISBN 1-55652-507-9

[3] *The Pet Sounds Sessions: "The Making Of Pet Sounds"* booklet

[4] Rock and Roll Hall of Fame "500 songs that shaped rock and roll" (http://www.rockhall.com/exhibithighlights/500-songs/)

[5] "200 Greatest Songs of the 1960s" (http://www.pitchforkmedia.com/article/feature/37901/The_200_Greatest_Songs_of_the_1960s/page_2). *Pitchfork*. . Retrieved August 18, 2006.

Goin' On

"Goin' On"	
Single by The Beach Boys	
from the album *Keepin' the Summer Alive*	
B-side	"Endless Harmony"
Released	March 11, 1980
Format	Vinyl
Genre	Pop
Length	3:00
Label	Caribou Records
Writer(s)	Brian Wilson, Mike Love
Producer	Bruce Johnston
The Beach Boys singles chronology	

"It's a Beautiful Day"/"Sumahama" (1979)	"Goin' On"/"Endless Harmony" (1980)	"Livin' with a Heartache"/"Santa Ana Winds" (1980)

"Goin' On" is a song written by Brian Wilson and Mike Love for the American pop band The Beach Boys. It was released on their 1980 album *Keepin' the Summer Alive*. The single reached number 83 on the *Billboard* Hot 100.

Performers

- Carl Wilson: Lead Vocals
- Mike Love: Lead Vocals

See also

- The Beach Boys
- Keepin' the Summer Alive
- List of songs by The Beach Boys

Goin' South

"Goin' South" is a song written by Carl Wilson and Geoffrey Cushing-Murray for the American pop band The Beach Boys. It was released on their 1979 album *L.A. (Light Album)*.

Details

- *Written by:* Carl Wilson/Geoffrey Cushing-Murray
- *Album:* L.A. (Light Album)
- *Time:* 3 min 16 sec
- *Produced by:* Bruce Johnston/The Beach Boys/James William Guercio

Performers

- *Carl Wilson:* Lead Vocals

See also

- The Beach Boys
- L.A. (Light Album)
- List of songs by The Beach Boys

Good Time

"Good Time"	
Song by The Beach Boys from the album *Love You*	
Released	April 11, 1977
Recorded	January 7, 1970 Brian Wilson's home studio
Genre	Rock and Pop music
Length	2:50
Label	Brother/Reprise
Composer	Brian Wilson and Al Jardine
Producer	Brian Wilson
Cover versions	
Spring	
***Love You* track listing**	
"Johnny Carson" (4) "**Good Time**" (5) "Honkin' Down The Highway" (6)	

"Good Time" is a song written by Brian Wilson and Al Jardine. It was recorded by The Beach Boys during the sessions for *Add Some Music*, but when that album was rejected and reconfigured into *Sunflower*, "Good Time" was not included. It was then recorded by Spring for their eponymous 1972 album.

The Beach Boys released their version of "Good Time" on *The Beach Boys Love You* in 1977.

The Beach Boys version

- written by - Brian Wilson/Al Jardine
- album - *The Beach Boys Love You*
- length - 2:50
- produced by - Brian Wilson
- lead vocals - Brian Wilson

Spring version

- album - *Spring*
- length - 2:50
- produced by - Brian Wilson/Stephen Desper/David Sandler
- lead vocals - Marilyn Wilson

The Spring recording of "Good Time" used the backing track recorded by The Beach Boys in 1970.

See also

- The Beach Boys
- Love You
- List of songs by The Beach Boys

Good Timin'

"Good Timin'"	
Single by The Beach Boys	
from the album *L.A. (Light Album)*	
Released	April 16, 1979
Format	Vinyl
Recorded	track: November 4, 1974 vocals: summer/fall 1978
Genre	Pop
Length	2:12
Label	Brother/Caribou/CBS
Writer(s)	Brian Wilson Carl Wilson
Producer	Bruce Johnston The Beach Boys James William Guercio

The Beach Boys singles chronology		
"Here Comes the Night"/"Baby Blue" (1979)	"**Good Timin'**"/"Love Surrounds Me" (1979)	"Lady Lynda"/"Full Sail" (1979)

"**Good Timin'**" is the second single that was released from the album *L.A. (Light Album)* in 1979 by The Beach Boys. The B-side of the single was "Love Surrounds Me".

"Good Timin'" reached number 40 in the U.S. during a stay of ten weeks on the *Billboard* Hot 100 singles chart. It was their first single to reach the Top 40 portion of the chart in nearly three years, since "It's OK" in October 1976. It also reached number 12 on the *Billboard* Adult Contemporary chart.

Performers

- *Carl Wilson:* Lead Vocals

See also

- List of The Beach Boys songs

Good Vibrations

"Good Vibrations"	
Single by The Beach Boys	
from the album *Smiley Smile*	
B-side	"Let's Go Away for Awhile"
Released	October 10, 1966
Format	7" single
Recorded	February–September 1966
Genre	Surf rock
Length	3:39
Label	Capitol
Writer(s)	Brian Wilson, Mike Love
Producer	Brian Wilson

The Beach Boys singles chronology		
"Wouldn't It Be Nice" (1966)	"Good Vibrations" (1966)	"Then I Kissed Her" (1967)

"**Good Vibrations**" is a song by American rock group The Beach Boys. Composed and produced by Brian Wilson, the song's lyrics were written by Wilson and Mike Love.

Released as a single on October 10, 1966 (backed with the *Pet Sounds* instrumental "Let's Go Away For Awhile"), it was The Beach Boy's third U.S. number-one hit, reaching the top of the *Billboard* Hot 100 chart in December 1966, as well as being their first British chart-topper. Initiated during the sessions for the *Pet Sounds* album, it was not taken from or issued as a lead single for an album, but as a stand-alone single, and later placed on the album *Smiley Smile* eleven months after its release.

Wilson's publicist Derek Taylor described "Good Vibrations" as a "pocket symphony". It featured instruments unusual for a pop song, including prominent use of the cello and an electro-theremin. It is number six on *Rolling Stone*'s list of the "500 Greatest Songs of All Time".[1] The song "Good Vibrations" is part of the The Rock and Roll Hall of Fame's 500 Songs that Shaped Rock and Roll list.[2]

Composition

Wilson recounted the genesis of the title "Good Vibrations" in his 1995 biopic, *I Just Wasn't Made for These Times*, and at other times. When he was a child, his mother told him that dogs could pick up "vibrations" from people, so that the dog would bark at "bad vibrations".[3] Wilson turned this into the general idea of vibrations (and Mike Love putting "good" in front of vibrations), and developed the idea of people being able to do the same with emotions.

Lyrics

Wilson first enlisted *Pet Sounds* lyricist Tony Asher for help in putting words to the idea. Soon after they met, Wilson asked his new writing partner Van Dyke Parks to pen lyrics for the song, but Parks declined. Beach Boys bandmate Mike Love supplied the final version of the lyrics around August 24, 1966.

According to Wilson, when he re-recorded "Good Vibrations" for his 2004 version of *Smile*, his wife, Melinda, suggested he use the original lyrics written by Tony Asher.

Recording

Originally composed during the Pet Sounds sessions with original lyrics by Tony Asher, Wilson recorded the song in sections, at different studios in order to capture the sound he heard in his head. Building upon the layered production approach he had begun to use with the *Pet Sounds* album, Wilson devoted months of effort to this single track.

The instrumental of the first version of the song was recorded on February 17, 1966. It was described in the session log as *#1 Untitled* (or as *Good, Good, Good Vibrations*), though on the tape Brian Wilson distinctly says "Good Vibrations, Take One". After 26 takes, a rough mono mix completed the session. Rough guide vocals were recorded the following day. By February 25, Wilson had placed the recording on hold in order to devote attention to the *Pet Sounds* album. The track was revisited on May 24, 1966, and worked on until June 18, at which time he put it aside again until August 24. The various sections of the song were edited together in a sort of musical collage, similar to The Beatles' later "Strawberry Fields Forever" and "A Day in the Life" records, both inspired by the works of Brian Wilson (according to Paul McCartney).

The distinctive high-pitched sliding electronic sound in the choruses and at the end of the track was created with an electro-theremin, played by Paul Tanner, and first used by Wilson on the track "I Just Wasn't Made for These Times".

The production of the song is reported to have spanned seventeen recording sessions at four different recording studios, and used over 90 hours of magnetic recording tape, with an eventual budget of $50,000. According to Wilson, the electro-theremin work itself cost $15,000.[4] Wilson is credited with developing the use of the recording studio as an instrument: He, the Beach Boys, and dozens of top studio musicians, including members of The Wrecking Crew, recorded and re-recorded seemingly unrelated musical and vocal sections for the song, then edited and mixed these sections into a 3:35 track.

The recording and production style used on the "Good Vibrations" single established Wilson's new method of operation: The recording and re-recording of specific sections of music, followed by rough mixes of the sections edited together, further recording as required, and the construction of the final mix from the component elements. This was the modular approach to recording that was next used on *Smile*.

David Leaf, author of the critically-acclaimed biography, *The Beach Boys and The California Myth*, said of the song, "Nothing but perfection here. The Beach Boys' first million-selling #1 hit...was a major technical breakthrough...the record that showed that anything was possible in the studio."

There has never been an official true stereo release of the final track, although bootlegs of this mix have been issued over the internet. In 2002 DSP (Disky Special Products) released in the Netherlands a various artist compilation CD named *The Radio's on - 40 echte radio hits* wich contains a stereo-mix of this song, probably using the stereo instrumental track mixed with the mono vocals. It has been said that not enough stems exist to actually create a new stereo mix (This is because the vocal tracks are currently missing; Bruce Johnston has stated that he believes they were accidentally destroyed in 1967 during a cleaning of the Capitol Records tape vault). However, a stereo version of the instrumental backing track was issued in 2006 on the 40th "Good Vibrations" EP.

Albums

Inspired by the success of the song and the positive reaction to *Pet Sounds*, and wanting to top The Beatles' recently-released *Revolver* album, Wilson and lyricist Van Dyke Parks embarked on the *Smile* project, intended as an entire album using the writing and production techniques devised for "Good Vibrations." That album was never released as Wilson descended into depression, drug use, and paranoia; several tracks salvaged from those sessions were re-recorded in greatly simplified versions for the *Smiley Smile* album instead, on which "Good Vibrations" made its first LP appearance.

In 2004, a re-recorded version of *Smile* was finally completed by Wilson, Parks, and Darian Sahanaja, with Wilson's touring band in place of the other Beach Boys and studio musicians. It was released in September of that year, to widespread critical acclaim. "Good Vibrations" was released as a single prior to the album, also featuring a live version of the song. In addition to incorporating most of the original Tony Asher lyrics, the Smile version also includes the "Hum-Be-Num" harmony section not included in the 1966 release.

Vinyl release of "Good Vibrations" from the album Smile.

Musicians

Original version

- Hal Blaine - drums, percussion
- Jimmy Bond - upright bass
- Glen Campbell - guitar
- Al de Lory - tack piano
- Jesse Ehrlich - cello
- Jim Gordon - drums
- Al Jardine - vocals
- Bruce Johnston - vocals
- Carol Kaye - bass guitar
- Larry Knechtel - Hammond organ
- Mike Love - lead vocals (chorus, bridge)
- Tommy Morgan - harmonica
- Ray Pohlman - bass guitar
- Don Randi - harpsichord
- Lyle Ritz - upright bass
- Paul Tanner - electro-theremin
- Brian Wilson - lead vocals (falsetto, chorus and bridge)
- Carl Wilson - lead vocals (verses), bass guitar, percussion
- Dennis Wilson - vocals, Hammond organ

Brian Wilson solo version

- Brian Wilson - vocals, and keyboards
- Scott Bennett - vocals, hammond organ
- Nelson Bragg - vocals, percussion
- Jeffrey Foskett - vocals, guitar
- Probyn Gregory - vocals, tannerin
- Jim Hines - drums
- Bob Lizik - bass
- Paul Mertons - flute, harmonica, baritone saxophone
- Taylor Mills - vocals, percussion
- Darian Sahanaja - vocals, keyboards
- Nick Walusko - vocals, guitar

Chart position/sales

According to Badman, the single sold over 230,000 copies in the first four days of its release, and entered the *Cash Box* chart at number six on October 22.

Critical response

Both the *New Musical Express* and *Melody Maker* gave positive reviews at the time of the single's release.

Praise was not universal, however, and Pete Townshend of The Who was quoted at the time as saying "'Good Vibrations' was probably a good record but who's to know? You had to play it about 90 bloody times to even hear what they were singing about", and feared that the single would lead to over-produced records in general.[5]

"Good Vibrations" earned The Beach Boys a Grammy nomination for Best Vocal Group performance in 1966 and the song was eventually inducted into the Grammy Hall of Fame in 1994. It has featured highly in many 'Top 100 Records of All Time' charts and was voted #1 in the Mojo Top 100 Records of All Time chart in 1997. *Rolling Stone* magazine ranked "Good Vibrations" as the sixth best song of all time [6]. The song was also voted #24 in the RIAA and NEA's listing of Songs of the Century. "Good Vibrations" is currently ranked as the #3 song of all time in an aggregation of critics' lists at acclaimedmusic.net.[7]

40th anniversary single

In celebration of its 40th year, the *Good Vibrations: 40th Anniversary Edition* single was released. The single includes five versions of "Good Vibrations" including:

- the original single version
- various session takes
- an alternate take (previously released on the Beach Boys' Rarities album)
- instrumental track in stereo (the only official stereo incarnation of this song)
- a live concert rehearsal (from Hawaii 08/1967).
- also included is the original B-side of the single, "Let's Go Away For Awhile" (stereo-mix).

Except as indicated, all tracks are in mono.

Charts

Chart (1966–67)	Peak position
Australian Singles Chart[8]	2
Belgian Singles Chart[9]	6
Dutch Singles Chart[10]	4
German Singles Chart[11]	8
Italian Singles Chart[12]	12
Malaysian Singles Chart[13]	1
New Zealand Singles Chart[14]	1
Norwegian Singles Chart[15]	2
Rhodesian Singles Chart[16]	1
UK Singles Chart	1
U.S. *Billboard* Hot 100	1

See Also

- Limbic resonance

References

- Badman, Keith. *The Beach Boys, The Definitive Diary of America's Greatest Band on Stage and in the Studio.* Backbeat Books. ISBN 0-87930-818-4.

External links

- Greg Panfile's Musical Analysis of "Good Vibrations" [17]
- List of Rankings of "Good Vibrations" [18]
- Sound on Sound article on the arrangement of "Good Vibrations" [19]
- BBC Radio 2: "Good Vibrations" [20]

References

[1] "The RS 500 Greatest Songs of All Time" (http://www.rollingstone.com/news/story/6595851/good_vibrations/1). *Rolling Stone*. . Retrieved 2008-09-21.
[2] Rock and Roll Hall of Fame "500 songs that shaped rock and roll" (http://www.rockhall.com/exhibithighlights/500-songs/)
[3] http://www.rollingstone.com/news/story/6595851/good_vibrations
[4] "Interview with Brian Wilson" (http://www.theaquarian.com/2005/08/10/brian-wilson-interview-with-brian-wilson/). theaquarian.com. . Retrieved 2009-11-22.
[5] *The Beach Boys*, Keith Badman, p. 156
[6] http://www.rollingstone.com/news/story/_/id/6595851/sort/rank?pageid=rs.RS500&pageregion=blob
[7] "Acclaimed Music Top 3000 songs" (http://www.acclaimedmusic.net). 27 May 2009. .
[8] "Australian Singles Charts" (http://www.mountvernonandfairway.de/charts10.htm). mountvernonandfairway.de. . Retrieved 4 May 2008.
[9] "Belgian Singles Charts" (http://www.mountvernonandfairway.de/charts7.htm). mountvernonandfairway.de. . Retrieved 4 May 2008.
[10] "Dutch Singles Charts" (http://www.mountvernonandfairway.de/charts6.htm). mountvernonandfairway.de. . Retrieved 4 May 2008.
[11] "German Singles Charts" (http://www.mountvernonandfairway.de/charts9.htm). mountvernonandfairway.de. . Retrieved 4 May 2008.

[12] "Italian Singles Charts" (http://www.mountvernonandfairway.de/charts3.htm). mountvernonandfairway.de. . Retrieved 4 May 2008.
[13] Priore, Domenic (1997). *Look! Listen! Vibrate! Smile!*. pp. 27.
[14] "New Zealand Singles Charts" (http://www.mountvernonandfairway.de/charts5.htm). mountvernonandfairway.de. . Retrieved 4 May 2008.
[15] "Norwegian Singles Charts" (http://www.mountvernonandfairway.de/charts4.htm). mountvernonandfairway.de. . Retrieved 4 May 2008.
[16] "Rhodesian Singles Charts" (http://www.mountvernonandfairway.de/charts2.htm). mountvernonandfairway.de. . Retrieved 4 May 2008.
[17] http://www.surfermoon.com/essays/mob3.html
[18] http://www.acclaimedmusic.net/S961.htm
[19] http://www.soundonsound.com/sos/1997_articles/oct97/arranging1.html
[20] http://www.bbc.co.uk/radio2/soldonsong/songlibrary/goodvibrations.shtml

Good to My Baby

"Good to My Baby"	
Song by The Beach Boys from the album *The Beach Boys Today!*	
Released	March 8, 1965
Recorded	track: January 13, 1965 vocals:January 19, 1965
Length	2:16
Label	Capitol
Composer	Brian Wilson/Mike Love
Producer	Brian Wilson
***The Beach Boys Today!* track listing**	
"Do You Wanna Dance" (1)	**"Good to My Baby"** (2)	"Don't Hurt My Little Sister" (3)

"Good to My Baby" is a song written by Brian Wilson and Mike Love for the American pop band The Beach Boys. It was released on their 1965 album *The Beach Boys Today!*.

The song was originally credited to only Wilson. Mike Love's name was added as a result of a lawsuit filed by him against Wilson in the 1990s.

Musicians

- Hal Blaine - drums
- Steve Douglas - tenor saxophone
- Al Jardine - backing vocals
- Plas Johnson - tenor saxophone
- Carol Kaye - bass guitar
- Mike Love - lead & backing vocals
- Jay Migliori - baritone saxophone
- Bill Pitman - guitar
- Don Randi - tack piano, organ
- Billy Strange - guitar
- Ron Swallow - tambourine
- Tommy Tedesco - guitar
- Julius Wechter - conga drums
- Brian Wilson - piano, lead & backing vocals
- Carl Wilson - guitar, backing vocals
- Dennis Wilson - backing vocals

See also

- List of songs by The Beach Boys

Got to Know the Woman

"Got To Know The Woman"	
Song by The Beach Boys from the album *Sunflower*	
Released	August 31, 1970
Recorded	February 13, 1969
Genre	Rhythm & Blues/Classic rock
Length	2:41
Label	Brother Records/Reprise Records
Composer	Dennis Wilson
Producer	The Beach Boys
***Sunflower* track listing**	
Add Some Music To Your Day (3) · **"Got To Know The Woman"** (4) · Deirdre (5)	

"Got to Know the Woman" is a song written by Dennis Wilson for the American pop band The Beach Boys. It was released on their 1970 album *Sunflower*.

Details

- *Written by:* Dennis Wilson
- *Album:* Sunflower
- *Time:* 2:41
- *Produced by:* The Beach Boys

Performers

- *Dennis Wilson:* Lead Vocals

See also

- The Beach Boys
- List of songs by The Beach Boys

H. E. L. P. Is on the Way

"H. E. L. P. Is on the Way" is a song written by Brian Wilson for the American pop band The Beach Boys. The song was written for the *Sunflower* album, which was scrapped before the album came out. It was later officially released on the band's 1993 box set *Good Vibrations: Thirty Years of The Beach Boys*.

The phrase, "Help is on the way" was also a campaign slogan for John Kerry's failed 2004 presidential bid.

See also

- List of songs by The Beach Boys

Had to Phone Ya

"Had to Phone Ya"	
Single by The Beach Boys	
from the album *15 Big Ones*	
Released	August 9, 1976
Format	Vinyl
Recorded	Unknown
Genre	Pop, Rock
Length	1:43
Label	Brother/Reprise
Producer	Brian Wilson
The Beach Boys singles chronology	

"Rock And Roll Music"/"TM Song" (1976)	"It's O.K."/"**Had to Phone Ya**" (1976)	"Everyone's in Love with You"/"Susie Cincinnati (1976)

"Had to Phone Ya" is a song written by Brian Wilson and Mike Love for the American pop band The Beach Boys. It was released on their 1976 album, *15 Big Ones*. The song was originally also credited to Diane Rovell, but her name was removed from the songwriting credit in later release albums.

All five members of the band take turns on lead vocals, with Mike Love and Carl Wilson handling the majority. Brian Wilson takes the closing segment, in which the key shifts from A to G. After an extended staccato vamp on a G Major Seventh, the final section begins with an unusual chord sequence of G Major Seventh, to B Flat Major Seventh, and E Flat Major Seventh, as Brian sings in a rough but passionate baritone, *"Come on / Come on and answer the phone / Come on, come on!"* (The listener is advised to turn the volume up as the song fades out.)

The song's instrumental backing track borrows some elements from the 1966 Pet Sounds outtake Trombone Dixie.

Performers

- Brian Wilson: Lead vocals, Backing vocals, Piano
- Carl Wilson: Lead vocals, Backing vocals
- Dennis Wilson: Lead vocals, Backing vocals, drums
- Mike Love: Lead vocals, Backing vocals
- Al Jardine: Lead vocals, Backing vocals
- Marilyn Wilson: Backing vocals
- Steve Douglas: Saxophone
- Jay Migliori: Saxophone
- Dennis Dreith: Clarinet
- Jules Jacobs: Clarinet
- Lyle Ritz: Bass
- Sidney Sharp: Violin
- Arnold Belnick: Violin
- Henry Ferber: Violin
- Bobby Shew: Trumpet
- Ed Carter: Guitar
- Billy Hinsche: Guitar

See also

- The Beach Boys
- 15 Big Ones
- List of The Beach Boys songs

Hang On to Your Ego

"Hang On to Your Ego" is a song written by Brian Wilson and Tony Asher for the American pop band The Beach Boys. The song was originally going to be released on their classic 1966 album *Pet Sounds*. Mike Love however objected to the title of the song and some of the lyrics and insisted that it be changed. "I was aware that Brian was beginning to experiment with LSD and other psychedelics," explained Love. "The prevailing drug jargon at the time had it that doses of LSD would shatter your ego, as if that were a positive thing... I wasn't interested in taking acid or getting rid of my ego." Jardine recalled that the decision to change the lyrics was ultimately Wilson's. "Brian was very concerned. He wanted to know what we thought about it. To be honest, I don't think we even knew what an ego was... Finally Brian decided, 'Forget it. I'm changing the lyrics. There's too much controversy.'" Terry Sachen, who co-wrote the revised lyrics to this song, was the Beach Boys' road manager in 1966.

The song was then renamed to "I Know There's an Answer" and it was released on *Pet Sounds* as the ninth track on the album. The lead vocal was sung by Mike Love and Alan Jardine with Brian Wilson singing lead on the choruses. The song was later covered by Frank Black on his eponymous 1993 album. The cover is a departure from the original in style as it is heavily influenced by 80s synthesizer work while staying true to the original. Black even tried singing like Brian on the song. Sonic Youth also did a cover of I Know There's an Answer in 1990. The song appears as a bonus track on the reissue of *Goo*. "Hang On to Your Ego" appears on the reissue of *Pet Sounds* as a bonus track.

Details

- *Written by:* Brian Wilson/Tony Asher
- *Time:* 3 min 08 sec
- *Produced by:* Brian Wilson
- *Instrumental track:* recorded February 9, 1966 at Western Recorders, Hollywood, California. Engineered by Chuck Britz.
- *Vocals track:* recorded February-March 1966 at Western Recorders, Hollywood, California.

Performers

- *Mike Love:* Lead Vocals
- *Alan Jardine:* Lead Vocals
- *Brian Wilson:* Lead Vocals on the choruses
- *Hal Blaine:* drums
- *Julius Wechter:* percussion
- *Lyle Ritz:* String Bass
- *Ray Pohlman:* Electric Bass
- *Glen Campbell:* Banjo
- *Barney Kessel:* Guitar
- *Al de Lory:* Tack Piano
- *Larry Knechtel:* Organ
- *Tommy Morgan:* Harmonica
- *Steve Douglas:* Tenor Saxophone
- *Jim Horn:* Tenor Saxophone
- *Paul Horn:* Tenor Saxophone
- *Bobby Klein:* Tenor Saxophone
- *Jay Migliori:* Baritone Saxophone

See also

- List of songs by The Beach Boys

Hawaii

"Hawaii" is a song written by Brian Wilson and Mike Love for the American pop band The Beach Boys. It was recorded in July 1963 and released on their 1963 album *Surfer Girl*. This song was also sung by Al and Matt Jardine on Al Jardine's live album released in 2001. In 1978, part of this song was used in the Beach Boys song "Kona Coast".

"Hawaii" was released in Australia as a single, where it charted during 1964.

Details

- *Written by:* Brian Wilson/Mike Love
- *Album:* Surfer Girl
- *Time:* 1 min 59 sec
- *Produced by:* The Beach Boys

Performers

- *Brian Wilson:* Lead Vocals (chorus)
- *Mike Love:* Lead Vocals (verse)

See also

- The Beach Boys
- Surfer Girl
- List of songs by The Beach Boys

He Come Down

"He Come Down" is a song written by Brian Wilson, Al Jardine and Mike Love for the American pop band The Beach Boys. It was released on their 1972 album *Carl and the Passions - "So Tough"*.

Details

- Written by: Brian Wilson/Al Jardine/Mike Love
- Album: Carl and the Passions - "So Tough"
- Time: 4 min 41 sec
- Produced by: The Beach Boys

Musicians

- Blondie Chaplin - bass guitar, lead and backing vocals
- Ricky Fataar - drums, backing vocals
- Billy Hinsche - organ
- Al Jardine - lead and backing vocals
- Mike Love - lead and backing vocals
- Brian Wilson - piano, organ, backing vocals
- Carl Wilson - ukulele, lead and backing vocals

See also

- List of songs by The Beach Boys

Heads You Win – Tails I Lose

"Heads You Win - Tails I Lose" is a song written by Brian Wilson and Gary Usher for the American pop band The Beach Boys. It was released on their 1962 album *Surfin' Safari*.

Details

- *Written by:* Brian Wilson/Gary Usher
- *Album:* Surfin' Safari
- *Time:* 2 min 17 sec
- *Produced by:* Nik Venet
- *Recording date:* September 6, 1962

Musicians

- Mike Love - lead vocal
- David Marks - guitar
- Brian Wilson - bass guitar, vocals
- Carl Wilson - guitar, vocals
- Dennis Wilson - drums, vocals

See also

- The Beach Boys
- Surfin' Safari
- List of songs by The Beach Boys

Help Me, Rhonda

"Help Me, Ronda"	
Song by The Beach Boys from the album *The Beach Boys Today!*	
Released	March 8, 1965
Recorded	track: January 8, 1965 vocals: January 19, 1965
Genre	Pop
Length	3:04
Label	Capitol
Writer	Brian Wilson/Mike Love
Producer	Brian Wilson
***The Beach Boys Today!* track listing**	

"When I Grow Up (To Be a Man)" (4)	**"Help Me, Ronda"** (5)	"Dance, Dance, Dance" (6)

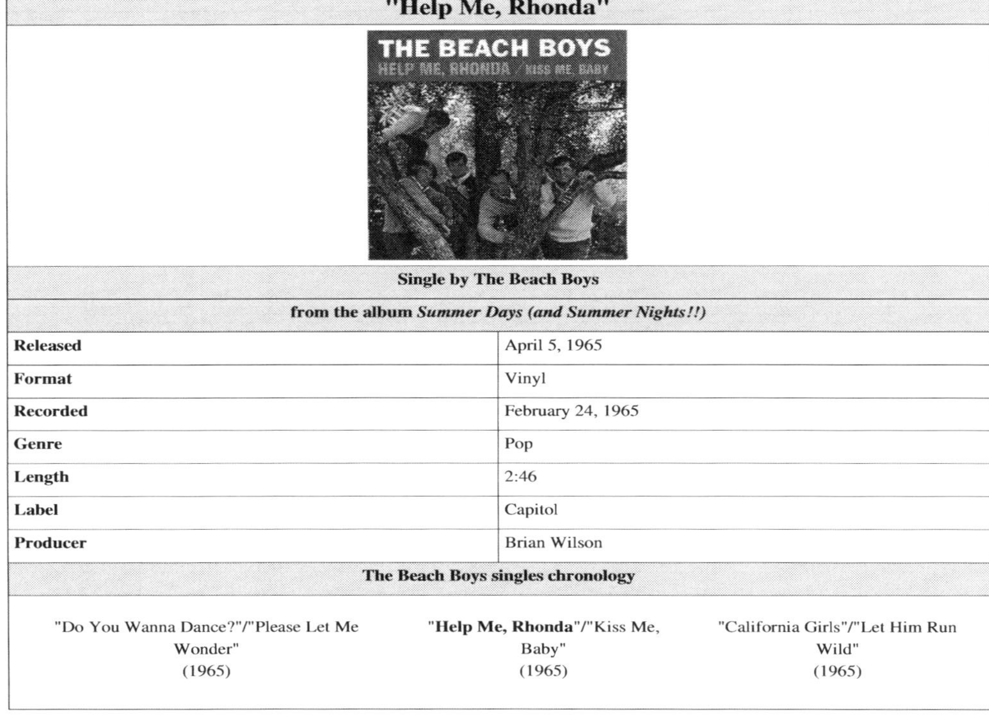

"Help Me, Rhonda"	
Single by The Beach Boys	
from the album *Summer Days (and Summer Nights!!)*	
Released	April 5, 1965
Format	Vinyl
Recorded	February 24, 1965
Genre	Pop
Length	2:46
Label	Capitol
Producer	Brian Wilson
The Beach Boys singles chronology	

"Do You Wanna Dance?"/"Please Let Me Wonder" (1965)	**"Help Me, Rhonda"**/"Kiss Me, Baby" (1965)	"California Girls"/"Let Him Run Wild" (1965)

"**Help Me, Rhonda**" is a song written by Brian Wilson and Mike Love for their American pop band The Beach Boys. The song is notable for being the first Beach Boys song (with the exception of their *Christmas Album*) to feature a lead vocal by Al Jardine. It was first released in March 1965 on the album *The Beach Boys Today!* as "**Help Me, Ronda**". By that time, it had already been re-recorded; this version was released as a single through Capitol Records in April 1965, re-titled with the more well-known "Rhonda" spelling.

The single peaked at number one in the United States, becoming their second U.S. number one single after "I Get Around". The song is featured on most Beach Boys hits compilations; typically the single version is used.

Recording

The original version of the song was recorded over two dates at Western Recording Studios in Hollywood on January 8 and 19, 1965, with Chuck Britz as the engineer and production by Brian Wilson.

The instrumental track has Carl Wilson, Bill Pitman, and Glen Campbell on guitar, Billy Strange on ukulele, Ray Pohlman on bass guitar, Leon Russell on piano, Hal Blaine on drums and timbales, Julius Wechter on claves, Billy Lee Riley on harmonica, Steve Douglas and Plas Johnson on tenor saxophone, and Jay Migliori on baritone saxophone. Al Jardine sang the lead vocal with backing vocals by Carl, Dennis and Brian Wilson, and Mike Love.

The song was originally considered to be an album cut only, but radio stations began to play the track and Brian decided to rework and re-record it. The single version of the song was recorded at Universal and Radio Recorders studios in Hollywood on February 24, 1965, again with Chuck Britz as the engineer and Brian Wilson as producer. Featured on the instrumental track were regular Wrecking Crew members such as Hal Blaine on drums and Carol Kaye on bass guitar. Beach Boys who contributed to the instrumental track were Carl Wilson (guitar) and Brian Wilson (acoustic piano and Hammond B-3). The single version features Al Jardine on lead vocals with backing vocals by Carl, Dennis and Brian Wilson, Mike Love, and Bruce Johnston.

Interruption by Murry Wilson

The recording session of this song was infamously interrupted by the Wilson brothers' father, Murry, who openly criticized the Boys' enthusiasm. His criticisms drove Brian Wilson to breaking point and Brian screamed an expletive, removed his headphones and confronted his father. Shortly after defending his actions, Murry Wilson left the studio and The Beach Boys continued with the session. The recording reel continued to roll and recorded the entire confrontation which circulates among fans.[1]

Versions and releases

The first version of the song appears on the 1965 album *The Beach Boys Today!* as "Help Me, Ronda", released March 8, 1965. This version runs over three minutes with no guitar solo, and has a number of false endings with the volume fading in and out; it is included on the *Endless Summer* compilation album.

The single version, which has a noticeably different arrangement, and one word changed in the lyrics, was released on April 5, 1965. In addition to topping the charts in the US, the single also reached #1 in Canada (on the *RPM* national chart), #5 in Sweden, #10 in Germany and Australia, #2 in Singapore, #3 in The Philippines, #5 in Hong Kong and #9 in Ireland. It peaked at number twenty-seven in the United Kingdom.

The new single version was subsequently included on the album *Summer Days (and Summer Nights!!)*, released June 28, 1965. The instrumental backing track of this version was released in 1968 on the band's *Stack-O-Tracks* album.

A slight variation, called "Help Me, Rhonda (Alternate Single Version)", is included on the 1998 *Endless Harmony Soundtrack* album. This version adds a wordless falsetto from Brian Wilson over the chorus.

Live versions

After becoming The Beach Boys second number one hit in the United States, it immediately became a regular in the band's live set. It has been released on two Beach Boys official live albums: 1973's *The Beach Boys In Concert* and *Good Timin': Live at Knebworth England 1980*. The song was also released by Brian Wilson on his own 2000 live album *Live at the Roxy Theatre*.

The song was performed by Ricky Martin at 2001's "An All-Star Tribute to Brian Wilson".

Cover versions

Johnny Rivers' cover in 1975 on his *New Lovers And Old Friends* album (with an assist from Brian Wilson on back-up vocals) reached #22 on the *Billboard* Hot 100.

A slow, reflective cover of the song appears on the 1998 album *Toxic Swamp And Other Love Songs* by Kenny Young And The Eggplants.

In pop culture

- On the 80s sitcom *Alf* and the spinoff cartoon series. Alf's girlfriend from his home planet Melmac was named Rhonda as a reference to this song.
- In the 1997 remake of *That Darn Cat*, the song is used to help Patti Randall figure out the riddle of the "Hell" watch realizing the message really means, "Help".
- In an episode of *Seinfeld*, "The Soul Mate", Jerry says, "Oh, help me Rhonda", in response to George's comment that his boss believes George killed Susan.
- One episode of season one of the CW series *90210* is titled "Help Me Rhonda". The episode is centered over a guest appearance of a character with that name.
- In a Honda commercial from the early 1990s, the tune is heard to the lyrics, "Help me Honda".
- In the *Full House* episode, "Road To Tokyo", Jesse tries to sing the song in Japanese, but then his interpreter drops the cue cards and Jesse starts naming Japanese related stuff (Honda, Godzilla, etc.) instead.

See also

- List of The Beach Boys songs

External links

- Recording Session of Help Me, Rhonda [2] Animated Version

References

[1] WFMU's Beware of the Blog: I'm A Genius, Too! The Murry Wilson Tapes (http://blog.wfmu.org/freeform/2005/10/im_a_genius_too.html)

[2] http://www.maniacworld.com/i-am-a-genius-too.html

Here Comes the Night

"Here Comes the Night"	
Single by The Beach Boys	
from the album *Wild Honey, L.A. (Light Album)*	
Released	February 19, 1979
Format	Vinyl
Genre	Rock, Disco(1979 version)
Length	2:41 (Original version), 10:51 (1979 album version)
Label	Capitol (1979 version), originally released in 1979 by Brother/Caribou/CBS
Writer(s)	Brian Wilson Mike Love
Producer	Bruce Johnston Curt Becher
The Beach Boys singles chronology	

"Peggy Sue"/"Hey, Little Tomboy" (1978)	**"Here Comes the Night"**/"Baby Blue" (1979)	"Good Timin'"/"Love Surrounds Me" (1979)

"Here Comes the Night" is a song written by Brian Wilson and Mike Love for the American pop band The Beach Boys. It was originally released on their 1967 album, *Wild Honey*. In 1979, the song was re-recorded and released on their 1979 album, *L.A. (Light Album)*, as a disco song lasting nearly eleven minutes.

The newer version of the song is over eight minutes longer than the original song. There are four edits of this disco version. The first edit appears on the *L.A. (Light Album)*, while the second edit was released on a 12" single release (Caribou/Brother/CBS 2Z8-9028). The third edit was the B-side of the 12" single, which is a slightly shorter instrumental (backing track) version of the song. The fourth and final version of the song is found on the 7" single release (Caribou/Brother/CBS ZS8 9026).

Details

Original Version

- Album: "Wild Honey"
- Time: 2 min 41 sec
- Produced by: The Beach Boys

Re-recording

- Album: *L.A. (Light Album)*
- Time: 10 min 51 sec (album version)
- Time: 10 min 36 sec (12" single edit)
- Time: 9 min 4 sec (12" instrumental edit)
- Time: 4 min 28 sec (7" single edit)
- Produced by: Bruce Johnston/Curt Becher

Performers

- Carl Wilson: Lead vocals
- Joe Chemay: Electric bass (disco version)

See also

- List of The Beach Boys songs

Here Today

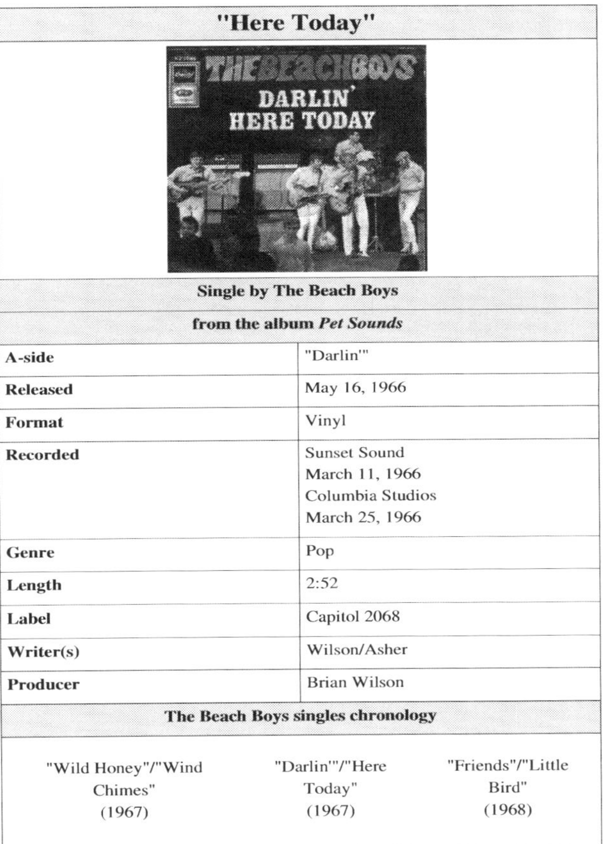

"Here Today"	
Single by The Beach Boys	
from the album *Pet Sounds*	
A-side	"Darlin'"
Released	May 16, 1966
Format	Vinyl
Recorded	Sunset Sound March 11, 1966 Columbia Studios March 25, 1966
Genre	Pop
Length	2:52
Label	Capitol 2068
Writer(s)	Wilson/Asher
Producer	Brian Wilson

The Beach Boys singles chronology		
"Wild Honey"/"Wind Chimes" (1967)	"Darlin'"/"Here Today" (1967)	"Friends"/"Little Bird" (1968)

Pet Sounds track listing

- "Wouldn't It Be Nice"
- "You Still Believe in Me"
- "That's Not Me"
- "Don't Talk (Put Your Head on My Shoulder)"
- "I'm Waiting for the Day"
- "Let's Go Away for Awhile"
- "Sloop John B"
- "God Only Knows"
- "I Know There's an Answer"
- "Here Today"
- "I Just Wasn't Made for These Times"
- "Pet Sounds"
- "Caroline, No"

"**Here Today**" is a song by the American pop band The Beach Boys, released on their 1966 album *Pet Sounds*. It is the tenth track on the album. The song was composed and produced by Brian Wilson with the lyrics by Tony Asher about love being "here today and gone tomorrow". The lead vocal was sung by Mike Love on the final release but some sessions have been released with Brian singing lead. Some studio chatter could be heard during the instrumental break (only in mono version release) and the subject matter was revealed to be about cameras in the 40th anniversary CD booklet. It was later released as the B-side to the 1967 single "Darlin'". Recently the song was re-recorded by Brian Wilson and his band in his 2002 live album *Pet Sounds Live*.

Performers

- Mike Love: Lead vocals
- Al Jardine: Vocals
- Bruce Johnston: Vocals
- Brian Wilson: Vocals
- Carl Wilson: Vocals
- Dennis Wilson: Vocals
- Nick Martinis: Drums
- Frank Capp: Percussion
- Terry Melcher: Tambourine
- Lyle Ritz: String bass
- Carol Kaye: Electric bass
- Al Casey: Guitar
- Mike Deasy: Guitar
- Don Randi: Piano
- Larry Knechtel: Organ
- Jay Migliori: Baritone saxophone
- Jack Nimitz: Baritone saxophone
- Gail Martin: Trombone
- Ernie Tack: Bass trombone

See also

- List of songs by The Beach Boys

Heroes and Villains

"Heroes and Villains"	
Single by The Beach Boys	
from the album *Smiley Smile*	
Released	July 24, 1967
Format	Vinyl
Recorded	October 20, 1966 (backing track of first two verses) February 27, 1967 (chorus backing track) June 12–14, 1967 (remainder)
Genre	Psychedelic pop, Psychedelic rock
Length	3:36
Label	Capitol
Writer(s)	Brian Wilson Van Dyke Parks
Producer	The Beach Boys
The Beach Boys singles chronology	

"Then I Kissed Her" (1967)	**"Heroes and Villains"**/"You're Welcome" (1967)	"Gettin' Hungry"/"Devoted to You" (1967)

"**Heroes and Villains**" is the title of a song co-written by Brian Wilson of The Beach Boys and Van Dyke Parks. It was originally intended as the centerpiece of the fabled but ill-fated *Smile* album (which was not completed until 2004 on Brian Wilson's solo release of the album). A number of versions of the song were recorded by The Beach Boys between 1966-67.

Composition

Composed in early 1966, mostly in a large sandbox holding a piano built in Wilson's living room, "Heroes and Villains" was the first collaboration between Wilson and Parks. It is reported that when Wilson first played the melody to him, Parks devised the opening line on the spot. Various musical themes in the song recur in numerous other songs and musical fragments which Wilson recorded for *Smile*.

The lyric for "Heroes and Villains" exemplify the allusive and playful nature of Parks' writing for *Smile*, evidently combining the experiences, feelings and preoccupations of both Wilson and Parks. Along with "Surf's Up" and "Cabinessence" it is lyrically among the most complex and ambiguous of all The Beach Boys recordings. The "heroes and villains" concept has often been suggested as referring to the conflicts between Wilson and the other members of The Beach Boys, but there are clear references to Parks' experiences as well.

"Heroes and Villains" is generally thought to have been the first song written specifically for *Smile*, although "Barnyard" and "I'm in Great Shape" might have been written at about the same time. "Good Vibrations" had been written earlier and was originally intended for *Pet Sounds*.

Recording

Despite its early genesis, the recording of the song was a difficult and protracted process. Wilson halted work on the other *Smile* tracks at the end of 1966 and concentrated on producing a version of "Heroes and Villains" for single release, but despite holding at least twenty recording sessions for the song over a period of several months and assembling several different edits of the track, he was apparently unable to complete the work to his satisfaction until after the May 1967 announcement that *Smile* had been shelved.

The song went through a number of transformations and at least one segment, the so-called "Cantina scene" was removed from the released versions. Carl Wilson often sang during live shows, a variation of "Do You Like Worms?" featured in the song the lyrics, "Bicycle rider, see, see what you've done" to give homage to some of the unreleased songs off *Smile*.

Releases

A number of different edits of the song exist; one was released as a single in July 1967 (Billboard #12, Cashbox Top Ten, UK #8) and appeared on their September 1967 LP *Smiley Smile*. The original *Smile* version was eventually released as a bonus track on the Beach Boys *Smiley Smile/Wild Honey* two-fer in 1990—this included the Cantina Scene and some additional lines ("At threescore and five, I'm very much alive, I've still got the jive to survive with the heroes and villains"). A 2001 stereo mix appears on the *Hawthorne, CA* album. On the Endless Harmony Soundtrack, there is a demo version of the song, which also incorporates two other songs: I'm in Great Shape and Barnyard.

There have been persistent rumors of a far longer two-part edit, reputedly running for six, seven or even ten minutes, and that this edit was intended for single release, split across the two sides of a single. However, it is possible that this rumoured long edit (if it exists) may in fact have been part of a trial assembly of the song and related fragments as part of the planned sequencing of the *Smile* tracks. Regardless, the intended "Heroes And Villains" single was originally assigned as Capitol 5826, issued with a white picture sleeve showing six pictures of the group members. However, Brian Wilson was still experimenting and creating further concepts for the song, thus the Capitol single was never pressed. By the time of the final single mix, the Beach Boys created their own Brother label and issued "Heroes And Villains" as its first single (Brother 1001) with the cartoon picture sleeve shown above. The picture sleeve for the unreleased Capitol single is very rare and considered a highly sought item among Beach Boys collectors.

Al Jardine believes that Brian underproduced the song for the *Smiley Smile* album. As he explains "We recorded a pale facsimile of 'Heroes And Villains', replete with discordant transitions...Brian re-invented the song for this record...He purposefully under-produced the song."

However, this version was good enough to place at No. 5 in Canada, No. 6 in New Zealand, No. 8 in Cash Box and Record World, No. 10 in Italy (their second biggest hit there) and Sweden, No. 11 in Australia, No. 24 in Germany and No. 30 in France; and at No. 8 in Holland, Switzerland and Malaysia, according to contemporary national charts sourced and sited by Billboard in fall 1967.

The Beach Boys have released four different live versions of the song: on *The Beach Boys in Concert*; on *Good Timin': Live at Knebworth England 1980*, as part of a medley with *Cotton Fields*; on the *Endless Harmony Soundtrack*, and also on the Beach Boys Concert/Live in London twofer, as a bonus track. It is also on Al Jardine's Live in Las Vegas album. While Brian was absent from the touring section of the group, Jardine sang lead on this song.

At his own tribute, Brian Wilson sang this after he was given a standing ovation, and how he spoke about the performers who sang that night.

The song was re-recorded in 2004 as part of Brian Wilson's new version of *Smile* with the original Brian Wilson lyrics and included the 'cantina' segment.

Musicians

Smile (Unreleased Original):

- Hal Blaine - drums
- Carol Kaye - bass guitar
- Lyle Ritz - string bass
- Don Randi - piano
- Billy Strange - guitar
- Brian Wilson - lead vocals, harmonies
- Mike Love, Al Jardine, Carl Wilson, Dennis Wilson, Bruce Johnston - backing vocals, laughter

Smiley Smile:

This list is incomplete.

- Hal Blaine - drums
- Al Jardine - vocals
- Bruce Johnston - vocals
- Carol Kaye - bass
- Mike Love - vocals
- Brian Wilson - lead vocal
- Carl Wilson - vocals
- Dennis Wilson - vocals

Brian Wilson's Smile Released Version:

- *Brian Wilson - Lead Vocals, and keyboards*
- *Scott Bennett - vocals, keyboards*
- *Nelson Bragg - vocals, percussion, whistle*
- *Jeffery Foskett - vocals, guitar*
- *Probyn Gregory - vocals, guitar*
- *Jim Hines - drums*
- *Bob Lizik - bass*
- *Paul Mertons - baritone saxophone, harmonica*
- *Taylor Mills - vocals, percussion*
- *Darian Sahanaja - vocals, keyboards*

- *Nick Walusko - vocals, guitar*
- Staffan Findin - bass trombone
- Andreas Forsman - violin
- Erik Holm - viola
- Anna Landberg - cello
- Malin-My Nilsson - violin
- Bjorn Samuelsson - trombone
- Victor Sand - saxophone, flute, clarinet
- Markus Sandlund - cello

Hey, Little Tomboy

"Hey, Little Tomboy" is a song written by Brian Wilson for the American pop band The Beach Boys for an untitled project in 1974. It was released on their 1978 album *M.I.U. Album*.

Details

- *Written by:* Brian Wilson
- *Album:* M.I.U. Album
- *Time:* 2 min 25 sec
- *Produced by:* Al Jardine/Ron Altbach

Performers

- *Brian Wilson:* Lead Vocals
- *Carl Wilson:* Lead Vocals
- *Mike Love:* Lead Vocals

See also

- The Beach Boys
- M.I.U. Album
- List of songs by The Beach Boys

Hold On Dear Brother

"Hold On Dear Brother"	
Single by The Beach Boys	
from the album *Carl and the Passions - "So Tough"*	
Released	June 26, 1972
Format	Vinyl
Genre	Pop, country, waltz
Length	4:43
Label	Brother/Reprise
Writer(s)	Ricky Fataar/Blondie Chaplin
Producer	The Beach Boys

The Beach Boys singles chronology		
"You Need a Mess of Help to Stand Alone"/"Cuddle Up" (1972)	"Marcella"/"**Hold On Dear Brother**" (1972)	"Sail On, Sailor"/"Only with You" (1973)

"**Hold On Dear Brother**" is a song written by Ricky Fataar and Blondie Chaplin for the American pop band The Beach Boys. It was released on their 1972 album, *Carl and the Passions - "So Tough"*, and as the B-side to the non-charting single, "Marcella".

Performers

- Blondie Chaplin: Lead Vocals

See also

- List of The Beach Boys songs

Honkin' Down the Highway

"Honkin' Down the Highway"	
Single by The Beach Boys	
from the album *Love You*	
Released	May 30, 1977
Format	Vinyl
Recorded	Unknown
Genre	Rock and Roll
Length	2:48
Label	Brother
Producer	Brian Wilson
The Beach Boys singles chronology	

"Everyone's in Love with You"/"Susie Cincinnati" (1976)	"Honkin' Down the Highway"/"Solar System" (1977)	"Peggy Sue"/"Hey, Little Tomboy" (1978)

"Honkin' Down the Highway" is a song written by Brian Wilson for the American pop band The Beach Boys. It was released on their 1977 album *Love You* with a lead vocal by Al Jardine. A remake is scheduled to appear on Jardine's album *A Postcard from California*, with Brian Wilson making a guest appearance.

A slightly edited version was released on a single, in which the drum machine intro is cut off. The same version erroneously appeared on the 1991 cassette and CD reissue of 'The Beach Boys Love You' on the Caribou label.

See also

- The Beach Boys
- Love You
- List of songs by The Beach Boys

Hot Fun in the Summertime

"Hot Fun in the Summertime"	
Single by Sly & the Family Stone	
from the album *Greatest Hits*	
B-side	"Fun"
Released	August 1969
Format	7" single
Recorded	1969
Genre	Psychedelic soul, funk, pop rock
Length	2:37
Label	Epic 5-10497
Writer(s)	Sly Stone
Producer	Sly Stone

Sly & the Family Stone singles chronology		
"Stand!"/"I Want to Take You Higher" (1969)	"Hot Fun in the Summertime"/"Fun" (1969)	"Thank You (Falettinme Be Mice Elf Agin)"/"Everybody is a Star" (1969)

"**Hot Fun in the Summertime**" is a 1969 hit single recorded by Sly & the Family Stone. The single was released in the wake of the band's high-profile performance at Woodstock, which greatly expanded their fanbase. It reached #2 on the U.S. pop chart and #3 on the U.S. R&B chart. Thematically, "Hot Fun in the Summertime" is a dedication to the fun and games to be had during the summer, although it has also been analyzed as a commentary on the race riots of the late-1960s. "Hot Fun in the Summertime" was intended to be included on an in-progress album with "Everybody Is a Star" and "Thank You (Falettinme Be Mice Elf Agin)"; the LP was never completed, and the three tracks were instead included on the band's 1970 *Greatest Hits* LP.

The B-side to this single is "Fun", a song taken from the group's third album (*Life*) from 1968.

It was performed on stage in HBO's 1981 television special *The Pee-wee Herman Show*.

The track was covered by The Beach Boys on their commercially and critically disastrous 1992 album *Summer in Paradise*. A video was made to accompany the song.

It was covered in 1982 with somewhat greater chart success by a funk outfit known as Dayton, and again in 1995 by The Manhattan Transfer featuring vocals by Chaka Khan.

Genesis vocalist and drummer Phil Collins cited the song as one of the musical inspirations for "Misunderstanding". The members of Toto have also cited it as an inspiration for "Hold the Line".

Rolling Stone ranked it #247 on their list of the 500 Greatest Songs of All Time.

Personnel

- Lead and Background Vocals by Sly Stone, Rose Stone, Freddie Stone, and Larry Graham
- Guitar by Freddie Stone
- Bass by Larry Graham
- Drums by Greg Errico
- Horns by Jerry Martini (tenor saxophone) and Cynthia Robinson (trumpet)
- Written and produced by Sly Stone

How She Boogalooed It

"How She Boogalooed It" is a song written by Mike Love, Bruce Johnston, Al Jardine and Carl Wilson for the American pop band The Beach Boys. It was the first non-instrumental original Beach Boys song not written or co-written by Brian Wilson. It was released on their 1967 album *Wild Honey*.

It was released as a single in Sweden, where it reached number 10 on the Swedish Radio channel 3 chart.

Details

- *Written by:* Mike Love/Bruce Johnston/Al Jardine/Carl Wilson
- *Album:* Wild Honey
- *Time:* 1 min 56 sec
- *Produced by:* The Beach Boys

Performers

- Carl Wilson - lead vocals [1]

See also

- List of songs by The Beach Boys

References

[1] Doe, Andrew G.: " ALBUMARCHIVE2 (http://www.btinternet.com/~bellagio/albumarchive2.html)." Bellagio 10452 (http://www.btinternet.com/~bellagio/). Retrieved on 2008-12-31.

Hully Gully

"Hully Gully"	
Song by The Beach Boys from the album *Beach Boys' Party!*	
Released	8 November 1965
Genre	Rock and roll
Length	2:22
Label	Capitol
Composer	Fred Sledge Smith, Clifford Goldsmith
Producer	Brian Wilson
***Beach Boys' Party!* track listing**	
• "Hully Gully" • "I Should Have Known Better" • "Tell Me Why" • "Papa-Oom-Mow-Mow" • "Mountain of Love" • "You've Got to Hide Your Love Away" • "Devoted to You" • "Alley Oop" • "There's No Other (Like My Baby)" • "Medley:I Get Around/Little Deuce Coupe" • "The Times They Are a-Changin'" • "Barbara Ann"	

"**(Baby) Hully Gully**" is a song written by Fred Sledge Smith and Clifford Goldsmith and recorded by The Olympics.[1] Released in 1959, the song peaked at number 72 on the *Billboard* Hot 100 in February 1960,[2] and sparked the Hully Gully dance craze.

Cover versions

"(Baby) Hully Gully" was covered by a number of different artists, sometimes under the name "Hully Gully (Baby)", "Hully Gully Baby" or simply "Hully Gully".

- Buddy Guy, *Stone Crazy! 1960–1967* (recorded 1960)
- Chubby Checker, *It's Pony Time* (1961)
- The Ventures, *Mashed Potatoes and Gravy* (1962)
- The Dovells, single (1962)
- Cliff Bennett and the Rebel Rousers (1962) (appears on some bootlegs miscredited as The Beatles)
- The Searchers, *At the Star Club*
- The Beach Boys, *Beach Boys' Party!* (1965)
- Jackie Lee, *The Duck* (1966)
- Hollywood Argyles, single (1960)
- Mike Bloomfield, *Junko Partner* and *Prescription for the Blues* (recorded 1977)
- The A-Bones, *Music Minus Five* (1993)

References

[1] BMI database (http://repertoire.bmi.com/title.asp?blnWriter=True&blnPublisher=True&blnArtist=True&page=1&keyid=72188&ShowNbr=0&ShowSeqNbr=0&querytype=WorkID)
[2] *Billboard* (http://www.billboard.com/bbcom/esearch/chart_display.jsp?cfi=379&cfgn=Singles&cfn=The+Billboard+Hot+100&ci=3069973&cdi=8779047&cid=03/28/1960)

Hushabye

"**Hushabye**" is a song written by Doc Pomus and Mort Shuman.[1]

The song was originally made famous in the summer of 1959 by New York doo wop group, The Mystics. The original plan was for them to record "A Teenager in Love," however, that song went to Dion and The Belmonts instead. "Hushabye" was their consolation prize. [2]

It was later covered by the American pop band The Beach Boys. It was released on their July 1964 album *All Summer Long* and it featured Brian Wilson and Mike Love on lead vocals. In the stereo version, Brian's vocals are in one channel and the rest of the group in the other. In 1993, two new versions of the song appeared on the Beach Boys' box set. One was a live version and the other was a split track with vocals in one channel and instruments in the other.

The follow up to "Hushabye" is "Hushabye Again", written by Mike Miller and performed by George Galfo's Mystics on the Collectables label.

External links

- George Galfo's Mystics (with Original Founding Mystic) [3]
- Original Mystics with Phil Cracolici-original voice of Hushabye [4]
- Mystic Memories featuring Hushabye video [5]
- review of Beach Boys album All Summer Long [6]
- Mike Miller Doo Wop Stylist http://www.harmonystreet.biz/

References

[1] "Doc Pomus Biography" (http://www.felderpomus.com/docpomus1.html#ShortBio). www.felderpomus.com. . Retrieved 2008-03-26.
[2] Hushabye Songfacts (http://www.songfacts.com/detail.php?id=16702)
[3] http://www.themystics.biz/
[4] http://www.originalmystics.com/
[5] http://www.johnnytunes.com/mystics.htm
[6] http://www.warr.org/brian.html#ASL

I Can Hear Music

"**I Can Hear Music**" is a pop song that was written by Jeff Barry, Ellie Greenwich and Phil Spector and originally performed by the Ronettes (1966). It was later covered by the Beach Boys (1969), then by Larry Lurex, which was the pseudonym of Freddie Mercury (1973), José Hoebee in (1983) and She & Him in (2010).[1]

Beach Boys version

"I Can Hear Music"	
Single by The Beach Boys	
from the album *20/20*	
Released	February 24, 1969
Format	Vinyl
Recorded	October 1, 1968
Genre	Pop
Length	2:36
Label	Capitol
Producer	Carl Wilson

The Beach Boys singles chronology		
"Bluebirds over the Mountain"/"Never Learn Not to Love" (1968)	"I Can Hear Music"/"All I Want to Do" (1969)	"Break Away"/"Celebrate the News" (1969)

"I Can Hear Music" was covered by the American pop band The Beach Boys. It was released on their 1969 album *20/20* with Carl Wilson on lead vocals.

With Brian Wilson increasingly losing interest in producing for the Beach Boys, his younger brother Carl took over the role of producer and lead Beach Boy. "I Can Hear Music" is considered by many to be Carl Wilson's first taste at being the "leader" of the group. Still, more than matching its top twenty peaks in the US charts of *Record World* and *Cash Box*, it placed #5 in Sweden, #6 in Holland and Malaysia, #7 in Poland, #10 in the UK, #13 in Germany and in Australia's *Go Set* chart, and #15 in Ireland.

Within the US it entered the top 10 playlists at #5 Boston, #7 New York, #7 Chicago (WCFL), San Diego, Seattle, Houston and Vancouver in order of success; #11 Chicago (WLS), #12 Los Angeles (KHJ), Columbus and Indianapolis; #14 Detroit.

In 1996, The Beach Boys re-recorded the song, with contemporary Christian singer Kathy Troccoli on lead vocals, for their country album *Stars and Stripes Vol. 1*. That recording was released as a single, and hit #16 on the US Adult Contemporary singles chart.

See also

- List of songs by The Beach Boys

References

[1] http://www.mergerecords.com/store/store_detail.php?catalog_id=694

I Do

"I Do" is a song written by Brian Wilson. Wilson originally produced a version for The Castells. But that record, released through Warner Brothers, never charted. The Beach Boys version of the song was first released on the Surfer Girl/Shut Down Volume 2 two-LP-on-one-CD format. It was recorded on 6 November 1963, between the recording of *Little Deuce Coupe* and *Shut Down Volume 2*.

Details

- *Written by:* Brian Wilson
- *Album:* released on Surfer Girl/Shut Down Volume 2 two-LP-on-one-CD format
- *Time:* 3 min 06 sec
- *Produced by:* Brian Wilson

Performers

- *Brian Wilson:* Lead Vocals
- *Mike Love:* Lead Vocals

See also

- The Beach Boys
- List of songs by The Beach Boys

I Do Love You

"**I Do Love You**" is a song written by Stevie Wonder for American pop band The Beach Boys. It was released on their 1985 album *The Beach Boys* with Carl Wilson and Al Jardine on lead vocals.

Details

- *Written by:* Stevie Wonder
- *Album: The Beach Boys*
- *Time:* 4:20
- *Produced by:* Steve Levine

Musicians

- Al Jardine - lead and backing vocals
- Bruce Johnston - backing vocals
- Steve Levine - synthesizer
- Julian Lindsay - piano
- Mike Love - backing vocals
- Brian Wilson - backing vocals
- Carl Wilson - lead and backing vocal
- Stevie Wonder - drums, bass, keyboard, harmonica

See also

- The Beach Boys
- The Beach Boys (album)
- List of songs by The Beach Boys

I Get Around

"I Get Around"	
Single by The Beach Boys	
from the album *All Summer Long*	
B-side	"Don't Worry Baby"
Released	May 11, 1964
Format	Vinyl
Recorded	Western Studios April 2, 1964 April 10, 1964
Genre	Pop music, Surf rock
Length	2:12
Label	Capitol 5174
Writer(s)	Wilson/Love
Producer	Brian Wilson

The Beach Boys singles chronology

"Fun, Fun, Fun"/"Why Do Fools Fall In Love" (1964)	**"I Get Around"**/"Don't Worry Baby" (1964)	"When I Grow Up (to be a man)"/"She Knows Me Too Well" (1964)

All Summer Long track listing

- "I Get Around"
- "All Summer Long"
- "Hushabye"
- "Little Honda"
- "We'll Run Away"
- "Carl's Big Chance"
- "Wendy"
- "Do You Remember?"
- "Girls on the Beach"

- "Drive-In"
- "Our Favorite Recording Sessions"
- "Don't Back Down"

Beach Boys' Party! track listing

- "Hully Gully"
- "I Should Have Known Better"
- "Tell Me Why"
- "Papa-Oom-Mow-Mow"
- "Mountain of Love"
- "You've Got to Hide Your Love Away"
- "Devoted to You"
- "Alley Oop"
- "There's No Other (Like My Baby)"
- "Medley:I Get Around/Little Deuce Coupe"
- "The Times They Are a-Changin' "
- "Barbara Ann"

"**I Get Around**" is a song written by Brian Wilson and Mike Love for The Beach Boys. The song features Love on lead vocal for the verse, and Wilson for the chorus. It is noteworthy for its back-to-front structure - it starts with a chorus and has two short verses. It was a single which was released in 1964 through Capitol Records; the B-side of the single was "Don't Worry Baby", which itself charted at number 24 in the United States. "I Get Around" was The Beach Boys' first number-one hit song in the United States. The single charted at number seven in the United Kingdom, and was the band's first top ten single there. The song's first album release was on *All Summer Long* in 1964.

Composition

In November 1969, the Wilsons' father, Murry Wilson, sold the copyrights to the band's songs to Irving Almo for approximately $700,000.[1] Many years later in April 1992, just after Brian Wilson had won a lawsuit which recovered many of the copyrights to his songs, Mike Love filed a lawsuit against Brian Wilson claiming that he had not been given credit, and therefore hadn't received royalties, on over thirty of the band's songs, many of them hit singles.[2] One of these songs was "I Get Around". The original credit only credited Wilson, but Love insisted that he had a hand in writing the lyrics. In an interview with Goldmine, published September 18, 1992, Love insisted that he and not Wilson "came up with 'round round get around'". Mike Love won the lawsuit and the song-writing credit was amended, therefore ensuring future royalties on all of the songs that he had claimed he had a hand in writing.

Recording

The instrumental track for "I Get Around" was recorded on April 2, 1964. The session, produced by Brian Wilson, was notable as being the session that most likely saw the sacking of the band's manager and the Wilsons' father, Murry Wilson. The bed instrumental track of the song without any instrumental overdubs was released on the 1993 five-disc box set *Good Vibrations: Thirty Years of The Beach Boys*.

The vocals were recorded during a session eight days later on April 10. The lead vocal features Mike Love on the verses and Brian Wilson on the choruses with backing vocals from Brian, Carl & Dennis Wilson, Mike Love and Alan Jardine (the soaring falsetto is Brian Wilson).

Single release

"I Get Around", backed with "Don't Worry Baby", was released as a single in the United States on May 11, 1964. The single entered the *Billboard* chart on June 6 at #17.[3] The song reached the #1 spot on the *Billboard* charts on July 4, replacing "A World Without Love" by Peter and Gordon and becoming the band's first #1 hit in the United States. The song remained at #1 for two weeks before being replaced by "Rag Doll" by The Four Seasons. The single also reached #1 on the United States *Variety* charts on July 1.[3]

According to Songfacts, Billboard and Cash Box magazines rated I Get Around 1964's fifth biggest selling song, and indicated it sold close to 2 million units in the U.S.[4]

Released in June 1964 in the United Kingdom the single peaked at #7 on the *Record Retailer* chart and thus becoming the band's first top ten hit in the United Kingdom. According to some sources, Mick Jagger, when appearing on the U.K. television show Ready Steady Go!, stated that he thought the song was a great record. This most likely played a part in boosting the singles success, while also helping the band become more popular in the United Kingdom.

In Germany the single peaked at #38 on the *Hit Bilanz* chart[5] , which was only the band's second single to chart in Germany.[6] The single was the band's first charting single in the Netherlands, charting at #38 on the Netherlands singles charts.[7] The single reached the top 10 in both the Canadian and Swedish singles charts, peaking at #10 in both countries.[8] [9]

Album and alternate releases

The song was first released on an album in 1964 on the band's *All Summer Long* album. In the following year, the band re-recorded the song as a medley along with "Little Deuce Coupe" for their 1965 *Beach Boys' Party!* album. The medley was a send-up of the original recording. The mock recording replaces lyrics such as "we always take my car cause it's never been beat" with "we always take my car although it's a heap". The original recording of the song was later re-released on the band's 1989 studio album *Still Cruisin'*. On the 1996 country styled studio release *Stars and Stripes Vol. 1* the band re-recorded the song for the album which featured country band Sawyer Brown as guests on the track who played several of the instruments on the recording as well as featuring a lead vocal by band member Mark Miller. The harmonies on the re-recorded track were provided by Brian & Carl Wilson, Alan & Matt Jardine, Mike Love and Bruce Johnston.

The song frequently appears on many of the groups Greatest Hits compilations including the 1974 #1 hit compilation album *Endless Summer*; the 1999 compilation *The Greatest Hits - Volume 1: 20 Good Vibrations*; the 2002 compilation *Classics Selected by Brian Wilson*, which was hand-picked by Brian Wilson himself; the 2003 compilation *Sounds of Summer: The Very Best of The Beach Boys* as well as the 1993 box set *Good Vibrations: Thirty Years of The Beach Boys*.

Live versions

After the song became the band's first United States number one hit song, it immediately became a regular in The Beach Boys live set. During the band's first British tour in 1964, they performed this song as well as "When I Grow Up (To Be a Man)" on their first television appearance in Britain on Ready Steady Go![10] Several live renditions of the song have been officially released on various Beach Boys releases. It was first released on their first live album *Beach Boys Concert* in 1964. A concert from Anaheim Stadium on July 3, 1976 which featured the song was filmed and produced by Lorne Michaels for a Beach Boys television special which first aired in the United States in August, 1976. The TV special was later released on video and DVD as *Good Vibrations Tour*. In 1980, a live rendition was recorded, though not released until 2002 on the *Good Timin': Live at Knebworth England 1980* live album. Footage from the concert was released on video and DVD format. Another live recording of the song from a concert in 1989 was released on the 2006 album Songs from Here & Back.

Cultural references

The first film in which the song appeared was the 1984 film *Surf II*. In 1986, the song was heard in the Disney science-fiction comedy, *Flight of the Navigator*. The song was later featured in two films in 1987, both *Good Morning, Vietnam* and *The Big Bang*. Two years later the song was used in the 1989 film *Look Who's Talking*. The 1990 film *Downtown* also used the song during the movie. It was also featured in the 1997 films *Bean* and *Toothless*. It was again used in the 1999 film *Three Kings*. More recently the song was used in the 2000 film *Last Resort*.[11]

A version of the song was featured on various Hoveround advertisements, advertising electronically powered wheelchairs.[12]

In one episode of *The Muppet Show*, Ms. Piggy along with other pig members of the cast, sing this song while riding Harley Davidson motorcycles.

In an episode of The Wonder Years, the song appears during the ending credits.

The song also featured in the Wii game, *Imagine Fashion Party*.

The song was also used by the Bondi Surf Club (Surf Life Saving Australia) for their march as a part of the Sydney Gay & Lesbian Mardi Gras parade in 2009.

In a Kidsongs video and DVD, "Let's Play Ball", the music video shows about driving race cars.

The song is also used in the Wes Anderson film, "Fantastic Mr. Fox".

The Song was used in the novel Boy's Life and was the song Reverend Blessett hated.

The song was used within a scene from the 1997 film Bean (film)

Charts

Chart (1964)	Peak position
Canadian RPM Singles Chart[13]	1
Dutch Singles Chart[7]	38
German Singles Chart[6]	38
Swedish Singles Chart[9]	10
UK Singles Chart	7
U.S. *Billboard* Hot 100	1

See also

- List of songs by The Beach Boys

References

[1] Beach Boys Timeline - 1969 (http://www.btinternet.com/~bellagio/1969.html)
[2] Beach Boys Timeline - 1992 (http://www.btinternet.com/~bellagio/1992.html)
[3] Badman, Keith (2004). *The Beach Boys: The Definitive Diary of America's Greatest Band on Stage and in the Studio*. p. 59.
[4] Songfacts.com (http://www.songfacts.com/detail.php?id=5373)
[5] Badman, Keith (2004). *The Beach Boys: The Definitive Diary of America's Greatest Band on Stage and in the Studio*. p. 62.
[6] German Singles Charts (http://www.mountvernonandfairway.de/charts9.htm)
[7] Dutch Singles Charts (http://www.mountvernonandfairway.de/charts6.htm)
[8] Canadian Singles Charts (http://www.mountvernonandfairway.de/charts8.htm)
[9] Swedish Singles Charts (http://www.mountvernonandfairway.de/charts1.htm)

[10] The Beach Boys Live on Ready Steady Go! in 1964 (http://www.youtube.com/watch?v=DCYouoLKxjo)
[11] The Beach Boys Filmography (http://movies.yahoo.com/movie/contributor/1809161623)
[12] Hoveround Commercial (http://www.youtube.com/watch?v=sC8x4UdSi50)
[13] "Canadian Singles Charts" (http://www.mountvernonandfairway.de/charts8.htm). mountvernonandfairway.de. . Retrieved 11 November 2007.

I Just Got My Pay

"I Just Got My Pay" is a song written by Brian Wilson for the American pop band The Beach Boys. The song was released on the band's 1993 box set *Good Vibrations: Thirty Years of The Beach Boys*.It involves money and singing. Parts of the melody were later used (with different lyrics) for the song Marcella, from Carl & The Passions. See also All Dressed Up For School.

See also

- List of songs by The Beach Boys

I Just Wasn't Made for These Times

"I Just Wasn't Made for These Times"	
Song by The Beach Boys from the album *Pet Sounds*	
Released	May 16, 1966
Recorded	Gold Star February 14, 1966 Columbia Studios March 10, 1966 April 13, 1966
Genre	Pop
Length	3:11
Label	Capitol
Composer	Wilson/Asher
Producer	Brian Wilson
***Pet Sounds* track listing**	
• "Wouldn't It Be Nice" • "You Still Believe in Me" • "That's Not Me" • "Don't Talk (Put Your Head on My Shoulder)" • "I'm Waiting for the Day" • "Let's Go Away for Awhile" • "Sloop John B" • "God Only Knows" • "I Know There's an Answer" • "Here Today" • "I Just Wasn't Made for These Times" • "Pet Sounds" • "Caroline, No"	

"**I Just Wasn't Made for These Times**" is a song by the Beach Boys from their album *Pet Sounds*. It is the eleventh song on the album. It is known as the first that features a keyboard-controlled variation on the theremin - later named the Electro-Theremin or Tannerin - in a rock record. Shortly after this track was recorded, Brian Wilson used the Tannerin on the "Good Vibrations" track.

Wilson stated: "It's about a guy who was crying out because he thought he was too advanced, and that he'd eventually have to leave people behind. All my friends thought I was crazy to do *Pet Sounds*."

The song has been covered by Wilson himself on *Pet Sounds Live*, by Sixpence None the Richer for the tribute album *Making God Smile*, by Patrick Wolf for *Do It Again: A Tribute To Pet Sounds*, by married couple Aimee Mann and Michael Penn for *A Tribute To Brian Wilson* (2001), and by the Japanese group Feelds for the tribute album *Smiling Pets*.

Details

- *Written by:* Brian Wilson/Tony Asher
- *Album:* Pet Sounds
- *Time:* 3 min 11 sec
- *Produced by:* Brian Wilson
- *Instrumental track:* recorded February 14, 1966 at Gold Star Recording Studios, Hollywood, California. Engineered by Larry Levine.
- *Vocal track:* recorded March through to April, 1966 at Columbia Studios, Hollywood, California. Engineered by Ralph Balantin.

Personnel

- Chuck Berghofer — upright bass
- Hal Blaine — drums, tympani, bongos
- Glen Campbell — guitar
- Frank Capp — tympani, latin percussion
- Steve Douglas — tenor saxophone
- Al Jardine — vocals
- Plas Johnson — tenor saxophone
- Barney Kessel — guitar
- Bobby Klein — tenor saxophone
- Mike Love — vocals
- Mike Melvoin — harpsichord
- Jay Migliori — baritone saxophone
- Tommy Morgan — harmonica
- Ray Pohlman — bass guitar
- Don Randi — piano
- Paul Tanner — tannerin
- Brian Wilson — lead vocal
- Carl Wilson — vocals
- Dennis Wilson — vocals

See also

- List of songs by The Beach Boys

I Know There's an Answer

"I Know There's an Answer"	
Song by The Beach Boys from the album *Pet Sounds*	
Released	May 16, 1966
Recorded	Western Studios February 9, 1966 March, 1966
Genre	Pop
Length	3:18
Label	Capitol
Composer	Wilson/Sachen/Love
Producer	Brian Wilson
***Pet Sounds* track listing**	
• "Wouldn't It Be Nice" • "You Still Believe in Me" • "That's Not Me" • "Don't Talk (Put Your Head on My Shoulder)" • "I'm Waiting for the Day" • "Let's Go Away for Awhile" • "Sloop John B" • "God Only Knows" • "I Know There's an Answer" • "Here Today" • "I Just Wasn't Made for These Times" • "Pet Sounds" • "Caroline, No"	

"**I Know There's an Answer**" is a song by the American pop band The Beach Boys, taken from their 1966 album *Pet Sounds*. It is the ninth track on the album. The song was composed and produced by Brian Wilson with the lyrics by Terry Sachen and Mike Love. The lead vocal was sung by Mike Love and Al Jardine with Brian Wilson singing lead on the choruses. The song features interesting use of a bass harmonica and a banjo.

The song was originally named "Hang On to Your Ego", but when the lyric of the chorus was changed after concerns that the LSD-related connotations of the phrase "Hang On to Your Ego" would be too controversial, the title of the song was also renamed. The subject of the revised song is the self-centeredness of people and how the singer tells them "...the way that they live could be better." The refrain of the song states "I know there's an answer/I know now but I have to find it by myself." Terry Sachen, who was the Beach Boys' road manager at the time, is given credit for co-writing the lyrics.

Details

- *Written by:* Brian Wilson/Terry Sachen/Mike Love
- *Album:* Pet Sounds
- *Time:* 3 min 18 sec
- *Produced by:* Brian Wilson
- *Instrumental track:* recorded February 9, 1966 at Western Recorders, Hollywood, California. Engineered by Chuck Britz.
- *Vocals track:* recorded February-March 1966 at Western Recorders, Hollywood, California.

Performers

- Hal Blaine - drums
- Glen Campbell - banjo
- Al de Lory - tack piano
- Steve Douglas - tenor saxophone
- Jim Horn - tenor saxophone
- Paul Horn - tenor saxophone
- Al Jardine - lead vocal
- Bruce Johnston - vocals
- Bobby Klein - tenor saxophone
- Barney Kessel - guitar
- Larry Knechtel - organ
- Mike Love - lead vocal
- Jay Migliori - baritone saxophone
- Tommy Morgan - harmonica
- Ray Pohlman - bass guitar
- Lyle Ritz - upright bass
- Julius Wechter - percussion
- Brian Wilson - lead vocal
- Carl Wilson - vocals
- Dennis Wilson - vocals

See also

- List of songs by The Beach Boys

I Love to Say Da-Da

"I Love to Say Da-Da" (aka **"In Blue Hawaii"**) is a song written by Brian Wilson and Van Dyke Parks. The song was originally intended to be on the famous unreleased *Smile* album before its sessions collapsed. It was the last major recording done for the ill-fated album.

The song was intended as the final portion of the "Elements" suite, originally recorded May 16–18, 1967. The Beach Boys resurrected elements of this song as "Cool, Cool Water" during sessions for their 1967 album *Wild Honey*, although it wasn't issued until 1970, on their album *Sunflower*.

When Brian Wilson reconstructed his version of the *Smile* album, he took the segment "Water Chant" (which would have been the second portion of the "Elements" suite) and combined it with "I Love to Say Da-Da" and a new orchestral coda to complete the song which he now called "In Blue Hawaii".

The original raw recording of "I Love to Say Da-Da" can be found on the Beach Boys' compilation box set *Good Vibrations: Thirty Years of The Beach Boys* along with other previously unreleased remnants of the *Smile* sessions.

(I Saw Santa) Rockin' Around the Christmas Tree

"(I Saw Santa) Rockin' Around the Christmas Tree" is a Christmas song written by Brian Wilson and Al Jardine. The song was recorded by the American pop band The Beach Boys and was released on their 1998 Christmas album *Ultimate Christmas*.

It should not be confused with Rockin' Around the Christmas Tree, written by Johnny Marks and first recorded by Brenda Lee.

See also

- List of songs by The Beach Boys

I Should Have Known Better

"I Should Have Known Better"	
Single by The Beatles	
from the album *A Hard Day's Night*	
A-side	"A Hard Day's Night"
Released	13 July 1964
Format	vinyl record (7", 12")
Recorded	Abbey Road Studios 25–26 February 1964
Genre	Pop
Length	02:44
Label	Capitol Records
Writer(s)	Lennon/McCartney
Producer	George Martin
The Beatles singles chronology	

"Can't Buy Me Love" (1964) — "Let it Be" (1970)	**"A Hard Day's Night"** (US-1964) — **"Yesterday"** (UK-1975)	"I'll Cry Instead" (1964) — "Back in the U.S.S.R." (1976)

***A Hard Day's Night* track listing**

13 tracks

Side one

1. "A Hard Day's Night"
2. "I Should Have Known Better"
3. "If I Fell"
4. "I'm Happy Just to Dance with You"
5. "And I Love Her"
6. "Tell Me Why"
7. "Can't Buy Me Love"

Side two

- "Any Time at All"

2. "I'll Cry Instead"
3. "Things We Said Today"
4. "When I Get Home"
5. "You Can't Do That"
6. "I'll Be Back"

"I Should Have Known Better"	
Song by The Beach Boys from the album *Beach Boys' Party!*	
Released	8 November 1965
Genre	Pop
Length	1:40
Label	Capitol
Composer	Lennon/McCartney
Producer	Brian Wilson
***Beach Boys' Party!* track listing**	

12 tracks
• "Hully Gully"
• **"I Should Have Known Better"**
• "Tell Me Why"
• "Papa-Oom-Mow-Mow"
• "Mountain of Love"
• "You've Got to Hide Your Love Away"
• "Devoted to You"
• "Alley Oop"
• "There's No Other (Like My Baby)"
• "Medley:I Get Around/Little Deuce Coupe"
• "The Times They Are a-Changin'"
• "Barbara Ann"

"**I Should Have Known Better**" is a song composed by John Lennon[1] [2] (credited to Lennon/McCartney), and originally released by The Beatles on the UK version of *A Hard Day's Night*, their soundtrack for the film of the same name.

The song is performed in the train compartment scene of *A Hard Day's Night*. It was in fact filmed in a van, with crew members rocking the vehicle to fake the action of a train in motion.[3]

An orchestrated version of the song conducted by George Martin appears on the U.S. version of the album.

Origin

In January 1964, during a three-week engagement at the Olympia Theatre in Paris, The Beatles first became aware of American singer and songwriter Bob Dylan and, when having acquired a copy of his album *Freewheelin' Bob Dylan*, began playing it continuously.[4] American journalist Al Aronowitz introduced them to Dylan when The Beatles visited New York in February 1964, and Dylan subsequently became a big influence on the group, especially Lennon, who even started wearing a copycat Huckleberry Finn cap.[5] One consequence of this "infatuation" (as Ian MacDonald later described it) was the song "I Should Have Known Better".[6] Paul McCartney said Dylan's songs were "great lyrically",[7] and Lennon credited Dylan with inspiring him to write more meaningful lyrics.[8]

Recording

The first recording session for the song was on 25 February 1964 at Abbey Road Studios when three takes were attempted, but only one was complete. Take 2 was aborted when Lennon broke into hysterics over his harmonica playing. The song was re-recorded the next day after making some changes to the arrangement.[9]

Lennon's harmonica playing opens the track, the last occasion The Beatles were to feature this instrument on an intro ("I'm a Loser", recorded 14 August 1964 has a harmonica solo) and thus draws a line under a significant period of their early music. The song's middle sixteen section features George Harrison's brand new Rickenbacker 360/12 12-string guitar.[6]

The mono and stereo versions have slightly different harmonica introductions. In the stereo version, the harmonica drops out briefly.[10] Also, a noticeably clumsy and audible tape edit is heard during the second middle eight between "You're gonna say you love me, too" and "And when I ask you to be mine".

Release

United Kingdom

In the UK, "I Should Have Known Better" appeared on *A Hard Day's Night* and was released on 10 July 1964. It was not released as a single at that time. In 1976, it was released as a B-side to "Yesterday".[11] [12]

United States

In the U.S., "I Should Have Known Better" was released on 13 July 1964 as the B-side to "A Hard Day's Night"[13] [14] and reached No. 53 in the Billboard Top 100. As part of the movie contract, United Artists acquired album rights for the American market.[15] They released a soundtrack album on 26 June 1964 with eight Beatles songs and four instrumentals. "I Should Have Known Better" was performed in the film, and it appears on the soundtrack. Capitol Records released *Something New* a month later with songs from the UK version of *A Hard Day's Night* that were not used in the film. It was later released by Capitol on the *Hey Jude* compilation album in 1970.[16]

Continental Europe

"I Should Have Known Better" was released as a single in a number of continental European countries, including Norway, where it reached number one,[17] and West Germany, where it reached number six.[18]

Personnel

- John Lennon – double-tracked vocal, acoustic rhythm guitar, harmonica
- Paul McCartney – bass
- George Harrison – 12-string lead guitar
- Ringo Starr – drums

Personnel per Ian MacDonald[6]

Cover versions

- The Beach Boys covered it on their 1965 album *Beach Boys' Party!*
- The Skatalites recorded an instrumental version under the name "Independence Anniversary Ska".
- She & Him covered the song on their 2008 debut album, *Volume One*, as a duet with both M. Ward and Zooey Deschanel singing.
- The Punkles did a punk cover of this song on their first album.
- Phil Ochs covered the song with Eric Andersen during a Greenwich Village concert in 1964; the live version can be heard on The Broadside Tapes 1.

References

- The Beatles (2000). *The Beatles Anthology*. London: Cassell& Co. ISBN 0-304-35605-0.
- Cross, Craig (2005). *The Beatles: Day-by-Day, Song-by-Song, Record-by-Record.* Lincoln, NE: iUniverse, Inc.. ISBN 0-595-34663-4.
- Dowlding, William (1989). *Beatlesongs*.
- "German Top 20 - The Chart of 1964" [19]. *Inifity Charts*. 2009. Retrieved 9 December 2009.
- Harry, Bill (2000). *The Beatles Encyclopedia: Revised and Updated*. London: Virgin Publishing. ISBN 0-7535-0481-2.
- Lewisohn, Mark (1988). *The Beatles Recording Sessions*. New York: Harmony Books. ISBN 0-517-57066-1.
- MacDonald, Ian (2005). *Revolution in the Head: The Beatles' Records and the Sixties* (Second Revised ed.). London: Pimlico (Rand). ISBN 1-844-13828-3.
- Miles, Barry (1997). *Paul McCartney: Many Years From Now*. New York: Henry Holt & Company. ISBN 0-8050-5249-6.
- Sheff, David (2000). *All We Are Saying: The Last Major Interview with John Lennon and Yoko Ono*. New York: St. Martin's Press. ISBN 0-312-25464-4.
- "Topp 20 Single uke 42, 1964" [20]. *MUSIKKEXTRA*. 2009. Retrieved 9 December 2009.

References

[1] Sheff 2000, p. 194.
[2] Miles 1997, p. 164.
[3] Dowlding 1989, p. 68.
[4] The Beatles 2000, p. 112.
[5] Harry 2000, pp. 357–359.
[6] MacDonald 2005, p. 109–110.
[7] Miles 1997, p. 195.
[8] Sheff 2000, p. 179.
[9] Lewisohn 1988, pp. 39–40.
[10] Cross 2005, p. 384.
[11] Cross 2005, p. 592.
[12] Lewisohn 1988, p. 200.
[13] Cross 2005, pp. 530–531.
[14] Lewisohn 1988, p. 201.
[15] Harry 2000, pp. 483–484.
[16] Lewisohn 1988.
[17] MUSIKKEXTRA 2009.
[18] Inifity Charts 2009.
[19] http://ki.informatik.uni-wuerzburg.de/~topsi/deu1964/deu_1964t.html
[20] http://lista.vg.no/show_list.php?ListsOp=showWeek&week=42&year=1964&listID=1

I Wanna Pick You Up

"I Wanna Pick You Up" is a song written by Brian Wilson for the American pop band The Beach Boys. It was released on their 1977 album *The Beach Boys Love You*.

Two decades later, the song was covered by Darian Sahanaja, who would later tour as a backup musician with Brian Wilson. Sahanaja's remake opens with a keyboard riff similar to the opening of The Beach Boys' "You Still Believe In Me," and ends with vocal harmonies borrowed from a "Heroes And Villains" outtake that were eventually used on the finished 'Smile' version of the song. Sahanaja's cover of "I Wanna Pick You Up" was released as a B-side of a vinyl single of a cover of Wilson's still-unreleased "Do You Have Any Regrets." The A-side was recorded in Brian Wilson's classic style, while Sahanaja interpreted the B-side as if it were part of The Beach Boys' *Smiley Smile* album. The rare single was pressed on blue vinyl with a label that was a parody of X Records, which was the label that released The Beach Boys' first single, "Surfin'" b/w "Luau."

Details

- *Written by:* Brian Wilson
- *Album:* The Beach Boys Love You
- *Time:* 2 min 39 sec
- *Produced by:* Brian Wilson

Performers

- *Brian Wilson:* Lead Vocals
- *Dennis Wilson:* Lead Vocals

I Was Made to Love Her

"I Was Made to Love Her"	
Single by Stevie Wonder	
B-side	"Hold Me"
Released	1967
Genre	Soul
Length	2:37
Label	Motown
Writer(s)	Stevie Wonder, Lula Mae Hardaway, Henry Cosby, Sylvia Moy
Producer	Henry Cosby
Stevie Wonder singles chronology	
"Hey Love" (1967) "I Was Made to Love Her" (1967) "I'm Wondering" (1967)	

"I Was Made to Love Her" is a hit single recorded by American soul musician Stevie Wonder for Motown's Tamla label in 1967 (see 1967 in music). The song was written by Wonder, his mother Lula Mae Hardaway, Sylvia Moy and producer Henry Cosby; and included on Wonder's 1967 album *I Was Made to Love Her*. Released as a single, "I Was Made to Love Her" peaked at number-two on the *Billboard* Pop Singles chart and spent four non-consecutive weeks at number-one on the Hot Rhythm & Blues Singles chart in the United States.[1]

The song was covered by the American band The Beach Boys on their 1967 album *Wild Honey*, by Jimi Hendrix (with Stevie Wonder on drums) on the BBC Sessions album, by the Jackson 5 on *Boogie*, and with minor changes, by American R&B singer Whitney Houston on her 1998 album *My Love Is Your Love* under the name "I Was Made To Love Him". Most recently, it was covered by Boyz II Men on their album *Motown Hitsville USA*.

Notes

[1] Whitburn, Joel (2004). *Top R&B/Hip-Hop Singles: 1942-2004*. Record Research. p. 635.

Interesting.

I Went to Sleep

"I Went to Sleep" is a song written by Brian Wilson and Carl Wilson for the American pop band The Beach Boys. It was released on their 1969 album *20/20*. The song was recorded in June, 1968.

Details

- Written by: Brian Wilson/Carl Wilson
- Album: *20/20*
- Time: 1:36
- Produced by: Brian Wilson

Performers

- *Brian Wilson:* Lead Vocals

See also

- List of songs by The Beach Boys

I'd Love Just Once to See You

"I'd Love Just Once to See You" is a song written by Brian Wilson and Mike Love for the American band The Beach Boys. It was released on their 1967 album *Wild Honey*.

Details

- *Written by:* Brian Wilson/Mike Love
- *Album:* Wild Honey
- *Time:* 1 min 48 sec
- *Produced by:* The Beach Boys

Performers

- *Brian Wilson:* Lead Vocals

Other versions

The song was covered in 2008 by Elastic No-No Band featuring Toby Goodshank, on the EP *The Meow Bits*. The same recording was later included on Elastic No-No Band's album *Fustercluck!!!*.

The last lines of this song are quoted in the song "Eisenhower is the Father" by Minneapolis band Best Friends Forever.

See also

- List of songs by The Beach Boys

I'll Be Home for Christmas

"**I'll Be Home for Christmas**" is a Christmas song, written by Buck Ram, Kim Gannon and Walter Kent.

In 1943, this song joined "White Christmas" to become one of America's most popular holiday songs. The recording by Bing Crosby shot to the top ten of the record charts that year and became a holiday musical tradition in the United States. The idea of being home for Christmas originated in World War I when soldiers at first thought that the war would be quick and they would return by Christmastime. This inevitably did not happen, hence the line "if only in my dreams".

A song titled "I'll Be Home for Christmas" was first copyrighted on August 24, 1943, by Kent (music) and James "Kim" Gannon (lyrics). The two revised and re-copyrighted their song on September 27, 1943, and it was this version that was made famous by Crosby. The label on Crosby's recording credits "I'll Be Home for Christmas" to Kent, Gannon, and Ram. Later recordings usually credit only Kent and Gannon. The discrepancy arose from the fact that on December 21, 1942 Buck Ram copyrighted a song titled "I'll Be Home for Christmas (Tho' Just in Memory)"—that song bore little or no resemblance, other than its title, to the Crosby recording.

According to Ram, who was primarily a lyricist, he had written the lyrics as a 16-year-old, homesick college student. Prior to his publishers planned release, he had discussed the song with two acquaintances in a bar. He left a copy with them, but never spoke to them about it again. Both he and his publisher were shocked when the song was released by a competing publishing house. Per news articles of the day, Ram's publisher, who had been holding the song back a year because they were coming out with "White Christmas," sued Gannon and Kent's publisher and prevailed in court.

On October 4, 1943, Crosby recorded "I'll Be Home for Christmas" with the John Scott Trotter Orchestra for Decca Records. Within about a month of Kent and Gannon's copyright the song hit the music charts and remained there for eleven weeks, peaking at number three. The following year, the song reached number nineteen on the charts. It touched a tender place in the hearts of Americans, both soldiers and civilians, who were then in the depths of World War II, and it earned Crosby his fifth gold record. "I'll Be Home for Christmas" became the most requested song at Christmas U.S.O. shows in both Europe and the Pacific and Yank, the GI magazine, said Crosby accomplished more for military morale than anyone else of that era.

"I'll Be Home for Christmas" was recorded by Perry Como (1946), Frank Sinatra (1957) and countless other artists. And the team of Kent and Gannon continued to write songs, although none attained the popularity of "I'll Be Home for Christmas." Kent also composed the hit song, "(There'll Be Bluebirds Over) The White Cliffs of Dover," with the lyricist Nat Burton. Buck Ram is one of the top five songwriters of BMI's first 50 years. His hits include: "Only You", "The Great Pretender", "The Magic Touch", "Twilight Time", "At Your Beck and Call", "Remember When", "Coma Prima", and dozens of others. He is a member of the Songwriter's Hall of Fame.

In December 1965, having completed the first U.S. space rendezvous and set a record for the longest flight in the U.S. space program, the astronauts Frank Borman and James Lovell hurtled back to earth aboard their Gemini 7 spacecraft. Asked by NASA communication personnel if they wanted any particular music piped up to them, the crew requested Bing Crosby's recording of "I'll Be Home for Christmas."

Versions

Recorded by:

- John Gary, 1964
- 98 Degrees
- Aqua Teen Hunger Force (*Have Yourself A Meaty Little Christmas*, 2009)
- Aly & AJ (*Acoustic Hearts of Winter*, 2006)
- Girl in a Coma (A Blackheart Christmas - *Blackheart Records, 2008) *Joan Jett's Record Label
- BarlowGirl (*Home for Christmas*, 2008)
- The Beach Boys (*The Beach Boys' Christmas Album*, 1964)
- Tony Bennett
- Ricky Van Shelton (*Ricky Van Shelton Sings Christmas*, 1989)
- Suzy Bogguss
- Pat Boone
- The Brothers Four , 1966 Billboard chart single
- Carl Brutananadilewski
- Peabo Bryson and Roberta Flack
- Michael Bublé
- Jimmy Buffett
- Glen Campbell
- The Carpenters
- Johnny Cash
- Harry Connick, Jr. (*Harry for the Holidays*, 2003)
- Kenneth Copeland
- Doris Day on The Doris Day Christmas Album, September 14, 1964
- Neil Diamond
- Placido Domingo, including a duet with Tony Bennett for a 2000 Christmas concert in Vienna, *Our Favourite Things: Christmas in Vienna*
- Fats Domino
- Gloria Estefan
- Sara Evans (*Hear Something Country - Christmas 2007*, 2007)
- Percy Faith
- Blue Blot
- Connie Francis
- The Forester Sisters
- Vince Gill
- Jackie Gleason
- Amy Grant
- Al Green
- Josh Groban (spent three weeks atop the *Billboard* Hot Adult Contemporary Tracks chart in December 2007/January 2008[1]
- Justin Guarini
- Hampton String Quartet
- Jillian Hall (*A Jingle with Jillian*, 2007)
- Gary Hoey
- Whitney Houston
- Brad Johner
- Wynonna Judd

- Toby Keith
- B.B. King
- Kokia (*Christmas Gift*, 2008)
- Lisa Leuschner
- Crystal Lewis Holiday!: "A Collection of Christmas Classics" 2002
- Lonestar
- Aimee Mann (*One More Drifter in the Snow*, 2006)
- Dean Martin
- Matchbook Romance (*A Santa Cause: It's a Punk Rock Christmas*)
- Johnny Mathis
- Martina McBride
- Reba McEntire
- Brian McKnight
- Sarah McLachlan
- Katharine McPhee - released as a digital single on November 17, 2009
- Tift Merritt
- Bette Midler
- Glenn Miller Orchestra
- Ronnie Milsap
- Dannii Minogue
- Anne Murray
- The Nylons
- The Oak Ridge Boys
- Jeffrey Osborne
- The Osmonds
- Overboard (Tidings, 2008)
- Brad Paisley
- Dolly Parton
- The Platters
- Elvis Presley (*Elvis' Christmas Album*, 1957)
- Eddie Rabbitt
- Rascal Flatts (*Greatest Hits Volume 1* Bonus Track, 2008)
- Leon Redbone
- Linda Ronstadt
- Art Paul Schlosser (I'll Be a Gnome for Christmas a parody from his 2003 recording Words of Cheese and Other Parrot Trees CD available at Apple iTunes)
- Diane Schuur
- Drew Seeley ("Disney Channel Holiday", 2007)
- Frank Sinatra
- Mindy Smith
- Jordin Sparks (*This Christmas* soundtrack, 2007)
- Spyro Gyra
- The Statler Brothers
- Barbra Streisand
- The Three Tenors
- Pam Tillis
- Garrett Gitchel

- Twisted Sister (*A Twisted Christmas*, 2006)
- Tierney Sutton with Erich Kunzel and the Cincinnati Pops Orchestra
- Carrie Underwood with Elvis Presley (*Christmas Duets* (Elvis Presley album), 2008)
- Jaci Velasquez
- Jennifer Warnes (*The Tradition of Christmas*, 1991)
- Slim Whitman
- Andy Williams
- Joe Williams
- Vanessa L. Williams
- Jackie Wilson (Merry Christmas From Jackie Wilson), 1963)
- Dwight Yoakam
- Kelly Clarkson in concert

References

[1] Groban version chart info (http://www.billboard.com/bbcom/esearch/chart_display.jsp?cfi=341&cfgn=Singles&cfn=Hot+Adult+Contemporary+Tracks&ci=3090294&cdi=9612972&cid=01/05/2008) Billboard.com. Retrieved 23 June 2009.

I'll Bet He's Nice

"I'll Bet He's Nice" is a song written by Brian Wilson for the American pop band The Beach Boys. It was released on their 1977 album *Love You*.

As Al Jardine put it in one of the demo sessions for the album "That [song] is a motherfucker!"

Details

- *Written by:* Brian Wilson
- *Album:* Love You
- *Time:* 2 min 36 sec
- *Produced by:* Brian Wilson

Performers

- *Brian Wilson:* Lead Vocals
- *Carl Wilson:* Lead Vocals (bridge)
- *Dennis Wilson:* Lead Vocals

See also

- The Beach Boys
- Love You
- List of songs by The Beach Boys

I'm Bugged at My Ol' Man

"I'm Bugged at My Ol' Man"		
Song by The Beach Boys from the album *Summer Days (and Summer Nights!!)*		
Released	June 28, 1965	
Recorded	May 24, 1965 Columbia Studios, Hollywood	
Genre	Pop music	
Length	2:17	
Label	Capitol	
Composer	Brian Wilson	
Producer	Brian Wilson	
***Summer Days (and Summer Nights!!)* track listing**		
Summer Means New Love (10)	**"I'm Bugged at My Ol' Man"** (11)	And Your Dream Comes True (12)

"**I'm Bugged at My Ol' Man**" is a song written by Brian Wilson for the American pop band The Beach Boys. It was released on their 1965 album *Summer Days (and Summer Nights!!)*. On the original back cover notes, the listed lead vocalist is: "Too embarrassed"

Details

- Written by: Brian Wilson
- Album: *Summer Days (and Summer Nights!!)*
- Time: 2 min 17 sec
- Produced by: Brian Wilson

Musicians

- Brian Wilson - piano, vocals
- Carl Wilson - vocals
- Dennis Wilson - vocals
- Marilyn Wilson - vocals

See also

- List of songs by The Beach Boys

I'm So Lonely

"I'm So Lonely" is a song written by Brian Wilson and Eugene E. Landy for the American pop band The Beach Boys. It was released on their 1985 album *The Beach Boys*.

Details

- *Written by:* Brian Wilson/Eugene E. Landy
- *Album:* The Beach Boys
- *Time:* 2:52
- *Produced by:* Steve Levine

Musicians

- John Alder - guitar
- Al Jardine - vocals
- Bruce Johnston - vocals
- Steve Levine - synthesizer, drum programming
- Julian Lindsay - synthesizer
- Mike Love - vocals
- Ian Ritchie - tenor saxophone
- Brian Wilson - keyboard, lead vocal
- Carl Wilson - vocals

See also

- The Beach Boys
- The Beach Boys (album)
- List of songs by The Beach Boys

I'm So Young

"I'm So Young" is a song written by William H. "Prez" Tyus, Jr., of Cincinnati, Ohio. While still in high school, Tyus wrote the songs "I'm So Young" and "Every Day of the Week" and gave them to a local African-American vocal group called the D'Italians. Once a recording contract with Chess Records was secured, the group changed its name to The Students, and it was under this name that Tyus's two classic doo-wop songs were recorded.

"I'm So Young" has been covered by the Rosie and the Originals, the The Del-Vikings, the Beach Boys, and, as "So Young," by The Ronettes and the Devil Dogs.

I'm Waiting for the Day

"I'm Waiting for the Day"	
Song by The Beach Boys from the album *Pet Sounds*	
Released	May 16, 1966
Recorded	track: March 6, 1966; Western Studios vocals: March 10, 1966; Columbia Studios
Genre	Pop
Length	3:03
Label	Capitol
Composer	Wilson/Love
Producer	Brian Wilson
***Pet Sounds* track listing**	
• "Wouldn't It Be Nice" • "You Still Believe in Me" • "That's Not Me" • "Don't Talk (Put Your Head on My Shoulder)" • "I'm Waiting for the Day" • "Let's Go Away for Awhile" • "Sloop John B" • "God Only Knows" • "I Know There's an Answer" • "Here Today" • "I Just Wasn't Made for These Times" • "Pet Sounds" • "Caroline, No"	

"**I'm Waiting for the Day**" is a song by the American pop band The Beach Boys, taken from their 1966 album *Pet Sounds*. It is the fifth track on the album. The song was written by Brian Wilson and Mike Love with Brian also the producer of the song. The lead vocal was sung by Brian Wilson. The Pet Sounds Sessions compilation included an alternate take featuring Mike on lead vocals. However Brian, frustrated with his band members' performance, dismissed their parts and sang all the vocals himself.

Details

- *Written by:* Brian Wilson/Mike Love
- *Album:* Pet Sounds
- *Time:* 3:03
- *Produced by:* Brian Wilson
- *Instrumental track:* recorded March 6, 1966 at Western Recorders, Hollywood, California. Engineered by H. Bowen David
- *String overdub:* recorded March 6, 1966 at Western Recorders, Hollywood, California. Engineered by H. Bowen David
- *Vocal track:* recorded March 10, 1966 at Columbia Studios, Hollywood, California. Engineered by Ralph Balantin.

Musicians

- Gary Coleman - timpani, bongos
- Al de Lory - piano
- Justin DiTullio - cello
- Bill Green - flute
- Jim Gordon - drums
- Leonard Hartman - English horn
- Jim Horn - flute
- Harry Hyams - viola
- Carol Kaye - bass
- Larry Knechtel - organ
- William Kurasch - violin
- Leonard Malarsky - violin
- Jay Migliori - flute
- Ray Pohlman - guitar
- Lyle Ritz - ukulele, upright bass
- Ralph Schaffer - violin
- Sid Sharp - violin
- Brian Wilson - lead and harmony vocals

See also

- List of songs by The Beach Boys

In My Room

"In My Room"	
Single by The Beach Boys	
from the album *Surfer Girl*	
Released	October 14, 1963
Format	Vinyl
Recorded	July 16, 1963
Genre	Pop
Length	2:11
Label	Capitol
Writer(s)	Brian Wilson Gary Usher
Producer	Brian Wilson
The Beach Boys singles chronology	

"Surfer Girl"/"Little Deuce Coupe" (1963)	"Be True to Your School"/"**In My Room**" (1963)	"Little Saint Nick"/"The Lord's Prayer" (1963)

"**In My Room**" is a song written by Brian Wilson and Gary Usher for the American pop band The Beach Boys. It was released on their 1963 album *Surfer Girl*. It was also released as the B-side of the "Be True to Your School" single. The single peaked at number six in the U.S. A remake by Usher's own band, Sagittarius, peaked at number eighty-six in 1969.

Writing the song

Gary Usher explained that

> "'In My Room' found us taking our craft a little more seriously. Brian and I came back to the house one night after playing 'over the line' (a baseball game). I played bass and Brian was on organ. The song was written in an hour... Brian's melody all the way. The sensitivity... the concept meant a lot to him. When we finished, it was late, after our midnight curfew. In fact, Murry [The Wilson brother's father] came in a couple of times and wanted me to leave. Anyway, we got Audree [The Wilson brothers' mother], who was putting her hair up before bed, and we played it for her. She said, 'That's the most beautiful song you've ever written.' Murry said, 'Not bad, Usher, not bad,' which was the nicest thing he ever said to me."

Gary Usher who co-wrote the lyrics with Brian Wilson further describes that "Brian was always saying that his room was his whole world." Brian seconds this opinion: "I had a room, and I thought of it as my kingdom. And I wrote that song, very definitely, that you're not afraid when you're in your room. It's absolutely true."

In 1990, Brian wrote,

> "I also enjoyed producing 'In My Room'. There is a story behind this song. When Dennis, Carl and I lived in Hawthorne as kids, we all slept in the same room. One night I sang the song 'Ivory Tower' to them and they liked it. Then a couple of weeks later, I proceeded to teach them both how to sing the harmony parts to it. It took them a little while, but they finally learned it. We then sang this song night

after night. It brought peace to us. When we recorded 'In My Room', there was just Dennis, Carl and me on the first verse...and we sounded just like we did in our bedroom all those nights. This story has more meaning than ever since Dennis' death."

Demo version and final release

The 1993 CD box set, *Good Vibrations: Thirty Years of The Beach Boys*, contains an early version of "In My Room" with a number of differences from the eventual official release. It is unclear if this fully developed demo was recorded the same day as the final version on July 16, 1963.[1] The tune features six Beach Boys: both Al Jardine (on vocals) and David Marks (whose strumming guitar backs up Carl Wilson's picked solo notes) are present.[2]

The demo begins with an intro that was later scrapped, and launches into the first verse with full group vocals, unlike the finished recording. There, as previously mentioned, the single brings in Brian Wilson's voice first, then his brother Carl Wilson and finally Dennis Wilson. Then the final version adds, in the title/hook, Al Jardine, and Mike Love's bass voicing which both join in to complete the vocal mix.[3]

Recognition and influence

"In My Room" remained on the Billboard Top 100 for 11 weeks, peaking at #23 in 1963.[4] In the UPI (United Press International) weekly survey it was #17 nationally, upheld by its widespead success across the country wherever it was treated as an A-side: #1 in Boston and Seattle; #2 San Francisco; and top ten Washington DC, Houston, Minneapolis, Pittsburgh, Columbus. *Rolling Stone* magazine named it #209 on its list of greatest songs of all-time. David Crosby of The Byrds and Crosby, Stills & Nash (and Young) admitted to being an admirer of the song, quoting "'In My Room' was the defining point for me. When I heard it, I thought 'I give up - I can't do that - I'll never be able to do that.'" He sang a trio cover version with Jimmy Webb and Carly Simon on "An All-Star Tribute to Brian Wilson (2001)." The song was among John Cale's selections for Desert Island Discs.

A recording by E.G. Daily & the Sydney Children's Choir appears in the animated film "Happy Feet" (2006).

Performers

- Brian Wilson: Lead Vocals, Bass
- Mike Love: Backing Vocals, Lead Vocals (bridge)
- Carl Wilson: Backing Vocals, Guitar
- Dennis Wilson: Backing Vocals, Drums
- Al Jardine: Backing Vocals
- David Marks: Guitar
- Hal Blaine: drums

See also

- List of The Beach Boys songs

External links

- Greg Panfile's Musical Analysis of "In My Room" [5]

References

[1] Badman, Keith- The Beach Boys: The Definitive Diary of America's Greatest Band on Stage and in the Studio- Pg. 39- 2004- Backstreet Books- San Francisco- ISBN 0-87930-818-4.
[2] Stebbins, Jon (2007). *The Lost Beach Boy*. London: Virgin Books Ltd. ISBN 978 1 8522 7391 0.
[3] Lambert, Philip (2007). *Inside the Music of Brian Wilson*. New York: Continuum International Publishing Group Inc. ISBN 13 978 0 8264 1877 7.
[4] Joel Whitburn's *Top Pop Singles 1955-2006* ISBN 089820-172-1 and ISBN 978-0-89820-172-7
[5] http://www.cabinessence.net/essays/mob7.html

In the Back of My Mind

"In the Back of My Mind" is a song written by Brian Wilson and Mike Love for the American pop band The Beach Boys. It was released on their 1965 album *The Beach Boys Today!*. The song seems to be going to some other theme at fadeout.

Details

- Written by: Brian Wilson/Mike Love
- Album: *The Beach Boys Today!*
- Time: 2 min 07 sec
- Produced by: Brian Wilson

Musicians

- Hal Blaine - temple blocks, timbales
- Steve Douglas - tenor saxophone
- Plas Johnson - tenor saxophone
- Carol Kaye - bass guitar
- Jay Migliori - baritone saxophone
- Bill Pitman - guitar
- Don Randi - organ
- Billy Lee Riley - harmonica
- Leon Russell - electric piano
- Billy Strange - guitar
- Tommy Tedesco - autoharp
- Julius Wechter - vibraphone
- Brian Wilson - vocals
- Carl Wilson - guitar, vocals
- Dennis Wilson - lead vocal

See also

- List of songs by The Beach Boys

External links

- "In the Back of My Mind" review [1] at Allmusic

References

[1] http://allmusic.com/cg/amg.dll?p=amg&sql=33:jifixqrrldke

In the Parkin' Lot

"In the Parkin' Lot"	
Song by The Beach Boys from the album *Shut Down Volume 2*	
Released	1964
Recorded	???
Genre	Pop Surf rock
Length	2:01
Label	Capitol Records
Writer	Brian Wilson/Roger Christian
Producer	Brian Wilson
***Shut Down Volume 2* track listing**	
• "Fun, Fun, Fun" • "Don't Worry Baby" • "In the Parkin' Lot" • "Cassius Love vs. Sonny Wilson" • "The Warmth of the Sun" • "This Car of Mine" • "Why Do Fools Fall in Love" • "Pom Pom Play Girl" • "Keep an Eye on Summer" • "Shut Down, Part II" • "Louie Louie" • "Denny's Drums"	

"In the Parkin' Lot" is a song written by Brian Wilson and Roger Christian for the American pop band The Beach Boys. It was released on their 1964 album *Shut Down Volume 2*.

Performers

- *Mike Love:* Lead Vocals

See also

- The Beach Boys
- Shut Down Volume 2
- List of songs by The Beach Boys

Island Fever

"Island Fever" is a song written by Mike Love and Terry Melcher for the American pop band The Beach Boys. It was released on their 1992 album *Summer In Paradise*.

Details

- *Written by:* Terry Melcher/Mike Love
- *Album:* Summer in Paradise
- *Time:* 3:26 (3:13 on European release)
- *Produced by:* Terry Melcher
- *Lead vocal*: Mike Love, Carl Wilson

Along with some other *Summer in Paradise* tracks, "Island Fever" was re-mixed and partially recorded for European release. On that version, Al Jardine takes the lead vocal lines that Carl Wilson had in the original.

See also

- List of songs by The Beach Boys

Island Girl

"Island Girl" is a song written by Al Jardine for the American pop band The Beach Boys. It was released on their 1989 album *Still Cruisin'*.

In the liner notes, the song is listed under the title "Island Girl (I'm Gonna Make Her Mine)", but on both the back cover and on the CD itself, it is listed as "Island Girl". Al Jardine's sons, Matt and Adam contribute to the backing vocals on this track. Matt would perform with The Beach Boys on tour in the 90s. Both Matt and Adam joined their father's band after he left The Beach Boys touring group in 1998.

Details

- *Written by:* Al Jardine
- *Album: Still Cruisin'*
- *Time:* 3:50
- *Produced by:* Al Jardine
- *Lead vocal*: Al Jardine, Mike Love, Carl Wilson

See also

- The Beach Boys
- Still Cruisin'
- List of songs by The Beach Boys

It's About Time

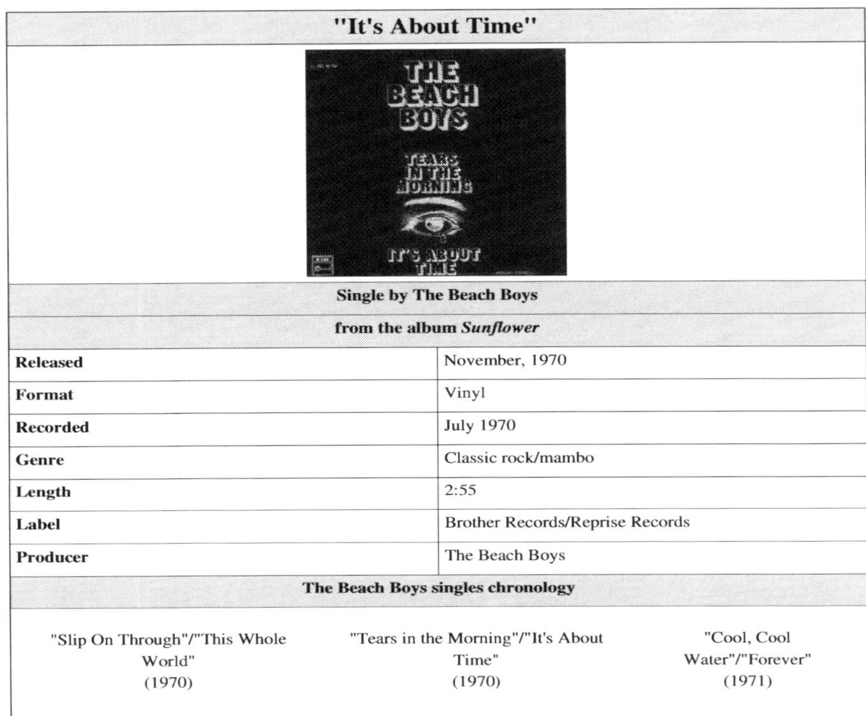

"It's About Time"	
Single by The Beach Boys	
from the album *Sunflower*	
Released	November, 1970
Format	Vinyl
Recorded	July 1970
Genre	Classic rock/mambo
Length	2:55
Label	Brother Records/Reprise Records
Producer	The Beach Boys

The Beach Boys singles chronology		
"Slip On Through"/"This Whole World" (1970)	"Tears in the Morning"/"It's About Time" (1970)	"Cool, Cool Water"/"Forever" (1971)

"It's About Time" is a song written by Dennis Wilson, Carl Wilson, Al Jardine and Bob Burchman for the American pop band The Beach Boys. It was released on their 1970 album *Sunflower*. It was also released as the B-side of the "Tears in the Morning" single although it never reached the charts in either the United States or in the United Kingdom.

Details

- *Written by:* Dennis Wilson/Al Jardine/Bob Burchman
- *Album:* Sunflower
- *Time:* 2:55
- *Produced by:* The Beach Boys

Performers

- *Carl Wilson:* Lead Vocals, Lead Guitar

See also

- The Beach Boys
- Sunflower
- List of songs by The Beach Boys

It's Gettin' Late

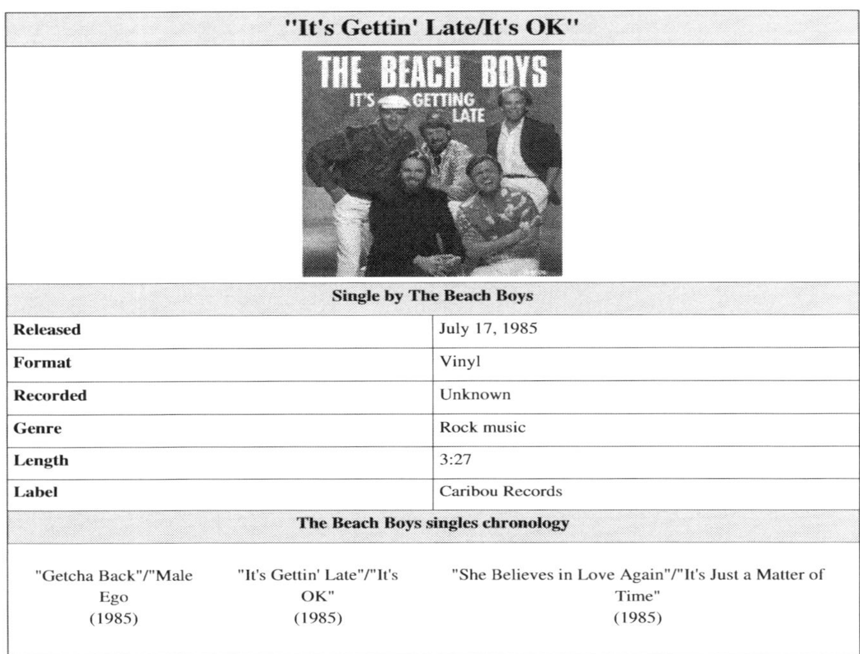

"It's Gettin' Late/It's OK"	
Single by The Beach Boys	
Released	July 17, 1985
Format	Vinyl
Recorded	Unknown
Genre	Rock music
Length	3:27
Label	Caribou Records

The Beach Boys singles chronology		
"Getcha Back"/"Male Ego" (1985)	"It's Gettin' Late"/"It's OK" (1985)	"She Believes in Love Again"/"It's Just a Matter of Time" (1985)

"It's Gettin' Late" is a song written by Carl Wilson, Myrna Smith Schilling and Robert White Johnson for the American pop band The Beach Boys. It was released on their 1985 album *The Beach Boys* and as a single with "It's OK".

The music video directed by Dominic Orlando, was filmed on location in Malibu, California, two months after Getcha Back.

Details

- *Written by:* Carl Wilson/Myrna Smith Schilling/Robert White Johnson
- *Album:* The Beach Boys
- *Time:* 3 min 27 sec
- *Produced by:* Steve Levine

Musicians

- Graham Broad - percussion
- Steve Grainger - baritone saxophone
- Al Jardine - vocals
- Bruce Johnston - vocals
- Steve Levine - synthesizer, drum programming
- Julian Lindsay - keyboards, synthesizers

- Mike Love - vocals
- Kenneth McGregor - trombone
- Ian Ritchie - tenor saxophone
- Dave Spence - trumpet
- Brian Wilson - vocals
- Carl Wilson - keyboard, guitar, lead vocal

See also

- The Beach Boys
- The Beach Boys (album)
- List of songs by The Beach Boys

It's Just a Matter of Time

"It's Just a Matter of Time"	
Song by The Beach Boys from the album *The Beach Boys*	
Released	10 June 1985
Length	2:23
Writer	Brian Wilson, Eugene E. Landy
Producer	Steve Levine
***The Beach Boys* track listing**	
Side one 1. "Getcha Back" 2. "It's Gettin' Late" 3. "Crack at Your Love" 4. "Maybe I Don't Know" 5. "She Believes in Love Again" Side two 1. "California Calling" 2. "Passing Friend" 3. "I'm So Lonely" 4. "Where I Belong" 5. "I Do Love You" 6. "It's Just a Matter of Time"	

"It's Just a Matter of Time" is a song written by Brian Wilson and Eugene E. Landy for the American pop band The Beach Boys. It was released on their 1985 album *The Beach Boys*.

Musicians

- John Alder - dobro
- Graham Broad - drums, percussion
- Al Jardine - vocals
- Bruce Johnston - vocals
- Judd Lander - harmonica
- Steve Levine - synthesizer
- Julian Lindsay - keyboard, bass
- Mike Love - lead vocal
- Brian Wilson - keyboard, lead vocal
- Carl Wilson - vocals

See also

- The Beach Boys
- The Beach Boys (album)
- List of songs by The Beach Boys

It's OK

"It's O.K."	
Single by The Beach Boys	
from the album *15 Big Ones*	
Released	August 9, 1976 July 17, 1985
Format	Vinyl
Recorded	1974
Genre	Rock
Length	2:12
Label	Brother/Reprise
Writer(s)	Brian Wilson Mike Love
Producer	Brian Wilson

The Beach Boys singles chronology		
"Rock and Roll Music"/"TM Song" (1976) ---- "Getcha Back/Male Ego" (1985)	**"It's O.K."**/"Had to Phone Ya" (1976) ---- "It's Gettin' Late"/"It's O.K." (1985)	"Everyone's in Love with You"/"Susie Cincinnati (1976) ---- "She Believes in Love Again"/"It's Just a Matter of Time" (1985)

"**It's OK**" is a song written by Brian Wilson and Mike Love for the American pop band The Beach Boys. It was released on their 1976 album *15 Big Ones*. It was released as a single on August 9, 1976 (with B-side "Had to Phone Ya") and climbed to number twenty-nine on the Billboard Hot 100 singles chart in the U.S. "It's OK" was subsequently released as the B-side to the single "It's Gettin' Late" on July 17, 1985.

Performers

- Mike Love: Lead vocals, Backing vocals
- Brian Wilson: Backing vocals, Piano, Organ, Moog Bass
- Carl Wilson: Backing vocals, Guitar
- Dennis Wilson: Backing vocals, drums
- Marilyn Wilson: Backing vocals
- Al Jardine: Backing vocals
- Ricky Fataar: Drums
- Dennis Dreith: Clavinet
- Jules Jacobs: Clavinet
- Roy Wood: Saxophone

See also

- The Beach Boys
- 15 Big Ones
- List of The Beach Boys songs

It's Over Now

"**It's Over Now**" is the title of a song written by Brian Wilson for The Beach Boys. The song was originally intended to be on the "Adult/Child" album although when the album was aborted the song sat in the archives for many years. It was eventually released on The Beach Boys' 1993 box set *Good Vibrations: Thirty Years of The Beach Boys* as the thirteenth track on disc four.

In order to make the performance sound more "mature" a la Frank Sinatra, the recording was slowed, giving Carl Wilson's voice a strange and haunting effect. Using most audio editing software, if you adjust the key one half-step higher (i.e., up one semitone, or +100 cents), you get the original key and Carl Wilson's normal singing voice comes across beautifully. Mike Love's vocals are featured on the song's bridge.

See also

- List of songs by The Beach Boys

It's a Beautiful Day

"It's a Beautiful Day"	
Single by The Beach Boys	
from the album *Ten Years of Harmony*	
Released	September, 1979
Format	Vinyl
Recorded	Unknown
Genre	Pop
Length	3 min 15 sec
Label	Caribou Records
Producer	Bruce Johnston
The Beach Boys singles chronology	

"Lady Lynda"/"Full Sail" (1979)	**"It's a Beautiful Day**"/"Sumahama" (1979)	"Goin' On"/"Endless Harmony" (1980)

"It's a Beautiful Day" is a song written by Mike Love and Al Jardine for the American pop band The Beach Boys. The song was never released on an original Beach Boys album; however, it was released on the soundtrack to the film *Americathon* and as a single in September 1979 with B-side, "Sumahama". The single charted at #45 in the United States but never charted in the United Kingdom. The song has also been released on the *Ten Years of Harmony* Beach Boys compilation album.

See also

- List of songs by The Beach Boys

Johnny Carson

"Johnny Carson" is a song written by Brian Wilson for the American pop band The Beach Boys. It was released on their 1977 album *Love You*.

Details

- *Written by:* Brian Wilson
- *Album:* Love You
- *Time:* 2 min 47 sec
- *Produced by:* Brian Wilson

Performers

- *Carl Wilson:* Lead Vocals (chorus)
- *Mike Love:* Lead Vocals (verses)

See also

- The Beach Boys
- Love You
- List of songs by The Beach Boys

Judy

"Judy" is a song written by Brian Wilson for The Beach Boys. It was recorded on February 8, 1962, during their second recording session. It was never officially released on a Beach Boys album. Its first release came in 1969 on an album called *The Beach Boys' Biggest Beach Hits*, which collected some of the songs from the first two Beach Boys sessions, with two songs by The Tornadoes filling out the album.

"Judy" was written about Brian's then-girlfriend Judy Bowles.

Musicians

- Al Jardine - guitar, vocals
- Mike Love - vocals
- Val Poliuto - vocals
- Brian Wilson - bass guitar
- Carl Wilson - lead guitar
- Dennis Wilson - drums

See also

- List of songs by The Beach Boys

Just Once in My Life

"Just Once in My Life"	
Single by The Righteous Brothers	
from the album *Just Once in My Life*	
B-side	"The Blues"
Released	1965
Format	7" single
Genre	Blue-eyed soul
Length	3:54
Label	Philles
Writer(s)	Gerry Goffin, Carole King, Phil Spector
The Righteous Brothers singles chronology	
"Bring Your Love to Me" (1965)	**"Just Once in My Life"** (1965)	"You Can Have Her" (1965)

"**Just Once in My Life**" is a song written by Gerry Goffin, Carole King and Phil Spector. The most popular version of the song was performed by The Righteous Brothers.

The Righteous Brothers released their version as a single in 1965. Their second release on the Philles label (the first being "You've Lost That Lovin' Feelin'"), the single was another big hit, making the top ten of the Billboard Hot 100, reaching number nine.

The song was remade by the American pop band The Beach Boys and released on their 1976 album *15 Big Ones*. Other artists to release versions include The Alan Price Set and The Action.

Beach Boys version

Details

- Album: *15 Big Ones*
- Length: 3 min 47 sec
- Produced by Brian Wilson
- Arranged by Brian Wilson

Performers

- Carl Wilson: Lead vocals, percussion
- Brian Wilson: Lead vocals, Backing vocals, Piano, Organ, Moog Bass, String Ensemble
- Al Jardine: Backing vocals
- Mike Love: Backing vocals
- Bruce Johnston: Backing vocals
- Dennis Wilson: drums
- Ed Carter: Guitar
- Billy Hinsche: Guitar
- Ricky Fataar: Percussion

Sources

- *15 Big Ones* reissue liner notes, written by Dennis Diken, 2000.

Keep an Eye on Summer

"Keep an Eye on Summer"	
Song by The Beach Boys from the album *Shut Down Volume 2*	
Released	1964
Recorded	???
Genre	Pop Surf rock
Length	2:21
Label	Capitol Records
Writer	Brian Wilson/Bob Norman
Producer	Brian Wilson
***Shut Down Volume 2* track listing**	
• "Fun, Fun, Fun" • "Don't Worry Baby" • "In the Parkin' Lot" • "Cassius Love vs. Sonny Wilson" • "The Warmth of the Sun" • "This Car of Mine" • "Why Do Fools Fall in Love" • "Pom Pom Play Girl" • "Keep an Eye on Summer" • "Shut Down, Part II" • "Louie Louie" • "Denny's Drums"	

"Keep an Eye on Summer" is a song written by Brian Wilson and Bob Norman for the American pop band The Beach Boys. It was released on their 1964 album *Shut Down Volume 2*. Wilson also recorded a version of the song on his 1998 album *Imagination*.

Performers

- *Brian Wilson:* Lead Vocals
- *Mike Love:* Lead Vocals

See also

- The Beach Boys
- Shut Down Volume 2
- List of songs by The Beach Boys

Keepin' the Summer Alive

"Keepin' the Summer Alive" is a song written by Carl Wilson and Randy Bachman for the American pop band The Beach Boys. It was released on their 1980 album *Keepin' the Summer Alive*.

Details

- *Written by:* Carl Wilson/Randy Bachman
- *Album:* Keepin' the Summer Alive
- *Time:* 3 min 43 sec
- *Produced by:* Bruce Johnston

Performers

- *Carl Wilson:* Lead Vocals

See also

- The Beach Boys
- Keepin' the Summer Alive
- List of songs by The Beach Boys

Kiss Me, Baby

"Kiss Me, Baby"	
Single by The Beach Boys	
from the album *The Beach Boys Today!*	
Released	April 5, 1965
Format	Vinyl
Recorded	December 16, 1964 & January 15, 1965
Genre	Pop
Length	2:35
Label	Capitol Records
Producer	Brian Wilson

The Beach Boys singles chronology		
"Do You Wanna Dance?"/"Please Let Me Wonder" (1965)	"Help Me, Rhonda"/"**Kiss Me, Baby**" (1965)	"California Girls"/"Let Him Run Wild" (1965)

"Kiss Me, Baby" is a song written by Brian Wilson and Mike Love. It was released as the B-side of the The Beach Boys number-one U.S. hit "Help Me, Rhonda". It was also released by The Beach Boys on their 1965 album *The Beach Boys Today!*.

Recording

The song was recorded over two dates at Western Recorders, both produced by Brian Wilson. Arranged by Brian Wilson, the instrumental track most likely was recorded on December 16, 1964, with Chuck Britz engineering. The vocals were most likely overdubbed at a session on January 15, 1965. On the verses it features the group singing in unison with Brian Wilson and Mike Love featured on lead vocals on the chorus. The backing vocals are provided by Brian, Carl & Dennis Wilson, Mike Love and Al Jardine. An A cappella mix of the song was released on the 2001 album *Hawthorne, CA*, allowing the listener to clearly hear the complex vocal arrangements and harmonies.

Musicians

- Hal Blaine - drums, temple block
- Peter Christ - English horn
- Steve Douglas - tenor saxophone
- David Duke - French horn
- Al Jardine - backing vocals
- Carol Kaye - bass guitar
- Barney Kessel - 12-string guitar
- Mike Love - lead and backing vocals
- Jay Migliori - baritone saxophone
- Bill Pitman - acoustic guitar
- Ray Pohlman - bass guitar
- Leon Russell - piano
- Billy Strange - electric guitar
- Julius Wechter - vibraphone, bell-tree
- Brian Wilson - piano, lead and backing vocals
- Carl Wilson - lead guitar, backing vocals
- Dennis Wilson - backing vocals

Single release

"Kiss Me, Baby" was released in April 1965 in the United States as the B-side of the band's second U.S. #1 hit, "Help Me, Rhonda". In the United Kingdom, the song was also released as the B-side of the "Help Me, Rhonda" single, which managed to chart at the number 27 position in Britain.

Album and alternate releases

The song was first released on an album in 1965 on the band's *The Beach Boys Today!* album. A stereo remix of the song was released on the 1998 *Endless Harmony Soundtrack*. A Dolby Digital 5.1 surround sound version of the song was released on the Endless Harmony DVD as a bonus track. The track, along with the other 5.1 surround sound mixes, were produced and mixed by Mark Linett. An A cappella mix of the song was released on the 2001 archival release *Hawthorne, CA*.

See also

- List of songs by The Beach Boys

External links

- "Kiss Me Baby" [1] review at Allmusic

References

[1] http://allmusic.com/cg/amg.dll?p=amg&sql=33:gifixqrrldke

Kokomo

"Kokomo"	
Single by The Beach Boys	
from the album *Still Cruisin'*	
Released	July 18, 1988 (US) October 1988 (UK)
Format	7" single 12" maxi
Recorded	March 22, 1988, April 5–6, 1988
Genre	Pop
Length	3:35
Label	Elektra Records Capitol (reissue)
Producer	Terry Melcher

The Beach Boys singles chronology		
"Happy Endings"/"California Girls" (1987) ---- "Kokomo"/"Tutti Frutti" (1988) ---- "Still Cruisin'"/"Kokomo" (1989)	"**Kokomo**"/"Tutti Frutti" (1988) ---- "Still Cruisin'"/"**Kokomo**" (1989) ---- "Somewhere Near Japan"/"**Kokomo**" (1990)	"Still Cruisin'"/"Kokomo" (1989) ---- "Somewhere Near Japan"/"Kokomo" (1990) ---- Wouldn't It Be Nice (1990)

"**Kokomo**" is a song written by John Phillips, Scott McKenzie, Mike Love and Terry Melcher and recorded by The Beach Boys in 1988. It was released as a single in 1988 by Elektra Records and became a No. 1 Hit in the United States, Japan and Australia (where it topped for about two months). The single was released to coincide with the release of the Tom Cruise movie *Cocktail*, and its subsequent soundtrack. It was nominated in the Grammy Award category: Best Song written specifically for a Motion Picture or Television in 1988, but lost to Phil Collins's "Two Hearts" (from the film "Buster").[1]

Composition and recording

The place referred to as "Kokomo" in the song is fictional.[2] The name was later used by resorts in Sandals Cay, Jamaica, and Grassy Key, Florida. The song also mentions many places in and around the Caribbean, including Aruba, Jamaica, Bermuda, Bahama(s), Key Largo, Montego, Martinique, Montserrat, and Port-au-Prince (Haiti).

In addition to the Beach Boys' signature layered-singing style, the song's instrumentation makes heavy use of steel drums played by Terry Melcher. Van Dyke Parks, who had worked on some of the group's earlier albums, played accordion, while session veteran Jim Keltner played drums.[3] Other players are Jeffrey Foskett (acoustic guitar), Ed Carter (bass), Joel Peskin (saxophone) and Stevie Heger (additional drums).

In the original version, lead vocals were performed by Mike Love and Carl Wilson. The harmonies include Al Jardine and Bruce Johnston. The only active Beach Boys member not involved with the recording was Brian Wilson, who, according to his autobiography, was given short notice of the recording session and unable to attend.[4] He was, however, included in concert recordings of the song, including a live concert filmed for the television show *Full House* (episode 028). The 2008 A&E Network *Biography* on Brian Wilson stated that Mike Love "bragged" about having a #1 hit without Wilson's help.

Release

The "Kokomo" single backed with "Tutti Frutti" by Little Richard was first released through Elektra Records in July 1988. It peaked at the #1 position on the *Billboard* charts on November 5, 1988 after knocking out "A Groovy Kind of Love" by Phil Collins. This meant that it was The Beach Boys' first #1 hit in the United States since "Good Vibrations" in 1966, making it the longest time span between two number one hits in America for a band (22 years). It is also their only #1 hit not written or produced by Brian Wilson. After spending just one week at the top of the charts, the single was knocked out of the number one spot by The Escape Club song "Wild, Wild West". After being signed to Capitol Records following the success of the initial single, Capitol issued the song in the United States for a second time. The song was re-released in July 1989 as the B-side of the "Still Cruisin'" single, which peaked at number 93 on the *Billboard* chart. Capitol again re-issued the song, just two months later, as the B-side of the "Somewhere Near Japan" single, but the single failed to chart.

In the United Kingdom, the single was first issued by Elektra in October 1988. The single peaked at number 25 on the charts. After Capitol had signed the band, as they had in the U.S., they released the single for the second time as the B-side of the "Still Cruisin'" single, however it failed to make any impact on the charts. In Australia the single became the band's third number one hit in Australia after "Do It Again" in 1968 and "Cottonfields" in 1970. In New Zealand the single peaked at the number 5 position. In the Dutch singles chart, the single peaked at the number 6 position. The song also peaked at number 19 in Belgium and at number 7 in Germany.

Album and alternative releases

"Kokomo" was first released on an album in 1989 on the band's *Still Cruisin'* album. The band had been given a one-off album contract by their former label Capitol Records after the song became a number 1 hit in both the United States and Australia. Brian Wilson, who did not perform on the original recording of the song, did later contribute vocals to a Spanish-language version.

In 2006, Beach Boys member Mike Love recorded a critically panned Christmas remake of the song, titled "Santa's Going To Kokomo".

Music video

The video for Kokomo was filmed at the then-recently opened Grand Floridian Resort at Walt Disney World in Florida. The members of the Beach Boys in the video are: Carl Wilson (playing guitar), Al Jardine (playing tambourine), Bruce Johnston (playing bass guitar), and Mike Love (playing saxophone). Actor and part time Beach Boys band member John Stamos can be seen playing the conga steel drums.

Appearances/References in other media

- The Muppets performed this song, with Kermit the Frog singing the lyrics. The lyrics "under a tropical island sky" replaced the lyrics "gave me a tropical contact high".
- In a *Yes Dear* episode, "Jimmy and the Amazing Technicolor Dream Boat," the song appears when Greg drives the boat.
- In a *Two Guys and a Girl* episode, "Two Guys and a Girl and a Vacation," the three main characters sing the song throughout the episode in celebration of their upcoming holiday.
- On an episode of *Scrubs*, Turk suggests Elliot and Keith honeymoon in Kokomo, but Elliot shoots down his fantasy, telling him blankly "For the last time, there is no such place as 'Kokomo'!", to which Turk angrily responds, "Then *where* did The Beach Boys shoot the video, huh?!" (there is a Kokomo in Arkansas, Indiana, Mississippi, and Texas)
- On the "Friends" episode "The One Where Rachel Tells..." in season 8 when Monica and Chandler are leaving for their honeymoon in the Caribbean, Chandler was singing the first line of "Kokomo" and Monica said "get it (the song) out your system while we are alone."
- In the *How I Met Your Mother* episode "Three Days of Snow," the song runs through Barney and Ted's Cocktail-like sequence while running the bar, and again in Barney's head during a telepathic conversation with Ted.
- In the *Family Guy* episode, "The Tan Aquatic with Steve Zissou," Stewie sings along to Kokomo while sunbathing in his sunbed.
- In the episode Office Spaceman, from the animated sitcom *American Dad!*, Roger the Alien (in disguise and working at the CIA) says he needs to go to Aruba, Jamaica, Key Largo, Montego and "a place called Kokomo" to follow leads on alien sightings. Deputy director of the CIA, Avery Bullock finishes the joke by saying "Book a flight, get there fast and then take it slow".
- Kokomo was also included in an episode of Full House when The Beach Boys visted the Tanner Family. Michelle's favorite song was Kokomo and begged for them to sing it at the end of the episode.
- Kokomo was also included in the *Spin City* season 5 episode "Burgers of Wrath"

Parodies

- A Norwegian group, The Shiptare Boys, performed a parody of the song called "Kosovo". It was originally done by Bob Rivers.
- Political satire group Capitol Steps has also recorded a parody called "Kosovo".
- There was a parody of the song referencing the characters of the anime *Ranma 1/2*.
- Bob & Tom parodied the song as Camel Toe.
- WWLS The Sports Animal in Oklahoma released a parody to celebrate the 2000 Oklahoma Sooner football team's trip to the National Championship game.
- In a 2001 episode of *Saturday Night Live*, host Derek Jeter owned a taco restaurant in one skit, "Derek Jeter's Taco Hole," whose theme song was a parody of "Kokomo."

Recognition and criticisms

"Kokomo" appeared on VH1's "40 Most Awesomely Bad No. 1 Songs". However, it received a Golden Globe nomination for Best Original Song - Motion Picture in 1989. The song also ranked at #12 on *Blender* magazine's list of the "50 Worst Songs Ever",[5] while the music video was named the #3 worst video of 1988 on MuchMoreMusic's Back In... '88.

Track listings

3" single

1. "Kokomo" — 3:34
2. "Tutti Frutti" by Little Richard — 2:23
3. "Hippy Hippy Shake" by The Georgia Satellites — 1:45

7" single

1. "Kokomo" — 3:34
2. "Tutti Frutti" by Little Richard — 2:23

12" maxi

1. "Kokomo" — 3:34
2. "Tutti Frutti" by Little Richard — 2:23
3. "Hippy Hippy Shake" by The Georgia Satellites — 1:45

Certifications

Country	Certification	Date	Sales certified
France[6]	Silver	1989	200,000
U.S.[7]	Platinum	January 10, 1989	1,000,000

Chart positions

Chart (1988–1989)	Peak position
Australian Singles Chart[8]	1
Belgian Singles Chart[9]	19
Canadian Singles Chart[10]	13
Dutch Singles Chart[11]	6
French SNEP Singles Chart[12]	6
German Singles Chart[13]	7
New Zealand RIANZ Singles Chart[14]	5
Swedish Singles Chart[12]	14
Swiss Singles Chart[12]	8

UK Singles Chart[15]	25
U.S. *Billboard* Hot 100[16]	1
U.S. *Billboard* Hot Adult Contemporary Tracks[16]	5

End of year chart (1989)	Position
Australian Singles Chart[17]	9

See also

- List of songs by The Beach Boys

References

[1] "Grammy Award" (http://www.metrolyrics.com/1989-grammy-awards.html#ixzz0bxi469dF). . Retrieved 7 January 2010.
[2] "Kokomo By The Beach Boys Songfacts" (http://www.songfacts.com/detail.php?id=505). . Retrieved February 18, 2010.
[3] Brown, Scott; Endleman, Michael (May 28, 2004). "Kokomo" (http://www.ew.com/ew/article/0,,640541,00.html). Entertainment Weekly. . Retrieved December 1, 2009.
[4] Wilson, Brian, *Wouldn't It Be Nice: My Own Story*. HarperCollins, 1991.
[5] Run for Your Life! It's the 50 Worst Songs Ever! (http://www.blender.com/guide/articles.aspx?id=819) from *Blender.com*. Retrieved on 4 May 2008.
[6] Elia Habib, *Muz hit. tubes*, p. 156 (ISBN 2-9518832-0-X)
[7] U.S. certifications riaa.com (http://www.riaa.com/goldandplatinumdata.php?table=SEARCH) (Retrieved August 19, 2008)
[8] "Australian Singles Charts" (http://www.mountvernonandfairway.de/charts10.htm). mountvernonandfairway.de. . Retrieved 12 November 2007.
[9] "Belgian Singles Charts" (http://www.mountvernonandfairway.de/charts7.htm). mountvernonandfairway.de. . Retrieved 12 November 2007.
[10] "Canadian Singles Charts" (http://www.collectionscanada.gc.ca/rpm/028020-119.01-e.php?brws_s=1&file_num=nlc008388.8683&volume=48&issue=26&issue_dt=October 15 1988&type=1&interval=24&PHPSESSID=ujgc075tlgv377braad2n1f9j5). collectionscanada.gc.ca. . Retrieved 1 August 2009.
[11] "Dutch Singles Charts" (http://www.mountvernonandfairway.de/charts6.htm). mountvernonandfairway.de. . Retrieved 12 November 2007.
[12] "French, Swedish and Swiss Singles Charts" (http://lescharts.com/showitem.asp?interpret=The+Beach+Boys&titel=Kokomo&cat=s). lescharts.com. . Retrieved 7 April 2008.
[13] "German Singles Charts" (http://www.mountvernonandfairway.de/charts9.htm). mountvernonandfairway.de. . Retrieved 12 November 2007.
[14] "New Zealand Singles Charts" (http://www.mountvernonandfairway.de/charts5.htm). mountvernonandfairway.de. . Retrieved 12 November 2007.
[15] "UK Singles Chart" (http://www.chartstats.com/songinfo.php?id=15929). chartstats.com. . Retrieved 7 April 2008.
[16] "Billboard" (http://www.allmusic.com/cg/amg.dll?p=amg&sql=11:3ifrxqw5ldse~T51). *Allmusic*. . Retrieved 7 April 2008.
[17] 1989 Australian Singles Chart aria.com (http://www.aria.com.au/pages/aria-charts-end-of-year-charts-top-50-singles-1989.htm) (Retrieved August 19, 2008)

Kona Coast

"Kona Coast" is a song written by Al Jardine and Mike Love for the American pop band The Beach Boys. It was released on their 1978 album *M.I.U. Album*. Parts of an earlier song "Hawaii" can be heard on this song. This was originally written as a Christmas song and new lyrics were written when a proposed Christmas album was rejected by Reprise.

Details

- *Written by:* Al Jardine/Mike Love
- *Album:* M.I.U. Album
- *Time:* 2 min 33 sec
- *Produced by:* Al Jardine/Ron Altbach

Performers

- *Mike Love:* Lead Vocals
- *Al Jardine:* Lead Vocals

See also

- The Beach Boys
- M.I.U. Album
- List of songs by The Beach Boys

Lady Liberty

"Lady Liberty"		
Single by The Beach Boys		
Released	September 1, 1986	
Format	Vinyl	
Genre	Pop	
Label	Capitol	
Writer(s)	Al Jardine, Ron Altbach	
The Beach Boys singles chronology		
"Rock 'n' Roll to the Rescue"/"Good Vibrations" (live) (1986)	"California Dreamin'"/"**Lady Liberty**" (1986)	"Happy Endings"/"California Girls" (1987)

"Lady Liberty" is a song written by Al Jardine and Ron Altbach for the American pop band The Beach Boys. The song is simply a varied version of "Lady Lynda" with completely different lyrics celebrating the Statue of Liberty. It was released as the B-side to their cover version of The Mamas & the Papas song, "California Dreamin'", in 1986.

See also

- List of The Beach Boys songs

Lady Lynda

"Lady Lynda"	
Single by The Beach Boys	
from the album *L.A. (Light Album)*	
Released	June 1979
Format	7"
Recorded	July-November 1978
Genre	Pop
Length	3:58
Label	Brother/Caribou/CBS
Writer(s)	Alan Jardine Ron Altbach
Producer	Bruce Johnston The Beach Boys James William Guercio

The Beach Boys singles chronology		
"Good Timin'"/"Love Surrounds Me" (1979)	**"Lady Lynda"**/"Full Sail" (1979)	"It's a Beautiful Day"/"Sumahama" (1979)

"Lady Lynda" is a song written by vocalist and guitarist Alan Jardine and Ron Altbach for the American pop band The Beach Boys. It was released on their 1979 album *L.A. (Light Album)*.

The music is derived from Johann Sebastian Bach's composition Jesu, Joy of Man's Desiring, with the opening harpsichord part being play by Sterling Smith. [1] The lyrics to the song refer to Jardine's then-wife, Lynda Jardine. After the two divorced, the song was rewritten as "Lady Liberty", a tribute to the Statue of Liberty.

The song hit #7 in the UK Singles Chart, although it was bereft of the harpsichord opening that was an important part in the album version . It also reached #39 on the U.S. adult contemporary chart.

Performers

- Al Jardine: Lead vocals

See also

- The Beach Boys
- L.A. (Light Album)
- List of The Beach Boys songs

References

[1] http://www.cabinessence.net/tracks/files/l/lady_lynda.shtml

Lahaina Aloha

"Lahaina Aloha" is a song written by Mike Love and Terry Melcher for the American pop band The Beach Boys. It was released on their 1992 album *Summer In Paradise*.

"Lahaina Aloha" is one of two songs on *Summer in Paradise* on which Van Dyke Parks plays accordion

Details

- *Written by:* Terry Melcher/Mike Love
- *Album:* Summer in Paradise
- *Time:* 3:44
- *Produced by:* Terry Melcher
- *Lead Vocal*: Mike Love, Carl Wilson

See also

- List of songs by The Beach Boys

Lana

"**Lana**" is a song written by Brian Wilson for the American pop band The Beach Boys. It was released on their 1963 album *Surfin' USA*.

Details

- *Written by:* Brian Wilson
- *Album:* Surfin' USA
- *Time:* 1 min 39 sec
- *Produced by:* Nik Venet
- *Recording date*: January 5 & January 31, 1963

Musicians

- Mike Love - vocals
- David Marks - guitar
- Brian Wilson - bass guitar, lead vocal
- Carl Wilson - guitar, vocals
- Dennis Wilson - drums, vocals

See also

- The Beach Boys
- Surfin' USA
- List of songs by The Beach Boys

Land Ahoy

"Land Ahoy" is a song written by Brian Wilson. The song was recorded by American pop band The Beach Boys. The song was never released on any of the band's albums. The song was however released on the band's 1983 compilation album *Rarities*. It also appeared as a bonus track on the two-fer *Surfin' Safari/Surfin' USA*.

Details

- *Written by*: Brian Wilson
- *Album*: *Rarities*
- *Time*: 1:43
- *Produced by*: Nik Venet
- *Recording date*: September 5, 1962

Musicians

- Mike Love - vocals
- David Marks - guitar
- Brian Wilson - bass guitar, vocals
- Carl Wilson - guitar, vocals
- Dennis Wilson - drums, vocals

See also

- List of songs by The Beach Boys

Lavender

For the Marillion song of the same name, see Lavender

"Lavender" is a song written by Dorinda Morgan. The song was recorded by American pop band The Beach Boys during their early years as a recording group. The song was never released on any of the band's albums. It was lost in the archives for many years until it was found and released on the band's 1991 compilation album *Lost & Found (1961-62)*.

Musicians

- Al Jardine - vocals
- Mike Love - vocals
- Brian Wilson - vocals
- Carl Wilson - vocals

Lavender was recorded September 15, 1961 in Hite Morgan's living room, along with Surfin' and Luau. Dennis Wilson was present for part of the session, but is not audible on Lavender.

See also

- List of songs by The Beach Boys

Leaving This Town

"Leaving This Town" is a song written by Ricky Fataar, Blondie Chaplin, Carl Wilson and Mike Love for the American pop band The Beach Boys. It was released on their 1973 album *Holland*. This song is considered by some to be an early example of progressive rock.

Details

- *Written by:* Ricky Fataar/Carl Wilson/Blondie Chaplin/Mike Love
- *Album:* Holland
- *Time:* 5 min 49 sec
- *Produced by:* Ricky Fataar

Performers

- *Blondie Chaplin:* Lead Vocals
- *Carli Munoz:* Hammond organ solo on The Beach Boys in Concert version 1973

See also

- The Beach Boys
- Holland
- List of songs by The Beach Boys

Let Him Run Wild

"Let Him Run Wild"	
Single by The Beach Boys	
from the album *Summer Days (and Summer Nights!!)*	
Released	July 12, 1965
Format	Vinyl
Recorded	Unknown
Genre	Sunshine pop, Baroque pop
Length	2:20
Label	Capitol
Writer(s)	Brian Wilson Mike Love
Producer	Brian Wilson
The Beach Boys singles chronology	
"Help Me, Rhonda"/"Kiss Me, Baby" (1965)	"California Girls"/"**Let Him Run Wild**" (1965)	"The Little Girl I Once Knew"/"There's No Other (Like My Baby)" (1965)

"**Let Him Run Wild**" is a song written by Brian Wilson and Mike Love for the American pop band The Beach Boys. It was released on their 1965 album *Summer Days (and Summer Nights!!)*.

Alternate releases

An instrumental version is found on the 1968 *Stack-O-Tracks* compilation.

The 1990–2001 reissue of *Summer Days (And Summer Nights!!)* includes among the bonus tracks a version of the song with alternate backing vocals.

Brian Wilson recorded a version of the song for his 1998 album *Imagination*.

The 2007 compilation *The Warmth of the Sun* features a new stereo mix of the song.

See also

- List of The Beach Boys songs

Let Us Go on This Way

"Let Us Go On This Way" is a song written by Brian Wilson and Mike Love for the American pop band The Beach Boys. It was released on their 1977 album *Love You*.

Details

- *Written by:* Brian Wilson/Mike Love
- *Album:* Love You
- *Time:* 1 min 58 sec
- *Produced by:* Brian Wilson

Performers

- *Carl Wilson:* Lead Vocals
- *Mike Love:* Lead Vocals (bridge)

See also

- The Beach Boys
- List of songs by The Beach Boys

Let the Wind Blow

"Let the Wind Blow" is a song written by Brian Wilson and Mike Love for the American pop band The Beach Boys. It was released on their 1967 album *Wild Honey*.

Details

- Written by: Brian Wilson/Mike Love
- Album: *Wild Honey*
- Time: 2 min 19 sec
- Produced by: The Beach Boys

Performers

- Brian Wilson: Lead Vocals
- Mike Love: Lead Vocals

See also

- List of songs by The Beach Boys

Let's Go Away for Awhile

"Let's Go Away for Awhile"		
Instrumental by The Beach Boys from the album *Pet Sounds*		
Released	May 16, 1966	
Recorded	January 18 & 19, 1966 Western Studios	
Genre	Pop	
Length	2:18	
Label	Capitol	
Composer	Brian Wilson	
Producer	Brian Wilson	
***Pet Sounds* track listing**		
"I'm Waiting for the Day" (5)	**"Let's Go Away for Awhile"** (6)	"Sloop John B" (7)

"**Let's Go Away for Awhile**" is an instrumental by the American pop band The Beach Boys, from their 1966 album *Pet Sounds*. It is the sixth track on the album. The track was composed and produced by Brian Wilson and was originally titled "The Old Man And The Baby". An early full working title was "Let's Go Away For Awhile (And Then We'll Have World Peace)" - the parenthetical being a reference to Del Close and John Brent's comedy album *How to Speak Hip*. "This is a great Burt Bacharach type of thing," Brian said in 1996.

Brian stated in 1967 that it was "the most satisfying piece of music I've ever made. I applied a certain set of dynamics through the arrangement and the mixing and got a full musical extension of what I'd planned during the earliest stages of the theme. I think the chord changes are very special. I used a lot of musicians on the track; twelve violins, piano, four saxes, oboe, vibes, a guitar with a coke bottle on the strings for a semi-steel guitar effect. Also, I used two basses and percussion. The total effect is Let's Go Away For Awhile, which is something everyone in the world must have said at some time or another. Nice thought; most of us don't go away, but it's still a nice thought."

It was included on the Neil Young soundtrack album *Journey Through the Past* as the closing track.

Details

- *Written by:* Brian Wilson
- *Album:* Pet Sounds
- *Time:* 2 min 18 sec
- *Produced by:* Brian Wilson
- *Instrumental track:* recorded January 18, 1966 at Western Studios, Hollywood, California. Engineered by Chuck Britz.
- *String and flute overdub:* recorded January 19, 1966 at Western Studios, Hollywood, California.
- *Single:* released October 10, 1966 as the B-side of Capitol single Good Vibrations.

Performers

- *Hal Blaine:* drums
- *Julius Wechter:* Tympani, Vibraphone
- *Lyle Ritz:* String Bass
- *Carol Kaye:* Electric Bass
- *Al Casey:* Guitar
- *Barney Kessel:* Guitar
- *Al de Lory:* Piano
- *Steve Douglas:* Tenor Saxophone
- *Plas Johnson:* Tenor Saxophone
- *Jim Horn:* Baritone Saxophone
- *Jay Migliori:* Baritone Saxophone
- *Roy Caton:* Trumpet

Overdub session

- *Arnold Belnick:* Violin
- *James Getzoff:* Violin
- *William Kurasch:* Violin
- *Leonard Malarsky:* Violin
- *Jerome Reisler:* Violin
- *Ralph Schaeffer:* Violin
- *Sid Sharp:* Violin
- *Tibor Zelig:* Violin
- *Joseph Di Fiore:* Viola
- *Harry Hyams:* Viola
- *Justin Di Tullio:* Cello
- *Joseph Saxon:* Cello

(The Sid Sharp Strings)

- *Steve Douglas:* Flute
- *Jules Jacob:* Flute

See also

- The Beach Boys
- Pet Sounds
- List of songs by The Beach Boys

Let's Go Trippin'

"Let's Go Trippin'"	
Single by Dick Dale and the Deltones	
from the album *Surfers' Choice*	
Released	September 1961
Format	vinyl record (7")
Recorded	1961
Genre	Surf rock
Length	2:10
Label	Deltone
Writer(s)	Dick Dale
Producer	Jim Monsour
Dick Dale and the Deltones singles chronology	
"Ooh-Wee Marie" (1961)	**"Let's Go Trippin"** (1961)
"Jungle Fever" (1962)	

"**Let's Go Trippin'**" is an instrumental by Dick Dale and the Del-Tones. It is often regarded as the first surf rock instrumental. It quickly reached #4 on influential Los Angeles station KFWB, and later reached #60 on the national charts.

The Beach Boys covered *Let's Go Trippin'* on their albums *Surfin' USA* and *Beach Boys Concert*.

The song was used as the theme tune to the BBC Radio 4 programme *Home Truths*, originally presented by John Peel.

Let's Put Our Hearts Together

"Let's Put Our Hearts Together" is a song written by Brian Wilson for the American pop band The Beach Boys. It was released on their 1977 album *Love You*.

Details

- *Written by:* Brian Wilson
- *Album:* Love You
- *Time:* 2 min 14 sec
- *Produced by:* Brian Wilson

Performers

- *Brian Wilson:* Lead Vocals
- *Marilyn Wilson:* Lead Vocals

See also

- The Beach Boys
- Love You
- List of songs by The Beach Boys

Little Bird

"Little Bird"	

Song by The Beach Boys from the album *Friends*	
Released	April 8, 1968
Recorded	Brian Wilson's home studio February 29, 1968
Genre	Pop
Length	1:57
Label	Capitol
Writer	Dennis Wilson/Steve Kalinich
Producer	The Beach Boys
***Friends* track listing**	
"Anna Lee, The Healer" (7) / **"Little Bird"** (8) / "Be Still" (9)	

"**Little Bird**" is a song written by Dennis Wilson, Steve Kalinich, and Brian Wilson (uncredited) for the American pop band The Beach Boys. It was released on their 1968 album *Friends* as well as being released as the B-side of the "Friends" single. The single peaked at #47 in the U.S. and #25 in the U.K.

Brian once said; "Dennis gave us 'Little Bird' which blew my mind because it was so full of spiritualness. He was a late bloomer as a music maker. He lived hard and rough but his music was as sensitive as anyone's."

Part of the chorus of "Little Bird" was written by Brian Wilson, taken from the 1966 track "Child Is Father To The Man" for the aborted *Smile* album. Early mixes of "Little Bird" included the muted trumpet featured in the Brian Wilson composition. "Child Is Father To The Man" was eventually rerecorded for the 2004 solo release Brian Wilson Presents *Smile*.

See also

- List of songs by The Beach Boys

External links

- Free song downloads (including "Little Bird") [1]

References

[1] http://www.stephenkalinich.com/dennis_wilson.html

Little Deuce Coupe

"Little Deuce Coupe"	
Song by The Beach Boys from the album *Surfer Girl*	
Released	July 22, 1963
Recorded	June 12, 1963 Western Studios
Genre	Surf rock
Length	1:38
Label	Capitol
Composer	Brian Wilson/Roger Christian
Producer	Brian Wilson
Surfer Girl **track listing**	
"The Rocking Surfer" (5) | **"Little Deuce Coupe"** (6) | "In My Room" (7)	
from the album *Beach Boys' Party!*	
Length	3:12 (medley)
Label	Capitol

- "Hully Gully"
- "I Should Have Known Better"
- "Tell Me Why"
- "Papa-Oom-Mow-Mow"
- "Mountain of Love"
- "You've Got to Hide Your Love Away"
- "Devoted to You"
- "Alley Oop"
- "There's No Other (Like My Baby)"
- "Medley:I Get Around/Little Deuce Coupe"
- "The Times They Are a-Changin' "
- "Barbara Ann"

"**Little Deuce Coupe**" is a song written by Brian Wilson and Roger Christian. The song first appeared as the b-side to The Beach Boys' 1963 single "Surfer Girl". It was released on the *Surfer Girl* album and then again as the title track of the album *Little Deuce Coupe*.

"Surfer Girl" reached #7 on the *Billboard* Hot 100, while "Little Deuce Coupe" became The Beach Boys' highest charting b-side, making it to #15. It was the first of the Beach Boys' b-sides to receive a million spins on US radio. Internationally, it was reported by a French internet publication to be the 20th biggest hit of 1963 in that country.

According to author Jon Stebbins in his book *The Lost Beach Boy*, while the group was on tour in July 1963 Mike Love hit on the idea to use short instrumental segments of the song in the Beach Boys' live set as a way to introduce the bandmembers to the audience, starting with Dennis Wilson on drums, then adding David Marks (and later Al Jardine) on rhythm guitar, Carl Wilson on lead guitar, and finally Brian on the bass, before launching song from the top.

Composition

The music was written by Brian Wilson with the lyric by local radio station DJ Roger Christian; it typified the Beach Boys' "car songs" which along with "surfing", glamourised the teenage 1960s Californian lifestyle. The car referred to is the Ford Model B; the 1932 model was referred to as a "deuce coupe". Model Bs were readily available and easily modified, as auto enthusiasts (or "hot rodders") removed spare weight and improved the engine.

Brian Wilson commented on the song in the liner notes of the 1990 CD re-release of the original *Surfer Girl* album: "We loved doing 'Little Deuce Coupe'. It was a good 'shuffle' rhythm, which was not like most of the rhythms of the records on the radio in those days. It had a bouncy feel to it. Like most of our records, it had a competitive lyric. This record was my favorite Beach Boys car song."

Recording

The song was recorded at Western Studios on June 12, 1963, at the same recording session as "Surfer Girl". The two songs were the first songs recorded for The Beach Boys' third album, *Surfer Girl*. This was the first Beach Boys recording session where Brian Wilson served as the official producer, and also one of the last sessions before Al Jardine rejoined the band.

Musicians

- Mike Love - lead vocals
- David Marks - guitar
- Brian Wilson - bass guitar, piano,vocals
- Carl Wilson - lead guitar, vocals
- Dennis Wilson - drums, vocals

Alternate versions

The Beach Boys have released four live versions of "Little Deuce Coupe", on *Beach Boys Concert*, *Good Timin': Live at Knebworth England 1980*, *Songs from Here & Back*, and as part of a medley on *Endless Harmony Soundtrack*. Al Jardine included this song on his solo album *Live in Las Vegas*.

A demo version surfaced on the 2001 compilation *Hawthorne, CA*.

It was also recorded as part of a medley with "I Get Around" on *Beach Boys' Party!*. On their 1996 album *Stars and Stripes Vol. 1*, the Beach Boys re-recorded this song with country music artist James House.

In the 2005 film, *War of the Worlds* directed by Steven Spielberg, Ray Ferrier (played by Tom Cruise) sings part of the song to his daughter (Dakota Fanning) as a lullaby when she is too afraid to sleep.

See also

- List of songs by The Beach Boys

Little Girl

"Little Girl (You're My Miss America)" is a song written by Vincent Catalano and Herb Alpert, and first recorded by Dante & His Friends.

In 1962 it was covered by the American band The Beach Boys. It is most notable for being Dennis Wilson's first lead vocal.

In the Surfin' Safari/Surfin' USA two-fer compilation the song was renamed to *Little Miss America*.

Beach Boys version

details

- *Written by*: Vincent Catalano/Herb Alpert
- *Album*: *Surfin' Safari*
- *Time*: 2:05
- *Produced by*: Nik Venet
- *Recording date*: September 5, 1962

Musicians

- Mike Love - vocals
- David Marks - guitar
- Brian Wilson - bass guitar, vocals
- Carl Wilson - guitar, vocals
- Dennis Wilson - drums, lead vocal

The Little Girl I Once Knew

"The Little Girl I Once Knew"	
Single by The Beach Boys	
B-side	"There's No Other (Like My Baby)"
Released	November 8, 1965
Format	7" vinyl
Recorded	October 13 & 24, 1965 Western Studios
Genre	Pop
Length	2:35
Label	Capitol
Writer(s)	Brian Wilson
Producer	Brian Wilson
The Beach Boys singles chronology	
"California Girls" (1965)	*"The Little Girl I Once Knew"* (1965)	"Barbara Ann" (1965)

"**The Little Girl I Once Knew**" is a song written by Brian Wilson for the American pop band The Beach Boys. It was released in November 1965 as a single 45 rpm, backed by "There's No Other (Like My Baby)", and reached #15 on the *Cash Box* chart, #20 on *Billboard*. On the UPI (United Press International) chart, quoted by newspapers across the United States, it placed at #4 -- the same position it peaked at the 'pirate' station Radio London serving the UK. In Canada it was #7 on the national chart cited by *Billboard* and #10 on the *RPM* chart. Across North America, of major markets, it was highly popular only in Minneapolis and Vancouver (both #3), Washington DC (#5), Boston (#8), Baltimore and Pittsburgh (both #9); also top ten across the South in Birmingham, Louisville, Orlando and St Joseph.

The last new original song the group produced before the album *Pet Sounds*, it was not included on any regular Beach Boys album, but has since been collected on several anthologies (its first LP appearance being volume 3 of the group's *Best Of* series) and as a bonus track on reissues of *Summer Days (and Summer Nights!!)*.

The song is notable for innovative use of two dramatic periods of near-silence lasting several seconds each. Although one of the Beach Boys' most exuberant songs, it was poorly received by radio stations preferring to avoid dead air time, which may account for its relatively low chart rating among their other singles of the period, including "California Girls" and "Barbara Ann". It is still rarely heard on oldies radio.

Capitol Records' rushed release of "Barbara Ann" in December ruined any chance "The Little Girl I Once Knew" had of continuing up the charts. Just after its release, John Lennon gave it a favorable review; another what-if for the Beach Boys.

Structurally, this song is one of Brian Wilson's greatest song writing achievements for a pre-*Pet Sounds* era composition. Although the lyrics may seem overly superficial, musically it shows the best of what the Beach Boys were able to do in a pop song single, incorporating incredible tags, dead stop timing breaks, repeating killer guitar hooks, lush choral arrangements, etc.

Little Honda

"**Little Honda**" is a song written by Brian Wilson and Mike Love for the American pop band The Beach Boys. It was released on their 1964 album *All Summer Long*, and it was also featured on their EP, *Four By the Beach Boys*. It was covered by The Hondells, whose recording peaked at #9 on the U.S. pop singles chart, and later by Jan & Dean, and Yo La Tengo. The song pays tribute to the small Honda motorcycle and its ease of operation, specifically the Honda Super Cub.

"Little Honda" peaked at #65 on the Billboard Hot 100 for the Beach Boys but became an international favorite, rising to #1 in Sweden and #8 in Norway in early 1965 as cited by a contemporary issue of Billboard, #15 on Canada's national RPM chart, and concurrently #44 in Germany.

In regional North American charts the Beach Boys' recording was particularly popular in Los Angeles, Washington DC and Minneapolis (all #2), Vancouver (#3), Richmond (#4), Montreal (#6), San Jose (#8), and came close to top ten in Miami, Cincinnati, Winnipeg and in Springfield and Manchester in New England.

Details

- Written by: Brian Wilson/Mike Love
- Album: All Summer Long
- Time: 1 min 52 sec
- Produced by: Brian Wilson

Performers

- Mike Love: Lead Vocals

Covered By

- Yo La Tengo, *I Can Hear the Heart Beating as One* (1997)
- The Queers, *Bubblegum Dreams* 7" (1996), Lookout!
- Expulsados, *Altoparlantes* (2003)
- Travoltas, *Party!* (2003)

See also

- The Beach Boys
- *All Summer Long*
- List of songs by The Beach Boys

Little Pad

"Little Pad" is a song written by Brian Wilson for the American pop band The Beach Boys. It was released on their 1967 album *Smiley Smile*. A psychedelic pop collage with elements of surf music, its only lyrics deal with the possibility of having a little house by the sea in Hawaii.

Details

- *Written by:* Brian Wilson
- *Album:* Smiley Smile
- *Time:* 2 min 30 sec
- *Produced by:* The Beach Boys

Performers

- *Mike Love:* Lead Vocals
- *Carl Wilson:* Lead Vocals

Other versions

A cover of this song was recorded by The Olivia Tremor Control, for the tribute release 'Smiling Pets'.

See also

- The Beach Boys
- Smiley Smile
- List of songs by The Beach Boys

Little Saint Nick

"Little Saint Nick"	
Single by The Beach Boys	
from the album *The Beach Boys' Christmas Album*	
Released	December 2, 1963
Format	Vinyl
Genre	Pop
Length	2:00
Label	Capitol
Producer	Brian Wilson

The Beach Boys singles chronology		
"Be True to Your School"/"In My Room" (1963)	"Little Saint Nick"/"The Lord's Prayer" (1963)	"Fun, Fun, Fun"/"Why Do Fools Fall In Love" (1964)

"**Little Saint Nick**" is a Christmas song written by Brian Wilson and Mike Love and originally performed by their group The Beach Boys. It was first released as a single in December 1963, reaching number three on the *Billboard* Christmas charts and peaking at #69 on the regular weekly sales chart surveyed by *Cash Box*. Despite a media-hushed Christmas in mourning for recently--assassinated President John F. Kennedy, the single went into the Top Tens of Los Angeles, San Diego, Sacramento, Milwaukee, Vancouver and Washington DC, and the Top Twenties of San Francisco, Seattle, Minneapolis, Houston, Miami, and Springfield MA. Eventually, over several more Christmases, it was credited as an unofficial (non-RIAA audited) million-seller.

"Little Saint Nick" reappeared on *The Beach Boys' Christmas Album* in 1964, minus the overdubbed sleigh bells from the original single mix. The song borrows its rhythm and structure from the group's 1963 hit "Little Deuce Coupe". (An alternate version, utilizing the melody from "Drive-In", was recorded for the album but remained unreleased until a 1991 CD reissue.)

The song is sometimes mistakenly called "Run Run Reindeer" because of the lyrics in the bridge [1]. In 2005, the song was re-recorded by Brian Wilson for his solo Christmas collection, *What I Really Want for Christmas*.

The song has been covered several times, including versions by John Denver and the Muppets (1979), Hanson (1997), Sugar Ray (2001), McFly (2004) and Overboard (2008). The song is also used in a Coca-Cola holiday commercial featuring a family of polar bears who stumble upon a festive penguin gathering. Some versions of the song include the usage of a xylophone.

References

[1] http://www.google.com/search?q=cache:r5mqPsuTYCkJ:www.musicsonglyrics.com/B/beachboyslyrics/beachboyslittlesaintnicklyrics.htm+run+run+reindeer+beach+boys%5C&hl=en&gl=us&ct=clnk&cd=3

Little Surfer Girl

"Little Surfer Girl" (not to be confused with the song **"Surfer Girl"** from the album of the same name, released in 1963), is a song written by Brian Wilson for the American pop band The Beach Boys. The song was released on the band's 1993 box set *Good Vibrations: Thirty Years of The Beach Boys*.

See also

- List of songs by The Beach Boys

Livin' with a Heartache

"Livin' with a Heartache"	
Single by The Beach Boys	
from the album *Keepin' the Summer Alive*	
Released	May 21, 1980
Format	Vinyl
Genre	Pop
Length	4:06
Label	Caribou Records
Writer(s)	Carl Wilson, Randy Bachman
Producer	Bruce Johnston

The Beach Boys singles chronology		
"Goin' On"/"Endless Harmony" (1980)	**"Livin' with a Heartache"**/"Santa Ana Winds" (1980)	"The Beach Boys Medley"/"God Only Knows" (1981)

"Livin' with a Heartache" is a song written by Carl Wilson and Randy Bachman for the American pop band The Beach Boys. It was released on their 1980 album *Keepin' the Summer Alive*. Released as a single backed with "Santa Ana Winds (song)", it failed to chart.

Performers

- Carl Wilson: Lead vocals

See also

- The Beach Boys
- Keepin' the Summer Alive
- List of The Beach Boys songs

Lonely Days

"Lonely Days"	
Single by Bee Gees	
from the album *2 Years On*	
Released	1970
Format	Vinyl record 7" 45rpm
Recorded	IBC Studios, London 1970
Genre	Rock
Length	3:45
Label	UK: Polydor, USA/CA: Atco
Writer(s)	Barry Gibb/Robin Gibb/Maurice Gibb
Producer	Robert Stigwood, Barry Gibb, Robin Gibb, Maurice Gibb
Bee Gees singles chronology	

If Only I Had My Mind on Something Else (1970)	*Lonely Days* (1970)	*How Can You Mend a Broken Heart?* (1971)

"**Lonely Days**" is a 1970 song by the Bee Gees, featured on their album *2 Years On*. The song incorporated the innovative structure and knack for changing tempos exemplified by the second side of The Beatles' *Abbey Road* album, released the previous year and a clear influence on this single. "Lonely Days" shifts back and forth between a piano-and-strings-dominated verse reminiscent of "You Never Give Me Your Money" and "Golden Slumbers," and an up-tempo stomping chorus that echoes "Carry That Weight;" perhaps as an acknowledgment of the debt, as the record approaches its fade-out, the lead singer's voice is filtered to sound like John Lennon's. The record's success helped establish the band as expert pop stylists. It was their first Top Five hit in the US, peaking at number three in the *Billboard* Hot 100 and reaching number one on the Cashbox and Record World charts.

In many interviews, the Bee Gees have said that they wrote this song and "How Can You Mend a Broken Heart?" in the same night that they reunited.

Chart performance

Chart	Peak position
Australia	9
Austria	15
Belgium	7
Brazil	2
Canada	1
Denmark	3
France	48
Germany	25
Netherlands	3
New Zealand	10
United Kingdom	33
United States	3

Lonely Sea

"**Lonely Sea**" is a song written by Brian Wilson and Gary Usher for the American pop band The Beach Boys. It was released on their 1963 album *Surfin' USA*.

Details

- *Written by:* Brian Wilson/Gary Usher
- *Album:* Surfin' USA
- *Time:* 2 min 21 sec
- *Produced by:* Murry Wilson
- *Recording date*: April 19, 1962

Musicians

- Mike Love - vocals
- David Marks - guitar
- Brian Wilson - bass guitar, lead vocal
- Carl Wilson - guitar, vocals
- Dennis Wilson - drums, vocals

See also

- The Beach Boys
- Surfin' USA
- List of songs by The Beach Boys
- Greg Panfile's Musical Analysis of "The Lonely Sea" [1]

References

[1] http://www.cabinessence.net/essays/mob2.html

Long Promised Road

"Long Promised Road"	
Single by The Beach Boys	
from the album *Surf's Up*	
B-side	Deirdre 'Til I Die
Released	May 24, 1971 October 11, 1971
Format	Vinyl
Recorded	April 3, 1971
Genre	Baroque Pop
Length	3:30
Label	Brother/Reprise
Writer(s)	Carl Wilson Jack Rieley
Producer	The Beach Boys

The Beach Boys singles chronology

"Wouldn't It Be Nice (live)" (1971)	"Long Promised Road"/"Deirdre" (1971)	"Long Promised Road"/""Til I Die" (1971)
"Long Promised Road"/"Deirdre" (1971)	"Long Promised Road"/""Til I Die" (1971)	"Surf's Up"/"Don't Go Near the Water" (1971)

"**Long Promised Road**" is a song written by Carl Wilson and Jack Rieley for the American pop band The Beach Boys. It was first released as a single in May 1971, and did not chart. It was then released on their 1971 album *Surf's Up*, and was rereleased as a single, with a different b-side, 'Til I Die, in October of the same year. This time it made it to #89 on the Billboard Hot 100. Aside from a few guitar solos written in the early days of the band, the song is Carl Wilson's first composition, and he handles the lead vocal on the track.

See also

- List of songs by The Beach Boys

Lookin' at Tomorrow

"Lookin' at Tomorrow (A Welfare Song)"	
Song by The Beach Boys from the album *Surf's Up*	
Released	August 30, 1971
Recorded	August 14, 1970
Genre	Pop
Length	1:55
Label	Brother/Reprise
Composer	Al Jardine/Gary Winfrey
Producer	The Beach Boys
***Surf's Up* track listing**	
Feel Flows (6)	**"Lookin' at Tomorrow (A Welfare Song)"** (7)
A Day in the Life of a Tree (8)	

"Lookin' at Tomorrow (A Welfare Song)" is a song written by Al Jardine and Gary Winfrey for the American pop band The Beach Boys. It was released on their 1971 album *Surf's Up*. The lead vocal is by Jardine.

See also

- List of songs by The Beach Boys

Loop de Loop (Flip Flop Flyin' in an Aeroplane)

"**Loop De Loop (Flip Flop Flyin' in an Aeroplane)**" is a song by American pop band The Beach Boys, written by Brian Wilson, Carl Wilson and Al Jardine. The song was released on the band's 1998 anthology album, the *Endless Harmony Soundtrack*.

It is unrelated to the Johnny Thunder hit, which was released as a single in 1963 and reached number four on the U.S. pop charts. However, his single was titled simply "Loop De Loop", without the parenthetical subtitle.

See also

- List of songs by The Beach Boys

The Lord's Prayer

"The Lord's Prayer"	
Single by The Beach Boys	
Released	December 2, 1963
Format	Vinyl
Recorded	Unknown
Genre	Pop music
Length	Unknown
Label	Capitol
Producer	Brian Wilson

The Beach Boys singles chronology		
"Be True to Your School"/"In My Room" (1963)	"Little Saint Nick"/"The Lord's Prayer" (1963)	"Fun, Fun, Fun"/"Why Do Fools Fall In Love" (1964)

"**The Lord's Prayer**" is a musical setting of the Lord's Prayer written by Albert Hay Malotte in 1935 and recorded by numerous singers including John Charles Thomas, Perry Como, Gracie Fields, Mahalia Jackson, Barbra Streisand, Elvis Presley, and Ronnie Milsap. The song's melody is very similar to that of Schubert's "Ave Maria" (a recording of which was issued as the B-side of Como's version).

"The Lord's Prayer" was also recorded by the American pop band The Beach Boys. It was released as the B-side of their single, "Little Saint Nick", on 2 December 1963. It was also released on the 1983 compilation album *Rarities*. In December 2009 Australian duo Generation Gap recorded a version of the song which was released on their album, A New Beginning, in December of that year.

References

- Elvis - Peace In The Valley (The Complete Gospel Recordings) (http://shop.elvis.com.au/prod423.html)
- Ronnie Milsap Music (http://www.ronniemilsap.com/music.html)
- Generation Gap Discography (http://www.generationgap.net.au/discography.html)

Louie Louie

"Louie Louie"	
Single by Richard Berry	
Released	April 1957[1]
Format	Vinyl single
Recorded	1957
Genre	R&B rock'n'roll garage rock
Length	2'09"
Label	Flip Records
Writer(s)	Richard Berry
Richard Berry singles chronology	
Take the Keys *Louie Louie* *Sweet Sugar*	

"**Louie Louie**" is an American rock 'n' roll song written by Richard Berry in 1955. It has become a standard in pop and rock, with hundreds of versions recorded by different artists. The song is written in the style of a Jamaican ballad; and tells, in simple verse-chorus form, the first-person story of a Jamaican sailor returning to the island to see his lady love. The singer brags of his "fine little girl" to the Louie of the title, presumably a bartender.

A recording by The Kingsmen in 1963 is the best-known version. The Kingsmen's edition was also the subject of an FBI investigation about the supposed but non-existent obscenity of the lyrics, an investigation that ended without prosecution.[2] The song is ranked #55 on the *Rolling Stone* magazine's list of The 500 Greatest Songs of All Time.

Original version

Richard Berry was inspired to write the song in 1955 after listening to and performing the song "El Loco Cha Cha" with Ricky Rillera and the Rhythm Rockers. The tune was written originally as "Amarren Al Loco" ("Tie up the crazy guy") by Cuban bandleader Rosendo Ruiz Jr. - also known as Rosendo Ruiz Quevedo - but became best known in the arrangement by René Touzet which included a rhythmic ten-note "1-2-3 1-2 1-2-3 1-2" riff. Touzet performed the tune regularly in Los Angeles clubs in the 1950s. In Berry's mind, the words "Louie Louie" superimposed themselves over the bass riff. Lyrically, the first person perspective of the song was influenced by "One for My Baby (and One More for the Road)", which is sung from the perspective of a customer talking to a bartender. Berry cited Chuck Berry's "Havana Moon" and his exposure to Latin American music for the song's speech pattern and references to Jamaica.[3]

Richard Berry released his version in April 1957 (Flip Records 321[1]), originally as a B-side, with his backing band The Pharaohs, and scored a regional hit on the west coast, particularly in San Francisco. When the group toured the Pacific Northwest, several local R&B bands began to adopt the song and established its popularity. The track was then re-released as an A-side.[4] However, the single never charted on *Billboard*'s national rhythm and blues or pop charts. Berry's label reported that the single had sold 40,000 copies. After a series of unsuccessful follow-ups, Berry sold his portion of publishing and songwriting rights for $750 to the head of Flip Records in 1959.

While the title of the song is often rendered with a comma ("Louie, Louie"), in 1988 Berry told *Esquire* magazine that the correct title of the song was "Louie Louie", with no comma.

Version by The Kingsmen

In the U.S. music industry of the 1950s and 1960s, mainstream white artists would often cover songs by black artists. On April 6, 1963, a rock and roll group from Portland, Oregon, called The Kingsmen, chose "Louie Louie" as their second recording, their first having been "Peter Gunn Rock."

The Kingsmen recorded the song at Northwestern, Inc., Motion Pictures and Recording [5] in Portland, Oregon. The group paid a small sum of $36 for a one-hour Saturday morning session. The session was produced by Ken Chase aka Mike Korgan. Chase was a local radio personality on the AM rock station 91 KISN and also owned the teen nightclub that hosted the Kingsmen as their house band. The engineer for the session was the studio owner, Robert Lindahl. The Kingsmen's lead singer Jack Ely based his version on a 1961 recording of Berry's tune by another band from the Pacific Northwest, Rockin' Robin Roberts and the Fabulous Wailers (no relation to The Wailers headed by Bob Marley years later), unintentionally introducing a change in the rhythm as he did. "I showed the others how to play it with a 1-2-3, 1-2, 1-2-3 beat instead of the 1-2-3-4, 1-2, 1-2-3-4 beat that is on the (Wailers') record," recalled Ely. The night before their recording session, the band played a 90-minute version of the song during a gig at a local teen club.

The Kingsmen's studio version was recorded in one take. They also recorded the "B" side of the release, an original instrumental by the group called "Haunted Castle".

A significant error on the Kingsmen's version occurs just after the lead guitar break. To some ears, singer Ely begins singing the verse in the correct place, but thinks he's come in too soon, and pauses for another cycle of the riff. To others, he comes in too soon and corrects himself but the band doesn't realize that he's done so. Either way, drummer Lynn Easton covers the pause with a drum fill. But then, before the verse has ended, the rest of the band goes into the chorus at the point where they expect it to be. They recover quickly, but the confusion would seem to indicate that the rest of the band couldn't hear the vocals while they were recording. This error is now so embedded in the consciousness of some groups that they deliberately duplicate it when performing the song. There is also a persistent and oft-repeated story that the microphone for Ely was mounted too high for him to sing without tilting his head back excessively, resulting in his somewhat pinched and strangled sound through most of his vocal. This seems unlikely, however, in view of the fact that it was recorded by professional personnel in a dedicated recording studio.

Regardless of accuracy or technique, the Kingsmen transformed Berry's relatively easy-going ballad into a raucous romp, complete with a twangy guitar, occasional background chatter, and almost completely unintelligible lyrics by Ely. A chaotic guitar break is triggered by the shout, "Okay, let's give it to 'em right now!", which first appeared in the Wailers' version. Critic Dave Marsh suggests it is this moment that gives the recording greatness: "[Ely] went for it so avidly you'd have thought he'd spotted the jugular of a lifelong enemy, so crudely that, at that instant, Ely sounds like Donald Duck on helium. And it's that faintly ridiculous air that makes the Kingsmen's record the classic that it is, especially since it's followed by a guitar solo that's just as wacky".[6]

Released in May 1963, the single entered the top ten on the Billboard Hot 100 chart for December 7, and peaked at number two the following week; it would remain in the top 10 through December and January before dropping off in early February.[7] In total, the Kingsmen's version spent 16 weeks on the Hot 100. (Singles by The Singing Nun, then Bobby Vinton, monopolized the top slot for eight weeks.) "Louie Louie" did reach number one on the Cashbox pop chart, as well as number one on the Cashbox R&B chart.[8] The version quickly became a standard at teen parties in the U.S. during the 1960s, even reappearing on the charts in 1966.

Another factor in the success of the record may have been the rumor that the lyrics were intentionally slurred by the Kingsmen. Allegedly, this was to cover the fact that it was laced with profanity, graphically depicting sex between the sailor and his lady. Crumpled pieces of paper professing to be "the real lyrics" to "Louie Louie" circulated among teens. The song was banned on many radio stations and in many places in the United States, including Indiana, where it was personally prohibited by the Governor, Matthew Welsh.

These actions were taken despite the small matter that practically no one could distinguish the actual lyrics. Denials of chicanery by Kingsmen and Ely did not stop the controversy. The FBI became involved in the controversy but concluded a 31-month investigation with a report that they were "unable to interpret any of the wording in the record."[9]

After a protracted lawsuit that lasted five years and cost $1.3 million dollars, The Kingsmen won the rights to their song "Louie Louie". The Supreme Court in November 1998, declined to hear an appeal by the record company of an earlier legal ruling giving the rights to the band.

Paul Revere & the Raiders also recorded a version of "Louie Louie" in April 1963 in the same Portland studio as The Kingsmen. This recording was paid for and produced by 91 KISN Radio Personality Roger Hart, who soon became Personal Manager for Paul Revere & The Raiders. Initially, their single was more successful locally, put out on Hart's SANDE label, then when signed to Columbia Records it was reissued in June 1963 nationally, where it went #1 in the West and Hawaii. The quick success of "Louie Louie" suddenly halted in the West. A few years later, Paul Revere & the Raiders learned why: Columbia Records A&R man Mitch Miller, who did not like rock n' roll, pulled the plug on Paul Revere & The Raiders' hit version.

Meanwhile, local sales of the Kingsmen record were so low (reportedly 600) that the group considered disbanding. Things changed when Boston's biggest DJ, Arnie Ginsburg, was given the record by a pitchman. Amused by its slapdash sound, he played it on his program as "The Worst Record of the Week." Despite the slam, listener response was swift and positive.

By the end of October, the Kingsmen's version was listed in Billboard as a regional breakout and a "bubbling under" entry for the national chart. Meanwhile, the Raiders' version, with far stronger promotion, was becoming a hit in California and was also listed as "bubbling under" one week after the Kingsmen's debut on the chart. For a few weeks, the two singles appeared destined to battle each other, but demand for the Kingsmen single acquired momentum and, by the end of 1963, Columbia had stopped promoting the Raiders' "Louie Louie", per Columbia Records Mitch Miller. But Paul Revere's band held the bragging rights in Portland, where they outsold the Kingsmen by a reported 10 to 1.

Robert Lindahl, then-president and chief engineer of NWI, and the sound engineer [10] on the Kingsmen's and Paul Revere & the Raiders' noted that the Raiders' version is not known for "garbled lyrics" or an amateurish recording technique. But despite these attributes, the single never seized the public's attention the way the less-polished Kingsmen version had.

By the time that the Kingsmen's "Louie Louie" had achieved national popularity, the band had split. Two rival editions — one featuring lead singer Ely, the other with Lynn Easton, who held the rights to the band's name — were competing for live audiences across the country.

Lyrics investigation

In February, 1964, an outraged parent wrote to Robert Kennedy, then the attorney general of the United States, alleging that the lyrics of "Louie Louie" were obscene. The Federal Bureau of Investigation investigated the complaint. In June, 1965, the FBI laboratory obtained a copy of the recording and, after two years of investigation, concluded that the recording could not be interpreted, that it was "unintelligible at any speed," and therefore the Bureau could not find that the recording was obscene. In September, 1965, an FBI agent interviewed one member of the Kingsmen. He denied that there was any obscenity in the song.

The lyrics controversy resurfaced briefly in 2005 when the superintendent of the school system in Benton Harbor, Michigan refused to let the marching band at one of the schools play the song in a parade. She later relented.[11] [12]

Motörhead version

"Louie Louie"	
Single by Motörhead	
from the album *Overkill (re-issue)*	
B-side	Tear Ya Down
Released	30 September 1978
Format	7"
Recorded	Wessex Studios London 1977
Genre	Hard rock
Length	2:47
Label	Bronze Records/EMI
Producer	Neil Richmond Motörhead

Motörhead singles chronology		
"Motorhead" (1977)	"**Louie Louie**" (1978)	"Overkill" (1979)

Louie Louie is the title track of Motörhead's third single. It was released as a 7" vinyl single in 1978 and reached number 68 on the UK Singles Chart.

The reverse cover carries the dog Latin motto "NIL ILLEGITIMUM CARBORUNDUM", which is humorously said to mean "Don't let the bastards grind you down".

The song is released with "Tear Ya Down" and appears later on the CD re-issues of *Overkill* and *The Best Of* Motörhead compilation.

On 25 October 1978, a pre-recording of the band playing this song was broadcast on the BBC show *Top of the Pops*.[13]

Track listing

1. "Louie Louie" (Richard Berry)
2. "Tear Ya Down" (Eddie Clarke, Ian Kilmister, Phil Taylor)

Personnel

- Fast Eddie Clarke – Guitars, vocals
- Philthy Animal Taylor – Drums
- Lemmy (Ian Kilmister) – Bass, lead vocals
- Photographs - Motorcycle Irene

Legacy

It is unknown exactly how many versions of "Louie Louie" have been recorded, but it is believed to be over 1,500, according to LouieLouie.net [14] [15].

The Kingsmen version has remained the most popular version of the song, retaining its association with wild partying. It enjoyed a comeback in 1978-79 and was associated with college fraternity parties when it was sung, complete with the supposedly obscene lyrics, by Bluto (John Belushi) and his fellow Delta House brothers in the movie *National Lampoon's Animal House* despite the anachronism of the film taking place in 1962, a year before the Kingsmen recording.

Following is a decade by decade survey of the song's popularity and influence across a broad spectrum of popular music. The song's continuing popularity helped Berry (who had retained his BMI rights) receive belated compensation for unpaid royalties.

1960s

After the Kingsmen and Raiders' versions, several other bands recorded the song:

- American soul singer Otis Redding for his 1964 debut album Pain in My Heart
- The Beach Boys recorded a rendition of "Louie Louie" for their 1964 album *Shut Down Vol. 2*.
- Ray Davies has stated that he wrote The Kinks' first hit, "You Really Got Me" (1964) while trying to work out the chords of "Louie Louie". The band recorded "Louie Louie" on 18 October 1964 and it was released in November on the "Kinksize Session" EP, but still the chords were not quite right.
- The Who were directed in their early recording career by the riff/rhythm of "Louie Louie". This was due to the song's influence on The Kinks, who, like the Who at the time, were produced by Shel Talmy, with the Kinks on the Pye label and the Who on Brunswick. Talmy wanted the successful sounds of The Kinks' 1964 hits "You Really Got Me", "All Day and All of the Night" and "Till the End of the Day" to be copied by The Who. As a result, Pete Townshend penned "I Can't Explain", released in March 1965. During a pre-song interview with host Brian Matthew on *Saturday Club* in May 1965, Pete explained that "I Can't Explain" was released to "introduce The Who to the charts" and that they were now trying to get away from all that and wanted to create the sort of sound they achieved on stage at present, hence their new single which they were about to sing live on *Saturday Club* now - the feedback-driven, Mod-inspired "Anyway, Anyhow, Anywhere". (In 1979 "Louie Louie" would be featured on the soundtrack album to *Quadrophenia*.)
- The American folk group The Sandpipers did a cover of the song in 1966 with a slower tempo and in Spanish.
- Prototype English punk/garage band The Troggs recorded a version of "Louie Louie" in 1966. Their cover version hit-single "Wild Thing" also uses a very similar riff to "Louie Louie".
- It underwent a psychedelic treatmeant courtesy of Friar Tuck on his 1967 album *Friar Tuck And His Psychedelic Guitar*

- "Louie Louie" repeatedly figured in the musical lexicon of Frank Zappa in the 1960s. An early live version of his original composition "Plastic People" (from his *You Can't Do That Onstage Anymore* series of live albums) was set to the melody of "Louie, Louie" (The official version was released on the album *Absolutely Free* in 1967). Also from the *Absolutely Free* album is the song "Son of Suzy Creamcheese", a song that has a melody that sounds like a sped-up version of "Louie Louie". Zappa reportedly fired guitarist Alice Stuart from The Mothers of Invention because she couldn't play "Louie Louie".[16] At a Zappa concert at the Royal Albert Hall in London, Mothers Of Invention keyboardist Don Preston climbed up to the legendary venue's pipe organ, usually used for classical works, and played the signature riff (this can be heard on the 1969 Zappa album *Uncle Meat*). Quick interpolations of "Louie Louie" also frequently turn up in other Zappa works.
- The Sonics also recorded a very rough, fuzz-tone-drenched version in the '60's.

1970s

By the 1970s the song was inspiring other songs and numerous other versions.

- In 1972, Berry released the song again as a single on the Happy Tiger label. This was the label's final release before it folded.[17]
- Also in 1972, The Stooges covered the song which was never released.
- In 1972, Led Zeppelin performed a version of the song in Los Angeles. It can be heard on bootleg recordings entitled *Burn Like a Candle*. The night of this performance is the source of most of their 2003 live album *How the West Was Won*, although "Louie Louie" was omitted from the official release.
- In 1973, Flash Cadillac & the Continental Kids performed the song in the film *American Graffiti* (1973). This recording was produced by Kim Fowley.
- Toots & the Maytals recorded a version for their album *Funky Kingston* (1973). It has been suggested that use of the Kingsmen's beat from this song may have thus helped lead to the invention of reggae music.[18]
- The 1973 song "Brother Louie" by the UK band Hot Chocolate was strongly inspired by "Louie Louie" and includes a minor-key reprise of the chorus. The song, about an interracial romance, became a No. 1 U.S. hit that same year in a cover version by the New York band Stories.
- "Louie Louie" was Motörhead's first single for Bronze Records in 1978. It was a relatively faithful cover of the song, with "Fast" Eddie Clarke's guitar emulating the Hohner Pianet electric piano riff.
- A version of "Louie Louie" performed by The Clash appears on a vinyl bootleg of the band called *Louie is a Punkrocker* (1977).[19]

1980s

Black Flag released its own version of "Louie Louie" in 1981 on Posh Boy Records, then reissued the single on its own SST label and as part of the anthology *The First Four Years*. It features Dez Cadena on vocals for the lead track, with Cadena improvising his own lyrics for the song;[20] an alternate version heard on the 1982 outtakes compilation *Everything Went Black*, recorded at a different session,[21] features a different set of lyrics.[22] A live recording of Black Flag's version from the 1986 live album *Who's Got the 10½?* features Henry Rollins following in the band's tradition of improvising new lyrics for the song.

Aside from the *Animal House* appearance, the song appeared in many other films, typically in raucous and humours contexts. An instrumental version is heard during the last scene and closing credits of *The Naked Gun* (1988). (In the film, the University of Southern California Marching Band is seen trampling Ricardo Montalban's character.)

The Grateful Dead covered the song live a few times in the 80's with Brent Mydland on vocals.

Animal House may have inspired various other real life pranks and tributes:

- In 1985, Ross Shafer, host and a writer-performer of the late-night comedy series *Almost Live!* on the Seattle TV station KING, spearheaded an effort to have "Louie Louie" replace "Washington, My Home" by Helen Davis as Washington's official state song.[23] Picking up on this initially prankish effort, Whatcom County Councilman Craig Cole introduced Resolution No. 85-12 in the state legislature, citing the need for a "contemporary theme song that can be used to engender a sense of pride and community, and in the enhancement of tourism and economic development". His resolution also called for the creation of a new "Louie Louie County". While the House did not pass it, the Senate's Resolution 1985-37 declared April 12, 1985, "*Louie Louie* Day". A crowd of 4,000, estimated by press reports, convened on the state capitol that day for speeches, singalongs, and performances by the Wailers, the Kingsmen, and Paul Revere and the Raiders. Two days later, a Seattle event commemorated the occasion with the premiere performance of a new, Washington-centric version of the song written by composer Berry.[24] [25]

The Fat Boys recorded a version of "Louie Louie" in 1988 on their album *Coming Back Hard Again*; their version features new lyrics written by the group about the history of the song and its original controversy.[26]

In the 1980s Rhino Records released *The Best of Louie Louie* in support of KFJC's Maximum Louis Louis event. The album features Richard Berry's original recording, the Kingsmen's influential version, Black Flag's version, and several other versions, some bizarre. These included a performance by the Rice University Marching Owl Band, and the a cappella "Hallalouie Chorus", in which the song's title was sung to the melody of Handel's "Hallelujah Chorus". Other volumes in this *Best of* series followed.

The song was mentioned in a 1984 cartoon of *The Far Side*.

The Kingsmen led the audience in a performance of "Louie Louie" at the end of Bud Clark's Inaugural Ball beginning his term as Mayor of Portland, Oregon in 1985.

1990s

Steve Plunkett of Autograph sang a hard rock version of "Louie Louie" in 1991. In the music video directed by Dominic Orlando, Louie is portrayed as Louis the XIV. The Kingsmen's version appears in the closing credits of *The Simpsons*' episode "Homer Goes to College", which included many references to *Animal House*.

"Louie Louie" also appeared in a number of films during the decade:

- Iggy Pop again recorded a version of the song, with political and satirical verses instead of obscenities, in his 1993 *American Caesar* album. This version was used during the opening credits of Michael Moore's *Capitalism: A Love Story* and as an ending song in Jim Jarmusch's *Coffee and Cigarettes* in which Pop took part as himself.
- Young MC 's take on the song was included in the 1990 film *Coupe de Ville*. The movie includes a lengthy scene where the three brother characters argue over the lyrics while the Kingsmen's version plays. The movie then returns to the topic in the final narration and Young MC 's version then plays as the credits roll.
- In *Dave* (1993), Kevin Kline's Dave Kovacs (impersonating the President of the United States) sings the first few lyrics of the song at a factory while controlling oversized robotic arms.
- A version of "Louie Louie" performed by Robert Plant is on the soundtrack of the 1993 film, *Wayne's World 2* (1993).
- The 1995 film *Mr. Holland's Opus* features a version of the song, played by a marching band led by Glenn Holland (Richard Dreyfuss).
- In the Chevy Chase film *Man of the House* (also 1995), Indian Scout members and their chaperones sing the song; when some of the younger children claim they don't know the lyrics, George Wendt's character explains that nobody does and thus it is acceptable to make up lyrics as they go along.
- In the 1996 movie *Down Periscope*, the crew of The Stingray sing the song to impersonate drunken fishermen.

- In the 1998-aired *Buffy the Vampire Slayer* episode "Band Candy" (3x06), after having eaten cursed chocolate bars and therefore behaving now like teenagers, a group of drunk adults/seniors sing, on stage at the Bronze, an a cappella chorus of "Louie, Louie".
- In 1999, The Three Amigos released a house version of the song.

2000s

In August 2003, 754 guitarists played a ten-minute rendition of "Louie Louie" at Cheney Stadium, in Tacoma, Washington, United States.[27]

The 2002 film, *24 Hour Party People* features two performances of "Louie Louie", the first time in a cappella form. Both performances are led by 'John the Postman'.

Played by Bruce Springsteen & The E Street Band within the song "Glory Days" during the 2009 Working On a Dream Tour.

Iggy Pop's version is played during the opening credits of Michael Moore's *Capitalism: A Love Story*.

The Smashing Pumpkins also released a cover of the song in their Live Smashing Pumpkins album series.

Sports

The New York Yankees played the song every time fan favorite Luis Sojo would get a hit or make a good play in the field.

The song is played when Martin St. Louis scores a goal for the Tampa Bay Lightning when playing at the St. Pete Times Forum.

The Seattle Mariners play "Louie Louie" at every home game during the bottom of the 7th inning. It was also a theme songs of sorts for Lou Pinella while he was manager for the team and was played during television commercials that featured him in this role.

Video games

The video game company Epyx used "Louie Louie" as the theme music to their hit title California Games, although the notes used in the Atari 2600 version were erroneous and bore little resemblance to the lead guitar part.

This song is playable on the 2004 North American release of *Donkey Konga*. It has also become one of the 32 song tracks you can dance to in Just Dance (video game).

Alternate versions and interpolations

Some bands have taken liberties with the lyrics, including attempts to record the supposed "obscene lyrics". It is believed the first artists to do so were The Stooges, whose version can be heard on their live album *Metallic K.O.* Iggy Pop later recorded a more civilized cover version of the song, with new lyrics composed by Pop, for his 1993 album *American Caesar*. He continues to play it live at shows.

In 1988, rap trio The Fat Boys covered the song for its album *Comin' Back Hard Again*, with new lyrics by the band that focused on the history of the song.

The old school rap group Ultramagnetic MC's have a song called "Traveling at the Speed of Thought" (1989) which contains a sample of the "Louie Louie" riff.

The Dave Matthews Band has been known to interpolate "Louie Louie" during live versions of *Warehouse*.

Further reading

- Marsh, Dave. *Louie Louie: The History and Mythology of the World's Most Famous Rock 'n' Roll Song*. Hyperion, 1993. ISBN 1-56282-865-7
- *Artforum* (Dec. 1993): untitled Adam Block review of *Louie Louie* by Dave Marsh [28]
- *The New York Times* (September 2, 1993): "Books of The Times: The Real Dirt About a Rock Hit of Ill Repute", by Margo Jefferson [29] (review of the book *Louie Louie* by Dave Marsh)
- Peterson, Dick. *Louie Louie Me Gotta Go Now*. Thalian Press, 2006. ISBN 1-4208-5610-3

External links

- Mikkelson, Barbara & David P. "Are the lyrics to 'Louie Louie' obscene?" [30] at *Snopes: Urban Legends Reference Pages*. [with original lyrics]
- Excerpts from the FBI file about the song [31], from The Smoking Gun
- 15 translations of *Louie Louie* in 13 languages from Afrikaans to Zulu [32]
- [33]
- "A brief history of Louie Louie and Richard Berry" [34], *The Louie Louie Pages* by "Theo"

The Kingsmen

- Classic Bands entry on The Kingsmen [35]

References

[1] *45 Discography for Flip Records* (http://www.globaldogproductions.info/f/flip.html), Global Dog Productions, accessed 2009-11-11
[2] The Smoking Gun The Lascivious 'Louie Louie' (http://www.thesmokinggun.com/louie/louie.html) Access Date: 2/18/2009
[3] Liner notes, Rhino Records re-release *The Best of Louie Louie* (1989; Rhino R1 70605)
[4] "Louie History" (http://www.xs4all.nl/~tdg/history.html), The Louie Louie pages, accessed 2009-11-11
[5] http://www.hynes-inc.com/~cindy/nwi/studioa.JPG
[6] Dave Marsh, 1989, *The Heart of Rock and Roll*, New American Library, p. 14. Marsh ranks the song as number eleven out of the 1001 greatest singles ever made.
[7] Whitburn, Joel (2001). *Joel Whitburn Presents Billboard Top 10 Singles Charts*. Menomonee, Wisconsin: Record Research, Inc.. pp. 69–72. ISBN 0-89820-146-2.
[8] Whitburn, Joel (2004). *Top R&B/Hip-Hop Singles: 1942-2004*. Record Research. p. 328.
[9] http://www.thesmokinggun.com/louie/louie.shtml
[10] http://www.louielouie.net/06-history.htm
[11] "Band Banned From Performing 'Louie Louie'" (http://www.foxnews.com/story/0,2933,155628,00.html). *Associated Press*. 2005-05-05. . Retrieved 2009-09-16.
[12] Seib, Laura (2005-05-06). "'Louie, Louie' gets go-ahead" (http://pqasb.pqarchiver.com/southbendtribune/access/840034681.html?FMT=ABS). *South Bend Tribune*. . Retrieved 2009-09-16.
[13] Burridge, Alan *Illustrated Collector's Guide to Motörhead* Published: 1995, Collector's Guide Publishing ISBN 0-9695736-2-6.
[14] http://louielouie.net
[15] LouieLouie.net (http://louielouie.net)
[16] The Incredible History Of The Mothers (http://www.wiki.killuglyradio.com/index.php/The_Incredible_History_Of_The_Mothers), from Zappa Wiki Jawaka. Originally written by Frank Zappa in June 1968.
[17] "45 Discography for Happy Tiger Records" (http://www.globaldogproductions.info/h/happy-tiger.html). Global Dog Productions. 2008. . Retrieved 2009-04-06.
[18] Marsh, p. 124.
[19] The Clash - Bootlegs & Rarities > Louie Is A Punkrocker (http://www.sharoma.com/clash/items/louie_is_a_punkrocker.htm)
[20] Black Flag, *The First Four Years*, SST Records, 1984.
[21] Spot with Chuck Dukowski, liner notes of Black Flag's *Everything Went Black*, SST Records, 1982
[22] Black Flag, *Everything Went Black*, SST Records, 1982
[23] *Seattle Weekly* (October 27, 1999) Music: "The State I'm In" (http://www.seattleweekly.com/music/9943/two-reighley.php), by Kurt B. Reighley
[24] *The Bellingham Herald* (Feb. 20, 2006): "What Would You Pick as State Vegetable?" (http://www.bellinghamherald.com/apps/pbcs.dll/article?AID=/20060220/COLUMNISTS01/602200320/1001/NEWS&theme=DEAN KAHN), by Dean Kahn

[25] Liner notes, *The Best Of Louie Louie Volume 2* (http://www.xs4all.nl/~tdg/dg/Comps/rhino2.html) (Rhino R1 70515), by Doc Pelzell
[26] The Fat Boys, *Coming Back Hard Again*, Tin Pan Alley/Polydor, 1988
[27] http://seattletimes.nwsource.com/html/localnews/2001608291_louie25m.html
[28] http://www.findarticles.com/p/articles/mi_m0268/is_n4_v32/ai_14890815
[29] http://query.nytimes.com/gst/fullpage.html?res=9F0CE6DB133EF931A3575AC0A965958260&sec=&pagewanted=print
[30] http://www.snopes.com/music/songs/louie.htm
[31] http://www.thesmokinggun.com/louie/louie.html
[32] http://www.xs4all.nl/~tdg/tr/transla.html
[33] http://seattletimes.nwsource.com/html/entertainment/2003643550_louietimeline01.html
[34] http://www.xs4all.nl/~tdg/history.html
[35] http://www.classicbands.com/kingsmen.html

Love Is a Woman

"Love Is a Woman" is a song written by Brian Wilson for the American pop band The Beach Boys. It was released on their 1977 album *Love You*.

Details

- *Written by:* Brian Wilson
- *Album:* Love You
- *Time:* 2 min 57 sec
- *Produced by:* Brian Wilson

Performers

- *Brian Wilson:* Lead Vocals (chorus)
- *Mike Love:* Lead Vocals (verses)
- *Al Jardine:* Lead Vocals (on the "counting" section)

See also

- List of songs by The Beach Boys

Love Surrounds Me

"Love Surrounds Me"	
Single by The Beach Boys	
from the album *L.A. (Light Album)*	
Released	April 16, 1979
Format	Vinyl
Recorded	Unknown
Genre	Pop
Length	3:41
Label	Caribou Records
Writer(s)	Dennis Wilson Geoffrey Cushing-Murray Producer = Bruce Johnston The Beach Boys James William Guercio

The Beach Boys singles chronology		
"Here Comes the Night"/"Baby Blue" (1979)	"Good Timin'"/"**Love Surrounds Me**" (1979)	"Lady Lynda"/"Full Sail" (1979)

"Love Surrounds Me" is the B-side of the single, "Good Timin'", released by the Beach Boys in 1979. The track also appears on the 30th Anniversary Edition of writer Dennis Wilson's album, *Pacific Ocean Blue*.

Performers

- Dennis Wilson: Lead vocals
- Christine McVie: backing vocals
- Bruce Johnston: backing vocals
- Carl Wilson backing vocals

See also

- L.A. (Light Album)
- List of The Beach Boys songs

Luau

"Luau"	
B-side by The Beach Boys	
Released	December 8, 1961
Recorded	October 3, 1961 World Pacific Studio
Genre	Surf music
Length	1:43
Label	Candix
Composer	Bruce Morgan
Producer	Hite Morgan

"Luau" is a song written by Bruce Morgan. The song was recorded by American pop band The Beach Boys during their early years as a recording group. The song was never released on any of the band's albums, although it was released as the B-side of the band's first ever single "Surfin'". The song was lost in the archives for many years until it was found and released on the band's 1991 compilation album *Lost & Found (1961-62)*.

Musicians

- Al Jardine - vocals
- Mike Love - vocals
- Brian Wilson - vocals, drum
- Carl Wilson - guitar, vocals
- Dennis Wilson - possibly vocals

Brian's 'drum' was the bottom of a garbage can with his shirt stretched across it. Dennis left the session early after an argument with his father, Murry Wilson, who was overseeing the session.

See also

- List of songs by The Beach Boys

Magic Transistor Radio

Magic Transistor Radio is the fourth track on the Mount Vernon and Fairway (A Fairy Tale) album. It was written by Brian Wilson for the American pop band The Beach Boys. The track features Jack Rieley on narration and Brian Wilson on lead vocals.

Details

- *Written by:* Brian Wilson
- *Album:* Mount Vernon and Fairway (A Fairy Tale)
- *Time:* 1 min 43 sec
- *Produced by:* The Beach Boys

Performers

- *Brian Wilson:* Lead Vocals

See also

- The Beach Boys
- Mount Vernon and Fairway (A Fairy Tale)
- List of songs by The Beach Boys

Make It Big

"Make It Big" is a song written by Mike Love, Bob House and Terry Melcher for the American pop band The Beach Boys. It was released on their 1989 album *Still Cruisin'*.

An alternate version of the song was used during the opening credits of the film Troop Beverly Hills, which was released that same year.

See also

- List of songs by The Beach Boys

Make It Good

"Make It Good"	
Song by The Beach Boys from the album *Carl and the Passions - "So Tough"*	
Released	May 15, 1972
Recorded	Brian Wilson's home studio: April 9, 1972 Sunset Studios: April 18, 1972
Genre	Pop
Length	2:36
Label	Brother/Reprise
Composer	Dennis Wilson/Daryl Dragon
Producer	Dennis Wilson and Daryl Dragon
***Carl and the Passions - "So Tough"* track listing**	
"Hold On Dear Brother" (5) **"Make It Good"** (6) "All This Is That" (7)	

"Make It Good" is a song written by Dennis Wilson and Daryl Dragon for the American pop band The Beach Boys. It was released on their 1972 album *Carl and the Passions - "So Tough"*. During the recording process, the song was titled "What I Feel".

Details

- Written by: Dennis Wilson/Daryl Dragon
- Album: Carl and the Passions - "So Tough"
- Time: 2 min 36 sec
- Produced by: The Beach Boys

Performers

- Toni Tennille - backing vocals
- Dennis Wilson - lead vocals

See also

- List of songs by The Beach Boys

Male Ego

"Getcha Back/Male Ego"	
Single by The Beach Boys	
from the album *The Beach Boys*	
Released	May 8, 1985
Format	Vinyl
Genre	Pop music
Length	2:32
Label	Brother Records
Writer(s)	Brian Wilson, Mike Love, Eugene E. Landy
Producer	Steve Levine
The Beach Boys singles chronology	

"Come Go with Me"/"Don't Go Near the Water" (1981)	"Getcha Back"/"**Male Ego**" (1985)	"It's Gettin' Late"/"It's O.K." (1985)

"**Male Ego**" is a song written by Brian Wilson, Mike Love, Eugene E. Landy for the American pop band The Beach Boys. It was released on their 1985 album, *The Beach Boys*, as a bonus track on all CD releases.

Musicians

- Al Jardine - vocals
- Bruce Johnston - vocals
- Steve Levine - synthesizer
- Julian Lindsay - bass, synthesizer
- Mike Love - lead vocal
- Ian Ritchie - baritone saxophone
- Brian Wilson - keyboards, lead vocal
- Carl Wilson - vocals

See also

- The Beach Boys
- The Beach Boys (album)
- List of The Beach Boys songs

Mama Says

"Mama Says" is a song written by Brian Wilson and Mike Love for the American pop band The Beach Boys. It was released on their 1967 album *Wild Honey*.

This a-capella fragment was originally part of "Vega-Tables" from *Smile*.

Details

- *Written by:* Brian Wilson/Mike Love
- *Album:* Wild Honey
- *Time:* 1 min 05 sec
- *Produced by:* The Beach Boys

See also

- List of songs by The Beach Boys

The Man with All the Toys

"The Man with All the Toys"	
Single by The Beach Boys	
from the album *The Beach Boys' Christmas Album*	
Released	November 16, 1964]
Format	Vinyl
Recorded	Unknown
Genre	Pop music
Length	1:32
Label	Capitol
Writer(s)	Brian Wilson Mike Love
Producer	Brian Wilson
The Beach Boys singles chronology	

"Dance, Dance, Dance"/"The Warmth of the Sun" (1964)	**"The Man with All the Toys"**/"Blue Christmas" (1964)	"Do You Wanna Dance?"/"Please Let Me Wonder" (1965)

"The Man with All the Toys" is a Christmas song written by Brian Wilson and Mike Love for the American pop band The Beach Boys. It was released on their 1964 album *The Beach Boys' Christmas Album*. As a single that year it had limited success (No. 6 on the *Billboard* Christmas chart), but built sales over successive Christmases and is listed by *Billboard* in the Top 100 selling Christmas songs in history, though well below the Beach Boys' 1963 Christmas single "Little Saint Nick".

Wilson re-recorded this song for his 2005 Christmas album, *What I Really Want for Christmas*.

Performers

- Brian Wilson: lead vocals, piano
- Mike Love: lead vocals
- Carl Wilson: lead guitar, rhythm guitar, harmony vocals
- Alan Jardine: bass guitar, harmony vocals
- Dennis Wilson: drums, harmony vocals

See also

- The Beach Boys
- *The Beach Boys' Christmas Album*
- List of The Beach Boys songs

Marcella

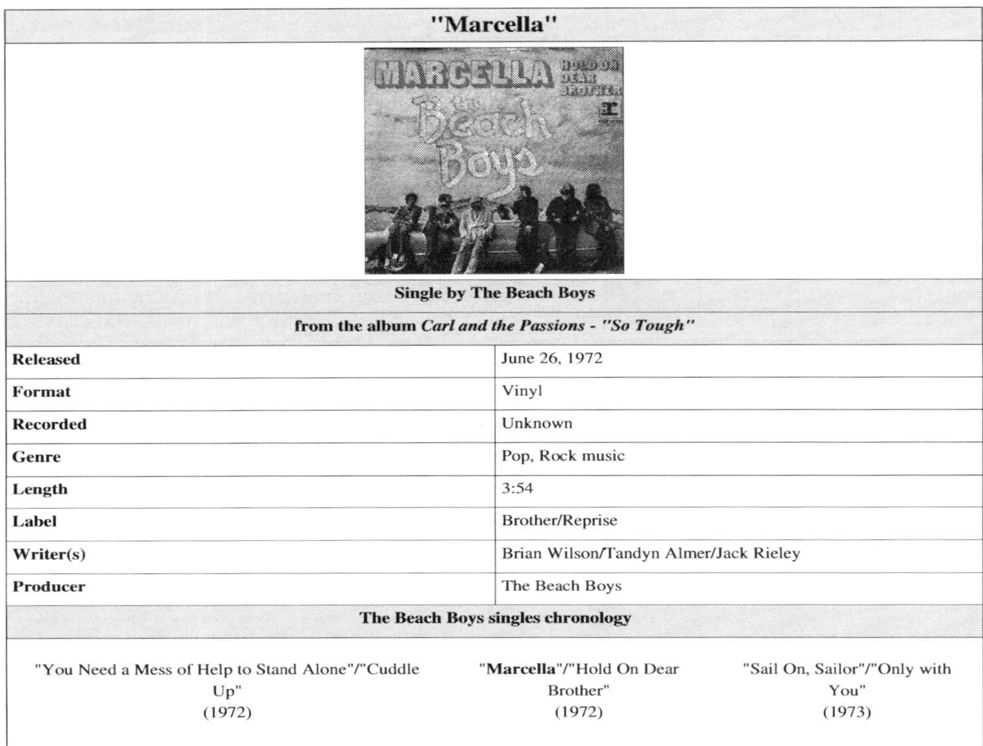

"Marcella"	
Single by The Beach Boys	
from the album *Carl and the Passions - "So Tough"*	
Released	June 26, 1972
Format	Vinyl
Recorded	Unknown
Genre	Pop, Rock music
Length	3:54
Label	Brother/Reprise
Writer(s)	Brian Wilson/Tandyn Almer/Jack Rieley
Producer	The Beach Boys
The Beach Boys singles chronology	

"You Need a Mess of Help to Stand Alone"/"Cuddle Up" (1972)	"**Marcella**"/"Hold On Dear Brother" (1972)	"Sail On, Sailor"/"Only with You" (1973)

"**Marcella**" is a song written by Brian Wilson, Tandyn Almer and Jack Rieley for the American pop band The Beach Boys. It was released on their 1972 album *Carl and the Passions - "So Tough"*. It is the last song to feature Bruce Johnston during his original tenure in the band.

Performers

- Tandyn Almer - keyboards
- Blondie Chaplin - backing vocals
- Ricky Fataar - drums, backing vocals
- Al Jardine - lead and backing vocals
- Bruce Johnston - bass guitar, backing vocals
- Mike Love - lead vocals (pre-chorus) and backing vocals
- Tony Martin Jr. - steel guitar
- Brian Wilson - piano, percussion, backing vocals
- Carl Wilson - guitar, lead vocals (verses) and backing vocals

See also

- The Beach Boys
- Carl and the Passions - "So Tough"
- List of The Beach Boys songs

Match Point of Our Love

"Match Point of Our Love" is a song written by Brian Wilson and Mike Love for the American pop band The Beach Boys. It was released on their 1978 album *M.I.U. Album*.

Details

- *Written by:* Brian Wilson/Mike Love
- *Album:* M.I.U. Album
- *Time:* 3 min 29 sec
- *Produced by:* Al Jardine/Ron Altbach

Performers

- *Brian Wilson:* Lead Vocals

See also

- The Beach Boys
- M.I.U. Album
- List of songs by The Beach Boys

Maybe I Don't Know

"Maybe I Don't Know" is a song written by Carl Wilson, Myrna Smith Schilling, Steve Levine, and Julian Lindsay for the American pop band The Beach Boys. It was released on their 1985 album *The Beach Boys*.

Details

- *Written by:* Carl Wilson/Myrna Smith Schilling/Steve Levine/Julian Lindsay
- *Album: The Beach Boys*
- *Time:* 3:53
- *Produced by:* Steve Levine

Musicians

- John Alder - guitar synthesizer
- Graham Broad - drums, percussion
- Al Jardine - vocals
- Bruce Johnston - vocals
- Steve Levine - synthesizer, drum programming
- Julian Lindsay - keyboard, bass
- Mike Love - vocals
- Gary Moore - guitars
- Brian Wilson - vocals
- Carl Wilson - lead vocal

See also

- The Beach Boys
- The Beach Boys (album)
- List of songs by The Beach Boys

Meant for You

"Meant for You" is a song written by Brian Wilson and Mike Love for the American pop band The Beach Boys. It was released on their 1968 album *Friends*. The song was recorded in April, 1968. It was also re-recorded for Wilson's 1995 solo album *I Just Wasn't Made for These Times*, with Wilson singing lead instead of Love. This song is a classical music, rock and pop ballad.

Details

- *Written by:* Brian Wilson/Mike Love
- *Album:* Friends
- *Time:* 0 min 38 sec
- *Produced by:* The Beach Boys

Performers

- *Mike Love:* Lead Vocals

See also

- List of songs by The Beach Boys

Merry Christmas, Baby

"Merry Christmas, Baby" is a Christmas song written by Brian Wilson for the American pop band The Beach Boys. It was released on their 1964 album *The Beach Boys' Christmas Album*.

Details

- *Written by:* Brian Wilson
- *Album:* The Beach Boys' Christmas Album
- *Time:* 2 min 20 sec
- *Produced by:* Brian Wilson

Performers

- *Mike Love:* Lead Vocals
- *Brian Wilson:* Harmony Vocals, Piano
- *Carl Wilson:* Harmony Vocals, Guitar
- *Alan Jardine:* Harmony Vocals, Bass Guitar
- *Dennis Wilson:* Drums, Harmony Vocals

Note: The above list of performers is assumed from the fact that this track was recorded on the same day as *The Man With All The Toys*, *Santa's Beard*, and *Christmas Day*, and that the former two tracks (and possibly the third as well) featured the Beach Boys playing the instruments themselves instead of hiring *The Wrecking Crew*. However, according to the liner notes for *The Beach Boys Ultimate Christmas*, Ray Pohlman may have played the bass guitar on this track instead of Jardine.

See also

- List of songs by The Beach Boys

Misirlou

Misirlou (Greek: Μισιρλού, "Egyptian Girl"; from Turkish *Mısırlı*, "Egyptian";[1] from Arabic مصر, *Mişr*, "Egypt"), is a popular Greek song with a cult-like popularity in five very diverse styles of music: Greek rebetiko, Middle-Eastern belly dancing, Jewish wedding music (Klezmer), American surf rock and international orchestral easy listening (Exotica).

History

The song was first performed by the Michalis Patrinos rebetiko band in Athens, Greece in 1927. As with almost all early rebetika songs (a style that originated with the Greek refugees from Turkey), the song's actual composer has never been identified, and its ownership rested with the band leader. The melody was most likely composed collaboratively by the group, as was often the case at the time; the initial lyrics were almost certainly written by Patrinos himself. Patrinos, who originally lived in Smyrna, named the song Mısırlı or Misirlou which means specifically a Muslim Egyptian girl, as opposed to Egyptian Christians who were referred to as 'Aigyptioi' in Greek.

Initially, the song was composed as a Greek (Asia Minor) tsifteteli dance, in the rebetiko style of music, at a slower tempo and a different key than the orientalized performances that most are familiar with today. This was the style of the first known recording by Michalis Patrinos in Greece, circa 1930 (which was circulated in the United States by Titos Dimitriadis' Orthophonic label); a second recording was made by Patrinos in New York, in 1931.

In 1941, Nick Roubanis, a Greek-American music instructor, released a jazz instrumental arrangement of the song, crediting himself as the composer. Since his claim was never legally challenged, he is still officially credited as the composer today worldwide, except in Greece where credit is variably given to either Roubanis or Patrinos. Subsequently S. Russell, N. Wise, and M. Leeds wrote English lyrics to the song. Roubanis is also credited with fine-tuning the key and the melody, giving it the oriental sound that it is associated with today. The song soon became an "exotica" standard among the light swing (lounge) bands of the day.

In 1944 maestro Clovis el-Hajj, an Arabic Lebanese musician, performed this song and called it "amal." This is the only Arabic version of this song.

In 1945, a Pittsburgh, Pennsylvania, women's musical organization asked Professor Brunhilde E. Dorsch to organize an international dance group at Duquesne University to honor America's World War II allies. She contacted Mercine Nesotas, who taught several Greek dances, including Syrtos Haniotikos (from Crete), which she called Kritikos, but for which they had no music. Because Pittsburgh's Greek-American community did not know Cretan music, Pat Mandros Kazalas, a music student, suggested the tune Misirlou, although slower, might fit the dance. The dance was first performed at a program to honor America's allies of World War II at Stephen Foster Memorial Hall in Pittsburgh on March 6, 1945. Thereafter, this new dance, which had been created by putting the Syrtos Kritikos to the slower Misirlou music, was known as "Misirlou" and spread among the Greek-American community, as well as among non-Greek U.S. folk-dance enthusiasts. The dance is also performed to instrumental versions of Never on Sunday by Manos Hadjidakis.

The song was rearranged as a solo instrumental guitar piece by Dick Dale in 1962. During a performance, Dale was bet by a young fan that he could not play a song on only one string of his guitar. Dale's father and uncles were Lebanese-Americans and musicians as well, and Dale remembered seeing his uncle play "Misirlou" on one string of the oud. He vastly increased the song's tempo to make it into rock'n'roll, and the result was the famous Dick Dale "Miserlou". It was Dale's version that introduced "Misirlou" to a wider audience in the United States as "Miserlou."

The song's oriental melody has been so popular for so long that many people, from Morocco to Iraq, claim it to be a folk song from their own country. In fact, in the realm of Middle Eastern music, the song is a very simplistic one, since it is little more than going up and down the *Hijaz Kar* or double harmonic scale (E-F-G#-A-B-C-D#).

The Beach Boys recorded a Dale-inspired "Miserlou" for the 1963 album *Surfin' USA*, forever making "Miserlou" a staple of American pop culture. Hundreds of recordings have been made to date, by performers as diverse as Agent Orange and Connie Francis (1965).

The Trashmen also recorded their "Miserlou" version.

In 1994, Dale's version of "Miserlou" was used on the soundtrack of the motion picture *Pulp Fiction*, thanks to a suggestion to Quentin Tarantino from his friend Boyd Rice. More recently, the song was selected by the Athens 2004 Organizing Committee as one of the most influential Greek songs of all time, and was heard in venues and at the closing ceremony--it was performed by Anna Vissi. In March 2005, *Q* magazine placed Dale's version at number 89 in its list of the 100 Greatest Guitar Tracks. In 2006, his version once again found popularity, this time as the basis of The Black Eyed Peas' single "Pump It." Also in 2006, a cover of Dale's version was included as a playable song in the rhythm game *Guitar Hero II*.

Lyrics

Greek

Μισιρλού μου, η γλυκιά σου η ματιά
Φλόγα μου 'χει ανάψει μες στην καρδιά.
Αχ, για χαμπίμπι, αχ, για λε-λέλι, αχ,
Τα δυο σου χείλη στάζουνε μέλι, αχ.
Αχ, Μισιρλού, μαγική, ξωτική ομορφιά.
Τρέλα θα μου 'ρθει, δεν υποφέρω πια.
Αχ, θα σε κλέψω μέσ' απ' την Αραπιά.
Μαυρομάτα Μισιρλού μου τρελή,
Η ζωή μου αλλάζει μ' ένα φιλί.
Αχ, για χαμπίμπι ενα φιλάκι,άχ
Απ' το γλυκό σου το στοματάκι, αχ.

Transliteration

Misirloú mou, i glukiá so i matiá
Phlóga mou'khi anápsi mes sten kardiá.
Akh, ya habíbi, akh ya le-léli, ah,
Ta dio sou khíli stázoune méli, ah.
Akh, Misirloú, magikí, ksotikí omorphiá.
Tréla tha mo'rthi then ipophéro pia.
Akh, tha se klépso més'ap'tin Arapiá.
Mavromáta Misirloú mou trelí,
I zoí mo allázi m'éna philí.
Akh, ya habíbi ena philáki, ah
Ap'to glikó sou to stomatáki, ah.

Translation

My Misirlou (*Egyptian girl*), your sweet glance
Has lit a flame in my heart.
Ah, ya habibi, Ah, ya leh-leli, ah (Arabic: *Oh, my love, Oh, my night*)[2]
Your two lips are dripping honey, ah.
Ah, Misirlou, magical, exotic beauty.
Madness will overcome me, I can't endure [this] any more.
Ah, I'll steal you away from the Arab land.
My black-eyed, my wild Misirlou,
My life changes with one kiss
Ah, ya habibi, one little kiss, ah
From your sweet little lips, ah.

Ladino lyrics (unrelated to original Greek lyrics)
No pretendas mas que
Ni te sforses a vartir lagrimas
Yo ya lo supe que era por enganyar
Este es un fakto que no puedes niegar
Ah... ahh... Missirlu
Es muy amargo, ah es muy amargo el sufrir.
Ma no por este uno deve murir.
Muchos anios te speri en vanedad
Creendo ke tu amor es verdad
Me amurcates propio con una flor
y me forsates a bivir con dolor
Ah... ahh... Missirlu
Es muy amargo, ah es muy amargo el sufrir
Ma no por este uno deve murir.
Algun dia sufrira tu korason

I konoseras lo que es la trahision
como yo yoro y tu yoraras,
Y konseulo nunca toparas

Other notable recordings

- The 1987 comedy film *Back to the Beach* features a surf-rock performance of Misirlou in front of wind machines by Dick Dale and Stevie Ray Vaughan.
- Ben Folds Five recorded a Piano/Bass/Drums/Strings song that interpolates the piece entitled "Theme from Dr. Pyser"
- A Ladino version of "Misirlou" was recorded by the Turkish-Jewish band Los Pasharos Sefaradis. Other Ladino recordings were made by Liliana Treves Alkalay and in sephardic speaking Salonika before and after World War 2.[3]
- In the late 1960s a recording of "Misirlou" was made by a group called The Devil's Anvil. Felix Pappalardi (who would go on to fame as producer for British super-group Cream, and as bassist for legendary guitarist Leslie West's hard rocking band Mountain) acted as producer on the album "Hard Rock from the Middle East" by the multi-cultural Devil's Anvil. Pappalardi, in fact, handled lead vocals on the track "Misirlou" according to the liner notes of a late 1990s re-release of the original album on CD. In 1967, the release of "Hard Rock from the Middle East", coincided almost exactly with the outbreak of the Arab-Israeli Six-Day War. As a result of this unfortunate coincidence, radio stations, record stores and The Devil's Anvil's record label, Columbia Records, all allowed the album to quickly sink into obscurity.
- Turkish singer Zeki Müren sang the melody as 'Yaralı Gönül'.
- Martin Denny and Arthur Lyman, founding fathers of Tiki and Exotica music, recorded two covers of the song.
- A Serbian version of this song titled *Vranjanka (The Girl from Vranje)* was created by Serbian singer Staniša Stošić. This version is widely sung across the territory of the former Yugoslavia; when *Pulp Fiction* appeared, to many it was a surprise to find out that the song was indeed Greek.
- The influential British Fingerstyle guitarist Davey Graham plays a fingerstyle guitar version on his albums Live at St Andrews' Folk Club 1966 and After Hours: Live at Hull University 1967. On the St Andrews' recording Graham introduces the song: 'I was in Greece last year, and I saw that the Greeks dance alone, which I thought was a bit queer at first; this is a tune, a song really, about a girl called Miserlou'.
- There is a Spanish version of "Misirlou" made by the Italian singer Caterina Valente with the Edmundo Ros Orchestra. This version appeared in the album called "Caterina Valente com Edmundo Ros", released in Brazil in 1961.
- French-Algerian rock star Rachid Taha recorded an Arabic, drum'n'bass-inspired version, titled "Jungle Fiction".
- Woody Herman and his Orchestra recorded a foxtrot version, published by Decca, which can be found as the b-side to "Blue Flame".
- British surf instrumental band The Thurston Lava Tube recorded a version on their 2006 album "The Thoughful Sounds of Bat Smuggling".
- The Greek garage rock band The Last Drive record an instrumental version of this song on its first album *Underworld Shakedown* (1986).
- American ethnomusicologist Harry Smith made several recordings of Naftali Zvi Margolies Abulafia, a prominent Jewish orthodox rabbi who lived on New York's Lower East Side as he sang and told stories in Yiddish. On January 1, 2006, NPR presented a story on the efforts of his grandson Lionel Ziprin to preserve these recordings and played some of them in their story. One of the pieces sounds identical to the melody of "Misirlou". (The melody can be heard, beginning at 4:13.) NPR: A Grandson's Quest To Preserve His Jewish Heritage [4]
- A version with Yiddish lyrics is often performed at weddings, and has been recorded by Klezmer Conservatory Band on their CD *Dancing in the Aisles*. The style is a hybrid of Ashkenazic Klezmer and Mizrahi (Jewish songs set to Arab melodies).

- NPR did a full report on the evolution and multiple versions of "Misirlou," which can be heard at [5].
- California Guitar Trio (with Tony Levin and Pat Mastelotto as special guests) covered Dale's version of the song on their album *Rocks the West* (2000).
- The song is featured in the opening sequence to the French film *Taxi*, released in 1998. The film, starring Samy Naceri, written by Luc Besson, and directed by Gérard Pirès forms part of one of the most successful French franchises ever. It also features in the sequel *Taxi 3*
- ECW in 1996 to 2001 used the "Misirlou" theme song for the promos at the end of each show along with the ending credits.
- The 2007 movie Ocean's Thirteen contains a version of the Misirlou melody.
- The Czech grindcore band Perversist recorded a cover for their album Machine Grind Surgery.
- The Kronos Quartet released a version of "Misirlou" on their album *Caravan*, called "Misirlou Twist."
- Fourplay often perform "Misirlou" during their live performances, using a Viola for the primary guitar. A recording of a live performance is in the first "Fourplay String Quartet" single.
- American jazz pianist Vince Guaraldi included a live version of the song on his 1963 album *In Person*.
- The United States Library of Congress holds two recordings created in 1939, each sung a cappella by a different woman. [6]
- In 1997, the band The Red Elvises recorded a version of Misirlou, which they retitled "Surfing in Siberia." It is on their album, also titled "Surfing in Siberia."
- In 1945 the song was also recorded by Jan August and Carl Frederick Tandberg.[7]
- Anita Darian, in 1960, released "Misirlou" on a self-titled album “Anita Darian” (later titled “East of the Sun”), Kapp Records KL-1168.
- Juan García Esquivel recorded "Misirlou" in 1959. It was rereleased on the compilation album "Watchamacallit!" in 2006.
- Harry Saroyan performed "Misirlou" on his album “Saroyan Sings 'Cairo'”, Saroyan Productions, Riverside, CA, 1994.
- Domino's Pizza, in 2000 used the song prominently in their television commercials; at one point featuring Dick Dale.
- Dale's version was also be used in the reggaeton song "Dame Un Kiss" by Franco "El Gorilla".
- Uruguayan surf rock band The Supersonicos released a medley of Misirlou and The Cure's Killing an Arab, in their album "Hola Estatica"; under the name "Killing An Arab/Miserlou".
- The Trashmen on their debut album, Surfin' Bird, in 1964
- A dance version of Misirlou was recorded in 1995 by Spaghetti Surfers. [8]
- Gallon Drunks 1992 version (on the album *Tonite ... The Singles Bar*) is utterly sick, depressed, both psychotic and pychedelic, actually anticipating Bohren & der Club of Gore's unique music style since the mid-90s.
- The song was sampled in the Black Eyed Peas song "Pump It."
- The Dick Dale version is used in the opening credits of the TV series Kitchen Nightmares.

Use in soundtracks

- In the opening scene of *Pulp Fiction*, a modified version of Misirlou was used.
- The Red Elvises' version "Surfing in Siberia" was featured in the surreal post-apocalyptic cult classic Six String Samurai.
- A version of the song was used in the opening scene of the French film Taxi
- "Misirlou" has been featured in Konami's *Guitar Freaks* and *Drummania* games.
- *Guitar Hero II*, released in 2006, features a cover of a Dale's alternate, faster rendition of Misirlou, also featured on Dale's Greatest Hits 1961-1976 album.
- "Misirlou" has also been featured as a song in *Rayman Raving Rabbids* in its rhythm mini-game, and in this game's advertising campaign.

- The sound track to the videogame *Command & Conquer: Red Alert* contains an homage as a secret track
- The Sega Saturn title *Guardian Force* features an homage to the *Pulp Fiction* rendition in level 3.
- A song similar in style to Dick Dale's version of "Misirlou" was featured in the PlayStation title *JetMoto*.
- The Xbox game Sega GT 2002 features a track similar to Dale's Misrilou
- The song in the first stage of *Metal Slug 2* and *Metal Slug X* uses some portions of Misirlou.
- The character theme for Bowser Jr. in Mario Strikers Charged is a variation of Misirlou.
- The dutch band New Cool Collective played a bigband-version of the song.
- The Dick Dale version appears in Space Jam.
- The Phil Woods Quartet on Into The Woods has a track called Misirlou attributed to Nicholas Roubanis

External links

- Original (MP3) versions of Greek Song Misirlou [9]
- Dick Dale's Extensive Explanation [10] (with guitar tabs and standard notation)
- Yiddish lyrics for Misirlou with English translation [11]
- Misirlou, from Klezmer to Surf Guitar [5] (NPR Weekend Edition Sunday, January 8, 2006). *(It should be noted that the program makes some patently incorrect statements - Rembetiko is not "a slow circle dance"; it does not have origins in Thraki; the Jews of Constantinople were Sephardim, not Askenazi, etc.)*
- Playlist of a KGNU broadcast [12] listing 25 performances of Misirlou.
- U.S. Library of Congress recordings. [6]

References

[1] "Mısırlı" (http://seslisozluk.com/?word=MÄ±sÄ±rlÄ±&sbT=Search&ssQBy=0). *SesliSozluk Online Dictionary*. Seslisozluk. . Retrieved 2009-11-10.

[2] The Arabic verse in the song is badly mispronounced - "ya leli" would be correct. This is probably because (a) Patrinos and his audience did not speak Arabic and/or (b) "ah ya *leh*-leli" has exactly the 5 syllables needed to fill the verse. The same sentence is very frequently used in Greek rembetiko songs (orientalism is a frequent theme).

[3] "Kimeni epi aktis thalasis" by Alberto Nar, p313-318

[4] http://www.npr.org/templates/story/story.php?storyId=5076613

[5] http://www.npr.org/templates/story/story.php?storyId=5134530

[6] http://memory.loc.gov/cgi-bin/query/S?ammem/flwpabib:@field(TITLE+@od1(Misirlou))

[7] "Bass Player Marking 11th Year at Ricky's". *Pasadena Star-News*. April 25, 1969. "Bass player Carl F. Tandberg is an 11-year man at Dick White's Rickey's Restaurant in Alhambra and a 42-year man in the music business. ... before recording "Miserlou" with Jan August in 1945."

[8] http://www.discogs.com/Spaghetti-Surfers-Misirlou/master/129609

[9] http://www.dinosaurgardens.com/archives/297

[10] http://www.fenderplayersclub.com/pdfs/artist_lessons/dale.pdf

[11] http://www.everything2.com/index.pl?node_id=797765

[12] http://playlist.kgnu.net/default.asp?show=7&from=03/02/2007&to=03/02/2007&ord=asc

Mona

"Mona"	
Song by The Beach Boys from the album *The Beach Boys Love You*	
Released	April 11, 1977
Recorded	October 21 and November 10, 1977 Brother Studios
Genre	Pop music and Rock music
Length	2:06
Label	Brother/Reprise
Composer	Brian Wilson
Producer	Brian Wilson
***The Beach Boys Love You* track listing**	
"Roller Skating Child" (2) "**Mona**" (3) "Johnny Carson" (4)	

"Mona" is a song written by Brian Wilson for the American pop band The Beach Boys. It was released on their 1977 album *Love You*. The lead vocal is sung by Dennis Wilson and Brian Wilson.

Details

- *Written by:* Brian Wilson
- *Album:* Love You
- *Time:* 2 min 06 sec
- *Produced by:* Brian Wilson

See also

- The Beach Boys
- Love You
- List of songs by The Beach Boys

Moon Dawg

Moon Dawg (often misspelled "Moon Dawn") is an instrumental written by Derry Weaver which was originally released in 1960 on World Pacific Jazz Records by Derry's band The Gamblers (Derry Weaver: lead guitar, Elliot Ingbar: rhythm guitar, Bruce Johnston: piano, Larry Taylor: bass, Rod Schaffer: drums). The song was covered on 30+ different recordings worldwide, which included the The Beach Boys (see details below), The Ventures, Paul Revere & the Raiders, and The Surfaris.

Details

- *Written by*: Derry Weaver
- *Album*: *Surfin' Safari*
- *Time*: 2:00
- *Produced by*: Nick Venet
- *Recording date*: September 6, 1962[1]

Other versions

Lineup for the cover version by the Beach Boys-

- David Marks - guitar
- Nick Venet - howling
- Brian Wilson - bass guitar
- Carl Wilson - guitar
- Dennis Wilson - drums

References

[1] http://www.secondhandsongs.com/song/80171

Morning Christmas

"Morning Christmas" is a Christmas song written by Dennis Wilson. The song was recorded by the American pop band The Beach Boys and was released on their 1998 Christmas album *Ultimate Christmas*.

See also

- List of songs by The Beach Boys

Mountain of Love

"Mountain of Love"	
Song by The Beach Boys from the album *Beach Boys' Party!*	
Released	8 November 1965
Genre	Rock and roll
Length	2:51
Label	Capitol
Composer	Harold Dorman
Producer	Brian Wilson
***Beach Boys' Party!* track listing**	
• "Hully Gully" • "I Should Have Known Better" • "Tell Me Why" • "Papa-Oom-Mow-Mow" • "Mountain of Love" • "You've Got to Hide Your Love Away" • "Devoted to You" • "Alley Oop" • "There's No Other (Like My Baby)" • "Medley:I Get Around/Little Deuce Coupe" • "The Times They Are a-Changin'" • "Barbara Ann"	

"**Mountain of Love**" is a song written by Harold Dorman (also known as Harold Kenneth Dorman). Dorman released his version as a single in 1960. It performed well, becoming a top forty hit on the *Billboard* Hot 100. It was the highest charting single of his career.

In 1964, Johnny Rivers released his remake as a single. This version also proved popular, charting at number nine on the *Billboard* Hot 100 [1] .

In 1968, singer Ronnie Dove had a minor hit when he released his version as a single on Diamond Records.

Other artists to record the song include The Beach Boys (on their 1965 album *Beach Boys' Party!*), Tommy Cash, Narvel Felts, and Jerry Lawson and Talk of the Town (on their 2007 album *Jerry Lawson Talk of the Town*. Bobby G. Rice took a rendition to #20 on the country music charts in 1971.[2]

Charley Pride version

"Mountain of Love"	
Single by Charley Pride	
from the album *Everybody's Choice*	
Released	1981
Genre	Country
Label	RCA
Charley Pride singles chronology	

"Never Been So Loved (In All My Life)" (1981)	"**Mountain of Love**" (1981)	"I Don't Think She's in Love Anymore" (1982)

In December 1981, Charley Pride released a cover version, which topped the Billboard Hot Country Singles chart in March 1982 [3] . Charley Pride's version of "Mountain of Love" would become his twenty-sixth number one on the country chart. Both Pride and Dorman are natives of Sledge, Mississippi.

Chart performance

Chart (1982)	Peak position
U.S. *Billboard* Hot Country Singles	1
Canadian *RPM* Country Tracks	1

References

[1] Whitburn, Joel (2004). *The Billboard Book of Top 40 Hits: Eighth Edition*. Record Research. p. 531.
[2] Whitburn, Joel (2008). *Hot Country Songs 1944 to 2008*. Record Research, Inc. p. 349. ISBN 0-89820-177-2.
[3] Whitburn, Joel (2004). *The Billboard Book Of Top 40 Country Hits: 1944-2006, Second edition*. Record Research. p. 277.

Mt. Vernon and Fairway (Theme)

"Mt. Vernon And Fairway (Theme)" is the first track on the Mount Vernon and Fairway (A Fairy Tale) extended play album. It was written by Brian Wilson for the American pop band The Beach Boys. The track features Jack Rieley on narration.

Details

- *Written by:* Brian Wilson
- *Album:* Mount Vernon and Fairway (A Fairy Tale)
- *Time:* 1 min 34 sec
- *Produced by:* The Beach Boys

See also

- The Beach Boys
- Mount Vernon and Fairway (A Fairy Tale)
- List of songs by The Beach Boys

My Diane

"My Diane"	
Song by The Beach Boys from the album *M.I.U. Album*	
Released	1978
Length	2 min 37 sec
Writer	Brian Wilson
Producer	Al Jardine/Ron Altbach

"My Diane" is a song written by Brian Wilson for the American pop band The Beach Boys. It was released on their 1978 album *M.I.U. Album*.

Performers

- *Dennis Wilson:* Lead Vocals

See also

- The Beach Boys
- M.I.U. Album
- List of songs by The Beach Boys

The Nearest Faraway Place

"The Nearest Faraway Place"	

Single by The Beach Boys	
from the album *20/20*	
Released	April 20, 1970
Format	Vinyl
Recorded	June 20, 1968
Genre	Pop music, instrumental rock and jazz
Length	2:39
Label	Capitol
Writer(s)	Bruce Johnston
Producer	Bruce Johnston
The Beach Boys singles chronology	

"Add Some Music to Your Day"/"Susie Cincinnati" (1970)	"Cottonfields"/"**The Nearest Faraway Place**" (1970)	"Slip On Through"/"This Whole World" (1970)

"**The Nearest Faraway Place**" is an instrumental written by Bruce Johnston for the American pop band The Beach Boys. It was released on their 1969 album *20/20*. The song was recorded on June 20, 1968.

See also

- The Beach Boys
- 20/20
- List of The Beach Boys songs

Never Learn Not to Love

"Never Learn Not to Love"	
Single by The Beach Boys	
from the album *20/20*	
Released	December 2, 1968
Format	Vinyl
Recorded	September 11, 1968
Genre	Pop
Length	2:31
Label	Capitol
Producer	Carl and Dennis Wilson

The Beach Boys singles chronology		
"Do It Again"/"Wake the World" (1968)	"Bluebirds over the Mountain"/"**Never Learn Not to Love**" (1968)	"I Can Hear Music"/"All I Want to Do" (1969)

"**Never Learn Not to Love**" is a song recorded by The Beach Boys. It was released on their 1969 album *20/20*. It was also released as the B-side of the "Bluebirds over the Mountain" single in 1968. On the Beach Boys album, the song is credited solely to Dennis Wilson.

However, the original song, titled "**Cease to Exist**", was written by Charles Manson.[1] Dennis Wilson, a former acquaintance of Manson's, took the original tune, changed some of the lyrics, and rewrote the melody. The Beach Boys version opens with the vaguely sexual come-on "Cease to resist," rather than Manson's more sinister "Cease to exist."

Performers

- Dennis Wilson: Lead vocals

See also

- List of The Beach Boys songs

References

[1] The Pop Culture Addict presents... Music (http://www.popcultureaddict.com/music/charlesmanson.htm)

The Night Was So Young

"The Night Was So Young" is a song written by Brian Wilson for the American pop band The Beach Boys. It was released on their 1977 album *Love You*.

Details

- *Written by:* Brian Wilson
- *Album:* Love You
- *Time:* 2 min 15 sec
- *Produced by:* Brian Wilson

Performers

- *Carl Wilson:* Lead Vocals

See also

- The Beach Boys
- Love You
- List of songs by The Beach Boys

No-Go Showboat

"No-Go Showboat" is a song written by Brian Wilson and Roger Christian for the American pop band The Beach Boys. It was released on their 1963 album *Little Deuce Coupe*. The song was covered a year later by Petula Clark, though with completely different lyrics, which she sang in French.

Details

- *Written by:* Brian Wilson/Roger Christian
- *Album:* Little Deuce Coupe
- *Time:* 1 min 54 sec
- *Produced by:* Brian Wilson

Performers

- *Brian Wilson:* Lead Vocals
- *Mike Love:* Lead Vocals

See also

- The Beach Boys
- Little Deuce Coupe
- List of songs by The Beach Boys

Noble Surfer

"**Noble Surfer**" is a song written by Brian Wilson and Mike Love for the American pop band The Beach Boys. It was released on their 1963 album *Surfin' USA*.

The song was originally credited to just Wilson. Mike Love's name was added as a result of a lawsuit filed by him against Wilson in the 1990s.

Details

- *Written by:* Brian Wilson/Mike Love
- *Album:* Surfin' USA
- *Time:* 1 min 51 sec
- *Produced by:* Nick Venet
- *Recording date*: February 11, 1963

Musicians

- Mike Love - lead vocal
- David Marks - guitar
- Brian Wilson - bass guitar, vocals
- Carl Wilson - guitar, vocals
- Dennis Wilson - drums, vocals

See also

- The Beach Boys
- Surfin' USA
- List of songs by The Beach Boys

Oh Darlin'

"Oh Darlin'" is a song written by Brian Wilson and Mike Love for the American pop band The Beach Boys. It was released on their 1980 album *Keepin' the Summer Alive*.

Details

- *Written by:* Brian Wilson and Mike Love
- *Album:* Keepin' the Summer Alive
- *Time:* 3 min 52 sec
- *Produced by:* Bruce Johnston

Performers

- *Carl Wilson:* Lead Vocals
- *Mike Love:* Lead Vocals

See also

- The Beach Boys
- Keepin' the Summer Alive
- List of songs by The Beach Boys

Ol' Man River

"**Ol' Man River**" (music by Jerome Kern, lyrics by Oscar Hammerstein II) is a song in the 1927[1] musical *Show Boat*, that contrasts African American hardship and struggles of the time with the endless, uncaring flow of the Mississippi River, from the view of a dock worker on a showboat.[2] [3] It is the most famous song from the show. It is sung complete, once, by the dock worker "Joe" who travels with the boat, and is re-sung three times more in brief reprises. Joe serves as a sort of musical one-man Greek chorus, and the song, when reprised, comments on the action, as if saying, "This has happened, but the river keeps rolling on anyway".

The song is notable for several aspects: the lyrical pentatonic-scale melody, the subjects of toil and social class, metaphor to the Mississippi, and as a bass solo (rare in musicals — solos for baritones or tenors being more common). To some, *Ol' Man River* is symbolically an American version of the famous Russian folksong The Song of the Volga Boatmen. Both songs tell the story of those who live and work on a river.

Various versions

The song was first performed in the original stage production of *Show Boat* on December 27, 1927 by Jules Bledsoe, who also sang it in the part-talkie 1929 film, although that film version had little to do with the stage musical. However, the most famous rendition of it, one that is still noted today, was sung by Paul Robeson in James Whale's classic 1936 film version of *Show Boat* (Robeson had first performed the song in the 1928 London production of the show and in the 1932 Broadway revival, and had even recorded it with Paul Whiteman's orchestra back in 1928). Many musicians and musical groups have covered the song, including Bing Crosby, Frank Sinatra, Sam Cooke, Al Jolson, Screaming Jay Hawkins, Django Reinhardt, Ray Charles, Jim Croce, Jimmy Ricks and the Ravens and The Beach Boys and it is considered an American classic. William Warfield sang it in the 1951 film version of *Show Boat*, another rendition which became very famous. (It became his signature song, and he performed it several times on television.) Famous bass singer of The Temptations, Melvin Franklin was known to sing this at most concerts, and it eventually became *his* signature song, as well. Judy Garland, one of the few female singers to attempt the song, sang a powerful rendition of it on her television show in 1963, and also recorded it.

Among less well-known singers who have performed the song on television, bass-baritone Dan Travis, Jr. sang it in the made-for-television biopic *Ziegfeld: The Man and His Women* (1978)[4] , and P.L. Brown sang it in the 1989 Paper Mill Playhouse version of *Show Boat*, which was televised by PBS.[5]

The song also has versions in the Indian languages Hindi, Bengali and Assamese sung by Bhupen Hazarika, who met Robeson while studying at Columbia University. The Assamese song is called Bistirno Parore, the Bengali version is Bistirno Dupare. The Hindi composition is known as "Ganga Behti Ho Kyon." Instead of the Mississippi, the song is dedicated to the Brahmaputra river in the Assamese version and the Ganges river in the Bengali and Hindi versions. Another excellent Bengali choral version is performed regularly on their concerts by Calcutta Youth Choir arranged by Ruma Guha Thakurta.

Second generation melody

From the show's song "Cotton Blossom", the notes in the phrase "Cotton Blossom, Cotton Blossom" are the same notes as those in the phrase "Ol' Man River, dat Ol' Man River," but inverted. However, "Cotton Blossom" was written first, and "Ol' Man River" was written only after Kern and Hammerstein realized they needed a song to end the first scene in the show. Hammerstein decided to use the idea of the Mississippi River as a basis for the song, and told Kern to use the melody that the stevedores sang in "Cotton Blossom" but invert some of it, and slow down the tempo. This inversion gave "Ol' Man River" a tragic quality.

The year was 1927, and few predicted the second-generation song would become so popular in the Roaring Twenties, which had lighter upbeat songs, such as "Yes, We Have No Bananas" (1923).

Paul Robeson's alterations to the song lyrics

Beginning about 1938, and continuing on to the end of his career, Paul Robeson changed a few of the lyrics of "Ol' Man River" when singing it at recitals, though never in actual stage performances of *Show Boat*.[2] (In addition to the 1928 and 1932 stage productions, he appeared in a Los Angeles stage revival in 1940). And except for the change in the lyrics of the word "niggers" to "darkies," the lyrics of the song as Robeson performed it in the 1936 film version of the show remain exactly as Oscar Hammerstein II originally wrote them in 1927. However, after 1938, Robeson would record the song only with the lyrics that he used in his post-1936 concert recitals.

In the 1978 one-man play *Paul Robeson*, by Phillip Hayes Dean, there is a (perhaps fictitious) reference to the change in the lyrics - an unseen interviewer asks Robeson (played by James Earl Jones) about the original lyrics, and he responds "No, I don't sing it that way anymore".[6]

In the 1951 film version of *Show Boat*, as well as the 1962 studio recording and the 1966 Lincoln Center revival of the show, William Warfield sang only the introductory verse and the lyrics to the main section of the song, but omitted the rest, in contrast to both Jules Bledsoe (who sang it in the prologue to the 1929 film version), and Robeson, who sang the whole song in the 1936 film. The section that Warfield omitted begins:

Niggers all work on de Mississippi,

Niggers all work while de white folks play...

In the 1936 film, the word "niggers" was changed to "darkies". Ever since the 1946 revival, the term has been changed to "colored folks", although there have been revivals that change the line to *Here we all work on de Mississippi*. Also, the phrase "feared of dyin' " (rather than "skeered" of dying) has been sung in some recordings[3], notably Lawrence Tibbett's 1930's version, Gordon MacRae's 1950's version (first heard on *The Railroad Hour*), and Frank Sinatra's 1946 performance, first heard in the film *Till the Clouds Roll By*. Al Jolson sang a version starting with "lots of folks work on the Missisippi."

Robeson's own 1938 changes in the lyrics of the song are as follows:

- Instead of "Dere's an ol' man called de Mississippi, / Dat's de ol' man that I'd like to be...", Robeson sang "There's an ol' man called the Mississippi, / That's the ol' man I don't like to be"..."
- Instead of "Tote that barge! / Lift that bale! / Git a little drunk, / An' you land in jail...", Robeson sang "Tote that barge and lift dat bale!/ You show a little grit and / You lands in jail..."
- Instead of "Ah gits weary / An' sick of tryin'; / Ah'm tired of livin' / An skeered of dyin', / But Ol' Man River, / He jes' keeps rolling along!" , Robeson sang "But I keeps laffin'/ Instead of cryin' / I must keep fightin'; / Until I'm dyin', / And Ol' Man River, / He'll just keep rollin' along!"

In recitals and in several of his many recordings of the song, Robeson also omitted the controversial section "Niggers all work on de Mississippi...", etc., with its middle portion "Don't look up/ An' don't look down/ You don't dast make / De white boss frown", etc., as well as its concluding "Lemme go ' way from de Mississippi/ Lemme go ' way from de white man boss, etc." . However, Robeson did include a portion of these lyrics in the 1932 4-record 78 RPM album of selections from *Show Boat*.

The changes in Robeson's concert renditions of the song shift the portrayal of Joe away from a resigned and sad character who is susceptible to the forces of his world, to one who is timelessly empowered and able to persevere through even the most trying circumstances.

Frank Sinatra famously changed the "Niggers all work on de Mississippi..." to "Here we all work on the Mississippi..." in a version of the song that he recorded post-1946. His 1946 performance of it omitted this section altogether.

The Temptations changed any references to the "white man boss" to "rich man boss", as well as "Here we all work while the white boys play" to "Here we all work while the rich boys play".

In 1988, EMI/Angel Records issued a 3-CD set of the complete score of *Show Boat*, starring Frederica Von Stade, Jerry Hadley, Teresa Stratas, and Bruce Hubbard, conducted by John McGlinn. On this album, the original 1927 lyrics of *Ol' Man River* were heard for the first time on a hi-fi stereo recording.

Gordon MacRae's version of the song, as performed on *The Railroad Hour*, changed the phrase *white man boss* to *big man boss*.[7]

Parodies and References

- A parody version was performed on CBS Radio by Stan Freberg and Daws Butler in 1957, entitled "Elderly Man River." The parody lampooned what would today be termed "political correctness" by featuring a prudish censor from the "Citizen's Radio Board" who repeatedly interrupts Freberg's performance of the song to criticize (and insist on changes to) the grammar and appropriateness of the song's lyrics.
- In an episode of the TV situation comedy *Maude*, the housekeeper Florida (played by Esther Rolle) sings "Darkies all work while de white folks play" as she does housework. Her politically correct and liberal employer Maude (Beatrice Arthur) scolds her and says that the words have changed, to which Florida sings "Coloured folks work on the Mississippi". Maude explains that the proper new lyrics to the song are "Here ***we*** all work on the Mississippi, here ***we*** all work while the straw boss plays." Florida replies that those may be the new lyrics, but the only problem is that "y'all still playing and we're still working".
- In *The Simpsons* episode "Simpsons Tall Tales", Doctor Julius Hibbert is featured as a steamboat captain singing "Ol' Man River".
- In *The Jackson Five* cartoon episode "Rasho-Jackson", all five brothers depict Jackie Jackson as a whip-wielding tyrant yelling "Tote that barge, lift that bale!". Jackie sees himself saying the same thing, but in a genteel, British accent.
- In an episode of *Everybody Loves Raymond*, Robert mentions that he sang this song in his high school chorus days.
- The Australian oddball pop group TISM produced in 1996 a hit single about River Phoenix and his death, entitled "(He'll Never Be An) Ol' Man River".
- Jimmy Velvit recorded a version titled "Old Man River Boogie" for his 1995 CD *Jimmy Velvit - The Original* (Collectables Records COL-5530).
- A popular, up-tempo British ballad of 1933, "Old Father Thames," mirrored some of the strains of "Ol' Man River" but celebrated stoicism over despair and resignation: Old Father Thames keeps rolling along, / Down to the mighty sea. / What does he know? What does he care? / Nothing for you or me.... (Words and music by Raymond Wallace & "Betsy O'Hogan" [Lawrence Wright]).
- In the animated short *Mississippi Hare*, some of which takes place on a Mississippi riverboat, a riverboat gambler named Colonel Shuffle threatens to throw Bugs Bunny into "Ol' Man River".
- In the 1947 film version of James Thurber's *The Secret Life of Walter Mitty*, Danny Kaye, during one of Mitty's fantasies, performs a number called "Fashions by Anatol", which contains the parodistic (and somewhat irrelevant) line "Tote dat barge! Lift dat veil!", referring of course, to a woman's veil. The film also contains a reference to *Show Boat*'s Gaylord Ravenal, by including a Mississippi riverboat sequence in which Mitty (Kaye) imagines himself as riverboat gambler Gaylord Mitty.
- In a politically incorrect Daffy Duck cartoon, Daffy suddenly appears as an old black slave, and in dialect, speaks the line "Tote dat barge! Lift dat bale!".
- In a Snagglepuss cartoon, Snagglepuss also says the line for no real reason (but not in dialect).
- In the *Family Guy* episode "Brian Goes Back to College", Ashlee Simpson is about to start miming a song when the song changes to "Ol' Man River".

- Singer Patti LuPone sang this song in her concert *Coulda, Woulda, Shoulda* stating "There were only two things standing between me and this role".
- In the *Futurama* episode "Fear of a Bot Planet", Bender complains about the amount of work he has to do, saying "Yes Miss Leela, no Miss Leela, tote that space barge, lift that space pail."
- In an episode of The Golden Girls, it is revealed that Dorothy (Bea Arthur) sang this song in high school. When prompted, she delivers the famous half-octave drop on the line, "Get a little drunk, and you land in jail".
- Tunis born and usually German language Singer Roberto Blanco sang it on the 70th anniversary of his birthday live on TV.
- On an episode of Martin entitled "Dead Men Don't Flush", the cast sings Ol' Man River around the supposedly dead plumber's body as he sits on the couch.
- In the first episode of *Boys from the Blackstuff*, Loggo (Alan Igbon) is seen walking down the street wearing fishing gear singing a few lines from the song.
- *Mad* Magazine published a parody about Hollywood movie stars and MGM studio boss Louis B. Mayer who went to great lengths to "collect more stars than the heavens".
- On an episode on the second season of the BBC sitcom *Grace & Favour*, Miss Brahms (Wendy Richard) and Mr. Humphries (John Inman) sing a version of the song while planting potatoes, featuring the lyrics *"Planting taters/Bake my bottom/And poor old Rumbold/Is soon forgotten/He just keeps plantin'/He just keeps plantin' along"*.
- Heath Ledger had the song title tatooed on his arm.[8]
- In the 76th Academy Awards, Billy Crystal sang a parody of "Ol' Man River" about *Mystic River* and its director, Clint Eastwood.
- During Michael Jordan's brief return to professional basketball playing for the Washington Wizards, the political satire group The Capitol Steps released a parody called "Old Man Wizard".
- In the movie Joe Versus The Volcano an edited version of Ray Charles's version of "Ol' Man River" plays while he hugs a Great Dane.
- In Leonard Bernstein's musical West Side Story, the character of Anybodys remarks "Whatta bunch of ol' man rivers; they don't know nothin', and they don't say nothin'."

External links

- 1927 lyrics to Ol' Man River [9]
- Ol' Man River in Hebrew [10]

Further reading

- The chapter "Ol' Man River" in the book *Stardust Memories: The Biography of Twelve of America's Most Popular Songs* by Will Friedwald (New York: Pantheon Books, 2002).

References

[1] http://www.ibdb.com/production.php?id=10538

[2] Amazon.com: Broadway: The American Musical: Books: Michael Kantor and Laurence Maslon (http://www.amazon.com/dp/0821229052)

[3] "Lesson: Ol' Man River" (school lesson for Mississippi River), Michael E. Marrapodi, New Covenant Christian School, Ashland, Massachusetts, 2006, webpage: MassGeo-River (http://www.massgeo.org/river.htm): shows phrase "feared of dyin' " (rather than "skeered" of dying) as sung in earlier recordings.

[4] http://www.imdb.com/title/tt0078526/

[5] http://www.imdb.com/title/tt0201928/

[6] http://www.amazon.com/Paul-Robeson-Phillip-H-Dean/dp/0822215152/ref=sr_1_20?ie=UTF8&s=books&qid=1273007935&sr=1-20
[7] http://www.otr.net/
[8] From Rolling Stone, March 23, 2006: "One day, his girlfriend, Michelle Williams, wrote a song title -- "Old Man River" -- on his forearm. Ledger got a tattoo artist to run the needles over her words, the way a shopkeeper will frame his first dollar. The song comes from a sad musical, and contains this key advice: "He must know somethin', but he don't say nothin'."
[9] http://lyricsplayground.com/alpha/songs/o/olmanriver.shtml
[10] http://zemer.co.il/song.asp?id=1655

Old Folks at Home

"Old Folks at Home", known also by the words of its first line, **"(Way Down Upon the) Swanee River"**, is a song written in 1851 by composer Stephen Foster, to be performed by the New York performing troupe Christy's Minstrels. The name of E. P. Christy, the troupe's leader, appears on early printings of the music as the song's creator, as shown in the illustration: Christy had paid Foster to be credited, something Foster himself had suggested though later regretted. It has been the official state song of Florida since 1935.[1]

"Old Folks at Home" as sung by Christy's Minstrels in 1851.

According to legend[1] , Foster had most of the lyrics but was trying to give a name to the river of the opening line and asked his brother to suggest one. The first suggestion was "the Yazoo" of Mississippi, which, despite fitting the melody perfectly, Foster rejected. The second suggestion was "the Pee Dee" of the Carolinas, to which Foster said, "Oh pshaw! I won't have that." His brother then consulted an atlas and called out "Suwannee!". Foster wrote it immediately in (misspelling it "Swanee" to fit the melody[2]), saying "That's it exactly!". Foster himself never saw the Suwannee or even visited Florida, but the popularity of the song initiated tourism to Florida to see the river.

Controversy

This song is claimed by some as being racist toward black Americans for its imitation of Black English Vernacular (the song is sung from the perspective of a black man), with its original lyrics referring to "darkies" and "a-longin' for the old plantation."[1] Foster himself supported the North during the American Civil War and sympathized with

African-Americans. In 1997, former state representative Willy Logan presented an unsuccessful motion to have the song replaced. For many public performances, words like "lordy," "mama," "darling," "brothers" or "dear ones" are often used in place of "darkies."

1904 postcard

As the official state song of Florida, it had become a tradition for the tune to be performed as part of the inauguration ceremony for incoming Florida governors. However, Charlie Crist decided not to include it in his 2007 inauguration ceremony. In its place, Crist decided upon "The Florida Song," a composition written by Charles Atkins, an African-American jazz musician born in Daytona Beach and who now lives in Tallahassee.

In May 2007, the Florida Music Educators Association began working in partnership with Senator Tony Hill and Representative Ed Homan to present an initiative in which all of Florida's citizens were invited to submit their entries for a new state song. From the press release: "The process officially begins Tuesday (May 15) for Florida's musicians to submit their entries for "Just Sing, Florida!", the search for a new state song." The Florida Music Educators' Association (FMEA) created a new web site, http://justsingflorida.org/, which contained rules and submission guidelines. On January 11, 2008, the song Florida (Where the Sawgrass Meets the Sky) [3] was selected as the winner and will be brought up before the state legislature as a possible replacement for "Old Folks At Home." [4]

Most authorities trace the success of "Old Folks at Home" to the same qualities shared by most of Foster's other well-known compositions: a memorable melody.

Lyrics

[5] Although this song may sometimes be performed with "modern" lyrics that some claim to be more sensitive racially, the song's original lyrics, included here, had been adopted officially as the lyrics of Florida's state song.[2] In 2008, the Florida Legislature adopted a version of the lyrics that has been revised by the Center for American Music at the University of Pittsburgh.[6]

Sheet music version

1st verse

Way down upon de Swanee ribber (river)
Far, far away,
Dere's wha my heart is turning ebber,
Dere's wha de old folks stay.
All up and down de whole creation
Sadly I roam,
Still longing for de old plantation
And for de old folks at home.

> **Chorus**
>
> All de world am sad and dreary,
> Ebry where I roam,
> Oh! darkies how my heart grows weary,
> Far from de old folks at home.

2nd verse

All round de little farm I wandered
When I was young,
Den many happy days I squandered,
Many de songs I sung.

When I was playing wid my brudder
Happy was I
Oh! take me to my kind old mudder,
Dere let me live and die.

Chorus

3rd verse

One little hut amond de bushes,
One dat I love,
Still sadly to my mem'ry rushes,
No matter where I rove
When will I see de bees a humming
All round de comb?
When will I hear de banjo tumming
Down in my good old home?

Popular culture

- Dvorak's Humoresque Number 7, written in the 1890s, is musically similar and is sometimes played along with "Old Folks at Home".
- The song is mentioned in Irving Berlin's "Alexander's Ragtime Band" (1911) in the line, "If you want to hear the 'Swanee River' played in ragtime" and featured in 1936's *Mr. Deeds Goes to Town*. Gershwin's "Swanee" (1919) is a takeoff on the Foster song, and even contains the line, "I love the old folks at home." The song was recorded by boogie woogie pianist Albert Ammons as "Swanee River Boogie" and by Ray Charles as "Swanee River Rock." Under the title "Swanee River," the song was recorded by Tony Sheridan in the early 1960s and is sometimes erroneously listed as an early recording by The Beatles due to their association with Sheridan at that time. The melody was used by The Beach Boys on their 1963 album Surfer Girl, for the song "South Bay Surfers", although there is no writing credit listed for anyone other than band members. The band also covered the song by connecting it with Old Man River; it can be found as a bonus song on their "Friends/20/20" double-LP.
- Science fiction writer John Wyndham's story *Pillar to Post* features a 20th century American marooned in the far future, who reminisces, "And the music which conjured a whole world from the aged dust? No, it was not a Beethoven symphony, nor a Mozart concerto; it was, I confess, 'The Old Folks at Home'...". The song is also a trivia question in an episode of *The Honeymooners* and is among the songs featured in an episode of *I Love Lucy*.[7]. The character Ed Norton of the Honeymooners must always play the first few bars of the song (much to Ralph Kramdens dismay) on piano before jumping into the song he actually intends to play.
- The song is referenced in the 1935 Rodgers and Hart musical, *Mississippi*. W. C. Fields asks a piano player what song he's playing. It is "Swanee River", which is "brand new" in the time the film is set. Fields disparages the song, saying its tune is unmemorable. He then finds himself singing the song as he walks away.
- Django Reinhardt recorded a version called Swanee River.
- Swanee River is also the name of an Irish rock group situated in Derry.
- In the Flintstones episode *The Flinstone Canaries*, the song was called *Stoney River*. Barney and Fred sing the chorus for an audition to land a spot on the musical TV series "Hum Along With Herman".
- In the Honeymooners episode *$99,000 Answer*, Ed Norton plays the song on his piano as a warmup before each song he plays for his friend Ralph Kramden to try to guess correctly in preparation for his appearance on a television quiz show.

- A remixed dance version of this song was included in the game *Dance Dance Revolution Mario Mix* for the Nintendo Gamecube called "Frozen Pipes".
- David Cross performs a piece of this song as Tobias Funke with his leather-daddy quartet in the ninth episode of Arrested Development, titled Storming the Castle.
- The Tuna Helpers recorded a version on their first album *Starring In... The Suspicious Fish*. It is a semi hidden track—it says "All songs by The Tuna Helpers except Old Folks at Home", but it is omitted from the track listing (it is track eight). Although the band acknowledges that they did not write the song, Foster's name is not listed in the album credits, a new surrealistic interlude with Easter imagery is the only portion of the lyrics included on the band's website.[8] Lead singer Adrienne Sneed continues to perform the song in her solo show after the band broke up.
- A reference is made by the character Roy Pitt to his wife April in Terrence McNally's play *Bad Habits*.
- Chuck Berry's rock adaptation of the song is on his 1975 self-titled Chess Records album.
- Bill Chase recorded a rock version of this song entitled "Swanee River" with his band on the album Ennea released in 1972. The song is credited as Stephen Foster/Bill Chase.
- On the 1951 Tom and Jerry cartoon entitled *Casanova Cat*, there is a scene where Tom blackens Jerry's face with cigar smoke and puts Jerry on a plate to dance while a musical rendition of "Old Folks at Home" plays in the background (it has to be noted that this scene has been deleted from this short on most TV broadcasts in the United States, but is reinstated in the VHS and DVD versions).
- During the third period of every men's hockey game, the Cornell Big Red Pep Band's tuba section plays a version of this song behind the opponents' bench, while the Lynah Faithful sing along with "Hey (opponent's school), die, drop dead, go home('you suck' if at an away game)!"[9]

This song also used to be printed on the red and white boxes used by Kentucky Fried Chicken back in the early 1960's before the company changed their image and also their name to "KFC".

External links

- Closeup of Foster's notebook page with first draft of "Old Folks at Home", including substitution of "Pedee" with "Swannee" [10]
- Old Folks at Home, from the Center for American Music, home of the Foster Hall Collection [11]
- New York Times article on Foster mentioning "Old Folks at Home" [12]
- www.negrophile.com article [13] on lyrics, alternate state songs
- Recording of "Old Folks at Home" at the 1955 Florida Folk Festival; made available for public use by the State Archives of Florida [14]
- Alternate recording by The 97th Regimental String Band [15]

References

[1] Center for American Music. "Old Folks at Home" (http://www.pitt.edu/~amerimus/ofah.htm). *Center for American Music Library*. . Retrieved 2007-04-29.
[2] "Florida State Song The Swanee River" (http://www.netstate.com/states/symb/song/fl_swanee_river.htm). *Netstate*. . Retrieved 2007-04-29.
[3] http://www.janhintonmusic.com/floridasongs.html
[4] "Lauderdale teacher wins state song vote" (http://www.miamiherald.com/news/breaking_news/story/375900.html). .
[5] source: Christy, E. P. [sic]. *Old folks at home : Ethiopian melody as sung by Christy's Minstrels.* New York : Firth, Pond & Co., [date obscured].
[6] *Florida Statutes* Section 15.0327
[7] http://www.amazon.ca/dp/product-description/B0007TKHF2
[8] The Words (http://www.thetunahelpers.org/words.html)
[9] "Cornell Hockey Chant" (http://www.youtube.com/watch?v=UGTRqfrY-h4). YouTube. . Retrieved 2009-12-18.
[10] http://images.library.pitt.edu/cgi-bin/i/image/getimage-idx?view=image;entryid=x-0000007v;viewid=0000007V.TIF;cc=sketchbook;c=sketchbook;quality=1
[11] http://www.pitt.edu/~amerimus/ofah.htm
[12] http://query.nytimes.com/gst/fullpage.html?res=9902E1DE1530F931A25752C0A9629C8B63&sec=&spon=&pagewanted=all
[13] http://www.negrophile.com/phile/articles/came_to_appreciate_the_wandering_brown_river_that_he_immortalized.html
[14] http://www.floridamemory.com/Collections/folklife/sound_folk.cfm
[15] http://www.iath.virginia.edu/utc/minstrel/oldfolksf.html

Only with You

"Only with You"	
Single by The Beach Boys	
from the album *Holland*	
Released	January 29, 1973 March 10, 1975
Format	Vinyl
Recorded	Unknown
Genre	Pop ballad and classic rock
Length	2:59
Label	Brother/Reprise
Writer(s)	Dennis Wilson, Mike Love
Producer	Dennis Wilson, Carl Wilson

The Beach Boys singles chronology

"Marcella"/"Hold On Dear Brother" (1972)	"Sail On, Sailor"/"**Only with You**" (1973)	"California Saga: California"/"Funky Pretty" (1973)
----	----	----
"Child of Winter"/"Susie Cincinnati" (1974)	"Sail On, Sailor"/"**Only with You**" (1975)	"Rock and Roll Music"/"The TM Song" (1976)

"**Only with You**" is a song written by Dennis Wilson and Mike Love for the American pop band The Beach Boys. It was released on their 1973 album *Holland*. A solo version was also recorded by Dennis Wilson during the sessions for his *Pacific Ocean Blue* album and released on the 2008 re-issue.

Performers

- Carl Wilson: Lead vocals

See also

- The Beach Boys
- Holland (album)
- List of The Beach Boys songs

Our Favorite Recording Sessions

"Our Favorite Recording Sessions" is a track on the American pop band The Beach Boys 1964 album *All Summer Long*. The track features all the group members engaging in studio banter (including the songs All Summer Long and Do You Remember?). Recording engineer Chuck Britz also briefly appears.

Details

- *Written by:* Brian Wilson/Dennis Wilson/Carl Wilson/Mike Love/Al Jardine
- *Album:* All Summer Long
- *Time:* 1 min 59 sec
- *Produced by:* Brian Wilson

See also

- The Beach Boys
- All Summer Long
- List of songs by The Beach Boys

Our Prayer

Clear vinyl release of "Our Prayer" remix.

"**Our Prayer**" is a song written by Brian Wilson for the American pop band The Beach Boys. It was released on their 1969 album *20/20* and was produced by The Beach Boys. The main vocals were recorded on October 4, 1966 with the additional vocals being recorded at Capitol Records Studios in Fall, 1968. The wordless, a cappella piece was originally supposed to be the opening track on the never-released *Smile* album. As Peter Reum explains "Brian intended for 'Our Prayer' to be the opening track, a spiritual invocation, for *Smile*."

Brian once said, "I was sitting at my piano thinkin' about holy music. I poked around for some simple but moving chords. Later I sat down and wrote 'Our Prayer' in sections. The boys were overtaken by the arrangement. I taught it to them in sections, the way I usually do. The purity of the blending of the voices made the listeners feel spiritual. I was definitely into rock church music."

An All-Star Tribute to Brian Wilson (2001) began with this song. The Boys' Choir of Harlem had performed "Our Prayer" at a live Radio City Music Hall concert on July 4, 2001.

The song was re-recorded and released on Brian Wilson's 2004 solo release of *Smile* although obviously without the other Beach Boys members.

See also

- The Beach Boys
- 20/20 (album)
- List of songs by The Beach Boys

Our Sweet Love

"Our Sweet Love"	
Song by The Beach Boys from the album *Sunflower*	
Released	August 31, 1970
Recorded	January 26, 1970
Genre	Pop
Length	2:38
Label	Brother Records/Reprise Records
Composer	Brian Wilson/Carl Wilson/Al Jardine
Producer	The Beach Boys
***Sunflower* track listing**	
"Forever" (9)	**"Our Sweet Love"** (10) · "At My Window" (11)

"Our Sweet Love" is a song written by Brian Wilson, Carl Wilson and Al Jardine for the American pop band The Beach Boys. It was released on their 1970 album *Sunflower*.

Details

- *Written by:* Brian Wilson/Carl Wilson/Al Jardine
- *Album:* Sunflower
- *Time:* 2:38
- *Produced by:* The Beach Boys

Performers

- *Carl Wilson:* Lead Vocals

See also

- The Beach Boys
- Sunflower
- List of songs by The Beach Boys

Our Team

"Our Team" is a song written by Brian Wilson, Carl Wilson, Dennis Wilson, Mike Love and Al Jardine for the American pop band The Beach Boys. The song was released on the band's 1993 box set *Good Vibrations: Thirty Years of The Beach Boys*.

See also

- List of songs by The Beach Boys

Palisades Park

"**Palisades Park**" is a song written by Chuck Barris and recorded by Freddy Cannon.

The original hit recording by Freddy Cannon

A tribute to New Jersey's Palisades Amusement Park, the song is an up-tempo tune led by a distinctive organ part. It also incorporates amusement park sound effects.

Released by Swan Records as a B-side to "June, July and August", "Palisades Park" broke in when a Flint, Michigan radio DJ played it by mistake. It peaked at #3 on the Billboard Hot 100 on 12 March 1962, the biggest hit of Cannon's career.[1]

It was covered by Shelley Fabares on her 1962 album *The Things We Did Last Summer*, Gary Lewis And The Playboys on their 1965 album *A Session With Gary Lewis And the Playboys*, The Beach Boys on their 1976 album *15 Big Ones*, and The Ramones on their 1989 album *Brain Drain*. It was also used as the stage introduction music for Bruce Springsteen and The E Street Band's Tunnel of Love Express Tour in 1988.

Cannon recorded "Kennywood Park" (which, unlike Palisades Park before it, is still in operation) in the mid-1980s, a reworking of the song about the Pittsburgh amusement park of the same name. It was issued as a limited edition 45 vinyl single and considered a collector's item.

Beach Boys version

Details

- *Album:* 15 Big Ones
- *Time:* 2:27
- *Produced by:* Brian Wilson
- *Arranged by:* Brian Wilson

Performers

- Ben Benay - guitar
- Hal Blaine - drums
- Jerry Cole - guitar
- Steve Douglas - saxophone
- Carl Fortina - accordion

- Al Jardine - vocals
- Plas Johnson - saxophone
- John J. Kelson Jr. - saxophone
- Mike Love - vocals
- Ray Pohlman - bass guitar
- Lyle Ritz - upright bass
- Julius Wechter - percussion
- Brian Wilson - piano, organ, vocals
- Carl Wilson - synthesizer, lead vocal

References

[1] Palisades Park - Mr. Freddy "BOOM BOOM" Cannon (http://www0.epinions.com/content_3383337092) Epinions.com Accessed 28 October 2008

Papa-Oom-Mow-Mow

"Papa-Oom-Mow-Mow"	
Original 45 rpm disc	
Single by The Rivingtons	
from the album *Doin' the Bird*	
B-side	Deep Water
Released	1962
Format	7" record
Genre	Novelty song, doo-wop
Length	02:17
Label	Liberty
Writer(s)	Carl White, Al Frazier, Sonny Harris, Turner Wilson Jr.
Producer	Adam Ross

"Papa-Oom-Mow-Mow"	
Song by The Rivingtons from the album *Doin' The Bird*	
Released	1962
Genre	Novelty song, Doo-Wop
Label	Liberty
Writer	Carl White, Al Frazier, Sonny Harris, Turner Wilson Jr.
***Doin' The Bird* track listing**	
• **Papa-Oom-Mow-Mow** • Love Pill • Long Tall Sally • Unchain My Heart • You Are My Sunshine • Happy Jack • Mama-Oom-Mow-Mow (The Bird) • Kickapoo Joy Juice • Slippin' and Slidin' • Old Time Love • Have Mercy, Mercy Baby • Standing in the Love Line	

"Papa-Oom-Mow-Mow"	
Song by The Beach Boys from the album *Beach Boys' Party!*	
Released	8 November 1965
Genre	Doo-Wop
Length	2:18
Label	Capitol
Composer	Carl White/Al Frazier/Sonny Harris/Turner Wilson Jr.
Producer	Brian Wilson
***Beach Boys' Party!* track listing**	
• "Hully Gully" • "I Should Have Known Better" • "Tell Me Why" • "Papa-Oom-Mow-Mow" • "Mountain of Love" • "You've Got to Hide Your Love Away" • "Devoted to You" • "Alley Oop" • "There's No Other (Like My Baby)" • "Medley:I Get Around/Little Deuce Coupe" • "The Times They Are a-Changin'" • "Barbara Ann"	

"**Papa-Oom-Mow-Mow**" is a 1962 novelty nonsensical doo-wop song by The Rivingtons. The song peaked at #48 on the Billboard Hot 100 [1] and #35 on the Cashbox charts.[2]

Cover versions

The song was later covered by The Beach Boys for their first live album, *Beach Boys Concert*, in 1964 -- this track entering the Philippines top 10 February 26th 1966 according to Billboard -- and, again sung by Brian Wilson, on their album *Beach Boys' Party!* in 1965.

In 1967, The Freshmen scored a Top 10 hit with the song in Ireland. Versions by both The Sharonettes and Gary Glitter made the UK Top 40 in 1975.

It was also covered in 1966 by The Thunderbirds, a Hong-Kong band headed by the brother of martial-arts star Bruce Lee, Robert Lee.

Garage rock band, Nobunny adds the songs lyrics at the end of "I am a girlfriend".

Other appearances of the song's lyrics

Together with The Rivingtons' 1963 novelty song, "Bird is the Word", "**Papa-Oom-Mow-Mow**" was the basis for the song "Surfin' Bird" by The Trashmen. Notably, a cover version of *Papa-Oom-Mow-Mow* by The Persuasions was briefly heard in the film *E.T. the Extra-Terrestrial*.

In 1964, surf rockers Jan and Dean morphed the song into "New Girl in School," with new lyrics and the refrain "Doo-ron-de-ron-de" substituted for "Papa-Oom-Mow-Mow". "New Girl in School" garnered significant U.S. airplay as the B-side of the Top 40 hit Dead Man's Curve.

In 1969 the song's distinctive titular nonsense lyrics appeared as a similarly-sung chorus in Giorgio Moroder's first single *Looky Looky* and The Oak Ridge Boys' 1981 hit *Elvira* has an "oom-papa-mow-mow" chorus, an element that existed in songwriter Dallas Frazier's 1967 original version of the song. (It should be noted that an Al Frazier was a member of The Rivingtons and is listed as a co-author of "Papa Oom Now Now." It has been erroneously reported over the years that he and Dallas Frazier were the same person.)

External links

- The Rivingtons [3] at Last.fm, featuring the songs *Papa-Oom-Mow-Mow* and *The Bird's the Word*

References

[1] *Top Pop Singles 1955-2002* by Joel Whitburn, Record Research Publications, Menomonee Falls, WI - ISBN 0898201551

[2] *Cashbox Pop Singles Charts 1950-1993* by Pat Downey, George Albert, and Frank Hoffmann, Libraries Unlimited, Englewood, CO - ISBN 1563083167

[3] http://www.last.fm/music/The+Rivingtons

Passing By

"Passing By" is a song written by Brian Wilson for the American pop band The Beach Boys. It was released on their 1968 album *Friends*. This song is a instrumental music, jazz rock and pop music with vocals.

Details

- *Written by:* Brian Wilson
- *Album:* Friends
- *Time:* 2 min 23 sec
- *Produced by:* The Beach Boys

Performers

- *Brian Wilson:* Lead Vocals
- *Carl Wilson:* Lead Vocals
- *Al Jardine:* Lead Vocals

See also

- List of songs by The Beach Boys

Passing Friend

"Passing Friend" is a song written by Boy George and Roy Hay, and recorded by the American pop band The Beach Boys. It was released on their 1985 album *The Beach Boys* with Carl Wilson singing lead vocals.

It was also released as a single in UK only.

Details

- *Written by:* George O'Dowd/Roy Hay
- *Album: The Beach Boys*
- *Time:* 4:59
- *Produced by:* Steve Levine

Musicians

- Steve Grainger - tenor saxophone
- Roy Hay - all other instruments
- Steve Levine - synthesizer, drum programming
- Al Jardine - vocals
- Bruce Johnston - vocals
- Mike Love - vocals
- Brian Wilson - vocals
- Carl Wilson - lead vocal

See also

- The Beach Boys
- The Beach Boys (album)
- List of songs by The Beach Boys

Peggy Sue

"Peggy Sue"	
Single by Buddy Holly and The Crickets	
from the album *Buddy Holly*	
B-side	"Everyday"
Released	September 20, 1957 November 15 1957 (UK)
Format	7" single
Recorded	June 29 and July 1, 1957, Clovis, New Mexico
Genre	Rock and Roll
Length	2:29
Label	Coral 61885
Writer(s)	Buddy Holly, Jerry Allison, Norman Petty
Buddy Holly and The Crickets singles chronology	
"Rock Around with Ollie Vee" (1957)	"Peggy Sue" (1957) · "Oh, Boy!" (1957)

"Peggy Sue" is a rock and roll song written by Buddy Holly, Jerry Allison, and Norman Petty, and originally performed, recorded and released as a single by Buddy Holly and the Crickets in early July of 1957. The song was also released on Buddy Holly's self-titled 1958 album. The song is ranked #194 on the *Rolling Stone* magazine's list of The 500 Greatest Songs of All Time.

The song was originally called "Cindy Lou", and was named for Buddy's niece, the daughter of his sister Pat Holley Kaiter. The title was later changed to "Peggy Sue" in reference to Crickets drummer Jerry Allison's girlfriend (and future wife), Peggy Sue Gerron, with whom he had recently had a temporary breakup.[1]

Appropriately, Allison played a prominent role in the production of the song, playing paradiddles on the drums throughout the song, the drums' sound rhythmically fading in and out as a result of real-time engineering techniques by the producer, Norm Petty. Many music critics regard this as Holly's all-time best recording.

The song went to #3 on the Billboard Hot 100 in 1957. The modal frame of the song is axial around the tonic, A:

The song is currently ranked as the 100th greatest song of all time, as well as the third best song of 1957, by Acclaimed Music.[2]

Sequel

Holly wrote a poignant sequel called "Peggy Sue Got Married", and recorded a demo or practice version in his New York City apartment on December 5, 1958, accompanied only by himself on guitar. The tape was discovered after his untimely death, and was "enhanced" for commercial release, by adding background vocals and an electric guitar track that drowned out Holly's own playing (and almost his voice as well). The rarely-heard original version was released on a vinyl collection called "The Complete Buddy Holly", and was later used over the opening credits of the 1986 Kathleen Turner film *Peggy Sue Got Married*.[3] After Holly's death The Crickets would also release their own cover single in 1960. They followed the original Peggy Sue arrangements with the only difference being David Box a Buddy Holly soundalike singing as the lead vocalist.[4]

Legacy

"Peggy Sue" vocal melody

- The Beatles were admirers of Holly and the Crickets. In addition to their straightforward remake of Holly's song "Words of Love", some analysts (Jonathan Cott, page 81), have suggested that one of their early songs, "P.S. I Love You", is a subtle reference to this song. Later, John Lennon would cover the song on his *Rock 'n' Roll* album in 1975.
- In his song "Old", Paul Simon indicates his age by singing "First time I heard Peggy Sue/I was 12 years old./Russians up in rocket ships /and the war was Cold."
- Julian Cope's 1991 album was called *Peggy Suicide*.
- In an episode of *Quantum Leap* ("How the Tess was won"), young Buddy Holly, working as a Texas farm boy, invents the song as a homage to a piglet, calling it *Piggy Sooey*. Sam Beckett suggests he calls it *Peggy Sue* instead and, after hearing this, he realizes that the teen, who he named "buddy", was in fact Buddy Holly.
- In blink-182's album *Cheshire Cat*, one of the songs is named "Peggy Sue". The song is also featured on a live album entitled "The Mark, Tom, and Travis Show: The Enema Strikes Back".
- In Myslovitz's album *Miłość w czasach popkultury*, one of the songs is named "Peggy Sue nie wyszła za mąż" (Peggy Sue did not get married).
- In *Almost Famous*, the lead guitarist of the fictional band Stillwater, Russell Hammond, begins to sing this song as the plane he and his bandmates are flying in encounters severe turbulence, a reference to Buddy Holly's own death in a plane crash.
- In 2004, the Norwegian band Trashcan Darlings released "Peggy Sue is Dead" on the "Tunes From The Trashcan EP".
- In a *Jimmy Neutron* episode, the Chinese princess is called Peggy Sue and Sheen is heard saying "Pretty, pretty pretty Peggy Sue"
- In Quentin Tarantino's *Pulp Fiction*, the waiter Buddy Holly is calling Mia Wallace as Peggy Sue, when taking her order in Jack Rabbit Slim's, a 1950s-themed restaurant staffed by lookalikes of the decade's pop icons.
- In the alternate history novel *Back in the USSA*, Peggy Sue is the name of a girl the young Holly knows and is attracted to.
- In the *Wild Cards* novels (another alternate history series), the song retains its original name, "Cindy Lou". In the fifth *Wild Cards* novel, *Down and Dirty*, it is explained that in this version of history, Jerry Allison's breakup with Peggy Sue Gerron was permanent, and thus the song's name was never changed.
- In his song "Saputnik", serbian singer Đorđe Balašević called his old highschool love Peggy Sue, even if he didn't saw her for fifteen years.
- The song is referenced in the Family Guy episode "Ocean's Three and a Half".
- The song is also referenced in a New Zealand children's songwriter named the Minstrel's song; "From Rock, to Roll to Rocket", in the line "Buddy Holly sang Peggy Sue".

Covers

- John Lennon covered the song on his 1975 album *Rock 'n' Roll* Rock 'n' Roll (John Lennon album)
- Country singer Billy "Crash" Craddock covered the song in 1973 on his album Mr. Country Rock.
- The Beach Boys covered the song on their 1978 "M.I.U. Album". The song was also a hit for them, charting at #59 in the United States.
- Tom Petty and the Heartbreakers have covered the song numerous times in concert.

References

[1] Amburn, p78
[2] "Acclaimed Music Top 3000 songs" (http://www.acclaimedmusic.net). 27 May 2009. .
[3] http://www.imdb.com/title/tt0091738/soundtrack
[4] http://www.buddyhollyonline.com/related/dbox.html

Literature

- Amburn, Ellis (1995). *Buddy Holly: a Biography*. St. Martins Press. ISBN 0-312-14557-8
- Jonathan Cott in *The Rolling Stone Illustrated History of Rock and Roll*. Rolling Stone Press Random House. (1976) ISBN 0-394-73238-3

External links

- http://www.pmoorcroft.freeserve.co.uk/disco.htm Discography
- List of Holly "covered" songs, including this one (http://home.online.no/~smpeders/ind-bud2.htm)
- BBC interview with Peggy Sue Gerron (http://news.bbc.co.uk/2/hi/uk_news/magazine/7861891.stm)

Pet Sounds

"Pet Sounds"	
Instrumental by The Beach Boys from the album *Pet Sounds*	
Released	May 16, 1966
Recorded	Western Studios November 17, 1965
Genre	Instrumental music, Pop
Length	2:20
Label	Capitol
Composer	Wilson
Producer	Brian Wilson
***Pet Sounds* track listing**	
• "Wouldn't It Be Nice" • "You Still Believe in Me" • "That's Not Me" • "Don't Talk (Put Your Head on My Shoulder)" • "I'm Waiting for the Day" • "Let's Go Away for Awhile" • "Sloop John B" • "God Only Knows" • "I Know There's an Answer" • "Here Today" • "I Just Wasn't Made for These Times" • "Pet Sounds" • "Caroline, No"	
Music sample	
Pet Sounds	

"**Pet Sounds**" is an instrumental composed and produced by Brian Wilson and is the twelfth track on the 1966 album *Pet Sounds* by the American pop band The Beach Boys. It was performed by Brian and several session musicians, with no other members of the Beach Boys.

Originally called "Run James Run", Brian intended it to be used as the theme of a James Bond movie.[1]

Pet Sounds was recorded on November 17, 1965 at Western Studios, with Chuck Britz engineering.[2]

Musicians

- Roy Caton - trumpet
- Jerry Cole - guitar
- Ritchie Frost - drums, percussion
- Bill Green - tenor saxophone, percussion
- Jim Horn - tenor saxophone
- Plas Johnson - tenor saxophone, percussion
- Carol Kaye - bass guitar
- Jay Migliori - baritone saxophone
- Lyle Ritz - upright bass
- Billy Strange - guitar
- Tommy Tedesco - guitar
- Brian Wilson - piano[3]

See also

- List of songs by The Beach Boys

References

[1] Lambert, Philip: *Inside the Music of Brian Wilson*, page 232. Continuum Publishing, 2007.
[2] Doe, Andrew G.: " GIGS65 (http://www.btinternet.com/~bellagio/gigs65.html)." Bellagio 10452 (http://www.btinternet.com/~bellagio/). Retrieved on 2009-10-11.
[3] "Sessionography". In *Pet Sounds: 40th Anniversary Edition* [CD booklet]. Los Angeles: Capitol Records

Pitter Patter

"Pitter Patter" is a song written by Brian Wilson, Mike Love and Al Jardine for the American pop band The Beach Boys. It was released on their 1978 album *M.I.U. Album*.

Details

- *Written by:* Brian Wilson/Mike Love/Al Jardine
- *Album:* M.I.U. Album
- *Time:* 3 min 14 sec
- *Produced by:* Al Jardine/Ron Altbach

Performers

- *Mike Love:* Lead Vocals
- *Al Jardine:* Lead Vocals

See also

- The Beach Boys
- M.I.U. Album
- List of songs by The Beach Boys

Please Let Me Wonder

"Please Let Me Wonder"	
Single by The Beach Boys	
from the album *The Beach Boys Today!*	
Released	February 8, 1965
Format	Vinyl
Recorded	January 7 & January 9, 1965
Genre	Sunshine pop/Pop
Length	2:45
Label	Capitol
Producer	Brian Wilson
The Beach Boys singles chronology	

"The Man with All the Toys"/"Blue Christmas" (1964)	"Do You Wanna Dance?"/"**Please Let Me Wonder**" (1965)	"Help Me, Rhonda"/"Kiss Me, Baby" (1965)

"**Please Let Me Wonder**" is a song written by Brian Wilson and Mike Love for American band The Beach Boys. The song was the B-side of the single "Do You Wanna Dance?" which was released by The Beach Boys in 1965 through Capitol Records. The song was first released on the band's 1965 album *The Beach Boys Today!*. As a B-side, it peaked at a number 52 in *Billboard* and number 46 in *Cash Box*. The contemporary Gilbert Youth Survey conducted nationally in April 1965 placed this song at number 9 in its chart one week.

Musicians

- Glen Campbell - guitar
- Steve Douglas - saxophone
- Al Jardine - vocals
- Plas Johnson - saxophone
- Carol Kaye - bass guitar
- Barney Kessel - guitar
- Mike Love - vocals
- Jack Nimitz - saxophone
- Earl Palmer - drums, timbales
- Don Randi - piano, organ

- Billy Lee Riley - harmonica
- Billy Strange - guitar
- Jerry Williams - vibraphone, timpani
- Brian Wilson - lead vocal
- Carl Wilson - vocals
- Dennis Wilson - vocals

Cover versions

- King's Singers
- Tatsuro Yamashita

See also

- List of The Beach Boys songs

External links

- "Please Let Me Wonder" [1] review at Allmusic

References

[1] http://allmusic.com/cg/amg.dll?p=amg&sql=33:difixqrrldke

Pom Pom Play Girl

"Pom Pom Play Girl"	
Song by The Beach Boys from the album *Shut Down Volume 2*	
Released	1964
Recorded	???
Genre	Pop Surf rock
Length	1:30
Label	Capitol Records
Writer	Brian Wilson/Gary Usher
Producer	Brian Wilson
***Shut Down Volume 2* track listing**	
• "Fun, Fun, Fun" • "Don't Worry Baby" • "In the Parkin' Lot" • "Cassius Love vs. Sonny Wilson" • "The Warmth of the Sun" • "This Car of Mine" • "Why Do Fools Fall in Love" • "Pom Pom Play Girl" • "Keep an Eye on Summer" • "Shut Down, Part II" • "Louie Louie" • "Denny's Drums"	

"Pom Pom Play Girl" is a song written by Brian Wilson and Gary Usher for the American pop band The Beach Boys. It was released on their 1964 album *Shut Down Volume 2*.

Performers

- *Carl Wilson:* Lead Vocals
- *Mike Love:* Lead Vocals

See also

- The Beach Boys
- Shut Down Volume 2
- List of songs by The Beach Boys

Punchline

"Punchline" is a song written by Brian Wilson for the American pop band The Beach Boys. The song was released on the band's 1993 box set *Good Vibrations: Thirty Years of The Beach Boys*.

See also

- List of songs by The Beach Boys

Radio King Dom

"Radio King Dom" is the sixth and final track on the Mount Vernon and Fairway (A Fairy Tale) album. It was written by Brian Wilson and Jack Rieley for the American pop band The Beach Boys. The track features Jack Rieley on narration.

Details

- *Written by:* Brian Wilson/Jack Rieley
- *Album:* Mount Vernon and Fairway (A Fairy Tale)
- *Time:* 2 min 38 sec
- *Produced by:* The Beach Boys

See also

- The Beach Boys
- Mount Vernon and Fairway (A Fairy Tale)
- List of songs by The Beach Boys

Remember (Walking in the Sand)

"Remember (Walking in the Sand)"	
Single by The Shangri-Las	
B-side	"It's Easier to Cry"
Released	1964
Format	7" single
Length	2:17
Label	Red Bird
Writer(s)	Shadow Morton
The Shangri-Las singles chronology	
"Remember (Walking in the Sand)" (1964)	"Leader of the Pack" (1964)

"Remember (Walking in the Sand)"		
Single by Aerosmith featuring Mary Weiss		
from the album *Night in the Ruts*		
B-side	"Bone to Bone"	
Released	1980	
Format	7" single	
Recorded	1979	
Length	4:04	
Label	Columbia	
Producer	Jack Douglas	
Aerosmith featuring Mary Weiss singles chronology		
"Chip Away the Stone" (1978)	**"Remember (Walking in the Sand)"** (1980)	"Lightning Strikes" (1982)

"Remember (Walking in the Sand)" is a song written by George "Shadow" Morton and originally recorded in 1964 by The Shangri-Las.

Original recording by The Shangri-Las

Morton was looking to break into the music business, and went to the Brill Building in New York City to see an old girlfriend, Ellie Greenwich, who had become a successful pop songwriter. Morton and Greenwich's writing partner, Jeff Barry, took a dislike to one another. Asked what he did for a living, Morton replied "I write songs", although he had never written one. When Barry asked him what kind, Morton retorted, "Hit songs!" Barry said he would love to hear one of Morton's tunes, and invited him to come back the following week with something.

Morton immediately wrote "Remember (Walking in the Sand)". He hired a teenage group from Queens, the Shangri-Las, to sing on the demo, which Morton produced himself. Barry was impressed and Red Bird Records picked up the song for release and signed Morton and the Shangri-Las to contracts. According to some accounts, the original version was nearly seven minutes long. In order to fit the AM radio format of the time, the song had to be cut in length, but rather than edit it, Morton simply faded it out after 2:10.

The song was released as the debut single on Red Bird Records by The Shangri-Las and became a number five hit on the Billboard Hot 100 and number nine on Cashbox Magazine's R&B chart [1] . It was also hit number fourteen on the UK Singles Chart, and became more successful in the UK when reissued on several occasions in the 1970s. Billy Joel, an unknown working as a session musician at the time, played piano on the original demo recording of the song and has playfully claimed that Morton failed to pay him his $67 union scale fee for the performance.

The Shangri-Las' recording placed #395 on Rolling Stone's 500 Greatest Songs of All Time list in 2004.

Cover versions

In 1965 the song was also covered by the Australian band 'Ray Columbus And The Invaders'

and released on the Australian 'Zodiac' label. As they didn't have access to sound effects of seagulls like the original the guitar player improvised and scraped his guitar pick across the strings to make the sound of seagulls crying.

In 1979, Louise Goffin remade the song. This version also became popular, charting in the top 50 of the Hot 100.

Aerosmith released a more rock version featuring uncredited backing by Mary Weiss of the Shangri-Las as a single in 1980. This charted on the Hot 100 at 67 .

Other artists to release versions include Mouth & MacNeal on the 1972 album *How Do You Do?*, The Nylons, and The Beach Boys on the 1992 album *Summer in Paradise*. The Go-Go's performed the song in their early days and a live version from 1981 is included on their 1994 album *Return to the Valley of the Go-go's*. Hillbilly Moon Explosion covered it on their album Introducing the Hillbilly Moon Explosion.

Little Jackie has covered the song in her live shows.

The Eden House covered this on the CD of their 2010 DVD/CD set 'The Looking Glass'

References

[1] Whitburn, Joel (2004). *Top R&B/Hip-Hop Singles: 1942-2004*. Record Research. p. 520.

Rock 'n' Roll to the Rescue

"Rock 'n' Roll To The Rescue"		
Single by The Beach Boys		
from the album *Made in U.S.A.*		
Released	1986	
Format	Vinyl	
Recorded	Unknown	
Genre	Rock	
Length	3:44	
Label	Capitol	
Writer(s)	Mike Love, Terry Melcher	
Producer	Terry Melcher and Brian Wilson (Uncredited)	
The Beach Boys singles chronology		
"She Believes in Love Again"/"It's Just a Matter of Time" (1985)	**"Rock 'n' Roll to the Rescue"**/"Good Vibrations" (live) (1986)	"California Dreamin'"/"Lady Liberty" (1986)

"Rock 'n' Roll to the Rescue" is a single released by The Beach Boys on June 9, 1986. It was recorded for their 1986 greatest hits compilation *Made in U.S.A.*. The single reached #68 on the U.S. Billboard pop singles chart. Brian Wilson sang most of the lead vocals, with Al Jardine, and Carl Wilson both having some lines. Mike Love and Bruce Johnston did backing vocals. The song has an autobiographical feel to it.

The 12" single of "Rock 'N' Roll to the Rescue" featured an extended remix of the song which has a lot more keyboard, heavier drum beat, and when Brian is singing, the music is basically led by the bass guitar, creating a more pop sounding version of the song, than mainstream rock like the album and 7" version. Also, on the master tapes labels, Brian Wilson is credited as co-producer, even though it doesn't list it on the single nor the album.

See also

- The Beach Boys
- Made in U.S.A.
- List of The Beach Boys songs

Rock and Roll Music

"Rock and Roll Music"	
Single by Chuck Berry	
from the album *One Dozen Berrys*	
B-side	"Blue Feeling"
Released	September 1957
Format	45 rpm, 78 rpm
Genre	Rock and roll
Length	2:30
Label	Chess 1671
Writer(s)	Chuck Berry
Producer	Leonard and Phil Chess
Chuck Berry singles chronology	

"Oh Baby Doll" (1957)	"Rock and Roll Music" (1957)	"Sweet Little Sixteen" (1958)

"Rock and Roll Music"	
Song by The Beatles from the album *Beatles for Sale*	
Released	4 December 1964
Recorded	Abbey Road 18 October 1964
Genre	Rock and roll
Length	2:30
Label	Parlophone
Writer	Chuck Berry
Producer	George Martin
***Beatles for Sale* track listing**	

14 tracks
Side one
1. "No Reply"
2. "I'm a Loser"
3. "Baby's in Black"
4. "Rock and Roll Music"
5. "I'll Follow the Sun"
6. "Mr. Moonlight"
7. "Kansas City/Hey-Hey-Hey-Hey!"
Side two
• "Eight Days a Week"
2. "Words of Love"
3. "Honey Don't"
4. "Every Little Thing"
5. "I Don't Want to Spoil the Party"
6. "What You're Doing"
7. "Everybody's Trying to Be My Baby"

"Rock and Roll Music/TM Song"	

Single by The Beach Boys	
from the album *15 Big Ones*	
Released	24 May 1976
Format	Vinyl
Recorded	Unknown
Genre	Rock music
Length	2:29
Label	Brother/Reprise
Writer(s)	Chuck Berry
Producer	Brian Wilson
The Beach Boys singles chronology	

"Sail On, Sailor"/"Only with You" (1975)	"Rock and Roll Music"/"The TM Song" (1976)	"It's OK"/"Had to Phone Ya" (1976)

"**Rock and Roll Music**" is a song written and originally recorded by Chuck Berry which became a hit single in 1957, reaching #8 in the U.S. chart, and was later covered by many artists, notably The Beatles and The Beach Boys.

The lyrics of the song extoll the virtues of rock and roll in comparison to other musical styles, and express the singer's resolve to dance only to this style of music. Berry's version is ranked number 128 on *Rolling Stone*'s list of the 500 Greatest Songs of All Time.

Berry performed his song on December 16, 1957, on ABC's short-lived variety program, *The Guy Mitchell Show*.

The song has been recorded by a number of other well-known artists, including Humble Pie, Manic Street Preachers, Bill Haley & His Comets, REO Speedwagon, Tenpole Tudor and Australian new wave band Mental As Anything.

The Beatles' version

The Beatles performed the song in many of their early Hamburg shows, and also played it on the BBC show *Pop Go The Beatles*. In late 1964, exhausted from non-stop touring and recording and short of original material, they decided to record several of their old rock and rhythm and blues favorites to fill out their LP release *Beatles for Sale*. Among these was a version of Berry's tune that eventually became as well-known as the original. The lead vocal in The Beatles' version was performed by John Lennon. In contrast to Berry's even-toned rendition, Lennon sang it as loudly and dynamically as his voice would permit. In the USA, it was released on the LP *Beatles '65*.

It also served as the title song to The Beatles' 1976 compilation album, *Rock 'n' Roll Music*.

The Beatles' version of "Rock and Roll Music" was released as a single in some countries, and topped the charts in Norway, The Netherlands (double a-side with "No Reply") and Australia.

Personnel

- John Lennon – vocals, rhythm guitar
- Paul McCartney – bass
- George Harrison – acoustic guitar
- Ringo Starr – drums
- George Martin – piano

Personnel per *The Beatles Bible*[1]

The Beach Boys' version

The Beach Boys' version is notable for the use of backing vocals which repeat the phrase "Rock, roll, rockin' and roll." There is a difference between the LP version and the single version in that the LP version has more synthesizer. Their version reached #5 in the US chart in 1976.

Personnel

- Mike Altschol – saxophone, clarinet
- Ed Carter – guitar
- Steve Douglas – saxophone
- Dennis Dreith – saxophone, clarinet
- Gene Estes – percussion
- Billy Hinsche – guitar
- Al Jardine – vocals
- John J. Kelson, Jr. – saxophone, clarinet
- Mike Love – lead vocal
- Carol Lee Miller – autoharp

- Jack Nimitz – saxophone, clarinet
- Brian Wilson – organ, piano, Moog bass, synthesizer
- Carl Wilson – vocals
- Dennis Wilson – drums, vocals
- Marilyn Wilson – vocals

References

[1] "The Beatles Bible: Rock and Roll Music" (http://www.beatlesbible.com/songs/rock-and-roll-music/). . Retrieved 2009-04-15.

The Rocking Surfer

"The Rocking Surfer" is a traditional song. It was most famously recorded by the American pop band The Beach Boys. It was released as an instrumental on their 1963 album *Surfer Girl*. **"The Rocking Surfer"** was released in Australia as a 'B' side single duing 1964.

Details

- *Written by:* Traditional. Arranged by Brian Wilson
- *Album:* Surfer Girl
- *Time:* 2 min 00 sec
- *Produced by:* Brian Wilson

See also

- The Beach Boys
- Surfer Girl
- List of songs by The Beach Boys

Roll Plymouth Rock

"**Roll Plymouth Rock**" is a song written by Brian Wilson and Van Dyke Parks in 1966 for the unreleased Beach Boys album *Smile*. The song was first released under the title "**Do You Like Worms?**" on *Good Vibrations: Thirty Years of The Beach Boys*, a boxed set which included much of the unreleased *Smile* material. In 2004, Brian Wilson completed *Smile*, with this song, under the title "Roll Plymouth Rock", included as the third track.

Beach Boys recording

"Do You Like Worms?"	
Song by The Beach Boys from the album *Good Vibrations: Thirty Years of The Beach Boys* originally intended for *Smile*	
Released	June 29, 1993
Recorded	Western Studios, October 18, 1966; Columbia Studios, December 21, 1966
Genre	Pop music
Length	4:00
Label	Capitol
Composer	Brian Wilson/Van Dyke Parks
Producer	Brian Wilson
Cover versions	
The Olivia Tremor Control	

In its original version, the song is in the form ABABCB'. The A sections feature a short instrumental section where the melody is carried by the timpani, then the lyrics "Rock, rock, roll, Plymouth Rock roll over" in two part harmony over the bass guitars. The B sections consist of the "Bicycle Rider" theme played on harpsichord. At the end of the song, the B' section, the harpsichord breaks down, only to start up again. The C section has Brian singing fake Hawaiian lyrics over backing vocals by the rest of the band and a sparse backing track.[1]

The instrumental track for the A and C sections of the song were recorded on October 18, 1966 at Western Studios. Brian also recorded some of his vocals at that session.[2] [3] The Beach Boys vocals were recorded at Columbia Studios, on December 21, 1966.[4] [5] The B sections of the song were recorded during sessions for "Heroes and Villains".

musicians

[6]

- Jerry Cole - guitar
- Gene Estes - percussion
- Jim Gordon - drums, conga drums
- Al Jardine - vocals
- Carol Kaye - bass guitar
- Mike Love - vocals
- Van Dyke Parks - unknown
- Lyle Ritz - upright bass
- Brian Wilson - vocals

- Carl Wilson - vocals
- Dennis Wilson - vocals

Brian Wilson version

"Roll Plymouth Rock"		
Song by Brian Wilson from the album *Smile*		
Released	September 28, 2004	
Recorded	Sunset Sound April 2004	
Genre	Pop music	
Length	3:48	
Label	Nonesuch	
Composer	Brian Wilson/Van Dyke Parks	
Producer	Brian Wilson	
***Smile* track listing**		
"Heroes and Villains" (2)	**"Roll Plymouth Rock"** (3)	"Barnyard" (4)

The 2004 Brian Wilson recording of "Roll Plymouth Rock" differs from the original Beach Boys recording in two ways. There are lyrics throughout the song; they were written by Van Dyke Parks in 1966 but never recorded by The Beach Boys.[7] The final sections of the song are not the same. The 2004 recording ends with a vocal siren which leads into the next song on the album, "Barnyard".

musicians

- Scott Bennett - keyboards, vocals
- Nelson Bragg - percussion, vocals
- Staffan Findin - bass trombone
- Jeff Foskett - guitar, ukulele, vocals
- Probyn Gregory - guitar, vocals
- Jim Hines - drums
- Anna Landberg - cello
- Bob Lizik - bass guitar
- Paul Mertons - bass flute
- Taylor Mills - vocals
- Bjorn Samuelsson - trombone
- Markus Sandlund - cello
- Darian Sahanaja - keyboards, vocals
- Nick Walusko - guitar
- Brian Wilson - keyboards, vocals

References

[1] Lambert, Philip: *Inside the Music of Brian Wilson*, page 273. Continuum Publishing, 2007.
[2] Doe, Andrew G.: " GIGS66 (http://www.btinternet.com/~bellagio/gigs66.html)." Bellagio 10452 (http://www.btinternet.com/~bellagio/). Retrieved on 2008-12-12.
[3] Shenk, Lou: " A Smile Primer (http://www.thesmileshop.net/index.php/A_SMiLE_Primer#Do_You_Like_Worms_.28B.Wilson_.E2.80.93_V.D.Parks.29)." The Smile Shop (http://www.thesmileshop.net/index.php/Main_Page). Retrieved on 2008-12-12.
[4] Doe, "GIGS66".
[5] Shenk, "A Smile Primer".
[6] Badman, Keith: *The Beach Boys*, page 152-153. Backbeat Books, 2004.
[7] Lambert, 2007. p. 273

Roller Skating Child

"Roller Skating Child" is a song written by Brian Wilson for the American pop band The Beach Boys. It was released on their 1977 album *Love You*.

Details

- *Written by:* Brian Wilson
- *Album:* Love You
- *Time:* 2 min 17 sec
- *Produced by:* Brian Wilson

Performers

- *Brian Wilson:* Lead Vocals (chorus, on the fadeout)
- *Carl Wilson:* Lead Vocals (chorus)
- *Mike Love:* Lead Vocals (verses)
- *Al Jardine:* Lead Vocals (chorus, bridge)

See also

- The Beach Boys
- Love You (The Beach Boys album)
- List of songs by The Beach Boys

Ruby Baby

"**Ruby Baby**" is a song written by Jerry Leiber and Mike Stoller. It was originally recorded by The Drifters and was a major R&B hit for them in 1956. It later became a number two Billboard Hot 100 hit when Dion released his remake as a single in 1962.

Covers

- It became a number one country hit when released by Billy "Crash" Craddock on the album Rub It In in 1974. It was also released on his 2009 live album *Live -N- Kickin'*.
- The song has been recorded by several other artists, including The Beach Boys. This version was released on the band's 1993 box set *Good Vibrations: Thirty Years of The Beach Boys* as an outtake from the 1965 *Beach Boys' Party!* album. There was also a version recorded for their 1976 "comeback" album, *15 Big Ones* which can be found on various bootlegs of that era.
- A young Miguel Ríos recorded a version on his 5th EP (1963).
- Björk Guðmundsdóttir & Tríó Guðmundar Ingólfssonar
- Ronnie Hawkins and The Hawks
- Del Shannon
- Tony Sheridan
- Donald Fagen, of Steely Dan, also recorded a version on his 1982 solo album, *The Nightfly*.
- Korean singer BoA uses elements of this song in her single, "Rock with You".
- Donald "Buck Dharma" Roeser covered a version of the song called "Rudy" available only on his Archive set of CDs.
- BWB performed an instrumental cover of the song on their album "Groovin'".

Advertising

Apple Inc. used the Dion cover of the song during its ad campaign for the new "Ruby" color of its July 19, 2000, revision of the iMac G3.

Sail On, Sailor

"Sail On, Sailor"	
Single by The Beach Boys	
from the album *Holland*	
B-side	Only with You
Released	January 29, 1973 March 10, 1975
Format	Vinyl
Recorded	Brian Wilson's home studio November 28, 1972
Genre	Pop
Length	3:18
Label	Brother/Reprise
Writer(s)	Brian Wilson, Van Dyke Parks, Tandyn Almer, Ray Kennedy, and Jack Rieley
Producer	Carl Wilson

The Beach Boys singles chronology		
"Marcella"/"Hold On Dear Brother" (1972)	"Sail On, Sailor"/"Only with You" (1973)	"California Saga: California"/"Funky Pretty" (1973)
----	----	----
"Child of Winter/Susie Cincinnati" (1974)	"Sail On, Sailor"/"Only with You" (1975)	"Rock And Roll Music"/"TM Song" (1976)

"Sail On, Sailor" was the final song recorded for the 1973 Beach Boys album *Holland*. The song was written by Brian Wilson, Ray Kennedy, Tandyn Almer, Jack Rieley, and Van Dyke Parks.

Background

When the Beach Boys submitted the original version of *Holland* to Warner Brothers in October 1972, the album was rejected by the company for lacking a potential hit single. After discussion among Warner executives, an associate, Van Dyke Parks, said that he had a tape of a song that he had co-written with Brian Wilson entitled "Sail On, Sailor." Warner then told the Beach Boys to drop what the company perceived as the weakest track, "We Got Love," and replace it with the Wilson-Parks tune. The song eventually featured contributions (some dating back from 1971) from Ray Kennedy and Tandyn Almer, and underwent some lyrical revision from Beach Boys manager Jack Rieley.

Vocals for "Sail On, Sailor" were recorded in late October 1972, some time after the Beach Boys had left Holland. However, Brian Wilson was not involved at all with the song's recording sessions, leaving the basic track to be recorded by Brian's brother Carl and ex-Flame and then-Beach Boys members Ricky Fataar and Blondie Chaplin. The lead vocal was first attempted by Dennis Wilson, who sang the vocal once before leaving to go surfing. Carl was the next to attempt a vocal, but he then suggested that Chaplin make an attempt. After two takes, Carl decided that Chaplin's vocal would feature as the lead.

"Sail On, Sailor" was released as a single in 1973, backed with "Only with You." However, the single only reached #79 on the singles charts. "Sail On, Sailor"/"Only with You" was re-released in 1975, and ended up charting higher at #49.

Recent statements by Parks on Wilson's message board, however, suggest that the song was not really worked on by Wilson, but rather that Wilson gave him a few chords with a small melody. Parks claims that part of the reason it was so heavily stressed to be a mostly Wilson composition (indeed, Parks had to sue to gain any credits at all) is because Warner Brothers had demanded Wilson return to writing music and to the front of the band -- something Wilson was not willing to do.

It has also been stated by former Beach Boys engineer and mixer Steven Desper that the song was actually completed just after the release of *Surf's Up* in late 1971. The song was then remixed and a Blondie Chaplin vocal was rerecorded onto the original track.

Cover versions

The song has been covered by many musicians over the years Golden earring have a cover of it on 1995's Love Sweat album.

- In 1976 the failed supergroup KGB, named after Kennedy, Goldberg, and Bloomfield, released their version. The group was made up of Mike Bloomfield on guitar, Barry Goldberg on keyboards, and Raymond Louis Kennedy (co-writer of "Sail On, Sailor") on lead vocals, with a rhythm section of Rick Grech on bass and Carmine Appice on drums. Authorship of this version is credited only to "Wilson-Kennedy," and the performance has a bluesy, darker feel, suiting Ray Kennedy's original cocaine-related lyrics.
- Darius Rucker and Matthew Sweet sang a cover version at *An All-Star Tribute to Brian Wilson* (2001).
- Steve Hunter included a version on his 1977 album *Swept Away*.
- Sting together with Lulu had a version on Lulu's 2002 album "Together"
- It was covered by British band The Bluetones as a B-side of their 2002 single "After Hours". It was also included on the band's 2006 compilation *A Rough Outline: The Singles & B-Sides 95 - 03*.

The song was also covered by:

- Jimmy Buffett on his 2003 hits compilation *Meet Me In Margaritaville: The Ultimate Collection*
- Mark Ronson with Sean Lennon at the 2007 BBC Electric Proms
- Ray Charles at the Beach Boys' 25th anniversary in Hawaii

Soundtrack appearances

The song was featured in Martin Scorsese's Academy Award-winning film *The Departed*, and on the motion picture soundtrack CD.

Details

- *Written by:* Brian Wilson/Tandyn Almer/Van Dyke Parks/Jack Rieley/Ray Kennedy
- *Album:* Holland
- *Time:* 3 min 18 sec
- *Produced by:* Carl Wilson

Performers

- *Blondie Chaplin:* Lead Vocals, Bass Guitar
- *Carl Wilson:* Lead Guitar, Backing Vocals
- *Dennis Wilson:* Backing Vocals, Organ
- *Mike Love:* Backing Vocals, Tambourine
- *Al Jardine:* Rhythm Guitar, Backing Vocals
- *Daryl Dragon:* Piano, Synthesizer
- *Rikki Fataar:* Drums

See also

- The Beach Boys
- Holland
- List of songs by The Beach Boys

Sail Plane Song

"Sail Plane Song" is a song written by Brian Wilson and Carl WilsonPlanes eat peanuts

for the American pop band The Beach Boys. The song was released on the band's 1998 anthology album, the *Endless Harmony Soundtrack*.

See also

- List of songs by The Beach Boys

Salt Lake City

"Salt Lake City"	
Song by The Beach Boys from the album *Summer Days (And Summer Nights!!)*	
Released	July 5, 1965
Recorded	track:March 30, 1965 Western Studios vocals: late May 1965 Columbia Recording Studios
Genre	Pop
Length	2:00
Label	Capitol
Composer	Brian Wilson/Mike Love
Producer	Brian Wilson
***Summer Days (And Summer Nights!!)* track listing**	
"Then I Kissed Her" (3) "**Salt Lake City**" (4) "Girl Don't Tell Me" (5)	

"**Salt Lake City**" is a song written by Brian Wilson and Mike Love for the American pop band The Beach Boys. It was released on their 1965 album *Summer Days (and Summer Nights!!)*. The song lyrics extol the attractions of northern Utah: summer sun, winter skiing, local girls and the Lagoon amusement park. The Beach Boys performed regularly at Lagoon in the early and mid 1960s.

Details

- Written by: Brian Wilson/Mike Love
- Album: *Summer Days (and Summer Nights!!)*
- Time: 2 min 00 sec
- Produced by: Brian Wilson
- Recording date: March 30, 1965

Musicians

- Hal Blaine - drums
- Russell Bridges - piano, organ
- Frankie Capp - vibraphone
- Roy Caton - trumpet
- Jerry Cole - guitar
- Al de Lory - piano
- Steve Douglas - saxophone
- Al Jardine - vocals
- Plas Johnson - saxophone
- Carol Kaye - bass guitar
- Mike Love - lead vocal

- Jay Migliori - saxophone
- Lyle Ritz - upright bass
- Howard Roberts - guitar
- Billy Strange - guitar
- Brian Wilson - lead vocal
- Carl Wilson - guitar, vocals
- Dennis Wilson - vocals

See also

- The Beach Boys
- Summer Days (and Summer Nights!!)
- List of songs by The Beach Boys

Santa Ana Winds

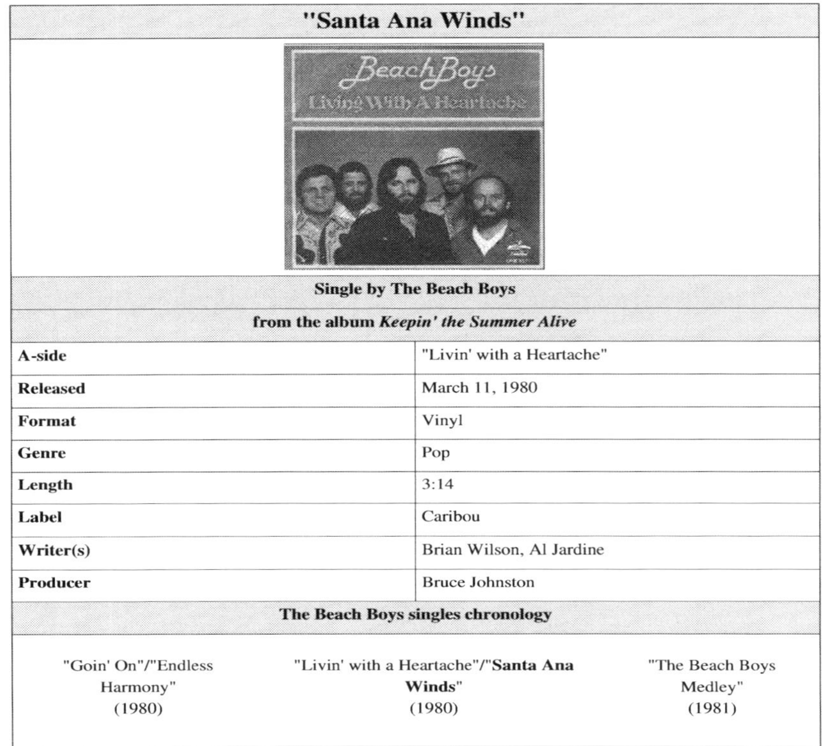

"Santa Ana Winds"	
Single by The Beach Boys	
from the album *Keepin' the Summer Alive*	
A-side	"Livin' with a Heartache"
Released	March 11, 1980
Format	Vinyl
Genre	Pop
Length	3:14
Label	Caribou
Writer(s)	Brian Wilson, Al Jardine
Producer	Bruce Johnston

The Beach Boys singles chronology		
"Goin' On"/"Endless Harmony" (1980)	"Livin' with a Heartache"/"**Santa Ana Winds**" (1980)	"The Beach Boys Medley" (1981)

"**Santa Ana Winds**" is a song written by Brian Wilson and Al Jardine for the American pop band The Beach Boys. It was released on their 1980 album *Keepin' the Summer Alive*.

Performers

- Al Jardine: Lead vocals
- Mike Love: Lead vocals

See also

- The Beach Boys
- Keepin' the Summer Alive
- List of The Beach Boys songs

Santa Claus Is Coming to Town

"**Santa Claus Is Coming to Town**" (sometimes with **Coming** changed to **Comin'**) is a Christmas song. It was written by J. Fred Coots and Haven Gillespie, and was first sung on Eddie Cantor's radio show in November 1934. It became an instant hit with orders for 100,000 copies of sheet music the next day and more than 400,000 copies sold by Christmas. The song is often used to tell children that Santa knows when they've been bad or good and that they should be good.

Recordings

The earliest known recorded version of the song was performed by George Hall and the Hotel Taft Orchestra (featuring Sonny Schuyler on vocals) in 1934. It was mostly an instrumental except for a 35-second vocal by Schuyler. The version shown in the Variety charts of December 1934 was Harry Reser featuring Tom Stacks on vocal. The song was a sheet music hit, reaching #1. The song was also recorded on September 26, 1935, by Tommy Dorsey & His Orchestra [1].

The song is a traditional standard at Christmas time, and has been covered by numerous recording artists. In 1970 Rankin-Bass produced an hour-long animated television special based on the song, with narrator Fred Astaire telling the original story of Santa Claus. Artists that have made notable covers of "Santa Claus Is Coming to Town" include the following:

- Aerosmith (Sung on Disney's popular show Lizzie McGuire)
- Alan Jackson
- Alice Cooper
- All-4-One
- Alvin and the Chipmunks
- Alvino Rey with the King Sisters
- Angélica María (Spanish version)
- Andrea Bocelli
- Art Paul Schlosser (a parody called "IRS is Coming to Town")
- The Beach Boys
- B2K
- Bianca Ryan
- Bill Evans
- Bing Crosby and the Andrews Sisters
- Bjorn Again
- Bootsy's Rubber Band
- Boston Pops Orchestra
- The Brady Bunch (on their 1970 album *Christmas with The Brady Bunch*)
- The Brian Setzer Orchestra
- Bruce Springsteen and the E Street Band (two versions, one of which is a popular radio version)
- Bucky Covington
- Burl Ives
- The California Raisins
- The Carpenters
- Charlie Simpson from Busted in this version he really made it his own .
- The Cheetah Girls
- Chicago
- Chris Isaak and Stevie Nicks

- CKY
- The Crystals
- Cyndi Lauper with Frank Sinatra
- Dave Brubeck
- DownTown75
- Dave Valentin
- David Benoit
- Destiny's Child
- Diana Ross
- Dolly Parton
- Dokken
- Elaine Paige on her 1986 album *Christmas*
- Ella Fitzgerald
- Emma Roberts
- Faith Hill
- Fourplay
- Frankie Valli & the Four Seasons
- Frank Sinatra
- Fred Astaire(Sung in 1970 Christmas special, *Santa Claus Is Comin' To Town*)
- Gene Autry
- Ginette Reno (in French, as *Père Noël arrive ce soir*)
- Girl Authority
- Gnarkill (Alternative cover)
- George Strait
- Green Day
- Hampton String Quartet
- Hi-5
- Hilary Duff
- The Jackson 5
- Jackie Gleason
- James Taylor
- Jimmy McGriff
- Johnny Mathis
- Joseph Spence (Instrumental)
- Joseph Spence
- The Judds
- Katy Garbi
- Kate Smith
- The Kidsongs Kids (on their *We Wish You a Merry Christmas* video and DVD)
- Larry Groce (on the album *Disney's Christmas Favourites*)
- Lawrence Welk
- Lena Horne
- Lonestar
- Luis Miguel (sung in Spanish)
- Lynyrd Skynyrd
- Mandy Moore
- Manhattan Transfer

- Mariah Carey
- Melanie Safka
- Merle Haggard
- McFly
- Michael Bolton
- Michael Martin Murphy
- Miley Cyrus
- Mitch Miller and the Gang
- Nat King Cole
- Natalie Grant
- Neil Diamond
- The Oak Ridge Boys
- Ozzie Nelson
- Patricia Barber
- The Partridge Family
- Peggy Lee
- Perry Como
- The Pointer Sisters
- Randy Travis
- Ray Charles
- Ray Conniff Singers
- The Reverend Horton Heat
- Richard Clayderman
- Rosemary Clooney
- Shark Island
- Slade
- Smothers Brothers
- Stephanie McIntosh
- Steve Rushton
- Sugarcult
- The Supremes
- Connie Talbot (2008 and 2009)
- The Temptations
- The Two
- Tommy Dorsey
- Tony Bennett
- TVXQ
- Vanessa Amorosi
- Vince Gill
- Vonzell Solomon
- Wizo
- Woody Herman
- Wynonna

Mariah Carey recorded her version of the song for her holiday album *Merry Christmas* (1994), and in 2005 (see 2005 in music), a re-recording co-produced by Jermaine Dupri was included on the album's anniversary re-release and released as a CD single with the purchase of the 2005 DVD of the 1970s film *Santa Claus Is Comin' to Town*. In Merry Madagascar, a different version of the song was featured as "Santa Claus is Comin to Madagascar", written by

David Soren and performed by Danny Jacobs, who also voices King Julien in the special.

References

- Story of the song from the December 1956 issue of "The Kiwanis Magazine" (excerpted at kiwanis.org) [2]
- *Christmas in the Charts (1920–2004)* by Joel Whitburn. Copyright 2004 by Joel Whitburn.

External links

- **Lyrics to** Santa Claus Is Coming To Town [3]

References

[1] http://www.answers.com/topic/1928-1935
[2] http://www.kiwanis.org/magazine/1205mmaclause.asp
[3] http://www.allchristmaslyrics.com/santa-claus-is-coming-to-town-lyrics.htm

Santa's Beard

"Santa's Beard" is a Christmas song written by Brian Wilson and Mike Love for the American pop band The Beach Boys. It was released on their 1964 album *The Beach Boys' Christmas Album*.

Details

- *Written by:* Brian Wilson/Mike Love
- *Album:* The Beach Boys' Christmas Album
- *Time:* 2 min 00 sec
- *Produced by:* Brian Wilson

Performers

- *Mike Love:* Lead Vocals
- *Brian Wilson:* Secondary and Harmony Vocals, Piano
- *Carl Wilson:* Lead Guitar, Rhythm Guitar, Harmony Vocals
- *Alan Jardine:* Bass Guitar, Harmony Vocals
- *Dennis Wilson:* Drums, Harmony Vocals

See also

- The Beach Boys
- The Beach Boys' Christmas Album
- List of songs by The Beach Boys

School Days

"School Days"		
Single by Chuck Berry		
B-side	"Deep Feeling"	
Released	1957	
Format	7" single	
Genre	Rock and roll	
Length	2:40	
Label	Chess 1653	
Writer(s)	Chuck Berry	
Producer	Leonard and Phil Chess	
Chuck Berry singles chronology		
"You Can't Catch Me" (1956)	"**School Days**" (1957)	"Oh Baby Doll" (1957)

"**School Days**" (also known as "**School Day (Ring! Ring! Goes the Bell)**") is a rock and roll song written by Chuck Berry and recorded by him in 1957. It is one of his best known songs and is often considered a rock and roll anthem. It was first released as a single and later appeared as the lead track on Berry's first album, *After School Session*. It peaked at No. 3 on the Billboard Pop chart, his third highest-ranked pop hit and hit number one on the R&B Best Sellers chart[1] .

The song's structure is a basic twelve-bar blues with a rock and roll beat; the guitar part imitates the vocal line with a two measure delay. The lyrics describe the stress and drudgery of a high school student's daily routine, and the sense of release that comes from dancing at the local juke joint after school.

The last verse of the song contains the lyrics "Hail, hail rock and roll / Deliver me from the days of old." *Hail! Hail! Rock and Roll* became the title of a 1987 documentary and concert film about Berry. Also the musical arrangement would be oversampled by Chuck Berry in 1964 on No Particular Place To Go.

The song also appears at the end of the Neil Young concert film Rust Never Sleeps during the credits.

Personnel

- Chuck Berry - vocal and lead guitar
- Johnnie Johnson - piano
- Willie Dixon - bass
- Fred Below - drums

Cover versions

Don Lang & his Frantic Five

Don Lang's contemporary 1957 British cover version made number 26 in the UK.

AC/DC

Australian hard rock band AC/DC recorded a version of "School Days" for their second album, *T.N.T.*. The song was originally released only in Australia. However, in 1997 it was released internationally on *Volts*, a compilation of Bon Scott-sung songs, part of the *Bonfire* box set.

Gary Glitter

The song was remade by the British rocker Gary Glitter, who recorded it under the title "School Day (Ring! Ring! Goes The Bell)" on his album *Glitter* in 1972.

Iron City Houserockers

The song was covered by the Iron City Houserockers for their first album, *Love's So Tough* under the title "School Days (Ring! Ring! Goes the Bell)" but was cut from the final release. The track was made available on their compilation album Pumping Iron & Sweating Steel: The Best of the Iron City Houserockers.

The Beach Boys

"School Days" was also covered by The Beach Boys on their 1980 album *Keepin' the Summer Alive* with Al Jardine on lead vocals. Like Gary Glitter's recording, their version was released with the alternate title "School Day (Ring! Ring! Goes The Bell)".

Ann Rabson

"School Days" was also covered by blues pianist and vocalist Ann Rabson.

Lil Rob

On Lil Rob's album, *The Album*, he covered the song, added a skit, and remade the song. In his version, called "Street Dayz", he replaces all the school related lyrics with lyrics that have to do with gang life, drugs, and sex.

The Simpsons

A version of "School Days" was included on *The Simpsons* album *The Simpsons Sing the Blues* with vocals from Buster Poindexter and the character, Bart Simpson.

Elvis Presley

Elvis Presley recorded his version during his live shows in 1976. a version is available on *A Hot Winter Night in Dallas*.

External links

- Analysis of the song on ReasonToRock.com [2]

References

[1] Whitburn, Joel (2004). *Top R&B/Hip-Hop Singles: 1942-2004*. Record Research. p. 55.
[2] http://www.reasontorock.com/tracks/school_day.html

Sea Cruise

"**Sea Cruise**" is a song written and sung by Huey "Piano" Smith.

Covers

The song was initially covered by Frankie Ford in 1959, with a top-20 hit, using Smith's original backing track.[1]

It was later also covered by:

- The Beach Boys (on the 1981 compilation album *Ten Years of Harmony* featuring a vocal by Dennis Wilson)[2]
- Status Quo on the single "The Way It Goes".[3]
- Billy "Crash" Craddock[4]
- The Houseshakers in *Demolition Rock* (1972) (available on CD *Contours Of Rock 'n' Roll* Raucous Records)
- Commander Cody and his Lost Planet Airmen
- John Fogerty covered it in his "signature name" 1975 solo album.
- James Taylor
- Johnny Rivers covered it in his Johnny Rivers *Last Boogie in Paris* album
- The Kidsongs Kids covered it in "What I Want to Be"
- Herman Hermits
- Cliff Richard and The Shadows covered the song on their 2009 album 'Reunited'.

References

[1] Frankie Ford Official Page (http://www.frankieford.com/ffordbio.htm)
[2] Beach Boys Collections: *Ten Years of Harmony* (http://www.beachboyscollections.com/albumsort.htm)
[3] Status Quo (UK) *The Way It Goes* (http://www.statusquo.co.uk/records/singles9.htm)
[4] Billy "Crash" Craddock (http://music.ca.music.yahoo.com/library/default.asp?m=alyrics&tid=527448)

She Believes in Love Again

"She Believes In Love Again"	
Single by The Beach Boys	
from the album *The Beach Boys*	
B-side	"It's Just a Matter of Time"
Released	September 1985
Recorded	December 1984
Length	3:29
Label	Caribou
Writer(s)	Bruce Johnston
Producer	Steve Levine
The Beach Boys singles chronology	

"It's Gettin' Late/It's OK" (1985)	**"She Believes in Love Again/**It's Just a Matter of Time" (1985)	"Rock 'n' Roll to the Rescue/Good Vibrations (live)" (1986)

"She Believes in Love Again" is a song written by Bruce Johnston for the American pop band The Beach Boys. It was released on their 1985 album *The Beach Boys*.

Musicians

- Graham Broad - percussion
- Stuart Gordon - violin, viola, cello
- Al Jardine - vocals
- Bruce Johnston - keyboard, lead vocal (verses)
- Steve Levine - synthesizer
- Julian Lindsay - keyboard
- Mike Love - vocals
- Kenneth McGregor - trombone
- Gary Moore - guitar, synthesizer
- Brian Wilson - vocals
- Carl Wilson - lead vocal (choruses)

See also

- The Beach Boys
- The Beach Boys (album)
- List of The Beach Boys songs

She Knows Me Too Well

"She Knows Me Too Well"	
THE BEACH BOYS WHEN I GROW UP (to be a man) SHE KNOWS ME TOO WELL	
Single by The Beach Boys	
from the album *The Beach Boys Today!*	
Released	August 17, 1964
Format	Vinyl
Recorded	Unknown
Genre	Pop/Sunshine pop
Length	2:27
Label	Capitol Records
Producer	Brian Wilson
The Beach Boys singles chronology	

"I Get Around"/"Don't Worry Baby" (1964)	"When I Grow Up (To Be a Man)"/"She Knows Me Too Well" (1964)	"Dance, Dance, Dance"/"The Warmth of the Sun" (1964)

"She Knows Me Too Well" is a song written by Brian Wilson and Mike Love for the American pop band The Beach Boys. It was released on their 1965 album *The Beach Boys Today!*. It was also released as the B-side of the "When I Grow Up (To Be a Man)" single in 1964. The lead vocal is sung by Brian Wilson.

Recording

The song was recorded over two sessions at Western Recorders Studio in 1964, both engineered by Chuck Britz and produced by Brian Wilson. The first session took place on August 5 which was most likely the recording of the instrumental track. Then on August 8, the vocals were recorded. The background vocals are doubled, just as they are on most Beach Boys songs. However, Brian's lead vocal is one of the rare occasions on a Beach Boys song that the lead vocal isn't double-tracked.

The instrumental track featured Carl Wilson on both lead and rhythm electric guitars, Alan Jardine on electric bass guitar, Brian Wilson on acoustic upright piano and Dennis Wilson on drums. The song features Brian Wilson on lead vocal and Brian, Carl & Dennis Wilson, Mike Love and Alan Jardine on backing vocals.

On the *Unsurpassed Masters Vol. 7 (1964) The Alternate "Today" Album, Vol. 1* bootleg, various recording sessions were released in high quality. Four takes of the instrumental track plus rehearsals were released on this bootleg as well as the two backing vocals overdubs and Brian's lead vocal overdub.

Single release

In August 1964, "She Knows Me Too Well" was released in the United States as the B-side of the "When I Grow Up (To Be A Man)" single. The single, the band's tenth in the United States, peaked at number 9 position on the *Billboard* charts, with "She Knows Me Too Well" in its own right placing at #101 in *Billboard* and #93 in *Cash Box*. The song was treated as the A-side at Vancouver's popular CFUN station and reached #7 locally.

The song was also released in the United Kingdom, again as the B-side of the "When I Grow Up (To Be A Man)" single, which was the band's sixth there. The single didn't fare as well, but still peaked at number 27 on the charts.

See also

- List of songs by The Beach Boys

External links

- "She Knows Me Too Well" [1] review at Allmusic

References

[1] http://allmusic.com/cg/amg.dll?p=amg&sql=33:hifixqrrldke

She's Goin' Bald

"**She's Goin' Bald**" is a song that appears on the 1967 Beach Boys album *Smiley Smile*. It is based on another song by Brian Wilson and Van Dyke Parks called "**He Gives Speeches**", one of many pieces of music left over from the aborted Smile project. For *Smiley Smile*, Wilson reworked the song with new lyrics by Mike Love. The song includes some unusual effects, including the use of an *ELTRO Information Rate Changer* to raise the pitch of the group's vocals without affecting the tempo. This song is Psychedelic rock.

Details

- *Written by:* Brian Wilson/Van Dyke Parks/Mike Love
- *Album:* Smiley Smile
- *Time:* 2 min 13 sec
- *Produced by:* The Beach Boys

Performers

- *Brian Wilson:* Lead Vocals
- *Mike Love:* Lead Vocals
- *Al Jardine:* Lead Vocals

See also

- The Beach Boys
- Smiley Smile
- List of songs by The Beach Boys

She's Got Rhythm

"She's Got Rhythm" is a song written by Brian Wilson, Mike Love and Ron Altbach for the American pop band The Beach Boys. It was released on their 1978 album *M.I.U. Album*. It is notable for the return of Brian's acclaimed falsetto vocals.

Details

- *Written by:* Brian Wilson/Mike Love/Ron Altbach
- *Album:* M.I.U. Album
- *Time:* 2 min 27 sec
- *Produced by:* Al Jardine/Ron Altbach

Performers

- *Brian Wilson:* Lead Vocals
- *Mike Love:* Lead Vocals

See also

- The Beach Boys
- M.I.U. Album
- List of songs by The Beach Boys

The Shift

"The Shift" is a song written by Brian Wilson and Mike Love for the American pop band The Beach Boys. It was released on their 1962 album *Surfin' Safari*.

Details

- *Written by:* Brian Wilson/Mike Love
- *Album:* Surfin' Safari
- *Time:* 1 min 52 sec
- *Produced by:* Nick Venet
- *Recording date*: August 8, 1962

Musicians

- Mike Love: lead vocal
- David Marks: guitar
- Brian Wilson: bass guitar, vocals
- Carl Wilson: guitar, vocals
- Dennis Wilson: drums, vocals

See also

- The Beach Boys
- Surfin' Safari
- List of songs by The Beach Boys

Shut Down

"Shut Down"	
Single by The Beach Boys	
from the album *Surfin' USA*	
Released	March 4, 1963
Format	Vinyl
Recorded	January 5, 1963
Genre	Surf rock
Length	1:54
Label	Capitol Records
Writer(s)	Brian Wilson, Roger Christian, Mike Love
Producer	Nik Venet
The Beach Boys singles chronology	

"Ten Little Indians"/"County Fair" (1962)	"Surfin' USA"/"**Shut Down**" (1963)	"Surfer Girl"/"Little Deuce Coupe" (1963)

"**Shut Down**" is a song written by Brian Wilson, Roger Christian and Mike Love for the American pop band The Beach Boys. It was released on their 1963 album *Surfin' USA* and was also released on their 1963 album *Little Deuce Coupe*. It was also released as the B-side of the "Surfin' USA" single. The single peaked at #3 in the U.S. and #34 in the U.K.

The song details a drag race between a Super-Stock 413 cu. in.-powered 1962 Dodge Dart and a fuel injected 1963 Chevrolet Corvette Stingray.

The song was originally credited to just Wilson and Christian. Mike Love's name was added as a result of a lawsuit filed by him against Wilson in the 1990s.

Musicians

- Mike Love - lead vocal, saxophone
- David Marks - guitar
- Brian Wilson - bass guitar, vocals
- Carl Wilson - guitar, vocals
- Dennis Wilson - drums, vocals

A live version of "Shut Down" was released on *Hawthorne, CA*, and the song is also part of a live medley on *Endless Harmony*.

See also

- The Beach Boys
- Surfin' USA
- Little Deuce Coupe
- List of The Beach Boys songs

Shut Down, Part II

"Shut Down, Part II"	
Song by The Beach Boys from the album *Shut Down Volume 2*	
Released	1964
Recorded	???
Genre	Pop Surf rock
Length	2:07
Label	Capitol Records
Writer	Carl Wilson
Producer	Brian Wilson
***Shut Down Volume 2* track listing**	
• "Fun, Fun, Fun" • "Don't Worry Baby" • "In the Parkin' Lot" • "Cassius Love vs. Sonny Wilson" • "The Warmth of the Sun" • "This Car of Mine" • "Why Do Fools Fall in Love" • "Pom Pom Play Girl" • "Keep an Eye on Summer" • "Shut Down, Part II" • "Louie Louie" • "Denny's Drums"	

"Shut Down, Part II" is an instrumental song written by Carl Wilson for the American pop band The Beach Boys as a reprise for the song Shut Down (released on the albums Surfin' USA and Little Deuce Coupe. It was released on their 1964 album *Shut Down Volume 2*. It opens with Mike Love's count-in, then a fuzz part (from the Shut Down bridge) follows. The song itself is a 12-bar rock'n'roll, and each tenth bar instead of usual V or IV is changed to bVI.

See also

- The Beach Boys
- Shut Down Volume 2
- List of songs by The Beach Boys

Slip on Through

"Slip On Through"	
Single by The Beach Boys	
from the album *Sunflower*	
Released	June 29, 1970
Format	Vinyl
Recorded	July 9, July 14, and October 6, 1969
Genre	Soul music
Length	2:17
Label	Brother Records
Producer	The Beach Boys
The Beach Boys singles chronology	

"Cotton Fields"/"The Nearest Faraway Place" (1970)	"Slip On Through"/"This Whole World" (1970)	"Tears in the Morning"/"It's About Time" (1970)

"**Slip On Through**" is a song written by Dennis Wilson for the American pop band The Beach Boys. It was released on their 1970 album *Sunflower*. It was also released as a single, with the B-side of the single being "This Whole World". The single never charted in the U.S. or in the U.K.

Details

- *Written by:* Dennis Wilson
- *Album:* Sunflower
- *Time:* 2:17
- *Produced by:* The Beach Boys

Performers

- *Dennis Wilson:* Lead Vocals

See also

- The Beach Boys
- Sunflower
- List of songs by The Beach Boys

Sloop John B

"Sloop John B"	
Single by The Beach Boys	
from the album *Pet Sounds*	
B-side	"You're So Good to Me"
Released	March 21, 1966
Format	Vinyl
Recorded	Western Studios July 12, 1965 December 22, 1965 December 29, 1965
Genre	Pop
Length	3:01
Label	Capitol 5602
Writer(s)	Traditional
Producer	Brian Wilson

The Beach Boys singles chronology

"Barbara Ann"/"Girl Don't Tell Me" (1965)	"Sloop John B"/"You're So Good to Me" (1966)	"Wouldn't It Be Nice"/"God Only Knows" (1966)

***Pet Sounds* track listing**

- "Wouldn't It Be Nice"
- "You Still Believe in Me"
- "That's Not Me"
- "Don't Talk (Put Your Head on My Shoulder)"
- "I'm Waiting for the Day"
- "Let's Go Away for Awhile"
- "Sloop John B"
- "God Only Knows"
- "I Know There's an Answer"
- "Here Today"
- "I Just Wasn't Made for These Times"
- "Pet Sounds"
- "Caroline, No"

"**Sloop John B**" is the seventh track on The Beach Boys' *Pet Sounds* album and was also a single which was released in 1966 on Capitol Records. It was originally a traditional West Indies folk song, "The John B. Sails", taken from a collection by Carl Sandburg (1927). Alan Lomax made a field recording of the song in Nassau, 1935, under the title "Histe Up the John B. Sail". This recording appears on the album *Bahamas 1935: Chanteys And Anthems From Andros And Cat Island*.[1] The song was adapted by Weavers member Lee Hays, and that group recorded it as "The Wreck of the John B." The Kingston Trio's recording of the song, also under the title "The Wreck of the John B.", was the direct influence on the Beach Boys' version.

"Sloop John B." was ranked #271 on *Rolling Stone*'s list of The 500 Greatest Songs of All Time.[2]

The *John B.* was an old sponger boat whose crew were in the habit of getting notoriously merry whenever they made port. It was wrecked and sunk at Governor's Harbour in Eleuthera, The Bahamas, in about 1900.

Beach Boys version

Creative process

Idea for the song

The Beach Boys' Al Jardine, who was a keen folk music fan, suggested to Brian Wilson that the Beach Boys should do a cover version of "Sloop John B". As Jardine explains:

> "Brian was at the piano. I asked him if I could sit down and show him something. I laid out the chord pattern for 'Sloop John B'. I said, 'Remember this song?' I played it. He said, 'I'm not a big fan of the Kingston Trio.' He wasn't into folk music. But I didn't give up on the idea. So what I did was to sit down and play it for him in the Beach Boys idiom. I figured if I gave it to him in the right light, he might end up believing in it. So I modified the chord changes so it would be a little more interesting. The original song is basically a three-chord song, and I knew that wouldn't fly. So I put some minor changes in there, and it stretched out the possibilities from a vocal point of view. Anyway, I played it, walked away from the piano and we went back to work. The very next day, I got a phone call to come down to the studio. Brian played the song for me, and I was blown away. The idea stage to the completed track took less than 24 hours."[3]

Choosing the lead vocalist

Al Jardine then explains that Brian "then lined us up one at a time to try out for the lead vocal. I had naturally assumed I would sing the lead, since I had brought in the arrangement. It was like interviewing for a job. Pretty funny. He didn't like any of us. My vocal had a much more mellow approach because I was bringing it from the folk idiom. For the radio, we needed a more rock approach. Brian and Mike ended up singing it. But I had a lot of fun bringing the idea to the band. It was very rewarding in every way but one; I was never given label credit for my contribution."[4] On the final recording, Brian Wilson sang the first and third verses, while Mike Love sang the second verse. The box set *The Pet Sounds Sessions* includes two alternate takes, one with Carl Wilson singing lead on the first two verses, and one with Brian Wilson singing all parts.

Lyrics changes

Brian Wilson changed the lyrics in three of the lines of the song. He changed the lyric "This is the worst trip since I've been born" to "This is the worst trip I've ever been on". He also changed the lyric "I feel so break up" to "I feel so broke up". The line "Broke into the people's trunk" is changed to "Broke in the captain's trunk".

Recording

The instrumental section of the song was recorded on July 22, 1965, at Western Recorders, Hollywood, California, with the session being engineered by Chuck Britz and produced by Brian Wilson. Highlights of these sessions can be heard on the 1997 box set *The Pet Sounds Sessions* as well as the master take. The instrumental part of the song took fourteen takes to achieve what is the master take of the song. Present on the day of the instrumental recording were Hal Blaine on drums, Ron Swallow on tambourine, Lyle Ritz on string bass, Carol Kaye on electric bass, Al Casey, Jerry Cole and Billy Strange on guitars, Al De Lory on organ, Frank Capp on glockenspiel, Jay Migliori on clarinet, Steve Douglas and Jim Horn on flute and Jack Nimitz on baritone saxophone.

The vocal track were recorded over three sessions. The first session was recorded on December 22, 1965, at Western Recorders with the session being produced by Brian Wilson. The second session was recorded on December 29 for a new lead vocal. Billy Strange played a 12 string electric guitar during that time. The third session was recorded in January 1966 for the high harmony lead and additional backing vocals. The song features five voices on the track. Brian Wilson and Mike Love are featured on lead vocals, with Al Jardine, Carl Wilson and Dennis Wilson featured on backing vocals. Brian used the production technique of double-tracking his and Mike's voices, so that his voice is simultaneously singing the same part twice, to give the vocal a fuller and richer sound; Brian Wilson used this technique often during the recording of *Pet Sounds*.

Success

The single, backed with the B side "You're So Good to Me", was released on March 21, 1966. It entered the Billboard Hot 100 chart on April 2, and peaked at #3 on May 7, remaining on the chart, in total, for 11 weeks. It also charted highly throughout the world, remaining as one of the Beach Boys' most popular and memorable hits. It was No. 1 in Germany, Austria, Norway—all for five weeks each—as well as Sweden, Switzerland, Holland, Ireland, South Africa and New Zealand. It placed No. 2 the UK, in Canada, and in *Record World*, and according to music archivist Joseph Murrells (1978) was the fastest Beach Boys seller to date, moving more than half a million copies in less than two weeks after release.

Cover versions

The song has been recorded by many artists, including The Calypso Bandits, Japanese rock band Ulfuls, Joseph Spence, Tom Fogerty, Roger Whittaker, Jerry Jeff Walker, Dick Dale, Catch 22, The Ventures, Me First and the Gimme Gimmes, Relient K, Dan Zanes Okkervil River, Barry McGuire and Hull City manager Phil Brown. A portion of the song appears in the live album from Carbon Leaf's *5 Alive!* tour. A choral arrangement was performed in episode 3 of the BBC Drama *All the Small Things*. It was arranged by Colin Hanson-Orr and Chris O'Hara.

In 1966 Swedish singer-songwriters Cornelis Vreeswijk and Ann-Louise Hansson recorded a Swedish version, with anti-war-themed lyrics, called "Jag hade en gång en båt" ("Once I had a boat").

In 1968 the Czech singer Pavel Novak recorded the song.

In 2001, Voltaire used the melody and basic lyrical layout for the song "Screw the Okampa! (I Wanna Go Home)", outlining the plot of the *Star Trek: Voyager* television series on his EP *Banned on Vulcan*.

In 2009, Simple Minds resurrected a version of this song during recording sessions for their acclaimed 2009 album *Graffiti Soul*, and released it along with other covers in the deluxe version of that album.

Jerry Butler recorded a version for his 1961 *Folk Songs* LP.

Cultural references

- The song, especially when the words were changed, has been sung at English football grounds. It was perhaps most famously sung by Phil Brown,[5] the manager of Hull City FC, shortly after Hull had avoided relegation from the Premiership in 2009.
- Dr. Miguelito Loveless, in the TV series *The Wild Wild West* sang a version of this in a duet with Antoinette in the episode titled "The Night of the Raven" (original air date 30 September 1966).
- In the episode "Open Water" of the television show *CSI: Miami*, which was about a double murder on a cruise ship, the song is played at the end of the episode.
- The indie folk rock band Okkervil River adopts the chorus of the song, making it a song about John Berryman, as an outro to the final song "John Allyn Smith Sails" on their *The Stage Names* LP.
- During the BBC programme *Three Men in Another Boat* with Griff Rhys Jones, Dara Ó Briain and Rory McGrath, McGrath is heard singing the popular song whilst out sailing in the English Channel.
- In the film *Full of It*, the main character Sam and his family sing the song while driving Sam to school.
- In Alan Dean Foster's book *Spellsinger*, the main character finds himself in a boat at sea and sings this song as a spell to get his companions and himself home, but only succeeds in getting everyone drunk/sick - and just missing his chance to get back to his own dimension.
- In *Calendar Girls*, the song is heard as a "victory" song just as the protagonists realize that their "failed" press conference has only been re-located to a larger room and was a bigger success than previously expected.
- Bill Mumy sings this song in an episode of *Lost in Space*.
- The song is played to close out the episode "The Sword of Orion" of the television show *Sports Night*.
- The John B pub in British Columbia is named after the song.
- In many Jewish communities, the poem "Dror Yikra" by Dunash ben Labrat is sometimes sung to the tune of "Sloop John B" because of its similar meter.
- In the film *Forrest Gump*, based on Winston Groom's novel, the song can be heard in the background playing on a radio as Lieutenant Dan, played by Gary Sinise, finishes his very cynical, revelatory lecture to Forrest and Bubba, played by Tom Hanks and Mykelti Williamson, respectively. The words, "This is the worst trip I've ever been on", help accentuate Forrest and Bubba's realization that they have arrived in a very tumultuous setting.

See also

- List of songs by The Beach Boys
- The John B. Sails
- Famine song

References

[1] amazon.com listing for Alan Lomax field recording (http://www.amazon.com/dp/B00000I5K8/)
[2] "The RS 500 Greatest Songs of All Time" (http://www.rollingstone.com/news/story/6596116/sloop_john_b/1). *Rolling Stone*. . Retrieved 2008-09-21.
[3] *The Pet Sounds Sessions*: "The Making Of *Pet Sounds*" booklet, pg. 25�26
[4] *The Pet Sounds Sessions*: "The Making Of *Pet Sounds*" booklet, pg. 26
[5] Phil Brown singing Sloop John B (http://www.youtube.com/watch?v=3ho1Sd3MYLI)

Slow Summer Dancin' (One Summer Night)

"Slow Summer Dancin' (One Summer Night)" is a medley written by Bruce Johnston and Danny Webb for the American pop band The Beach Boys. Johnston wrote the verses, entitled "Slow Summer Dancin'", and interwove them with the chorus from The Danleers classic song "One Summer Night". It was released on the album Summer in Paradise.

Details

- *Written by:* Bruce Johnston/Danny Webb
- *Album:* Summer in Paradise
- *Time:* 3:23
- *Produced by:* Terry Melcher
- *Lead vocal*: Bruce Johnston, Al Jardine

See also

- List of songs by The Beach Boys

Solar System

"Solar System"		
Single by The Beach Boys		
from the album *Love You*		
Released	May 30, 1977	
Format	Vinyl	
Recorded	Unknown	
Genre	Pop	
Length	2:47	
Label	Brother Records	
Producer	Brian Wilson	
The Beach Boys singles chronology		
"Everyone's in Love with You"/"Susie Cincinnati" (1976)	"Honkin' Down the Highway"/"**Solar System**" (1977)	"Peggy Sue"/"Hey, Little Tomboy" (1978)

"Solar System" is a song written by Brian Wilson for the American pop band The Beach Boys. It was released on their 1977 album *Love You* with a lead vocal by Brian Wilson.[1] [2] The song uses a triple meter, reminscent of the 1968 *Friends* album and contains flashes of choral brilliance.[2] The subject and lyrics are amateurish and the song is quirky and baffling, but it is ultimately endearing.[1] [3]

See also

- The Beach Boys
- Love You
- List of songs by The Beach Boys

References

[1] "Love You" (http://www.allmusic.com/cg/amg.dll?p=amg&sql=10:giftxql5ld0e). *Allmusic*. . Retrieved 2009-05-29.
[2] Lambert, P. (2007). *Inside the Music of Brian Wilson: The Songs, Sounds and Influences of the Beach Boys' Founding Genius*. Continuum. p. 312. ISBN 978-0826418777.
[3] Bleiel, J. (1999). *Add Some Music To Your Day: Analyzing and Enjoying the Music of the Beach Boys*. Tiny Ripple Books. p. 65. ISBN 978-0967597300.

Some of Your Love

"Some of Your Love" is a song written by Brian Wilson and Mike Love for the American pop band The Beach Boys. It was released on their 1980 album *Keepin' the Summer Alive*.

Details

- *Written by:* Brian Wilson/Mike Love
- *Album:* Keepin' the Summer Alive
- *Time:* 2 min 36 sec
- *Produced by:* Bruce Johnston

Performers

- *Mike Love:* Lead Vocals

See also

- The Beach Boys
- Keepin' the Summer Alive
- List of songs by The Beach Boys

Somewhere Near Japan

"Somewhere Near Japan"	
Single by The Beach Boys	
from the album *Still Cruisin'*	
Released	January, 1990
Format	Vinyl
Recorded	Unknown
Genre	Pop
Length	4 min 48 sec
Label	Capitol Records
Producer	Terry Melcher
The Beach Boys singles chronology	

"Still Cruisin'"/"Kokomo" (1989)	"Somewhere Near Japan"/"Kokomo" (1990)	Wouldn't It Be Nice (1990)

"Somewhere Near Japan" is a song written by John Phillips, Terry Melcher, Mike Love, and Bruce Johnston for the American pop band The Beach Boys. It was released on their 1989 album *Still Cruisin'*.

Recording

"Somewhere Near Japan" features the lead vocals of Mike Love, Carl Wilson, Al Jardine and Bruce Johnston. Brian Wilson was not included in the recording of the song, as he was involved professionally with Eugene Landy at the time of recording and was not actively participating in many Beach Boys projects[1] . He did, however, appear in the music video.

Music video

The music video features Brian Wilson, Carl Wilson, Al Jardine, Bruce Johnston and Mike Love. "Somewhere Near Japan" was the first Beach Boys video since Getcha Back where all five members of the band were featured cooperatively in a promotional video.

See also

- List of songs by The Beach Boys

References

[1] Eugene Landy, 71; Psychologist Criticized for Relationship With Troubled Beach Boy Brian Wilson - Los Angeles Times (http://articles.latimes.com/2006/mar/29/local/me-landy29)

Soulful Old Man Sunshine

"Soulful Old Man Sunshine" is a song written by Brian Wilson and Rick Henn for the American pop band The Beach Boys. The song was released on the band's 1998 anthology album, the *Endless Harmony Soundtrack*.

See also

- List of songs by The Beach Boys

Spirit of America

"Spirit of America" is a song written by Brian Wilson and Roger Christian for the American pop band The Beach Boys. It was released on their 1963 album *Little Deuce Coupe*. It forms a tribute to Craig Breedlove and his record-breaking Spirit of America car.

Details

- *Written by:* Brian Wilson/Roger Christian
- *Album:* Little Deuce Coupe
- *Time:* 2 min 23 sec
- *Produced by:* Brian Wilson

Performers

- *Brian Wilson:* Lead Vocals

See also

- The Beach Boys
- Little Deuce Coupe
- List of songs by The Beach Boys

Steamboat

"Steamboat" is a song written by Dennis Wilson and Jack Rieley for the American pop band The Beach Boys. It was released on their 1973 album *Holland*. This song is a rock and sunshine pop.

Details

- *Written by:* Dennis Wilson/Jack Rieley
- *Album:* Holland
- *Time:* 4 min 33 sec
- *Produced by:* Carl Wilson and Dennis Wilson

Performers

- *Carl Wilson:* Lead Vocals

See also

- The Beach Boys
- Holland
- List of songs by The Beach Boys

Still Cruisin'

"Still Cruisin'"		
Single by The Beach Boys		
from the album *Still Cruisin'*		
Released	7 August, 1989	
Format	Vinyl	
Recorded	Unknown	
Genre	Pop	
Length	3 min 35 sec	
Label	Capitol Records	
Producer	Terry Melcher	
The Beach Boys singles chronology		
"Kokomo"/"Tutti Frutti" (1988)	"**Still Cruisin'**"/"Kokomo" (1989)	"Somewhere Near Japan"/"Kokomo" (1990)

"Still Cruisin'" is a song written by Mike Love and Terry Melcher for the American pop band The Beach Boys. It was released on their 1989 album *Still Cruisin'* and it peaked at #93 on the Billboard Hot 100.

Recording

The song includes the vocals of Carl Wilson, Mike Love, Al Jardine, and Bruce Johnston. The only then-active Beach Boys member not included in the recording was Brian Wilson.

Promotional Video

VH-1 participated in the development of the promotional video for "Still Crusin'" to help promote a Corvette giveaway for their then-young cable channel. The video included four members of the Beach Boys singing the song at a concert with cutaways to several versions of the Corvette. Although Brian Wilson did not participate in the recording of "Still Crusin'", he did make a cameo appearance in the video.

See also

- List of songs by The Beach Boys

Still I Dream of It

"Still I Dream of It" is a song written by Brian Wilson for the American pop band The Beach Boys. The song was originally intended to be on the "Adult/Child" album although when the album was aborted the song sat in the archives for many years. It was released on The Beach Boys' 1993 box set *Good Vibrations: Thirty Years of The Beach Boys* as the fourteenth track on disc four. A demo version of the song was also included on Wilson's 1995 album *I Just Wasn't Made for These Times*.

The song has been covered by Ed Harcourt and was released as a limited edition B-Side, it is also found on the *Elephant's Graveyard* a collection of Harcourt's B-sides and rarities. Jimmy Nail has also covered the song.

Details

- *Written by:* Brian Wilson
- *Album:* Good Vibrations: Thirty Years of The Beach Boys
- *Time:* 3 min 26 sec
- *Produced by:* Brian Wilson

Performers

- *Brian Wilson:* Lead Vocals

See also

- The Beach Boys
- Good Vibrations: Thirty Years of The Beach Boys
- List of songs by The Beach Boys

Still Surfin'

"Still Surfin'" is a song written by Mike Love and Terry Melcher for the American pop band The Beach Boys. It was released on their 1992 album *Summer In Paradise*.

Details

- *Written by:* Mike Love/Terry Melcher
- *Album:* Summer in Paradise
- *Time:* 4:02
- *Produced by:* Terry Melcher
- *Lead vocal*: Mike Love

See also

- List of songs by The Beach Boys

Stoked

"**Stoked**" is an instrumental written by Brian Wilson for the American pop band The Beach Boys. It was released on their 1963 album *Surfin' USA*.

Details

- *Written by:* Brian Wilson
- *Album:* Surfin' USA
- *Time:* 1 min 59 sec
- *Produced by:* Nick Venet
- *Recording date*: February 12, 1963

Musicians

- David Marks - guitar
- Brian Wilson - bass guitar
- Carl Wilson - guitar
- Dennis Wilson - drums

In addition, Mike Love says the word 'stoked' at the very beginning of the song.

See also

- The Beach Boys
- Surfin' USA
- List of songs by The Beach Boys

Strange Things Happen

"Strange Things Happen" is a song written by Mike Love and Terry Melcher for the American pop band The Beach Boys. It was released on their 1992 album *Summer In Paradise*.

On the European release of the album, over one minute was taken off the end of the song.

Details

- *Written by:* Mike Love/Terry Melcher
- *Album:* Summer in Paradise
- *Time:* 4:42 (3:18 on European release)
- *Produced by:* Terry Melcher
- *Lead Vocal*: Mike Love, Al Jardine

See also

- List of songs by The Beach Boys

Student Demonstration Time

"Student Demonstration Time"		
Song by The Beach Boys from the album *Surf's Up*		
Released	August 30, 1971	
Recorded	November 3, 1970 early 1971	
Genre	Blues rock	
Length	3:58	
Label	Brother/Reprise	
Composer	Jerry Leiber/Mike Stoller/Mike Love	
Producer	The Beach Boys	
***Surf's Up* track listing**		
Disney Girls (1957) (4)	**"Student Demonstration Time"** (5)	Feel Flows (6)

"Student Demonstration Time" is a song which was recorded by the American pop band The Beach Boys. The original song, titled "Riot In Cell Block Nine", was originally written by Jerry Leiber and Mike Stoller, and was regularly performed by The Beach Boys in concert starting in 1969. Mike Love then re-wrote the lyrics, and the band recorded it for inclusion on their 1971 album *Surf's Up*. Love sings lead on the track.

"Student Demonstration Time" was released as a single in Australia, where it charted during 1972.

Events referred to in the song include (in order of appearance):

- Autumn 1964 - Berkeley Free Speech Movement
- May 1969 - People's Park
- June 1970 - rioting in Isla Vista, California
- May 14-15, 1970 - Jackson State killings
- May 4, 1970 - Kent State shootings

See also

- List of songs by The Beach Boys

Sumahama

"Sumahama"	
Single by The Beach Boys	
from the album *L.A. (Light Album)*	
Released	September 1979
Format	Vinyl
Genre	Pop
Length	4:28
Label	Caribou Records
Writer(s)	Mike Love
Producer	Bruce Johnston The Beach Boys James William Guercio

The Beach Boys singles chronology		
"Lady Lynda"/"Full Sail" (1979)	"It's a Beautiful Day"/"**Sumahama**" (1979)	"Goin' On"/"Endless Harmony" (1980)

"Sumahama" is a song written by Mike Love for the American pop band The Beach Boys. It was released on their 1979 album *L.A. (Light Album)*. The original United States LP release of the *L.A. (Light Album)* featured a version of "Sumahama" that faded out early during the final Japanese verse and did not feature the instrumental ending present on the later released 45 or the re-released CD version of the album. The original LP version of the song was approximately four minutes and seven seconds.

Performers

- *Mike Love:* Lead Vocals

See also

- List of songs by The Beach Boys

Summer Means New Love

"Summer Means New Love"	
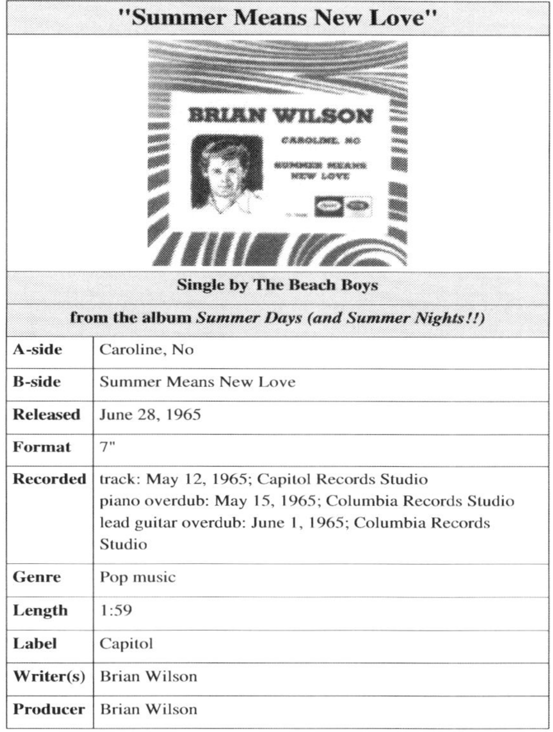	
Single by The Beach Boys	
from the album *Summer Days (and Summer Nights!!)*	
A-side	Caroline, No
B-side	Summer Means New Love
Released	June 28, 1965
Format	7"
Recorded	track: May 12, 1965; Capitol Records Studio piano overdub: May 15, 1965; Columbia Records Studio lead guitar overdub: June 1, 1965; Columbia Records Studio
Genre	Pop music
Length	1:59
Label	Capitol
Writer(s)	Brian Wilson
Producer	Brian Wilson

"**Summer Means New Love**" is an instrumental written by Brian Wilson for the American pop band The Beach Boys. It was released on their 1965 album *Summer Days (and Summer Nights!!)*. It was also released as the b-side to Brian Wilson's first single, "Caroline, No", but this was not until 1966 ("Caroline, No" also appearing on the "Pet Sounds" album).

Musicians

- Israel Baker - violin
- Arnold Belnick - violin
- Hal Blaine - drums
- Frank Capp - vibraphone
- Joseph DiFlore - viola
- Steve Douglas - tenor saxophone
- James Getzoff - violin
- William Hinshaw - French horn
- Harry Hyams - viola
- Carol Kaye - bass guitar

- Bernard Kundell - violin
- Leonard Malarsky - violin
- Jay Migliori - baritone saxophone
- Ralph Schaeffer - violin
- Sid Sharp - violin
- Billy Strange - guitar
- Tommy Tedesco - lead guitar
- Brian Wilson - piano
- Tibor Zelig - violin

See also

- The Beach Boys
- Summer Days (and Summer Nights!!)
- List of songs by The Beach Boys

Summer in Paradise

"Summer in Paradise" is a song written by Mike Love, Terry Melcher and Craig Fall for the American pop band The Beach Boys. It was released on their 1992 album *Summer in Paradise*.

Details

- *Written by:* Mike Love/Terry Melcher/Craig Fall
- *Album:* Summer in Paradise
- *Time:* 3:52 (3:30 on European release)
- *Produced by:* Terry Melcher
- *Lead Vocal*: Mike Love

See also

- List of songs by The Beach Boys

Summer of Love

Not to be confused with the B-52's song of the same name, "Summer of Love".

"**Summer of Love**" is a song written by Mike Love and Terry Melcher for the American pop band The Beach Boys. It was released on their 1992 album *Summer In Paradise*. Originally, it was written to be performed on The Simpsons Sing the Blues as a duet with Bart Simpson.

Some of the background vocals are similar to the background vocals of an earlier Beach Boys song, 1980's "Some of Your Love".

The song was featured on a 1995 episode of Baywatch.

Details

- *Written by:* Mike Love/Terry Melcher
- *Album:* Summer in Paradise
- *Time:* 2:50
- *Produced by:* Terry Melcher
- *Lead Vocal*: Mike Love

See also

- List of songs by The Beach Boys

Summertime Blues

"Summertime Blues"

Single by Eddie Cochran

Released	June 11, 1958
Genre	Rock and roll, Blues
Length	1:53
Label	Liberty Records 55144
Writer(s)	Eddie Cochran Jerry Capehart

"**Summertime Blues**" is a 1958 song recorded by Eddie Cochran about the trials and tribulations of teenage life in America.

It was written in the late 1950s by Eddie Cochran and his manager Jerry Capehart. Originally a single B-side, it peaked at #8 on the Billboard Hot 100 on September 29, 1958 and #18 on the UK Singles Chart. The handclapping is performed by Sharon Sheeley, and the deep vocals at the end of each verse are done by Cochran. The drummer on that recording date was Earl Palmer.

The song was used in the 1980 movie *Caddyshack*. In March 2005, *Q* magazine placed it at #77 in its list of the 100 Greatest Guitar Tracks.

The song is ranked #73 in Rolling Stone's 500 Greatest Songs of All Time.

Part of its lyrics address the controversy surrounding the voting age, which at the time was 21. Such protests would lead to the 26th Amendment, lowering the age to 18.

Cover versions

Beach Boys' version

The Beach Boys's version appears on their album *Surfin' Safari*.

Blue Cheer's version

Blue Cheer recorded it for their 1968 album *Vincebus Eruptum*. Their version, which omits all of the response lyrics heard in Cochran's version in favor of instrumental responses by each member of the band, was featured as one of the first heavy metal recordings in the 2005 documentary *Metal: A Headbanger's Journey*.

During the '80s MTV played a black & white video for the song, taken from a TV program, in their *Closet Classics* segment. The song was also featured in the 1986 movie *Troll* and the 1991 movie *Night on Earth* and the 1996 movie *I Shot Andy Warhol*.

The Who's version

"Summertime Blues"	

Single by The Who	
from the album *Live at Leeds*	
B-side	"Heaven and Hell"
Released	June 1970
Format	7" 45 RPM
Genre	Rock
Length	3:22
Label	Track (UK) Decca (US)
Producer	Kit Lambert, Chris Stamp

The Who singles chronology		
"The Seeker" (1970)	**"Summertime Blues"** (1970)	"See Me, Feel Me" (1970)

The Who's version appears on the 1970 album *Live at Leeds*. Their version is done in a more aggressive style than the original. It is played in the key of A major and on the 3rd verse modulates up to B major. The single peaked at number 37 in the UK and number 28 in the US.

This version features John Entwistle singing the vocal parts of the boss, the father, and the congressman in his trademark baritone growl, doubling Roger Daltrey's lead vocals in his normal voice in the verses, and singing the falsetto part in the chorus, in addition to playing the bass guitar . The track features the original four-man Who lineup of Roger Daltrey, John Entwistle, Keith Moon, and Pete Townshend.

Other live versions from The Who are featured in the concert and documentary film *Woodstock* and the *Monterey Pop Festival* box set.

"Summertime Blues" was a staple of Who concerts between 1967 and 1976, with intermittent appearances thereafter, but has not been played since Entwistle's death in 2002.

Other Who versions can be found on *Live at the Isle of Wight Festival 1970*, *Odds & Sods*, and the CD release of *Live at the Royal Albert Hall*.

Olivia Newton-John's version

On her *Clearly Love* album, 1975.

T. Rex's version

On their *T. Rex* album, 1970. Originally a single 'B' side.

Brian Setzer version

Played by Setzer on the *La Bamba* soundtrack (and on the film in which he performs as Eddie Cochran). Another version appears on *Rockin' by Myself*, released in 1998.

Cheech Marin's version

- Played in the 1987 movie *Born in East L.A.*

Nathan Cavaleri's version

- Played in the 1994 movie *Camp Nowhere*.

Alan Jackson's version

"Summertime Blues"		
Single by Alan Jackson		
from the album *Who I Am*		
B-side	"Hole in the Wall"	
Released	July 4, 1994[1]	
Format	CD Single	
Recorded	January 11, 1994[2]	
Genre	Country	
Length	3:13 (album version)	
Label	Arista Nashville	
Producer	Keith Stegall	
Alan Jackson singles chronology		
"(Who Says) You Can't Have It All" (1993)	"**Summertime Blues**" (1994)	"Livin' on Love" (1994)

- Recorded on his 1994 album *Who I Am*, Alan Jackson's version reached Number One on the U.S. *Billboard* Hot Country Singles & Tracks chart and #4 on the Bubbling Under Hot 100 (equivalent to #104 on the Billboard Hot 100).

While so many versions of this song have been recorded, Alan was inspired by Buck Owens' version.[2]

Music Video

The video was directed by Michael Salomon and was released in June 1994.

Chart positions

Chart (1994)	Peak position
U.S. *Billboard* Hot Country Singles & Tracks	1
U.S. *Billboard* Bubbling Under Hot 100	4
Canadian *RPM* Country Tracks	1

Gary Allan's version

- Played in the 1999 TV miniseries *Shake, Rattle and Roll: An American Love Story.*

Rush's version

"Summertime Blues"	

Single by Rush	
from the album *Feedback*	
Released	June 2004
Format	promo CD
Genre	Rock
Length	3:52
Label	Anthem (CAN) Atlantic Records (US)
Producer	Rush & David Leonard
Rush singles chronology	
"Secret Touch" (2002) "Summertime Blues" (2004) "Far Cry" (2007)	

- **Like the Blue Cheer version, the line "I'd like to help you son..." is not spoken.**
- Played as the theme song for the World Wrestling Entertainment (WWE)'s *SummerSlam* pay per view in 2004.
- In A major like the Who's version (3rd verse likewise modulates up to B major), but guitar intro is that of the Blue Cheer version, transposed to fit new key

The Black Keys' version

- B-side on the *10 A.M. Automatic* single
- bonus track on the Japanese release of their 2004 album *Rubber Factory*

References

[1] Alan Jackson Discography at LP Discographies.com link (http://lpdiscography.com/elpe.htm)
[2] (1995) Album notes for *The Greatest Hits Collection* by Alan Jackson [CD]. Arista Records (07822 18801).

Sunshine

"Sunshine" is a song written by Brian Wilson and Mike Love for the American pop band The Beach Boys. It was released on their 1980 album *Keepin' the Summer Alive*.

Details

- *Written by:* Brian Wilson/Mike Love
- *Album:* Keepin' the Summer Alive
- *Time:* 2 min 52 sec
- *Produced by:* Bruce Johnston

Performers

- *Mike Love:* Lead Vocals

See also

- The Beach Boys
- Keepin' the Summer Alive
- List of songs by The Beach Boys

Surf Jam

"**Surf Jam**" is an instrumental written by Carl Wilson for the American pop band The Beach Boys. It was released on their 1963 album *Surfin' USA*.

Details

- *Written by:* Carl Wilson
- *Album:* Surfin' USA
- *Time:* 2 min 10 sec
- *Produced by:* Nick Venet

See also

- The Beach Boys
- Surfin' USA
- List of songs by The Beach Boys

Surfer Girl

"Surfer Girl"	
Single by The Beach Boys	
from the album *Surfer Girl*	
Released	July 22, 1963
Format	Vinyl
Recorded	June 12, 1963
Genre	Pop music
Length	2:26
Label	Capitol Records
Producer	Brian Wilson
The Beach Boys singles chronology	

"Surfin' U.S.A"/"Shut Down" (1963)	**"Surfer Girl"**/"Little Deuce Coupe" (1963)	"Be True to Your School"/"In My Room" (1963)

"Surfer Girl" is the title of a song written and sung by Brian Wilson for The Beach Boys. It was released as a single and it then appeared on the 1963 album of the same name, *Surfer Girl*. The B-side of the single was Little Deuce Coupe. The single was the first Beach Boys record to have Brian Wilson officially credited as the producer.

Composition

Written solely by Brian Wilson, the song is one of his very first compositions. Although the song is sometimes referred to as a tribute to his then girlfriend Judy Bowles, this is untrue as the song wasn't written with anyone particular in mind. The meter of the song is identical to "When You Wish upon a Star".

Brian explained the genesis of the song: "Back in 1961, I'd never written a song in my life. I was nineteen years old. And I put myself to the test in my car one day. I was actually driving to a hot dog stand, and I actually created a melody in my head without being able to hear it on a piano. I sang it to myself; I didn't even sing it out loud in the car. When I got home that day, I finished the song, wrote the bridge, put the harmonies together and called it 'Surfer Girl'."

Recording

The band first recorded the song at World Pacific Studios on February 8, 1962 which was one of the band's first ever recording sessions. However, the recordings from that session, engineered by Hite Morgan, would ultimately remain unreleased until later archival releases.

The instrumental track as well as the vocals for the officially released version were recorded at Western Recorders on June 12, 1963. The session was produced by Brian; the first song, along with "Little Deuce Coupe", to be credited as a Brian production. The musicians on the track are David Marks and Carl Wilson on guitar; Brian Wilson on bass guitar and Dennis Wilson on drums. The finished instrumental track can be heard on the 1968 release *Stack-O-Tracks*. The song is sung by the group - Mike Love, Carl & Dennis Wilson - with a prominent vocal by Brian. Also recorded during that session was "Little Deuce Coupe".

Single release

The "Surfer Girl" single backed with "Little Deuce Coupe" was released under Capitol Records in the United States on July 22, 1963. The single entered the *Billboard* chart on August 3 and it would then hit the Top 40 on August 17 at the number 28 position. After the single had been on the charts for six weeks it peaked at number 7 on September 14, 1963. It placed at number 5, for three weeks, in *Cash Box* and number 3 in the UPI weekly survey used by newspapers. Its regional performances belie even these higher national peaks, having risen to #1 in playlists in Los Angeles (four weeks), San Francisco (six weeks), Philadelphia, Boston and Dallas -- all major markets where it was among the very biggest hits that year; and runner-up or top three in Washington DC, Toronto, Montreal, Sacramento, Minneapolis, Columbus, Pittsburgh. The single also peaked in the U.S. *Billboard* R & B chart at number 18 in September 1963. Internationally, it was number 1 on New Zealand's *Teen Scene* chart and number 8 in Australia (2UE).

In 1969 the World Pacific Studios sessions recording of the song was issued on Era Records as a single with another artist on the B-side, thus seeing the first official release of the early Surfer Girl recording. The single however failed to make any impact on the charts. Years later, in May 2003, the song was released on an EP under Capitol Records along with "Surfin' USA", "Don't Worry Baby" and "The Beach Boys Medley". However the record failed to chart.

In Australia the single peaked at number 8 on the charts in October 1963 and thus became the band's second top 10 hit in Australia.

Album and alternate releases

The song was first released on an album in 1963 on the band's *Surfer Girl* album.

The early World Pacific Studios recordings of the song were eventually released on CD in 1991 on the archival release *Lost & Found (1961-62)* as well as subsequent re-issues of that album which featured alternate album titles. A binaural mix of the song was released on the 1998 compilation *Endless Harmony Soundtrack*. This mix featured the instrumental recording on one channel and the vocal recording on the other channel.

Live versions

The first live version of the song to be released was on the band's 1973 live album *The Beach Boys in Concert* which featured Alan Jardine on lead vocal and Billy Hinsche on the falsetto vocal. In 1980, a live rendition was recorded, though not released until 2002 on the *Good Timin': Live at Knebworth England 1980* live album. Footage from the concert was also released on video and DVD format. Another live recording of the song from a concert in 1989 was released on the 2006 album *Songs from Here & Back*. There is also a live rehearsal of the song on the *Good Vibrations box set*.

The band performed a live version of the song at the NBC Television Studios in Burbank, California which was filmed on March 14, 1964. Footage of the concert was later released on the DVD *The Lost Concert*. The band also performed the song on The T.A.M.I. Show which was filmed at the Santa Monica Civic Auditorium on October 28 and 29, 1964 and featured other top artists of the day such as Chuck Berry, Marvin Gaye, The Supremes, James Brown & The Famous Flames and The Rolling Stones. The concert was released as a film in 1964 featuring the Beach Boys performance. However, After the initial showing of the film Brian insisted that the band's performance be cut from the film. Because of a rights dispute the footage of the Beach Boys' performance does not appear in most versions of The T.A.M.I. Show. The footage was eventually released on the DVD Sights of Summer included with the special 2004 edition of *Sounds of Summer: The Very Best of The Beach Boys*.

Brian Wilson released a live version of the song on his 2000 live album Live at the Roxy Theatre. Al Jardine also released a live version of the song on his *Live In Las Vegas* solo album.

Cover versions

- The Sentinals on their 1964 album *Surfer Girl*
- Hollyridge Strings covered the song instrumentally on their 1966 album *The Beach Boys Song Book, Volume 2*
- The Fantastic Baggys on their 1966 album *Ride The Wild Surf*
- Little Joe Shaver & Devil Dog on their 1976 album *Sing the Hits of the Beach Boys*
- Papa Doo Run Run on their 1985 album *California Project*
- Phranc on her 1991 album *Positively Phranc*
- Cathedral City Project in 1994
- Pere Ubu on the 1995 album Ray Gun Suitcase
- Don Grusin on the 1997 tribute album *Wouldn't It Be Nice: A Jazz Portrait Of Brian Wilson*
- Philip Aaberg & Scott Mathews on the 1997 various artists compilation *Summer Solstice: A Windham Hill Collection*
- Fred Simon on his 1998 album *Fred Simon's Interpretation of The Beach Boys*
- John B. & The Surfin´ Safaris on their 2002 album *A Tribute to the Beach Boys*
- Scott Cain on his 2004 album *Roller Coaster*

Paul Simon sang a cover version of the song at *An All-Star Tribute to Brian Wilson* in 2001, which was later released on DVD.

OC Times caused consternation at the 2007 International convention of the Barbershop Harmony Society by singing a barbershop arrangement of this song.

In popular culture

- The song featured the film Surf's Up.

Charts

Chart (1963)	**Peak position**
Australian Singles Chart[1]	8
U.S. *Billboard* Hot 100	7
U.S. *Billboard* R&B Best Sellers	18

See also

- List of songs by The Beach Boys

References

[1] "Australian Singles Charts" (http://www.mountvernonandfairway.de/charts10.htm). mountvernonandfairway.de. . Retrieved 12 November 2007.

The Surfer Moon

"The Surfer Moon" is a song written by Brian Wilson for "Bob and Sheri". It was released in October 1962. The next year, Wilson recorded the song with the American pop band The Beach Boys. It was released on their 1963 album *Surfer Girl*.

Details

- *Written by:* Brian Wilson
- *Album:* Surfer Girl
- *Time:* 2 min 11 sec
- *Produced by:* Brian Wilson
- *Recording date*: July 14, 1963 & July 16, 1963

Musicians

- David Marks - guitar
- unknown string players - strings
- Brian Wilson - bass guitar, lead vocal
- Carl Wilson - guitar
- Dennis Wilson - drums

This is the first Beach Boys recording which features a string section.

See also

- The Beach Boys
- Surfer Girl
- List of songs by The Beach Boys

Surfin'

"Surfin'"	
Single by The Beach Boys	
from the album *Surfin' Safari*	
Released	December 8, 1961
Format	Vinyl
Recorded	October 3, 1961 World Pacific Studio
Genre	Surf music
Length	2:10
Label	Candix
Producer	Hite Morgan
The Beach Boys singles chronology	
"Surfin'"/"Luau" (1961)	"Surfin' Safari"/"409" (1962)

"Surfin'" is the title of a song written by Brian Wilson and Mike Love for The Beach Boys. It was first released as a single on December 8, 1961 on Candix Records and it later appeared on the 1962 album *Surfin' Safari*. The B-side of the single was "Luau". It was The Beach Boys first ever released single and it is therefore an important part of The Beach Boys' history. The Beach Boys were trying to think of something original and creative that they could write a song about. Brian Wilson remembers that "One day, my brother Dennis came home from the beach and said, 'Hey, surfing's getting really big. You guys ought to write a song about it."[1] Surfing was becoming the latest craze in California and Dennis himself was an avid surfer.

The song features Mike Love on lead vocals with Carl Wilson on backing vocals and guitar, Al Jardine on backing vocals and stand-up bass, Brian Wilson on backing vocals and percussion and Dennis Wilson on backing vocals. The single peaked at #75 in the United States and it was never released in the United Kingdom as a single.

Origins of the song

Brian Wilson remembers that "I began noodling around the piano singing 'surfin', surfin', surfin''. It sounded stupid. But then Mike [Love] sang 'ba-ba-dippity-dippity-ba-ba.' He was fooling around, trying to spark a new idea with the same bass sounds he'd sung countless times before. From some reason, though, this time when he sang I pounded out a few chords to accompany him and then he took up the chant I'd been singing, 'surfin', surfin''."[1]

Brian continues that "twenty seconds later, I had the opening for the song that would become the Beach Boys' first hit single. A couple of hours later, I finished the song and called it "Surfin'".[1]

Audree Wilson, the Wilson brothers' mother, remembers that they "had guests from England. We took them to Mexico City for a three-day trip, and left the refrigerator stocked. We left them adequate money if they chose to eat out."[1] Carl Wilson continues that "the day after they left, we all went down to a music store and got instruments with our food money...I was gonna play guitar, Alan could play stand up bass, Brian could play keyboards already...Dennis just chose the drums. And then Brian said, 'I'm gonna play bass and you play guitar and then it'll be a rock sound, be rock and roll'. Michael [Mike Love] didn't play anything but he got a saxophone, he thought he'd play sax, but Mike never practiced. The group really learned how to play after we made records."[1]

Audree Wilson continues that she and her husband, Murry Wilson, "barely got in the door, and they said, 'We've got something to play for you.' Well, we saw all this stuff...and they had an act...and that's when Surfin' was born, that's when they sang it and put it together...It was a lot of fun, but they were serious about it. They were having fun, but yet they wanted to do something with it. They were just very excited."[1]

Recording

Brian Wilson recalls that "the five of us arrived at the Morgans' Melrose Avenue office."[1] The group sang a cover version of "Sloop John B" (a song which they'd later record), though Hite Morgan's response was "these days you need something original. You've gotta have an angle. The music business is all about selling a product."[1] Brian remembers that "there was a long, awkward moment of silence that caught us looking at our shoelaces."[1]

Dennis Wilson then surprised the other group members by responding, "Yeah, we got an original. It's called 'Surfin''."[1] Hite Morgan then asked them to play the song but as Brian recalls he responded, "Well, it's not finished. We've got the song, and its original. But it's not done yet."[1]

When it came time to record their new song, the group went back to the Morgans' studio for a second time. Audree Wilson remembers that Brian, Mike, Carl and Al were at the Morgan's studio recording a demo when they said, "We want to play this for you."[1] So they played the demo of 'Surfin'' to Dorinda Morgan and Hite Morgan of Hite Morgan's Recording Studio. Dorinda Morgan was excited by the demo as Audree recalls "Immediately, she said, 'Drop everything, we want to record that.' He [Hite] wasn't so much in favour of it, but she heard something she thought would click."[1]

Brian remembers that "we were at the Morgans' all day; twelve takes of 'Surfin''...tried everyone's patience. I was to blame. I wanted the song to sound perfect."[1] Brian remembers that they "did it all live. Our mix wasn't as good [as today's mix], it wasn't as balanced. You couldn't hear the guitar playing...you didn't hear the bass notes as well...some of the vocals were a little buried. It wasn't mixed and balanced very well. And my father was critical of the first thing we did, he said, 'Well, look, you don't hear the guitar, you don't hear this, what is going on here? Listen, I'm going to have to take over as producer', which he did. He took over as producer."[1]

Radio play

Brian recalls that "Hite [Morgan] announced that he was going to turn our demo into a record, press up a small quantity, and see how it did on local radio."[1]

Dennis Wilson remembers "the first time we ever heard our record played [on the radio], We [Carl, Brian, Dennis and David Marks] were all on Hawthorne Boulevard in Brian's 1957 Ford...they said, 'Here's a group from Hawthorne, California, The Beach Boys, with their song, 'Surfin''. It was a contest; they played three songs and the one that got the most requests over the phone was the one they would add to the playlist. We were screamin' in the street, and knockin' on everybody's door, 'We got a record on the radio!'...That was the biggest high ever. Nothing will ever top the expression on Brian's face. Ever...THAT is the all-time moment."[1]

Dennis remembers that they "got so excited hearing our record on the radio that Carl threw up." Brian recalls that he "ran down the street screaming."[1] Russ Regan, the man who gave The Beach Boys their name, remembers that 'Surfin'' "actually exploded here in the city of Los Angeles. Their record was a big record here. It was just a natural Southern California record."[1]

Alternate versions from 1961

The first recorded demo version of the song is available on CD (both the 1993 *Good Vibrations – Best of The Beach Boys* box, and the 2001 *Hawthorne, CA* two CD set) featuring a portion of "Surfin' " recorded on Brian's home Wollensak tape recorder "sometime in early September 1961, between the Labor Day weekend get-together and the group's first recording session with the Morgans on September 15th" according to Peter Ames Carlin's 2006 book *Catch a Wave*.

A later demo version of "Surfin'" was recorded at the aforementioned session at Hite and Dorinda Morgan's home studio September 15; this version is available on the *Lost & Found (1961–62)* CD released in 1991. (Both these versions are in a different key and lack the musical introduction of the tracks recorded October 3, 1961, among other differences.) This archival CD also features an alternate take of "Surfin'" recorded the same day as the eventual master take released on three different labels (X-301, Candix-301 and Capitol LP T-1081, the *Surfin' Safari* album.) The master take was subsequently sped up for release in the 60's, but is restored to the original speed on *Lost and Found* as well as the 1993 *Good Vibrations* box set.

Cover versions

Jan and Dean, with instrumental and vocal help from The Beach Boys, covered the song on their album *Jan & Dean Take Linda Surfin'*. The Beach Boys also rerecorded the song for their 1992 album Summer in Paradise.

See also

- List of songs by The Beach Boys

References

[1] *The Beach Boys and the California Myth* by David Leaf. Published by Grosset & Dunlap, 1978. ISBN 0-448-14626-6

Surfin' Safari

"Surfin' Safari"	
Single by The Beach Boys	
from the album *Surfin' Safari*	
A-side	"Surfin' Safari"
B-side	"409"
Released	June 4, 1962
Format	Vinyl
Recorded	April 19, 1962
Genre	Rock
Length	2:05
Label	Capitol Records
Writer(s)	Brian Wilson and Mike Love
Producer	Murry Wilson
The Beach Boys singles chronology	

"Surfin'"/"Luau" (1961)	**"Surfin' Safari"**/"409" (1962)	"Ten Little Indians"/"County Fair" (1962)

"**Surfin' Safari**" is a song written by Brian Wilson and Mike Love for The Beach Boys. It was released as a single with "409" in 1962. The song also appeared on the 1962 album of the same name, *Surfin' Safari*.

Recording

The band first recorded the song at World Pacific Studios on February 8, 1962 in what was one of the band's first ever recording sessions. However, the recordings from that session, engineered by Hite Morgan, would ultimately remain unreleased until later archival releases. The only difference instrumentally on this early version as opposed to the officially released version was the presence of Al Jardine on guitar instead of David Marks.

The instrumental track as well as the vocals for the officially released version were recorded at Western Recorders on April 19, 1962. The session, produced by Brian, featured David Marks and Carl Wilson on guitar; Brian Wilson on bass guitar and Dennis Wilson on drums. The song features Mike Love on lead vocals with backing vocals by Brian, Carl & Dennis Wilson and Mike Love. Also recorded during that session were "409", "Lonely Sea" and "Their Hearts Were Full Of Spring". This session was recorded and given to Capitol Records as a demo tape. The label was impressed and immediately signed the band to their first major label. "Surfin' Safari" and "409" would be the band's first single to be issued under Capitol Records.

Single release

The "Surfin' Safari" single backed with "409" was the band's second single and the first single to be released on the band's new label Capitol Records in the United States in June, 1962.

Originally Capitol Records felt "409" should be the 'A' Side, and first promoted the car song (according to Beach Boys biographers Badman, Gaines and Carlin) instead of 'Surfin Safari'. However, as noted in the booklet to the 1993 "Good Vibrations- Thirty Years of the Beach Boys" CD box-set, radio station airplay in Phoenix, Arizona jump-started the 'B' side into a major nationwide hit. The *Billboard* issue of July 14, 1962 cited Detroit as the major market of its national 'break out'.

The single peaked at the number 14 position on the *Billboard* Hot 100 chart, with "409" also charting at number 76, making it the band's first double-sided hit single. It placed at number 10 on the *Cash Box* sales chart, and number 5 on UPI's national weekly survey used by newspapers. According to music journalist Joseph Murrells in *The Book of Golden Discs*, 1978 edition, it placed number 3 on another national chart. Certainly its regional sales backed up these higher placings (than *Billboard*). As well as its Capitol-record sales in New York, it was No. 1 in Los Angeles, San Diego, Dallas, Minneapolis and Hartford; and top five in Chicago, San Francisco, Phoenix, Tucson, Nashville, Cincinnati, Columbus, Dayton, Springfield MASS.

Capitol A&R executive Nick (Nik) Venet, who signed the group and is listed as producer on their first two albums, is quoted in the Steven Gaines book as saying regarding the release that "The biggest order Capitol had from a single market all year [1962] was from New York City - where there was no surfing. It sold approximately nine hundred thousand records, but not enough for a gold."

In January 1970, the World Pacific Studios sessions recording of the song was issued on Trip Records as the B-side of a "Surfin'" single re-issue. This was the first official release of the early Surfer Girl recording. The single however failed to make any impact on the charts.

In October 1962, the "Surfin' Safari" single was the first to be released by the band in the United Kingdom. However, given mediocre reviews at best, the single failed to make any impact on the charts. It did qualify as the Beach Boys' first international chart-topper, however. By the end of September it had peaked at No. 7 in Australia's *Music Maker* chart -- only to reach the Billboard top 20 the following week -- then in November spent three weeks at No. 1 in Sweden (both charts cited by contemporary issues of *Billboard*). In Germany, the World Pacific Studios recording of the song was used as the single release instead of the more well-known version. The single failed to chart.

Album and alternate releases

The song was first released on an album in 1962 on the band's debut *Surfin' Safari* album, and on a number of later 'greatest hits' compilations.

The 1993 *Good Vibrations - Thirty Years of the Beach Boys* box set includes the original Capitol "Surfin' Safari" single with a notable difference from other releases: the track does not fade out, but instead continues well beyond the original fade until the vocals, then the guitars, and finally drums stop playing.

Three takes of the early World Pacific Studios recordings of the song were eventually released on CD in 1991 on the archival release *Lost & Found (1961-62)* as well as subsequent re-issues of that album which featured alternate album titles.

1962 filmed performance

A live concert performance of the tune "Surfin' Safari" is featured in the short documentary "One Man's Challenge", written and directed by Dale Smallin. Filmed July 28, 1962 (with the same lineup as the official Capitol single) at the Azuza Teen Club, this particular visual version of the song is, according to author Jon Stebbins in 'The Lost Beach Boy', "The only known performance footage of the Pendleton-shirt era Beach Boys."

In popular culture

- The original recording by The Beach Boys is featured in the film *American Graffiti* (1973).

See also

- List of The Beach Boys songs

Surfin' USA

"Surfin' U.S.A."	
Single by The Beach Boys	
from the album *Surfin' USA*	
Released	March 4, 1963
Format	Vinyl
Recorded	January 5, 1963
Genre	Surf rock
Length	2:27
Label	Capitol Records
Writer(s)	Chuck Berry, Brian Wilson
Producer	Nick Venet

The Beach Boys singles chronology		
"Ten Little Indians"/"County Fair" (1962)	**"Surfin' USA"**/"Shut Down" (1963)	"Surfer Girl"/"Little Deuce Coupe" (1963)

"**Surfin' U.S.A.**" is the title of a song with lyrics written by Brian Wilson for The Beach Boys, set to the melody from Chuck Berry's *Sweet Little Sixteen*. Berry has sole credit for composing the song.[1] "Surfin' USA" was recorded by The Beach Boys released as a single on March 4, 1963 and it also appeared on the 1963 album of the same name. It debuted on network television via *The Steve Allen Show* broadcast two days before release with the band lip-synching it. It peaked at #2 in the chart of the *Music Vendor* trade paper (within a year renamed *Record World*) and according to several sources was the biggest seller in the US in 1963. The B-side of the single is "Shut Down". The song features Mike Love on lead vocals.

It was revived in 1977 by teen idol Leif Garrett, who also had a top 20 hit with it in the USA.

The song was famously featured in the hit 1985 Michael J. Fox comedy *Teen Wolf*.

Composition

The songwriting credit for the song was eventually given entirely to Chuck Berry, as "Surfin' USA" is similar to Berry's song "Sweet Little Sixteen" in many respects, including melody, rhythm, and lyrics.

Brian Wilson claims the song was merely influenced by Berry, as well as Chubby Checker and Jimmy Bowles, the little brother of Wilson's girlfriend Judy. Bowles came up with the list of surf spots which were included in the song.[2]

Surfing spots

At the time that the song was written, Brian Wilson was dating a girl named Judy Bowles. Her brother, Jimmy Bowles, was an avid surfer. Brian thought to himself "what about doing surf lyrics and mentioning every surf spot in the state? They're doing it here, there, in this city and that, like Chubby Checker's 'Twistin' U.S.A.'."[2] According to Brian, "I asked [Jimmy] to make a list of every surf spot he knew, and by God he didn't leave one out."[2]

In the song the following surfing spots are mentioned, the majority of places being situated in California, two in Hawaii and one in Australia:

- "Del Mar" - Del Mar, San Diego County, California
- "Ventura County Line" - Ventura County, California
- "Santa Cruz" - Santa Cruz, Santa Cruz County, California
- "Trestles" - San Onofre State Park, San Diego County, California
- "Australia's Narrabeen" - Narrabeen, New South Wales
- "Manhattan" - Manhattan Beach, Los Angeles County, California
- "Doheny" - Doheny Beach, Dana Point, Orange County, California
- "Haggerty's" - Palos Verdes Estates, Los Angeles County, California
- "Swami's" - Swami's Beach, Encinitas, San Diego County, California
- "Pacific Palisades" - Pacific Palisades, Los Angeles County, California
- "San Onofre" - San Onofre State Park, San Diego County, California
- "Sunset" - Sunset Beach, Oahu, Hawaii - or - Sunset Beach, Orange County, California
- "Redondo Beach" - Redondo Beach, Los Angeles County, California
- "LA" - Los Angeles, Los Angeles County, California
- "La Jolla" - La Jolla, San Diego County, California
- "Waimea Bay" - Waimea Bay, Hawaii

Single release

The "Surfin' USA" single backed with "Shut Down" was released under Capitol Records in the United States in March 1963. The song peaked on the *Billboard* pop chart at number three, the band's first top ten hit in the United States. The B-side also charted at number 23. The song was re-issued in the U.S. as a single in July 1974 backed with "The Warmth of the Sun". That single also hit the *Billboard* Top 40 charts, peaking at the number 36 position.

In the United Kingdom the single was released in June 1963. The third single by the band to be issued in the UK, it became the first single to actually chart. It would go on to peak at the number 34 position (#28 in the New Musical Express).

In Australia the single was released in 1963 and peaked at number 9, thus becoming the band's first single to chart in Australia. The single was re-released in Australia in 1974 and again charted, peaking at number 66. In Sweden, the single was released in 1963 and peaked on the charts at the number 6 position. In Canada, the single was released in 1963 and peaked at the number 6 position on the charts. In national charts cited by contemporary Billboard issues, in July 1963 it peaked at #9 in Hong Kong, #8 in Austria the following month, and #9 (for two weeks) in Japan, delayed until August 1964.

Chart performance summary

Chart (1963)	Peak position
U.S. *Billboard* Hot 100	3
Australian Singles Chart[3]	9
Canadian Singles Chart[4]	1
Swedish Singles Chart[5]	6
UK Singles Chart	34
Chart (1974)	**Peak position**
U.S. *Billboard* Hot 100	36
Australian Singles Chart	66

Songwriting credit disputes

When the song was released in 1963, the original pressing listed Brian Wilson as the sole composer of the song. Wilson has written that, after the song became a hit, "Chuck Berry claimed the melody was his, an inadvertent copy of 'Sweet Little Sixteen'."[2] Wilson also wrote there are "plenty of musicologists who'd argue otherwise."[2] Murry Wilson turned the copyright over to Berry without ever informing his son Brian.[2] Brian Wilson didn't realize for more than twenty-five years that Murry also "gave away [Brian's] royalties for writing the lyrics"[2] , possibly because Wilson's lyrics list several geographical locations in a very similar fashion to Berry's original lyrics. Berry still has sole songwriting credit for the song.[1]

Despite there being tensions over the incident at the time, Carl Wilson says the Beach Boys "ran into Chuck Berry in Copenhagen and he told us he loves 'Surfin' USA'."[6]

Musicians

- Frank DeVito - drums
- Mike Love - lead vocal
- David Marks - guitar, vocals
- Brian Wilson - bass guitar, organ, vocals
- Carl Wilson - guitar, vocals
- Dennis Wilson - vocals, drums

Album and alternate releases

The song was first released on an album as the title track on the band's 1963 album *Surfin' USA*. In July 1963, a month after the song had been issued as a single in the United States, Capitol issued the *Surfin' USA EP* featuring "Surfin' USA" & "Shut Down" on the A-side and "Surfer Girl" & "Surfin' Safari" on the B-side. The EP however, failed to chart. In May, 2003 Capitol again issued the song on an EP along with "Surfer Girl", "Don't Worry, Baby", and "The Beach Boys Medley". However, the record failed to make an impact on the charts.

A demo version of the song featuring only Brian Wilson singing and playing piano was released on the 1993 box set, *Good Vibrations: Thirty Years of The Beach Boys*. A different demo version, in which Wilson is joined by drums was released on the 2001 archival release *Hawthorne, CA*. Both demos feature similar minor lyrical differences from the final recording. Both demos are played in the key of E major, in contrast to the final recording which was pitched in Eb.

The instrumental track of the final recording was also released on the *Hawthorne, CA* album. This version of the cut does not 'fade out', but continues on well past the original ending of the song until it ends abruptly.

Live versions

After being released the song became a concert regular for the band. The band recorded live versions of "Surfin' USA" on several Beach Boys albums. It was first released on *The Beach Boys in Concert* album. A concert from Anaheim Stadium on July 3, 1976 which featured the song was filmed and produced by Lorne Michaels for a Beach Boys television special which first aired in the United States in August, 1976. The TV special was later released on video and DVD as *Good Vibrations Tour*. In 1980, a live rendition was recorded, though not released until 2002 on the *Good Timin': Live at Knebworth England 1980* live album. Footage from the concert was also released on video and DVD format. A live version was also released on the band's 1993 box set *Good Vibrations: Thirty Years of The Beach Boys*.

The band also performed a live version of the song at the NBC Television Studios in Burbank, California which was filmed on March 14, 1964. Footage of the concert was later released on the DVD *The Lost Concert*. The band performed the song on The T.A.M.I. Show which was filmed at the Santa Monica Civic Auditorium on October 28 and 29, 1964 and featured other top artists of the day such as Chuck Berry, Marvin Gaye, The Supremes, James Brown & The Famous Flames and The Rolling Stones. The concert was released as a film in 1964 featuring the Beach Boys performance. However, after the initial showing of the film Brian insisted that the band's performance be cut from the film. Because of a rights dispute the footage of the Beach Boys' performance does not appear in most versions of The T.A.M.I. Show. The footage was eventually released on the DVD Sights of Summer included with the special 2004 edition of *Sounds of Summer: The Very Best of The Beach Boys*.

Also, Alan Jardine included the song on his *Live In Las Vegas* album.

Cover versions

Papa Doo Run Run covered the song on their 1985 album *California Project*. The Jesus and Mary Chain covered the song, which appears on their 1988 album *Barbed Wire Kisses*, a compilation of B-sides and rare tracks. Typical for early style of The Jesus and Mary Chain the song features large amounts of feedback. The power metal band Blind Guardian covered the song on their 1996 album *The Forgotten Tales*. Noise punk band Melt Banana covered the song on their album *13,000 Miles At Light Velocity*. Pre-teen pop singer Aaron Carter performed a cover of the song. It was released as a single in 1998, and also appeared on the 1998 re-release of his self titled debut album. John B. & The Surfin´ Safaris covered the song on their 2002 album *A Tribute to the Beach Boys*.

Frank Sidebottom recorded a verion as *Surfin Timperley* (Timperley being nowhere near the sea, and therefore not a place where surfing is possible). Redgum parodied this track as "Servin' USA". Alvin and the Chipmunks also released a cover version of the song. Pennywise have also covered the song at various live performances.

Serbian rock band Eva Braun covered the song with lyrics in Serbian language entitled "Zviždi Srbija" in 1997, but the song had not been officially released until 2008 on the compilation album *Off the Record*.

See also

- List of songs by The Beach Boys

References

[1] http://www.arcmusic.com/searchresults.aspx?track=81367

[2] *Wouldn't It Be Nice: My Own Story* by Brian Wilson and Todd Gold. Published by Harpercollins, 1991. ISBN 0-06-018313-6

[3] "Australian Singles Charts" (http://www.mountvernonandfairway.de/charts10.htm). mountvernonandfairway.de. . Retrieved 12 November 2007.

[4] "Canadian Singles Charts" (http://www.mountvernonandfairway.de/charts8.htm). mountvernonandfairway.de. . Retrieved 12 November 2007.

[5] "Swedish Singles Charts" (http://www.mountvernonandfairway.de/charts1.htm). mountvernonandfairway.de. . Retrieved 12 November 2007.

[6] *Good Timin': Live at Knebworth England 1980* DVD, 2002.

Surf's Up

"Surf's Up"	
Single by The Beach Boys	
from the album *Surf's Up*	
Released	November 8, 1971
Format	Vinyl
Recorded	1966–1967, 1971
Genre	Baroque pop, sunshine pop
Length	4:12
Label	Brother/Reprise
Producer	The Beach Boys
The Beach Boys singles chronology	

"Long Promised Road"/"'Til I Die" (1971)	**"Surf's Up"**/"Don't Go Near the Water" (1971)	"You Need a Mess of Help to Stand Alone"/"Cuddle Up" (1972)

"Surf's Up" is the title of a song written by Brian Wilson and Van Dyke Parks. The song was intended as one of the centrepieces for the aborted Beach Boys' album *Smile*, which was begun in late 1966 but shelved in mid-1967. It was reworked and used as the title track for the twenty-second official album by The Beach Boys, *Surf's Up*, released in 1971. It also appears as the tenth track in Brian Wilson's re-recorded *Smile*, released in 2004.

1966-67 recording

Studio version

"Surf's Up" was written in a single night at Brian Wilson's piano in his sandbox. Brian believes; "the lyrics for 'Surf's Up' were very Van Dyke; only he could have done that - only Van Dyke could have written those lyrics. We wrote that at my Chickering piano, I think, in my sandbox and it took us about an hour at most to write the whole thing. We wrote it pretty fast; it all happened like it should." In *Beautiful Dreamer: Brian Wilson and the Story of Smile*, when asked by Van Dyke Parks what Wilson was feeling when he wrote the music for "Surf's Up," he responded with, "I just felt some love, I felt a whole lot of love, there was a whole lot of love going on at the time." An apparently complete backing track for the first (2:20) section was recorded and mixed in November 1966, but vocals and other overdubs were still to be added, and work on the middle and closing sections was either never undertaken, or never finished. It is notable that the flourishes played on muted trumpet in the verses of "Surf's Up" are almost identical to the familiar 'laughing' refrain of the theme for the *Woody Woodpecker* cartoon series. This musical reference recurs in the instrumental piece "Fall Breaks And Back To Winter" on the album *Smiley Smile*, (which was in fact subtitled "Woody Woodpecker Symphony").

The original studio recording of the song was never completed. A fully finished (or near-complete) backing track for the first section was recorded in late 1966 and early 1967 under the production of Brian Wilson, and other vocal and instrumental segments were also recorded, but a final edit was apparently never made. Although the second section of the song features the demo version of the song from 1966-67, with Brian Wilson on lead vocals, the entire demo version remained unreleased until it was included on the Beach Boys 1993 box set release *Good Vibrations: Thirty Years of The Beach Boys*.

CBS News version

The song was certainly fully composed by November 1966, when Brian Wilson was filmed performing a complete 'demo' solo version of the song on piano for a CBS News special on popular music. The show was hosted by Leonard Bernstein, who expressed his admiration for the song:

Brian Wilson's performance of "Surf's Up"

> There is a new song, too complex to get all of first time around. It could come only out of the ferment that characterizes today's pop music scene. Brian Wilson, leader of the famous Beach Boys, and one of today's most important musicians, sings his own 'Surf's Up.' Poetic, beautiful even in its obscurity, 'Surf's Up' is one aspect of new things happening in pop music today. As such, it is a symbol of the change many of these young musicians see in our future.

The demo version of the song obviously does not feature any additional vocal or instrumental overdubs, and, at the conclusion of the song, Brian can be heard singing the original ending to the "Surf's Up" song without the "Child is Father of the Man" vocal overdubs.

1971 recording

A later composite version of the song was completed by The Beach Boys under the supervision of Carl Wilson in 1971. The song was credited as being produced by The Beach Boys, though most of the production for the new instrumental sections of the song was done by Carl. The first section featured a new lead vocal by Carl dubbed over the original 1966 backing track, as well as additional instrumentation. It's said that the band asked Brian to do the lead vocal as he would have originally, but he was unwilling to or possibly felt he was unable to perform it at this point in time.

The second section ("Dove nested towers"...) featured mainly Brian's vocal and piano from the demo recording plus new vocal and instrumental overdubs. The third section combined the closing section of Brian's demo with newly-recorded vocals and other additions, with the lead vocal ("A children's song, have you listened as they play?") being done by Al Jardine. Oddly enough, despite being completely unwilling to work on the rest of the song and do the lead vocal, the new ending of the 1971 version was entirely Brian's work. It is based on another *Smile* era track, "Child is the Father of the Man". It is unknown whether the song was originally to end this way or if it was a newer addition by Brian. An additional line to this section, "The father's life is done, and the children carry on," was written but was removed at Brian's request.

The newly-finished song was released as a single and also appeared on the 1971 album of the same name, *Surf's Up*. The B-side of the single was "Don't Go Near the Water". Evidently referring to the solo 'demo' version, Brian stated, "The vocal on that [Surf's Up] was a little bit limited. It's not my favorite vocal I ever did, but it did have heart. Nevertheless, it'll be out there again with this reissue, and I'll be naked to the world!"

Critical reception

Writing for *The Guardian* in October 1971, Geoffrey Cannon praised the song's music and the group's vocal harmonies, highlighting it as a standout track from *Surf's Up*, despite his criticism of its co-writer, Van Dyke Parks;[1]

> Van Dyke Parks, who writes pretentious words, messed Brian up in 1967, particularly on the album Smiley Smile. The title track of Surf's Up was written by Van Dyke Parks around that period, and Brian sat on it until now... It's delicacy is close to Pet Sounds, released in 1966, especially to "You Still Believe In Me" and "I Just Wasn't Made For These Times" on that album. Its subtle shifts of pace and timing, and delicate harmony singing, put it in the top flight of Beach Boys' numbers.

2004 version

On Brian Wilson's 2004 recording of *Smile*, the musical arrangement is very similar to the 1971 release, but with the clarity of modern recording technology. The vocal arrangement is slightly altered for the highest parts. This melody runs a full octave plus a minor third, sweeping up a minor sixth (five whole steps) at one point, and peaking at the second F above Middle C. As Brian Wilson was then 62, with a naturally reduced vocal range, the part was rearranged for harmonies, with additional voices blending in smoothly, allowing Wilson to sing a lower part. In the concert performances, this approach was used many other times during the *Smile* material, with his younger backup singers doubling many of his parts in unison (similar to the recording technique of doubletracking), blending in and taking over for the high parts that were more difficult for Wilson to reach on stage than in the studio.

Personnel

- Brian Wilson – lead vocals, and keyboards
- Scott Bennett – vocals, keyboards, xylophone
- Nelson Bragg – vocals, percussion
- Jeffery Foskett – vocals, percussion
- Probyn Gregory – trumpet, french horn
- Jim Hines – drums
- Bob Lizik – bass
- Paul Mertons – flute, harmonica
- Taylor Mills – vocals
- Darian Sahanaja – vocals, keyboards
- Nick Walusko – vocals, guitar
- Stockholm Strings 'N' Horns

Other releases

A Dolby Digital 5.1 surround sound version of the song was released on the *Endless Harmony* DVD as a bonus track. The track, along with the other 5.1 surround sound mixes, were produced and mixed by Mark Linett. On *An All-Star Tribute to Brian Wilson* (2001), a cover version was made by David Crosby, Vince Gill, Jimmy Webb. Gill sang the first part, Webb & Gill sang the second, and David Crosby sang the coda in an extended version.

Some fan mixes and bootlegs sync Brian's original vocal demo with the original 1967 backing track.

See also

- List of songs by The Beach Boys

References

[1] Cannon, Geoffrey. "Feature: *Out of the city*". *The Guardian* (Guardian Media Group) (October 29, 1971): 10.

Susie Cincinnati

"Susie Cincinnati"	
Single by The Beach Boys	
from the album *15 Big Ones*	
Released	February 23, 1970 December 23, 1974 November 1, 1976
Format	Vinyl
Recorded	Unknown
Genre	Rock music
Length	2 min 57 sec
Label	Brother/Reprise
Producer	The Beach Boys

The Beach Boys singles chronology

"Break Away"/"Celebrate the News" (1969)	"Add Some Music to Your Day"/"Susie Cincinnati" (1970)	"Cottonfields"/"The Nearest Faraway Place" (1970)
----	----	----
"California Saga: California"/"Funky Pretty" (1973)	"Child of Winter"/"Susie Cincinnati" (1974)	"Sail On, Sailor"/"Only with You" (1975)
----	----	----
"It's O.K."/"Had to Phone Ya" (1976)	"Everyone's in Love with You"/"Susie Cincinnati" (1976)	"Honkin' Down the Highway"/"Solar System" (1977)

"Susie Cincinnati" is a song written by Al Jardine for the American pop band The Beach Boys. It was released as a B-Side to three singles over six years. First, it was released as the B-side of Add Some Music to Your Day on February 23, 1970, then as the B-side of Child of Winter on December 23, 1974, and finally as the B-side of Everyone's in Love with You on November 1, 1976.

It was also released their 1976 album *15 Big Ones*.

A single mix from 1970, which is slightly different from the mix on 15 Big Ones, was released on Greatest Hits Volume Three: Best of the Brother Years 1970-1986.

Details

- *Written by:* Al Jardine
- *Album:* 15 Big Ones
- *Time:* 2 min 57 sec
- *Produced by:* The Beach Boys (*15 Big Ones credits production to Brian Wilson*)

Performers

- *Al Jardine:* Lead Vocals, Backing Vocals, Guitar
- *Brian Wilson:* Backing Vocals, Bass, Harmonica
- *Carl Wilson:* Backing Vocals, Guitar
- *Dennis Wilson:* Backing Vocals, drums
- *Mike Love:* Backing Vocals
- *Bruce Johnston:* Backing Vocals
- *Daryl Dragon:* Clavinet

See also

- The Beach Boys
- 15 Big Ones
- List of songs by The Beach Boys

Sweet Sunday

"Sweet Sunday" is a song written by Brian Wilson and Mike Love for the American pop band The Beach Boys. It was released on their 1978 album *M.I.U. Album*.

Details

- *Written by:* Brian Wilson/Mike Love
- *Album:* M.I.U. Album
- *Time:* 2 min 42 sec
- *Produced by:* Al Jardine/Ron Altbach

Performers

- *Carl Wilson:* Lead Vocals

See also

- The Beach Boys
- M.I.U. Album
- List of songs by The Beach Boys

Take a Load Off Your Feet

"Take a Load Off Your Feet"		
Song by The Beach Boys from the album *Surf's Up*		
Released	August 30, 1971	
Recorded	January 1970 early 1971	
Genre	Pop	
Length	2:29	
Label	Brother/Reprise	
Composer	Al Jardine, Brian Wilson, Gary Winfrey	
Producer	The Beach Boys	
***Surf's Up* track listing**		
Long Promised Road (2)	**"Take a Load Off Your Feet"** (3)	Disney Girls (1957) (4)

"Take a Load Off Your Feet" is a song written by Al Jardine, Brian Wilson and Gary Winfrey for the American pop band The Beach Boys. It was projected to be released on *Add Some Music*, an album which was to be released in 1970. After that album was reworked into *Sunflower*, "Take a Load Off Your Feet" was released on the next Beach Boys album, *Surf's Up*.

Composition

Gary Winfrey returned to California, after serving in the Air Force, in 1968. He and Al Jardine quickly rekindled a friendship that had begun back when both were in high school. Winfrey's wife Sandi was pregnant at the time, and her ankles were swollen. With the song Hair being popular at the time, somebody suggested writing a similar song about ankles. That song turned into "Take a Load Off Your Feet". Brian Wilson would later add some lyrics and help with the melody.

Recording

The first session for the song was during the *Add Some Music* sessions in January 1970. The song was then put on hold until the early part of the next year. All of the sessions were held at Brian Wilson's home studio. Brian did the lead vocal on the first verse, before giving way to Jardine, who sang the rest of the song and also played bass guitar. The Beach Boys, with help from Winfrey, sang the backing vocals, and Brian added the sound effects.

See also

- List of songs by The Beach Boys

Talk to Me

"Talk to Me", or **"Talk to Me, Talk to Me"**, is a song written and originally recorded by Joe Seneca.[1] It was also covered by Little Willie John (1958), Sunny & the Sunglows (1963), and The Beach Boys, whose version was released on their 1976 album *15 Big Ones*, with Carl Wilson singing lead vocals.

Cover versions

- 1958 Little Willie John
- 1961 Bobby Vee, on *Bobby Vee*
- 1963 Sunny & the Sunglows
- 1967 The Avons
- 1969 Al Green, on *Green Is Blues*
- 1973 Johnnie Taylor, on *Taylored in Silk*
- 1976 The Beach Boys, on *15 Big Ones*
- 1978 Freddy Fender, on *Swamp Gold*
- 1978 Ray Stevens, on *There Is Something on Your Mind*
- 1982 Mickey Gilley, who had his fifteenth number one country hit [2] .
- 1983 Colorblind James Experience (single)

Beach Boys version

Details

- *Album:* 15 Big Ones
- *Time:* 2 min 14 sec
- *Produced by:* Brian Wilson
- *Arranged by:* Brian Wilson

Performers

- *Carl Wilson:* Lead Vocals, Backing Vocals, Bass
- *Brian Wilson:* Backing Vocals, String Ensemble, Piano, Organ Moog Bass
- *Dennis Wilson:* Backing Vocals, drums
- *Mike Love:* Backing Vocals
- *Al Jardine:* Backing Vocals
- *Billy Hinsche:* Guitar
- *Ed Carter:* Guitar

See also

- The Beach Boys
- 15 Big Ones
- List of songs by The Beach Boys

References

[1] ""La Onda Chicano: Sunny Ozuna, still talking – to you, me, and Texicans everywhere" by Greg Beets" (http://www.austinchronicle.com/gyrobase/Issue/story?oid=oid:388445). *The Austin Chronicle*. 2006-07-21. . Retrieved 2008-03-31.

[2] Whitburn, Joel (2004). *The Billboard Book Of Top 40 Country Hits: 1944-2006, Second edition*. Record Research. p. 137.

Tears in the Morning

"Tears in the Morning"	
Single by The Beach Boys	
from the album *Sunflower*	
B-side	"It's About Time"
Released	November 1970
Format	7" vinyl
Recorded	November 18, 1969, and January 26 & 28, 1970
Genre	Sunshine Pop
Length	4:07
Label	Brother/Reprise
Writer(s)	Bruce Johnston
Producer	The Beach Boys
The Beach Boys singles chronology	

"Slip on Through" (1970)	**"Tears in the Morning"** (1970)	"Cool, Cool Water" (1971)

***Sunflower* track listing**

Side one

1. "Slip on Through"
2. "This Whole World"
3. "Add Some Music to Your Day"
4. "Got to Know the Woman"
5. "Deirdre"
6. "It's About Time"

Side two

1. "**Tears in the Morning**"
2. "All I Wanna Do"
3. "Forever"
4. "Our Sweet Love"
5. "At My Window"
6. "Cool, Cool Water"

"**Tears in the Morning**" is a song written by Bruce Johnston for the American pop band The Beach Boys. It was released on their 1970 album *Sunflower*. It was also released as a single, with the B-side of the single being "It's About Time". The single never charted in the U.S. or in the U.K., but reached the top 10 in the Netherlands.

Personnel (incomplete)

- Bruce Johnston – lead vocals
- Michel Colombier – arrangement

Chart performance

Chart (1971)	Peak position
Dutch GfK chart[1]	4
Dutch Top 40[2]	6

Cover versions

Norwegian stoner rock band Thulsa Doom recorded a cover version of this song in 2005 for their album *Keyboard, Oh Lord! Why Don't We?*.

See also

- List of songs by The Beach Boys

References

[1] "dutchcharts.nl - The Beach Boys - Tears In The Morning" (http://dutchcharts.nl/showitem.asp?interpret=The+Beach+Boys&titel=Tears+In+The+Morning&cat=s). . Retrieved 24 February 2009.
[2] "De Nederlandse Top 40, week 2, 1971" (http://www.radio538.nl/web/show/id=44685/chartid=6438). . Retrieved 24 February 2009.

Tell Me Why

"Tell Me Why"	
Song by The Beatles from the album *A Hard Day's Night*	
Released	10 July 1964
Recorded	27 February 1964 Abbey Road Studios
Genre	Rock
Length	2:10
Label	Parlophone
Writer	Lennon/McCartney
Producer	George Martin
***A Hard Day's Night* track listing**	

13 tracks

Side one

1. "A Hard Day's Night"
2. "I Should Have Known Better"
3. "If I Fell"
4. "I'm Happy Just to Dance with You"
5. "And I Love Her"
6. "Tell Me Why"
7. "Can't Buy Me Love"

Side two

- "Any Time at All"

2. "I'll Cry Instead"
3. "Things We Said Today"
4. "When I Get Home"
5. "You Can't Do That"
6. "I'll Be Back"

"Tell Me Why"	
Song by The Beach Boys from the album *Beach Boys' Party!*	
Released	8 November 1965
Genre	Rock and roll
Length	1:46
Label	Capitol
Composer	Lennon/McCartney
Producer	Brian Wilson
***Beach Boys' Party!* track listing**	

"I Should Have Known Better" (2)	**"Tell Me Why"** (3)	"Papa-Oom-Mow-Mow" (4)

"Tell Me Why" is a song by The Beatles from their album *A Hard Day's Night*. In the US, it was released on both the US version of *A Hard Day's Night* and the album *Something New*. Credited to Lennon/McCartney, it was written by John Lennon in either Paris or New York[1] [2] and recorded in eight takes on 27 February 1964 at Abbey Road Studios.[3]

Background

Paul McCartney said:

> "I think a lot of these [Lennon's] songs like "Tell Me Why" may have been based in real experiences or affairs John was having, or arguments with Cynthia [Lennon's wife] or whatever, but it never occurred to us until later to put that slant on it all."[4]

Lennon described the song as resembling "a black New York girl-group song".[5] Its basic structure of simple doo-wop chord changes and block harmonies over a walking bass line "creates an illusion of sincerity through its sheer attack."[2]

"Tell Me Why" was performed in The Beatles' debut feature film, *A Hard Day's Night*. The song was part of the 'studio performance' sequence, which was filmed at the Scala Theatre, London, on 31 March 1964. Lennon's lead vocals in the film differ from either the mono or stereo studio versions.[6]

Releases

- Included on the British LP *A Hard Day's Night*.
- Included on the British EP *Extracts from the Film A Hard Day's Night*.
- Included on the US LP *A Hard Day's Night*.
- Included on the US LP *Something New*.
- B-side of the UK single "If I Fell".[7]

Personnel

- John Lennon – vocal, rhythm guitar
- Paul McCartney – harmony vocal, bass
- George Harrison – harmony vocal, lead guitar
- Ringo Starr – drums

Personnel per MacDonald[2]

Covers

- In 1965, the Beach Boys covered "Tell Me Why" on their *Beach Boys' Party!* album.
- In 1982, April Wine covered it on their album *Power Play*.
- In 2002, The Punkles did a cover of this song on their second album, *Punk!*.

References

- Calkin, Graham (2002). "The Beatles - If I Fell" [8]. *JPGR*.
- Harry, Bill (2000). *The Beatles Encyclopedia: Revised and Updated*. London: Virgin Publishing. ISBN 0-7535-0481-2.
- Lewisohn, Mark (1988). *The Beatles Recording Sessions*. New York: Harmony Books. ISBN 0-517-57066-1.
- MacDonald, Ian (2005). *Revolution in the Head: The Beatles' Records and the Sixties* (Second Revised ed.). London: Pimlico (Rand). ISBN 1-844-13828-3.
- Miles, Barry (1997). *Paul McCartney: Many Years From Now*. New York: Henry Holt and Company. ISBN 0-8050-5249-6.
- Spitz, Bob (2005). *The Beatles: The Biography*. Boston: Little, Brown. ISBN 0-316-80352-9.
- "Tell Me Why" [9]. *The Beatles Bible*. 2009. Retrieved 15 April 2009.

References

[1] Harry 2000, p. 1067.
[2] MacDonald 2005, p. 110.
[3] Lewisohn 1988, p. 40.
[4] Miles 1997, p. 164.
[5] Spitz 2005, p. 489.
[6] The Beatles Bible 2009.
[7] Calkin 2002.
[8] http://www.jpgr.co.uk/dp562.html
[9] http://www.beatlesbible.com/songs/tell-me-why/

Ten Little Indians

"Ten Little Indians"	
Single by The Beach Boys	
from the album *Surfin' Safari*	
Released	November 19, 1962
Format	Vinyl
Recorded	August 8, 1962
Genre	Rock
Length	3:41 for both songs
Label	Capitol
Producer	Nick Venet
The Beach Boys singles chronology	
"409"/"Surfin' Safari" (1962)	**"Ten Little Indians"**/"County Fair" (1962)	"Surfin' USA"/"Shut Down" (1963)

"Ten Little Indians" is a song written by Brian Wilson and Gary Usher for the American pop band, The Beach Boys. It was released on their 1962 album, *Surfin' Safari*. It was the second single from that album, and was The Beach Boys' lowest charting single (#49 U.S. Pop) until "Bluebirds over the Mountain" in 1968.

Released as a single by Capitol to keep their newest, youngest stars spotlighted, it featured at No. 6 on the Swedish national chart. It was ignored on the group's native West Coast as well as the Northeast (excepting No. 21 at Atlantic City-Philadelphia's WIBG) and South, but across the Midwest it made top thirty in Chicago, Dallas and Pittsburgh and went as high as No. 9 in Minneapolis (KDWB) in a New Year 1963 chart still dominated by "Surfin' Safari".

Musicians

- Mike Love - vocals
- David Marks - guitar
- Brian Wilson - bass guitar, vocals
- Carl Wilson - guitar, vocals
- Dennis Wilson - drums

See also

- The Beach Boys
- Surfin' Safari
- List of songs by The Beach Boys

That Same Song

"That Same Song" is a song written by Brian Wilson and Mike Love for the American pop band The Beach Boys. It was released on their 1976 album *15 Big Ones*.

Details

- *Written by:* Brian Wilson/Mike Love
- *Album:* 15 Big Ones
- *Time:* 2 min 16 sec
- *Produced by:* Brian Wilson
- *Arranged by:* Brian Wilson

Performers

- *Brian Wilson:* Lead Vocals, Piano, Organ
- *Carl Wilson:* Lead Vocals
- *Mike Love:* Lead Vocals
- *Al Jardine:* Lead Vocals
- *Marilyn Wilson:* Lead Vocals
- *Dennis Wilson:* drums, Vibes
- *Steve Douglas:* Saxophone
- *Jay Migliori:* Saxophone
- *Ron Altbach:* Accordion
- *Gene Estes:* percussion
- *Tim Drummond:* Bass
- *Ed Carter:* Guitar
- *Sidney Sharp:* Violin
- *Tiber Zelig:* Violin
- *Lori Klass:* Violin
- *Murry Adler:* Violin
- *William Kurasch:* Violin

See also

- The Beach Boys
- 15 Big Ones
- List of songs by The Beach Boys

That's Not Me

"That's Not Me"	
Song by The Beach Boys from the album *Pet Sounds*	
Released	May 16, 1966
Recorded	February 15, 1966
Genre	Rock music, Art rock
Length	2:27
Label	Capitol
Composer	Wilson/Asher
Producer	Brian Wilson
***Pet Sounds* track listing**	
• "Wouldn't It Be Nice" • "You Still Believe in Me" • "That's Not Me" • "Don't Talk (Put Your Head on My Shoulder)" • "I'm Waiting for the Day" • "Let's Go Away for Awhile" • "Sloop John B" • "God Only Knows" • "I Know There's an Answer" • "Here Today" • "I Just Wasn't Made for These Times" • "Pet Sounds" • "Caroline, No"	
Music sample	
That's Not Me	

"That's Not Me" is a song by the American pop band The Beach Boys, taken from their 1966 album *Pet Sounds*. It is the third track on the album. The song was composed and produced by Brian Wilson with the lyrics by Tony Asher. The lead vocal was sung by Brian Wilson and Mike Love.

Brian stated "This showcased Mike Love's voice. Listen for the twelve-string guitar right after the lyric "I'm a little bit scared 'cause I haven't been home in a long time."

Unlike all of the other songs on *Pet Sounds*, this track actually featured the Beach Boys playing the instruments; Brian had been using session musicians since *The Beach Boys Today!*. Brian Wilson plays organ, Carl Wilson plays guitar, and Dennis Wilson plays drums. Alan Jardine has also been credited as playing tambourine, while Mike Love sings the lead vocal with the whole band singing background vocals. The whole band is featured on this one track as the liner notes imply:

> The AFM contract for this date lists Brian, Carl, Dennis, Alan and Bruce as having played on this track. However, on the surviving session tape, only Brian, Carl and Dennis are clearly audible on the basic track, which includes just drums, organ, one guitar, and tambourine. As Brian was on the studio floor. Bruce was in the control booth, helping Chuck Britz direct the session. The tambourine apparently was played by Alan Jardine or an uncredited Terry Melcher; Brian has named the latter on at least one occasion.

Although it is unclear who is playing the tambourine, highlights from the session imply that it could be Alan Jardine who is playing the tambourine with them. An overdub session came later.

Details

- *Written by:* Brian Wilson and Tony Asher
- *Album: Pet Sounds*
- *Time:* 2 min 27 sec
- *Produced by:* Brian Wilson
- *Basic track:* recorded February 15, 1966 at United Western Recorders, Hollywood, California. Engineered by Chuck Britz.
- *Additional Instrumentation:* recorded February–March 1966 at Western Recorders, Hollywood, California
- *Vocal track:* recorded February–March 1966 at Western Recorders, Hollywood, California.

Musicians

- Glen Campbell - twelve string guitar
- Frank Capp - percussion
- Al Jardine - vocals
- Bruce Johnston - vocals
- Carol Kaye - bass guitar
- Mike Love - lead vocal
- Terry Melcher - tambourine
- Lyle Ritz - upright bass
- Brian Wilson - organ, vocals
- Carl Wilson - guitar, vocals
- Dennis Wilson - drums, vocals

It is unknown whether the tambourine was played by Al Jardine or Terry Melcher.

See also

- List of songs by The Beach Boys

Then I Kissed Her

"Then I Kissed Her"	
Single by The Beach Boys	
from the album *Summer Days (And Summer Nights!!)*	
B-side	"Mountain of Love"
Released	May 1967
Format	7" vinyl
Recorded	May 5, 1965
Genre	Pop
Length	2:15
Label	Capitol
Writer(s)	Phil Spector, Ellie Greenwich, Jeff Barry
Producer	Brian Wilson

The Beach Boys singles chronology		
"Good Vibrations"/"Let's Go Away for Awhile" (1966)	"Then I Kissed Her"/"Mountain of Love" (1967)	"Heroes and Villains"/"You're Welcome" (1967)

"Then I Kissed Her" is a song written by Phil Spector, Ellie Greenwich and Jeff Barry as "Then He Kissed Me". This was a major hit for The Crystals. The song was re-worded to the title "Then I Kissed Her" when it was covered by the American pop band The Beach Boys. It was released on their 1965 album *Summer Days (And Summer Nights!!)* with Al Jardine on lead vocals and with production by Brian Wilson. The song was also released as a single in April 1967 in the United Kingdom, where it charted at number four. The B-side of the single was "Mountain of Love", a song off the band's 1965 *Beach Boys' Party!* album.

The original song was used in the films *Goodfellas* and *Adventures in Babysitting*.

The 10cc song "The Dean and I" features a section parodying "Then I Kissed Her" most notable in the line *"And then I kissed her - it's a wonderful world when you're rolling in kisses"*

Chart performance

Chart (1967)	Peak position
Dutch Top 40[1]	2
German Singles Chart[2]	39
Irish Singles Chart[3]	4
Norwegian Singles Chart[4]	10
UK Singles Chart[5] [6]	4

According to contemporary national charts sourced and cited by *Billboard* in 1967, it reached No. 2 in Sweden and South Africa and No. 9 in Belgium. It was No. 12 in Australia's *Go Set* chart and No. 6 in New Zealand.

Musicians

- Al Jardine - lead vocal
- Mike Love - vocals
- Ron Swallow - tambourine
- unknown - castanets
- Brian Wilson - piano, bass guitar, vocals
- Carl Wilson - guitar, vocals
- Dennis Wilson - drums, vocals

See also

- List of songs by The Beach Boys

References

[1] "De Nederlandse Top 40, week 26, 1967" (http://www.radio538.nl/web/show/id=44685/chartid=6574). . Retrieved January 10, 2009.
[2] "charts-surfer.de search results" (http://www.charts-surfer.de). . Retrieved January 10, 2009.
[3] "irishcharts.ie search results" (http://www.irishcharts.ie). . Retrieved January 10, 2009.
[4] "norwegiancharts.com" (http://norwegiancharts.com/showitem.asp?interpret=The+Beach+Boys&titel=Then+I+Kissed+Her&cat=s). . Retrieved January 10, 2009.
[5] "everyhit.com search results" (http://www.everyhit.com). . Retrieved January 10, 2009.
[6] "Chart Stats - Beach Boys - Then I Kissed Her" (http://www.chartstats.com/songinfo.php?id=4593). . Retrieved January 10, 2009.

There's No Other (Like My Baby)

"There's No Other (Like My Baby)" is a song written by Phil Spector and Leroy Bates, first recorded by legendary girl group The Crystals.

Beach Boys version

"There's No Other (Like My Baby)"		
Single by The Beach Boys		
from the album *Beach Boys' Party!*		
Released	November 8, 1965	
Format	Vinyl	
Recorded	Unknown	
Genre	Pop	
Length	3:05	
Label	Capitol Records	
Producer	Brian Wilson	
The Beach Boys singles chronology		
"California Girls"/"Let Him Run Wild" (1965)	"The Little Girl I Once Knew"/"There's No Other (Like My Baby)" (1965)	"Barbara Ann"/"Girl Don't Tell Me" (1965)

***Beach Boys' Party!* track listing**

- "Hully Gully"
- "I Should Have Known Better"
- "Tell Me Why"
- "Papa-Oom-Mow-Mow"
- "Mountain of Love"
- "You've Got to Hide Your Love Away"
- "Devoted to You"
- "Alley Oop"
- "There's No Other (Like My Baby)"
- "Medley:I Get Around/Little Deuce Coupe"
- "The Times They Are a-Changin' "
- "Barbara Ann"

"There's No Other (Like My Baby)" was covered by the American pop band The Beach Boys. It was released on their 1965 album *Beach Boys' Party!* It features the whole group on lead vocals, but mainly Brian Wilson. The song was also released on November 8, 1965 as the B-side of the "The Little Girl I Once Knew" single. It charted at #20 in the United States and it never charted in the United Kingdom.

Details

- *Album:* Beach Boys' Party!
- *Time:* 3 min 05 sec
- *Produced by:* Brian Wilson

Performers

- *Brian Wilson:* Lead Vocals

See also

- The Beach Boys
- Beach Boys' Party!
- List of songs by The Beach Boys

A Thing or Two

"**A Thing or Two**" is a song written by Brian Wilson and Mike Love for the American pop band The Beach Boys. It was released on their 1967 album *Wild Honey*.

Details

- *Written by:* Brian Wilson/Mike Love
- *Album:* Wild Honey
- *Time:* 2 min 40 sec
- *Produced by:* The Beach Boys

Performers

- *Brian Wilson:* Lead Vocals
- *Carl Wilson:* Lead Vocals
- *Mike Love:* Lead Vocals

See also

- List of songs by The Beach Boys

This Car of Mine

"This Car of Mine"	
Song by The Beach Boys from the album *Shut Down Volume 2*	
Released	1964
Recorded	???
Genre	Pop Surf rock
Length	1:35
Label	Capitol Records
Writer	Brian Wilson/Mike Love
Producer	Brian Wilson
***Shut Down Volume 2* track listing**	
• "Fun, Fun, Fun" • "Don't Worry Baby" • "In the Parkin' Lot" • "Cassius Love vs. Sonny Wilson" • "The Warmth of the Sun" • "This Car of Mine" • "Why Do Fools Fall in Love" • "Pom Pom Play Girl" • "Keep an Eye on Summer" • "Shut Down, Part II" • "Louie Louie" • "Denny's Drums"	

"**This Car of Mine**" is a song written by Brian Wilson and Mike Love for the American pop band The Beach Boys. It was released on their 1964 album *Shut Down Volume 2*.

Performers

- *Dennis Wilson:* Lead Vocals

See also

- The Beach Boys
- Shut Down Volume 2
- List of songs by The Beach Boys

This Whole World

"This Whole World"	
Single by The Beach Boys	
from the album *Sunflower*	
Released	June 29, 1970
Format	Vinyl
Recorded	November 13, 1969
Genre	Classic rock
Length	1:56
Label	Brother Records
Producer	The Beach Boys

The Beach Boys singles chronology		
"Cotton Fields"/"The Nearest Faraway Place" (1970)	"Slip On Through"/"This Whole World" (1970)	"Tears in the Morning"/"It's About Time" (1970)

"This Whole World" is the title of a song written by Brian Wilson for The Beach Boys, and was released on their 1970 album Sunflower. The song features Carl Wilson on lead vocals (with Brian singing the first line) and is credited as a Beach Boys production. Earlier in the year, it had been included on the Warner Brothers promotional sampler album *The Big Ball*, and as a single, backed with "Slip On Through", but did not make the US or UK pop charts. This song was recorded in November 1969 and features numerous chord and key changes. The song also features stunning background vocals making use of improved sound technology.

Brian Wilson re-recorded the song for his 1995 solo album *I Just Wasn't Made for These Times*.

See also

- List of songs by The Beach Boys

'Til I Die

"'Til I Die"	
Single by The Beach Boys	
from the album *Surf's Up*	
A-side	"Long Promised Road"
Released	October 11, 1971
Format	Vinyl
Recorded	Brian Wilson's home studio August 15, 1970 July 30, 1971
Genre	Baroque Pop
Length	2:41
Label	Brother-Reprise 1047
Writer(s)	Wilson
Producer	Brian Wilson & Carl Wilson

The Beach Boys singles chronology		
"Long Promised Road"/"Deirdre" (1971)	"Long Promised Road"/"'Til I Die" (1971)	"Surf's Up"/"Don't Go Near the Water" (1971)

***Surf's Up* track listing**

- "Don't Go Near the Water"
- "Long Promised Road"
- "Take a Load Off Your Feet"
- "Disney Girls"
- "Student Demonstration Time"
- "Feel Flows"
- "Lookin' at Tomorrow"
- "A Day in the Life of a Tree"
- "'Til I Die"
- "Surf's Up"

This article refers to the song by The Beach Boys. For the Potshot album, see Til I Die (album).

"'**Til I Die**" is the title of a song written by Brian Wilson for The Beach Boys. It is one of the few songs in which both the words and music were written solely by Wilson. The song was first released on the band's 1971 album *Surf's Up* and was subsequently released as the B-side of the "Long Promised Road" single.

Inspiration

According to Brian in the press material for the *Surf's Up* album, the song was inspired after a late night trip to the beach. Wilson recalled the events prior to him writing the song:

> "Lately, I'd been depressed and preoccupied with death...Looking out toward the ocean, my mind, as it did almost every hour of every day, worked to explain the inconsistencies that dominated my life; the pain, torment, and confusion and the beautiful music I was able to make. Was there an answer? Did I have no control? Had I ever? Feeling shipwrecked on an existential island, I lost myself in the balance of darkness that stretched beyond the breaking waves to the other side of the earth. The ocean was so incredibly vast, the universe was so large, and suddenly I saw myself in proportion to that, a little pebble of sand, a jellyfish floating on top of the water; traveling with the current I felt dwarfed, temporary. The next day I began writing "'Til I Die", perhaps the most personal song I ever wrote for The Beach Boys...In doing so, I wanted to re-create the swell of emotions that I'd felt at the beach the previous night."[1]

Composition

The song was written over the course of several weeks as Wilson tried to express the feelings he had experienced on that night he had spent alone at the beach. As he himself explains, "I struggled at the piano, experimenting with rhythms and chord changes, trying to emulate in sound the ocean's shifting tides and moods as well as its sheer enormity. I wanted the music to reflect the loneliness of floating a raft in the middle of the Pacific. I wanted each note to sound as if it was disappearing into the hugeness of the universe.[1]

After asking Brian how he came up with the chords, Don Was recalls that "he told me that he was sitting at a piano, creating geometric patterns with his fingers, trying not to move the fingers on the outside of the patterns, but limiting changes to internal movements. When he landed on a shape that both looked cool and sounded good, he wrote it down. So, essentially he created this masterpiece by contorting his fingers into really groovy shapes." However, Was goes on to say "I've absolutely no idea whether this story has any basis in truth or whether he was just making it up on the spot to entertain me."[2]

According to some sources, one certain member of the band was less than impressed with Brian's new song [3] [4] . Bruce Johnston remembers Brian "playing it for the band and one member of the band didn't understand it and put it down, and Brian just decided not to show it to us for a few months. He just put it away. I mean, he was absolutely crushed. This other person just didn't like it."[5] It has been speculated by several sources that it was Mike Love who initially criticized the song.[6] Love has, however, praised the song in retrospect, calling it "phenomenal."[7]

Wilson has stated that the line *"I'm a cork on the ocean"* was the first thing lyrically that came to him.[7] In the lyrics, Wilson compares himself to a cork on the ocean, a rock in a landslide, and a leaf on a windy day—seeing himself as a small, helpless object, being moved inconceivable distances by forces beyond his comprehension. *"How deep is the ocean? How long will the wind blow?"* The hopeless conclusion is given in the song's title. At one stage, due to the criticism the song had received from the band, Wilson changed the lyrics from "It kills my soul" to "It holds me up" or "It fills my soul" and "I lost my way" to "I found my way". However, the rest of the group insisted that the original lyrics be kept as the new lyrics contradicted the lyrics in the verses.

Despite the criticism, Bruce Johnston in particular has praised the song on several occasions by calling it the last great Brian Wilson song[5] [8] as well as describing it as Wilson's "heaviest song."[5] Johnston has also stated that "the words absolutely fit his mindset".[7] Wilson also felt this was the case when he stated that "the song summed up everything I had to say at the time."[1]

Recording

The song was first attempted during the recording of the *20/20* album[9] although due to the negative reactions from a fellow band member, Brian wouldn't work on the song again for several months. The first dated session for the song was at Brian Wilson's home studio on August 15, 1970. Brian would record five takes of the song although the song would be left only partially completed. On August 26, the partially completed track was mixed although very little work would be done on the recording until later the following year when it became a full blown production.

The finished backing track features organ, guitar, vibraphone, an RMI electra-piano, bass guitar and a Maestro Rhythm King drum machine.

Years later Alan Jardine reminisced, "I love the use of the keyboards...but extraordinary use of the vocals. And it's really a good vocal sound, I think Desper [the engineer] deserves all the credit on that one, I mean we just had the best microphones, the best microphone technique and engineering on that particular piece and that particular time. It was just a wonderful piece of music."[7] Bruce Johnston has also expressed similar feelings towards the song as he states that "the track is very simple...and the great, great vocal arrangement that he wrote. Really, a great piece of work."[7]

Album and alternate releases

The song was first released on the bands album *Surf's Up* on August 30, 1971. However, in February of the previous year an alternate version of the song with a different backing track was played on the WPLJ FM radio station in New York.[9] The song has also appeared on several greatest hits compilations over the years including the 1981 album *Ten Years of Harmony*; the 1993 *Good Vibrations box set* and the 2002 release *Classics Selected by Brian Wilson*. An extended mix of the original recording, created by engineer Steve Desper, was included on the 1998 *Endless Harmony Soundtrack*. It is notable for having each instrumental layer come in after the other as an introduction and features more prominent vibraphone and organ throughout. The mix was reportedly done only for the engineer's self-interest with no intent for the song to see an official release. As Desper himself explains:

> "[the band] went out for lunch or something like that and since the song was already mounted and a mix up, I put together what I thought was a structure that better showcased the harmonic beauty of Brian's writing. Somewhere thereafter I did play the track for Carl, but only in the interest of disclosure, not to sway him to change the structure that Brian intended."

A remake of the song was recorded - along with an accompanying video - by Brian Wilson for inclusion in the 1995 documentary *I Just Wasn't Made for These Times* and it would later appear on the films soundtrack. This version, produced by Brian and Don Was, is much more sparse than the original. In 2000, over a period of two days on April 7 and 8, Brian and his band recorded a live version of the song—based on Desper's extended mix—for inclusion on Brian's 2000 live album *Live at the Roxy Theatre*.

Single release

On October 11, 1971, the song was released in the United States as the flip-side of the "Long Promised Road" single, which had also been released earlier that year in May with a different B-side. The single entered the Billboard charts on October 30 in the #93 position. It would peak three weeks later at #89 on the Billboard charts, where it would remain for one more week until the single dropped off the charts altogether.[10] It was the first single by the group in 19 months to chart. However, at the time it was the lowest charting single in the group's history and it would remain so for a further eighteen years.[11]

Brian's re-recording of the song, which was featured in the *I Just Wasn't Made For These Times* documentary, was released as the second track on a relatively rare UK single in 1995. However, the single failed to make any impact on the charts.

Cover versions

The song has been covered by several artists in recent years. The band Medicine covered the song in 1993 on their "Never Click" single release. In 1996 The Josephine Wiggs Experience covered the song on their *Bon Bon* album. Brian's daughters Carnie and Wendy covered the song on their 1997 album simply titled *The Wilsons*, with Brian co-producing and co-mixing the track as well as guesting on vocals. Two cover versions by The Elements and Clark Burroughs Group appeared on the 1997 tribute album *Wouldn't It Be Nice: A Jazz Portrait of Brian Wilson*. Christy McWilson covered the song on her 2000 album *The Lucky One*. Marty Rudnick covered the song on his 2006 album *More Songs About Cars and Girls*. Doug Powell covered the song on the 2002 tribute album *Making God Smile: An Artists' Tribute to the Songs of Beach Boy Brian Wilson*. In 2005 on February 11, the Barenaked Ladies performed an acoustic version of the song at a MusiCares concert honoring Brian Wilson. This performance was later released on DVD.

See also

- List of songs by The Beach Boys

References

[1] Badman, Keith (2004). *The Beach Boys: The Definitive Diary of America's Greatest Band on Stage and in the Studio*. p. 288.
[2] Williams, Paul (2003). *How Deep is the Ocean?*. pp. 212–13.
[3] White, Timothy (1996). *The Nearest Faraway Place*. p. 286.
[4] Granata, Charles L. (2003). *I Just Wasn't Made For These Times*. p. 211.
[5] Leaf, David (1978). *The Beach Boys And The California Myth*. p. 144.
[6] Carlin, Peter Ames (2006). *Catch A Wave: The Rise, Fall, and Redemption of the Beach Boys' Brian Wilson*. p. 162.
[7] The Warmth of the Sun podcast series: Episode 9 (http://boss.streamos.com/download/emicat/beachboys/warmth_podcasts/episode_9.mp3)
[8] Boyd, Alan (Director). (1998). *Endless Harmony: The Beach Boys Story*. [Documentary]. Eagle Eye Media.
[9] Elliott, Brad (2003). *Surf's Up: The Beach Boys On Record 1961-1981*. p. 183.
[10] Elliott, Brad (2003). *Surf's Up: The Beach Boys On Record 1961-1981*. p. 421.
[11] Badman, Keith (2004). *The Beach Boys: The Definitive Diary of America's Greatest Band on Stage and in the Studio*. p. 300.

Time to Get Alone

"**Time to Get Alone**" is a song written by Brian Wilson for the American pop band The Beach Boys. It was released on their 1969 album *20/20* and was produced by Carl Wilson.[1] It is a waltz.

Recording

Brian was originally planning to give the song to Redwood (later to become known as Three Dog Night) as he was friends with Danny Hutton. Redwood actually began recording the song on the October 14 and 15. Brian wanted Redwood to become artists on the Beach Boy's label Brother Records but according to Chuck Negron it was clear that "Mike Love and the other Beach Boys wanted Brian's immense songwriting and producing talents used strictly to enhance their own careers".[2] Negron explained the time when Brian's career producing Redwood came to a crashing halt:

> "It all came to a head...when Mike Love, Carl Wilson and Al Jardine came to the studio and heard our version of 'Time To Get Alone'...They manoeuvred Brian into the control booth and reduced him to tears. It was a cruel and pathetic scene. Danny, Cory and I were in the studio and could see it all happening through the control-booth window. It was as if Brian had turned into a little boy. The conversation appeared quiet and calm, but we could tell it was emotional and intense. The others were doing most of the talking, like overbearing, controlling parents. Brian would move away, and they would block his escape. We couldn't hear what was being said, but I think a good lip-reader would have picked up something like, 'We don't give a shit about these guys, and we want those songs for us.' We could actually feel Brian crumbling, and when he came out of the booth, a tear dropped down his cheek. His head was lowered and his shoulders sagged. It was the body language of a child who had just been scolded and punished. And this brilliant musical icon - whose songs defined one generation and influenced another - weepingly told us, 'We can't do this. I have to give the songs to them. They're family and I have to take care of my family. They want the songs. I'll give you any amount of money you want to finish an album, but I can't produce it. They won't let me.'"[2]

The song was eventually recorded by The Beach Boys around a year later in 1968 on October 2, October 4 and November 21 at Brian's home studio. The song features Carl Wilson singing lead vocals on the verses and Brian and Alan Jardine singing lead vocals on the chorus.

See also

- List of songs by The Beach Boys

References

[1] 20/20 Credits (http://www.btinternet.com/~bellagio/albumarchive2.html)
[2] Priore, Domenic (2007). *Smile: The Story of Brian Wilson's Lost Masterpiece*. p. 129.

A Time to Live in Dreams

"**A Time to Live in Dreams**" is a song written by Dennis Wilson and Stephen Kalinich. The song was first discovered in The Beach Boys tape archive around 2000. It was first released on The Beach Boys 2001 anthology album *Hawthorne, CA*. In December 2000, Brian Wilson was able to hear the song for the first time and according to Alan Boyd said "Wait - I don't remember this one. What album was this done for?"[1] Later on in the song when the organ begins to play and Dennis sings the line "in this new day, change your heart, forgive your brother...", Brian sat up straight and said softly, "Wow. What a great song." [1]

Details

- Written by: Dennis Wilson/Stephen Kalinich
- Album: *Hawthorne, CA*
- Time: 1 min 50 sec
- Produced by: The Beach Boys

Performers

- Dennis Wilson: Lead Vocals

See also

- List of songs by The Beach Boys

External links

- Free song downloads (including "A Time To Live In Dreams") [2]

References

[1] "Dennis Wilson & Stephen Kalinich" article (http://www.stephenkalinich.com/sjkdennis.html), URL retrieved 12th July 2006.

The Times They Are a-Changin'

"The Times They Are a-Changin'"	
Single by Bob Dylan	
from the album *The Times They Are a-Changin'*	
Released	1964
Format	7"
Recorded	October 24, 1963 at Columbia Studios, New York City
Genre	Folk
Length	3:15
Label	Columbia
Writer(s)	Bob Dylan
Producer	Tom Wilson

Bob Dylan singles chronology		
"Blowin' in the Wind" (1963)	**"The Times They Are a-Changin'"** (1965)	"Maggie's Farm" (1965)

***The Times They Are a-Changin'* track listing**

Side one

1. **"The Times They Are a-Changin'"**
2. "Ballad of Hollis Brown"
3. "With God on Our Side"
4. "One Too Many Mornings"
5. "North Country Blues"

Side two

1. "Only a Pawn in Their Game"
2. "Boots of Spanish Leather"
3. "When the Ship Comes In"
4. "The Lonesome Death of Hattie Carroll"
5. "Restless Farewell"

"The Times They Are a-Changin'" is a song written by Bob Dylan and released as the title track of his 1964 album, *The Times They Are a-Changin'*. The song was ranked #59 on *Rolling Stone*'s 2004 list of The 500 Greatest Songs of All Time.

Inspiration and composition

Dylan appears to have written the song in September and October 1963. He recorded it as a Witmark publishing demo that month, a version that was finally released on *The Bootleg Series Volumes 1–3 (Rare & Unreleased) 1961–1991*. The song was then recorded at the Columbia studios in New York on October 23 and 24,[1] and the latter session yielded the version that became the title song of Dylan's third album.[2]

Dylan recalled writing the song as a deliberate attempt to create an anthem of change for the moment. In 1985, he told Cameron Crowe: "This was definitely a song with a purpose. It was influenced of course by the Irish and Scottish ballads ...'Come All Ye Bold Highway Men', 'Come All Ye Tender Hearted Maidens'. I wanted to write a big song, with short concise verses that piled up on each other in a hypnotic way. The civil rights movement and the folk music movement were pretty close for a while and allied together at that time."[3]

Dylan biographer Clinton Heylin recounts how Tony Glover stopped by Dylan's apartment in September 1963, picked up a page of the song Dylan was working on and read a line from it: "'Come senators, congressmen, please heed the call.' Turning to Dylan, Glover said, 'What is this shit, man?' Dylan shrugged his shoulders and replied, 'Well, you know, it seems to be what the people want to hear.'"[4]

Dylan critic Michael Gray called it "the archetypal protest song." Gray commented, "Dylan's aim was to ride upon the unvoiced sentiment of a mass public—to give that inchoate sentiment an anthem and give its clamour an outlet. He succeeded, but the language of the song is nevertheless imprecisely and very generally directed."[2] Gray suggests that the song has been outdated by the very changes that it gleefully predicted, and hence the song was politically out of date almost as soon as it was written.

Literary critic Christopher Ricks suggests that the song transcends the political preoccupations of the time in which it was written. Ricks argues that Dylan is still performing the song, and when he sings "Your sons and your daughter/Are beyond your command", he sings inescapably with the accents not of a son, no longer perhaps primarily a parent, but with the attitude of a grandfather. Ricks concludes: "Once upon a time it may have been a matter of urging square people to accept the fact that their children were, you know, hippies. But the capacious urging could then come to mean that ex-hippie parents had better accept that their children look like becoming yuppies. And then Republicans..."[5]

Critic Andy Gill points out that the song's lyrics echo lines from the Book of Ecclesiastes which Pete Seeger adapted to create his anthem "Turn, Turn, Turn!". The climactic line about the first later being last, likewise, is a direct scriptural reference to Mark 10:31: "But many that are first shall be last, and the last first."[6]

Less than a month after Dylan recorded the song, President John F. Kennedy was assassinated in Dallas, Texas, on November 22, 1963. The next night, Dylan opened a concert with "The Times They Are a-Changin'"; he told biographer Anthony Scaduto: "I thought, 'Wow, how can I open with that song? I'll get rocks thrown at me.' But I had to sing it, my whole concert takes off from there. I know I had no understanding of anything. Something had just gone haywire in the country and they were applauding the song. And I couldn't understand why they were clapping, or why I wrote the song. I couldn't understand anything. For me, it was just insane."[7]

Cover versions

The song has been covered by many other artists, most notably Joan Baez, The Seekers, The Byrds, Judy Collins, The Hollies, Marc Bolan, Peter Paul & Mary, James Taylor & Carly Simon, Phil Collins, Simon and Garfunkel, Tracy Chapman, U2, Eddie Vedder, Bruce Springsteen and Nina Simone (on 1969's *To Love Somebody*), and recently by Blackmore's Night and Les Fradkin.

The Byrds covered the song on their 1965 album *Turn! Turn! Turn!*[8]

The Beach Boys recorded a cover of the song for their 1965 album *Beach Boys' Party!*.

Odetta recorded the song in 1965 on the album *Odetta Sings Dylan*, RCA LSP3324.

The Hollies released an album of Dylan covers including this song. Graham Nash disagreed with the band's decision to perform an album of Dylan covers. As a result of leaving, he joined David Crosby & Stephen Stills to form Crosby, Stills & Nash which eventually became Crosby, Stills, Nash & Young

Flatt & Scruggs performed the song, with 3 other Dylan covers, on their album (LP) *Nashville Airplane*.

James Taylor & Carly Simon covered the song at the No Nukes benefit concert in 1979.

Keb' Mo' covered this song in his 2004 album *Peace...Back by Popular Demand*. This version of the song was used in episode 8, season 5 of *Boston Legal*.

Bruce Springsteen covered the song, with Dylan in attendance, in a concert to honor the artist at The Kennedy Center.[9]

Burl Ives covered the song on his 1968 album *The Times They Are A-Changin'*, named after Dylan's song.

Billy Joel was another famous artist who covered this song. The track can be found on the Russian concert album *КОНЦЕРТ* and the 5-disc compilation *My Lives*.

Richie Havens covered the song on his 1994 album *Cuts to the Chase*.

John Mellencamp made a home-video recording of the song on a web-cam on September 2, 2008 and posted it on his website the next day as a statement about the possible change the 2008 Presidential Election could bring to America.

Damien Leith also covered this song for his 2008 album *Catch the Wind: Songs of a Generation*.

Me First and the Gimme Gimmes recorded the song in their EP *Turn Japanese*.

A Whisper in the Noise covered this song for the movie *Lady In The Water*.

Josephine Baker performed the song at her concert at Carnegie Hall in 1973. The concert was recorded and released on the LP *Joséphine Baker recorded live at Carnegie Hall*.

Filmmaker Michael Moore sang the third verse of the song live on *The Jay Leno Show* after being told that he had to "earn" a clip from his film *Capitalism: A Love Story* to be shown.

Dutch musician Boudewijn de Groot made a Dutch version named "Er komen andere tijden"

U2 covered the song on the last day of the Point Depot concerts of the Lovetown Tour in 1989. This show was broadcast on radio and became one of the most widely bootlegged U2 concerts before it received an official online release via iTunes.[10]

Whilst performing at a fundraising event for Ralph Nader at Madison Square Gardens for the 2000 elections, Eddie Vedder delivered a "true to the original" performance of the song. There are a number of amateur videos of the song on the web, showing the unmistakable Vedder vocals.

Bryan Ferry turned this into a "driving song" on his album of Dylan covers, *Dylanesque*. The lead guitar work is by Oliver Thompson.

The "Dylan Covers Database"[11] listed 436 recordings, including bootlegs, of this song as of 19 Oct 2009, including 85 versions of it by "Bob Walkenhorst", recorded live between March 2004 and September 2009, at "Molly's Irish Pub" in Kansas City. According to the same data base, the song has been recorded in Catalán, Czech, Dutch, Finnish,

French, German, Hungarian, Italian, Japanese, Norwegian, Polish, Serbian, Spanish (Castellano) & Swedish.

The song has been used in a television advertisement for insurance company Kaiser Permanente[12] as well as in the opening credits of the *Watchmen* film (it is also available for sale as part of the film soundtrack). It has also been licensed for advertisements for the auditing and accountancy firm Coopers & Lybrand, (as performed by Richie Havens) and the Bank of Montreal (performed by Pete Seeger).[13] The song was also referenced in the popular Japanese manga *One Piece* as the title of chapter 572, written out in English.

Jibjab, a humorous website, parodied the song in their "Election '08" video.

References

- Bjorner, Olof (2002). *Olof's Files: A Bob Dylan Performance Guide (Bob Dylan all alone on a shelf)*. Hardinge Simpole. ISBN 1843820242.
- Gill, Andy (1999). *Classic Bob Dylan: My Back Pages*. Carlton. ISBN 1-85868-599-0.
- Gray, Michael (2006). *The Bob Dylan Encyclopedia*. Continuum International. ISBN 0-8264-6933-7.
- Heylin, Clinton (2003). *Bob Dylan: Behind the Shades Revisited*. Perennial Currents. ISBN 0-06-052569-X.
- Ricks, Christopher (2003). *Dylan's Visions of Sin*. Penguin/Viking. ISBN 0-670-80133-X.

External links

- Lyrics at official Bob Dylan site [14]

References

[1] Bjorner, Olof (2004-10-08). "The Times They Are A-Changin' sessions" (http://dir.salon.com/story/books/review/2004/10/08/dylan/index.html?pn=1). Bjorner.com. . Retrieved 2009-01-10.

[2] Gray, 2006, *The Bob Dylan Encyclopedia*, p. 662.

[3] *Biograph*, 1985, Liner notes & text by Cameron Crowe.

[4] Heylin, *Bob Dylan: Behind the Shades Revisited*, p. 126.

[5] Ricks, 2003, *Dylan's Visions Of Sin*, pp. 260–271.

[6] Gill, 1999, *My Back Pages*, pp. 42–43.

[7] Scaduto, 1971, *Bob Dylan*, p. 160.

[8] "Turn! Turn! Turn! review" (http://www.allmusic.com/cg/amg.dll?p=amg&sql=10:difyxqw5ld6e). Allmusic. . Retrieved 2009-12-09.

[9] Bob Dylan Honored at Kennedy Center (http://www.mtv.com/news/articles/1428464/19971209/dylan_bob.jhtml), MTV.com, accessed on 2008-06-24

[10] http://www.u2gigs.com/show1070.html Details of the last U2 concert at Point Depot, Dublin Ireland

[11] * Dylan Covers Database (http://baseportal.com/cgi-bin/baseportal.pl?htx=/dylancov/main)

[12] http://www.kaiserthrive.org/media-coverage/#AdPulp

[13] Gray, *The Bob Dylan Encyclopedia*, p. 152.

[14] http://bobdylan.com/songs/times.html

TM Song

Not to be confused with the song "Transcendental Meditation", also by The Beach Boys.

"Rock And Roll Music/The TM Song"	
Single by The Beach Boys	
from the album *15 Big Ones*	
Released	May 24, 1976
Format	Vinyl
Recorded	Unknown
Genre	Rock music
Length	1:34
Label	Brother/Reprise
Writer(s)	Brian Wilson
Producer	Brian Wilson
The Beach Boys singles chronology	

"Sail On, Sailor"/"Only with You" (1975)	"Rock and Roll Music"/"**TM Song**" (1976)	"It's O.K."/"Had to Phone Ya" (1976)

"TM Song" is a song written by Brian Wilson, a member of the American pop band The Beach Boys.

The song

TM Song was released on the Beach Boys 1976 album *15 Big Ones*. The song features Al Jardine on lead vocals plus each band member featured as part of the spoken introduction. An improvised, five-way, discussion goes on in the background while one of the band members "approaches" the microphone, and says "*Whew!* Time for me to meditate!" Then the music starts. The lyrics of the song mention Maharishi Mahesh Yogi.

Performers

- Al Jardine: Lead vocals, Backing vocals
- Brian Wilson: Backing vocals, Organ
- Mike Love: Backing vocals
- Dennis Wilson: drums
- Steve Douglas: Saxophone, Flute
- Jay Migliori: Saxophone, Flute
- Ed Carter: Guitar
- Billy Hinsche: Guitar

See also

- "Transcendental Meditation (song)"
- The Beach Boys
- 15 Big Ones
- List of The Beach Boys songs

The Trader

"The Trader" is a song written by Carl Wilson and Jack Rieley for the American pop band The Beach Boys. It was released on their 1973 album *Holland*. This song is a rock music and sunshine pop.

Details

- *Written by:* Carl Wilson/Jack Rieley
- *Album:* Holland
- *Time:* 5 min 04 sec
- *Produced by:* Carl Wilson

Performers

- *Carl Wilson:* Lead Vocals, Guitar, Backup Vocals, Electric Piano
- *Alan Jardine:* Guitar, Backup Vocals
- *Mike Love:* Backup Vocals
- *Dennis Wilson:* Backup Vocals, Moog Bass
- *Ricky Fataar:* Drums, Flute, Backup Vocals
- *Blondie Chaplin:* Guitar, Backup Vocals
- *Daryl Dragon:* Piano, Electric Piano
- *Jonah Wilson:* "Hi!"

See also

- The Beach Boys
- Holland
- List of songs by The Beach Boys

Transcendental Meditation

Not to be confused with "TM Song", also by The Beach Boys.

"Transcendental Meditation" is a song written by Brian Wilson, Mike Love and Al Jardine for the American pop band The Beach Boys.

The song

Transcendental Meditation, the song, was released on the Beach Boys 1968 album *Friends*. The song is has a loud, dissonant, horns and a rhythm section. It is an experimental rock or jazz rock song.

Details

- *Written by:* Brian Wilson/Mike Love/Al Jardine
- *Album:* Friends
- *Time:* 1 min 49 sec
- *Produced by:* The Beach Boys
- *Lead Vocals:* Brian Wilson

See also

- "TM Song"
- List of songs by The Beach Boys

Vegetables

"**Vegetables**" (or "**Vega-Tables**") is a song written by Brian Wilson and Van Dyke Parks for the American pop band The Beach Boys. It was released on their 1967 album *Smiley Smile* with Al Jardine and Brian Wilson on lead vocals.

The song was originally composed and recorded during the infamous *Smile* sessions. After the shelving of the *Smile* album, it was re-arranged and simplified for its eventual release on *Smiley Smile*, as were the songs "Heroes and Villains", "Wind Chimes" and "Wonderful". A discarded bridge section from "Vegetables" was later reused as "Mama Says" on the album *Wild Honey*. This song is psychedelic rock.

In 1993, the original version of "Vegetables" was finally given an official release, along with a slew of other *Smile* material, on the *Good Vibrations* boxset. A new recording of the song (based on the original version) was made for the 2004 release of *Brian Wilson Presents Smile*.

Recording

All versions of the song feature the novel use of vegetable chewing as percussion. During the *Smile* sessions, Paul McCartney was recorded chewing celery. Al Jardine remembers that "the night before a big tour, I was out in the studio recording the vocal [for 'Vegetables'] when, to my surprise, Paul McCartney walked in and joined Brian at the console. And, briefly, the two most influential musical Geminis in the world had a chance to work together. I remember waiting for long periods of time between takes to get to the next section or verse. Brian [seemed to have] lost track of the session. Paul would come on the talkback and say something like 'Good take, Al.'"[1]

Details

- Written by: Brian Wilson/Van Dyke Parks
- Album: *Smiley Smile*
- Time: 2 min 07 sec
- Produced by: The Beach Boys

Alternately:

- Album: *Smile*
- Time: 2 min 19 sec
- Produced by: Van Dyke Parks

Performers

- *Brian Wilson:* lead vocals
- *Al Jardine:* lead vocals

Cover versions

The song was covered by Jan and Dean (under the name Laughing Gravy) on a single released in 1968.

Terry Scott Taylor covered the song on the 2002 tribute album *Making God Smile: An Artists' Tribute to the Songs of Beach Boy Brian Wilson*.

It was also covered by Canadian group The Old Soul in 2005, though the lyrics don't entirely match. This cover includes a portion of "Mama Says", similar to the *Smile* version.

While not a cover, the song "Receptacle for the Respectable" from the album *Rings Around the World* by Super Furry Animals also features Paul McCartney chewing celery and carrots.

See also

- List of songs by The Beach Boys

References

[1] *Smiley Smile/Wild Honey* CD booklet notes, David Leaf, c.1990.

Wake the World

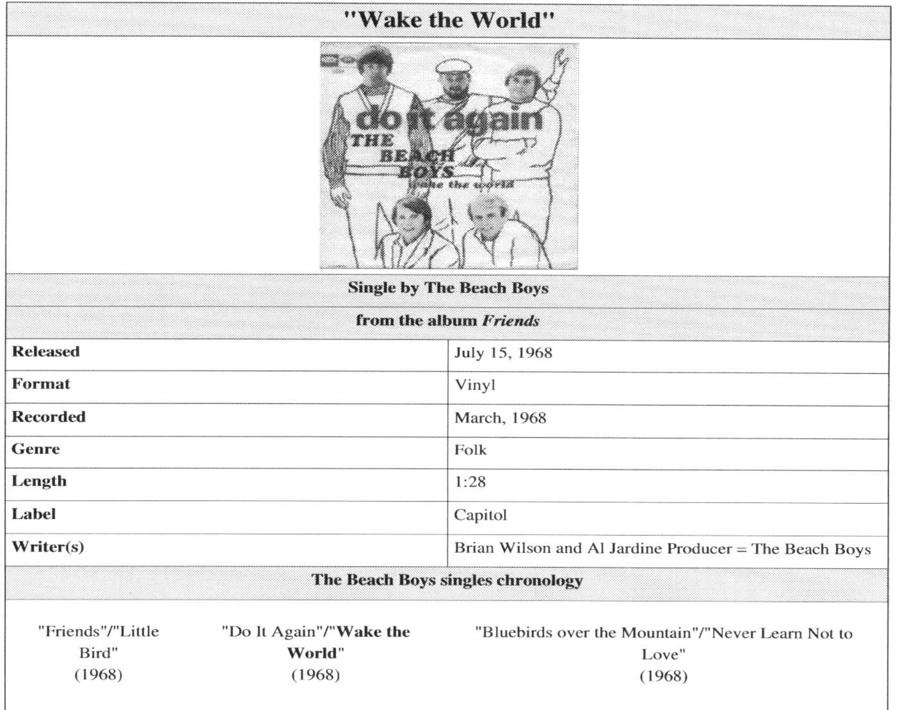

"Wake the World"	
Single by The Beach Boys	
from the album *Friends*	
Released	July 15, 1968
Format	Vinyl
Recorded	March, 1968
Genre	Folk
Length	1:28
Label	Capitol
Writer(s)	Brian Wilson and Al Jardine Producer = The Beach Boys
The Beach Boys singles chronology	

"Friends"/"Little Bird" (1968)	"Do It Again"/"**Wake the World**" (1968)	"Bluebirds over the Mountain"/"Never Learn Not to Love" (1968)

"**Wake the World**" is the B-side of the single "Do It Again", which was released by The Beach Boys in 1968 through Capitol Records. The song was recorded in March 1968.

"Wake the World" was the first original song that Brian Wilson and Al Jardine wrote together. As Wilson later stated, "'Wake the World' was my favorite cut. It was so descriptive to how I felt about the dramatic change from day to night...'one by one, stars appear, the light of the day is no longer here'."

Personnel

- Brian Wilson: Lead vocals
- Carl Wilson: Lead vocals

See also

- List of The Beach Boys songs

The Warmth of the Sun

"The Warmth of the Sun"	
Single by The Beach Boys	
from the album *Shut Down Volume 2*	
Released	October 26, 1964
Format	Vinyl
Recorded	January 1, 1964 January 8, 1964
Genre	Rock
Length	2:51
Label	Capitol Records
Writer(s)	Brian Wilson, Mike Love
Producer	Brian Wilson

The Beach Boys singles chronology		
"When I Grow Up (To Be a Man)"/"She Knows Me Too Well" (1964)	"Dance, Dance, Dance"/"The Warmth of the Sun" (1964)	"The Man with All the Toys"/"Blue Christmas" (1964)

"**The Warmth of the Sun**" is a song written by Brian Wilson and Mike Love for the American pop band The Beach Boys. It was released on their 1964 album *Shut Down Volume 2* and as the B-side of the "Dance, Dance, Dance" single, which charted at number eight in the United States and number twenty-four in the United Kingdom. Brian Wilson produced the song, and the rest of the album. He also sang lead vocals on the song, which was written on the evening of President John Kennedy's assassination at the now-defunct Hotel El Dorado in Sacramento, California.

It was featured on the soundtrack of *Good Morning, Vietnam* (1987), the comedy-drama feature film starring Robin Williams, along with other Beach Boys hits "I Get Around" and "Don't Worry, Baby".

Cover versions

The song was covered by the Wilsons' (Brian, Carl and Dennis) father on his one and only album, *The Many Moods of Murry Wilson*, which was released in 1967 under Capitol Records.

In 2006, it was covered by Matthew Thiessen and the Earthquakes, the solo side project of Relient K singer Matt Thiessen.

Vince Gill performed a cover version at "An All-Star Tribute to Brian Wilson (2001)" concert.

In 2006, Matthew Sweet and Bangles lead singer Susanna Hoffs recorded the song for their collaboration, *Under the Covers, Vol. 1*.

See also

- List of The Beach Boys songs
- Greg Panfile's Musical Analysis of "Warmth of the Sun" [1]

References

[1] http://www.cabinessence.net/essays/mob6.html

We Three Kings

"**We Three Kings**", also known as "**We Three Kings of Orient Are**" or "**The Quest of the Magi**", is a Christmas carol written by Reverend John Henry Hopkins, Jr., who wrote both the lyrics and the music. It is suggested to have been written in 1857 but did not appear in print until his *Carols, Hymns and Song* in 1863. John Henry Hopkins, Jr., then an ordained deacon in the Episcopal Church,[1] was instrumental in organizing an elaborate holiday pageant (which featured this hymn) for the students of the General Theological Seminary in New York City in 1857 while serving as the seminary's music director. In 1872 Hopkins was ordained an Episcopal priest and later served as rector at Christ Episcopal Church, Williamsport, Pennsylvania. (which still stands at the corner of Fourth and Mulberry Streets).[2]

Recordings

- The Beach Boys recorded a version with an orchestral arrangement by Dick Reynolds on their 1964 album *The Beach Boys' Christmas Album*.
- The Barenaked Ladies and Sarah McLachlan did a version of this song which they combined with another carol, "God Rest Ye Merry Gentlemen," for their 2004 Christmas album *Barenaked for the Holidays*.
- Harry Connick, Jr. on his 2008 album *What a Night! A Christmas Album*.
- Odds originally recorded a version of the song on the 1991 A Lump of Coal compilation. It reappeared most recently on their 2000 greatest hits album *Singles: Individually Wrapped*.
- Kamelot played an instrumental of "We Three Kings" on their first live album.
- Burl Ives sings this song on his album *Christmas at the White House* (1972).
- Aly & AJ did a cover of this song on their 2006 Christmas album *Acoustic Hearts of Winter*.
- Toby Keith covered the song on his 2007 album *A Classic Christmas*.
- Patti Smith - *A Very Special Christmas 3* album, (1997)
- Bradley Joseph - solo piano arrangement on his 2008 album, *Classic Christmas*.
- Andrew Parrott and the Taverner Consort on their 1993 EMI album The Carols Album 2, using the original arrangement.
- John Rutter and the Cambridge Singers on their 1997 album Christmas Star

- Martin Neary and the Choir of Westminster Abbey on their 1997 album Christmas Carols from Westminster Abbey
- Antony Pitts and Tonus Peregrinus on the 2003 album The Naxos Book of Carols[3]
- Lycia on their 2001 release Compilation Appearances Volume 2
- Jonas Brothers recorded "Joyful Kings," a combination of this song and "Joy to the World" for the Target exclusive Christmas album All Wrapped Up.
- Blackhawk covered the song in 1998 on the "Country Cares for Kids" album.
- Overboard recorded a dance remix version for their 2008 holiday album, "Tidings".
- Steve Ouimette recorded an instrumental version of "We Three Kings" as a playable track in the video game *Guitar Hero III: Legends of Rock*.
- Rob Halford covers this song for his solo album *Halford III - Winter Songs*
- Tori Amos recorded a version of the carol for her solstice album, *Midwinter Graces*
- Percy Faith included the song in his 1954 "Music Of Christmas" LP.
- Ella Fitzgerald in the 1967 religious standards LP "Ella Fitzgerald's Christmas".
- Blondie recorded the song in 2009
- The Toasters recorded a ska version of the song on the 1996 Moon Ska Records compilation "Christma-Ska"

See also

- Three Wise Men

Further reading

- Fuld, James (1966). *The Book of World Famous Music Classical, Popular and Folk.*

External links

- Images of early editions of the carol and historical information[4]
- Free typeset sheet music [5] from *Cantorion.org*
- **Lyrics to** We Three Kings [6]

References

[1] John Henry Hopkins (http://www.hymntime.com/tch/bio/h/o/p/hopkins_jh.htm) at CyberHymnal
[2] "Biography of Rev. John Henry Hopkins" (http://poetry.poetryx.com/poets/108/bio/). . Retrieved 2008-11-27.
[3] www.naxoscarols.com (http://www.naxoscarols.com/,)
[4] http://www.hymnsandcarolsofchristmas.com/Hymns_and_Carols/we_three_kings_of_orient_are.htm
[5] http://cantorion.org/musicsearch/title/We%20Three%20Kings
[6] http://www.allchristmaslyrics.com/we-three-kings-of-orient-are-lyrics.htm

We'll Run Away

"We'll Run Away" is a song written by Brian Wilson and Gary Usher for the American pop band The Beach Boys. It was released on their 1964 album *All Summer Long*. The song is a doo-wop ballad in 12/8 time. The lyrics are about a young couple wishing to elope, and their respective parents are warning them against such an impulse:

"We know they're right / When they say / We're not ready / But all we care / Is how we feel / Right now / . . . We'll run away / And get married / Anyhow"

The lyrics come to a twist ending by revealing the parents' hypocrisy:

"But one thing they're forgetting / A thing they're not regretting / They ran away and got married / Anyhow"

Details

- *Written by:* Brian Wilson/Gary Usher
- *Album:* All Summer Long
- *Time:* 2 min 00 sec
- *Produced by:* Brian Wilson

Performers

- *Brian Wilson:* Lead Vocals

See also

- The Beach Boys
- All Summer Long
- List of songs by The Beach Boys

We're Together Again

"**We're Together Again**" is a song written by Brian Wilson and Ron Wilson. The song was recorded by the American pop band The Beach Boys. The song was released on the re-release of the *Friends/20/20* albums.

See also

- List of songs by The Beach Boys

Wendy

"Wendy"	
Song by The Beach Boys from the album *All Summer Long*	
Released	July 13, 1964
Recorded	April 29, 1964 Western Studios
Genre	Pop
Label	Capitol Records
Composer	Brian Wilson/Mike Love
Producer	Brian Wilson
***All Summer Long* track listing**	
"Carl's Big Chance" (6) "**Wendy**" (7) "Do You Remember?" (8)	

"Wendy" is a song written by Brian Wilson and Mike Love for the American pop band The Beach Boys. It was released on their 1964 album *All Summer Long*. It was also featured on their EP, *Four by The Beach Boys*. "Wendy" peaked at No. 44 on the *Billboard* Hot 100, at No. 36 in Germany and at No. 5 in Switzerland in July 1967 when it was nominally the B-side of "Good Vibrations" -- as it was everywhere outside the US. In regional North American charts it made the top ten in Washington DC, Louisville, Vancouver, Minneapolis, Denver (rising to #2 at KBTR), and Tucson; top twenty in Toronto, San Francisco, San Diego, Miami, Columbus, and Cincinnati.

The opening has an ominous feel to it and a cough is audible during the song's middle eight. The song was originally credited to just Wilson. Mike Love's name was added as a result of a lawsuit filed by him against Wilson in the 1990s.

Details

- Written by: Brian Wilson/Mike Love
- Album: *All Summer Long*
- Time: 2 min 16 sec
- Produced by: Brian Wilson

Performers

- Brian Wilson: Lead Vocals
- Mike Love: Lead Vocals

See also

- List of songs by The Beach Boys

When Girls Get Together

"When Girls Get Together" is a song written by Brian Wilson and Mike Love for the American pop band The Beach Boys. It was released on their 1980 album *Keepin' the Summer Alive*.

Details

- *Written by:* Brian Wilson/Mike Love
- *Album:* Keepin' the Summer Alive
- *Time:* 3 min 31 sec
- *Produced by:* Bruce Johnston

Performers

- *Brian Wilson:* Lead Vocals
- *Mike Love:* Lead Vocals

See also

- The Beach Boys
- Keepin' the Summer Alive
- List of songs by The Beach Boys

When I Grow Up (To Be a Man)

"When I Grow Up (to Be a Man)"	
Single by The Beach Boys	
from the album *The Beach Boys Today!*	
Released	August 24, 1964
Format	Vinyl
Recorded	track: August 5, 1964 vocals & guitar solo: August 10, 1964
Genre	Sunshine pop
Length	2:01
Label	Capitol Records
Producer	Brian Wilson
The Beach Boys singles chronology	
"I Get Around"/"Don't Worry Baby" (1964)	**"When I Grow Up (To Be a Man)"**/"She Knows Me Too Well" (1964)	"Dance, Dance, Dance"/"The Warmth of the Sun" (1964)

"When I Grow Up (to Be a Man)" is a song written by Brian Wilson and Mike Love for the American pop band The Beach Boys. It was released on their 1965 album *The Beach Boys Today!* and as a single the previous year hit number nine on the *Billboard* Hot 100 chart, number seven in *Cash Box*. It spent two weeks at number one in Canada's national RPM chart. The B-side of the single was "She Knows Me Too Well" and stopped one place under the *Hot 100*.

The lead vocal is shared by Brian Wilson and Mike Love.

Recording

The song was recorded over two sessions in 1964 at Western Recorders. The instrumental track was most likely recorded on August 5 with the vocals being overdubbed five days later on August 10. The instrumental track, arranged by Brian Wilson, features Carl Wilson on lead and rhythm guitars; Al Jardine on electric bass guitars; Brian Wilson on acoustic piano & harpsichord; Carrol Lewis on harmonica and Dennis Wilson on drums. The song features both Mike Love and Brian Wilson on the lead vocals with backing vocals by Brian, Carl & Dennis Wilson, Mike Love and Al Jardine.

Album and alternate releases

The song was first released on an album in 1965 on the band's *The Beach Boys Today!* album. A binaural mix of the song was released on the 1993 box set *Good Vibrations: Thirty Years of The Beach Boys*. This mix featured the instrumental recording on one channel and the vocal recording on the other channel allowing the listener to hear the complexity of both the instrumental and vocal track.

Live versions

During the band's first British tour in 1964, they performed this song as well as "I Get Around" on their first television appearance in Britain on Ready Steady Go.[1] However, the song was rarely performed live by the band.

Pop Culture References

- The song is used during the opening credits of American comedy-drama Men of a Certain Age.

See also

- List of The Beach Boys songs

External links

- "When I Grow Up (To Be a Man)" [2] review at Allmusic

References

[1] Live on Ready Steady Go! 1964 (http://www.youtube.com/watch?v=DCYouoLKxjo)
[2] http://allmusic.com/cg/amg.dll?p=amg&sql=33:aifuxqrrldke

When a Man Needs a Woman

When a Man Needs a Woman is a song written by Brian Wilson, Carl Wilson, Dennis Wilson, Al Jardine, Steve Korthof and Jon Parks for the American pop band The Beach Boys. It was released on their 1968 album *Friends*.

Details

- *Written by:* Brian Wilson/Dennis Wilson/Carl Wilson/Al Jardine/Steve Korthof/Jon Parks
- *Album:* Friends
- *Time:* 2 min 06 sec
- *Produced by:* The Beach Boys

Performers

- *Brian Wilson:* Lead Vocals

See also

- List of songs by The Beach Boys

Where I Belong

"Where I Belong"	
Song by The Beach Boys from the album *The Beach Boys*	
Released	May 1985
Genre	Pop music
Length	2:55
Label	Caribou
Composer	Carl Wilson/Robert White Johnson
Producer	Steve Levine
***The Beach Boys* track listing**	
"I'm So Lonely" (8)	**"Where I Belong"** (9)	"I Do Love You" (10)

"Where I Belong" is a song written by Carl Wilson and Robert White Johnson for the American pop band The Beach Boys. It was released on their 1985 album *The Beach Boys*.

Details

- Written by: Carl Wilson/Robert White Johnson
- Album: *The Beach Boys*
- Time: 2:55
- Produced by: Steve Levine

Musicians

- Al Jardine - vocals
- Bruce Johnston - vocals
- Steve Levine - synthesizer
- Julian Lindsay - all other instruments
- Mike Love - vocals
- Brian Wilson - vocals
- Carl Wilson - keyboard, lead vocal

See also

- The Beach Boys
- *The Beach Boys*
- List of songs by The Beach Boys

Whistle In

"Whistle In" is a song written by Brian Wilson for the American pop band The Beach Boys. It was released on their 1967 album *Smiley Smile*.

Details

- *Written by:* Brian Wilson
- *Album:* Smiley Smile
- *Time:* 1 min 04 sec
- *Produced by:* The Beach Boys

Performers

- *Carl Wilson:* Lead Vocals
- *Mike Love:* Lead Vocals

See also

- The Beach Boys
- Smiley Smile
- List of songs by The Beach Boys

White Christmas

"**White Christmas**" is an Irving Berlin song reminiscing about an old-fashioned Christmas setting. The version sung by Bing Crosby is the best selling single of all time.[1]

Accounts vary as to when and where Berlin wrote the song.[1] One story is that he wrote it in 1940, poolside at the Biltmore hotel in Phoenix, Arizona. He often stayed up all night writing — he told his secretary, "Grab your pen and take down this song. I just wrote the best song I've ever written — heck, I just wrote the best song that anybody's ever written!"[2]

White Christmas, 1995 re-release CD album cover

Bing Crosby version

The first public performance of the song was also by Crosby, on his NBC radio show *The Kraft Music Hall* on Christmas Day, 1941 and the recording is not believed to have survived.[1] [3] He recorded the song with the John Scott Trotter Orchestra and the Ken Darby Singers for Decca Records in just 18 minutes on May 29, 1942, and it was released on July 30 as part of an album of six 78-rpm songs from the film *Holiday Inn*.[1] [3] At first, Crosby did not see anything special about the song. He just said "I don't think we have any problems with that one, Irving."

The song initially performed poorly and was overshadowed by the film's first hit song: "Be Careful, It's my Heart".[3] By the end of October 1942, however, "White Christmas" topped the "Your Hit Parade" chart. It remained in that position until well into the new year.[3] (It has often been noted that the mix of melancholy — "just like the ones I used to know" — with comforting images of home — "where the treetops glisten" — resonated especially strongly with listeners during World War II. The Armed Forces Network was flooded with requests for the song.[3])

In 1942 alone, Crosby's recording spent eleven weeks on top of the *Billboard* charts. The original version also hit number one on the Harlem Hit Parade for three weeks[4] , Crosby's first-ever appearance on the black-oriented chart. Re-released by Decca, the single returned to the #1 spot during the holiday seasons of 1945 and 1946 (on the chart dated January 4, 1947), thus becoming the only single with three separate runs at the top of the U.S. charts. The recording became a chart perennial, reappearing annually on the pop chart twenty separate times before Billboard Magazine created a distinct Christmas chart for seasonal releases.

Following its prominence in the musical *Holiday Inn*, the composition won the Academy Award for Best Original Song. In the film, Bing Crosby sings "White Christmas" as a duet with actress Marjorie Reynolds, though her voice was dubbed by Martha Mears. This now-familiar scene was not the moviemakers' initial plan; in the script as originally conceived, Reynolds, not Crosby, was to sing the song.[3]

The familiar version of "White Christmas" most often heard today is not the one Crosby recorded in 1942. He was called to Decca studios on March 18, 1947, to re-record the track; the 1942 master had become damaged due to its frequent use. Efforts were made to exactly reproduce the original recording session, and Crosby was again backed by the Trotter Orchestra and the Darby Singers.[2] Even so, there are subtle differences in the orchestration, most notably the addition of a celesta and flutes to brighten up the introduction.

Crosby was dismissive of his role in the song's success, saying later that "a jackdaw with a cleft palate could have sung it successfully." But Crosby was associated with it for the rest of his career. Another Crosby vehicle — the 1954 musical *White Christmas* — was the highest-grossing film of 1954.

Sales figures

Crosby's "White Christmas" single has been credited with selling 50 million copies, the most by any release. The *Guinness Book of World Records* lists the song as a 100-million seller, encompassing all versions of the song, including albums.[1] Crosby's holiday collection *Merry Christmas* was first released as an LP in 1949, and has never been out-of-print since. However, due to incomplete record keeping before 1958, "White Christmas" is officially listed as the second best-selling single worldwide.

Historic influence

"ItsRanked" ranked Crosby's "White Christmas" as the number one Christmas song on its Top 40 Christmas Songs of all time.[5] In 1999, National Public Radio included it in the "NPR 100", which sought to compile the one hundred most important American musical works of the 20th century. In 2002, the original 1942 version was one of 50 historically significant recordings chosen that year by the Library of Congress to be added to the National Recording Registry.

The recording was broadcast on the radio on April 30, 1975, as a secret, pre-arranged signal precipitating the U.S. evacuation of Saigon (see Fall of Saigon).

Original introduction

Irving Berlin's opening bars are often dropped in many recordings, but are included on *A Christmas Gift for You from Phil Spector*, sung by Darlene Love.[2]

> The sun is shining, the grass is green,
> The orange and palm trees sway.
> There's never been such a day
> in Beverly Hills, L.A.
> But it's December the twenty-fourth,—
> And I am longing to be up North—
>
> —Verse dropped from original version[6]

Keane's version also did include the introduction, but changed lyrics to give the song a melancholic feeling:

> The sun's been hiding, the streets are gray,
> The rain has been falling down.
> Seems everyone wears a frown
> for Christmas in London town
> It reminds me each time I roamed.
> I'm longing to be back home
>
> —Keane version of the introduction

Other versions

The Drifters' 1954 cover of "White Christmas" showcased the talents of lead singer Clyde McPhatter and the bass of Bill Pinkney. Their recording of the song peaked at #2 on *Billboard*'s R&B chart in December 1954, and returned to the same chart in the next two years. In December 1955, "White Christmas" became the Drifters' first of 34 singles to register in the mainstream Hot 100 chart.[7] For decades, the Drifters' version was primarily heard on R & B radio stations, getting little exposure elsewhere. The song received a boost in the early 1990s, when it was prominently featured in the film *Home Alone* during a scene in which the lead character Kevin is applying his father's aftershave while mouthing the lyrics. Radio stations formats as diverse as oldies, adult contemporary, Top 40, and country began playing the Drifters' version. The song was later featured in the film *The Santa Clause*.

Andy Williams charted on the Christmas Singles chart in 1963 (#1) and 1967 (#22) with his version. The B-Side was his version of *The Christmas Song*.

In 1963, Jimmy McGriff recorded the song for his album "Christmas With McGriff".

Michael Bolton covered the song on his 1992 album *Timeless: The Classics*.

In 2006 was covered by Twisted Sister feat Doro Pesch and was released on their album *A Twisted Christmas*, with German/English lyrics.[8]

Andrea Bocelli recorded the song for his first holiday album, *My Christmas*, in 2009. The song debuted at No. 30, on the *Portuguese Singles Chart*, spent the 2 following weeks at No. 19, then rose to No. 18, on its forth week, before reaching No. 16 on its fifth.[9] The song also debuted at No. 7 on the Hungarian Singles Chart.[10]

Stiff Little Fingers Covered the song as part of their Silly Encores B-Side and also appeared on their USA release album - Hanx!.

Boy George did make a cover of the song in 2009 and released as a single in digital download format.

References

[1] Roy J. Harris, Jr. (December 5, 2009). "The Best-Selling Record of All. 'White Christmas' and the reasons it endures" (http://online.wsj.com/article/SB10001424052748703499404574561734246276554.html). *Wall Street Journal*. . Retrieved 2009-12-06. "It was a peaceful song that became a wartime classic. Its unorthodox, melancholy melody—and mere 54 words, expressing the simple yearning for a return to happier times—sounded instantly familiar when sung by America's favorite crooner. But 67 years after its introduction, some still are surprised to learn that Bing Crosby's recording of the Irving Berlin ballad "White Christmas" became not only the runaway smash-hit for the World War II holidays, but the best-selling record of all time."

[2] White Christmas (http://www.hymnsandcarolsofchristmas.com/Hymns_and_Carols/white_christmas.htm)

[3] John Mueller (1986). *Astaire Dancing - The Musical Films*. London: Hamish Hamilton. pp. 204, 425. ISBN 0-241-11749-6.

[4] Whitburn, Joel (2004). *Top R&B/Hip-Hop Singles: 1942-2004*. Record Research. p. 139.

[5] Top 40 Christmas Songs (Lyrical) - ItsRanked! (http://itsranked.com/rankings/2007/11/christmas-songs-top-40.html)

[6] *White Christmas* piano solo, Hal Leonard

[7] CD sleeve: Billboard Greatest Christmas Hits (1955 - Present), 1989 Rhino Records Inc.

[8] laut.de | Twisted Sister - "A Twisted Christmas" (CD-Kritik) (http://www.laut.de/lautstark/cd-reviews/t/twisted_sister/a_twisted_christmas/index.htm)

[9] "White Christmas-bianco Natale" on acharts.com (http://acharts.us/song/52351)

[10] "White Christmas-bianco Natale" Hungary Top 10 (http://mahasz.hu/m/?menu=slagerlistak&menu2=single_track_top_10), Week 51/2009

Why Do Fools Fall in Love

"**Why Do Fools Fall in Love**" is a song that was originally a hit for early New York City-based rock and roll group Frankie Lymon & The Teenagers in 1956. It reached No. 1 on the R&B chart,[1] No. 6 on *Billboard*'s Pop Singles chart, and number one on the UK Singles Chart.[2] The song was ranked #307 on the *Rolling Stone* magazine's list of The 500 Greatest Songs of All Time.

The song helped to make Frankie Lymon a household name and would make him a rock and roll pioneer, paving the way for later teen prodigies like Stevie Wonder and Michael Jackson, whose careers also took off at the age of 13.

Writing credits

In late 1955, The Teenagers (at that time calling themselves The Premiers) auditioned a song called "Why do Birds Sing So Gay?" for George Goldner, recording producer and owner of Gee Records. Jimmy Merchant, tenor of the group, had written the song based on a line from some love letters given to the guys by a tenant in bassist, Sherman Garnes' apartment building. One of them featured the words "Why do birds sing so gay?," which fit in with lyrics of other songs that Jimmy had been writing based on a 1-6-2-5 chord pattern. So Jimmy worked with it, creating a song for Herman Santiago to lead, and adjusting the harmony to take advantage of Frankie Lymon's high tenor/soprano. Along the way, Herman changed some of the lyrics. During the audition Frankie's voice stood out and, at Goldner's suggestion, the lead in subsequent recording sessions was given to Frankie. Frankie did some improvising and re-created the melody to match his own style. According to Jimmy Merchant, what happened at the recording session was a combination of "Frankie's singing ability coupled with George Goldner's special ability to bring out the best in Frankie."[3]

Although early vinyl single releases of "Why Do Fools Fall in Love" credit Frankie Lymon, Herman Santiago, and Jimmy Merchant as co-writers of the song, later releases and cover versions were attributed to Lymon and record producer George Goldner. Goldner's name was later replaced by Morris Levy when Levy bought Goldner's interest in Gee Records, the Teenagers' record company.

After a lengthy court battle, song-writing credits were awarded to original Teenagers members Herman Santiago and Jimmy Merchant in December 1992.[4]

However, four years later in 1996, this ruling was overturned by the Court of Appeals for the 2nd Circuit under the statute of limitations and authorship, because Santiago and Merchant did not bring the case to court soon enough.

This gave the song rights back to Lymon and Levy.[4] The current publisher of the song is EMI Music Publishing, which still lists these as the songwriters.[5]

Cover versions

The song was used as a B-side for the Beach Boys single *Fun, Fun, Fun*, which reached #5 on the Billboard Hot 100 in 1964. It had only appeared in mono since the release of the single back in 1964. The only release that was heard through the 90's and 2001 was the album mono mix. The single mix of the song was found and used on the 2007 Warmth of the Sun Compilation and on 2008 Singles Boxset. The 2008 Boxset also used a recently found mono Single Edit mix. In 2009, a new stereo mix was created with an amazing newly discovered intro thanks to the discovery of the original multitrack masters by Jon Stebbins. That version is featured on the band's new compilation *Summer Love Songs*. Diana Ross released a cover version on the RCA label in 1981, peaking at #7 on *Billboard*'s Pop Singles Chart, and number four in the UK Singles Chart[2] . The success of Ross' cover helped reintroduce a new generation of audiences to Lymon. A remix of Ross' cover peaked at #36 on the UK charts in July, 1994[2] .

Why Do Fools Fall in Love has also been covered by Kenny Rankin, Gale Storm, Marion Ryan, Alma Cogan, Voices of Theory, Frankie Valli and the Four Seasons and Joni Mitchell. The Gale Storm version on Dot Records was recorded shortly after the Frankie Lymon original was released. It sold well and many white radio listeners of the time had heard only the Storm version and had no idea another version existed. Storm had a light soprano voice, and sounded classically trained; she had nearly no feel for rhythm and blues and yet her record in its way is as significant as the Lymon original. She approaches the song ironically and playfully. Virtually all of Storm's hits were covers of other artists' songs, but, she never simply copied the originals. She always brought her own qualities to them.

The Diamonds also did a more traditional Doo Wop version that came out the week after Lymon's version. This version spent 19 weeks on the charts, topping out at #12.

It's notable that both Diana Ross and Ronnie Bennett Spector said they had wanted to sound like Frankie Lymon and had been inspired by the tone and texture of his voice and particularly its clear, ringing quality. At the time of releasing her version of "Why" as her first RCA Victor single and the title track on her premier RCA album, Ross paid tribute to Lymon's inspiration.

In popular culture

The recording by Frankie Lymon & The Teenagers features in the film "American Graffiti" (1973).

References

[1] Whitburn, Joel (2004). *Top R&B/Hip-Hop Singles: 1942-2004*. Record Research. p. 368.
[2] EveryHit.com (search for songs called "Why Do Fools Fall In Love") (http://www.everyhit.com/)
[3] Marv Goldberg's R&B Notebooks, "The Teenagers", based on interviews with Jimmy Merchant.
[4] Frankie Lymon, Find A Grave Memorial (http://www.findagrave.com/cgi-bin/fg.cgi?page=gr&GRid=9929)
[5] Fools_Fall_In_Love EMI Song Details - Why Do Fools Fall in Love (http://search.emimusicpub.com/client/search.html?q=Why_Do_)

Wild Honey

"Wild Honey"	
Single by The Beach Boys	
from the album *Wild Honey*	
Released	October 23, 1967
Format	Vinyl
Recorded	Brian Wilson's home studio September 26 & 27, 1967
Genre	Psychedelic rock
Length	2:37
Label	Capitol Records
Producer	The Beach Boys

The Beach Boys singles chronology		
"Gettin' Hungry"/"Devoted To You" (1967)	**"Wild Honey"**/"Wind Chimes" (1967)	"Darlin'"/"Here Today" (1967)

"Wild Honey" is a song written by Brian Wilson and Mike Love for the American pop band The Beach Boys. It was released on their 1967 album *Wild Honey*. It was also released as a single, with the B-side of the single being "Wind Chimes". The single peaked at #31 in the U.S. and #29 in the U.K.

Composition

In a 1992 issue of Goldmine, Mike Love explained the idea for the lyrics of the song:

> "Brian was doing this track with a theremin and we were doing the song. I went into the kitchen and we were in this health food thing and wild honey was all natural. So there's this can of wild honey and we're making some tea. So I said, I'll write the lyrics about this girl who was a wild little honey. And I wrote it from the perspective that that album was Brian's R&B-influenced album, in his mind. It may not sound like it to a Motown executive but that was where he was coming from on that record. In that particular instance I wrote it from the perspective of Stevie Wonder singing it."[1]

Recording

Recording for the song began on September 26, 1967 at Brian's home studio in Bel Air, California with Jim Lockert engineering the session. The song would be almost completely recorded in one day. The band would initially record organ and electric bass guitar courtesy of Bruce Johnston, percussion, tambourine and piano and following that Carl Wilson's lead vocal was overdubbed onto the basic track. The band then recorded instrumental inserts including bongos, percussion and drums, in which Dennis Wilson's bass drum was purportedly recorded in a hallway.[2] The session then concluded with the band doing further vocal and organ overdubs.[3]

Work was resumed on the track the following day with Paul Tanner overdubbing his theremin - again at Brian's home studio - over the otherwise finished track. This was the third song in the Beach Boys catalogue - after "I Just Wasn't Made For These Times" and "Good Vibrations" - to feature the theremin.

Album and alternate releases

The song was first released as a single on October 18, 1967. It was then released as the first track on *Wild Honey* in December of the same year. The following year, the song's backing track was released on the *Stack-O-Tracks* album. The song has appeared on several of the groups Greatest Hits compilations including the 1999 compilation album *The Greatest Hits - Volume 2: 20 More Good Vibrations*; the 2003 compilation *Sounds of Summer: The Very Best of The Beach Boys* as well as the 1993 box set *Good Vibrations: Thirty Years of The Beach Boys*.

Charts

Chart (1968)	Peak position
Australian Singles Chart[4]	10
Dutch Singles Chart[5]	26
New Zealand Singles Chart[6]	11
UK Singles Chart	29
U.S. *Billboard* Hot 100	31

The single peaked at No. 22 in Cash Box and No. 14 in Canada. It featured in the top 10 in playlists of many large markets including Philadelphia, Detroit, Dallas, Minneapolis, Kansas City, Cleveland and the rest of Ohio, Portland, Phoenix, Vancouver, and lodged at No. 2 in Washington DC for three weeks, kept out only by the Monkees; No. 20 in New York. The following year, the song's backing track was released on the *Stack-O-Tracks* album.

See also

- List of songs by The Beach Boys

References

[1] Sharp, Ken (1992-09-18). "Love Among The Ruins". Goldmine. p. 19.

[2] Doe, Andrew G, Tobler, John (2004). *Brian Wilson and the Beach Boys: the Complete Guide to their Music*. p. 63.

[3] Badman, Keith (2004). *The Beach Boys: The Definitive Diary of America's Greatest Band on Stage and in the Studio*. pp. 200–01.

[4] "Australian Singles Charts" (http://www.mountvernonandfairway.de/charts10.htm). mountvernonandfairway.de. . Retrieved 13 November 2007.

[5] "Dutch Singles Charts" (http://www.mountvernonandfairway.de/charts6.htm). mountvernonandfairway.de. . Retrieved 13 November 2007.

[6] "New Zealand Singles Charts" (http://www.mountvernonandfairway.de/charts5.htm). mountvernonandfairway.de. . Retrieved 13 November 2007.

Wind Chimes

"Wind Chimes"	
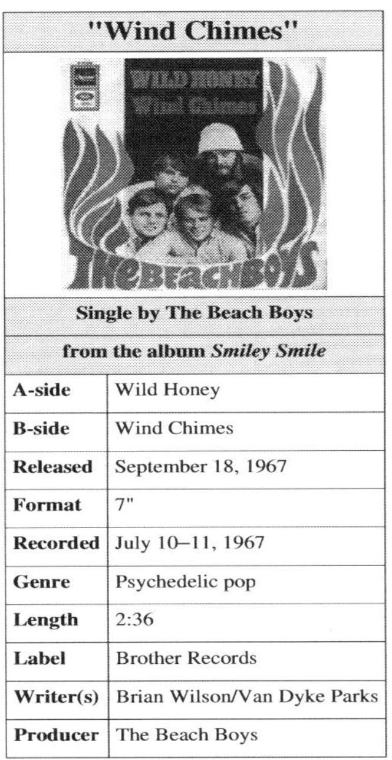	
Single by The Beach Boys	
from the album *Smiley Smile*	
A-side	Wild Honey
B-side	Wind Chimes
Released	September 18, 1967
Format	7"
Recorded	July 10–11, 1967
Genre	Psychedelic pop
Length	2:36
Label	Brother Records
Writer(s)	Brian Wilson/Van Dyke Parks
Producer	The Beach Boys

"**Wind Chimes**" is a song written by Brian Wilson and Van Dyke Parks for the American pop band The Beach Boys, and was intended to be on the aborted 1966 album *Smile*. The band completely re-recorded the song for inclusion on their next album, *Smiley Smile*. That version was released on the b-side of "Wild Honey", their 1967 single which charted at #31 on the Billboard Hot 100 chart.

When Brian Wilson returned to finish *Smile* as a solo project in 2004, he would record the song again. This version was also used as a b-side, this time for Wilson's solo recording of Wonderful which charted at #29 in the UK.

Original version

"Wind Chimes" was originally written and recorded for the *Smile* project. It is one of the few songs that was completely finished for the album and was included as one of the previously unreleased tracks on the *Good Vibrations: Thirty Years of The Beach Boys* boxset released in 1993.

In its original version, "Wind Chimes" was in AAB form. The A sections feature Carl Wilson on lead vocals, singing over a backing track consisting of vibraphones, percussion, and bass guitar. The B section consists of variations on the bass line from the A section, first sung by the whole group over a full backing track, and then, much more quietly, by three pianos.

The song was recorded in three sessions. On August 3, 1966 at Gold Star Studios, Brian Wilson produced the backing track. Two months later, on October 5, the A sections of the backing track were redone with a much smaller band, and the band recorded their vocals on October 10. The October recording sessions were at Western Studios and were engineered by Chuck Britz.

musicians

- Charles C. Berghofer - upright bass
- Hal Blaine - drums
- Frank Capp - percussion
- Al de Lory - piano
- William Green - clarinet
- Sam Glenn - saxophone
- James Horn - clarinet
- Al Jardine - vocals
- Carol Kaye - bass guitar
- Larry Knechtel - organ
- Mike Love - vocals
- Jay Migliori - saxophone
- Van Dyke Parks - unknown
- Don Randi - piano
- Lyle Ritz - upright bass
- Brian Wilson - vocals
- Carl Wilson - guitar, lead vocal
- Dennis Wilson - vocals

Smiley Smile version

After *Smile* was abandoned, the group quickly recorded an album, to be released in its place. *Smiley Smile* would be released in September 1967 and featured both new songs and new recordings of songs originally intended for *Smile*. The new version of "Wind Chimes" was recorded by the band on July 10 & 11 at Brian Wilson's home studio. It starts with 2 A sections, just like the original version, but the rest of the song is different, ending with a vocal tag based on a *Smile* track called "Holidays".

As with the other *Smile* songs that were re-recorded for *Smiley Smile*, the arrangement is much sparser than the original recording. Brian Wilson, Carl Wilson, Mike Love, and Dennis Wilson all take turns on the lead vocals.

See also

- The Beach Boys
- Smiley Smile
- List of songs by The Beach Boys

Winds of Change

"Winds of Change" is a song written by Ron Altbach and Ed Tuleja. The song was recorded by the American pop band The Beach Boys. It was released on their 1978 album *M.I.U. Album* which featured Al Jardine, Mike Love and Brian Wilson on lead vocals. The song ends with the "won't last forever" line from "When I Grow Up (To Be a Man)."

Wipe Out

"Wipe Out"	
Single by The Surfaris	
Released	1962
Recorded	1962, Cucamonga's Pal Recording Studio
Genre	Surf music, hard rock
Writer(s)	Bob Berryhill, Pat Connolly, Jim Fuller and Ron Wilson
Music sample "Wipeout"	

"**Wipe Out**" is a tune written by Bob Berryhill, Pat Connolly, Jim Fuller and Ron Wilson. The tune was first performed and recorded by The Surfaris, who were elevated to international status with the release of the "Surfer Joe" and "Wipe Out" single. The tune also featured in the films *Flipper* and *Dirty Dancing*.

The term 'wipeout' refers to a fall from a surfboard, especially one that looks painful.

Recording and single release

Bob Berryhill, Pat Connolly, Jim Fuller and Ron Wilson wrote the tune almost on the spot as a suitable B-side was needed for the intended "Surfer Joe" single. In late 1962, while the band was in Cucamonga's Pal Recording Studio recording the single, one of the band members suggested that a gimmick sound indicating a wipe out off a surfboard be emulated. The suggestion was made that during the introduction before the music starts, a cracking sound, imitating a breaking surfboard, should be made.

Also in the introduction is a manic voice babbling, "ha ha ha ha ha wipe out". The spoken voice at the beginning of the song is the voice of the band's manager of the time, Dale Smallin.

Ron Wilson's energetic drum solo (a sped up version of his Charter Oak High School marching band's drum cadence) was beaten out on malt-shop tables all over the country which also helped "Wipe Out" to become one of the best-remembered instrumental tunes of the period. The afterthought track spent four months on the national Billboard chart in the autumn of 1963, reaching #2 and kept out of the top slot only by Stevie Wonder's *Fingertips*. The smash hit returned to the Hot 100 in 1966, reaching #16 in its second national chart run. Meanwhile, original A-side "Surfer Joe" only attracted airplay in the wake of *Wipe Out*'s success, and peaked at #62 during its six-week run.

Another Southern Californian surf group calling themselves the Surfaris had formed around the same time. They renamed themselves the Original Surfaris following the popularity of "Wipe Out".

Following the death of television personality Morton Downey, Jr., news reports and obituaries incorrectly credited him as the composer of "Wipe Out".[1] [2] As of 2009, Downey's official website continues to make this claim.[3]

In September 2009, it was used for the Local on the 8s segment on The Weather Channel.

Cover versions

The tune has been covered by several artists including the American rap group The Fat Boys in which the tune was released on their 1987 album *Crushin'* making guest appearances with the pop group The Beach Boys on the track. A promo clip was also filmed for The Fat Boys version of the tune. This cover version reached #12 in the U.S. charts and #2 in the UK charts in 1987.

Rock and roll revival act Sha Na Na performed *Wipe Out* at the 1969 Woodstock Festival.

The Saints, an English band covered the tune (produced by Joe Meek) in the mid-1960s.

Joe Piscopo featured the tune on his 1985 album *New Jersey* as "Music Minus One," a parody of the play-along recording series. The drums are the "minus one," which means that this version frequently goes silent for a few seconds.

The 2006 Dancehall riddim "Wipe Out" is based on the Surfaris tune. Several well known Jamaican musicians (Lady Saw, T.O.K., Elephant Man, Beenie Man and others) recorded vocals over this instrumental.[4]

Gary Hoey covered this tune on his *Monster Surf* album in 2005.

The Queers performed a cover of "Wipe Out" on the *Acid Beaters* split-cd with The Manges in 2003.

The Korean rhythm video game *Pump It Up* featured a track called "Mr. Larpus" that was based on this tune.

The Ventures covered the tune on their live album *The Ventures on Stage* in 1965.

The Toy Dolls also covered the tune with an additional video made in 1984.

Ce'Cile Flava covered this tune with the title "Goody" on her album *Bad Gyal* in 2008.[5]

Serbian doo wop band Vampiri recorded a cover version on their 1992 album *Tacno u ponoc*.

In the video game *Final Fantasy VII*, one of the game's music tracks, "Electric de Chocobo", contains most of the melody of the tune about a minute into the cut.

In November, 1998, Phish played a cover of the tune and then from that point, jokingly, throughout the duration of the show, slipped back into the tune in the middle or between other tunes, and then encored with it. The show was released on *Live Phish Volume 6*.

Steve Vai has also done a cover, but with a new twist to the tune. It is featured on his album *Mystery Tracks Vol. 3* as well as *Radio Disney: Kid Jams*.

Sacred Reich has included a part of the tune (including the drum solo) in their tune "Surf Nicaragua".

New Model Army has been known to play the tune live, often seguing from their song "Inheritance" during a show.

Two covers feature in the film *Surf's Up*. One by The Queers and another by Big Nose.

"Wipe Out" was used in a medley arranged for band, titled Rock N' Roll Hall of Fame.

In the middle of the 1990s, Animal from The Muppet Show recorded a version of *Wipe Out*.

In the 1970s a band called "Timothy P. and The Rural Route Three" performed an a cappella version of the song, closely imitating the sound of the instruments in the original.

The Smashing Pumpkins also released a cover of the tune in their Live Smashing Pumpkins album series.

"Wipe Out" was one of the many songs parodied by The Residents on their 1975 album *The Third Reich 'n Roll*.

The Adventures of Super Mario Bros. 3 episode " Mind Your Mummy Mommy Mario" has a cover version playing when Luigi, Toad, and Princess Toadstool retrieve the prince's mummy tomb and escape with it from King Koopa's castle. The song was removed in later runs, most DVD/VHS releases, etc. to avoid copyright issues. It is intact, though, on the "King Koopa Katastrophe" VHS/DVD release.

References

[1] "Wiping Out a Myth" (http://www.buriedlede.com/journalism/wipeout.html). *Orange County Register*. 2002. . Retrieved 2007-06-24.
[2] "Morton Downey Jr. Dies, Combative Talk Show Host Was An Icon Of The 1980s" (http://www.cbsnews.com/stories/2001/03/13/entertainment/main278395.shtml). *CBS News*. .
[3] Morton Downey Jr.'s Home Page (http://mortondowneyjr.com/mortondowney.html)
[4] Review : Various - Riddim Driven ~ Wipe Out (http://www.reggae-vibes.com/rev_var/wwipeout.htm)
[5] Video : Goody by Ce'Cile (http://www.youtube.com/watch?v=rd-se1s5rsw)

With Me Tonight

"With Me Tonight" is a song written by Brian Wilson for the American pop band The Beach Boys. It was released on their 1967 album *Smiley Smile*.

At about 0:26, one can here a voice say "good." This was caused by an accident when Arnie Geller, a friend of Brian Wilson's, said it during the vocal take. The grouped liked it so much, that they left it in there.

Details

- Written by: Brian Wilson
- Album: *Smiley Smile*
- Time: 2 min 17 sec
- Produced by: The Beach Boys

Performers

- Carl Wilson: Lead Vocals

See also

- List of songs by The Beach Boys

Wonderful

"Wonderful"	
Single by Brian Wilson	
from the album *SMiLE*	
B-side	Wind Chimes
Released	September 20, 2004
Format	7" single
Genre	Baroque pop
Label	Nonesuch Records
Writer(s)	Brian Wilson, Van Dyke Parks
Producer	Brian Wilson
Brian Wilson singles chronology	

Your Imagination (1998)	**Wonderful** (2004)	"Good Vibrations" (2004)

"**Wonderful**" is a song written by Brian Wilson and Van Dyke Parks for the American pop band The Beach Boys. It was to be included on the ill-fated 1966-1967 *Smile* album. A reworked version was released on their 1967 album *Smiley Smile*. A subsequent recording was later released for the 2004 album *Smile*. This song is a baroque pop on psychedelic music.

History

The original version was based around a harpsichord. The *Smiley Smile* version contains sustained organ chords as nearly the only accompaniment. It also includes an interlude not found on the original version.

The *Smile* version was completed and performed with the rest of the finally completed *Smile* songs, live in February 2004 by Brian Wilson and his band, consisting mostly of members of the Wondermints with prior Beach Boys guitarist/vocalist Jeff Foskett. A studio version of the *Smile* arrangement was subsequently recorded and included on the *Smile* studio album when it was released later in 2004. The song was released as a limited 7" single backed with "Wind Chimes" totaling 5,000 copies on blue, green, and yellow vinyl.

Brian Wilson claims that he and Van Dyke Parks wrote the song along with "Heroes and Villains" "Cabin Essence" and "Surf's Up" in a giant sandbox with a piano in it that Wilson had built in his living room.

Credits

- **Written by:** Brian Wilson/Van Dyke Parks
- **Album:** *Smiley Smile* 1967 / *Smile* 2004
- **Time:** 2 minutes 21 seconds
- **Produced by:** The Beach Boys (*Smiley Smile*)/ Brian Wilson (*Smile*)
- Carl Wilson: Lead vocals (*Smiley Smile*)

Performers: *Smile* Version:

- Brian Wilson - lead vocals, keyboards
- Scott Bennett - vocals, keyboards
- Nelson Bragg - vocals, percussion
- Jeffery Foskett - vocals
- Probyn Gregory - trumpet
- Jim Hines - drums
- Bob Lizik - bass
- Paul Mertons - clarinet
- Taylor Mills - vocals
- Darian Sahanaja - vocals, keyboards
- Nick Walusko - vocals, guitar
- Stockholm Strings 'N' Horns

See also

- List of songs by The Beach Boys

Wontcha Come out Tonight?

"Wontcha Come Out Tonight?" is a song written by Brian Wilson and Mike Love for the American pop band The Beach Boys. It was released on their 1978 album *M.I.U. Album*.

Details

- *Written by:* Brian Wilson/Mike Love
- *Album:* M.I.U. Album
- *Time:* 2 min 30 sec
- *Produced by:* Al Jardine/Ron Altbach

Performers

- *Brian Wilson:* Lead Vocals
- *Mike Love:* Lead Vocals

See also

- The Beach Boys
- M.I.U. Album
- List of songs by The Beach Boys

Wouldn't It Be Nice

"Wouldn't It Be Nice"	
Single by The Beach Boys	
from the album *Pet Sounds*	
B-side	"God Only Knows"
Released	July 11, 1966
Format	Vinyl
Recorded	Gold Star Studios January 22, 1966 Columbia Studios March 10, 1966 April 11, 1966
Genre	Pop, soft rock
Length	2:22
Label	Capitol 5706
Writer(s)	Wilson/Asher/Love
Producer	Brian Wilson

The Beach Boys singles chronology

"Sloop John B"/"You're So Good to Me" (1966) ---- "Cool, Cool Water"/"Forever" (1971)	"Wouldn't It Be Nice"/"God Only Knows" (1966) ---- "Wouldn't It Be Nice" (live at the Big Sur Folk Festival) (1971)	"Good Vibrations"/"Let's Go Away For Awhile" (1966) ---- "Long Promised Road"/"Deirdre" (1971)"

Pet Sounds track listing
• "Wouldn't It Be Nice" • "You Still Believe in Me" • "That's Not Me" • "Don't Talk (Put Your Head on My Shoulder)" • "I'm Waiting for the Day" • "Let's Go Away for Awhile" • "Sloop John B" • "God Only Knows" • "I Know There's an Answer" • "Here Today" • "I Just Wasn't Made for These Times" • "Pet Sounds" • "Caroline, No"
Music sample
"Wouldn't It Be Nice"

"**Wouldn't It Be Nice**" is the opening track on the 1966 album *Pet Sounds* and one of the most widely recognized songs by the American pop group The Beach Boys. It was composed and produced by Brian Wilson, with lyrics by Tony Asher and Brian Wilson, and the lead vocal was sung by Brian Wilson with Mike Love singing lead vocals on the bridge and the end tag, 'Good night my baby, Sleep tight my baby'.

In the *Endless Harmony* documentary, Brian Wilson described the song as "what children everywhere go through... wouldn't it be nice if we were older, or could run away and get married".

Wilson was quoted as saying:

> Listen for the rockin' accordions and the ethereal guitars in the introduction. Tony and I had visualized a scene. We had a feeling in our hearts, like a vibration. We put it into music, and it found its way onto tape. We really felt good about that record.

In a 1996 interview, Wilson stated, "'Wouldn't It Be Nice' was not a real long song, but it's a very 'up' song. It expresses the frustrations of youth, what you can't have, what you really want and you have to wait for it."

Wilson also used the title of the song for the title of his autobiography.

Composition

In November 1969, the Wilsons' father Murry Wilson sold the copyrights to the band's songs to Irving Almo for approximately $700,000. In April 1992, just after Brian Wilson had won a lawsuit in which he received $25M for damages but failed to recover his claims to ownership of the copyrights, Mike Love filed a lawsuit against Brian Wilson for $13M claiming that he had not been given credit, and therefore hadn't received royalties, on over thirty of the band's songs, many of them hit singles and was therefore entitled to some of the reward. One of these songs was "Wouldn't It Be Nice". The original credit read "Wilson/Asher" but Mike Love claimed that he had a hand in writing the lyrics, specifically the tag lines "Good night my baby, sleep tight my baby". Mike Love won the lawsuit and the song-writing credit was amended, therefore ensuring future royalties on all of the songs that he had claimed he had a hand in writing.

Tony Asher has questioned Love's involvement in the song claiming that his involvement was "none, whatsoever"[1] as the song "was one of the few songs [he] wrote the entire lyric to by [himself] at home".[1]

Recording

The instrumental track was recorded in Los Angeles, California at Gold Star Studios on January 22, 1966. The session was engineered by Larry Levine and produced by Brian Wilson. It took 21 takes of recording the instrumental track before Brian Wilson decided that it was good enough to be the master take. Highlights of these sessions can be heard on the 1997 box set *The Pet Sounds Sessions* as well as the master take. The full recording of the instrumental track, all 21 takes, can be heard on the Sea Of Tunes Unsurpassed Masters series Vol. 13 box set.[2]

The musicians present on the day of the instrumental recording were Hal Blaine on drums; Frank Capp on percussion; Roy Caton on trumpet; Jerry Cole on guitar; Al de Lory on piano; Steve Douglas on saxophone; Carl Fortina on accordion; Plas Johnson on saxophone; Carol Kaye on bass guitar; Barney Kessel on a specially built 12-string mandolin; Larry Knechtel on organ; Frank Marocco on accordion; Jay Migliori on saxophone; Bill Pitman on guitar; Ray Pohlman on mandolin and Lyle Ritz on upright bass.[3]

The vocals were recorded over two sessions at Columbia engineered by Ralph Balantin. The first vocal session took place on March 10, which also saw vocal work on "I'm Waiting for the Day", "God Only Knows" and "I Just Wasn't Made for These Times".[4] This session was almost certainly for recording the backing vocals of "Wouldn't It Be Nice" as there is a recording of the instrumental track with the backing vocals that was released on *The Pet Sounds Sessions* box set. The next session around a month later on April 11 was most likely the session at which the lead vocal for the song was recorded. Vocals for "God Only Knows" were also worked on at that particular session.[4]

On *The Pet Sounds Sessions* box set, two alternate mixes of the song can be heard. On one of the mixes, the song begins with the line "wouldn't it be nice to live together, in the kind of world where we belong", instead of the finished version of the song which opens with the line "wouldn't it be nice if we were older, then we wouldn't have to wait so long" and follows with the aforementioned lyric.

Single release

On July 11, 1966, "Wouldn't It Be Nice" was released backed with "God Only Knows" in the United States, which was the third single from the *Pet Sounds* album. It entered the *Billboard* chart on July 30 and remained there for 11 weeks, peaking at number 8 on September 17. The single also peaked at number 7 on the *Cashbox* chart and #5 in *Record World*. It was No. 4 on Canada's RPM national chart. In Australia, the song was released in August 1966 as the A-side with "God Only Knows" as the B-side of the single. It entered the charts on August 24 at number 39 and spent 17 weeks on the charts, peaking at number 2.[5] The song was also released as the A-side in New Zealand where it peaked at number 12.[6] In July 1966 in the United Kingdom the song was released as the B-side of the "God Only Knows" single,[7] which reached number 2.

In April 1971, a live version of the song from the *Live In London* album was released in the United States as the A-side of a single which featured a different artist on the B-side. However, the single failed to make any impact on the charts just as many of the other Beach Boys singles from that period had failed to chart.

In July 1976, the song was released in the United Kingdom as the B-side of the re-issued "Good Vibrations" single. The single peaked at number 18.

In June 1990, a different recording of the song from 1966 that had appeared on the 1989 *Still Cruisin'* album was released in the United Kingdom as a single with the B-side featuring a Beach Boys Medley as well as the original recording of "I Get Around", which had also been released on the *Still Cruisin'* album.

Alternate releases

The song first appeared in monophonic sound on The Beach Boys album *Pet Sounds* which was released on May 16, 1966 in the United States and in June 1966 in the United Kingdom. The song was later released in November 1966 in the United Kingdom on the *God Only Knows EP*.[7] Live versions also appear on two of the band's live albums. The 1970 release *Live In London* and the 1973 release *The Beach Boys in Concert*. On the 1986 *Made in U.S.A.* compilation, an alternate version with different vocals was used. That same version was also released on the 1989 Beach Boys album *Still Cruisin'*.

The song appears on several occasions from different stages of the recording process and in different formats on *The Pet Sounds Sessions* box set, including the song in its original monophonic mix; the first ever original stereo mix of the song, which was remastered by Mark Linett; over seven minutes of highlights from the tracking date, which documents the progress of the recording of the instrumental track; the finished instrumental track; the stereo track with the background vocals; an a cappella mix of the song; and two alternate mixes of the song one of which has a slight difference lyrically.

Cover versions

- Anni-Frid Lyngstad in 1975
- Mike Post in 1975
- Papa Doo Run Run on their 1985 album *California Project*
- Jeffrey Osborne on the 1997 tribute album *Wouldn't It Be Nice: A Jazz Portrait Of Brian Wilson*

At the 2001 special *An All-Star Tribute to Brian Wilson*, Wilson sang a duet with Elton John to the song.

Cultural references

Wouldn't It Be Nice was played over the opening scene and end credits of Hal Ashby's 1975 *Shampoo*. It was also featured during the end credits of Michael Moore's 1989 documentary *Roger & Me* and the 1994 *Seinfeld* episode "The Hamptons". It was also featured in the 1989 *The Wonder Years* episode "Summer Song", the 1997 *King of the Hill* episode "Plastic White Female," and in the 2003 *Angel* episode "The Magic Bullet". It was also featured in the 2001 Blair Hayes film *Bubble Boy*. It was also featured at the end of the 1997 Will Ferrell film *Men Seeking Women*. It was featured throughout the film *50 First Dates* as the song that the character Lucy (Drew Barrymore) constantly sang and that Henry Roth (Adam Sandler) sang sadly and tearfully to himself but humorously to the audience. It was used in the teaser trailer for the film adaption of the Bret Easton Ellis novel *American Psycho*.

In 1990, the song was portrayed in the comic strip *Doonesbury* upon the death of Andy Lippincott from AIDS.[8]

It has also been featured in two advertisements in Australia and New Zealand, the first also shown in Canada - a Cadbury chocolate advertisement ("Wouldn't it be nice if the world were Cadbury")[9] and a lottery advertisement ("Wouldn't it be nice to win a million?").

The end of the "Weird Al" Yankovic song "Pancreas" (a style parody of Brian Wilson) sounds similar to the main chorus of "Wouldn't It Be Nice".

Charts

Chart	Peak position
Australian Singles Chart[10]	2
New Zealand Singles Chart[11]	12
UK Singles Chart[12]	2
U.S. *Billboard* Hot 100[13]	8

See also

- List of songs by The Beach Boys

External links

- Making of the studio recording [14]

References

[1] Tony Asher Interview from April 4, 1996 (http://surfermoon.com/interviews/asher.html)
[2] Unsurpassed Masters Vol.13 track listing (http://www.beachboys.com/SOT13.txt)
[3] *The Pet Sounds Sessions: "The Making Of Pet Sounds"* booklet
[4] Beach Boys 1966 Recording Sessions (http://www.btinternet.com/~bellagio/gigs66.html)
[5] Abbott, Kingsley (2003), *Back To The Beach*, Helter Skelter Publishing, ISBN 1900924463
[6] New Zealand Single Charts (http://www.mountvernonandfairway.de/charts5.htm)
[7] UK 1960's Singles Charts (http://www.btinternet.com/~bellagio/45uk60s.html)
[8] Carey, Anna (2000-06-25). "Not so loony these old 'toons" (http://www.tribune.ie/archive/article/2000/jun/25/not-so-loony-these-old-toons/). *Sunday Tribune*. . Retrieved 2008-08-02. "The heartbreaking strip showing his death-- a thin shape huddled under a blanket, bald head showing, 'Wouldn't It Be Nice' coming from the stereo-- was stuck to the door of our fridge for ages."
[9] Cadbury Ad (http://www.youtube.com/watch?v=xo2wRvJ04ss)
[10] "Australian Single Charts" (http://www.mountvernonandfairway.de/charts10.htm). . Retrieved 9 November 2007.
[11] "New Zealand Single Charts" (http://www.mountvernonandfairway.de/charts5.htm). . Retrieved 9 November 2007.
[12] http://www.chartstats.com/songinfo.php?id=4361
[13] "US Singles Charts" (http://www.btinternet.com/~bellagio/60ssingles.html). . Retrieved 9 November 2007.
[14] http://www.youtube.com/watch?v=ofByti7A4uM&NR=1

You Need a Mess of Help to Stand Alone

"You Need a Mess of Help to Stand Alone"	
Single by The Beach Boys	
from the album *Carl and the Passions - "So Tough"*	
Released	May 15, 1972
Format	Vinyl
Recorded	Unknown
Genre	Country soul
Length	8 min 57 sec for both songs
Label	Brother/Reprise
Producer	The Beach Boys

The Beach Boys singles chronology		
"Surf's Up"/"Don't Go Near the Water" (1971)	"You Need a Mess of Help to Stand Alone"/"Cuddle Up" (1972)	"Marcella"/"Hold On Dear Brother" (1972)

"You Need a Mess of Help to Stand Alone" is a song written by Brian Wilson and Jack Rieley for the American pop band The Beach Boys. It was released on their 1972 album *Carl and the Passions - "So Tough"*.

Details

- *Written by:* Brian Wilson/Jack Rieley
- *Album:* Carl and the Passions - "So Tough"
- *Time:* 3 min 27 sec
- *Produced by:* The Beach Boys

Performers

- *Carl Wilson:* Lead Vocals

See also

- The Beach Boys
- Carl and the Passions - "So Tough"
- List of songs by The Beach Boys

You Still Believe in Me

"You Still Believe in Me"	
Song by The Beach Boys from the album *Pet Sounds*	
Released	May 16, 1966
Recorded	track: November 1, 1965 & January 24, 1966 vocals: early 1966
Genre	Pop
Length	2:30
Label	Capitol
Composer	Wilson/Asher
Producer	Brian Wilson
***Pet Sounds* track listing**	

- "Wouldn't It Be Nice"
- "You Still Believe in Me"
- "That's Not Me"
- "Don't Talk (Put Your Head on My Shoulder)"
- "I'm Waiting for the Day"
- "Let's Go Away for Awhile"
- "Sloop John B"
- "God Only Knows"
- "I Know There's an Answer"
- "Here Today"
- "I Just Wasn't Made for These Times"
- "Pet Sounds"
- "Caroline, No"

"**You Still Believe in Me**" is a song by the American pop band The Beach Boys, taken from their 1966 album *Pet Sounds*. It is the second track on the album. The song was composed and produced by Brian Wilson with the lyrics by Tony Asher.

Information

This was the first song on Pet Sounds to which Asher wrote lyrics. The lead vocal was sung by Brian Wilson. The song was originally titled "In My Childhood" and a bicycle horn and bell from "In My Childhood" can be heard at the end of the song because they could not be edited out of the final track. This song "compositionally embodies the unique manner in which Brian writes his music. In a sense, Brian created a new way of using the scale. His progressions are always going up, then pausing before they go up again, like they're going towards God."[1]

In the original mono version of the song, the lead is shared by Brian and Carl Wilson. The 1997 stereo version, due to inability to locate the source material for Carl's vocal overdub, has only a single-tracked lead by Brian.

To achieve the unique sound in the introduction, Tony Asher explains that "one of us had to get inside the piano to pluck the strings, while the other guy had to be at the keyboard pushing the notes so that they would ring." Brian in 1966 explained that this song is "A little 'Boys Choir'-type song with me doing the soprano. Very, very spiritual."

This song has been covered by M. Ward and also appears on the Beach Boys' *In Concert* album. Brian recorded this song for his 2002 album *Pet Sounds Live*.

Details

- *Written by:* Brian Wilson/Tony Asher
- *Album:* Pet Sounds
- *Time:* 2 min 30 sec
- *Produced by:* Brian Wilson
- *Instrumental track:* recorded November 1, 1965 at Western Studios, Hollywood, California. Engineered by Chuck Britz.
- *Vocals track:* recorded January-February 1966 at Western Studios, Hollywood, California.

Musicians

- Hal Blaine - drums
- Jerry Cole - guitar
- Al de Lory - harpsichord
- Steve Douglas - clarinet
- Bill Green - saxophone
- Jim Horn - saxophone
- Al Jardine - vocals
- Plas Johnson - saxophone
- Bruce Johnston - vocals
- Carol Kaye - bass guitar
- Barney Kessel - guitar
- Mike Love - vocals
- Jay Migliori - bass clarinet
- Lyle Ritz - upright bass
- Billy Strange - guitar
- Julius Wechter - percussion, incl. timpani
- Jerry Williams - percussion
- Brian Wilson - lead vocal
- Carl Wilson - vocals
- Dennis Wilson - vocals

See also

- List of songs by The Beach Boys

References

[1] Michael deMartin on "Pet Sounds" (http://www.maths.dundee.ac.uk/~sanderso/music/petsndsrev.htm)

You're So Good to Me

"You're So Good to Me"	
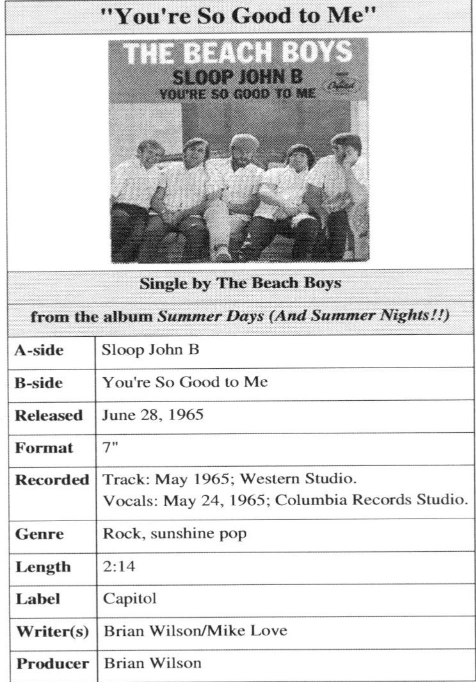	
Single by The Beach Boys	
from the album *Summer Days (And Summer Nights!!)*	
A-side	Sloop John B
B-side	You're So Good to Me
Released	June 28, 1965
Format	7"
Recorded	Track: May 1965; Western Studio. Vocals: May 24, 1965; Columbia Records Studio.
Genre	Rock, sunshine pop
Length	2:14
Label	Capitol
Writer(s)	Brian Wilson/Mike Love
Producer	Brian Wilson

"**You're So Good to Me**" is a song by The Beach Boys, originally released on the 1965 album, *Summer Days (And Summer Nights!!)*, and later included as the B-side of the group's single, "Sloop John B", released by Capitol Records on March 21, 1966.

Chart performance

"Sloop John B" entered the *Billboard* "Hot 100" on April 2, 1966, and remained on the chart for eleven weeks, peaking at #3 in the U.S. on May 7, 1966.

Personnel

The Beach Boys

- Al Jardine – bass guitar, guitar, vocals
- Bruce Johnston – organ, vocals
- Mike Love – vocals
- Brian Wilson – piano, handclaps, lead vocals
- Carl Wilson – guitar, vocals
- Dennis Wilson – drums

Additional musicians

- Ron Swallow – tambourine
- Marilyn Wilson – vocals

Cover versions

On *An All-Star Tribute to Brian Wilson* (2001), Wilson Phillips sang a cover version and mentioned the love that Wendy and Carnie have for their father, and for Chynna Phillips. "You're So Good to Me" was covered by Math and Physics Club on their 2005 EP, *Movie Ending Romance*. It was also covered by Velocity Girl on their Merge Records 7" from 1994. It was the B-side to "Your Silent Face", a cover of the song by New Order.

See also

- The Beach Boys

You're Welcome

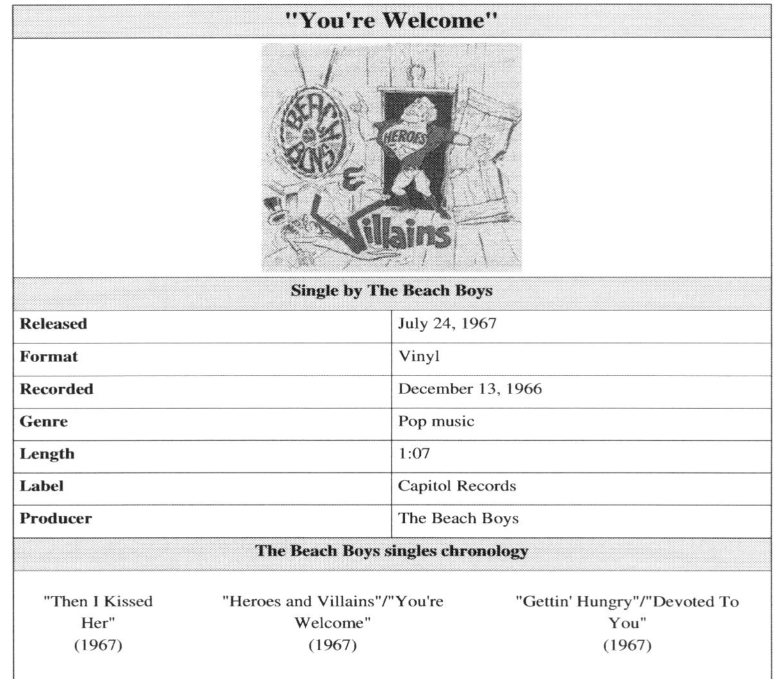

"You're Welcome"	
Single by The Beach Boys	
Released	July 24, 1967
Format	Vinyl
Recorded	December 13, 1966
Genre	Pop music
Length	1:07
Label	Capitol Records
Producer	The Beach Boys

The Beach Boys singles chronology		
"Then I Kissed Her" (1967)	"Heroes and Villains"/"You're Welcome" (1967)	"Gettin' Hungry"/"Devoted To You" (1967)

"You're Welcome" is a song written by Brian Wilson for the American pop band The Beach Boys. The a cappella chant was released on July 24, 1967 as the B-side of the "Heroes and Villains" single. It was later released on the Smiley Smile/Wild Honey re-release.

Details

- *Written by:* Brian Wilson
- *Album:* Smiley Smile/Wild Honey re-release
- *Time:* 1 min 07 sec
- *Produced by:* The Beach Boys

See also

- List of songs by The Beach Boys

You've Got to Hide Your Love Away

"You've Got to Hide Your Love Away"	
Song by The Beatles from the album *Help!*	
Released	6 August 1965
Recorded	18 February 1965 Abbey Road Studios
Genre	Folk rock
Length	2:11
Label	Parlophone
Writer	Lennon/McCartney
Producer	George Martin
***Help!* track listing**	

14 tracks

Side one

1. "Help!"
2. "The Night Before"
3. "You've Got to Hide Your Love Away"
4. "I Need You"
5. "Another Girl"
6. "You're Going to Lose That Girl"
7. "Ticket to Ride"

Side two

- "Act Naturally"

2. "It's Only Love"
3. "You Like Me Too Much"
4. "Tell Me What You See"
5. "I've Just Seen a Face"
6. "Yesterday"
7. "Dizzy Miss Lizzy"

Music sample

"You've Got to Hide Your Love Away"

"You've Got to Hide Your Love Away"	
Song by The Beach Boys from the album *Beach Boys' Party!*	
Released	8 November 1965
Genre	Rock
Length	2:56
Label	Capitol
Composer	Lennon/McCartney
Producer	Brian Wilson
***Beach Boys' Party!* track listing**	

12 tracks
• "Hully Gully"
• "I Should Have Known Better"
• "Tell Me Why"
• "Papa-Oom-Mow-Mow"
• "Mountain of Love"
• "You've Got to Hide Your Love Away"
• "Devoted to You"
• "Alley Oop"
• "There's No Other (Like My Baby)"
• "Medley: I Get Around / Little Deuce Coupe"
• "The Times They Are a-Changin' "
• "Barbara Ann"

"**You've Got to Hide Your Love Away**" is a song by The Beatles. It was written and sung by John Lennon (credited to Lennon/McCartney) and released on the album *Help!* in August 1965.

Composition and recording

The song shows the influence of the American singer Bob Dylan. The song "is just basically John doing Dylan", McCartney later said.[1] Lennon seems to mimic Dylan's gruff vocal style: the song is in a folkish strophic form and uses a Dylanesque acoustic guitar figure in compound time, chiefly acoustic accompaniment, no backing voices and light percussion from brushed snare, tambourine and maraca. The lyrics of Dylan's 1964 song "I Don't Believe You (She Acts Like We Have Never Met)" open with a strikingly similar image: "I can't understand, she let go of my hand, and left me here facing the wall", as compared with Lennon's "Here I stand head in hand, turn my face to the wall".

"You've Got To Hide Your Love Away" was the first Beatles song to feature an outside musician (apart from "Love Me Do", the group's first EMI recording, in which producer George Martin had engaged a session drummer to substitute for the then-untried Ringo Starr). The basic rhythm track was recorded first, followed by Harrison's guitar and some extra percussion. John Scott recorded a tenor flute in the spaces in Lennon's vocal track and an additional alto flute part, in harmony with the first, on the last available track of the four-track machine.[2]

Musician/singer Tom Robinson connected the lyric to Brian Epstein, the group's manager, who was homosexual (homosexuality was a criminal offence in Britain at the time).[3] When Lennon made a mistake during the recording, singing "two foot small" instead of "two foot tall", he is reported to have said: "Let's leave that in, actually. All those pseuds will really love it."[3]

Performance in the film

In the film *Help!*, at the opening of the song, the head of the cult, Clang (Leo McKern), appears from underneath a manhole cover in the middle of Ailsa Avenue, London, where parts of the film were shot. He stays there for the whole song, which the Beatles play in Lennon's fourth of the Beatles' shared flat. The flute part of the song is performed by George's in-house gardener (who also trims his grass carpet with chattery teeth). They are watched by Ahme (Eleanor Bron), and at the end of the song, George Harrison passes out after Ahme produces a giant needle for Ringo Starr, who is wearing the ring the cult is seeking.

Other studio tracks

There is an alternative take included on Anthology 2. Before the song proper begins, a montage of chatter associated with several other takes is presented. In this sequence, Lennon counts off the song, then stops to readjust his guitar pickup. After a glass shatters, Lennon sings "Paul's broken a glass, broken a glass. Paul's broken a glass. A glass, a glass he's broke today."

Personnel

- John Lennon — double-tracked vocal, twelve-string rhythm guitar
- Paul McCartney — bass, acoustic guitar
- George Harrison — acoustic lead guitar
- Ringo Starr — tambourine, maracas
- John Scott — tenor & alto flutes

Cover versions

Artists who have covered this song include the following, listed alphabetically:

- The Beach Boys, on their *Beach Boys' Party!* album, with the lead vocal by Dennis Wilson
- The Beau Brummels on their album *Beau Brummels '66*.
- The Grass Roots
- Joe Cocker
- Chris Cornell
- Elvis Costello
- Gary Lewis and the Playboys
- Government Mule
- Howie Day, with Dispatch
- Daniel Johnston, live shows
- The Kentucky Headhunters
- Oasis, as a B-side
- Perry Rose
- Tim Rose
- The Silkie, produced by The Beatles
- The Subways
- Travis
- Type O Negative Peter Steele performed the song live, solo, on bass and vocals while on tour supporting "Dead Again (Type O Negative album)" .
- U2 has performed a snippet of the song during various tours [4], usually towards the end of the song, "Bad".

- Eddie Vedder, on the movie soundtrack of *I Am Sam*, also popular during Pearl Jam concerts
- Pearl Jam
- Julieta Venegas
- Ronnie Von

External link

- Alan W. Pollack's *Notes on* "You've Got To Hide Your Love Away" [5]

References

[1] Dowling, William J. (1989). *Beatlesongs*. New York: Simon & Schuster Inc.. p. 554. ISBN 0-671-68229-6.
[2] Spitz, Bob (2005). *The Beatles: The Biography*. Boston: Little, Brown. ISBN 0-316-80352-9.
[3] "You've Got To Hide Your Love Away" (http://www.beatlesbible.com/songs/youve-got-to-hide-your-love-away/). *The Beatles Bible*. 2008. . Retrieved 29 November 2008.
[4] http://www.u2gigs.com/Youve_Got_To_Hide_Your_Love_Away-s285.html
[5] http://www.icce.rug.nl/~soundscapes/DATABASES/AWP/ygthyla.shtml

A Young Man Is Gone

"A Young Man Is Gone" is a song recorded by the American pop band The Beach Boys and released on their 1963 album *Little Deuce Coupe*. It is performed a cappella by Brian Wilson, Carl Wilson, Dennis Wilson, Mike Love, David Marks and Al Jardine.

Based on the melody of *Their Hearts Were Full of Spring*, (written by Bobby Troup and earlier recorded by The Four Freshmen), its new lyrics, written by Mike Love to fit the car/racing theme of *Little Deuce Coupe*, are a eulogy to actor James Dean, who died in a car accident while en route to a car race in which he intended to compete.

The Beach Boys later recorded the original *Their Hearts Were Full of Spring* in both live and studio versions. The singing style of the Four Freshmen was a major early influence on the band's musical leader Brian Wilson.

Discography and lists

The Beach Boys discography

The Beach Boys are an American rock band that were formed in Hawthorne, California in 1961.[1] Initially rising to become the most popular surf rock band in the U.S. during the early 1960s, the band's mastermind and chief songwriter, Brian Wilson, took The Beach Boys' music to ever increasing levels of sophistication and artistry between 1964 and 1966. This resulted in the band becoming one of most popular international acts of the decade and arguably the only group to effectively challenge the success of The Beatles in terms of mainstream appeal and critical recognition.[1] Following a nervous breakdown, Brian retreated from the spotlight and relinquished his role as musical leader, leaving the other band members to continue on through the 1970s, 1980s, and 1990s with Brian as an inconsistent participant.[1] In the 21st century, The Beach Boys continue as a touring band under the stewardship of original member, Mike Love.[1]

The Beach Boys' discography from 1961 to 1984 was originally released on the vinyl format, with the 1985 album, *The Beach Boys*, being the group's first CD release. Over the years, The Beach Boys catalogue has been released on reel-to-reel, 8-track, cassette, CD, MiniDisc, and most recently, as music downloads from a number of digital media vendors. This article lists all of the band's studio albums, live albums, official compilations, and singles.

Studio albums

Year	Album	Chart positions			Certifications	
		US 200[2]	UK[3]	AUS[4]	US[5]	UK[6]
1962	*Surfin' Safari*	32	—	—	—	—
1963	*Surfin' USA*	2	17	—	Gold	—
1963	*Surfer Girl*	7	13	—	Gold	—
1963	*Little Deuce Coupe*	4	—	—	Platinum	—
1964	*Shut Down Volume 2*	13	—	—	Gold	—
1964	*All Summer Long*	4	—	—	Gold	—
1964	*The Beach Boys' Christmas Album*	6	—	—	Gold	—
1965	*The Beach Boys Today!*	4	6	—	Gold	—
1965	*Summer Days (and Summer Nights!!)*	2	4	—	Gold	—
1965	*Beach Boys' Party!*	6	3	—	—	—
1966	*Pet Sounds*	10	2	—	Platinum	—
1967	*Smiley Smile*	41	9	—	—	—
1967	*Wild Honey*	24	7	—	—	—
1968	*Friends*	126	13	—	—	—
1969	*20/20*	68	3	—	—	—
1970	*Sunflower*	151	29	—	—	—
1971	*Surf's Up*	29	15	32	—	—
1972	*Carl and the Passions - "So Tough"*	50	25	42	—	—

1973	*Holland*	36	20	37	—	Silver
1976	*15 Big Ones*	8	31	17	Gold	—
1977	*Love You*	53	28	90	—	—
1978	*M.I.U. Album*	151	—	70	—	—
1979	*L.A. (Light Album)*	100	32	70	—	—
1980	*Keepin' the Summer Alive*	75	54	64	—	—
1985	*The Beach Boys*	52	60	67	—	—
1989	*Still Cruisin'*	46	—	24	Platinum	—
1992	*Summer in Paradise*	—	—	53	—	—
1996	*Stars and Stripes Vol. 1*	101	—	—	—	—

Live albums

Year	Album	Chart positions		Certifications
		US 200[2]	AUS[4]	US[5]
1964	*Beach Boys Concert*	1	3	—
1970	*Live in London*	75	—	—
1973	*The Beach Boys in Concert*	25	29	Gold
2002	*Good Timin': Live at Knebworth England 1980*	—	—	—

Compilations

Year	Album	Chart positions			Certifications	
		US[2]	UK[3]	AUS[4]	US[5]	UK[6]
1966	*Best of The Beach Boys*	8	2	—	2x Multi-Platinum	Platinum
1967	*Best of The Beach Boys Vol. 2*	50	3	—	2x Multi-Platinum	Platinum
1968	*Best of The Beach Boys Vol. 3*	153	9	—	—	—
1968	*Stack-O-Tracks*	—	—	—	—	—
1970	*Greatest Hits*	—	5	—	—	—
1974	*Endless Summer*	1	—	23	3x Multi-Platinum	—
1975	*Spirit of America*	7	—	79	Gold	—
1975	*Good Vibrations - Best of The Beach Boys*	25	—	—	—	—
1976	*20 Golden Greats*	—	1	26	—	Platinum
1981	*Ten Years of Harmony*	156	—	—	—	—
1982	*Sunshine Dream*	180	—	—	—	—
1983	*Rarities*	—	—	—	—	—
1983	*The Very Best of The Beach Boys*	—	1	8	—	Gold

1986	*Made in U.S.A.*	96	—	67	2x Multi-Platinum	—
1990	*The Complete Beach Boys 50 Greatest Hits (3CDs)Digital Assembly by Ron McMaster*	—			—	—
1990	*Summer Dreams - 28 Classic Tracks*	—	2	10	—	—
1991	*Lost & Found (1961–62)*	—	—	—	—	—
1993	*Good Vibrations: Thirty Years of The Beach Boys*	—	—	—	Gold	—
1995	*The Best of The Beach Boys*	—	25	—	—	—
1998	*Endless Harmony Soundtrack*	—	—	—	—	—
1999	*The Greatest Hits - Volume 1: 20 Good Vibrations*	95	28	—	2x Multi-Platinum	—
1999	*The Greatest Hits - Volume 2: 20 More Good Vibrations*	192	—	—	—	—
2000	*The Greatest Hits - Volume 3: Best of The Brother Years 1970-1986*	—	—	—	—	—
2001	*Hawthorne, CA: Birthplace of a Musical Legacy*	—	—	—	—	—
2001	*The Very Best of The Beach Boys*	—	—	—	—	—
2002	*Classics Selected by Brian Wilson*	159	112	—	—	—
2003	*Sounds of Summer: The Very Best of The Beach Boys*	16	46	—	2x Multi-Platinum	—
2007	*The Warmth of the Sun*	40	—	—	—	—
2008	*The Original US Singles Collection The Capitol Years 1962-1965*	—	—	—	—	—
2009	*Summer Love Songs*	—	—	—	—	—

Singles

Date of release	Title	Label	Chart position[7] [3]						RIAA certification[8]
			US	US AC	UK	AUS[4]	Nor[9]	Swe[10]	
Oct., 1961	"Surfin'"/"Luau"	X Records							
Nov., 1961	"Surfin'"/"Luau"	Candix Records	75						
June 4, 1962	"Surfin' Safari"/ (A-side)	Capitol Records	14			48		1	
	→ "409" (B-side)	Capitol Records	76						
Nov. 19, 1962	"Ten Little Indians"/"County Fair"	Capitol Records	49					8	
March 4, 1963	"Surfin' USA"/ (A-side)	Capitol Records	3		34	12		8	
	→ "Shut Down" (B-side)	Capitol Records	23						
July 22, 1963	"Surfer Girl"/ (A-side)	Capitol Records	7			17			

	→ "Little Deuce Coupe" (B-side)	Capitol Records	15			17			
Oct. 14, 1963	"Be True to Your School"/ (A-side)	Capitol Records	6			78		16	
	→ "In My Room" (B-side)	Capitol Records	23			78			
Dec. 2, 1963	"Little Saint Nick"/"The Lord's Prayer"	Capitol Records							
Feb. 1, 1964	"Hawaii"/"The Rocking Surfer"[11]	Capitol Records				9			
Feb. 3, 1964	"Fun, Fun, Fun"/"Why Do Fools Fall in Love"	Capitol Records	5			17			
May 11, 1964	"I Get Around"/ (A-side)	Capitol Records	1		7	33		19	Gold
	→ "Don't Worry Baby" (B-side)	Capitol Records	24			33			
Aug. 17, 1964	"When I Grow Up (To Be a Man)"/"She Knows Me Too Well"	Capitol Records	9		27	39			
Sept. 21, 1964	"Four by The Beach Boys" (EP) / "Little Honda"/"Wendy"	Capitol Records	44		11		8	1	
Oct. 26, 1964	"Dance, Dance, Dance"/ (A-side)	Capitol Records	8		24	52		13	
	→ "The Warmth of the Sun" (B-side)	Capitol Records							
Nov. 16, 1964	"The Man with All the Toys"/"Blue Christmas"	Capitol Records							
Feb. 8, 1965	"Do You Wanna Dance?"/ (A-side)	Capitol Records	12			95		18	
	→ "Please Let Me Wonder" (B-side)	Capitol Records	52						
April 5, 1965	"Help Me, Rhonda"/"Kiss Me, Baby"	Capitol Records	1		27	16		7	
July 12, 1965	"California Girls"/ (A-side)	Capitol Records	3		26	58		18	
	→ "Let Him Run Wild" (B-side)	Capitol Records							
Nov. 8, 1965	"The Little Girl I Once Knew"/"There's No Other (Like My Baby)"	Capitol Records	20						
Dec. 20, 1965	"Barbara Ann"/ (A-side)	Capitol Records	2		3	2	1	2	
	→ "Girl Don't Tell Me" (B-side)	Capitol Records							
March 7, 1966	"Caroline No"/"Summer Means New Love" (A "Brian Wilson" single)	Capitol Records	32						
	"Sloop John B"/ (A-side)	Capitol Records	3		2	17	1	4	

March 21, 1966	→ "You're So Good to Me" (B-side)	Capitol Records				17			
July 11, 1966	"Wouldn't It Be Nice"/ (A-side)	Capitol Records	8			17			
	→ "God Only Knows" (B-side)	Capitol Records	39		2	17	6		
Oct. 10, 1966	"Good Vibrations"/"Let's Go Away for Awhile"	Capitol Records	1		1	1	2	3	Gold
May, 1967	"Then I Kissed Her"/"Mountain of Love"	Capitol Records			5	14	10	4	
July 24, 1967	"Heroes and Villains"/"You're Welcome"	Brother Records	12		8	13		7	
Aug. 28, 1967	"Gettin' Hungry"/"Devoted to You" (A "Brian Wilson and Mike Love" single)	Brother Records							
Oct. 23, 1967	"Wild Honey"/"Wind Chimes"	Capitol Records	31		29	25			
Dec. 11, 1967	"Darlin'"/"Here Today"	Capitol Records	19		11	28			
April 8, 1968	"Friends"/"Little Bird"	Capitol Records	47		25				
July 15, 1968	"Do It Again"/"Wake the World"	Capitol Records	20		1	2	5	8	
Dec. 2, 1968	"Bluebirds over the Mountain"/"Never Learn Not to Love"	Capitol Records	61		33	90			
Feb. 24, 1969	"I Can Hear Music"/"All I Want to Do"	Capitol Records	24		10	10		15	
June 23, 1969	"Break Away"/"Celebrate the News"	Capitol Records	63		6	83			
Feb. 23, 1970	"Add Some Music to Your Day"/"Susie Cincinnati"	Brother Records	64						
April 20, 1970	"Cottonfields"/"The Nearest Faraway Place"	Capitol Records	103		5	1	1	2	
June 29, 1970	"Slip On Through"/"This Whole World"	Brother Records							
Nov., 1970	"Tears in the Morning"/"It's About Time"	Brother Records							
Feb., 1971	"Cool, Cool Water"/"Forever"	Brother Records							
April, 1971	"Wouldn't It Be Nice" (live)/"The Times They Are a-Changin'"	Ode Records							
May 24, 1971	"Long Promised Road"/"Deirdre"	Brother Records							
Oct. 11, 1971	"Long Promised Road"/"'Til I Die"	Brother Records	89						
Nov. 8, 1971	"Surf's Up"/"Don't Go Near the Water"	Brother Records							

Jan. 31, 1972	"Student Demonstration Time"/"Don't Go Near the Water"	Stateside Records				62			
May 15, 1972	"You Need a Mess of Help to Stand Alone"/"Cuddle Up"	Brother Records							
June 26, 1972	"Marcella"/"Hold On Dear Brother"	Brother Records	110						
Jan. 29, 1973	"Sail On, Sailor"/"Only with You"	Brother Records	79						
April 16, 1973	"California Saga: California"/"Funky Pretty"	Brother Records	84		37				
Aug. 17, 1974 (US chart date)	"Surfin' USA"	Capitol Records	36			66			
Dec. 23, 1974	"Child of Winter"/"Susie Cincinnati"	Brother Records							
March 10, 1975	"Sail On, Sailor"/"Only with You"	Brother Records	49						
May 24, 1976	"Rock And Roll Music"/"The TM Song"	Brother Records	5		36	35			
Aug. 9, 1976	"It's O.K."/"Had to Phone Ya"	Brother Records	29	33					
Nov. 1, 1976	"Everyone's in Love with You"/"Susie Cincinnati"	Brother Records							
May 30, 1977	"Honkin' Down the Highway"/"Solar System"	Brother Records							
Aug. 28, 1978	"Peggy Sue"/"Hey, Little Tomboy"	Brother Records	59	46		97			
Feb. 19, 1979	"Here Comes the Night"/"Baby Blue"	Caribou Records	44		37	90			
April 16, 1979	"Good Timin'"/"Love Surrounds Me"	Caribou Records	40	12					
June, 1979	"Lady Lynda"/"Full Sail"	Caribou Records		39	7	54			
Sept., 1979	"It's a Beautiful Day"/"Sumahama"	Caribou Records			45				
March 11, 1980	"Goin' On"/"Endless Harmony"	Caribou Records	83						
May 20, 1980	"Livin' with a Heartache"/"Santa Ana Winds"	Caribou Records							
Oct., 1981	"The Beach Boys Medley"	Caribou Records	12	20		16			
Nov. 2, 1981	"Come Go with Me"/"Don't Go Near the Water"	Caribou Records	18	11					
Sept. 1984	"East Meets West" (with The 4 Seasons)	FBI Records							
May 8, 1985	"Getcha Back"/"Male Ego"	Caribou Records	26	2		81			

July 17, 1985	"It's Gettin' Late"/"It's O.K."	Caribou Records	82	20					
Oct. 2, 1985	"She Believes in Love Again"/"It's Just a Matter of Time"	Caribou Records		26					
June 9, 1986	"Rock 'n' Roll to the Rescue"/"Good Vibrations" (Live in London)	Capitol Records	68			79			
Sept. 1, 1986	"California Dreamin'"/"Lady Liberty"	Capitol Records	57	8					
July 1987	"Wipe Out" (with The Fat Boys)	Tin Pan Apple Records	12						
Nov., 1987	"Happy Endings" (with Little Richard) /"California Girls"	Critique Records							
July 18, 1988	"Kokomo"/"Tutti Frutti" (with Little Richard)	Elektra Records	1	5	25	1			Platinum
December 1988	"Don't Worry Baby" (with The Everly Brothers)	Capitol Records							
Aug. 7, 1989	"Still Cruisin'"/"Kokomo"	Capitol Records	93	9		33			
Jan., 1990	"Somewhere Near Japan"/"Kokomo"	Capitol Records							
June, 1990	"Wouldn't It Be Nice"/"The Beach Boys Medley"	Capitol Records				58			
July, 1990	"Problem Child"/"Tutti Frutti" (with Little Richard)	RCA Records		38					
July, 1992	"Hot Fun in the Summertime"/"Summer of Love"	Brother Records		17					
Dec. 28 1992	"Forever (with John Stamos)"	Brother Records				97			
Aug., 1996	"I Can Hear Music" (w/Kathy Troccoli)	River North Records		16					

See also

- List of songs by The Beach Boys

External links

- Extended Beach Boys Discography [12]
- The Ones That Got Away - a guide to the Beach Boys' lost albums [13]

References

[1] "The Beach Boys Biography" (http://www.allmusic.com/cg/amg.dll?p=amg&sql=11:3ifrxqw5ldse~T1). Allmusic. . Retrieved 2010-01-11.

[2] allmusic (((The Beach Boys > Charts & Awards > Billboard Albums))) (http://www.allmusic.com/cg/amg.dll?p=amg&sql=11:3ifrxqw5ldse~T5)

[3] Everyhit.com - UK album and singles database (http://www.everyhit.com/)

[4] Australian Chart Books 1940-2005 (David Kent). Album chart position details prior to 1970 are limited.

[5] RIAA Gold and Platinum Search for albums by The Beach Boys (http://www.riaa.com/goldandplatinumdata.php?table=SEARCH_RESULTS&artist=Beach Boys&format=ALBUM&go=Search&perPage=50)

[6] BPI certification database (http://www.bpi.co.uk/)
[7] allmusic (((The Beach Boys > Charts & Awards > Billboard Singles))) (http://www.allmusic.com/cg/amg.dll?p=amg&sql=11:3ifrxqw5ldse~T51)
[8] RIAA Gold and Platinum Search for singles by The Beach Boys (http://www.riaa.com/goldandplatinumdata.php?table=SEARCH_RESULTS&artist=Beach Boys&format=SINGLE&go=Search&perPage=50)
[9] "http://lista.vg.no/artist_info.php?ArtistOp=show&artistId=2117"> The Beach Boys at norwegian VG-lista
[10] Hallberg, Eric (1993). *Kvällstoppen i P3* (1th ed.). Sweden: Drift Musik. ISBN 91-630-2140-4.
[11] Australia only release
[12] http://www.sergent.com.au/beachboys/
[13] http://www.esquarterly.com/bellagio/unreleased.html

List of The Beach Boys songs

List of songs by **The Beach Boys**
The Beach Boys Songs
Brian Wilson Songs | Carl Wilson Songs | Dennis Wilson Songs | Mike Love Songs

This list is an attempt to document every song released by The Beach Boys. It does not include songs released only separately by the individual members. Lead vocals by the official members of the group (Brian Wilson, Carl Wilson, Dennis Wilson, Al Jardine, Mike Love, Bruce Johnston, Blondie Chaplin, and Ricky Fataar) are listed by first name only. Guest lead vocals show full names.

Studio recorded

Song	Author	Recorded	Album	Time	Producer	Lead Vocal
409	Brian Wilson Mike Love Gary Usher	April 19, 1962	Surfin' Safari (1962) Little Deuce Coupe (1963)	1:59	Nick Venet	Mike
4th of July	Dennis Wilson	April 3, June 20, & July 1971	Good Vibrations Box Set (1993)	2:44	Dennis Wilson	Carl
Add Some Music to Your Day	Brian Wilson Joe Knott Mike Love	October 28 & December 1969 Jan 1970	Sunflower (1970)	3:34	The Beach Boys	Mike/Bruce/Carl/Brian/Al
Airplane	Brian Wilson	Autumn 1976 January 12, 1977	Love You (1977)	2:41	Brian Wilson	Mike/Brian/Carl
All Alone	Carli Muñoz	June 13, 1979	Endless Harmony Soundtrack (1998)	3:36	Carli Muñoz	Dennis
All Dressed Up for School	Brian Wilson	September 16, 1964	Little Deuce Coupe/All Summer Long (Re-Issue)	2:23	Brian Wilson	Carl/Brian
All I Wanna Do	Brian Wilson Mike Love	March 19, 1969	Sunflower (1970)	2:34	The Beach Boys	Mike/Brian

All I Want to Do	Dennis Wilson Stephen Kalinich	November 21, 1968	20/20 (1969)	2:02	The Beach Boys	Mike
All Summer Long	Brian Wilson Mike Love	May 7, 1964	All Summer Long (1964)	2:06	Brian Wilson	Mike/Group
All This Is That	Al Jardine Carl Wilson Mike Love	April 1972	Carl and the Passions - "So Tough" (1972)	4:00	Al Jardine Carl Wilson	Carl/Al/Mike
Alley Oop	Dallas Frazier	September 16, 1965	Beach Boys' Party! (1965)	2:56	Brian Wilson	Mike
Amusement Parks USA	Brian Wilson Mike Love	May 5, 1965	Summer Days (and Summer Nights!!) (1965)	2:29	Brian Wilson	Mike/Brian
And Your Dream Comes True	Brian Wilson Mike Love	May 24, 1965	Summer Days (and Summer Nights!!) (1965)	1:04	Brian Wilson	group
Angel Come Home	Carl Wilson Geoffrey Cushing-Murray	January 13, 14, & November 15, 1978	L.A. (Light Album) (1979)	3:39	Bruce Johnston The Beach Boys James William Guercio	Dennis
Anna Lee, the Healer	Brian Wilson Mike Love	April 2, 1968	Friends (1968)	1:51	The Beach Boys	Mike
Aren't You Glad	Brian Wilson Mike Love	November 1967	Wild Honey (1967)	2:16	The Beach Boys	Mike/Brian/Carl
At My Window	Brian Wilson Al Jardine	November 11, 1969	Sunflower (1970)	2:30	The Beach Boys	Bruce
Auld Lang Syne	Traditional	June 25, 1964	The Beach Boys' Christmas Album (1964)	1:19	Brian Wilson	group
Baby Blue	Dennis Wilson Gregg Jakobson Karen Lamm	Unknown (1977?)	L.A. (Light Album) (1979)	3:25	Bruce Johnston The Beach Boys James William Guercio	Carl/Dennis
Back Home	Brian Wilson Bob Norberg	September 1975 May 1976	15 Big Ones (1976)	2:49	Brian Wilson	Brian

The Baker Man	Brian Wilson	March 7, 1963	Surfin' Safari/Surfin' USA (Re-Release)	2:34	Murry Wilson	Brian
Ballad of Ole' Betsy	Brian Wilson Roger Christian	September 2, 1963	Little Deuce Coupe (1963)	2:15	Brian Wilson	Brian
Barbara	Dennis Wilson	April 1971	Endless Harmony Soundtrack (1998)	2:58	Dennis Wilson	Dennis
Barbara Ann	Fred Fassert	September 23, 1965	Beach Boys' Party! (1965)	3:23	Brian Wilson	Brian/Dean Torrence
Barbie	Bruce Morgan	March 8, 1962	Lost & Found (1961-62) (1991)	2:23	Hite Morgan	Brian
Be Here in the Mornin'	Brian Wilson Carl Wilson Dennis Wilson Mike Love Al Jardine	March 29 & 31, 1968	Friends (1968)	2:16	The Beach Boys	Al/Brian/Carl
Be Still	Dennis Wilson Stephen Kalinich	April 13, 1968	Friends (1968)	1:22	The Beach Boys	Dennis
Be True to Your School	Brian Wilson Mike Love	September 2, 1963	Little Deuce Coupe (1963)	2:06	Brian Wilson	Mike
Be with Me	Dennis Wilson	November 2 & 11, 1968	20/20 (1969)	3:08	The Beach Boys	Dennis
Beach Boys Stomp	Carl Wilson	February 8, 1962	Lost & Found (1961-62) (1991)	2:15	Hite Morgan	instrumental
Bells of Christmas	Al Jardine Ron Altbach Mike Love	November 18, 1977	Ultimate Christmas (1998)	2:44	Al Jardine	Al
Belles of Paris	Brian Wilson Mike Love Ron Altbach	November 18, 1977 February 22, 1978	M.I.U. Album (1978)	2:27	Al Jardine Ron Altbach	Mike
Better Get Back in Bed	Brian Wilson	1972	Mount Vernon and Fairway (A Fairy Tale) (1973)	1:39	The Beach Boys	Jack Rieley (narration)/Carl
Blue Christmas	Billy Hayes Jay W. Johnson	June 18, 1964	The Beach Boys' Christmas Album (1964)	3:09	Brian Wilson	Brian
Blueberry Hill	Vincent Rose Al Lewis Larry Stock	January 31 & March 25, 1976	15 Big Ones (1976)	3:01	Brian Wilson	Mike

Bluebirds over the Mountain	Ersel Hickey	29 September 1967 October 16, 1968	20/20 (1969)	2:51	The Beach Boys	Mike/Carl/Bruce
Boogie Woodie	Nikolai Rimsky-Korsakov Brian Wilson	July 16, 1963	Surfer Girl (1963)	1:56	Brian Wilson	instrumental
Break Away	Brian Wilson Reggie Dunbar	March 31, April 2, 10 & 23, 1969	Friends/20/20 (Re-Release)	2:56	The Beach Boys	Carl/Al/Brian/Mike
Brian's Back	Mike Love	Unknown (1976?)	Endless Harmony Soundtrack (1998)	4:07	Paul Fauerso	Mike/Carl
Bull Session with the "Big Daddy"	Brian Wilson Carl Wilson Dennis Wilson Mike Love Al Jardine	January 13, 1965	The Beach Boys Today! (1965)	2:10	Brian Wilson	group
Busy Doin' Nothin'	Brian Wilson	March 26 & April 11, 1968	Friends (1968)	3:04	The Beach Boys	Brian
Cabinessence	Brian Wilson Van Dyke Parks	October 11 & December 11, 1966 November 20, 1968	20/20 (1969)	3:34	The Beach Boys	Carl/Mike
California Calling	Al Jardine Brian Wilson	ca. June 1984 - March 1985	The Beach Boys (1985)	2:50	Steve Levine	Mike/Al
California Dreamin'	John Phillips Michelle Phillips	October 1982 & November 12, 1982	Best of the Brother Years (2000)	3:12	Terry Melcher	Al/Carl
California Feelin'	Brian Wilson Stephen Kalinich	2002?	Classics selected by Brian Wilson (2002)	2:49	Brian Wilson	Brian
California Girls	Brian Wilson Mike Love	April 6, 1965	Summer Days (and Summer Nights!!) (1965) Still Cruisin' (1989)	2:38	Brian Wilson	Mike
California Saga: Big Sur	Mike Love	July 27, 1972	Holland (1973)	2:56	The Beach Boys	Mike
California Saga: California	Al Jardine	August 15, 1972	Holland (1973)	3:21	The Beach Boys	Mike
California Saga: The Beaks of Eagles	Robinson Jeffers Al Jardine Lynda Jardine	August 15, 1972	Holland (1973)	3:49	The Beach Boys	Mike/Al
Can't Wait Too Long	Brian Wilson	October 28 & November 1, 1967 July 25 & 26, 1968	Good Vibrations Box Set (1993)	3:51	Brian Wilson	group/Brian

Car Crazy Cutie	Brian Wilson Roger Christian	September 2, 1963	Little Deuce Coupe (1963)	2:47	Brian Wilson	Brian
Carl's Big Chance	Brian Wilson Carl Wilson	April 29, 1964	All Summer Long (1964)	2:25	Brian Wilson	instrumental
Caroline, No	Brian Wilson Tony Asher	January 31, 1966	Pet Sounds (1966)	2:52	Brian Wilson	Brian
Cassius Love vs. Sonny Wilson	Mike Love Brian Wilson	February 20, 1964	Shut Down Volume 2 (1964)	3:30	Brian Wilson	Brian/Mike
A Casual Look	Ed Wells	March 17 & 25, 1976	15 Big Ones (1976)	2:45	Brian Wilson	Mike/Al
Catch a Wave	Brian Wilson Mike Love	July 16, 1963	Surfer Girl (1963)	2:07	Brian Wilson	Mike/Brian
Celebrate the News	Dennis Wilson Gregg Jakobson	February 25, 1969	Friends/20/20 (Re-release)	3:07	The Beach Boys	Dennis
Chapel of Love	Jeff Barry Ellie Greenwich Phil Spector	March 17 & 25, 1976	15 Big Ones (1976)	2:34	Brian Wilson	Brian
Chasin' the Sky	Randy Bishop	mid-January 1984	Up the Creek soundtrack	2:40	Spenser Proffer	Carl
Cherry, Cherry Coupe	Brian Wilson Roger Christian	September 2, 1963	Little Deuce Coupe (1963)	1:47	Brian Wilson	Mike
Child of Winter	Brian Wilson Stephen Kalinich	November 18, 1974	Ultimate Christmas (1998)	2:48	Brian Wilson	Brian/Mike
Christmas Day	Brian Wilson	June 25 & 27, 1964	The Beach Boys' Christmas Album (1964)	1:47	Brian Wilson	Al
Christmas Time Is Here Again	Buddy Holly Jerry Allison Norman Petty Al Jardine	November 1977	Ultimate Christmas (1998)	3:01	Al Jardine	Al
Chug-A-Lug	Brian Wilson Gary Usher Mike Love	August 8, 1962	Surfin' Safari (1962)	1:59	Nick Venet	Mike
Cindy, Oh Cindy	B. Barons B. Long	September 13, 1962	Surfin' Safari/Surfin' USA (Re-Release)	2:08	Nick Venet	Brian
Come Go with Me	C.E. Quick	Unknown (1977?)	M.I.U. Album (1978)	2:06	Al Jardine Ron Altbach	Al
Cool, Cool Water	Brian Wilson Mike Love	October 29, 1967 & July 1970	Sunflower (1970)	5:03	The Beach Boys	Brian/Mike

Cotton Fields (The Cotton Song)	Huddie Ledbetter	November 18, 1968 & August 15, 1969	20/20 (1969)	2:21	The Beach Boys	Al
Country Air	Brian Wilson Mike Love	November 14, 1967	Wild Honey (1967)	2:20	The Beach Boys	group
County Fair	Brian Wilson Gary Usher	September 6, 1962	Surfin' Safari (1962)	2:15	Nick Venet	Mike
Crack at Your Love	Brian Wilson Al Jardine	ca. June 1984 - March 1985	The Beach Boys (1985)	3:40	Steve Levine	Al/Brian
Crocodile Rock	Elton John Bernie Taupin	1991?	Two Rooms: Celebrating the Songs of Elton John and Bernie Taupin (1991)	3:56	Gus Dudgeon	Al/Carl
Cuckoo Clock	Brian Wilson Gary Usher	September 6, 1962	Surfin' Safari (1962)	2:08	Nick Venet	Brian
Cuddle Up	Dennis Wilson Daryl Dragon	April 9, 1972	Carl and the Passions - "So Tough" (1972)	5:30	Dennis Wilson Daryl Dragon	Dennis
Custom Machine	Brian Wilson Mike Love	September 2, 1963	Little Deuce Coupe (1963)	1:38	Brian Wilson	Mike
Dance, Dance, Dance	Brian Wilson Carl Wilson Mike Love	October 9, 1964	The Beach Boys Today! (1965)	1:59	Brian Wilson	Mike/Brian
Darlin'	Brian Wilson Mike Love	October 27, 1967	Wild Honey (1967)	2:12	The Beach Boys	Carl
A Day in the Life of a Tree	Brian Wilson Jack Rieley	April, June, & July 26, 1971	Surf's Up (1971)	3:07	The Beach Boys	Jack Rieley/Van Dyke Parks/Al
Deirdre	Bruce Johnston Brian Wilson	February 21, 1969	Sunflower (1970)	3:27	The Beach Boys	Bruce
Denny's Drums	Dennis Wilson	January 7, 1964	Shut Down Volume 2 (1964)	1:56	Brian Wilson	instrumental
Devoted to You	Boudleaux Bryant	September 16, 1965	Beach Boys' Party! (1965)	2:13	Brian Wilson	Mike/Brian
Diamond Head	Al Vescovo Lyle Ritz Jim Ackley Brian Wilson	April 12, 1968	Friends (1968)	3:37	The Beach Boys	instrumental
Ding Dang	Brian Wilson Roger McGuinn	Autumn 1973	Love You (1977)	0:56	Brian Wilson	Mike/Carl
Disney Girls	Bruce Johnston	June 3, 1971	Surf's Up (1971)	4:07	The Beach Boys	Bruce

Do It Again	Brian Wilson Mike Love	May 26 & June 6, 1968	20/20 (1969)	2:25	The Beach Boys	Mike/Carl
Do You Like Worms	Brian Wilson Van Dyke Parks	October 18 & December 21, 1966	Good Vibrations Box Set (1993)	4:00	Brian Wilson	Brian
Do You Remember?	Brian Wilson Mike Love	May 6 & 18, 1964	All Summer Long (1964)	1:37	Brian Wilson	Mike/Brian
Do You Wanna Dance?	Bobby Freeman	January 11, 1965	The Beach Boys Today! (1965)	2:19	Brian Wilson	Dennis
Don't Back Down	Brian Wilson Mike Love	April 29, 1964	All Summer Long (1964)	1:44	Brian Wilson	Mike/Brian
Don't Go Near the Water	Mike Love Al Jardine	April 3 & July 30, 1971	Surf's Up (1971)	2:39	The Beach Boys	Mike/Al
Don't Hurt My Little Sister	Brian Wilson Mike Love	June 22, 1964	The Beach Boys Today! (1965)	2:07	Brian Wilson	Mike/Brian
Don't Talk (Put Your Head on My Shoulder)	Brian Wilson Tony Asher	April 3, 1966	Pet Sounds (1966)	2:51	Brian Wilson	Brian
Don't Worry Baby	Brian Wilson Roger Christian	January 7, 1964	Shut Down Volume 2 (1964)	2:47	Brian Wilson	Brian
Drive-In	Brian Wilson Mike Love	October 18, 1963 April 29, 1964	All Summer Long (1964)	1:51	Brian Wilson	Mike
East Meets West	Bob Gaudio/Bob Crewe	December 24, 1983	single (1984)	4:03	Bob Gaudio	Mike/Al/Carl/Frankie Valli/Brian
Endless Harmony	Bruce Johnston	November 1, 2, 6, 11, 13, 15, & 30, December 14 & 20, 1979	Keepin' the Summer Alive (1980)	3:10	Bruce Johnston	Bruce/Carl
Everyone's in Love with You	Mike Love	September 1975 April 1976	15 Big Ones (1976)	2:42	Brian Wilson	Mike
Fall Breaks and Back to Winter (Woody Woodpecker Symphony)	Brian Wilson	June 29, 1967	Smiley Smile (1967)	2:15	The Beach Boys	instrumental
Farmer's Daughter	Brian Wilson Mike Love	January 5 & 31, 1963	Surfin' USA (1963)	1:49	Nick Venet	Brian
Feel Flows	Carl Wilson Jack Rieley	July 29, 1971	Surf's Up (1971)	4:44	The Beach Boys	Carl
Finders Keepers	Brian Wilson Mike Love	February 12, 1963	Surfin' USA (1963)	1:38	Nick Venet	Mike/Brian
Forever	Dennis Wilson Gregg Jakobson	January 9 & March 17, 1969	Sunflower (1970)	2:40	The Beach Boys	Dennis

Forever	Dennis Wilson Gregg Jakobson	ca. Autumn 1991 - Spring 1992	Summer in Paradise (1992)	3:05	Terry Melcher	John Stamos
Friends	Brian Wilson Carl Wilson Dennis Wilson Al Jardine	March 13, 1968	Friends (1968)	2:30	The Beach Boys	Carl
Frosty the Snowman	Steve Nelson Jack Rollins	June 24, 1964	The Beach Boys' Christmas Album (1964)	1:54	Brian Wilson	Brian
Full Sail	Carl Wilson Geoffrey Cushing-Murray	September 18, November 13, & November 27, 1978	L.A. (Light Album) (1979)	2:56	The Beach Boys James William Guercio	Carl
Fun, Fun, Fun	Brian Wilson Mike Love	January 1 & 8, 1964	Shut Down Volume 2 (1964)	2:03	Brian Wilson	Mike
Funky Pretty	Brian Wilson Mike Love Jack Rieley	January 21, June 3-June 22, June 28-August 2, 1972	Holland (1973)	4:09	The Beach Boys	Carl/Al/Blondie Ricky/Mike
Games Two Can Play	Brian Wilson	October 20, 1969	Good Vibrations Box Set (1993)	2:01	Brian Wilson	Brian
Getcha Back	Mike Love Terry Melcher	ca. June 1984 - March 1985	The Beach Boys (1985)	3:02	Steve Levine	Mike
Gettin' Hungry	Brian Wilson Mike Love	July 14, 1967	Smiley Smile (1967)	2:27	The Beach Boys	Mike/Brian
Girl Don't Tell Me	Brian Wilson	April 30, 1965	Summer Days (and Summer Nights!!) (1965)	2:19	Brian Wilson	Carl
The Girl from New York City	Brian Wilson Mike Love	May 24, 1965	Summer Days (and Summer Nights!!) (1965)	1:54	Brian Wilson	Mike
Girls on the Beach	Brian Wilson	April 10 & May 19, 1964	All Summer Long (1964)	2:24	Brian Wilson	Brian/Dennis
God Only Knows	Brian Wilson Tony Asher	March 9, 1966	Pet Sounds (1966)	2:49	Brian Wilson	Carl
Goin' On	Brian Wilson Mike Love	November 20, 21, 26, & December 10, 1979 January 3, 4, 22, February 4, & 14, 1980	Keepin' the Summer Alive (1980)	3:00	Bruce Johnston	Mike/Carl

Goin' South	Carl Wilson Geoffrey Cushing-Murray	September 18, October 2, & December 18, 1978	L.A. (Light Album) (1979)	3:16	The Beach Boys James William Guercio	Carl
Good Time	Brian Wilson Al Jardine	January 7, 1970	Love You (1977)	2:50	Brian Wilson	Brian
Good Timin'	Brian Wilson Carl Wilson	November 4, 1974	L.A. (Light Album) (1979)	2:12	The Beach Boys James William Guercio	Carl
Good to My Baby	Brian Wilson Mike Love	January 13, 1965	The Beach Boys Today! (1965)	2:16	Brian Wilson	Brian/Mike
Good Vibrations	Brian Wilson Mike Love	February 17, May 4 & 24, June 2 & 12, September 1, 12, & 21, 1966	Smiley Smile (1967)	3:36	The Beach Boys	Carl/Mike/Brian
Got to Know the Woman	Dennis Wilson	February 13 & 14, 1969	Sunflower (1970)	2:41	The Beach Boys	Dennis
Graduation Day	Joe Sherman Noel Sherman	May 5, 1965	Summer Days (and Summer Nights!!) (1965)	2:21	Brian Wilson	group
Had to Phone Ya	Brian Wilson Mike Love Diane Rovell	March 30, 1976	15 Big Ones (1976)	1:43	Brian Wilson	Mike/Al/Dennis/Carl/Brian
Hang On to Your Ego	Brian Wilson Terry Sachen	January 24, 1966	Pet Sounds (Re-Release)	3:01	Brian Wilson	Brian
Happy Endings	Bruce Johnston Terry Melcher	1987?	Non-LP single, song from the Motion Picture The Telephone (1987)	4:02	Terry Melcher	Little Richard/Carl/Mike/Al
Hawaii	Brian Wilson Mike Love	July 16, 1963	Surfer Girl (1963)	1:59	Brian Wilson	Mike/Brian
He Come Down	Brian Wilson Al Jardine Mike Love	December 1971 April 18, 1972	Carl and the Passions - "So Tough" (1972)	4:41	The Beach Boys	Mike/Blondie/Al/Carl
Heads You Win - Tails I Lose	Brian Wilson Gary Usher	September 6, 1962	Surfin' Safari (1962)	2:17	Nick Venet	Mike
H. E. L. P. Is on the Way	Brian Wilson	August 17, 1970	Good Vibrations Box Set (1993)	2:30	Brian Wilson	Mike
Help Me, Rhonda	Brian Wilson Mike Love	February 24, 1965 March 4 & 21, 1965	Summer Days (and Summer Nights!!) (1965)	2:46	Brian Wilson	Al

Help Me, Ronda	Brian Wilson Mike Love	January 8, 1965	The Beach Boys Today! (1965)	3:08	Brian Wilson	Al
Here Comes the Night	Brian Wilson Mike Love	October 26, 1967	Wild Honey (1967)	2:41	The Beach Boys	Brian
Here Comes the Night	Brian Wilson Mike Love	October 12 & 16 November 10 December 7, 18-20, 22-23, & 27-29, 1978 January 4, 1979	L.A. (Light Album) (1979)	10:51	Bruce Johnston Curt Becher	Carl/Al
Here She Comes	Ricky Fataar Blondie Chaplin	December 4–10, 1971 April 3–13, 1972	Carl and the Passions - "So Tough" (1972)	5:10	The Beach Boys	Ricky/Blondie
Here Today	Brian Wilson Tony Asher	March 10, 1966	Pet Sounds (1966)	2:52	Brian Wilson	Mike
Heroes and Villains	Brian Wilson Van Dyke Parks	June 12–14, 1967	Smiley Smile (1967)	3:37	The Beach Boys	Brian/Al
Hey Little Tomboy	Brian Wilson	Autumn 1976	M.I.U. Album (1978)	2:25	Al Jardine Ron Altbach	Mike/Brian/Carl
Hold On Dear Brother	Ricky Fataar Blondie Chaplin	April 12, 1972	Carl and the Passions - "So Tough" (1972)	4:43	The Beach Boys	Blondie
Honkin' Down the Highway	Brian Wilson	October 13, 1976	Love You (1977)	2:48	Brian Wilson	Al
Honky Tonk	Bill Doggett Billy Butler Clifford Scott Shep Shepherd	February 11, 1963	Surfin' USA (1963)	2:01	Nick Venet	instrumental
Hot Fun in the Summertime	Sylvester Stewart	ca. Autumn 1991 - Spring 1992	Summer in Paradise (1992)	3:29	Terry Melcher	Mike/Carl
How She Boogalooed It	Mike Love Bruce Johnston Al Jardine Carl Wilson	November 15, 1967	Wild Honey (1967)	1:56	The Beach Boys	Carl
Hully Gully	Fred Smith Cliff Goldsmith	September 8, 1965	Beach Boys' Party! (1965)	2:22	Brian Wilson	Mike
Hushabye	Doc Pomus Mort Shuman	April 29, 1964	All Summer Long (1964)	2:40	Brian Wilson	Brian/Mike
I Can Hear Music	Jeff Barry Ellie Greenwich Phil Spector	October 1, 1968	20/20 (1969)	2:36	The Beach Boys	Carl
I Do	Brian Wilson	November 6, 1963	Surfer Girl/Shut Down Volume 2 (Re-Release)	2:09	Brian Wilson	Mike/Brian
I Do Love You	Stevie Wonder	ca. June 1984 - March 1985	The Beach Boys (1985)	4:20	Steve Levine	Carl/Al

I Get Around	Brian Wilson Mike Love	April 2 & 10, 1964	All Summer Long (1964) Still Cruisin' (1989)	2:12	Brian Wilson	Brian/Mike
I Just Got My Pay	Brian Wilson	January 5, 1970	Good Vibrations Box Set (1993)	2:20	Brian Wilson	Mike/Bruce
I Just Wasn't Made for These Times	Brian Wilson Tony Asher	February 14, March 10, & April 13, 1966	Pet Sounds (1966)	3:11	Brian Wilson	Brian
I Know There's an Answer	Brian Wilson Terry Sachen Mike Love	February 9 & March, 1966	Pet Sounds (1966)	3:08	Brian Wilson	Mike/Al/Brian
I Love To Say Da-Da	Brian Wilson	May 16–18, 1967	Good Vibrations Box Set (1993)	1:32	Brian Wilson	Mike
(I Saw Santa) Rockin' Around the Christmas Tree	Brian Wilson Al Jardine	November 1977	Ultimate Christmas (1998)	2:22	Brian Wilson Al Jardine	Al/Matt Jardine/Adam Jardine
I Should Have Known Better	John Lennon Paul McCartney	September 14, 1965	Beach Boys' Party! (1965)	1:40	Brian Wilson	Carl/Al
I Wanna Pick You Up	Brian Wilson	October 13, 1976	Love You (1977)	2:39	Brian Wilson	Dennis/Brian
I Was Made to Love Her	Henry Cosby Sylvia Moy Lola Mae Hardaway Stevie Wonder	October 28, 1967	Wild Honey (1967)	2:05	The Beach Boys	Carl
I Went to Sleep	Brian Wilson Carl Wilson	June 4 & November 18, 1968	20/20 (1969)	1:36	The Beach Boys	Brian/Carl
I'd Love Just Once to See You	Brian Wilson Mike Love	November 13, 1967	Wild Honey (1967)	1:48	The Beach Boys	Brian
I'll Be Home for Christmas	Kim Gannon Walter Kent Buck Ram	June 30, 1964	The Beach Boys' Christmas Album (1964)	2:44	Brian Wilson	Brian
I'll Bet He's Nice	Brian Wilson	October-November, 1976	Love You (1977)	2:36	Brian Wilson	Dennis/Brian/Carl
I'm Bugged at My Ol' Man	Brian Wilson	May 24, 1965	Summer Days (and Summer Nights!!) (1965)	2:17	Brian Wilson	Brian
I'm So Lonely	Brian Wilson Eugene Landy	ca. June 1984 - March 1985	The Beach Boys (1985)	2:52	Steve Levine	Brian/Carl
I'm So Young	William H. Tyrus Jr.	January 18, 1965	The Beach Boys Today! (1965)	2:30	Brian Wilson	Brian

I'm the Pied Piper	Brian Wilson Carl Wilson	1972	Mount Vernon and Fairway (A Fairy Tale) (1973)	2:09	The Beach Boys	Jack Rieley (narration)/Brian
I'm the Pied Piper (Instrumental)	Brian Wilson Carl Wilson	1972	Mount Vernon and Fairway (A Fairy Tale) (1973)	2:20	The Beach Boys	Jack Rieley (narration)
I'm Waiting for the Day	Brian Wilson Mike Love	March 6, 1966	Pet Sounds (1966)	3:03	Brian Wilson	Brian
In My Car	Brian Wilson Eugene Landy Alexandra Morgan	June 17 & 18, 1989	Still Cruisin' (1989)	3:21	Brian Wilson Eugene Landy	Brian/Carl/Al
In My Room	Brian Wilson Gary Usher	July 16, 1963	Surfer Girl (1963)	2:11	Brian Wilson	Brian
In the Back of My Mind	Brian Wilson Mike Love	January 13, 1965	The Beach Boys Today! (1965)	2:07	Brian Wilson	Dennis
In the Parkin' Lot	Brian Wilson Roger Christian	January 7, 1964	Shut Down Volume 2 (1964)	2:01	Brian Wilson	Mike
In the Still of the Night	F. Parris	March 11, 1976	15 Big Ones (1976)	3:03	Brian Wilson	Dennis
Island Fever	Mike Love Terry Melcher	ca. Autumn 1991 - Spring 1992	Summer in Paradise (1992)	3:27	Terry Melcher	Mike/Carl
Island Girl	Al Jardine	ca. 1987-1989	Still Cruisin' (1989)	3:49	Al Jardine	Carl/Al/Mike
It's a Beautiful Day	Mike Love Al Jardine	June 15 & 17, 1979	Ten Years of Harmony (1981)	3:15	Bruce Johnston	Carl/Al/Mike
It's About Time	Dennis Wilson Carl Wilson Bob Burchman Al Jardine	July 1970	Sunflower (1970)	2:55	The Beach Boys	Carl
It's Gettin' Late	Carl Wilson Myrna Smith Schilling Robert White Johnson	ca. June 1984 - March 1985	The Beach Boys (1985)	3:27	Steve Levine	Carl
It's Just a Matter of Time	Brian Wilson Eugene Landy	ca. June 1984 - March 1985	The Beach Boys (1985)	2:23	Steve Levine	Brian/Mike
It's OK	Brian Wilson Mike Love	early 1976	15 Big Ones (1976)	2:12	Brian Wilson	Mike
It's Over Now	Brian Wilson	April 25 & March 11, 1977	Good Vibrations Box Set (1993)	2:50	Brian Wilson	Carl/Brian/Marilyn
Johnny Carson	Brian Wilson	November 10, 1976	Love You (1977)	2:47	Brian Wilson	Mike/Carl

Judy	Brian Wilson	February 8, 1962	Lost & Found (1961-62) (1991)	2:21	Hite Morgan	Mike/Brian
Just Once in My Life	Gerry Goffin Carole King Phil Spector	March 16, 1976	15 Big Ones (1976)	3:47	Brian Wilson	Carl/Brian
Keep an Eye on Summer	Brian Wilson Bob Norman	February 19, 1964	Shut Down Volume 2 (1964)	2:21	Brian Wilson	Brian/Mike
Keepin' the Summer Alive	Carl Wilson Randy Bachman	August 27–29 October 30 & 31 November 2, 6, & 13 December 3–5, 1979 January 28 & February 5, 1980	Keepin' the Summer Alive (1980)	3:43	Bruce Johnston	Carl
Kiss Me, Baby	Brian Wilson Mike Love	December 16, 1964	The Beach Boys Today! (1965)	2:35	Brian Wilson	Mike/Brian
Kokomo	Mike Love Scott McKenzie Terry Melcher John Phillips	March 22, April 5 & 6, 1988	Still Cruisin' (1989)	3:35	Terry Melcher	Mike/Carl
Kona Coast	Al Jardine Mike Love	November 18, 1977	M.I.U. Album (1978)	2:33	Al Jardine Ron Altbach	Mike/Al
Lady Liberty	Al Jardine Ron Altbach	Unknown (1986?)	single only	Unknown	Unknown	Al/Carl
Lady Lynda	Al Jardine Ron Altbach	September 19, October 11 & 16, & November 27, 1978	L.A. (Light Album) (1979)	3:58	The Beach Boys James William Guercio	Al
Lahaina Aloha	Mike Love Terry Melcher	ca. Autumn 1991 - Spring 1992	Summer in Paradise (1992)	3:44	Terry Melcher	Mike/Carl
Lana	Brian Wilson	January 5 & 31, 1963	Surfin' USA (1963)	1:39	Nick Venet	Brian
Land Ahoy	Brian Wilson	September 5, 1962	Rarities (1983)	1:42	Nick Venet	Mike
Lavender	Dorinda Morgan	October 3, 1961	Lost & Found (1961-62) (1991)	2:31	Hite Morgan	group
Leaving This Town	Ricky Fataar Blondie Chaplin Carl Wilson Mike Love	July 31, 1972	Holland (1973)	5:49	The Beach Boys	Blondie
Let Him Run Wild	Brian Wilson Mike Love	March 30, 1965	Summer Days (and Summer Nights!!) (1965)	2:20	Brian Wilson	Brian

Let the Wind Blow	Brian Wilson Mike Love	November 1967	Wild Honey (1967)	2:19	The Beach Boys	Mike/Brian/Carl
Let Us Go On This Way	Brian Wilson Mike Love	October 27, 1976	Love You (1977)	1:58	Brian Wilson	Carl/Mike
Let's Go Away For Awhile	Brian Wilson	January 18, 1966	Pet Sounds (1966)	2:18	Brian Wilson	instrumental
Let's Go Trippin'	Dick Dale	February 11, 1963	Surfin' USA (1963)	1:57	Nick Venet	instrumental
Let's Put Our Hearts Together	Brian Wilson	Autumn 1976	Love You (1977)	2:14	Brian Wilson	Brian/Marilyn Wilson
The Letter	Wayne Carson	September 11, 1967	Rarities (1983)	1:47	Brian Wilson	Brian
Little Bird	Dennis Wilson Stephen Kalinich	February 29, 1968	Friends (1968)	1:57	The Beach Boys	Dennis
Little Deuce Coupe	Brian Wilson Roger Christian	June 12, 1963	Surfer Girl (1963) Little Deuce Coupe (1963)	1:38	Brian Wilson	Mike
The Little Girl I Once Knew	Brian Wilson	October 13, 1965	The Beach Boys Today!/Summer Days (and Summer Nights!!) (Re-Release)	2:36	Brian Wilson	Brian/Al
Little Girl (You're My Miss America)	Vincent Catalano Herb Alpert	September 5, 1962	Surfin' Safari (1962)	2:04	Nick Venet	Dennis
Little Honda	Brian Wilson Mike Love	April 10, 1964	All Summer Long (1964)	1:52	Brian Wilson	Mike
Little Pad	Brian Wilson	June 28, 1967	Smiley Smile (1967)	2:30	The Beach Boys	Brian/Carl/Mike
Little Saint Nick	Brian Wilson Mike Love	October 18 & 20, 1963	The Beach Boys' Christmas Album (1964)	2:00	Brian Wilson	Mike
Little Surfer Girl	Brian Wilson	c. 1962-1963	Good Vibrations Box Set (1993)	0:31	Brian Wilson	Brian
Livin' with a Heartache	Carl Wilson Randy Bachman	August 27–29, November-December, 1979 January-February, 1980	Keepin' the Summer Alive (1980)	4:06	Bruce Johnston	Carl
Lonely Days (Beach Boys song)	Unknown	October 28, 1967	Hawthorne, CA (2001)	0:49	The Beach Boys	Carl/Bruce/Al
Lonely Sea	Brian Wilson Gary Usher	April 19, 1962	Surfin' USA (1963)	2:21	Nick Venet	Brian

Long Promised Road	Carl Wilson Jack Rieley	April 3, 1971	Surf's Up (1971)	3:30	The Beach Boys	Carl
Lookin' at Tomorrow (A Welfare Song)	Al Jardine Gary Winfrey	August 14, 1970	Surf's Up (1971)	1:55	The Beach Boys	Al
Loop De Loop (Flip Flop Flyin' In An Aeroplane)	Brian Wilson Carl Wilson Al Jardine	March 5, 6, 8, & 11, 1969 July 3 & 4, 1998	Endless Harmony Soundtrack (1998)	2:56	Al Jardine	Al/Mike
The Lord's Prayer	Albert Hay Malotte	October 20, 1963	Rarities (1983)	2:31	Brian Wilson	group
Louie, Louie	Richard Berry	February 20, 1964	Shut Down Volume 2 (1964)	2:17	Brian Wilson	Carl/Mike
Love Is a Woman	Brian Wilson	October 28, 1976	Love You (The Beach Boys album) (1977)	2:57	Brian Wilson	Mike/Brian/Al
Love Surrounds Me	Dennis Wilson Geoffrey Cushing-Murray	Unknown (1977?)	L.A. (Light Album) (1979)	3:41	The Beach Boys James William Guercio	Dennis
Luau	Bruce Morgan	October 3, 1961	Lost & Found (1961-62) (1991)	1:49	Hite Morgan	Mike/Dennis/Brian
Magic Transistor Radio	Brian Wilson	1972	Mount Vernon and Fairway (A Fairy Tale) (1973)	1:43	The Beach Boys	Jack Rieley (narration)/Brian
Make It Big	Mike Love Bob House Terry Melcher	March 9, 1989	Still Cruisin' (1989)	3:08	Terry Melcher	Carl/Mike/Al/Brian
Make It Good	Dennis Wilson Daryl Dragon	April 9 & 18, 1972	Carl and the Passions - "So Tough" (1972)	2:36	Dennis Wilson Daryl Dragon	Dennis
Male Ego	Brian Wilson Mike Love Eugene Landy	ca. June 1984 - March 1985	The Beach Boys (1985)	2:32	Steve Levine	Brian/Mike
Mama Says	Brian Wilson Mike Love	November 1967	Wild Honey (1967)	1:05	The Beach Boys	group
The Man with All the Toys	Brian Wilson Mike Love	June 25, 1964	The Beach Boys' Christmas Album (1964)	1:32	Brian Wilson	Brian/Mike
Marcella	Brian Wilson Tandyn Almer Jack Rieley	February 17, 1972	Carl and the Passions - "So Tough" (1972)	3:54	The Beach Boys	Carl/Mike

Match Point of Our Love	Brian Wilson Mike Love	November 8, 18, & December 2, 1977	M.I.U. Album (1978)	3:29	Ron Altbach	Brian
Maybe I Don't Know	Carl Wilson Myrna Smith Schilling Steve Levine Julian Lindsay	ca. June 1984 - March 1985	The Beach Boys (1985)	3:54	Steve Levine	Carl
Meant for You	Brian Wilson Mike Love	April 1, 1968	Friends (1968)	0:38	The Beach Boys	Mike
Melekalikimaka	Al Jardine Mike Love	November 18, 1977	Ultimate Christmas (1998)	2:34	Al Jardine	Mike/Al
Merry Christmas, Baby	Brian Wilson	June 30, 1964	The Beach Boys' Christmas Album (1964)	2:20	Brian Wilson	Mike
Misirlou	Fred Wise Sidney Keith Russell Michalis Patrinos Milton Leeds Nick Roubanis	February 11, 1963	Surfin' USA (1963)	2:03	Nick Venet	instrumental
Mona	Brian Wilson	October 21, 1976	Love You (The Beach Boys album) (1977)	2:06	Brian Wilson	Dennis
Moon Dawg	Derry Weaver	September 6, 1962	Surfin' Safari (1962)	2:00	Nick Venet	instrumental
Morning Christmas	Dennis Wilson	November 22, 1977	Ultimate Christmas (1998)	3:23	Dennis Wilson	Dennis
Mt. Vernon And Fairway (Theme)	Brian Wilson	1972	Mount Vernon and Fairway (A Fairy Tale) (1973)	1:34	The Beach Boys	Jack Rieley (narration)
Mountain of Love	Harold Dorman	September 14, 1965	Beach Boys' Party! (1965)	2:51	Brian Wilson	Mike
My Diane	Brian Wilson	Autumn 1976 December 13, 1977 February 22, 1978	M.I.U. Album (1978)	2:37	Al Jardine Ron Altbach	Dennis
The Nearest Faraway Place	Bruce Johnston	20 June 1968	20/20 (1969)	2:39	The Beach Boys	instrumental
Never Learn Not to Love	Dennis Wilson	11 September 1968	20/20 (1969)	2:31	The Beach Boys	Dennis
The Night Was So Young	Brian Wilson	Autumn 1976	Love You (1977)	2:15	Brian Wilson	Carl
Noble Surfer	Brian Wilson Mike Love	February 11, 1963	Surfin' USA (1963)	1:51	Nick Venet	Mike

No-Go Showboat	Brian Wilson Roger Christian	2 September 1963	Little Deuce Coupe (1963)	1:54	Brian Wilson	Brian/Mike
Oh Darlin'	Brian Wilson Mike Love	Unknown (1979?)	Keepin' the Summer Alive (1980)	3:52	Bruce Johnston	Carl/Mike
Old Folks at Home (Swanee River)/Ol' Man River	Stephen Foster/ Jerome Kern Oscar Hammerstein II	June 10, 1968	Friends/20/20 (Re-Release)	2:53	Brian Wilson	Brian/Mike/Carl/Al
Only with You	Dennis Wilson Mike Love	August 4, 1972	Holland (1973)	2:59	The Beach Boys	Carl
Our Car Club	Brian Wilson Mike Love	16 July 1963	Surfer Girl (1963) Little Deuce Coupe (1963)	2:22	Brian Wilson	Brian/Mike
Our Favorite Recording Sessions	Brian Wilson Carl Wilson Dennis Wilson Mike Love Al Jardine	May 6, 1964	All Summer Long (1964)	1:59	Brian Wilson	group
Our Prayer	Brian Wilson	4 October 1966 November 17, 1968	20/20 (1969)	1:07	The Beach Boys	group
Our Sweet Love	Brian Wilson Carl Wilson Al Jardine	November 6, 1969 January 26, 1970	Sunflower (1970)	2:38	The Beach Boys	Carl
Our Team	Brian Wilson Carl Wilson Dennis Wilson Mike Love Al Jardine	November 15 & December 4, 1977	Good Vibrations Box Set (1993)	2:33	Al Jardine Ron Altbach	Al/Brian
Palisades Park	C. Barris	January 30 & March 25, 1976	15 Big Ones (1976)	2:27	Brian Wilson	Carl
Papa-Oom-Mow-Mow	Carl White Al Frazier Sonny Harris Turner Wilson Jr.	September 14, 1965	Beach Boys' Party! (1965)	2:18	Brian Wilson	Brian/Mike
Passing By	Brian Wilson	March 1968	Friends (1968)	2:23	The Beach Boys	Brian/Al
Passing Friend	George O'Dowd Roy Hay	ca. June 1984 - March 1985	The Beach Boys (1985)	5:00	Steve Levine	Carl
Peggy Sue	Buddy Holly Jerry Allison Norman Petty	Unknown (1977?)	M.I.U. Album (1978)	2:15	Al Jardine Ron Altbach	Al
Pet Sounds	Brian Wilson	17 November 1965	Pet Sounds (1966)	2:20	Brian Wilson	instrumental

Pitter Patter	Brian Wilson Mike Love Al Jardine	November 18 & December 4, 1977	M.I.U. Album (1978)	3:14	Al Jardine Ron Altbach	Mike/Al
Please Let Me Wonder	Brian Wilson Mike Love	7 January 1965	The Beach Boys Today! (1965)	2:45	Brian Wilson	Brian/Mike
Pom Pom Play Girl	Brian Wilson Gary Usher	February 19, 1964	Shut Down Volume 2 (1964)	1:30	Brian Wilson	Carl/Mike
Problem Child	Terry Melcher	April 12, 1990	single (1990)	4:22	Terry Melcher	Carl/Mike/Al
Punchline	Brian Wilson	2 January 1963	Good Vibrations Box Set (1993)	1:51	Nick Venet	instrumental
Radio King Dom	Brian Wilson Jack Rieley	1972	Mount Vernon and Fairway (A Fairy Tale) (1973)	2:38	The Beach Boys	Jack Rieley (narration)
Remember "Walking In The Sand"	George Morton	ca. Autumn 1991 - Spring 1992	Summer in Paradise (1992)	3:31	Terry Melcher	Carl
Rock 'n' Roll to the Rescue	Mike Love Terry Melcher	March 17, 18, 24 & April 6, 1986	Made in U.S.A. (1986)	3:44	Terry Melcher	Brian/Carl/Al/Mike
Rock and Roll Music	Chuck Berry	March 16, 1976	15 Big Ones (1976)	2:29	Brian Wilson	Mike
The Rocking Surfer	Traditional	16 July 1963	Surfer Girl (1963)	2:00	Brian Wilson	instrumental
Roller Skating Child	Brian Wilson	November 2, 1976	Love You (1977)	2:17	Brian Wilson	Mike/Al/Brian
Ruby Baby	Jerry Leiber Mike Stoller	September 8, 1965	Good Vibrations Box Set (1993)	2:10	Brian Wilson	Brian
Sail On, Sailor	Brian Wilson Tandyn Almer Ray Kennedy Jack Rieley Van Dyke Parks	28 November 1972	Holland (1973)	3:19	The Beach Boys	Blondie
Sail Plane Song	Brian Wilson Carl Wilson	June 8, 1968	Endless Harmony Soundtrack (1998)	2:12	Brian Wilson	Brian
Salt Lake City	Brian Wilson Mike Love	30 March 1965	Summer Days (and Summer Nights!!) (1965)	2:00	Brian Wilson	Mike/Brian
San Miguel	Dennis Wilson Gregg Jakobson	January 9, 13, 22, 24, 27, & 29, 1969	Good Vibrations Box Set (1993)	2:26	Dennis Wilson	Carl
Santa Ana Winds	Brian Wilson Al Jardine	November 1979-January 1980 February 1 & 4, 1980	Keepin' the Summer Alive (1980)	3:14	Bruce Johnston	Al/Mike/Carl

Santa Claus Is Comin' To Town	J. Fred Coots Haven Gillespie	18 June 1964	The Beach Boys' Christmas Album (1964)	2:20	Brian Wilson	Brian/Mike
Santa's Beard	Brian Wilson Mike Love	25 June 1964	The Beach Boys' Christmas Album (1964)	2:00	Brian Wilson	Mike
Santa's Got an Airplane	Al Jardine Brian Wilson Mike Love	November 14, 1977	Ultimate Christmas (1998)	3:09	Al Jardine	Mike/Al
School Day (Ring! Ring! Goes The Bell)	Chuck Berry	July 24, 1979 November 1979-January 1980 February 6, 1980	Keepin' the Summer Alive (1980)	2:52	Bruce Johnston	Al
Sea Cruise	Huey P. Smith	March 9, 1976	Ten Years of Harmony (1981)	3:23	Brian Wilson	Dennis
She Believes in Love Again	Bruce Johnston	ca. June 1984 - March 1985	The Beach Boys (1985)	3:29	Steve Levine	Carl/Bruce
She Knows Me Too Well	Brian Wilson Mike Love	8 June 1964	The Beach Boys Today! (1965)	2:27	Brian Wilson	Brian
She's Goin' Bald	Brian Wilson Van Dyke Parks Mike Love	July 5, 1967	Smiley Smile (1967)	2:13	The Beach Boys	Mike/Brian/Dennis/Al
She's Got Rhythm	Brian Wilson Mike Love Ron Altbach	November 7, 14, & December 3, 1977	M.I.U. Album (1978)	2:27	Al Jardine Ron Altbach	Brian/Mike
The Shift	Brian Wilson Mike Love	August 8, 1962	Surfin' Safari (1962)	1:52	Nick Venet	Mike
Shortenin' Bread	Traditional	November 12 & 13, 1979	L.A. (Light Album) (1979)	2:49	Bruce Johnston The Beach Boys James William Guercio	Carl/Dennis
Shut Down	Brian Wilson Roger Christian	January 5, 1963	Surfin' USA (1963) Little Deuce Coupe (1963)	1:49	Nick Venet	Mike
Shut Down, Part II	Carl Wilson	February 20, 1964	Shut Down Volume 2 (1964)	2:07	Brian Wilson	instrumental
Slip On Through	Dennis Wilson	July 9, 14, & October 6, 1969	Sunflower (1970)	2:17	The Beach Boys	Dennis
Sloop John B	Traditional	July 12, December 22, & 29, 1965	Pet Sounds (1966)	2:56	Brian Wilson	Brian/Mike

Slow Summer Dancing (One Summer Night)	Bruce Johnston Danny Webb	ca. Autumn 1991 - Spring 1992	Summer in Paradise (1992)	3:23	Terry Melcher	Bruce/Al
Solar System	Brian Wilson	October 26, 1976	Love You (1977)	2:47	Brian Wilson	Brian
Some of Your Love	Brian Wilson Mike Love	November 29, 1979 December 1979-January 1980 February 1, 1980	Keepin' the Summer Alive (1980)	2:36	Bruce Johnston	Mike/Carl
Somewhere Near Japan	Bruce Johnston Mike Love Terry Melcher John Phillips	ca. 1987-1989	Still Cruisin' (1989)	4:48	Terry Melcher	Mike/Carl/Al/Bruce
Soulful Old Man Sunshine	Brian Wilson Rick Henn	August 29 & September 5, 1969	Endless Harmony Soundtrack (1998)	3:25	Brian Wilson Rick Henn	Carl
South Bay Surfer	Stephen Foster Brian Wilson Carl Wilson Al Jardine	16 July 1963	Surfer Girl (1963)	1:45	Brian Wilson	Brian/Mike
Spirit of America	Brian Wilson Roger Christian	2 September 1963	Little Deuce Coupe (1963)	2:23	Brian Wilson	Brian
Steamboat	Dennis Wilson Jack Rieley	July 19, 1972	Holland (1973)	4:33	The Beach Boys	Carl
Still Cruisin'	Mike Love Terry Melcher	ca. 1987-1989	Still Cruisin' (1989)	3:35	Terry Melcher	Mike/Carl/Al/Bruce
Still I Dream of It	Brian Wilson	February 9 & March 11, 1977	Good Vibrations Box Set (1993)	3:26	Brian Wilson	Brian
Still Surfin'	Mike Love Terry Melcher	ca. Autumn 1991 - Spring 1992	Summer in Paradise (1992)	4:03	Terry Melcher	Mike
Stoked	Brian Wilson	February 12, 1963	Surfin' USA (1963)	1:59	Nick Venet	instrumental
Strange Things Happen	Mike Love Terry Melcher	ca. Autumn 1991 - Spring 1992	Summer in Paradise (1992)	4:42	Terry Melcher	Mike/Al
Student Demonstration Time	Jerry Leiber Mike Stoller Mike Love	July 23, 1971	Surf's Up (1971)	3:58	The Beach Boys	Mike
Sumahama	Mike Love	December 18, 1978	L.A. (Light Album) (1979)	4:30	Bruce Johnston The Beach Boys James William Guercio	Mike
Summer in Paradise	Mike Love Terry Melcher Craig Fall	ca. Autumn 1991 - Spring 1992	Summer in Paradise (1992)	3:52	Terry Melcher	Mike

Summer Means New Love	Brian Wilson	15 May 1965	Summer Days (and Summer Nights!!) (1965)	1:59	Brian Wilson	instrumental
Summer of Love	Mike Love Terry Melcher	ca. Autumn 1991 - Spring 1992	Summer in Paradise (1992)	2:51	Terry Melcher	Mike
Summertime Blues	Eddie Cochran Jerry Capeheart	September 5, 1962	Surfin' Safari (1962)	2:09	Nick Venet	Carl/David/Mike
Sunshine	Brian Wilson Mike Love	July 23 & November 1, 1979 December 1979-February 1980	Keepin' the Summer Alive (1980)	2:52	Bruce Johnston	Mike/Brian/Carl
Surf Jam	Carl Wilson	February 12, 1963	Surfin' USA (1963)	2:10	Nick Venet	instrumental
Surfer Girl	Brian Wilson	12 June 1963	Surfer Girl (1963)	2:26	Brian Wilson	Brian
The Surfer Moon	Brian Wilson	13 September 1962	Surfer Girl (1963)	2:11	Brian Wilson	Brian
Surfers Rule	Brian Wilson Mike Love	16 July 1963	Surfer Girl (1963)	1:54	Brian Wilson	Dennis/Brian
Surfin'	Brian Wilson Mike Love	October 3, 1961	Surfin' Safari (1962)	2:10	Nick Venet	Mike
Surfin'	Brian Wilson Mike Love	ca. Autumn 1991 - Spring 1992	Summer in Paradise (1992)	3:45	Terry Melcher	Mike
Surfin' Safari	Brian Wilson Mike Love	April 19, 1962	Surfin' Safari (1962)	2:05	Nick Venet	Mike
Surfin' USA	Brian Wilson Chuck Berry	January 5, 1963	Surfin' USA (1963)	2:27	Nick Venet	Mike
Surf's Up	Brian Wilson Van Dyke Parks	November 4 & December 15, 1966 June 18, 1971	Surf's Up (1971)	4:12	The Beach Boys	Carl/Brian
Susie Cincinnati	Al Jardine	December 24, 1969 January 7 & February 2, 1970	15 Big Ones (1976)	2:57	Brian Wilson	Al
Sweet Sunday Kinda Love	Brian Wilson Mike Love	November 18 & December 2, 1977	M.I.U. Album (1978)	2:42	Al Jardine Ron Altbach	Carl
Take a Load Off Your Feet	Al Jardine Brian Wilson Gary Winfrey	January 17, 26, 1970 July 26, 1971	Surf's Up (1971)	2:29	The Beach Boys	Al/Brian
Talk to Me	Joe Seneca	March 19, 1976	15 Big Ones (1976)	2:14	Brian Wilson	Carl
Tears in the Morning	Bruce Johnston	November 18, 1969 January 26 & 28, 1970	Sunflower (1970)	4:07	The Beach Boys	Bruce
Tell Me Why	John Lennon Paul McCartney	September 8, 1965	Beach Boys' Party! (1965)	1:46	Brian Wilson	Carl/Al

Ten Little Indians	Brian Wilson Gary Usher	August 8, 1962	Surfin' Safari (1962)	1:26	Nick Venet	Mike
That Same Song	Brian Wilson Mike Love	April 28, 1976	15 Big Ones (1976)	2:16	Brian Wilson	Brian
That's Not Me	Brian Wilson Tony Asher	February 15, 1966	Pet Sounds (1966)	2:27	Brian Wilson	Mike
Their Hearts Were Full of Spring	Bobby Troup	25 August 1967	Smiley Smile/Wild Honey (Re-Issue)	2:48	The Beach Boys	group
Then I Kissed Her	Phil Spector Ellie Greenwich Jeff Barry	May 5, 1965	Summer Days (and Summer Nights!!) (1965)	2:15	Brian Wilson	Al
There's No Other (Like My Baby)	Phil Spector Leroy Bates	September 16, 1965	Beach Boys' Party! (1965)	3:05	Brian Wilson	Brian
A Thing or Two	Brian Wilson Mike Love	October 27, 1967	Wild Honey (1967)	2:40	The Beach Boys	Mike/Carl/Brian
Things We Did Last Summer	J. Styne S. Cahn	September 24, 1963	Good Vibrations Box Set (1993)	2:27	Brian Wilson	Mike/Brian/Carl
This Car of Mine	Brian Wilson Mike Love	February 7, 1964	Shut Down Volume 2 (1964)	1:35	Brian Wilson	Dennis
This Whole World	Brian Wilson	November 13, 1969	Sunflower (1970)	1:56	The Beach Boys	Brian/Carl
'Til I Die	Brian Wilson	August 15, 1970 July 30, 1971	Surf's Up (1971)	2:41	The Beach Boys	Brian/Carl/Mike
Time to Get Alone	Brian Wilson	4 October 1968	20/20 (1969)	2:40	The Beach Boys	Carl/Brian/Al
A Time to Live in Dreams	Dennis Wilson Stephen Kalinich	1 November 1968	Hawthorne, CA (2001)	1:50	Dennis Wilson	Dennis
The Times They Are A-Changin'	Bob Dylan	September 23, 1965	Beach Boys' Party! (1965)	2:23	Brian Wilson	Al
TM Song	Brian Wilson	March 18, 1976	15 Big Ones (1976)	1:34	Brian Wilson	Al
The Trader	Carl Wilson Jack Rieley	Autumn 1972	Holland (1973)	5:04	The Beach Boys	Carl
Transcendental Meditation	Brian Wilson Mike Love Al Jardine	April 4, 1968	Friends (1968)	1:49	The Beach Boys	Brian/Al
Trombone Dixie	Brian Wilson	November 1, 1965	Pet Sounds (Re-Issue)	2:53	Brian Wilson	instrumental

Under the Boardwalk	Mike Love Artie Resnick Kenny Young	ca. Autumn 1991 - Spring 1992	Summer in Paradise (1992)	4:07	Terry Melcher	Mike/Carl
Unreleased Backgrounds	Brian Wilson	February 11, 1966	Pet Sounds (Re-Issue)	0:50	Brian Wilson	Brian
Vegetables	Brian Wilson Van Dyke Parks	April, June 3, 5-7, & 15, 1967	Smiley Smile (1967)	2:07	The Beach Boys	Al/Brian/Mike
Wake the World	Brian Wilson Al Jardine	March 1968	Friends (1968)	1:28	The Beach Boys	Brian/Carl
Walk On By	Burt Bacharach Hal David	26 May 1968	Friends/20/20 (Re-Issue)	0:52	The Beach Boys	Brian/Dennis
The Warmth of the Sun	Brian Wilson Mike Love	January 1 & 8, 1964	Shut Down Volume 2 (1964)	2:51	Brian Wilson	Brian
We Three Kings of Orient Are	John Henry Hopkins	18 June 1964	The Beach Boys' Christmas Album (1964)	4:03	Brian Wilson	Brian/Mike
Wendy	Brian Wilson Mike Love	April 29, 1964	All Summer Long (1964)	2:16	Brian Wilson	Mike/Brian
We'll Run Away	Brian Wilson Gary Usher	May 18, 1964	All Summer Long (1964)	2:00	Brian Wilson	Brian
We're Together Again	Brian Wilson Ron Wilson	11 September 1968	Friends/20/20 (Re-Release)	1:48	The Beach Boys	Dennis/Brian
What Is A Young Girl Made of?	Bruce Morgan	March 8, 1962	Lost & Found (1961-62) (1991)	2:18	Hite Morgan	Brian
When a Man Needs a Woman	Brian Wilson Carl Wilson Dennis Wilson Al Jardine Steve Korthof Jon Parks	March 18, 1968	Friends (1968)	2:06	The Beach Boys	Brian
When Girls Get Together	Brian Wilson Mike Love	November 4, 1969	Keepin' the Summer Alive (1980)	3:31	Bruce Johnston	Al/Mike/Carl
When I Grow Up (To Be a Man)	Brian Wilson Mike Love	5 August 1964	The Beach Boys Today! (1965)	2:01	Brian Wilson	Mike/Brian
Where I Belong	Carl Wilson Robert White Johnson	ca. June 1984 - March 1985	The Beach Boys (1985)	2:58	Steve Levine	Carl/Al
Whistle In	Brian Wilson	July 13, 1967	Smiley Smile (1967)	1:04	The Beach Boys	Carl/Mike

White Christmas	Irving Berlin	18 June 1964	The Beach Boys' Christmas Album (1964)	2:29	Brian Wilson	Brian
Why Do Fools Fall In Love	Frankie Lymon M. Levy	January 7, 8, & 10, 1964	Shut Down Volume 2 (1964)	2:07	Brian Wilson	Brian
Wild Honey	Brian Wilson Mike Love	September 26–27, 1967	Wild Honey (1967)	2:37	The Beach Boys	Carl
Wind Chimes	Brian Wilson	July 10–11, 1967	Smiley Smile (1967)	2:36	The Beach Boys	Mike/Brian/Carl/Dennis
Winds of Change	Ron Altbach Ed Tuleja	November 23, 1977 June 28, 1978	M.I.U. Album (1978)	3:14	Al Jardine Ron Altbach	Al/Mike
Winter Symphony	Brian Wilson	November 15, 21, & 22, 1977	Ultimate Christmas (1998)	2:59	Brian Wilson Al Jardine	Brian
Wipe Out	Bob Berryhill Pat Connolly Jim Fuller Ron Wilson	February 27, 1987	Still Cruisin' (1989)	4:00	Albert Calbrera Tony Moran The Beach Boys	The Fat Boys/Brian
With a Little Help from My Friends	John Lennon Paul McCartney	September 23, 1967	Rarities (1983)	2:22	The Beach Boys	Bruce
With Me Tonight	Brian Wilson	June 30, 1967	Smiley Smile (1967)	2:17	The Beach Boys	Carl
Wonderful	Brian Wilson Van Dyke Parks	July 12, 1967	Smiley Smile (1967)	2:21	The Beach Boys	Carl
Wontcha Come Out Tonight	Brian Wilson Mike Love	November 7, 17, & December 3, 1977	M.I.U. Album (1978)	2:30	Al Jardine Ron Altbach	Brian/Mike
Wouldn't It Be Nice	Brian Wilson Tony Asher Mike Love	19 January 1966, March 10, & April 11, 1966	Pet Sounds (1966) Still Cruisin' (1989)	2:22	Brian Wilson	Brian/Mike
You Need a Mess of Help to Stand Alone	Brian Wilson Jack Rieley	December 1971 April 1972	Carl and the Passions - "So Tough" (1972)	3:27	Carl Wilson	Carl
You Still Believe in Me	Brian Wilson Tony Asher	1 November 1965 January-February 1966	Pet Sounds (1966)	2:30	Brian Wilson	Brian

A Young Man is Gone	Bobby Troup Mike Love	2 September 1963	Little Deuce Coupe (1963)	2:15	Brian Wilson	Brian/Carl/Mike/Al
Your Summer Dream	Brian Wilson Bob Norberg	16 July 1963	Surfer Girl (1963)	2:27	Brian Wilson	Brian
You're So Good to Me	Brian Wilson Mike Love	May 1965	Summer Days (and Summer Nights!!) (1965)	2:14	Brian Wilson	Brian
You're Welcome	Brian Wilson	13 December 1966	Smiley Smile/Wild Honey (Re-Release)	1:07	Brian Wilson	Brian
You're With Me Tonight	Brian Wilson	Unknown (1967?)	Hawthorne, CA (2001)	0:49	Brian Wilson	
You've Got to Hide Your Love Away	John Lennon Paul McCartney	23 September 1965	Beach Boys' Party! (1965)	2:56	Brian Wilson	Dennis

Live recordings

This list is an attempt to document every live recording that has been released by the Beach Boys, whether on an album, single, compilation or anthology album.

Song	Author	Recorded	Album	Time	Producer
409	Brian Wilson Gary Usher Mike Love	March 27, 1965 Chicago, IL	U.S. Singles Collection: The Capitol Years 1962-1965 (2008)	2:29	Brian Wilson
All I Want to Do	Dennis Wilson	December 8, 1968 London, England	Rarities (1983)	2:30	The Beach Boys
Aren't You Glad	Brian Wilson Mike Love	December 8, 1968 London, England	Live In London (1970)	3:09	The Beach Boys
Barbara Ann	Fred Fassert	December 8, 1968 London, England	Live In London (1970)	2:32	The Beach Boys
		June 20, 1980 Knebworth, England	Good Timin': Live at Knebworth England 1980 (2002)	2:46	The Beach Boys
Be True to Your School	Brian Wilson Mike Love	August 1, 1964 Sacramento, CA	Good Vibrations Box Set (1993)	2:29	Brian Wilson
		June 20, 1980 Knebworth, England	Good Timin': Live at Knebworth England 1980 (2002)	2:27	The Beach Boys
Bluebirds over the Mountain	Ersel Hickey	December 8, 1968 London, England	Live In London (1970)	2:53	The Beach Boys

California Girls	Brian Wilson Mike Love	December 8, 1968 London, England	Live In London (1970)	2:19	The Beach Boys
		August 19, 1973 Uniondale, NY	The Beach Boys In Concert (1973)	2:57	The Beach Boys
		June 20, 1980 Knebworth, England	Good Timin': Live at Knebworth England 1980 (2002)	3:10	The Beach Boys
Caroline, No	Brian Wilson Tony Asher	1972–1973	The Beach Boys In Concert (1973)	3:04	The Beach Boys
Dance, Dance, Dance	Brian Wilson Carl Wilson Mike Love	November 4, 1989 Los Angeles, CA	Songs From Here & Back (2006)	2:08	Mark Linett Alan Boyd
Darlin'	Brian Wilson Mike Love	December 8, 1968 London, England	Live In London (1970)	2:41	The Beach Boys
		1972–1973	The Beach Boys In Concert (1973)	2:21	The Beach Boys
		June 20, 1980 Knebworth, England	Endless Harmony Soundtrack (1998)	2:26	The Beach Boys
		June 20, 1980 Knebworth, England	Good Timin': Live at Knebworth England 1980 (2002)	2:37	The Beach Boys
Do It Again	Brian Wilson Mike Love	December 8, 1968 London, England	Live In London (1970)	2:47	The Beach Boys
		June 20, 1980 Knebworth, England	Good Timin': Live at Knebworth England 1980 (2002)	3:08	The Beach Boys
Don't Worry Baby	Brian Wilson Roger Christian	August 1, 1964 Sacramento, CA	Beach Boys Concert/Live In London (re-release)	???	Brian Wilson
		1972–1973	The Beach Boys In Concert (1973)	3:11	The Beach Boys
Fun, Fun, Fun	Brian Wilson Mike Love	August 1, 1964 Sacramento, CA	Beach Boys Concert (1964)	2:26	Brian Wilson
		1972–1973	The Beach Boys In Concert (1973)	3:16	The Beach Boys
		June 20, 1980 Knebworth, England	Good Timin': Live at Knebworth England 1980 (2002)	4:49	The Beach Boys
Funky Pretty	Brian Wilson Jack Rieley Mike Love	1972–1973	The Beach Boys In Concert (1973)	4:04	The Beach Boys
God Only Knows	Brian Wilson Tony Asher	December 8, 1968 London, England	Live In London (1970)	3:27	The Beach Boys
		June 20, 1980 Knebworth, England	Good Timin': Live at Knebworth England 1980 (2002)	2:51	The Beach Boys

Good Vibrations	Brian Wilson Mike Love	December 8, 1968 London, England	Live In London (1970)	4:36	The Beach Boys
		1972–1973	The Beach Boys In Concert (1973)	4:49	The Beach Boys
		October 22, 1966 Ann Arbor, MI	Good Vibrations Box Set (1993)	5:14	Brian Wilson
		December 8, 1968 London England (soundcheck)	Endless Harmony Soundtrack (1998)	3:40	The Beach Boys
		August 25, 1967 Honolulu, HI (soundcheck)	Hawthorne, CA (2001)	4:09	The Beach Boys
		June 20, 1980 Knebworth, England	Good Timin': Live at Knebworth England 1980 (2002)	6:03	The Beach Boys
		1974	Songs From Here & Back (2006)	4:38	The Beach Boys
Graduation Day	Joe Sherman Noel Sherman	August 1, 1964 Sacramento, CA	Beach Boys Concert (1964)	3:29	Brian Wilson
Hawaii	Brian Wilson Mike Love	August 1, 1964 Sacramento, CA	Beach Boys Concert (1964)	1:51	Brian Wilson
Help Me, Rhonda	Brian Wilson Mike Love	1972–1973	The Beach Boys In Concert (1973)	4:59	The Beach Boys
		June 20, 1980 Knebworth, England	Good Timin': Live at Knebworth England 1980 (2002)	4:05	The Beach Boys
Heroes and Villains	Brian Wilson Van Dyke Parks	August 25, 1967 Honolulu, HI	Beach Boys Concert/Live In London (re-release)	???	Brian Wilson
		1972–1973	The Beach Boys In Concert (1973)	3:51	The Beach Boys
		October or November, 1972	Endless Harmony Soundtrack (1998)	3:40	The Beach Boys
Hushabye	Doc Pomus/Mort Shuman	August 1, 1964 Sacramento, CA	Good Vibrations Box Set (1993)	3:56	Brian Wilson
I Get Around	Brian Wilson Mike Love	August 1, 1964 Sacramento, CA	Beach Boys Concert (1964)	2:42	Brian Wilson
		June 20, 1980 Knebworth, England	Good Timin': Live at Knebworth England 1980 (2002)	2:14	The Beach Boys
		November 4, 1989 Los Angeles, CA	Songs From Here & Back (2006)	2:26	Mark Linett Alan Boyd
In My Room	Brian Wilson Gary Usher	August 1, 1964 Sacramento, CA	Beach Boys Concert (1964)	2:25	Brian Wilson
Johnny B. Goode	Chuck Berry	August 1, 1964 Sacramento, CA	Beach Boys Concert (1964)	1:56	Brian Wilson

Keepin' the Summer Alive	Carl Wilson Randy Bachman	June 20, 1980 Knebworth, England	Good Timin': Live at Knebworth England 1980 (2002)	3:42	The Beach Boys
Kokomo	Mike Love Scott McKenzie Terry Melcher John Phillips	November 4, 1989 Los Angeles, CA	Songs From Here & Back (2006)	4:33	Mark Linett Alan Boyd
Lady Lynda	Al Jardine Ron Altbach	June 20, 1980 Knebworth, England	Good Timin': Live at Knebworth England 1980 (2002)	5:01	The Beach Boys
Leaving This Town	Carl Wilson Ricky Fataar Blondie Chaplin Mike Love	1972–1973	The Beach Boys In Concert (1973)	6:59	The Beach Boys
Let the Wind Blow	Brian Wilson Mike Love	1972–1973	The Beach Boys In Concert (1973)	4:22	The Beach Boys
Let's Go Trippin'	Dick Dale	August 1, 1964 Sacramento, CA	Beach Boys Concert (1964)	2:34	Brian Wilson
Little Deuce Coupe	Brian Wilson Roger Christian	August 1, 1964 Sacramento, CA	Beach Boys Concert (1964)	2:27	Brian Wilson
		June 20, 1980 Knebworth, England	Good Timin': Live at Knebworth England 1980 (2002)	2:14	The Beach Boys
		November 4, 1989 Los Angeles, CA	Songs From Here & Back (2006)	1:46	Mark Linett Alan Boyd
The Little Old Lady from Pasadena	Don Altfield Jan Berry Roger Christian	August 1, 1964 Sacramento, CA	Beach Boys Concert (1964)	3:00	Brian Wilson
Long Promised Road	Carl Wilson Jack Rieley	November 23, 1972 New York, NY	Endless Harmony Soundtrack (1998)	4:17	Carl Wilson
Long, Tall Texan	Henry Strezlecki	August 1, 1964 Sacramento, CA	Beach Boys Concert (1964)	2:32	Brian Wilson
Marcella	Brian Wilson Tandyn Almer Jack Rieley	1972–1973	The Beach Boys In Concert (1973)	3:55	The Beach Boys
medley: Surfin' Safari/Fun, Fun, Fun/Shut Down/Little Deuce Coupe/Surfin' USA	Brian Wilson Mike Love Roger Christian Chuck Berry	October 22, 1966 Ann Arbor, MI	Endless Harmony Soundtrack (1998)	3:33	Brian Wilson
medley: Cotton Fields/Heroes and Villains	Huddie Ledbetter Brian Wilson Van Dyke Parks	June 20, 1980 Knebworth, CA	Good Timin': Live at Knebworth England 1980 (2002)	5:19	The Beach Boys
Monster Mash	Boris Pickett Lenny Capizzi	August 1, 1964 Sacramento, CA	Beach Boys Concert (1964)	2:27	Brian Wilson

Papa-Oom-Mow-Mow	Carl White Al Frazier Sonny Harris Turner Wilson Jr.	August 1, 1964 Sacramento, CA	Beach Boys Concert (1964)	???	Brian Wilson
Rock and Roll Music	Chuck Berry	June 20, 1980 Knebworth, England	Good Timin': Live at Knebworth England 1980 (2002)	2:22	The Beach Boys
Sail On, Sailor	Brian Wilson Tandyn Almer Ray Kennedy Jack Rieley Van Dyke Parks	1972–1973	The Beach Boys In Concert (1973)	3:21	The Beach Boys
School Days	Chuck Berry	June 20, 1980 Knebworth, England	Good Timin': Live at Knebworth England 1980 (2002)	3:26	The Beach Boys
Shut Down	Brian Wilson Roger Christian	March 26, 1965 Chicago, IL	Hawthorne, CA (2001)	1:56	Brian Wilson
Sloop John B	Trad. arr. Brian Wilson	December 8, 1968 London, England	Live In London (1970)	2:30	The Beach Boys
		1972–1973	The Beach Boys In Concert (1973)	3:12	The Beach Boys
		June 20, 1980 Knebworth, England	Good Timin': Live at Knebworth England 1980 (2002)	3:04	The Beach Boys
Surfer Girl	Brian Wilson	1972–1973	The Beach Boys In Concert (1973)	2:35	The Beach Boys
		August 1, 1964 Sacramento, CA	Good Vibrations Box Set (1993)	2:52	Brian Wilson
		August 25, 1967 Honolulu, HI (soundcheck)	Good Vibrations Box Set (1993)	2:18	The Beach Boys
		June 20, 1980 Knebworth, England	Good Timin': Live at Knebworth England 1980 (2002)	2:39	The Beach Boys
		November 4, 1989 Los Angeles, CA	Songs From Here & Back (2006)	3:01	Mark Linett Alan Boyd
Surfin' USA	Brian Wilson Chuck Berry	1972–1973	The Beach Boys In Concert (1973)	2:49	The Beach Boys
		August 1, 1964 Sacramento, CA	Good Vibrations Box Set (1993)	3:15	Brian Wilson
		June 20, 1980 Knebworth, England	Good Timin': Live at Knebworth England 1980 (2002)	2:54	The Beach Boys
The Trader	Carl Wilson Jack Rieley	1972–1973	The Beach Boys In Concert (1973)	4:46	The Beach Boys
The Wanderer	Ernest Maresca	August 1, 1964 Sacramento, CA	Beach Boys Concert (1964)	2:00	Brian Wilson

Their Hearts Were Full of Spring	Bobby Troup	December 8, 1968 London, England	Live In London (1970)	2:49	The Beach Boys
		August 25, 1967 Honolulu, HI (soundcheck)	Smiley Smile/Wild Honey (twofer)	2:32	The Beach Boys
Wake the World	Brian Wilson Al Jardine	December 8, 1968 London, England	Live In London (1970)	2:26	The Beach Boys
We Got Love	Ricky Fataar Blondie Chaplin Mike Love	August 19, 1973 Uniondale, NY	The Beach Boys In Concert (1973)	5:25	The Beach Boys
What'd I Say	Ray Charles	January 24, 1964 Sydney, Australia	Beach Boys/Brian Wilson Rarities (1981)	unk.	Brian Wilson
Wonderful/Don't Worry, Bill	Brian Wilson Van Dyke Parks/ Ricky Fataar Blondie Chaplin Steve Fataar Brother Fataar	November 23, 1972 New York, NY	The Beach Boys In Concert (1973)	???	Carl Wilson
Wouldn't It Be Nice	Brian Wilson Tony Asher Mike Love	December 8, 1968 London, England	Live In London (1970)	1:53	The Beach Boys
		October 3, 1970 Monterey, CA	single (1971)	unk.	Lou Adler
		1972–1973	The Beach Boys In Concert (1973)	2:45	The Beach Boys
		1974	Songs From Here & Back (2006)	2:42	The Beach Boys
You Are So Beautiful	Billy Preston Bruce Fisher	June 20, 1980 Knebworth, CA	Good Timin': Live at Knebworth England 1980 (2002)	3:13	The Beach Boys
You Still Believe in Me	Brian Wilson Tony Asher	1972–1973	The Beach Boys In Concert (1973)	2:58	The Beach Boys

Notes and references

- Badman, Keith (October 2004). *The Beach Boys: The Definitive Diary of America's Greatest Band on Stage and in the Studio*. Backbeat Books. ISBN 978-0879308186.
- Elliott, Brad (November 2003). *Surf's Up! The Beach Boys on Record, 1961-1981*. Surf's Up Books. ISBN 978-0972768610.

See also

- The Beach Boys discography

External links

- Extended Beach Boys Discography [12]

The Beach Boys solo discography

Many solo albums have been released by members of **The Beach Boys**: Brian Wilson, Carl Wilson, Dennis Wilson, Mike Love, Bruce Johnston and Blondie Chaplin have all produced solo albums. Bruce Johnston had two album releases prior to joining the band, and one while on hiatus from the group in 1977, *Going Public*. The same year Dennis Wilson released *Pacific Ocean Blue*. Carl Wilson also released two albums, *Carl Wilson* in 1981 and *Youngblood* in 1984. Mike Love released *Looking Back with Love* in 1981. In 1988, Brian Wilson released his first solo album, *Brian Wilson*. He has since released a further six studio albums and two live albums. Blondie Chaplin, a member of the band from 1972 to 1973, released two studio albums in 1977 and 2006.

Dennis Wilson

Albums

Pacific Ocean Blue (August 22, 1977) Caribou Records – US: #96 (1977) UK: #16 (2008) Norway: #5 (2008) Tracks: River Song; What's Wrong; Moonshine; Friday Night; Dreamer; Thoughts of You; Time; You and I; Pacific Ocean Blues; Farewell My Friend; Rainbows; End of The Show

Singles

Date of release	Title	Label	Chart positions
December, 1970, UK	"Sound of Free"/"Lady"	Stateside Records	never charted
September, 1977, Europe	"River Song"/"Farewell My Friend"	Caribou Records	never charted
October, 1977, US	"You and I"/"Friday Night"	Caribou Records	never charted

Carl Wilson

Albums

Carl Wilson (1981) Caribou Records – US: #185 Tracks: Hold Me; Bright Lights; What You Gonna Do About Me?; The Right Lane; Hurry Love; Heaven; The Grammy; Seems So Long Ago
Youngblood (1983) Caribou Records – never charted Tracks: What More Can I Say; She's Mine; Givin' You Up; One More Night Alone; Rockin' All Over The World; What You Do To Me; Young Blood; Of The Times; Too Early To Tell; If I Could Talk To Love; Time

U.S. Singles

Date of release	Title	Label	Chart positions
March, 1981	"Hold Me"/"Hurry Love"	Caribou Records	never charted
June, 1981	"Heaven"/"Hurry Love"	Caribou Records	never charted
March, 1983	"What You Do To Me"/"Time"	Caribou Records	#72 – Billboard Hot 100
July, 1983	"Givin' You Up"/"It's Too Early to Tell"	Caribou Records	never charted

U.K. Singles

Date of release	Title	Label	Chart positions
April, 1981	"Heaven"/"The Right Lane"	Caribou Records	never charted
May, 1983	"What You Do to Me"/"Time"	Caribou Records	never charted

Mike Love

Albums

Looking Back With Love (October 8, 1981) Boardwalk Records – never charted
Tracks: Looking Back With Love; On And On And On; Runnin' Around The World; Over And Over; Rockin' The Man In The Boat; Calendar Girl; Be My Baby; One Good Reason; Teach Me Tonight; Paradise Found

Unreleased albums

In late 1978, Mike Love made his first attempts at a solo album, recording *First Love* and *Country Love* simultaneously. Only one song has been released from these sessions, "Brian's Back", on the 1998 compilation album *Endless Harmony*. Recently, Love has recorded another album, first titled *Unleash The Love*, which then changed to *Mike Love, Not War*. One song from this album has also been released, "Cool Head, Warm Heart", in 2006 on *Songs from Here & Back*, a Beach Boys album which was only available at Hallmark stores. "Cool Head, Warm Heart" has been performed by The Beach Boys in concert.

Singles

Date of release	Title	Label	Chart positions
September, 1981, U.S.	"Looking Back With Love"/"One Good Reason"	Boardwalk Records	never charted
November, 1983, U.K.	"Jingle Bell Rock"/"Let's Party"	Creole Records	never charted

Brian Wilson

Albums

Brian Wilson (July 12, 1988) Sire Records – US: #54

Tracks: Love And Mercy; Walkin' The Line; Melt Away; Baby Let Your Hair Grow Long; Little Children; One For The Boys; There's So Many; Night Time; Let It Shine; Meet Me In My Dreams Tonight; Rio Grande *I Just Wasn't Made for These Times* (August 15, 1995) MCA Records – UK: #59[1]

Tracks: Meant for You; This Whole World; Caroline, No; Let the Wind Blow; Love And Mercy; Do It Again; The Warmth of the Sun; Wonderful; Still I Dream of It; Melt Away; 'Til I Die*Orange Crate Art* (with Van Dyke Parks) (October 24, 1995) Warner Bros. Records – never charted

Tracks: Orange Crate Art; Sail Away; My Hobo Heart; Wings of A Dove; Palm Tree And Moon; Summer In Monterey; San Francisco; Hold Back Time; My Jeanine; Movies Is Magic; This Town Goes Down At Sunset; Lullaby *Imagination* (June 16, 1998) Giant Records – US: #88; UK: #30[1]

Tracks: Your Imagination; She Says That She Needs Me; South American; Where Has Love Been?; Keep an Eye on Summer; Dream Angel; Cry; Lay Down Burden; Let Him Run Wild; Sunshine; Happy Days *Live at the Roxy Theatre* (June, 2000) Brimel Records – UK: #199[1]

Tracks: Little Girl Intro; The Little Girl I Once Knew; This Whole World; Don't Worry Baby; Kiss Me, Baby; Do It Again; California Girls; I Get Around; Back Home; In My Room; Surfer Girl; The First Time; This Isn't Love; Add Some Music to Your Day; Please Let Me Wonder; Band Intro; Brian Wilson; 'Til I Die; Darlin'; Let's Go Away For Awhile; Pet Sounds; God Only Knows; Lay Down Burden; Be My Baby; Good Vibrations; Caroline No; All Summer Long; Love And Mercy; Sloop John B; Barbara Ann; Interview With Brian *Pet Sounds Live* (June 11, 2002) Sanctuary Records – UK: #107[1]

Tracks: Show Intro; Wouldn't It Be Nice; You Still Believe in Me; That's Not Me; Don't Talk (Put Your Head on My Shoulder); I'm Waiting for the Day; Let's Go Away For Awhile; Sloop John B; God Only Knows; I Know There's an Answer; Here Today; I Just Wasn't Made for These Times; Pet Sounds; Caroline No*Gettin' in Over My Head* (June 22, 2004) Warner Bros. Records – US: #100; UK: #53[1]

Tracks: How Could We Still Be Dancin'?; Soul Searchin'; You've Touched Me; Gettin' In Over My Head; City Blues; Desert Drive; A Friend Like You; Make A Wish; Rainbow Eyes; Saturday Morning In The City; Fairy Tale; Don't Let Her Know She's An Angel; The Waltz*Smile* (September 28, 2004) Nonesuch Records – US: #13; UK: #7[1]

Tracks: Our Prayer/Gee; Heroes and Villains; Roll Plymouth Rock; Barnyard; The Old Master Painter/You Are My Sunshine; Cabin Essence; Wonderful; Song For Children; Child Is Father of The Man; Surf's Up; I'm In Great Shape/I Wanna Be Around/Workshop; Vega-Tables; On A Holiday; Wind Chimes; Mrs. O'Leary's Cow; In Blue Hawaii; Good Vibrations*What I Really Want for Christmas* (October 18, 2005) Arista Records – US: #200

Tracks: The Man with All the Toys; What I Really Want For Christmas; God Rest Ye Merry Gentlemen; O Holy Night; We Wish You a Merry Christmas; Hark the Herald Angels Sing; It Came Upon a Midnight Clear; The First Noel; Christmasey; Little Saint Nick; Deck the Halls; Auld Lang Syne; On Christmas Day; Joy to the World; Silent Night*That Lucky Old Sun* (September 2, 2008) Capitol Records – US: #21; UK: #37[2]

Tracks: That Lucky Old Sun; Morning Beat; narrative: Room with a View; Good Kind of Love; Forever She'll Be My Surfer Girl; narrative: Venice Beach; Live Let Live; Mexican Girl; narrative: Cinco de Mayo; California Role; narrative: Between Pictures; Oyxgen to the Brain; Can't Wait Too Long (excerpt); Midnight's Another Day; Going Home; Southern California

Singles

Date of release	Title	Label	UK	US Hot 100	US AC
March, 1966	"Caroline, No"/"Summer Means New Love"	Capitol Records		32	
April, 1987	"Let's Go to Heaven in My Car"/"Too Much Sugar"	Sire Records			
July 11, 1988	"Love and Mercy"/"He Couldn't Get His Poor Old Body To Move"	Sire Records			
January 19, 1989	"Melt Away"/"Being With The One You Love"	Sire Records			40
November 24, 1995	"Do It Again"/"'Til I Die"/"This Song Wants To Sleep With You Tonight"	MCA Records			
May 19, 1998	"Your Imagination"/"Happy Days"	Giant Records			20
September 20, 2004	"Wonderful"/"Wind Chimes"	Nonesuch Records	29[1]		
2004	"Good Vibrations"/"In Blue Hawaii"	Nonesuch Records	30[1]		
2004	"Good Vibrations"/"Our Prayer" (Live)/"Good Vibrations" (Live)	Nonesuch Records			
2004	"Our Prayer" (Freeform Reform mix)	Nonesuch Records	124[1]		
December 5, 2005	"What I Really Want For Christmas"/"We Wish You a Merry Christmas"/"Brian's Christmas Message"	Sony BMG	66[1]		29
December 5, 2005	"Deck the Halls"				8
August 19, 2008	"Midnight's Another Day"/"That Lucky Old Sun"/"Morning Beat"	Capitol Records			
July, 2009	"What Love Can Do"	429 Records			

Sources: Billboard and Allmusic.com

Al Jardine

Albums

Live in Las Vegas (2001) Tracks: Dance, Dance, Dance; Do You Wanna Dance; Catch a Wave; Hawaii; Do It Again; Darlin'; Wild Honey; Come Go With Me; Surfer Girl; Don't Worry, Baby; Shut Down; Little Deuce Coupe; I Get Around; In My Room; Girl Don't Tell Me; Break Away; Sail On Sailor; God Only Knows; Sloop John B; Wouldn't It Be Nice; Good Vibrations; Heroes & Villains; Help Me, Rhonda; Surfin' USA; Barbara Ann; Fun, Fun, Fun; California Energy Blues

Singles

Date of release	Title	Label	Chart positions
December 2002	"PT Cruiser"/"PT Cruiser" (a capella)/"PT Cruiser" (track)	CQ	never charted

Bruce Johnston

Albums

Surfers' Pajama Party (1962) Del-Fi Records

Tracks: Surfer's Delight; Kansas City; Mashin' the Popeye; Gee But I'm Lonesome; Green Onions; Ramrod; Last Night; Surfer Stomp; What'd I Say; Something On Your Mind

Surfin' Round the World (1963) Columbia Records

Tracks: Surfin' Round the World; Maksha at Midnight; Down Under; Cape Town; Biarritz; Jersey Channel Islands, Pt. 7; The Hamptons; Virginia Beach; Surf-A-Nova; Hot Pastrami, Mashed Potatoes, Come on to Rincon-Yeah!!; Malibu; Surfin's Here to Stay

Going Public (1977) Columbia Records

Tracks: I Write the Songs; Deirdre; Thank You Baby; Rendezvous; Won't Somebody Dance With Me; Disney Girls; Rock and Roll Survivor; Don't Be Scared; Pipeline

Singles

Date of release	Title	Label	Chart positions
February 1962	"Do the Surfer Stomp (Part One)"/"Do the Surfer Stomp (Part Two)"	Donna	never charted
April, 1962	"Soupy Shuffle Stomp"/"Moon Shot"	Donna	never charted
March, 1963	"The Original Surfer Stomp"/"Pajama Party"	Del-Fi	never charted
August, 1977 (UK)	"Pipeline"/"Disney Girls"	CBS Records	#33 (UK)
September, 1977	"Pipeline"/"Disney Girls" + "Pipeline"/"Deirdre" (12")	Columbia Records	never charted
1977	"Rendezvous"/"I Write the Songs"	Columbia Records	never charted

David Marks

Albums

Work Tapes (1992)

Tracks: Siren Song; Ocean Liner; I Wanna Be Your Driver; Fool's Guarantee; Over My Head; Doctor Of Love; Bamboo Shack; Early In The Morning; Have Love Will Travel; Hollywood Joe

Something Funny Goin' On (2003) Quiver Records

Tracks: Second Wind; Stowaway; Put Yourself In My Place (live); Mixed Drinks & High Emotions; High Side Of Normal; Crenshaw Blvd.; You Can't Talk To Me; The Legend; Put Yourself In My Place; Still Life In Motion; Land Of Opportunity

I Think About You Often (2006) Quiver Records

Tracks: Like 1969; Bamboo Shack; Light Of The Spirit; I Fall Into The Grace; Big Wave; Stowaway; I'm So Clever; Pretty Eyes; Dancin' In The Mirror; I Ain't Goin' Surfin'; Have You Ever Been Duped; I Think About You Often

Blondie Chaplin

Albums

Blondie Chaplin (album) (1977) Asylum Records Tracks: Bye Bye Babe; Can You Hear Me; Crazy Love; Woman Don't Cry; Loose Lady; Be My Love; Lonely Traveller; Riverboat Queen; Say You Need Me; For Your Love; Gimme More Rock 'N' Roll
Between Us (Blondie Chaplin album) (2006) Big Karma Records Tracks: Between Us; Heal The Rage; Hurricane; So Hard; Mother Smother; Children Of War; Love Power; Heads On Fire; Love You Till I Die; Crawl

See also

- List of songs by Brian Wilson
- List of songs by Carl Wilson
- List of songs by Dennis Wilson
- List of songs by Mike Love
- List of songs by The Beach Boys
- The Beach Boys discography

References

[1] Zobbel (June 16, 2007). "Chart Log UK" (http://www.zobbel.de/cluk/CLUK_W.HTM). Zobbel. . Retrieved September 10, 2008.
[2] "The Official Album Chart for the week ending September 13, 2008". *ChartsPlus* (Milton Keynes: IQ Ware Ltd) (368): 5–8.

The Beach Boys lineups

The Beach Boys lineups

1961 - 1962	• Mike Love - lead vocals, saxophone • Carl Wilson - lead guitar, vocals, bass, percussion • Al Jardine - bass, rhythm guitar, vocals • Dennis Wilson - drums, vocals • Brian Wilson - keyboards, bass, percussion, vocals
1962 - 1963	• Mike Love - lead vocals, saxophone • Carl Wilson - lead guitar, vocals • David Marks - guitar, vocals • Dennis Wilson - drums • Brian Wilson - bass, keyboards, vocals
1963	• Mike Love - lead vocals, saxophone • Carl Wilson - lead guitar, vocals • David Marks - guitar, vocals • Dennis Wilson - drums • Al Jardine - bass, vocals (tour replacement for Brian Wilson) • Brian Wilson - keyboards, bass, percussion, vocals
1963 - 1964	• Mike Love - lead vocals • Carl Wilson - lead guitar, vocals • Al Jardine - guitar, vocals • Dennis Wilson - drums • Brian Wilson - bass, keyboards, vocals
1964 - 1965	• Mike Love - lead vocals • Carl Wilson - guitar, vocals • Al Jardine - guitar, vocals • Dennis Wilson - drums • Glen Campbell - bass guitar, keyboards, lead guitar, vocals (tour replacement for Brian Wilson) • Brian Wilson - keyboards, bass, vocals (only in the studio)
1965 - 1972	• Mike Love - lead vocals • Carl Wilson - lead guitar, vocals • Al Jardine - guitar, vocals • Dennis Wilson - drums • Bruce Johnston - bass, keyboards, vocals (replaced Brian Wilson on tours and Johnston will be involved in the studio) • Brian Wilson - keyboards, bass, vocals (only in the studio)
1972 - 1973	• Mike Love - lead vocals • Carl Wilson - lead guitar, vocals • Blondie Chaplin - bass, vocals • Al Jardine - guitar, vocals • Dennis Wilson - keyboards, vocals • Ricky Fataar - keyboards, drums, vocals • Brian Wilson - keyboards, bass, vocals (only in the studio)
1973-1974	• Mike Love - lead vocals • Carl Wilson - lead guitar, vocals • Al Jardine - guitar, vocals • Dennis Wilson - keyboards, vocals • Ricky Fataar - keyboards, drums, vocals • Brian Wilson - no longer involved in the studio

1974 - 1978	• Mike Love - lead vocals • Carl Wilson - lead guitar, vocals • Al Jardine - guitar, vocals • Brian Wilson - keyboards, bass, vocals • Dennis Wilson - keyboards, vocals, drums
1978 - 1983	• Mike Love - lead vocals • Carl Wilson - lead guitar, vocals • Al Jardine - guitar, vocals • Bruce Johnston - bass, keyboards, vocals • Brian Wilson - bass, keyboards, vocals • Dennis Wilson - keyboards, vocals, drums
1983 - 1985	• Mike Love - lead vocals • Carl Wilson - lead guitar, vocals • Al Jardine - guitar, vocals • Brian Wilson - bass, keyboards, vocals • Bruce Johnston - bass, keyboards, vocals
1986 - 1995	• Mike Love - lead vocals • Carl Wilson - lead guitar, vocals • Al Jardine - guitar, vocals • Bruce Johnston - bass, keyboards, vocals
1995 - 1996	• Mike Love - lead vocals • Carl Wilson - lead guitar, vocals • Al Jardine - guitar, vocals • Brian Wilson - bass, keyboards, vocals • Bruce Johnston - bass, keyboards, vocals
1997 - 1999	• Mike Love - lead vocals • David Marks - lead guitar, vocals • Al Jardine - guitar, vocals • Bruce Johnston - bass, keyboards, vocals
1999 - 2007	• Mike Love - lead vocals • Bruce Johnston - keyboards, vocals with supporting musicians • Adrian Baker • Chris Farmer - bass • Scott Totten - guitar • Randell Kirsch - guitar • Tim Bonhomme - keyboards • John Cowsill - keyboards, vocals • Mike Kowalski - drums
2007 - Present	• Mike Love - lead vocals • Bruce Johnston - keyboards, vocals with supporting musicians • Scott Totten - guitar, vocals • Randell Kirsch - bass, vocals • Tim Bonhomme - keyboards • John Cowsill - drums, vocals • Christian Love - electric and acoustic guitars, vocals

From the start, The Beach Boys have undergone many variations in composition, being represented by fill-ins onstage as often as not. Wilson neighbor David Marks appeared on their first four albums, played with the group in its formative stages, and was a member from 1962 to 1963 as a replacement for Jardine, who had left the group to attend college. Jardine returned to the band in 1963 as an onstage fill-in for Brian Wilson, who was already feeling the stresses of touring. Marks rejoined the band in 1997, during Carl Wilson's last illness, and remained with them for two years.

Glen Campbell toured for several months with the group in 1965, as a touring replacement for Brian, who had played bass in concert. Campbell was subsequently replaced by Bruce Johnston, who later became a permanent member. In 1972 drummer Ricky Fataar and guitarist Blondie Chaplin joined the band, as Johnston left the band. In 1973 and 1974 Fataar and Chaplin left. In 1978, Johnston returned.

Though not corporate members of The Beach Boys, supporting players have featured many notable musicians over the years. Keyboard players Daryl Dragon & Toni Tennille, later famous as the pop duo The Captain & Tennille, toured with the band. Carli Muñoz, who had been playing keyboards with the band since 1970, in 1971 replaced Daryl Dragon as keyboard player until 1979. Mike Meros took over the position from May 1, 1979 to July 4th, 2000. Drummer Mike Kowalski and bassist/guitarist Ed Carter were two of the first outside musicians to join the group in 1969. Percussionist/drummer Bobby Figueroa was added in the mid-seventies until the end of 1987. Adrian Baker joined the band in 1981 as a vocalist/guitarist and left sometime in mid-1982. Jeff Foskett came aboard in early 1982 as a guitarist and vocalist and played his last show with the group on the night of July 4th, 1990. There was a stretch of time in 1981 and 1982 where both Jeff Foskett and Adrian Baker were in the band. Foskett was generally filling in for Carl's harmony parts, while he was away, while Baker did the falsetto vocals. Foskett is currently a member of Brian Wilson's group. Adrian Baker re-joined the band in 1989 to 1993 as a vocalist/guitarist. Saxman John Renner was added in the Summer of 1991 for live sax on Kokomo and others. John Renner was replaced in 1992 by Ritchie Cannata, one of Billy Joel's early live band and record saxophone players. Billy Hinsche, of Dino, Desi, & Billy fame, was also a longtime member of the supporting band throughout the '70s, '80s and '90s. Matt Jardine, son of Beach Boy Al Jardine also joined the band in 1989 through 1998 as singer / percussionist. In 1998, Adrian Baker re-joined the band (for a record-breaking third time) in 1998 until 2004. Randell Kirsch replaced Baker in 2004 to present as falsetto vocalist/guitarist. Nashville musician John Foster temporarily filled in on falsetto vocals and guitar between Baker's tenure and the addition of Kirsch. John Cowsill, an original member of the 1960s pop band The Cowsills, has been a vocalist/keyboardist since 1999. John Cowsill, replaced Mike Kowalski as the group's full time drummer in late 2007, leaving his secondary keyboard spot vacant.

Some of the changes in The Beach Boys' organization were less formal. They enjoyed a casual collaboration with fellow Southern Californians Jan and Dean. Much to the consternation of other band members, Wilson composed "Surf City" and gave the song, without compensation, to Dean Torrence. Jan and Dean, at the time not nearly as popular as The Beach Boys, recorded the song and scored their first number one single, a year before the Beach Boys finally reached the same milestone. Years later, Torrence happened upon the studio where the Beach Boys were recording their *Beach Boys' Party!* album. He joined in the singing, and can be heard singing harmony in the "Barbara Ann" (sample) cut from that album.

To the surprise and delight of fans around the world, Wilson has mounted several major tours under his own name with a band containing members of The Wondermints and led by former Beach Boys guitarist Jeff Foskett plus other supporting musicians. Their note-perfect live performances of the entire *Pet Sounds* album earned some of the most glowing concert reviews of Wilson's career, with some commentators calling the shows "the concert of a lifetime". In 2003 and 2004, he and Van Dyke Parks reunited to complete the unfinished sections of *Smile*, and in 2004 Wilson and his band toured the world performing a live concert version of the album. They then recorded a new studio version of *Smile* using vintage recording equipment and including sessions at the fabled Sunset Sound Studios in Hollywood, where some of the original recordings were made.

Jardine toured for a while with the Beach Boys Family & Friends (which for legal reasons quickly became Alan Jardine Family & Friends Beach Band, then Al Jardine's Endless Summer Band), featuring his sons Matt and Adam, Wilson's daughters Carnie and Wendy, and Carl's brother-in-law Billy Hinsche, among others. Jardine now tours as the Endless Summer Band which includes his two sons, Hinsche, and several other performers. He also tours with other artists, including Stevie Heger and members of the pop/rock band Tripsitter. Most recently, in late 2006 and early 2007, Brian Wilson and Jardine performed several joint shows in honor of *Pet Sounds*' 40th anniversary.

Litigation between Jardine and Love was resolved in 2009. Both Love and Brian Wilson have made guest appearances on Jardine's upcoming solo album *A Postcard From California*.

Current touring band

The Beach Boys

- Mike Love - lead vocals (1961-present)
- Bruce Johnston - keyboards, vocals (1965-1972, 1978-present)

Backing band

- Tim Bonhomme - keyboards (1996-present) [1]
- Scott Totten - guitar, vocals (1999-present)
- John Cowsill - keyboards, vocals (1999-2007); drums, vocals (2007-present)
- Randell Kirsch - guitar, vocals (2004-2007); bass, vocals (2007-present)
- Christian Love - electric and acoustic guitars, vocal (2007-present)

References

[1] http://www.beachboysband.net/MEMPAGES/TB_PAGES/TB_H-PAGE.htm

Article Sources and Contributors

The Beach Boys *Source*: http://en.wikipedia.org/w/index.php?oldid=364417157 *Contributors*: 17Drew, 1gus1, 1jrb, 1zackman, 23skidoo, 2D, 500channels, 75pickup, A no-knee mouse, Abluescarab, AbsolutDan, Abstrator, Acather96, Adamthebamf, Addshore, Administration, Adrianhula, Ahoerstemeier, AjaxSmack, Akirn, Alan Liefting, Alansohn, Alcuin, AlexWaelde, AlexiusHoratius, AlfredNWhitehead, Amazon10x, Analogdemon, Anazgnos, AndperseAndy, Andre666, Andreasegde, Andres, Andrewa, Andrewlp1991, Anger22, Anna Lincoln, Anstormning, Anthonylombardi, Antmusic, Antodav2007, ArglebargleIV, Arjun01, Art Markham, Artrush, Ash, Ashl, Ashlie123, Astral, Atlantik, AyaK, AzaToth, BGC, BRG, BabuBhatt, Bachrach44, Barrettmagic, Baseball Bugs, Bearcat, Bearic1, Beat 768, Beetstra, Belovedfreak, Bender235, Betacommand, Betty kerner, Bissinger, Blatkinson, BloodDoll, Bob9999999, Bobblewik, Bobby H. Heffley, Bobo192, Bojars, Booyah 007, Bortis, Braitman, Brentt, Bri4daz, Brianhenke, Brutannica, Bsadowski1, Bubba73, Burndownthedisco, Byates5637, Byrial, C-squared, CAPS LOCK, CBDunkerson, CCRoxtar, Calbaer, Calor, CambridgeBayWeather, CapitalQ, CardinalDan, Catcoe6, Cath0de, Cdc, Celardore, Cgilbert76, Chadcole74, Chensiyuan, Cheung1303, Chovain, Chowbok, Chris9086, Chu.chris, Coasting, Cody574, Commander Keane, CommonsDelinker, Conchita23, Conversion script, Cookage, Coolman230, Cootiequits, Corker1, Cosprings, CradBris, Cruzich, Crystallina, DBeardauthor, DCEdwards1966, DJ Clayworth, DONOVAN, DR04, Dale Arnett, Daniel challam, Danielmea, Danio, Bibliophylax, Dantesque1, Darrenhusted, DavidOaks, DavidWBrooks, Dcandeto, Ddespie@san.rr.com, Deadlightbulb, Deathshine, Delldot, Demomoke, DerHexer, Destineerox12, Digitize, Digresser, Dissolve, Djsasso, Doc Strange, DocWatson42, Doctormelodious, Domino42, Don1962, Dondt1, Doogle93, Doorbang, DropDeadGorgias, Dsreyn, Dudesleeper, Dunks58, Durin, E-Kartoffel, E0steven, EKindig, EagleFan, Easytoremember, Ebyabe, Ecki, EdTrist, Eddhurt, Edison, Edvhou812, Eeekster, Egg Creations, Eivind F Øyangen, Elaich, Elinnea, Epbr123, Ericamandy, Escape Orbit, Esprit15d, Everyking, EvocativeIntrigue, Extraordinary Machine, Facts707, Favonian, Fcumpassion, Feelingthevibe, Fenderfreak03, Fenwayguy, Fiercewolf1119, Fisherjs, Fixer88, Flixnpix, Floaterfluss, Fluteboy, Footprintx, FotoPhest, Franksieradzki, Frecklefoot, Funnybunny, Furrykef, Gaius Cornelius, Gareth Owen, Gawaxay, GeneMosher, Gephart, Germancarr, Gershwinrb, Getmoreatp, Ghmyrtle, Gillyweed, Giraffedata, Godlord2, Gogo Dodo, Goochelaar, GoogleMe, Gorosaurus, Goteamsnake, Gpietsch, Gr8white, Gracenotes, Graham87, Gregory Shantz, GripTheHusk, Gtrmp, Gunmetal Angel, Gurch, Guruz, Hall Monitor, HamburgerRadio, Hamiltondaniel, Happyme22, Hardylane, Heaven's Wrath, Hell in a Bucket, Hertz1888, Hiphats, Hippie Metalhead, Hl, Hottentot, Hraefen, Hu12, Hugh Mason, Hulmem, Hwonder, Hydrargyrum, Hyukan, IBook of the Revolution, IRP, Iambret, Ianblair23, IbLeo, Icarus071, Igoldste, IllaZilla, Improv, Infrogmation, Insanephantom, Interested2, Into The Fray, Inviernoh, IonescoIsaRhino, Iridescent, IrisKawling, J.delanoy, J.smith, JBC3, JFreeman, JGabbard, JPX7, JRHorse, JSF23, Jamespnugent, Jan van Male, JayHenry, Jayron32, Jbl1975, JediScougale, Jeff G., Jemiller226, Jessiejames, Jgm, Jiy, Jmlk17, Jmw0000, JoBrLa, Joebrell, Jogers, John of Lancaster, JohnInDC, JohnOwens, Jojhutton, Jolsonmhd, Jpers36, Jpetsounds, Jpjrocks, Jrgilb, Jsmaye, Jtnelson, Jubella, Jusdafax, Just64helpin, Justzisguy, Jweed, K1Bond007, Kaihoku, Kameejl, Kbdank71, Kbh3rd, Keithbob, Ketsuekigata, Kevin j, KevinMichaels, Keyser Söze, Kgrad, Khatru2, Kingboyk, Kingofallwhites, Kinkyturnip, Kintetsubuffalo, Kitagz, Kl4m, Konczewski, Korg, Kramertron, Kukini, Kungfuadam, Kuru, Kwantus, Kyrintethron, Laalalla, Lalli, Levineps, Lightdarkness, LilHelpa, Little Mountain 5, Liyster, Lofighost, Lukobe, Luna Santin, Luna1, M.C. Brown Shoes, M412k, MER-C, MKoltnow, MacGyverMagic, Macg4cubeboy, Madchester, Magi Media, Magnus.de, Mago266, Majorly, Mamour, Marcus2, Mariusds, Marked1234, Martarius, Martin451, Martpol, MattTC1028, Mattbr, Mattbrundage, Matthewn, Matveims, Mdoc7, Meegs, MegX, Mendaliv, Mensuur, Merope, Metstotop333, Michaelfool, MilborneOne, Mintleaf, MisfitToys, Mooco2000, MookieZ, MosheA, Moxy, Mqduck, MrMurph101, Mthteh, Muggmag, MusicaBaroque, Musicbbbtom, Musicpvm, NHRHS2010, Nagytibi, Natalie Erin, Neon5162, Nips, Niteowlneils, No Guru, NobodyImportant, Nortino, Notahippie76, Novel Concept, Number87, Nv8200p, Oakshade, Oanabay04, Ore4444, Oscarthecat, Ossmann, Oxymoron83, PJtP, PL290, Pallavimty, Panhandleman, Parapazzi, Paul Magnussen, Pbr2000, Pedro, Pekinpekin, Pele Merengue, Penmachine, Peregrine Fisher, PetSounds, Peter Fleet, Philip Trueman, Piper108, Pizza1512, Pjoef, Poland1918, Politepunk, PranksterTurtle, Prince-fan, Professor marginalia, ProfessorFokker, Proofreader77, Proteus71, PseudoSudo, Pseudorious, Qqq3123, Quadgirl10, QuasyBoy, Qxz, R27182818, Rachel Essien, Rachelej, RadioKirk, Radioinfoguy, Radzewicz, RainbowOfLight, RandomP, RandySavageFTW, RattleandHum, RedWolf, Redvers, Registered user 92, Relianiana, Reserching, Retraité, ReversionOne, RicDod, Rich Farmbrough, Rikstar, Riotrocket8676, Ritchie333, Riverman19, Rjwilmsi, Road Wizard, Robbie314, Robert K S, Roberta F., Robomaeyhem, Ronanfeely, Ronline, RottweilerCS, Roygbiv666, Rp, Rrburke, Runt, RxS, Rycho, S19991002, SCEhardt, SECProto, SJP, SNIyer12, Sahafan, Salavat, Salmar, Saltywood, Samuel Blanning, Sandman, Sandmountainslim, Santa Claus of the Future, Schumi555, Scienceman123, Scooby1970, Scorpion0422, Scottmsg, Scratchy, Sdcoates, SelfStudyBuddy, Serpent-A, Sfahey, Shadowjams, Shamrox, Sharkface217, Shatfield96, ShelfSkewed, Shell Kinney, Shmelsey, Sietse Snel, Sigma 7, SilkTork, Sir Isaac Lime, Siroxo, Sjoerd visscher, Sjones23, Sk8punk3d288, Skinsmoke, Sky Attacker, Slark, SlayerXT, Sleeming88, Slon02, Slysplace, Snow1215, Snowolf, Soakologist, Solitude, Sopoforic, Spacebirdy, Spicoli, Spitfire, Spoonpwner, SpuriousQ, Srikeit, Srsrsr, Stardust8212, Steelbeard1, Stephan KŒNIG, Steventhomas42, Stewgunn, Stonerose84, Stormie, Studioghiblitotoro, Stwalkerster, Subseven26, Sueyen, Superwesman, Surfmalc, Swinterich, Szyslak, T-borg, THE evil fluffyface, TUF-KAT, Tabletop, Tangotango, Tassedethe, Tastywheat, Tbone, Tbone0204, Tcncv, Ted Wilkes, Tema, Tempodivalse, TenPoundHammer, TexasDex, The Rogue Penguin, The Squicks, TheHYPO, TheKMan, TheMatty, TheScotch, Thebowser, Theofan, Thingg, Thivierr, Tide rolls, Tikitown, Tim1357, Tinton5, Tktktk, TomFriend08, Tomcwheeler, TommyStardust, Tony1, Tregoweth, Trekphiler, Trezjr, Triage, Tusho, Tweetsabird, Ukexpat, Ulyssesmsu, Un4v41l4l3, UpTooLate, Uriah is Boss, UserVOBO, Vague Rant, Vandymorgan, Versucher, Veyklevar, Viriditas, Virus on the tissue, Vorash, WJetChao, Wallstreethotrod, Wasted Time R, Wegngis, WereSpielChequers, WesleyDodds, Wether B, WhichOne'sPink?, Whiskey in the Jar, WhisperToMe, Whotookthatguy, Wiki alf, Wiki libs, WikiPro81, Wikimachine, Wildheartedoutsider, Wimt, Witchwooder, Wmahan, Wolbo, Wtmitchell, Wyckyd Sceptre, Y2kcrazyjoker4, Yerauy, Yerpo, Zazaban, Zendonut, Zeno Gantner, Zephyrad, ZhaoHong, Zoe, Zoe Goddard, Zoicon5, Zone46, Zr123, Zsinj, Zundark, 1327 anonymous edits

Blondie Chaplin *Source*: http://en.wikipedia.org/w/index.php?oldid=358380170 *Contributors*: Bobdc, CCRoxtar, Caerwine, DukeB-120th, Earshear34, Ethanepstein, F4280, Flappleton, Fram, Gazpacho, Irishninja1980, J04n, Koavf, Leahtwosaints, LoserTalent, Mike Selinker, Mild Bill Hiccup, Monni1995, Mrceleb2007, NHRHS2010, No Guru, Nymf, Ronfrankl, Santa Claus of the Future, Tassedethe, TheHYPO, TomGreen, UkPaolo, Valentinian, Waacstats, Wasted Time R, Wiki libs, Wikipediarules2221, Woohookitty, Yerauy, 49 anonymous edits

Ricky Fataar *Source*: http://en.wikipedia.org/w/index.php?oldid=364198142 *Contributors*: Ashley Pomeroy, Bawtyshouse, Bceglowski, Bobo192, Bobyllib, Canley, Chiquitabanana93, Crablogger, D6, Democraticmacguitarist, DukeB-120th, Erik Henning Edvardsen, Erik9, Foxearth, Gaius Cornelius, Geniac, Hullaballoo Wolfowitz, Johnnyrememberme, Leahtwosaints, MacRusgail, Metstotop333, Mike Selinker, Mowens35, Namiba, No Guru, Otto4711, Rich Farmbrough, Richhoncho, Sahafan, Shirimasen, Tassedethe, Templarion, Thecurran, Tinton5, Varlaam, VolatileChemical, Wasted Time R, Woodenthomas, Woohookitty, 27 anonymous edits

Al Jardine *Source*: http://en.wikipedia.org/w/index.php?oldid=357615006 *Contributors*: AarHan3, Alcuin, All Hallow's Wraith, AndrewHowse, Artrush, Ary29, Aspects, Avilena, Beachboy7545, Beetstra, Bobo192, Cabinessence67, Calvin08, Crystallina, D6, DLA75, Dale Arnett, David Gerard, Derek R Bullamore, Dhawk1964, Dsreyn, E-Kartoffel, E. Sn0 =31337=, Edvhou812, FMAFan1990, FallOfFingolfin, Folajimi, Hoof Hearted, Howcheng, Jamesontai, JesseW, Jogers, John, Jusdafax, Kamezuki, King of Hearts (old account 2), KittenKlub, Koavf, Laraspal00, Lukobe, Marcus2, Mike Selinker, Minesweeper.007, Musicbbbtom, Oh maestro, Orbst, Otrfan, PM800, Phantompie, PrahladKrishna, Redf0x, SJP, Sahafan, Santa Claus of the Future, ShelfSkewed, Sjones23, Spike Wilbury, Srsrsr, Stealth Munchkin, Stephen, Stonerose84, Surfmalc, Tbone0204, Thaurisil, Tiburon, Tinton5, TonyW, Wafulz, Wiki libs, Yerauy, Zone46, 56 anonymous edits

Bruce Johnston *Source*: http://en.wikipedia.org/w/index.php?oldid=363502550 *Contributors*: Amchow78, AntonioMartin, Aspects, Atthebeach, BGC, Bearcat, Bill37212, Bobo192, Boleyn2, Bovineboy2008, Cdw1952, Closeapple, D6, DS1953, David Gerard, Derek R Bullamore, Elaich, Fences and windows, Frecklefoot, Funktim, Garion96, Gilliam, Gontroppo, Gurch, Hall Monitor, Hyju, J04n, Jimmiefoxx, Jmw0000, Jubella, Junjk, Jwissick, Karaboom, Kingboyk, Latics, LoserTalent, M.C. Brown Shoes, MPLX, Metstotop333, Mike Dillon, Mike Selinker, MookieZ, Mr.Z-man, Musicbbbtom, No Guru, Pugs Malone, R. fiend, Rich Farmbrough, Richhoncho, Rklawton, Rosenzweig, Roygbiv666, Runnerupnj, Sahafan, Sandahl, Shalom S., SloopJohnB, Sounddude, Srsrsr, Stealth Munchkin, Tiburon, Tobit2, TonyW, Veyklevar, Wafulz, Wasted Time R, Wyckyd Sceptre, 125 anonymous edits

Mike Love *Source*: http://en.wikipedia.org/w/index.php?oldid=359383732 *Contributors*: A Raider Like Indiana, Abstrator, Acroterion, Afterwriting, All Hallow's Wraith, Alvis, Amazon10x, Andrzejbanas, Artrush, AtYourService100, BabuBhatt, Bapples81, Barachel001, Bdve, Beckettwatt, Beetstra, Beijomacio, Beve, Bigturtle, Bigweeboy, Billdescoteaux, Blransom, Bobo192, BurnDownBabylon, C-squared, Catachresis, Cesarpermanente, Charolastra charolo, Chowbok, Clawson, Crystallina, D6, DH85868993, Dale Arnett, DelusionOfGrandeur, Design, DiggyG, Dunks58, Ebyabe, Edvhou812, EnakoNosaj, EngineerScotty, Esprqii, Fabiform, Feelingthevibe, Fosnez, Fram, Fratrep, GeneMosher, Gershwinrb, GreatWhiteNortherner, Heracles31, Herostratus, Insanity Incarnate, Irishguy, J.R. Hercules, J.delanoy, Jimfbleak, Jmw0000, Jogers, Jubella, Jusdafax, Kbh3rd, Keithbob, Kingboyk, KittenKlub, Korny O'Near, Ksy92003, Laraspal00, Layla12275, LoserTalent, Lupin, M.C. Brown Shoes, Marcus2, MegX, Mendaliv, Metstotop333, Mhvolsky, Mike Selinker, Mkilly, MookieZ, MrSnow, Musicbbbtom, NellieBly, OS2Warp, Osmodiar, Pax:Vobiscum, Peruvianllama, Piper108, Ppntori, QuasyBoy, RandallJones, Registered user 92, Rex49, RickK, Ronhjones, Rynosoft, Sahafan, Saltywood, Samar, Santa Claus of the Future, Scooby1970, Sean William, Secretlondon, Sjones23, Skibum8713, Speedboy Salesman, Stealth Munchkin, Stefan, Stonerose84, Stupid Corn, Surfmalc, Tiburon, Tide rolls, TonyW, TurboCat, Vipinhari, ViresetHonestas, Wafulz, Waikikihulagirl, Ward3001, Wasted Time R, Whotookthatguy, Wiki libs, Will Beback, Yerauy, 260 anonymous edits

David Marks *Source*: http://en.wikipedia.org/w/index.php?oldid=364453927 *Contributors*: Acjelen, Ahkond, Anthropocentrism, Artrush, BocoROTH, BuddyOfHolly, Crystallina, Crzrussian, D6, DLA75, David marks, DearPrudence, Dljone9, Dsreyn, Edvhou812, Fish and karate, Geoff Whistle, Guanaco, Handmanad62, Iridescent, Jane Bennet, Jusdafax, Kbdank71, KittenKlub, Koavf, Levineps, Linuxbeak, Macg4cubeboy, Mahahahaneapneap, Malber, Marcus2, Mattbrundage, Mike Selinker, Muhand, Oknazevad, PDD, QYV, Richfife, Scarian, Shimmera, Signalhead, Sk8punk3d288, Smallweed, Srsrsr, Surfmalc, Sverdrup, Tabletop, TheKMan, Warpozio, Whotookthatguy, Wiki libs, Yerauy, Zephyrad, 57 anonymous edits

Brian Wilson *Source*: http://en.wikipedia.org/w/index.php?oldid=364596087 *Contributors*: (jarbarf), -- April, 75pickup, Abu badali, Adem89, Alansohn, Alers, Alextwa, Alicia85, All Hallow's Wraith, Andre Engels, Andyluciano, Anetode, Angr, Arnoldlover, Arthuralee, Artrush, Ashadeofgrey, AuburnPilot, Auximines, BGC, Bananatalk, Barrettmagic, Bartledan, Bchboy4091, Bdve, Bearcat, Beckettwatt, Beetstra, Bender235, Bigbluefish, Bigdaddy1999, BillyJack193, BitterMilton, Bjones, Bjrbbhaw81, BlankVerse, Blm07, Blokeski, Bluekahuna, Bobo192, Bovineboy2008, Brain seltzer, Brenont, Brian G. Wilson, Briandavies80, Brighterorange, BrokenSegue, Bullius, BurnDownBabylon, Cali232, Can't sleep, clown will eat me, Caspian, Cassiewebb, CatherineMunro, CattleGirl, Cbrown285, ChewyMcMittens, Cholmes75, Chris83, ChrisWilker, Ckatz, Clarifier19, Clawson, Claymcc, ColdShine, CommonsDelinker, Cosprings, Cungaro, D6, Dadc7, Dah31, Dale Arnett, DaltreyEntwistleMoonTownshend, Dan Harkless, Dark jedi requiem, Dasani, Davemarshall70, David Newton, David Shankbone, DavidWBrooks, Dbs, DearPrudence, Demps88, DiggyG, Discospinster, Dissident, Djsasso, Dkanaga, Docob5, Doczilla, Doktor Who, Domino42, Don1962, Dr who1975, Dsp13, Dunks58, E-Kartoffel, Eastpaw, El C, Elaich, Electronique, Eliz81, Erik9, Erxnmedia, Esprit15d, Everyking, Experimental Hobo Infiltration Droid, Falconus, Ferdinand Pienaar, Fiercewolf1119, Figureground, Flewis, Flexiblehead,

Flowerparty, Flydpnkrtn, Flyguy33, Fortdj33, Foxhound66, Frecklegirl, Funkyvoltron, Furrykef, Fuzzform, GTBacchus, GammaShade, Garion96, Gcranston, Ghghghghnineif, Gilliam, Gogh, Gorillaenvelope, Graham87, GregU, Hall Monitor, Hankthehero, Hardylane, Hatto, Hede2000, Hercule Was A Berkule, HexaChord, Hiphats, HisSpaceResearch, Howcheng, Hulmem, Humanriff, Hydrargyrum, Idigworms, Iheartravis, Indopug, Information yes, J.delanoy, J.smith, JKrantoski, James086, Jaxl, Jaysweet, Jeffreykopp, Jeffreyn77, Jeronimo, Jiy, Jmw0000, Joe Yippee, John Cardinal, Johnfos, Jpjrocks, Jtj608, Jubella, Jump Guru, Jusdafax, Just64helpin, Jóna Þórunn, Kaiba, Kalki, Karaboom, Karl Palmen, Kathryn NicDhàna, Katr67, Kellishelli, Kelly Martin, KittenKlub, Koavf, Konczewski, Leahtwosaints, Lectonar, Leopold Stotch, Levineps, LittleOldMe, Lolo123456, LoserTalent, Luckystrike99, Lukobe, Lynnfay, MER-C, MZMcBride, Maartenvdbent, Marcus Brute, Marcus2, Mattbrundage, Mazdapickup89, McCune, Mdhowe, Meg marx, Megamanic, Melissa Never Wears Socks, Michaelfool, Mihoshi, Mike Payne, Mike Selinker, Mike.pratt, Mike65535, Mindme, Mississippienne, Mooco2000, MookieZ, Moxy, Mrstonky, Mtmelendez, Murrax, Musicbbbtom, NFAN3, Nairobiny, NawlinWiki, Nohat, NonvocalScream, Northoltjohn, NuclearWarfare, Oanabay04, Oleskok, Omicronpersei8, Omphaloscope, Ori.livneh, PEJL, Pardy, Pariah23, Patstuart, PaulVIF, PennyDreadfulness, PetSounds, Phbasketball6, Picapica, Pietaster, PigFlu Oink, Pikahomie, Pinkadelica, Piper108, Pizzabob18, Polly, Prince-fan, Proteus71, ProveIt, PseudoSudo, Radiosonde, Radon210, Rainmtn53, Rainwarrior, Realm of Shadows, Registered user 92, Rich Farmbrough, Rjwilmsi, Rlei1130, RoryS89, Roygbiv666, Rsm99833, Ryulong, Saganaga, Sahafan, Salavat, Salimi, Saltywood, Sam Korn, Sandmountainslim, Santa Claus of the Future, Saule97, Schweiwikist, Scooteristi, Scott Paeth, Sculptorjones, Seaeagle04, Secretlondon, Seduisant, Shamrox, Shanemcd, ShelfSkewed, Sjones23, Sneller2, Sourcecode, Spebudmak, Speedboy Salesman, Srikipedia, Stealth Munchkin, Suffusion of Yellow, Tabletop, Tagrich1961, Talensis, TamYum, Tarcieri, Tassedethe, Tbsdy lives, Tdrtdr, TextAlchemist, The monkeyhate, The stuart, The wub, TheHYPO, TheScotch, Thebanjohype, Thewod, Threeafterthree, Thu, Thutton67, Tiburon, Tide rolls, Tjkorzun1, Tlogmer, TonyW, Tooke, TorbenFrost, Tremspeed, Treybien, Trödel, Twas Now, UkPaolo, Uncle Dick, Vague Rant, Veemonkamiya, Vianello, Vicvroom, Wachholder0, Wafulz, Ward3001, Weyes, Whotookthatguy, WikHead, Wiki libs, Wikipelli, Willondon, Winick88, Witchwooder, Woman Man, Wwwhhh, Y2kcrazyjoker4, Yagsian Asked, Yamla, YellowMonkey, Yerauy, Zapptastic, Zenohockey, Zone46, 爆笑連合, 593 anonymous edits

Carl Wilson *Source*: http://en.wikipedia.org/w/index.php?oldid=363217939 *Contributors*: Abstrator, Ace Class Shadow, AndrewHowse, Aranel, BD2412, BGC, BabuBhatt, Balok, Bbsrock, Beetstra, Binary TSO, Bobby H. Heffley, Bobo192, BuddyOfHolly, Cabinessence1, Can't sleep, clown will eat me, Charles Matthews, Chase me ladies, I'm the Cavalry, Chills42, ChrisCork, Cirt, Clarahamster, D6, David Newton, Deltabeignet, Deodar, Dina, Dsreyn, E-Kartoffel, Earshear34, Edvhou812, EoGuy, Everyking, Fortdj33, GeneMosher, Good Olfactory, Gurch, Hakanand, Herostratus, Howcheng, Igno2, Imnotminkus, Janetvekteris, Jayron32, Jogers, John M., JonHarder, Jusdafax, KF, KittenKlub, Koavf, Lonely Summer, Mago266, Marcus2, Mike Selinker, MookieZ, Musicbbbtom, Myoho5, Oanabay04, Oli Filth, Pd THOR, Peter Fleet, Piper108, Richfife, Risker, SU Linguist, Sahafan, Santa Claus of the Future, Scooteristi, Sjones23, Spearhead, Srsrsr, Stealth Munchkin, Stewgunn, TMC1982, Tassedethe, TheHYPO, Tiburon, TonyW, Twas Now, Uvaduck, Wafulz, Wasted Time R, WikHead, Wiki libs, Wikipe-tan, Wolfer68, Yerauy, 139 anonymous edits

Dennis Wilson *Source*: http://en.wikipedia.org/w/index.php?oldid=362087819 *Contributors*: 75pickup, ABF, Alexius08, Ali, Aranel, Artrush, Athene cunicularia, BGC, Bbsrock, Beetstra, Beryll, Betelgeuse, BigHeadFred, Bobo192, BorisAndDoris, Bumm13, Chris 73, Chuq, Cmoonshine, D6, Dale Arnett, Dantesque1, Demomoke, Devatipan, Djsasso, Dwilz, Edvhou812, Edwr, Elaich, Emma591, Emoscopes, Erpy83, Esanchez7587, Estiv, Frankly speaking, Gaius Cornelius, Getmiy, Giplee, Good Olfactory, Guidedbyalan, HANDBONE, Hafsabadsha, Hakanand, Hettta, Hiphats, Howcheng, IbLeo, Imnotminkus, Irishguy, J S Ayer, JHunterJ, Japandcaffben, Jeff3000, Jeffmar, Jgm, Jimmcguire, Joe Suggs, Jonesgang6, Jusdafax, Kintetsubuffalo, Kinu, Kitten b, KittenKlub, Kittybrewster, Kudinurse, Kuru, Leon..., Lightmouse, Littleolive oil, Localboy, Longhair, LoserTalent, Luminifer, Marcus2, Martarius, Mike Selinker, Miketm, Mikew100, Mississippienne, Modulatum, MookieZ, Musicbbbtom, Mythirdhouse, No Guru, Noirish, Oanabay04, Paloma Walker, Pdar, Piper108, Poco a poco, PrahladKrishna, Ramennooodles, Registered user 92, Res2216firestar, Rjwilmsi, Rklawton, Rockfang, SJP, Sahafan, Saltywood, Sandwich Eater, Sanfranman59, Santa Claus of the Future, Scooteristi, Secretlondon, Shamrox, Sjones23, Slatkin, Speedboy Salesman, Srsrsr, Stan Simmons, Stegop, Surfmalc, Swastikasekkks, Swinterich, Tassedethe, Tdl185, TenPoundHammer, The monkeyhate, TheHYPO, Tiburon, TonyW, Tramps like us, UnitedMartialArtist, UtherSRG, VMS Mosaic, WAvegetarian, Wafulz, WagByName, Ward3001, Wesley M. Curtus, Wiki libs, Wikipelli, Wildhartlivie, WizardOfTheCDrive, Wknight94, Xenophrenic, Yerauy, Zoicon5, Zone46, 227 anonymous edits

15 Big Ones *Source*: http://en.wikipedia.org/w/index.php?oldid=357830144 *Contributors*: 1jrb, A Knight Who Says Ni, Airproofing, Analogdemon, Ary29, BGC, Bathysphere, Betacommand, Bmicomp, Bobblewik, Bobo192, Bryan Derksen, CanisRufus, Chairman S., E-Kartoffel, Gamaliel, Jbacardi, JeffyJeffyMan2004, Jogers, Jonas Franck, Kbh3rd, Koavf, Kohoutek1138, Laurapinto, Metstotop333, Monicasdude, MookieZ, MysteryDog, Netoholic, Pcg13, PetSounds, Redhotwheels, Rich Farmbrough, Roygbiv666, Saga City, Sahafan, Santa Claus of the Future, ScudLee, ShelfSkewed, Somebody in the WWW, SteinbDJ, Tassedethe, The6969, Zone46, 37 anonymous edits

20/20 *Source*: http://en.wikipedia.org/w/index.php?oldid=364568681 *Contributors*: A Knight Who Says Ni, Airproofing, Alansohn, Analogdemon, Ary29, BGC, Bathysphere, Beckettwatt, Betacommand, Biograph1985, Bisbis, Bluerincon, Bmicomp, Bobo192, Bryan Derksen, CanisRufus, CattleGirl, Chairman S., Chyll, Cmdrjameson, Copybara, Cowbellcity45, Curps, Dekimasu, Docu, Dunks58, Hyju, J.R. Hercules, JeffyJeffyMan2004, Jiy, Jmw0000, Jogers, Jonas Franck, Kevinloy, KingPenguin, Koavf, Laurapinto, Mago266, Me-tan, MegX, Metstotop333, Monicasdude, MookieZ, Mrceleb2007, Muntfish, NPswimdude500, Nach0king, Nagle, Neilc, Noahdabomb3, Pcg13, PetSounds, Rich Farmbrough, Roygbiv666, Sahafan, Santa Claus of the Future, ShelfSkewed, Snigbrook, Somebody in the WWW, TenPoundHammer, Tom-, Twas Now, Warpozio, Zoicon5, 57 anonymous edits

All Summer Long *Source*: http://en.wikipedia.org/w/index.php?oldid=364681919 *Contributors*: A Knight Who Says Ni, Airproofing, Always Absent, Andrzejbanas, Ary29, BGC, Bathysphere, BillyH, Bobblewik, Chairman S., Chowbok, Commander Cyclops, Copernicium, Fortdj33, GaryColemanFan, Gertlex, Harryboyles, Igodard, Jaydec, JessBr, Jogers, Jonas Franck, Jusdafax, Ketiltrout, Kralizec!, Mago266, Martpol, Mikeblas, MookieZ, PetSounds, Phyte, Rich Farmbrough, Rjwilmsi, Roygbiv666, Sahafan, Santa Claus of the Future, Seano1, Ss112, Sublimefan97, Surfmalc, TheHYPO, 22 anonymous edits

The Beach Boys *Source*: http://en.wikipedia.org/w/index.php?oldid=346469453 *Contributors*: A Knight Who Says Ni, Analogdemon, BGC, Bathysphere, Bmicomp, Bobo192, Bryan Derksen, CanisRufus, Chairman S., Cmdrjameson, Crackpottheorist, Cureden, Curps, Docob5, Fayenatic london, Gamaliel, GassyGuy, Hapsiainen, Hyju, JeffyJeffyMan2004, Jogers, JustASimpleMonk, Koavf, Kwib, LeaveSleaves, Marysunshine, Mel Etitis, Monicasdude, MookieZ, NuclearWarfare, Pcg13, PetSounds, Rich Farmbrough, Sahafan, Santa Claus of the Future, ScudLee, Somebody in the WWW, Spin Boy 11, Starblind, Swanrizla, Tassedethe, TenPoundHammer, Wolfer68, 33 anonymous edits

Beach Boys Concert *Source*: http://en.wikipedia.org/w/index.php?oldid=363685783 *Contributors*: A Knight Who Says Ni, Airproofing, Andrzejbanas, Ary29, BGC, Bmicomp, Bobo192, Bryan Derksen, CanisRufus, Chairman S., Classicrockfan42, Dabomb87, DaveGorman, Econrad, Gertlex, Googuse, Hyju, J 1982, JeffyJeffyMan2004, Jmw0000, Jogers, Koavf, LeaveSleaves, Loukoum, Mlsquad, Netoholic, PetSounds, Rich Farmbrough, Rowleyites, Santa Claus of the Future, ScudLee, Somebody in the WWW, Surfermoon, The Thing That Should Not Be, TheHYPO, Ulric1313, Zidane tribal, 27 anonymous edits

The Beach Boys Today! *Source*: http://en.wikipedia.org/w/index.php?oldid=363492245 *Contributors*: 2Pac, A Knight Who Says Ni, Airproofing, Andrzejbanas, Ary29, BGC, Bathysphere, Bmicomp, Bobo192, Brewcrewer, Bryan Derksen, CanisRufus, Cbing01, Chairman S., Cmdrjameson, Cowbellcity45, DCEdwards1966, Dale Arnett, Ffirehorse, Gamaliel, Gertlex, Hyju, JeffyJeffyMan2004, Jmw0000, Jogers, Jonas Franck, Just64helpin, Kohoutek1138, Leevclarke, Leopold Stotch, Mago266, MajorB, MookieZ, Mralexreynolds, NewChampion, Omarcheeseboro, PetSounds, Rich Farmbrough, RobinCarmody, Roygbiv666, ST47, Sahafan, Santa Claus of the Future, Sean Whitton, Shamrox, Somebody in the WWW, Superpeer, Ufinne, Wasted Time R, Whotookthatguy, Zellin, 68 anonymous edits

The Beach Boys in Concert *Source*: http://en.wikipedia.org/w/index.php?oldid=361878669 *Contributors*: A Knight Who Says Ni, After Midnight, Airproofing, BGC, Bmicomp, Bobo192, CanisRufus, Chairman S., Cmdrjameson, Crslowin, E-Kartoffel, Gamaliel, J 1982, Jogers, Koavf, Mdhowe, Michaelfool, Pcg13, PetSounds, Rich Farmbrough, Santa Claus of the Future, Seth slackware, Tassedethe, TheHYPO, Ybbor, Zidane tribal, 19 anonymous edits

The Beach Boys' Christmas Album *Source*: http://en.wikipedia.org/w/index.php?oldid=363711201 *Contributors*: A Knight Who Says Ni, Airproofing, Andrzejbanas, Ary29, Awilgus, BGC, Bmicomp, Bobo192, Bryan Derksen, CanisRufus, Chairman S., Cmdrjameson, DCEdwards1966, Dancon7, Gertlex, Hyju, J 1982, JeffyJeffyMan2004, Jmw0000, Jogers, Loukoum, Marcus Brute, Mdumas43073, MookieZ, Nickflavor, PetSounds, Rich Farmbrough, Sahafan, Santa Claus of the Future, ScudLee, T3hpez, TheHYPO, Ulric1313, 22 anonymous edits

Beach Boys' Party! *Source*: http://en.wikipedia.org/w/index.php?oldid=363685829 *Contributors*: A Knight Who Says Ni, Airproofing, Andrzejbanas, Ary29, BGC, Betty kerner, Big Smooth, Billwikstrom, Bmicomp, Bobo192, Bobyllib, Brain seltzer, Bryan Derksen, CanisRufus, Cbing01, Chairman S., CheckeredFlag200, Chilly Penguin, Cmdrjameson, Fauxuser782, Hyju, JeffyJeffyMan2004, Jmw0000, Jogers, Jonas Franck, Kohoutek1138, Lairor, Monicasdude, MookieZ, MrGater, OnBeyondZebrax, PetSounds, Poco a poco, Rich Farmbrough, Robbie314, Roygbiv666, Sahafan, Santa Claus of the Future, Sfahey, Somebody in the WWW, Spiby, Stt13, Titoxd, Twas Now, Ufinne, Ulric1313, Varlaam, Zidane tribal, Zone46, 46 anonymous edits

Best of The Beach Boys Vol. 2 *Source*: http://en.wikipedia.org/w/index.php?oldid=361109450 *Contributors*: A3oertENG, Airproofing, BGC, Bluerincon, CanisRufus, Chairman S., Cmdrjameson, Everyking, Fritz Saalfeld, Harryboyles, Hiphats, Jaydec, Jiy, Jmw0000, Jogers, Koavf, Mm40, MookieZ, PetSounds, Poco a poco, Rich Farmbrough, Santa Claus of the Future, Zidane tribal, 7 anonymous edits

Best of The Beach Boys *Source*: http://en.wikipedia.org/w/index.php?oldid=360970768 *Contributors*: A3oertENG, Airproofing, BGC, Bluerincon, Bmicomp, Bobblewik, CanisRufus, Chairman S., Cmdrjameson, Curps, Dom Kaos, Everyking, Harryboyles, Jaf7965, Jaydec, Jmw0000, Jogers, Koavf, Monicasdude, MookieZ, Okki, PetSounds, Rich Farmbrough, Santa Claus of the Future, Ste900R, Zidane tribal, 5 anonymous edits

Best of The Beach Boys Vol. 3 *Source*: http://en.wikipedia.org/w/index.php?oldid=364409635 *Contributors*: Airproofing, Artrush, BGC, Bluerincon, Bobo192, CanisRufus, Chairman S., Cmdrjameson, Everyking, Gaius Cornelius, Jaydec, Jmw0000, Jogers, Koavf, Nickflavor, PetSounds, Rich Farmbrough, Santa Claus of the Future, ScudLee, Zidane tribal, 12 anonymous edits

The Capitol Years *Source*: http://en.wikipedia.org/w/index.php?oldid=364738007 *Contributors*: E-Kartoffel, Efe, Ericorbit, Jogers, Koavf, MookieZ, ShelfSkewed, Sixsevenfive, Tassedethe, W guice, Waacstats, Wolfer68, Yeahbutnobut92, 1 anonymous edits

Carl and the Passions – "So Tough" *Source*: http://en.wikipedia.org/w/index.php?oldid=364729218 *Contributors*: A Knight Who Says Ni, Airproofing, Analogdemon, Ary29, BGC, Bathysphere, Beckettwatt, Bobo192, Bryan Derksen, Calliopejen1, CanisRufus, Chairman S., David S, space nerd, Docob5, Gamaliel, Holiday56, Hyju, Iridescent, JeffyJeffyMan2004, Jmw0000, Jogers, Jonas Franck, Koavf, Lairor, Mago266, Metstotop333, Monicasdude, MookieZ, Nach0king, Pcg13, PetSounds, Rich Farmbrough, Rjwilmsi, Roygbiv666, Sahafan, Santa Claus of the Future, ShelfSkewed, Somebody in the WWW, The Keymaster, Thebogusman, Whotookthatguy, WikHead, Yorkshiresky, Zidane tribal, Ælfgar, 56 anonymous edits

Classics Selected by Brian Wilson *Source*: http://en.wikipedia.org/w/index.php?oldid=364413541 *Contributors*: Airproofing, BGC, CanisRufus, Chairman S., Cmdrjameson, Jiy, Jogers, Koavf, MookieZ, PetSounds, Phthoggos, Rich Farmbrough, Santa Claus of the Future, ShelfSkewed, Srsrsr, Tassedethe, Zidane tribal, 4 anonymous edits

Endless Harmony Soundtrack *Source*: http://en.wikipedia.org/w/index.php?oldid=330849072 *Contributors*: Airproofing, BGC, Bmicomp, Bobyllib, CanisRufus, Chairman S., Cmdrjameson, Drbuzzard, Enchanter, Jiy, Jogers, Michaelfool, PetSounds, Rich Farmbrough, Sahafan, 5 anonymous edits

Endless Summer *Source*: http://en.wikipedia.org/w/index.php?oldid=364417241 *Contributors*: ACSE, Airproofing, BGC, Classicrockfan42, DR04, Fourohfour, Jaydec, Jdcooper, Jogers, Koavf, LSK, Mooco2006, MookieZ, NeilDespres, PetSounds, Phthoggos, Piano non troppo, Pr0t0type, Rich Farmbrough, Santa Claus of the Future, Sayler, ScudLee, Seaduck79, ShelfSkewed, Splash, Srsrsr, Swanrizla, TUF-KAT, Thewhiteswan9, Vague Rant, Wasted Time R, Zone46, 25 anonymous edits

Four by The Beach Boys *Source*: http://en.wikipedia.org/w/index.php?oldid=356987122 *Contributors*: Airproofing, Cosprings, Fantailfan, Jaydec, KearF, Kubigula, Mike Selinker, Ore4444, Rich Farmbrough, Sahafan, Santa Claus of the Future, Skier Dude

Friends *Source*: http://en.wikipedia.org/w/index.php?oldid=353133625 *Contributors*: A Knight Who Says Ni, Airproofing, Ary29, BGC, Bathysphere, Beckettwatt, Bisbis, Bluerincon, Bmicomp, Bobo192, BurtonM, C777, Chairman S., Cmdrjameson, Cowbellcity45, Curps, Cymi, Dunks58, E-Kartoffel, Ericorbit, Graham87, Herostratus, Hyju, JLaTondre, Jaydec, JeffyJeffyMan2004, Jmw0000, Jogers, John M., Jonas Franck, Mago266, MegX, Metstotop333, Monicasdude, MookieZ, Ms2ger, Namrevlis, Pcg13, PetSounds, Rich Farmbrough, Sahafan, Salavat, Sallymcvegas, Santa Claus of the Future, SlubGlub, Somebody in the WWW, Sun King, Taras, Tassedethe, Thue, WikHead, Woohookitty, 37 anonymous edits

Good Timin': Live at Knebworth England 1980 *Source*: http://en.wikipedia.org/w/index.php?oldid=361878789 *Contributors*: Airproofing, Alcuin, BGC, BabuBhatt, Bmicomp, CanisRufus, Chairman S., Cmdrjameson, Harro, J 1982, Jogers, Mike Selinker, PetSounds, Rich Farmbrough, Srsrsr, 5 anonymous edits

Good Vibrations – Best of The Beach Boys *Source*: http://en.wikipedia.org/w/index.php?oldid=364419477 *Contributors*: Airproofing, Analogdemon, BGC, Bmicomp, CanisRufus, Chairman S., Cmdrjameson, DR04, E-Kartoffel, Jogers, Koavf, Kohoutek1138, MegX, MookieZ, PetSounds, Rich Farmbrough, Srsrsr, Truthanado, 3 anonymous edits

Good Vibrations: Thirty Years of The Beach Boys *Source*: http://en.wikipedia.org/w/index.php?oldid=364741589 *Contributors*: Airproofing, Alcuin, Aldejerph, Analogdemon, BGC, Bobo192, CanisRufus, Chairman S., Cmdrjameson, Don1962, E-Kartoffel, Everyking, Hakanand, Jiy, Jmw0000, Jogers, Koavf, MegX, MookieZ, Mutt1343, Orat Perman, Pcg13, PetSounds, Rich Farmbrough, Santa Claus of the Future, ShelfSkewed, Srsrsr, Ste900R, Swanrizla, Tassedethe, The monkeyhate, TheHYPO, Ulric1313, 23 anonymous edits

The Greatest Hits – Volume 1: 20 Good Vibrations *Source*: http://en.wikipedia.org/w/index.php?oldid=364519011 *Contributors*: Airproofing, BGC, CanisRufus, Chairman S., Cmdrjameson, Ddespie@san.rr.com, Everyking, Green lantern40, Joedeshon, Jogers, Koavf, MookieZ, PetSounds, Pig de Wig, PigsCanFly2day, Rich Farmbrough, Srsrsr, Swanrizla, Tascena, Tassedethe, The monkeyhate, 5 anonymous edits

The Greatest Hits – Volume 2: 20 More Good Vibrations *Source*: http://en.wikipedia.org/w/index.php?oldid=364519086 *Contributors*: Airproofing, Alcuin, BGC, CanisRufus, Chairman S., Cmdrjameson, Ddespie@san.rr.com, E-Kartoffel, Jogers, Koavf, Laurapinto, MegX, PetSounds, Pig de Wig, Rich Farmbrough, ShelfSkewed, Srsrsr, Tascena, 2 anonymous edits

Greatest Hits Volume Three: Best of the Brother Years 1970–1986 *Source*: http://en.wikipedia.org/w/index.php?oldid=364423036 *Contributors*: Airproofing, BGC, Bluerincon, CanisRufus, Chairman S., Cmdrjameson, Jogers, JuPitEer, Koavf, MookieZ, PetSounds, Rich Farmbrough, Swanrizla, Tassedethe, 8 anonymous edits

Hawthorne, CA *Source*: http://en.wikipedia.org/w/index.php?oldid=360856655 *Contributors*: Airproofing, Alcuin, BGC, Bmicomp, CanisRufus, Chairman S., Cmdrjameson, Jaydec, Jogers, JuPitEer, Nach0king, PetSounds, Rich Farmbrough, Santa Claus of the Future, ScudLee, Welsh, 5 anonymous edits

Holland *Source*: http://en.wikipedia.org/w/index.php?oldid=359107931 *Contributors*: A Knight Who Says Ni, Ajax-and-Achilles, AyaK, BGC, Bathysphere, Bmicomp, Bobblewik, Bobo192, Bryan Derksen, CanisRufus, Chairman S., Chilly Penguin, Darklilac, David S, space nerd, Fnorp, Gamaliel, GassyGuy, Gidonb, Hyju, JeffyJeffyMan2004, Jmw0000, Jogers, Jonas Franck, Liuzhou, Mago266, Monicasdude, MookieZ, Nach0king, Netoholic, No Guru, Pcg13, PetSounds, Rich Farmbrough, Rothorpe, Roygbiv666, Saga City, Sahafan, Santa Claus of the Future, ScudLee, Somebody in the WWW, Surfmalc, TheHYPO, WikHead, Zoicon5, 49 anonymous edits

Keepin' the Summer Alive *Source*: http://en.wikipedia.org/w/index.php?oldid=359307875 *Contributors*: A Knight Who Says Ni, Analogdemon, Ary29, BGC, Bathysphere, Bmicomp, Bobo192, Bryan Derksen, CanisRufus, Chairman S., Cmdrjameson, Curps, E-Kartoffel, Estoy Aquí, Fayenatic london, Hapsiainen, Hyju, JeffyJeffyMan2004, Jogers, John M., Mel Etitis, Monicasdude, MookieZ, No Guru, Pcg13, PetSounds, Rich Farmbrough, Sahafan, Santa Claus of the Future, ScudLee, ShelfSkewed, Somebody in the WWW, Unionsoap, Wgfinley, 15 anonymous edits

L.A. *Source*: http://en.wikipedia.org/w/index.php?oldid=355276516 *Contributors*: A Knight Who Says Ni, Analogdemon, BGC, Bathysphere, Bmicomp, Bobo192, Bryan Derksen, CanisRufus, Chairman S., Chilly Penguin, Cmdrjameson, Commander Cyclops, Curps, DiggyG, E-Kartoffel, Fayenatic london, Gamaliel, Geniac, Hapsiainen, Hyju, JeffyJeffyMan2004, Jmw0000, Jogers, Mel Etitis, Meredyth, Metstotop333, Mike Eder, Monicasdude, MookieZ, Pcg13, PetSounds, R. fiend, Rich Farmbrough, Rothorpe, Sahafan, Santa Claus of the Future, ScudLee, Somebody in the WWW, Starblind, Swanrizla, Taestell, Tassedethe, Violncello, William Bowe, 33 anonymous edits

Little Deuce Coupe *Source*: http://en.wikipedia.org/w/index.php?oldid=354131785 *Contributors*: A Knight Who Says Ni, Airproofing, Ary29, BGC, Bmicomp, Bobo192, Bryan Derksen, Chairman S., Cmdrjameson, Curps, Dmeyferth21, Dsreyn, E-Kartoffel, GSlicer, Gephart, Gertlex, Greg221b, Gwen Gale, Hyju, JamesMadison, Jaydec, JeffyJeffyMan2004, Jerry warriner, Jmw0000, Jogers, John, John M., Jonas Franck, Jusdafax, Karaboom, Lightsup55, Lukobe, M1ss1ontomars2k4, Mattbrundage, Maximus Rex, Monicasdude, MookieZ, Nitcowlneils, Pedro, PetSounds, Rfc1394, Rich Farmbrough, Richwales, Roygbiv666, Sahafan, Sam Hocevar, Santa Claus of the Future, ScudLee, Shawh, SheeEttin, Stephen Turner, Surfmalc, Tinton5, Tony1, Twsx, Verne Equinox, Wasted Time R, 36 anonymous edits

Live in London *Source*: http://en.wikipedia.org/w/index.php?oldid=361878246 *Contributors*: Airproofing, Alai, Ary29, BGC, Biograph1985, Bmicomp, Bobo192, Bryan Derksen, CanisRufus, ChicXulub, Cmdrjameson, EsonLinji, Gtrmp, J 1982, JeffyJeffyMan2004, Jogers, Loukoum, Michaelfool, MookieZ, Owen, PetSounds, Rich Farmbrough, Rjwilmsi, Santa Claus of the Future, ScudLee, Seth slackware, Somebody in the WWW, Tassedethe, Warpozio, 39 anonymous edits

Lost & Found (1961–62) *Source*: http://en.wikipedia.org/w/index.php?oldid=364554634 *Contributors*: Alcuin, Bobo192, E-Kartoffel, Koavf, Nach0king, Rich Farmbrough, Rubikonchik, Sahafan, TubularWorld

Love You *Source*: http://en.wikipedia.org/w/index.php?oldid=355276799 *Contributors*: 5theye, A Knight Who Says Ni, Airproofing, Analogdemon, Antandrus, Artrush, BGC, Bathysphere, Bjones, Bluerincon, Bmicomp, Bobblewik, Bobo192, Bryan Derksen, Bumm13, CambridgeBayWeather, CanisRufus, Chairman S., Cmdrjameson, Curps, E-Kartoffel, Gamaliel, Gtrmp, Hapsiainen, Hraefen, Hyju, JeffyJeffyMan2004, Joe M'Geek, Jogers, Jonas Franck, Keith D, Kevin143, Koavf, Krash, Kuru, Kzollman, LoveVirus, Mago266, Mel Etitis, Monicasdude, MookieZ, Pcg13, PetSounds, Qxz, Rich Farmbrough, Roygbiv666, Sahafan, Santa Claus of the Future, Somebody in the WWW, TheoClarke, Wasted Time R, , 58 anonymous edits

M.I.U. Album *Source*: http://en.wikipedia.org/w/index.php?oldid=362039941 *Contributors*: A Knight Who Says Ni, Analogdemon, Artrush, BGC, Bathysphere, Bigweeboy, Bluerincon, Bmicomp, Bobo192, Bryan Derksen, CanisRufus, Chairman S., Cmdrjameson, Curps, Dekimasu, E-Kartoffel, Gamaliel, Hapsiainen, JeffyJeffyMan2004, Joedeshon, Jogers, Kjm914a, Madchester, Mattbrundage, Mazdapickup89, Mel Etitis, Monicasdude, PetSounds, Rich Farmbrough, Rjwilmsi, Rothorpe, Sahafan, Santa Claus of the Future, ScudLee, Somebody in the WWW, Ste900R, William Bowe, 30 anonymous edits

Made in U.S.A. *Source*: http://en.wikipedia.org/w/index.php?oldid=364429101 *Contributors*: Docob5, Fourdee, Iain.dalton, Koavf, Lola Voss, Mattbrundage, MookieZ, PEJL, Santa Claus of the Future, ShelfSkewed, Swanrizla, Tassedethe, Wmcgarry, Wolfer68, 6 anonymous edits

The Original US Singles Collection The Capitol Years 1962–1965 *Source*: http://en.wikipedia.org/w/index.php?oldid=364747727 *Contributors*: Crazysane, Drbreznjev, GrahamHardy, Koavf, Koopatroopa89, Marsilies, Postcard Cathy, Skier Dude, Valentinejoesmith, Victor Lopes, 3 anonymous edits

Pet Sounds *Source*: http://en.wikipedia.org/w/index.php?oldid=363480124 *Contributors*: 0dd1, 23skidoo, 75pickup, A Knight Who Says Ni, Adan torres, Addit, AdorableRuffian, Airproofing, Analogdemon, Andman8, Andreasegde, Andrzejbanas, Anger22, ArglebargleIV, Artrush, Avram Fawcett, BGC, Bathysphere, Bdve, Betty kerner, Beyond My Ken, Bmicomp, Bobo192, Bojars,

Bovineone, Bruce1ee, Byrial, Cbing01, Chairman S., ChicXulub, Chilly Penguin, Chowbok, Chyll, Citymovement, Cmdrjameson, Complex Wisdom, Cowbellcity45, Curps, DCEdwards1966, Danio, Bibliophylax, David Johnson, Dcqec111, Design, Dmeyferth21, Dremora, DropShadow, Dunks58, Eligius, Equal, Everyking, Faithlessthewonderboy, Fenderfreak03, Frehley72, Freshacconci, Furste, Gamaliel, Ghindo, Ghmyrtle, Glassbreaker5791, Goethean, Grstain, Grunge6910, Heyimpauly, Hiphats, Ian Rose, Indopug, Infrogmation, Insomniastan, IonescoIsaRhino, J Milburn, JJBunks, JPX7, Jacobolus, James Epstein, James599, Jamespoky, Jaxl, Jayron32, Jazz77, Jennica, Jimregan, Jmw0000, Jogers, John Reaves, JohnRussell, Jonas Franck, Jtgotsjets, Just64helpin, Kafziel, Karl Palmen, KirbyMaster14, Koavf, Konczewski, Lenoxus, LightningMan, Limmerine, Ling.Nut, Lupin, Mago266, Markkawika, Martpol, Mattbrundage, MeltBanana, Metstotop333, Michael Snow, Monicasdude, Mooco2006, MookieZ, Movabletype, Mrperson27, Mtmtmt, Mulad, Mumby, Omarcheeseboro, Omicronpersei8, Onresume, Ortolan88, Orwellson, Palaciopalermo12, Papa November, Passport90, Paul A, Pele Merengue, PetSounds, Pinoy Pride, Piper108, Polizzi, Pomtidom, Prince-fan, Q8-falcon, Radagast83, Rainmtn53, Rc251, Redheylin, Registered user 92, Rhobite, Rich Farmbrough, Ridernyc, RockAndBowler, Rodhullandemu, Rorschach567, Roygbiv666, ST47, Sahafan, Salix alba, Sam Hocevar, SamuelMaglor, Sanfranman59, Santa Claus of the Future, SchfiftyThree, SeanO, Shamrox, Slysplace, Soakologist, Soarhead77, SplitGuy, Spysquirrel, StevenHW, Strabismus, Sublimefan97, Suddenly There Is a Valley, Sweetness46, THollan, TODAYxTHExPOND, TUF-KAT, Tarquin, Teiladnam, Tezero, The Thing That Should Not Be, TheHYPO, TheLeopard, Thebogusman, TherealslimMarxtoneReturns, Thom, Tim1357, Tinmanic, Tlogmer, Tofu Tim, Trivialist, Tsinfandel, Ulmanor, UtherSRG, Uucp, Vague Rant, Varlaam, Vivenot, WalrusOct9, Walshga, Wether B, Wiki libs, Willy91, Witchwooder, Wolfer68, Woohookitty, Yamamoto Ichiro, Yardcock, ZPM, Zazaban, Zenohockey, Zoicon5, Zone46, 285 anonymous edits

The Pet Sounds Sessions *Source*: http://en.wikipedia.org/w/index.php?oldid=364748001 *Contributors*: Airproofing, Akawalrus, BGC, Bmicomp, CanisRufus, Chairman S., DiggyG, Jogers, Koavf, Kohoutek1138, LoserTalent, Mandarax, Mattbrundage, Michaelfool, PetSounds, Rich Farmbrough, Teklund, TheHYPO, 3 anonymous edits

Rarities *Source*: http://en.wikipedia.org/w/index.php?oldid=360797134 *Contributors*: Airproofing, Alcuin, Bluerincon, FuriousFreddy, Jogers, Koavf, MookieZ, Rich Farmbrough, Sahafan, TenPoundHammer, 1 anonymous edits

Shut Down Volume 2 *Source*: http://en.wikipedia.org/w/index.php?oldid=355376273 *Contributors*: A Knight Who Says Ni, Airproofing, Andrzejbanas, Armchair Potentate, Ary29, BGC, Bathysphere, Bmicomp, Bobo192, Bryan Derksen, Caligulaimp, Chairman S., Cmdrjameson, DabMachine, E-Kartoffel, F-22 Raptored, Gertlex, GreatWhiteNortherner, Hyju, JeffyJeffyMan2004, Jmw0000, Jogers, Jonas Franck, Jusdafax, Magioladitis, Metstotop333, MookieZ, PetSounds, Rich Farmbrough, Roygbiv666, Sahafan, Santa Claus of the Future, ScudLee, Surfmale, Twsx, Verne Equinox, Wafulz, Zone46, 22 anonymous edits

Smile *Source*: http://en.wikipedia.org/w/index.php?oldid=359076292 *Contributors*: Airproofing, Alextking, BGC, Betty kerner, Big Smooth, Billwikstrom, Calmypal, CapitalQ, Cmichael, Dale Arnett, Decorativeedison, Donor, Dunks58, E-Kartoffel, Farfendugle, Gaius Cornelius, Gohst, Gongshow, Gotham23, Hiphats, Hu12, Indefatigable, J.smith, Jak86, Jogers, Just64helpin, Koavf, Leopold Stotch, MWB1138, Mablanco, Marcus Brute, Meisterkoch, Million dollar honk, MookieZ, MuzikJunky, Mydogtrouble, Number87, Ossmann, Piper108, Poco a poco, Quentinisgod, Ridernyc, Rjwilmsi, Salamurai, Santa Claus of the Future, ScatteredFrog, Schavira, Shamrox, Some jerk on the Internet, Starfighter Pilot, Steven J. Anderson, The Squicks, TheHYPO, Tothebarricades.tk, Twas Now, Vladsinger, Warchef, Warpozio, WhatGuy, Zone46, 105 anonymous edits

Smiley Smile *Source*: http://en.wikipedia.org/w/index.php?oldid=361856899 *Contributors*: A Knight Who Says Ni, Airproofing, Artrush, Ary29, BGC, BTLizard, Bathysphere, Bjrbbhaw81, Bmicomp, Bobo192, BurnDownBabylon, Calmypal, Cheekyal, Chilly Penguin, Chowbok, Clarahamster, Cmdrjameson, Cowbellcity45, Curps, DCEdwards1966, Dale Arnett, Davidpatrick, Dmeyferth21, Dunks58, Dusti, E-Kartoffel, Egpetersen, Greendaylad196, Hiphats, Hyju, Izehar, Jaydec, Jiy, Jmw0000, Jogers, John M., Jonas Franck, Just64helpin, Kauczuk, Konczewski, Lukobe, M.C. Brown Shoes, Macg4cubeboy, Magnus Manske, Mago266, Mazdapickup89, Mboverload, Monicasdude, MookieZ, Night Gyr, Nilfanion, Oanabay04, PetSounds, Rich Farmbrough, Roope, Roygbiv666, Sahafan, Santa Claus of the Future, ScudLee, Shamrox, Slysplace, Surfmale, Swinterich, Teewikitoo, Thebogusman, Tony Sidaway, Warchef, Zone46, 85 anonymous edits

Songs from Here & Back *Source*: http://en.wikipedia.org/w/index.php?oldid=362368431 *Contributors*: Alcuin, Analogdemon, BGC, BabuBhatt, Bobo192, Koavf, NobodyImportant, Srsrsr, Whotookthatguy, 5 anonymous edits

Sounds of Summer: The Very Best of The Beach Boys *Source*: http://en.wikipedia.org/w/index.php?oldid=364507171 *Contributors*: Airproofing, Analogdemon, BGC, Bmicomp, CanisRufus, Chairman S., Cmdrjameson, E-Kartoffel, Everyking, Foolishgrunt, InnocuousPseudonym, JBellis, Joedeshon, Jogers, Kingboyk, Koavf, Laurapinto, MegX, MookieZ, PetSounds, Rajiv Varma, Rich Farmbrough, Rob Ruiz Anderson, Santa Claus of the Future, Srsrsr, Swanrizla, TheHYPO, Traxinet, 14 anonymous edits

Spirit of America *Source*: http://en.wikipedia.org/w/index.php?oldid=364507490 *Contributors*: Abstrator, Airproofing, Analogdemon, BGC, Bmicomp, Cmdrjameson, DR04, Jogers, John Cardinal, Koavf, Laurapinto, Mattbrundage, Mooco2006, MookieZ, PetSounds, Rich Farmbrough, Santa Claus of the Future, Srsrsr, Swanrizla, THollan, Thewhiteswan9, 8 anonymous edits

Stack-O-Tracks *Source*: http://en.wikipedia.org/w/index.php?oldid=364697538 *Contributors*: Airproofing, BGC, Bmicomp, CanisRufus, Chairman S., Cmdrjameson, Estoy Aquí, Gregory Shantz, Jaydec, Jmw0000, Koavf, PetSounds, Rich Farmbrough, ScudLee, ShelfSkewed, Tassedethe, TheHYPO, Wgfinley, 6 anonymous edits

Stars and Stripes Vol. 1 *Source*: http://en.wikipedia.org/w/index.php?oldid=363749048 *Contributors*: 1zackman, BGC, Bathysphere, Bmicomp, Bobo192, Bryan Derksen, CanisRufus, Catgut, Chairman S., Cmdrjameson, Docob5, Editor14, Eric444, Ghostwords, JeffyJeffyMan2004, Jogers, Koavf, Laurapinto, MajorCrespo, Nach0king, PetSounds, Pseudomonas, Rich Farmbrough, Rothorpe, ScudLee, Somebody in the WWW, Taestell, TenPoundHammer, WODUP, WikiSpaceboy, 15 anonymous edits

Still Cruisin' *Source*: http://en.wikipedia.org/w/index.php?oldid=357542103 *Contributors*: A Knight Who Says Ni, Airproofing, Analogdemon, BGC, Barticus88, Bathysphere, Bmicomp, Bobblewik, Bobo192, Brettalan, Bryan Derksen, CanisRufus, Carefree Highway, Chairman S., Cmdrjameson, Curps, DOHC Holiday, Docob5, DropDeadGorgias, Faulmacca, GassyGuy, Gongshow, Griffles, Hapsiainen, Hyju, Jaydec, Jmw0000, Lexor, LoserTalent, Markaci, Martpol, MegX, Mel Etitis, Monicasdude, MookieZ, Pcg13, PetSounds, Propaniac, Rebecca, Rich Farmbrough, Rjwilmsi, Sahafan, Salamurai, Santa Claus of the Future, ScudLee, StevenHW, Sw2442, Swanrizla, Thenewdeal87, Whotookthatguy, Zone46, 37 anonymous edits

Summer Days (And Summer Nights!!) *Source*: http://en.wikipedia.org/w/index.php?oldid=363685912 *Contributors*: A Knight Who Says Ni, Airproofing, Andrzejbanas, BGC, Bathysphere, Betty kerner, Bmicomp, Bobo192, Bryan Derksen, Camw, CanisRufus, Cbing01, Chairman S., ChrisStupak, Cmdrjameson, Cowbellcity45, Dream out loud, GTBacchus, Gertlex, Hyju, Jaydec, JeffyJeffyMan2004, Jmw0000, Jogers, John M., Jonas Franck, Kevin Forsyth, Koavf, Lord mortekai, M.C. Brown Shoes, Mago266, Marcus Brute, MookieZ, PetSounds, Rich Farmbrough, Rjwilmsi, Roygbiv666, Sahafan, Santa Claus of the Future, Shamrox, Somebody in the WWW, Tangotango, Ufinne, Ulric1313, 54 anonymous edits

Summer in Paradise *Source*: http://en.wikipedia.org/w/index.php?oldid=351626399 *Contributors*: 1zackman, 24ip, A Knight Who Says Ni, Airproofing, Analogdemon, BCKILLa, BGC, Bathysphere, Bmicomp, Bobo192, Brettalan, Bryan Derksen, CanisRufus, Carefree Highway, Chairman S., Cmdrjameson, Djsasso, Dmanning, E-Kartoffel, FuriousFreddy, Ghmyrtle, J Milburn, JeffyJeffyMan2004, Joedeshon, Jogers, Just64helpin, Macg4cubeboy, Mattbrundage, Mel Etitis, Miki-121, MookieZ, Nooby god, PetSounds, Phaota, Rich Farmbrough, Rjwilmsi, Rxdxt, Sahafan, Santa Claus of the Future, ScudLee, Seduisant, Slysplace, Surfmale, Swanrizla, Taestell, TimBentley, UnhandledException, Warpozio, Whotookthatguy, Xihix, 40 anonymous edits

Sunflower *Source*: http://en.wikipedia.org/w/index.php?oldid=361756895 *Contributors*: 2Pac, A Knight Who Says Ni, AKGhetto, Airproofing, Alcuin, BGC, Bathysphere, Betty Kerner, Biograph1985, Bisbis, Bjrbbhaw81, Bluerincon, Bmicomp, Bobo192, Bryan Derksen, Chowbok, Chyll, Cowbellcity45, Curps, Drsmoo, Dunks58, Erogul, Foozao, Gamaliel, Hyju, IonescoIsaRhino, Jiy, Jmw0000, Jogers, Jonas Franck, Macg4cubeboy, Mago266, Mattbrundage, Metstotop333, Monicasdude, MookieZ, Pcg13, PetSounds, Prolvman, Rich Farmbrough, Rigadoun, Rjwilmsi, Roygbiv666, ST47, Sahafan, Santa Claus of the Future, ScudLee, Surfmale, Tassedethe, TenPoundHammer, TheoClarke, Warpozio, Wdfarmer, WikHead, William Bowe, Woohookitty, 185 anonymous edits

Sunshine Dream *Source*: http://en.wikipedia.org/w/index.php?oldid=364509013 *Contributors*: Airproofing, Alcuin, Analogdemon, DR04, Jogers, Koavf, Rich Farmbrough, Sahafan, 2 anonymous edits

Surf's Up *Source*: http://en.wikipedia.org/w/index.php?oldid=353718524 *Contributors*: A Knight Who Says Ni, Airproofing, Applemask, Ary29, BGC, Bathysphere, Beckettwatt, Billwikstrom, Biograph1985, Bisbis, Bluerincon, Bmicomp, Bobo192, Bobyllib, Bryan Derksen, CanisRufus, Chairman S., Chilly Penguin, Chowbok, Clarityfiend, Cowbellcity45, Curps, David S, space nerd, DocWatson42, E-Kartoffel, Esn, Everyking, Faulmacca, Gamaliel, Gtrmp, Heather, Hiphats, Holly25, Hyju, JeffyJeffyMan2004, Jiy, Jmw0000, Jogers, John M., Jonas Franck, Kevin, Kvaks, Light current, M.C. Brown Shoes, MJSkia1, Mago266, Mattisse, Mdumas43073, Micha69, Michael Rogers, Monicasdude, MookieZ, Pcg13, PetSounds, Radiojon, Rgreed, Rich Farmbrough, Rossami, Roygbiv666, Sahafan, Santa Claus of the Future, SlubGlub, SugarKane, Surfmale, TheTruthiness, Twas Now, Tygrrr, Xndr, 124 anonymous edits

Surfer Girl *Source*: http://en.wikipedia.org/w/index.php?oldid=355277212 *Contributors*: A Knight Who Says Ni, Airproofing, Alvis, Analogdemon, Andrzejbanas, Ary29, BGC, Bathysphere, BlueTyson, Bmicomp, Bobo192, Bobyllib, Bryan Derksen, Chairman S., Dsreyn, E-Kartoffel, Feydey, Jaydec, Jiy, Jmw0000, Jogers, John M., Jonas Franck, Jusdafax, LoserTalent, MookieZ, PetSounds, Phaleux, Rich Farmbrough, Roygbiv666, Sahafan, Santa Claus of the Future, ScudLee, Surfmale, TUF-KAT, TheHYPO, Thue, Twsx, Zone46, 32 anonymous edits

Surfin' Safari *Source*: http://en.wikipedia.org/w/index.php?oldid=357539523 *Contributors*: A Knight Who Says Ni, Airproofing, Andrzejbanas, BGC, Bmicomp, Bobo192, Bryan Derksen, Cmdrjameson, Colonies Chris, Curps, Dmeyferth21, Drutt, Dsreyn, E-Kartoffel, Estoy Aquí, Fortdj33, Hqb, Insanity Incarnate, JeffyJeffyMan2004, Jmw0000, Jogers, Jonas Franck, Jukejar, Jusdafax, Ketiltrout, Martpol, Mattbrundage, Monicasdude, MookieZ, Otrfan, PetSounds, Piper108, Rich Farmbrough, Richhoncho, Roygbiv666, Sahafan, Santa Claus of the Future, ScudLee, Shoaler, Stassats, Surfmale, Swanrizla, Szyslak, Thom, Zackfeld52, 48 anonymous edits

Surfin' USA *Source*: http://en.wikipedia.org/w/index.php?oldid=346467529 *Contributors*: A Knight Who Says Ni, Airproofing, Andrzejbanas, Ary29, BGC, Bmicomp, Bobo192, Bryan Derksen, Canadaworker, Chairman S., Cmdrjameson, Dmeyferth21, E-Kartoffel, Econrad, Eric444, JJasper123, Jaydec, JeffyJeffyMan2004, Jmw0000, Jogers, Jusdafax, Karaboom, Kohoutek1138, Labalius, Leopold Stotch, Mark 2000, MookieZ, Mysdaao, PetSounds, Phil Boswell, Pie.er, Pitoutom, R'n'B, Rich Farmbrough, Roygbiv666, Sahafan, Santa Claus of the Future, Surfmale, Swanrizla, Truthanado, Twsx, 49 anonymous edits

Ten Years of Harmony *Source*: http://en.wikipedia.org/w/index.php?oldid=364509896 *Contributors*: Analogdemon, BGC, Bmicomp, Bobo192, CanisRufus, Chairman S., Cmdrjameson, Curps, Dima6, E-Kartoffel, Fayenatic london, Grafen, Hapsiainen, IbLeo, Koavf, Mel Etitis, Monicasdude, MookieZ, PetSounds, Piniricc65, Rich Farmbrough, Santa Claus of the Future, Srsrsr, Swanrizla, TenPoundHammer, Tregoweth, 10 anonymous edits

Ultimate Christmas *Source*: http://en.wikipedia.org/w/index.php?oldid=361629650 *Contributors*: Airproofing, Alcuin, Alvestrand, BGC, Bmicomp, Bobo192, CanisRufus, Chairman S., Cmdrjameson, DerHexer, Jogers, Koavf, Mdumas43073, PetSounds, Rich Farmbrough, ScudLee, Srsrsr, Île flottante, 11 anonymous edits

The Very Best of The Beach Boys *Source*: http://en.wikipedia.org/w/index.php?oldid=364513318 *Contributors*: Akujy, E-Kartoffel, Fratrep, Java13690, Jogers, JuPitEer, Karaboom, Koavf, Michael Devore, Michaelfool, Rothorpe, ShelfSkewed, Warpozio, WikHead, 4 anonymous edits

The Warmth of the Sun *Source*: http://en.wikipedia.org/w/index.php?oldid=364512682 *Contributors*: Airproofing, Anticipation of a New Lover's Arrival, The, BGC, Everyking, Fisherjs, Giraffedata, Karaboom, Koavf, Lotje, Mooco2006, MookieZ, Rob Ruiz Anderson, Santa Claus of the Future, Spellcast, Subwayguy, Swanrizla, Tassedethe, Tjwells, 7 anonymous edits

Wild Honey *Source*: http://en.wikipedia.org/w/index.php?oldid=346468412 *Contributors*: A Knight Who Says Ni, Airproofing, BGC, Bathysphere, Bjones, Bluemask, Bmicomp, Bobo192, Bryan Derksen, CanisRufus, Chairman S., Chilly Penguin, Cmdrjameson, Cowbellcity45, Curps, Dugwiki, E-Kartoffel, Gamaliel, Gogol999, GreatWhiteNortherner, Hyju, J.R. Hercules, Jaydec, JediScougale, JeffyJeffyMan2004, Jfpierce, Jinman, Jiy, Jmw0000, Jogers, John M., Jonas Franck, Knoxville ITA, Mago266, Mikemoto, Mild Bill Hiccup, Monicasdude, MookieZ, Nickflavor, Open2universe, Pcg13, PetSounds, Rich Farmbrough, Roygbiv666, Sahafan, Santa Claus of the Future, Sixsevenfive, Somebody in the WWW, Squids and Chips, Surfmale, Zone46, 45 anonymous edits

409 *Source*: http://en.wikipedia.org/w/index.php?oldid=341463346 *Contributors*: Billdescoteaux, Durova, E-Kartoffel, Eldumpo, GaryDe, Jogers, Kaiba, Kosunen, MarkJablonski, MookieZ, Rich Farmbrough, Richhoncho, Runt, Sahafan, Sb26554, Slysplace, 12 anonymous edits

4th of July *Source*: http://en.wikipedia.org/w/index.php?oldid=346344681 *Contributors*: Black Kite, Cyanolinguophile, Deletion Mutation, Jogers, Juvenile Deletionist, Koavf, Master of Puppets, MookieZ, NuclearWarfare, Rich Farmbrough, Richhoncho, Sahafan, Santa Claus of the Future, Waacstats, 2 anonymous edits

Add Some Music to Your Day *Source*: http://en.wikipedia.org/w/index.php?oldid=336165231 *Contributors*: AyaK, Bobo192, Chowbok, GaryDe, Jogers, Lightmouse, Metstotop333, MookieZ, Pianoman001, Rich Farmbrough, Richhoncho, Sahafan, Suddenly There Is a Valley, TenPoundHammer, 3 anonymous edits

Airplane *Source*: http://en.wikipedia.org/w/index.php?oldid=364619657 *Contributors*: E-Kartoffel, Iansal94, MookieZ, Rich Farmbrough, Richhoncho, Sahafan, Santa Claus of the Future, 2 anonymous edits

All Alone *Source*: http://en.wikipedia.org/w/index.php?oldid=331982632 *Contributors*: MookieZ, Sahafan

All Dressed Up for School *Source*: http://en.wikipedia.org/w/index.php?oldid=344005108 *Contributors*: Bobyllib, Jogers, Koavf, MookieZ, Oo7565, Rich Farmbrough, Richhoncho, Sahafan, 2 anonymous edits

All I Wanna Do *Source*: http://en.wikipedia.org/w/index.php?oldid=343073232 *Contributors*: Ahha3289, John Broughton, Koavf, Mago266, Mattbrundage, MookieZ, Rich Farmbrough, Richhoncho, Sahafan, ShelfSkewed, 3 anonymous edits

All I Want to Do *Source*: http://en.wikipedia.org/w/index.php?oldid=343073374 *Contributors*: Chowbok, Eric444, Jogers, Kaldari, Koavf, Mago266, MookieZ, Richhoncho, Sahafan, ShelfSkewed, Tassedethe, TenPoundHammer, 3 anonymous edits

All Summer Long *Source*: http://en.wikipedia.org/w/index.php?oldid=361422434 *Contributors*: ABF, Euchiasmus, GaryDe, MookieZ, Noneforall, Prudentius, Rich Farmbrough, Richhoncho, Sahafan, Salamurai, Santa Claus of the Future, Schavira, 9 anonymous edits

All This Is That *Source*: http://en.wikipedia.org/w/index.php?oldid=331982963 *Contributors*: Kafziel, Kimchi.sg, Richhoncho, Sahafan, Suddenly There Is a Valley, 4 anonymous edits

Alley Oop *Source*: http://en.wikipedia.org/w/index.php?oldid=357348867 *Contributors*: AarHan3, Brianhenke, Chris Capoccia, Clarityfiend, Dinosauria, Ericorbit, Goustien, Jjmandel, Jorge Stolfi, Justinkrivers, Lithium.plateau, MookieZ, ObtuseAngle, Rich Farmbrough, Sahafan, Santa Claus of the Future, Spiby, TenPoundHammer, True Pagan Warrior, Vchimpanzee, Webetuck, Wolfer68, Xoloz, 7 anonymous edits

Amusement Parks USA *Source*: http://en.wikipedia.org/w/index.php?oldid=348616044 *Contributors*: Djsasso, ESkog, Jaydec, Jogers, Mago266, MookieZ, Rich Farmbrough, Richhoncho, Sahafan, Santa Claus of the Future, Slysplace, 3 anonymous edits

And Your Dream Comes True *Source*: http://en.wikipedia.org/w/index.php?oldid=343452524 *Contributors*: Infracaninophile, Jaydec, Jogers, Mago266, MookieZ, Rich Farmbrough, Richhoncho, Sahafan, Santa Claus of the Future, Stusutcliffe, 1 anonymous edits

Angel Come Home *Source*: http://en.wikipedia.org/w/index.php?oldid=331987690 *Contributors*: Bretonbanquet, Maxshenk, Richhoncho, Sahafan, 1 anonymous edits

Anna Lee, the Healer *Source*: http://en.wikipedia.org/w/index.php?oldid=331988502 *Contributors*: Chowbok, Jogers, Mago266, Richhoncho, Sahafan, ShelfSkewed, 3 anonymous edits

Aren't You Glad *Source*: http://en.wikipedia.org/w/index.php?oldid=332004007 *Contributors*: E-Kartoffel, Richhoncho, Sahafan, 2 anonymous edits

At My Window *Source*: http://en.wikipedia.org/w/index.php?oldid=332103182 *Contributors*: Bobo192, Koavf, MookieZ, Rich Farmbrough, Richhoncho, Sahafan

Baby Blue *Source*: http://en.wikipedia.org/w/index.php?oldid=353913225 *Contributors*: E-Kartoffel, Jogers, Putnam269, Richhoncho, Sahafan, Tassedethe, TenPoundHammer, XxTimberlakexx, 1 anonymous edits

Back Home *Source*: http://en.wikipedia.org/w/index.php?oldid=355359042 *Contributors*: Docob5, JHunterJ, Koavf, Mago266, Mattbr, Ouedbirdwatcher, Richhoncho, Sahafan, Santa Claus of the Future, ShambhalaFestival, Slysplace, Tassedethe, TubularWorld, 1 anonymous edits

The Baker Man *Source*: http://en.wikipedia.org/w/index.php?oldid=333140399 *Contributors*: Koavf, MookieZ, Richhoncho, Sahafan, Slysplace

Ballad of Ole' Betsy *Source*: http://en.wikipedia.org/w/index.php?oldid=332013813 *Contributors*: E-Kartoffel, Franklindonovan, Jogers, Karaboom, Richhoncho, Sahafan, 2 anonymous edits

Barbara *Source*: http://en.wikipedia.org/w/index.php?oldid=331991593 *Contributors*: Jj137, Leofric1, Richhoncho, Sahafan, Waacstats

Barbara Ann *Source*: http://en.wikipedia.org/w/index.php?oldid=363821676 *Contributors*: 0dd1, Aitias, Akujy, BD2412, Bobo192, Cabinessence1, Can't sleep, clown will eat me, Carptrash, Drumgillette, Durova, E-Kartoffel, Endosmk, Erikadianne, Errandir, ForDorothy, GPHemsley, GaryDe, Gimmetrow, Giovannii84, Hoary, Hoplon, Ibbn, IlSoge, Indopug, Insanity Incarnate, J'onn J'onzz, Jaydec, Jesscatena, JustAGal, Kmolnar, Kneebiter42, Koavf, Koncorde, Leowatson, Marcus Brute, Mastaclocksetta, Mattbrundage, Metalman780, Mezigue, Mfishrules, Mooco2006, MookieZ, Nicholas Tan, Peregrine Fisher, Porges, RobinCarmody, Sag1738, Sahafan, Salamurai, Santa Claus of the Future, SeventhSon777, SimpsonDG, Smeagol90, Sonia, Spiby, Tabletop, Tahondi, Tide rolls, Tree Hugger, White 720, WizardOfTheCDrive, ZX81, 91 anonymous edits

Barbie *Source*: http://en.wikipedia.org/w/index.php?oldid=330951391 *Contributors*: Goyington, Jedik801, NuclearWarfare, PamD, Sahafan, Stephenb, 3 anonymous edits

Be Here in the Mornin' *Source*: http://en.wikipedia.org/w/index.php?oldid=332017813 *Contributors*: Chowbok, Jogers, Mago266, Pianoman001, Richhoncho, Sahafan, ShelfSkewed

Be Still *Source*: http://en.wikipedia.org/w/index.php?oldid=340110245 *Contributors*: Cricket02, Ericorbit, Extraordinary Machine, Flappychappy, Jaydec, Jogers, Mago266, Richhoncho, Riderncyc, Sahafan, ShelfSkewed, Steveweiser, Tinton5, 1 anonymous edits

Be True to Your School *Source*: http://en.wikipedia.org/w/index.php?oldid=344376243 *Contributors*: Armyyour, Bobo192, Carptrash, Chowbok, Durova, E-Kartoffel, GaryDe, Jogers, Karaboom, Mago266, Mattbrundage, NHRHS2010, PaladinWhite, Rich Farmbrough, Richhoncho, Sahafan, Sb26554, ScatteredFrog, Skopelos-slim, SolveigNL, Whotookthatguy, WikiJefeDos,

WordyGirl90, Zone46, 10 anonymous edits

Be with Me *Source*: http://en.wikipedia.org/w/index.php?oldid=335858048 *Contributors*: Chowbok, Drt45, Jaydec, Jogers, MookieZ, Rich Farmbrough, Richhoncho, Sahafan, Tassedethe

The Beach Boys Medley *Source*: http://en.wikipedia.org/w/index.php?oldid=343757260 *Contributors*: ChuckCrane, EoGuy, Wolfer68, 2 anonymous edits

Belles of Paris *Source*: http://en.wikipedia.org/w/index.php?oldid=363335613 *Contributors*: Jogers, Richhoncho, Sahafan, Santa Claus of the Future

Bells of Christmas *Source*: http://en.wikipedia.org/w/index.php?oldid=332019100 *Contributors*: Richhoncho, Sahafan

Better Get Back in Bed *Source*: http://en.wikipedia.org/w/index.php?oldid=313412401 *Contributors*: Chowbok, Jogers, Rettetast, Richhoncho, Sahafan

Blue Christmas *Source*: http://en.wikipedia.org/w/index.php?oldid=347435912 *Contributors*: Abog, Academic Challenger, AsherMusic, BKP, Bca71185, Blue*skies*ahead*, Brianhenke, BurnDownBabylon, CambridgeBayWeather, Carl.bunderson, Cason eat world., Chris the speller, Chris83, Coffee, CzechChristian, DKSpencer, Discographer, East718, Epbr123, Eric444, EulerOperator, Fisherjs, Fratrep, GRboss, IdleOz, Iridescent, Izzy007, JJLatWiki, JMyrleFuller, Jogers, Killiondude, Korky Day, Kvetsh, LonesomeMoon, Lurker, Max24, MegX, Mlaffs, Nickellmusic, Oldiesmann, Philip Stevens, Rich Farmbrough, Rob Shanahan, Rocket000, Rwggs, Ryanbstevens, Sahafan, Salamurai, Scottandrewhutchins, TRTX, Talkingbirds, Tassedethe, TenPoundHammer, Thaurisil, Thelegacyoftruth, Thingg, WSteG, Warofdreams, WikHead, Xeno, Zzyzx11, 111 anonymous edits

Blueberry Hill *Source*: http://en.wikipedia.org/w/index.php?oldid=364134259 *Contributors*: 23skidoo, Alansohn, Analogdemon, Aquarius Rising, BRG, BigT2006, Carlossfsu, Chubbles, Darwinek, Derek Parnell, Design, Doczilla, Durova, Eco84, Edelmand, Fishwristwatch, Foffo 93, Hermitage, Howard352, Hyju, Infrogmation, InnocuousPseudonym, IrisKawling, Izzy007, JzG, Marcus Brute, Mark83, MarkBuckles, Mike Selinker, Moochocoogle, Nickellmusic, Paul A, S@lo, ST47, Sahafan, Sky Attacker, Steve Pastor, Tapeworm420, Tassedethe, Trivialist, Ælfgar, 34 anonymous edits

Bluebirds over the Mountain *Source*: http://en.wikipedia.org/w/index.php?oldid=334129146 *Contributors*: Douglasr007, GaryDe, Jogers, Koavf, Mago266, MegX, MookieZ, Nickellmusic, Pianoman001, Sahafan, Samorchard, Santa Claus of the Future, Tassedethe, TenPoundHammer, WikHead, Wolfer68, 2 anonymous edits

Boogie Woodie *Source*: http://en.wikipedia.org/w/index.php?oldid=304850101 *Contributors*: Jafeluv, NHRHS2010, Richhoncho, Sahafan

Break Away *Source*: http://en.wikipedia.org/w/index.php?oldid=349859931 *Contributors*: Analogdemon, Bobo192, DslSWF, Extraordinary Machine, GaryDe, Jaydec, Jennavecia, Jmw0000, Jogers, JonMiller, Mago266, Melsaran, Mike Eder, Mike Halterman, Mild Bill Hiccup, Miss perfect x, Pinirice65, Rich Farmbrough, Richhoncho, Sahafan, Santa Claus of the Future, ShelfSkewed, TenPoundHammer, Trackerseal, Waltloc, William Bowe, 20 anonymous edits

Brian's Back *Source*: http://en.wikipedia.org/w/index.php?oldid=332021450 *Contributors*: Dreamafter, GregorB, Jmw0000, Jrisbara, Richhoncho, Sahafan, 1 anonymous edits

Bull Session with the "Big Daddy" *Source*: http://en.wikipedia.org/w/index.php?oldid=332033909 *Contributors*: Chowbok, Mooco2006, Sahafan, 1 anonymous edits

Busy Doin' Nothin' *Source*: http://en.wikipedia.org/w/index.php?oldid=332035515 *Contributors*: Mago266, Richhoncho, Sahafan, ShelfSkewed, 1 anonymous edits

Cabinessence *Source*: http://en.wikipedia.org/w/index.php?oldid=364146463 *Contributors*: Bobyllib, Glovefish, Gorosaurus, Hiphats, Mago266, Mooco2000, Mooco2006, MookieZ, Nagle, Number87, Richhoncho, Rickbolger, Ridernyc, Sahafan, Tassedethe, Twas Now, Wiki alf, Zone46, 24 anonymous edits

California Calling *Source*: http://en.wikipedia.org/w/index.php?oldid=332038508 *Contributors*: Chowbok, Mooco2006, MookieZ, Richhoncho, Sahafan, Witchwooder, 2 anonymous edits

California Dreamin' *Source*: http://en.wikipedia.org/w/index.php?oldid=364371840 *Contributors*: *drew, AbsoluteDann, Acegikmoq, AjAldous, Ajd, Albrozdude, Aldejerph, Andrewlp1991, Atlasvan, Aurigas, Autiger, Avengerx, Baseball Bugs, Biruitorul, Black Falcon, Bobo192, Bobsmith84, Bonalaw, Bravogolfhotel, Brwombat, Bseker, Carptrash, CesarB, Cezza44, Cgingold, ChKa, Chaddy, Chanlyn, Chininazu12, Citydoctor, Colorfulharp233, ConradPino, DJ Ujuin, Daviedoodle, Dawnseeker2000, Dbl2010, Dekimasu, Djungelurban, Doniago, DuncanHill, Durova, EMTQueen, Eaglizard, Earle Martin, Europe22, Fram, Frecklefoot, GassyGuy, Geni, Giovannii84, Grm wnr, Gurch, Gwguffey, Hucz, Idosedthekoolaid, Impasse, InnocuousPseudonym, Interiot, Invitamia, J 1982, J.T., JavelinTiger, JaymanJohn, Jayteecork, Jmsofia, Jochen Kiene, John Cardinal, Juryen, KingGerbille, KingMorpheus, Klow, Kwiki, Labalius, Lyght, M30W, MHS1976, Malik Shabazz, Manbemel, Mareino, Marius01, Marnanel, Masaruemoto, Matchups, Matthew Fennell, Mattisse, Mercs07, Midnight Madness, Mike Selinker, Milosppf, Miquonranger03, Mooco2006, Moosh88, Morshem, Mr Tan, Mr. Laser Beam, Musicfan9999999, Musik-chris, Nbarth, Nemobius, Neosophist, Nicknitro6969, Nintendude, Nixeagle, OP8, OllieFury, Pashpaw, Pbr2000, Penale52, PhilOak, PhilipBembridge, PhilipO, Putnam269, Raafman, Radon210, Ridesim, Rissole, Rjwilmsi, Rl, Ronbo76, Ronline, Sahafan, SamuelTheGhost, Sandius, Satoshi32, Schlagwerk, Settler14, Sevey13, SidP, Skooma2112, Slinga, Smmurphy, SnapSnap, Stassats, Stikko, TUF-KAT, Tassedethe, Teknocrat123, The Obento Musubi, TheSubtleDoctor, Tinton5, Tony Keen2, Tregoweth, Tritecode, Tsinfandel, Twsx, Ufwuct, Unyoyega, Uwaine, Val1005, Vivalasvegas1907, Voidxor, Warpflyght, Whizkid 0000, Wikid77, Will Beback, Wl219, Woman Man, WordyGirl90, Yorkshiresky, Ziadelgamal, 250 anonymous edits

California Feelin' *Source*: http://en.wikipedia.org/w/index.php?oldid=294811459 *Contributors*: Pixletwin, Richhoncho, Rjwilmsi, Sahafan, ScatteredFrog, 1 anonymous edits

California Girls *Source*: http://en.wikipedia.org/w/index.php?oldid=363301360 *Contributors*: Amcbride, AnonMoos, Azior, Bedient, Black Falcon, Bobo192, Branddobbe, Cammoore, Carptrash, Chanlyn, Cholmes75, CmdrTaco, Cruccone, D lovell, DWaterson, Dale Arnett, Darth Maddolis, Djsasso, Dream out loud, Durova, Evil Monkey, Foot Dragoon, GaryDe, Geelcat, Ghirlandajo, Grutness, Hailfellowwellmet, Holiday56, Hyacinth, Iansal94, InnocuousPseudonym, IronGargoyle, Jackie Stuntmaster, Jaydec, Jesscatena, Jmw0000, John Cardinal, Killing Vector, Lexein, Lint Roll, Llosoc, M35Plus, Mago266, Martarius, Matchups, Metstotop333, Michael93555, Middkylee16, MookieZ, Ndugu, Night Time, Pgaru, PhilipBembridge, Pie.er, Pimlotte, Putnam269, Rbb l181, Rich Farmbrough, Richhoncho, ST47, Sahafan, Santa Claus of the Future, Sintaku, Sjones23, Slysplace, Smmurphy, Steveprutz, Suduser85, Svivian, TMC1982, TUF-KAT, Template namespace initialisation script, TenPoundHammer, TheHYPO, Tiburon, Tinton5, Valtter92, Viriditas, Wl219, Wolfer68, Xnux, Yeff, YeshuaDavid, 63 anonymous edits

California Saga: California *Source*: http://en.wikipedia.org/w/index.php?oldid=334149765 *Contributors*: DslSWF, Emeraude, Famer1, GaryDe, Jogers, Mago266, MookieZ, Rich Farmbrough, Richhoncho, Ridernyc, Sahafan, Santa Claus of the Future, WordyGirl90, 9 anonymous edits

California Saga: The Beaks of Eagles *Source*: http://en.wikipedia.org/w/index.php?oldid=332038585 *Contributors*: Chowbok, Mago266, MookieZ, Richhoncho, Sahafan, Whotookthatguy, 1 anonymous edits

Can't Wait Too Long *Source*: http://en.wikipedia.org/w/index.php?oldid=312099378 *Contributors*: Abstrator, Booyabazooka, Canadaworker, Fleebo, Genev766, Malcolma, Michaelfool, MookieZ, Signalhead, 7 anonymous edits

Car Crazy Cutie *Source*: http://en.wikipedia.org/w/index.php?oldid=353848085 *Contributors*: E-Kartoffel, Karaboom, Richhoncho, Sahafan, ShelfSkewed, 4 anonymous edits

Carl's Big Chance *Source*: http://en.wikipedia.org/w/index.php?oldid=332043695 *Contributors*: Richhoncho, Sahafan, 1 anonymous edits

Caroline, No *Source*: http://en.wikipedia.org/w/index.php?oldid=363478645 *Contributors*: 66richardson, Ary29, Ashley Pomeroy, BD2412, Canadaworker, Chowbok, Djsasso, ElbridgeGerry, Equal, Freshacconci, GaryDe, Glassbreaker5791, Hiphats, John Cardinal, LoserTalent, Mago266, Mattbrundage, MookieZ, Night Time, Nn123645, Oudeis23, Polizzi, Richhoncho, Rigadoun, Roygbiv666, Sahafan, Santa Claus of the Future, Sb26554, Sjones23, SloopJohnB, Slysplace, Spike iron, TKD, Teemu08, Tomp01, Ufinne, Walloon, Zackfeld52, Zone46, 27 anonymous edits

Cassius Love vs. Sonny Wilson *Source*: http://en.wikipedia.org/w/index.php?oldid=329689313 *Contributors*: CloudNine, Koavf, P. S. Burton, PigFlu Oink, Richhoncho, Rocket000, Sahafan, Tentu, Twsx, 1 anonymous edits

A Casual Look *Source*: http://en.wikipedia.org/w/index.php?oldid=262325074 *Contributors*: Koavf, Kukini, Sahafan, Slysplace, 3 anonymous edits

Catch a Wave *Source*: http://en.wikipedia.org/w/index.php?oldid=335509204 *Contributors*: Cherrydude, Chowbok, Jaydec, Jogers, Jusdafax, Mooco2006, MookieZ, Rich Farmbrough, Richhoncho, Rigadoun, Runt, Sahafan, Slysplace, TheHYPO, Tinton5, WJetChao, 7 anonymous edits

Celebrate the News *Source*: http://en.wikipedia.org/w/index.php?oldid=332047290 *Contributors*: Chowbok, Jogers, Richhoncho, Sahafan, ShelfSkewed, Tassedethe, TenPoundHammer, Wolfer68

Chapel of Love *Source*: http://en.wikipedia.org/w/index.php?oldid=347446150 *Contributors*: 2Pac, Debresser, Derek R Bullamore, Design, Durova, Ericorbit, Ghirlandajo, Jogers, Ludmila Pilecka, Mike Selinker, MookieZ, Petepait, Rich Farmbrough, Richhoncho, ST47, Sahafan, Santa Claus of the Future, Slysplace, Steelbeard1, Sunny910910, The JPS, 35 anonymous edits

Cherry, Cherry Coupe *Source*: http://en.wikipedia.org/w/index.php?oldid=332053080 *Contributors*: Karaboom, Richhoncho, Sahafan, 2 anonymous edits

Child of Winter *Source*: http://en.wikipedia.org/w/index.php?oldid=332054492 *Contributors*: Bdknocks, Jmw0000, Jogers, Mattbrundage, Metstotop333, MookieZ, PigFlu Oink, Richhoncho, Sahafan, 5 anonymous edits

Christmas Day *Source*: http://en.wikipedia.org/w/index.php?oldid=343073396 *Contributors*: Americanfreedom, Koavf, Richhoncho, Sahafan, TheWreckingCrew

Christmas Time Is Here Again *Source*: http://en.wikipedia.org/w/index.php?oldid=334043334 *Contributors*: Black Kite, Brettalan, Juvenile Deletionist, Koavf, Oldiesmann, Richhoncho, Sahafan, Salamurai, 6 anonymous edits

Chug-A-Lug *Source*: http://en.wikipedia.org/w/index.php?oldid=343073406 *Contributors*: Koavf, MookieZ, PubliusFL, Richhoncho, Sahafan, TenPoundHammer, Tiburon, Witchwooder, 2 anonymous edits

Cindy, Oh Cindy *Source*: http://en.wikipedia.org/w/index.php?oldid=340458404 *Contributors*: BRG, Calico1947, Durova, Europe22, InnocuousPseudonym, Lillygirl, MookieZ, Sahafan, ShelfSkewed, Slysplace, Wendy2010

Come Go with Me *Source*: http://en.wikipedia.org/w/index.php?oldid=362995745 *Contributors*: Angels4lyfe, Antodav2007, Bbrose10, Betty kerner, BigT2006, Buried Alien, Chowbok, Dawnseeker2000, Elephantissimo, Ghirlandajo, InnocuousPseudonym, NHRHS2010, Naze nani p4ul., Paul20070, Runt, Sahafan, Santa Claus of the Future, Sojambi Pinola, SteinbDJ, Waacstats, ZPM, Zephyrnthesky, 17 anonymous edits

Cool, Cool Water *Source*: http://en.wikipedia.org/w/index.php?oldid=332079475 *Contributors*: Domino42, Durova, EHonkoop, Jaxl, Jmw0000, Jogers, Lightmouse, M.C. Brown Shoes, Mattbrundage, MookieZ, Papa November, PigFlu Oink, Richhoncho, Sahafan, Santa Claus of the Future, Soakologist, Tassedethe, TenPoundHammer, 6 anonymous edits

Cotton Fields *Source*: http://en.wikipedia.org/w/index.php?oldid=357934881 *Contributors*: A Nobody, Abstrator, Affyarmy, AkeHolm, Alabamaxslim, Altenmann, AndyReid56, Angusmclellan, Avinic1, Bobo The Ninja, Bobo192, Cuchullain, Derek R Bullamore, Donkey92, E-Kartoffel, Face, GaryDe, Hifihitman, Hihkite, InnocuousPseudonym, JRP61, Jogers, Kbdank71, Lillygirl, Mago266, Merovingian, MookieZ, Nickellmusic, Pustelnik, Putnam269, R. fiend, Rahulkamath, Rbb l181, Rich Farmbrough, Richhoncho, RobinCarmody, Rockear, SMeeds, Sahafan, Santa Claus of the Future, ShelfSkewed, Stevey7788, Tassedethe, TenPoundHammer, Tom3605, Treybien, Wbkelley, Westbury28, Wolfer68, 64 anonymous edits

Country Air *Source*: http://en.wikipedia.org/w/index.php?oldid=335417007 *Contributors*: E-Kartoffel, Jaydec, Richhoncho, Sahafan

County Fair *Source*: http://en.wikipedia.org/w/index.php?oldid=332802753 *Contributors*: E-Kartoffel, Jogers, MookieZ, Richhoncho, Sahafan, Santa Claus of the Future, Tiburon, Whotookthatguy, Wolfer68, 3 anonymous edits

Crack at Your Love *Source*: http://en.wikipedia.org/w/index.php?oldid=332145149 *Contributors*: Chowbok, GassyGuy, MookieZ, Richhoncho, Sahafan

Cuckoo Clock *Source*: http://en.wikipedia.org/w/index.php?oldid=333046178 *Contributors*: KazakhPol, Ketiltrout, MookieZ, Richhoncho, Sahafan, Slysplace, 1 anonymous edits

Cuddle Up *Source*: http://en.wikipedia.org/w/index.php?oldid=339190894 *Contributors*: AyaK, Clarityfiend, Jogers, Kafziel, Mago266, Metstotop333, Olliyeah, Richhoncho, Sahafan, ShelfSkewed, Woohookitty, 2 anonymous edits

Custom Machine *Source*: http://en.wikipedia.org/w/index.php?oldid=332149781 *Contributors*: GassyGuy, Richhoncho, Sahafan

Dance, Dance, Dance *Source*: http://en.wikipedia.org/w/index.php?oldid=356508557 *Contributors*: Andrzejbanas, Carptrash, EHonkoop, GaryDe, InnocuousPseudonym, Jogers, John Cardinal, Mago266, Mooco2006, MookieZ, Richhoncho, Runt, Sahafan, Sb26554, Slysplace, Tinton5, 6 anonymous edits

Darlin' *Source*: http://en.wikipedia.org/w/index.php?oldid=364187481 *Contributors*: Derekbill, Docob5, Douglasr007, Durova, E-Kartoffel, EHonkoop, Ericorbit, GaryDe, Jogers, Just64helpin, Justinbivona, Koavf, Ktappe, Mago266, MookieZ, Richhoncho, Sahafan, Santa Claus of the Future, Sb26554, WikHead, 15 anonymous edits

A Day in the Life of a Tree *Source*: http://en.wikipedia.org/w/index.php?oldid=336807128 *Contributors*: BananaFiend, Btilm, D6, Jmw0000, Jogers, Koavf, MookieZ, PoprocksCk, Rich Farmbrough, Richhoncho, Sahafan, Spin Boy 11, Tmac380, VBerrini, 8 anonymous edits

Deirdre *Source*: http://en.wikipedia.org/w/index.php?oldid=357935037 *Contributors*: EHonkoop, GraemeL, Jogers, MegX, MookieZ, Pianoman001, Richhoncho, Sahafan, Santa Claus of the Future, Treybien, 7 anonymous edits

Denny's Drums *Source*: http://en.wikipedia.org/w/index.php?oldid=336217033 *Contributors*: MookieZ, P. S. Burton, PigFlu Oink, Radiopathy, Richhoncho, Sahafan, Twsx, 4 anonymous edits

Devoted to You *Source*: http://en.wikipedia.org/w/index.php?oldid=356494066 *Contributors*: BRG, Chowbok, Durova, E-Kartoffel, GassyGuy, Grstain, Jaydec, Jogers, Lightmouse, MookieZ, Rbsjrx, Sahafan, Spiby, TenPoundHammer, Wasted Time R, 5 anonymous edits

Diamond Head *Source*: http://en.wikipedia.org/w/index.php?oldid=343726601 *Contributors*: Artrush, Mago266, Richhoncho, Sahafan, ShelfSkewed, TubularWorld, Ucucha, WikHead, 1 anonymous edits

Ding Dang *Source*: http://en.wikipedia.org/w/index.php?oldid=335257964 *Contributors*: E-Kartoffel, Mago266, Newfraferz87, Richhoncho, Sahafan, 3 anonymous edits

Disney Girls *Source*: http://en.wikipedia.org/w/index.php?oldid=347417609 *Contributors*: Bobyllib, Garion96, GregorB, Hulmem, Lairor, MookieZ, PigFlu Oink, Richhoncho, Sahafan, Timwi, 2 anonymous edits

Do It Again *Source*: http://en.wikipedia.org/w/index.php?oldid=357918057 *Contributors*: Anticipation of a New Lover's Arrival, The, Captain Quirk, Domino42, E-Kartoffel, EEMIV, EHonkoop, Ericorbit, Fenrir2000, GaryDe, GregorB, Iridescent, Jaydec, Jogers, Jpjrocks, Koavf, Lewvalton, Locano, Luschen, Mago266, Mazdapickup89, Mdkats, Metstotop333, MookieZ, NHRHS2010, Rich Farmbrough, Richhoncho, Sahafan, Tassedethe, Thebrid, Thincat, Ungvichian, Wasted Time R, Ynhockey, 10 anonymous edits

Do You Remember? *Source*: http://en.wikipedia.org/w/index.php?oldid=343073432 *Contributors*: Deb, Don1962, Koavf, Milnivri, Richhoncho, Sahafan, 1 anonymous edits

Do You Wanna Dance? *Source*: http://en.wikipedia.org/w/index.php?oldid=355822948 *Contributors*: AveOK, Bashereyre, BirdDog23, BlueMoonlet, Bobo192, Cvanhasselt, DSJH, Durova, E-Kartoffel, Eric444, Ericgoldman, GaryDe, GassyGuy, Giovannii84, Guroadrunner, Hes Quadraphonic, Highwayman91, Hstfreak, Jogers, John Asfukzenski, Julianhall, Kingboyk, Kmell, Mago266, Michaelfool, Mnealon, MookieZ, Oliviahenry, Rray, Sahafan, Salamurai, Santa Claus of the Future, Sb26554, Sk8skanj, Slysplace, Soetermans, Tjmayerinsf, Walloon, Wasted Time R, Wolfer68, Woohookitty, 40 anonymous edits

Don't Back Down *Source*: http://en.wikipedia.org/w/index.php?oldid=345264334 *Contributors*: Aboringstory, Copernicium, Mooco2006, Richhoncho, Sahafan, 4 anonymous edits

Don't Go Near the Water *Source*: http://en.wikipedia.org/w/index.php?oldid=343073486 *Contributors*: Chowbok, Clarityfiend, Jogers, Koavf, MookieZ, PigFlu Oink, Rich Farmbrough, Richhoncho, Ron Ritzman, Sahafan, Santa Claus of the Future, TenPoundHammer, Tresiden, Wehwalt, 9 anonymous edits

Don't Hurt My Little Sister *Source*: http://en.wikipedia.org/w/index.php?oldid=333190401 *Contributors*: MookieZ, PigFlu Oink, Richhoncho, Sahafan, Slysplace

Don't Talk (Put Your Head on My Shoulder) *Source*: http://en.wikipedia.org/w/index.php?oldid=335765602 *Contributors*: Bobo192, Freshacconci, Fugreena, Jogers, Koavf, Mago266, Mattbr, MookieZ, Richhoncho, Rlendog, Rpyle731, Sahafan, Slysplace, Zombiebaron, Zone46, 8 anonymous edits

Don't Worry Baby *Source*: http://en.wikipedia.org/w/index.php?oldid=348033093 *Contributors*: Armyyour, Bobyllib, Conquistador2k6, Durova, Eric444, Fabrictramp, Frankly speaking, Fratrep, Graham87, Jesscatena, Jogers, Karaboom, Longhair, Mardruck, Mattbrundage, MaurizioBochum, MookieZ, Mysdaao, Patriarch, Pie.er, Pinodario, Pkmntrainerred, Q8-falcon, Radiohawk, Rholton, Rich Farmbrough, Richhoncho, Roygbiv666, Sahafan, Supermd, Wolfer68, Woodywoodpeckerthe3rd, Xiner, Zackfeld52, 41 anonymous edits

Drive-In *Source*: http://en.wikipedia.org/w/index.php?oldid=332180611 *Contributors*: Ketiltrout, Richhoncho, Sahafan

The Elements *Source*: http://en.wikipedia.org/w/index.php?oldid=348052309 *Contributors*: Calmypal, Hiphats, Jogers, Koavf, MookieZ, Pentasyllabic, Richhoncho, Sahafan, Santa Claus of the Future, 4 anonymous edits

Endless Harmony *Source*: http://en.wikipedia.org/w/index.php?oldid=360877189 *Contributors*: Jogers, MookieZ, Papa November, Sahafan, Unionsoap, Wolfer68, 2 anonymous edits

Everyone's in Love with You *Source*: http://en.wikipedia.org/w/index.php?oldid=333790932 *Contributors*: BD2412, Design, E-Kartoffel, Jogers, Koavf, Mago266, Mooco2006, Papa November, Richhoncho, Sahafan, Sazabirules, Slysplace, Wolfer68, Woohookitty, 2 anonymous edits

Fall Breaks and Back to Winter (Woody Woodpecker Symphony) *Source*: http://en.wikipedia.org/w/index.php?oldid=348051663 *Contributors*: Bobo192, Chowbok, GassyGuy, Hiphats, Mago266, Nach0king, Richhoncho, Sahafan, Santa Claus of the Future, 2 anonymous edits

Feel Flows *Source*: http://en.wikipedia.org/w/index.php?oldid=353456357 *Contributors*: BD2412, Edenbeast, Kafziel, Lew19, Mbroderick271, MookieZ, PigFlu Oink, Richhoncho, Sahafan, Santa Claus of the Future, Slysplace, Tiburon, 6 anonymous edits

Finders Keepers *Source*: http://en.wikipedia.org/w/index.php?oldid=343073525 *Contributors*: E-Kartoffel, Jogers, Koavf, MookieZ, Richhoncho, Sahafan, Slysplace, 1 anonymous edits

Forever *Source*: http://en.wikipedia.org/w/index.php?oldid=343073944 *Contributors*: Another Believer, Antandrus, Anthonylombardi, Aspects, Docob5, EHonkoop, East 99 187killum, Faulmacca, Icairns, Jaydec, Jmw0000, Jogers, Just64helpin, Koavf, Mago266, MookieZ, Papa November, Richhoncho, Sahafan, Tassedethe, TenPoundHammer, TheHYPO, WAVY 10 Fan, Woohookitty, 25 anonymous edits

Friends *Source*: http://en.wikipedia.org/w/index.php?oldid=343073980 *Contributors*: Artrush, E-Kartoffel, Ericorbit, Jogers, Koavf, Mago266, McB, MegX, PigFlu Oink, Richhoncho, Sahafan, Wolfer68, 2 anonymous edits

Frosty the Snowman *Source*: http://en.wikipedia.org/w/index.php?oldid=363455546 *Contributors*: ***Ria777, 23skidoo, 2over0, AEMoreira042281, Academic Challenger, Accurizer, AlecStewart, Alvis, Andrea105, Andy, Angr, AngrySliver, Apple1013, B, Banana04131, Beano, Bearcat, Bib, Blehfu, Bossyboots221, Brian Kendig, Bwilkins, CR85747, CambridgeBayWeather, Camw, Can't sleep, clown will eat me, Canthusus, Capricorn42, Champ wwe johncena, Chris Capoccia, CiTrusD, Circlejerk1000, Cmdrjameson, Cuchullain, December21st2012Freak, Dfoy, Dfrg.msc, Dkg, Doc Strange, Drake Clawfang, Dumana, Duncan, DuoDeathscyther 02, Eaglizard, Eccentricpurple, Elvenscout742, Enviroboy, Epbr123, Eric444, Everyking, Fastily, Fayenatic london, Foofbun, Fractyl, Fratrep, Fru1tbat, Furrykef, Gaius Cornelius, Gigi head, Gilliam, Glane23, Glow-in-the-Dark Guy, GraemeL, Graham87, Granpuff, Heavens To Betsy, Hiphats, Hotdog1000, Huntster, Ianthegecko, Inferno, Lord of Penguins, Infrogmation, J.delanoy, JACK5555, JMyrleFuller, Jengod, Jmchuff, Joeyinlancaster, Kaibabsquirrel, Kbdank71, Kcordina, Killerbern, Knowledgeum, Krustyandhomer, KsTap, Leo Tomcat, Lowk, Luk, MER-C, MY MOM WONT LET ME EAT AT THE TABLE WITH A SWORD., Maddie!, Mailer diablo, Marek69, MarkGallagher, Masaruemoto, MattieTK, Maxis ftw, Mayumashu, Mike Selinker, Mike Teavee, Mikeewen 19, Mitch keo, Modemac, NHSavage, NawlinWiki, Nickellmusic, Nintendo Maximus, Nixw, NoseNuggets, Oatmeal batman, Ohnoitsjamie, Onondagas, Ougrad1764, Paxse, Peniceman, Pnkrockr, Postdlf, Pyrospirit, Reaper111089, Redrocketboy, Remember, ReverendLogos, Rjd0060, Rtkat3, Sahafan, Samwb123, SaraCSF, Searchme, Shirik, Sky Attacker, Somsack, Srikeit, Stc2999, SteveCrook, Surfeit of palfreys, Tassedethe, Tearsdonttfall, TerraFrost, Theleftorium, Theriusthechronicler, Timer8, Trancer78, Tregoweth, Twoe gappes, Ulric1313, Varitek, Venu62, WOSlinker, Wafulz, Wahkeenah, WarioLoaf, Washburnmav, Whitebox, Wmahan, Wolfman100, Woohookitty, Yellowstone County Girl, Yip1982, Zzyzx11, 259 anonymous edits

Full Sail *Source*: http://en.wikipedia.org/w/index.php?oldid=333272190 *Contributors*: E-Kartoffel, Jogers, MookieZ, Richhoncho, Sahafan

Fun, Fun, Fun *Source*: http://en.wikipedia.org/w/index.php?oldid=346730403 *Contributors*: Alansohn, Andy, AnonMoos, Azior, Bjh21, Bobo192, Carptrash, Cbustapeck, Craig Adams, Derek R Bullamore, Discospinster, Dkorn, Editor99, Fredd the Redd, GaryDe, Ike9898, Jay Firestorm, Jesscatena, Joe Gatt, Kingboyk, Martarius, Metstotop333, Moochocoogle, MookieZ, Murflak, PSIMagnet17, Prodego, Rich Farmbrough, Richhoncho, Roygbiv666, Sahafan, Sango123, Santa Claus of the Future, SchnitzelMannGreek, ShelfSkewed, Smmurphy, TheHYPO, Twsx, Wahoofive, Wolfer68, ZPM, Zone46, 55 anonymous edits

Funky Pretty *Source*: http://en.wikipedia.org/w/index.php?oldid=350560678 *Contributors*: Jogers, Mago266, MookieZ, Richhoncho, Sahafan, Wolfer68, 3 anonymous edits

Games Two Can Play *Source*: http://en.wikipedia.org/w/index.php?oldid=332227186 *Contributors*: Richhoncho, Sahafan

Getcha Back *Source*: http://en.wikipedia.org/w/index.php?oldid=355743061 *Contributors*: AndrewHowse, Clarityfiend, E-Kartoffel, Jogers, MookieZ, Richhoncho, Sahafan, TenPoundHammer, Totophi, Trevor MacInnis, VirtualDelight, Wolfer68, 10 anonymous edits

Gettin' Hungry *Source*: http://en.wikipedia.org/w/index.php?oldid=333317636 *Contributors*: Durova, E-Kartoffel, Jogers, Mago266, Metstotop333, MookieZ, Richhoncho, Ridernyc, Sahafan, Santa Claus of the Future, Wolfer68, 2 anonymous edits

Girl Don't Tell Me *Source*: http://en.wikipedia.org/w/index.php?oldid=349706967 *Contributors*: Bobo192, Cjc13, Durova, E-Kartoffel, Jaydec, Jogers, Mick Earl, Mooco2006, MookieZ, Porges, Raellie, Rbb l181, Richhoncho, Sahafan, Santa Claus of the Future, 11 anonymous edits

The Girl from New York City *Source*: http://en.wikipedia.org/w/index.php?oldid=363083295 *Contributors*: Jaydec, Jogers, Koavf, Kransky, MookieZ, Richhoncho, Sahafan, Slysplace, Whotookthatguy, 3 anonymous edits

Girls on the Beach *Source*: http://en.wikipedia.org/w/index.php?oldid=347001255 *Contributors*: Chowbok, Jogers, Richhoncho, Sahafan, Tinton5, 4 anonymous edits

God Only Knows *Source*: http://en.wikipedia.org/w/index.php?oldid=363959205 *Contributors*: -Anthony-, Andycjp, Another Believer, Aranel, Arcadian, BD2412, BMo2xl, Barnt001, Bobyllib, Briggsy9, Carlossfsu, CmdrTaco, Colmillo, Cyfal, DJ Clayworth, DLA75, Dancomono, DearCatastropheWaitress, Domino42, DropDeadGorgias, Durova, Elaich, Engineer Bob, Equalpants, Ethanepstein, Ezramirez, Firsfron, Freshacconci, Frokor, Fuddle, Gaius Cornelius, Gareth Owen, Garion96, GaryDe, Hornplease, Hulmem, Hushpuckena, Indopug, Jackgill06, James599, Jellypuzzle, Jguk 2, Jmw0000, Jogers, John Cardinal, Jpgordon, Mago266, MarkBuckles, Mattbrundage, Maxkillen, Mayathemayan, McTavidge, Metstotop333, Milton Stanley, Mkortela, MookieZ, Nbk87, Night Time, Nihilumrob, Oanabay04, Otrfan, Paul A, Paulo cavalcanti, Pie.er, Pimlottc, Prince-fan, R. fiend, Richhoncho, Rjwilmsi, Rocket000, RoyFocker, Roygbiv666, RxS, ST47, Sahafan, Santa Claus of the Future, Sarabreak, Sb26554, ScramGravy, Shindo9Hikaru, SilkTork, Sjones23, Slysplace, Smmurphy, Softparade, Sposato, Stuart1000, Supercrazy99, Tbone762, Terminatorr69, That Guy, From That Show!, The monkeyhate, The stuart, TheHYPO, TheHelper91, TheLeopard, TheSubtleDoctor, Tiburon, Timerrill, Tinton5, Trampikey, TrumpetMan202, Valerio79, Viriditas, Vytal, Waqcku, WesleyDodds, WikHead, Williamnilly, Wmahan, YonDemon, Zhmusicgeek, Zone46, 172 anonymous edits

Goin' On *Source*: http://en.wikipedia.org/w/index.php?oldid=332232163 *Contributors*: Jogers, MookieZ, Papa November, Richhoncho, Sahafan, Unionsoap, Wolfer68

Goin' South *Source*: http://en.wikipedia.org/w/index.php?oldid=332232169 *Contributors*: Richhoncho, Sahafan

Good Time *Source*: http://en.wikipedia.org/w/index.php?oldid=343073989 *Contributors*: Koavf, Mago266, MookieZ, Rich Farmbrough, Richhoncho

Good Timin' *Source*: http://en.wikipedia.org/w/index.php?oldid=353913966 *Contributors*: Analogdemon, E-Kartoffel, Jogers, Koavf, Linuxlad, MookieZ, Richhoncho, Sahafan, Tassedethe, Wolfer68, 2 anonymous edits

Good Vibrations *Source*: http://en.wikipedia.org/w/index.php?oldid=364350720 *Contributors*: 23skidoo, 6SJ7, 97198, Alers, Amberrock, AnonMoos, Another Believer, Aoi, Art1991, AxelBoldt, Azumanga1, BGC, BeeArkKey, Big Brother is Watching, Blainster, Bobo192, Bobyllib, C colorado, Carptrash, Chamal N, Chancegordon, Chilly Penguin, Cjeffrey17, CmdrTaco, D-Day, DAMurphy, Dale Arnett, Dapsv, Dfluker, Dick van Aggelen, Domino42, Droll, DropDeadGorgias, Dunks58, Ericorbit, Gaius Cornelius, GassyGuy, Gershwinrb, Giftednumber10, Graham87, Grstain, Gurch, Halo, Hiphats, Ikespirit, Im.a.lumberjack, Indopug, Inter, Iridescent, Jeneral28, Jesscatena, Jgm, Jiy, Jmw0000, Jogers, John Cardinal, Josephabradshaw, Kirby8371, Klippa, Koavf, Kww, Lakeyboy, Lukobe, Lyta79, MadFunk, Madhero88, Madmardigan53, Mago266, Mangobanan, Manoridius, Martarius, MegX, Metstotop333, Michaelas10, Michaelmeltzer1, MookieZ, Mrh30, Nickflavor, Night Time, Nixdorf, No Guru, Number87, PJtP, PRRfan, Petepait, Phatkid56, Piano non troppo, Pie.er, Pitoutom, RL0919, Razorflame, Richhoncho, Rjwilmsi, Roadstaa, Rocket000, Rodhullandemu, Roygbiv666, Rrose Selavy, Rsiapmps, SDC, ST47, Sahafan, Sam Hocevar, SamuraiClinton, Santa Claus of the Future, Sb26554, Sdornan, Seduisant, Seraphim, ShaneCavanaugh, SilkTork, Slowslow, Slysplace, Sublimefan97, T, TakuyaMurata, The monkeyhate, TheFBH, TheHYPO, Themfromspace, Tregoweth, Valerio79, Vince50, Warchef, WesleyDodds, Wiki alf, Willers, Witchwooder, Wolfer68, Woman Man, Wutschwlllm, Xtreambar, Y2kcrazyjoker4, Zeno Gantner, Zone46, Zurairi, 136 anonymous edits

Good to My Baby *Source*: http://en.wikipedia.org/w/index.php?oldid=335769799 *Contributors*: Jaydec, Jogers, Koavf, MookieZ, Mr Stephen, PigFlu Oink, Richhoncho, Sahafan, Slysplace

Got to Know the Woman *Source*: http://en.wikipedia.org/w/index.php?oldid=332029915 *Contributors*: Amalas, David Humphreys, Jogers, Koavf, Mago266, MookieZ, Richhoncho, Sahafan

H. E. L. P. Is on the Way *Source*: http://en.wikipedia.org/w/index.php?oldid=350003990 *Contributors*: EmilyWolff, Jogers, Koavf, Richhoncho, Sahafan, 2 anonymous edits

Had to Phone Ya *Source*: http://en.wikipedia.org/w/index.php?oldid=347989335 *Contributors*: AyaK, Bobo192, Design, E-Kartoffel, Jogers, Koavf, Mago266, Richhoncho, Sahafan, Slysplace, Wolfer68, Woohookitty, 5 anonymous edits

Hang On to Your Ego *Source*: http://en.wikipedia.org/w/index.php?oldid=346119664 *Contributors*: Bradywahl, David Edgar, Jogers, Koavf, Kransky, Richhoncho, Sahafan, Slysplace, Snowolf, 15 anonymous edits

Hawaii *Source*: http://en.wikipedia.org/w/index.php?oldid=331993732 *Contributors*: Bluegum Bill, Geelcat, Mooco2006, Phthoggos, Richhoncho, Sahafan

He Come Down *Source*: http://en.wikipedia.org/w/index.php?oldid=347448371 *Contributors*: Kafziel, MookieZ, Richhoncho, Sahafan, Santa Claus of the Future, 5 anonymous edits

Heads You Win – Tails I Lose *Source*: http://en.wikipedia.org/w/index.php?oldid=335174265 *Contributors*: MookieZ, Richhoncho, Sahafan, Slysplace, 1 anonymous edits

Help Me, Rhonda *Source*: http://en.wikipedia.org/w/index.php?oldid=357540975 *Contributors*: Art1991, Bigjimr, Bobo192, Carptrash, Cherrydude, DLA75, Declark, Djsasso, Drew R. Smith, Durova, GaryDe, Gilliam, Jaydec, Jesscatena, JimVC3, Jogers, John Cardinal, Kevrhon, Koavf, Leopold Stotch, LoserTalent, Lowellian, Mago266, Marcus Brute, Matt Heard, Metstotop333, MookieZ, PL290, Petepait, Rbb l181, Rhondawikigirl, Richhoncho, Rjwilmsi, Sahafan, Santa Claus of the Future, Schmendrick, Slysplace, Smokegreen, Srsrsr, Subwayguy, THollan, TenPoundHammer, TheHYPO, Ufinne, Wasted Time R, Wolfer68, Zntrip, 46 anonymous edits

Here Comes the Night *Source*: http://en.wikipedia.org/w/index.php?oldid=364188081 *Contributors*: ABMDavidson, B.Wind, Bobo192, E-Kartoffel, Jogers, Kazak, Koavf, Lendorien, Mago266, Richhoncho, Sahafan, Santa Claus of the Future, Tassedethe, TorontoDrew, Whotookthatguy, Wolfer68, 4 anonymous edits

Here Today *Source*: http://en.wikipedia.org/w/index.php?oldid=355899312 *Contributors*: Domino42, E-Kartoffel, Freshacconci, Girylive, Jogers, Just64helpin, Koavf, Leopold Stotch, LoserTalent, Mago266, Mattbr, Mooco2006, MookieZ, Paul A, Phyte, PigFlu Oink, Richhoncho, Sahafan, Santa Claus of the Future, Slysplace, Whotookthatguy, Zone46, 7 anonymous edits

Heroes and Villains *Source*: http://en.wikipedia.org/w/index.php?oldid=360958349 *Contributors*: BGC, Bizket, Bobo192, Brianhe, CmdrTaco, Decorativeedison, Deltabeignet, Docob5, Dunks58, Earle Martin, Elleaware, Gaius Cornelius, GaryDe, Gtrmp, Hiphats, Jesscatena, Jmw0000, Jogers, LorenzoB, MSGJ, Mago266, Marcus Brute, MookieZ, Mutt, Nach0king, Nickellmusic, Number87, Pele Merengue, Richhoncho, Rjwilmsi, Rocket000, Rootmoose, Sahafan, Santa Claus of the Future, Seth slackware, Sjones23, Slysplace, SteveO, TheHYPO, Wiki alf, Wolfer68, Zackfeld52, Zone46, 60 anonymous edits

Hey, Little Tomboy *Source*: http://en.wikipedia.org/w/index.php?oldid=362995972 *Contributors*: Jmw0000, Richhoncho, Rjwilmsi, Sahafan, Santa Claus of the Future, 1 anonymous edits

Hold On Dear Brother *Source*: http://en.wikipedia.org/w/index.php?oldid=332000269 *Contributors*: AyaK, Jogers, Kafziel, Koavf, Mago266, MookieZ, Sahafan, ShelfSkewed, WikHead, Wolfer68

Honkin' Down the Highway *Source*: http://en.wikipedia.org/w/index.php?oldid=332001514 *Contributors*: Dmanning, E-Kartoffel, Jaxl, Jogers, Koavf, Mago266, MookieZ, Richhoncho, Sahafan, 6 anonymous edits

Hot Fun in the Summertime *Source*: http://en.wikipedia.org/w/index.php?oldid=364226611 *Contributors*: 2Pac, BigT2006, Dan56, EHonkoop, Engineer Bob, FuriousFreddy, Jogers, John Cardinal, Mike Halterman, Nach0king, Putnam269, Richhoncho, ST47, Sahafan, Sanguinity, Sb26554, Slysplace, Stonemason89, Synchronism, Tinton5, TomFriend08, Whotookthatguy, 15 anonymous edits

How She Boogalooed It *Source*: http://en.wikipedia.org/w/index.php?oldid=294950502 *Contributors*: E-Kartoffel, John M., MookieZ, Richhoncho, Sahafan, Sixsevenfive, Wenili3a, 3 anonymous edits

Hully Gully *Source*: http://en.wikipedia.org/w/index.php?oldid=333613521 *Contributors*: Black Kite, Juvenile Deletionist, Sahafan, Spiby, TheJazzDalek, 1 anonymous edits

Hushabye *Source*: http://en.wikipedia.org/w/index.php?oldid=321785959 *Contributors*: Annabells, Mattisse, Mooco2006, Oldiesmann, Sahafan, Thegoddamnbatman, 21 anonymous edits

I Can Hear Music *Source*: http://en.wikipedia.org/w/index.php?oldid=353110866 *Contributors*: Abstrator, Acélan, Candyfloss, Daisykc, Donny, Durova, Freshacconci, GaryDe, JarlaxleArtemis, Jogers, MookieZ, OlliffeObscurity, RalphRuiz, Ramurf, Richhoncho, Rjwilmsi, Sahafan, Santa Claus of the Future, Sb26554, Sec906, Shyguy1991, Tassedethe, TenPoundHammer, Tiburon, Wolfer68, 14 anonymous edits

I Do *Source*: http://en.wikipedia.org/w/index.php?oldid=329703218 *Contributors*: E-Kartoffel, Hippi ippi, Hraefen, Pedro, Richhoncho, Sahafan, Super Rad!

I Do Love You *Source*: http://en.wikipedia.org/w/index.php?oldid=348782582 *Contributors*: Altenmann, Artrush, Brucelee, InnocuousPseudonym, MookieZ, PiMaster3, Richhoncho, Sahafan, Santa Claus of the Future, Slysplace, Starcheerspeaksnewslostwars, 1 anonymous edits

I Get Around *Source*: http://en.wikipedia.org/w/index.php?oldid=360118248 *Contributors*: Art1991, Bobo192, CalicoCatLover, Captain-tucker, Carptrash, Deelano, Don1962, Dra, E-Kartoffel, Father McKenzie, GaryDe, Gilliam, GregorB, Iridescent, James599, Jesscatena, Johnl, Ka Faraq Gatri, Koavf, License2Kill, Lundgren8, Mago266, Metstotop333, MookieZ, Petepait, Richhoncho, Rjwilmsi, Roygbiv666, Sahafan, Santa Claus of the Future, Sir Grant the Small, Sjones23, Spiby, Tangytoad, Ted87, TheHYPO, Ufinne, Wolfer68, Woodywoodpeckerthe3rd, 40 anonymous edits

I Just Got My Pay *Source*: http://en.wikipedia.org/w/index.php?oldid=332005925 *Contributors*: Richhoncho, Sahafan, 3 anonymous edits

I Just Wasn't Made for These Times *Source*: http://en.wikipedia.org/w/index.php?oldid=360146087 *Contributors*: Bubba hotep, Datadata, Design, Foetusized, Freshacconci, Ghmyrtle, Jesscatena, Jogers, Jtgotsjets, Karada, Koavf, Kralizec!, LightningMan, LoserTalent, Mago266, Marcus Brute, Martarius, MookieZ, Passitivity, Richhoncho, Sahafan, Santa Claus of the Future, Slysplace, Sublimefan97, Zone46, 18 anonymous edits

I Know There's an Answer *Source*: http://en.wikipedia.org/w/index.php?oldid=334534034 *Contributors*: Design, Freshacconci, IonescoIsaRhino, Jehfes, Jogers, Koavf, Kransky, Mago266, Mattbr, Mattbrundage, Mooco2006, MookieZ, Petchboo, Pianoman001, Richhoncho, Sahafan, Schavira, Slysplace, Snowolf, Traxinet, Zone46, 17 anonymous edits

I Love to Say Da-Da *Source*: http://en.wikipedia.org/w/index.php?oldid=334534165 *Contributors*: Chowbok, Hiphats, Minesweeper.007, MookieZ, Number87, Richhoncho, Sahafan, TenPoundHammer, Wiki alf, 1 anonymous edits

(I Saw Santa) Rockin' Around the Christmas Tree *Source*: http://en.wikipedia.org/w/index.php?oldid=364806167 *Contributors*: Alvestrand, Cesium 133, Discospinster, Eeekster, Jogers, Richhoncho, Sahafan, Underneath-it-All, 2 anonymous edits

I Should Have Known Better *Source*: http://en.wikipedia.org/w/index.php?oldid=357145127 *Contributors*: Agahnim, AntoinePancakes, Ashadeofgrey, Bancroftian, Bobblehead, CuriousEric, Democraticmacguitarist, Discographer, Dpr, DykiousMaximus, EdGl, Emperornortonx, Ewlyahoocom, FMAFan1990, Goldom, Ibenjamin, Idols of Mud, Jenmoa, Jogers, John Cardinal, Kingboyk, Koavf, Leolaursen, Martarius, Martpol, Mclay1, Mikeblas, Mooco2006, Nouse4aname, Patthedog, Paulito, Qirex, RL0919, Redwolf24, Richhoncho, Rjwilmsi, RobinCarmody, Sahafan, Schavira, ShelfSkewed, Speedboy Salesman, Spiby, Tassedethe, Velvetron, Vera, Chuck & Dave, Ward3001, Wolfer68, Xholyrelicx, Zone46, 53 anonymous edits

I Wanna Pick You Up *Source*: http://en.wikipedia.org/w/index.php?oldid=332006277 *Contributors*: E-Kartoffel, Richhoncho, Sahafan, 2 anonymous edits

I Was Made to Love Her *Source*: http://en.wikipedia.org/w/index.php?oldid=355563840 *Contributors*: Admc2006, Ary29, Brand s, Bstct, Carlossfsu, ChicJanowicz, Durova, E-Kartoffel, Eucommia, Flowerparty, FuriousFreddy, Jogers, KnowledgeOfSelf, Kww, Light current, Night Time, PJtP, Piotr127, Richhoncho, Sahafan, Seraphim, Starcheerspeaksnewslostwars, Tchernomush, Valerio79, Wiccalrish, 22 anonymous edits

I Went to Sleep *Source*: http://en.wikipedia.org/w/index.php?oldid=335860175 *Contributors*: Jaydec, Jogers, Koavf, MookieZ, Richhoncho, Sahafan, Tassedethe

I'd Love Just Once to See You *Source*: http://en.wikipedia.org/w/index.php?oldid=333092956 *Contributors*: Arthurpewty, E-Kartoffel, Jogers, Koavf, Richhoncho, Sahafan, 2 anonymous edits

I'll Be Home for Christmas *Source*: http://en.wikipedia.org/w/index.php?oldid=364384476 *Contributors*: 1cookiegs2, AlbertSM, All Hallow's Wraith, AndrewHowse, Andy, Arpt, Auntof6, Baberlp, Bib, BravesFan2006, Builtbyanimals, Bwilkins, CambridgeBayWeather, Captain Cornflake, Carl.bunderson, Charlie White, DavidBrooks, Dethme0w, Discographer, Durova, Egorock, Eric444, Gareth E Kegg, Gobonobo, Goofy94101, Hattrem, Hmains, IAngelofFuryI, JaeRae, Johndburger, KevinMeghan, Koavf, LilHelpa, Maxime9232, Nickellmusic, P Carn, Peter2012, Preslethe, Prosperosity, Quentin X, Rdsmith4, Richhoncho, Rjwilmsi, Rosabas, Ryanbstevens, Sahafan, Shaq26, ShelfSkewed, Suddenly There Is a Valley, SyncopatorSyncopator, TIL34, Tassedethe, Thaimissions2006, TubularWorld, Utcursch, Vkennedy, Wmcewenjr, Yip1982, Zephyrnthesky, 71 anonymous edits

I'll Bet He's Nice *Source*: http://en.wikipedia.org/w/index.php?oldid=332006559 *Contributors*: E-Kartoffel, Richhoncho, Sahafan, 4 anonymous edits

I'm Bugged at My Ol' Man *Source*: http://en.wikipedia.org/w/index.php?oldid=335540843 *Contributors*: BGC, Djsasso, Gillyweed, Jaydec, Jogers, Koavf, Mago266, MookieZ, Richhoncho, Ridernyc, Sahafan, 2 anonymous edits

I'm So Lonely *Source*: http://en.wikipedia.org/w/index.php?oldid=332006771 *Contributors*: Coughinink, DslSWF, MookieZ, Richhoncho, Sahafan, Supertigerman, 1 anonymous edits

I'm So Young *Source*: http://en.wikipedia.org/w/index.php?oldid=362632156 *Contributors*: Andrzejbanas, Artrush, Magichands, Runt, Sahafan, Seduisant, 3 anonymous edits

I'm Waiting for the Day *Source*: http://en.wikipedia.org/w/index.php?oldid=361315844 *Contributors*: Freshacconci, JTCBlues, Jogers, Koavf, Kralizec!, Mago266, Mattbr, MookieZ, Richhoncho, Sahafan, Slysplace, Sublimefan97, Zone46, 6 anonymous edits

In My Room *Source*: http://en.wikipedia.org/w/index.php?oldid=359287148 *Contributors*: Bri4daz, Carptrash, D6, Feydey, GaryDe, GassyGuy, Giovannii84, Jesscatena, Jogers, Jusdafax, Keith D, MookieZ, Richhoncho, Rjwilmsi, Roygbiv666, Sahafan, Santa Claus of the Future, ShaneCavanaugh, ShelfSkewed, Thedeepend1, Tjmayerinsf, Trivialist, Ville Siliämaa, Wolfer68, 13 anonymous edits

In the Back of My Mind *Source*: http://en.wikipedia.org/w/index.php?oldid=363491963 *Contributors*: Andrzejbanas, Bhadani, Jaydec, Jogers, Koavf, MookieZ, Richhoncho, Sahafan, 1 anonymous edits

In the Parkin' Lot *Source*: http://en.wikipedia.org/w/index.php?oldid=329703706 *Contributors*: Jogers, Karaboom, Koavf, P. S. Burton, PigFlu Oink, Richhoncho, Sahafan, Twsx

Island Fever *Source*: http://en.wikipedia.org/w/index.php?oldid=332016469 *Contributors*: Bobo192, Einstein145, Godcast, MookieZ, Pichoscosama, Richhoncho, Run4fun, Sahafan, 4 anonymous edits

Island Girl *Source*: http://en.wikipedia.org/w/index.php?oldid=349086013 *Contributors*: Koavf, MookieZ, Richhoncho, Santa Claus of the Future

It's About Time *Source*: http://en.wikipedia.org/w/index.php?oldid=343073771 *Contributors*: Bull-Doser, EHonkoop, JTCBlues, Jogers, Koavf, MJD86, Mago266, MookieZ, Randywombat, Rich Farmbrough, Richhoncho, Sahafan, TenPoundHammer, 1 anonymous edits

It's Gettin' Late *Source*: http://en.wikipedia.org/w/index.php?oldid=333347612 *Contributors*: Artrush, E-Kartoffel, Jogers, LilHelpa, Metstotop333, MookieZ, Richhoncho, Sahafan, Tassedethe, VirtualDelight, 2 anonymous edits

It's Just a Matter of Time *Source*: http://en.wikipedia.org/w/index.php?oldid=332017277 *Contributors*: Briguy52748, E-Kartoffel, MookieZ, PigFlu Oink, Richhoncho, Sahafan, Slysplace, Tassedethe, TenPoundHammer

It's OK *Source*: http://en.wikipedia.org/w/index.php?oldid=343073760 *Contributors*: AyaK, Bobo192, E-Kartoffel, Jogers, Koavf, Mago266, Martin H., Mattbr, Mattisse, Mezaco, Richhoncho, Sahafan, Slysplace, Wolfer68, 1 anonymous edits

It's Over Now *Source*: http://en.wikipedia.org/w/index.php?oldid=347037041 *Contributors*: Blackjays1, Fuhghettaboutit, Mrmusic16, Richhoncho, Sahafan, ShelfSkewed, Yellowstan, 8 anonymous edits

It's a Beautiful Day *Source*: http://en.wikipedia.org/w/index.php?oldid=332241127 *Contributors*: Elonka, Jogers, Koavf, MER-C, MookieZ, Oakshade, Papa November, Richhoncho, Sahafan, Wolfer68, Woodshed

Johnny Carson *Source*: http://en.wikipedia.org/w/index.php?oldid=340671605 *Contributors*: E-Kartoffel, Pianoman001, Richhoncho, Sahafan, Uncle Dick, Wolfer68, 2 anonymous edits

Judy *Source*: http://en.wikipedia.org/w/index.php?oldid=343073755 *Contributors*: D6, Koavf, LilHelpa, Mattbrundage, MookieZ, Richhoncho, Slysplace, 2 anonymous edits

Just Once in My Life *Source*: http://en.wikipedia.org/w/index.php?oldid=335427423 *Contributors*: Durova, GassyGuy, Hellobeatle, Jogers, Kbdank71, Koavf, LA2, Mattbr, Paul20070, Richhoncho, Sahafan, Slysplace, Wolfer68, 2 anonymous edits

Keep an Eye on Summer *Source*: http://en.wikipedia.org/w/index.php?oldid=337043576 *Contributors*: Centrx, D6, Jogers, Koavf, P. S. Burton, PigFlu Oink, Richhoncho, Sahafan, Santa Claus of the Future, Twsx, 2 anonymous edits

Keepin' the Summer Alive *Source*: http://en.wikipedia.org/w/index.php?oldid=332033344 *Contributors*: Jogers, Koavf, Occuli, Richhoncho, Sahafan

Kiss Me, Baby *Source*: http://en.wikipedia.org/w/index.php?oldid=349704998 *Contributors*: Andrzejbanas, Iridescent, Jogers, LilHelpa, MookieZ, Richhoncho, Sahafan, Slysplace, Wolfer68, 3 anonymous edits

Kokomo *Source*: http://en.wikipedia.org/w/index.php?oldid=363414750 *Contributors*: 4twenty42o, Anais82, Angeldeb82, Ardric47, Artrush, Ary29, Atlant, Atropos, Bedford, Bensin, Bluejay Young, Bobo192, Brettalan, C777, Calbaer, Chensiyuan, CmdrTaco, Dajagr, Dale Arnett, Danga, Dannerz, Darrenhusted, December21st2012Freak, DepressedPer, Dmn, Doc Strange, Docob5, Drilnoth, DropDeadGorgias, Eldaran, Ericorbit, Esrever, Europe22, Fortdj33, Fyyer, Gary2863, General Eisenhower, Glickmam, Gongshow, Grutness, IllaZilla, Iridescent, J.R. Hercules, JBellis, JSarek, Jbl1975, John Cardinal, Just64helpin, Killertu, Kokomokid, Larrymep, Lightmouse, Lillygirl, Littlebum2002, Love vigilante, Lucio, Lukobe, Merovingian, Michael Snow, Mishmash8, MookieZ, Nerditron, Night Gyr, Njbob, Nonagonal Spider, Outlanderssc, Paul "The Wall", Paul Magnussen, PaulHanson, Paulisdead, Pimlottc, Qirex, RandomCritic, Rast, Rich Farmbrough, Richhoncho, Rjwilmsi, Roadstaa, Rob T Firefly, Robert Brockway, SDC, Saberwyn, Sahafan, Santa Claus of the Future, Scyker, Seamus the Leprechaun, Sen67, Seven Genres, Statler&Waldorf, Subwayguy, Svivian, Teknocrat123, TenPoundHammer, TheHYPO, TheSmuel, Tiburon, Toddst1, Trilliumz, Tutsuro, Varlaam, Wasted Time R, WesleyDodds, Whiner01, Whotookthatguy, Williamnilly, Yath, Zone46, Zscout370, 135 anonymous edits

Kona Coast *Source*: http://en.wikipedia.org/w/index.php?oldid=362996012 *Contributors*: Chris Capoccia, Mooco2006, Richhoncho, Sahafan, Santa Claus of the Future, Stephenb, Utcursch, 1 anonymous edits

Lady Liberty *Source*: http://en.wikipedia.org/w/index.php?oldid=332049029 *Contributors*: Mooco2006, Paine Ellsworth, Papa November, Richhoncho, Station1, TenPoundHammer, Tiburon, Wolfer68

Lady Lynda *Source*: http://en.wikipedia.org/w/index.php?oldid=345995746 *Contributors*: Ajffrwd, E-Kartoffel, Jogers, MookieZ, Nach0king, Richhoncho, Sahafan, Sjones23, Wolfer68, 8 anonymous edits

Lahaina Aloha *Source*: http://en.wikipedia.org/w/index.php?oldid=332049486 *Contributors*: MookieZ, Richhoncho, Sahafan

Lana *Source*: http://en.wikipedia.org/w/index.php?oldid=332050814 *Contributors*: Jogers, Lanax, MookieZ, Richhoncho, Sahafan, Slysplace, 4 anonymous edits

Land Ahoy *Source*: http://en.wikipedia.org/w/index.php?oldid=333425957 *Contributors*: Bobo192, MookieZ, Richhoncho, Sahafan, Slysplace, 3 anonymous edits

Lavender *Source*: http://en.wikipedia.org/w/index.php?oldid=332054106 *Contributors*: MookieZ, Rubikonchik, Sahafan, Vipers8993, 2 anonymous edits

Leaving This Town *Source*: http://en.wikipedia.org/w/index.php?oldid=341142963 *Contributors*: J'onn J'onzz, Koavf, Mago266, MookieZ, Richhoncho, Sahafan, Skier Dude, 1 anonymous edits

Let Him Run Wild *Source*: http://en.wikipedia.org/w/index.php?oldid=341567434 *Contributors*: Bobyllib, Jaydec, Jogers, Mago266, Metstotop333, Mild Bill Hiccup, RJaguar3, Rbb l181, Richhoncho, Sahafan, Sixsevenfive, Starcheerspeaksnewslostwars, 8 anonymous edits

Let Us Go on This Way *Source*: http://en.wikipedia.org/w/index.php?oldid=332059966 *Contributors*: E-Kartoffel, Koavf, Pianoman001, Richhoncho, Sahafan, Skier Dude

Let the Wind Blow *Source*: http://en.wikipedia.org/w/index.php?oldid=335860789 *Contributors*: E-Kartoffel, Jaydec, Jogers, Koavf, Richhoncho, Sahafan

Let's Go Away for Awhile *Source*: http://en.wikipedia.org/w/index.php?oldid=335601072 *Contributors*: 66richardson, Allynfolksjr, Betty kerner, Design, Domino42, Dunks58, Flewis, Freshacconci, Indopug, Jafeluv, Jeepday, Jogers, Koavf, Kralizec!, Mago266, MookieZ, Paul A, Richhoncho, Sahafan, Shmelsey, Slysplace, Ss112, Sublimefan97, Zone46, 10 anonymous edits

Let's Go Trippin' *Source*: http://en.wikipedia.org/w/index.php?oldid=341583541 *Contributors*: Aranel, Crystallina, D6, Durova, Econrad, Emyr42, Jafeluv, Moochocoogle, MookieZ, Parsa, Qirex, RFBailey, Richhoncho, Sahafan, Sheled Umlal, Slysplace, Starcheerspeaksnewslostwars, Stt13, The stuart, Twsx, Wolfer68, 5 anonymous edits

Let's Put Our Hearts Together *Source*: http://en.wikipedia.org/w/index.php?oldid=332060089 *Contributors*: E-Kartoffel, Richhoncho, Sahafan

Little Bird *Source*: http://en.wikipedia.org/w/index.php?oldid=343073743 *Contributors*: Can't sleep, clown will eat me, E-Kartoffel, Ericorbit, Jaydec, Jogers, Koavf, Mago266, Mattbrundage, MegX, Richhoncho, Ridernyc, Sahafan, Santa Claus of the Future, Seanickaye, ShelfSkewed, Wolfer68, 6 anonymous edits

Little Deuce Coupe *Source*: http://en.wikipedia.org/w/index.php?oldid=342863555 *Contributors*: Bobo192, Bobyllib, Davehi1, Deltabeignet, E-Kartoffel, GaryDe, Jaydec, Jogers, Jusdafax, Kaisershatner, Karaboom, Lightsup55, Mago266, Mattbrundage, MookieZ, Mushroom, Pearle, Qirex, Richhoncho, Sahafan, Santa Claus of the Future, Schroeder74, Slysplace, Spiby, TenPoundHammer, Timvasquez, Tinton5, Wolfer68, 13 anonymous edits

Little Girl *Source*: http://en.wikipedia.org/w/index.php?oldid=333507723 *Contributors*: MookieZ, Sahafan, Slysplace, Tiburon, 2 anonymous edits

The Little Girl I Once Knew *Source*: http://en.wikipedia.org/w/index.php?oldid=342862284 *Contributors*: Abstrator, Bobyllib, Durova, EHonkoop, GaryDe, Jaydec, Mattbrundage, Philnppn, Richhoncho, Sahafan, Santa Claus of the Future, Sb26554, 9 anonymous edits

Little Honda *Source*: http://en.wikipedia.org/w/index.php?oldid=345818371 *Contributors*: Bigjimr, Carptrash, Copernicium, DocteurCosmos, GaryDe, InnocuousPseudonym, Longhair, M.nelson, Maralex334, Mathmannix, Putnam269, Richhoncho, Sahafan, Santa Claus of the Future, Sissyneck, 9 anonymous edits

Little Pad *Source*: http://en.wikipedia.org/w/index.php?oldid=340892733 *Contributors*: Mago266, Richhoncho, Riffic, Sahafan, 2 anonymous edits

Little Saint Nick *Source*: http://en.wikipedia.org/w/index.php?oldid=346993244 *Contributors*: Americanfreedom, Awilgus, Bobo192, Craig Adams, GaryDe, Hraefen, Jogers, Justme89, Mdumas43073, Papa November, Richhoncho, Riverdanceman, Sahafan, Sb26554, Smmurphy, Sorcha, Suddenly There Is a Valley, Vkennedy, Whotookthatguy, Wolfer68, Zoe, Zzyzx11, 13 anonymous edits

Little Surfer Girl *Source*: http://en.wikipedia.org/w/index.php?oldid=332187059 *Contributors*: Bri4daz, Classicrockfan42, Richhoncho, Sahafan, 1 anonymous edits

Livin' with a Heartache *Source*: http://en.wikipedia.org/w/index.php?oldid=333518956 *Contributors*: Jogers, Koavf, Metstotop333, MookieZ, Occuli, Papa November, Richhoncho, Sahafan, Unionsoap, Wolfer68, 2 anonymous edits

Lonely Days *Source*: http://en.wikipedia.org/w/index.php?oldid=358729580 *Contributors*: BigT2006, Durova, ESkog, Ghirlandajo, Hyju, InnocuousPseudonym, Jaydec, Lou72JG, Oanabay04, Rapaa3001, Richhoncho, RobinCarmody, Rogerd, Sahafan, Sd-100, TenPoundHammer, Wolfer68, 5 anonymous edits

Lonely Sea *Source*: http://en.wikipedia.org/w/index.php?oldid=354806740 *Contributors*: Jogers, MookieZ, Richhoncho, Roygbiv666, Sahafan, Slysplace, 2 anonymous edits

Long Promised Road *Source*: http://en.wikipedia.org/w/index.php?oldid=334104161 *Contributors*: Clarityfiend, Durova, Jogers, Kafziel, Mattbrundage, MookieZ, Richhoncho, Sahafan, Santa Claus of the Future, 2 anonymous edits

Lookin' at Tomorrow *Source*: http://en.wikipedia.org/w/index.php?oldid=333461536 *Contributors*: D6, Jogers, Kafziel, Kingboyk, Koavf, MookieZ, Richhoncho, Sahafan

Loop de Loop (Flip Flop Flyin' in an Aeroplane) *Source*: http://en.wikipedia.org/w/index.php?oldid=332413760 *Contributors*: InnocuousPseudonym, Koavf, Putnam269, Richhoncho, Sahafan, Wolfer68

The Lord's Prayer *Source*: http://en.wikipedia.org/w/index.php?oldid=354436132 *Contributors*: Babsdude, Durova, Ericorbit, IHeartAshleigh, InnocuousPseudonym, Jogers, Koavf, Papa November, Sahafan, Spiderdoggy, Wally903, Wolfer68, Zootropic, 6 anonymous edits

Louie Louie *Source*: http://en.wikipedia.org/w/index.php?oldid=364719471 *Contributors*: 121a0012, 1zackman, ACT1, Alansohn, AlexCharyna, Alexbrewer, Andrew Levine, Angusmclellan, Anwiyayoukhanna, Argcar519, Ashley Pomeroy, BD2412, Beachbabydarragh, Benc, Betaeleven, Bgruber, BigT2006, Billdescoteaux, Binary TSO, Bjimba, Blanchardb, Blueminute, Bobblehead, Brian Crawford, Brick Wall, Btyner, CAVincent, Carlossfsu, ChadRLarson, Chadbryant, Charolastra charolo, Chicken0895, Chris Henniker, Chris the speller, Chubbles, Chuckiesdad, Cigarette, Cjmarsicano, Clarityfiend, Clmen, Cofax48, Coneslayer, Craig Adams, Cuyaken, D4g0thur, DBaba, DHN, DJ Clayworth, DMCer, Damaged again, Daniel Case, Danjoman, Dave.Dunford, DaveDixon, David spector, Deke42, Derek R Bullamore, Design, DrRevXyzzy, Dravecky, E-Kartoffel, ESkog, Edcolins, ElectraShore, Esprit15d, Ezeu, FMAFan1990, FlyingPenguins, Foo.themusical, Fortdj33, Frecklefoot, Frschoonover, Gavinatkinson, GaylordHopscotch, Geoduck, Ghmyrtle, Giovanni84, Glennwells, Gogo Dodo, GoingBatty, Gongshow, Gregory T. Glading, Grizzly ripper, Gzornenplatz, H2oldies, Hadal, Haruo, HeretiKc, Heron, HoichitheEarless, Hux, Hyacinth, Ibji, IllaZilla, Im.a.lumberjack, J.H, J.delanoy, Jailerdaemon, Jerry, Kaibabsquirrel, KarlM, Karlhahn, Katr67, Kbdank71, Kdammers, Keraunoscopia, Kittyslasher, Koavf, Krtdive, LFaraone, Lfh, Lilac Soul, LizardJr8, Luiluiely, M.thoriyan, Mapsax, Marcus Brute, Mario777Zelda, Markjoseph125, Markus randall, Martin451, Martpol, Master of Puppets, Mattg82, Matty-chan, Max Schwarz, Mechla, Michael Snow, Mike Rosoft, Mike Selinker, Mike hintze, Miller17CU94, MindstormsKid, Misiekuk, MissingNOOO, Mlaffs, Moochocoogle, MyrddinEmrys, Mysolution10311970, Naniwako, Ncsaint, Nick Dillinger, Niteowlneils, Noozgroop, Nytiend, Oburger, Ortolan88, Oxymoron83, Phil Boswell, Pigman, Pjoef, Q8-falcon, REVOL, Rain1222, Ram sos, Redmegtheavenger, Renaissongsman, Rexter101, Richhoncho, Rjanag, Rnewson, RobinCarmody, Rock15, Rocket000, Rothorpe, Saemikneu, Sahafan, Scooter, Shadowjams, Shocking Blue, ShootFrank, Skomorokh, Smithbcs, Soap, Spellmaster, Staxringold, Stusutcliffe, Surferbeto, TUF-KAT, Tbone, Technopat, TenPoundHammer, The Myst, The fantastic dark, The wub, TheRedPenOfDoom, TheSubtleDoctor, Themindset, Thomengel, Tlatseg, Tony Myers, Travisl, Trivialist, Trontonian, Unicycledude42, Upsiditus, VernKlukas, Verne Equinox, Virginia Dutch, Wafulz, Wereon, Wiki alf, Wolfer68, Yossarian, Zoicon5, 326 anonymous edits

Love Is a Woman *Source*: http://en.wikipedia.org/w/index.php?oldid=332072573 *Contributors*: E-Kartoffel, Koavf, Richhoncho, Sahafan, 1 anonymous edits

Love Surrounds Me *Source*: http://en.wikipedia.org/w/index.php?oldid=359006691 *Contributors*: Bobyllib, E-Kartoffel, Jogers, Richhoncho, Sahafan, Tassedethe, Wolfer68, 2 anonymous edits

Luau *Source*: http://en.wikipedia.org/w/index.php?oldid=332073561 *Contributors*: Bobo192, E-Kartoffel, LoserTalent, MookieZ, Sahafan, 2 anonymous edits

Magic Transistor Radio *Source*: http://en.wikipedia.org/w/index.php?oldid=332080378 *Contributors*: Captadam, Julesd, Richhoncho, Roger Apple, Sahafan

Make It Big *Source*: http://en.wikipedia.org/w/index.php?oldid=332086716 *Contributors*: Richhoncho, Sahafan, 1 anonymous edits

Make It Good *Source*: http://en.wikipedia.org/w/index.php?oldid=343074003 *Contributors*: Holiday56, Kafziel, Koavf, Richhoncho, Sahafan, Santa Claus of the Future

Male Ego *Source*: http://en.wikipedia.org/w/index.php?oldid=332208101 *Contributors*: Clarityfiend, E-Kartoffel, I am Tux, Jogers, MookieZ, Richhoncho, Sahafan, Wolfer68, 2 anonymous edits

Mama Says *Source*: http://en.wikipedia.org/w/index.php?oldid=332089647 *Contributors*: E-Kartoffel, Richhoncho, Sahafan, 2 anonymous edits

The Man with All the Toys *Source*: http://en.wikipedia.org/w/index.php?oldid=338314800 *Contributors*: Americanfreedom, Emeraude, Fisherjs, GaryDe, Iridescent, Jogers, Koavf, MJD86, Mike Selinker, Richhoncho, Sahafan, Sir Bradfordshire, TheWreckingCrew, Wolfer68, 2 anonymous edits

Marcella *Source*: http://en.wikipedia.org/w/index.php?oldid=356465850 *Contributors*: AyaK, Bobo192, Durova, Jogers, KOHLJOE, Mago266, MookieZ, Richhoncho, Sahafan, Santa Claus of the Future, Wolfer68, 5 anonymous edits

Match Point of Our Love *Source*: http://en.wikipedia.org/w/index.php?oldid=363335905 *Contributors*: Richhoncho, Sahafan, Santa Claus of the Future

Maybe I Don't Know *Source*: http://en.wikipedia.org/w/index.php?oldid=332103224 *Contributors*: GassyGuy, MookieZ, Richhoncho, Sahafan, Slysplace

Meant for You *Source*: http://en.wikipedia.org/w/index.php?oldid=332104839 *Contributors*: Jogers, Koavf, Mago266, Richhoncho, Sahafan, ShelfSkewed, 3 anonymous edits

Merry Christmas, Baby *Source*: http://en.wikipedia.org/w/index.php?oldid=338315232 *Contributors*: Egpetersen, Esasus, Richhoncho, Sahafan, Sir Bradfordshire, TheWreckingCrew, Zzyzx11, 3 anonymous edits

Misirlou *Source*: http://en.wikipedia.org/w/index.php?oldid=364139832 *Contributors*: 21655, 3tesas, 404notfound, A Powerful Weakness, Aaronbrick, Abravanel GR, Aizawa Yuuichi, Alanraywiki, Albany NY, Alvis, Amchow78, Amrstation, AndSalX-WWECR, Antrophica, ArthurDenture, BRG, BSveen, Badagnani, Badseed, Bigjimr, Billdescoteaux, BillionSix, Billstewart, CRocka05, Cammoore, CannedLizard, Cat's Tuxedo, Cath sal, Chapultepec, Cherlin, Cholmes75, Ckey13, CyberSkull, Ddrane, DragonflySixtyseven, Dromioofephesus, Drummer8510, Dyfsunctional, Etz Haim, EvKnight13, EvilCouch, F4e.iNC, Fdssdf, Flohrm, FordPrefect42, Gargaj, Geniac, Gokmenf, Golbez, Hairy Dude, Handstu, Hyacinth, Ianb, Ihcoyc, Iustinus, J21, JMyrleFuller, JackMcJiggins, JingaJenga, Josepheh, Jpbrenna, Jpgordon, Just64helpin, Kicking222, Kieff, Kizzuwatna, Kmbear, Kyros, Lordmagnusen, MPD01605, Macrakis, Maggas, Maotx, Martpol, Masem, Matia.gr, Mauls, Mcpusc, MegX, Michael Hardy, Milant, Miskin, Misterlevel, Moochocoogle, Myscrnnm, N. Harmonik, Natsyl, Nehrams2020, Ntsimp, Organizing, Pelister, Philwelch, Phso2, Pmills48, Poiuyt Man, Pollard666, Ptricky, R'n'B, RWyn, Rastapopoulos, Richard Arthur Norton (1958-), Richard Jackson, Richhoncho, Ruby Queen, Ruthfulbarbarity, RyanGerbil10, Rydia, SMC, Sahafan, Schwarzschachtel, Somebodyfamous, Stusutcliffe, Swi4life, Sysin, TShilo12, Tassedethe, The Gnome, The Real Walrus, The.Modificator, Thibbs,

Tubesship, Twingoman, Ubername, Wathiik, Whatsit14, Y2kcrazyjoker4, Yosephus, Zdlo, Zoukboy, Φοίνιξ, 238 anonymous edits

Mona *Source*: http://en.wikipedia.org/w/index.php?oldid=332140084 *Contributors*: E-Kartoffel, Mago266, MookieZ, Rich Farmbrough, Richhoncho, Sahafan, 4 anonymous edits

Moon Dawg *Source*: http://en.wikipedia.org/w/index.php?oldid=330485177 *Contributors*: Alynna Kasmira, DMG413, Eelatom, MookieZ, OlEnglish, Pinkadelica, Sahafan, Santa Claus of the Future, Shapular, Slysplace, Thegamblers, Usien6, 3 anonymous edits

Morning Christmas *Source*: http://en.wikipedia.org/w/index.php?oldid=332143021 *Contributors*: Richhoncho, Sahafan

Mountain of Love *Source*: http://en.wikipedia.org/w/index.php?oldid=352781457 *Contributors*: Briguy52748, Carlossfsu, Carptrash, David829, Download, Eric444, GassyGuy, Jaydec, Mm354200, Nickellmusic, Putnam269, Sahafan, Spiby, TenPoundHammer, Tonyloyals, Umlemmesee, Wasted Time R, 6 anonymous edits

Mt. Vernon and Fairway (Theme) *Source*: http://en.wikipedia.org/w/index.php?oldid=332146423 *Contributors*: Fenwayguy, Koavf, Richhoncho, Sahafan

My Diane *Source*: http://en.wikipedia.org/w/index.php?oldid=362997288 *Contributors*: Bobo192, MookieZ, Pwimageglow, Richhoncho, Sahafan, Santa Claus of the Future, TubularWorld, 4 anonymous edits

The Nearest Faraway Place *Source*: http://en.wikipedia.org/w/index.php?oldid=342996089 *Contributors*: Alcuin, Jafeluv, Jogers, Mago266, MookieZ, Richhoncho, Sahafan, Starcheerspeaksnewslostwars, Tassedethe, 1 anonymous edits

Never Learn Not to Love *Source*: http://en.wikipedia.org/w/index.php?oldid=353032355 *Contributors*: Alzorn, Andrewaskew, Bobo192, Deb, Douglasr007, Dsims209, Freshacconci, InvertedSaint, Jogers, M.C. Brown Shoes, Mago266, Marcus Brute, MegX, Mlsquad, MookieZ, Pearle, Richhoncho, Sahafan, Serpent-A, Super Rad!, Tassedethe, TenPoundHammer, Timcrrill, Trivialist, Wolfer68, Woodenthomas, 21 anonymous edits

The Night Was So Young *Source*: http://en.wikipedia.org/w/index.php?oldid=332170030 *Contributors*: E-Kartoffel, Koavf, Richhoncho, Sahafan

No-Go Showboat *Source*: http://en.wikipedia.org/w/index.php?oldid=332172203 *Contributors*: Karaboom, Richhoncho, Sahafan, 1 anonymous edits

Noble Surfer *Source*: http://en.wikipedia.org/w/index.php?oldid=332172431 *Contributors*: Jogers, MookieZ, Richhoncho, Sahafan, Slysplace, 1 anonymous edits

Oh Darlin' *Source*: http://en.wikipedia.org/w/index.php?oldid=343074015 *Contributors*: E-Kartoffel, Koavf, MookieZ, Richhoncho, Sahafan, Unionsoap, Wikalliz

Ol' Man River *Source*: http://en.wikipedia.org/w/index.php?oldid=363605847 *Contributors*: 1111wtG, Acq3, Alan Canon, Alan Liefting, AlbertSM, Allen rosenthal@msn.com, Aranel, Aspects, Awh, BRG, Bachrach44, Birajghosh, Bogey97, Brwombat, CRKingston, DrSamba, Durova, Ekem, Emoll, FredrikT, FuriousFreddy, Gareth E Kegg, Gohst, Gravidef, Grm wnr, Grstain, Hayford Peirce, Igordebraga, JGKlein, Jam32nd, Jimgleeson, John Wilcox, Jpgordon, JustPhil, Korossyl, Kransky, Krawunsel, Leger, Leopea, MONGO, Mbakkel2, Mdb1370, Mikhailovich, Minglex, Moochocoogle, Nigelquinine, Oatmeal batman, Ondewelle, Pinethicket, Pirxhh, Poccil, Protase, Quebec99, Raven4x4x, SDC, Sahafan, SalomonCeb, Seneca91, Shawn allen@hotmail.com, Smmurphy, SpeedyS, Stephen Burnett, Steven J. Anderson, Subwayguy, TMC1982, Thebine, Thryduulf, Trolls are involved, Tstrobaugh, UltimatePyro, Wikid77, Woohookitty, Zgystardst, 98 anonymous edits

Old Folks at Home *Source*: http://en.wikipedia.org/w/index.php?oldid=362419151 *Contributors*: 0dd1, 23skidoo, ABCD, Adam Keller, Aetzkorn, Amcaja, Baseball Bugs, Bigtop, Bovineboy2008, Caerwine, Carinemily, Ccradio, Cuchullain, Dulcem, Eliot Rosewater, Excirial, Experimental Hobo Infiltration Droid, Facep, Firsfron, Fz0, Gaius Cornelius, Ghmyrtle, Graham87, Hmains, Hoary, Horologium, Hydrargyrum, Infrogmation, Interestingstuffadder, JDG, Jcp1925, Jengod, Jevansen, Jg325, Jimknut, Jmabel, Jogers, Jokestress, Kbdank71, Ketiltrout, Longlivefolkmusic, Luatha, Ludivine, MakeRocketGoNow, Mike Halterman, Mindspillage, Moochocoogle, Neutrality, Nonenmac, Oanabay04, Ogdred, Open2universe, Ortolan88, Pharos, Poccil, RattleMan, Rdsmith4, Renice, Revolución, Rhesusmonkeyboy, Ridinbai, Roadrunner, Rockedaz, SDC, Sahafan, Schrei, Scottandrewhutchins, ShelfSkewed, Sylfred1977, Teiladnam, Tetraminoe, TheCustomOfLife, Tjmayerinsf, Tmol42, Zer0Nin3r, Zscout370, 84 anonymous edits

Only with You *Source*: http://en.wikipedia.org/w/index.php?oldid=343074022 *Contributors*: AyaK, Diego Grez, Ericorbit, Jogers, Koavf, Mago266, MookieZ, Richhoncho, Robsinden, Sahafan, Wolfer68

Our Favorite Recording Sessions *Source*: http://en.wikipedia.org/w/index.php?oldid=332263345 *Contributors*: Sahafan, Santa Claus of the Future, 2 anonymous edits

Our Prayer *Source*: http://en.wikipedia.org/w/index.php?oldid=346740670 *Contributors*: Freakofnurture, Hiphats, Jesscatena, Koavf, Number87, Richhoncho, Sahafan, Santa Claus of the Future, Stusutcliffe, Tassedethe, TheHYPO, Wiki alf, 4 anonymous edits

Our Sweet Love *Source*: http://en.wikipedia.org/w/index.php?oldid=332263420 *Contributors*: MookieZ, Richhoncho, Sahafan, Santa Claus of the Future

Our Team *Source*: http://en.wikipedia.org/w/index.php?oldid=332263428 *Contributors*: Richhoncho, Sahafan

Palisades Park *Source*: http://en.wikipedia.org/w/index.php?oldid=338871447 *Contributors*: Bashereyre, Design, Durova, InnocuousPseudonym, Joniafeliece, Konczewski, Mattbr, MookieZ, Radiohawk, RussBlau, Sahafan, Sisyph, Slysplace, Steelbeard1, Suddenly There Is a Valley, Tjmayerinsf, Wasted Time R, Worc63, 13 anonymous edits

Papa-Oom-Mow-Mow *Source*: http://en.wikipedia.org/w/index.php?oldid=362599151 *Contributors*: Archaeolojae, Bill Detty, CS42, Chris83, Euchiasmus, GaryDe, Jim Bruce, Kikprog, Mugs2109, Piano non troppo, Runt, Sahafan, Seduisant, Sin-man, SoSaysChappy, Spiby, Textus, Thebarbes, 38 anonymous edits

Passing By *Source*: http://en.wikipedia.org/w/index.php?oldid=332267510 *Contributors*: Mago266, Richhoncho, Sahafan, ShelfSkewed

Passing Friend *Source*: http://en.wikipedia.org/w/index.php?oldid=332267516 *Contributors*: Crystallina, InnocuousPseudonym, MookieZ, Sahafan, 2 anonymous edits

Peggy Sue *Source*: http://en.wikipedia.org/w/index.php?oldid=361104869 *Contributors*: 999, Alan Liefting, Antaeus Feldspar, Berek, CLW, Clicketyclack, DragonflySixtyseven, Durova, E-Kartoffel, EHonkoop, Elynnia, Esasus, Georgia guy, Holothurion, HopeSeekr of xMule, Hyacinth, InnocuousPseudonym, Izzy007, Jafeluv, John Vandenberg, Johnny Spasm, Kbdank71, Kuralyov, L4E Monkey, Longhair, MacGyverMagic, Marchelo88, Marcushamblett, Mattisse, Mlaffs, Moochocoogle, Oren0, Ossmann, PTSE, Pennyforth, Q8-falcon, Quuxplusone, Richhoncho, Ricky81682, Rjwilmsi, Sahafan, Salix alba, Sarge55, Seth Whales, Silpol, Smmurphy, TJRC, TheSubtleDoctor, Trivialist, Tunads, Victor Lopes, Wahkeenah, WichitaQ, 71 anonymous edits

Pet Sounds *Source*: http://en.wikipedia.org/w/index.php?oldid=343727483 *Contributors*: Abstrator, Betty kerner, Freshacconci, Ghmyrtle, Glassbreaker5791, Indopug, Jafeluv, Mago266, MookieZ, Richhoncho, Sahafan, Santa Claus of the Future, Sjones23, Srice13, Sublimefan97, Ucucha, WesleyDodds, WikHead, Woohookitty, Zone46, 5 anonymous edits

Pitter Patter *Source*: http://en.wikipedia.org/w/index.php?oldid=363335831 *Contributors*: Billbong1322bong, Dangherous, Metstotop333, Richhoncho, Sahafan, Santa Claus of the Future, Tinsley, Tonywalton, 1 anonymous edits

Please Let Me Wonder *Source*: http://en.wikipedia.org/w/index.php?oldid=334107485 *Contributors*: Andrzejbanas, GaryDe, Jogers, Mago266, MookieZ, Richhoncho, Sahafan, Santa Claus of the Future, Slysplace, Wolfer68, 3 anonymous edits

Pom Pom Play Girl *Source*: http://en.wikipedia.org/w/index.php?oldid=329975940 *Contributors*: P. S. Burton, Richhoncho, Sahafan, Twsx

Punchline *Source*: http://en.wikipedia.org/w/index.php?oldid=340965907 *Contributors*: Richhoncho, Sahafan, 1 anonymous edits

Radio King Dom *Source*: http://en.wikipedia.org/w/index.php?oldid=294834188 *Contributors*: Dialectric, Richhoncho, Sahafan

Remember (Walking in the Sand) *Source*: http://en.wikipedia.org/w/index.php?oldid=364555654 *Contributors*: Abog, Carlossfsu, Ephemeraldog, FutureNJGov, GassyGuy, Genevieve-Tamerlaine, Ghmyrtle, Janadore, Koavf, Larakid, Les woodland, Marcus Brute, Putnam269, Sahafan, Shiai, Wolfer68, 14 anonymous edits

Rock 'n' Roll to the Rescue *Source*: http://en.wikipedia.org/w/index.php?oldid=297428890 *Contributors*: C777, Mattbrundage, Rascaly, Richhoncho, Wolfer68, 7 anonymous edits

Rock and Roll Music *Source*: http://en.wikipedia.org/w/index.php?oldid=356699879 *Contributors*: 23skidoo, 2Pac, Angmering, Aranel, AyaK, Billy Hathorn, Bjones, Bobo192, BrentS, Cammoore, Chris 42, CowboyNeal, CrystalRecords, Democraticmacguitarist, Design, Durova, E-Kartoffel, Edison, George cowie, Georgia guy, GoingBatty, Goldom, Grstain, Hayesgm, Huntster, Ianblair23, InnocuousPseudonym, Iothiania, Jaranda, Jgm, Jogers, John Cardinal, Kaiba, KevinCuddeback, Khoikhoi, Kingboyk, Koavf, MarkBuckles, Mooco2006, MookieZ, N5iln, Nimravus, Otisjimmy1, PEJL, Putnam269, Qirex, Richhoncho, Rmerik, RobinCarmody, Rocket000, ST47, Sahafan, Shirik, Slysplace, The monkeyhate, Thetriangleguy, Wahkeenah, Wolfer68,

Zakco, 46 anonymous edits

The Rocking Surfer *Source*: http://en.wikipedia.org/w/index.php?oldid=332287112 *Contributors*: Billdescoteaux, Bluegum Bill, Koavf, Sahafan

Roll Plymouth Rock *Source*: http://en.wikipedia.org/w/index.php?oldid=342169077 *Contributors*: MookieZ, Richhoncho, Santa Claus of the Future, SoWhy, 1 anonymous edits

Roller Skating Child *Source*: http://en.wikipedia.org/w/index.php?oldid=332260230 *Contributors*: E-Kartoffel, MookieZ, Richhoncho, Sahafan, 1 anonymous edits

Ruby Baby *Source*: http://en.wikipedia.org/w/index.php?oldid=347449145 *Contributors*: 1000Faces, Blutfink, Briguy52748, Carlossfsu, Durova, DéRahier, E-Kartoffel, Eric444, GassyGuy, InnocuousPseudonym, Izzy007, Lullabud, Mattbrundage, Putnam269, Sahafan, TenPoundHammer, Vapidjerk, Wasted Time R, 11 anonymous edits

Sail On, Sailor *Source*: http://en.wikipedia.org/w/index.php?oldid=356467510 *Contributors*: Abstrator, Ajax-and-Achilles, AyaK, Bill Conn, Bobo192, ChrisB, Csutula77, Ctoddv, Dale Arnett, Egpetersen, Gyrofrog, Hiphats, Jesscatena, Jiy, Jogers, Koavf, Lox, Mago266, Martarius, MookieZ, Mrstonky, No Guru, Quentin X, Richhoncho, Robina Fox, SRHPalace, Sahafan, Santa Claus of the Future, Sb26554, Suddenly There Is a Valley, TheHYPO, Timerrill, Walrus655321, 41 anonymous edits

Sail Plane Song *Source*: http://en.wikipedia.org/w/index.php?oldid=361262480 *Contributors*: Calahan4, Richhoncho, Sahafan

Salt Lake City *Source*: http://en.wikipedia.org/w/index.php?oldid=335539119 *Contributors*: Jaydec, Jogers, Meservy, MookieZ, Richhoncho, Rockford1963, Sahafan, Santa Claus of the Future, Slysplace

Santa Ana Winds *Source*: http://en.wikipedia.org/w/index.php?oldid=333371318 *Contributors*: A Nobody, Jogers, Metstotop333, MookieZ, Papa November, Richhoncho, Sahafan, Thehelpfulone, Unionsoap, Wolfer68, 2 anonymous edits

Santa Claus Is Coming to Town *Source*: http://en.wikipedia.org/w/index.php?oldid=358026657 *Contributors*: "D", Alensha, Alium, Andycjp, ArCgon, B Touch, B.Wind, BRG, Bearcat, Beardo, Bellhalla, Bib, Bluestuf, CALR, CambridgeBayWeather, Carl.bunderson, Cdyson37, Chironomia, Chris7cn, Colonies Chris, Dcelano, Deltabeignet, Dethme0w, Eclecticology, Editor510, Eduemoni, El Zoof, Eric444, Esn, Evice, Extraordinary Machine, Firesky, Fratrep, FreakyFlyBry, FredRys, Freshyill, FuriousFreddy, Gameaddict30, Gareth E Kegg, Georgia guy, Getcrunk, Giovannii84, GorillaWarfare, Graham87, Hailey C. Shannon, Hiphats, Hnsampat, Iridescent, Izzy007, J.delanoy, JACK5555, Jackgill06, Janke, Jellyj5, Jimfbleak, Jogers, Joseon, Kbthompson, Lmarbury, LordLiberation, Lucyricardo, Magiciandude, MasterA113, Matthew R Dunn, Mazca, Mbakkel2, Mervyn, Michel565, Mike Selinker, Moochocoogle, Nickellmusic, Pdpp, Phreppen, Pittsburgh Poet, Polo Muncher, Pumpkinbootz, Raine r pierre, RandomStringOfCharacters, Raul654, Realist2, Remember, Ryguy88games, SNIyer12, Sahafan, Schweiwikist, Scorpiusdiamond, ShelfSkewed, Sir Paul, Sliv812, Suddenly There Is a Valley, Sweetie candykim, TenPoundHammer, Tetraedycal, TheLetterM, Thelb4, Tinton5, Tomlizjamal, UnitedStatesian, Unplugging, Ville Siliämaa, WFinch, Wasted Time R, Yip1982, Zzyzx11, 142 anonymous edits

Santa's Beard *Source*: http://en.wikipedia.org/w/index.php?oldid=332268266 *Contributors*: Americanfreedom, Richhoncho, Sahafan, TheWreckingCrew, 1 anonymous edits

School Days *Source*: http://en.wikipedia.org/w/index.php?oldid=363475427 *Contributors*: Ac-dcfreak785, After Midnight, Bretonbanquet, Carlossfsu, Crystallina, Dover 5, Durova, E-Kartoffel, East 99 187killum, Ghmyrtle, IShadowed, Ianblair23, InnocuousPseudonym, Jailbreaker22, JoeSmack, Lisatwo, Michal Nebyla, MookieZ, NJGW, Nouse4aname, Pawnkingthree, Richhoncho, Rothorpe, Sahafan, Sam Blacketer, Starcheerspeaksnewslostwars, Svivian, The Phantom of Wikipedia, Thehelpfulone, Tokek, Tsporr93, Twsx, Unionsoap, Zackarcher, 23 anonymous edits

Sea Cruise *Source*: http://en.wikipedia.org/w/index.php?oldid=350422160 *Contributors*: AjaxSmack, Dcelano, InnocuousPseudonym, Izzy007, Kingboyk, LanceBarber, Mbakkel2, Mild Bill Hiccup, Neelix, Nunquam Dormio, Piano non troppo, Rehevkor, Rothorpe, Sahafan, Shark96z, Wasted Time R, 8 anonymous edits

She Believes in Love Again *Source*: http://en.wikipedia.org/w/index.php?oldid=332294973 *Contributors*: E-Kartoffel, Jogers, Koavf, Mattbrundage, MookieZ, Richhoncho, Sahafan, Tassedethe, Wolfer68, X96lee15, 2 anonymous edits

She Knows Me Too Well *Source*: http://en.wikipedia.org/w/index.php?oldid=349705340 *Contributors*: Andrzejbanas, Chaser, GaryDe, Iridescent, Jogers, Mago266, Mild Bill Hiccup, Pigman, Richhoncho, Sahafan, Surfer4life, TenPoundHammer, 3 anonymous edits

She's Goin' Bald *Source*: http://en.wikipedia.org/w/index.php?oldid=348051558 *Contributors*: Bobo192, Cheekyal, Domino42, Mago266, Richhoncho, Sahafan, Santa Claus of the Future, Thinkerchanger

She's Got Rhythm *Source*: http://en.wikipedia.org/w/index.php?oldid=363335784 *Contributors*: Richhoncho, Sahafan, Santa Claus of the Future, 2 anonymous edits

The Shift *Source*: http://en.wikipedia.org/w/index.php?oldid=333659643 *Contributors*: MookieZ, Richhoncho, Sahafan, Slysplace, 1 anonymous edits

Shut Down *Source*: http://en.wikipedia.org/w/index.php?oldid=343074030 *Contributors*: Billdescoteaux, Jogers, Karaboom, Koavf, Metstotop333, MookieZ, MosheA, NHRHS2010, Richhoncho, Sahafan, Slysplace, Wolfer68, 4 anonymous edits

Shut Down, Part II *Source*: http://en.wikipedia.org/w/index.php?oldid=349693691 *Contributors*: MookieZ, P. S. Burton, Richhoncho, Sahafan, Twsx, 2 anonymous edits

Slip on Through *Source*: http://en.wikipedia.org/w/index.php?oldid=333631142 *Contributors*: Douglasr007, EHonkoop, Fisherjs, Jogers, MJD86, Mago266, MookieZ, Richhoncho, Sahafan, Tassedethe, 1 anonymous edits

Sloop John B *Source*: http://en.wikipedia.org/w/index.php?oldid=361291871 *Contributors*: AMCKen, Brian14leonard, Brighterorange, Bwarx, CPMcE, Carcharoth, Carptrash, Charles Matthews, CharlotteWebb, Cometstyles, Davefish23, Dead-or-Red, Design, DocWatson42, Drastic quench, Earthlyreason, EunuchOmerta, F.E., Figureground, Flominator, Freshacconci, GaryDe, Genelazerman, Gorosaurus, HBKFan75, HDCase, HPRappaport, Hangosloopyjohnb, Hugo999, JJR512, James Penghelly, Jaydec, Jevansen, Jogers, John Cardinal, K1da42, KirbyMaster14, Lemonade51, Lightmouse, LoserTalent, ML5, Mago266, MarcTheStringsPlayer, Marcus Brute, Martarius, Mattbr, Matthew Slater, Mattinbgn, Mild Bill Hiccup, Misterajc, MookieZ, Nick, Night Time, Nikos Bonanos, Paraparanormal, Paul A, Paunaro, Phthoggos, Putnam269, RHaworth, Rjwilmsi, RobinCarmody, Sahafan, Santa Claus of the Future, Sensei48, SidP, Sjones23, Slinga, Slysplace, Stevouk, Sublimefan97, Super Rad!, TauntTheMoose, Thincat, Tzviari, Vera, Chuck & Dave, WikHead, WilliamThweatt, Woohookitty, Work permit, Zone46, 110 anonymous edits

Slow Summer Dancin' (One Summer Night) *Source*: http://en.wikipedia.org/w/index.php?oldid=294952852 *Contributors*: Kukini, Midwest Peace, MookieZ, Richhoncho

Solar System *Source*: http://en.wikipedia.org/w/index.php?oldid=357009888 *Contributors*: E-Kartoffel, Jogers, John Cardinal, Koavf, MacGyverMagic, Mago266, MookieZ, Richhoncho, Ridernyc, Rlendog, Sahafan, Uncle Dick, Wolfer68, 1 anonymous edits

Some of Your Love *Source*: http://en.wikipedia.org/w/index.php?oldid=332295149 *Contributors*: MookieZ, Richhoncho, Sahafan, Unionsoap

Somewhere Near Japan *Source*: http://en.wikipedia.org/w/index.php?oldid=345140388 *Contributors*: Docob5, Lightmouse, MookieZ, Papa November, Richhoncho, Roygbiv666, Shirik, Sixsevenfive, Tassedethe, Tiburon, Tricky Victoria, 2 anonymous edits

Soulful Old Man Sunshine *Source*: http://en.wikipedia.org/w/index.php?oldid=332297254 *Contributors*: Richhoncho, Sahafan

Spirit of America *Source*: http://en.wikipedia.org/w/index.php?oldid=332236804 *Contributors*: Emoscopes, Karaboom, Richhoncho, Sahafan

Steamboat *Source*: http://en.wikipedia.org/w/index.php?oldid=332242259 *Contributors*: Atavi, Captain Bird, Mago266, MookieZ, Richhoncho, Sahafan, Woohookitty

Still Cruisin' *Source*: http://en.wikipedia.org/w/index.php?oldid=345112436 *Contributors*: Docob5, MookieZ, Richhoncho, Roygbiv666, TenPoundHammer, Tiburon, 1 anonymous edits

Still I Dream of It *Source*: http://en.wikipedia.org/w/index.php?oldid=332243280 *Contributors*: DiggyG, Richhoncho, Sahafan, Skagedal, 3 anonymous edits

Still Surfin' *Source*: http://en.wikipedia.org/w/index.php?oldid=332243306 *Contributors*: MookieZ, Richhoncho, Sahafan, 2 anonymous edits

Stoked *Source*: http://en.wikipedia.org/w/index.php?oldid=343727708 *Contributors*: Jogers, MookieZ, Richhoncho, Sahafan, Slysplace, Ucucha, 1 anonymous edits

Strange Things Happen *Source*: http://en.wikipedia.org/w/index.php?oldid=332244137 *Contributors*: Anticipation of a New Lover's Arrival, The, Artrush, Bobo192, Broxyibrox, MookieZ, Philip Trueman, Richhoncho, Sahafan, 2 anonymous edits

Student Demonstration Time *Source*: http://en.wikipedia.org/w/index.php?oldid=341899440 *Contributors*: Badagnani, Bluegum Bill, Bobyllib, Centrx, D6, Gamerpanda, Mago266, Mattisse, MookieZ, PigFlu Oink, Richhoncho, Sahafan, 3 anonymous edits

Sumahama *Source*: http://en.wikipedia.org/w/index.php?oldid=332298970 *Contributors*: Jogers, Mike Eder, Papa November, Richhoncho, Sahafan, Tiburon, TorontoDrew, Wolfer68, 1 anonymous edits

Summer Means New Love *Source*: http://en.wikipedia.org/w/index.php?oldid=363479039 *Contributors*: Djsasso, Gillyweed, Jaydec, Jogers, Koavf, MookieZ, NHRHS2010, Rbb l181, Richhoncho, Sahafan, Scchipli, Slysplace, 3 anonymous edits

Summer in Paradise *Source*: http://en.wikipedia.org/w/index.php?oldid=332298843 *Contributors*: Bobo192, Jogers, Koavf, Richhoncho, Sahafan, 1 anonymous edits

Summer of Love *Source*: http://en.wikipedia.org/w/index.php?oldid=332298772 *Contributors*: Holiday56, MookieZ, Rettetast, Richhoncho, Sahafan, 2 anonymous edits

Summertime Blues *Source*: http://en.wikipedia.org/w/index.php?oldid=362916007 *Contributors*: Alana Smithy, Alphachimp, AnonMoos, Antheii, Argylexsoul, Ashley Pomeroy, Bevo, BigT2006, Bmpower, Bobo192, CS42, Caldorwards4, Canadaolympic989, CanisRufus, Carptrash, Clarahamster, Coma1976, Crimson123, Dino, Durga2112, Durova, E-Kartoffel, Eagle eyes, Eric444, Evanreyes, Funeral, GSequoia, GassyGuy, Geat, Gershom, GoingBatty, Gtreisman, HairyWombat, Hollycochran, Indopug, JYelof, Jam425, James Epstein, Jc1033, Jukejar, Justme89, K1darkknight, Kaiketsu, Kenyon, Konczewski, LarrisM, Leftfoot69, Leger, Leonidas 480E, LonesomeMoon, Marcus Brute, Martin4647, Martpol, Matt d84, MegX, Metnever, Metsman, Mick Jones, Mike Selinker, Mjm mn, Moochocoogle, Mulad, Nach0king, Nahallac Silverwinds, Nintendude, Nitrofest, Nuclearlehder, Number87, Oakster, Ortolan88, Publichall, Pxma, Qirex, RHolecko, RafaAzevedo, Raskalx, RedWolf, Retromaniac, Richhoncho, Rock'N'More, Rockgenre, Rockyrococco, Rolling, ST47, Sahafan, Saltywood, Sb26554, ShelfSkewed, Siege72, Slowtiger, Spalding, TenPoundHammer, The Rogue Penguin, TheSubtleDoctor, Thegeneralpublic, Thryduulf, Tim Long, Tinton5, Tolivero, Travelling Tragition, Ume, Unschool, Wasted Time R, WesleyDodds, WhiteHatLurker, Wolfer68, Wutsje, Xnux, Z00ropean, 163 anonymous edits

Sunshine *Source*: http://en.wikipedia.org/w/index.php?oldid=343074392 *Contributors*: Bibhu heaven 123, Koavf, MookieZ, Richhoncho, Sahafan, ShelfSkewed, Unionsoap, 1 anonymous edits

Surf Jam *Source*: http://en.wikipedia.org/w/index.php?oldid=332271299 *Contributors*: Jafeluv, Jogers, Richhoncho, Sahafan

Surfer Girl *Source*: http://en.wikipedia.org/w/index.php?oldid=344376583 *Contributors*: Bobo192, Carptrash, GaryDe, Giovannii84, Jesscatena, Jogers, MookieZ, Rich Farmbrough, Richhoncho, Sahafan, Sam Fike, TheHYPO, Wolfer68, 13 anonymous edits

The Surfer Moon *Source*: http://en.wikipedia.org/w/index.php?oldid=333669732 *Contributors*: MookieZ, Richhoncho, Sahafan, Slysplace, 5 anonymous edits

Surfin' *Source*: http://en.wikipedia.org/w/index.php?oldid=345134463 *Contributors*: Armyyour, Bobo192, E-Kartoffel, Jaydec, Jogers, LilHelpa, LoserTalent, Mattbrundage, MookieZ, Redspork02, Richhoncho, Rjwilmsi, Sahafan, Santa Claus of the Future, Shirik, Sixsevenfive, Tiburon, 14 anonymous edits

Surfin' Safari *Source*: http://en.wikipedia.org/w/index.php?oldid=341477488 *Contributors*: Armyyour, Bashereyre, E-Kartoffel, GaryDe, Giovannii84, Jogers, Jusdafax, MookieZ, Richhoncho, Runt, Sahafan, Santa Claus of the Future, Sb26554, Tiburon, Wolfer68, Zone46, 11 anonymous edits

Surfin' USA *Source*: http://en.wikipedia.org/w/index.php?oldid=354789480 *Contributors*: 0dd1, Aeluwas, Armyyour, Artrush, Boffy b, Carptrash, Dsutton, E-Kartoffel, Erasrhed, Evanreyes, FrancoGG, Fratrep, Furrykef, GaryDe, Gilliam, Gogo Dodo, Insanity Incarnate, J 1982, Jeff79, Jjb, Jjmcspooh, Jogers, Jusdafax, Martarius, Matt Heard, Mattbrundage, Metstotop333, Milosppf, MookieZ, Pitoutom, Rich Farmbrough, Richhoncho, Roman Dog Bird, Sahafan, Samuel Sol, Santa Claus of the Future, Scratchdawg, SigmaEpsilon, Slysplace, Surfin' USA (song), TheContralto, TheHYPO, Thrane, Tim Long, Wolfer68, 49 anonymous edits

Surf's Up *Source*: http://en.wikipedia.org/w/index.php?oldid=346740225 *Contributors*: AyaK, BananaFiend, Bobo192, Clarityfiend, Doodledoo, Dunks58, Durova, GregorB, Hiphats, Impy4ever, Jesscatena, Jogers, Lairor, LilHelpa, Mago266, Mattbrundage, Michaelfool, Mjperen, MookieZ, Number87, Percenttwenty, Phthoggos, Pianoman001, Richhoncho, Rjwilmsi, Sahafan, Santa Claus of the Future, SloopJohnB, Stefan, TenPoundHammer, Themightyquill, Wiki alf, 35 anonymous edits

Susie Cincinnati *Source*: http://en.wikipedia.org/w/index.php?oldid=345134586 *Contributors*: Abstrator, AyaK, Bobo192, E-Kartoffel, Jmw0000, Jogers, Mago266, MookieZ, Richhoncho, Sahafan, Shirik, Slysplace, 8 anonymous edits

Sweet Sunday *Source*: http://en.wikipedia.org/w/index.php?oldid=362996540 *Contributors*: Dialectric, Richhoncho, Sahafan, Santa Claus of the Future

Take a Load Off Your Feet *Source*: http://en.wikipedia.org/w/index.php?oldid=333676229 *Contributors*: BananaFiend, Koavf, MookieZ, PigFlu Oink, Richhoncho, Rjwilmsi, Sahafan, Santa Claus of the Future, Twas Now, 3 anonymous edits

Talk to Me *Source*: http://en.wikipedia.org/w/index.php?oldid=351228026 *Contributors*: Carlossfsu, E-Kartoffel, Koavf, Mattbr, Richhoncho, Sahafan, ShelfSkewed, Slysplace, 2 anonymous edits

Tears in the Morning *Source*: http://en.wikipedia.org/w/index.php?oldid=313262389 *Contributors*: Douglasr007, EHonkoop, Jogers, Koavf, MJD86, Mago266, Metstotop333, MookieZ, PigFlu Oink, Richhoncho, Sahafan, Tassedethe, TenPoundHammer, 13 anonymous edits

Tell Me Why *Source*: http://en.wikipedia.org/w/index.php?oldid=357191168 *Contributors*: Ashadeofgrey, BRG, Bancroftian, Bobyllib, BostonMA, Bryan Earnest, Cammoore, Chris 42, CuriousEric, Das Ansehnlisch, Democraticmacguitarist, DykiousMaximus, Emperornortonx, Goldom, John Cardinal, JohnInDC, Kaiba, KeithD, Klippdass, Lou72JG, Matthew Fennell, Nareek, Patthedog, Qirex, Redwolf24, Richhoncho, Sahafan, Seb35, Sebeat, ShelfSkewed, Signinstranger, Speedboy Salesman, Spiby, Surachit, TheOnlyOne12, Velvetron, Vera, Chuck & Dave, Waggers, Xiglofre, 14 anonymous edits

Ten Little Indians *Source*: http://en.wikipedia.org/w/index.php?oldid=343074390 *Contributors*: Bobo192, E-Kartoffel, GaryDe, Iain99, Jogers, Koavf, MookieZ, Richhoncho, Sahafan, Slysplace, Tiburon, Triwbe, Wolfer68, Yamamoto Ichiro, 16 anonymous edits

That Same Song *Source*: http://en.wikipedia.org/w/index.php?oldid=332233806 *Contributors*: Design, Mattbr, Richhoncho, Sahafan, Slysplace, 2 anonymous edits

That's Not Me *Source*: http://en.wikipedia.org/w/index.php?oldid=347087657 *Contributors*: Betty kerner, JTCBlues, John of Reading, M.C. Brown Shoes, Mago266, Mattbr, Mdumas43073, Mild Bill Hiccup, MookieZ, Richhoncho, Rlendog, Sahafan, Slysplace, The Guilty Undertaker, Trilliumz, Zone46, 8 anonymous edits

Then I Kissed Her *Source*: http://en.wikipedia.org/w/index.php?oldid=358053905 *Contributors*: Artrush, Barneyboot, Djsasso, EHonkoop, Eggman64, GaryDe, HeWhoLifeCanNoLongerSurprise, Jaydec, Jogers, Matt Heard, Mattbrundage, MookieZ, Mrceleb2007, Rbb l181, Richhoncho, Sahafan, Santa Claus of the Future, Slysplace, 6 anonymous edits

There's No Other (Like My Baby) *Source*: http://en.wikipedia.org/w/index.php?oldid=345138274 *Contributors*: Richhoncho, Rothorpe, Sahafan, Shirik, Spiby, 5 anonymous edits

A Thing or Two *Source*: http://en.wikipedia.org/w/index.php?oldid=332224807 *Contributors*: Chowbok, E-Kartoffel, Jogers, Koavf, Richhoncho, Sahafan

This Car of Mine *Source*: http://en.wikipedia.org/w/index.php?oldid=329985349 *Contributors*: Jogers, P. S. Burton, PigFlu Oink, Richhoncho, Sahafan, Twsx

This Whole World *Source*: http://en.wikipedia.org/w/index.php?oldid=342395332 *Contributors*: EHonkoop, Jogers, Mago266, Metstotop333, Mooco2006, MookieZ, Papa November, Richhoncho, Sahafan, Tassedethe, 3 anonymous edits

'Til I Die *Source*: http://en.wikipedia.org/w/index.php?oldid=352517419 *Contributors*: Bobo192, Clarityfiend, Jogers, Ling.Nut, Martarius, Marturo54, Meisterkoch, Merovingian, MookieZ, Mumby, Papa November, Rich Farmbrough, Richhoncho, Rjwilmsi, Sahafan, SunCreator, Tassedethe, TheHYPO, 16 anonymous edits

Time to Get Alone *Source*: http://en.wikipedia.org/w/index.php?oldid=335859272 *Contributors*: Jaydec, Jogers, Koavf, MookieZ, Pianoman001, Richhoncho, Sahafan, Tassedethe, 4 anonymous edits

A Time to Live in Dreams *Source*: http://en.wikipedia.org/w/index.php?oldid=353308930 *Contributors*: Chowbok, Domino42, Jaydec, Jogers, Koavf, LoserTalent, Richhoncho, Sahafan, 3 anonymous edits

The Times They Are a-Changin' *Source*: http://en.wikipedia.org/w/index.php?oldid=363784895 *Contributors*: 66richardson, AkeHolm, Alanraywiki, Alexignatiou, Allreet, Ary29, Bdude, Berenlazarus, Biruitorul, Blah3, Cfortunato, Chironomia, Colin MacLaurin, Crito2161, Dawson1066, Denito19, Duke nut, E-Kartoffel, Elvrum, GassyGuy, Geg, Gimboid13, GoingBatty, Gprateek, Hrududu, I.M.S., INDREAMS, J 1982, James Epstein, John Cardinal, Kirjtc2, Koavf, Kohoutek1138, Kollision, Kuralyov, Llewelyn MT, Marcel flaubert, Mick gold, Moormand, Mrlopez2681, Ode2joy, Q8-falcon, Rajah, Richhoncho, Rjwilmsi, Robertsteadman, Royboycrashfan, SECProto, Sahafan, Signinstranger, Sillyfolkboy, Spiby, Steamboat28, Stephan Leeds, Thatother1dude, Tmanflys, Tomásomaonaigh, Uglinessman, Weeliljimmy, Wellesradio, WikiCroon, WikipedianMarlith, Writtenright, 85 anonymous edits

TM Song *Source*: http://en.wikipedia.org/w/index.php?oldid=333864572 *Contributors*: AyaK, Bigweeboy, Bobo192, Design, E-Kartoffel, Jogers, Keithbob, Koavf, Mattbr, Mooco2006, MookieZ, Richhoncho, Sahafan, Slysplace, Ss112, Wolfer68, 2 anonymous edits

The Trader *Source*: http://en.wikipedia.org/w/index.php?oldid=332226240 *Contributors*: Mago266, MookieZ, Richhoncho, Sahafan, 1 anonymous edits

Transcendental Meditation *Source*: http://en.wikipedia.org/w/index.php?oldid=332393405 *Contributors*: Keithbob, Koavf, Mago266, Richhoncho, Sahafan, ShelfSkewed, 1 anonymous edits

Vegetables *Source*: http://en.wikipedia.org/w/index.php?oldid=352475047 *Contributors*: Aaronite, Ahkond, Barek, Bobyllib, BurnDownBabylon, Calmypal, CapitalQ, Crazynas, Domino42, E-Kartoffel, Jan.Smolik, Jaydec, Konczewski, Mago266, MookieZ, Neilka, Nickflavor, Number87, Proofreader77, Richhoncho, Rigadoun, Sahafan, Walter Görlitz, Wiki alf, 16 anonymous edits

Wake the World *Source*: http://en.wikipedia.org/w/index.php?oldid=341796354 *Contributors*: Douglasr007, Ericorbit, Jogers, Mago266, MegX, Metstotop333, Richhoncho, Sahafan, ShelfSkewed, Starcheerspeaksnewslostwars, WikHead, 1 anonymous edits

The Warmth of the Sun *Source*: http://en.wikipedia.org/w/index.php?oldid=345826268 *Contributors*: 8 Ball Corner Pocket, BGC, Danjoshmass, GaryDe, Jesscatena, Jogers, Koavf, Michaelfool, MookieZ, Peege, Richhoncho, RoryS89, Roygbiv666, Sahafan, Santa Claus of the Future, Stevie2810, Tbonnie, Wolfer68, Zoe, Zondi, 15 anonymous edits

We Three Kings *Source*: http://en.wikipedia.org/w/index.php?oldid=361138337 *Contributors*: A Powerful Weakness, Alltheusernamesiwantedwerealreadyinuse, Amphytrite, Andrei Iosifovich, Angmering, Bib, Caldorwards4, CambridgeBayWeather, Chironomia, Clariosophic, Cmaryon, Cricket02, Crumley, Daleks Rule, David.Mestel, Deaghaidhcjjd, Douglas Seth Gordon, Earfetish1, Ectomorpheus, Ed g2s, Eric444, Everwyck, Feline Hymnic, Felixalleycat, Firefox2023, Georgia guy, Gongshow, Graeme Bartlett, HowardBerry, Hutcheson, Implovious, JCO312, JHunterJ, Jbshryne, Lightsup55, Lozarithm, Lucid, Man vyi, Marcus Brute, Maris stella, Metatron's Cube, Miss Pippa, Montrealais, Mwanner, Nickellmusic, Odin of Trondheim, Phil Boswell, Pne, PollyNim, Postdlf, Proxy User, Quadell, Randomtime, RickK, Rockhopper10r, Rtiztik, SNIyer12, Sahafan, Samw, Shaile, Srhanna, Srleffler, Stanselmdoc, The JumpStation, The Watusi, Travis Wells, Twsx, Vkennedy, Wahoofive, Walloon, Wtstanford, Yip1982, Zzyzx11, 120 anonymous edits

We'll Run Away *Source*: http://en.wikipedia.org/w/index.php?oldid=332184540 *Contributors*: Richhoncho, Sahafan, 1 anonymous edits

We're Together Again *Source*: http://en.wikipedia.org/w/index.php?oldid=332184505 *Contributors*: Richhoncho, Sahafan, ShelfSkewed, Tassedethe, 1 anonymous edits

Wendy *Source*: http://en.wikipedia.org/w/index.php?oldid=335770182 *Contributors*: Copernicium, DAK4Blizzard, GaryDe, Jaydec, MookieZ, Richhoncho, Sahafan, Santa Claus of the Future, Wolfer68, 1 anonymous edits

When Girls Get Together *Source*: http://en.wikipedia.org/w/index.php?oldid=332180563 *Contributors*: MookieZ, Richhoncho, Sahafan, Unionsoap

When I Grow Up (To Be a Man) *Source*: http://en.wikipedia.org/w/index.php?oldid=349705197 *Contributors*: Andrzejbanas, Don1962, Durova, GaryDe, Iridescent, Jogers, Josephabradshaw, Koavf, MookieZ, Richhoncho, Sahafan, Santa Claus of the Future, Sb26554, Wolfer68, Wschart, 9 anonymous edits

When a Man Needs a Woman *Source*: http://en.wikipedia.org/w/index.php?oldid=294836354 *Contributors*: Jogers, Koavf, Richhoncho, Sahafan, ShelfSkewed, Truthanado, ^demon, 1 anonymous edits

Where I Belong *Source*: http://en.wikipedia.org/w/index.php?oldid=343074479 *Contributors*: Koavf, MookieZ, Richhoncho

Whistle In *Source*: http://en.wikipedia.org/w/index.php?oldid=332180199 *Contributors*: Richhoncho, RyanCross, Sahafan

White Christmas *Source*: http://en.wikipedia.org/w/index.php?oldid=363290257 *Contributors*: Abderitestatos, Abrazame, Aezram, After Midnight, Ahmad123987, Aivazovsky, Alanjohns, Alpha Ralpha Boulevard, Andromeda321, Andycjp, Apple1013, Appraiser, ApprenticeFan, Ashill, Babsdude, BambooBanga, Betaeleven, Biglovinb, Boffob, Boffomusic, Boxter1977, BrotherFlounder, Buckdj, C colorado, CBM, CambridgeBayWeather, Carlossfsu, Cgbraschi, Charlie White, Chironomia, CorreXDa, Cuchullain, Cyclone77, D7240, DabMachine, Dahveed76, Daveschrader, Djarra, Dravecky, Dreamer.se, Dsp13, Dutzi, Dynamite XI, Emmo827, Epolk, Eric444, Esasus, Fanficgurl, Farmerman, Firesky, Fluence, FordPrefect42, Fortdj33, Free Mind301, Free-encyclopedia, Gaius Cornelius, Gamaliel, Georgia guy, Giovannii84, Godards, GoingBatty, Hargrimm, HiFiGuy, Hydrargyrum, InnocuousPseudonym, JeanColumbia, Jeff Fries, Jeffhrsn, JoanneB, John of Reading, JohnDoe0007, Kbdank71, KeltieMartinFan, Kidshare, Kimwildefan, Kintetsubuffalo, Koalajump, Ld100, Lewismaster, Lilac Soul, Lindmere, MJEH, Maestrosync, Mandarax, Marianoherreroa, Martin451, Martin4647, MaryGW, Mattbrundage, Mbakkel2, MegX, Mervyn, Miguelg, Mike Bags, Mike Selinker, Miles Carter, Milnivlek, Mimihitam, Myname808, Nez202, Nickellmusic, Parjor, Pd THOR, Peeperman, Pfalstad, Pga1965, Pianoman2, PlutoYellow, ProhibitOnions, RBBrittain, Raul654, Rees11, Richard Arthur Norton (1958-), Rigadoun, Riverstepstonegirl, Rogerd, Rsolermo, Ryanbstevens, SDC, SPKx, Sahafan, Salamurai, Schweiwikist, Shadowjams, Shaq26, ShawnMcCann, Sluzzelin, Squiggyfm, Stimpy9337, Stormwatch, Supernatural02, Teklund, That Guy, From That Show!, The wub, TheListUpdater, TheRetroGuy, Tregoweth, Trekphiler, Ventura, Wagimawr, Wahkeenah, Walloon, Well, girl, look at you!, WikHead, WikiPedant, Wikid77, WindAndConfusion, Wooddoor, Wykebjs, YUL89YYZ, Yip1982, ZPM, Zephyrnthesky, Zombie433, 山田晴通, 248 anonymous edits

Why Do Fools Fall in Love *Source*: http://en.wikipedia.org/w/index.php?oldid=363295572 *Contributors*: Amalthea, AntonioMartin, Avicennasis, BRG, Carlossfsu, Cecropia, Chubbles, Cleftonefan, Colonies Chris, Daffdaemon, Discographer, DividedByNegativeZero, Draggleduck, E-Kartoffel, FuriousFreddy, GentlemanGhost, Giovannii84, GoingBatty, Harrisbp, Jessibird, Jogers, Leevclarke, Marine 69-71, Mike Selinker, MookieZ, Palm Highwayville, QzDaddy, Rich Farmbrough, Sahafan, Shimmera, Simple Bob, Sir Grant the Small, Steelbeard1, TKD, Tabletop, TheoMorgan, Titoxd, Tvoz, Wolfer68, 34 anonymous edits

Wild Honey *Source*: http://en.wikipedia.org/w/index.php?oldid=353677894 *Contributors*: December21st2012Freak, E-Kartoffel, GaryDe, Jogers, Koavf, Mago266, MookieZ, Pianoman001, Rich Farmbrough, Richhoncho, Sahafan, Santa Claus of the Future, ShelfSkewed, Wolfer68, 4 anonymous edits

Wind Chimes *Source*: http://en.wikipedia.org/w/index.php?oldid=347007427 *Contributors*: BurnDownBabylon, E-Kartoffel, Hiphats, Jogers, Koavf, Mago266, Mattbrundage, MookieZ, Number87, Plrk, Richhoncho, Rjwilmsi, Sahafan, Santa Claus of the Future, Slysplace, Wiki alf, Zone46, 2 anonymous edits

Winds of Change *Source*: http://en.wikipedia.org/w/index.php?oldid=362997655 *Contributors*: E-Kartoffel, Koavf, Mooco2006, Sahafan, Santa Claus of the Future, ShelfSkewed, Ste900R

Wipe Out *Source*: http://en.wikipedia.org/w/index.php?oldid=362115898 *Contributors*: Ahuebner2004, Baswerkhoven, Cheesechimp, Colonies Chris, D, DOHC Holiday, Darkpower, Dawnseeker2000, DrGaellon, E-Kartoffel, Giovannii84, Gloriamarie, Guroadrunner, HaeB, Hoponpop69, HumanFrailty, IllaZilla, InnocuousPseudonym, J04n, Jabbathenut, John Cardinal, KingRaven44, Koavf, LilHelpa, Marcus Brute, Microchip08, Milosppf, MookieZ, NHRHS2010, Nickellmusic, Ortolan88, Paul Magnussen, Pichpich, Pretzelpaws, Putnam269, Sahafan, Scharb, Seven Genres, Shadowjams, Sherick, Simsimius, Sleigh, Starcheerspeaksnewslostwars, Surfbum, Thibbs, Trblhdfun, Tslocum, Ucucha, Waynecha, WesleyDodds, Woohookitty, 73 anonymous edits

With Me Tonight *Source*: http://en.wikipedia.org/w/index.php?oldid=357589612 *Contributors*: Dialectric, Jaydec, Richhoncho, Sahafan, 1 anonymous edits

Wonderful *Source*: http://en.wikipedia.org/w/index.php?oldid=364147845 *Contributors*: Andrei Iosifovich, BGC, Bobyllib, Colonies Chris, Just64helpin, Koavf, Kukini, Mago266, Number87, Richhoncho, Rjwilmsi, Sahafan, Santa Claus of the Future, Wiki alf, 20 anonymous edits

Wontcha Come out Tonight? *Source*: http://en.wikipedia.org/w/index.php?oldid=363335525 *Contributors*: Koavf, Richhoncho, Sahafan, Santa Claus of the Future

Wouldn't It Be Nice *Source*: http://en.wikipedia.org/w/index.php?oldid=361579071 *Contributors*: Andycjp, Art1991, Betty kerner, Bobo192, Bruce1ee, Carptrash, Cbrown285, Cdm113, Design, Drysarcasm, Echuck215, EncMstr, Everything counts, Fisheatsteel, Freshacconci, GaryDe, GoingBatty, Ian-turner77, Irfanmp, Iridescent, JarlaxleArtemis, Jayron32, JeffBillman, Jesscatena, Jogers, John Cardinal, Josephabradshaw, Lord Bodak, Mago266, Martarius, Mattbr, Mattbrundage, Mboverload, MegX, Metstotop333, Mister sparky, MookieZ, Pimlottc, Qviri, Rich Farmbrough, Richhoncho, RyanCross, Sahafan, Santa Claus of the Future, Sb26554, Scott87, Sjones23, Slysplace, Svivian, Synergy, TenPoundHammer, That Guy, From That Show!, TheHYPO, Tim Long, Timerrill, Tnxman307, Trotter, VolatileChemical, Wadems, Wesley M. Curtus, Williamnilly, Xiong Chiamiov, Zone46, 83 anonymous edits

You Need a Mess of Help to Stand Alone *Source*: http://en.wikipedia.org/w/index.php?oldid=333749462 *Contributors*: AyaK, Clarityfiend, Jogers, Koavf, Mago266, Metstotop333, MookieZ, Richhoncho, Sahafan, Silence of the Yams, 1 anonymous edits

You Still Believe in Me *Source*: http://en.wikipedia.org/w/index.php?oldid=340140010 *Contributors*: Design, Domino42, Equal, Freshacconci, Jogers, Koavf, Mago266, Mooco2006, MookieZ, Richhoncho, Rjwilmsi, Rlendog, Sahafan, Sanremofilo, Sjones23, Slysplace, Zone46, 11 anonymous edits

You're So Good to Me *Source*: http://en.wikipedia.org/w/index.php?oldid=346993274 *Contributors*: Arthurpewty, Berlyant, Djsasso, Douglasr007, Firien, Jaydec, Jesscatena, Jogers, Koavf, Lotje, Mago266, Michaelfool, MookieZ, Rbb1181, Richhoncho, Sahafan, Slysplace, 7 anonymous edits

You're Welcome *Source*: http://en.wikipedia.org/w/index.php?oldid=332160536 *Contributors*: E-Kartoffel, Josiah Rowe, Mira, MookieZ, Musicman378, Richhoncho, Sahafan, Santa Claus of the Future, Synergy, 1 anonymous edits

You've Got to Hide Your Love Away *Source*: http://en.wikipedia.org/w/index.php?oldid=363997569 *Contributors*: -5-, AdorableRuffian, Alcuin, Allstarecho, Allwham, Apanuggpak, Ashadeofgrey, Audiori, Beatlescool, Bjones, Burkedavis, Cammoore, CherryFlavoredAntacid, CrnkMnky, Daniellcb32, Design, Discospinster, Dsims209, Duprass, Fenian Swine, Fratrep, GPHemsley, Garion96, Gestackmoney, Gemcaranguian, Goldom, GregorB, Helpsloose, Huntster, Indopug, Jemd4185, John Cardinal, Jsl83, Justnin9, Kaiba, Kartik Agaram, Kingboyk, Kingcrimson2, Koavf, Lew19, Liverpool Scouse, Lowellian, MicroProf, Mrshock13, Nareek, Nscheffey, OutbackKidd, PEJL, Preslethe, Qirex, Que-Can, Qworty, RMc, Red dwarf, Redheylin, Redwolf24, Richhoncho, Rocket000, Rodhullandemu, Sahafan, Spiby, TOGASHI Jin, TenPoundHammer, Thadius856, Undrwood9098, Urbanus1234, Velvetron, Vern69, Ward3001, XSG, ZhaoHong, 100 anonymous edits

A Young Man Is Gone *Source*: http://en.wikipedia.org/w/index.php?oldid=332386527 *Contributors*: Dsreyn, Koavf, Mattbrundage, Richhoncho, Sahafan, Suddenly There Is a Valley, 3 anonymous edits

The Beach Boys discography *Source*: http://en.wikipedia.org/w/index.php?oldid=357538146 *Contributors*: 1jrb, AjaxSmack, Artrush, Ary29, BGC, Bluegum Bill, Bobo192, Boobah1111, Braitman, Clarityfiend, Cosprings, DR04, Don1962, E-Kartoffel, Ed g2s, Ericorbit, Ernie Scribner, Esprit15d, Guettarda, Holiday56, Ingman, Java13690, Jogers, Karaokegod, Ketiltrout, Koavf, Kohoutek1138, Lairor, Linnix, Magioladitis, Mago266, Mattbrundage, MegX, Metstotop333, MookieZ, Moxy, Muskmellon, Nogravity, Odin's Beard, Ore4444, Oskar71, Pbr2000, PeterCanthropus, Rjwilmsi, Sahafan, Santa Claus of the Future, Scchipli, ShelfSkewed, Slicoliver, Snow1215, SonjiCeli, Spakatak, Ss112, Stlyter, Tails 2009, Tassedethe, TenPoundHammer, Tiburon, Yeahbutnobut92, 83 anonymous edits

List of The Beach Boys songs *Source*: http://en.wikipedia.org/w/index.php?oldid=357533059 *Contributors*: Abstrator, Akrabbim, Beat 768, Bobo192, Bobyllib, Bonnmusik, Candyfloss, Chris the speller, ChristTrekker, Circeus, Clarityfiend, Deb, Docu, E-Kartoffel, EdJohnston, Eric444, Ericorbit, Fratrep, GoingBatty, Holiday56, Howard352, Hqb, JIP, James Epstein, Jeffmilner, Jogers, John Cardinal, Karaboom, Ketiltrout, Koavf, Macg4cubeboy, Magioladitis, Mattbrundage, Mdumas43073, MegX, Metstotop333, Mooco2006, MookieZ, Moxy, Nagle, NeoChaosX, Quentin X, Rich Farmbrough, Richhoncho, Rubikonchik, Sahafan, Santa Claus of the Future, ShelfSkewed, Spakatak, TJRC, Tassedethe, TenPoundHammer, Tiburon, Wafulz, Warofdreams, Wiki alf, Wildfire burn, Wolfer68, 92 anonymous edits

The Beach Boys solo discography *Source*: http://en.wikipedia.org/w/index.php?oldid=364797253 *Contributors*: Artrush, BGC, Bleddynefans, Cosprings, Don1962, E-Kartoffel, Fratrep, J Milburn, Jogers, Koavf, Lairor, LoserTalent, Marcus Brute, Martpol, MegX, Metstotop333, MookieZ, Redrkr, Rich Farmbrough, Sahafan, Samalamalamdam, Santa Claus of the Future, ShelfSkewed, Sk8punk3d288, TenPoundHammer, Tony1, Warpozio, YUL89YYZ, 12 anonymous edits

The Beach Boys lineups *Source*: http://en.wikipedia.org/w/index.php?oldid=363247553 *Contributors*: ACupOfCoffee, Ary29, BD2412, Belsen, Carefree Highway, CoastTOcoast533, D6, Dale Arnett, DollyD, E-Kartoffel, Jfoster4189, Jusdafax, Mattbrundage, Metstotop333, MookieZ, Santa Claus of the Future, Sk8punk3d288, The Elfoid, Whotookthatguy, 33 anonymous edits

Image Sources, Licenses and Contributors

Image:The Beach Boys 1965.jpg *Source*: http://en.wikipedia.org/w/index.php?title=File:The_Beach_Boys_1965.jpg *License*: unknown *Contributors*: Angusmclellan, Calmer Waters, FotoPhest, 1 anonymous edits

Image:Beach boys X label 301.jpg *Source*: http://en.wikipedia.org/w/index.php?title=File:Beach_boys_X_label_301.jpg *License*: GNU Free Documentation License *Contributors*: Cool Hand Records / Yoshi Takeuchi - Koki Kobayashi

Image:Beachboys-ariola.jpg *Source*: http://en.wikipedia.org/w/index.php?title=File:Beachboys-ariola.jpg *License*: GNU Free Documentation License *Contributors*: Cool Hand Records / Yoshi Takeuchi - Koki Kobayashi

Image:Beachboys smile cover.jpg *Source*: http://en.wikipedia.org/w/index.php?title=File:Beachboys_smile_cover.jpg *License*: unknown *Contributors*: Analogdemon, BGC, Jiy, Koavf, Lukobe, Melesse, Yoursvivek

File:The Beach Boys concierto.jpg *Source*: http://en.wikipedia.org/w/index.php?title=File:The_Beach_Boys_concierto.jpg *License*: Creative Commons Attribution 2.0 *Contributors*: Wonker Wonker

Image:Reagans with the Beach Boys.jpg *Source*: http://en.wikipedia.org/w/index.php?title=File:Reagans_with_the_Beach_Boys.jpg *License*: Public Domain *Contributors*: White House Photo Office

Image:Blondie chaplin 79.jpg *Source*: http://en.wikipedia.org/w/index.php?title=File:Blondie_chaplin_79.jpg *License*: Creative Commons Attribution-Sharealike 3.0 *Contributors*: User:Rtsanderson

Image:Ricky Fataar 2008.JPG *Source*: http://en.wikipedia.org/w/index.php?title=File:Ricky_Fataar_2008.JPG *License*: Public Domain *Contributors*: User:Svickova

Image:Jardinenj.jpg *Source*: http://en.wikipedia.org/w/index.php?title=File:Jardinenj.jpg *License*: Public Domain *Contributors*: Original uploader was DLA75 at en.wikipedia

Image:Bruce Johnston 2006 Birmingham.jpg *Source*: http://en.wikipedia.org/w/index.php?title=File:Bruce_Johnston_2006_Birmingham.jpg *License*: Creative Commons Attribution 2.0 *Contributors*: Brian Peters

Image:Mike_Love.jpg *Source*: http://en.wikipedia.org/w/index.php?title=File:Mike_Love.jpg *License*: Creative Commons Attribution 2.0 *Contributors*: Photo taken by Brian Peters Original uploader was Chowbok at en.wikipedia

Image:marks.jpg *Source*: http://en.wikipedia.org/w/index.php?title=File:Marks.jpg *License*: Public Domain *Contributors*: DLA75

Image:Brian Wilson Jan 2007.jpg *Source*: http://en.wikipedia.org/w/index.php?title=File:Brian_Wilson_Jan_2007.jpg *License*: Creative Commons Attribution 3.0 *Contributors*: User:Richard King

Image:Carl Wilson.jpg *Source*: http://en.wikipedia.org/w/index.php?title=File:Carl_Wilson.jpg *License*: unknown *Contributors*:

Image:Dennis_Wilson.jpg *Source*: http://en.wikipedia.org/w/index.php?title=File:Dennis_Wilson.jpg *License*: Public Domain *Contributors*: User:75pickup, User:Yamla

Image:15BigOnesCover.jpg *Source*: http://en.wikipedia.org/w/index.php?title=File:15BigOnesCover.jpg *License*: unknown *Contributors*: Analogdemon

File:Star full.svg *Source*: http://en.wikipedia.org/w/index.php?title=File:Star_full.svg *License*: Public Domain *Contributors*: User:Conti, User:RedHotHeat

File:Star half.svg *Source*: http://en.wikipedia.org/w/index.php?title=File:Star_half.svg *License*: Creative Commons Attribution-Sharealike 2.5 *Contributors*: User:Conti

File:Star empty.svg *Source*: http://en.wikipedia.org/w/index.php?title=File:Star_empty.svg *License*: Creative Commons Attribution-Sharealike 2.5 *Contributors*: User:Conti, User:RedHotHeat

Image:2020Cover.jpg *Source*: http://en.wikipedia.org/w/index.php?title=File:2020Cover.jpg *License*: unknown *Contributors*: Analogdemon, Tassedethe

Image:AllSummerLongCover.jpg *Source*: http://en.wikipedia.org/w/index.php?title=File:AllSummerLongCover.jpg *License*: unknown *Contributors*: Analogdemon

Image:BeachBoys85Cover.jpg *Source*: http://en.wikipedia.org/w/index.php?title=File:BeachBoys85Cover.jpg *License*: unknown *Contributors*: Analogdemon

Image:BBConcertCover.jpg *Source*: http://en.wikipedia.org/w/index.php?title=File:BBConcertCover.jpg *License*: unknown *Contributors*: Analogdemon

Image:BeachBoysTodayCover.jpg *Source*: http://en.wikipedia.org/w/index.php?title=File:BeachBoysTodayCover.jpg *License*: unknown *Contributors*: Analogdemon

Image:BBInConcertCover.jpg *Source*: http://en.wikipedia.org/w/index.php?title=File:BBInConcertCover.jpg *License*: unknown *Contributors*: Analogdemon

Image:BBXmasCover.jpg *Source*: http://en.wikipedia.org/w/index.php?title=File:BBXmasCover.jpg *License*: unknown *Contributors*: Analogdemon

Image:BeachBoysParty.album.cover.jpg *Source*: http://en.wikipedia.org/w/index.php?title=File:BeachBoysParty.album.cover.jpg *License*: unknown *Contributors*: Analogdemon

Image:BestOfBBVol2.jpg *Source*: http://en.wikipedia.org/w/index.php?title=File:BestOfBBVol2.jpg *License*: unknown *Contributors*: Analogdemon

Image:BestOfBB.jpg *Source*: http://en.wikipedia.org/w/index.php?title=File:BestOfBB.jpg *License*: unknown *Contributors*: Analogdemon

Image:BestofbbV3.jpg *Source*: http://en.wikipedia.org/w/index.php?title=File:BestofbbV3.jpg *License*: unknown *Contributors*: Analogdemon

Image:Capitol_Years_Album_Cover.jpg *Source*: http://en.wikipedia.org/w/index.php?title=File:Capitol_Years_Album_Cover.jpg *License*: unknown *Contributors*: Rettetast, Skier Dude, Yeahbutnobut92

Image:CarlPassionsSoToughCover.jpg *Source*: http://en.wikipedia.org/w/index.php?title=File:CarlPassionsSoToughCover.jpg *License*: unknown *Contributors*: Analogdemon, PetSounds, RedWolf, Strangerer

Image:ClassicsBWCover.jpg *Source*: http://en.wikipedia.org/w/index.php?title=File:ClassicsBWCover.jpg *License*: unknown *Contributors*: Analogdemon, PetSounds, RedWolf, Strangerer

Image:Endless1Cover.jpg *Source*: http://en.wikipedia.org/w/index.php?title=File:Endless1Cover.jpg *License*: unknown *Contributors*: Analogdemon, PetSounds, WCX

Image:Endless2Cover.jpg *Source*: http://en.wikipedia.org/w/index.php?title=File:Endless2Cover.jpg *License*: unknown *Contributors*: Analogdemon, PetSounds, WCX

Image:EndlessSummerBBCover.jpg *Source*: http://en.wikipedia.org/w/index.php?title=File:EndlessSummerBBCover.jpg *License*: unknown *Contributors*: Analogdemon, PetSounds, WCX

Image:BeachBoysFriends.jpg *Source*: http://en.wikipedia.org/w/index.php?title=File:BeachBoysFriends.jpg *License*: unknown *Contributors*: Analogdemon

Image:BBKnebworthCover.jpg *Source*: http://en.wikipedia.org/w/index.php?title=File:BBKnebworthCover.jpg *License*: unknown *Contributors*: Analogdemon

Image:GoodVibesBestOfCover.jpg *Source*: http://en.wikipedia.org/w/index.php?title=File:GoodVibesBestOfCover.jpg *License*: unknown *Contributors*: Analogdemon, PetSounds, RedWolf

Image:30YearsBBCover.jpg *Source*: http://en.wikipedia.org/w/index.php?title=File:30YearsBBCover.jpg *License*: unknown *Contributors*: Admrboltz, Analogdemon, BGC, OldakQuill, OsamaK, 2 anonymous edits

Image:BBGV1Cover.jpg *Source*: http://en.wikipedia.org/w/index.php?title=File:BBGV1Cover.jpg *License*: unknown *Contributors*: Analogdemon

Image:BBGV2Cover.jpg *Source*: http://en.wikipedia.org/w/index.php?title=File:BBGV2Cover.jpg *License*: unknown *Contributors*: Analogdemon

Image:BBGH3.jpg *Source*: http://en.wikipedia.org/w/index.php?title=File:BBGH3.jpg *License*: unknown *Contributors*: Analogdemon

Image:HawthorneCover.jpg *Source*: http://en.wikipedia.org/w/index.php?title=File:HawthorneCover.jpg *License*: unknown *Contributors*: Analogdemon, PetSounds, RedWolf

Image:HollandCover.jpg *Source*: http://en.wikipedia.org/w/index.php?title=File:HollandCover.jpg *License*: unknown *Contributors*: Analogdemon, Caesura, PetSounds

Image:KTSACover.jpg *Source*: http://en.wikipedia.org/w/index.php?title=File:KTSACover.jpg *License*: unknown *Contributors*: Analogdemon, PetSounds, RedWolf

Image:LALightCover.jpg *Source*: http://en.wikipedia.org/w/index.php?title=File:LALightCover.jpg *License*: unknown *Contributors*: Analogdemon, PetSounds, RedWolf

Image:LittleDeuceCover.jpg *Source*: http://en.wikipedia.org/w/index.php?title=File:LittleDeuceCover.jpg *License*: unknown *Contributors*: Analogdemon, E-Kartoffel, Geschichte, PetSounds, Sfan00 IMG

Image:BBLiveLondonCover.jpg *Source*: http://en.wikipedia.org/w/index.php?title=File:BBLiveLondonCover.jpg *License*: unknown *Contributors*: Analogdemon

Image:LoveYouCover.jpg *Source*: http://en.wikipedia.org/w/index.php?title=File:LoveYouCover.jpg *License*: unknown *Contributors*: Analogdemon, E-Kartoffel, Geschichte, Keith D, PetSounds, Sfan00 IMG

Image:MIUCover.jpg *Source*: http://en.wikipedia.org/w/index.php?title=File:MIUCover.jpg *License*: unknown *Contributors*: Analogdemon, Dbenbenn, PetSounds

Image:MadeinUSACover.jpg *Source*: http://en.wikipedia.org/w/index.php?title=File:MadeinUSACover.jpg *License*: unknown *Contributors*: Admrboltz, Analogdemon, PetSounds

Image:PetSoundsCover.jpg *Source*: http://en.wikipedia.org/w/index.php?title=File:PetSoundsCover.jpg *License*: unknown *Contributors*: Analogdemon, Casey Abell, Jecrabman, Northoltjohn, PetSounds, RedWolf

Image:PetBoxCover.jpg *Source*: http://en.wikipedia.org/w/index.php?title=File:PetBoxCover.jpg *License*: unknown *Contributors*: Analogdemon, PetSounds, RedWolf

Image:Beach Boys - Rarities.jpg *Source*: http://en.wikipedia.org/w/index.php?title=File:Beach_Boys_-_Rarities.jpg *License*: unknown *Contributors*: Analogdemon, Sahafan

Image:ShutDownVol2Cover.jpg *Source*: http://en.wikipedia.org/w/index.php?title=File:ShutDownVol2Cover.jpg *License*: unknown *Contributors*: Analogdemon, PetSounds, RedWolf

Image:Beachboys smile cover.jpg *Source*: http://en.wikipedia.org/w/index.php?title=File:Beachboys_smile_cover.jpg *License*: unknown *Contributors*: Analogdemon, BGC, Jiy, Koavf, Lukobe, Melesse, Yoursvivek

Image:SmileySmileCover.jpg *Source*: http://en.wikipedia.org/w/index.php?title=File:SmileySmileCover.jpg *License*: unknown *Contributors*: Analogdemon, PetSounds, RedWolf

Image:SongsFromHereAndBack.jpg *Source*: http://en.wikipedia.org/w/index.php?title=File:SongsFromHereAndBack.jpg *License*: unknown *Contributors*: Analogdemon

Image:SOSBBCover.jpg *Source*: http://en.wikipedia.org/w/index.php?title=File:SOSBBCover.jpg *License*: unknown *Contributors*: Analogdemon, PetSounds, WCX

Image:SpiritBBCover.jpg *Source*: http://en.wikipedia.org/w/index.php?title=File:SpiritBBCover.jpg *License*: unknown *Contributors*: Analogdemon, DR04, PetSounds, Sfan00 IMG, Supercoop

Image:StackTracksCover.jpg *Source*: http://en.wikipedia.org/w/index.php?title=File:StackTracksCover.jpg *License*: unknown *Contributors*: Analogdemon, PetSounds, Supercoop

Image:BBStarsCover.jpg *Source*: http://en.wikipedia.org/w/index.php?title=File:BBStarsCover.jpg *License*: unknown *Contributors*: Analogdemon

Image:StillCruisinCover.jpg *Source*: http://en.wikipedia.org/w/index.php?title=File:StillCruisinCover.jpg *License*: unknown *Contributors*: Analogdemon, Dbenbenn, PetSounds

Image:SummerDaysandSummerNights.album.cover.jpg *Source*: http://en.wikipedia.org/w/index.php?title=File:SummerDaysandSummerNights.album.cover.jpg *License*: unknown *Contributors*: Analogdemon, Cbing01

Image:SummerParadiseCover.jpg *Source*: http://en.wikipedia.org/w/index.php?title=File:SummerParadiseCover.jpg *License*: unknown *Contributors*: Analogdemon, PetSounds, RedWolf

Image:SummerInParadiseUK.jpg *Source*: http://en.wikipedia.org/w/index.php?title=File:SummerInParadiseUK.jpg *License*: unknown *Contributors*: Analogdemon

Image:SunflowerCover.jpg *Source*: http://en.wikipedia.org/w/index.php?title=File:SunflowerCover.jpg *License*: unknown *Contributors*: Analogdemon, Melesse, PetSounds, RedWolf

Image:SunshineDreamBBCover.jpg *Source*: http://en.wikipedia.org/w/index.php?title=File:SunshineDreamBBCover.jpg *License*: unknown *Contributors*: Analogdemon

Image:SurfsUpCover.jpg *Source*: http://en.wikipedia.org/w/index.php?title=File:SurfsUpCover.jpg *License*: unknown *Contributors*: Analogdemon, PetSounds, RedWolf

Image:SurferGirlCover.jpg *Source*: http://en.wikipedia.org/w/index.php?title=File:SurferGirlCover.jpg *License*: unknown *Contributors*: Analogdemon, PetSounds, RedWolf

Image:Surfin'SafariCover.jpg *Source*: http://en.wikipedia.org/w/index.php?title=File:Surfin'SafariCover.jpg *License*: unknown *Contributors*: Analogdemon, PetSounds, RedWolf

Image:Surfin'USACover.jpg *Source*: http://en.wikipedia.org/w/index.php?title=File:Surfin'USACover.jpg *License*: unknown *Contributors*: Analogdemon, Melesse, PetSounds, RedWolf

Image:TenYearsHarmonyCover.jpg *Source*: http://en.wikipedia.org/w/index.php?title=File:TenYearsHarmonyCover.jpg *License*: unknown *Contributors*: Analogdemon, PetSounds, RedWolf

Image:UltimateXCover.jpg *Source*: http://en.wikipedia.org/w/index.php?title=File:UltimateXCover.jpg *License*: unknown *Contributors*: Analogdemon, PetSounds, Stezton

Image:Very Best of The Beach Boys cover.jpg *Source*: http://en.wikipedia.org/w/index.php?title=File:Very_Best_of_The_Beach_Boys_cover.jpg *License*: unknown *Contributors*: Java13690

Image:wild_honey_beach_boys.jpg *Source*: http://en.wikipedia.org/w/index.php?title=File:Wild_honey_beach_boys.jpg *License*: unknown *Contributors*: Analogdemon, E-Kartoffel, Gogol999, J3ff

File:Beach Boys - Here Comes The Night.jpg *Source*: http://en.wikipedia.org/w/index.php?title=File:Beach_Boys_-_Here_Comes_The_Night.jpg *License*: unknown *Contributors*: Melesse, Metstotop333, Tassedethe

File:Beach Boys - Barbara Ann.jpg *Source*: http://en.wikipedia.org/w/index.php?title=File:Beach_Boys_-_Barbara_Ann.jpg *License*: unknown *Contributors*: Metstotop333

File:Beach Boys - Be True To Your School.jpg *Source*: http://en.wikipedia.org/w/index.php?title=File:Beach_Boys_-_Be_True_To_Your_School.jpg *License*: unknown *Contributors*: GentlemanGhost, Sahafan

File:Beach Boys - Bluebirds Over The Mountain.jpg *Source*: http://en.wikipedia.org/w/index.php?title=File:Beach_Boys_-_Bluebirds_Over_The_Mountain.jpg *License*: unknown *Contributors*: Melesse, Metstotop333

File:Beach Boys - Break Away.jpg *Source*: http://en.wikipedia.org/w/index.php?title=File:Beach_Boys_-_Break_Away.jpg *License*: unknown *Contributors*: Sahafan, Skier Dude

File:Beach boys california girls.PNG *Source*: http://en.wikipedia.org/w/index.php?title=File:Beach_boys_california_girls.PNG *License*: unknown *Contributors*: Melesse, Metstotop333

File:California Girls David.jpg *Source*: http://en.wikipedia.org/w/index.php?title=File:California_Girls_David.jpg *License*: unknown *Contributors*: Holiday56

File:Beach Boys - Caroline No.jpg *Source*: http://en.wikipedia.org/w/index.php?title=File:Beach_Boys_-_Caroline_No.jpg *License*: unknown *Contributors*: Melesse, Metstotop333

File:The_Beach_Boys_Child_Of_Winter.PNG *Source*: http://en.wikipedia.org/w/index.php?title=File:The_Beach_Boys_Child_Of_Winter.PNG *License*: unknown *Contributors*: Metstotop333

File:Beach Boys - Cottonfields.jpg *Source*: http://en.wikipedia.org/w/index.php?title=File:Beach_Boys_-_Cottonfields.jpg *License*: unknown *Contributors*: AWeenieMan, Metstotop333

File:Beach Boys - You Need A Mess Of Help To Stand Alone.JPG *Source*: http://en.wikipedia.org/w/index.php?title=File:Beach_Boys_-_You_Need_A_Mess_Of_Help_To_Stand_Alone.JPG *License*: unknown *Contributors*: Melesse, Metstotop333, ShelfSkewed

File:Beach Boys - Dance, Dance, Dance.jpg *Source*: http://en.wikipedia.org/w/index.php?title=File:Beach_Boys_-_Dance,_Dance,_Dance.jpg *License*: unknown *Contributors*: Melesse, Metstotop333

File:Beach Boys - Darlin'.jpg *Source*: http://en.wikipedia.org/w/index.php?title=File:Beach_Boys_-_Darlin'.jpg *License*: unknown *Contributors*: Douglasr007, Melesse, Metstotop333

File:Beach Boys - Long Promised Road & Deirdre.jpg *Source*: http://en.wikipedia.org/w/index.php?title=File:Beach_Boys_-_Long_Promised_Road_&_Deirdre.jpg *License*: unknown *Contributors*: Melesse, Metstotop333

File:Beach Boys - Do It Again (single).JPG *Source*: http://en.wikipedia.org/w/index.php?title=File:Beach_Boys_-_Do_It_Again_(single).JPG *License*: unknown *Contributors*: Melesse, Metstotop333

File:Beach Boys - Do You Wanna Dance?.jpg *Source*: http://en.wikipedia.org/w/index.php?title=File:Beach_Boys_-_Do_You_Wanna_Dance?.jpg *License*: unknown *Contributors*: Melesse, Metstotop333

File:Beach Boys - I Get Around.jpg *Source*: http://en.wikipedia.org/w/index.php?title=File:Beach_Boys_-_I_Get_Around.jpg *License*: unknown *Contributors*: Melesse, Metstotop333

File:Beach Boys - Friends (single).jpg *Source*: http://en.wikipedia.org/w/index.php?title=File:Beach_Boys_-_Friends_(single).jpg *License*: unknown *Contributors*: Melesse, Metstotop333

File:The Beach Boys - Fun, Fun, Fun.PNG *Source*: http://en.wikipedia.org/w/index.php?title=File:The_Beach_Boys_-_Fun,_Fun,_Fun.PNG *License*: unknown *Contributors*: Metstotop333

File:Beach Boys - Getcha Back.jpg *Source*: http://en.wikipedia.org/w/index.php?title=File:Beach_Boys_-_Getcha_Back.jpg *License*: unknown *Contributors*: Melesse, Metstotop333

File:Beach boys gettin' hungry.PNG *Source*: http://en.wikipedia.org/w/index.php?title=File:Beach_boys_gettin'_hungry.PNG *License*: unknown *Contributors*: Metstotop333, Qst

File:Beach boys god only knows.PNG *Source*: http://en.wikipedia.org/w/index.php?title=File:Beach_boys_god_only_knows.PNG *License*: unknown *Contributors*: Melesse, Metstotop333

File:Beach Boys - Good Timin'.jpg *Source*: http://en.wikipedia.org/w/index.php?title=File:Beach_Boys_-_Good_Timin'.jpg *License*: unknown *Contributors*: E-Kartoffel, Melesse, Metstotop333

File:Good Vibrations single.jpg *Source*: http://en.wikipedia.org/w/index.php?title=File:Good_Vibrations_single.jpg *License*: unknown *Contributors*: Buckeyeblogger, Sahafan, Xtreambar

Image:Brian Wilson - Good Vibrations.jpg *Source*: http://en.wikipedia.org/w/index.php?title=File:Brian_Wilson_-_Good_Vibrations.jpg *License*: unknown *Contributors*: Koavf

File:Beach Boys - It's OK.jpg *Source*: http://en.wikipedia.org/w/index.php?title=File:Beach_Boys_-_It's_OK.jpg *License*: unknown *Contributors*: Melesse, Metstotop333

File:Beach Boys - Help Me, Rhonda.jpg *Source*: http://en.wikipedia.org/w/index.php?title=File:Beach_Boys_-_Help_Me,_Rhonda.jpg *License*: unknown *Contributors*: Melesse, Metstotop333

File:Beach Boys - Heroes and Villains.jpg *Source*: http://en.wikipedia.org/w/index.php?title=File:Beach_Boys_-_Heroes_and_Villains.jpg *License*: unknown *Contributors*: Melesse, Metstotop333, Mfko

File:Beach Boys - Marcella.jpg *Source*: http://en.wikipedia.org/w/index.php?title=File:Beach_Boys_-_Marcella.jpg *License*: unknown *Contributors*: Melesse, Metstotop333

File:Beach Boys - I Can Hear Music.jpg *Source*: http://en.wikipedia.org/w/index.php?title=File:Beach_Boys_-_I_Can_Hear_Music.jpg *License*: unknown *Contributors*: Melesse, Metstotop333, TenPoundHammer

File:StevieWonderIWasMadeToLoveHer7InchSingleLabel.jpg *Source*: http://en.wikipedia.org/w/index.php?title=File:StevieWonderIWasMadeToLoveHer7InchSingleLabel.jpg *License*: unknown *Contributors*: User:Tchernomush

File:Beach Boys - Tears In The Morning.jpg *Source*: http://en.wikipedia.org/w/index.php?title=File:Beach_Boys_-_Tears_In_The_Morning.jpg *License*: unknown *Contributors*: Melesse, Metstotop333

File:The_Beach_Boys_It's_Gettin'_Late.PNG *Source*: http://en.wikipedia.org/w/index.php?title=File:The_Beach_Boys_It's_Gettin'_Late.PNG *License*: unknown *Contributors*: E-Kartoffel, Metstotop333

File:JustOnceInMyLife.jpg *Source*: http://en.wikipedia.org/w/index.php?title=File:JustOnceInMyLife.jpg *License*: unknown *Contributors*: GassyGuy

File:Kokomo.jpg *Source*: http://en.wikipedia.org/w/index.php?title=File:Kokomo.jpg *License*: unknown *Contributors*: Europe22, Geniac, 1 anonymous edits

File:Let's Go Trippin' (single).jpg *Source*: http://en.wikipedia.org/w/index.php?title=File:Let's_Go_Trippin'_(single).jpg *License*: unknown *Contributors*: Econrad

Image:Beach Boys - Friends (single).jpg *Source*: http://en.wikipedia.org/w/index.php?title=File:Beach_Boys_-_Friends_(single).jpg *License*: unknown *Contributors*: Melesse, Metstotop333

File:Beach Boys - The Little Girl I Once Knew.jpg *Source*: http://en.wikipedia.org/w/index.php?title=File:Beach_Boys_-_The_Little_Girl_I_Once_Knew.jpg *License*: unknown *Contributors*: Harej, Sahafan

File:Lonely Days.jpg *Source*: http://en.wikipedia.org/w/index.php?title=File:Lonely_Days.jpg *License*: unknown *Contributors*: Lou72JG, Melesse, Skier Dude, Wknight94

File:Louie Louie Motorhead.jpg *Source*: http://en.wikipedia.org/w/index.php?title=File:Louie_Louie_Motorhead.jpg *License*: unknown *Contributors*: User:Wiki alf

File:Oldfolksathome.jpg *Source*: http://en.wikipedia.org/w/index.php?title=File:Oldfolksathome.jpg *License*: Public Domain *Contributors*: E.P. Christy

File:SuwanneeRiverPostcard.jpg *Source*: http://en.wikipedia.org/w/index.php?title=File:SuwanneeRiverPostcard.jpg *License*: Public Domain *Contributors*: AEMoreira042281, Albertomos, Ebyabe, Infrogmation

File:8_Old_Folks_at_Home.png *Source*: http://en.wikipedia.org/w/index.php?title=File:8_Old_Folks_at_Home.png *License*: Public Domain *Contributors*: User:Aetzkorn

File:Beach Boys - Sail On, Sailor.jpg *Source*: http://en.wikipedia.org/w/index.php?title=File:Beach_Boys_-_Sail_On,_Sailor.jpg *License*: unknown *Contributors*: Melesse, Metstotop333, MockieZ

Image:Brian Wilson - Our Prayer.jpg *Source*: http://en.wikipedia.org/w/index.php?title=File:Brian_Wilson_-_Our_Prayer.jpg *License*: unknown *Contributors*: Koavf

Image:Palisadespark45.jpg *Source*: http://en.wikipedia.org/w/index.php?title=File:Palisadespark45.jpg *License*: unknown *Contributors*: Steelbeard1

File:Rivingtons Papa-Oom-Mow-Mow.gif *Source*: http://en.wikipedia.org/w/index.php?title=File:Rivingtons_Papa-Oom-Mow-Mow.gif *License*: unknown *Contributors*: Archaeolojae

Image:Peggy Sue vocal melody.png *Source*: http://en.wikipedia.org/w/index.php?title=File:Peggy_Sue_vocal_melody.png *License*: unknown *Contributors*: User:Hyacinth

File:Beach Boys - Rock and Roll Music.jpg *Source*: http://en.wikipedia.org/w/index.php?title=File:Beach_Boys_-_Rock_and_Roll_Music.jpg *License*: unknown *Contributors*: FotoPhest, John Cardinal, Sahafan

File:Beach Boys - Living With A Heartache.JPG *Source*: http://en.wikipedia.org/w/index.php?title=File:Beach_Boys_-_Living_With_A_Heartache.JPG *License*: unknown *Contributors*: Melesse, Metstotop333, PhilKnight

File:Beach Boys - When I Grow Up (to be a man).jpg *Source*: http://en.wikipedia.org/w/index.php?title=File:Beach_Boys_-_When_I_Grow_Up_(to_be_a_man).jpg *License*: unknown *Contributors*: Melesse, Metstotop333

File:Beach boys surfin' usa.PNG *Source*: http://en.wikipedia.org/w/index.php?title=File:Beach_boys_surfin'_usa.PNG *License*: unknown *Contributors*: Melesse, Metstotop333

File:Beach Boys - Sloop John B.jpg *Source*: http://en.wikipedia.org/w/index.php?title=File:Beach_Boys_-_Sloop_John_B.jpg *License*: unknown *Contributors*: Melesse, Metstotop333

File:Summertime Blues Eddie Cochran.jpg *Source*: http://en.wikipedia.org/w/index.php?title=File:Summertime_Blues_Eddie_Cochran.jpg *License*: unknown *Contributors*: Canadaolympic989

File:SummertimeBlues45.jpg *Source*: http://en.wikipedia.org/w/index.php?title=File:SummertimeBlues45.jpg *License*: unknown *Contributors*: Sb26554

File:Summertime blues.jpg *Source*: http://en.wikipedia.org/w/index.php?title=File:Summertime_blues.jpg *License*: unknown *Contributors*: Canadaolympic989

File:RUSH summertimeblues.jpg *Source*: http://en.wikipedia.org/w/index.php?title=File:RUSH_summertimeblues.jpg *License*: unknown *Contributors*: RUSH

File:Beach boys X label 301.jpg *Source*: http://en.wikipedia.org/w/index.php?title=File:Beach_boys_X_label_301.jpg *License*: GNU Free Documentation License *Contributors*: Cool Hand Records / Yoshi Takeuchi - Koki Kobayashi

Image:Brianonleonardbernstein.jpg *Source*: http://en.wikipedia.org/w/index.php?title=File:Brianonleonardbernstein.jpg *License*: unknown *Contributors*: Sahafan

File:Beach Boys - Then I Kissed Her.jpg *Source*: http://en.wikipedia.org/w/index.php?title=File:Beach_Boys_-_Then_I_Kissed_Her.jpg *License*: unknown *Contributors*: Sahafan, Skier Dude

Image:Music album record white christmas.jpg *Source*: http://en.wikipedia.org/w/index.php?title=File:Music_album_record_white_christmas.jpg *License*: unknown *Contributors*: After Midnight, Bender235, Dreamer.se, Jdforrester, Jusjih, Sherool, Skier Dude, Steelbeard1, Zanimum

File:Beach Boys - Wild Honey (single).jpg *Source*: http://en.wikipedia.org/w/index.php?title=File:Beach_Boys_-_Wild_Honey_(single).jpg *License*: unknown *Contributors*: E-Kartoffel, Melesse, Metstotop333

License

Made in the USA
Lexington, KY
04 February 2012